THE CAMBRIDGE HISTORY OF
ENGLISH ROMANTIC LITERATURE

The Romantic period was one of the most creative, intense and turbulent periods of English literature, an age marked by revolution, reaction and reform in politics, and by the invention of imaginative literature in its distinctively modern form. This *History* presents an engaging account of six decades of literary production around the turn of the nineteenth century. Reflecting the most up-to-date research, the essays are designed both to provide a narrative of Romantic literature, and to offer new and stimulating readings of the key texts. One group of essays addresses the various locations of literary activity – both in England and, as writers developed their interests in travel and foreign cultures, across the world. A second set of essays traces how texts responded to great historical and social change. With a comprehensive bibliography, chronology and index, this volume will be an important resource for research and teaching in the field.

JAMES CHANDLER is Barbara E. and Richard J. Franke Distinguished Service Professor and Director of the Franke Institute for the Humanities at the University of Chicago. He is the General Editor of Cambridge Studies in Romanticism and has written and edited many books in the field, including *Romantic Metropolis: The Urban Scene in British Romanticism, 1780–1840* (editor, with Kevin Gilmartin, Cambridge, 2005) and *The Cambridge Companion to Romantic Poetry* (editor, with Maureen N. McLane, 2008).

The New Cambridge History of English Literature is a programme of reference works designed to offer a board synthesis and contextual survey of the history of English literature through the major periods of its development. The organisation of each volume reflects the particular characteristics of the period covered, within a general commitment to providing an accessible narrative history through a linked sequence of essays by internationally renowned scholars. The History is designed to accommodate the range of insights and fresh perspectives brought by new approaches to the subjects, without losing sight of the need for essential exposition and information. The volumes include valuable reference features, in the form of a chronology of literary and political events, extensive primary and secondary bibliographies and a full index.

The Cambridge History of Medieval English Literature
EDITED BY DAVID WALLACE

The Cambridge History of Early Modern English Literature
EDITED BY DAVID LOEWENSTEIN AND JANEL MUELLER

The Cambridge History of English Literature 1660–1780
EDITED BY JOHN RICHETTI

The Cambridge History of English Romantic Literature
EDITED BY JAMES CHANDLER

The Cambridge History of Twentieth-Century English Literature
EDITED BY LAURA MARCUS AND PETER NICHOLLS

IN PREPARATION

The Cambridge History of Victorian Literature
EDITED BY KATE FLINT

THE CAMBRIDGE HISTORY OF
ENGLISH ROMANTIC LITERATURE

*

Edited by
JAMES CHANDLER

CAMBRIDGE
UNIVERSITY PRESS

CAMBRIDGE UNIVERSITY PRESS
Cambridge, New York, Melbourne, Madrid, Cape Town, Singapore, São Paulo, Delhi

Cambridge University Press
The Edinburgh Building, Cambridge CB2 8RU, UK

Published in the United States of America by Cambridge University Press, New York

www.cambridge.org
Information on this title: www.cambridge.org/9780521790079

First published 2009

Printed in the United Kingdom at the University Press, Cambridge

A catalogue record for this publication is available from the British Library

Library of Congress Cataloguing in Publication data
The Cambridge history of English romantic literature / [edited by] James Chandler.
p. cm. – (New Cambridge history of English literature)
Includes bibliographical references and index.
ISBN 978-0-521-79007-9 (hardback)
1. English literature–History and criticism.   2. Romanticism–England.
I. Chandler, James, 1948–   II. Title: History of English romantic literature.
III. Title: English romantic literature.   IV. Series.
PR146.C335 2008
820.9'007–dc22   2008033151

ISBN 978-0-521-79007-9 hardback

Contents

Contents

Contents

Contributors

JOHN BARRELL *University of York*

JOHN BREWER *California Institute of Technology*

JULIE CARLSON *University of California at Santa Barbara*

JAMES CHANDLER *University of Chicago*

IAN DUNCAN *University of California at Berkeley*

SIMON DURING *The Johns Hopkins University*

MARY A. FAVRET *Indiana University*

FRANCES FERGUSON *The Johns Hopkins University*

INA FERRIS *University of Ottawa*

MARGOT FINN *University of Warwick*

CATHERINE GALLAGHER *University of California at Berkeley*

LUKE GIBBONS *University of Notre Dame*

KEVIN GILMARTIN *California Institute of Technology*

JAN GOLINSKI *University of New Hampshire*

PAUL HAMILTON *Queen Mary, University of London*

ANNE JANOWITZ *Queen Mary, University of London*

ADRIAN JOHNS *University of Chicago*

NIGEL LEASK *University of Glasgow*

DEIDRE LYNCH *University of Toronto*

SAREE MAKDISI *University of California at Los Angeles*

SUSAN MANNING *University of Edinburgh*

JEROME MCGANN *University of Virginia*

List of contributors

W. J. T. MITCHELL *University of Chicago*

TILOTTAMA RAJAN *University of Western Ontario*

ESTHER SCHOR *Princeton University*

DAVID SIMPSON *University of California at Davis*

CLIFFORD SISKIN *New York University*

KATIE TRUMPENER *Yale University*

SUSAN J. WOLFSON *Princeton University*

Acknowledgements

Like most books of such length and logistical complexity, this one was long in the planning and even longer in the making. Beyond the extraordinary roster of contributors whose work is represented here, a number of other colleagues and friends have helped in ways that demand special recognition. The volume was commissioned by Josie Dixon, and it was in extensive consultation with her that the basic scheme of the book was developed. Generously helping to finish what she helped to start, she produced detailed and helpful comments on a late draft of the Introduction. Through most of its own history, the in-house editorial work on this history was shouldered by Linda Bree. She vetted the entire manuscript at a late stage, providing helpful comments on every chapter; her patience and perspicuity have been remarkable throughout. My heartiest thanks go to them both, and also to Maartje Scheltens, who presided over the final stages of preparation and production. At the University of Chicago, I benefited from the impressive endurance and steadfast aid of Gina DeGiovanni, research assistant for the project. Her skills in organization and editing were invaluable. She and Michael Meeuwis did the lion's share of work on the detailed Chronology that appears toward the end of this volume. Two work-study assistants, John Maki and Mollie Godfrey, stepped in to provide needed help at various points along the way. Andrew Yale has shouldered much of the work in the final stages. Janel Mueller and David Wallace, editors of two early volumes in this new *Cambridge History of English Literature*, delivered some sage advice in the early going. Maureen McLane and Nigel Leask offered useful suggestions about the Introduction. Philip Gossett, former Dean of Humanities at Chicago, not only encouraged me to undertake this project but also provided some assistance with its execution. Finally, I would like to thank Barbara and Richard Franke, who sponsor the eponymous faculty chair that has supported me through most of the years I have worked on this volume.

Introduction

JAMES CHANDLER

Like the other volumes of the new *Cambridge History of English Literature*, this one offers a collaborative account for one of the recognized periods of a rich and complex literary history – one far richer and more complex, indeed, than the compromise category of 'English Literature' can capture. Like the other volumes, it builds on the extensive scholarship that has been undertaken in the field since the publication of the first *History of English Literature* by Cambridge early in the twentieth century. Like the others, too, it is responsive to major shifts in critical frameworks and historiographical assumptions over recent decades. Finally, like the others, and in keeping with the Press's own directive for the new *History* as a whole, it is organized and executed in a way that 'reflects the particular characteristics of the period covered'. In that last consideration, logically enough, lies a key to this volume's special place and character among the other volumes.

By comparison with periods traditionally defined by century demarcations, or by the reigns of monarchs, the Romantic age has often been marked off in ways that are at once less arbitrary and more so. Some of its characteristic boundaries – 1789, 1783 and 1776, on the early side, and 1832 on the far side – are dates primarily of political significance, years associated with rebellion and revolution on the one hand, and with reform on the other. It is especially fitting that the literary history of this period should be bracketed by events of such political and social impact, since English writers at this time so often assumed their work to carry serious political weight in a contentious sphere of public sentiment and opinion. This assumption often seems to inform even the simplest of nature lyrics, even the most abstruse of poetic meditations. Indeed, part of what has made the literature of this period so intriguing for so many of its students is that many writers aspired to political and ethical influence indirectly – often, paradoxically, by way of a new assertion of the aesthetic claims of their work. In the decades that straddle the turn of the eighteenth century, the categories of 'aesthetics' and 'poetics' both underwent serious transformation in ways that still matter in the early twenty-first century.

This paradox can be reformulated in slightly different terms. On the one hand, the defining political developments of this age were recognized, even by many contemporaries, as unprecedented in their magnitude. 'All circumstances taken together', wrote Edmund Burke in 1790, 'the French Revolution is the most astonishing that has hitherto happened in the world.'[1] On the other hand, the Romantic age is the only major period of British literary history that is named for a literary category. 'Romance', of course, designates both a literary genre and a major European language group, as well as a style or mode of artistic expression, a kind of atmosphere. This is a period, furthermore, that is often strongly identified with the emergence of what might be called a cultural idiom, a whole way of being in the world, one sometimes understood in contradistinction to the 'classical' idiom. This polarity of 'classic' and 'romantic' is not, however, a simple one. Marilyn Butler, among others, once showed that British Romanticism is hard to distinguish in certain respects from ongoing forms of neo-classicism, and further complications of these categories can be found in many of the chapters to follow.[2]

However we label them, the period saw the emergence of an exceptional number of poets now recognized among the finest in British history – many of them working in relations of personal and literary intimacy with one another. For most of the century since the first *Cambridge History of English Literature* was published, the works of Blake, Wordsworth, Coleridge, Byron, Shelley and Keats have stood prominent in even the briefest anthologies of British poetry. All these poets – and they were not alone – were explicit about their engagement with what would later be called 'the condition of England' in their time. Some tried, like Wordsworth in his Preface to *Lyrical Ballads* (1800), to come to terms with 'the present state of the public taste in this country, and to determine how far this taste is healthy or depraved'.[3] And many, too, like Wordsworth, considered that these important matters 'could not be determined, without pointing out,

1 Edmund Burke, *Reflections on the Revolution in France*, ed. Conor Cruise O'Brien (Harmondsworth: Penguin, 1968), p. 92.
2 Marilyn Butler, *Rebels, Romantics and Reactionaries* (New York: Oxford University Press, 1982).
3 Preface to *Lyrical Ballads*, in *Prose Works of William Wordsworth*, ed. W. J. B. Owen and Jane Worthington Smyser, 3 vols. (Oxford: Clarendon Press, 1974), vol. I, p. 120. Subsequent references cited by page number in the text.

in what manner language and the human mind act and react on each other, and without retracing the revolutions not of literature alone but likewise of society itself' (p. 120). Most of them would therefore also have agreed with Wordsworth when he specified that 'a multitude of causes unknown to former times are now acting with a combined force' (p. 128) on the experience of British and Irish subjects. These causes included both 'the great national events which are daily taking place' and the more gradual processes of modernity, such as 'the encreasing accumulation of men in cities, where the uniformity of their occupations produces a craving for extraordinary incident which the rapid communication of intelligence hourly gratifies' (ibid.). A central task for any history of British literature in this period, therefore, is to chart the impact both of this perception and the facts that lay behind it on the practices of writing and reading.

The Romantic period has long been distinguished by the quality of its verse, but its poetic canon has recently been expanded to include (or reinclude): the work of women poets like Anna Barbauld, Laetitia Elizabeth Landon, Charlotte Smith, Mary Robinson and Felicia Hemans; the work of Scottish and Irish poets such as Robert Burns, Sir Walter Scott and Thomas Moore; and the working-class poetry of John Clare. Each of these reconfigurations of the field of Romantic poetry has had its effects on how we understand a given text's exemplary status for the age, and many of these shifts are registered, even addressed, in the chapters that follow. Most of these poets – male or female, English or Scottish or Irish, well-born or low-born – found themselves confronting a wider world than most of their poetic predecessors: a world where issues such as slavery and abolition, empire and settlement, were far more on the minds of readers than ever before. These were precisely the sorts of issues that circulated with 'the rapid communication of intelligence' of which Wordsworth wrote in the Preface.

The impact of this new literary culture on the writers of the period certainly extended beyond poetry itself. These decades witnessed the transformation of the English novel – from the impressive but miscellaneous productions of Richardson, Fielding and Sterne in the mid-eighteenth century into the more comprehensive and comprehensible Victorian novel form that took shape in the years that followed Dickens's Pickwick Papers (1837). This segment of the novel's history once seemed to be a fairly barren time identified chiefly by two dominant figures in fiction: on the one hand, what Scott referred to as the 'exquisite touch' of Austen's novels and, on the other, by the 'big bow-wow' of his own Waverley series.[4] Now, however, it is recognized as the fertile period in which sentimental and Gothic fiction achieved their astoundingly durable forms, and in which both science fiction and the modern detective novel had their first emergence. It is recognized, too, as the time when experiments by Maria Edgeworth and others helped to shape an enlightened ethnographic impulse into a new kind of fiction, and with this recognition comes a new sense of the contributions of the Celtic strain of Irish and Scottish literature in the making of the great Victorian social novels. Finally, we now see this as a period when 'philosophy', often with a Continental turn, gained new authority in and through fiction writing.

Thus, whereas Mary Shelley's *Frankenstein* once stood for all that was idiosyncratic (not to say monstrous) in 'the Romantic novel', we now have a new appreciation for the fiction of William Beckford, Frances Burney, Susan Ferrier, John Galt, William Godwin, Mary Hays, James Hogg, Elizabeth Inchbald, Charles Maturin, Lady Morgan, Clara Reeve, Charlotte Smith and Mary Wollstonecraft. Even such a preliminary list reminds us that the novel of this period brought women into literature not only as readers but also as writers in unprecedented numbers. And while feminist scholarship continues to exhume important writing by women from decades earlier, the explosion of work by and for women in the later eighteenth century was remarked upon at the time and remains unquestionably striking in retrospect. Again, Maria Edgeworth emblematizes much about the novel in the period, a cosmopolitan woman writing from Ireland who did much to reshape British fiction, much to foster *both* the 'big bow-wow' historical novel of Scott *and* the intellectual domestic novel of Austen.

While there was no shortage of critics or reviewers in the increasingly active public sphere of eighteenth-century Britain, most observers would grant that criticism took on a new and more aggressively institutionalized function during the decades around the turn of that century. The great reviewing establishments, and the aesthetic and political camps that formed around them, generated an increasingly distinct reaction among poets, dramatists and novelists. Much of what became of the 'Lake School' of poetry can be understood in reaction to the critiques of Francis Jeffrey in the *Edinburgh Review*, beginning with his remarks on the new 'sect' in a review of Southey's *Thalaba the Destroyer* in October 1802. Keats's anticipation of

---

4 Sir Walter Scott, *The Journal of Sir Walter Scott*, ed. David Douglas, 2 vols. (New York: Burt Franklin, 1970), vol. I, p. 155.

the reviewer's critique became a defining characteristic and even an explicit theme of his poetry almost from the beginning of his more ambitious work. And the positions staked out in the great controversies of this period – positions on the value, meaning and political effects of what we still call 'imaginative literature' – continue to structure much debate in our time. The notion of poetic autonomy was born in the same historical moment as the specialized institutions of criticism on which it paradoxically depends.

The Romantic period did not invent the idea of the modern, but it did modernize it. No longer understood in terms of an opposition between the contemporary vernacular and its ancient classical antecedent, the 'modern' now assumed its place in a specifically national story. In this new story, the primitive could be revisited in a polite mode, and experimental ballads could be produced (as Wordsworth put it in his Preface) in the spirit 'of our elder writers' (p. 128) – i.e., English elder writers. Virginia Woolf recognizes the full implication of this new story for the history of the modern novel when she points to her forebear, Sir Walter Scott (whose historical fiction makes a significant appearance in *To the Lighthouse*), as a novelist whose paradoxical accomplishment can be emblematized in the fantastical neo-gothic home he built for himself at Abbotsford on the River Tweed in the 1820s. It is a home, she points out, that, though stuffed with antiquarian books and artifacts, was nonetheless the first domestic residence in Britain to be fitted with modern gas fixtures.[5]

In narrating these developments, telling the stories of Romanticism and the story of romanticisms, this volume of the new *Cambridge History* must willy-nilly come to terms with a peculiarly Janus-faced moment in the history of literary history itself. And herein lies an important source of the shaping pressure that this period itself exerts on its representation in such a history. For it is indeed in Britain's Romantic period that many of the informing concepts for projects of this sort underwent a crucial formation or transformation. I mean concepts such as 'literature', 'criticism', 'culture' and indeed 'period' itself – though certainly, as John Richetti suggests in introducing the 1660–1780 volume in this *History*, intimations of these changes were earlier afoot. Thus, while Janel Mueller and David Lowenstein, editors of the Early Modern volume, astutely cite Raymond Williams's *Keywords* to authorize their broadening of the notion of 'literature', Williams and others

---

5 Virginia Woolf, 'Gas at Abbotsford', in *Collected Essays* (New York: Harcourt, Brace and World, 1925), pp. 134–9.

have noted that the period when the concept of 'the literary' was modified toward its still dominant sense of 'creative' or 'imaginative' literature was precisely that of Romanticism. And thus, too, David Wallace, editor of the medieval volume of the *History*, shrewdly resolves the antinomy between detail and comprehensiveness in literary history ('true' microhistory vs. 'grand' general narrative) by multiplying the possibilities for true but different grand narratives of the medieval period. But again, this sort of pluralism about general historical narrative emerged with singular éclat in the wake of the French Revolution, and it was revisited in the debates over Sir Walter Scott's new form of fictionalized history as practised in the Waverley novels. It is a sense that a historian's narrative is inevitably produced in a certain style and plot form, what the French called 'histoire Walter Scotteé'.

It is something of a cliché among historians that all researchers see their own period as decisive for the story of the really important things about our modernity. It is this sort of recognition that leads some wits to insist that we have never been modern, or else that we always already were. But it is not for nothing that a thinker of the eminence of Hannah Arendt (by no means a Romanticist and even less a romantic) identifies what we call the Romantic period as the age of the 'pathos of novelty' or that the period is so routinely labelled with some variation on Karl Polanyi's phrase, 'the Great Transformation'.[6] To be sure, Polanyi was writing about 'the political and economic origins of our time', and even Arendt was concerned primarily with the theory and practice of politics and the new forms of modern statehood. At the same time, however, one of the most important historical points to recognize about this period is how literary activity became so crucial, so quickly, to national (and indeed international) affairs – how poets could come to seem legislators.

The full maturation of what Jürgen Habermas has termed the literary public sphere of the long eighteenth century would ultimately elevate writers to positions of great influence, both real and imagined. Here we discover one of the enabling conditions for the seemingly outlandish claim by Shelley in 1819 that 'poets and philosophers are the unacknowledged legislators of the world'.[7] To understand the extent to which Shelley's

---

6 Hannah Arendt, *On Revolution* (Harmondsworth: Penguin, 1965), p. 34; Karl Polanyi, *The Great Transformation: The Political and Economic Origins of our Time* (New York: Rinehart & Company, 1944), pp. 3–19.
7 Percy Bysshe Shelley, *Shelley's Poetry and Prose*, ed. Donald Reiman and Neil Fraistat, 2nd edn (New York: W. W. Norton, 2002), p. 535.

sentiment was shared by his contemporaries is to begin to grasp what would otherwise seem inexplicable. It would not be difficult to show, for example, how Britons talented in other ways consistently gravitated toward writing as the primary work of their lives in this period, precisely out of a sense that writing had become a medium of extraordinary potency. Among the group of six male Romantic poets who until recently tended to dominate the anthologies, all of them initially set out pursuing other careers: Blake in the visual arts, Wordsworth in law, Coleridge in the ministry, Byron in politics and Keats in medicine. Percy Shelley, Alfred North Whitehead observed, might have been a 'Newton among chemists' if he had pursued his interests in science instead of turning to poetry and letters.[8]

In this connection it is worth noting that there is also another, subtler way in which our way of naming this period signals its distinction. For other periods we employ a different grammar. We say, for example, 'Medieval English Literature', not 'English Medieval Literature'; and we say 'Early Modern English Literature', not 'English Early Modern Literature'. It sounds odd to say 'Romantic English Literature' – so much so that the pattern for titling volumes of the *Cambridge History* was broken for this volume. Why this grammatical idiosyncrasy? How is it that English Romantic Literature does not jar on the ear? The explanation may lie in the defensible claim that 'Romantic literature' forms a category so powerfully intelligible in itself that it makes more sense to speak of the English variety of that literature than of the 'Romantic age' as one among many in a series of periods. Is it not the case that the adjectival phrase 'English-Romantic' has a kind of coherence that 'English-Medieval' or (for a different reason) 'English-Victorian' does not? (The decision to name the subject for these volumes as 'English' literature in the first place had more to do with identifying a language than a nation, though 'literature in English' would have misled by being too comprehensive for the volumes' actual scope.)

The explanation may well have to do with the period's association with the concept of a *movement*, one named by the eventually nominalized form of the adjective Romantic: Romanticism. The category of Romanticism has been debated since its coinage during the period in question. In the century since the last *Cambridge History*, 'Romanticism' has had perhaps as many as three cycles of ups and downs, though they overlap in complex ways. F. H. Bradley and W. B. Yeats helped rehabilitate Romanticism after the sort of critique lodged in Thomas Hardy's brilliant anti-Romantic lyric of 1900,

8 A. N. Whitehead, *Science and the Modern World* (New York: Macmillan, 1925), p. 84.

'The Darkling Thrush', in which Hardy subverted the vatic landscape of Keats's 'Ode to a Nightingale' and Shelley's 'To a Skylark' with a sketch of his thrush's gloomy response to a scene identified as 'the century's corpse outleant'.[9] Irving Babbitt and T. S. Eliot discredited Romanticism sternly in the period between the Wars. But then, in the period after the Second World War, Northrop Frye and a group of scholars clustered at Yale, including Frederick Pottle and his student Harold Bloom, revived interest in the movement. Two decades later, deconstructive criticism, also largely anchored at Yale, sustained this renewed interest, perhaps even intensified it: the major Romantics were special objects of attention for the school of Paul de Man. Another cycle commenced in the 1970s and 1980s. Both new historicism (with its nominalist approach to periodization more generally) and feminist criticism (with its powerful critique of a canon centred so insistently on six male poets) spelled trouble for the hegemony of Romanticism as an organizing principle in the last quarter of the century. Just in the past few years, however, one finds that 'Romantic' and 'Romanticism' remain more durable terms than we might have imagined as recently as the 1990s. There seems to be a fascination with matters Romantic – and indeed a utility in the very category itself – that will not go away.

It may well be that 'Romanticism' survives because it captures something important about the other '-isms' of the period that it names. The '-ism' form came into frequent and often self-parodic vogue in the nineteenth century. Think of Matthew Arnold's mocking references to the various 'isms' of 'hole-in-corner' splinter groups in his *Culture and Anarchy*.[10] To be sure, *Romanticism* was not the first '-ism' to appear in English, nor was the period we call Romantic the era in which the '-ism' form was coined. The '-ism' form derives from a Latin suffix (*-ismus*) and, as a way of naming a doctrinal position, it can be traced in English usage before the Early Modern period, where it mainly refers to positions in ancient philosophy: Stoicism, Epicureanism and the like. By the seventeenth century, the form has begun to be used for positions in the spectrum of modern religious positions. The *OED* cites John Milton as the first citation for 'Protestantism' in 1649. By the 1680s, one already finds an instance of the quasi-noun form, 'ism', in the characterization of a man

---

9 Thomas Hardy, *Complete Poetical Works*, ed. Samuel Hynes, 5 vols. (Oxford: Clarendon Press, 1982–95), vol. 1, p. 187.
10 Matthew Arnold, *Works*, ed. George W. E. Russell, 15 vols. (London: Macmillan, 1903–4), vol. VI, p. xxi.

who 'was the great Hieroglyphick of Jesuitism, Puritanism, Quaquerism, and of all the Isms from Schism'.[11]

Something changes, however, with the '-ism' form as it evolves through the eighteenth century and into the Romantic period. It more and more often assumes the sense of an ideological movement, and some of these movements would come to be identified with the Romantic period itself, as has been explained by work in the 'historical semantics' of the age by scholars such as Reinhart Koselleck.[12] Hence the special appositeness of Thomas Carlyle's 1837 description of the moral vacuum left by the French Revolution and of all the 'isms that make up Man in France' that he sees 'rushing and roaring in that gulf'.[13] Three years later, taking aim at modern women and their place in 'the system of society', and more particularly at Socialism and Owenism, *Fraser's Magazine* prophesied that 'All the untidy *isms* of the day shall be dissipated.'[14] One of the early and powerful -isms of the period, Jacobinism, may well have been Edmund Burke's coinage of the early 1790s, but it was probably a back-formation from 'Jacobitism', a term that appeared in the title of a pamphlet as early as the 1690s.[15] Still, the -ism form acquires a peculiar sense of urgency and intensity in the writings of the Romantic age, as writers come to believe that the state of society can be shown, and in being shown, altered.[16]

Evidence – both qualitative and quantitative – of this peculiar intensity in the writing of the Romantic period is not hard to find. The Romantic era has traditionally been the shortest of the literary periods to take its place in the sequence of epochs that structure anthologies and literary histories, and it is typically granted representation out of all proportion to its duration. The first *Cambridge History of English Literature* did not have a volume on

---

11 Heraclito Democritus [Edward Pettit], *The Vision of Purgatory* (London: Printed by T. N. for Henry Brome, 1680), p. 46.

12 Reinhart Koselleck, '"Neuzeit": Remarks on the Semantics of the Modern Concepts of Movement', in *Futures Past: On the Semantics of Historical Time*, trans. Keith Tribe (Cambridge, MA: The MIT Press, 1985), pp. 231–66.

13 Thomas Carlyle, *Works*, 30 vols. (New York: C. Scribner's Sons, 1896–1901), vol. IV, p. 205.

14 'Woman and the Social System', *Fraser's Magazine for Town and Country* 21:126 (June 1840), 689.

15 *The Spirit of Jacobitism: or, Remarks upon a Dialogue Between K[ing] W[illiam] and Benting [Bentinck, Earl of Portland] in a Dialogue between Two Friends of the Present Government* (London: J. Whitlock, 1695).

16 In his historical survey of the 'Ism' form H. M. Höpfl describes the early nineteenth-century awareness of 'a plague of -isms', and he distinguishes this moment from the other great surge of -isms, in the late sixteenth and early seventeenth centuries, in terms not dissimilar from those I have used here – 'Isms', *British Journal of Political Science* 13:1 (January 1983), 1–17.

Romanticism as such but it did have one on 'the Period of the French Revolution' (1789–1815). That volume, moreover, included neither the work of the later eighteenth-century 'Age of Sensibility' nor that of Scott, Byron, Hazlitt, Mary Shelley or Percy himself. Likewise, *two* of the twelve volumes in the mid-century *Oxford History of English Literature* (eds. Dobree, Davis and Wilson) were dedicated, respectively, to two brief and consecutive periods, one volume on 1789–1815, the other on 1815–1832. The same pattern has held true for the standard anthologies. In the widely used *Norton Anthology of English Literature*, for example, a similar disproportion has long been apparent between the duration of the Romantic period and the amplitude of representative writings included.

How does one best address these special features and dimensions of the age of Romanticism in a volume of this sort? Looking back at the original *Cambridge History of English Literature*, one notes that three kinds of headings tend to be used for chapter titles in the eighteenth- and nineteenth-century volumes: single authors ('Keats'), classes of authors ('Letter Writers'), or kinds of writing ('The Literature of Dissent'). The primary or at least default approach governing all these volumes is that of literary biography, individual or collective. There are obviously great advantages to this kind of approach, especially for those periods in which sufficient biographical record survives for the authors in question. If one wished to find something about Jane Austen, or *Ivanhoe*, or Byron's Oriental tales, one had a pretty good idea of where to look and of what kind of discussion to expect. There was very little risk of overlap and, in a way, a fairly good principle for ensuring coverage. This kind of model served those volumes very well, as is clear from their extraordinary shelf life.

It must be recalled, however, that the first *Cambridge History* was undertaken after a century of practice in the art of biographical criticism. The twentieth century did not much advance this art, nor whet the taste that calls for it. To rehearse an oft-told tale: for several decades after the 1910s, the study of English literature was characterized by an uneasy yoking of unhistorical formal analysis, the New Criticism, and exhaustive 'background' scholarship into matters of literary, intellectual, social, political and cultural history relevant to reading works of the past. In the last quarter of the twentieth century, the disciplines of English study have become far more splintered, more dependent on other fields of study for their research paradigms. It sometimes seems that the 'boundaries' of fields and disciplines are there only to be overleapt, straddled, traversed, transgressed or otherwise disrespected. As difficult a task as literary history has always been – R. S. Crane illustrated its near impossibility in his failure even to complete *The Principles of Literary History* back in the 1950s – today it is a more eclectic and more uncertain project than ever. Not that the resort to literary biography could at any point be accepted as a fully satisfactory solution to it. Indeed, in so far as the volumes in the new *Cambridge History of English Literature* have been conceived precisely as *histories* rather than 'handbooks' or 'companions', the literary-biographical or encyclopedic approach would appear to be particularly unhelpful, though Iain McCalman's compendious *Oxford Companion to the Romantic Age* is an impressive example of what can be accomplished in the companion format.

As David Wallace has explained, a number of new models have been proposed in recent years for attacking the task of comprehensive and large-scale literary history in the academic circumstances of recent decades. Of these, Denis Hollier's non-continuous array of articles arranged by date has been one of the most inventive and experimental, and one of the most debated. David Wellbery follows a similar method in his superb *New History of German Literature*. This approach was a tempting one for the present volume, not least because, as I have explained in detail elsewhere, there is a peculiarly intimate relationship between the practice of 'dating' culture in this way and the kind of cultural historicism that developed in Walter Scott's Britain: think of the first of the Waverley novels, subtitled "Tis Sixty Years Since', as a study of 'Britain in 1745'.[17] In the end, I resisted the temptation. It is not just that the choice of which dates is inevitably somewhat arbitrary. In addition, it is difficult in such a format to register both the processes of historical change and the locations of historical activity, and these seemed major desiderata for this volume.

From the perspective of the current volume, the peculiar editorial challenge of a collaborative history of Romanticism at the present time is, broadly, threefold. First, one must find a way to do justice to the burgeoning array of writings worthy of critical and historical interest in the period. This is not even easy to do under formats that assign the period multiple volumes; it is all the more difficult in a single volume. Secondly, one must acknowledge the self-consciousness of the Romantic period as such – the sense that, as J. S. Mill said (in 1831) about the 'spirit of the age', this was an age not simply of *change* but of a change in the manner of

---

17 James Chandler, *England in 1819: The Politics of Literary Culture and the Case of Romantic Historicism* (Chicago: University of Chicago Press, 1998), pp. 105–35.

change.[18] Thus, one must also reckon with the extraordinary precedent that this age establishes for subsequent periods of English literary history. And finally, one must trace the linkages between the wealth of writings and the period's self-consciousness, thus showing the value of such a notion as 'the Romantic period' in the first place. This task becomes particularly timely since the self-evidence of that value may be at a particularly low ebb at the turn of the twenty-first century, a time when the period concept of Romanticism remains under some suspicion. Difficult as this last challenge might seem, it may also be the case that in attempting to meet it one is positioned to address some of the larger challenges of literary history in the present critical environment. To historicize a set of practices – including the practice of reading certain texts as if they might be representative of past literary culture – is not necessarily to debunk or to discredit them.

The present volume, then, has been structured by means of an interlocking set of organizational rubrics that provide a loose narrative ordering, a conceptually flexible framework of analysis, and a set of topics that have proven appropriately rich and relevant. This scheme negotiates between sometimes competing goals: coverage and innovation, authority and interest. The volume is organized into four parts: two brief framing sections and two large sections comprising the body of the materials. The two framing sections – Part I: The ends of Enlightenment and Part IV: The ends of Romanticism – aim to demarcate the literature of Romanticism chronologically, thematically and ideologically by considering key topics framed centrally in terms of these two familiar period categories. The play on the term 'ends' is deliberate, of course, since the point was to allow the authors of these chapters to consider both the problem of how to determine the beginning and end of Romanticism and the problem of how to determine its shape or putative *telos* (problematic as that notion might seem), and to do so in part by comparison with the temporally prior but grammatically parallel notion of 'Enlightenment'. The section on 'The ends of Enlightenment' includes accounts of the transition from Enlightenment to Romanticism, as well as of their interdependence as categories. The particular topics – sensibility, sentiment, antiquarianism, political economy, and system – are all key concepts of the British Enlightenment that

---

18 J. S. Mill, 'The Spirit of the Age', in Mill's *Essays on Literature and Society*, ed. J. B. Schneewind (New York: Collier, 1965), p. 31. Mill was echoing the title of Hazlitt's important collection of literary portraits, *The Spirit of the Age* (1825).

importantly set the terms of debate for the age to come. The final section, 'The ends of Romanticism', looks at some ways in which Romanticism set the terms for posterity. Chapters in this section assess the changes wrought in the central and multi-faceted concept of 'representation', survey Britain's newly developed project in cultural imperialism, reflect on the relation of Romanticism and modern secularism, and ultimately weigh the question of whether, to the degree we consider Romanticism itself as a movement, we should consider it over.

The two larger sections that comprise the body of the volume also mirror each other, but do so chiastically. Part II, 'Geographies', proceeds on the assumption that the age can be defined by a sense of writing as having a particularized (though often very grand) historical 'scene'. The literature of this period is distinguished, in part, by its marked sense of place, and it is precisely this distinctive feature that makes such a rubric especially apposite for this particular volume. The great scenes of the age's writing often supply crucial conditions for its production and interpretation. Sometimes, though, these scenes seemed to be all but produced by the writers who inhabit them. This was, after all, the time when it became fashionable to associate geographies with particular writers: the Trossachs as 'Scott Country', the Lake District with the 'Lake Poets'. The geographies in question thus involve more than one kind of relationship to the literary production of the period, and more than one scale of 'scene'. Some deal with regions of the so-called British Isles, some with places of Britons' exile (such as Italy), and others with places (such as France, Germany and America) that shaped British literature rather as a matter of distant influence or image. Some of these locations even stretch our sense of 'geography' – chapters dealing with what Felicia Hemans called 'the Homes of England', for example, or with the period's theatres of war. Finally, since cultural geography as a category was itself partly a product of this period, some chapters in this section (e.g. Chapter 10, 'Country matters') explore the conceptual and terminological issues involved.

According to the dictum (revived by Anna Barbauld in the early nineteenth century) that 'geography and chronology' are the two eyes of history, it might be expected that Part III would address 'Chronologies'. But even apart from the fact that the volumes in the History attend to 'chronology' with a special appendix, it seemed helpful, rather in the spirit of the 'ratios' developed in Kenneth Burke's framework of 'dramatism', to exploit a corresponding sense of complementarity between the notions of 'scene' and 'activity'.[19] In the case

19 Kenneth Burke, *A Grammar of Motives* (New York: Prentice-Hall, 1945), pp. 7–9.

of the Romantic period, as noted earlier, the most significant activities in question typically involve some sense of 'novelty' (in Arendt's formulation) – that is, of innovation, transformation and (in Koselleck's sense) historical movement. Thus, the third section approaches the Romantic period by focusing on different aspects of literary activity and its relation to cultural, social, and political transformation. It stresses how, contra Marx's later antinomy between interpretation and transformation, writers in this period helped to change the world in the very work of interpreting it. This section tracks changes within the major genres as well as in the very idea of genre itself. It considers how changes in the kinds of writing we associate with 'imaginative literature' relate to changes in other kinds of writing, such as the new literature of science. It looks at how changes in the worlds of which literature forms a part in this period – publishing, for example – are imbricated with the kinds of transformations traced within the period's fascinating body of literary production.

As I suggested earlier, traditional considerations of 'coverage' have in this volume been balanced against those of new interests and paradigms for writing and reading the history of literary culture. Such considerations have not, however, been abandoned. There is no getting around the fact that, under such a principle of organization, a writer such as Wordsworth will tend to appear in multiple entries rather than enjoying the privilege of an entry of his own, or one he shares with, say, Coleridge and Southey. The cross-hatching structure of chapters in this volume provides an additional boon in fostering discussion of a given writer or issue from multiple angles. Thus, Wordsworth and Coleridge's experiments with balladry are dealt with proleptically in the chapter 'Antiquarianism, balladry and the rehabilitation of romance' more directly in the chapters on 'Country matters' and 'The new poetries', and from another more surprising angle in the chapter on 'Romantic cultural imperialism'. Keats appears under several of these same headings, but also under 'Regency London' and 'The "warm south"'. Mary Wollstonecraft is discussed in some detail both in 'Rebellion, revolution, reform' and in 'Romantic cultural imperialism'. Jane Austen appears under 'The homes of England' and 'Romanticism and the wider world', and of course she has a central place, along with Scott and Edgeworth, in 'Transformations of the novel – II'. In turn, Scott gains attention in the chapter on 'Edinburgh and Lowland Scotland', Edgeworth in the chapter on 'Romantic Ireland', and so on. There are some delightfully fresh angles of approach to familiar authors along the way, an account of the urban poet Blake in 'Country matters', for example, and of Felicia Hemans in 'The "warm south"'. And there are chapters, such as the two on London or the chapter on the making of child readers, that discuss very few major authors in detail but do other kinds of work for the volume instead. The London chapters provide a thick description of cultural, social and political life in two of the great metropolis's most fascinating decades. The chapter on child readers is grounded in new research on a neglected development in British publishing.

I have deliberately avoided the resort to a separate heading for 'Women writers', on the twofold grounds that they should not be ghettoized and that they would be fully integrated into the volume as a whole. This is not to say that women writers might not appear more prominently under some entries than others. Women writers figure prominently in 'Sentiment and sensibility', 'The homes of England', 'The "warm south"', 'Writing, reading and the scenes of war', 'Rebellion, revolution, reform', 'The new poetries', both chapters devoted to the transformation of the novel, 'Theatre, performance and urban spectacle' and 'Romantic cultural imperialism'. There could be no doubt that the distinguished cast of contributors for this volume would not fail to do convincing justice to the literary work women contributed to make the Romantic period what it was. They have not disappointed in this respect – nor, I believe, in any other.

One of the women writers to have resurfaced in recent years is Anna Barbauld, whose career as a poet began with a fine volume of verse in 1771 and closed four decades later with a remarkable poem entitled *Eighteen Hundred and Eleven*. Barbauld's last poem dared to comment publicly and politically under a woman's name on the state of the British nation. For her troubles she was attacked in baldly misogynist terms by the reviewing establishment, and though she continued writing she herself published no more during her lifetime. Her case thus dramatically stages the fate of many women writers in this period. The poem itself looks back on Britain in 1811 from the point of view of an observer living decades hence. It thus exemplifies the new Romantic sense of 'futurity', a favourite notion of the Shelleys. Indeed, Percy Shelley would reprise the terms of Barbauld's futuristic retrospect in his Preface to *Peter Bell the Third* (1819) and Mary Shelley would later produce an epic novel about 'futurity' with *The Last Man* (1826). Because writers of the Romantic period reconceived the relation of the present to the past, they could scarcely help doing their part to reconceive the relation of the present to the future. They were the heirs to a new, secular notion of 'posterity' that Carl Becker once explained as part of the work of the eighteenth-century philosophes.[20] When they imagined the 'future state', it was typically not in the heaven of heavens but rather in a new phase of human history. When they imagined the gigantic shadows that futurity casts upon the present, as Percy Shelley proposed, they were not thinking primarily of Christian Revelation.

The implicit location of Barbauld's historical retrospective on Britain in 1811 is North America. The poem imagines visitors from 'the blue mountains, or Ontario's lake' scanning the ruins of what once was a seat of Empire, a nation whose apparent prosperity gave the lie to its fatally misguided policies.[21] Barbauld may have been prophetic in suggesting that the future of empire was in North America, but this is no cause for gloating on the part of those who now live there. It would not be difficult to outline a poem along similar lines for, say, 'Two Thousand and Eleven', in which the contemporary North American empire is subjected to a similarly externalized critique in a yet more distant future. Contemporary Britain has of course not been reduced to rubble, but Barbauld did accurately predict North America's keen interest in the cultural achievements of Britain's past. Half the contributors to the new Cambridge History tend to come from outside Britain and by far the largest number of those from North America. This volume is no exception.

This circumstance reflects, among other things, the longstanding importance of British literary history, and more recently Scottish and Irish literary history, in North American higher education – that is, in those departments, programmes, and curricula that still go by the name of 'English'. But support for the humanities is not growing in North American universities (nor in many other places), and other claims are being made on English programmes everywhere – claims on behalf of cultural studies, gender studies, ethnic studies, cinema and media studies, creative writing, and, of course, studies in North American literature. Shakespeare will surely remain a central figure in North American undergraduate education, and so will a number of other crucial authors. It is not clear, however, that the twenty-first century will sustain the interest in the field narrowly known as 'English literary history', not in the way in which the twentieth century generally did in spite of the decades-long hegemony of the New Criticism.

---

20 Carl Becker, *The Heavenly City of the Eighteenth-Century Philosophers* (Cambridge, MA: Harvard University Press, 1932), pp. 119–68.
21 Anna Laetitia Barbauld, *Eighteen Hundred and Eleven* (London: J. Johnson, 1812), p. 10.

It is therefore a matter of extreme uncertainty what we might expect of a *Cambridge History of English Literature* a century hence. It is possible, with the spread of English-language use around the world, that even more of its contributors might come from an even greater number of places abroad. Then again, it is also possible, if 'English literary history' is not nourished outside Britain, that many fewer contributors will come from abroad. There is of course no assurance that such a History will actually be undertaken again in a century's time – nor, if it is, that it will appear in books like this one. Needless to say, none of us who have worked on this History will be around to find out. Our hope, I suppose, is less that we will have produced the last word on these matters than that we will have stimulated new interest in them for future generations of readers.

PART I

★

THE ENDS OF ENLIGHTENMENT

Sentiment and sensibility

JOHN BREWER

For much of the second half of the eighteenth century the language of feeling, with its key terms of sentiment, sympathy and sensibility, was central to the discussion of man and society, manners, ethics and aesthetics. In its concern with interiority – with feeling, the human psyche and the creative imagination – its emphasis on the ethical and psychological power of literature, its concern with everyday life, and the debate it provoked about the effects – chiefly malign – of the publishing industry, critics and the literary system, the literature of sentiments and sensibility rehearsed many of the issues and deployed some of the language we tend to associate with 'Romanticism'. At the same time sensibility has its own history, anchored, as we shall see, in the material conditions of the production, dissemination and consumption of literature in the period between the mid-eighteenth century and the French Revolution. To apprehend both this history and its possible relations to what subsequently was called Romanticism, we need to characterize sensibility less as a body of ideas or as a discourse deployed across a series of texts than as the site of a major dispute about how to understand, express and affect man's capacity for moral deliberation and action. This debate about man's moral consciousness and its relations to literary technology – both in the sense of a poetics of sentiment and of mechanisms of literary production – was sensibility's inheritance to Romanticism.

But let me begin with some working definitions. Before mid-century, sentiments, as Chambers Encyclopedia explained, were seen merely as 'thoughts which several persons express; whether they relate to matters of opinion, passion, business or the like'. 'But of late years', it adds, '[sentiment] has been much used by some writers to denote an internal impulse of passion, affectation, fancy or intellect, which is considered rather as the cause or occasion of forming an opinion, than as the real opinion itself.'[1] Hence the attachment

---

1 Ephraim Chambers, *Cyclopedia: or an Universal Dictionary of Arts and Sciences*, 5 vols. (London: W. Strahan, 1778–88), vol. IV, s.v. 'Sentiments'.

of the adjective 'sentimental' to different views and thoughts, as a way of locating their origin. Qualifying a magazine, journey, novel history, comedy or educational tract as 'sentimental', a practice that became common in the 1770s, alerted the reader both to its style and content – its attention to and deployment of the language of feeling. Sympathy, a concept developed by David Hume and most memorably elaborated by Adam Smith in his *The Theory of Moral Sentiments* (1759), was the means by which sentiments were communicated; it was the psychological and emotive transaction which placed them at the heart of social life. As Hume put it, 'No quality of human nature is more remarkable, both in itself and its consequences, than that propensity we have to sympathize with others, and to receive by communication their inclinations and sentiments, however different from, or even contrary to our own.'[2] Sensibility, in turn, alluded to the capacity to feel and exert sympathy; it was, according to *The Monthly Magazine* 'that peculiar structure, or habitude of mind, which disposes a man to be easily moved, and powerfully affected, by surrounding objects and passing events'.[3] These definitions emphasize the psychological and social nature of man – they seem like an analytic and descriptive account of the person of feeling – but the terminology was also prescriptive and ethical. Crucially, sentimental feeling, the exercise of sympathy, was seen as a form of moral reflection. Society was imagined, as in Smith's analysis in *The Theory of Moral Sentiments*, as a body of people who had the capacity for sympathy with others and also knew that they themselves might or might not be the objects of sympathy from others. These circumstances inform individuals' moral deliberations which depended upon their ability to exercise sympathy. They also affected their taste.

These preliminary definitions should not be seen as fixed or definitive – there was always a debate about their meaning (notably in the 1770s and 1780s) and of their value (in the 1790s) – but as pointing to the wide range of contexts and discourses – philosophical, psychological and social, as well as literary – in which the language of feeling was deployed. Scholarly recognition of this fact has meant that over the last ten years accounts of sentimentalism have both pushed back in time and expanded the scope of what Northrop Frye memorably (and sardonically) described as an age when literature 'moved from a reptilian Classicism, all cold and dry reason,

2 David Hume, *A Treatise of Human Nature*, ed. David Fate Norton and Mary J. Norton (Oxford: Oxford University Press, 2000), Section xi, 'Of the Love of Fame'.
3 *The Monthly Magazine* 2:706 (October 1796).

to a mammalian Romanticism, all warm and wet feeling'. Thus much scholarship has been determined to trace the roots of sentimentalism to late-seventeenth-century sensationalist psychology, seventeenth- and eighteenth-century physiology and medical theory, Scottish common sense philosophy, and – more controversially – the benevolent views of Latitudinarian theologians. Recognizing the diverse origins of sensibility has also encouraged discussion of a more generalized 'culture of sentiment' or 'culture of sensibility', treated either as a spirit of the times or as an overriding motor of history. Two factors are crucial here: the growing recognition of the centrality of theories of sympathy to the development of the first developmental accounts of the history of society by Hume, Smith, John Millar and a whole body of what became known as conjectural history; and the growth of benevolent and humanitarian reform movements – for the reform of prostitutes, the better treatment of lunatics, the improvement of gaols, the ending of such child labour practices as the use of climbing boys to sweep chimneys, the nurturing of orphans and foundlings, and the abolition of slavery – which made sentimental appeals for public patronage and support. Such studies provide insight into the genealogy and scope of 'the premise of feeling' but they lack the sort of specificity that is possible when considering particular sites or genres of sensibility such as late-eighteenth-century Lowland Scotland or the novel. How then can we write a history of sensibility which is neither tied to a single genre or place (and therefore too narrow) nor forced to assert a ubiquity which both the apologists and critics of sensibility sometimes claimed but of which we should rightly be sceptical?

In the following discussion of sensibility, I combine intellectual history with the material conditions of its production, connecting debates about the ethical and aesthetic effects of particular ways of story-telling, writing and reading to the literary and publishing system that underpinned them. I begin, therefore, with an account of how sensibility was figured both as a universal human attribute and as the particular feature of modern, late eighteenth-century society. The emergence of this sort of analysis was necessary in order to recognize the power, limits and dangers of sentiment and the need to understand the literary techniques by which sentimental story-telling could excite sympathy. I therefore discuss the ways in which a whole range of genres used sentimentalism to excite sympathy and assess the implications of these strategies for notions of authorship, readership and the public. In the third section I anchor these developments to the remarkable changes that occurred in the system of literary circulation as it developed between 1750 and the 1780s. Finally I look at the debate about sensibility in its shifting manifestations between the 1770s, when it first became a generalized object of concern, and the politicized discussion in the wake of the French Revolution.

Physiology, philosophy and society: the making of modern sensibility

Sensationalist philosophers, physiologists and physicians constructed the foundations on which theories of sensibility were built. John Locke's *Essay concerning Human Understanding* (1690), Thomas Willis's *The Anatomy of the Brain and Nerves* [*Cerebri anatome, cui accessit nervorum descriptio et usus.*] (1664), George Cheyne's *The English Malady* (1733), Albrecht von Haller's *De Partibus Corporis Humani Sensibilibus et Irritabilius* (English translation 1755) and Robert Whytt's *Observations on the Sensibility and Irritability of the Parts of Men and other Animals* (1768) established a view of man as a sentient being, whose body and mind – corporeal formation and psychic state – were indissolubly intertwined. Mental states always had their bodily formation and symptoms: sensibility was signed through its palpitations, blushes, swoons and, above all, through its tears. (Indeed, it was a common claim of sentimental literature that true sentiment was a phenomenon beyond language.) The basis of this view was a theory of human nervousness, which saw the self as a creature of sensibility (as opposed to plants which were irritable not sensible) whose feelings were transmitted through fibres or nerves to the mind or soul. The precise physiology of this phenomenon was a source of considerable dispute, though more important was the growing consensus that the feeling body consisted of a series of organs which were connected to one another by their collective sympathy to one another. The physician Thomas Trotter, whose *A View of the Nervous Temperament* brought together a development account of society with a medical analysis of nerves, believed the nervous system to be centered on the 'GREAT SYMPATHETIC NERVE ... whose office directs the most important operation in the animal economy, and binds together in one great circle of feeling, actions and motions both distant and opposite'.[4] The body, like society and the economy, was envisaged as a natural *system*, one that,

4 Thomas Trotter, *A View of the Nervous Temperament; being a practical Enquiry into the increasing prevalence, prevention and treatment of those diseases*, 2nd edn (Newcastle, 1807), in *Radical Food: The Culture and Politics of Eating and Drinking 1790–1820*, ed. Timothy Morton, 3 vols. (London: Routledge, 2000), vol. III, p. 641.

because it was natural, could be neither removed nor suppressed; rather, it required government or management.

Such theories of nervous sensibility were both material accounts of the universal human condition and the basis on which a system of human distinction was made. This tension can be clearly seen in the two entries on sensibility from the French Encyclopedie. The first, written by the physician Fouquet, is concerned with a strictly material condition: 'the faculty of sensing, the cause of feeling, or feeling itself in the organs of the body, the basis of life and what assures its continuance, animality par excellence, the finest, the most singular phenomenon of nature, &c . . . It consists essentially in a purely animal awareness of physical objects, which distinguishes between what is useful and what is harmful.'[5]

This is the necessary but not sufficient condition of moral sensibility (*sensibilité morale*) which is not equally available to all: this is a

> Tender and delicate disposition of the soul which renders it easy to be moved and touched. Sensibility of soul, which is rightly described as the source of morality, gives one a kind of wisdom concerning matters of virtue and is far more penetrating than the intellect acting alone. People of sensibility because of their liveliness can fall into errors which men of the world would not commit; but these are greatly outweighed by the amount of good they do. Men of sensibility live more fully than others: the good and bad things of their life are increased as far as they are concerned. Reflection can produce a man of probity: but sensibility makes a man virtuous. Sensibility is the mother of humanity, of generosity; it is at the service of merit, lends its support to the intellect, and is the moving spirit which animates belief.[6]

Sensibility, then, was both sufficient and excessive, necessary for humanity but a luxury found in its most highly developed forms only among certain privileged people.

Sensibility was both a moral and an aesthetic category. Alexander Gerard in his influential *An Essay on Taste* published in the same year as Smith's *The Theory of Moral Sentiments* explained that the man of taste needed, 'such a *sensibility of heart*, as fits a man for being easily moved, and for readily catching, as by infection, any passion, that a work is fitted to excite'.[7] Burke, Kames and a host of popular writers in the magazines followed Gerard's

---

5 Denis Diderot and Jean le Rond d'Alembert, *Encyclopédie, ou Dictionnaire raisonné des sciences, des arts, et des métiers*, 17 vols. (Paris, 1765), vol. XV, p. 38.
6 *Encyclopédie*, vol. XV, p. 38.
7 Alexander Gerard, *An Essay on Taste* (Edinburgh, 1764), p. 81.

lead in connecting good taste to sensibility, and effective creative work to the power to evoke sympathy. Taste, like sensibility, was found in all humans, but was only effectively deployed by a few.

What then affected the uneven distribution of the natural phenomenon of sensibility? Some explanations seem to emphasize basic physiology. Thus Trotter, reiterating many other commentators both medical and literary, argued that the youth of both sexes and especially women were more prone to sensibility because of their constitutions: 'Nature has endued the female constitution with greater delicacy and sensibility than the male, as destined for a different occupation in life . . . . the female constitution, therefore, [is] furnished by nature with peculiar delicacy and feeling, soft in its muscular fibre, and easily acted upon by stimuli.'[8] But more usually critics offered environmental explanations, portraying sensibility above all as a symptom of modern life. As Trotter put it, 'The *nervous system*, that organ of sensation, amidst the untutored and illiterate inhabitants of a forest, could receive none of those fine impressions, which, however they may polish the mind and enlarge its capacities, never fail to induce delicacy of feeling, that disposes alike to more acute pain, as to more exquisite pleasure.'[9] Acute sensibility was the result of modern commerce, urban life and the manners they promoted – Montesquieu's *doux commerce* – which created new, peaceful forms of mutual dependence among strangers (webs of credit and debt, contract and exchange) led to the better treatment and greater regard for women, and encouraged the arts of politeness and refinement. Commercial society encouraged greater sympathy and sensibility; this distinguished modern societies both from the ancients and the primitives.

At the same time not all moderns were equally sentimental. George Cheyne, physician and friend of Samuel Richardson, believed those with 'more delicate and *elastic Organs of Thinking and Sensibility*' were '*Genii, Philosophers* and *Lawgivers*', a governing elite replete with sensibility, while Hume famously remarked that the 'skin, pores, muscles, and nerves of a day labourer are different from those of a man of quality: So are his sentiments, actions and manners.'[10] Gilbert Stuart, for one, did not hesitate to draw a distinction between 'Readers of the lower classes' and 'those who have

---

8 *Nervous Temperament*, vol. III, p. 575.
9 *Ibid.*, vol. III, p. 566.
10 George Cheyne, *The Natural Method of Cureing the Diseases of the Body and the Disorders of the Mind Depending on the Body* (London: Geo. Strahan, 1742), p. 83; David Hume, *A Treatise of Human Nature*, p. 259.

sensibility'.[11] Sensibility, though largely a consequence of environment, was nevertheless an important sign of social distinction.

One figure repeatedly characterized as the victim of an excessive sensibility was the author or literary man. As Mrs Donnellan sycophantically commented to Samuel Richardson 'the misfortune is, those who are fit to write delicately, must think so; those who can form a distress must be able to feel it; and as the mind and body are so united as to influence one another, the delicacy is communicated, and one too often finds softness and tenderness of mind in a body equally remarkable for those qualities'.[12] *Literati* ... who indulge themselves too much in Study, continual Meditations, and Lucrubrations', were singled out in Robert James's *Medicinal Dictionary* (1743–5) as especially prone to HYPERCHONDRIACUS MORBUS. Samuel Auguste Tissot devoted an entire treatise to literary illness in his *Essay on the Diseases incident to literary persons* (1768) which Herbert Croft, the author of the epistolary novel, *Love and Madness* (1780), used in one of the first full-blown accounts of the sensitive genius of boy poet and forger Thomas Chatterton. No wonder that when Trotter, at the end of the century, listed 'moderns' as especially susceptible to nervous diseases, he began with 'Literary Men ... endued by nature with more than usual sensibility in the nervous system'.[13]

The analysis of sensibility as modern had two rather different registers. The Scottish attempts to account for modern societies tended to emphasize interdependence as the source of modern polish and refinement. Though they voiced their doubts and misgivings about some aspects of modernity, as well as providing the tools for its analysis, they usually saw eighteenth-century man and society as an improvement or innovation. But some social commentators and physicians, stoics, civic humanists and conservative clerics saw modernity as being about the proliferation of desire, the elevation of feeling and heightening of sensibility into forms that were socially and individually pathological. Thus Trotter writes,

> as the ambition or ingenuity of man finds out for him new employments; these, while they draw forth latent talents, call forth new passions and desires: so that however much he may be styled a *creature of habit*, he is in many respects the *creator* of his own temperament ... A large city or town

---

11 *Monthly Review* 44:418 (May 1771).
12 *The Correspondence of Samuel Richardson*, ed. Anna Laetitia Barbauld, 6 vols. (London, 1804), vol. IV, p. 30.
13 *Nervous Temperament*, vol. III, p. 570–1.

may be truly called a hot-bed for the passions . . . Where the savage feels one want, the civilized man has a thousand. Devoted either to love or ambition, these impress all his actions with extraordinary vehemence, perseverance, and enterprise . . . Everything within his view is calculated to prompt his desires and provoke his passions; no antidote is opposed to suppress the one or to moderate the other.[14]

This is the root of those modern disorders which manifest themselves as diseases of nervousness.

Thus sensibility was figured as virtuous, social, modern, youthful and feminine but also as readily pathologized by the very forces – modernity, politeness, good taste, sociability, commerce, feminization – that brought it into being. It was, as many verses and essays on sensibility commented, both a virtue and a source of distress, a sign of moral superiority, but also of weakness. As a contributor to the *Lady's Magazine* in 1775 exclaimed,

Sensibility – thou source of human woes – thou aggrandiser of evils! – Had I not been possessed of thee – how calmly might my days have passed! – Yet would I not part with thee for worlds. We will abide together – both pleased and pained with each other. Thou shalt ever have a place in my heart – be the sovereign of my affections, and the friend of my virtue.[15]

And because Britain was the exemplary case of a modern commercial society, excessive sensibility came to be seen as an English disease, one that took the form of melancholia in men and hysteria in women. Doctors, clerics and, as we shall see, critics stepped forward to police the fine boundary between a healthy and diseased sensibility, to patrol the medical, social and literary environment.

Whether they saw sensibility as the necessary consequence or moral affliction of modernity, historians, political economists and physicians were agreed on the power of sentiment in modern society. But if those who pathologized sensibility, particularly the doctors who had a professional interest in doing so, emphasized its extraordinary strength and prevalence, a number of figures of the Scottish Enlightenment, notably Adam Smith and Lord Kames, were also conscious of the limits of sympathy. Both Smith and Kames, in their different ways, were interested in the workings of social relationships between strangers. Both commented on the relative ease with which sympathy could work in the face-to-face world of the household, kith

14 *Ibid.*, vol. III, p. 568.
15 *Lady's Magazine* 3:251–5 (May 1775).

and kin and close friends, and on the difficulty in sympathizing with those with whom we are unacquainted. As Kames put it, 'it is remarkable in human nature, that though we always sympathize with our relations, and with those under our eye, the distress of persons remote and unknown affects us very little'.[16]

Literary technology

How was such sympathy to be achieved? The answer, I want to suggest, has to do with telling stories (though in a distinctively sentimental way) and with the technologies of publishing which could bring the tale of Sterne's Maria or of a dying slave to a distant public. Sentimental story-telling was believed to set in train the sympathetic reaction that proliferates sensibility, uniting narrator, narrated and listener/reader. It elaborated a complex chain of interdependence effected through feeling, but this sentimental bond was supplemented by the additional consciousness that achieving sensibility affirmed the humanity and morality of those who accomplish it. The key physical sign of sensibility – a spontaneous lachrymosity – also became a sign of humanity. Thus *Man: A Paper for Ennobling the Species* (1755) commented: 'that it may be questioned whether those are properly men, who never wept upon any occasion . . . What can be more nobly human than to have a tender sentimental feeling of our own and others' misfortunes?'[17]

Robert Whytt, the physician, commented on the effect of 'doleful, or moving stories' in producing nervous complaints brought on by an excess of sensibility.[18] Smith in *The Theory of Moral Sentiments* also depicted a mutual sympathy created by narration: 'by relating their misfortunes [the unfortunate] in some measure renew their grief. Their tears accordingly flow faster than before . . . They take pleasure, however, in all this, and it is evident are sensibly relieved by it, because the sweetness of the bystander's sympathy, more than compensates for their anguish.'[19] And in sentimental literature, though a sentimental response is often triggered by sight (as in Smith's spectatorial view of sympathy), it is nurtured to maturity and sometimes to excess by a story.

16 Henry Home, Lord Kames, *Principles of Equity* (Edinburgh, 1767), p. 17.
17 *Man: A Paper for Ennobling the Species* 43:4 (22 October 1755).
18 Robert Whytt, *Observations on the nature, causes, and cure of those disorders which have been commonly called nervous, hypochondriac, or hysteric* (Edinburgh: J. Balfour, 1765), p. 212.
19 Adam Smith, *The Theory of Moral Sentiments*, ed. D. D. Raphael and A. L. Macfie (Indianapolis: Liberty Fund, 1982), p. 15.

Yorick's response to Maria, Goethe's to Charlotte, and Thomas Day's white woman to a negro slave are all elaborated by story-telling; sentimental fiction is full of stories within stories – both as narratives and in the physical form of the fragment, letter or document.

A large number of critical works produced in the 1750s and 1760s – Gerard and Burke on taste, Adam Smith and Hugh Blair's lectures on rhetoric, first delivered in respectively 1748 and 1759, and Kames's *Elements of Criticism* of 1762 – all explored the sentimental mechanisms, the story-telling techniques, by which sensibility could be produced. Their broad assumption was Hugh Blair's, made in one of his sermons: 'Moral and Religious instruction derives its efficacy not so much from what men are taught to know, as from what they are brought to feel'; or as William Craig put it in an essay in *The Lounger*, 'The cold and selfish may be warmed and expanded by the fiction of distress or the eloquence of sentiment; the coarse and the rude may receive polish and refinement from the delineation of elegant manners and of delicate feelings.'[20] The relationship between narrator and reader is not formed by the imparting of knowledge or the use of exemplary instruction but by the engagement of the reader's feelings. Writing and reading become performances of affect. Jerome McGann captures this perfectly in his characterization of Macpherson's Ossian: 'Macpherson treats language as a dynamic and volatile order, more performative than referential. Indeed, the world of Ossian appears to subsist as a complex affective system rather than a machine for transmitting information. Its language builds knowledge by developing sympathetic relations, not by labelling, storing, sending and receiving data.'

The object, as William Enfield explained in the *Monthly Review* was 'by the whole narrative, to fix virtuous impressions upon the heart of the reader, without the aid of sententious reflections and a formal application'.[21] Thus Henry Brooke in *The Fool of Quality* (1763): 'I related to them a thousand entertaining stories, and passages occasionally recollected from the poets and historians of antiquity; and a secret emotion, and inward ardour of pleasing, gave me, fluently, to intersperse sentimental observations and pertinent digressions, more delightful to my auditory than all my quoted authorities.'[22] As Clara Reeve pointed out in her history of romance

---

20 Hugh Blair, *Sermons*, 3 vols. (London, 1750), vol. III, p. 106; *The Lounger* 27:112 (13 August 1785).
21 *Monthly Review* 52:361 (April 1775).
22 Henry Brooke, *The Fool of Quality, or, the history of Henry Earl of Moreland*, 2 vols. (London, 1767), vol. I, pp. 246–7.

and the novel, fiction should therefore 'deceive us into a persuasion (as least while we are reading) that all is real, until we are affected by the joys or distresses, of the persons in the story, as if they were our own'.[23] Realism is not an end but the means of capturing and moving the reader.

But as a technique this was in no way confined to fiction. Smith and Blair were as much concerned with the rhetorical devices of non-fiction (especially history) as with the novel and verse. Both singled out the classical historian Tacitus for his effects on the reader. Blair describes him as possessing 'beyond all Writers, the talent of painting, not to the imagination merely, but to the heart'.[24] For Smith, Tacitus exemplified the strategy of indirect narration in which events are conveyed 'by the Effects they produce either on the Body or the mind'. 'He leads us', says Smith, 'far into the sentiments and mind of some of the actors that they are some of the most striking and interesting passages to be met with in any history', an observation that prompts him, in a self-consciously provocative way, to compare Tacitus to the French novelists Marivaux and Crebillon.[25] Tacitus engages the reader by revealing the feeling and sentiment of historical actors provoked by their circumstances. Effective history depends on conveying the interiority of historical actors. Put another way, we might see it as the encouragement of intimacy, a fictive closeness with those far away, what Mark Salber Phillips has called 'the poetics of presence and distance'.

This is how Kames conceptualized the problem of shaping literary response in his *Elements of Criticism*. Literary representations, he argued, could have the same effect as real experience through the creation of what he called 'ideal presence', the ability of the text to get the reader to envisage what he read as if it were really there: 'ideal presence supplies the want of real presence'. The reader is 'thrown into a kind of reverie; in which state, losing the consciousness of self, and of reading, his present occupation, he conceives every incident as passing in his presence, precisely as if he were an eye-witness'.[26] In Clara Reeve's words, 'there is not a better Criterion of the merit of a book, than our losing sight of the Author'.[27] Reading becomes a form of transport, a vehicle to move the reader closer either to a distant

23 Clara Reeve, *The Progress of Romance*, 2 vols. (Colchester, 1785), vol. I, p. iii.
24 Hugh Blair, *Lectures on Rhetoric and Belles Lettres*, ed. Linda Ferreira–Buckley and S. Michael Halloran (Carbondale, IL: Southern Illinois University Press, 2005), p. 407.
25 Adam Smith, *Lectures on Rhetoric and Belles Lettres*, The Glasgow Edition of the Works of Adam Smith, 6 vols. (Indianapolis: Liberty Fund, 1985), vol. IV, pp. 162, 67, 64.
26 Henry Home, Lord Kames, *Elements of Criticism*, ed. Peter Jones, 2 vols. (Indianapolis: Liberty Fund, 2005), vol. I, p. 69.
27 *The Progress of Romance*, vol. II, p. 25.

(historical) past or into an imaginary realm. As Kames puts it the reader enters the text as a spectator.

How then to bring the reader closer, to excite their sympathy and therefore to shape their moral sensibility? Exploring the interior feeling and not just external action of those represented was, as we have seen, one important means of achieving this. At the same time the portrayal in memoirs, biographies, novels, collections of letters and verses and even histories of the quotidian, ordinary, private and mundane was more likely to excite the reader's sympathy, because of their closeness to their own experience. In Blair's words, 'It is from private life, from familiar, domestic, and seemingly trivial occurrences, that we most often receive light into the real character.'[28] Sensibility was best staged in the intimate theatre of the home and family, and its most characteristic plots concerned the joys and misfortunes of everyday life – romantic and conjugal love, amatory disappointment, misfortunes brought on by intemperance and improvidence, the pleasures of familial companionship in a circle of virtue. The sympathetic moral response that sentimental literature evoked in the reader depended on particularity, specificity, a sense of face-to-faceness, that engaged the reader rather than on moral lessons or grand abstractions which appealed only to the intellect. Laurence Sterne, whose consciousness of every sentimental trick was unsurpassed, ironized the technique in *A Sentimental Journey* (1768). Having failed to free a starling in a cage, Yorick returns to his room – 'the bird in his cage pursued me' – 'to figure to myself the miseries of confinement'. He begins with the big picture: 'I was going to begin with the millions of my fellow creatures born to no inheritance but slavery: but finding, however affecting the picture was, that I could not bring it near me, and that the multitude of sad groups in it did but distract me' he switches tactics in a way that would have heartened Kames: 'I took a single captive, and having first shut him up in his dungeon, I then look'd through the twilight of his grated door to take his picture.'[29]

The authorial, editorial and reading techniques of literary sentimentalism, identified and analysed by critics in the 1750s and 1760s, spread with astonishing swiftness in the third quarter of the century. Newspaper reporting, pamphlets advocating reform and improvement such as Hanway's *Sentimental History of a Chimney-sweep*, biographies and memoirs like Goldsmith's *Life of Beau Nash* or

---

28 Hugh Blair, *Lectures on Rhetoric*, p. 411.
29 Laurence Sterne, *A Sentimental Journey and Other Writings*, ed. Ian Jack and Tim Parnell (Oxford: Oxford University Press, 2003), p. 61.

Boruwlaski's *Memoirs of the Celebrated Dwarf* – 'I not only mean to describe my size and its proportions, I would likewise follow the unfolding of my sentiments, the affections of my soul' – travel literature such as Bank's account of Cook's voyage, histories such as those of Hume and sermons of which the most popular were those of Hugh Blair, literary forgeries, advice literature, plays and periodical essays – as well as a raft of sentimental novels and verses – used the techniques of literary sentimentalism, even when they were not sentimental literature as such.[30]

Older works were re-read sentimentally. As we have seen, Smith and Blair – and later Arthur Murphy – read Tacitus, previously thought one of the toughest-minded realists, as a sentimental historian. Joseph Warton in his *Essay on the Writing and Genius of Pope* (1756) re-read Pope and his contemporaries, searching them for the 'tender and pathetic', in the process elevating the previously marginal 'Elegy on the Death of an Unfortunate Lady' and 'Eloisa and Abelard' to the greatest works in Pope's canon. Even the gospels were reinterpreted, praised for their ability to soften the heart 'into sympathy and the tenderest affections', while Christ became a man of feeling: 'the sensibility of his nature was tender and exquisite'.[31] When the young Boswell read the Bible he wept. 'This forenoon I read the history of Joseph and his brethren, which melted my heart and drew tears from my eyes. It is simply and beautifully told in the Sacred Writings.'[32] Biblical tales retold in sacred histories and storybooks for children were shaped as sentimental stories.

One effect of this sentimental view of texts and readers was to erode the distinctions between genres: their form was less important than their general capacity to move the reader. When Kames wrote about 'fiction' he did not mean the novel, but any literary representation and explicitly connected history and fable as both needing to solve the problem of 'ideal presence'. Hugh Blair called novels 'fictitious histories'. Later in the century both William Godwin and James Mackintosh emphasized the similarities between fictional genres and true story-telling. As Mackintosh put it,

> history and fiction are on a footing. Both present distress not occurring in our own experience. The effect does not at all depend on the particular or historical Truth, but on that more general and philosophical Truth of

30 Joseph Boruwlaski, *Memoirs of the Celebrated Dwarf Joseph Boruwlaski, a Polish Gentleman*, 2nd edn, trans. S. Freeman (Birmingham: J. Thompson, 1792), p. 46.
31 Hugh Blair, *Sermons, Volume the Second* (London, Edinburgh: W. Strahan, 1780), p. 122.
32 James Boswell, *Boswell's London Journal, 1762–63*, 2nd edn, ed. Frederick A. Pottle (Edinburgh: Edinburgh University Press, 2004), p. 196.

which Aristotle speaks, and which consists in conformity to human nature. The effect of the death of Clarissa, or of Mary Stuart on the heart by no means depends on the fact that the one really died, but on the vivacity of the exhibition by the two great pathetic painters, Hume and Richardson.[33]

This emphasis on the power of literary effect rather than on the factual truth of what was represented was troubling. But it opened a space which was quickly filled by the likes of James Macpherson and Thomas Chatterton, creators of powerful moving historical and literary texts (claiming to be documents) capable of transporting their readers back to Celtic Scotland or medieval Bristol. The status of these works may have worried antiquarians and critics, but it is a sign of how prevalent sentimental reading had become, that many of their readers were indifferent to the issue. The provincial poet Anna Seward brushed aside the question of whether the poems of Ossian were written by ancient bards or Macpherson himself; she was only inter-ested in enjoying their effect: 'Never yet have I opened the Erse volumes without a poignant thrill of pensive transport. The lonely scenery of a barren and mountainous country rises before me. By turns I see the blue waves of their seas . . . I view the majestic and melancholy graces, in the persons of their warriors and mistresses, walking over the silent hills.'[34]

In creating a chain of sentimental feeling, by achieving sensibility, the sentimental text created a new set of relationships between authors, readers and texts, binding them closer together with bonds of affect. On one level it encouraged an intimacy with texts. Books became familiar close compan-ions. 'The first time I read an excellent book', wrote Oliver Goldsmith, 'it is to me just as if I have gained a new friend: when I read over a book, I have perused before, it resembles the meeting with an old one.'[35] It also encouraged a powerful identification of readers with characters, bound as they were by sympathy. Richardson complained about Clarissa of 'every one putting him and herself into the Character they read, and judging of it by their own Sensations'. And paradoxically, though the transport of the sentimental reader should have erased their consciousness of the author, it also excited the desire to establish a sympathetic relationship with the person responsible for exciting their sensibility. Both Richardson and Sterne

---

33 James Mackintosh, journal entry for August and September 1811, BL Add. MSS 132r–132v.
34 Anna Seward to Dr Gregory, 25 March 1792, in *Letters of Anna Seward written between the years 1784 and 1807*, 6 vols. (Edinburgh, 1811), vol. III, p. 128.
35 Oliver Goldsmith, *The Citizen of the World; or, letters from a Chinese philosopher*, 2 vols. (Dublin, 1762), vol. II, p. 86.

exploited this to the full. As John Mullan remarks of Richardson, 'Quite obsessively, he attempted to reconstruct in his relations with a select group of appreciative friends the bonds of delicacy and feeling which he celebrated in his fiction, and to exploit a literary notoriety for the creation of a social identity.'[36] Sterne worked assiduously at acting out his sentimental character before friends and correspondents. The private lives and feelings of authors became increasingly important to readers.

The poetics of sensibility depended upon the opening up of the private realm – interior feelings, emotional affect, intimate and familial friendship, the transactions of the home, the business of the closet, parlour, even bedroom – to public view. And it also privileged intimate and personal expression as true feeling untainted by a worldly desire for wealth or fame – hence the fiction of the editor employed by novelists like Richardson who posed as those who did not so much write as bring into the world a private, familiar correspondence. Their privileged status also explains why authors of memoirs and biographies stressed the importance of quoting diaries and private letters. Job Orton, introducing his *Memoirs of the life, character and writings of the late reverend Philip Doddridge* (1766), informed his readers: 'I have made such Extracts from his Diary and other Papers, written solely for his own Use, and his Letters to his intimate Friends in which he laid open his whole Heart, as I judged most proper to give my Readers a just Idea of his inward Sentiments, and the grand Motives, on which he acted thro' Life.' But Orton ended on a note of unease: 'I am sensible, it hath been objected, that what was principally written for a Person's own Use, ought not to be made public.'[37] Exciting a reader's sympathy by revealing a man's sentiments was a strategy of intimacy. Could they legitimately be thrust before the reading public?

Between 1750 and 1780 critics, authors and readers became fully conscious of what I have termed a new literary technology, a sentimental mechanism to establish bonds of sympathy and excite sensibility among authors and readers alike. This technology impressed contemporaries with its power – its ability to transport the reader, to transform the relations between authors, texts and readers. But like any powerful mechanism, it was also regarded with some apprehension and fear. If the physicians and critics were right, what happened when sentimental techniques were misused? How

---

36 John Mullan, *Sentiment and Sociability: The Language of Feeling in the Eighteenth Century* (Oxford: Clarendon Press, 1988), p. 4.

37 Job Orton, *Memoirs of the Life, Character and Writings of the Late Reverend Philip Doddridge* (Salop, 1766), p. vi.

could it be certain that they were used to moral ends? How could those who were most susceptible to sensibility be protected? And what happened when the intimate world the sentimental style evoked and created ended up in the public sphere? These anxieties became focused on the effects of the commercialization of literature – the growth of the literary system – and on the power of sentiment over readers, especially those who were young and female.

The literary system

It is not until the period between the 1750s and 1780s that we can first speak of a national system of literary production, one that first covered England but which soon extended to cover the whole of Britain. This development is not simply an artifact of hindsight. During the debates and legal cases which challenged and eventually overthrew the de facto perpetual copyright of London booksellers in 1774, critics of the monopoly – including Lord Kames – sketched out a literary system, 'a vast Superstructure', which they saw as flourishing because of the free national circulation of texts, ideas and sentiments.

They were able to envisage this in large part because of two connected developments: the full integration of a national postal system, thanks in large part to Ralph Allen, the friend of Henry Fielding and the putative model for Squire Allworthy, and the growth of the newspaper press not just in London but in the provinces. The reform of the postal system made it possible to distribute printed information rapidly into the provinces. This in turn led to the founding of provincial newspapers – more than fifty were operating by the 1780s. The distribution of printed news was dominated by organs owned by booksellers, printers and circulating library owners; they used the networks they set up to distribute not only news but to advertise and sell every sort of published material. New title book production, which had faltered between the 1730s and late 1750s, began to increase rapidly. Genres that depicted the quotidian, the domestic and the inner life of the human heart – memoirs, biographies, collections of familiar letters as well as novels and verse – were among the most popular sorts of literature. Much of this expansion seems to have been the result of a larger provincial readership.

The literary scene between the 1750s and 1790s came to include large numbers of provincial authors and critics. Sterne came from York, Anna Seward, Thomas Day and Erasmus Darwin from Lichfield; the most popular English poet of the 1780s, William Hayley, dismissed by Byron – 'His style in youth or age is still the same / For ever feeble, for ever tame' – and now only remembered as the patron of William Blake, lived in rural retreat outside Chichester.[38] Amateurs, women, provincials – writing verses and reading novels, contributing essays to reviews, recording their thoughts and feelings in journals with one eye to publication, and gaining literary sustenance through networks of familiar correspondence – they were able to acquire a national reputation and audience, thanks to the metropolitan literary system they often defined themselves against or affected to despise. Both authorship and readership – often embodied in one and the same person – were expanding.

The relations between newspapers and other printed genres changed in other ways. A loophole in the 1757 duties on newspapers made it more economical to increase the size of each issue. Papers suddenly had more columns to fill. They responded not by increasing the quantity of news but by filling their pages with letters (some written by readers, others by hacks and staff) not just on politics but on literary, moral, philosophical and sentimental subjects, and by publishing essays and commentary of the sort which had earlier been found only in the periodical papers. Thus Edinburgh's *Caledonian Mercury* published essays, extracts of works on history and political economy, verses and sermons. The *Mercury* was, of course, the premier paper of the Scottish Enlightenment, but its general contents did not differ much from most of the London and some of the provincial papers. It did not, however, offer its readers a diet of gossip and scandal that was to become a staple of the metropolitan press.

At the same time the 1760s and 1770s saw the proliferation of new periodicals and magazines, some political, others sentimental or satirical but most emanating from a group of booksellers and printers (some newspaper proprietors) who, for political reasons, had set out to link their scandalous private lives with the public depravity of government officials and courtly aristocrats. Deriding 'the doctrine, that a man may be possessed of public virtue, who is destitute of that quality in private life', booksellers and printers like George Kearsley and John Wheble made the personal political.[39] The exposure of private life, especially in high places, was justified as being in the public interest. Adultery Trials and scandalous true-life

---

38 Lord Byron, 'English Bards and Scotch Reviewers' (1809), in *Byron: Poetical Works*, ed. Frederick Page (Oxford, 1970).

39 *Caledonian Mercury* (13 December 1769).

stories thinly veiled as fictions revealed the private pecadillos of major public figures. Periodicals like the *Town and Country Magazine* (1769–96), *The Sentimental Magazine* (1773–7) and *The Lady's Magazine* (1770–1838), though not overtly political, took up this material, directed it at sentimental and female readers, mixing gossip and scandal, sentimental story-telling (much of it written by readers) and didactic essays. Together with the novel, these magazines were probably the chief means by which sentimental reading was encouraged.

A mixture of zealous politics, the promotion of scandal, gossip and sensationalism, and a hard-hearted commercialism fuelled the expansion of publishing. Nowhere was this more apparent than in the production and consumption of the novel. Novel publication was dominated by a small number of large well-run firms which combined the commissioning and sale of novels with the business of a circulating library. Their distribution networks relied on the provincial posts and newspapers; their publicity, circulated by the same means, often encouraged controversy and scandal to boost sales. John and Francis Noble dominated novel publishing in the 1760s and 1770; by the 1780s they had been outstripped by Thomas Hookham, the Robinsons and William Lane of the Minerva Press. (Lane published one third of all novel titles in the 1790s; six of the 'horrid novels' praised by the vapid Isabella Thorpe in Austen's *Northanger Abbey* came from Lane's presses.) After 1774, when perpetual copyright collapsed, novels were reprinted and extracted in profusion. In 1779 James Harrison began the weekly and highly successful *Novelists Magazine*, followed two years later by the *New Novelists Magazine*. Fiction was in the hands of what some critics called 'novel manufacturers'.

The expansion of the literary system was marked by two contradictory trends. On the one hand it involved extensive commercialization and fragmentation, an increased commodification of writing; on the other it saw the beginnings of the consolidation of a literary canon, policed in several different ways by critics and commentators. The debate about sensibility lies at the heart of the tension between these two developments. The end of perpetual copyright meant that any publisher could put together a volume of literary bits and pieces. Hannah More complained, 'the swarms of *Abridgements, Beauties*, and *Compendiums* . . . This extract reading . . . illustrates the character of the age in which we live.'[40] *The Beauties of Sterne*, first

---

40 Hannah More, *Strictures on the Modern System of Female Education. With a view of the principles and conduct prevalent among women of rank and fortune*, 2 vols. (London: T. Cadell, 1799), vol. I, pp. 173–5.

published in 1782, offered the reader his most pathetic episodes 'Selected for the Heart of Sensibility'. Judicious editing excised most of Sterne's irony, making his work an unproblematic example of unalloyed sensibility rather than a complex and witty reflection on its strategies. Such examples seemed to confirm that commercial packaging made for bland – what most critics described as 'insipid' – literature.

On the other hand – and not far removed from fragmentation – there was critical consolidation: the selection and putting together of groups of texts which claimed to represent British literature. John Bell's *British Theatre* and *British Poets* were the best known of many of these projects which included John Cooke's series of classic novels and poets which were to feed the literary appetite of Leigh Hunt and Hazlitt. Though fuelled by commerce, many of the attempts at canon formation also purported to be attempts at literary regulation. Clara Reeve's *The Progress of Romance*, usually described as the first history of the novel, was primarily concerned to identify a list of properly moral fictions that could be read by the young reader. She even proposed censoring Rousseau's *Nouvelle Eloise*, producing an abridgement in which all sexual innuendo would be removed. Similarly *The Beauties of the English Drama*, published in four volumes in 1774 'endeavoured to avoid the introduction of any subjects that were either of too great an extent, or that tended to obscenity, immorality, or vice; preferring such as were concise, that enforce virtue, liberty, morality and patriotism, and that decry vice in all its various forms'.[41]

The coincidental expansion of the literary system and the recognition that sentimental poetics were an exceptional literary tool, especially capable of shaping those more prone to the potentially diseased excesses of sensibility, provoked a debate which began in earnest in the 1770s but which continued into the nineteenth century. By the 1770s, and not least because of the extraordinary popularity of Sterne's *A Sentimental Journey*, sentimental writing had become both fashionable and highly commercialized. The domain of sensibility in literature – domestic, feminine, playful – may have been, as John Mullan emphasizes, 'constituted, in various ways, out of an opposition to a "world" of masculine desire, commercial endeavour, and material ambition',[42] but it had become both modish and commodified. When sensibility became a part of fashion it was appropriated by the very thing it was supposed to stand against; when it was commodified its moral

---

41 *The Beauties of the English Drama, digested alphabetically according to the date of their performances*, 4 vols. (London, 1777), vol. I, 'Preface'.
42 Mullan, *Sentiment and Sociability*, p. 213.

purpose was subordinated to profit. Anxieties about sentimentalism had been present from its inception but grew in intensity and changed in character after the 1760s, not least because they were expressed not only by those who had been troubled all along by a poetics of feeling but also by those who embraced sensibility itself.

Sensibility's appropriation as a fashionable indulgence, a product of what Trotter called 'wealth, luxury, indolence and intemperance', made it appear an artificial, transitory artifact, a superficial and false want (rather than a deeply felt human need), a modish sentiment whose moral status was unclear. And its commodification – epitomized in the circulating library novel, 'those mushroom romances', as the *Monthly Review* put it, 'which our expert novel Spinners will manufacture in a week' – rendered feeling an object and end for its own sake rather than a means to moral sympathy.[43] The critics of the 1750s and 1760s had laid bare the mechanics of sentimental literature; Sterne's playful brilliance had made these even more apparent. Now the production of transport appeared to have become more important than its moral destination.

The anxieties these developments provoked are to be seen repeatedly in the discussions of sensibility in these decades: the fear that enacting sensibility is an empty performance; the anxiety that false tears can hide an 'unfeeling heart'; the discussion in the Edinburgh press of the 1770s about the spread of 'false refinement'; the sentimentalization of the trivial object criticized in essays such as that on 'lady Love Puppy', and the growing fear that fine feeling would not, as was often assumed, produce moral action.

To a remarkable degree these worries focused on the novel and the youthful female reader. In the 1770s the reviewers in *The Monthly Review* and *The Critical Review* mapped out a critical history of the novel that was to survive into the twentieth century. Novels had become 'manufactures', either marked by a common insipidity – 'every track has become beaten', most contain 'the usual distressful incidents' – or by a contrived improbability: 'the virtuous characters are elevated to a degree of perfection, and the vicious sunk to a depth of villainy, scarcely to be supposed: incidents are related too extraordinary to be credited; and events are brought about, which, though they surprise by their novelty, evidently appear to be the creation of fancy'.[44] As the *Critical Review*, discussing Roger's *The History of Miss Temple* (1777), complained,

43 *Monthly Review* 42:72 (June 1770).
44 *Monthly Review* 55:157 (August 1776).

The abuse of novel writing is so great, that it has almost brought that species of entertainment into discredit. Meager stories, flatly told, and drawled through many tedious volumes with no other view than a little dirty emolument, have overwhelmed us like a flood; and the names of Richardson, Fielding and Smollett have often been cruelly tortured by their imitators.[45]

Lack of literary skill – a frequent complaint – was attributed either to the conveyor-belt-like manufacture of the product and/or the lack of education of the author. Commerce and the pursuit of profit destroyed sensibility.

Even more pernicious were those novels that failed to harness sympathy and right moral conduct. When an English translation of *Les Liaisons dangereuses* by Laclos, *Dangerous Connections*, was published in 1784, it was condemned as 'an improper story, or the insinuations of a depraved heart'.[46] 'The pretence of *"instruction"*', wrote Samuel Badcock, 'is an insult on the understanding of the public, as the work itself is a daring outrage on every law of virtue and decorum.'[47] Other novels were condemned as 'in the highest degree, disgusting'; others were given a health warning: 'we are firmly convinced of the bad tendency of putting such decorated pictures of vice into the hands of young persons'.[48] In novels, according to Ralph Griffith, the editor of the *Monthly Review*, 'the moral is the main object and end of the piece'.[49] Works that failed to fulfil this obligation or, even worse, subverted it, should be condemned to literary oblivion.

Such critiques were not attacks on sensibility but signs that, thanks to its enemies, pecuniary greed and sexual desire, it had fallen from grace. Indeed novels that were praised, were almost invariably lauded for their sentimental power. 'Our sensibility', wrote the *Critical Review* of *The School for Husbands, Written by a Lady* (1774) 'has been greatly affected by the perusal of this performance, which is calculated to promote the interests of virtue.'[50] Similarly praised were Jane Warton's 'chasteness and delicacy of imagination, as well as pathetic and moral sentiment', while Madame de Genlis' *Tales of the Castle*, translated by Thomas Holcroft, must, wrote Enfield, 'captivate every heart, whose virtuous sensibility has not been dampened by a fastidious philosophy, or debased by criminal passions'.[51] Much of the

---

45 *Critical Review* 43:473 (June 1777).
46 *Critical Review* 57:473–4 (June 1784).
47 *Monthly Review* 71:149 (August 1784).
48 *Critical Review* 31:315 (April 1771).
49 *Monthly Review* 50:176–82 (March 1774).
50 *Critical Review* 37:317–18 (April 1774).
51 *Critical Review* 56:476 (December 1783); *Monthly Review* 73:92–6 (July 1785).

debate about sensibility was therefore prompted by a regretful sense that it had become debased and corrupted.

Readers were as much an object of criticism as authors and publishers. Most critics, following Dr Johnson in his essay on the novel in *The Rambler* (31 March 1750), characterized novel readers as 'the young, the ignorant and the idle', and just as many depicted the typical novel reader as young and female. (This despite the fact that surviving evidence on circulating library borrowing and on novel authorship puts male readers and writers in the majority, and that diaries and journals reveal men as eager consumers of fiction.) Such fears were based on the assumption, well put by Anna Seward, that 'it cannot be doubted that the understanding, and virtue, the safety, and happiness, of those branches of Society which are raised above the necessity of mechanic toil, depend much upon the early impressions they receive from books which captivate the understanding, and interest the heart'.[52] Mature men, it was assumed, could resist the worst excesses of sensibility provoked by literature, and see through the guile of authors using sentiment to wicked ends. But 'young persons whose passions are more mature than their powers of reflection, and whose dispositions are pliable to the most alluring bias', and young women easily swayed by tales of romance, could be misled into error and wickedness.[53] The strength of sentimental story-telling was premised on the readers' sensibility which, though a sign of potential virtue, was also one of weakness. The vulnerability of fictional characters endowed with sensibility was mirrored in conceptions of the reader. Just as many fictional plots were narratives of the exposure of domestic and familial innocence to external evil forces (notably sexual and financial predators), so the novel, leaving the circulating library and ending up in the closet or parlour, could prey on innocent readers. Like Lovelace's rape of Clarissa, the novel could, said Johnson, possess the reader 'by a kind of violence'. So Thomas Trotter, when discussing attempted suicides by fallen women, writes 'Thus the dose of opium concludes what was begun in the circulating library.'[54] It is no wonder that sentimental novels themselves feature as vehicles of seduction in some fictions.

---

52 Anna Seward, 'On the Clarissa of Richardson, and Fielding's Tom Jones', in *Variety: a Collection of Essays. Written in the year 1787*, ed. Humphry Repton (London: T. Cadell, 1788), pp. 213–21: 213.
53 *Critical Review* 31:315 (April 1771).
54 *Nervous Temperament*, vol. III, p. 607.

But fear for the (youthful and female) reader was as much fear of a certain sort of reading. In the 1770s and 1780s critics repeatedly worried that a virtuous book with evil characters or scenes of depravity would be misread. Writing of *The Wedding Ring*, a three-volume novel published by the Nobles in 1779, William Enfield wrote, 'The bad effect of the exhibition of such characters [as the abandoned libertine], is by no means counter-balanced by the good impression that may arise from the execution of poetic justice in the catastrophe of the tale, in which the contemptible hero is punished, and the innocent object of his machinations escapes into the arms of a virtuous lover.'[55] Similar criticisms were made of Richardson. Vicesimus Knox conceded that 'Richardson's Novels were written with the purest intent' but feared that 'youthful' readers would concentrate on the 'lively description of love'.[56] James Beattie condemned Lovelace as an altogether too attractive character; and Richard Cumberland, though concurring that Richardson's intentions were virtuous, regarded 'the novel of *Clarissa* as one of the books which a prudent parent will put under interdiction'.[57] There seems to have been a general recognition in these years that authors, though powerful, could not determine how their texts were read. The reader's response, explored earlier by the likes of Kames, became a pressing issue, and the last quarter of the century saw a plethora of advice books, essays and reading manuals which prescribed not only the content but the manner of reading, seeking to contain sentimental poetics within the bounds of a limited sensibility.

Thus, even before the French Revolution politicized the debate about sensibility and inflamed its harshest critics, there was a strong feeling that it had become both corrupted by fashion and commerce – and therefore diminished – and yet, paradoxically, that sentimentalism had proved excessively powerful, producing a surplus of sensibility. The effect of the debates both before and during the French Revolution was to bring into sharp relief questions that the success of sentimental poetics engendered, but which sensibility, at least in its commercial forms, did not answer. If the power and sensibility of authors – their capacity, if you like, to be legislators – was made abundantly clear, how were they to escape the insipidity or overwrought forms of the three-volume novel and the verses of the Della Cruscans? How could 'everyday life' and everyday language make

55 *Monthly Review* 60:324 (April 1779).
56 Vicesimus Knox, *Essays Moral and Literary*, 2 vols. (London, 1779), vol. II, p. 187.
57 Richard Cumberland, *The Observer: being a collection of moral, literary and familiar essays*, 4 vols. (London, 1787), vol. II, p. 156.

their proper appearance? How could the relations between authors and a new body of readers be better fashioned? And how was the author and critic to position him (or less frequently) herself in relation to the metropolitan literary system? These were the issues that the contradictory inheritance of sensibility – its weaknesses and strengths – bequeathed to the Romantics.

Antiquarianism, balladry and the rehabilitation of romance

SUSAN MANNING

Antiquarianism

In 1699, *A New Dictionary of the Terms Ancient and Modern of the Canting Crew* defined an antiquary as a 'curious Critick in old Coins, Stones and Inscriptions, in Worm-eaten Records and ancient Manuscripts; also one that affects and blindly doats, on Relicks, Ruins, old Customs, Phrases and Fashions'.[1] Notwithstanding the widening range of antiquarian activities and their increasing cultural authority, it was a reputation hard to shake off; ridicule is in the air almost as often as the subject is mentioned – and it is ubiquitous – throughout eighteenth-century writing. Thomas Love Peacock drew on a fully-fledged anti-antiquarian discourse when he created the figures of Reverend Dr Folliott, Mr Chainmail, the roaring Welsh bard Seithenyn and Mr Derrydown.[2] It is not immediately obvious what, at the height of the Romantic era, made such figures worth the repeated flourish of a satirist's pen. But the significance of antiquarian activities reaches right into the quiddity of Romantic writing. Indeed, it has been suggested that 'English literature', understood in its broadest sense, 'constitutes itself in the late eighteenth and early nineteenth centuries through the systematic imitation, appropriation and political neutralization of antiquarian and nationalist literary developments in Scotland, Ireland and Wales'.[3] This is a claim that requires a great deal of unpacking.

Antiquarian researches were certainly politically charged, though their implications often remained unarticulated beneath a wealth of accumulated

---

1 *A New Dictionary of the Terms Ancient and Modern of the Canting Crew, in its several Tribes, of Gypsies, Beggers, Thieves, Cheats, &c. with An Addition of some Proverbs, Phrases, Figurative Speeches, &c.* By B. E. Gent. (London: Hawes, 1699), n.p.

2 In *Crotchet Castle* (1831), *The Misfortunes of Elphin* (1829) and *Melincourt* (1817); *The Novels of Thomas Love Peacock*, ed. David Garnett (London: Rupert Hart-Davis, 1948).

3 Katie Trumpener, *Bardic Nationalism: The Romantic Novel and the British Empire* (Princeton, NJ: Princeton University Press, 1997), p. xi.

data. The patriotism impelling James Thomson was broadly manifest, however, when his 'Rule, Britannia' appeared in a celebratory masque of a heroic national past, *King Alfred* (1740). Thomson's 'Spring' in *The Seasons* (1728) naturalized ancient British ruins in a peaceful pastoral landscape of the present: 'sportive lambs' 'now . . . sprightly race' over decayed, ruinous remains of 'ancient barbarous times' without any interest being indicated about what processes (other than the imaginative synthesis of the Spenserian shepherd / poet) might connect them.[4] The bleeding world of 'disunited Britain' is recovered as the playground of a new British harmony created by political union between Scotland and England in 1707. Following the enthusiastic researches of William Stukeley (1687–1765), secretary and co-founder of the Society of Antiquaries, the Druids, too, were invoked by Thomson and his later contemporaries William Collins and Thomas Gray, as ancient upholders of British liberty against Imperial Rome. Through the century the evidence of antiquity would be deployed as a calming measure in response to external threat and to anti-Unionist sentiment from within Britain; the Scottish jurist, agriculturalist, philosopher and essayist Henry Home, Lord Kames (1696–1782) composed his *Essays on Antiquities* in the shadow of 'our late Troubles': the 1745 Jacobite rising against the Hanoverian monarchy. The author hoped 'to raise a Spirit among his Countrymen, of searching into their Antiquities', in the belief that 'nothing will more contribute . . . to eradicate a Set of Opinions, which, by Intervals, have disquieted this Island for a Century and an Half'.[5]

Explicit political tractability apart, amateur pursuit of antiquarian interests performed a number of socially cohesive functions. Though predominantly a pastime for the gentry (country squires, parish ministers and those of independent means were amongst the most notable collectors), a shared passion for collection and classification brought men of widely divergent social status and political sympathies into friendly – and sometimes rivalrous – correspondence: the Earl of Buchan, the Bishop of Dromore and the wealthy beneficiary of commerce Richard Gough found themselves on common ground with, and often indebted for information to, those of humbler birth like Joseph Ritson, David Herd and John Nichols. Neither academic nor metropolitan in origin, antiquarian activities were characteristically locale- and region-based: Thomas Percy (later Bishop of

---

4 *The Seasons and the Castle of Indolence*, ed. James Sambrook (Oxford: Clarendon Press, 1972), lines 836–44 (pp. 25–6).

5 Henry Home, Lord Kames, *Essays Upon several Subjects Concerning British Antiquities* (Edinburgh: A. Kincaid, 1747), n.p.

Dromore) was a Northamptonshire vicar when he published *Reliques of Ancient English Poetry* in 1765, Herd was born in Kincardineshire and Ritson in Stockton-on-Tees.

Mutual enthusiasms encouraged collaboration: collectors built up pictures of local history and topography, collected and translated ancient texts and solidified a regionally based sense of cultural continuity. In the field of Welsh literary antiquities, for example, George Ellis supported William Owen's projected translation of the Welsh epic *Mabinogion*; later the Poet Laureate Robert Southey would encourage editions of the epic, and of Malory's *Le Morte d'Arthur*; his own antiquarian long poem *Madoc* (1805) brought a uniquely Welsh past to national prominence. Antiquarianism accumulated a form of national history based in particularities rather than theories, in artifacts as 'collectables' rather than decipherable evidence; it recovered the kind of past in which communities and individuals might possess a direct stake. Local societies of antiquaries established 'County Histories'; the first historical geographies were undertaken, and chorographic inquiries such as Sir John Sinclair's *Statistical Account of Scotland* (1791 et seq.) produced systematic accounts of landmarks, customs and local conditions. Topography and ethnography awakened tourism, not least as an indirect result of the extensive travels undertaken by many antiquaries in pursuit of their material. Accounts such as the English antiquary and naturalist Thomas Pennant's *A Tour in Scotland* (1769) prompted subsequent travellers to substitute collection of 'sights' for acquisition of objects.

If antiquarian research might uphold and quicken British patriotism, antiquaries (particularly those from the peripheries) were well aware that there was no *necessary* connection between their activities and Unionism: as William Smellie put it, 'till we were happily united to England, not in government only, but in loyalty and affection to a common Sovereign, it was not, perhaps, altogether consistent with political wisdom, to call the attention of the Scots to the antient honours and constitution of their independent monarchy'.[6] There were many ways in which accumulating the objects of material culture might act as occluded expression of resistance to the political *status quo*. The valency of antiquarian endeavours was rarely fixed or clear: Thomson or Kames might claim their findings for protestant, patriotic Hanoverian 'Britishness'; researches into Druidic culture also served to evoke a genealogy of nation at odds with eighteenth-century

---

6 William Smellie, *Account of the Institution and Progress of the Society of Antiquaries of Scotland* (Edinburgh: William Creech; London: Thomas Cadell, 1782), p. 2.

metropolitan versions of Britishness. 'Antiquities' readily acquired the taint of Jacobitism or the 'secret allurement' of Catholicism experienced by Gray when he encountered the relics of the oratory of Mary Queen of Scots in Hardwick Hall.[7] The collection of artifacts, a progressive enterprise that supported the empirical principles of Enlightenment and by increasing local knowledge of antiquities, folk customs and material phenomena contributed to the mapping of Britain's regions and districts, also awakened interest in popular culture, and articulated – through sympathetic recovery of a more 'credulous' past – aspects of experience not favoured by Enlightened discourse.

It was a pursuit that certainly seemed to attract unmalleable and *recherché* characters: fanaticism, eccentricity and bitter territoriality made antiquarians a gift to caricature and satire, weapons frequently employed to serve antagonisms founded in class and denominational differences. Ritson embarked on a personal vendetta against his fellow ballad-collectors Bishop Percy and John Pinkerton, questioning the former's editorial skills and triumphantly exposing the 'ignorance', 'blunders' and 'criminal parts' of the latter's 'literary and moral character'.[8] William Combe's *Dr Syntax* (1812) and *Dr Prosody* (1821) continued a tradition of ridicule that stretched back well into the fifteenth century. Francis Grose (?1731–1791), known as 'the antiquarian Falstaff', edited *The Antiquarian Repertory: a miscellany, intended to preserve and illustrate several valuable remains of old times. Adorned with elegant sculptures* (1775 et seq.). A collector of customs, idioms and popular manners, Grose had a particular interest in spoken language and is now regarded as one of the founders of studies in popular culture and ethnography. His indefatigable endeavours produced *A Classical Dictionary of the Vulgar Tongue* (1785); an antiquarian lexicography of local dialect words with etymologies and variants that stimulated ethnographic and linguistic interest in Britain's regions, the *Provincial Dictionary* (1787); a material record of *The Antiquities of England and Wales* (6 vols., 1773–87); *The Antiquities of Ireland* (2 vols., 1791–5); and *The Antiquities of Scotland* (1789 and 1791). Grose prompted Robert Burns not only to affectionate caricature, but to the composition of his greatest poem: when collecting for his *Scottish Antiquities*, Grose 'applied to Mr. Burns . . . to write him an account of the Witches Meetings at Aloway Church near Ayr'; the result was 'Tam O'Shanter', a

---

7 Jayne Elizabeth Lewis, *Mary Queen of Scots: Romance and Nation* (London and New York: Routledge, 1998), p. III.

8 Joseph Ritson to George Paton, 21 July 1795; *The Letters of Joseph Ritson, Esq.*, 2 vols., ed. Sir Harris Nicolas (London: William Pickering, 1833), vol. II, p. 93.

poem that reaches from 'illustration' through reconstruction of locale and community to an uncanny realm of shifting emotional and expressive registers, memories and nightmares.[9] In an idiomatic range that encompasses vernacular narrative and enlightened commentary, 'Tam O'Shanter' compounds tradition from the remaindered bits and pieces of the past.

The ridicule which surrounded antiquaries issued as much from cultural anxiety about the nature, epistemological status and purpose of their activities as from any inherent risibility in the practitioners. It is worth looking more closely into what it was that antiquaries did that made their activities suspect, and the objects of their research so productive of ambiguity. In the seventeenth century, and earlier, 'antiquity' (the material evidence of the past) and history (philosophy taught through example, as Philip Sidney had put it) inhabited different and antagonistic conceptual spaces. They shared, however, an essentially a-chronological attitude to the past. In the course of the eighteenth century, in a climate of increasing speculation about societal development, their spheres came closer together. As collectors of the fragmentary remains of the past antiquaries inhabited the boundary between two prevailing, and complementary, models of Enlightenment historiography: the empirical, analytic 'Newtonian' tradition which accumulated evidence and inferred social organization from it, and the conjectural modes of Scottish Enlightenment philosophical or 'stadialist' history which posited the universal progress of all societies through a uniform set of 'stages' from primitive hunter-gatherers, through a pastoral existence to civil society and (ultimately) decadence and disintegration. Continental interest in 'natural' and 'primitive' states, most tendentiously explored by Jean-Jacques Rousseau, reinforced these stadialist views. Each of these models (and sometimes both simultaneously) had an impact not only on the traditional activities of material antiquarianism, but also on its literary manifestation in ballad collection and the eighteenth-century retrieval of 'romance' forms from obscurity and degradation. But though valuable for its provision of 'raw materials' for higher forms of history, antiquarianism's uncertain conceptual placing and primary rationale in the accumulation of material without subordination to system or theory rendered its implications ideologically promiscuous and therefore politically suspect.

---

9 'On the Late Captain Grose's Peregrinations thro' Scotland, collecting the Antiquities of that Kingdom', *The Poems and Songs of Robert Burns*, ed. James Kinsley, 3 vols. (Oxford: Oxford University Press, 1968), vol. I, p. 494.

The fragmented relics partially recuperated in assemblages of antiquities offered access to a kind of unsyntaxed past, whose unarticulated elements stimulated imaginative contemplation released from the pressures of context and the controls of social hierarchy. They described the thickness, the texture of the past, rather than its meaning. Investing meaning in the process of acquisition rather than in the settled interpretation of the accumulated outcome, the obsessive accumulations of antiquaries seemed to testify to the essentially insufficient nature of all inquiry. Objects, often in decayed or ruinous form, overwhelmed the interpretative offices of the human mind. A true antiquary's collection, whatever its object, was never, could never be, complete: a set of practices characterized by repeated activity, by accretion rather than interpretation, it shunned the *measure*, the discrimination and the habit of conceptualization prized by civil society. The presence, indeed the prevalence, of a taste for antiquarian collections amongst booksellers, clergymen, squires and earls, suggested that the middle and upper echelons of society might be pervaded by an unarticulated discontent (across denominational, political and educational boundaries) with the adequacy of the cultural system to which they subscribed and contributed. The prized acquisitions of the antiquarian collections embodied longing for possession of the past, a kind of commodification of history which moved into the public domain as private 'cabinets of curiosities' were reflected in the eclectic cultural repositories of the new national museums.[10]

Antiquarianism, then, supplied at once object-cluttered commentary on, and resistance to, the great Enlightenment historiographic visions of progressive societal development. David Hume's *History of Great Britain* (1754–62) was deeply antipathetic to the unphilosophical aspect of 'domestic antiquities', although both his enterprise and that of his compatriot William Robertson shared with the antiquarians at least the aim of illustrating the manners and customs of the past. Where the antiquarian's world was a static and fragmented one, that of the philosophical historians was developmental and illustrative of progressive cultural advancement. The complex historiographic and emotional valencies of antiquarianism embraced

10 Walter Benjamin, *Illuminations* (1931; rpt London: Fontana, 1973), p. 60; see also Werner Muensterberger, *Collecting: An Unruly Passion: Psychological Perspectives* (Princeton, NJ: Princeton University Press, 1994), and Susan Stewart, *On Longing: Narratives of the Miniature, the Gigantic, the Souvenir, the Collection* (1993; rpt Durham, NC: Duke University Press, 1999). The British Museum originated in 1753 when the private collections of Sir Hans Sloane were acquired by the government.

the raw material of meaning, and its waste or detritus. So the antiquary's objects, the real matter of popular or of past culture, were simultaneously the building blocks of reconstruction and melancholy survivals, imbued with loss, fragmentariness and the elusive possibility of integrity. Their disturbingly paradoxical 'presence' signified absence. In this sense too, they offered Enlightenment in a minor key, audibly dragging its feet against the 'MARCH OF MIND'.[11] Anxieties about the historical status and cultural authority of antiquarian activities frequently expressed itself, too, in terms of gender, either in relation to the antiquary or the 'manliness' of his activity. Reconstruction of the past based on its fragmented material remains was even imagined as the kind of reanimation of dead body-parts that would later form the raw matter of Dr Frankenstein's unhallowed experiments in Mary Shelley's novel: Scott's fictional antiquarian Rev. Dr Jonas Dryasdust FAS declared the romancing activities of his creator akin to those of 'Lucan's witch, at liberty to walk over the recent field of battle, and to select for the subject of resuscitation by his sorceries, a body whose limbs had recently quivered with existence, and whose throat had but just uttered the last note of agony'.[12] To the 'true' antiquarian (Dryasdust himself), the past was not only dead but buried; one of the satisfactions of retrieval was the immutability of the exhumed fragments, their resistance to connecting narratives. Searching for remnants of the past sometimes quite literally meant digging downwards; many antiquarians were also (in modern terminology) archaeologists. Temporal and vertical co-ordinates were readily superimposed and helped to generate the layered discourse of depth psychology developed in the Edinburgh professor Thomas Brown's *Lectures on the Philosophy of the Human Mind* (1810). A century later, Sigmund Freud's disquisition on '*the psychological differences between the conscious and the unconscious*' would turn on 'the fact' that 'everything conscious was subject to a process of wearing-away, while what was unconscious was relatively unchangeable'.[13] Illustrating his comments 'by pointing to the antiques standing about in [his] room', Freud described them as 'only objects found in a tomb, and their burial had been their preservation; the destruction of Pompeii was only beginning now that it had been dug up'. Emotionally, the

11 Peacock, *Crotchet Castle*, p. 655.
12 'Dedicatory Epistle', *Ivanhoe* (1820), ed. Graham Tulloch (Edinburgh: Edinburgh University Press, 1998), p. 7.
13 'Notes Upon a Case of Obsessional Neurosis (the "Rat Man"), 1909', in Sigmund Freud, *Case Histories*, vol. II, ed. Angela Richards (Harmondsworth: Penguin Books, 1979), p. 57. (Italics in the original.)

exhumed remnants of the past articulated a sense of lost integrity, disrupted cultural and personal continuity.

The relationship between accumulation of evidence and imaginative interpretation were not only issues for historiography, philosophy, topography and psychology; they also structured a running debate about the relationship between 'taste' and 'scholarship' in aesthetics. Warton's encyclopaedic *History of English Poetry* 1100–1603 (1774–81), began to formulate a national canon and may be considered as part of a cultural project of 'nation-building'. In another respect, though, it was read by contemporaries less as a history than as a quarry for the imagination – in Scott's words 'an immense commonplace-book of *memoirs to serve for such an history*. No antiquary can open it, without drawing information from a mine which, though dark, is inexhaustible in its treasures.'[14] Warton was 'not a mere collector of dry and minute facts which the general historian passes over with disdain'; he carried 'the torch of genius, to illustrate the ruins'.[15] Literary antiquaries tended to be described as 'imaginative' in proportion as their collections betrayed the impress of their own personalities and enthusiasms in interpreting their fragmentary finds. In the conceptually and emotionally compounded discourse of antiquarianism the backward-facing nostalgic mood is complicated always by the reconstructive potential of retrieval and collection.

Ballad collection

Ballad collectors were the antiquaries of poetic culture, their 'artifacts' were recovered remnants of ancient poetry, valued initially for their glimpses into 'the arts, usages and modes of living, of our forefathers, both in war and in peace', and increasingly for their poetic qualities.[16] Joseph Addison's much-quoted praise of 'Chevy Chase' as 'full of the majestick Simplicity which we admire in the greatest of the ancient Poets' ratified the cultural value of ballad collection.[17]

---

14 'On Ellis's Specimens of the Early English Poets' (*Edinburgh Review*, April 1804), p. 153; *The Miscellaneous Prose Works of Sir Walter Scott*, 28 vols. (Edinburgh: Robert Cadell, 1834–6), vol. XVII, p. 4. (Scott's italics.)

15 'Memoir of Horace Walpole', *Prose Works*, vol. III, p. 306.

16 Edward King, President of the Society of Antiquaries, quoted by Sweet, 'A Social Tie', unpublished paper presented to the University of Edinburgh History seminar, January 2001, p. 3.

17 *The Spectator* 74 (25 May 1711), in *The Spectator*, ed. and intro. Donald F. Bond, vol. I, p. 316.

Percy's *Reliques* was neither the first nor by any means the only Enlightenment anthology of early British balladry: following the Union with England in 1707, poetic antiquaries strove to preserve and revive Scottish national feeling in James Watson's *Choice Collection of Comic and Serious Scots Poems* (1706–11) and Allan Ramsay's *The Ever Green* (1724) and *The Tea-Table Miscellany* (1724–37).

But the *Reliques* was the fullest and also the most carefully presented and theorized collection of the mid-century. Eliding under the designation 'English' the heterogeneous provenance of his collection (many contributions arrived from Scottish correspondents), Percy contributed to the synthesis of a 'national history' from the literary remains of regional enmities. His extensive prefatory material, and the controversial mythologizing of the essays 'On the Ancient Minstrels' and 'On the Ancient Metrical Romances' added to later editions, offered a primer of reading practices to assure their enthusiastic reception by a polite audience (a tactic Wordsworth would later adopt for the second edition of *Lyrical Ballads* and in *Poems* (1815)). Percy defended the simplicity of his ballads against the sensibility of 'a polished age'; their matter was far from 'polite', and he employed a range of familiarizing strategies to introduce tales of bloody warfare, violent revenge and obscenity. The Preface positioned the Editor carefully as antiquary, as man of taste and as necessary adjunct to the 'defective or corrupted' remains of 'the Bard'.

The *Reliques of Ancient Poetry*, as their title suggests, imply veneration for these quasi-sacral remnants; an attitude apparently not incompatible with substantial 'making good' which allowed their classical standing to re-emerge: 'These mutilated antiques thus perfected and restored by Dr. Percy', wrote the Edinburgh printer Wotherspoon to George Paton, 'will give us a pleasure resembling that which we should feel from beholding the injuries of time on a statue of Phidias or Polycetus repaired by the hand of Buonaruoti'.[18] A stake in 'British' tradition was signalled by positioning 'The Ancient Ballad of Chevy Chase', prefaced by Philip Sidney's praise (also quoted by Addison), at the head of the *Reliques*. The ballads themselves were presented in a sequence designed to illustrate society's advancement towards refinement: 'cruder' examples could thus be 'explained' as belonging to more primitive times. They embodied a paradoxical primitivism: purer, more 'natural' in expression, it required also the progress to civility to 'recover' its true value. When Ritson's combative *Ancient Metrical*

---

18 British Library Add. MS 32,332 f. 77; letter of 29 August 1774.

Romances (1802) printed transcripts of material from Percy's manuscripts in parallel with the published versions, his harsh appeal to the superiority of primitive texts implied an aggressive series of binary oppositions: the 'authentic' against the fabricated, the 'raw' against the culturally cooked, 'scholarship' against 'taste', a dissenting voice against Establishment hegemony.

The ballad-collecting practices of Percy and his extensive network of correspondents carried a complex and not easily reducible emotional charge, however. Most obviously, they provided additional evidence for the aesthetic dimension of 'stadialist' theory in works like Thomas Blackwell's *Letters Concerning Mythology* (1748) and Hugh Blair's *Lectures on Rhetoric and Belles Lettres* (1783). Poetry, according to Blair, was 'child of imagination . . . frequently most glowing and animated in the first ages of society'; his lectures quoted and endorsed Addison's praise of the classical standing of ancient British ballads.[19] Scott, whose own *Minstrelsy of the Scottish Border* (1801–3; 1830) explicitly acknowledged Percy's influence, evoked a history of balladry that closely mirrored Blair's account of linguistic evolution in primitive society, to offer a Scottish dimension to the flowering of poetry in an idealized British barbarian past. Wordsworth's 'Appendix' to *Lyrical Ballads* would offer a similar stadialist rationale for the already well-tried 'experiment' of the poems *Lyrical Ballads*. Progress, in this model, was predicated upon loss and it invoked longing as a measure of resistance. The attraction of Percy's poems (as some at least of them must be styled) was not and cannot now be separated from their illusion of stark, primitive reality, their contrast with the elaborate poetic diction and literary convention of the milieu into which they emerged:

> Then Solemnlye he made a vowe,
>   Before the companìe:
> That he would neither eat nor drinke,
>   Until he did her see.
>
> O then bespake the scullion-boye,
>   With a loud voice so hye:
> If now you will your daughter see,
>   My lord, cut up that pye:
>
> Wherein her fleshe is minced small,
>   And parched with the fire;

---

19 Hugh Blair, 'A Critical Dissertation on the Poems of Ossian' (1765 edn), in *The Poems of Ossian*, ed. Howard Gaskill (Edinburgh: Edinburgh University Press, 1996), p. 346.

> All caused by her step-mothèr,
> Who did her death desire.
> ('Lady Isabella's Tragedy',
> Reliques III: 158)[20]

Their subject-matter attenuated, these ballad rhythms infuse Wordsworth's 'Lucy' poems; their diction and their voices permeate Scott's verse narratives, Coleridge's Rime of the Ancyent Marinere and the sinister complicities of Christabel and Keats's 'La Belle Dame sans Merci. A Ballad':

> O what can ail thee, knight-at-arms
> Alone and palely loitering?
> The sedge has wither'd from the lake,
> And no birds sing.

More than a coincidence of names connects it to the gruesome plot of 'Isabella, or the Pot of Basil', whose narrator, lingering over the 'wormy circumstance' of decapitation in the tomb, longs 'for the gentleness of old Romance, / The simple plaining of a minstrel's song!'[21] Its lyric counterpart, as in 'Waly, Waly, Love be Bonny' (from 'a modern copy', Percy's version), prepared the ground for national collections along similar lines, such as Charlotte Brooke's Reliques of Irish Poetry (1789) and Robert Burns's and James Johnson's Scots Musical Museum (1787–96). Percy's ballads inhabit emotional extremes, from the tender presence of 'My heart is rent sith we maun part, / My handsome Gilderoy' (Reliques I: 340), to the off-hand, off-stage brutality and appetite of

> Hee cutt the pappes beside her brest,
> And did her body spille;
> He cutt the eares beside her heade,
> And bade her love her fille.
> ('Old Robin of Portingale', Reliques III: 53)

The excessive, disjunctive moods of the ballads, like the sanctioned behavioural quirks of their collectors, expanded late Enlightenment discursive registers beyond the idioms of measure, order and continuous development.

As with more material forms of antiquarianism, balladry's unfixed historical and ontological standing and the heterogeneous principles of

---

20 Thomas Percy, Reliques of Ancient English Poetry, 3 vols. (London: J. Dodsley, 1765), vol. III, p. 158. Abbreviated references to Reliques will be given in the text hereafter.
21 John Keats, Poetical Works, ed. H. W. Garrod (Oxford: Oxford University Press, 1956; rpt 1973), pp. 350, 191.

collection facilitated covert communication of resistance to cultural cohesion. Percy's correspondent and supplier of source material David Herd (like Ritson, George Ellis, Richard Heber and Scott's fictional antiquary the Laird of Monkbarns) participated in the pervasive homosocial culture of antiquarianism. Herd was an accountant's clerk and a member of the Edinburgh club of 'Knights Companions of the Cape', whose meetings had a cast of distinctly antiquarian or romance pageantry. He accumulated the largest manuscript collection of ballads in the eighteenth century; not all of these were published in his lifetime, but they were known to Percy, to Ritson, Burns and Scott. Misogyny surfaces alongside love fairly frequently in these songs: 'Fye on ye, ill woman, the bringer o' shame, / The abuser o' love the disgrace o' my name . . .'[22] Anti-feminist sentiment characterized Ritson's collection, too, though hardly Burns's; nonetheless, Herd's 'popular songs' included several adapted or re-written by Burns, as well as a section of Robin Hood ballads and Irish songs. His manuscripts furnished an important source for synthesizing 'national recollections' in Romantic historical writing. In a different register, many Scottish productions, in particular, expressed crypto-Catholic sympathies through scholarly retrieval of Jacobite songs. Ballad collection, particularly in Scotland and Wales, allowed for the simultaneous expression of tradition-based cultural difference and a new construction of Britishness.

Less readily recuperable for the processes of nation-formation were a series of 'Nursery Songs and Popular Rhymes' and (anticipating William Blake's *Songs of Innocence and Experience*) pared-down, laconic lyrics such as 'The Nurse's Song'. Their diction stripped of literary sophistication and resistant to hermeneutic translation, recovered ballad verses were naturalized as poetic embodiments of pure presence available to an earlier state of society and subsequently lost in the process of refinement, a belief invoked in Wordsworth's Preface to the second edition of the *Lyrical Ballads* and mocked in Peacock's *Melincourt* (1817), in which Mr Derrydown, having expended 'a great quantity of midnight oil, over ponderous tomes of ancient and modern learning', 'found, or fancied he found, in the plain language of [Percy's *Reliques*], glimpses of the truth of things, which he had vainly sought in the vast volumes of philosophical disquisition'.[23]

22 'Fragment', in H. Hecht, ed. and intro., *Songs From David Herd's Manuscripts* (Edinburgh: William J. Hay, 1904), p. 108.
23 Peacock, *Melincourt*, p. 145.

Orality, print and authenticity

Translation of the oral ballads into printed collections opened chasms of classification and interpretation. Possible in theory, distinction between collection, editing, improvement, imitation (what Scott called 'the fair trade of manufacturing modern antiques') and – at the extreme – forgery, was elusive in practice.[24] 'Authenticity' became an issue when oral performance was consigned to print. Collected and printed ballads became what Jon Klancher in a different context has called 'a representation instead of a practice': marking orality on the printed page, they replaced the temporality and fluidity of performance with the static entity of 'text'.[25] Indicators of performance and change appeared in the inclusion of multiple 'versions' of the 'same' ballad, a convention that Coleridge would follow in the successive revisions of his *Ancyent Marinere* and Keats in multiple versions of the 'Belle Dame'. Scott's 'Essay on Imitations of the Ancient Ballads' prefaced to the 1829 edition of *Minstrelsy* encompassed the close alignment of the roles of editor and synthesizer; the third volume contained a number of 'Imitations' of the ancient ballad, some of Scott's own composition. In 1825 he had confessed that 'in endeavouring to make the best possible set of an ancient ballad out of several copies obtained from different quarters . . . if I improved the poetry, I spoiled the simplicity of the old song'.[26]

The question of how print might and should represent the fragmentary survival of past culture was troublesome and much-contested; theory and practice evolved from collection to collection through accusations and recriminations. Semantic and syntactic approaches to the genre (the analysis of ballads on the basis of their 'meaning', or in terms of their 'mechanisms' or structure) supplied different and sometimes antagonistic criteria of authenticity. Preference for the 'semantic' favoured interpretative reconstruction and 'completion' of fragmentary remains and corresponded to the 'conjectural' modes of historiography. 'Syntactic' or structural principles prompted collection of elements by type; their corollary was antiquarian methodology operating on paratactic accumulations that resisted

---

24 'Essay on Imitations of Ancient Ballad', *Minstrelsy of the Scottish Border* (1830), 4 vols. (Edinburgh and London: William Blackwood and Sons, 1902), vol. IV, p. 13.
25 Jon Klancher, *The Making of English Reading Audiences, 1790–1832* (Madison, WI: University of Wisconsin Press, 1987), p. 24.
26 3 May 1825, in *Letters of Sir Walter Scott*, ed. H. J. C. Grierson, 12 vols. (Edinburgh: Edinburgh University Press, 1932–7), vol. IX, p. 101.

imposition of taxonomic explanations derived from historical origins or social conditions. Furthermore, Enlightenment debate demonstrated the extent to which 'the Ballad' is not an essential but a cultural category. Controversy surrounding ballad and romance retrieval in the late Enlightenment period ventilated not only anxieties about principles of collection and interpretation and uncertain relationships between oral and print culture, but wider issues of literary ownership. Textual instability and the processes of 'fixing' it for print also generated a discourse of 'authenticity' and 'forgery' which became intrinsic to articulating 'tradition'.

The *Reliques* were essentially and insistently *literary* relics: their survival in material form was a cornerstone of Percy's enterprise. His reconstructions ensured that the ballads began and ended like 'proper' poetry; but the editorial apparatus offered the evidence of textual distress – the *need* for an editorial hand – in support of the ballads' authenticity. Miscellaneity protected the multiple and anonymous authorship of the 'originals', while uniting them in the scholarly domain. The 'Advertisement' to the fourth edition (1794) countered charges of forgery by appealing to the indisputable existence of the original manuscript. Percy's strategy set his scholarly enterprise definitively apart from James Macpherson's claim to have discovered and translated the literary remains of the poems of the third-century Celtic bard Ossian. Macpherson's *Fragments of Ancient Poetry, Collected in the Highlands of Scotland* was published as a slender volume in 1760 and (capitalizing on an unexpected celebrity which rapidly spread across Europe) succeeded by further and more substantial recovery of ancient national poetry; by 1765 the *Poems of Ossian* included two fragmentary epics, *Fingal* and *Temora*, positioned somewhere between translation, re-creation and fabrication. Macpherson stitched together fragments of oral Gaelic poetry still current with the highlanders amongst whom he had lived and now travelled again, creating the kind of Homeric and Virgilian epic cycle which stadialist history expected to find as the historical record of a 'classical' society in its early stages. His researches were sponsored by Edinburgh writers materially interested in the recovery of evidence about Britain's (and particularly Scotland's) national past that would help to supply the detail of conjectural theory; Hugh Blair composed an extended 'Critical Dissertation on the Poems of Ossian' for the edition of 1763, defending their authenticity on a mixture of Classical and primitivist justifications.

The experiential extremes inhabited by the ancient ballads are claimed for the martial universe of the recovered third-century Celtic epic, but their emotional presence is obscured and occluded by the melancholy patina of nostalgia which characterizes the omnipresent voice of the Bard Ossian:

> Wrathful the brothers frowned. Their flaming eyes in silence met. They turned away. They struck their shields. Their hands were trembling on their swords. They rushed into the strife of heroes for long-haired Srina-dona.
> Corcul-suran fell in blood. On his isle raged the strength of his father.[27]

The attenuated denotative register of this poeticized prose banishes action to an ever-mourned, never-to-be-redeemed past world, glorious exploits reduced to the dying fall of sibilant leaves, echoing hills and whispering brooks. Struggling to articulate his sense of the poems' spuriousness, Wordsworth invoked their antiquarian ethos, their retrieval of dismembered elements denied the combinatory powers of 'nature' and 'presence' and – therefore – condemned to the empty register of absence and inauthenticity: 'everything (that is not stolen) is defined, insulated, dislocated, deadened – yet nothing distinct. It will always be so when words are substituted for things.'[28] Which was precisely Macpherson's point. The world of which Ossian sang was emotionally compounded of nostalgia and desire; the Gaelic Bard ventriloquized the decapitated plight of the Jacobite Highlands in the wake of the Culloden massacre (1746) and the flight of Charles Edward, Stuart Pretender, to France. The printed embodiment of this idealized version of Britain's primitive origins has, appropriately and perhaps necessarily, neither beginning nor end. It is narrative process repeatedly testifying to its own ruination. Inditing (in the sense of setting down on the page) the oral record of cultural annihilation, Macpherson's Ossian indicted the conditions to which his translator subscribed and inaugurated the first phase of European Romanticism. This appropriation of the paradoxical space of antiquarianism was revolutionary; it conjured new expressive possibilities for both poetry and prose. The fragmentary 'translations' embrace the theory that transference from performance to text, like that between linguistic media, introduces a distance (embodied in the space of the printed page) as speaker and hearer become writer and reader, with a consequent and lamentable loss of emotional presence. Truncation and severance substitute for narrative progression as the collected fragments repeatedly re-enact the moment of loss. The oral world was

---

27 'Cath-Loda', *Poems of Ossian*, p. 315.
28 'Essay, Supplementary to Preface, Poems, 1815', in *Wordsworth's Literary Criticism*, ed. N. C. Smith (Bristol: Bristol Classical Press, 1980), p. 191.

characteristically represented as being on the point of self-destruction, passing out of being into memory and superseded by a written culture of which it was paradoxically at once the product and the victim. Surviving in mutilated form into print, the absent–present voice from the periphery assumed enormous cultural power for a civil society construing itself on the cusp of that inevitable 'Corruption incident to Polished Nations'.[29]

Samuel Johnson, the most articulate antagonist of orality, engaged himself on the side of 'civility' and of written evidence and dismissed the authenticity of the Ossianic poems unless the manuscripts from which they purported to have been translated could be produced. His belief, reported by Boswell, that 'All that is really *known* of the ancient state of Britain is contained in a few pages. We *can* know no more than what the old writers have told us',[30] implicitly denied the historical value of any evidence that did not base its authority on the survival of the past in verifiable material form, a view that was already being energetically challenged by the field-work of Grose and other antiquaries of popular culture. Topographically, the oral was construed as marginal, located at the periphery; epistemologically, it occupied an equivocal area of contingency and transience; jurisprudentially, its immaterial nature protected it from the reach of law. All of these contributed to these broken relics' cultural potential for regeneration. Orality claimed a kind of double authenticity: as performance, a direct interaction between a speaker and his audience, it possessed the authority of the speaking voice; that voice uttered from lived experience. On the page, both were lost in the distance between writer and reader; endorsement became dependent on the printed or manuscript page itself. Only when it manifested itself materially could orality's authenticity be challenged. Antiquarian activity collided with literary convention in the recovery and collection of ancient manuscripts: the possibility of fiction or forgery was by the mid-eighteenth century implicit in every apparently serious 'discovery'.

Thomas Chatterton (1752–70) produced at the age of seventeen several voluminous manuscripts purporting to be the output of Thomas Rowley, a medieval monk, which were forgeries in a technical sense evaded by Macpherson's redactions of oral reminiscence. In 1769, Chatterton sent Horace Walpole (who had recently brought out the first volumes of *Anecdotes of Painting in England* (1762)), a 'transcript' of 'The Ryse of

---

29 Adam Ferguson, *An Essay on the History of Civil Society* (1767), ed. and intro. Duncan Forbes (Edinburgh: Edinburgh University Press, 1966), pp. 248 et seq.
30 *Boswell's Life of Johnson*, ed. George Birkbeck Hill, rev. L. F. Powell, 6 vols. (Oxford: Oxford University Press, 1931; 1971), vol. III, p. 333.

Peyncteynge yn Englãde, wroten bie T. Rowlie' along with some verse purporting to come from the same hand. To Walpole an *authentic* 'Curious Manuscript' of this kind would have held the same importance as the discovery of an ancient Celtic epic for Scottish historians; initially his anti-quarian enthusiasm got the better of his judgement. Habitual scepticism prevailed, and a relationship which might have turned to patronage ended in acrimony. Chatterton had forged the currency of antiquarianism and the tools of the antiquarian, fittingly, detected the imposture: 'the pigment that had been employed to stain the parchment, in order to give it the appear-ance of antiquity, was literally speaking both visible and palpable: It came off with a moistened finger [that revealed] it to be yellow ochre.'[31]

But Walpole himself, scourge of pedantic antiquaries, had created an experimental *rifacimento* of pastness in The Castle of Otranto (1764), 'Trans-lated by William Marshal, Gent. From the Original ITALIAN OF ONUPHRIO MURALTO, Canon of the Church of St. Nicholas at OTRANTO.' The Preface announced its discovery 'in the library of an ancient catholic family in the north of England. It was printed at Naples, in the black letter, in the year 1529.'[32] The following year, Percy described his rescue of the 'very curious Old Manuscript' on which the *Reliques* were based in terms reminiscent of the opening of a novel. Henry Mackenzie invoked tensions between progress and resistance in antiquarian manuscript recoveries when he based the distinctive fragmentary form of The Man of Feeling (1771) on discarded wadding from a curate's gun, a 'bundle of little episodes, put together without art, and of no importance on the whole'.[33] The rationale for the fragment in Romantic-period writing as the material embodiment of nostalgia and lament emerged in late Enlightenment anti-quarianism; in the end, debates about forgery and authenticity, too, were merely part of the enabling ground for articulating the 'lostness' of all pasts.

Warton expressed the mixed feelings of many about Chatterton's impersonation:

Ancient remains of English poetry, unexpectedly discovered, and fortunately rescued from a long oblivion, are contemplated with a degree of fond

---

31 Robert Chambers to Thomas Percy, 7 Nov. 1789, reprinted in A. Watkins-Jones, 'Bishop Percy, Thomas Warton, and Chatterton's Rowley Poems 1773–1790 (Unpublished Letters)', *PMLA* 50(1) (1935), 777.

32 Horace Walpole, *The Castle of Otranto*, ed. W. S. Lewis (Oxford: Oxford University Press 1964; 1981), pp. xix, 3.

33 *The Works of Henry Mackenzie, Esq*, 8 vols. (1808), intro. Susan Manning (London and Bristol: Thoemmes Press, 1996), vol. I, p. 6.

enthusiasm: exclusive of any real or intrinsic excellence, they afford those pleasures, arising from the idea of antiquity, which deeply interest the imagination. With these pleasures we are unwilling to part. But there is a more solid satisfaction, resulting from the detection of artifice and imposture.[34]

The unmasking of these charming poems' inauthenticity represented the kind of necessary but grievous disillusionment later associated by Scott with his hero Waverley's 'fall' from the world of romance into that of reality.

Denied the imprimatur of authenticity, the young poet from the provinces poisoned himself in a London garret and became a Romantic icon of neglected genius, a figure of displaced poetic self-projection in Wordsworth's 'marvellous Boy', Coleridge's gay 'Minstrel', 'Fated to heave sad Disappointment's sigh' and Keats's 'Dear child of sorrow – son of misery!'[35] Keats's diction, particularly, was repeatedly drawn back to the imagistic and emotional density of Rowleian verse. The extraordinary lyric episodes of *Ælla*, a drama set in Saxon England, suggest what made Keats 'always somehow associate Chatterton with autumn':

> Whann the fayre apple, rudde as even skie,
> Do bende the tree unto the fructyle grounde;
> When joicie peres, and berries of black die,
> Doe daunce yn ayre, and call the eyne arounde;
> Thann, bee the even foule, or even fayre,
> Meethynckes mie hartys joie ys steynced wyth somme care.[36]

The Chatterton / Rowley poems' Gothic strangeness of diction and medieval trappings, their apparent emotional spontaneity and their alternation of melancholy self-regard and striking action, exploded the tensions in neo-classical tonalities into a dazzling range of alternative rhetorical registers. This poetry referred its reader to authority located not in material or conceptual verifiability but in 'poetic presence': the effervescence of voice in language. Despite Chatterton's insistent and influential medievalizing, the affective power of this diction initiated a reaction against the 'dry, sapless, mouldering and disjointed bones' of antiquity, as public interest focused more on the singer than the

---

34 Thomas Warton, *The History of English Poetry*, Section 26, p. 424.
35 W. Wordsworth, 'Resolution and Independence', in *Wordsworth's Poems of 1807* (Poems in Two Volumes), ed. Alun R. Jones (London: Macmillan, 1987), lines 43–4; S. T. Coleridge, 'Monody on the Death of Chatterton (First Version)', in *Poetical Works*, ed. E. H. Coleridge (Oxford: Oxford University Press, 1912, rpt 1988), lines 25, 40, 77; John Keats, 'To Chatterton', in *Poetical Works*, p. 375.
36 *The Letters of John Keats 1814–1821*, ed. Hyder Edward Rollins, 2 vols. (Cambridge: Cambridge University Press, 1958), vol. II, p. 167; Thomas Chatterton, *Ælla*, lines 302–7, in *Selected Poems*, ed. Grevel Lindop (Manchester: Carcanet Press, 1986), p. 50.

song.[37] Wordsworth's antipathy to Macpherson's dislocated and deadened diction did not prevent him from responding warmly to the notional figure of the bard Ossian. Relocation of cultural authority away from material towards vocative presence reflected developing discussion of the *immaterial* nature of copyright, in which the author was understood to be the creator and ultimate source of literary property.

Bards and minstrels

Ælla's minstrels were astutely placed. Four years previously Percy's Dedi-cation of the *Reliques* to the Countess of Northumberland figured their Editor as the Minstrel of that ancient noble house, preserving through his songs the illustrious inheritance of the gallant Percys of yore. He re-created the vulgar 'minstrel-jongleur' figure of medieval literature as a respectable representative and recorder of the lost world in process of piecemeal retrieval; literary antiquaries found their own projection-reflection in these minstrels, 'the genuine successors of the ancient Bards, who united the arts of Poetry and Music, and sung verses to the harp, of their own composing'.[38] Scott's own obsequious dedications to the family of Buccleuch clothed his poetic persona in the latter-day garb of clan bard.

The Minstrel-Bard was figured as the historian of society in its infancy, a crucial connecting term between past and present whose voice established a community's temporal continuity by catching (as Scott astutely suggested) 'somewhat the refinement of modern poetry, without losing the simplicity of his original model'.[39] Following Percy's lead, and in the light of the furore over the Gaelic-Scots Ossianic poems, the Welsh antiquary Edward Jones (who was also a harpist) attempted to cover all ideological bases in his *Musical and Poetical Relicks of the Welsh Bards, Preserved by Tradition, and Authentic Manuscripts, From Remote Antiquity* (1784). Jones invoked a bardic stance explicitly identified with resistance to English national tradition; he deliberately evaded the stadialist logic of its inevitable supersession by invoking an earlier, independent and highly developed national culture. The

---

37 *Ivanhoe*, p. 7. The refracting perspectives of Lawrence Templeton and Dryasdust protect Scott's own position in the dispute; the reaction referred to, though widespread, co-existed in the Romantic period with a vogue for medieval pastiche.

38 Thomas Percy, 'An Essay on the Ancient English Minstrels', in *Reliques of Ancient English Poetry*, 3 vols. (London: J. Dodsley, 1765), vol. I, p. xv.

39 Walter Scott, Preface to 'The Lay of the Last Minstrel', in *Poetical Works*, p. 1; Dafydd Moore, 'Ossian, Chivalry and the Politics of Genre', *British Journal of Eighteenth Century Studies* 23:1 (Spring 2000), 23.

history of Wales, in this explicitly politicized version, conformed not to the comforting gradual progress of 'civil society', but to a violent, disrupted story of conquest and forced colonization. The dying bard of the Irish novelist Charles Maturin's *Milesian Chief* (1812) 'poured out his grief to his harp' in words, significantly, of 'intranslateable [sic] beauty' that expressed the underlying historical and epistemological pessimism that threatened to undo the optimistic empirical endeavours of Enlightened antiquarians and cohesive nationalists.[40] With an intriguing anticipation of Freud's analogy, the narrative imaged resistance to continuity and cultural assimilation in terms of archaeological layering.

Earlier, and much more equivocally, Thomas Gray's celebrated Pindaric Ode 'The Bard' had ventriloquized the voice of Welsh national glory in the idiom of neo-classical English; only one conclusion could be envisaged for oral culture's ancient spokesman:

> '. . . . With joy I see
> The different doom our Fates assign.
> Be thine Despair, and scept'red Care,
> To triumph and to die, are mine.'
> He spoke, and headlong from the mountain's height
> Deep in the roaring tide he plung'd to endless night.[41]

In this suicidal leap, the Bard symbolically took to himself the cultural violence practised by the integrative forces of progress to the way of life he represented. Gray's Bard combined the roles of proponent and antagonist for his culture; the experimental blend of the poem's diction employed the highest poetic resources of 'civil society', in the cause of emotional primitivism. The bardic stance, as recovered by Welsh, Irish and Scots antiquaries, generated ample discursive space for a new figure of poetic genius and played into late Enlightenment debates about the standing of the 'national bard' Shakespeare; the synthesizing powers of this voice redeemed the disaggregated retrievals made by antiquaries of popular culture, thereby releasing both reader and scholar from the burden of ordering an unintelligible bundle of fragments.[42]

---

40 Charles Maturin, *The Milesian Chief*, 4 vols. (Facsimile edn, New York: Garland, 1979), vol. I, p. 184.
41 Roger Lonsdale (ed.), *Thomas Gray and William Collins: Poetical Works* (Oxford: Oxford University Press, 1977), p. 58.
42 It has been argued that the bardic figure recuperated by nationalist antiquaries as a cultural spokesman was re-imagined by English imitators as 'an inspired, isolated and peripatetic figure' (Trumpener, *Bardic Nationalism*, p. 6).

Another isolated minstrel-bard assumed contemporary pastoral guise in James Beattie's *The Minstrel* (1770), whose anti-scholastic hero, born 'in a solitary and mountainous country' sports an 'imagination ... wild and romantick; but in the first part of his life he has hardly any opportunity of acquiring knowledge, except from that part of the book of nature which is open before him'.[43] Where Thomson's shepherd–poet had inhabited a conceptual landscape of neo-classical peace and plenty based on poetical stability, Beattie's equally 'British' Spenserian stanzas looked to a timeless landscape as the direct source of poetic inspiration. The minstrel-bard was at once a conserving force and a revolutionary one, fundamentally individualistic and anti-populist, an embodied figure of poetic imagination integral to the development of Romantic ideology.

Romance

Clara Reeve 'reckon[ed] *Ossian* among the Romances', on the basis of 'its strong marks of genius and Originality'.[44] Samuel Johnson's *Dictionary* had defined the term as a 'military fable of the middle ages; a tale of wild adventure in war and love', but also as 'a lie; a fiction'; Blair's defence of *Ossian* grounded the poems' authenticity on the historical truth of their heroic representation; their 'gallantry and generosity' was precisely *not* that of 'romance'. Scott (whose own historical interests combined stadialist historiographic influences with a strongly antiquarian pull towards the relics of popular culture) described Fingal as possessing 'the strength and bravery of Achilles, with the courtesy, sentiment, and high-breeding of Sir Charles Grandison'.[45] Early controversy had centred on whether *Ossian* was third-century epic or thirteenth-century romance; by 1805 it was possible to assign it a new kind of authenticity founded in romantic affect rather than antiquity. The process of rehabilitation was complex.

The chimeras of romance and chivalry were held to have been exploded by Cervantes' *Don Quixote*; but their demise was prematurely announced: Charlotte Lennox's *The Female Quixote; or, The Adventures of Arabella* (1752)

---

43 Letter from Beattie to Thomas Gray (November 1769), *The Correspondence of Thomas Gray*, ed. Paget Toynbee and Leonard Whibley, 3 vols. (Oxford: Clarendon Press, 1935), vol. III, p. 1084.
44 *The Progress of Romance, Through Times, Countries and Manners*, 2 vols. (in one) (Colchester: W. Keymer, 1785), p. 67.
45 Hugh Blair, 'Critical Dissertation', in Gaskill (ed.), *The Poems of Ossian*, p. 376; Walter Scott, *The Edinburgh Review* 6 (July 1805), 446.

was premised on romance modes' continuing power to seduce the reason from judgement to fantasy. After a series of disastrous episodes brought on by her persistent reading of 'reality' as though it were 'romance', the novel's eponymous heroine is finally brought to recognize that she has 'trifled away' her time, to the point of colluding in 'Violence and Revenge'.[46] Lennox's warning sentiments were echoed in innumerable prefaces, periodical articles and essays before Austen's *Northanger Abbey*, as the genre's reputation reached its critical nadir. Dangerous fantasy-inducing romances were frequently tracked back to the ethically bankrupt French *ancien régime*; they offered questionable pleasures without instructive guidance or moral truth and they were deeply inimical to the masculinist tradition of British novelists from Fielding to Smollett.

Historians and antiquarians were already recuperating medieval quest romance (from which these degenerate examples were believed to have sprung) for the evidence they provided about life in the past. Richard Hurd's *Letters on Chivalry and Romance* (1762) located romance and chivalry in the feudal constitution of medieval society, explaining the apparent absurdities of its conventions in terms of the needs of the society which generated them. The *Letters* offered detailed historical 'conjecture' about '*the rise and genius* of knight-errantry', taken from 'it's proper Source, the *old Romances*'.[47] His rehabilitation exceeded merely vindicating romances as sources for historical deduction about medieval conditions; offering Homeric parallels he asserted, by association, the romances' classical standing. Homer and the old romance writers wrote of their respective societies at similar stages; chivalry was the new classicism: 'the resemblance between the heroic and Gothic ages is very great . . . . the parallel would hardly have held so long and run so closely, if the *civil* condition of both had not been much the same' (p. 38). The exotic world of Gothic medievalism and chivalry, in Hurd's view, also manifested the primitive virtues of our own society in its heroic age.

Furthermore, Hurd insisted that read according to their own proper conventions rather than by inappropriate Aristotelian rules of action, the design of the romances of the Gothic age would emerge, purged of deformity and monstrosity. His detailed analysis of *The Faery [Faerie] Queene* revealed its aesthetic complexity and incidentally claimed for quest romance

---

46 *The Female Quixote, or, The Adventures of Arabella*, ed. Margaret Dalziel (Oxford: Oxford University Press, 1989), p. 381.
47 *Letters on Chivalry and Romance* (London: A. Millar, 1762), p. 10.

the endorsement of British literary tradition. A stance of historical impartiality and conjectural investigation failed to conceal Hurd's enthusiasm for the 'enchanted ground' of romance. His readings were allegorical, metaphorical and imaginative, and his closing peroration, with its familiar acquiescence in and lament for progress, was celebrated:

> Thus at length the magic of the old romances was perfectly dissolved . . .
> What we have gotten by this revolution, you will say, is a great deal of good sense. What we have lost, is a world of fine fabling; the illusion of which is so grateful to the charmed Spirit . . .   (pp. 118, 120)

In a further discussion of the constitutive power of lost pastness to the self-definition of the present, Hurd's friend Warton argued that the institutions and traditions of the Middle Ages were peculiarly favourable to poetry, and that their imaginative modes had been subdued by the 'modern' spirit of reason and inquiry. Ballad collectors, too, involved themselves in retrieving and theorizing larger romance narratives: in an essay added to the third volume of the *Reliques*, Percy supplied an antiquarian genealogy for 'Metrical Romances' which justified a place in the canon of British poetry for previously derided popular tales of King Arthur and Robin Hood, as originary fictions of ancient Britain. An explosion of retrieved romances in the first decade of the nineteenth century included Scott's 'Sir Tristrem' in 1804 and Ritson's *Ancient English Metrical Romances*. Theories about the origins of romance became the conventional opening to 'modern' histories of fiction such as John Moore's *Works of Smollett* (1797) and Anna Barbauld's *The Origin and Progress of Novel-Writing*, prefaced to *The British Novelists* (1810).

Their prototype was Clara Reeve's *The Progress of Romance, through Times, Countries and Manners . . .* (1785), which claimed that romances are universal and associated their 'enchantments' with bardic culture at a specific stage of societal development.[48] Her account elaborated an alternative world with a strong imaginative link to the real, an ethical version of Walpole's intention 'of leaving the powers of fancy at liberty to expatiate through the boundless realms of invention, and thence of creating more interesting situations'.[49] Romance embodied the history of human experience, rather than of events: 'From the romance', as Scott would later put it, 'we learn what [people]

---

48 *Progress of Romance*, p. 18.
49 'Preface to Second Edition', in *The Castle of Otranto*, p. 7.

were; from the history, what they did'.[50] There is discernible slippage – which the Romantic novel would exploit – between a paradigmatic version of romance as *fiction* (any non-factual narrative in prose) and a historicist version which located it at various particular 'moments' in the stadialist sequence which linked the barbarous past to modernity.

Clara Reeve's own romance, *The Old English Baron* (1777) explicitly declared its derivation from *The Castle of Otranto* and aimed 'to unite the most attractive and interesting circumstances of the ancient Romance and modern Novel'.[51] Supernatural agency delivers her characters from oppression and arbitrary authority to understanding with a very 'Enlightened' flavour. The romance's medievalism was signalled in chivalrous behaviour and Gothic furniture which substitute for cultural density, until the striking intrusion of a Rowleyesque inscription thickens the verbal texture and claims antiquarian authenticity for the Romance's resolution. In Ann Radcliffe's *Gaston de Blondeville, or The Court of Henry III. Keeping Festival in Ardenne: A Romance* (written 1802) a series of temporally receding narrative perspectives from 'the present' through Shakespeare's Arden to a tale of medieval chivalry supplied an illusion of historical density and played on both senses of 'Romance'. A rustic 'aged historian' imparts the discovery of an ancient oaken chest containing 'old parchments . . . and some old books, dropping to pieces with the worms', from which a 'modernised copy', presenting 'somewhat of the air of the old style, without its dryness', is recovered by an amateur antiquary who is nonetheless 'compelled to regret, that much of the effect of the story was lost, with the simplicity, brevity and quaintness of the ancient manner'.[52] Scott's *Ivanhoe* lurks in the wings.

Like antiquarianism, the political valencies of romance and chivalry were initially unfixed and multiple, though characteristically linked to notions of subordination, whether gendered, class-based or geographical (as in 'the Highlands' as location). Their strangeness offered the possibility, as Fredric Jameson has put it, 'of sensing other historical rhythms, and of demonic or

50 Walter Scott, 'Specimens of early English Metrical Romances, chiefly written during the early Part of the Fourteenth Century. By George Ellis, Esq. And Ancient Engleish Metrical Romanceës, selected and published by Joseph Ritson', *Edinburgh Review* 7:14 (January 1806), 388; *Prose Works*, vol. XVII, p. 18.

51 'Preface to the Second Edition', in *The Old English Baron: A Gothic Story*, ed. James Trainer (Oxford: Oxford University Press, 1977), pp. 3, 4.

52 *Gaston de Blondeville, or, The Court of Henry III. Keeping Festival in Ardenne: a romance; St. Alban's Abbey: a metrical tale with some poetical pieces, to which is prefixed a memoir of the author with extracts from her journals* (London: H. Colburn, 1826), vol. I, pp. 27, 40, 75.

Utopian transformations of a real now unshakably set in place'.[53] From an 'Enlightened' point of view, this provoked an increasingly strong negative association of romance with the forces of absolutism, Catholicism and Jacobitism. Edmund Burke's celebrated fantasy of the plight of Marie Antoinette directed subsequent connection of romance modes with forces of conservatism; the terms of chivalry and romance retrieved from anti-quarian discourse, with all their magical associations, were irreversibly politicized by antagonists on both sides in dispute over the French Revo-lution to offer newly charged versions of Britishness. By the beginning of the nineteenth century 'romance' seemed to be tied firmly to a reconsti-tuted past; the 'simple plaining of a minstrel song' was – as it had always been – construed as no longer available. But the complex interplay of romance images, themes and narrative motifs through works as diversely radical as Scott's *Waverley* (et seq.), Shelley's *Alastor* and *The Revolt of Islam*, Keats's *St Agnes Eve* and Austen's *Sense and Sensibility*, warns (as with the discursive currencies of balladry and antiquarianism) against reductionist or polarized ideological reading of the mode.

With its questing connotations of desire and indefinite deferral, romance became the province of imagination, a realm not so much politically neu-tralized as politically suspended, of enchantment and entrapment whose seductions and dangers the poetry of Coleridge and Keats, in particular, would inhabit, and the prose of William Hazlitt elaborate:

> It is the undefined and uncommon that gives birth and scope to the imagination; we can only fancy what we do not know. As in looking into the mazes of a tangled wood we fill them with what shapes we please, with ravenous beasts, with caverns vast, and drear enchantments, so in our ignorance of the world about us, we make gods or devils of the first object we see, and set no bounds to the wilful suggestions of our hopes and fears.[54]

The very malleability of romance forms and their equivocal association with both history and the imagination opened capacious possibilities to nineteenth-century historical novels. In the layered discourse of personhood and psychology which was one of the furthest reaching Ends of Enlight-enment, 'romance' might be construed as the pre-historical 'dream' from

---

53 Fredric Jameson, *The Political Unconscious: Narrative as a Socially Symbolic Act* (London: Methuen, 1981), p. 104.
54 William Hazlitt, 'On Poetry in General', 'Lectures on the English Poets (1818)', in Geoffrey Keynes (ed.), *Selected Essays of William Hazlitt* (London: Nonesuch Press, 1930), p. 397.

which the self or society 'must' awaken into adulthood or civility; Beattie's *Minstrel* offered a paradigm for the moment when, his chivalric dreams realized in grim and bloody defeat, Waverley felt himself 'entitled to say firmly, though perhaps with a sigh, that the romance of his life was ended, and that its real history had now commenced'.[55] But in the compound emotional and evidential discourse of the past these binary oppositions could not hold, and the hero would rapidly find himself called upon to 'justify' his too-ready pretension to the analytic certitudes of 'reason and philosophy'.

---

55 Walter Scott, *Waverley; or, 'Tis Sixty Years Since* (1814), ed. Claire Lamont (Oxford: Clarendon Press, 1981), p. 283.

3

The Romantics and the political economists

CATHERINE GALLAGHER

The field of political economy assumed its initial shape over the course of the eighteenth century in Britain, especially in the work of Adam Smith, and had become a powerful influence on a wide range of writers even before the revisions and reconceptions of the field by William Godwin, Thomas Robert Malthus, David Ricardo and Thomas De Quincey. Concepts basic to the developing discipline, such as the labour theory of value, the necessity of letting markets grow and change organically, and the importance of population size as an indicator of a nation's well-being, were widely accepted at the close of the century, even by those who later turned into the 'Lake Poets'. In 1800, for example, Coleridge defended Adam Smith's opinion that grain markets will eventually 'find their own level' (like rivers) and so should not be artificially manipulated (like pumps).[1] As this example indicates, eighteenth-century British political economy, which was a product of the Scottish Enlightenment, and nascent Romanticism emphasized the natural processes that bring humans and their environments into reciprocal relations. Both thought the life of the nation was constituted by the accumulated daily experiences and choices of common people, rather than the decisions of the powerful; both looked beyond the rational faculties (favoured by French *philosophes*) to emotions and sensations for the deepest springs of human motivation; and both tended to rely on free individuals and their instincts, rather than changes imposed by the state, to bring about social progress. Their similarities, indeed, reached all the way into Romantic aesthetics, for there is a close kinship between Adam Smith's labour theory of value and Edmund Burke's concept of sublimity. In the last decades of the eighteenth century, both early political economists and the Romantics-to-be

1 See his 'Letter to the Morning Post: 14 October 1800', *Essays on His Times*, ed. David V. Erdman, in *Collected Works of Samuel Taylor Coleridge*, vol. III (Princeton: Princeton University Press, 1978), p. 255.

aimed to let loose the creative and productive energies of the majority of the British people – hampered, in their view, by censorship, repressive laws, unequal taxes and other forms of state oppression – without touching off a violent and bloody revolution.

Many of the ideas they held in common at the close of the eighteenth century were destined to become the common sense of the nineteenth, the almost inescapable (if often unconscious) first premises for reasoning about social organization and human well-being. They worked their way into most aspects of nineteenth-century thought by confirming and advancing the precedence of the bodily (as distinct from the spiritual) welfare of humanity. Certainly, they helped shift the social discourse from one centred on religious values to one centred on secular values. But, perhaps more importantly, they linked both kinds of value to the needs of biological and social man taken in the mass. Political economy's influence thus extended far beyond those who consciously adhered to its principles, and those who became its critics in the new century – including the Lake Poets – continued to share its basic tenets.

And yet political economy came to have a dreadfully bad odour among the most prominent literary figures of the early nineteenth century. How did they come to see it as a tissue of errors?[2] That's one question this chapter will answer by sketching the development of hostilities, from the outraged reaction occasioned by the first editions of Thomas Robert Malthus's *Essay on Population*, through disagreements about the national economy during the Napoleonic War years, and into disputes (some might say misunderstandings) about the nature of labour, value and happiness. In this survey of the major controversies, I will proceed in a loosely chronological order, taking up topics as they were first urged by one side or the other, although within the discussion of each topic ((1) population; (2) fiscal and monetary

---

2 Answering this question has lately proved more difficult than literary historians previously believed, for they used to be content to generalize about the natural antagonism between 'organic' and 'mechanistic' ways of thinking, or to gesture toward the rift between 'enlightenment empiricism' and 'Romantic idealism'. Now literary and intellectual historians are piecing together a complex picture, which relies less heavily on the self-representations of the 'Lake Poets', especially Samuel Taylor Coleridge and Robert Southey. Philip Connell's *Romanticism, Economics and the Question of Culture* (Oxford: Oxford University Press, 2001) is the most authoritative and detailed examination of the topic. For a general analysis of the original proximity between British (primarily Scottish) aesthetic and economic thought in the 1700s and their developing discordance at the end of the century, see Howard Caygill, *Art of Judgement* (London: Basil Blackwell, 1989).

policy; (3) labour, value and class conflict). I will often discuss texts out of their chronological sequence.

In addition to explaining their divergences, I will also urge an awareness of the unacknowledged continuity of shared premises, the larger discursive agreements that made the terms of the controversies intelligible to both sides. Romanticism and political economy should be thought of as competing forms of 'organicism',[3] flourishing alike in British radical thought at the turn of the eighteenth century and fostering scepticism toward what they presented as their immediate predecessors' unrealistic faith in an idealized human rationality. As they travelled their separate paths in the nineteenth century, they continued to foster organicist thinking: the political economists, like the Romantics, privileged natural processes, operating according to intrinsic and lifelike dynamics, over what they regarded as artificial ones, mechanically constructed and wilfully directed from without. Moreover, vital and natural processes increasingly served not only as analogies in the social visions of political economists and Romantics but also as the literal forces driving human behaviour. Romantics and political economists attributed cohesion, conflict, change and stability not to political direction from above but to the embodied experiences of the mass of the people: their lives and deaths, desires and frustrations, pains and pleasures. Romantic notions of aesthetic value, as well as Romantic social commentary, connected and clashed with classical political economy's theories of value because corporeal and sensational experience were central to both. Each posited necessary conjunctures between the expense of life and the production of value, between suffering and owning, between investing vital energy in an object and making it transferable to others, but they described the connections in irreconcilable ways. This chapter will look at several explanations for the collision between Romantic writers and

---

3 The meaning and history of 'organicism' and 'organism' in social and economic thought have been much analysed. For a general discussion of the terms, see Raymond Williams, *Keywords* (New York: Oxford University Press, 1985). Immanuel Kant is said to have been the first to establish criteria for 'organic' or natural entities, which, taken together, differentiate them from machines: (1) the whole determines the form and the relation of parts; (2) parts mutually form each other; and (3) the whole reproduces itself (*Critique of Judgment*, Part II, Analytics of Teleological Judgment). For descriptions of the uses of biological sciences and natural metaphors in the history of economic thought, as well as analyses of economies as physiological organizations, see *Natural Images in Economic Thought: Markets Red in Tooth and Claw*, ed. Philip Mirowski (New York: Cambridge University Press, 1994). For the sources of political economy's organicism in Scottish Enlightenment thought, see Catherine Packham, 'The Physiology of Political Economy: Vitalism and Adam Smith's Wealth of Nations', *Journal of the History of Ideas* 63 (2002), 465–81.

political economists over these issues – for example, the Romantics tended to take a peculiar form of work (their own) as paradigmatic of labour in general – but the first thing to notice is that the conflict could never have been so sharp if they had not been fighting over common ground.

Population: sex and food

The earliest overt controversy between the two groups clearly reveals their joint preoccupation with organic life, for it concerns the basic bodily issues of sexuality, reproduction and food.[4] When Thomas Robert Malthus's *An Essay on Population* (first published in 1797) provoked their indignation on these topics, Coleridge and Southey were not yet called 'Romantics' and Malthus was not yet known as a political economist. Indeed, the resemblances among the three men might have seemed more obvious to contemporaries than their differences, for although the social thought of each was in flux, they were all affiliated with those circles loosely designated 'radical'. In 1800, Coleridge may have abandoned his faith in the French Revolution, but Southey had not, and both men still hoped for democratic change in Britain, as did Malthus's family and friends. His *Essay* was also the fruit of British radicalism, albeit of a different strain.

In the 1790s, while support for franchise reform was the definitive marker of radicalism, many varieties of the species flourished in relative harmony. Christians like Coleridge and Southey took inspiration from secularists like William Godwin, while Godwin, advocating an eventual voluntary sharing of wealth, seemed to resemble Jeremy Bentham, who put his trust in self-interest, because both supported the widest possible franchise on utilitarian grounds. In the new century, however, divisions among radicals were to become more fixed and obtrusive. In particular, the brand that came to be called 'philosophical radicalism', the Benthamite variety championing parliamentary reform while stressing self-interest, was increasingly distinguished from more communitarian radicalisms. And, although the classical canon of political economy was largely unwritten when the century began,

---

4 Secondary works that discuss the Romantics and Malthus's population principle include the following: Connell, *Romanticism*, pp. 13–41, 210–12; Maureen N. McLane, *Romanticism and the Human Sciences: Poetry, Population, and the Discourse of the Species* (Cambridge: Cambridge University Press, 2000); Frances Ferguson, 'Malthus, Godwin, Wordsworth, and the Spirit of Solitude', in *Literature and the Body: Essays on Population and Persons*, ed. Elaine Scarry (Baltimore: Johns Hopkins University Press, 1988), pp. 106–24; David Kaufman, *The Business of Common Life: Novels and Classical Economics Between Revolution and Reform* (Baltimore: Johns Hopkins University Press, 1985).

its line of development in the next three decades continually intertwined the discipline with Benthamite presuppositions. Malthus (and the political economists who were to follow), therefore, advanced one tendency within British radicalism, Coleridge and Southey advanced another, and the growing antipathy between Romanticism and political economy can partly be traced to their earlier political commonality.

Malthus's *An Essay on Population* and the reaction to it reveal not only that the antagonism between proto-political economy and incipient Romanticism was internal to British radicalism at the turn of the century but also that several varieties of radical thought were placing a new emphasis on the lived experience, especially the sensational life, of the common people. The *Essay* was conceived inside this radical tradition and drew entirely from its stock of ideas, but it partly framed itself as a quarrel with one of radicalism's greatest heroes, William Godwin. Malthus set out to prove that, contrary to some fatuous remarks made by Godwin in the *Enquiry Concerning Political Justice and Its Influence on Morals and Happiness* (1793),[5] there are known limits to the 'future improvement of society' – a thesis that, as many early reviewers noted, was hardly controversial. But Malthus's way of supporting his thesis and the practical consequence he drew from it were provocative, some would say inflammatory, in their challenge to expectations of human progress. His assertion that population increases always outstrip increases in the food supply unless they are brought into equilibrium through misery (starvation, sexual abstinence, late marriage) or vice (prostitution, birth control, infanticide) went directly against Godwin's prediction that people would someday become so reasonable and temperate in their passions that they would be able to control reproduction at will. Godwin forecast a time when men and women, without the prodding of a government, would divide their wealth equitably, form virtuous attachments without the need for patriarchal marriage, and consider their offspring (whose numbers would be limited by the relative passionlessness of the prevailing manners) to be the responsibility of the community as a whole.

Instead of accusing Godwin of sedition and impiety, as conservative critics had, Malthus calmly demonstrated that Godwin's utopian vision was impossible because it rested on the unsubstantiated premise that truly

---

5 The immediate irritant was 'Essay II' of Godwin's *The Enquirer: Reflections on Education, Manners, and Literature* (1789), but, Malthus tells us in the 'Preface', his objections to that essay 'started the general question of the future improvement of society' and led him to formulate his own views in opposition to those articulated by Godwin in the *Enquiry*.

rational social arrangements would diminish the passion between the sexes. Malthus argued that sexual desire is as constant a feature of human nature as the need for food, and he is one of the first modern thinkers to insist that sexual intercourse is both ineradicable and essential to human happiness. Malthus strengthened the side of British radicalism that emphasized the motivating force of bodily pleasure and made the needs of desiring bodies the basis of economic thought. Healthy, procreative sexual passion, he insisted, 'seems to be that sort of mixture of sensual and intellectual enjoyment particularly suited to the nature of man, and most powerfully calculated to awaken the sympathies of the soul and produce the most exquisite gratifications'.[6] Godwin, he charged, was a desiccated, heartless repressor of this legitimate enjoyment (p. 76).

Malthus's intention, historians now claim, was to refute Godwin within the assumptions of latitudinarian English natural theology,[6] but many of his contemporaries were scandalized by what appeared to be his sensual materialism, and he was immediately accused of adopting a base and irreligious view of human nature. That accusation, indeed, is reiterated four times in Robert Southey's angry review of the second edition of the *Essay*. The review appeared in 1803, and it closely follows marginal notes that Coleridge made in his copy of Malthus, so it seems to reflect the views of both poets and exposes another fissure that had earlier been present within English radicalism between those whose social thought was religiously inflected and those who kept their discourse within secular confines. Even in their most revolutionary youth, Coleridge and Southey had spoken in the idiom of Protestant Dissenting radicalism, modelling their activities on those of the early Christian church, and advocating 'The republic of God's own making.'[7] They made common cause with secularists in the eighteenth century because both opposed the Anglican Church Establishment, but as early as 1796, Godwin's sexual politics had already drawn a reproof from Coleridge, who accused him of pandering to sensuality[8] – just the reverse of Malthus's critique. And the rifts between Christian and free-thinking radicals became more apparent in the next century. Coleridge and Godwin

---

6 Thomas Malthus, *An Essay on the Principle of Population: Text, Sources and Background, Criticism*, ed. Philip Appleman (New York: Norton, 1976), p. 77. Subsequent page references will be given in the text.

7 *Letters of Samuel Taylor Coleridge*, ed. Bart Winer (London: Routledge and Kegan Paul, 1970), p. 196.

8 *Watchman*, in *The Collected Works of Samuel Taylor Coleridge*, vol. II, ed. Bart Winer (London: Routledge and Kegan Paul/Princeton: Princeton University Press, 1970), p. 196.

became friends again in the 1800s, but by that time, Godwin was moving away from his earlier hostility toward organized religion. So, although Southey's review excoriates Godwin's as well as Malthus's thoughts on reproduction and sexuality, showing signs of disaffection from all godless radicals, it continues a tendency from within British radicalism that sought social change in conformity with a reformed and purified Christianity.

How, then, can I claim that Southey and Coleridge helped locate the happiness of the common body at the centre of social discourse? The evidence, at first glance, would tend to point in the opposite direction, toward the promotion of spiritual over physical well-being. 'The whole [of Malthus's argument]', Southey claimed, 'proceeds upon the assumption, that lust and hunger are alike passions of physical necessity, and the one equally with the other independent of the reason and the will.'[9] He hammered away at the *Essay*'s apparent biological determinism, opposing it to a belief in the active power of Christian virtue:

> There lives not a wretch corrupt enough of heart, and shameless enough of front to say that this is so: there lives not a man who can look upon his wife and his daughter, who can think upon his sister, and remember her who bore him, without feeling indignation and resentment that he should be insulted by so infamous an assertion. (p. 296)

Malthus's sensualism, he insisted, is not only lewd but also blasphemous because it implies that God created human beings who are helplessly in the grip of an overpowering instinct and doomed either to misery or sinfulness. Southey the Christian radical sided with Godwin in blaming corrupt human institutions for the existence of misery and vice, for to blame the human organism is only, by extension, to blame God: 'it remains to be seen . . . whether we are to complain of the folly of man, or of the will of God, for this is the alternative. Let not the impiety of the question be imputed to us!' (p. 297).

The opposition between Christian free will[10] and materialist determinism that Southey framed in this review may have obscured Malthus's theological intentions, but it remained a continuous underlying current in the

---

9 Rev. of *An Essay on the Principles* [sic] *of Population*, in *The Annual Review and History of Literature for 1803*, vol. II (London: Printed for T. N. Longman and O. Rees by T. Gillet, 1804), p. 296.

10 Not all Christians held this tenet. For a map of the various Christian positions on this topic and their impact on nineteenth-century social controversies, see Gallagher, *The Industrial Reformation of English Fiction: Social Discourse and Narrative Form, 1832–67* (Chicago: University of Chicago Press, 1985), chapter 1.

stream of attacks on political economy that flowed from the first generation of Romantic writers. It should not, however, lead us to underestimate the Romantics' own commitments to increasing the material welfare, comfort and pleasure of the general population. Southey accused Malthus of over-stating the role of sexual feeling in human happiness, but he did not dis-count earthly pleasure as a primary goal or recommend that the poor should transcend their desires. Indeed, he censured Malthus's pessimism about making significant improvements in the physical lives of the poor. Ironically, Malthus's seemingly scientific sensualism (however integrated into a meliorist theodicy) guided him to bleak conclusions about the material advantages of political reform, whereas the poets' volunteerism gave them faith in a more general future abundance. So in addition to attacking his sexual determinism in 1803, Southey excoriates Malthus's seeming indifference to the physical plight of the poor. Malthus acknow-ledged that propertyless labourers (the vast majority of the population) suffered the miseries attending the pressure of population dis-proportionately. It was they who lacked the resources to raise healthy children and whose offspring went hungry or died in infancy. The vices of the rich (prostitution and birth control, for example, which acted as 'pre-ventive checks' to population) were too expensive for them, so their passion often had no outlet other than in reproductive sexuality, which resulted in the 'positive checks' of starvation, disease or infanticide. To decrease the burden of their misery, Malthus argued that they should be discouraged from marrying and bearing children; he thought they should be encouraged to suffer the unhappiness of abstinence instead of the greater wretchedness of starvation and death. Consequently, he opposed the practice of giving impoverished couples extra relief for each child they had, noting that, in the long term, such a policy only lowered wages by producing a supply of labour in excess of demand, and he also suggested the eventual abolition of parish relief for able-bodied labourers and their families.

Southey responded to these proposals with all the fervour of a radical who fashioned himself as the defender of the poor, one whose duty was not only to secure more political rights but also to protect certain traditional rights of the propertyless, such as the right to parish relief from destitution. His 1803 review demonstrates how wide the gap was between such com-munitarian radicals and the incipient philosophical radicals, who were often sceptical about the benefits of state interference in the economy and thought that traditional rights sometimes stood in the way of economic progress. Southey's radicalism had a material aim – the redistribution of wealth – inconsistent with Malthus's (and that of the political economists generally) – the augmentation of the sum total of the wealth of the nation. The poor, according to classical political economy, would share in that wealth up to a point, for the total wealth of the country would grow, and the level of subsistence itself would rise. But the law of wages would ensure that the labouring population would normally earn little more than their subsistence, since it was thought that the labour supply would expand when wages were high, bringing the supply up to demand and lowering wages again. Southey countered that the rich were not compelled by some economic law but instead *chose* to keep labourers' wages down to a minimum. Paying parish rates (taxes on property that would be distributed to the needy poor) was the only way of transferring some additional portion of the wealth they had created back to the labourers' tables. Malthus, according to Southey, did not offer sound advice to the poor but merely sided with the rich, who 'have found a place at the table of nature; and why should they be disturbed at their feast?' (pp. 300–1). Malthus's treatment of food thus seemed as abominable as his treatment of sexual passion, for the *Essay* apparently promoted sex as an individual necessity while denying that a share in the community's food is everyone's birthright.

Through all of these substantial disagreements between Malthus and Southey, though, there persisted a similarity of emphasis on the organic lives of the poor, on their miseries and enjoyments, as indices of the commonweal's vitality, as forces propelling its movements, and as sources of its equilibrium. Both parties presented themselves as champions of natural man, whose feelings are as powerful as his thoughts, rejecting the tepid, artificial creature imagined by rationalists like Godwin. Both insisted that only actual experiences of observing ordinary life can serve as a basis for social diagnosis. 'Life', 'experience', 'passion' and 'nature': these are their common objects and their common values.

As Southey's political radicalism waned, he nevertheless maintained and nurtured his anti-Malthusianism, which hardened into a generalized opposition to political economy at the core of what has been called 'Romantic conservatism'.[11] Southey and Coleridge gave up the new-fangled radical idea of equality, but they clung all the more strenuously to their

---

11 'Romantic Conservatism', writes David Eastwood, 'might be defined negatively as the rejection of political economy.' See 'Robert Southey and the Intellectual Origins of Romantic Conservatism', *English Historical Review* 411 (April 1989), 308–31. See also Geoffrey Carnall, *Robert Southey and His Age: The Development of a Conservative Mind* (Oxford: Clarendon Press, 1960).

defence of the traditional rights of the poor, especially their right to an adequate share of the food they produced. The critique of Malthus served as a bridge between radicalism and conservatism, making it fundamental to their social vision in both political phases. Philip Connell has astutely analysed the context of Southey's review and has linked it to William Wordsworth's use of anti-Malthusian rhetoric in the 1805 *Prelude*, showing that both texts helped the Lake Poets to suppress their earlier affiliations with Godwin. Indeed, Connell demonstrates, Wordsworth even began the 'Romantic' habit of disparaging Malthus almost as another Godwin, a thinker who considered passion dangerous, or at least dangerous for the poor. Malthus actually went to considerable rhetorical lengths to propound both the rightness and necessity of sexual feeling, but, according to Connell, he was nevertheless referred to in the 1805 *Prelude* as among 'those who think that strong affections, love / Known by whatever name, is falsely deem'd / A gift . . . / Of vulgar Nature, that its growth requires / Retirement, leisure . . .' (XII. 185–9).[12] Anti-Malthusianism allowed the Lake Poets to salvage what they wanted to preserve from their earlier radicalism while projecting the hyper-rationalism of Godwin onto Malthus and, later, political economy.

The success of the strategy seems apparent if we look ahead into the next decade and note that Percy Bysshe Shelley, reviving Romantic radicalism after the first generation had abandoned it, takes up the cry against Malthus in 1816:

> A writer of the present-day (a priest of course, for his doctrines are those of a eunuch and a tyrant) has stated that the evils of the poor arise from an excess of population, and that . . . the soothing, elevating and harmonious gentleness of the sexual intercourse and the humanizing charities of domestic life which are its appendages, – that is to be obliterated.[13]

Absent from Shelley's violent diatribe is any sense of Malthus's sexual radicalism, which had been so prominent a feature of Southey's review; for the later Romantic, Malthus only threatens 'to deprive [the poor] of that

---

12 Connell, *Romanticism*, pp. 41–61.
13 'A Philosophical View of Reform', in *The Complete Works of Percy Bysshe Shelley*, vol. VII (New York: Scribner's, 1930), pp. 32–3. For a discussion of this text in relation to political economy, see James Chandler, 'Ricardo and the Poets: Representing Commonwealth in the Year of Peterloo', *The Wordsworth Circle* 25 (Spring 1994), 82–6. For a discussion of Malthus and Mary Shelley's *Frankenstein*, see Maureen McLane, *Romanticism*, pp. 84–108.

property which is as strictly their birthright as a gentleman's land is his birthright, without giving them any compensation but the insulting advice to conquer . . . a propensity which persons of the most consummate wisdom have been unable to resist, and which it is difficult to admire a person for having resisted.' Shelley here repeats the charge earlier made against Malthus's denial of the 'birthright' of parish relief, but he does not at all share the other half of Southey's anti-Malthusianism. Instead, he magnifies Wordsworth's claim that Malthus hoped to suppress passion. Malthus, indeed, becomes an anti-sexual icon for Shelley, a eunuch and a tyrant dispensing a sentence of celibacy on the poor without understanding the misery entailed in sexual abstinence. The last phrase of this passage, in which Shelley expresses his contempt for chastity ('a propensity . . . it is difficult to admire a person for having resisted'), indicates the high value that he, in contradistinction to Southey, placed on sexual activity, and, ironically, it recalls Malthus's criticism of Godwin, Shelley's own father-in-law, for devaluing sexual passion. Without even realizing it, Shelley follows in Malthus's footsteps, propounding, against a putatively unsexed adversary, the necessity as well as the goodness of the passion between the sexes. Romanticism, to be sure, kept defining itself against Malthus, but not against the same Malthus.

As Shelley's unwitting repetition of Malthus indicates, underlying the substantial causes for antipathy, there remained common premises that he, too, shared with the author of *An Essay on Population*. Shelley also writes as if the state of labouring bodies is the key factor in the commonweal and depicts the common body as generally miserable. The populousness of a nation had long been thought to indicate its overall prosperity, but the economic instability of the post-war years helped focus attention not only on the *fact* that higher wages bring more babies and lower wages shrink the population but also on the *lived experience* of that generalization. The actual processes by which life ebbed and flowed were earlier not thought a fit object of study. But the late eighteenth century had seen a flood of representations of common rural existence, in which writers like Wordsworth and Southey had participated. Malthus had only repeated a leading idea to which radicals in both the 1790s and the post-war period subscribed: the poor lived in relative misery even in fairly good times, and that fact was central, not peripheral, to the polity. His most important contribution to the population debate is his claim that the pressure of population operates constantly instead of coming into play in some distant future when the country will be fully inhabited. Population pressure is the daily, oppressive burden felt by ninety per cent of the people. Both Southey and Shelley fully conceded that Malthus had not exaggerated either the degree or the significance of national suffering; their agreement on this fundamental issue, indeed, made it seem all the more outrageous for Malthus to claim that there was no political remedy.

A second strong connection between Shelley and Malthus was that both were essentially eudemonic or 'utilitarian' moralists, maintaining that the best social system, like the best individual action, is that which yields the greatest happiness to the greatest number. The doctrine is most famously associated with Jeremy Bentham, whom Shelley idolized, and the philosophical radicals, but there were also Christian utilitarians, like William Paley, who had a great influence on Malthus. Indeed, eudemonism was standard in both English natural theology and Scottish Enlightenment philosophy. And this broadly conceived 'principle of utility' was a mainstay of radical reasoning (both Thomas Paine and William Godwin frequently appealed to the greatest happiness principle in elucidating their ethical systems), for it seemed to lead to the conclusion that political institutions should be democratized to reflect the interests, and therefore promote the happiness, of the majority. Of course, 'happiness' is a notoriously difficult term to define, and there were deep disagreements over its meaning as well as debates over its value. But those very debates disseminated the idea that the felicity of the multitude – the question of how they *feel* – as a collection of sensitive individuals, rather than, for example, the glory of God or the power of the State, was the purpose of civil arrangements.

War: money, debt and taxes

The next phase of the Romantics' encounter with political economy was determined by the Napoleonic wars, which drastically changed the immediate intellectual environment. They shifted the focus of economic thought to fiscal and monetary policy – taxes, the national debt and paper money – on the face of it not topics that seem likely to generate passion or stimulate fundamental thinking about the nature of collective human life. But they were as hotly contested as the Malthusian controversy, and they served as the platform on which David Ricardo reformulated the discipline's bases and made it a political force. It was in the debates over these topics, moreover, that the competing models of the social organism emerged that would dominate nineteenth-century thought.

Whether closer in analytic framework to William Cobbett or to Bentham, radicals were generally critical of the war economy, but after 1802 their reasons for disapproval became increasingly divergent. Those who shared William Cobbett's point of view placed themselves in opposition to political economy in the later years of the decade, whereas previously, when radicals were usually pacifists, they had relied on Adam Smith's argument that warfare was a drain on the productive capacities of the nation. Radicals had not only tacitly accepted Smith's analysis but also claimed that war enriched the Crown and its allies at the expense of the middle and lower classes. However, as free trade became a moot issue, Napoleon's Continental System making it impossible, and the war effort gained radical support, many reconciled their patriotism with their attack on the war economy by accusing commercial interests, especially those involved in foreign trade, of encouraging military mismanagement and corrupt administration. William Cobbett, Major John Cartwright and Sir Francis Burdett attacked the financial system based on high taxes, national debt and paper money, not as the outcome of financing any war, but as the result of ineffectual generalship, fraud and profiteering. Developing a form of Little Englandism *avant la lettre*, radical parliamentary reformers of this new stripe maintained that the country needed no foreign trade or empire, no national debt or paper money, and that only a reformed Parliament could deliver the people from administrations principally beholden to commercial interests.

Anti-commercial radicalism strongly influenced those Romantics who remained within the radical fold. Witness, for example, Shelley's post-war diatribe against the national debt: an 'execrable contrivance of misrule', which multiplies 'the number of those who are idle in proportion to those who work, while it increases, through the factitious wants of those indolent, privileged persons, the quantity of work to be done'.[14] Shelley apparently swallowed Cobbett's view of the wartime economy whole and, in 'A Philosophical View of Reform', waxed as irate about the suspension of payment on banknotes as about the existence of the debt. The Bank of England (then a private corporation) had been instructed by the government to suspend cash (that is coin) redemption of its banknotes in 1797 as a temporary expedient to quell panics resulting from rumours of invasion, and the suspension was afterwards continued because it helped the government to finance the war, a practice Shelley equated with outright deceit and theft:

14 'Philosophical View of Reform', p. 25.

> They declared subsequently that these pieces of paper were the legal coin of the country. Of this nature are all such transactions of companies and banks as consist in the circulation of promissory notes to a greater amount than the actual property possessed by those whose names they bear. They have the effect of augmenting the prices of provision, and of benefitting at the expense of community the speculators in this traffic.   (p. 27)

His long-term solution was the widest possible franchise, but he also offered a short-term solution to the problem of the national debt, proposing that, since it consists in 'a debt contracted by the whole mass of the privileged classes towards one particular portion of those classes', the propertied class should pay only the principal to the investors, who would include some among themselves. 'It would be a mere transfer among persons of property' (p. 35), he claimed, and the nation would then be able to rid itself of the parasites that drain its vitality. To be sure, Shelley did not, like some other popular radicals of the time, waste soft words on the monarchy, but he attributed its power to the existence of a 'fictitious paper currency' (p. 39), so that the financial revolution, as in Cobbett's analysis, was said to be the source of modern oppression. By identifying public credit as the main enemy, Shelley implicitly places those who live by financial transactions outside the legitimate national community.

Meanwhile, David Ricardo was using political economy to mount a very different critique of the war economy. Between the publication of the second edition of Malthus's *Essay* in 1803 and that of Ricardo's *Principles of Political Economy and Taxation* in 1817, no widely read book in the new discipline appeared. Malthus entered into debates over the nature of value and formulated a theory of rent that became a basic tenet of the developing discipline; he also began calling himself a political economist, a fact that may have further alienated the Romantics from the whole enterprise. As the economy underwent dramatic changes, David Ricardo wrote articles and pamphlets criticizing the government's wartime fiscal policies, especially the suspension of specie payments by the Bank of England and the concomitant growth of the national debt. But he did not encourage the conspiracy theorists of paper money or use the national debt as an excuse for attacking commercial interests. Recognizing the necessity of raising taxes in order to support the war, Ricardo thought it would be better to tax subjects directly than to expand the national debt as a form of financing. His concern, unlike that of Shelley and the anti-commercial radicals, was not that an idle elite deceived the honest people, exercising undue influence over the government and siphoning off the country's wealth. Indeed, he maintained that paying the interest on the national debt had no effect on the national wealth, but the debt should nevertheless be speedily liquidated because 'the system of borrowing . . . to defray the extraordinary [wartime] expenses of the state' 'blind[s] us to our real situation'. Called upon to pay only the interest on the debt, the taxpayers forget that they are spending millions and put off the day of reckoning until the end of the war, setting aside no savings to meet their collective obligation. As he later phrased his position in *The Principles*, if people had to pay directly their shares of the cost of the war, 'as soon as the war ceased taxation would cease, and we should immediately fall into a natural state of prices'.[15]

To Ricardo, therefore, war financing was no fraud perpetrated by a swindling elite against the true nation, but only a form of self-delusion. Ricardo was interested in finding a money form that would allow the relative values of commodities to appear; establishing the gold standard was intended to remove an obstructing, artificial fiscal system, to neutralize money and make it a transparent medium for exchange values, which originated in the amount of labour required in their production. Whereas Shelley seemed to maintain that paper money and credit were necessarily fraudulent, Ricardo simply wanted them properly regulated so they would not interfere with trade. He achieved his goal in the immediate post-war period; in 1817, consciously appealing to the desire for a scientific under-standing of monetary policy but probably also buoyed by popular prejudice against paper money and bankers in general, he led Parliament to reinstate cash redemption of banknotes. Ricardo, too, based his proposals on a hol-istic, organic understanding of the nation, but unlike Cobbett's or Shelley's, Ricardo's social organism was driven by the commercial urge, although it contained internal resistances. The economy, he thought, should be encouraged to achieve a homoeostatic balance independently. A faulty currency could misrepresent the organism's well-being and might also attract investment into ultimately unproductive channels, threatening the health of the entire entity.

Inside these general wartime transformations of radical thought – in which, on the one hand, commercial interests were portrayed as cynically profiteering while patriots paid their way, and, on the other, commercial freedom was said to be threatened by wartime expediency – many British

---

15 *The Principle of Political Economy and Taxation*, ed. Donald Winch (London: J. M. Dent and Sons, 1973), p. 163. On the post-war development of political economy, see Cary F. Langer, *The Coming of Age of Political Economy, 1815–1825* (New York: Greenwood, 1987), p. 230.

writers found themselves with new allies and new grudges. Just as the former Tory anti-Jacobin William Cobbett came around to supporting Parliamentary reform, making a convert of Shelley, Coleridge and Southey became more nationalistic and bellicose, and in the second decade of the century, they became unorthodox Tories themselves. Coleridge, especially, found a distinctive political vantage point from which to attack both anti-commercial and pro-commercial radicals.

It has often been said that Coleridge counterposed an organic model of the nation against competing mechanistic models, and certainly he strove to give that impression. But in fact one would be hard-pressed to find political and economic commentators who refrained from organic metaphors in those years. Certainly political economists and other radicals as well scrambled to line up behind Edmund Burke's attack on the French Revolution for trying to substitute an artificial social and political system for a living legacy of national feeling deeply rooted in a distinctive way of life. The ubiquity of holistic and naturalist social thought during the war posed something of a rhetorical challenge for Coleridge, and his reflections on political economy during those years reveal an attempt to wrest organicist rhetoric from both anti-commercial radicals and political economists. In an 1809 essay in *The Friend*, Coleridge actually defended the war's financing, and his most surprising display of metaphoric virtuosity is an organicist defence of the national debt:

> What has rendered Great Britain . . . with more than metaphorical propriety a BODY POLITIC, our Roads, Rivers, and Canals being so truly the veins, arteries, and nerves, of the state; that every pulse in the metropolis produces a correspondent pulsation in the remotest village on its extreme shores! . . . I answer without hesitation, that the cause and mother principle of this unexampled confidence, of this *system* of credit, which is as much stronger than mere positive possessions, as the soul of man is than his body . . . has been our NATIONAL DEBT.[16]

However, it was not enough merely to develop his own bodily analogies, supplemented by references to credit as the 'soul' of the nation; he also needed to denigrate his enemies' organic rhetoric. Therefore, returning to the body-state metaphor in another essay, he associated it with 'the sect of Economists' – by which he meant not only the eighteenth-century French

---

16 *The Friend*, in *The Collected Works of Samuel Taylor Coleridge*, vol. IV, ed. Barbara E. Rooke (London: Routledge and Kegan Paul/Princeton: Princeton University Press, 1969), p. 230.

économistes but also Sir James Steuart and, one might suggest, Adam Smith – and accused them of mistaking their verbal construct of the body politic for an actual living being and of sacrificing real bodies to its merely fictive vigour. As much as the real patriot desires to make a 'body politic' out of separate individuals, Coleridge claimed, 'he places limits even to this wish', whereas the 'sect of Economists' allow concrete individuals to become 'diseased and vicious, in order that each may become useful to *all*, or the State, or the Society', which is a mere 'non-entity under the different words' (p. 299). Hence, his insistence that such metaphors be 'more than metaphoric', that they describe economic systems that nourish individual lives. What the political economists called a social body, he complained, was merely 'a self-regulating economic machine',[17] the workings of which severely injured actual people.

Coleridge's desire to gain a monopoly on true organicism is perhaps best demonstrated by the fact that the political economist he reviled most was the very thinker who worried most about the physical well-being of the poor: Malthus.[18] Unfolding a theory of rent and of the rising costs of production in agriculture, Malthus's wartime writings also expressed the concern that capital might abandon agriculture for manufacturing and that the food supply might therefore be threatened. As a consequence of these fears, he supported policies to protect and encourage the landed interests, including the Corn Law of 1815. The economic body politic had to adjust actual bodies to their available nutrients, Malthus insisted: abolish the poor laws to keep down the population and protect the landed interests to keep up food production. Although Coleridge opposed those measures, the two writers similarly demanded a constant attention to the health and vitality of labouring bodies.

The post-war period: value, labour and class conflict

As political economy coalesced in the post-war period around Ricardo's analyses, it increasingly became a kind of life science: the quantity of vital

---

17 *Lay Sermons*, in *The Collected Works of Samuel Taylor Coleridge*, vol. VI, ed. R. J. White (London: Routledge and Kegan Paul/Princeton: Princeton University Press, 1972), p. 205.
18 For more on the similarities between Coleridge and Malthus, see Donald Winch, *Riches and Poverty: An Intellectual History of Political Economy in Britain, 1750–1834* (Cambridge: Cambridge University Press, 1996), pp. 289–306, 396–404, and Connell, *Romanticism*, pp. 16–17, 30–47.

human energy exerted in its production – that is to say, the quantity of labour – was acknowledged to be the only source of a commodity's exchange value, a fact which led to an inevitable conflict between classes over the division of wealth. And the resulting unresolvable tension between the elements of the social organism was further thought to require constant economic expansion. Far from seeming a machine with a fixed input and output, the national capitalist economy was imagined to be a creature facing the distinctly lifelike alternatives of either growing or dying. In the post-war period, political economy was increasingly used to explain the relations among labour, value and life, as well as the peculiarly conflicted relations among various parts of the social organism. After briefly summarizing the main points of Ricardo's argument, I will discuss, first, some Romantic perspectives on the issue of labour and value, and, second, Coleridge's understanding of the inevitability of class conflict.[19]

Ricardo's *Principles of Political Economy and Taxation* opens with the question of how a society's wealth is distributed among the three parties involved in its production: labour (or the working class), capital (or the owners of the means of production), and rent (or the land-owning class). He did not ask how it should be distributed or how statesmen intend that it be distributed, but how it is distributed, following the internal and natural dynamics of capitalism, without any premeditation. His first step in answering this question was to explain how things acquire their exchangeable value in the first place, distinguishing the origin of value from its measurement. Ricardo clarified and developed the labour theory of exchange value, which his predecessors had confusingly and ambivalently indicated. Forty years earlier, in *The Wealth of Nations*, Adam Smith had taken labour to be the source and measure of exchange value and often calculated the value of labour by the value of the commodities (primarily the food) necessary to replenish the body for the hours of labour expended on another commodity. Thus he rooted the exchange value of any commodity in biological need; the worker's body was the primary nexus of exchange through which the value of those commodities that reproduce its labour largely determine the value of all other commodities. Ricardo cleared up many inconsistencies in Smith's formulations, distinguishing

---

19 For an account of the differences between Coleridge's social vision and that of the political economists, see David P. Calleo, *Coleridge and the Idea of the Modern State* (New Haven: Yale University Press, 1966); see also William F. Kennedy, *Humanist versus Economist: The Economic Thought of Samuel Taylor Coleridge* (Berkeley: University of California Press, 1958).

especially between labour as the origin and labour as the measure of value, and his corrections had the effect of rendering value even more definitively biological. For by insisting that the *quantity* of labour, the measurable sum of the workers' lives, is the sole determinate of a commodity's 'natural' exchange value,[20] he further literalized the older metaphors of the economy as an animated being. In the Ricardian theory, human vitality pulses through every exchange. After establishing this essential rule, Ricardo's *Principles* returns to the question of who gets what share of the produce of labour. The wealth, he explained, is allocated by the vital needs of the economy itself, especially by the imperative that it constantly *grow* in order to stay alive. The shares of the produce of labour, he held, are apportioned by the constant struggle among the three contending classes in the context of the varying conditions retarding or advancing the rate of profit and contracting or expanding economic activity.

The easiest part of Ricardo's book for contemporaries to accept and assimilate to various agendas was its apparent restatement of the labour theory of value, with its echoes not only of Adam Smith but also of John Locke, or, for that matter, the Bible. The theory could be taken to buttress commonplace bourgeois pieties: labour is virtuous and should be cheerfully sought; one should work as hard as possible; the industrious are superior to the idle. Work was increasingly valorized, even idealized, as a good in itself, not only a means to an end but also a process through which one realized oneself. Moreover, as the economic distress deepened instead of lifting in the 1820s, a new radical working-class movement used the theory to press its own claims: if labour alone created value then labourers deserve the whole produce of their efforts. These moral and political uses of the theory, though, operated at a great distance from the political economists' intentions. They were by no means touting the independent virtues of work, which for them remained mere toil. In fact, they assumed it was a *painful* necessity, certainly not a joyful activity or a means of self-realization, and it is only as pain that labour factors into the pain/pleasure calculation that economic agents make when deciding how to spend their time. 'Aversion', explained Jeremy Bentham, 'is the emotion, the only emotion, which

---

20 Several other factors, including the ratio of supply to demand, might influence the market price of a commodity, but these would act as temporary modifications of the 'natural' value. On Ricardian economics, see Mark Blaug, *Ricardian Economics: A Historical Study* (New Haven: Yale University Press, 1958); and D. P. O'Brien, *The Classical Economists* (Oxford: Clarendon Press, 1975).

labour, taken by itself, is qualified to produce.'[21] 'Aversion' leads to the division of labour in the first place and then motivates people to keep track of the time spent in various tasks. Although the labour theorists of value seldom dwelt on the quality of exertion expended in production, they nevertheless assumed as axiomatic that everyone strives to counterbalance the affliction of labour by the pleasures of remuneration and consumption. If work were intrinsically pleasurable, economic calculations would be unmotivated, and one would not be able to tell the difference between labour and leisure. The labour theory of value, in short, rested on certain naturalistic assumptions about how our individual sensations, our sensitivity to pain and pleasure, are aggregated into complex economic systems.

Coleridge noted early on that political economists viewed labour from this peculiar vantage-point, although he seems to have missed the reason for their self-imposed limitation. Since the publication of *The Wealth of Nations*, political economists had explained that they were primarily concerned with the labour that created *exchange* value; such labour would have to be performed inside a market economy and produce a surplus over the subsistence (or reproduction) of the labour itself. This sort of labour, which yields a profit as well as a wage, Smith called 'productive' to distinguish it from other kinds of work which might nevertheless be both necessary and creative: in his list,

> The sovereign, for example, with all the officers both of justice and war who serve under him, the whole army and navy, are unproductive labourers . . . In the same class must be ranked, some both of the gravest and most important, and some of the most frivolous professions: churchmen, lawyers, physicians, men of letters of all kinds; players, buffoons, musicians, opera-singers, opera-dancers; &c.   (p. 295)

The division of the population into kinds of labourers was both an extraordinary innovation (since previously many of the people on Smith's list weren't imagined to be labouring at all) and a neutral analytical tool by which those who built up the nation's capital could be distinguished from those who did not. Later political economists disputed the boundaries and usefulness of these categories, but the distinction was never intended to separate valid from invalid, or useful from useless occupations.

---

21 *Deontology, Together with a Table of the Springs of Action, and the Article on Utilitarianism,* ed. Amnon Goldworth (Oxford: Clarendon Press, 1983), p. 104.

But Coleridge, like many other critics of political economy, seemed to think that it was, and he chose to base his critique of the political economists' logic on an early, and superseded, iteration of the distinction, by James Steuart (1767), in which what would later be termed 'productive' is called 'useful to society' and 'unproductive' is identified as 'useful only to oneself'. Steuart used the example of a vine-dresser who spends half his day growing enough grain to feed himself and his family and the other half growing grapes for the market, to be exchanged for other commodities. Using this example to demonstrate the difference between 'Agriculture exercised *as a trade*, and *as a direct means of subsisting*', Coleridge quotes Steuart as concluding 'that as to the last part he is only useful to himself; but as to the first, he is useful to the society and becomes a member of it; consequently were it not for his trade the State would lose nothing, although the vine-dresser and his land were both swallowed up by an earthquake'.[22] Influenced, perhaps, more by the closing image than by the logic of the entire passage (in which Steuart is articulating the levels of market, society and state), Coleridge took Steuart to mean that the man's life is useless, that he is a cipher unworthy to live, and Coleridge goes on to claim that this narrow definition of value in labour can distort and corrupt social existence. Devising a contrasting idyll, Coleridge imagines a countryman who, after spending half the day in subsistence farming, 'endeavoured to provide for his moral and intellectual appetites, by physical experiments and philosophical research, by acquiring knowledge for himself, and communicating it to his wife and children'. 'Would he be useful then?' Coleridge asks, and imagines the negative reply of the political economist: '*He* useful! The state would lose nothing although [he] and his land were both swallowed up by an earthquake!' (p. 300).

It was Coleridge, of course, not Steuart, who moralized the issues; Steuart said only that a man living in complete economic isolation would not be missed by the state if he disappeared, whereas Coleridge seems to think he was being condemned to perdition, cast into some sort of hell. Moreover, Coleridge's competing idyll has all the unreality of the genre: if the man were truly labouring only for subsistence, how could he have the means for 'physical experiments and philosophical research?' Steuart's point was that such things come from surplus, exchangeable produce, whereas Coleridge apparently thought that they were just given in the state of nature. He is really picturing an idealized version of himself, a man of

---

22 *The Friend*, I, 299.

middle-class means doing light labour in the morning and spending the afternoon in scholarly pursuits, or in being 'neighbourly', like the author of *The Friend*.

And that, indeed, was typical of the Romantic train of thought. Coleridge's mind ran so quickly and defensively to a situation like his own – to the value of providing for 'his moral and intellectual appetites' and 'acquiring knowledge for himself and communicating it' – because political economy seemed to denigrate intellectual and authorial labour. What, after all, does it add to the wealth of the nation? Assuming its paltry contribution to capital and its usual inability even to support the writer's household, what sort of labour is it? It seems neither 'useful to society' nor sufficiently 'useful to himself'. 'Men of letters of all kinds' are definitely on Adam Smith's list of 'unproductive' workers, to use the terminology later employed by most classical political economists; and even though the mixed nature of the company (ranging from the sovereign to the buffoon) should make it clear that 'unproductive' is not a term of moral condemnation, it nevertheless resonated negatively.

It is hard to determine whether political economy created an anxious defensiveness about authorial – especially literary – production or merely provided a focus for a worry engendered by the larger sea change in the general attitude toward labour, but nineteenth-century writers, starting with the Romantics, certainly felt compelled to describe their labours, while expanding the concept of productivity in ways that countered the economists' apparent reduction. Some, like Coleridge, developed vitalistic accounts of their literary products, which resembled but also exceeded the labour theory of value's accent on the amount of *life* (the quantity of labour) that goes into a product. Literary labour might not appear to be exertion at all, might, as in Coleridge's version of the composition of 'Kubla Khan', be accomplished in one's sleep, but for that very reason be the conduit of a powerful visionary force. Just as Coleridge broke down the distinction between acting and recuperating, Wordsworth also confounded the border between leisure and labour, indolence and industry. In contrast to labour's normal, externally coerced condition, its poetic state is unwilled and unconstrained, as implied in Wordsworth's famous formulation from the 'Preface' to the Lyrical Ballads (1798) – 'the spontaneous overflow of powerful feelings'.

The emotion of the poetic worker, like that of the political economists' labourer, is apposite to the product's value as well, but here, too, we see a striking contrast. Unhappiness may subtend labour in political economy and may therefore condition exchange value, but the commodity itself isn't painful; indeed, it is normally pleasurable. In contrast, the poetic product actually *is* the superabundance of powerful, unsubdued feeling, which might indeed be painful and yet mingled with the pleasurable effects of the medium when read or heard. The intermixing of pain and pleasure in both the production and consumption of poetry would, moreover, seem to place it in a realm far from the Benthamite calculus on which exchange value rests, in which the two kinds of sensation must be easily told apart so that we will know what, in Bentham's terms, to 'minimize' and what to 'maximize'. The Romantics, one might *almost* say, might have claimed that their work made a clean contrast with Ricardian labour by being an unalienated expression of the superabundance of affective being (Shelley's 'best and happiest moments of the happiest and best minds'[23]) in which emotional states are often complex wholes and products are inseparable from producers.

But that is only one side of the Romantics' representation of their labour. On the other side, we should note their emphasis on the suffering of creative work, especially in Coleridge and De Quincey, which seems to share in the labour theory of value's implicit reliance on unhappy work. The very absence of a resistant material medium, which might seem the condition of unconstrained labour, also threatened to mire the poet in fanciful delusions. The precarious state of the poet, his desolation or harrowing experiences in the terrifying depths of the imagination, are a sensational version of the labourer's intimacy with mortality, the constant pressure of necessity in his existence. And the writer's vocational challenges, as Wordsworth's *Prelude* attests, are recurrent themes, as is the complex relation between his own labour and the often economically marginal labouring lives he depicted.[24] Although not highly productive in an economic sense, the lives of Wordsworth's country people receive a different kind of value through their representation, and the poet might be said to 'live', through the

---

23 'Defense of Poetry', *Shelley's Poetry and Prose*, ed. Donald H. Reiman and Sharon B. Powers (New York: Norton, 1977), p. 504.
24 For discussions of these topics and further elaboration of Romantic poetic labour, see Gary Harrison, *Wordsworth's Vagrant Muse: Poetry, Poverty, and Power* (Detroit: Wayne State University Press, 1994); Clifford Siskin, *The Work of Writing: Literature and Social Change in Britain, 1700–1830* (Baltimore: Johns Hopkins University Press, 1998); Willard Spiegelman, *Majestic Indolence: English Romantic Poetry and the Work of Art* (New York: Oxford University Press, 1995); Thomas Pfau, *Wordsworth's Profession: Form, Class, and the Logic of Early Romantic Cultural Production* (New York: Cambridge University Press, 1993).

sympathetic understanding instantiated in the poems, their accumulated struggles. The poet, in other words, came up with a competing answer to the question of how labourers produce value, and he made himself the centre of that process; but as in the political economists' account, value still seems to rely on deprivation.

Romanticism, we might say, activated a latent contradiction between eighteenth-century aesthetics, which often privileged the desirable pain of sublimity, and utilitarianism, which assumed all pain to be undesirable. In his *Philosophical Enquiry into the Origin of Our Ideas of the Sublime and the Beautiful* Edmund Burke had already linked, while differentiating, toil and the terror of the sublime: 'as common labour, which is a mode of pain, is the exercise of the grosser, a mode of terror is the exercise of the finer parts of the system . . .'[25] And yet the aestheticians were no more paradoxical than the economists in preferring the pain-born product; indeed, it is a striking coincidence that the sublime was elevated above the beautiful in the same decades that labour, old Adam's affliction and the bane of human existence, was discovered to be the source of value. By linking the agony of the poet to the unhappiness of the labourer, Romanticism further solidified this kinship between the economists' and the aestheticians' concepts of value.

The Romantics, that is, defended literary labour in two, incommensurate ways: (1) they presented it as an idealized, perhaps utopian, contrast to the economists' miserable but 'productive' labour, and (2) they stressed that they felt as alienated in their work, as jeopardized or engulfed in suffering as any productive worker. Their representation of labour crossed that of the political economists sometimes and at others ran parallel to it. The deeper similarity, though, was that both groups undertook the description of the relations among life, labour, feeling and value; despite the huge differences between them, both felt professionally dedicated to that task. To be sure, most political economists paid short shrift to their own labour or to that of any professional men and/or writers, for they all fell outside of the 'productive' fold. Smith, for example, did not seem at all bothered by the fact that he belonged to his own 'unproductive' category. The poets, however, looked to their own work as paradigmatic for understanding the right relations among life, labour and value, and what they found there was no harmonious enterprise, but a seemingly contradictory juxtaposition of

---

25 *Philosophical Enquiry into the Origin of Our Ideas of the Sublime and the Beautiful*, Part 4, Section vi. For more on feeling, labour and poetry, see Kevis Goodman, *Georgic Modernity and British Romanticism: Poetry and the Mediation of History* (Cambridge: Cambridge University Press, 2004).

states, which eluded the available ideological frameworks. Eventually it would come to seem a free-standing discourse, the one we call 'Romanticism', which drew on the earlier idea of the sublime and featured the fusion of pain and pleasure in the creator and his product.

We should not leave the topic of value without mentioning the contribution of the one Romantic writer who aspired to be something of a political economist himself and who subscribed to the Ricardian position: Thomas De Quincey. He wrote two important works on the subject; the first, *Dialogues of Three Templars on Political Economy, Chiefly in Relation to the Principles of Mr. Ricardo* (1824), explicates and defends Ricardo, stressing his superiority to Smith and Malthus; the second, *The Logic of Political Economy* (1844), attempts to clarify the theory of value by paying special attention to the concept of 'use value'. Like Ricardo, De Quincey ignored the emotional state of the producer; the very category of labour assuming that which people generally wish to avoid. The subjective state of the purchaser was *normally* likewise inapposite to exchange value, but De Quincey claimed that the strength of desire can have an effect on the value of an item whenever supply and demand are not in equilibrium. Then, he argued, exchange value can be shown to consist not only of what he calls the 'negative' value of the cost of production (labour) but also the 'positive' value of 'use', or the value of the commodity to a particular purchaser at a particular time. Use value may normally be submerged in exchange value, but in eccentric markets it reveals itself to be part of the market value.

De Quincey is careful to point out that he is not talking about *intrinsic* usefulness, or some objective utility in the commodity; in order to obviate such misunderstandings, he goes so far as to discuss the market value of a rare poison for one who might want to kill himself. Use value seems altogether personal; it is 'the utmost sacrifice to which you would ever submit ... under the known alternative of losing [the commodity] if you refuse [to pay]'.[26] The extreme subjectivity of the origin of use value, therefore, requires an inordinate amount of narrative; we cannot, for example, conceive the economic logic of a man who pays one hundred times the 'natural' price for a music box unless we know where he is, where he's going, and what his personal tastes are. There is, indeed, so much circumstantial narrative in De Quincey's explication of use value that it

---

26 *The Logic of Political Economy*, in *The Works of Thomas De Quincey* (New York: Hurd and Houghton, 1878), vol. X, p. 81. For more on De Quincey and political economy see Josephine McDonagh, *De Quincey's Disciplines* (Oxford: Clarendon Press, 1994).

overwhelms his abstract point: use value is always there in market value even when the equilibrium of the market keeps it identical with exchange value. And even if one were willing to cede the point – John Stuart Mill thought it had been anticipated from the beginning – it is difficult to know how it could be applied on any but an individual, narrative basis.

The significance of De Quincey's book, therefore, lay less in its direct contribution to the discipline than in its impulse to draw out and examine the issue of individual desire in political economy. In doing so, he anticipated the political economy of the end of the century, which would try to understand the relation between value and what came to be called the 'marginal utility' of a commodity to the consumer. Moreover, unlike most Romantics, De Quincey also broached the question of aesthetic value from the point of view of the receiver of the art work. For example, in describing the relation between what he called 'affirmative value' (what someone is willing to pay) and 'negative value' (the quantity of labour invested or needed to reproduce the identical item), he seized on an aesthetic instance: '. . . a genuine picture of Da Vinci's or Raphael's, sells always on the principle of value in use, or teleologic value' (p. 82). The uniqueness of the works of the dead artist are what take them altogether out of the purview of the labour theory of value; they cannot be reproduced through any amount of labour, and yet they clearly have a market value. That value must be put there entirely by the potential purchasers.

This is one of De Quincey's highly unusual instances of a market value made up entirely of a use value, one that completely escapes from the logic of the labour theory of value. In De Quincey's scheme, therefore, the specialness of the value of certain aesthetic works has nothing whatever to do with the agony or the ecstasy of the artist but arises wholly from the desire and the wherewithal of the beholder. It may seem odd that a Romantic who was also a good Ricardian would conclude that the rare aesthetic commodity receives none of its market value in production, but Ricardo himself had excepted 'some commodities, the value of which is determined by their scarcity alone' from the general rule that production is the source of value. Like De Quincey, he gave 'rare statues and pictures, scarce books and coins, wines of a peculiar quality', as instances because 'no labour can increase the quantity of such goods'.[27] Ricardo's exclusion of such rarities from the behaviour of normal commodities has been identified by John Guillory as a significant indication of the dissociation between

27 *The Principles of Political Economy and Taxation*, p. 6.

economics and aesthetics,[28] but it should also be noted that Ricardo and De Quincey were giving *economic* explanations for these anomalies, and De Quincey was trying to extend the reach of political economy to include such eccentric markets. It should be noted as well that the exceptions would not include any works capable of mere mechanical reproduction, such as printed literature; 'scarce books' are items in the book market, not the literary market. Nevertheless, such commodities do direct our attention to the buyer's desire, and De Quincey's *Logic of Political Economy* therefore allows us to see that even Ricardian political economy was forced to acknowledge the limits of the labour theory of value.

And the labour theory of value was the least controversial part of Ricardo's thought. The social implications of his argument, especially his configurations of class interests and antipathies, were less familiar and more painful to contemplate. He not only divided the nation into two sectors of economic activity, agriculture and industry, but also presented those spheres as opposed. The interests of the owners of land, because their rents increased as the rate of profit declined and stagnation threatened, especially conflicted with the economic interests of all 'productive' classes: farmers, agricultural labourers, industrial capitalists and industrial workers. And the interests of capital and labour in both spheres were also necessarily antagonistic, for any increase in wages led to a drop in profits and vice versa. Ricardo's theories seemed, if not to encourage, then at least to tolerate class conflict as an inevitability, and his body politic was composed of parts that only worked in tension with each other; certainly each part contributed to the whole, but not in a blithely harmonious manner.

Some working-class radicals in the period (for example Thomas Hodgskin, John Gray and William Thompson) may have taken sustenance from Ricardo's ideas[29] or may have built directly on earlier radicals inspired by Adam Smith, but there is no doubt that the popularization of political economy accompanied the growth of trade unionism and the legitimation

---

28 John Guillory, *Cultural Capital: The Problem of Literary Canon Formation* (Chicago: University of Chicago Press, 1993), p. 315. Guillory's persuasive and influential argument uses Caygill's account of the original connection between aesthetics and political economy in the discourse of moral philosophy to explain the incoherence of attempts by aestheticians to construct a concept of 'aesthetic value' in the art object that would be wholly independent of economic value.

29 See Noel W. Thompson, *The People's Science: The Popular Political Economy of Exploitation and Crisis, 1816–1834* (Cambridge: Cambridge University Press, 1984), pp. 83–110, for the historiographic debate over the amount of influence Ricardo actually had on the thinking of so-called 'Ricardian socialists'.

of contesting class interests. A significant portion of the population began to identify, subjectively, with the social categories that Ricardo had outlined as competing economic classes. Especially in industrial areas of Britain, class consciousness became a primary mode of self-understanding.[30]

Coincidentally, in the same year that Ricardo published *The Principles of Political Economy and Taxation*, Coleridge also published a view of the nation's economic forces and their interactions in his *A Lay Sermon, Addressed to the Higher and Middle Classes on the Existing Distresses and Discontents*. In many regards, the two works form an instructive contrast. Coleridge identified 'Commerce' and 'Agriculture' as separate sectors, but he argued that the 'Spirit of Commerce' has slowly infiltrated and overwhelmed the true purposes of Agriculture, 'which ultimately are the same as those of the State of which it is the offspring'.[31] Commerce, he admitted, has propelled the nation's progress and continues to open avenues for industry and talent, but it also encourages speculative behaviour, confuses ends and means, and fails to acknowledge a difference between 'Things and Persons' (p. 220). Land owners, however, because they hold their estates 'in trust' for the State, should put the moral, physical and mental well-being of their dependants ahead of all commercial considerations. Coleridge, therefore, did not believe landowners to be a separate economic class primarily; they were, rather, intrinsic units of the State itself, who should resist acting in their own commercial interest. Only because they had surrendered their true purpose and identity to the spirit of commerce, which should properly be confined to its own sphere, had they pursued enclosures, depopulation of the countryside, and impoverishment of their labourers.

Thus Coleridge reversed Ricardo. Instead of regarding the landholders as the most specialized and unproductive of economic classes, Coleridge insisted that, in their deepest essence, they were not an economic class at all, but local instantiations of the Whole which is the State. Instead of basing the good of the nation on the unimpeded activity of the most vigorous elements of commerce, Coleridge concluded that 'Our manufacturers must consent to regulations' (p. 229) and asked 'Agriculture' to provide a counterweight to commerce as a cure for the post-war distress, which had been visited mainly on the labouring populations of both the towns and agricultural districts.

---

30 E. P. Thompson describes this process in detail in his *Making of the English Working Class* (New York: Vintage, 1966).
31 *Lay Sermons*, p. 216.

And yet the very neatness of the contrast between the two works attests to their deep structural congruity. In both, the nation is divided into two sectors (or spheres). For Ricardo, these were agriculture and industrial production, while for Coleridge they were Agriculture (with a capital 'A') and what he calls 'Commerce'. Ricardo's 'industry' looked forward to nineteenth-century discourse, whereas Coleridge's 'commerce' maintained continuity with eighteenth-century social thought, especially that of Edmund Burke. But despite their differences in orientation, Ricardo and Coleridge name roughly similar divisions. Moreover, each imagined three classes: landowners, capitalists and labourers, even though Coleridge insisted that the first of these was more than a class. Finally, and most surprisingly, both envisioned the relations among these groups to be anti-pathetic; neither thinks that landlord and capitalist can act harmoniously in concert, and both point to the strife between capital and labour. To be sure, the antipathy arose for different reasons in the two writers' accounts, but both thought it natural for the possessors of the land and the owners of capital to counteract each other, and both believed that the 'commercial spirit' automatically instrumentalizes the labouring population. Ricardo may have fretted less than Coleridge about the necessity of a society in conflict, and Coleridge may have hoped to reform 'our Agricultural system' into an island of amicable paternalism in a sea of expanding commercial strife, but in confronting the post-war realities of industrializing Britain they both depicted a nation whose vitality depended on the contention of opposing forces. Indeed, Coleridge's hopes for Agriculture were belied by his later call for the artificial creation of a special order, a 'clerisy',[32] that could transcend all interests and represent the State in its entirety.

In the immediate post-war period, though, the organicism of both thinkers resembled less the early modern hierarchical model of a smoothly coordinated body-politic, with an undisputed head and numerous subor-dinate parts, than the model that Darwin (with Malthus's help) would come to articulate in the 1850s. With the substantial prodding of political econ-omy, British organicism, even in its Romantic form, underwent a transition from imagining the nation on the model of a unified single organism to imagining it as a vital autotelic system, not only tolerating but also requiring dynamic conflict.

32 Coleridge develops the idea of a clerisy in *On the Constitution of the Church and State: According to the Idea of Each*, in *The Collected Works of Samuel Taylor Coleridge*, vol. X, ed. John Colmer (London: Routledge and Kegan Paul/Princeton: Princeton Uni-versity Press, 1969).

By the 1830s, the controversies I've described here had themselves come to seem 'natural'. It appeared that a 'humanist' literary sensibility instinctively opposed the scientific objectification of human activity; or, conversely, it appeared that an empirical understanding of the optimal modes of accumulating and distributing social wealth came under fire from moralists who wanted to interfere with those processes. And yet both sides promoted the nineteenth-century apotheosis of 'Life' as an ultimate good, and both looked to the feelings of the mass of people to measure the success of a way of 'Life'. As Michel Foucault argued in *The Order of Things*, the nineteenth-century 'episteme' (the ordering principles of its knowledge) initially organized the world according to biological models: '. . . man, his psyche, his group, his society, the language he speaks – all these exist in the Romantic period as living beings'.[33] And the prevailing models of knowledge throughout the century remained biological; even in the twentieth century, Alfred Marshall remarked that 'the Mecca of the economist is economic biology'.[34] The seemingly intractable controversies we've been examining over the competing *varieties* of 'organicism' helped establish its ubiquity and laid the basis for many of the distinctive traits of Victorian literary realism and social science.

33 Michel Foucault, *The Order of Things: An Archeology of the Human Sciences* (New York: Random House, 1970), p. 359.
34 Foucault argued that the biological model in the Human Sciences was followed by economic and anthropological models, but he also recognized that both of these built on certain premises about life. Moreover, Foucault names Ricardo not just as an author of the discourse of economics but also as the thinker who located the source of value in physiological labour, thereby rooting it in the productive body. See *The Order of Things*, pp. 253–63. Alfred Marshall's remark is in *The Memorials of Alfred Marshall*, ed. Alfred Pigou (London, Macmillan, 1925), p. 318.

4

The problem of periodization: Enlightenment, Romanticism and the fate of system

CLIFFORD SISKIN

What is Enlightenment?

When Immanuel Kant answered the question 'What is Enlightenment?' in 1784, he defined it not only as a philosophical concept but as a particular moment in history. Looking back *from* the 1780s – over decades of debate regarding reason and religion, scepticism and idealism – he had no trouble naming his period: 'we do live in an age of enlightenment'.[1] Looking back *to* the 1780s, however, is another matter. The irony, for us, of Kant's confident assertion is that he made it at precisely the moment that has since come to mark the start of another age: the period we call Romantic. Kant's certainty about his own age is now a central *un*certainty of our own: the problem of periodization.

Was there a period shift in the late eighteenth century? Do the terms 'Enlightenment' and 'Romanticism' describe it? The progressive agenda of Enlightenment complicates the confusion. If, for example, history followed the developmental logic of Kant's vision – he argued that his present 'age of enlightenment' would lead to 'an enlightened age' – Romanticism as the next period would realize rather than reject what came before. But what we call Romanticism came with its own baggage – claims of difference, of a turn from the past. In that scenario, Romanticism has been either celebrated as a remedy – a cleansing new 'Spirit of the Age' – or blamed as a reaction – an emotionally charged retreat from the rational means and ends of Enlightenment.

---

1 Immanuel Kant, 'An Answer to the Question: 'What is Enlightenment?'' in *Kant's Political Writings*, ed. Hans Reiss (Cambridge: Cambridge University Press, 1970), p. 58. My thanks to my research assistants at the University of Glasgow, Anthony Jarrells and then Thomas Mole, for their considerable help with this project.

Since this problem began, in a sense, with Kant's answer, I will begin by reposing the question: 'What is Enlightenment?' Given that the query is as old as the object it interrogates, there is an easy answer: the Enlightenment is that which asks itself what it is. But instead of a self-reflexive, philosophical response, our goal here of period specificity demands a concrete one – one that pins the object down to a time, a place, a technology. If the evidence that Enlightenment *has* been practised is the knowledge it produces, then how is it produced? With what tools? Using which procedures? How does Enlightenment materialize?

The technology of Enlightenment is *writing*;[2] the tools are the forms that writing assumed in the eighteenth century; the procedures are the characteristic ways those forms mixed. Those mixtures, as we shall see, took knowledge in the different directions we call disciplines. Enlightenment thus materialized *in* writing *as* disciplinarity; it transported us into the modern organization of knowledge.

However, when you are along for the ride – as Einstein has told us – it is hard to detect the motion. Fortunately, such travelling leaves traces – and the trace that is the calling card of Enlightenment is the palimpsest. It not only figures the confusion of Enlightenment and Romanticism; even when we use the term 'Enlightenment' *alone*, two different versions seem to overwrite each other. One version is of a historically specific phenomenon in the past – the Enlightenment as a moment confined to the eighteenth century, as in the Scottish Enlightenment; the other is of Enlightenment as the condition of modernity, that is, something that we are all still in. It is tempting to blame the Enlightenment itself for this apparent confusion, but doing so would be to give in to what Foucault called the intellectual 'blackmail' of the Enlightenment – the feeling that we must be either for or against it.[3]

My strategy is not to choose but to explain – explain the very propensity to blame by linking Enlightenment to that which we have come to blame habitually for just about everything: the System, which, in its most popular form, works both too well – 'you can't beat the System' – and not well

<hr />

2 This claim to writing's centrality in Enlightenment does not deny the importance of other forms of expression and communication, such as the visual; rather, it highlights the ways that the interrelated practices of writing, reading and print both frame and inform – as when we 'read' a painting – those other forms. See Raymond Williams's argument for a 'history of writing' in *Writing in Society* (London: Verso, 1983), pp. 1–7.
3 Michel Foucault, 'What is Enlightenment?', in Paul Rabinow (ed.), *The Foucault Reader* (New York: Pantheon, 1984), pp. 42–3.

enough – it always seems to 'break down'. In the twenty-first century, we 'blame the System' even as we admit systems of all kinds – operating systems, support systems, ecosystems, telephone systems – into our lives. In the eighteenth century, systems were also powerful and ubiquitous, but the technology that embodied them then was different: writing was the new technology and system was not just an idea but a *genre* – a form of writing that competed with other forms, particularly the essay, to become a central means of knowledge production. As a genre with an important function in the past – and newly important functions today – system can serve as an index to change: pointing across the history of writing to how the Enlightenment world of learning, in which writers used systems, became today's knowledge-driven society, in which we feel that the System uses us.

For students of the Enlightenment, this turn to system will not surprise – its centrality to the period confirmed in the debate over its use famously epitomized by Ernst Cassirer:

> In renouncing, and even in directly opposing, the 'spirit of systems' (*esprit de système*), the philosophy of the Enlightenment by no means gives up the 'systematic spirit' (*esprit systématique*); it aims rather to further this spirit in another and more effective manner.[4]

System's spirit was Enlightenment's goal: comprehensive knowledge of a world that could be known. Both the actual genre of 'system', as well as the manifestations of its spirit in similarly ambitious attempts at comprehensiveness from encyclopedias to treatises, are widely recognised markers of Enlightenment aspiration.

Students of Romanticism, however, will be on less familiar terms with system, in part because our standard literary histories have fixed upon a different set of terms and genres to signal and embody the spirit of this age: genius and imagination, fragment and lyric. A few uses have surfaced, however, that at least sound Romantic, notably the 'howl[ing]' battlecry of Blake's Los in *Jerusalem*:

> I must Create a System, or be enslav'd by another Mans
> I will not Reason & Compare: my business is to Create
>
> (1.10.20–1)[5]

---

4 Ernst Cassirer, *The Philosophy of Enlightenment*, trans. Fritz C. A. Koelin and James P. Pettegrove (Boston: Beacon Press, 1955), p. vii.
5 William Blake, *The Poetry and Prose of William Blake*, ed. David V. Erdman with commentary by Harold Bloom (New York: Doubleday, 1970), p. 151.

As so often in Blake, seemingly High Romantic features – the 'I' that 'must Create' – exhibit their Enlightenment underpinnings: 'Creat[ion]' is defined in opposition to 'Reason'. The turn to 'System' is similarly revealing. Los's creative 'business' is – in fact and out of necessity – the business of Enlightenment: the making of Systems.

My point is not that all references to system are Enlightenment holdovers or that Romanticism is relatively bereft of them – precisely the opposite is the case – but that, for specific historical reasons, we do not know where and how to look. It is hard, of course, to miss Blake at full rhetorical throttle, and thus in regard to system he appears, as usual, to be an exception – but an exception that can help to clarify the larger picture. System is as crucial to Romantic writing as Blake's embattled declaration makes it sound; in fact, invocations of, and accusations regarding, system are the discursive weapons with which Romanticism configured itself.

Take, for example, the dividing up of writing into 'schools'. 'Mr. Wordsworth is a System maker' bellowed the *Poetical Register* reviewer of *Poems in Two Volumes*,[6] an attack famously echoed by Francis Jeffrey: 'With Mr. Wordsworth and his friends, it is plain that their peculiarities of diction are things of choice, and not of accident. They write as they do upon principle and system.'[7] Grouped under the rubric of system, these writers became easy targets of withering attacks; in the very manoeuvre feared by Los, they were 'enslav'd' by another man's system: the critical system of grouping under system. Taking Los's advice and, in defence, creating a system of one's own did not, of course, end such strife, but provoked it. Thus Leigh Hunt defended his 'vulgarisms' to Byron by asserting that 'his style was a system', only to be dismissed systematically as a system-maker: 'when a man talks of system', wrote Byron, 'his case is hopeless'.[8] As case after case followed the principle articulated in *Don Juan* – 'One system eats another up' (XIV.2.5)[9] – the discursive map of Britain was redrawn, with a 'Lake School' now at one end and a 'Cockney School' at another.

---

6 Review of *Poems in Two Volumes* in the *Poetical Register*, cited in Robert Woof (ed.), *William Wordsworth: The Critical Heritage*, vol. I (London and New York: Routledge, 2001), p. 231.

7 Review of *Poems* (1807) by Francis Jeffrey in the *Edinburgh Review*, cited in Woof (ed.), *Critical Heritage*, pp. 185–201.

8 *Byron's Letters and Journals*, ed. Leslie A. Marchand, 13 vols. (London: John Murray, 1973–94), vol. VI, p. 46.

9 *Lord Byron: The Complete Poetical Works*, ed. Jerome J. McGann, 7 vols. (Oxford: Clarendon Press, 1980–93), vol. V, *Don Juan* (1986), p. 559.

Many other features of that map, from generations to genres, were similarly inscribed. In system, then, lies the secret history of Romanticism – its tale of self-configuration and thus its continuities with and departures from Enlightenment. To hear it we have to follow system's fate through both periods, tracking it not just as an idea, but as a genre. Blake again points the way here, for he consistently gives system weight, reminding the reader that ideas take form:

> . . . I saw the finger of God go forth
> Upon my Furnaces, from within the Wheels of Albions Sons:
> Fixing their Systems, permanent: by mathematic power
> Giving a body to Falshood that it may be cast off for ever.
>
> (1.12.10–13)

By recovering the history of system as something embodied – as something that embodies things – we can cast off some of the confusion surrounding the Enlightenment/Romanticism divide: 'you cannot behold him', wrote Blake, 'till he be reveald in his System' (2.43.10).

System as a genre

And all depends on keeping the mind's eye fixed on things themselves, so that their images are received exactly as they are.
(Bacon, *The Great Instauration* (1620)[10])

The question now afloat in the world respecting *Things As They Are* is the most interesting that can be presented to the human mind.
(Godwin, Preface to *Caleb Williams* (1794)[11])

During the seventeenth and eighteenth centuries in Western Europe, systems were written to answer a basic 'question' about the real world – what Bacon termed 'things' 'as they are'. How do we know them? Induction used things as the means to an end: observation and experiment were expected to yield knowledge in the forms of principles or descriptive laws. Deduction, however, put principles first as the means for knowing things. For Bacon, the systematical was a particularly pernicious form of deduction, for he saw

10 Francis Bacon, *Novum Organum With Other Parts of The Great Instauration* (1620), trans. Peter Urbach and John Gibson (Chicago: Open Court, 1994), pp. 29–30.
11 William Godwin, *Things As They Are; or, The Adventures of Caleb Williams* (1794), ed. Maurice Hindle (London: Penguin, 1988), p. 3.

putting principles *before* things as an 'anticipation of nature' that prevented the proper 'fix[ation]' of mind.[12]

What troubled Bacon was that particular use of system, but *not* system itself as a written form of inquiry. In fact, he insisted that his own plan for the 'restoration' of science 'must only be made by a natural history, and that of a new kind and compiled on a new *system*' (p. 24). Thus even as the idea of system as an epistemological procedure was critiqued, the *genre* of system remained a primary vehicle for the production of knowledge. Although this distinction resembles Cassirer's between '*esprit de système*' and '*esprit systématique*', there is a crucial difference of emphasis. In both versions, the reaction to the dangers of system-making was the desire for form. Cassirer, however, stresses the Platonic nature of the quest: 'Enlightenment wants philosophy to move freely and in this immanent activity to discover the fundamental form of reality, the form of all natural and spiritual being'.[13] Bacon also wanted to know the real, but his focus was always on things – in this case, on forms materialized *in* writing; he sought the proper genres for his undertaking.

Bacon recognized, however, that even a desirable genre such as system – precisely because it was the product of desire – could reproduce the problem of anticipating nature; it might define what science could be, rather than what, at that time, it actually was. In the early stages of restoration, Bacon realized, system might easily be deployed as 'method', with rhetoric[14] – rather than knowledge of things – 'fill[ing] out' the initially 'empty' spaces. His solution was again generic: claiming to follow the 'first and earliest seekers after truth', he wrote 'short' and 'scattered' aphorisms, a form that conveyed, he argued, the sense of 'knowledge in growth' (pp. 96, xii). The alternative that proved most popular, however, was the 'essay', for that genre was not then understood as a finished piece of knowledge but as an irregular attempt.

In the next century, Bacon's experimental tools became the genres of Enlightenment. In fact, in the 122 times that system and its variants appear in the first edition of Johnson's *Dictionary* that is its most telling guise.[15] The second quotation under the term 'systematical', for example, explains system by setting up what is to us a surprising, but – with Bacon in

---

12 Bacon, *Novum Organum*, pp. 29–30, 50.
13 Cassirer, *Philosophy of Enlightenment*, p. vii.
14 See the explanation of 'method' as 'rhetoric' in Bacon, *Novum Organum*, p. 96, n. 81.
15 Samuel Johnson, *A Dictionary of the English Language*, ed. Anne McDermott, 1st and 4th edns, CD-ROM (Cambridge: Cambridge University Press, 1996).

mind – historically compelling contrast: 'Now we deal much in essays', wrote Isaac Watts in *The Improvement of the Mind* (1741), 'and unreasonably despise *systematical* learning; whereas our fathers had a just value for regularity and systems'.[16]

'Systems' *versus* 'essays' – Watt's implication, seized upon by Johnson in defining system as the 'reduc[tion]' of 'many things' into a 'regular' and 'uni[ted]' 'combination' and 'order', is that essays entail a less regular ordering or reduction of things than systems do. In another of Johnson's quotations, from Boyle, that distinction is echoed in the form of a prefer-ence: 'I treat of the usefulness of writing books of essay, in comparison of that of writing systematically.' Since we know that essays rapidly became, during the eighteenth and nineteenth centuries, one of the most important forms – if not the most important form – for knowledge production and circulation, we might expect to find a turn away from systems in the later 1700s.

Such expectations would appear to be particularly true of the 1790s given Britain's changing political climate. System, grouped with 'theory' and 'method', was linked to France – in opposition to English 'common sense' and 'empiricism' – and thus became a weapon in the discursive wars of English nationalism, particularly the conservative assault on radical thinking after the French Revolution.[17] Faced with such political hostility, system – as an idea – should have been in eclipse by the time of *Lyrical Ballads*. And, even if we do address it as a genre, the competition with essay also suggests that systems and system-writing should have been on the run. But the turn to genre also provides us with ways to ascertain what did happen: we can, for example, *count* how many self-proclaimed systems appeared in print. The results belie these expectations in startling ways. Not only do *English Short Title Catalogue* figures show that there was no decline at the end of the century; 1798 was actually a watershed year for published systems in Eng-land. Through most of the century, the number of works that explicitly called themselves 'systems', or invoked 'system' in their titles, trailed – in a ratio of 1 to 3 (or higher) – the number of those efforts self-identified as, or with, essays. After 1798, however, production of self-described

---

16 Isaac Watts, *The Improvement of the Mind: or, A supplement to the Art of logick: containing a variety of remarks and rules for the attainment and communication of useful knowledge, in religion, in the sciences, and in common life* (London: J. Brackstone, 1741).

17 See David Simpson's argument in *Romanticism, Nationalism, and the Revolt Against Theory* (Chicago: University of Chicago Press, 1993), p. 170.

systems – particularly specialized stand-alone systems, such as the system of the income tax – regularly outpaces essay output.[18]

In addition to counting, we can also look for the other indicator of generic prominence: how often the genre, in whole or in part, is embedded in other genres. The power of satire in the early eighteenth century, for example, is indexed both by the number of satires published and by the incorporation of satiric features in other forms – thus Pope's 'Arbuthnot' as a satiric epistle.[19] To the question 'Where did systems go under the political pressures of the 1790s?' we might therefore answer 'The most vulnerable took cover *within* other genres'. As I shall argue, that is precisely what happened – think, for example, of Godwin's system of political justice embedded in the novel he called – echoing Bacon's quest for a more exact way to know the world – *Things As They Are*. Together with the *ESTC* productivity figures, these embeddings make a case for a newly empowered genre.[20]

Enlightenment(s) and system

To understand what was new and powerful about system during Romanticism, we need to clarify further its earlier usages. Throughout the eighteenth century, writers maintained a Baconian caution regarding the use of system. However, the rise of Newtonianism both in England and on the Continent convinced even the wary that the universe could be known

---

18 These counts, of course, are not by themselves conclusive evidence of the importance of system at the turn into the nineteenth century. I offer them as numerical readings that signal the need for other kinds of readings of other kinds of evidence. By calling them 'readings', I wish to emphasize that – even with the *ESTC* – counts of this kind are a very inexact science. As I've indicated, they are limited by self-description: the keywords 'system' and 'essay' must be in the title or subtitle. In addition, *ESTC* contains and finds more than one copy or edition of the same title; should they be treated as extras, and cut out of the counts, or kept as evidence of the pervasiveness or influence of particular texts? Since this problem occurred with both systems and essays, and my concern is with establishing a shift in their relative importance over a number of years, I have not altered the counts to address the existence of multiple copies or editions. For details of my procedures and results – and an extended version of this history of system – see Clifford Siskin, 'The Year of the System', in *1798: The Year of Lyrical Ballads*, ed. Richard Cronin (Basingstoke: Macmillan, 1998), pp. 9–31.
19 For a discussion of this aspect of genre theory, see Clifford Siskin, *The Historicity of Romantic Discourse* (New York: Oxford University Press, 1988), pp. 9–14.
20 I am arguing that this empowerment of system takes two mutually reinforcing forms: the increase in specialized, stand-alone systems *and* the increase in the embedding of systems in other forms.

precisely because it was a system – what Newton called the 'System of the World'. As a whole ordered by rules, argued the Abbé de Condillac,

> each part of it having the least complexity is a system: man himself is a system. If, then, we renounce systems, how can we explore anything deeply? I agree that in general philosophers are wrong. They invent systems, but systems should not be invented. We should discover those which the author of nature has made.[21]

Writers of systems, that is, needed to be good readers – both of the divine author and of the deductive 'errors that the craze for systems led to'.[22] The former told of man's place *in* nature as part of things as they are, while the latter detailed his departures from it when pressed to explain those things.

Readers, of course, managed to disagree, filling the pages of eighteenth-century journals with repetitive debate. A letter to the *Gentleman's Magazine* in 1777, for example, began with an obligatory bow to Bacon and then proceeded to turn a discussion about inoculating the poor into a debate over system: when men's

> opinions are warped in favour of a *System*, all future experiments must be made to fit it. Thus from some successful experience of the benefit of tar-water, Bp. Berkeley erected a fanciful and elaborate theory, which attributed to it the essence of all medical virtues.[23]

A writer in the *Monthly Review*, however, turned to precisely the same figure not to attack but to extol the 'spirit of system':

> To the discerning enquirer after philosophy and science, the speculations of a Berkeley or a Hume, notwithstanding the absurdities with which they may be chargeable, are infinitely more valuable than the collective mass of the dissertations and essays that have been written against them.[24]

---

21 Abbé de Condillac, *Dictionnaire des synonymes*, ed. Georges LeRoy, *Oeuvres philosophiques de Condillac*, vol. III, Paris: Presses Universitaires de France, 1947–51, pp. 511–12. For the translation and a discussion of true and false systems, see Isabel F. Knight, *The Geometric Spirit: The Abbé de Condillac and the French Enlightenment*, Yale Historical Publications, Miscellany 89 (New Haven: Yale University Press, 1968), pp. 52–78.

22 Abbé de Condillac, 'A Treatise on Systems', in *Philosophical Writings of Etienne Bonnot, Abbé de Condillac* (1746), trans. Franklin Philip and Harlan Lane (Hillsdale, NJ: Lawrence Erlbaum, 1982), p. 10.

23 *Gentleman's Magazine* 47 (March 1777), 105.

24 Review of *Essays Moral, Philosophical, and Political* in *Monthly Review* 46 (1772), 382–3.

Notice how a disagreement that appears to be about the work of an individual turns out to be about the *form* of that work: the systematic speculations of Berkeley versus the essays of his critics.

Hume's career enacted that debate. When his systematic *Treatise of Human Nature* (1739–40) 'fell dead-born from the press', he switched genres, fragmenting it into separate enquiries into 'understanding' (1748), 'morals' (1751), 'passions' (1757) and 'religion' (1755), and then arranged to have them published together posthumously as *Essays and Treatises on Several Subjects* (1777). The status of 'system' played a crucial role in the content as well as the form of those efforts. He used system both to explain how scepticism works – focusing on the conditions under which we should 'embrace a new system with regard to the evidence of our senses' – and to clarify its purpose. Scepticism, he argued, is not a turn from the production of knowledge, but a 'necessary preparative' to do it well: 'though by these means we shall make both a slow and a short progress in our systems; [they] are the only methods, by which we can ever hope to reach truth'.[25]

The Enlightenment use of systems and the discourse about it consistently carried this mixed message of affirmation and critique – optimism regarding what could be known through system and the sceptical record of efforts that fell short. In generic terms, it was a feature enacted formally through the embedding of systems within SYSTEMS. Here, for example, is Benjamin Martin in 1747:

> Having read and consider'd the Design of the several Books hitherto published for the Explanation of the NEWTONIAN PHILOSOPHY, under the titles of *Commentaries, Courses, Essays, Elements, Systems*, &c. I observed not one of them could be justly esteemed a TRUE SYSTEM, or COMPLEAT BODY of this science.[26]

Martin's response demonstrated the ongoing power of system, for the above is from a Preface to a book entitled *A New and Comprehensive SYSTEM of the Newtonian PHILOSOPHY, ASTRONOMY and GEOGRAPHY*. The solution to failed systems, and other forms of generic inadequacy, was system itself – a SYSTEM ambitious enough to comprehend the embedded remains of its predecessors.

25 David Hume, *Enquiries Concerning the Human Understanding and Concerning the Principles of Morals*, ed. L. A. Selby-Bigge and P. H. Nidditch, 3rd edn (Oxford: Clarendon Press, 1902, 1975), section 12, pp. 150–2.
26 Benjamin Martin, *Philosophia Britannica or A New and Comprehensive SYSTEM of the Newtonian PHILOSOPHY, ASTRONOMY and GEOGRAPHY*, 2 vols. (London: C. Micklewright and Co., 1747).

In pursuing this particular form of comprehensiveness, writers like Martin were indebted not only to Newton's ideas, but to his *generic* innovations. The latter's strange publication record sets this formal drive to system in dramatic relief. Newton first published on optics in a 1672 article in the *Transactions of the Royal Society*, an effort that elicited a wide range of criticisms requiring detailed rebuttal. For Newton, that kind of debate was *not* healthy, for it left the knowledge he produced looking like old knowledge – the unconvincing result of deductive hypothesizing and Scholastic debate. His reaction was absolute. Newton, with only one minor exception, never again published *anything* in a journal. He was to present his major physical findings only within books – the complete and comprehensive *systems* of the *Opticks* and the *Principia*, forms that reduced opposing arguments from debatable differences 'to error'.[27] All other arguments became parts of the new master SYSTEM.

With that generic tool in hand, no question was out of the question: everything could be known. Adam Smith, for example, took as the task of his very first book (1759) an explanation of the principles of human behaviour. Of the seven parts of *The Theory of the Moral Sentiments* ('theory', according to Johnson, being a *'system* yet subsisting only in the mind'), the longest is the final one; there we find embedded the 'particular system[s]' formed out of the 'different theories' of his predecessors.[28] My point is not that earlier writers neglected to review their competition, nor that other genres did not turn upon themselves, but that the genre of system was the specific historical site for a particularly powerful mixture – a mixture of extraordinary intellectual aspirations and, thanks to the practice of embedding system within SYSTEM, sustained attention paid to the very genre that articulated them.

The Wealth of Nations proceeds in precisely the same fashion. Following his own formula for system – in which one principle is 'found to be sufficient to bind together all the discordant phenomena that occur as a whole species of things' – Smith foregrounded the 'division of labour'. And, within that overarching system, he embedded an entire book (one of five) on the various 'Systems of political Oeconomy' in 'different ages and nations'

---

27 See Charles Bazerman, *Shaping Written Knowledge: The Genre and Activity of the Experimental Article in Science* (Madison, WI: University of Wisconsin Press, 1988), pp. 82–3, 119.

28 Adam Smith, *The Theory of Moral Sentiments* (1759), ed. D. D. Raphael and A. L. Macfie, Glasgow Edition of the *Works and Correspondence of Adam Smith*, 6 vols. (Oxford: Clarendon Press, 1976), vol. I, p. 265.

(p. 428). The power and unrelenting optimism of *The Wealth of Nations* – the sense that those systems have been productively reconciled in this age and in this nation – are in large part effects of that embedding.

That specific mode of producing knowledge in writing – systems within a master SYSTEM – was the Enlightenment – that is, the astonishing, but temporally and geographically localized Enlightenment that did not make it out of the eighteenth century. The reason it remained bounded is, in generic terms, rather obvious: more writing of more systems made reconciliation into a single SYSTEM less and less likely. Efforts continued to be made, of course, but they tended to sink under their own weight. In 1798, for example, William Belcher wrote *Intellectual Electricity, Novum Organum of Vision, and Grand Mystic Secret*. Described in the subtitle as 'an experimental and practical *system* of the passions, metaphysics and religion, *really* genuine', Belcher's claim to the real was grounded in the same generic procedure that served Smith so well: he embedded extracts of other systems by, in order, 'Sir Isaac Newton, Dr. Hartley, Beddoes, and others'. Those systems are all generically subordinated within the 'grand' scope of Belcher's own SYSTEM – a SYSTEM so undone by its own ambition that it is still, to use his word, a 'secret' to most of us 200 years later.[29]

The generic alternative to such excess was to embed systems in *other* forms. In the same year as *Intellectual Electricity*, for example, Malthus put a principle of population into an essay: 'Population, when unchecked, increases in a geometrical ratio. Subsistence increases only in an arithmetical ratio.'[30] This is the phenomenon of population reduced to the regular ordering of system, and if it had become part – through critique or affirmation – of an encompassing master SYSTEM, then the whole work would have either followed Belcher over the top, or secured some of the same *kind* of ongoing power as *The Wealth of Nations*.

Malthus's first and second paragraphs both begin, however, by emphasizing that the work is an 'essay', and, as such, 'might undoubtedly have been rendered much more complete' (p. 15). The work of essays is in some way preliminary or partial and thus gestures outside of itself – Johnson

---

29 William Belcher, *Intellectual Electricity, Novum Organum of Vision, and Grand Mystic Secret* . . . : *being an experimental and practical system of the passions, metaphysics and religion, really genuine: accompanied with appropriate extracts from Sir Isaac Newton, Dr. Hartley, Beddoes, and others: with medical observations rising out of the subject / by a rational mystic* (London: Lee and Hurst, 1798).

30 Thomas Robert Malthus, *An Essay on the Principle of Population* (1798), ed. Philip Appleman (New York: Norton, 1976), p. 20.

defined it as a 'loose sally' – while the logic of systems is self-contained: a system is anything that talks to itself, points out Kevin Kelly; 'a thermostat system', for example, 'has endless internal bickering' about whether to turn the furnace on or off.[31] Can the commands of an embedded system carry their authority into the adventures of essay? Does the principle *travel* to produce more knowledge?

That is how Enlightenment, in its most capacious sense as the condition of modernity, materialized. *That* Enlightenment is the travel narrative we tell when the technology of writing takes the form of embedded systems. In Malthus, this travelling question poses the particular problem of whether his particular thermostat – the on and off of growth governed by the population principle – can and should *extend* into and dictate the main concern of his *essay*, human behaviour – specifically, the moral issue of whether men who find themselves naturally turned on ('the passion between the sexes is necessary and will remain nearly in its present state', p. 19) should, with the misery of overpopulation in mind, turn their desires off. The answer is that the commands travelled, but not all that well: Malthus had to revise the *Essay*'s morality substantially between 1798 and the next edition in 1803. The particular combination of systems-in-essays produced, that is, a specific *formal* effect: the certainty of system extended into essay resulted in a sense of expansive *but* attenuated authority.

Exercised in this manner, Enlightenment now worked both too well – the principles of the system adventuring into all kinds of questions – and not well enough – they didn't always quite fit. Knowledge was thus successfully extended in new disciplinary directions, but the extensions also had a subsidiary effect. Travelling, by making system newly pervasive yet *always* short of the Truth, gave us the experience of form we now blame as 'the System'.

That sense is the occasion, then, for the palimpsest of Enlightenments: the tendency, in Julie Hayes's words, 'to blur the distinction between a historically locatable phenomenon and a particular intellectual stance'.[32] My argument is that the blurring is not, at root, a dialectical or interpretative issue – they're in no sense two sides of the same coin – but a historical one. The two Enlightenments actually refer to two *different*

31 Kevin Kelly, *Out of Control: The Rise of Neo-Biological Civilization* (Reading, MA: Addison-Wesley, 1994), p. 125.
32 Julie C. Hayes, 'Fictions of Enlightenment: Sontag, Süskind, Norfolk, Kurzweil', *Bucknell Review: A Scholarly Journal of Letters, Arts and Sciences* 41:2 (1998), p. 22.

uses of the technology of writing, each deployed during a different period of time. The 'historically locatable' Enlightenment *is* historically locatable in the eighteenth century because it *ended* back then. Its generic marker is the monumental efforts to contain systems within master SYSTEMS that flourished, particularly in Scotland, from roughly 1740 to 1780. During the last two decades of the eighteenth century, that procedure gave way not just to a different 'stance' but to a different procedure – to the dispersing of systems into *other* forms, particularly the specialized essays of the modern disciplines. It is that practice that has continued to the present day, drawing Enlightenment's shadow over all of modernity. Faced with both forms of knowledge production but unable to theorize and identify the *material* shift, we have been left asking 'What is Enlightenment?'

We have had to ask that question again and again because – and here is where literary historians must shoulder the blame – something has stayed stubbornly in the way of our seeing that shift. In a palimpsest of a palimpsest, the term Romanticism has overwritten the difference between Enlightenments. When we look for change in the late eighteenth century, it has persistently claimed our attention – not because it is a clear and precise marker, but because, as all Romanticists know, it is not. That is particularly true in regard to issues of generic change – such as the fate of system – where it functions both to highlight and to downplay issues of form. On the one hand, Romanticism has been conventionally hailed as an Age of Lyric; on the other, its discourse of authorial creativity characteristically subordinates formal concerns to psychological arguments about genius and imagination. While we hash out these differences, the Enlightenments I have described slip in and out of view, enough of them revealed to make us ask what Enlightenment is, and enough obscured to force us to repeat the question.

Enlightenment(s)/Romanticism

Kant gave his answer to that question at the moment of transition between Enlightenments, and that is the key to the problem of periodization I posed at the start of this chapter. 1784 was both Enlightenment *and* the start of another age, for it was the moment that Enlightenment started to work in a new way. To call that age a second Enlightenment is to stress the continuity underlying that change – the centrality of system. But how, then, can we fit the term 'Romanticism' into the picture? Is the apparent overlap just a problem in classification itself – a notoriously sticky task – or, in this case, did something happen – something that *made* overlap possible?[33]

What happened, strangely enough, was Enlightenment #2. By extending knowledge in new disciplinary directions, Kant's 'age of Enlightenment' created the possibility of *other* histories of that age. In a sense, it invited palimpsest, change producing the new rubrics in which that change came to be understood. To be more specific, events in the history of writing – particularly the embedding of system in other forms – helped to shape the modern disciplines and the histories *they* tell about their object of knowledge.

What is Romanticism? It is our label for the tales literary study tells about the period in which it became a discipline. During the late eighteenth and early nineteenth centuries, the first courses in English Literature were taught, the first departments of English were formed, the essay and the review – as well as the periodicals that contained them – assumed their modern forms, and our current disciplinary distinction between the humanistic and the scientific was first instituted.[34] As a volume in the history of literature, Romanticism thus has a special relationship to all of the other volumes, for it is where the history of that history can be told. I emphasize 'can' because that has not previously been the norm. Histories of Romanticism have often tended to universalize, treating the particularities of this period as if they applied across all of them – including the writer's own period and practice. The result was the de-historicizing of the category of literature, as critics repeated the Romantic under the guise of interpreting it.

That is why so much of the Romantics scholarship leading up to this new Cambridge history has focused so intensely on issues of 'historicism' and 'historicity' – and on the professional problem of how to write about Romanticism without being Romantic. Whether seen as a feature of

---

33 The possibilities for explaining overlap, I am arguing, are straightforward. Either there are two labels vying for space within a single history – in which case our only task is to choose the 'best' one – or there are different histories at issue. The most likely scenarios of difference are geographical versions of disciplinary difference: Enlightenment as French and philosophical versus Romanticism as English and literary. But those disciplinary histories *have* a history – the history of disciplinarity itself – thus opening up the possibility pursued here.

34 For discussions of the formation of this disciplinary difference and of the historical change in the meaning of the term 'literature', see Clifford Siskin, *The Work of Writing: Literature and Social Change in Britain 1700–1830* (Baltimore: Johns Hopkins University Press, 1998), pp. 5–12.

ideology or discourse,[35] such repetition is inevitable as long as Romanticism is treated as just another period *in* literature; the alternative is to acknowledge its paradoxical historical status: the reason Romantic discourse so thoroughly penetrates the study of literature is that literature emerged in its presently narrowed – but thus 'deep' and disciplinary – form during that period and thus *in* that discourse.

The historicizing of Romanticism thus has been – and is – part of the process of historicizing literature, and thus a way of providing a touchstone for all of the volumes of the New Cambridge History. Negotiating the Enlightenment/Romanticism divide is a crucial step towards that end, but one made treacherous by the shift in Enlightenments I have identified.[36] The genre of system, however, materially marks the way; uses of it and references to it configure not only that shift and both periods, but even those features of Romanticism with which we think we are most familiar.

Romanticism and system

So pervasive is system in the period, that it effectively functions as Romanticism's familiar, haunting it from its forebears to its finish. Claims for Rousseau's paternal status as the father of Romanticism, for example, have been based on features supposedly inherited from his work, such as confession, emotion and a focus on childhood. But when those confessions turn to the figure who becomes his surrogate mother, another form comes to the fore: he remembers his beloved 'Mama' as 'She who brought everything to system' ('Elle, qui mettait toute chose en système').[37] His rebelliousness is conventionally understood as a turn from social convention, but what he actually turned to was not the wilds of nature but

---

35 See Jerome McGann, *The Romantic Ideology: A Critical Investigation* (Chicago: University of Chicago Press, 1983) and Clifford Siskin, *The Historicity of Romantic Discourse* (New York: Oxford University Press, 1988).

36 The path from the first Enlightenment to Romanticism is the one we expect to find: a chronological journey between centuries with some late-eighteenth-century switchbacks along the way. But the second Enlightenment poses problems of a different kind: chronological switchbacks become conceptual overlaps – knots in knowledge tied by the turn to the disciplines that I have described. Among the efforts to sort out the terms without making this distinction, the most comprehensive is Marshall Brown's 'Romanticism and Enlightenment', in *The Cambridge Companion to British Romanticism*, ed. Stuart Curran (Cambridge: Cambridge University Press, 1997), pp. 195–219.

37 Jean-Jacques Rousseau, *The Confessions of Jean-Jacques Rousseau newly translated into English*, 2 vols. (Philadelphia and London: J. B. Lippincott Company, 1891), vol. I, p. 238.

system – something he found only in a cherished few, such as Mama and M. Salomon, 'who spoke tolerably well on the system of the world' (p. 241).

In fact, Rousseau plots the entire *Confessions* as a journey from system to system. That form is the focal point; his feeling subjects act upon each other *through* systems:

> It is, therefore, at this period that I think I may fix the establishment of a system, since adopted by those by whom my fate has been determined, and which ... will seem miraculous to persons who know not with what facility everything which favours the malignity of men is established.
>
> (pp. 163–4)

Even Rousseau's celebrated turn to himself is mediated through the secret spring of system. His first sense of himself as capable of 'effecting a revolution' was his 'system of music' (p. 297), the fortunes of which take us from Book Six through most of Book Seven, and take him – in his dreams – back 'to the feet' of Mama, 'restored to herself' (p. 290). When he walks 'alone', he confesses, there is always one thing in his 'pocket': 'my grand system'. For Rousseau, the writing of system is his primary connection to writing: a turn 'back to literature ... as a means of relieving my mind' (p. 23).

Hume's literary career and analytic practice were, as noted earlier, similarly informed by system. His sceptical centring of philosophical doubt did call 'grand' systems into question, but only to enable system to do other kinds of work. Rather than turning from the Enlightenment dream of knowledge, he enabled new ways to realize it – ways that were naturalized in Romanticism and were his signal contributions to it. His most notorious bout of doubting, for example – the attack on miracles – was occasioned by the redeployment of system that shaped his career: the shift from the self-contained systematizing of the *Treatise* to the dispersal of system into the open-ended 'attempts' of essay and enquiry. The *Enquiry Concerning Human Understanding*, unconstrained by a master SYSTEM's imperative to totalize, could open up to illustration and digression, including proto-disciplinary ventures into new areas of knowledge.

Hume thus added entirely new sections to those carried over from the *Treatise*, including one that pioneered the comparative history of religions – a comparison based on the principle that the purpose of a 'miracle' 'is to establish the particular system to which it is attributed'.[38] Not only did this

---

38 Hume's editor, L. A. Selby-Bigge, finds the addition of 'Miracles' a mystery. Arguing that 'they do not add anything to his general speculative position', he concludes that 'their insertion in the Enquiry is due doubtless rather to other considerations than to

anticipate Blake's conjectural history of religion in *The Marriage of Heaven and Hell* – 'Till a system was formed' – it elaborated a logic and vocabulary of system that linked Hume at his most doubtful with Los at his most defiant. Since every miracle is generative of a particular religious system, argued Hume, it has

> the same force, though more indirectly, to overthrow every other system. In destroying a rival system, it likewise destroys the credit of those miracles, on which that system was established; so that all the prodigies of different religions are to be regarded as contrary facts. (pp. 121–2)

This rhetorical resemblance to Blake, I must emphasize, is not the most critical connection to Romanticism; more consequential is what made it possible: system appearing in two complementary ways – redeployed as form and thematized as content.

That is the precise combination at work when Godwin inserts his system of things as they are into the fictitious adventures of Caleb Williams. In the original ending, Caleb goes to prison and Falkland flourishes. Godwin portrays this defeat in a rather astonishing way – one that makes sense *only* within the history of genre I have been describing. Back in prison and writing only in 'short snatches', Caleb retreats from system to its eight-eenth-century rival: he struggles, Godwin *specifies*, 'to proportion' an 'essay' (p. 344). For a true believer in system like Caleb, the psychological equivalent of this generic fall from complete system into fragmented essay is madness.

In the revised and published version, however, Godwin gives us what he called simply the 'new catastrophe'. Caleb realizes – at the very moment he triumphs – that his system of vindication has worked, but too well – Falkland dies – and thus not well enough – Caleb has nothing to live for. Embedded in the novel, system becomes a vehicle not for rational explanation but for habitual blame. In the original ending, Falkland remains a tyrant and is clearly the reason for Caleb's descent into madness. Read the revision and you've entered what I have termed the condition of modernity – a world in which we know that it is no one's fault and everyone's; thanks to the pervasiveness of embedding, we have the System to blame.

---

a simple desire to illustrate or draw corollaries from the philosophical principles laid down in the original work', Hume, *Enquiries*, p. xix.

By the 1790s, then, blame is already becoming a marker for the workings of system, illuminating its presence in apparently unlikely places. Two particularly telling instances occur in 1798, the year often cited as the start of Romanticism – but also the year that systems numerically overtake essays. Embedded within *Lyrical Ballads and Other Poems* are the basic components of a system: explanatory principles and 'things' to be known. All of the reviewers of the 1798 edition read the poems *through* the frame of the Advertisement,[39] and, in critiques of subsequent editions and other volumes, Wordsworth was explicitly portrayed, as we have seen, as writing 'upon' system.[40]

Embedded within an Advertisement – like an essay, a loose sally likely to promise more than it delivers – Wordsworth's principles posed the problem of fit, of how far their authority would travel: in this case, do theory and practice coincide? The answer for most readers was, at best, 'maybe'. For Wordsworth, as for Malthus and Godwin, it was revision. The Advertisement became a Preface – also, like the essay, promising but incomplete. Its very suggestiveness only raised the stakes, challenging the system to explain 'the revolutions not of literature alone but likewise of society itself' (p. 243). The embedding induced, that is, more revision, leading, finally, out of the preface itself into another form of incompletion: an appendix. Its concluding sentence uncannily enacts the phenomenon of embedding it describes: Wordsworth writes that he is tempted 'here to add a sentiment which ought to be the pervading spirit of a system, detached parts of which have been imperfectly explained in the Preface' (p. 318).

Imperfect explanations, of course, invite others; much of the criticism written about the Romantics has been an effort to address that particular gap. That is why Romanticism, far from being a nightmare turn from the dream of Enlightenment knowledge, is the moment in which the reorganization of that knowledge leads to unprecedented productivity. In an effort to escape the shadow of Mary Wollstonecraft, for example, Mary Hays directs her *Appeal to the Men of Great Britain* to 'all classes', and addresses systematic behaviours by men as well as by women.[41] This

---

39 See the examples provided in William Wordsworth, *Lyrical Ballads* (1798), ed. R. L. Brett and A. R. Jones (London: Methuen, 1965), pp. 319–26.
40 See, for example, the review of *Poems, in Two Volumes* published in the *Edinburgh Review* 11 (October 1807), 214–31, reprinted in John Louis Haney, *Early Reviews of English Poets* (New York: Burt Franklin/Lenox Hill, 1904; 1970), p. 29.
41 Mary Hays, *Appeal to the Men of Great Britain in Behalf of Women* (1798), ed. Gina Luria (New York: Garland, 1974), pp. 239, 47, 90.

essayistic attempt to extend the authority of systematic analysis in new directions, meets the same imperfect end of Wordsworth's Preface, Godwin's novel, and Malthus's revised essay. When it ventures into 'what women ought to be', the whole structure of the work comes into question and Hays positions her self to catch the blame:

> Though I have not certainly, the vanity to believe myself equal to the task of fulfilling the title of this chapter . . . I shall retain it, as it expresses exactly what I wish to accomplish, however I may fail in the execution. (p. 125)

The result, Hays writes, using generic terms, may not be a 'regular system', but it will at least be a 'bold . . . outline'.

This slippage between 'system' and 'outline' produces very specific effects – effects that became characteristic features of the writing we call Romantic. When systems are extended so that they can no longer, in Kevin Kelly's thermostatic terms, talk to themselves, another *kind* of self must do the talking. In just the one sentence of the *Appeal* quoted above, the first-person pronoun 'I' appears *four* different times. Hays herself is clearly surprised by what has expressively filled the gap between the authority of system and her 'free' outline. She concludes her appeal with six pages of 'apology for a fault which is perhaps too obvious to escape notice':

> It must be confessed, that, 'the monosyllable' alleged to be 'dear to authors' – that the proscribed little personage – I – unfortunately occurs, remarkably often, in the foregoing pages.   (p. 298)

What is most remarkable to us today – after so many 'I's in so much writing – is that such an extended apology would have seemed necessary. Hays speculates that vanity might be at work – and adds, in one last satiric jab, that men may be less susceptible – but just consider Godwin's admission that he started his embedded system – *Caleb Williams* – in the third person, but had to switch to the first, and Wordsworth's apology for the 'unprecedented'[42] 'I' we call *The Prelude* – an effort to embed a philosophical system into poetry. The Romantic subject, I am suggesting, is, importantly, a formal effect of the fate of system.

---

42 William Wordsworth and Dorothy Wordsworth, *The Letters of William and Dorothy Wordsworth: The Early Years, 1787–1805*, ed. Ernest de Selincourt and rev. Chester L. Shaver, 2 vols. (Oxford: Oxford University Press, 1967), vol. II, p. 586.

Periods and systems

To call such effects 'Romantic' is also to recall our attention to the ways in which the period itself is such an effect. Here is Francis Jeffrey's initial attempt to order the writing of his time according to schools or sects. It appeared in the very first issue of the periodical designed to shift that genre's goal from comprehensive description to the mapping of critical difference – the *Edinburgh Review*:

> The author who is now before us [Southey], belongs to a *sect* of poets, that has established itself in this country within these ten or twelve years . . ..
> The peculiar doctrines of this sect, it could not, perhaps, be very easy to explain; but, that they are *dissenters* from the established systems in poetry and criticism, is admitted, and proved indeed, by the whole tenor of their compositions.[43]

Imperfect explanation, again occasioned by dispatching system in different directions, was again enabling. It opened the way for a new kind of disciplinary knowledge, providing some of our earliest 'facts' about the period we call Romantic: a starting point of roughly 1790 for the initial break from what was 'established', as well as a framework of 'peculiar[ities]' upon which differences could be mapped. The resulting map of sects/schools, as we have seen, was drawn in terms of the issue of writing 'upon system'.

The historical roots of that accusation lay in the distrust of deduction already documented; adherence to a system also suggested a lack of the gentlemanly virtue of disinterestedness. However, as the disciplinary distinction between the science and the humanities took hold during the Romantic period, the negatives metamorphosed: within science, interested errors of deduction became lack of objectivity; within the humanities, interest, whether in school or party, became a challenge to a newly idealized subjectivity: the sincerity and thus authority of the creative individual.

Arguments about schools, therefore, have not been incompatible with the emphasis on individual writers that still preoccupies the period study of literature – particularly the study of Romanticism as the 'Big Six' – but productive of it. A period, that is, can map its differences using many grids,

---

43 Francis Jeffrey, review of *Thalaba the Destroyer: A Metrical Romance* in *Edinburgh Review* 1 (October 1802) in Donald Reiman (ed.), *The Romantics Reviewed: Part A, The Lake Poets*, 2 vols. (New York and London: Garland, 1972), vol. II, pp. 415–25. For the intentions of its founders see Alvin Sullivan (ed.), *British Literary Magazines: The Romantic Age, 1789–1836* (Westport, CT: Greenwood Press, 1983), pp. 139–42.

and system was a parameter in more than one. In fact, it played a substantial role in drawing the other lines that have made Romanticism into a recognizable whole: generations, gender and genre.

Schools and generations can be superimposed, of course – the first generation linked to the Lakes and the second identified either in opposition to the first or configured by internal rivalries, such as the attacks on Hunt's Cockney School. However, the first generation is also identified with a specific project, one that has been seen as Romantic in the grand scope of its ambition – Wordsworth compared it to a 'Gothic church' – but, upon closer look, was Enlightenment (the second kind) in its conceptual architecture. That church was the great *'Philosophical Poem'* which Coleridge demanded of Wordsworth. The charge to embed philosophy into poetry was not only a matter of content, but, Coleridge specified, a matter of form: Wordsworth was 'to deliver upon authority a system of philosophy . . . in substance, what I have been all my life doing in my system of philosophy'.[44]

The purpose of embedding system into other forms was once again to allow its principles to travel into new areas of inquiry; in fact, that was precisely the metaphor that Wordsworth himself adopted in his prospectus to the project: he 'must tread on shadowy ground, must sink / Deep, and ascend aloft' in order to go philosophically where no man has gone before: 'into' *man* ('Prospectus', pp. 16–17, 1–2). Although *The Recluse* remained largely unwritten, Wordsworth was identified with this procedure, for purposes of praise or of blame, throughout his career. 'Your poems', wrote John Wilson in 1802, 'are of very great advantage to the world, from containing in them a system of philosophy'.[45]

Two decades later, however, that act of containment (including the travel metaphor) became the means by which generational difference was solidified:

> And Wordsworth, in a rather long 'Excursion',
> (I think the quarto holds five hundred pages),

---

44 Samuel Taylor Coleridge, *The Collected Works of Samuel Taylor Coleridge*, ed. Kathleen Coburn, 16 vols., Bollingen Series, vol. XIV, *Table Talk*, ed. Carl Woodring (2 vols.) (Princeton, NJ: Princeton University Press/London: Routledge, 1971–2001), vol. II, p. 177 (entry number 403). To grasp the consequences of this chapter's periodization argument for our understanding of the careers of Wordsworth (and Coleridge), see 'William Wordsworth' in *The Oxford Encyclopedia of British Literature*, vol. V, ed. David Kastan (Oxford: Oxford University Press, 2006), pp. 326–34.

45 See Wordsworth, *Early Years*, vol. I, pp. 352–8; *Lyrical Ballads*, ed. Brett and Jones, p. 334.

> Has given a sample from the vasty version
> Of his new system to perplex the sages;[46]

Byron did not publish these lines, but his discretion in not wishing to 'attack the dog in the dark' did not save him from the intragenerational warfare that used the same kind of weapon. *Don Juan* was assailed not just for its 'profanity' and 'indecency', but for how these had been 'embodied into the compactness of a system'.[47]

Byron, however, was already used to such attacks, and three years earlier had momentarily stepped back from the fray to make an eerily prophetic act of periodization:

> With regard to poetry in general I am convinced the more I think of it – that he [Moore] and all – Scott – Southey – Wordsworth – Moore – Campbell – I – are all in the wrong – one as much as another – that we are upon a wrong revolutionary poetical system – or systems – not worth a damn in itself – & from which none but Rogers and Crabbe are free – and that the present & next generations will finally be of this opinion.[48]

These claims are now very familiar ones, for they are claims about a period – the period we now call Romantic – and they are familiar even to the extent of raising Crabbe as an exception. What is less familiar – but should not be surprising given the Enlightenments/Romanticism connection I have recovered – is that the argument is cast in terms of 'system'.

One consequence of that casting – one that has now occasioned a recasting – is the exclusion of women writers from this period portrait. It is important to stress that this exclusion was not done after the fact – as an effect of labelling the period 'Romantic' or of criticism under that label – though such activities have certainly reinforced it. This was exclusion done *during* the period of time in question. Many factors played a role – including the formation of a two-tier market, the rise of anthologies, the reshaping of the working lives of women, and the professionalization of criticism[49] – but the deployment of system as an analytic tool (often in the service of that new professionalism) clearly contributed. Arguing about system helped to construct a system of exclusion.

---

46 Byron's unpublished Dedication to *Don Juan*, lines 25–8 in *Complete Poetical Works*, ed. McGann, vol. V, p. 4.
47 Review of *Don Juan* I and II in the *Edinburgh Monthly Review* (1819) cited in Moyra Haslett, *Byron's* Don Juan *and the Don Juan Legend* (Oxford: Clarendon Press, 1997), p. 119.
48 Letter to John Murray (1816), *Byron's Letters and Journals*, ed. Marchand, vol. V, p. 265.
49 See Siskin, *Work of Writing*, pp. 210–27.

This does not mean that writing by women did not refer to system – Austen calls the Churchill–Fairfax engagement a 'system of secrecy and concealment'[50] – nor does it mean that their writing was not configured by the disciplinary travels of system as a genre – Hays's slippage from system to outline is precisely such a configuration. Rather it means that the pervasiveness of system – through embedding and in the rhetoric of criticism – made it available as a tool with which to discriminate. That is why Anna Barbauld, perhaps trying to defend the generic ground held by women during the period, introduced her collection of novels by trying to appropriate some of system's power: 'Let me make the novels of a country', she wrote in 1810, 'and let who will make the systems.'[51]

Two decades later, however, the *Edinburgh Review* tried to reclaim the novel's glory in its own preferred generic terms, bringing system back to bear on the argument. The novel, it announced, had now reached its maturity.[52] A mature male writer, Scott, is singled out for praise, but that praise forms the basis of a larger claim: his incorporation of history exemplifies a new generic strategy – a strategy of embedding that has given the novel a new function.[53] The learning and experience that previously would have been contained in less entertaining genres is now, argues the *Review*, being conveyed *in* a more appealing form. The reform-minded public of 1832 wanted 'facts', and fiction was now valued as a practical way of meeting the demand.[54]

'In consequence of this newly-enlarged view of the principles on which fiction should be written', declared the *Review*,

> we have, since the appearance of *Waverley*, seen the fruits of varied learning and experience displayed in that agreeable form; and we have even received

---

50 Jane Austen, *Emma*, ed. Terry Castle, World's Classics (Oxford: Oxford University Press, 1998), p. 361.
51 Anna Laetitia Barbauld, 'On the Origin and Progress of Novel-Writing', in *The British Novelists*, ed. Anna Laetitia Barbauld (London: F. C. & J. Rivington, 1810), vol. I, pp. 61–2. For an extended treatment of the relationship between novel and system in the long eighteenth century see Clifford Siskin, 'Novels and Systems', *Novel* 34:2 (Spring 2001), 202–15.
52 Anon., Review of the *Waverley Novels* and *Tales of My Landlord*, *Edinburgh Review* (January 1832), pp. 61–79.
53 Since the *Review*'s primary purpose is to extol Scott as 'the greatest master' (p. 62) – the genre of the article is an encomium – it dates the change from *Waverley*; I am suggesting that our historical perspective allows us to see him as part of an era of embedding systems of knowledge.
54 See Daniel Born's argument in *The Birth of Liberal Guilt in the English Novel: Charles Dickens to H. G. Wells* (Chapel Hill, NC: University of North Carolina Press, 1995), pp. 31–2.

from works of fiction what it would once have been thought preposterous to expect – information . . . We have learnt, too, how greatly the sphere of the Novel may be extended, and how capable it is of becoming the vehicle almost of every species of popular knowledge. (p. 77)

Using philosophical terms and mechanistic images that echo back through the Enlightenment to Newton and Bacon, the *Review* describes the 'extended' novel as beginning to behave like a system: new 'principles' allow it to be the 'vehicle' for more things. In the terms I have suggested, the embedding of systems in other forms transformed their hosts – in this case, giving the novel a role in the work traditionally performed by system: the production and circulation of knowledge. To the surprise of the *Review*, novels began to become 'information' systems.

To assert the novel's maturity in 1832 is yet another sign of how the period, through the use of system, configured itself. That is, of course, still our standard endpoint for the period. But what kind of end? 'Maturity' does not suggest either an absolute end or a radical change, but rather something that has, at least for the moment, stabilized. Vast amounts of critical energy have been expended, however, under the very different assumption that an end must be a break of some kind – that we need to argue about whether Romanticism *stopped*.

To begin our periodization with the Enlightenment/Romanticism connection allows for a different picture. The period can then be seen to emerge from the late eighteenth-century proliferation of print – a proliferation that turned the Enlightenment production of knowledge in the direction of the disciplines. As our discipline's label for that transformation, Romanticism can be said to end but by no means stop when the destination was reached: when knowledge settled into disciplinarity and the modern modes of literary production became standard. By the 1830s we have clear signals of the pace of change reaching a kind of watershed – a normalization: the processes of print are completely mechanized, the mass market established, English Literature is institutionalized. Beyond that point lies the modern – in Raymond Williams's terms, fully 'naturalized' – world of print.

At that moment, the period becomes, in a sense, a system capable of talking to itself,[55] of sustaining the discipline's now familiar dialogues of the creative and the critical, and of high and low culture. To hear this

---

55 For a discussion of literature itself as a system, see Claudio Guillen, *Literature as System: Essays Toward the Theory of Literary History* (Princeton, NJ: Princeton University Press, 1971).

conversation as a historical *norm* is to become more, not less, sensitive to subsequent variations – variations that have invited other claims of historical difference – such as the Victorian – that do not *need* to be construed as absolute departures. This is not to call into question all other arguments for the shape of Romanticism, but to underwrite them with a literary history of writing itself – of the genres of Enlightenment and of the work they do.

PART II

★

GEOGRAPHIES: THE SCENES OF LITERARY LIFE

London in the 1790s

JOHN BARRELL

Perambulation

Caleb Williams, fleeing from Fernando Falkland and his creature, his all-seeing spy Gines, repeatedly determines to conceal himself in London, which, by reason of its huge population and 'the magnitude of its dimensions', he believed would offer him 'an inexhaustible reservoir of concealment'. In the event, of course, when at last he manages to reach the metropolis, he discovers that within the limits of that apparently limitless space, news travelled faster than he, a country boy, had ever imagined. When Gines causes his description to be circulated by means of a halfpenny handbill sold in the streets, Caleb suddenly finds himself trapped in 'the gaze of indiscriminate curiosity'; his pursuer had multiplied himself until 'a million of men', in every quarter, every house of the vast city, would now be looking with a 'suspicious eye' on 'every solitary stranger'.[1]

Inexhaustible though Caleb believed London to be, there was nothing new at all, nothing specific to the 1790s, about the hyperbole by which London is prefigured in his imagination before his arrival there. We can read this language of vastness, of limitlessness, of the inexhaustibility, so reminiscent of Burke's definitions of the sublime, as evidence of a kind of late eighteenth-century metropolitan sublime. It is as if an aesthetic developed primarily – at least as far as it was a *visual* aesthetic – to describe wild landscape that resisted the taming, the domesticating power of civilization, has suddenly collided with a new kind or degree of civilization itself, a city, as Wordsworth described it, of 'streets without end', thronged with 'face after face' in an endless parade of anonymity.[2] But to see it in these terms, or simply in these terms, is to ignore the fact that throughout the

---

1 William Godwin, *Caleb Williams*, ed. David McCracken (London: Oxford University Press, 1970), pp. 262, 254, 270.
2 *The Prelude* (1805 version), Book VII, lines 133, 173.

century, and well before 1700, London had been repeatedly described as a place indescribable except by hyperbole.

If this is true of how the size and extent of London had been represented, it was equally true of another of the defining characteristics attributed to eighteenth-century London, though not as it happens by Caleb, that it was a place of endless change. The character of its various districts, the extent of its trade, the social status of its individual inhabitants, their appearance and that of the streets they walked through, were all apparently subject to alteration, year by year, month by month. But as Alison O'Byrne has pointed out, there is a paradox in literary representations of London in the eighteenth century – she has in mind especially topographical descriptions of the capital and guide-books of various kinds – that while they describe London in terms of a modernity characterized by ceaseless change, by novelty ever renewed, they remain themselves relatively unchanged throughout the period. She explains this partly in terms of what seems to us (as it did to Caleb Williams) one of the most salient features of eighteenth-century metropolitan modernity, the extraordinary proliferation of commercial print culture. Commercial publishers satisfied an ever-increasing demand for descriptive accounts of London by repeatedly recycling earlier texts and passing them off as so new as to render out-of-date every publication that preceded them. But partly too, she argues, the idea of London as a place above all of endless novelty and ceaseless change was so deeply imprinted on contemporary ideas of the city that change became reified, became a simple fact so often repeated as to become too inert to exert much pressure on the genre, form, discourse, style, even the content of the stream of publications by which it was handed down.[3] The gasps of awe and wonder at the population, the size, the novelty of London were thoroughly familiar, and must have lost their power to intimidate or excite, long before William Godwin and William Wordsworth – whatever else they had to say about London – repeated them.

So how big was London in the 1790s? According to the first decennial census in 1801 the population of London was a little less than 800,000, but this figure was based on a strangely unhelpful notion of where London was. Throughout the eighteenth century, for the purposes of calculating its population, the metropolitan area of London was taken to include all the

---

3 Alison O'Byrne, 'Walking, Rambling, and Promenading in Eighteenth-Century London: A Literary and Cultural History' (unpublished Ph.D. thesis, University of York, 2003), pp. 19–20, 47–8.

parishes included in the Bills of Mortality – the records of births and deaths in 109 parishes in and around London kept by the Company of Parish Clerks. The area included in the bills, however, had been defined in the sixteenth century, and had not grown as London had grown. It included, as well as the City of London, the City and Liberties of Westminster, and the Borough of Southwark – the area usually regarded as 'London' for the purposes of local government – a wedge of urban Middlesex, including Clerkenwell; Lambeth in Surrey; and a number of villages to the East, most notably Hackney and Bethnal Green and Limehouse, which were cut off from or barely joined to the central built area. To the west it excluded the five Middlesex parishes collectively known as 'the parishes beyond the bills': St Pancras and St Marylebone, which in the eighteenth century had attached their huge developments of genteel housing to the built-up area, as well as Chelsea, Kensington and Paddington. According to the 1801 census, the population of London, including the parishes beyond the bills, had reached 900,000.

There are reasons to be suspicious of these figures, but they are now widely thought to be only about five per cent too low; and they are no doubt immeasurably more reliable than the widely divergent estimates produced by statisticians over the preceding decades. In 1795, Patrick Colquhoun estimated the population at one and a quarter million; Richard Price, just fifteen years earlier, calculated it at barely over half a million, including the whole of Middlesex.[4] Such estimates were saturated in controversy, not only about the numbers and the means by which they were calculated, but because they were produced in support of conflicting theses about the tendency of commercial, urbanized societies to flourish or to degenerate. Was the population of London increasing or diminishing? Through most of the century, it was recognized that more people died in London than were born, but was the deficit replenished by inward migration? To engage these questions, population estimates were produced with the aim of comparing them with earlier estimates, and so were obliged to confine themselves to the same area, the bills of mortality, and to omit from their calculations the greatest area of population increase.

It is probable that the population of the City of London remained static or even declined in the last fifty years of the century; that in Westminster and

4 See Patrick Colquhoun, *A Treatise on the Police of the Metropolis*, 3rd edn (London: C. Dilly, 1796), p. 375; for Price, see his *Essay on the Population of England*, 2nd edn (London: T. Cadell, 1780), p. 5.

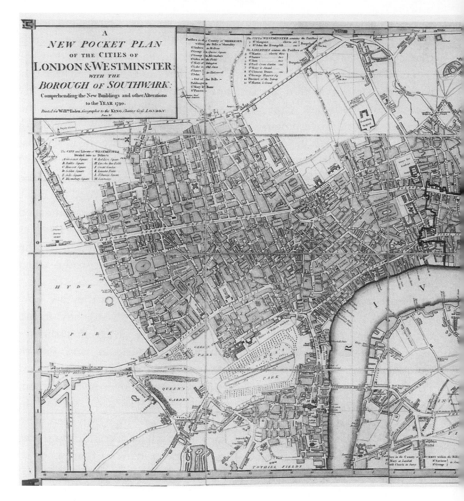

1 *A New Pocket Map of the Cities of London and Westminster; with the Borough of Southwark, Comprehending the new Buildings and other Alterations*, 3rd edn (London: William Faden, 1790).

the Borough it increased only slightly; and that the main increase within the bills occurred at the suburban edge. But the greatest increase between 1750 and 1801 occurred elsewhere, south of the river, and in the 'five parishes beyond the bills' where the population may have grown by 600 per cent in that time, in suburbs that were mainly excluded from most maps of London. In short, though it was clear in the 1790s that London was many times larger than any other city in Britain, it was not at all clear how much

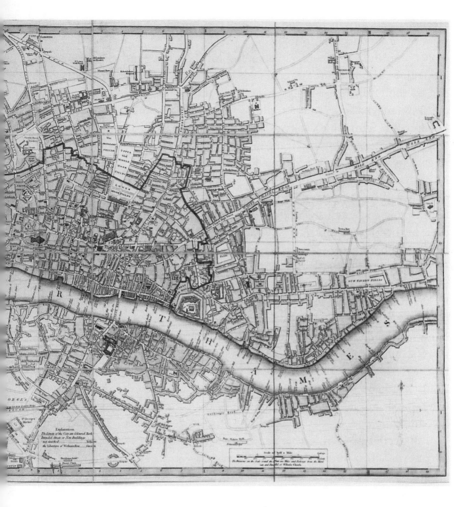

larger. When in early 1793 Britain found itself yet again at war with France, this uncertainty was fed by the continuing British anxiety about the size, the wealth, the military potential of its oldest, its 'natural' enemy. Was London more or less populous than Paris?[5] It is now believed that at the end of the century London was eleven times more populous than Liverpool, the

5 See for example John Aikin, quoted in *Ambulator: or, a Pocket Companion in a Tour round London* (London: J. Scratcherd, 1796), p. 24.

second largest city in England, and twice as populous as Paris; but in the 1790s there was no way to tell.

By contrast, the frequent mapping of London, and especially the immensely detailed surveys conducted in the 1790s by Richard Horwood and by the Ordnance Survey, meant that the extent of London was very precisely understood.[6] And for all the hyperbolic accounts of the extent of London, 'the illimitable walk', as Wordsworth put it, through those 'streets without end',[7] it was not larger in area by 1790 than many middle-sized English towns, like York, are now. From east to west the continuously built up area was in most places no more than four miles wide; from south to north it was rarely more than two. On the north bank of the Thames, the limit of this continuously built-up area reached no further, at the western edge of town, than Horseferry Road which feeds into the river crossings where Lambeth Bridge is now, a few hundred yards south of the Houses of Parliament. This boundary curved west and north up St James's Park, then as now a long tongue of green reaching eastward almost to Charing Cross. It skirted the eastern edges of Green Park and Hyde Park up to Tyburn at the western end of Oxford Street, and reached a few hundred yards up Edgware Road, ending well short of Paddington, which for a few years more would keep the character of a separate suburban village. From the Edgware Road it turned north-east towards the junction of Tottenham Court Road and what is now the Marylebone Road, and then turned south where fields ran all the way to the rear of the British Museum. Thus from the museum end of the newly built Store Street, where in 1792 Mary Wollstonecraft was writing her *Vindication of the Rights of Woman*, you could look north across a miscellaneous foreground – gravel pits, the field under the present Malet Street where the members of the Toxophilite Society practised archery,[8] pasture-land criss-crossed with paths made by Sunday

---

6 This and the following paragraphs are based on various maps including William Faden's *A New Pocket Map of the Cities of London and Westminster; with the Borough of Southwark, Comprehending the new Buildings and other Alterations* (London: for William Faden, 1790); *Horwood's Plan of London, Westminster, Southwark & Parts Adjoining 1792–1799* (London: London Topographical Society Publication No. 106, 1966); and (for 1800) Yolande Hodson (ed.), *Facsimile of the Ordnance Surveyor's Drawings of the London Area 1799–1808* (London: London Topographical Society publication no. 144, 1991).

7 *The Prelude* (1805 version), Book VII, lines 133, 159. There is a superb account of Wordsworth's walks through the long arterial streets of London in Kenneth R. Johnston, *The Hidden Wordsworth: Poet, Lover, Rebel, Spy* (New York and London: W. W. Norton, 1998), pp. 235–63.

8 Richard Tames, *Bloomsbury Past: A Visual History* (London: Historical Publications, 1993), p. 17.

walkers in search of country air – up to the suburban construction site, over half a mile away, that was Somers Town, where in 1797 Wollstonecraft would live and die.

From the museum the boundary ran east to the Foundling Hospital, to Gray's Inn Road and to the higher fields, watered by the River Fleet and pierced by chalybeate springs, which still formed a green belt between Clerkenwell and the small town of Islington. North of the City itself, the City with a large 'C', the boundary of the continuously built-up area reached barely further than Old Street. On the eastern side of town, it ran from Hoxton, still just about a separate village, along a zig-zag line dividing the streets from pastures and market gardens, to the Whitechapel Road, where ribbon development reached as far as the village of Mile End. East of Whitechapel and Wapping, more ribbon development followed the line of the Thames to Poplar at the virtually unpopulated Isle of Dogs. This eastward riverside development was matched across the river, the built-up area bulging southward to include Southwark, but from there westward to the river at Vauxhall Gardens the streets lay among a patchwork of pasture, market-garden and marshland, which gave Lambeth, where Blake lived throughout the 1790s, if not quite a rural, at least a grubbily verdant look. It was in Lambeth, and in the fields to the north-west of the city bounded by the Edgware and Marylebone Roads, that the continuously built-up area would grow most during the 1790s – elsewhere, it would hardly grow at all.

'Off the stones', in the contemporary Cockney expression,[9] beyond the limit of the paved roads, this continuously built-up area was fringed by villages and small towns, suburbs still physically separate from London unless joined by a ribbon of houses along the major roads. Even by 1800, as well as Paddington, Islington, Hoxton, Mile End, these suburbs included Chelsea, Kensington, Knightsbridge, Hampstead, the developing Camden Town – where in 1801 the satirical poet John Wolcot, 'Peter Pindar', would move in the hope that the rural air would improve his asthma[10] – Stoke Newington, Hackney, Bethnal Green, Stepney, Deptford, Peckham, Newington Butts, Camberwell, Clapham. Many of these places, and many places beyond them, have since come to be regarded as belonging to the 'inner city', though the policy of selling off public housing to private buyers,

---

9 *Metropolitan Grievances; or, A Serio-Comic Glance at Minor Mischiefs in London and its Vicinity . . . By One who thinks for Himself* (London: Sherwood, Neely, and Jones, 1812), p. 75.

10 See Tom Girtin, *Doctor with Two Aunts: A Biography of Peter Pindar* (London: Hutchinson, 1959), p. 218.

and the continued inflation of house prices, is making the term, with its connotations of deprivation, more and more inappropriate.

Throughout the eighteenth century, London had become an increasingly divided city, as those who could afford to do so moved into the squares and wide streets of the West End, most of them bearing the names of royalty or of great aristocratic families, that continued to be built throughout the century. For relatively impoverished 'jacobin' novelists, such as Charlotte Smith, perhaps especially in *Desmond* (1792) and *The Young Philosopher* (1798), or Elizabeth Inchbald, whose novel of West End life, *A Simple Story* (1791), was written in a dingy second-floor flat in Frith Street, Soho, this fashionable ghetto seemed a place of frivolity and corruption. The threshold of the West End moved, during the century, from Temple Bar to Charing Cross; further north and west it came to be marked by Swallow Street, which earlier in the next century would be redeveloped as Regent Street with the express intention of marking a grand symbolic boundary between east and west, or drawing, as John Nash put it, a 'Line of Separation' between 'the Streets and Squares occupied by the Nobility and Gentry' and 'the narrow Streets and meaner houses occupied by mechanics and the trading part of the community'.[11] In the 1790s, pockets of London remained, for example in the fading grandeur of Soho Square, where the polite still lived in neighbourhood with tradesmen. There were places too where the dwellings of the abject poor were all but next door to those of the very rich. In what would come to be called in the next century the St Giles 'rookery' – centered on Dyott Street, south of Great Russell Street and north of St Giles's Church – some houses in the tangled network of tiny courts and narrow alleys were let twelve to a room. This area was within 200 yards of Bloomsbury Square, where until 1800 the great house of the Dukes of Bedford still stood, and only 100 yards from the iron gates that protected Bedford Square, which according to the 'young philosopher' of Smith's novel was the address of choice for city merchants who had become immensely rich.[12]

On the rookeries of London the fiction of the 1790s is virtually silent. An exception is one of Hannah More's 'Cheap Repository Tracts' (1795–8), *Betty Brown; or, the St Giles's Orange Girl*, in which Betty lodges with Mrs Sponge, 'not far from the Seven-Dials', one or two hundred yards south of the

11 Quoted in Rodney Mace, *Trafalgar Square: Emblem of Empire* (London: Lawrence and Wishart 1976), p. 33.
12 Charlotte Smith, *The Young Philosopher*, ed. Elizabeth Kraft (Lexington: University Press of Kentucky, 1999), p. 67.

'rookery' near Bedford Square. Here she lives in a tiny windowless garret-room, one of nine people sharing three beds. There were small pockets of poverty and squalor even in the West End, at least in its oldest quarter, St James's.[13] By contrast however with the rest of London, and especially as you moved further west and north-west towards Mayfair and Marylebone, the West End was overwhelmingly inhabited by the aristocracy and gentry, along with the servants and shopkeepers who took care of their needs. The *Universal British Directory* of 1791 lists the London addresses of 231 members of the House of Lords who divided their year between residence in the country during summer and in town during the season. Of these, 218, nearly 95 per cent, lived west of Charing Cross: in St James's, Mayfair, Whitehall, or in the grand squares and streets of Marylebone, north of Oxford Street, still being developed at the end of the century. No less than fourteen lived in the grandest square of all, Grosvenor Square, where in *A Simple Story* Inchbald placed the house of Lord Elmwood, and where Camilla, in the novel of that name by Fanny Burney (1796), stayed in a 'mansion the most splendid' belonging to the posh faroholic Mrs Berlinton; the very spellin' of her name is intended to suggest pure Mayfair.[14] The addresses of the 456 members of the House of Commons listed in the 1791 directory followed a similar pattern: 414, over 90 per cent, lived in the West End, nine of these in Grosvenor Square. Eight lived in semi-fashionable Bloomsbury, and six in the luxurious riverside Adelphi development south of the Strand.[15]

To most members of both Houses of Parliament, and to many members of the politest classes residing in the West End, London east of Charing Cross must have been, if not exactly a *terra incognita*, then still much of it

13 For example the 'rookery' in Duke's Court, St James's, inhabited by Rhynwick Williams, the supposed London 'monster', in the late 1780s, and described by Jan Bondeson in *The London Monster: A Sanguinary Tale* (London: Free Association Books, 2000), pp. 207–9.

14 Fanny Burney, *Camilla: or, A Picture of Youth*, eds. Edward A. and Lillian D. Bloom (Oxford: Oxford University Press, 1983), p. 793. Of the remainder, five lived in fashionable parts of Bloomsbury and six were bishops or lawyers with professional reasons for living further east. One lived in King Street off Covent Garden, the only member of the aristocracy and gentry still living in a once-fashionable area now abandoned by people of fashion. See *Directory to the Nobility, Gentry, and Families of Distinction in London, Westminster, &c. . . . for 1793* (London: J. Wilkes, n.d.), p. 25.

15 Based on *The Universal British Directory of Trade, Commerce, and Manufacture* (London: Champante and Whitrow, 1791), pp. lxxi–lxxxvi. Fifteen, for professional reasons, lived in legal precincts, and fourteen in the City. Of the remaining MPs listed, two lived in Holborn, one off the Strand, and one at an address I cannot identify. Henry Dundas, a member of the cabinet in different capacities throughout the 1790s, gives his address as Somerset House, where he may sometimes have stayed when he could not get back to his suburban home at Wimbledon.

largely unexplored except for the routes along the Strand, Oxford Street and Holborn to the shops, the City, the courts, the theatres, the Royal Academy. To such people the 'knowledge' (I am using the taxi-driver's term) of the labyrinth of streets of the inner city – linked, as Caleb describes them, 'by narrow lanes and alleys, with intricate insertions and sudden turnings'[16] – must have seemed impossible to acquire; the geography must have seemed, by contrast with the broad streets and squares of St James's, St George's, Marylebone, almost designed to frustrate the acquisition of that knowledge. If they came across them at all, the poorest inhabitants of 'the lanes and back streets of the metropolis' may have struck them as members of another species altogether, as they did Maria in Wollstonecraft's *Wrongs of Woman* (1798), who found herself 'mortified at being compelled to consider them as my fellow-creatures, as if an ape had claimed kindred with me'.[17] No wonder, then, that on occasions when the 'mob' invaded the West End, as it had done in the Gordon Riots of 1780, and would do on several occasions in the 1790s, the shock could be tremendous.

East and West

By the end of 1792, France, newly declared a republic, was at war with Austria and Prussia, and the movement for parliamentary reform had revived in Britain, no longer, as it had been in the early 1780s, a concern mainly of the polite classes, but now chiefly of artisans and tradesmen. The government began suppressing publications it considered seditious. The following year Louis XVI was executed, and Britain entered the war with France. In 1794 the Whig party split, with the majority going into coalition with Pitt, leaving a handful of Whigs led by Charles James Fox to oppose the war with France and the government's attacks on freedom of speech. These and other developments opened new fissures throughout British society, and especially in some of the largest cities: Edinburgh, Birmingham, Manchester, Sheffield and London.

Late in 1792 the 'Association for the Preservation of Liberty and Property against Republicans and Levellers', a society dedicated to prosecuting the publishers of seditious writings and the makers of seditious speeches, was founded in London, and a miasma of suspicion enveloped the city. The

16 Godwin, *Caleb Williams*, p. 265.
17 Mary Wollstonecraft, *Mary and The Wrongs of Woman*, ed. Gary Kelly (Oxford: Oxford University Press, 1980), p. 168.

largest popular reform group, the London Corresponding Society, campaigning for universal manhood suffrage, was heavily infiltrated by spies and informers, and the surviving reports of its meetings, themselves written by government spies, are full of anxieties about who might be spying on them;[18] as many have pointed out, *Caleb Williams* itself is partly a product of this anxiety. In many places the owners and tenants of taverns and coffee-houses were threatened with the loss of their licences and so of their livelihoods if they allowed popular reform societies to meet on their premises. In Blake's Lambeth, as Michael Phillips has shown, the local loyalist association required every householder to sign a pledge of loyalty, declaring their attachment to the constitution of Great Britain and their abhorrence of all attempts to subvert it. This abhorrence was to be shown by refusing to subscribe to newspapers, 'manifestly . . . in the pay of France', which supported any degree of parliamentary reform, and by reporting the names of all foreigners residing in the parish, so that, to repeat Caleb's words, a 'suspicious eye' was now to be cast on 'every solitary stranger'. Those who refused to sign this pledge were to be reported to the association, along with their reasons for refusing. As Phillips points out, it would have taken great courage for Blake to have withheld his signature; it is likely that, with however great reluctance, he signed.[19]

Thus for most of the 1790s London was a city divided politically, but the division was as unequal as were the economic, cultural and geographic divisions: by far the majority of all classes supported the war with republican France and opposed a reform of parliament which was represented by loyalists as certain to lead to the establishment of a republic in Britain. This political fissure, however, ran vertically rather than horizontally, and it divided public space in a new way. Of the two patent theatres, for example, Covent Garden came to be regarded as much more loyalist than Drury Lane, managed by Fox's closest ally, the Irish dramatist and politician Richard Brinsley Sheridan, who was reluctant to stage the patriotic dramas more favoured at Covent Garden, who twice in the decade recommended that Pitt should be hanged,[20] and who was known to be sympathetic to those demanding political freedom for Ireland. To many London

---

18 Mary Thale (ed.), *Selections from the Papers of the London Corresponding Society 1792–1799* (Cambridge: Cambridge University Press, 1983), *passim*.

19 Michael Phillips, 'Blake and the Terror 1792–93', *The Library*, 6th ser., 26:4 (December 1994), 263–97, especially pp. 274–8 and plate 1.

20 See John Barrell, *Imagining the King's Death: Figurative Treason, Fantasies of Regicide 1793–1796* (Oxford: Oxford University Press, 2000), pp. 415, 593.

theatregoers, Sheridan's political views, however shocking to them, were not so evident in the productions of Drury Lane as to keep them away, but the king himself encouraged them to do so, by refusing to visit the theatre from 1794 until, in 1798, when the political fissure was beginning to close, he attended a performance of Sheridan's new, ambiguously patriotic tragedy *Pizarro*.[21]

In the highest levels of the political world, the breakdown of cordiality between the supporters of Pitt's government and the Foxite Whigs was confirmed in the clubs of St James's Street: White's became the favoured drinking and gambling joint of the one group, Brooks's, across the street, of the other.[22] The split is depicted in James Gillray's brilliant caricature of late 1796, *Promis'd Horrors of the French Invasion, – or – Forcible Reasons for Negotiating a Regicide Peace* (Fig. 2). It imagines a peace negotiated with the French republic as tantamount to a surrender to be followed by an invasion. A regiment of French soldiers has just set fire to St James's Palace, the residence of the king in London. Now it is marching up St James's Street towards Piccadilly, leaving a detachment to break into White's and purge its members. Several cabinet members and supporters of Pitt have already been killed; the Prince of Wales is being hurled from the balcony. But the effects of the invasion are represented in the favourite haunts not only of those with most to lose by it, but of others, so Gillray pretends, with the most to gain. The hostility of the Foxite Whigs to the war with France leads Gillray to pretend, as did much of the government-funded press, that they were Jacobins and virtually agents of the republic. Accordingly Pitt, tied to a hastily-erected liberty tree, is being scourged by the eager and determined Fox. Sheridan, his money-troubles at last over, has plundered the treasury and sneaks into Brooks's with his swag. The radical political activist John Thelwall is goading a huge bull – who stands in for the agriculturally minded Duke of Bedford – to toss Edmund Burke, the greatest enemy of the revolution in France. On Brooks's balcony, the liberal barrister Thomas Erskine announces a new code of laws, the nature of which is made clear by the guillotine behind him, which has already been used on the Lord Chancellor and other government notables.

Gillray's *Promis'd Horrors* is so powerful an image not simply because of what it fantasizes, with his characteristic mixture of revulsion and

---

21 See George Taylor, *The French Revolution and the London Stage 1789–1805* (Cambridge: Cambridge University Press, 2000), pp. 172–7.

22 For more on this, see Ralph Nevill, *London Clubs: their History and Treasures* (London: Chatto and Windus, 1911), chs. 3 (White's) and 4 (Brooks's).

2 James Gillray, *Promis'd Horrors of the French Invasion, – or – Forcible Reasons for Negotiating a Regicide Peace* (London: H. Humphrey, 20 October 1796; BM 8826), reproduced courtesy of the Lewis Walpole Library, Yale University.

carnivalesque gusto, as an imminent possible future, but because of memories it conjures up of the very recent past: memories of invasion by the alien London poor of the purlieus of the civilized rich. The most recent such invasion had taken place eleven months before the caricature was published, and featured some of those who appear in it. On 16 November 1795, in Old Palace Yard Westminster, Fox and a number of his closest associates, including Sheridan and the Duke of Bedford, addressed a huge public meeting to protest and petition against the passing of the 'two bills', two repressive pieces of legislation intended to destroy the popular radical movement, in part indeed by making it almost impossible to organize petitioning meetings to protest against the government. Following the meeting Fox, Sheridan and the Duke walked with the crowd up Whitehall and engaged a hackney coach at the stand in Charing Cross. Their supporters, however, were not content to let them be driven away. In a scene reminiscent of the inversion rituals that had mocked state power and ceremonial in the days of Wilkes and Liberty, they unloosed the horses, and dragged the coach in triumph up Cockspur Street to Pall Mall and St James's Street to Brooks's, 'the properest place', snarled the tory *True Briton*, 'for such demagogues to rest after their degrading labours'. The newspaper chose to lose sight of them there, but in fact the procession continued along Piccadilly, through Berkeley Square, down Hill Street to Fox's house in South Street off Park Lane.[23] The affair had apparently passed off in good order, but the sight and sound of hundreds or thousands of what the *True Briton* described as 'dirty ruffians' huzzaing and parading through the heart of the West End may indeed have looked to the polite inhabitants like a foretaste of 'the promis'd horrors' Gillray would depict.

Two similar such invasions had occurred in late 1794, when the treason trials, by which the government had hoped to break the influence of the London Corresponding Society, ended in the triumphant acquittals of the defendants. Throughout the long trial of Thomas Hardy, the secretary of the LCS, in October and November 1794, large crowds had gathered in the City outside the Old Bailey. When Hardy was finally acquitted, the crowd followed him as far as Somerset House in the Strand, where they unhitched the horses from his coach and pulled it themselves at the head of a triumphal procession, thousands strong, to Charing Cross. Here they chose to

---

23 My description of this incident is based on the reports published in *TB*, the *Oracle*, *MC*, the *Courier* and *MP* on 17 November 1795. See also *Account of the Proceedings of a Meeting of the Inhabitants of Westminster, in Palace-Yard, Monday, Nov. 26, 1795* (London: Citizen Lee [1795]) (which mistakes the date of the meeting).

take the scenic route through the aristocratic heartlands of the West End: up Cockspur Street to Pall Mall, where the Prince of Wales was lavishing public money on the magnificent Carlton House which, as soon as it was completed, he would demolish; on to St James's Palace and past the fine shops and magnificent clubs of St James's Street, as if in a jovial rehearsal for Gillray's caricature; then back along Piccadilly, down the Haymarket to Cockspur Street again and through Charing Cross to the Strand where Hardy alighted. The meaning of this route was unmistakable: to the crowd, the acquittal was a victory for those living east of Charing Cross over the inhabitants of the West End, especially the king and the members of both houses of the corrupt parliament which Hardy had been tried for attempting to reform. When Thelwall, his alleged co-conspirator, was acquitted a month later, the crowd chose a route no less circuitous and provocative for his triumph: at Charing Cross they turned south down Whitehall, dragging the coach up Downing Street and down again to show it to Pitt, then back to Charing Cross and along Piccadilly before setting Thelwall down in Bloomsbury.[24]

Other invasions of the West End in the 1790s, or skirmishes on its border, were less peaceful, and though certainly political in nature seem to have had little to do with organized politics, whether the parliamentary politics of Whig and Tory or the extra-parliamentary politics of the reform movement. The best place to concentrate on is Charing Cross, precisely because, as the threshold of the West End, the various fracas that took place there threatened the social and geographical separation of rich and poor, aristocratic and vulgar. Charing Cross combined the politeness of St James's with the squalor of the alleys of St Giles's or St Martin's. It was formed by the junction of Whitehall, Cockspur Street, and the Strand. Whitehall, leading south to its junction with Downing Street, then as now the residence of the Prime Minister, was lined by great office buildings of the state: the Treasury, the Admiralty, Horse Guards, the Banqueting Hall. Carlton House was 300 yards up Cockspur Street, at its junction with Pall Mall. The Strand was at this period the greatest shopping street in London, if not quite as fashionable as Oxford Street: a parade of some 230 shops,[25] becoming more fashionable the nearer they approached Charing Cross, and mainly selling

---

24 *Oracle* and *Morning Chronicle* (6 November 1794); *Morning Post* (6 December 1794); *State Trials for High Treason, embellished with Portraits. Part Third* (London: B. Crosby [1795]).

25 Calculated from *The General London Guide; or, a Tradesman's Directory for the Year 1794* (London: P. Boyle, n.d.), pp. 1–132.

luxury goods or the products of the polite culture industry. Charing Cross itself was centred on the towering plinth supporting Herbert Le Sueur's equestrian statue of Charles I, the royal martyr to republican ferocity, and dominated by the great Jacobean palace of the Duke of Northumberland which stood on the south side of the junction with the Strand. Opposite, on the site of the present Trafalgar Square, was the King's Mews, where the king's horses and the state coach were kept in the grand stables designed by William Kent, now buried under the National Gallery. On the third corner of the Cross were Spring Gardens and New Street, short rows of elegant houses backing on to St James's Park. Many of the shops and businesses at Charing Cross had the same character as those in the Strand: three gold-smiths and jewellers, two perfumers and perruquiers, a sword-cutler, the fashionable Drummond's Bank, the equally fashionable Cannon Coffee House, and so on.

Francis Place, however, the radical tailor and political agitator, who had been brought up in the Strand and in 1799 opened a shop at 29 Charing Cross, gave a very different account of the area as it had been in the earlier 1790s (Fig. 3). In his autobiography, perhaps the most vivid account we have of London in the 1790s, he wrote that the Cross

> was then an infamous neighbourhood. There were some highly respectable people living there, but there was also a much larger number of very disreputable people. There were Five notorious houses of ill-fame – three of which were in the main street. Seven public Houses, three of which were gin shops, all of them frequented by common soldiers and common women of the lowest description, and other vagabonds.

The soldiers – 'excessively gross' in their 'language and manners', and barracked in a wooden building at the narrow mouth of Middle Scotland Yard – were the main problem. In front of the Treasury and the Horse Guards, those going on guard in the morning 'were shaved, weather per-mitting – had their heads well greased and flowered – and their pigtails tied'. Across the road, the wall of the Privy Garden (where lived a Duke, two Earls, and sundry other aristocrats) was hung all day with obscene ballads and pornographic images for sale; at night it was patrolled by prostitutes who for twopence would climb over the wall with their military clients. Behind the shopfronts on the eastern side of Charing Cross itself was a place 'which could not be outdone in infamy and indecency by any other place in London': the bifurcated, winding alley made by Johnson's Court and Angel Court, where once elegant old houses crumbled in the shadow of

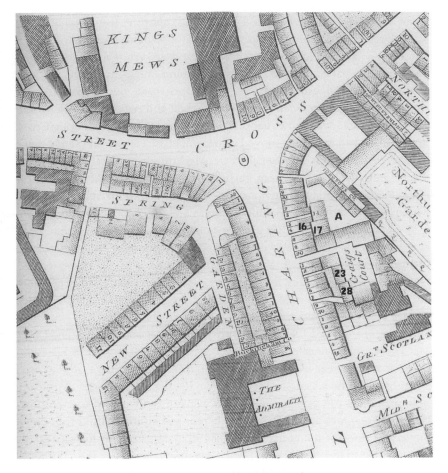

3 Detail (Charing Cross) from sheet 23 of Richard Horwood, *Plan of the Cities of London and Westminster, the Borough of Southwark, and Parts Adjoining, Shewing Every House* (London: Horwood, 1792–9). Marked in bold are the Turk's Head or Rummer (nos. 16 and 17) rented from 1799 by Francis Place; the King's Arms (23 and 28), and Angel Court (A).

Northumberland House.[26] 'There were 13 houses in this court, all in a state of great dilapidation, in every room in every house excepting only one lived one or more common prostitutes of the most wretched discription . . . The house excepted was a kind of public house and a Crimping house of the very

26 See *Horwood's Plan* (above, n. 6), sheet C3, for Johnson's Court, the adjoining Angel Court (not named on the plan), and all individual houses and house numbers mentioned in the following account of Charing Cross.

worst sort.' This house was the Turk's Head, *alias* the Rummer, *alias* the Royal Bagnio, a brothel fitted up with hot and cold baths and attracting, if not a respectable, at least an aristocratic clientele. Probably at the start of the war with France, it had become a 'crimping house', into which young men were decoyed, usually by prostitutes. Once inside they were then plied with drink, locked up when insensible, robbed and enlisted into the army. The Turk's Head was at the rear of a print-seller's shop at 16 Charing Cross. In 1801 Place and his family moved into number 16. He sub-let the brothel – in 1802 the great but impoverished geologist William Smith had a room there – and, by his own account, turned the print-shop into one of the most elegant and fashionable menswear shops in London, with huge plate-glass windows lit by brilliant oil-lamps.[27]

Seven years earlier, in July 1794, a young journeyman baker had been dragged into the Turk's Head and apparently disappeared. Believing that he had been forcibly enlisted, a crowd gathered and a minor riot ensued.[28] Over the next weeks, cries for assistance, cries of 'murder', had been heard out in Charing Cross itself. On Friday 15 August, a young man named George Howe appeared on the roof of a crimping house, one of a row of six which all but divided Johnson's Court from Angel Court, all owned by a Mrs Hanna, all connected with each other by 'secret avenues'. He stood there, frozen in fear as the crimps approached him, then 'threw himself from the tiles, and was dashed to pieces on the flags of the court'. His dying sigh must have run in blood down the walls of the Duke of Northumberland's palace. Once again a crowd gathered, and attempted to break down the locked door of the house; when Sheridan appeared, in his capacity as a local magistrate, another suspected crimping house in the court was searched; and there, in a locked room, a young man was discovered dying of smallpox. At Sheridan's request, the crowd departed; it collected again at evening but was dispersed by horse guards summoned from Whitehall.[29]

Early on Saturday morning a crowd gathered for the third time, broke into several of Mrs Hanna's houses, and threw all the bedding out of the windows, making a summer snowstorm of feathers in Charing Cross.

27 Mary Thale (ed.), *The Autobiography of Francis Place* (Cambridge: Cambridge University Press, 1972), pp. 213–15, 227–9. For the Royal Bagnio/Rummer/Turk's Head see Bryant Lillywhite, *London Coffee Houses: A Reference Book of Coffee Houses of the Seventeenth, Eighteenth and Nineteenth Centuries* (London: George Allen and Unwin, 1963), p. 611; for Smith in Charing Cross, see Simon Winchester, *The Map that Changed the World* (London: Penguin, 2002), pp. 206–7.
28 *Morning Chronicle* (18 August 1794).
29 *Ibid.* (18 August 1794).

All that day and the next, the angry crowd hung around the Cross under the eye of patrolling horse guards and footguards. On both days a group of rioters, estimated at between 40 and 100, attacked another suspected crimping house, the King's Arms, at 23 and 28 Charing Cross.[30] They smashed the door to pieces and hurled the fragments, along with stones and half-bricks, through the windows. The crowd and the horse guards gathered again and angrily faced each other down. At some point the windows of the sword-cutler's shop at the entrance to Johnson's Court were broken, prompting fears that the crowd intended to arm themselves. For a long summer weekend Charing Cross was under siege.[31]

Over the next few days the trouble moved east and north. There were attacks on crimping houses and recruiting offices in Whitcomb Street, Drury Lane, Fleet Street, Holborn, Shoe Lane, Bride-Lane near St Paul's Cathedral, Long Lane, Smithfield, Barbican, Golden Lane, Moorfields, Whitechapel Green, Gray's Inn Lane and Clerkenwell.[32] Driven from one district by the military, the crowd reassembled elsewhere and rioted again. Here and there fires were started; in some places whole buildings were pulled down. One contemporary described the rioters as 'the most alarming mob since [the Gordon Riots in] 1780'.[33] More damage was done in and around the City than at Charing Cross, but because the riots began there, because there they lasted a long four days, and because of its strategic position at the threshold of the West End, it was the riots at Charing Cross that received the bulk of the coverage and caused most outrage in the newspapers. In September Joseph Strutt, the alleged leader of those who attacked the King's Arms, was sentenced to death; in October Mrs Hanna, who had eventually been charged with keeping a disorderly house, was acquitted.[34]

Protests and riots against crimping houses continued sporadically through the early months of 1795, their bitterness sharpened by the food

---

30 *Ibid.* (22 September 1795).
31 *Ibid.* (18, 19, 20, 22 August 1794). For the attack on the sword-cutler's shop, see John Stevenson's invaluable essay 'The London Riots of 1794', *International Review of Social History* 16 (1971), 40–58. To this, and to Stevenson's *Popular Disturbances in England 1700–1780* (London and New York: Longman, 1979), esp. ch. 8, my own essay is much indebted. See also Francis Plowden, *A Short History of the British Empire during the Year 1794* (London: G. G. and J. Robinson, 1795), pp. 255–62.
32 *Morning Chronicle* (20, 21, 22 August 1794); Stevenson, 'London Riots', pp. 45–50.
33 The diary of William Goodwin, a Suffolk surgeon, transcribed by Mrs J. Rothery, at www.earl-soham.suffolk.gov.uk/history/Goodwin1794.htm
34 *Morning Chronicle* (22 September, 25 October 1794).

shortages caused by the failure of the 1794 harvest. Then, on 12 July, the King's Arms in Charing Cross was attacked again. A guardsman, John Lewis, entered the house accompanied by a young boy called Hollis, and began to behave so obstreperously that a burly soldier showed him into the street. He started to shout to a gathering crowd that Hollis had been seized and chained to the floor in the back kitchen. A constable searched the house and reported to the crowd that he could find no men in irons. The crowd, however, were not convinced, and, once again, the door and windows of the King's Arms were shattered; every stick of furniture was destroyed, and another feathery blizzard hit the Cross. The riot lasted for five hours until, at dusk, the horse and foot guards were called out.[35]

Next evening the rioters gathered again, now according to one (probably exaggerated) report 12,000 strong, and marched down Whitehall. In Downing Street they threw stones through the windows of the Prime Minister's house, where the Earl of Mornington was a dinner guest. According to the radical *Telegraph* Mornington, a member of cabinet and elder brother of the future Duke of Wellington, was hit a violent blow on the shoulder; Pitt fled to Henry Dundas's house in Wimbledon. Driven off by the military, the crowd streamed over Westminster Bridge to St George's Fields, where, to chants of 'Pitt's Head and a Quartern Loaf for Sixpence', they attacked a suspected crimping house and a butcher's shop, nearly demolishing both and burning furniture in the street. Some of the rioters were trampled by the cavalry, and two died.[36] Lewis was eventually hanged in Charing Cross, at the entrance to the alley leading to the King's Arms.[37]

But what seemed to many – and in particular the king and his government – the most horrific plebeian invasion of the West End occurred at the end of October 1795, when, after a summer of near-famine and a year of defeats by France, the king travelled in the state coach from St James's Palace to Westminster for the opening of Parliament. His route, along the Mall in St James's Park, through the Horse Guards, and down Whitehall and Parliament Street to the House of Lords, was lined by what was estimated

---

35 See *Morning Chronicle* (13, 22 July 1795); *True Briton* (14, 16, 20 July 1795); note that the radical newspapers the *Courier* (13 July) and the *Telegraph* (14 July) both insist that chained men were found within the King's Arms. The report of Lewis's trial, however, in the *Morning Chronicle* (22 July) makes this seem unlikely.
36 *Telegraph* (14, 16 July 1795).
37 *Autobiography*, pp. 228–9.

to be as many as 200,000 spectators, many of whom, however, had not come simply to stare and wonder. The coach was mobbed, greeted with hisses, groans, and demands for bread and peace; in Whitehall a stone broke one of the coach windows; in Old Palace Yard another window was broken by what the king insisted was a bullet, though it was probably another stone. On the return journey the crowds were still waiting, and as the coach arrived at the palace gate, a stone and an oyster shell were thrown, and one of the horses, frightened by the mob, reared up and knocked down a groom; the coach ran him over and he later died. The king got safely inside the palace, and, when the coast seemed clear, left in a private coach for Buckingham House, now Buckingham Palace. His route lay again through the park, but here remnants of the crowd grabbed at the wheels of the coach to bring it to a halt, and (in the words of a radical pamphleteer) they 'were proceeding to lay their Harpy hands on *The Representative of the King of Heaven*, when a party of life-guards came trotting up, . . . and rescued (without any bloodshed) their royal Master from the hands of the hungry Rabble'.[38] Meanwhile the state coach had started up Pall Mall to be returned to the King's Mews in Charing Cross. From Carlton House to the mews it was pelted with stones again, until every window and door panel was smashed. Like hauling heroes in triumph or pulling down the houses of villains, destroying the coaches of the aristocracy was a crowd activity with a long provenance – during the Gordon Riots the vehicles of four lords, two bishops and one baronet had been demolished or badly damaged.[39] To tear the king's coach to pieces, however, was different: it went beyond the mockery of official power and ceremony in the inversion rituals we looked at earlier; it was a direct attack on the ceremonial by which the sovereign power performed its sovereignty, and amounted almost to a metonymic dismembering of the king himself. The broken fragments changed hands in the street for threepence and sixpence, according to size.[40] It was this riot that led to the introduction of the two bills, which led in turn to the meeting at Old Palace Yard.

---

38 *Truth and Treason! Or a Narrative of the Royal Procession to the House of Peers, October the 29th, 1795* (no imprint, 1795), p. 4.

39 Thomas Holcroft, *A Plain and Succinct Narrative of the Gordon Riots* (1780), ed. Garland Garvey Smith, (Atlanta, GA: Emory University Library, 1944).

40 This account of the events of 29 October 1795 is based on writing in the *True Briton*, *The Times*, the *Oracle*, *Morning Post* and *Morning Chronicle* printed on 30 October 1795; [John Reeves?], *A Narrative of the Insults offered to the King, on his Way to the House of Lords, on Thursday last* (London: J. Owen, 1795); *Truth and Treason!*; and Francis Place's essay on the two bills in BL Add. MS 27,808.

Two cultures

The government joined with loyalist opinion in blaming the LCS also for the outrages of 29 October 1795: three days earlier the society had held a huge general meeting at the Copenhagen tea-house north of Islington where it issued a provocative warning to the king about the need for famine-relief, peace with France and a reform of parliament, and a handbill had been sold, by the radical bookseller 'Citizen' Richard Lee, entitled *King Killing*.[41] The government responded to the attack on the king's coach by introducing two bills greatly limiting the society's freedom to meet and to publish. Many loyalists had blamed the LCS for the crimping riots too, and though the LCS adopted a policy of peaceful protest and reiterated that policy at every opportunity, in August 1794 two members of the society, including the life-long radical Dr Robert Watson, had been found in a London coffee-house with handbills urging the rioters to continue their efforts. The ultra-loyalist Lord Mayor, Paul Le Mesurier, believed these bills had been published by another LCS member, the bookseller Daniel Isaac Eaton.[42] In 1795 Thelwall had been reported to the Home Office as leader of the rioters at St George's Fields, though he had been on the Isle of Wight at the time.[43]

41 *Account of the Proceedings of a Meeting of the London Corresponding Society, held in a Field near Copenhagen House, Monday, Oct. 26, 1795* (London: Citizen Lee [1795]); *King Killing* (London: Citizen Lee [1795]). For Lee and *King Killing*, see Jon Mee, 'The Strange Career of Richard Citizen Lee: Poetry, Popular Radicalism and Enthusiasm in the 1790s', in Timothy Morton and Nigel Smith (eds.), *Radicalism in British Literary Culture, 1650–1830* (Cambridge: Cambridge University Press, 2002), pp. 151–66; Barrell, *Imagining the King's Death*, ch. 17, and Barrell (ed.), *Exhibition Extraordinary!! Radical Broadsides of the mid 1790s* (Nottingham: Trent Editions, 2001), pp. 74–5.
42 Conversations at LCS committee meetings in August 1794, reported to the government by the spy William Metcalfe, make it clear that though individual members of the LCS were thoroughly sympathetic to the rioters, and though perhaps a few had been rioters themselves, the LCS itself had had no organizing role in the riots: see Thale (ed.), *Papers of the London Corresponding Society*, pp. 211–13. Early in September the society published a pamphlet, *Reformers No Rioters* (London: London Corresponding Society [1794]), the title of which adequately sums up its policy. Eaton's teenage son claimed to have participated in the 1794 riots (Thale (ed.), *Papers of the London Corresponding Society*, pp. 211–12), and for evidence of Eaton senior's sympathy with the riots, see 'Henry Martin Saunders', *The Crimps, or the Death of poor Howe: A Tragedy in One Act* (London: D. I. Eaton, 1794. For Watson and the handbills, see Stevenson, 'London Riots', p. 50; for more on Watson, see Iain McCalman, 'Controlling the Riots: Dickens and Romantic Revolution', *History* 84 (July 1999), 458–74.
43 See John Thelwall, *The Tribune, A Periodical Publication, consisting chiefly of the Political Lectures of John Thelwall*, 3 vols. (London: D. I. Eaton, J. Smith, J. Burks, 1795), vol. II, pp. 183–4.

Both loyalists and radicals agreed that the greatest weapon of the reformers was their access to the printing press,[44] not only via established booksellers of a liberal or radical character, such as Joseph Johnson, James Ridgway and Henry Symonds, but via the emergence, in the 1790s, of more or less plebeian booksellers, like Lee, Eaton and Thomas Spence. The LCS often published their many addresses to the nation, to other reform societies, and so on, in sympathetic newspapers, and as pamphlets with a print run of many thousands. The reform movement was to an important degree an effect of the astonishing growth of print culture in the eighteenth century, and in London especially, where the volume of publication was huge compared with anywhere else in the English-speaking world; among the other effects of that growth was the emergence of monthly periodicals or 'reviews', which sifted the vast pile of books and pamphlets published every month, and summarized and judged them (or some of them) for the convenience of their subscribers. The circulation figures of the most successful of these reviews, the *Monthly*, the *Critical*, the *Analytical* and the *British Critic*, were impressive, between 1,500 and 5,000; they sold well to circulating libraries outside the capital and were widely influential.[45] All this activity led to increasing possibilities of all kinds: for publishers to make fortunes and occasionally to lose them, for new small publishers to emerge and often fail, for professionals such as clerics and physicians to supplement their incomes by writing, and for some writers to risk living entirely on the fees they received from publishers.

London newspapers too had flourished in the great expansion of print culture. By 1793 there were fourteen daily newspapers published in London, thirteen papers publishing two or three times a week, and eleven weeklies; ten years earlier there had been only eight daily newspapers and nine bi- or tri-weeklies.[46] One of the main functions of late eighteenth-century newspapers was to carry the front-page advertisements, a vital source of revenue, which gave notice of theatrical shows, new publications, products and services for

---

44 See for example [John Bowles], *Letters of the Ghost of Alfred, addressed to the Hon. Thomas Erskine, and the Hon. Charles James Fox* (London: J. Wright, 1798) esp. pp. 105–7; [Arthur O'Connor], *The Measures of Ministry to prevent a Revolution are the certain Means of bringing it on*, 3rd edn (London: D. I. Eaton, 1794); *The Pernicious Effects of the Art of Printing upon Society, exposed. A Short Essay. Addressed to the Friends of Social Order* (London: Daniel Isaac Eaton [1793]).

45 See Derek Roper, *Reviewing before the Edinburgh* (London: Methuen, 1978), pp. 24–5.

46 Figures for 1783 from A. Aspinall, *Politics and the Press c. 1780–1850* (London: Home and Van Thal, 1949), p. 6 (corrected); for 1793 from *The Universal British Directory of Trade, Commerce, and Manufacture*, 3rd edn (London: Champante and Whitrow [1794]).

sale and so on. Advertisements in the London newspapers are an important feature of such novels as Holcroft's *Hugh Trevor* (1794–7), Wollstonecraft's *The Wrongs of Woman* and Smith's *The Young Philosopher*; in the latter two novels they concern missing persons, and like Gines's handbill in *Caleb Williams* communicate a sense not only of how possible it was for people to lose themselves in the vast metropolis, but also of how the saturation of the city in print might make it harder for them to hide. As well as advertisements and news, the papers frequently carried long feature articles which were sometimes later published as books or pamphlets. The number of such features increased as, from 1792 onwards, newspapers became increasingly divided between those subsidized by the Treasury on behalf of the government and those which opposed Pitt's ministry. This added to the opportunities available for professional writers – for Coleridge, for example, who moved to London and began writing for the *Morning Post* late in 1799.

The divisions between the various groups of writers feeding and trying to feed off the publishing industry were as marked as any other in the divided London of the 1790s. Leaving aside the output of the plebeian booksellers, the most salient division for most of the decade was probably that between the group of writers contributing to the *British Critic*, and those more or less closely affiliated to the overlapping 'circles' surrounding Godwin and Johnson, the publisher of the *Analytic Review*. The *British Critic* was conceived under the auspices of the Society for the Reformation of Principles by Appropriate Literature, founded by the arch-tory Suffolk clergyman William Jones of Nayland. Its mission was to expose the supposed international conspiracy which had brought about the French Revolution, and to counteract the *'monopoly of the press'* by those Whig, or radical, or dissenting writers and booksellers who had been responsible for circulating Paine's *Rights of Man* and whose 'Jacobin' principles found expression every month in the *Analytical*, and, to a lesser extent, in the *Critical* reviews.[47] It was first published in 1793, probably with a small secret float from the Treasury[48], and was co-owned by Rivingtons, the Tory booksellers, and by two youngish Tory clergyman of the Church of England who co-edited its early numbers. One of these was the philologist Robert Nares, the Oxford-educated and well-connected son of the composer and organist to the king, and nephew of an anti-Wilkesite MP who later became a judge. The other was the classical scholar and miscellaneous

---

47 See Roper, *Reviewing*, p. 23; Emily Lorraine de Montluzin, *The Anti-Jacobins, 1798–1800: The Early Contributors to the Anti-Jacobin Review* (New York: St Martin's, 1988), pp. 1–2, 21, 111.
48 See Roper, *Reviewing*, p. 265, n. 50.

writer William Beloe, the son of a Norwich tradesman, educated (unhappily) under the Whig Samuel Parr at Stanmore and later at Cambridge. Many of the contributors were in holy orders, and many, like Beloe, of relatively unprivileged birth, though mostly Oxbridge-educated. John Brand, the economist, was the son of a tanner, also from Norwich; the astronomer John Hellins was the son of a Devonshire labourer, and had been apprenticed to a cooper before being taken on as an assistant at the Royal Observatory and entering the church. John Whitaker, an antiquarian, was the son of a Manchester innkeeper; the father of William Vincent, educationalist, was a packer and Portugal merchant; the poet and orientalist Thomas Maurice, a probable contributor[49] and certainly part of the social circle around the review, was the son of a headmaster in Hertford.

It was by no means unusual in the eighteenth century for men of fairly humble origins to become clergymen of the established church, or for clergymen to supplement their incomes by writing or even to work entirely as professional writers. What is striking, however, about this group is how many of them, by virtue of their strict orthodoxy and of their work for the *British Critic* and the connections it enabled them to form, were very well rewarded by the church itself and by patrons who had the right of presentation to ecclesiastical livings. Preferments in the church were showered on Nares and Vincent especially, pluralists whose numerous ecclesiastical sources of income it would take a long paragraph to list. Beloe, who had given up schoolteaching to become a writer in London, was made rector of Allhallows, London Wall, in 1796, a living which at his death in 1817 passed, inevitably, to Nares; he became a prebendary of Lincoln and of St Pauls, where, inevitably, Nares was already installed. Brand was rewarded with the rectory of St George's Southwark; Maurice with a number of livings all of which he kept until he died. Maurice, Beloe and Nares were all found valuable employment at the British Museum, Nares eventually as keeper of manuscripts, Beloe as keeper of printed books until his inability to prevent their being stolen in large numbers led to his resignation. Only Whitaker of those I have mentioned seems to have made nothing out of his connection with the review. From 1777 until his death he lived on the income from his Cornish rectory and his other writings, and asked no fee for his contributions, wishing, as he put it, 'merely to support it as an orthodox and constitutional journal of literature'.[50]

---

49 *Ibid.*, pp. 23 and 265, n. 60.
50 *Ibid.*, p. 25.

The group formed around the *British Critic* was far from a closed one. Along with its connections to the established church, it had, through Nares, who was chaplain to the Duke of York, and William Vincent, chaplain-in-ordinary and sub-almoner to the king, connections with the court; through Brand with the government economists at the Board of Trade; through Hellins with the Royal Society; through Nares again (he was assistant preacher at Lincoln's Inn) with the legal profession. These Tory intellectuals were enmeshed in, supported and sustained by some of the most powerful and influential institutions in Britain. By contrast, the 'circles' of Godwin and Johnson were both composed largely of dissenters of one kind or another (Godwin himself, Hays, Anna Barbauld and her brother John Aikin), many of them unitarians or with strong unitarian connections (Johnson himself, William Frend, Thomas Christie, Gilbert Wakefield, Amelia Alderson), some of them members of fringe sects (Blake, William Sharp). They included liberal catholics (Inchbald, Alexander Geddes, James Barry), and they welcomed women writers (Hays, Alderson, Barbauld, Wollstonecraft, Inchbald, Eliza Fenwick), though some on more nearly equal terms than others.

Such connections as they had with professional faculties and institutions were often short-lived or precarious. Among them are an academic banished from his university (Frend); physicians who have given up medicine (Aikin, Wolcot); dissenting, Catholic and Church of England clergy who have abandoned the ministry (Godwin, Geddes, Wakefield, John Horne Tooke, Wolcot again). Though the painters among them (Barry, Henry Fuseli, John Opie) were all Royal Academicians, in 1799 Barry would be expelled from the Academy, partly on account of his declared admiration for the French republic, partly perhaps, following the Irish rebellion of 1798, because of his suspected sympathy for the United Irishmen. Through Inchbald and Holcroft in particular, the Godwin circle had connections with the theatre, but it took years for Holcroft to re-establish himself as a dramatist following his arrest and acquittal on a charge of high treason in 1794. Otherwise they were excluded from the formal and informal institutions of the state and the polite national culture, by virtue of their political beliefs, their gender, and the 'disabilities' (the legal abridgement of civil rights) imposed on Catholics and dissenters. Many adhered instead to institutions – dissenting chapels and academies – which emphasized their exclusion. We have come to regard the Godwin and Johnson circles as constituting a radical critical public sphere; but loyalists would have seen them as precisely the kind of unpropertied, disaffiliated, extra-institutional intellectuals whom Burke held in large part responsible for initiating the revolution in France.[51]

Though some members of the Johnson and Godwin circles, Inchbald, for example, and Wolcot, and to a lesser degree Holcroft, were able to remain on good terms in the 1790s with a wide and politically diverse group of friends, others – partly by choice, partly by necessity – seem to have associated almost exclusively with other members of those circles; when the British Critic reviewed Hays's Emma Courtney (1796), it advised her to widen her acquaintance.[52] It is difficult to imagine Godwin and Wollstonecraft in particular forming the kind of friendships of the kind that develop simply as a result of living in a particular neighbourhood; one is reminded by them of what Wordsworth had been expecting to find in London prior to his first visit there in 1791:

> Above all, one thought
> Baffled my understanding, how men lived
> Even next-door neighbours, as we say, yet still
> Strangers, and knowing not each other's names.[53]

Godwin, in the last two decades of the century during which he was almost continuously in London, lived at fourteen different addresses – in the City, off Long Acre, in the Strand, in Covent Garden, in Soho, off Oxford Street, in fashionable and less fashionable parts of Marylebone, and in Somers Town. In 1807 he moved back to the City. In the last ten years of her life, of which she spent about seven in London, Mary Wollstonecraft had eight different addresses there, in Southwark, in Bloomsbury, off Oxford Street, in Finsbury Square and Finsbury Place just north of the City, in Pentonville and in Somers Town. These moves are not simply signs of a metropolitan restlessness and there were no doubt good reasons for all of them. Both writers sometimes leave London and, on their return, take new lodgings. Godwin's few months' sojourn in the West End were made possible by sudden literary success, and his subsequent eastward retreat enforced by his inability to sustain it. Wollstonecraft's move from Southwark to Store Street was also partly the result of relative success; her stay in Finsbury

51 Burke, Reflections on the Revolution in France, in The Works of the Right Honourable Edmund Burke, new edn, 14 vols. (London: F. and C. Rivington, 1815–22), vol. V, pp. 207ff.; see also Burke's attack on men of 'talents' in Three Letters Addressed to a Member of the Present Parliament, on the proposals for peace with the regicide Directory of France, in Works, vol. VIII, p. 170.
52 British Critic, vol. IX (March 1797), p. 315.
53 The Prelude (1805 version), Book VII, lines 117–20.

Square was immediately after her attempted suicide, when the Christies offered her shelter; her later moves may have been motivated by the desire to be nearer Godwin, but may possibly have been prompted also by a predictable hostility in her lodging-keepers to a woman of advanced views, with a baby, claiming to be married but with no visible husband. But the effect of this constant mobility may have been that, though they lived *in* London they were not *of* it, except insofar as London meant to them the circles, with their very specific character, in which they socialized.

In an essay published in 1797, Godwin offers to distinguish in a paragraph between 'the man of talent and the man without', by describing how each of them might pass the time during a walk from Temple Bar to Hyde Park Corner. The point is to show the generalizing, the abstracting, the imaginative power of men such as himself, as compared with the impoverished intellect of ordinary men, but it can be read also as an account of how Godwin himself responds to street life in London, and how he supposes other men respond to it. 'The dull man', he suggests,

> goes straight forward; he has so many furlongs to traverse. He observes if he meets any of his acquaintance; he enquires respecting their health and their family. He glances perhaps [at] the shops as he passes; he admires the fashion of a buckle, and the metal of a tea-urn. If he experience any flights of fancy, they are of short extent; of the same nature as the flights of a forest-bird, clipped of his wings, and condemned to spend the rest of his life in a farm-yard.

This man is not to be taken as showing an appropriately lively interest in the health and well-being of his friends and in the window displays of the shops. As far as Godwin is concerned, all that is mere distraction from the inner life of the intellect. If the heavy imagination of this dullard ever leaves the ground, it soon bumps to earth as he becomes distracted once again by some glittering object for sale or by some equally trivial social encounter. It is imprisoned in the London streets; the thick-and-fast sense impressions of the man without talent are the walls of its cell.

The man of talent, on the other hand, is entirely indifferent to the contents of shop windows and apparently meets no acquaintances. If any of the passers-by on the streets do briefly catch his attention, he 'reads their countenances, conjectures their past history, and forms a superficial notion of their wisdom or folly, their vice or virtue, their satisfaction or misery'. If he does observe the shifting scenery of the walk, it is in order to reconstruct it aesthetically, 'with the eye of a connoisseur or an artist'. For the most part, however, he is quite 'unindebted to the suggestions of surrounding objects', for 'his whole soul is employed' with his own thoughts.

> He laughs and cries. . . . He enters into nice calculations; he digests saga-cious reasonings. In imagination he declaims or describes, impressed with the deepest sympathy, or elevated to the loftiest rapture. He makes a thousand new and admirable combinations. He passes through a thousand imaginary scenes, tries his courage, tasks his ingenuity, and thus becomes gradually prepared to meet almost any of the many-coloured events of human life. He consults by the aid of memory the books he has read, and projects others for the future instruction and delight of mankind.

How well the man of talent improves the hour! 'The time of these two persons in one respect resembles; it has brought them both to Hyde-Park-Corner. In almost every other respect it is dissimilar.'[54] Nowhere can be a prison for the man of talent, for *his* imagination, at one bound, escapes all confinement, as Caleb's did in his cell.[55]

But however admirable Godwin intends his man of talent to appear, it seems evident that he might as well have walked from Temple Bar to anywhere, for all the difference it made to him. Indeed he might as well have remained in his study. T. J. Mathias, a well-connected Tory satirist, Treasurer to the Queen, friend and admirer of Nares and Vincent of the *British Critic* if not himself a contributor to the periodical, quoted Godwin's comparison in full in his anonymous *Pursuits of Literature*, garnishing it throughout with incredulous italics. It was, he sneered, '*very instructive*. No man can ever again be at a loss to know a man of talents, from a man without, *in the streets*. I had often been puzzled, till I met with this instructive volume.'[56] Judging by what he italicized – '*if* he observes the passers-by, for example, or '*if*' he notices the scenery – what Mathias found most extraordinary about the passage was not the willingness of the man of talent 'to meet almost any of the many-coloured events of human life' but his determination to avoid meeting almost everything outside himself.

It is to the members of the Johnson and Godwin circles, and to others like Wordsworth and Charlotte Smith who briefly adhered to them or shared many of their political attitudes, that we owe most of the sense we derive

---

54 William Godwin, *The Enquirer: Reflections on Education, Manners, and Literature* (London: G. G. and J. Robinson, 1797), pp. 31–2.
55 This passage is closely related to the chapter in which Caleb describes how he employed his mind when imprisoned (Godwin, *Caleb Williams*, pp. 185–7).
56 T. J. Mathias, *The Pursuits of Literature, A Satirical Poem in Four Dialogues*, 8th edn (London: T. Becket, 1798), pp. 374–6.

from contemporary literature of what London was like in the 1790s. The experiences that constitute Caleb's brief stay in the capital – the constant moving, the sense of exclusion, the attempt to survive by writing in an expanding but overstocked literary market, being vilified in print, being watched by an authority removed and difficult to confront – these experiences were Godwin's also, but many of them characterize the London that appears in the poems of Blake and Wordsworth and in the novels of Wollstonecraft, Hays, Inchbald, Holcroft and Smith. Above all however is the sense of exclusion, the sense of being not a participant in the busy life of the city unless as victim, or of observing its corruption at a distance, baffled and angry, or of inhabiting a city of ideas superimposed upon and occluding the city of brick and stone and its strange inhabitants. Some like Wordsworth may represent themselves or their characters as so distracted by everything they see in the streets that London becomes for them an unintelligible chaos of meaningless stimuli; other writers or their characters may seem, like Godwin's man of talent, to pass from place to place entirely oblivious to the people and objects that surround them. Either way, London in the 1790s seems to produce, and be produced by, a new kind of metropolitan intellectual, marginalized by its economic and political divisions, alienated from its commercial values, wandering its chartered streets with a blank, or an appalled, sense of estrangement. Had the authors of the *British Critic* written fiction, or poems of more interest than those of Thomas Maurice, or had Mathias offered us his own version of the route from Temple Bar to Hyde Park Corner, London in the 1790s might look to us a very different place.

6

Edinburgh and Lowland Scotland

IAN DUNCAN

Enlightenment and Romance

In the century between David Hume's *A Treatise of Human Nature* (1739) and Thomas Carlyle's *The French Revolution* (1837) Lowland Scotland became one of the advanced centres of European and North Atlantic literary culture. Scottish innovations in moral philosophy, history, the social sciences, rhetoric, poetry, periodical journalism and the novel outweighed their English counterparts in the balance of an emerging imperial world order. The intellectuals of the so-called Scottish Enlightenment – Hume, Adam Smith, Adam Ferguson, John Millar, William Robertson, Lord Kames, Thomas Reid, Dugald Stewart and their peers – developed a new, synthetic account of human nature, social organization, economic activity and historical process in a cosmopolitan or universal order of modernity. At the same time, antiquarian scholars and poets began to invoke the national past, ancestral origins and regional popular traditions in an influential series of attempts to reimagine cultural identity in a post-national age. In the early 1760s, James Macpherson's collections of the 'Poems of Ossian' founded European Romanticism upon a scandalous invention of lost national origins. A quarter-century later, Robert Burns fashioned the first decisively modern vernacular style in British poetry. In the first three decades of the nineteenth century Walter Scott's historical romances combined those distinctively Scottish inventions, universal modernity and a national past, to define the governing form of Western narrative for the next 100 years. Meanwhile the Edinburgh periodicals – *The Edinburgh Review, Blackwood's Edinburgh Magazine, Chambers's Edinburgh Journal* – recast the main medium of the nineteenth-century public sphere.

The Scottish contribution to European Romanticism awaits an adequate assessment. For one thing, its achievements make up a history quite different from the English model to which they are typically subordinated. In Scotland, 'Enlightenment' and 'Romantic' cultural formations occupy the same epoch, and the same institutional base, rather than articulating a succession. The simultaneous appearance of the Ossian epics and the scientific projects of Scottish philosophy defies the English schema of a teleological development of Romanticism proper from Augustan neo-classicism via a liminal 'pre-Romanticism' and the paradigm-shifting fulcrum of the French Revolution. The routine dismissal of Macpherson's works as forgeries has tended to reinforce, instead, a wholesale 'Ossianic' diagnosis of Scottish literature, from Macpherson to Scott, as an inauthentic mutation of Romanticism, symptomatic – alongside the contemporaneous anti-Romanticism of 'Scotch philosophy' (from *The Wealth of Nations* to *The Edinburgh Review*) – of the pathological failure of an 'organic' national development.

Yet it is not hard to read a cultural logic shared by the projects of poetry and the human sciences in eighteenth-century Scotland. The objective, materialist discourse of Smith's *Wealth of Nations* offers an at once descriptive and prescriptive account of 'commercial society', the socio-economic form of modernity, under the rubric of 'improvement', meaning moral and cultural development as well as economic progress; while the Ossian epics recall a heroic Gaelic past that is not just extinct but imaginary, unreal, in a declension that undoes the historical materiality of the poem itself. Both projects represent a secular condition of modernity defined by a radical temporal break, a historical or metaphysical dislocation from origins. The poems of Ossian unfold the subjective and ontological relation between past and present in the new order of universal history, projected by Smith's science as a succession of distinct cultural stages, each of which cancels the one preceding it – from savage prehistory to civil society, the vantage point of the modern reader. Enlightenment history calls modernity into being upon that obliteration of ancestral worlds which constitutes the imaginary time and space of *Fingal*.

The representation of this temporal structure was made possible by objective historical conditions, in the form of a series of political and cultural revolutions in national life. Scotland's entry into modernity followed its dissolution into 'North Britain' at the 1707 Union of Parliaments: a loss of sovereignty preceded by the drastic change of religion at the Reformation, the departure of the king at the Union of Crowns, and the religious and dynastic civil wars of the seventeenth century, and followed by the after-shock of Jacobite insurgency. The destruction of Highland clan society in the wake of the 1745 rising, enforced by government legislation as well as military conquest, was only the most drastic instance of a logic of modernization that entailed the abolition of ancient national formations lingering in the uneven political geography of the country. The internal division between primitive Highlands and improving Lowlands underlined, in turn, Scotland's anomalous – yet typical – status: politically a province, ruled from Westminster, yet part of the economic core of the ascendant 'United Empire', bearing within itself the logic of a new world order.

More thoroughly than their counterparts elsewhere, Lowland Enlightenment intellectuals were able to conceptualize a 'great divide' – a range of effects of disconnection from origins – bearing upon the phenomenological and psychological as well as socio-historical conditions of modernity. Hume's deconstruction of the metaphysical foundations of causality in the *Treatise of Human Nature*, the most radical of these conceptualizations, provided an epistemic matrix for schemes of national and universal history as well as for poetic invocations of a vanishing Scotland. Humean moral philosophy frames a dialectical relation between principles of 'enlightenment' and 'romance', in the discovery of a metaphysically denuded, ruined reality by the work of reason, and that reality's replenishment by the work of imagination. The dialectic governs the conceptual structure of modern – 'Romantic' – Scottish writing. In the high decades of Enlightenment, from the Seven Years' War to the French Revolution, it articulates the relation between the objective accounts of modernity in philosophical history and its discourses, such as political economy, sociology and anthropology, as these emerge (not yet separated into disciplines) in the general field of the human sciences, and the various literary revivals and reclamations of pre-modern cultural forms.

The French Revolution marked a turning point in Scotland as in England, although with different dynamics. The anti-Jacobin reaction of the 1790s, especially vehement in Scotland, broke up the popular radical movement (transporting its leaders) and chilled the Whig Moderate consensus that had sustained the ideological climate of Enlightenment. Scottish literary production shifted its institutional base, from the university curriculum (supplying cultural capital for the London and Edinburgh booksellers) to an industrializing literary marketplace. In the first third of the nineteenth century Edinburgh became the British centre for innovative publishing in the booksellers' genres of periodicals and fiction. A 'Post-Enlightenment' cultural revival got under way in 1802 (the year of the Peace of Amiens), with the founding of *The Edinburgh Review* by a set of young Whig lawyers. The political contestation of the post-war decade drove the principles of Enlightenment and Romance into partisan opposition, when the *Edinburgh*

Review and its adversary *Blackwood's Magazine* (from 1817) formulated antithetical ideologies of (Whig, reformist) political economy and (Tory) cultural nationalism. At the same time, Scott's Waverley novels gave the dialectic a fully narrative and retrospective development, as they made modernization their grand theme, in the potent formal combination of fiction and history. And even as the Waverley novels tested and renegotiated the synthesis, it was broken apart in rival fictional projects, notably by the Blackwood authors James Hogg and John Galt.

Scotland's literary eminence declined sharply after the 1830s, despite an influential spate of liberal and radical periodicals encouraged by Reform (*Tait's Edinburgh Magazine, Chambers's Edinburgh Journal*). Nationalist critics used to ascribe the decline to an organic fatality or decadence – the consequences of the Union, or of the ideological–aesthetic compromise of Scott.[1] It seems clear however that a combination of political, economic and social transformations undermined the regional institutions that sustained Scotland's metropolitan literary culture. The 1825–6 financial crash that ruined Scott and his publishers depressed the book trade throughout Great Britain, and when it recovered it was decisively London-based. Modernizing transport and financial technologies brought Edinburgh too close to London for it to retain the gravitational integrity of a rival centre. The 1832 Reform measures rationalized Scottish institutions, including the universities, bringing them into line with English models and eroding their local autonomy. London emerged as the definitive world-city, the undisputed centre of literary as of other markets, and Scottish cultural capital (the great periodicals and publishing houses) and ambitious intellectuals (like Carlyle) went south. The London serialization of Carlyle's *Sartor Resartus* (1833–4) marks the end of a century of Scottish literary modernization for which Romanticism may provide the title.

Frontiers of the Republic of Letters

In 1707 Scotland lost its parliament, as a century earlier it had lost its court (and the apparatus of royal and aristocratic patronage). The articles of Union preserved, however, the national religion (the Presbyterian Church

---

1 Examples of this critical tradition include Edwin Muir, *Scott and Scotland: The Predicament of the Scottish Writer* (London: Routledge, 1936); David Craig, *Scottish Literature and the Scottish People, 1680–1830* (London: Chatto & Windus, 1961). For a critique see Cairns Craig, *Out of History: Narrative Paradigms in Scottish and English Culture* (Edinburgh: Polygon, 1996), pp. 82–118.

of Scotland) and autonomous legal, banking and educational establishments. These provided the institutional base for a public sphere, and an
official modernity, separate from the political formation of the state, which
Enlightenment intellectuals theorized as 'civil society', a liberal domain of
economic and moral improvement. At the same time, the church, law-
faculties and universities continued to regulate a distinctively national
system of codes, doctrines and traditions governing daily life – in other
words, a culture. Practically and institutionally, in the absence of political
sovereignty, culture supplied the terms of a Scottish national identity that
flourished within the cosmopolitan or imperial framework of civil society.

Scottish intellectuals were the products of these institutions. (In contrast,
as John Brewer has emphasized, English literature in the 'Age of Johnson'
was overwhelmingly commercial and entrepreneurial, with its main institutional base in booksellers' shops.[2]) In the absence of court and parliament,
lawyers and university professors, many of the latter also clergymen, made
up a social elite in the Lowland cities, especially Edinburgh, which
accommodated a prototypical formation of professional-class intellectuals,
regulated (however) by powerful patronage networks. Philosophical
autonomy was fostered by the sheer distance from London, by cultural as
well as commercial links with France, Germany and the Netherlands, and
the ascendancy of a 'Moderate' party in the Church of Scotland. Literacy
rates in Lowland Scotland were among the highest in Europe in the later
eighteenth century, thanks to parish schools, while the five universities
were demographically more accessible than Oxford and Cambridge and
offered far more innovative curricula. The accumulation of urban wealth
through colonial trade, agricultural improvement and early industrialization financed the institutions that comprised the republic of letters of the
Lowland Scottish Enlightenment: the Edinburgh-based legal profession, the
colleges of Aberdeen (King's and Marischal), St Andrews, Glasgow and
Edinburgh, a proliferation of literary, scientific and debating societies
catering to men (but rarely women) of all classes, and booksellers and
printing presses, dispersed throughout the Lowland burghs in the latter part
of the eighteenth century, increasingly centred in Edinburgh in the nineteenth. The development of the Edinburgh New Town after 1767 provided
this republic of letters with a spectacular urban habitat.

---

2 John Brewer, *The Pleasures of the Imagination: English Culture in the Eighteenth Century*
(London: HarperCollins, 1997), pp. 44–50, 125–66.

James Macpherson, raised in one of the Jacobite clans, had studied at Aberdeen, where research into 'primitive' cultural conditions (cf. Thomas Blackwell, *An Enquiry into the Life and Writings of Homer*, 1735) reflected the city's proximity to the Highlands. Macpherson's translations of ancient Gaelic poetry were patronized by intellectuals such as Hugh Blair, the first Regius Professor of Rhetoric and Belles Lettres at the University of Edinburgh. The new discipline (founded by Adam Smith) promoted anglicization through the techniques of literacy, as part of a larger programme of cultural assimilation to the British state. Its professors set English linguistic and literary standards of improvement for Scottish students, equipping them for careers in imperial administration and business; in doing so, they banished native traditions from the trajectory of improvement – defining them as archaic, 'rustic' and 'barbarous', embedded in pre-modern times and spaces.[3] The discourse of improvement, in other words, produced the category of a cultural pre-modernity – a past recognized in order to be renounced – as its enabling antithesis, its own negative origin. The ambiguity of this relation is evident in Blair's scholarly defence of Ossian. The Gaelic epic limns the historical otherness of an extinct ancestral world: an absence that frames, at the same time, the image of an abiding human nature, in which ancient heroic and modern sentimental virtues merge.[4]

A quarter-century after Ossian the Edinburgh literati discovered Robert Burns, whose rural working-class origins made him (more reliably than Macpherson) the embodiment of a universal yet vexingly fugitive 'nature'. Even while they applauded the 'Heaven-taught ploughman', the literati urged him to submit to the disciplines of improvement and write in English. Far from being a Schillerian 'naive poet', Burns (as Scott would later observe) had a better education than many a gentleman, and his relationship to the primitivist cultural formation Katie Trumpener has called 'Bardic

---

3 On these developments see Robert Crawford (ed.), *The Scottish Invention of English Literature* (Cambridge: Cambridge University Press, 1998); Janet Sorensen, *The Grammar of Empire in Eighteenth-Century British Writing* (Cambridge: Cambridge University Press, 2000).

4 See Hugh Blair, 'A Critical Dissertation on the Poems of Ossian', in *The Poems of Ossian and Related Works*, ed. Howard Gaskill (Edinburgh: Edinburgh University Press, 1995), pp. 343–99; John Dwyer, 'The Melancholy Savage: Text and Context in the Poems of Ossian', in Howard Gaskill (ed.), *Ossian Revisited* (Edinburgh: Edinburgh University Press, 1991), pp. 164–206; Adam Potkay, *The Fate of Eloquence in the Age of Hume* (Ithaca, NY: Cornell University Press, 1994), pp. 196–200.

Nationalism' is accordingly problematic.[5] The 1786 volume of *Poems, Chiefly Written in the Scottish Dialect* was published not in Edinburgh but Kilmarnock; far from lying outside modernity, Ayrshire was the home of rich indigenous traditions of religious and political radicalism. In an early series of poems Burns confronts, with aggressive sophistication, the different literary discourses that intersected his poetic identity: regional popular tradition, both literary and oral; a 'high' (courtly, humanist) Scots tradition, eclipsed at the Union of Crowns but recently revived by Allan Ramsay and Robert Fergusson; and the imperial Anglo-British tradition currently undergoing canonization – as official discourse of the republic of letters – in college rhetoric courses. The 'Epistle to J. L*****k, An Old Scotch Bard' opens with a bold remapping of these domains:

> On Fasteneen we had a rockin,
> To ca' the crack and weave our stockin;
> And there was muckle fun and jokin,
>   Ye need na doubt;
> At length we had a hearty yokin,
>   At *sang about*.

> There was ae *sang*, amang the rest,
> Aboon them a' it pleas'd me best,
> That some kind husband had addrest,
>   To some sweet wife:
> It thirl'd the heart-strings thro' the breast,
>   A' to the life.

> I've scarce heard ought describ'd sae weel,
> What gen'rous, manly bosoms feel;
> Thought I, 'Can this be *Pope*, or *Steele*,
>   Or *Beattie's* wark;'
> They told me 'twas an odd kind chiel
>   About *Muirkirk*.[6]

Burns rewrites the topology of national culture to reclaim his local place from an expulsion to social, geographical and temporal margins. The traditional Shrovetide 'sang about', the neighbourly exchange of songs and verses, constitutes a nexus of production and transmission no less 'central' than the salons of London or Edinburgh: the effusions of the 'chiel about

---

5 See Donald A. Low (ed.), *Robert Burns: The Critical Heritage* (London: Routledge and Kegan Paul, 1974), pp. 67–71, 81–2, 258; Katie Trumpener, *Bardic Nationalism: The Romantic Novel and the British Empire* (Princeton: Pinceton University Press, 1997), pp. 2–34.

6 Burns, *Poems and Songs*, ed. James Kinsley (Oxford: Oxford University Press, 1968), p. 85.

Muirkirk' mingle with, and rank beside, the British neo-classical works, models of official style, by Pope (a Catholic), Steele (an Irishman) and Beattie (the tradition's Anglo-Scots representative).[7] Poetic production is figured as democratic homosocial exchange (rather than lost Bardic origination), dispersed across a synchronous network of male heterosexual friendship, which casts the poet as emphatically living, proximate, familiar and embodied.

In 'The Vision', Burns more forcefully invokes Scots – rather than Anglo-British – national models: the poem is divided into 'Duans', after one of the Ossian fragments; the dream-vision imitates a late-medieval Makars' genre; the 'Scottish Muse' is green-mantled, like the fairy queen of Border ballads. The poem seeks a synecdochic equivalence between an intensively particular, local representation and an abstract, 'Augustan' national system; but the synthesis is compromised by the poet's melancholy acceptance of a diminished, domesticated role as mere 'rustic bard'. Elsewhere, in the 'Address to the Deil', Burns restores a satiric, dissident energy to the 'bardie', who rewrites Milton and the Bible into the demotic, sceptical and sentimental expression of a radical ideal of *fraternité*. The latter part of Burns's career found him undertaking a fascinating solution to the bardic predicament of lost origins: becoming the anonymous donor of texts to the living corpus of national airs, in collaborative projects such as *The Scots Musical Museum* (1787–1803). Burns found himself by losing himself, disappearing into the archive of national popular tradition, reconstituting it as a collective textual body. In a magnanimous wager, Burns granted the national airs cultural priority: his words would last so long as performers consented to remember them – to embody them, in breath and voice – as the lyrics best fitted to the music.[8]

Burns's would be, by definition, a hard act to follow. His most enterprising heir, in the next generation, was James Hogg – although the attempt to literalize the succession (he changed his birthday to make the claim) yielded diminishing returns in Hogg's career, as he moved from the rustic, 'bardic' genres of ballad, lyric and folk-tale to the modern, metropolitan genres (established as 'national' by Scott) of metrical romance and novel.

---

7 See Leith Davis, 'At "Sang About": Robert Burns, Music and the Scottish Challenge to British Culture', in *Scotland and the Borders of Romanticism*, ed. Leith Davis, Ian Duncan and Janet Sorensen (Cambridge: Cambridge University Press, 2004), pp. 195–6.
8 See Robert Crawford, 'Robert Fergusson's Robert Burns', in Crawford (ed.), *Robert Burns and Cultural Authority* (Edinburgh: Edinburgh University Press, 1997), pp. 16–20; Mary Ellen Brown, *Burns and Tradition* (Urbana: Illinois University Press, 1984), pp. 27–70.

Hogg established his reputation as 'The Ettrick Shepherd', a more self-consciously primitive persona than Burns's, with cultural capital more heavily invested in local oral tradition – Hogg's maternal grandfather was the last man in the Borders to have conversed with the fairies. At the same time, Hogg too was formed in the thoroughly modern crucible of local literary clubs, both in the countryside and in Edinburgh, a democratic milieu that generated the remarkable weekly periodical with which he attempted to take the city in 1810–11, *The Spy*.[9] The Tory intellectuals, however, preferred to confine Hogg to the ideologically useful role of primitivist mascot, the personification of an 'organic' Scotland. When Hogg braved discouragement to write a series of experimental and subversive fictions in the early 1820s, the literati of *Blackwood's Magazine* brazenly carried on inventing the comic sayings and antics of 'the Shepherd' in the satiric serial symposium *Noctes Ambrosianae*.

Conjectured worlds

Encouraged by the reception of his *Fragments of Ancient Poetry, Collected in the Highlands of Scotland* (1760), Macpherson published what he claimed were translations from a third-century Gaelic epic cycle (*Fingal*, 1761; *Temora*, 1763). While the Ossian poems celebrate a heroic Celtic past, the significance of the epos lay in its inclusiveness and portability. Macpherson's native epic would supply all Scots, not only Highlanders, with a mythology of virtuous ancestors. And not just the Scots: 'Ossian' provided the modern prototype of an aboriginal high culture that could challenge an imperial classicism on its own terms. The poems' sensational success charts the temporal and geographical reach of the cultural movement later to be called Romanticism, across Europe and North America and well into the next century – except in England and Ireland, where Macpherson's translations came under attack on the grounds of their inauthenticity.

Recent scholarship has begun to replace the vulgar consensus that Macpherson faked the Ossian poems with a more nuanced understanding of an ideologically complex act of synthesis. The authenticity scandal, in any case, should be read as measuring rather than annulling the historical force of Macpherson's achievement. The 'translations' opened up new expressive and mythopoeic possibilities, which would be fundamental to the culture of

---

9 James Hogg, *The Spy*, ed. Gillian K. Hughes (Edinburgh: Edinburgh University Press, 2000), 'Introduction', pp. xvii–xlii.

modernity over the next 200 years. While a discourse of feeling would constitute the 'authentic' legacy of Ossian – a sentimental and psychological representation, separable from the antiquarian controversy – the poems' 'inauthentic' achievement was no less crucial: not least, for specifying authenticity itself as a key term in the conceptualization of culture. Far from flouting some already existing discourse of authenticity, in other words, the Ossian scandal did much to precipitate such a discourse. Blurring the distinction between scholarly recovery and poetic invention, Macpherson defined a new cultural position, between translation and forgery, which would become the classic address of an 'invented tradition'. Inauthentic inventions prepared the way for authentic ones, in that they opened up a Romantic (eventually Modernist) conceptual space of 'myth' as a designation of immaterial, imaginary, deep-structural schemes and figures underlying the textual surfaces of history and everyday life. The Ossian controversy would issue, on the one hand, in the scientific account of oral tradition, which Macpherson and his supporters lacked; and, on the other, in an affirmation of invention itself – of fiction-making, *poesis* – as the imaginary mode of production of national mythologies.

The affective power of the Ossian poems (reshaping European taste over half a century) did not mainly reside, meanwhile, in their antiquarian or ethnological evocation of an ancestral Scottish culture, so much as in the expressive dynamic of loss itself, generalized to encompass an entire society. The glamour of the world of *Fingal* derives less from its ideological associations (although those were locally important) than from the datum of its extinction. The poems generate an overwhelming melancholy in the breach between their heroic past and British modernity, a breach so absolute as ontologically to engulf both past and modern conditions. 'Songs of other times', they invoke Gaelic culture as a ghostly presence that turns out, at its own moment of historical being and in its own expressive utterance, to be fading away into some yet remoter anteriority. The gap between then and now – the temporality of extinction – constitutes our activity as readers, since to read the poems is to find our own subjective present caught recursively in the elegiac logic of the Ossianic bards and heroes, as they mourn their extinction in a future occupied by nothing except our act of reading. Macpherson's act of translation obliterates the Gaelic original in order to recreate it as a dead poetic language embalmed in English prose: not just the poem's world, but its sites of production and reception undergo a grievous dematerialization. The flaw that discredited Macpherson's enterprise followed his insistence that the poems referred to something substantial, literal, real, an authentic world of life on the far side of modernity – rather than recognizing that the poems' achievement was to have discovered the gulf itself as the matrix of a peculiarly modern form of subjectivity, in which we contemplate a lost past from the viewpoint of an ever-vanishing present.[10]

This representation of the subjective form of modernity provides the strong link between Ossian and Enlightenment philosophy, with its commitment to the objective formation of modernity as a historical category. Both poetic and scientific projects, as suggested earlier, elaborate the temporal structure of a dislocation from origins. The desolation of the Highlands after the '45, the primary historical referent for the Ossian poems, was only the latest in the series of catastrophic breaks that constituted Scottish history. Eighteenth-century Scottish historiography narrated the ideological displacement of the national past by the Anglo-British constitution of 1689, which became Scotland's political inheritance at the Union. This narrative asserted a qualitative breach between British modernity and that national past, now repudiated as impoverished, violent, fanatical, backward – the antithesis of post-Union civil society.[11]

The empirical narrative of national history, as a serial disconnection from origins, informed another, more ambitious historiographic order: the theoretical narrative of universal history as an evolutionary sequence of discrete socio-economic stages, from hunter-gatherer tribalism through nomadic pastoralism and agricultural settlement to modern commercial society. The 'stadial' scheme of history, developed in Adam Smith's university jurisprudence course in the 1750s, informs (with varying degrees of flexibility) such projects as Ferguson's *History of Civil Society* (1767), Millar's *Origin of the Distinction of Ranks in Society* (1771), Kames's *Sketches of the History of Man* (1778), and the works of Robertson, as well as Smith's own *Wealth of Nations* (1776). This so-called conjectural history seeks to overcome the discontinuous

---

10 See Peter Osborne, *The Politics of Time: Modernity and Avant-Garde* (London: Verso, 1995); Peter Womack, *Improvement and Romance: Constructing the Myth of the Highlands* (Basingstoke: Macmillan, 1989), pp. 78–108; Trumpener, *Bardic Nationalism*, pp. 67–127. On orality and authenticity in eighteenth-century and Romantic writing, see also Penny Fielding, *Writing and Orality: Nationality, Culture, and Nineteenth-Century Scottish Fiction* (Oxford: Clarendon Press, 1996), pp. 9–10; Susan Stewart, *Crimes of Writing: Problems in the Containment of Representation* (New York: Oxford University Press, 1991), pp. 102–106; Margaret Russett, *Fictions and Fakes: Forging Romantic Authenticity, 1760–1845* (Cambridge: Cambridge University Press, 2006), pp. 155–191.

11 On eighteenth-century Scottish historiography and Whig ideology see Colin Kidd, *Subverting Scotland's Past: Scottish Whig Historians and the Creation of an Anglo-British Identity, 1689–c. 1830* (Cambridge: Cambridge University Press, 1993), passim.

structure of a particular national history by reconstituting the universal, synchronic field which contains it and gives it meaning. Attuned to Scotland's modern geopolitical status, conjectural history produces a new conceptual specificity of time and place, informed by an imperial horizon of world history and a concomitant logic of 'uneven development'. Its narrative tends to overdetermine modernity as the universal end of history, at the same time as it admits a dynamic contemporaneity of social formations, juxtaposing different cultural times and spaces (adjacent or competing 'historical stages') within a singular global horizon.[12] Conjectural history thus schematizes that discursive production of cultural formations outside the metropolitan core already noted in the practices of Scottish poetry. In defining a historical as well as geographical difference of certain locations from the sites of modernity, conjectural history performs a double, sometimes contradictory function: it marks those locations as temporally and spatially peripheral within the imperial political economy of modernity, predicting their (eventual) absorption; but it also recognizes the integrity of their difference as the sign of an autonomous cultural system, another world of life, making its own kinds of sense in relation to its own material conditions.

Dugald Stewart (Smith's biographer, teacher of Scott and the Edinburgh Reviewers) outlines the methodological principles of conjectural history:

> In examining the history of mankind, as well as in examining the phenomena of the material world, when we cannot trace the process by which an event has been produced, it is often of importance to be able to show how it may have been produced by natural causes. . . . To this species of philosophical investigation, which has no appropriated name in our language, I shall take the liberty of giving the title of *Theoretical or Conjectural History*; an expression which coincides pretty nearly in its meaning with that of *Natural History*, as applied by Mr Hume[.][13]

'Nature' supplies the universal constant which allows the historian to fill in evidential gaps and bind particular data into a total system of laws. The historian is able to extend his representation beyond the scientific record by resorting to the art of analogy – that is, the imaginary construction of a symbolic system by the interpretation of associative schemes of correspondence. As Stewart notes, conjectural history follows the

---

12 On the Romantic legacy of Scottish representations of 'uneven development' see James Chandler, *England in 1819: The Politics of Literary Culture and the Case of Romantic Historicism* (Chicago: University of Chicago Press, 1998), pp. 127–51.

13 Dugald Stewart, 'Account of the Life and Writings of Adam Smith, LL.D.', in Adam Smith, *Essays on Philosophical Subjects*, ed. I. S. Ross (Oxford: Clarendon Press, 1980), p. 293.

philosophical terms set by Hume: not only in the appeal to 'nature', but in the cognitive turn to the imagination.

Hume himself produced the most thoroughgoing of the paradigms of disconnection, in the epistemological break from metaphysical foundations. The *Treatise of Human Nature* performs a secularization of the faculties that licenses the subsequent projects of Enlightenment. Hume's logic exposes all the relations by which we construct our knowledge of the world, and ourselves, to be fictions: an economy of the imagination generates the figures of cause and effect, of temporal and spatial continuity, in a kind of associative grammar. Yet the revelation need not condemn us to a melancholy solipsism, since we take part in a collective, social fiction – Hume calls it 'common life' – produced by ongoing transactions of linguistic, economic and sympathetic exchange, which regulate the perilous impulses of the individual passions and fancy. The specification of these domains of exchange occupies the philosophical project of Adam Smith, in his lecture courses and the books that grew out of them (*The Theory of Moral Sentiments*, *The Wealth of Nations*). In the absence of a metaphysical basis, the associative grammar that sustains empirical effects is anchored in 'nature', that is, human nature: Hume posits a universal framework of desire and feeling, fixed in the (gendered) body, which Smith makes the ground for his social regime of exchange in *The Theory of Moral Sentiments*. In short, Hume makes the imagination the primary and normative faculty of cognition, not an aberration from it. In establishing the imagination's positivity in social terms – as the medium of a continuous, collective invention of the world – Hume thus differentiates it from the radically alienated, individualist faculty adumbrated in the English Romantic lyric.

History as fiction

Hugh Blair buttressed his defence of the antiquity of *Fingal* with the appeal to conjectural history, in an argument that exposed its circular, fictive logic. Details from the poem are adduced as evidence of a world in which the poem has its origins: so that the cultivation of polite manners among ancient Celtic warriors, far from being anachronistic, must be due to the institutional situation of the bards, 'highly respected in the state, and supported by a public establishment'.[14] Samuel Johnson grasped the Humean logic at work here – the imaginary filling of a 'vacuity': 'If we know little of

14 Blair, 'Critical Dissertation on the Poems of Ossian', p. 350.

the ancient highlanders, let us not fill the vacuity with Ossian.' Out of a vague association of names and proverbial sentiments, Macpherson and his allies 'coin a resemblance without an original'.[15] There were two solutions to Johnson's critique. One was a more rigorously scientific commitment to the recovery of original forms, through genealogical (philological and anthropological) accounts of culture. The other was a sceptical – Humean – insistence on the act of invention that coins a resemblance *as* an original. It would be the solution pursued by Scott: intensifying the rhetoric of historicism, on the one hand, and on the other – dialectically, no less crucially – intensifying the rhetoric of fiction. In the wake of the Ossian scandal, the nation and its accessories – tradition, culture, history – would be recovered and circulated in the forms of romance, founded on the shared associations, articulated in aesthetic categories and sustained by acts of exchange, of a modern reading public.

A strong tradition of commentary has recovered Scott's intellectual roots in Enlightenment philosophical history – encouraging a tendency, perhaps, to read the historical novels as novelized histories rather than as novels.[16] In the 'Dedicatory Epistle' to *Ivanhoe* (1819), Scott's editorial persona likens the author of the Waverley Novels to 'a second M'Pherson' – characterized as a poet who supplemented his invention with antiquarian data, rather than as an antiquary who forged historical evidence. Scott's poems and novels incessantly remind the reader of their rhetorical status as inventions, as works of fiction, and so evade the authenticity trap Macpherson fell into. Both Scott's first metrical romance, *The Lay of the Last Minstrel* (1805), and his first novel, *Waverley* (1814), are allusively steeped in Ossian – not just the Ossianic poems, but the Ossian affair, which they swallow whole, scandal and all, by insisting on their own fictionality, at the same time as they insist (with superior sophistication in *Waverley*) on their historicity. The historicity of *Waverley* comprehends more than the history woven into the romance plot – the chronicle of the 1745 rising, the antiquarian details of Scottish life sixty years since. It comprehends also the novel's own genealogy and presence in modern culture, in Scotland, in Great Britain and

---

15 Samuel Johnson and James Boswell, *A Journey to the Western Islands of Scotland and The Journal of a Tour to the Hebrides*, ed. P. Levi (Harmondsworth and New York: Penguin, 1984), pp. 118–19.

16 See, e.g., Peter Garside, 'Scott and the "Philosophical" Historians', *Journal of the History of Ideas* 36 (1975), 497–512; Graham McMaster, *Scott and Society* (Cambridge: Cambridge University Press, 1981), pp. 49–69; Cyrus Vakil, 'Walter Scott and the Historicism of Scottish Enlightenment Philosophical History', in J. H. Alexander and D. Hewitt (eds.), *Scott in Carnival* (Aberdeen: Aberdeen University Press, 1991), pp. 404–18.

Europe in 1814, as a work of fiction – encoded, for instance, in an allegory of the novel's emergence as modern national form. This historicization touches not just literary form but the role of the reader. The apparent simplicity of an enlightenment scheme in which archaic 'romance' must give way to 'real history' accompanies a simultaneous insistence on the condition of the novel as a novel, a work of fiction, exposing the provisional, 'romantic' character of the historical reality it sets in place.

Invoking the delusions of romance to characterize Edward Waverley's involvement in the 1745 rising, Scott's narrative draws an equivalency between psychological immaturity, old-regime Jacobite politics, Highland clan society, and the pre-modern narrative forms that preceded the rise of the novel. In other words, Scott totalizes the scheme of conjectural history by writing it in cultural and psychological as well as economic and social terms. This total-ization draws the book – as material nexus of author, reader and a complex of social and economic relations of production – into the historical scheme, rather than keeping it aloof, invisible, transcendent. The novel itself, which mediates our act of reading, constitutes the vantage point of modernity, reflexively producing the plot of its own production. The Jacobite defeat, the decisive settlement of modernity, allows Waverley 'to say firmly, though perhaps with a sigh, that the romance of his life was ended, and that its real history had now commenced'.[17] For the reader, however, that settlement means an 'end of history' and a reassertion of the devices of romance: an occult work of plotting delivers Waverley from the charge of treason, rewards him with bride, estate and fortune out of the rebellion's wreck, and so on. With his entry into civil society the hero blends into the time and space of our reading, as the novel has hinted all along: a subjective standpoint of modernity from which 'real history' can be accessed through the customary associations, the imaginative grammar, of romance. The difference between Waverley's mystified, reactionary or primitivist investment in romance, and our modern, sophisticated, critical investment, falls in the melancholy recognition of defeat and loss that has intervened between the historical experience and its repre-sentation. The imaginary discipline of that elegiac and sceptical knowledge delivers us to the post-historical domain of civil society and private life.

The nation is recovered through a knowledge of historical loss that frames the very opening of consciousness onto modernity. Thus the his-torical novel absorbs history into the cognitive work of fiction, in a dialectic

---

17 Walter Scott, *Waverley; or, 'Tis Sixty Years Since*, ed. Claire Lamont (Oxford: Clarendon Press, 1981), p. 283.

for which Hume provided philosophical authority. Ten years later (1824) *Redgauntlet*, the most Humean of Scott's novels, recapitulates not just the major genres of eighteenth-century writing – letter, journal, Burnsian lyric and 'folk' tale, Gothic novel, family history, law case, rogue's memoir, stage comedy – but the Waverley novels that have preceded it, as it rewrites the plot of Jacobite rebellion entwined with family romance first related in *Waverley* itself. Here, though, a 1765 Jacobite rising dissolves comically, melancholically, into anticlimax and non-event: a failure to re-enter history confirmed in the rising's status as a fabrication of Scott's own. As it affirms an ambiguous dominion of the novelistic in modern life, the novel brings its reader to recognize the imaginary, socially and textually constructed condition of historical reality, in the present as well as in the past. Although the author may have wanted the recognition to bind us more closely to that reality, the novels themselves do not guarantee a particular ideological outcome, as their reception history shows.

From political economy to national culture

It was after the British victory over Napoleon, according to Henry Cockburn, 'that the foolish phrase, "The Modern Athens," began to be applied to the capital of Scotland'.[18] A post-war boom of public works and civic improvements, fuelled by deficit spending, ceased with the Edinburgh Town Council's bankruptcy in 1833 – one year after Scott's death and the Reform bill. Cockburn's discomfort with the 'foolish phrase' stems from its currency as a political slogan in the journalistic wars of the Post-Enlightenment. An 1819 essay in *Blackwood's Edinburgh Magazine*, 'On the Proposed National Monument at Edinburgh', argues that Edinburgh can reconstitute its ancient national status precisely through Scotland's modern role as a province within the core of a worldwide 'United Empire'. This national recovery occurs through a division of ideological labour: if London is Rome, the political and financial capital of Empire, Edinburgh may be another Athens, its cultural and aesthetic capital.[19] The aesthetic representation of Edinburgh as a metropolis of national culture was

---

18 Henry Cockburn, *Memorials of His Time*, ed. Karl Miller (Chicago: University of Chicago Press, 1974), p. 277.

19 [Archibald Allison], 'On the Proposed National Monument at Edinburgh', *Blackwood's Edinburgh Magazine* 28 (July 1819), 377–87. On Edinburgh as 'Modern Athens' see Ian Duncan, *Scott's Shadow: The Novel in Romantic Edinburgh* (Princeton: Princeton University Press, 2007), pp. 8–20.

promoted by the Tory intellectuals of *Blackwood's* in their post-war campaign to seize the ideological high ground from the *Edinburgh Review* Whigs. Such a representation was plausible because of Edinburgh's renewed eminence, between 1802 and 1832, as a European centre of literary production. Scott's poems and novels and the Edinburgh periodicals were the most conspicuous products of a publishing, printing, editing and reviewing industry that rivalled if not outdid London's. Edinburgh's literary formations – the historical novel, the quarterly review, monthly miscellany and weekly journal of 'useful knowledge', the entrepreneurial publisher, an ethos of literary professionalism, the ideological opposition between a materialist political economy and an idealist national culture – these would retain their paradigmatic authority throughout the nineteenth century.

The Edinburgh formations of literary production were agitated by a bitter partisan warfare between Whigs and Tories. This politicization helped drive the paradigm shift to a 'Romantic' discursive order in Scottish writing, systematized and broadcast in the great periodicals, as they debated the institutional status and social function of 'literature' in relation to the totalizing forces of politics and commerce in modern society. The debate traces the theoretical collapse of the eighteenth-century republic of letters and its replacement with a new symbolic domain, 'national culture'. *The Edinburgh Review* flaunted a late-Enlightenment redaction of political economy as the ideological standard for Whig Reform policy, a by-product of which was the attempt to establish an ideology of professionalism for literary production. The Tory counter-attack involved both the renovation of a genre, the monthly miscellany *Blackwood's*, and a new ideology, Romantic cultural nationalism, which received its first, full-blown theorization in English in *Blackwood's* and its satellites. A systematic mystification of cultural production, focused on the figure of Scott, provided the basis for this ideology – so forcefully mounted, that the conflation of Scott's novels with their Blackwoodian reduction remains a persistent critical fallacy.

The French Revolution shivered the conceptual base of the Enlightenment republic of letters, a liberal domain of civil society separate from politics. Whig critics as well as Tories theorized the revolution as a catastrophic convulsion of the whole of social life by politics. Intellectuals had contributed to the catastrophe irrespective of their intentions, according to Francis Jeffrey in the inaugural article of *The Edinburgh Review*. The structural complexity of modern historical process, in which 'events are always produced by the co-operation of complicated causes', will subvert any claim upon a field of agency outside politics.[20] Accordingly, *The Edinburgh Review* promotes the rational infusion of the public sphere by political ideas as a project of scientific management. Political economy undertakes a rationalizing realignment of politics with the socio-economic forces of modernization, designed to forestall a revolutionary eruption. At the same time, the *Edinburgh Review* addresses its own contingency within the predicament it diagnoses. In a later article, 'On Literature, Considered in its Relationship to Social Institutions' (1813), Jeffrey develops a conservative (Burkean) critique of modern culture. Commercial society has reduced literature and science to commodities, available without labour of invention or research in the new periodicals and encyclopaedias; market-driven technologies of reproduction and distribution threaten to make obsolete the intellectual work of consumers as well as of producers. The *Edinburgh Review* participates in these conditions, as only the most eminent of those mercenary machines that are reducing literature to a paper currency.[21]

The response, if not solution, to the predicament was to reformulate it as a problem of authority. The notorious judicial strictness of the *Edinburgh Review* exalts critical judgement as the faculty that restores intellectual agency and distinction in a levelling age. The trope of judicial authority invokes the disinterested ideal of the Scots legal profession, and the local site of the Edinburgh Court of Session, occupying the former Parliament-house (many of the reviewers were advocates). Just as the law regulates civil society in post-Union North Britain, so the *Edinburgh Review* will constitute a literary legislature, monitoring the domain of culture. High fees and authorial anonymity signified a new, professional formation of cultural authority. Tory critics complained that the *Edinburgh Review's* commitment to Whig Reform policy subverted that formation. John Gibson Lockhart accused the *Edinburgh Review* of being partisan because it remained commercial: a set of hired advocates posing disingenuously as judges. Such criticism exposed the instability of professionalism as a social figure at this moment of its ideological assembly – a determined assault could push it back into the abyss of 'trade'.[22]

20 [Francis Jeffrey], 'Mounier, De l'influence des Philosophes, Francs-Maçons, et Illuminées, sur la Revolution de France', *Edinburgh Review* 1 (1802), 1–18 (13).
21 [Francis Jeffrey], 'Mad. De Stael, De la Littérature considérée dans ses Rapports avec les Institutions Sociales', *Edinburgh Review* 41 (1813), 1–25.
22 See Ina Ferris, *The Achievement of Literary Authority: Gender, History, and the Waverley Novels* (Ithaca, NY: Cornell University Press, 1991), pp. 19–27; [John Gibson Lockhart], 'Remarks on the Periodical Criticism of England, by the Baron von Lauerwinkel', *Blackwood's Edinburgh Magazine* 2 (1818), 670–79 (675).

The critical debate over the institutional relations of literature to politics and commerce thus yields a prototypical formation of the Victorian (humanist and pedagogic) concept of culture, clarifying its genealogical link with eighteenth-century Scottish philosophy. The early appearance of professionalized literary production in *The Edinburgh Review* marks the institutional reconfiguration of Enlightenment discourse as it descends from its traditional site, the academy (now monopolized by Tory patronage), into the marketplace, and claims autonomy over its production there. Together, the sociological trope of professionalism and the aesthetic trope of critical judgement begin to constitute an etiology of disinterested value. 'The real and radical difficulty', wrote Jeffrey, 'is to find some pursuit that will permanently interest – some object that will continue to captivate and engross the faculties': since modernity has replaced the ideological vectors of 'enthusiasm' and 'enchantment' not merely with 'knowledge' but with a restless, rootless, commodified desire.[23] *Blackwood's* was quick to locate that pursuit, that object, in the aesthetic connection with works of art. In an argument derived from German Romanticism (Lockhart had translated Friedrich Schlegel), works of art acquire sacral status as relics of a past ancestral virtue and an organic relation between individual subject and national tradition. Yet it is not immediately apparent how literary production can fill that ancient imaginary space in a modern culture: especially since the Blackwoodians – ignoring the role of their own magazine in the politicization and commodification of culture – refrain from any sociological or institutional analysis.

Tory reviewers would identify the domain of national culture, instead, with masterful figures of great authors, most of all with Scott, who personified Scottish literature (romance and history) for a wider public. Lockhart hailed that generative figure, 'the Patriarch of the National Poetry of Scotland', in his book *Peter's Letters to his Kinsfolk* (1819), a *Blackwood's* spin-off which gives the first programmatic account in English of the ideological formation of cultural nationalism. *Peter's Letters* marks the doctrinal emergence of the aesthetic field of national culture, represented by the symbolic techniques of romance revival, and defined in antithesis to the Jacobin-tainted Enlightenment heritage of *The Edinburgh Review*. National culture, in Lockhart's account, is a virtual construct, posed somewhere else than the present scene – in an ancestral and legendary time and space – and associated with the mythopoeic authority of Scott. A visit to Abbotsford

23 [Jeffrey], 'Mad. De Stael', p. 17.

reveals Scott as the modern avatar of national tradition: an uncanny cross between antiquary and bard, curator and necromancer, prophet and impresario, at once collecting material relics of the past and channelling the national *Geist*.[24] Scott represents a potent hybrid of Ossianic and Coleridgean formations of the Romantic artist, combining powers of mechanical reproduction and demiurgic creation. Indeed, Scott functions as an allegorical figure for modern industrial production itself, imagined as archaic magical invention in its character as symbolic production.

Scott appears to have authorized Lockhart's appropriation of his persona, which would be decisive in the later fortunes of his reputation. Lockhart misconstrued the cultural-historical formation of Scott's writing, nevertheless, by severing it from the Enlightenment genealogy it shared with the *Edinburgh Review*. Scott's role as tutelary genius of national culture emerges through a systematic clouding of the distinction between scientific historicism and poetic invention, rather than the articulation of a dialectic between them. Lockhart casts Scott, in short, as an up-to-date, sophisticated, successful version of Macpherson. Scott's romances evade the charge of inauthenticity by grasping – as mere (Whig) history cannot – the inner, spiritual truth of historical experience. Lockhart silently reattaches the Waverley Novels to the Ossianic project, reading them as the 'authentic' achievement of the revivalist project Macpherson could only fake, and cutting out the crucial, intervening, dialectical figure, whom Lockhart has spent the early part of *Peter's Letters* exorcizing from the national tradition, of David Hume. The Blackwoodian claim upon Scott, reprocessing the Waverley novels for a purely ideological enunciation of official nationalism, thus systematically inverts their Humean activation of the rhetoric of fiction through the epistemological field of 'inauthenticity'.

Unwriting Scottish Romanticism

Scott's centrality was at once a resource and a burden for his contemporaries. The unprecedented commercial and critical success of his fiction stimulated a vast literary industry, much of it managed or patronized by Scott himself. The new prestige of the novel as national historical form, as well as the profits it could realize, encouraged a host of imitators and

---

24 J. G. Lockhart, *Peter's Letters to his Kinsfolk*, 3 vols. (Edinburgh: Blackwood, 1819), vol. II, pp. 295–362.

rivals. 'Scotch novels' dominated the British literary market in the early 1820s. If Scott himself, at the height of his popularity, had turned away from the making of modern Scotland in *Ivanhoe* and its successors, James Hogg, John Galt, Susan Ferrier, J. G. Lockhart, John Wilson and Christian Isobel Johnstone (all published by William Blackwood) addressed the theme. The most ambitious of these resisted, even as they exploited, Scott's example. Thus Ferrier strategically ignored historical romance and worked a moral, satiric and increasingly evangelical vein of national domestic fiction, derived from Maria Edgeworth's Irish and 'fashionable life' tales: a model already imported into Scotland by Elizabeth Hamilton and Mary Brunton, before Scott's epochal transmutation of the National Tale in *Waverley*. Christian Johnstone undoes Scott's and Edgeworth's Unionist synthesis with an explosive collision between Scottish domestic romance and Irish colonial and revolutionary violence in her 1827 Blackwood novel *Elizabeth de Bruce*. (Johnstone then abandoned the novel for the other leading Edinburgh genre of the day, and became the *de facto* editor of the radical-reformist *Johnstone's Edinburgh Magazine* and its successor, *Tait's*.)

The most original of the Blackwood authors, who established the strongest critical alternatives to the Waverley novels, were Hogg and Galt. Although they shared certain techniques, such as the narrative promotion of vernacular Scots, they wrote strikingly different kinds of fiction. Galt claimed that his most characteristic works, *Annals of the Parish* (1821) and *The Provost* (1822), were not novels at all but essays in 'a kind of local theoretical history'. In other words, Galt eschewed the Scott model of plot-intensive romance for a different fictional development of conjectural history, a *trompe-l'oeil* representation of historical change in the micropolitics of everyday life. In 1823 Galt developed the vein to challenge Scott on his own ground, in two powerful historical novels: *The Entail* (reworking the national, domestic and legal romance of Scott's *The Heart of Mid-Lothian*, 1818) and *Ringan Gilhaize* (reclaiming radical Presbyterianism from Scott's enlightened-romantic redaction in *Old Mortality*, 1816).

The comparison with Hogg charts a striking triangulation in the institutional ecology of the novel in early 1820s Edinburgh. Galt challenges the Humean dialectic at work in the Waverley novels with a strong development of one of its terms, materialist social history, and a refusal of the other, antiquarian romance. Hogg, in contrast, asserts vernacular and literary principles of storytelling in defiance of an Enlightenment cultural teleology. Hogg's experimental narratives offended polite taste by disrupting the conventions within which 'folk' material was expected to be packaged, and by laying presumptuous claim to metropolitan styles and genres. *The Three Perils of Man: War, Women and Witchcraft* (1821), a romance of the medieval Borders, rebuts Scott's brilliant antiquarian entertainments (*Ivanhoe*, *The Monastery*) with a fiercely comical performance of what can only be called proto-postmodern magic realism. *The Three Perils of Woman: Love, Leasing and Jealousy* (1823) enacts the dissolution, rather than development, of the domestic national tale into the historical romance of *Waverley*: its issue a traumatic meltdown of cultural meaning. *The Private Memoirs and Confessions of a Justified Sinner* appeared simultaneously with *Redgauntlet* (June 1824); both novels share striking formal and thematic features, including an elaborate self-reflexiveness about their material and cultural status as 'tales of the eighteenth century', fictional narratives of Scottish modernization, and as printed books, published at the end of the decade of historical fiction inaugurated with *Waverley*. The novels provide, thus, competing analyses of 'Scottish Romanticism' of remarkable power and subtlety. While *Redgauntlet* reaffirms, with virtuosic complexity, the Humean paradigm of historical romance, *Confessions of a Justified Sinner* decomposes the ingredients of Scottish cultural modernity into a waste material residue – represented through the metonymic identification, in the final pages, of the sinner's unhallowed corpse with the text we are reading. A nauseating disintegration of meaning touches the identity of the author, his work and the reader – and indeed, Hogg's masterpiece would remain all but unreadable until the twentieth century.

The most drastic unwriting of Scottish Romanticism occurred, however, in a sequence of works that effectively terminated the post-Enlightenment era of national literature in Edinburgh. The young Thomas Carlyle began his career translating German fiction, experimenting with a novel of his own, and contributing to the *Edinburgh Review*. His first major original work, *Sartor Resartus*, is an anti-novelistic experiment in the Blackwoodian manner which systematically dismantles the narrative complex of history, fiction, *Bildung* and national character set in place by Scott. Darkly announcing the author's own departure from Scotland, *Sartor Resartus* marks the liquidation of a tradition as well as of the local conditions that sustained it. *The French Revolution* (1837), published in London in the year of Victoria's accession, mounts a radically anti-Enlightenment, vatic and oratorical mode of historical narration upon the wreck of Scottish Romanticism. Carlyle takes for his theme, as Scott had done, the history of the last age: except that Revolution is now revealed as the sublime historical condition – the breach itself – that Scottish writing had sought to close, or at least to cover up. Ventriloquizing the abyss, Carlyle's great book initiates the apocalyptic narrative of perpetual crisis – an Ossianism of the future – that will enunciate modern conditions.

Romantic Ireland: 1750–1845

LUKE GIBBONS

One of the emblematic moments of Irish Romanticism occurs in Sydney Owenson's pioneering novel, *The Wild Irish Girl* (1806), when Horatio, a jaded libertine, travels from London to the west of Ireland in pursuit of primitive simplicity and the noble savage, only to find that the natives are already reading Rousseau.[1] *The Wild Irish Girl* can be seen as ushering in the 'myth of the West' of Ireland that was to preside over Irish Romanticism and, indeed, the images of the western seaboard promulgated by W. B. Yeats and John Millington Synge during the Literary Revival at the turn of the twentieth century. Central to this romantic vision was the idea that the further west one travelled – whether to Kerry, Connemara or Sligo – the more one came into contact with the 'real' Ireland, uncontaminated by the influence of the city or, at another remove, empire. Yet from the outset, Romantic Ireland contained within itself its own counter-currents, at once staging and contesting the 'images for the affections' (in Yeats's phrase) that drew countless visitors and travellers to the periphery. In Lady Morgan's novel, well-stocked libraries in crumbling castles compete with the awe-inspiring scenery for the attention of local inhabitants, and Glorvina, the daughter of a Gaelic chieftain and eponymous heroine of the novel, is as attuned to debates in the Enlightenment salons of mainland Europe as she is to the 'woodnotes wild' of her Irish harp.[2] At one point in the novel – following an exchange with the local priest, Father John, on such usual topics of Irish rural small talk as Locke's distinction between innate and acquired ideas – a mention of the ancient Irish hero Oscar prompts a lengthy discussion of James Macpherson and the Ossian controversy, complete with scholarly quotations, footnotes and learned asides.

---

1 Sydney Owenson [Lady Morgan], *The Wild Irish Girl* (1806), ed. Claire Connolly and Stephen Copley (London: Pickering & Chatto, 2001), p. 139. In Lady Morgan's *O'Donnel*, the eponymous Gaelic hero is also given to quoting Rousseau: *O'Donnel* (1814) (London: Downey & Co, 1895), p. 98.
2 *Wild Irish Girl*, p. 102. Scholarly libraries on the wild western coast also feature in *O'Donnel*, pp. 81–2.

In this, Horatio is left in no doubt as to the Irish genealogy of the great warrior bard and of the achievements of Irish antiquity for, as Father John points out:

> Ireland, owing to its being colonized from Phoenicia, and consequent early introduction of letters there, was at that period esteemed the most enlightened country in Europe; and indeed Mr Macpherson himself avers, that the Irish, for ages antecedent to the Conquest, possessed a competent share of that kind of learning which prevailed in Europe.[3]

For Rousseau, and for certain key strands of romantic primitivism, the invention of letters was part of the fall from grace into civilization, a sundering of human experience from its immersion in its original, Edenic surroundings. Though Ireland, as we shall see, was central at many important junctures to the rise of Romanticism – it was, after all, the home of the Celt, one of the few 'primitives' extant *within* Europe – apologists for native culture contested the very basis of Romantic primitivism, being more determined to assert the Enlightenment credentials of Gaelic Ireland, and its claim to be considered among the civilizations of antiquity. From this perspective, barbarism and a 'state of nature' were the unwelcome consequences of colonization, rather than the brute condition of society before the conquest. The desire to trace the ancestry of ancient Ireland to Phoenicia was motivated, among other things, by the conviction that the Phoenicians invented letters – and, indeed, spoke a language not dissimilar to Irish, if the Borgesian speculations of the antiquarian scholar, General Charles Vallancey (1726–1812) were to be believed. The more modest contention that the Irish possessed literacy before the coming of St Patrick (and, by extension, Roman civilization) was advanced by pioneering national historians such as Charles O'Conor (1710–91) and Sylvester O'Halloran (1728–1807), and was considered central to establishing ancient Ireland's claims to civility.

From the outset, therefore, Ireland's precarious position within European Romanticism in the late eighteenth and early nineteenth century challenged many of the oppositions between Enlightenment and counter-Enlightenment (i.e. Romantic) discourses – or, for that matter, between Romanticism and modernity, as that periodization later evolved in critical timelines. Viewed from the metropolitan centre, the Celtic periphery was the outpost of one of Europe's most exotic, dying cultures, but in the eyes of

---

3 *Wild Irish Girl*, p. 104.

its own enthusiasts, it was a culture awaiting its re-entry into the modern world. 'It is new strung, and shall be heard', declared the motto of the United Irishmen movement over the emblem of a maiden harp in 1791, a resonant symbol of the radical alliance between advanced republicanism and a resurgent Gaelic, Catholic Ireland. As early as 1762, the Irish republican painter James Barry (1741–1806) sought to give expression in painting to this conception of a vernacular Enlightenment by depicting St Patrick's crowning of Aengus, the pagan King of Munster, in a setting that established visual links between the Doric columns of a building in the foreground, and megalithic, Stonehenge-type dolmens on a romantic landscape overlooking the scene. This painting represents one of the earliest attempts to elevate an antiquity other than Judaic or Greco-Roman to the status of history painting, and as such is a harbinger of Herderian cultural nationalism: but as the architectural reminders of classical republicanism indicate, it also situated Romantic localism within an Enlightenment frame. Romanticism on this reading was preoccupied not only with a past but with a *future* that was lost, and is thus closer to a form of proto-modernity than the backward look which became the fate of doomed races, or others excluded from the pale of civilization.

The extent to which the romantic emblem of the harp, with its sympathetic, vibrant strings, struck the jarring chords of an Irish Enlightenment sensibility in the 1790s is clear from the engagement of the United Irishmen, and the radical intelligentsia, with the forces of indigenous, Gaelic culture. This was exemplified by the Belfast Harp Festival of 1792, which acted as a catalyst for the first Irish cultural revival, and the publication of the first magazine in the Irish language, *Bolg an tSolair*, in Belfast in 1795. In keeping with the Romantic appropriation of the past, there was indeed nostalgia for a vanquished order but this was not for a cultural imaginary beyond retrieval, or an ancient order lost in the mists of time. The true exemplar of the glories of the bardic past was not, as in Scotland, the distant, nebulous Ossian but the near contemporary figure of Turlough O'Carolan (1670–1738), the so-called 'last of the Irish bards', who performed within the living memory of the Romantic period: 'In the summer of 1797', Sydney Owenson relates in a characteristic footnote in *The Wild Irish Girl*, 'the Author conversed with an old peasant in Westmeath, who had frequently listened to the tones of Carolan's harp in his boyish days'.[4] O'Carolan's

---

4 *Ibid.*, p. 88. As Liam McIlvanney suggests, there is an important sense in which the equivalent of the bard as a vital force in Scottish Romanticism may be Robert Burns

music was performed on the Dublin stage by Robert Owenson (1744–1812), the novelist's father, who was also the first to introduce the Irish language to theatre-going audiences. For the United Irishmen, the Irish language was deemed appropriate for commerce as well as poetry, and it is in this sense, as *The Wild Irish Girl* describes it, that the filigree of the past is threaded into the base-metal of everyday life: it resembles the 'peculiar property of gold, which subtilely insinuates itself through the most minute and various particles, without losing anything of its own intrinsic nature by the amalgamation'.[5] The underlying metaphor here has as much to do with commerce and mineralogy as with a mythic golden age, thus relating the untapped potential of Ireland's cultural past to an emergent discourse of political economy, often seen as the antithesis of Romanticism. Perhaps 'national economy' might be a more accurate term, as the debate on Ireland's undeveloped natural resources, and the demand for free trade to regenerate an economy stifled under colonialism, stemmed from a new consciousness of Ireland's status as an independent nation with its own distinctive claim to civilization.

Instead of being an out-take from, or a consolation for, the relentless march of progress, Irish Romanticism was placed on a collision course with Britishness and the ideology of empire, thus accentuating a major difference with Scotland or Wales often masked by the myth of an undifferentiated 'Celtic' periphery. Ireland's ambivalent position on the periphery is captured in the critical reputation of Maria Edgeworth's *Castle Rackrent* (1800), welcomed on the one hand as the first 'regional' novel and the inspiration for Sir Walter Scott's integrationist fictions, and on the other as the progenitor of the more turbulent Irish 'National Tale'. Edgeworth's regional idiom was bound up with the mapping of the Irish countryside in Whig, reformist terms of agricultural improvement and its aesthetic cognate, the 'picturesque', but in the 1790s this landscape was rent by nationalist energies more in keeping with the convulsions of the 'sublime', and which found expression in the Gothic fiction of Charles Maturin and the later Lady

rather than the remote figure of Ossian. (Liam McIlvanney, *Burns the Radical: Poetry and Politics in Late Eighteenth-century Scotland* (East Linton: Tuckwell Press, 2002), pp. 220–4). Burns, however, was not seen as the exemplar of an antiquarian or Gaelic tradition, but owed his fame, in the eyes of Irish contemporaries, to writing in the English language: O'Carolan shared his contemporary (or near contemporary) status, while yet staking Irish claims to a separate language and national past. (See James Hardiman's comments on Burns in his *Irish Minstrelsy, or Bardic Remains of Ireland* (1831) (Shannon: Irish University Press, 1971), pp. i , xxiv.)

5 Ibid., p. 67.

Morgan. For Edmund Burke, it was not just mineral resources that lay beneath the soil but volcanic deposits, awaiting the tremors that would set off a political conflagration: the Protestant Ascendancy, he wrote to his son, Richard, in 1792, think they are 'dealing with a credulous mob, soon inflamed, soon extinguished. No such thing, as you know as well as I. The igneous fluid has its lodging in a solid mass.'[6]

The Celtic sublime

The concept of 'the sublime' was one of the most important formative influences on the rise of a new romantic sensibility in the late eighteenth century. Introduced into the critical lexicon by translations of the first century AD treatise *On the Sublime* by Longinus, it owed its widespread popularity to Edmund Burke's treatise, conceived while still a student at Trinity College, Dublin, *A Philosophical Enquiry into the Origin of our Ideas of the Sublime and Beautiful* (1757).[7] Burke's *Enquiry* is generally credited with helping to shift artistic endeavour from the formal designs of 'beauty' (order, symmetry, decorum) to the call of the wild (danger, obscurity, vastness) – in effect, removing the artist, like Horatio in *The Wild Irish Girl*, from the comforts of the garden to the ordeal in the wilderness. In the eyes of some acerbic English critics such as Richard Payne Knight, Burke's upbringing in Ireland gave him a head start on such matters,[8] and it was not surprising to find Ireland itself portrayed as an outpost of the 'natural sublime' in the emergent genres of travel writing and Romantic literature. According to Raymond Immerwahr, some of the earliest uses of the term 'romantic' to describe a heightened response to scenery date from the opening up of Killarney as a beauty spot in the 1750s,[9] and this is echoed in Robert Rosenblum's *Modern Painting and the*

6 Edmund Burke to Richard Burke, 21 November 1792, in *The Correspondence of Edmund Burke*, vol. VII, ed. P. J. Marshall and John A. Woods (Cambridge: Cambridge University Press, 1968), p. 301.

7 Edmund Burke, *A Philosophical Enquiry into the Origin of our Ideas of the Sublime and Beautiful* (1757) (London: Routledge & Kegan Paul, 1958).

8 See Payne Knight's dismissal of the *Enquiry*'s preoccupation with terror as 'a stout instance of confusion even with every allowance that can be made for the ardour of youth in an Hibernian philosopher of five and twenty'. (Richard Payne Knight, *An Analytical Enquiry into the Principles of Taste* (London: T. Payne, 1808), p. 379.)

9 Raymond Immerwahr, ' "Romantic" and its Cognates in England, Germany and France before 1790' in Hans Eichner (ed.), *Romanticism and its Cognates: The European History of a Word* (Manchester: Manchester University Press, 1972), p. 33.

Northern Romantic Tradition, with a shift of scene to Powerscourt Waterfall closer to Dublin:

> Already by the 1760s and 1770s . . . there were artists as far afield as Ireland and Switzerland, who suddenly turned to specific sites in wild nature that seemed to elicit at the least, curiosity, and at the most, divine revelation. Undoubtedly inspired by another Irishman, Edmund Burke, whose *Philosophical Enquiry into the Origins of our Ideas of the Sublime and the Beautiful* (1756) [sic] was to become a major aesthetic source for the first generation of Romantic artists in search of overwhelming and fear-inspiring experiences, the painter George Barret could record on his native soil the Powerscourt Waterfall and exhibit this topographical fact of sublime nature to a London audience of the 1760s.[10]

Though the newly found taste for Irish scenery was framed in terms of innocence, spontaneity and solitude, such responses to nature were as much textual productions as works of art themselves. Not least of the texts that authorized such 'natural' feelings was Burke's own *Enquiry*, which became the bible of the discerning, romantic traveller: 'I will now conduct you to one of the greatest beauties, of its kind, perhaps, in the world', wrote John Bush of the Irish landscape in *Hibernia Curiosa* (1764), before proceeding to praise the 'lofty and sublime curiosities of nature' exemplified by Powerscourt waterfall, and the more variegated splendours of Killarney.[11] In the Romantic fiction of the period, passages from the *Enquiry* are often inserted without acknowledgement into 'spontaneous' effusions on natural scenery, as if the modality of the visible was mediated from the outset by the inscriptions of language and storytelling on the landscape. As Lady Llanberis, a visiting aristocrat, remarks to Colonel O'Donnel of his native landscape in Lady Morgan's *O'Donnel* (1814):

> I know you are a worshipper of the picturesque: – I hear there is nothing so beautiful as your descriptions; and I expect, after seeing Longlands with you, that I shall have a better opinion of it; for, I am told, you give interest to the most trifling object by your mode of detailing it . . . . I really long, Colonel O'Donnel, to hear some of your beautiful Irish stories. I love stories beyond everything, and I hear you are a *raconteur* of the very first order.[12]

10 Robert Rosenblum, *Modern Painting and the Northern Romantic Tradition: Friedrich to Rothko* (London: Thames and Hudson, 1975), p. 17.

11 [John Bush], *Hibernia Curiosa: A Letter from a Gentleman in Dublin to his Friend at Dover in Kent* (1764) (London: W. Flexney, 1769).

12 *O'Donnel*, p. 133.

Though the romantic tourist is in pursuit of the uninterrupted view, native informants place themselves between the spectator and Nature, bringing with them all their attendant local associations and narrative trappings.

This interception of vision by language, unacknowledged or otherwise, is in keeping with the logic of Burke's treatise, for notwithstanding the visual pleasures of scenery, and the illusion of communion with nature, the *Enquiry* asserts the primacy of words over images in evoking the intensity of the sublime. Burke's *Enquiry* did not concern itself solely with the sublime, however: as its title indicates, it also elaborated a theory of beauty, making provision, moreover, for ominous crossovers between the two, as in the 'fatal beauty' of certain women, or the unrestrained violence of 'Furies'.[13] It was not long before this combination of beauty and terror, sentimentalism and savagery, came to be associated with Gaelic culture itself, under the new generic rubric of 'Celticism'. The term 'Celt' first gained popular currency in a Breton context through the writings of the Cistercian monk, Paul-Yves Pezron (1639–1706), whose *Antiquity of the Celts* (1703) confined the term for the most part to Gaulish or Breton civilization. This omission – or exclusion – of Gaelic culture did not go unnoticed, and it was largely through the outstanding philological researches of the great Welsh antiquarian, Edward Lhuyd (1660–1709), and the Irish polymath and republican John Toland (1670–1722), that the idea of a common cultural genealogy linking Gaelic, Welsh and Breton culture took root, based primarily on linguistic affinities between their respective languages. The romance of the Enlightenment with the Celtic periphery began perhaps with Toland, for by identifying himself as a *pantheist* (a term which he coined), Nature-worship and spirituality were introduced into the nebulous world of Celticism. Toland's notion of early society was no primitive, pre-social wilderness, however, for as his preoccupation with ritual and hermeticism in his *History of the Druids* (1726) shows,[14] even the civic sphere shared some of the encryption of ritual: 'Secrecy, together with Resolution, are the Life and Soul of great Actions'.[15] Civic in spirit, this clandestine

---

13 Burke, *Enquiry*, p. 171; Edmund Burke, *Reflections on the Revolution in France* (1790), ed. Conor Cruise O'Brien (Harmondsworth: Penguin, 1975), pp. 164–5.

14 'A Specimen of the Critical History of the Celtic Religion and Learning, Containing an Account of the Druids', in *A Collection of Several Pieces of Mr. John Toland* (London, 1726).

15 John Toland (ed.), *A Collection of Letters Written by his Excellency General George Monk* (London: J. Roberts, 1714), vol. VI, cited in Stephen H. Daniel, *John Toland: His*

public sphere was no austere brotherhood based on abstract ideals, but was embedded in the rituals of everyday life: 'It is a known observation, that there can never be any hearty fellowship, where people do'nt [sic] eat and drink together', hence 'partaking of the sweetest kind of sauce, viz., philosophizing over the meal.'[16] This prospect of high talk in low places may account for the familiarity with Lockean distinctions among the inhabitants of the west of Ireland in *The Wild Irish Girl*, noted above, and also for the manner in which the daily conversation of the Gaelic chieftain King Corny in Maria Edgeworth's *Ormond* (1817) is peppered with references to Socrates and the Stoics – a penchant for philosophy which does not rule out a comparison a few pages later to a savage American Indian. At one point in the novel, King Corny's young nephew and protégé Harry Ormond, who has been rusticated on the backward Black Islands with his wayward uncle, interrupts an exchange with a returned French cosmopolite, M de Connel, to make a distinction between pleasures and sensations:

> 'A sensation! [replied M. de Connel], and you are not sure whether you should call it a pleasure. Do you know you have a genius for metaphysics?'
> 'I!' exclaimed Ormond.
> 'Ah! now I have astonished you again. Good! Whether pleasurable or not, trust me, nothing is so improving to a young man as to be well astonished. Astonishment I conceive to be a sort of electric shock – electric fire; it opens at once and enlightens the understanding; and really you have an understanding so well worth enlightening – I do assure you, that your natural acuteness will, whenever and wherever you appear, make you *un homme marquant* . . .' The electric shock of astonishment did operate in a salutary manner in opening Harry's understanding: the materials for thinking were not thrown away: he *did* think – even in the Black Islands.[17]

Theory, critical reflection, even the shock of modernity, are already a feature of the Irish periphery, for all its quaint appeal to the romantic imagination.

This preoccupation with secrecy, furtiveness and high talk in taverns found expression not only in the countryside but in descriptions of Dublin as a city of shadows, in keeping with its conspiratorial role in the

---

Method, Manners and Mind (Kingston and Montreal: McGill-Queen's University Press, 1984), p. 209.

16 John Toland, *Nazarenus* (London: J. Brown, 1718), 43; John Toland, *Panthesisticon* (1720) (London: Sam Paterson, 1751), p. 110, cited in Daniel, *John Toland*, p. 217.

17 Maria Edgeworth, *Ormond* (1817), ed. Claire Connolly (London: Penguin, 2000), pp. 126–7.

1798 and 1803 rebellions. Not least of the innovations of Charles Maturin's *The Milesian Chief* (1812), *Women: or Pour et Contre* (1818), and Lady Morgan's *The O'Briens and the O'Flahertys*, are the remarkable, almost film noir renditions of the city as a site of fear and suspicion, the shocks attending the 'proto-modern' colonial *flâneur* giving rise to shudders rather than the distraction of his (or her) later metropolitan counterpart:

> It was now a dark and foggy twilight; the sun, which sets with so fine and picturesque an effect behind the last bridge over the Liffey, had sunk portentously in black and lurid clouds. A premature obscurity had already involved the worst lighted city in the empire. The shops and house of the neighbourhood of the riot, had been shut up at an early hour, and the mob and the military . . . had so completely cleared the streets of pedestrians and carriages, that the capital at nine o'clock had the desolate and deserted aspect, which it was wont to assume in troubled times.[18]

As Ina Ferris has perceptively argued, the self-consciousness of the shudder can be interpreted as a mode of *thinking* or psychic shivering, 'not simply a matter of involuntary somatic response but a function of cerebral processes'.[19] The most distinctive aspect of this reflexiveness, however, is that it eschews psychological interiority, being registered on the public domain of the body rather than the inner life of the mind. Such depth as the mind possesses marks cultural rather than individual attainment: attempting to persuade her endangered beau, Connal, to leave his wild habitat on the western seaboard, Armida, the Italianate heroine of *The Milesian Chief*, sighs, or rather shudders, at his response: 'Armida trembled at the difference of their characters, and at the little hope she had of entire influence over a mind so national'.[20]

The national tale and peripheral modernity

Contrary to the Enlightenment assumption that reflective thought is the preserve of the advanced European mainland, the effect of the sublime in the Irish romantic novel is to galvanize the inhabitants of remote regions – next in line for colonial subjugation – into an acute awareness of their predicament; into a kind of modernity before its time. Though not

---

18 Morgan, *The O'Briens and the O'Flahertys: A National Tale*, intro. Mary Campbell (London: Pandora Press, 1988), pp. 120–1.
19 Ina Ferris, *The Romantic National Tale and the Question of Ireland*, p.119.
20 Charles Robert Maturin, *The Milesian Chief: A Romance* (1812) (New York: Garland Publishing, 1979), vol. III, p. 119.

philosophical in the Hegelian sense, this jolt – or 'shudder' – was sufficient to awaken a desire to enter the modern world on their own terms, and to challenge the premature exit from history predestined for the Celt. It was not that the pre-modern had to give way to the modern: both cohabited and occupied the same deeply contested, cultural spaces. A number of factors in the Irish national tale facilitated the introduction of cosmopolitan Europe into the romantic periphery, primary among them being the narrative device of a returned exile – most notably a Gaelic/Catholic figure of distinguished Jacobite ancestry who, fallen into hard times under the Penal Laws, was educated in France (preferably at St Omar), or else gained military service in the Austrian army, thereby acquiring an uncouth, albeit sophisticated, civility. The connections between the western seaboard and global modernity pre-date the eighteenth century, however, for there is a continual awareness on the thwarted commercial development of a native Gaelic economy that once enjoyed regular trade with the Continent. In *The O'Briens and the O'Flahertys*, the Spanish architecture of Galway – 'the second city of the country' – is frequently alluded to: a character speaks 'in the drawling French accent, acquired in her paternal castle in Connaught, from her mother's Swiss maid' and remains of vineries are visible in the landscape, though claret now comes from cousins in Bordeaux. Bog Moy, the residence of the eccentric Miss Mac Taffs in Connemara, is described as 'isolated by [its] topographical situation' with all but two habitual visitors; yet its social soirées feature 'a display of French silks, and point lace, of fashions from Bordeaux, and flowers from Oporto . . . which might have put the *petites maitresses* of the capital to the blush'.[21] Ostensibly turning on a clear-cut opposition between centre and periphery – as if bearing out Joep Leerssen's succinct formulation that 'to go into Gaelic Ireland means leaving Europe, leaving civilization as we know it'[22] – the disjointed temporality of Irish national narratives throws the whole genre of the romantic novel into question.[23]

In his insightful discussion of the mutations of the romantic novel, Leerssen draws on Sir Walter Scott's celebrated distinction between the *novel* and the *romance* to elucidate the characteristics of both Irish and Scottish fiction. For Scott, romance 'turns upon marvellous and uncommon

21 *Ibid.*, pp. 405, 90, 418, 427, 440.
22 J. Th. Leerssen, 'Fiction, Poetics and Cultural Stereotype: Local Colour in Scott, Morgan, and Maturin', *Modern Language Review*, 86:2 (April 1991), 282.
23 For illuminating discussions of the uneven temporalities of the Irish national tale, see Trumpener, *Bardic Nationalism*, and Ferris, *The Romantic National Tale*.

incidents', whereas the novel accommodates itself 'to the ordinary train of human events, and the modern state of society' – being more concerned, in Leerssen's word's, with 'its plausibility, its being true to life: more precisely, true to "life as we know it" '.[24] The difficulty with this formulation is that plausibility, what is considered normal and everyday, is itself historically situated and culturally specific, so that what is marvellous to a citizen of London in the early nineteenth century may not necessarily be so to an Irish rural dweller. Generic structures are themselves bound up with wider belief systems or life worlds: though ghosts and witches feature in *Hamlet* and *Macbeth*, this does not make Shakespeare a Gothic writer.[25] For the genre to take effect, there has to be a willed suspension of belief, whereas in the earlier Elizabethan period, belief in apparitions and visitations from the other world was still commonplace in society. Likewise in the culture of Gaelic Ireland as manifested in the national tale: incidents that struck the metropolitan observer as out of the ordinary were part of everyday life for natives, and much of the narrative texture of the genre was devoted to the clash between these competing perspectives on the world. As several scholars have pointed out, the 'meta-fictional' scholarly apparatus deployed in the novels of Edgeworth or Morgan is partly designed to negotiate these fault-lines, as the more implausible the events, the greater the reliance on authorial footnotes to give eye-witness veracity, or archival authority, to the narration. There is, perhaps, a sliding scale of irrationality here, for what started out as a distinction between romance and the novel addressed to questions of ontology and belief – the marvellous in the sense of *supernatural* occurrences – extended imperceptibly to *ethnography*, as if the strangeness of certain customs and practices was sufficient to relegate them to a civic otherworld. If so, that otherworld was not content to stay in its place, but was likely – in keeping with the intrusions of peasant superstition – to make regular, unsettling interventions into everyday life, disrupting the improving designs of a polite, imperial civility.

It is striking that in accounts of supernatural events, first-hand testimony on the part of the author gives way to the (more dubious) authority of the *community*, as in the footnotes on the 'leprechaun' and – more implausibly even by Irish standards – the 'transmigration of souls' in Lady Morgan's *O'Donnel*, the latter of which is glossed as follows: 'A belief in this sort of

24 Leerssen, 'Fiction, Poetics and Cultural Stereotype', p. 273.
25 E. J. Clery, *The Rise of Supernatural Fiction, 1762–1800* (Cambridge: Cambridge University Press, 1995).

transmigration, is a common superstition in Ireland. Lefanu refers to this superstition in one of his humorous tales.'[26] What comes across as a problem of form – the porous boundaries between novel and romance – is, perhaps, a transmigration of history into aesthetics, insofar as the genre of romance was based on an understanding of *temporality* that consigned its moral universe to the past.[27] Romantic Ireland, however, was not dead and gone, and did not lend itself to the premature closure of historical fiction. As originally conceived, *O'Donnel* was set in Elizabethan times and purported to deal with the struggle of the rebel Chieftain, Red Hugh O'Donnell, against English rule in Ireland. Having acquainted herself with the raw materials of the story, Morgan 'found it necessary to forego [her] original plan' as the violence of even two centuries earlier could not be contained – 'events which the interests of humanity require to be forever buried in oblivion'.[28] Accordingly the chronology was switched to the contemporary period, with a descendant of Red Hugh, the dispossessed exile Colonel O'Donnel, taking centre stage in an attempt to regain his lost rights and family estates. Through the narrative conventions – or sleight of hand – of the marriage plot, O'Donnel pledges his devotion to a former governess, Miss O'Halloran, who turns out to be the widow of the Duke of Belmont, a scion of the Williamite family that had usurped his estate. That such an ending lacks conviction surfaces in the text itself, as even O'Donnel is not wholly convinced by the denouement that brings about his good fortune:

> Yet still, over these joyous emotions, some feeling of melancholy would at times throw its shadow. He was willing to owe his best felicity to the hand of love; but he would have wished to have obtained the repossession of his rights by means more consonant to the spirit of the gentleman, the dignity of the man, and the general interests of his country.[29]

– in a word, through *justice*.

Not least of the ironies in Walter Scott's distinction between the novel and the romance is that insofar as it addresses the political realities of Ireland, the novel itself is forced to deploy a range of narrative conceits, such as the marriage plot, that stretch the credibility of the most far-fetched romance. Superstition may have been evicted from the natural world, but it

26 Morgan, *O'Donnel*, p. 288.
27 Leerssen, 'Fiction, Poetics, and Cultural Stereotype', p. 283.
28 Lady Morgan, *O'Donnel: A National Tale*, 3 vols. (London, 1814), vol. I, pp. x–xi, cited in Leerssen, 'Fiction, Poetics and Cultural Stereotype', p. 277.
29 Morgan, *O'Donnel*, p. 269.

re-enters history in modes of wishful thinking and happy endings that owe more to magic than to the material realities of post-Union Ireland. Neither the healing powers of marriage nor of time are sufficient to seal off the injuries of the past from the present. Emotions may have been recollected in tranquillity but as the poetry of the period made clear, this tranquillity was itself, as Burke averred, invariably 'ting'd with terror'.[30] Instead of affording a private solution to a public problem, romantic love was absorbed into an obsession with genealogy, the bitterly contested memories of confiscation that cut across affairs of the heart. As Lady Morgan herself described the opening pages of *The O'Briens and the O'Flahertys*, which risked losing the reader in a maze of legal disputes and labyrinthine family trees:

> This volume is a faithful transcript of the manners, style, & habits of the Provincial Irish (particularly in Connaught) 60 years ago – Terrence O'Brien & the Miss Mac Taafs are portraits of originals long passed away – and tho for the English reader the *busy facility* of the first 100 pages, will render them tedious – In Ireland, they made the fortune of the book –[31]

The early collapse of the marriage plot is seen, perhaps, to starkest effect in Maturin's *The Milesian Chief* in which the cross-cultural attachments of both love stories in the plot – between the 'Milesian' rebel, Connal, and the refined beauty, Armida, on the one hand, and the equally doomed affair between Connal's delinquent brother, Desmond (a British army officer), and Armida's sister, Ines (who passes as a young boy, Endymion) – are violently sundered in the bloody denouement of another Irish rebellion.

Avant-bardism: Moore and radical nostalgia

The fascination of the Enlightenment with the Celtic periphery took on a decidedly different political cast in the mid eighteenth century when, under the aegis of the Ossian controversy, a new typology of the Celt took shape. In keeping with emergent racist notions of national character, the Celt's inability to answer the demands of pure reason led to his portrayal as a creature of impulse, at the mercy of irrational forces of either violence, on the one hand, or incapacitating displays of melancholy, fatalism and nostalgia on the other. The ethnocidal purges that followed the battle of Culloden in Scotland in 1746 provided an all too real basis for bloodshed

---

30 Burke, *Enquiry*, p. 136.
31 Lady Morgan, handwritten dedication to Lord Adolphus Fitzclarence, 10 February 1830, in presentation copy of *The O'Briens and the O'Flahertys* (private collection).

and lamentation, and it was thus that the enemy within the British polity – the persistent threat presented by Catholicism, the Highlands and the old Gaelic order – was re-incarnated as the Celtic Jekyll and Hyde, the embodiment of both tenderness and terror. It is for this reason that extermination was never really on the cards, for despite the revulsion towards 'popery', Gaelic barbarism and clan society, the able bodied male was too valuable as a foot-soldier, or as a menial labourer, in the service of empire.

Purged from the civil sphere, 'the Celt' enjoyed a new aesthetic afterlife in the Ossian poems (1760–5) of James Macpherson, as the warrior culture of the Scottish Highlands was rehabilitated for the metropolitan reading public of London and, indeed, Europe and the United States, by projecting it onto a distant past, safely removed from the exigencies of the present. What is seldom appreciated in accounts of the cult of Ossian is the link between this yearning for a lost warrior ethos, and the need for a shattered culture to redeem its wounded pride on the battlefields of empire. Coinciding with the Seven Years' War and the unprecedented expansion of the British Empire, the ideology of the sighing, warlike Celt can be seen as an aesthetic call to arms, preparing the injured masculinity of the 'Celtic races' for what lay in store for them on the battlefields of America, Africa or India. 'They went forth to war, but they always fell' wrote Macpherson, in what became for Matthew Arnold a valedictory credo for Celticism itself in the Victorian era. It was perhaps this theme of 'the last of the race' that prompted Thomas Jefferson's fascination with Ossian in the early 1770s, for the analogies with the imminent destruction of native American culture were all too clear.[32] Like their Celtic counterparts, Indians were admired for their bravery, martial valour and eloquence but, as in the case of Jefferson's salutation to the speech of Chief Logan, this was essentially elegiac in tone as if, like the Thane of Cawdor in *Macbeth*, nothing became defeated races in life like their leaving it.

It is against this backdrop of militarism and defeat that the extraordinary success of Thomas Moore's *Irish Melodies* (1808–34), written in the bitter aftermath of the rebellion of 1798, is thrown into relief. Moore's romantic nostalgia is often compared to the Ossianic glorification of the Highlands, or its later reincarnation in the novels of Sir Walter Scott, a matter of eulogizing an exotic culture while ensuring its sell-by date had passed. But while

---

32 Paul J. Degategno, ' "The Source of Daily and Exalted Pleasure": Jefferson Reads the Poems of Ossian' in Howard Gaskill (ed.), *Ossian Revisited* (Edinburgh: Edinburgh University Press, 1991).

Moore does indeed pine for a world that was lost, and registers the catastrophic effect of the rebellion, defeat does not give way to dejection. 'The
tone of defiance' as he describes it in the 1810 preface to his *Irish Melodies*,
may 'be succeeded by the languor of despondency', but there is still enough
to 'alarm with advantage' those in high places 'from whom more is to be
gained by their fears than could ever be expected from their justice'.[33]
During his student years at Trinity College, when Robert Emmet was one
of his closest friends, the young Moore confronted directly the gloomy
pessimism of Macpherson in his own idiosyncratic Ossianic fragment,
published anonymously in the United Irishman paper, *The Press*. Instead of
locating Ossian's tale of woe in the dim mists of time or the regions of
romance, the travails of his Irish counterpart are brought into the contemporary world of everyday life and the novel – except, in the Ireland of
the 1790s, this world was riven by the Gothic horror of hulks, prisons and
the scorched earth of a countryside on the verge of revolt. Moore's sentiments were couched in the windy, inflated diction of Macpherson's original
with due emphasis on futility and passivity, but there is nothing vague about
the forces of oppression, and this gives rise to a change of mood and a call
for resistance at the end:

> Tyranny strides o'er our land dreadful as the gloom on his brow; and
> the pangs of despair are beneath him he treads the subjected soil . . . O!
> children of Erin! you'r robbed; why not rouse from your slumber of Death? –
> Oh! why not assert her lov'd cause, and strike off her chains and your
> own – and hail her to freedom and peace? Oh! that Ossian now flourished . . .
> for his Harp flow'd a torrent around, and incitement enforc'd as the stream –
> but silence now reigns o'er its wires – it met the fate of Jura![34]

Though imbued with longing and regret, Moore's melodies do not succumb to the fatalism and despair that characterized so-called 'Celtic melancholia'. There is a constant acknowledgement that the failure of rebellion
will be attributed to fate, but this is offset by the claim that disaster could
have been avoided if the Irish people had reclaimed their collective moral
agency and resolve in the face of tyranny. Mourning and desolation are

---

33 Thomas Moore, 'Prefatory Letter on Music', to *Irish Melodies* (1807–28), *The Poetical
Works of Thomas Moore* (London: Frederick Warne, n.d.), p. 194.
34 [Thomas Moore], 'Extract for a Poem in Imitation of Ossian', *The Northern Star*
[Belfast], 12 May 1797/ *The Press* [Dublin], 19 October 1797, reprinted in Mary Helen
Thuente, *The Harp Re-Strung: The United Irishmen and the Rise of Literary Nationalism*
(Syracuse: Syracuse University Press, 1994), p. 248.

indeed in evidence, but there is no sense that fate is invincible, still less that it vanquishes all traces of hope:

> Let Fate do her worst; there are relics of joy,
> Bright dreams of the past, which she cannot destroy;
> Which come in the night time of sorrow and care
> And bring back the features that joy used to wear.[35]

Hence the pervasiveness of the optative mood, the continual awareness of what might have been to forestall the hand of fate:

> The string that now languishes loose o'er the lyre,
> *Might* have bent a proud bow to the warrior's dart;
> And the lip, which now breathes but the song of desire,
> *Might* have poured the full tide of a patriot's heart.[36]

'Might', as it were, is 'right', but in this sense it is a weapon of the weak rather than the all-conquering sword of empire. In 'Forget not the Field', Moore develops Robert Emmet's suggestion in his famous speech from the dock that under a different dispensation, and more favourable circumstances, the outcome of history may have been reversed. This, of course, is the kind of 'fancy' associated with romance and Moore's more escapist reveries, but given the lure of Celtic melancholia, and the pressure in the aftermath of 1798 and 1803 to follow in the wake of Culloden, Moore's counter-factual fantasies might be construed more profitably as scenes from an unrequited past, a time whose moment has yet to come. At several points in Maturin's *The Milesian Chief*, the hero Connal (whose rebellion is overtly compared to Emmet's insurrection) is actually energized by despair: 'Then springing forward with the enthusiasm of despair, "I will offer this last sacrifice to my country," he exclaimed, "though the temple is in ruins, and the priest himself the victim"'.[37] Despair shares with desperation the capacity to increase the resolve of the rebels, even in the heat of battle:

> Bodily strength and mere despair at length obtained the victory . . . Connal perceived them [the redcoats] approaching, and remembering the event of the engagement in 1798, in which Lords O'Neil and Mountjoy fell, drew his wounded and scattered ranks in as close order as the broken ground admitted, and received the charge upon their extended pikes.[38]

35 'Farewell!–But Whenever you Welcome the Hour', *Poetical Works*, p. 227.
36 'Oh! Blame, Not the Bard', in *ibid.*, p. 209 (my italics).
37 Maturin, *The Milesian Chief*, vol. IV, p. 94.
38 *Ibid.*, vol. III, pp. 108–9.

'An Amalgamation of Incompatibles': From Jacobite to Jacobin

> He is gone on a wild hope; but to the desperate, only desperate things can give hope. — Charles Maturin, *The Milesian Chief* [39]

The gesturing towards alternative futures in evocations of the past suggests that it was not a spent force, a bygone era awaiting the embalming of romantic nostalgia. On visiting the ramshackle home of his aged aunts, the Miss Mac Taffs, in Connemara, Murrough O'Brien, the protagonist of *The O'Briens and the O'Flahertys*, notices that there are no hands on their large silver watches – an indication 'that their owners had taken as little account of time, as time had taken of them'.[40] Though they had undergone conversion to Protestantism to maintain what they could of their land in the wildest regions, 'by the great Protestant authorities the Miss Mac Taffs were looked upon, like other very old Protestant families, as half papist and whole Jacobites (a race in these remote regions, even then not quite extinct)'. O'Brien himself has inherited a Jacobite title, Lord Arranmore, on his return to Ireland, but not least of the anomalies of his social elevation is that it coincides with his expulsion from Trinity College for his involvement with the anti-aristocratic republican politics of the United Irishmen. 'A worshipper of Lafayette' and 'a disciple of Mirabeau', O'Brien, the narrative informs us, was present at both the fall of the Bastille in Paris, and the revolutionary assembly at the Jeu de Paume in Versailles – yet, as a descendant of the great High King family of the O'Briens, he was also 'deeply read in O'Flaherty, and in Keating, in O'Connor, and all the celebrated genealogists and senacchies, ancient and modern'. For all his investment in Enlightenment tenets of universal reason, O'Brien was 'still unconsciously partaking in his father's prejudices and sentiments, while he had stood opposed to him in his political and religious opinions':

> Now, however, he was struck even to sorrowful amazement, on the life nerve of that family pride, so curiously mingled with his democratic opinions, – an amalgamation of incompatibles, which forms the weakness of almost all the liberal descendants of the great feudal families, both of the Scotch and Irish.[41]

---

39 *Ibid.*, vol. III, 122.
40 Morgan, *The O'Briens and the O'Flahertys*, p. 420.
41 *Ibid.*, pp. 436, 212, 209.

Instead of defusing the energies of the Enlightenment, the amalgamation of Jacobite visionary politics with Jacobin democratic ideals helped to instill notions of hope and deliverance into the history of defeat that over-shadowed romantic nationalism. In the aftermath of the American Revo-lution, George Washington was celebrated by Gaelic poets in Jacobite terms as delivering the new world from British oppression; in a similar vein, the republican abolition of ranks in the French Revolution was welcomed as a portent that the end was nigh for another hated aristocracy in Ireland, that of the Anglo-Irish Ascendancy.[42] It only remained for Napoleon Bonaparte to assume the role of a deliverer from France, a re-routing of residual Jacobite millennial sentiments into popular culture and poetry to keep alive the shattered dreams of the 1798 rebellion (the fact that Robert Emmet actually met Napoleon in France while preparing for his abortive rising of 1803 indicated that such hopes of deliverance did not belong entirely to a dream world).[43]

It may be that the future oriented longings of Irish Romanticism owed as much to the unresolved cultural energies of the Jacobite Gaelic Ireland as to more overt Enlightenment utopian thinking. As James Joyce noted of the millennial poetry of James Clarence Mangan (1803–49), one of the few Irish writers he was prepared to acknowledge as a precursor:

> The old national soul that spoke during the centuries through the mouths of fabulous seers, wandering minstrels, and Jacobite poets disappeared from the world with the death of James Clarence Mangan, With him, the long tradition of the old Celtic bards ended; and today other bards, animated by other ideals, have the cry.[44]

Joyce may have been somewhat premature in noting the end of this genealogy, for Mangan himself acted as a lightning conductor in relaying a turbulent visionary poetics to a paralysed, post-Famine Ireland. As Bakhtin noted of carnival, disruptive or oppositional forces relegated to a

---

42 Breandán Ó Buachalla, 'From Jacobite to Jacobin', in Thomas Bartlett, David Dickson, Daire Keogh, Kevin Whelan (eds.), *1798: A Bicentenary Perspective* (Dublin: Four Courts, 2003), pp. 81–3.

43 *Ibid.*, p. 83. For popular ballads relating to Bonaparte, see Georges Denis Zimmerman, *Songs of Irish Rebellion: Political Street Ballads and Rebel Songs* (Dublin: Figgis, 1967), pp. 32–3, 183–92.

44 James Joyce, 'Ireland, Island of Saints and Sages', in *The Critical Writings of James Joyce*, ed. Ellsworth Mason and Richard Ellmann (London: Faber and Faber, 1959), pp. 173–4. See also Joyce's two extended essays on Mangan in same volume, pp. 73–83, 175–86.

cultural underground may often re-emerge in more concentrated, stylistic form in literature, bringing with them an intensified self-awareness and purpose.[45] Mangan's own reworking of Jacobite motifs owed much to the Irish language poet Micheal Óg Ó Longáin (1766–1837), in whose work the transition from Jacobite to Jacobin was given its most forceful expression during the early Romantic period. Establishing a reputation as a writer of visionary *aisling* poetry in the 1780s, Ó Longáin became an active United Irish organizer in Cork in the 1790s, complete with cropped hair. Instead of the Stuarts, it was now the people of Ireland who were due their rights – a use of the past more in keeping with forward-looking democratic demands than a restorationist Royalist discourse. Ó Longáin's primary attachment was to the Catholic cause, but it was a commitment tempered by republican notions of religious tolerance: '[I]f he's a Protestant or a Quaker, do not envy or hate him but let ye all rise up together as they smite the enemy.'[46] Ó Longáin's inclusion of the 'Marseilles' in both English and French in one of his Irish language compilations indicated that vernacular cosmopolitanism was not confined to the Anglophone world but was also part of Gaelic culture, for all its displacement on the periphery.

Though considered an outpost of all that was authentic in Romanticism, Ireland presented the prospect of landscape without 'Nature', indigenous culture without primitivism, intensity without interiority, and emotion recollected without tranquillity. 'I have pleasure in nothing', wrote James Clarence Mangan, 'and I admire nothing. I hate scenery and suns. I see nothing in creation but what is fallen and ruined.'[47] Taking him at his word, his contemporary Thomas Davis (1814–45), the poet and cultural nationalist, urged all patriots to abjure nature: 'not to live influenced by wind and sun and tree, but by the passion and deeds of the past'.[48] The

---

45 What Bakhtin writes of the 'defiance' of carnival could equally be said of Jacobitism in late eighteenth-century Ireland, and its aesthetic re-constitution in nineteenth-century poetry: 'Its wide popular character, its radicalism and freedom, soberness and materiality were transferred from an almost elemental tradition to a state of artistic awareness and purposefulness' (Mikhail Bakhtin, *Rabelais and his World*, trans. Helene Iswolsky (Cambridge, MA: Harvard University Press, 1968), p. 73. One critical difference, however, is that a high 'state of artistic awareness and purposefulness' already co-existed with more popular forms before the political demise of Jacobitism in 1760s with the ending of Papal recognition of the Stuart cause.

46 Ó Buachalla, 'From Jacobite to Jacobin', p. 90.

47 James Clarence Mangan, 'Autobiography' in *Prose* (Dublin: Irish Academic Press, 2003), p. 269.

48 Cited in Geoffrey Taylor, 'Some Irish Naturalists as Men of Letters', *Irish Monthly* (November 1949), 514. For a comprehensive overview of competing Irish perspectives

past was not relayed solely through texts – 'bardic remains' – and oral tradition, moreover: it also assumed a tangible, fragmented presence in the ruins that embossed the Irish landscape. As several commentators on the trope of the ruin attest, much of the Romantic response to the mouldering remains of other eras looked to them as evidence of nature's inexorable revenge over the futility of human endeavour – nature, in this abstract sense, as the silent operation of Divine providence or fate on the fallen, material world. In *The Milesian Chief*, Connal, the son of the dispossessed Gaelic family, guides a visiting party over the ancestral site of his ancestors on the west coast, and expresses his impatience with the generalized cult of ruins promoted by Volney's *Revolutions of Empire*, as opposed to the more visceral lived attachments of local memory: 'The nameless ruins . . . amid which fancy sits down at leisure to dream of what its tenants might have been; such may suggest and abstract and indefinite melancholy – a melancholy without passion, an without remembrance'. But then, 'his voice trembled as he added', pointing to the ruins of his own disinherited family:

> Here is a local genius; a spirit of eloquence and mortality seems to have taken up his residence between the living and the dead, and to interpret to one the language of the other. I feel who lies below: every step I take awakes the memory of him on whose tomb I tread, and every hour seems weary till I lie down with them, and are [sic] forgotten.[49]

In Wordsworth's 'Lines written a few miles above Tintern Abbey', the decay of the ruin – which is not even present to the eye – is 'restored' through the creative powers of the imagination and a retreat into inwardness that for many critics marks the emergence of Romanticism as a revolutionary literary and wider aesthetic movement. Yet, as M. H. Abrams among others has observed, this radical interiority was itself founded on a failure of revolution in the outside world as disillusionment with events in France forced visionary poets such as Wordsworth and Coleridge in on themselves: 'Having given up the hope of revolutionizing the social and political structure, Wordsworth . . . [sought] to effect through his poetry an egalitarian revolution of the spirit' so that readers 'may share his revelation of the equivalence of souls, the heroic dimension of common life, and the

on nature, see John Wilson Foster, ed., *Nature in Ireland: A Scientific and Cultural History* (Dublin: Lilliput Press, 1997)

49 Maturin, *The Milesian Chief*, vol. I, p. 187.

grandeur of the ordinary and the trivial in Nature.'[50] In Harold Bloom's pithy formulation, revolution gave way to revelation, revelation itself emanating from an internalization of the kind of external forces, 'sometimes magical', that obtained in the pre-modern world.[51] In Ireland, as we have seen, this process of internalization never took place, whether in politics, religion or intimate life: 'a private happiness becomes impossible when nations break', as Katie Trumpener acutely observes of the devastation of the love story at the end of *The Milesian Chief*. What is not so evident, however, is the conclusion Trumpener draws from this, namely, that it is 'a new institutional reorganization of power, so impersonal that it cannot be embodied allegorically, which renders obsolete the local loyalties of Connal's forces' – and by extension, the resurgence of Irish culture.[52] It was precisely the retention of allegory as a formative social agency, a means of mobilizing sentiment in the outer as well as the inner world that reclaimed Romanticism for the fragmented 'proto-modernity' of the colonial periphery. One of the constant refrains of Connal in *The Milesian Chief* is the Ossianic theme that he is the last of the race, and the death wail of the banshee attends not only individuals but entire cultures: 'Such is the tale of the Benshi', he laments, and 'the curtain of futurity . . . only waits for a feeble old man, and two unknown young ones [Connal and Desmond], to close on the last of the race'.[53] Connal does indeed meet his fate but not least of the anomalies of the novel is that while the death of the heroic individual is described at length, the defeat of the rebel forces in the background is drawn out to the point where closure becomes all but impossible. The incommensurability of two modes of warfare is such that *both* are reduced to savagery:

> The conflict had not ceased, and so totally unlike to modern war, that it seemed like the contest of two savage nations in their deserts: there was no array, no regularity, no conducted charge, no disciplined retreat . . . At first it was rather a rout than an engagement, rather a slaughter than a victory, but as the night advanced, the superior knowledge and activity of the rebels in their wild recesses, and the contempt of the military for these fugitive savages, was fatal to multitudes of the former, who pursued their victory

50 M. H. Abrams, 'English Romanticism: the Spirit of the Age' in Northrop Frye (ed.), *Romanticism Reconsidered* (New York: Columbia University Press, 1963), pp. 68–9, cited in Aidan Day, *Romanticism* (London: Routledge, 1996), p. 100.
51 Harold Bloom, 'The Internalization of Quest-Romance', *The Yale Review* (1969), pp. 5–6, cited in Day, *Romanticism*, p. 104.
52 Trumpener, *Bardic Nationalism*, p. 332.
53 Maturin, *The Milesian Chief*, vol. 1, pp. 177–8.

too far; and before midnight, though the soldiers claimed the victory, the loss had been nearly equal.[54]

In Yeats's later valedictory terms, the romantic hero may have been in the grave but it was far from clear that romantic Ireland was dead and gone, or safely interred in the pages of the literary canon.

54 *Ibid.*, vol. IV, pp. 85–6.

8

France, Germany, America

DAVID SIMPSON

Describing the nation

Self-consciousness about being *English* can be traced very early in the national literature, although it is often hard to be sure whether the reference is to a political, racial, social or linguistic category, or to some unspoken measure of each. Chaucer's Anglo-Norman literary language is very different from that of his equally English (and some say more English) contemporaries in the midlands and the north. Richard Helgerson has proposed that by the sixteenth century we can see in place a coherent national consciousness and a sense of occupying the heart of an empire among writers and intellectuals seeking to consolidate their interests within a professional and vocational elite.[1] But the point at which such circumstances can be called a fully developed *nationalism* has been a topic of some debate among historians and political scientists. Benedict Anderson's influential book restricts the term to nineteenth-century liberation or unification movements motivated primarily by an emergent bourgeoisie with the resources of print capitalism at their disposal,[2] while Hans Kohn sees the origins of modern nationalism in the English seventeenth century, when Puritan England 'regarded itself as the new Israel'.[3] During the early eighteenth century, as Gerald Newman and Howard Weinbrot have shown in some detail, several varieties of self-ascribed Englishness came into prominence: the new Rome, the Protestant bastion, the abiding enemy of all things French.[4] The huge expansion of the empire during the eighteenth

---

1 Richard Helgerson, *Forms of Nationhood: The Elizabethan Writing of England* (Chicago and London: University of Chicago Press, 1992).
2 Benedict Anderson, *Imagined Communities: Reflections on the Origins and Spread of Nationalism*, rev. edn (London and New York: Verso, 1991).
3 Hans Kohn, *Nationalism, its Meaning and History*, rev. edn (New York: Van Nostrand, 1971), p. 16.
4 Gerald Newman, *The Rise of English Nationalism: A Cultural History, 1740–1830* (New York: St Martin's Press, 1987) and Howard D. Weinbrot, *Britannia's Issue: The Rise of British Literature from Dryden to Ossian* (Cambridge: Cambridge University Press, 1993).

century involved not just fiscal, military and administrative reform on a massive scale, but also a heightened attention to the mostly virtuous features of the English national character, lampooned indeed from the first by Defoe in his 'True Born Englishman' (1700) but celebrated by a host of other willing writers.

The traditional cosmopolitan alliance between the French and English aristocracies meant that for much of the eighteenth century the campaign against things French (neo-classicism, highly codified manners, worldly sophistication) could also double as a protest against the luxurious habits and political corruptions of the English ruling families themselves. The celebration of Shakespeare and Milton as national poets, the antiquarian revival of all things British and the trumpeting of the Anglo-Saxon commonwealth as the original English parliament similarly contributed as much to class politics within the nation as to any coherent assault on the integrity of foreigners. By the 1790s, however, this pattern had been scrambled by Burke and his supporters who sought to estrange the French (who had revolted against their own aristocracy) as the enemy of *all* things English. The term *patriotism*, which for much of the century had been the declared identity of opposition groups (Tories against Whigs, radicals against wealth and commerce), became, beginning with the American war and resoundingly after 1789, the property of the conservative loyalists. After the contested and controversial union with Scotland in 1707 the term *British* had also become newly self-conscious, designating (according to Linda Colley and Robert Crawford) a nation-state identity that was supposed to include the Scots in whatever benefits political assimilation had to offer.[5] The awkward and opportunistic relations of identity and difference between the terms *British* and *English* which continue to inform modern usage (as for example in the title to this very series) were thus in place well before 1800.

Any account of English (or British) Romantic attitudes to foreigners – their cultures, writers, political systems and racialized national characters – must then recognize that the available stereotypes were employed to serve interests that were local and partisan and not simply monolithically national. This sometimes produced obscurities and displacements, reactions whose significance is not at all obvious now that we are so far removed in place and time. In the late 1790s, for example, we know that England was in

5 Linda Colley, *Britons: Forging the Nation, 1707–1837* (New Haven and London: Yale University Press, 1992) and Robert Crawford, *Devolving English Literature* (Oxford: Clarendon Press, 1992).

the middle of a protracted war with France, and some of us know about the major preoccupation with the Irish rebellion. The great quarrel in literary and dramatic circles, however, was over the virtues or vices of German drama, and particularly of the plays of Kotzebue. These questions seem to have nothing in common. But there was a major conspiracy theory circulating at the time, put about by the Abbé Barruel and others, which attributed the French Revolution to the machinations of a German secret society, the Illuminati, who were said to have subsequently infiltrated European freemasonry, including most particularly the Irish lodges. So the recent French and threatened Irish revolutions were made to look like German inventions, causing widespread concern about the taste for German plays and their libertine sex-gender doctrines. Other displacements explain why Rousseau, who had died in 1778, was of more urgent interest to British conservatives in the 1790s than any living French writer. And the enormous success of Walter Scott's *Waverley*, published in 1814 but describing events during the Jacobite rebellion of 1745, may (as Katie Trumpener has argued) have significantly depended upon its silent inclusion and occlusion of the more recent and unresolved disturbances in Ireland, which were not so readily open to portrayal as part of a progressive modernization guided by the spirit of tolerant bourgeois nationalism.[6] Scott, indeed, acknowledged the precedence of the Irish writer Maria Edgeworth in developing the novel of national history.

The predominance of France and Germany and eventually of America as the Romantic period's most commonly discussed foreign places (though Spain, Italy, Scandinavia and others also make appearances) does not then reflect any single or self-evident set of historical circumstances. France was of course the old enemy, with whom England had been at war for much of the previous century, and the cultural coordinates of their rivalry were established long before 1789, though they were modified in the 1780s and again after the Revolution. France after 1789 transformed itself rapidly from a monarchy to a republic to an empire and then, after 1815, back again to a monarchy, though it began as and remained throughout an independent nation state. The United States of America, in contrast, declared itself a new nation with its history all before it, though many British observers and interested parties as well as many Americans were unwilling to admit to this in 1776–83. Germany throughout the Romantic period was no nation at all,

---

6 Katie Trumpener, *Bardic Nationalism: The Romantic Novel and the British Empire* (Princeton: Princeton University Press, 1997).

but a collection of states, monarchies and principalities more or less held together by language and geography, though even these could not be taken for granted. France and England were competing for global empire; America and Germany were not, although America began its own continental expansion very early in the nineteenth century. Debating the attributes of these three national characters takes up most of the rhetorical space allotted to the assessment of what is foreign during a period when the major historical tendency was to worldwide empire. By 1815 England controlled Canada, most of the West Indies and India, and had settlements at Cape Town and in Australasia and the South Pacific. There is a wider consciousness evident in Romantic literature: poems like *Lalla Rookh, Gebir, Prometheus Unbound, Thalaba* and *The Curse of Kehama* all reflect the eastward course of empire, and the huge debate about slavery and the slave trade responds to the enormous (though diminishing) economic importance of the West Indies to the national economy. The Romantics may be performing an ideological displacement in limiting their main assessment of things foreign to two European 'nations' and one anglophone ex-colony, as if they and they alone were the significant alternatives. At the same time these discussions had a historical vitality of their own which was not independent of the global situation.

Empirical estimates of other national characters were not easy to make during the French wars: extensive contact between civilian populations was not practical for a quarter of a century after 1790, and commercial and literary relations were limited. There were few literary connections between France and England during the war, owing to the sheer difficulty of contact and the force of the economic blockade. De Sade's work appeared, but did not much register even inside France; Chénier's poetry was mostly not published until 1819; and French Romanticism (Lamartine, de Vigny, Hugo) came late, during the decade of the 1820s. De Staël and Chateaubriand, writing from exile, made some impact in the 1800s, but principally as oppositional writers, 'not French', as Napoleon himself said of De Staël (though Chateaubriand was rehabilitated after the alliance between the emperor and the pope). Wordsworth, Coleridge and Crabb Robinson, among others, were able to visit Germany in the late 1790s, but all Continental travel became harder as the scope of the war extended. After 1815 German culture came more and more to be typified in the English mind by philosophy – at first received as unintelligible and possibly revolutionary, then welcomed (even when it was not understood) as a source of profound spiritual guidance and as a corrective to the utilitarian and materialist tendencies of the national culture. German literature correspondingly came to be treated as itself a philosophical medium. America and its literature were throughout the Romantic period somewhat minor objects of attention in British literary circles, although the American urge to cultural independence picked up during the war of 1812 and began to seem convincing within the following decade as Irving and Cooper started to market their novels in England and to comment explicitly on the relations between the two cultures. As James Chandler has shown, there was by about 1820 an increasing emigration of the British artisan and middle classes to the United States, which produced a more complex image of the new world than had often obtained before, in contrast to the completely negative prospect rendered by Goldsmith at the end of *The Deserted Village* (1770) and there intended to cut short the consoling fantasy of a satisfactory world elsewhere.[7] Let us now move to a closer account of how British writers construed the respective identities of France, Germany and America.

The example of France

. . . was largely a warning to England, as Arthur Young put it in the title to one of his pamphlets. The aristocratic–cosmopolitan consensus that had received Voltaire and Montesquieu as honorary Englishmen and that looked to France as the repository of good taste and polite culture had weakened dramatically by the end of the eighteenth century. The conservative patriots effectively blamed the bloody violence of the Terror on the anticlerical bias of the French Enlightenment philosophers – easy to do at a time when both sides were very willing to believe in the historical force of ideas managed by exemplary intellectuals. For Burke and his followers, Enlightenment materialism was seen to have sponsored both an overestimation of the powers of unassisted human reason, cutting people off from the unanalyzed, inherited habits that sustained them, and a dangerous approval of the pleasurable rights of human passion and the powers of sentiment and sensation. The Frenchman of Burke's *Reflections on the Revolution in France* and of his later writings is a bifurcated creature, by turns uncontrollably libidinous and coldly rational, but never in a state of rest: you can trust him neither with your wives and daughters nor with the

7 James K. Chandler, *England in 1819: The Politics of Literary Culture and the Case of Romantic Historicism* (Chicago and London: University of Chicago Press, 1998), pp. 441–80.

machinery of the state. Nor could you trust him with your savings, since the fiscal profligacy of the republic was seen to have further intensified an already parlous prerevolutionary economic predicament. The French national character occupies the extreme ends of the spectrum of personality, between which it oscillates without ever dwelling comfortably in the middle. It is this middle ground which is the natural territory of the Englishman, committed to what Burke called the 'method of nature'.[8] The 'cold sluggishness' and 'sullen resistance to innovation' of Burke's typical Englishman may seem socially primitive and uncivil but they are the guarantee of political stability and peaceful continuity and they keep him from being tempted by the 'new conquering empire of light and reason'[9] that is embodied in the French constitution. Arthur Young, the voice of agricultural 'improvement', wrote in a similar vein against the pretensions of 'French theory'.[10] The scientific and technological revolution that began in the seventeenth century was by now seen as justifying the conviction that all things useful to mankind were to be discovered by experimental diligence and common sense, and the English thought themselves particularly adept at such discoveries. The French, in contrast, were far too persuaded by the claims of abstract ideas and purely rational paradigms. The new American republic had its declarations and constitutions, but it was the French who were, as Seamus Deane and David Simpson have shown, deemed guilty of a fatal disregard for precedent and of a deranged faith in mathematical and metaphysical principles.[11] Many felt that the American colonists had backed into a revolution, or been pushed into it, whereas the French Revolution appeared to be the planned implementation of radical and coherent principles, the inadvisability of which seemed to be proven by the course of its subsequent history. These principles were seen as the natural outgrowth of a culture which worshiped the likes of Descartes, Laplace and Condorcet, and which had pursued philosophical materialism to the point of a fine art.

The course of the French Revolution could then be seen as being negatively predetermined by an established national character, whereas that of

---

8 Edmund Burke, *Reflections on the Revolution in France*, ed. Conor Cruise O'Brien (Harmondsworth: Penguin, 1976), p. 120.
9 *Ibid.*, pp. 181, 171.
10 Arthur Young, *The Example of France, a Warning to Britain* (Dublin, 1793), p. 9.
11 Seamus Deane, *The French Revolution and Enlightenment in England, 1789–1832* (Cambridge and London: Harvard University Press, 1988) and David Simpson, *Romanticism, Nationalism, and the Revolt Against Theory* (Chicago and London: University of Chicago Press, 1993).

the Americans was either deemed a residually English evolution or as something yet to be born. The French character, as I have said, was typified by excessive passion as well as by overbearing reason, the two extremes abiding together in a volatile mix of fire and ice. The stereotyped French-man's cynical and superficial attitude to sexual morality rendered him antithetical to the developing English cult of domesticity and family soli-darity which was the narrative goal of *Pamela* and the narrative target of so many Gothic novels, and which was further reified by British responses to the events of 1789. Hugh Blair preached a sermon responding to the dec-laration of war against France in April, 1793, titled 'On the Love of our Country', in which he identified hearth and home as the foundations of the national religion and the state. For many of his peers, the greatest individual threat to the evolving celebration of domesticity was Rousseau, whose *Social Contract* only became influential a decade after his death in 1778, and whose notoriety as a founding father of Jacobin political science rekindled the earlier controversies over his novel *Julie* and his educational treatise *Émile*, at the same time as the posthumous publication of the two volumes of the *Confessions* (1782, 1789) publicized its author as sexually disreputable and even, in the eyes of many, perverted.[12] Rousseau's statue was erected in Paris in 1790, after his grave had already become a popular shrine. In October 1794 the remains of both Voltaire and Rousseau were placed in the Panthéon in an act of national homage: corrosive reason and uncontrolled passion enshrined together. William Blake always refers to them as a pair, perfectly reproducing the national paradigm. Burke (in his 'Letter to a Member of the National Assembly' of 1791) had already fastened on the case of Rousseau as symptomatic of the disastrous course of French politics and culture. In obedience to his peculiar notion of sincerity Rousseau had revealed far too much about himself and had thereby provided the British commentators with an arsenal of anecdotes demonstrating the depravity of

---

12 See Edward Duffy, *Rousseau in England: The Context for Shelley's Critique of the Enlightenment* (Berkeley, Los Angeles, London: University of California Press, 1979); Joan McDonald, *Rousseau and the French Revolution, 1762–1791* (London: Athlone Press, 1965); Deane, *The French Revolution*; and Simpson, *Romanticism*. On the continuing importance of *Julie* to debates about the novel, see Nicola J. Watson, *Revolution and the Form of the British Novel, 1790–1825: Intercepted Letters, Interrupted Seductions* (Oxford: Clarendon Press, 1994). On Rousseau's reception by British women writers, see Annette Cafarelli, 'Rousseau and British Romanticism' in *Cultural Interactions in the Romantic Age*, ed. Gregory Maertz (Albany, NY: SUNY Press, 1998). Voisine and Roddier offer bibliographical studies of Rousseau's English imprints. See Jacques Voisine, *J-J en Angleterre à l'époque romantique: les écrits autobiographiques et la légende* (Paris, 1956); Henri Roddier, *J-J Rousseau en Angleterre au XVIIIe siècle* (Paris, 1947).

the French national character. Some English writers, Hazlitt chief among them, kept faith with what they felt to be an integrity at the heart of Rousseau's work, and it has been recently argued that the turn against it was far less widespread or complete than had been previously assumed.[13] Byron (in Canto III of *Childe Harold*) and Shelley (in 'The Triumph of Life'), who were by no means hostile, still found a fatal incoherence in the Rousseavian character, a mixture of sympathetic and antithetic emotions disarrayed by a besetting megalomania. Mary Wollstonecraft's *Vindication of the Rights of Woman* takes strong issue with his subjugation and domestication of the female sex, and with the emotionalism that she reasonably perceives as negatively gendered. Her treatise in many ways exemplifies the complex response to the revolution that radical women writers experienced once the French themselves turned against extending the rights of women in their various constitutions.[14] The expansion of Wordsworth's *Prelude* may well have been significantly conceived as a critical response to Rousseau's educational theories, although there is no explicit naming of names.[15] And Coleridge, who read and delivered opinions on almost everything and everyone, has little to say (and nothing good) about Rousseau at any point in his career. Rousseau's appeal to British radicals and reformers was seldom less than ambivalent; with the end of hostilities in 1815, writers and intellectuals who were disposed to look beyond the seas were for the most part also looking beyond France, either to Germany or America or to the Mediterranean cultures of Greece and Rome where, as Marilyn Butler has shown, the beginnings of national liberation movements seemed to offer, at least to the liberals, a release from a patriotism that had been captured by

13 Gregory Dart makes a persuasive case for the continued positive response among British liberals and radicals to the anti-modernizing strain in Rousseau and (in a more qualified way) in Robespierre (*Rousseau, Robespierre and English Romanticism* (Cambridge: Cambridge University Press, 1999)). In a similar spirit Simon Bainbridge describes a commonly favourable British view of Napoleon enduring until 1802–4 (*Napoleon and English Romanticism* (Cambridge: Cambridge University Press, 1995)). Both of these critics, incidentally, present a view of Wordsworth as much less conservative than many readers have previously decided.

14 The importance and variety of women writers' experiences of and responses to the revolution is only now being explored in adequate detail: see, among others, Gary Kelly, *Women, Writing and Revolution, 1790–1827* (Oxford: Clarendon Press, 1993), and Adriana Craciun and Kari Lokke (eds.), *Rebellious Hearts: British Women Writers and the French Revolution* (Albany, NY: SUNY Press, 2001).

15 See James K. Chandler, *Wordsworth's Second Nature: A Study of the Poetry and Politics* (Chicago and London: University of Chicago Press, 1984), pp. 93–119; and, on the repression of references to Rousseau, W. J. T. Mitchell, 'Influence, Autobiography and Literary History: Rousseau's *Confessions* and Wordsworth's *The Prelude*', ELH 57 (1990), 643–64.

the reactionaries and a conservative spiritualism that was being attributed to the Germans.[16] The lineaments of the French national character that had been established before 1789 were able to be deployed to explain most of what happened during the revolution. Those more or less favourable to reform made just as much use of the inherited paradigms as did the conservatives who rallied round the defence of throne and altar. Thus Hazlitt, as late as 1828 in his *Life of Napoleon*, could regard the positive historical tendency that ended the old regime as doomed to failure by its appearance among a people least able to carry it through: 'there is no absurdity of speculation, no disgusting rodomontade or wildness of abstraction, into which they will not run once thrown off their guard'.[17] Such great events required a people habituated to 'strength of character' and 'solidity of judgement', usually imagined as the property of Protestant culture, although Hazlitt himself did not recommend the Germans for this role, mostly because so many of his more conservative contemporaries were turning to Germany as an example of a prepolitical society whose spiritual identity had no natural home in the world of ordinary experience. But this had not always been the case.

The appearance of Germany

Writing in 1833, Bulwer Lytton (as Lytton Bulwer) proposed that 'Wordsworth's genius is peculiarly German', and that 'his poetry has repaired to us the want of an immaterial philosophy – it *is* philosophy, and it is of the immaterial school'.[18] John Stuart Mill felt the appeal of that same immateriality, although in Matthew Arnold's famous judgement it would be transposed out of philosophy and back into nature, so that Wordsworth would become canonized as the least philosophical of our major poets. Nonetheless the fact that one of the most visibly English of poets could be identified as 'German' tells us much about the cult of German philosophy at the point of Romanticism's transition into Victorianism. There was in the 1830s still no political entity called Germany, which was another thirty years away. The declared German 'national' identity had

---

16 Marilyn Butler, *Romantics, Rebels and Reactionaries: English Literature and its Background, 1760–1830* (Oxford and New York: Oxford University Press, 1982).
17 *The Complete Works of William Hazlitt*, ed. P. P. Howe, 21 vols. (New York: AMS Press, 1967), vol. XIII, p. 55.
18 Edward Lytton Bulwer, *England and the English*, ed. Stanley Meacham (Chicago and London: University of Chicago Press, 1970), pp. 282, 284.

hitherto been continuously cultural rather than political, a way of holding together some 300 territories and 1,500 'minor principalities' into some sort of imagined whole.[19] The effort at legitimating a national literary language gave writers and intellectuals an ideal form for a German language, but it has been estimated that the *Hochsprache* was spoken by fewer than half a million people in the eighteenth century.[20]

The Teutonic or Gothic languages and histories, of which some or other version of German was the most widespread, had functioned in the eighteenth century as an item in the 'culture wars' disputing whether the origins and best elements of Englishness came from the culture of chivalry and civility associated with France and the Latin civilizations or from the primitive but energetic inhabitants of the northern forests. Given that modern English had visible elements of both, and that the British Isles had successively experienced invasions by Romans, Saxons and Normans, the only sensible answer had to be a complex one, which left considerable room for disputing the relative scope and merits of each ingredient of the national history and character. For much of the eighteenth century, for example, it was commonplace to consider Shakespeare as a genius indeed, but one whose talents were marred by flourishing in a culture heavily marked by Gothic barbarism. Gibbon, with his usual eye for paradox, declared that 'the most civilized nations of modern Europe issued from the woods of Germany', but noted that the 'liberty' thence derived depended upon poverty rather than principle, the outgrowth of a primitive and uncivilized society.[21] Thomas Warton's *History of English Poetry*, first published in 1774–81, took the position that the Norman conquest (and thus the French connection) was the major civilizing influence on what had previously been an 'unformed and unsettled race'[22]: the Crusades produced contact with the 'Arabian' romance that, Warton thought, filtered through French into English literature and made it imaginatively rich and worthwhile. Richard

19 See Hanno Segeberg, 'Germany', in Otto Dann and John Dinwiddy (eds.), *Nationalism in the Age of the French Revolution* (London and Ronceverte: Hambledon Press, 1988), pp. 137–56.
20 E. J. Hobsbawm, *Nations and Nationalism Since 1780: Programme, Myth, Reality* (Cambridge: Cambridge University Press, 1990), p. 61. On the history of the German language in the eighteenth century, see Eric A. Blackall, *The Emergence of German as a Literary Language, 1770–1775*, 2nd edn (Ithaca and London: Cornell University Press, 1978).
21 Edward Gibbon, *The History of the Decline and Fall of the Roman Empire*, 7 vols. (London: Bell and Daldy, 1872), vol. I, p. 272.
22 Thomas Warton, *The History of English Poetry*, ed. Richard Price, 3 vols. (London: Thomas Tegg, 1840), vol. I, p. 7.

Price's variorum edition of Warton's book, from which I am quoting here, took up the alternative defence of the 'northern genius' thesis made popular by Percy and Mallet among other antiquarians, along with a pan-European anthropological model offering an apparent key to all mythologies. Arthur Murphy's 1793 translation of Tacitus's *Germania* stimulated interest in what he called 'the seminary of the modern European nations, the VAGINA GENTIUM'.[23] And, since the Protestant victory of the late seventeenth century, various political intellectuals had been promoting the Anglo-Saxon commonwealth as the source of an English liberty threatened by a 'Norman yoke'.[24]

Toward the end of the eighteenth century contemporary German literature began to feature in its own right in British literary circles: Goethe and Schiller especially gave evidence of a culture that was no longer immured in the dark forests of the north. Goethe's *Werther* (1779), like Rousseau's *Julie*, was an international success and scandal, and according to F. W. Stokoe one of its English translations had reached a seventh edition by 1788.[25] Enthusiasm for German ballads seems to have peaked around 1795–6, with seven translations of Bürger's 'Lenore' in 1796 alone; and by the end of the decade German drama, and above all the plays of Kotzebue, had cornered the market. The year 1799 saw at least twenty-seven translations or adaptations of his plays in England.[26] But by this time the responses were not all positive. German literature, and above all Kotzebue's plays, had come to be associated with a dangerous libertinism and a collapse of sexual and domestic conventions, so that the image of Germany came to be very closely akin to that of France. Gibbon had pronounced the ancient German women to have been chaste and virtuous, though not exactly out of choice; in the late 1790s modern German women were coming to be regarded as apologists of free love, easy divorce and cross-class love affairs. The best known occurrence of Kotzebue in English literature comes much later, in the narrative of Austen's *Mansfield Park*; but there the perceived impropriety

---

23 *Tacitus: Historical Works*, trans. Arthur Murphy, 2 vols. (London and New York: Dent and Dutton, 1907), vol. II, p. 309.

24 The classic survey of this debate is by Christopher Hill ('The Norman Yoke', in *Puritanism and Revolution* (London: Secker and Warburg, 1958)). Popular Saxonism also influenced Noah Webster's efforts at distinguishing American from British English: see David Simpson, *The Politics of American English, 1776–1850* (Oxford and London: Oxford University Press, 1986), pp. 81–90.

25 F. W. Stokoe, *German Influence in the English Romantic Period, 1788–1818. With Special Reference to Scott, Coleridge, Shelley and Byron* (1926) (New York: Russell and Russell, 1963), p. ix.

26 *Ibid.*, pp. 48–9.

of performing *Lover's Vows* harks back to an earlier controversy. Some of the energy behind the Kotzebue debate undoubtedly came from the Irish situation, to which I have already alluded; and some perhaps emanated from the fact that these same plays had been enormously popular in France in the early 1790s. But issues of gender and class were also prominent in the writings of British 'Jacobin' feminists of the 1790s (Wollstonecraft and Hays), and in simultaneous efforts in France in the early phases of the revolution to advance the cause of women's rights. One critic, William Preston, responded adversely to German drama's celebration of 'the loves and heroic acts of beggars and bunters, of thieves and cutpurses, of tailors and seamstresses', and to its tendency to 'moralize on the inequality of human conditions'.[27] Preston's terms are very similar to those appearing in the negative responses to Wordsworth after 1800 complaining about his dignifying the likes of pedlars, ploughboys and strolling bedlamites; no wonder, then, that Wordsworth had sensed the need to distance himself from any association with 'sickly and stupid German Tragedies'.[28]

The idea of the German national character that supported the controversies of the 1790s was one made up of melancholy, sentimentality and passionate excess. Those who admired it saw there an honest delineation of 'the passions and the feelings of the human heart',[29] to borrow the words of John Britton, one of Kotzebue's defenders. Some of the same enthusiasm would be aroused by Wordsworth's poetry. Those who did not, including at this time most of the political conservatives, found only the licentious ravings of disordered imaginations believed to derive from the lack of a civilizing metropolitan centre and a coherent nation-state identity. Early responses to Kant and to the increasing volume of serious philosophical writing in German were also starting to be registered in the later 1790s, although they were at first (as René Wellek has shown) quite ill-informed,

27 William Preston, 'Reflections on the Peculiarity of Style and Manner in the Late German Writers whose Works have appeared in English, and on the Tendency of their Productions', *Transactions of the Royal Irish Academy*, vol. VIII (Dublin, 1802), p. 24.
28 *Prose Works of William Wordsworth*, 3 vols., ed. W. J. B. Owen and Jane Worthington Smyser (Oxford: Clarendon Press, 1974), vol. I, p. 128. For a fuller account of the image of Germany in the period, see Simpson, *Romanticism*, pp. 84–103. Julie A. Carlson discusses the gendered dimension of the image of Germany (*In the Theatre of Romanticism: Coleridge, Nationalism, Women* (Cambridge: Cambridge University Press, 1994)); and Michael Gamer argues that Joanna Baillie sought to introduce a recognizably British model of the supernatural, one that would be free of Germanic associations (*Romanticism and the Gothic: Genre, Reception, and Canon Formation* (Cambridge: Cambridge University Press, 2000), pp. 144–62).
29 John Britton, *Sheridan and Kotzebue* (London, 1799), p. 68.

and necessarily so given the difficulty that the new philosophical language presented to anglophone readers among whom even basic German was uncommon. Most of the responses complained of the obscurity of these abstract speculations, and sometimes of their wild and visionary nature; they were therefore, in the polemical shorthand of the times, assumed to be atheistic and Jacobinical. F. A. Nitsch and A. F. M. Willich, who were Kant's earliest interpreters in English (publishing in 1796 and 1798 respectively), had no very detailed understanding of the critical philosophy and could not convincingly argue for, although they did assert, its religious orthodoxy. The internal disputes among German thinkers – Kant's quarrel with Herder, Schiller's effort to render the aesthetic a more capacious category than Kant had appeared to endorse – were not significantly noticed by British readers. Crabb Robinson's relatively well-informed reports may have had some influence upon those who knew and read him, but it was Germaine de Staël who was most directly responsible for creating a positive response to German philosophy with the publication in England and in English of *On Germany* (1813). De Staël had more or less made a career out of refining models of the European national characters. Her novel *Corinne* (1807) was an extended narrative of the personality conflicts between England and Italy, and her earlier *On Literature* (1800) had set out a detailed distinction between the cultures of north and south, typified by Homer and Ossian respectively, which closely anticipates the one that Hegel would later adapt into an evolutionary historical explanation of the progress of spirit. Northern literatures, including the German, are imaginative, transcendental and melancholy, and place a high value on freedom; they are naturally at home with the Protestant religion. *On Germany* devoted three volumes to developing this case. The book (written in 1810 but suppressed by Napoleon) is in part an exhortation to the Germans to resist French imperialism, military and cultural, and it consequently complains that they are as yet too lacking in 'national prejudices' and in a proper 'love of liberty'.[30] The book is not simply an encomium; it complains about the high divorce rate, the absence of metropolitan culture, and the political obedience of the Germans. But above all and in a very positive sense the Germans differ from the French, with whom they compose 'two extremes of the moral chain'[31]; they are idealistic and spiritual where the French are empirical and materialist, and

---

30 Germaine de Staël, *Germany*, 3 vols. (London: John Murray, 1813), vol. I, pp 13, 32.
31 *Ibid.*, vol. I, p. 4.

the English too preoccupied with the merely 'useful'.[32] The whiff of scandal barely touches de Staël's account of Kotzebue, who now seems completely rehabilitated.[33] The essence of the German genius is philosophical, and the entire third volume is given over to a presentation of German philosophy as an inward, anti-materialist movement – the author seems happy to make all the simplifications necessary to such a conclusion. Thus Kant is imaged as one who 'always connects the evidence of the heart with that of the under-standing', though this was precisely the topic on which he most stringently differed from Schiller, while Fichte, who had lost his professorship after accusations on atheism in 1799, 'makes everything spring from the soul'. Kant and his successors are said to have sponsored a literature built on 'inward conviction and spontaneous feeling'– exactly what Kant had in fact opposed in his case against the Romantics.[34]

We should not of course expect a disinterested account of German cul-ture from de Staël or anyone else at this time: the debates about the vices and virtues of the various national characters were always responsive to polemic pressures and local events. Presenting German philosophy as restoring 'the empire of religion' makes it a contributor to the emerging 'condition of England' debate, a means of addressing the educated elite (the class that Coleridge called the clerisy) in order to propel it in a less utilitarian direction than it might otherwise have gone. These ideas are unlikely ever to become 'common': they are too abstruse for general acceptance. Their function is thus to energize an elite; they are 'inadequate to form a nation', a task only to be fulfilled by political institutions . . . like the ones to be found in England.[35] De Staël's capture of the German genius for criticism and philosophy as a model for training leaders is taken over by Carlyle, who is (along with De Quincey and with the complicated case of Coleridge) the most devoted British importer of German ideas. Carlyle's *Past and Present* (1843) repeats all of Burke's platitudes about the English national character as a naturally conservative one, and those theorists of nationalism who see its doctrines as expressions of the self-interest of the professional intellectual would find ample confirmation of their position in Carlyle's work. Fichte, for example, is credited in one of Carlyle's essays with the doctrine that 'Literary Men' are the 'appointed interpreters' of a 'Divine Idea'; and Kotzebue's brief popularity is now produced as an instance of the

---

32 *Ibid.*, vol. I, p. 222.
33 *Ibid.*, vol. II, p. 251–9.
34 See *ibid.*, vol. III, pp. 87, 115, 135.
35 See *ibid.*, vol. III, pp. 302, 170, 172.

inadequacy and impermanence of mass culture: 'the loudest roar of the million is not fame . . . the multitude of voices is no authority'.[36] By 1823 De Quincey felt able to dismiss at last the commonplace request that Kant's terminology must be lacking something if it cannot be translated into 'good old mother-English'.[37] New ideas need new words, and the judgement of a common reader is not significant. In their appeal to German philosophy the British critics had found a support against the threats of utilitarianism and popular literature; they had come a long way since Germany was associated with throngs of excitable theatre-goers soaking up sexual freedoms and political protests. They had also laid to rest the challenges of the French Enlightenment and revolution. In 1800 the loyalist scaremonger William Hamilton Reid had worried about the availability of sets of Voltaire's works in 'sixpenny numbers', with single volumes thence remaindered 'at no more than a penny a number', which he chose to see as putting the nation in grave danger.[38] By 1829 Carlyle was confident that there was not 'one great thought' in all of Voltaire's 'six-and-thirty quartos'.[39]

The emergence of America

Anna Barbauld's 'Eighteen Hundred and Eleven' was not popular with the critics. At the height of the gathering of nations against Napoleon it dared to imagine a time when Europe as a whole and England in particular might look like one huge deserted village commemorated only 'by the grey ruin and the mouldering stone' and visited by tourists from the new world in search of their personal and cultural roots.[40] The spirit of historical progress would then reside in the Americas, north and south. But in the United States they would still be reading Locke, Paley, Milton and Thomson rather than or as well as a literature of their own: Barbauld does not raise the issue of American writers. A decade later Sydney Smith asked his famous question: 'In the four quarters of the globe, who reads an American book?'.[41] The

---

36 Thomas Carlyle, *Critical and Miscellaneous Essays*, 5 vols. (London: Chapman and Hall, 1905), vol. I, pp. 58, 360, 422.
37 Thomas De Quincey, *The Collected Writings of Thomas De Quincey*, ed. David Masson, 14 vols. (Edinburgh: Adam and Charles Black, 1890), vol. X, p. 75.
38 William Hamilton Reid, *The Rise and Dissolution of Infidel Societies in this Metropolis* (London: J. Hatchard, 1800), p. 88.
39 Carlyle, *Essays*, vol. I, p. 414.
40 *The Works of Anna Laetitia Barbauld, with a Memoir by Lucy Aikin*, 2 vols. (Boston: David Reed, 1826), vol. I, p. 168.
41 Smith's *Edinburgh Review* essay is reprinted in Richard Ruland, *The Native Muse: Theories of American Literature*, vol. I (New York: Dutton, 1976), p. 157.

response was, by the modest standards of literary controversies, deafening, at least among the group of American writers competing in the international literary marketplace and those sympathetic to them. By the mid 1820s, lots of people were reading American books, some of which still disguised their national origins but many of which were now visibly proud of their new world pedigree. Indeed, it could be argued that the job of evaluating national characters had passed from the European writers to James Fenimore Cooper, whose *Notions of the Americans* (1828) and various volumes of *Gleanings in Europe* took up the task of comparative cultural journalism for the next generation.

But for many British readers and critics before about 1820, American culture and literature was merely an accidental extension of an English tradition – they read what we write, their writers are our writers. America had long been imaged as the place for criminals, fortune hunters and noble savages. It was seen as an unpromising site for the development of any new or worthwhile national culture, having no history or legends, no learned class, and a distinct preoccupation only with trade and profit. As early as 1679 Aphra Behn had feared 'the reproach of being American . . . The Muses seldom inhabit there; or if they do, they visit and away'.[42] The Americas, north and south, tended to be seen as one, represented in a familiar icon as a befeathered Indian darker than the European but lighter than the African. The war of 1776–83 did not produce a radical or abiding cultural schism between Britain and the United States, partly because it was seen as a version of an ongoing war with France (from 1778), and partly because the thirteen colonies had considerable support among British politicians: a general revolution in the West Indies would have been much more economically and ideologically threatening. The war of 1812 and the emergence of writers like Irving, Paulding and Cooper did much to publicize American cultural independence. But while these authors were indeed busy explaining and defending American landscapes and social habits to their British readers, they were also recording and adjudicating the rivalries and diversities among their own citizens – northern and southern, New Yorkers and New Englanders, English, Irish, Scots, Dutch, German, and of course the interactions of all of these with the native Americans. Cooper's *The Pioneers* (1823) is typical of the genre. As Benjamin Lease and David Simpson have

---

42 *The Works of Aphra Behn*, ed. Janet Todd (Columbus: Ohio State University Press, 1996), vol. VII, p. 83.

shown, nothing as simple or single as an American *nation* could be derived from these books.[43]

During the 1790s the popular response to Thomas Paine was to the radical Jacobin rather than to the American citizen and author of *Common Sense*. The *Rights of Man* was dedicated to George Washington and looked forward to a time when the new world might regenerate the old: William Blake's *America* and his unpublished 'The French Revolution' made the same connection between 1776 and 1789. And Richard Price, in 1785, wrote of the American revolution as opening a 'new aera in the history of mankind' and as 'the most important step in the progressive course of improvement' since the introduction of Christianity.[44] The text to which Burke so famously responded, Price's *Discourse on the Love of our Country* (1789), ends with words that Blake would poeticize almost verbatim: 'Behold, the light you have struck out, after setting America free, reflected to France and there kindled into a blaze that lays despotism in ashes and warms and illuminates Europe.'[45] But this deterministic pattern was not one that hugely influenced the popular rhetoric; even Burke, the master of conspiracy theorists, had little interest in raising the issue, not least because the American Revolution was one that he himself had supported. To the degree that the British reformers looked to the authority of a historical prototype, it was to the so-called 'glorious' revolution of 1688, rather than to 1649 or 1776. America did exist in the imagination as a place to begin again: Southey and Coleridge once planned for a utopian community on the banks of the Susquehanna, and Imlay's *The Emigrants* (1793), though it is visibly deficient in any first hand knowledge of the places it describes, presents the new world as 'the asylum of all unfortunate people', a place free from despotism and from the abuse of women.[46] Paine, Priestley, Daniel Isaac Eaton and Cobbett, as well as Wolfe Tone and many other radicals and reformers, all lived or visited there at various times. But the oddity that needs explaining is that the United States did not figure more prominently in the political rhetoric of the 1790s, given its obvious appeal as a (largely) English-speaking republic. The loyalists perhaps had little incentive to recall a revolution that had

---

43 Benjamin Lease, *Anglo-American Encounters: England and the Rise of American Literature* (Cambridge: Cambridge University Press, 1981); Simpson, *Politics*.
44 Richard Price, *Political Writings*, ed. D. O. Thomas (Cambridge: Cambridge University Press, 1991), pp. 117, 119.
45 *Ibid.*, p. 196.
46 Gilbert Imlay, *The Emigrants*, ed. Robert R. Hare (Gainesville: Scholars' Facsimiles and Reprints, 1964), p. 64. The modern editor, Robert Hare, strongly believes that Wollstonecraft wrote the novel.

succeeded, but radicals and reformers might have been encouraged by this, and by the traditional friendliness between America and France. America was however no mere welcoming refuge for European radicals. The 1798 Alien and Sedition Acts were specifically designed to keep them out, and John Thelwall probably spoke for many others in finding that the new republic had too much respect for religion, property and law, and too much of a habit of 'looking up to *affluence* as an honourable distinction, instead of proportioning our esteem to the talents and virtues of mankind'.[47] Tom Moore, publishing in 1806 a poetic record of his own sojourn in America, claimed to have anticipated an 'elysian Atlantis'[48] and to have found only a hotbed of vicious party politics. When Shelley wrote 'To the Republicans of North America' in 1812, he seems (like Anna Barbauld) to have had Mexico and South America in mind as the most likely sites for hopeful new beginnings. The manuscript reads *Nouth*, as if South has almost been altered to North, but not quite. The images and references in the poem are not of or to the United States.[49]

The most widely read Romantic literary treatment of the Americas was probably Thomas Campbell's enormously popular *Gertrude of Wyoming*, published in 1809. Southey had written his 'Songs of the American Indians' (1799) and set his ambitious epic *Madoc* (1805) in the Mississippi-Missouri valley, but it was Campbell's poem that attracted the wider readership. Its topic is an Indian massacre in 1778 which destroyed a utopian community in Pennsylvania made up of exiles from all over the world living together in peace. The tragedy is occasioned by the British alliance with the Indians, who thus murder the new, non-native Americans; but the poem also harks back to an earlier massacre in the Seven Years' War, when presumably those same natives were being encouraged by the French. The effect is thus to defuse and confuse the question of blame, and much of the poem is taken up with anthropological and zoological footnotes explaining the place and its native peoples – a sort of encyclopedia of the new world in the Scottish

---

47 *The Politics of English Jacobinism: The Writings of John Thelwall*, ed. Gregory Claeys (University Park: Penn State University Press, 1995), p. 55. For a detailed account of Anglo-American relations in the 1790s, see Michael Durey, *Transatlantic Radicals and the Early American Republic* (Lawrence: University Press of Kansas, 1997).

48 *The Poetical Works of Thomas Moore*, ed. A. D. Godley (Oxford: Oxford University Press, 1915), p. 94.

49 Percy Bysshe Shelley, *The Esdaile Notebook*, ed. Kenneth Neil Cameron (London: Faber and Faber, 1964), pp. 201–4. The first title in the notebook was 'To the Republicans of New Spain'.

Enlightenment tradition.[50] Partly an anti-war poem and partly a guidebook, *Gertrude* is a poem that deserves further study, as do Southey's *Tale of Paraguay* and Hemans's *The Forest Sanctuary*, both published in 1825. But by the 1820s, when emigration began to increase significantly, American writers were beginning in greater numbers to write their own literature, and to stand as themselves both instances and analysts of an American national character.

Conclusion

Many of the poets and novelists of the period were not obsessed with addressing the national characters of foreign countries. Crabbe, Clare, Austen and Wordsworth are largely silent about the French, the Germans and the Americans, but of course their localism can be seen as a deliberate gesture at a time when the matter of Englishness was very much under discussion. Blake has a moment of comic spleen against Klopstock and some famous poems on France and America, but in his later career he becomes more aggressively British in his allusions and associations. Keats is a classicizing Englishman. Byron, Shelley and Hemans remain cosmopolitan in their poetical subjects and sympathies, but not in simply judgemental ways. Coleridge is the figure who most thoroughly takes up the critical adjudication of foreign paradigms, and his rejection of the French in favour of the Germans is, as we have seen, symptomatic of the domestication of metaphysics after 1815. It is often the critics, politicians and intellectuals who most vigorously carry on the business of defining a marketable form of Englishness by denigrating or selectively appropriating foreign influences. In 1817 Hazlitt set about demystifying the omnipresent John Bull, the surly embodiment of the national character, noting that his countrymen 'are too apt to mistake the vices of others for so many virtues in themselves'.[51] The mythology of Englishness throughout the eighteenth century had been one

---

50 See Robert Crawford, *Devolving English Literature* (Oxford: Clarendon Press, 1992), pp. 176–215. There is a good deal of this anthropological and geographical summary in eighteenth-century writing on America – in Smollett's *Humphry Clinker*, for example, and in William Robertson's *History of America*. Campbell was a Scotsman whose father had lost money in Virginia as a result of the War of Independence.

51 Hazlitt, *Complete Works*, vol. IV, p. 98. The figure of John Bull appeared much more frequently after 1789, although he had been on the scene since the early eighteenth century: see Jeannine Surel, 'John Bull', in Raphael Samuel (ed.), *Patriotism: The Making and Unmaking of British National Identity*, 3 vols. (London and New York: Routledge, 1989), vol. III, pp. 3–25. I thank James Chandler, Nigel Leask, Sarah Maza and Bradford Mudge for valuable help with this chapter.

of common sense and steady habits, respectful and productive of genius (Milton and Shakespeare) but impervious to abstract theory, rule-bound procedures, and violent passions. The French Revolution further solidified the myth, and placed it at the service of conservative and loyalist propaganda. During the Romantic period the Germans and the Americans joined the French as popular yardsticks by which the national character could measure itself. Unlike the French, the Germans were seen to have something to teach us, while the Americans left us somewhat undecided. Some restless spirits, like the Shelleys and the Brownings, opted for the warm south, perhaps in part because (despite the popularity of *Corinne*) the Italian character had not been exhausted by efforts at defining Englishness. One would scarcely call any of this a global consciousness; but it was perhaps enough to guarantee that the recourse to a deliberately narrower perspective would be defined in critical rather than approving terms: it would be a turn to *Little England*.

9

The 'warm south'

ESTHER SCHOR

O, for a draught of vintage! That hath been
  Cool'd a long age in the deep-delved earth,
Tasting of Flora and the country green,
  Dance, and Provençal song, and sunburnt mirth!
O for a beaker full of the warm South! . . .
      John Keats, 'Ode to a Nightingale' (1819)

The 'cult of the south'

For Britons of the Romantic era, the 'warm south' was many things: an imaginary elsewhere of lemon trees and olive groves; a place of refuge and exile; a sensuous landscape of desire; a living gallery of the picturesque; a ruined monument to lost liberties; a nidus of revolutionary fervour; and a region halted on the far side of enlightenment, fatally in thrall to superstition. It is hard to imagine British Romanticism uninvested by the sun and shadows of this 'world elsewhere', not least because this interfusion of British and Mediterranean cultures had been centuries in the making. In the sixteenth century, when Sir Philip Sidney and Lord Henry Wotton ventured to Italy, it became fashionable for young men (often aides to aristocrats or official attachés) to undertake what came to be called the 'Grand Tour'. Two centuries later, the rise of Napoleon halted the routines of the Grand Tour, though some brave travellers would invent their own grand alternatives: for Wollstonecraft in 1796, Scandinavia; for Byron in 1809, Greece, Albania and Turkey. After Napoleon's incarceration on Elba in 1814, Mediterranean travel resumed with a vengeance. The era of the Grand Tour did not end so much as persist, in a somewhat democratized form, until well into the nineteenth century. The sentimental rake of Sterne's *Sentimental Journey* (1768) became the philistine traveller, alternately grumpy and enthusiastic, unable to overcome what Mary Shelley wryly diagnosed as a phrenological bump of 'stayathomeativeness'.

My epigraph from Keats's 'Ode to a Nightingale', however, speaks for those Romantics who understood the 'warm south' to be something far other than a commodity or cultural capital. In Keats's famous phrase, the south is a scene figured as a fluid empowered to alter consciousness; to taste it is to be possessed, and its after-effects are lasting, profound, haunting. Some quaffed Keats's beaker among the Euganean hills or the baths of Caracalla; others drew it from the fluid vowels of Italian poetry or music; some drank it in through the eye, in the nubile madonnas of Renaissance painting. Many, of course, sipped the south from English teacups, poring over the numerous travel diaries, essays and poems published by returning tourists. For Percy Shelley, Mary Shelley, Byron and Hemans, the most potent draught was that of history, and its effect was to broach the political consciousness of a subject people. In their tragedies of resistance, the poet's beaker brims with tears of pain, rage and betrayal.

If the 'warm south' is not wholly a metaphor, but more than a map, how best then to approach it? This chapter plies between literal and literary geographies, taking up both the material aspect of crossings between Britain and the Mediterranean and the myriad of crossings undertaken in the aesthetic realm. Sometimes these crossings involved turning away from other imposing sources of influence. For writers of the second generation of Romantics, turning away from the generation of Wordsworth and Coleridge opened the way for new fathers; such writers sought and found a new, liberal style of literary paternity in Italian literature. As we will see, the adoption of Italian fathers masculinized 'la bella Italia', characterized since the early modern period alternately as mother, lover and siren. Another imposing influence for writers seeking a southern alternative to northern modes and mores was Romantic Hellenism, exemplified by Shelley's Homeric Hymns and translations of Plato, Aeschylus and Euripides; Peacock's *Rhododaphne*; Keats's *Ode to Psyche* and *Lamia*; and Mary Shelley's mythological dramas. Such works bespeak the atheistical tone of comparative mythography propounded by William Drummond who, in turn, developed the earlier arguments of Sir William Hamilton and Sir Richard Payne Knight.[1] With modern Greece degenerate ('hereditary bondsmen', 'eastern Irish Papists'), for example, Byron's Childe Harold finds comfort

---

1 Marilyn Butler, *Romantics, Rebels and Reactionaries: English Literature and its Background 1760–1830* (Oxford: Oxford University Press, 1982), p. 124; Martin Priestman, *Romantic Atheism: Poetry and Freethought, 1780–1830* (Cambridge: Cambridge University Press, 1999), pp. 44–79.

in the Greek landscape, which retains a numinous, mythological presence: 'Where'er we tread 'tis haunted, holy ground . . .' (*Childe Harold's Pilgrimage* 2:88).[2]

But if *Childe Harold's Pilgrimage* is a reliable indicator, the Romantics' investments in later periods of Italian history far outstripped their investments in classical Rome. Byron's Italy, where Harold encounters the feverish, decadent vitality of Venice; the Florentine shrines of Galileo, Alfieri and Machiavelli; the legacies of Dante, Petrarch and Boccaccio; and the sublime cataracts of the Appenines, far exceeds the ruined Harold's subsidence to classical Roman ruins. Moreover, Harold's tour of Rome generates centrifugal energies, with stanzas hurtling in time and space; Canto IV culminates in Byron's extensive notes on the present state of Italian letters. Though Harold's ruined destination is Rome, Byron's is Italy, a site of – and occasion for – redemption and regeneration. But as we shall see, such optimism, though a major strain in the immediate wake of Waterloo, becomes eclipsed after 1820 by tragic reckonings.

Escape, encounter, exile

The Revolutionary–Napoleonic period left Britain's watery contours untouched, but it drastically redrew the island nation's imaginary geography. Throughout the eighteenth century, though France remained the papal menace in the popular imagination, Paris had become a world capital, and its cosmopolitan allure drew countless Britons to its salons, theatres, operas and museums. During the so-called Revolution controversy, this ambivalence to things French became difficult to sustain; some Britons, like Wollstonecraft, Helen Maria Williams and the young Wordsworth, rejoiced in the Revolution; others, like Edmund Burke, warned that violence would soon follow. When England declared war on France in 1793, few suspected that an entire generation would come of age without ever setting foot on French soil – nor, as Napoleon moved eastward, on much of the Continent. Though many Britons' imaginations were captured by the ermined emperor, France was widely considered an intractable, implacable enemy, and that nation's privileged role as the cultural complement to Britain was an early casualty of the war. Even as the imperial eagle took wing in France,

2 George Gordon, Lord Byron, *Byron: The Complete Poetical Works*, 7 vols., ed. Jerome McGann (Oxford: Clarendon Press, 1980–92), vol. II, p. 73.

German intellectuals had begun to theorize nationhood from the ground up: Herder's theory of a *volksgeist*, the folk spirit of a people as distinct from a nation-state or principality, became broadly elaborated by Goethe, Schiller and Friedrich Schlegel as a theory of northern and southern characters. Where Rousseau placed *l'homme sauvage* in a vague past, Schiller located this past in bucolic Greece, a region of unselfconscious '*naïveté*' lived out in the bosom of nature; by contrast, Schiller describes sentimental consciousness as a reflexive, melancholy yearning. With a debt to Montesquieu, Germaine de Staël would render both the northern aesthetic, in *De L'Allemagne* (1810), [3] and the southern, in her 1807 novel *Corinne, or Italy*: 'In the warm countries, nature puts us in touch with external objects, and feelings spread gently outward . . . . Elsewhere, life as it is proves inadequate to the soul's powers; here the soul's powers are inadequate to life . . .'[4] In the tragic story of the Anglo-Italian *improvisatrice* Corinne and the English Lord Nelvil, south and north come together – and then part – in a clash of instinct and convention. In Corinne's fatal ordeal of romance and rejection, the decks are stacked in favour of the masculine northerner, 'a man who could only thwart her natural self, and repress rather than stimulate her gifts . . .'[5] Once all manner of difficulty could be construed as *malaise du nord*, the 'warm south' came to appear an ideal escape. Even during the violent decade of Austerlitz, the Peninsular War and Borodino, both Coleridge and Byron escaped from messy entanglements in Mediterranean travel. On the face of it, their experiences abroad could not have been more different: whereas Coleridge between 1804 and 1806 essayed the life of an aide to the Governor of Malta (with occasional forays into the underworlds of eros and art),[6] Byron and his retinue of servants, companions, lovers, hangers-on and pets scaled the mountains of Albania for a meeting with the notorious Ali Pasha. During his voluptuous interval in Greece, where homosexual relations between mature men and young boys were commonplace, Byron asked in a cancelled stanza from *Childe Harold's Pilgrimage*, 'Fair Greece! . . . Who now shall call thy scatter'd children forth' – and scrawled his own interlinear answer: 'Byron'.[7] But both men took risks, Byron dallying in Portugal

---

3 Butler, *Romantics*, p. 120.
4 Germaine de Staël, *Corinne, or Italy*, trans. Avriel H. Goldberger (New Brunswick: Rutgers University Press, 1987), p. 195.
5 *Ibid.*, p. 303.
6 Richard Holmes, *Coleridge: Darker Reflections, 1804–1834* (New York: Pantheon, 1998), pp. 1–83.
7 Benita Eisler, *Byron: Child of Passion, Fool of Fame* (New York: Knopf, 1999), p. 228.

during the height of the Peninsular campaign, Coleridge lazing under the ceiling of the Sistine Chapel during the winter of 1806, while French soldiers paced the aisles. Undaunted when Britons were declared *personae non gratae* in occupied Italy, Coleridge posed as an American on a quick trip to Pisa. Joseph Forsyth was not as lucky. Caught in Italy when the Peace of Amiens collapsed, he was arrested in Turin in 1803 and after a forced march of 600 miles, imprisoned in France.[8] Remarkably, he survived to write one of the period's two indispensable guidebooks to Italy, *Remarks on Antiquities* (1813). The other, which also appeared in 1813, was J. C. Eustace's *Classical Tour through Italy* (1813).

Once news of Napoleon's incarceration in 1814 reached Britain, the packet boats began to teem with tourists. Among the first were W. S. Landor, on the run from creditors, and the banker-poet Samuel Rogers (soon followed by J. M. W. Turner, whose 1830 illustrations for Rogers's *Italy* would vastly impress an eleven-year-old boy named Ruskin). Mary Shelley, writing in the mid-1820s, reminisced, 'a new generation . . . poured, in one vast stream, across the Pas De Calais into France: in their numbers, and their eagerness to proceed forward, they might be compared to the Norwegian rats . . . .'[9] If her picture is grim, so were the conditions these tourists faced. Travel was slow and arduous; a sea voyage to Italy would take five to six weeks; overland, two to four. The most affluent travelled by private coach and the most straitened in a 'diligence', a large, long-reined vehicle that traversed at about five miles per hour. The most popular, if galling, mode of travel was the vettura (or vetturino), owned by Italian driver/guides who doubled as booking agents for meals and accommodation. At a daily cost of fifteen shillings, vetturini covered only thirty-five miles per day. Travelling with the post or a courier was about twice as fast but less commodious. Most travellers to Italy, arriving via the Simplon pass in autumn, stopped at Turin, Milan and Bologna; sojourned briefly at Florence; spent Christmas in Rome; then ventured south to Naples, where stories of *banditti* kept most from going further. And most returned to Rome for the pageantry of Holy Week, and then (increasingly throughout the century) stayed briefly in Venice.[10] By summer, though the lion's share of Britons had already

8 See introduction by J. R. Hale in Samuel Rogers, *Italian Journal* (London: Faber and Faber, 1956), p. 57.
9 Mary Shelley, 'The English in Italy', in *The Mary Shelley Reader*, ed. Betty T. Bennett and Charles E. Robinson (Oxford: Oxford University Press, 1990), p. 341.
10 Hale in Rogers, *Italian Journal*, pp. 56–92; C. P. Brand, *Italy and the English Romantics* (Cambridge: Cambridge University Press, 1957), pp. 7–25.

returned home, upper-floor apartments were taken to avoid *la malaria*; carriage windows were tightly shut.

Outside of larger towns and cities, British travellers endured squalid accommodation and frequent requests to surrender passports, show documents, obtain signatures. Hotel registers were routinely perused by the Austrian police; when a weary Byron, registering late one night, recorded his age as '100', the hosteller anxiously followed him to his bed for confirmation.[11] In major cities, however, comfortable rooms could be had cheaply. The cost of an eight-month tour has been estimated at approximately 100 pounds; in Sicily this figure would buy an entire year's stay.[12] In Italy, even meagre funds could buy the trappings of gentility.

Byron departed for Italy in April, 1816, when his notorious affair with his half-sister, Augusta Leigh, prompted his wife Annabella to request a separation. In Venice, he composed the final canto of *Childe Harold's Pilgrimage* and *Beppo: A Venetian Tale*, punctuating the writer's life with prodigious sexual exploits. The Shelleys, children and nurses in tow, joined Byron in Italy in 1818. Between their arrival and Percy's death four years later, they would live in over a dozen locales from Pisa to Naples and all this movement had dire costs. The infant Clara contracted dysentery and died in Venice on 24 September. Byron's abysmal neglect of his own child, forbidden ever after to see her mother, would lead to her death in a Venetian convent at age five. The Shelleys' remaining son, William, would die in Rome the following May, 1819, at age three. Thereafter, the Shelleys (along with their new baby, Percy Florence) contracted the circle of their travels, settling in the environs of Pisa in January of 1820.

Three weeks earlier, Byron had relocated to Ravenna to be close to the young Countess Teresa Gamba Ghiselli Guiccioli; Teresa's middle-aged husband notwithstanding, Byron became drawn deeper and deeper into her life, as he composed the nacreous stanzas of *Don Juan*. Byron both revelled in and balked at the role of Teresa's *cavaliere servente* – 'I should not like to be frittered down into a regular cicisbeo'[13] – and they considered elopement. But as so often for Byron, circumstances intervened, now in the guise of threats to Teresa's Carbonarist family. During the spring of 1820 (the year of the Cato Street Conspiracy), Byron attended secret meetings of the

---

11 Eisler, *Byron*, p. 546.
12 Hale in Rogers, *Italian Journal*, pp. 88–91.
13 Byron to Hobhouse, 6 April 1819, *Byron's Letters and Journals*, 13 vols., ed. Leslie Marchand (Cambridge, MA: Harvard University Press, 1973–94), vol. VI, p. 107.

Carbonari in Ravenna, helping to plan and fund an uprising for early 1821. But when the short-lived Neapolitan revolution was quashed by the Austrians that March, northern hopes fell as well; exasperated, needing a refuge from his Carbonarist activities and rattled by the prospect of casting his lot in with Teresa, Byron joined Shelley in Pisa late in 1821.

Together, they invited the radical writer and publisher Leigh Hunt to come to Italy and collaborate with them on a new journal, *The Liberal*, only four numbers of which would appear. For only days after the arrival of Hunt and his family (including his wife Marianne, six children and a goat)[14] in June 1822, Shelley and Edward Williams drowned in a sailing accident, their bodies washing ashore some days later. These events brought the gradual dispersal of the short-lived Pisan colony. The next year, in July 1823, Mary Shelley would return to England; the same week, Byron departed for Greece, along with Teresa's brother Pietro Gamba – but not, of course, the distraught Teresa.

Pisa was a mecca for Greek exiles;[15] there Prince Alexander Mavrocordato, who later became the first president of the Greek republic, taught Mary Shelley Greek, garnering her sympathy for his cause against the Turks. Percy Shelley, who had translated fragments from Aeschylus and Euripides, written *Prometheus Unbound* (1820) and celebrated the Greek cause in *Hellas* (1822), was a committed philhellene, as was Trelawny. But in Byron the philhellenic cause would find its most ardent – and most renowned – supporter. After numerous flattering letters from the nascent London Greek Committee, Byron, together with Trelawny, set out for Cephalonia, plumed helmets at the ready; at the end of December, Byron continued on to the mainland, his entourage reduced to three men and two dogs. As is well known, Byron's brief tenure as Commander in Chief of Western Greece ended with his death at Missolonghi, probably of malaria, on 19 April 1824. But in the case of both Greece and Italy, no matter how deep sympathies ran, no matter how many diplomats read Greek or spoke Italian, the business of the Foreign Office was carried out in the language of balance-of-power diplomacy. Only the threat of French intervention – and the capturing of markets for British goods – would provoke the Government to intervene on behalf of either cause.

---

14 Leigh Hunt, *Autobiography*, ed. J. E. Morpurgo (London: Cresset, 1969), p. ix.
15 William St Clair, *That Greece Might Still Be Free: The Philhellenes in the War of Independence* (London: Oxford University Press, 1972), pp. 138–54.

Fair Ausonia: exchanging Matria for Patria

Given the government's policy of non-intervention, sympathy for Italy among the British public remained within the realm of letters, often in strains of benign condescension. Central to this attitude was the proverbial feminization of Italy, rendered in tones at once pathetic and damning.[16] The locus classicus of such laments, is a sonnet by the seventeenth-century Florentine poet Filicaja, 'Italia, Italia, o tu coi feo la sorte', rendered by Byron in these lines from *Childe Harold's Pilgrimage*: 'Italia! oh Italia! Thou who hast / The fatal gift of beauty, which became / A funeral dower of present woes and past, / On thy sweet brow is sorrow plough'd by shame, / And annals graved in characters of flame' (*CHP* 4:42). Traduced, yet culpable, Italy sometimes finds her assorted qualities split among various locales. Byron, famously, figures Rome as 'the Niobe of Nations! ... Childless and crownless . . .' (*CHP* 4:79). Anna Jameson declares that 'Naples wears on her brow the voluptuous beauty of a syren.'[17] Wordsworth laments Venice, no longer 'a maiden City, bright and free'[18] while Hemans (who also translated Filicaja's sonnet) invokes 'Fair Florence! Queen of Arno's lovely vale!'[19] 'Widow'd Genoa' and 'fair Milan' are asked by Shelley to watch how Florence 'blushes within her power for Freedom's expectation'.[20] No wonder Italy was feminized both by liberal sympathizers and by those who blamed Italy for her own degradation.[21] Critics of the Della Cruscans, a circle of English poets in the 1790s who claimed for themselves an 'Italian' style, linked their theatricality to the 'vacuousness' of its female proponents, who included the playwright Hannah Cowley and the illustrious actress and poet Mary Robinson.[22] Yet another victim of this figure is the *vir* in Italian virtue: laments for an effeminized Italy shade seamlessly into complaints about the effeminacy of Italy's men. Gothic novels such as

---

16 Sandra M. Gilbert, 'From *Patria* to *Matria*: Elizabeth Barrett Browning's Risorgimento', in *Victorian Women Poets: A Critical Reader*, ed. Angela Leighton (Oxford: Blackwell, 1996), p. 27.

17 Anna Jameson, *Diary of an Ennuyée* (Boston: Osgood, 1875), p. 269.

18 William Wordsworth, *The Poems*, 2 vols., ed. John O. Hayden (Harmondsworth: Penguin, 1982), vol. I, p. 571.

19 Felicia Hemans, *Felicia Hemans: Selected Poems, Letters, Reception Materials*, ed. Susan J. Wolfson (Princeton: Princeton University Press, 2000), p. 22.

20 Percy Bysshe Shelley, *Complete Poetical Works*, ed. Thomas Hutchinson (London: Oxford University Press, 1929), p. 613.

21 Maura O'Connor, *The Romance of Italy and the English Political Imagination* (New York: St Martin's, 1998), p. 20.

22 Judith Pascoe, *Romantic Theatricality: Gender, Poetry and Spectatorship* (Ithaca: Cornell University Press, 1997), p. 88.

Ann Radcliffe's *The Italian* (1797), featuring androgynous, fiendish monks, contributed to the British habit of figuring Italian men as unreliable, fickle, superstitious and dim. Greek men were similarly impugned; even Byron depicts them as 'unmann'd' (*CHP* 2:74), having forfeited 'their father's heritage' (*CHP* 2:75). While blaming this unmanning on three centuries of captivity, Byron relentlessly contrasts the Greeks with the fierce Albanians and the barely civil Turks. But a powerful countertrope to 'povere bella Italia' emerges in the Romantic cult of Italian poet-fathers, which stakes Italian regeneration on a regendering of Italy. The key figure, of course, is Dante, but partial credit goes to Coleridge who, after a chance meeting with the Rev. H. F. Cary at the seaside in 1817, retrieved the minister's blank verse *Vision of Dante* (1814) from near-oblivion. In his *Lectures on European Literature* (Lecture 10, February 1818), Coleridge presents Dante as a 'religious-metaphysical' poet whose Christian symbolism invests Platonic infinitude with Aristotelian clarity.[23] Appearing at the same moment, Ugo Foscolo's favourable review of Cary in *The Edinburgh Review* champions Dante as an anticlerical patriot, excoriating the Jesuitical readings that dominated Italian criticism.[24] The Dante embraced by Shelley, Byron, Keats and Hunt would draw elements from both approaches; from Foscolo, Dante the antipapal liberator; from Coleridge, Dante the visionary who recognized the power of images. Perhaps the most remarkable fusion of these figures appears in Blake's engravings, where the heroic poet is surrounded by the pulsating images of his poem.[25] In Coleridge's view, Dante's choice of Italian rather than Latin evoked far better than Wordsworth 'the real language of men'. *This*, for Byron, made Dante 'The Great Poet-Sire of Italy'.

For Shelley in the *Defence of Poetry*, as for Coleridge, Dante was a pivotal figure in European literature: 'The poetry of Dante may be considered as the bridge thrown over the stream of time, which unites the modern and antient world.'[26] Shelley's Dante, like his Homer, was an epic poet whose work is a summa of his age, yet he faces firmly forward, a poet of Enlightenment: 'Dante was the first awakener of entranced Europe . . . the Lucifer of that starry flock which . . . shone forth from republican Italy, as

---

23 Edoardo Zuccato, *Coleridge in Italy* (Cork: Cork University Press, 1996), pp. 87–90.
24 *Ibid.*, p. 89.
25 Ralph Pite, *The Circle of our Vision: Dante's Presence in English Romantic Poetry* (Oxford: Oxford University Press, 1994), pp. 64–7.
26 Percy Bysshe Shelley, *Shelley's Poetry and Prose*, ed. Donald H. Reiman and Neil Fraistat (New York: Norton: 2002), p. 526.

from a heaven, into the darkness of the benighted world.'[27] To Shelley's mind, Dante taught Milton epic heresy. Not only was he 'the first religious reformer',[28] but a reformer also of relations between men and women: 'Dante understood the secret things of love even more than Petrarch. His *Vita Nuova* is an inexhaustible fountain of purity of sentiment and language . . .'[29] While Shelley drew on, alluded to, or translated from all three *cantiche* of the *Commedia*, he preferred the *Paradiso*, 'a perpetual hymn of everlasting love'.[30] In Dante's lines, love renders 'men more amiable, more generous, and wise, and lift[s] them out of the dull vapours of the little world of self'.[31]

Leaving behind the self's 'dull vapours' for the vapours of vision, Shelley, Byron and Keats all composed their own Dantesque visions. Shelley's final, unfinished *Triumph of Life* finds him in Dante's role of sympathetic, urgently interrogating observer, with the Virgilian role played by the errant, miserable Rousseau. Here, as in 'Prince Athanase' and *Ode to the West Wind*, Shelley recreates *terza rima*, the intertwined rhyming tercets perfected by Dante, as a remarkably supple form. Unlike Dante, Shelley does not endstop about half his tercets, rhyming different parts of speech with abandon; like Dante, on the other hand, Shelley accommodates dialogue with dashes, exclamations and interruptions, a technique Byron would use to more awkward effect in 'The Prophecy of Dante'.[32] Keats alone among the major Romantic poets did not know Italian, but when he toured Scotland in 1818, Cary's translation was in his pack.[33] And in *The Fall of Hyperion*, one sip from a 'cool vessel of transparent juice' – yet another 'beaker full of the warm south' – transforms his own epic parent, Milton, into the visionary Dante: 'That full draught is parent of my theme.'[34] Epic in ambition, though not in execution, *The Triumph of Life* and *The Fall of Hyperion* exemplify the Romantic fragmentation of Dante's vision. Cary being an exception, most who translated the *Commedia* undertook discrete episodes, usually from the *Inferno*. The two most popular were the episode of Ugolino (*Inf.* 33) and that of the doomed lovers – and readers – Paolo and Francesca (*Inf.* 2). Leigh

27 *Ibid.*, p. 528.
28 *Ibid.*, pp. 527–8.
29 *Ibid.*, p. 525.
30 *Ibid.*, p. 526.
31 *Ibid.*, p. 525.
32 Pite, *The Circle of our Vision*, p. 184.
33 Brand, *Italy and the English Romantics*, p. 55.
34 John Keats, *Complete Poems*, ed. Jack Stillinger (Cambridge, MA: Harvard University Press, 1982), p. 362.

Hunt's four-book version of this episode, *The Story of Rimini* (1816), stands at the expansive pole of this fragmentary tradition; at the pole of contraction, we find Keats's sonnet, 'On a Dream', whose ninth-line turn catapults him into the lovers' whirlwind.

Though Hunt spent only three years in Italy, his sustained involvement in Italian letters for more than nearly four decades played an important role in the shaping of English tastes. Attacked in Blackwood's in 1817 as a member of the so-called 'Cockney School', Hunt had already drawn attention in *The Examiner* to a group of 'young poets' – Keats, Shelley and John Hamilton Reynolds – whose 'aspiration after real nature and original fancy'[35] was a sign that they had rejected French influence. What Byron called Hunt's 'Italianism'[36] was a strategy designed to distance Hunt and his circle from both neo-classicism and the pieties of the 'Lake School' of Wordsworth and Coleridge. But Hunt's 'Italianism' was also a positive programme, designed to challenge class-based, effete values with erotic, sensuous subjects, and a diction liberated by proximity to the Italian language. Not by accident did he subtitle his journal *The Liberal*, 'Verse and Prose from the South'. So conspicuous were the Cockneys' prose and verse translations (in some cases, free renderings) of Dante, Ariosto, Boccaccio and Tasso, that several anti-Cockney attacks came to centre on the parvenu temerity of translating without knowing Italian. If Hunt's Italian was mostly learned to hand during his sojourns in Genoa, Florence and Maiano (where Boccaccio, 'that many-hearted writer'[37] had set the *Decameron*), he lived to become the premier Italianist of his age, translating more than a score of Italian poets and dramatists. (Charles Cowden Clarke, who introduced Hunt – and, earlier, his Examiner – to Keats, would marry the daughter of Italian composer Vincent Novello; later, the couple settled permanently in Genoa.[38]) Hunt's manifesto against stilted, academic translations of Italian works by those trained in the classics appears in his preface to his 1846 prose work, *Stories of the Italian Poets*: 'Now if I had no acquaintance with the Italian language, I confess I would rather get any friend who had, to read to me a passage out of Dante, Tasso, or Ariosto, into the first simple prose that offered itself, than go to any of the above translators for a taste of it . . .'[39]

35 Leigh Hunt, 'Young Poets', *The Examiner*, 1 December 1816.
36 Byron to Leigh Hunt, 30 October 1815; *Byron's Letters and Journals*, 13 vols., ed. Leslie Marchand (Cambridge, MA: Harvard University Press, 1973–94), vol. IV, p. 326.
37 Hunt, *Autobiography*, p. 371.
38 *The Novello-Cowden Clarke Collection* (Leeds: Brotherton Library, 1955), pp. 5–6.
39 Hunt, *Stories from the Italian Poets* (Paris: Galignani, 1846), p. xi.

Boccaccio was an especially favoured source, probably because his narratives enabled the Cockneys to admit a degree of vulgarity that they defended, in part, by appeal to the robust Middle English narratives of Chaucer. Keats and Reynolds never did fulfil their plan to collaborate on a volume of poems based on the *Decameron*, though Reynolds composed two poems and Keats, more famously, *Isabella, or The Pot of Basil*, which Lamb deemed the highlight of Keats's 1820 volume. Though Keats later disparaged his 'Story from Boccaccio', *Isabella* spoke to another generation of readers; Arnold and the Pre-Raphaelites found in it much to praise, and no wonder:[40] for *Isabella* reminds us that a crucial dimension of Hunt's 'Italianism' was its criticism not only of hoarded cultural capital, but also of the hoarded wealth of industrial capitalism. If *Isabella's* searing indictment of the proud, greedy, exploitative 'ledger men' bespeaks the early, radical phase of Cockney poetry, Hunt's Italianate poetics of fancy would endure to become a staple of bourgeois taste during the first several decades of Queen Victoria.[41] When Hunt died at Putney in 1859, Shelley and Keats had already been dead for three decades, but Joseph Severn, who nursed Keats during his final weeks in Rome, and Edward Trelawny, who had watched the corpse of Shelley burn on the beach near Viareggio, both attended his funeral.[42] Shelley's remains came to lie in the Protestant Cemetery at Rome, not far from the graves of his son William and Keats.

If Dante parented dream-visions and love lyrics, and Boccaccio played the role of bawdy, indulgent uncle, the Italian progenitor of romance was the worldly Ariosto. Wordsworth took *Orlando Furioso* to the Alps in 1790, translating his favourite passages, while Southey credited 'The first of my epic dreams' to Ariosto.[43] Though Keats based his *Isabella* on an episode from Boccaccio, he pored over Ariosto, stanza by stanza, in an attempt to learn Italian. In 1818, the same season Coleridge lectured on Dante and Milton, Hazlitt was lecturing on Ariosto and Spenser. Hunt's 1846 prose rendering of 'The Adventures of Angelica' in *Stories from the Italian Poets*, reminds us that in 1820, even before going to Italy, Hunt translated some sixty stanzas of the *Furioso*. In Scott's *Waverley* and *Ivanhoe*, Ariosto

---

40 See Stillinger's commentary on *Isabella* in Keats, *Complete Poems*, p. 442.
41 Against the views of Hunt as a radical, held by Nicholas Roe and Jeffrey N. Cox, Ayumi Mizukoshi views Hunt primarily as a maker of a 'bourgeois cultural revolution'; see *Keats, Hunt and the Aesthetics of Pleasure* (Basingstoke: Palgrave, 2001), p. 19.
42 James R. Thompson, *Leigh Hunt* (Boston: Twayne, 1977), p. 25.
43 Brand, *Italy and the English Romantics*, p. 74.

overtakes Spenser as the presiding genius of romance; as Scott writes in his 1824 'Essay on Romance', 'Ariosto ... delights us ... by the extreme ingenuity with which he gathers up the broken ends of his narrative, and finally weaves them all handsomely together in the same piece.'[44]

Not surprisingly, Tasso's Jesuitical epic, *Gerusalemme Liberata*, had no such ardent following; Clorinda's sword was nothing to Angelica's charms. Though Shelley read the *Gerusalemme* in Italian before he ever came upon Dante, most who perused it were uninspired. On the other hand, Goethe's tragedy *Torquato Tasso* (1790) led Shelley, Byron, Hemans and Landor each to recreate their own imprisoned poet-hero, betrayed, mad and doomed. Though he abandoned a drama about Tasso in 1818, Shelley used the legend of Tasso's demise as the basis for his poem of 1819, *Julian and Maddalo; A Conversation*. The philosophical Julian and the haughty (though 'gentle, patient, and unassuming') Count Maddalo, are thinly veiled versions of Shelley and Byron. Their genial debate between Julian's idealism and Maddalo's barely tempered nihilism mediates between the paradisal backdrop of Venice and the hellish suffering of the Maniac. Or rather, *should* mediate; for neither Maddalo's generosity nor Julian's anguished sympathy avail to 'reclaim him from his dark estate'. The Maniac, a man betrayed by both his mistress and his philosophy, becomes for Julian a secular martyr, refusing the temptations of bitterness and scepticism. But though Tasso, the epic poet, is the putative model for this heroic figure, the Maniac speaks most resonantly in the voices of two Continental *heroines*: in the anguished cadences of Pope's cloistered Eloisa, and in the incandescent speeches of the imprisoned Beatrice Cenci, over whom Shelley laboured even as he completed *Julian and Maddalo*.

The Italians provided a genealogy not only for Romantic poet-heroes, but for antiheroes as well. Where Ariosto fancifully takes Orlando to the moon, Pulci's *Il Morgante Maggiori* takes him into the realms of high camp, escorted by an ungainly giant who converts to Christianity and vows to serve him. That Byron scoured Pulci is apparent in his translation of Canto I of *Il Morgante Maggiore*, which appeared in the first number of *The Liberal* (1822) with the Italian text on facing pages.[45] In *Beppo: A Venetian Story* (1818), Byron at last accommodates the autobiographical impulse that eclipsed the nominal hero of *Childe Harold's Pilgrimage*. Oscillating between reflection

---

44 Sir Walter Scott, 'Essay on Romance', *Prose Works*, 3 vols. (Edinburgh: Cadell, 1841), vol. I, p. 570.
45 Brand, *Italy and the English Romantics*, p. 85.

and deflection, the narrator frames a louche Venetian tale with a satirical commentary on contemporary British writers, politics, social customs, as well as its own mock-inept poetics. *Beppo* also provides a prototype of the eponymous antihero of *Don Juan*, not to mention its bouncing ottava rima stanzas. For the comic 'passing' of the Venetian-as-Turk who reclaims 'wife, religion, house and Christian name',[46] foreshadows Juan's ability to move deftly among the people of Spain, Greece, Turkey, Russia and finally England. *Beppo*'s comical resolution of fidelity, both marital and religious, acquires considerable irony in *Don Juan*, where Juan's self-fashionings leave him progressively farther from his point of origin and faithful, yes – but to several women.

In Byron's hands, the 'warm south' becomes an eroticized landscape scorched by 'that indecent sun/Who cannot leave alone our helpless clay/ But will keep baking, broiling, burning on . . .' (*DJ* 1:62). These 'sun-burnt nations' discipline sexuality by ritualizing, displaying and performing, not by repressing it: 'What men call gallantry, and gods adultery / Is much more common where the climate's sultry'(*DJ* 1:63). Yet Byron's capacious epic contrasts the crypto-Venetian decadence of Seville with the warm pastoral of Greece. The lengthy Haidée episode of Cantos II, III and IV is paradoxically both a retreat *from* instinct (following the famous stanzas of cannibalism) and a retreat *into* instinct; either way, this is no Edenic point of origin, at least not for Juan. Though what transpires between Juan and Haidée is passion, not dalliance, Byron bumps his lovers against the cult of pure, naive antiquity: 'And thus they form a group that's quite antique / Half naked, loving, natural and Greek' (*DJ* 2:194). On the other hand, although Byron warns that nationalism is a collective narcissism, the pulsing blood of Juan and Haidée floods the blood-and-soil paean to Greek freedom in Canto III ('The isles of Greece, the isles of Greece!').

In the so-called English cantos, Byron, who finally abandoned all plans to return to England in December 1819, sends Juan as his surrogate. These cantos are a fevered thought-experiment in cultural introjection: what would happen were England to embrace southern vitalism? Juan confronts in English womanhood a ferocious vortex: he is swept under the wing of Lady Adeline Amundeville and (most likely) seduced by Lady Fulke-Greville, in the guise of the ghostly Black Friar. Notwithstanding the open drawing room of Lady Adeline – and the open arms of Lady Fulke-Greville – Juan's perverse campaign for the virginal (and resistant) Aurora Raby

46 George Gordon, Lord Byron, *Byron: The Complete Poetical Works*, vol. IV, p. 159.

anticipates something other than an easy, comic embrace – perhaps even the seduction of chilly English maidenhood by the 'sun-burnt' child of the south. In the English cantos Byron, as ever, was looking for trouble.

Mediating sympathy

Don Juan sustains the Romantic regendering of the 'warm south': in lieu of a myth of Italian poet-fathers, we find an allegory of Britain embracing the south as a virile force. But the troubling, incomplete embrace of the English cantos echoes in the Romantic failure to sustain a poetics of identification with liberal causes in Italy and Greece. Shelley, writing *Hellas* in the heady days of the Greek revolt of 1821, declares, 'We are all Greeks.'[47] Yet turning to poems that explicitly embrace these causes, we find instead that the poetics of sympathy compromises, rather than enables, such ardourous identifications.

Felicia Hemans's *Restoration of the Works of Art to Italy* (1816) and *Modern Greece* (1817) both hinge on a problem central to the poetics of sensibility: can art supply an adequate consolation for loss? Whereas the lachrymose sonnets of Charlotte Smith answer this question negatively, Hemans answers positively. What remains to 'degraded Rome' is the sovereignty of art, who has 'rear'd her throne o'er Latium's trophied tomb.' (*RWAI* lines 322–3). Turning to Greece, the fancy's 'bright illusions' (*MG* line 272) must work overtime to envision gods and heroes. Art is not restored to Greece, but rather transferred to England, in the celebrated Elgin marbles. To read the *Restoration* and *Modern Greece* in sequence, however, is to find that the Elgin marbles are not a displacement of Greek glory, but a restoration of lost glory to Britain. For as the closing stanzas of *Modern Greece* imply, they provide restitution for the British lives sacrificed at Waterloo: 'And who can tell how pure, how bright a flame, / Caught from these models, may illume the west? / What British Angelo may rise to fame' (*MG* lines 981–3). Taken together, Hemans's poems powerfully shine the glories of Greek and Italian art on the island nation who 'hast power to be what Athens e'er hath been' (*MG* line 990).

Hemans, eschewing the *mise en abyme* of sentimental effusion, allows the splendours of art to mitigate the degradation of Greece and Italy. For Wordsworth, Shelley and Byron, however, the enthralment of Venice is mediated by the gloom of decay. A mere five years after Napoleon's

---

47 Shelley, *Shelley's Poetry and Prose*, p. 431.

occupation, Wordsworth's 1802 'Sonnet on the Extinction of the Venetian Republic' elides the conquest entirely. Once a 'Child of Liberty . . . a maiden City, bright and free' (lines 4–5), Venice has never been compromised, certainly not by her espousal of 'the everlasting Sea' (line 8). Instead, in cadences that anticipate his sonnet 'Mutability', Wordsworth represents the decline of the Venetian republic as a sublimation, a fading, a vanishing, a decay. Its final extinction, then, is a second-order disappearance, the passing of 'the Shade / Of that which once was great . . .' (line 14).

For both Byron and Shelley, laments for Venice hew to the grotesque, rather than the sublime. Shelley's 'Lines Written among the Euganean Hills' figures Venice – 'Once Ocean's child, and then his queen' (line 116) and finally 'his prey' (line 118) – in grim metaphors of incest and murder. Whereas Venice on her 'watery bier' (line 120) is anthropomorphized, her human occupants are 'Pollution-nourished worms' (line 147) who 'to the corpse of greatness cling . . .' (line 148). Shelley hedges his bets, never wholly surrendering the revolutionary cause, but his admonition to the Venetians is severe: unless 'Freedom' loosens 'the Celtic Anarch's hold' (line 152), Venice is better off beneath the waves. The central conceits of Byron's 'Ode on Venice' correspond to Shelley's: where Shelley's Venetians are vermiform, Byron's are crustaceans who 'creep, / Crouching and crab-like, through their sapping streets' (lines 12–13).[48] And like Shelley, Byron depicts the corpse of Venice *in extremis*, as 'the cold staggering race which Death is winning / Steals vein by vein and pulse by pulse away . . .' (line 40). To Venice, 'a sick man in his sleep' (line 153), Byron contrasts the American Esau, raising its 'red right hands' (line 147) of revolutionary violence. Byron, who forsook the paralyzed Carbonari for the patriotic gore of Greece (where, ironically, his life ended on a sickbed), could only imagine bloody self-sacrifice as an alternative to Venice's watery grave.

Whereas Byron's 'Ode on Venice' erupts in blood, Shelley's odes on the insurrections of 1820–1 disembody the struggle through allegories of liberty and apocalypse. In the 'Ode to Liberty', Shelley invokes not infant nations, but the revival and accomplishment of Jacobin ideals mowed under by Napoleon: that 'human thoughts might kneel alone, / Each before the judgement-throne / Of its own awless soul . . .' (lines 231–3). In the demise of kings and priests, Shelley emphasizes individual conscience, not the *volk*, not the nation. Nor does the 'Ode to Naples', written to celebrate the newly

---

48 George Gordon, Lord Byron, *Byron: The Complete Poetical Works*, vol. IV, p. 201.

granted constitution, explore the particulars of its freedoms. As in the 'Ode to Liberty', the poet traces an oracular voice – 'I felt that Earth out of her deep heart spoke'[49] (line 8) – to Spain, then Naples, then other regions of Italy. The rapidity and fluency with which liberation occurs – without armies, without 'red right hands' – bypasses revolutionary violence in an apocalypse that echoes the closing hymn of *Hellas*: 'faiths and empires gleam / Like wrecks of a dissolving dream'.[50]

In these poems by Hemans, Wordsworth, Shelley and Byron, sympathy describes so great an ambit that the human object of sympathy – put differently, the human subject – is entirely obscured. Whether subject peoples are disembodied, as in Shelley's odes; dismembered, as in Byron's 'Ode on Venice'; sublimated, as in Wordsworth's sonnet; or, as in Hemans's poems, shadowed by the splendour of art, idealization of the object of sympathy cancels the representation of human sufferers. Clearly this idealization occurs across an ideological spectrum, whether we construe the deflections of Hemans and Wordsworth as conservative endorsements of the status quo, or as aesthetic deflections of liberal ideals.

Exactly what this elision of persons means is difficult to say. It may suggest that liberalism, in its very origins, is haunted by the internationalist ideals of the Enlightenment, for we find here a marked resistance to the category of 'the nation'. Alternatively, it may suggest a more complex sense of human psychology than the Germanic theory of national types could support. Less optimistically, it reminds us of the condescension with which both Greeks and Italians were regarded, even by those who spent years among them. But the absence of individual sufferers may also signal a scruple, shared as much by Hemans as the male poets, lest the poem be read – and diminished – as a sentimental effusion. The logic of the English cantos seems to prevail: to embrace these adolescent nations as virile powers feminizes the British subject. Thus, we can interpret the divorcement of political sympathies from sentimentalism as another regendering, this time of the lamenting subject, rather than of the southerners.

As a counterpoint to these idealizing poems of political sympathy, several Romantic writers confront, in Shelley's words, the 'sad reality' of Italian history. Most of these works are composed in the shadow of the failed risings of 1820–1, when both Italians and Greeks took up arms on their own behalf. These tragedies (in which category I include Mary Shelley's novel,

---

49 Shelley, *Shelley's Poetical Works*, p. 611.
50 *Ibid.*, p. 460.

Valperga, and Hemans's tragic monologues) leave behind the effeminizing Germanic notion of Italy as an earthy, naive complement to the brooding, cerebral north. Invoking tragedy, they partake of an alternative, masculine tradition in which heroics and emotion are inextricable. At the same time, they bring the writer's subjectivity in line with that of individual subjects – in line, that is, with subject individuals. In these tragedies of resistance, the simmering beaker of 'warm south' comes to a boil.

Tragedies of resistance: the 'sad reality' of Italian history

During the Regency period, in J. C. de Sismondi's *Histoires des Républiques Italiennes* (1809–18), the historiography of Italy itself becomes a work of resistance. Parrying Gibbon's *Decline and Fall of the Roman Empire* (1776), Sismondi locates the republican ideal in medieval, rather than classical Rome: 'The pre-eminent object of this study – the science of governing men for their advantage, of developing their individual faculties, intellectual and moral, for their great happiness . . . began . . . only with the Italian republics of the middle ages.'[51] Mary Shelley and Byron, in particular, read Sismondi but bypassed Gibbon in favour of earlier Italian sources – Muratori, Villani, Sanuto, Sandi, Navagero and Morelli, among others – while Percy Shelley researched the Cenci story in an unidentified seventeenth-century manuscript, a portrait of Beatrice Cenci and other Cenci 'Monuments' in Rome. In their conspicuous use of early, indigenous, even unpublished, sources, these writers strove for fresh, unmediated encounters with Italian history from an Italian perspective.

My purpose is not to map these tragedies of resistance directly onto the constitutional crises and insurrections in Naples, Piedmont and the Peleponnesus in the early 1820s. Certainly these tragic heroes, male and female, resist too wide an array of powers to make such assignments possible. But in their focus on resistance, Romantic writers make two crucial recognitions. First, for agents in the throes of national or dynastic crises, the politics of gender and family are always implicated. Hence, in each of these works, identity is multifarious and malleable, a crucial, ongoing crisis. Second, acts of resistance are not only represented as simultaneously free and determined, but also their agents experience them as such. Each protagonist veers between a rich sense of his or her own agency, and a keen

---

51 J. C. L. de Sismondi, *History of the Italian Republics* (London: Longman, 1832), p. 1.

sense of being subject to a field of forces beyond one's control, whether cultural, historical or providential.

In Shelley's *The Cenci* (1820), the rape of Beatrice and her parricide – both of which occur offstage – are vortices around which swirl the discourses of public and private, fate and freedom. In the Preface, Shelley notes that 'the fit return to make to the most enormous injuries is . . . a resolution to convert the injurer from his dark passions by peace and love'.[52] But the play gives ample evidence to the contrary, as Beatrice scales tiers of paternal abuse in her vain appeal for justice: priest, pope, patricians and finally, God alike are deaf to her appeal. Temporarily shattered by madness, Beatrice recovers her agency in a pivotal moment of conversion – not her father's, but her own. For Beatrice's parricidal act arises from the belief that 'though wrapped in a strange cloud of crime and shame' she nonetheless '[Lives] ever holy and unstained' (*Cenci* 5.4.148–9). Despite Shelley's shrewd analysis of Catholicism as a culture, rather than a religion, he endorses Beatrice's claim to be 'universal as the light' (*Cenci* 4.4.48); her 'moral deformity' is simply 'the mask and mantle in which circumstances clothed her for her impersonation on the scene of the world'.[53] But it is by these 'cloudy' garments, rather than by her luminous consciousness, that she is known to the tribunal that condemns her to death. When Beatrice's incandescence makes apparent 'the most dark and secret caverns of the human heart',[54] it only deepens the darkness.

The eponymous hero of Byron's *Marino Faliero* (1821) careers between resolving on action and (to borrow a phrase from *The Cenci*) 'self-anatomizing' his own dark heart. When Byron denies in the preface that Faliero is motivated by jealousy, he fatally inflects Faliero's wounded honour as a sexual assault. The sexual wound elaborates in Faliero's forfeiture of both his ducal patrimony and his paternity, his only son, slain on the battlefield defending Venice. Unlike Beatrice Cenci, whose dismantled identity is radically reconstituted, Faliero attempts to restore himself through numerous identifications. He is alternately warrior, noble, rebel against the aristocratic 'Hydra' (*MF* 3.2.238),[55] citizen of Venice, representative of the people and martyr. In his overtures to his wife, identities redouble, as he invokes his 'patriarchal love' (*MF* 2.1.363) for her and 'the violated majesty of Venice' (*MF* 2.1.407). For her part, Angiolina replies

52 Shelley, *Shelley's Poetry and Prose*, p. 142.
53 *Ibid.*, p. 144.
54 *Ibid.*, p. 141.
55 George Gordon, Lord Byron, *Byron: The Complete Poetical Works*, vol. IV, p. 374.

cannily, 'something has stung your pride, not patriotism' (*MF* 2.1.205).[56] (In *The Two Foscari*, Marina makes a similar retort to Jacopo: 'This love of thine / For an ungrateful and tyrannic soil / Is passion, and not patriotism' (*Foscari* 3:1:141–3)). Faliero's resistance fails not because it is hollow, but because it collapses under the weight of its own complex motivation – and who better than Byron to 'anatomize' an overdetermined resistance?

If *The Cenci* and *Marino Faliero* feature the tyrannical abuses of corrupt aristocrats, the tragedies of Mary Shelley and Felicia Hemans adumbrate tragedies of imperialism. In *Valperga; or, the Life and Adventures of Castruccio, Prince of Lucca* (1823), Shelley divides her attention between the Florentine Euthanasia dei Admirari, countess of Valperga, and Castruccio Castracani, a Lucchese condottiere whom Percy Shelley described as 'a little Napoleon' with 'all the passions and the errors of his antitype'.[57] Euthanasia's betrothal to Castruccio founders on the opposition between her vision of a peaceful, civil republic and his autocratic regime of pitiless conquest. But her resistance to both matrimony and political alliance entails an austere transformation of identity; it 'schooled her to the pain and anguish which were afterwards her portion'.[58] Complicating this moralized, gendered standoff, Shelley creates two female figures who parody Euthanasia's power and passion, respectively: Fior di Mandragola, a witch, and the self-described prophet Beatrice, whose fanatical love for Castruccio has left her utterly abject. When Euthanasia allegorizes the 'inner cave' of the soul – a darkness beyond the purview of conscience, the provenance of virtue and vision, madness and sin – we know that her own darkest spaces are, tragically, beyond illumination. Only when she joins a conspiracy against Castruccio does her vitality return, but she is soon taken prisoner and dies a watery death en route to exile.

Similarly, a woman's heroic resistance to imperialism – specifically, the French occupation of Sicily in the late thirteenth century – is the focus of Felicia Hemans's tragedy, *The Vespers of Palermo* (1821). Here, too, betrothal is the nexus of betrayal, now a ruse by which Vittoria, still mourning her beloved Sicilian hero Conradin, delivers her Provençal groom to his death. Appropriately, the vesper bell of her marriage doubles as the call for insurrection in Act III. Like Euthanasia, Vittoria becomes a victim of the violence her conspiracy brings about. But in the final two acts, this tragedy

---

56 *Ibid.*, p. 169.
57 Mary Shelley, *Valperga: Or, the Life and Adventures of Castruccio, Prince of Lucca*, ed. Michael Rossington (Oxford: Oxford University Press, 2000), p. ix.
58 *Ibid.*, p. 114.

is oddly subsumed by another transacted between father and son. In the story of Procida and his son Raimondo, a suspected traitor, Hemans explores in detail how violence disrupts the domestic affections. Procida's love for his son, however shattering, is no match for his stern love of Sicily; once acquitted, Raimondo goes straight to his death in battle, another boy on the burning deck of patriotism. In one sense, the Procidas' story supplies the elided story of Vittoria's great loss of Conradin; indeed, Vittoria sends Raimondo to battle enjoining him to 'Be – Conradin' (Vespers 5.3).[59] But instead of restoring Conradin, the Procida subplot merely augments the damage to the domestic affections, and in Act V, Raimondo's successful liberation of Sicily dissolves in gore and tears.

From the impasse of this tragedy, Hemans would develop the poetics of her dramatic monologues of the 1820s. For Hemans understood that the voice of tragic resistance would gain *gravitas*, rather than lose it, in isolation. Writing monologues in lieu of tragedies (many framed by a third-person speaker), Hemans augments her theme without resort to iterative subplots. Of the thirty-one poems collected in her 1828 volume *Records of Women: With Other Poems*, nearly one-third centre on Italian or Greek female subjects. But in these monologues, Hemans is no less ambivalent about the nationalist cause than she is in *The Vespers of Palermo*. In most cases, she makes no distinctions among the causes of 'mail-clad men' who pursue, in the words of *Costanza*'s dying Cesario, 'the gauds of pride / Whose hollow splendor lured me from her side . . . .'[60] But when Hemans draws lines of identity through gender *instead of nation*, her heroines become resisters of the imperium of male prerogatives. Redescribing resistance for an English audience – an audience weary of foreign wars, domestic unrest and economic depression – Hemans displaces nationalism from homeland to home. Hemans's 'The Sicilian Captive' appears to be an exception, since the bereft Sicilian bride yearns for the 'green land' of Sicily. And yet this poem offers a sharp riposte to Keats's conceit of the 'warm south' in 'Ode to a Nightingale'. For whereas the voice of the Nightingale escapes to 'other glades', the voice of the Sicilian Captive is entirely vanquished by her terrifying ordeal.

Hemans's cautionary tale reminds us what was at stake in taking in 'the warm south': the autonomy not only of sovereignty and culture but also of consciousness. But as these tragedies of resistance suggest, for

---

59 Felicia Hemans, *Poetical Works* (Philadelphia: Grigg and Elliot, 1844), p. 95.
60 *Felicia Hemans: Selected Poems*, p. 394.

the Romantics, the 'warm south' was far more than a frail lyric voice. If anything, their efforts ensured that Britain would remain conscious of the causes of Greece and Italy throughout the century. Indeed, these Romantic writers transformed the cult of the south by bringing gender, class, culture and agency to bear on the phenomenon of subjection. And this transformation prefigures, both politically and culturally, the centrality of the Mediterranean to Victorian culture. From the fostering of Italian refugees, including Mazzini; to the Pre-Raphaelite Brotherhood; to the young men of the Oxford movement; to Bulwer and the Brownings, Ruskin, George Eliot and Swinburne; to the tireless Society of the Friends of Italy, the beaker of Keats would pass on and on. As the momentum for Italian and Greek nationhood increased in the coming decades, Britons at home and abroad would refract their own national crucibles through those of the 'warm south': crucibles of class, cult and gender on the one hand; crucibles of empire, on the other. Most likely, the popularity of the Italian cause with Britons of the late 1840s and 1850s – despite the crown's refusal to intercede – hastened the unification of Italy. But the results for Britain, if less dramatic, were as deeply felt: in the Romantic cult of the south, the 'place elsewhere' relocates to the heart of the British nation, opening up new and liberating possibilities – and with them, new liabilities and dangers.

Country matters

W. J. T. MITCHELL

An enormous amount of British Romantic literary production is situated in the countryside, as a setting for narrated action, a scene for poetic meditation, or a place to write. One thinks immediately of Wordsworth's relation to the Lake District, indeed of a whole school called 'the Lakers' (Wordsworth, Coleridge and Southey); or of a writer like John Clare, identified with the peasantry, or of William Cobbett, a keen and critical observer of the changing character of the countryside in his *Rural Rides*. Landscape painting, most famously exemplified by Constable and Turner, displaces portraiture and history painting in the hierarchy of the visual arts in the Romantic period. The cult of the Picturesque in tourism and landscape gardening becomes a fad and an object of satire in the caricatures of Rowlandson and the novels of Jane Austen. When one thinks of England in the Romantic period, then, one thinks of the country, and it is difficult to imagine what would be left of Romantic literature if it were divested of its natural objects and rural settings, if it lacked flowers, trees, birds, fields, rivers, mountains, seashores and the innumerable 'prospects' that invite the traveller to stop and stare at the countryside. Beyond the literary domain, the country becomes the object of a newly intensified attention in the Romantic period. Local histories, the study of rural customs, folklore and peasant life, antiquarian research into the traces of vanished civilizations, from the Druids to the Romans to the Normans, and scientific inquiries such as geology, archaeology, paleontology and other forms of natural history make the English countryside in this period into an object, not just of nostalgia, sentimentality and aesthetic contemplation, but of new sciences, technologies and industries.

But why does the country matter so much to the Romantics? What is at stake in the obsession with rural scenes? The short answer is perhaps the most telling: the country is *not* the city; it is what stands in contrast to the city, providing an alternative scene of cultural value, a place of retreat and retirement from the metropolis where undisturbed writing can go on, and

where numerous other values can be tapped: cleaner air, quieter surroundings, open spaces, the 'beauteous forms' of unchanging natural
objects such as mountains, rivers, valleys and above all the 'one green hue'
that pervades the English imaginary from Robin Hood's Sherwood Forest
to Shakespeare's Forest of Arden to Andrew Marvell's 'green thoughts in a
green shade'.

But the supposedly non- or anti-urban character of the country is only
one dimension of its use in a variety of discourses that pervade literature,
the arts and the sciences in the Romantic period. The second answer is that
'the country' is not just one thing, but many things – many places and many
kinds of places. In order to see this clearly, we need to reflect on the very
idea of the country, beyond its specific formulation in the Romantic period.

'Country' is, in the vocabulary of cultural geography, the term in which
the dialectics of space, place and landscape are most vividly captured. The
country may be thought of as a specific place or location, as a social 'space'
in which certain human activities are carried on, or as a 'landscape' to be
seen, described or depicted.[1] The word originates in a sense of opposition
and contrariety, stemming from the Latin 'contra', 'against, opposite . . .
that which lies opposite or fronting the view, the landscape spread out
before one' (OED; cf. the German word 'Gegend', against, meaning 'region').
The countryside is thus the locus of difference and resistance, from the
peasant revolt to the Nicaraguan 'contras'. But the countryside as landscape
presents an abject, supine resistance: it does not *stand*, but '*lies* opposite' to
the viewer, like a reclining figure, 'spread out' in a horizontal display as
country-*side*. As such, it is a feminized counterpart to an implicitly erect,
masculine viewer. In its pure, natural, untouched condition it is thus known
as 'virgin country', and is viewed as a beautiful, passive space for fertilization
by the plough of the 'husbandman' and farmer.[2] When *Hamlet* jokes
about lying in the virgin Ophelia's lap, the pun on 'country matters' comes
naturally to his lips (*Hamlet* III.ii.115). The feminized country can, on the
other hand, unpredictably transform itself into its contrary, a phallic,

---

1 The distinction between 'space' and 'place' is elaborated in Michel de Certeau's *The
Practice of Everyday Life* (University of California Press, 1984), pp. 117–18. On the concept
of 'social space', see Henri Lefebvre, *The Production of Space* (London: Blackwell, 1991).
For a discussion of the distinctions among the conceptual triad, 'space, place,
and landscape', see the preface to the 2nd edition of *Landscape and Power*, ed.
W. J. T. Mitchell (Chicago: University of Chicago Press, 2002).
2 See Darby Lewes, *Nudes from Nowhere: Utopian Sexual Landscapes* (New York: Rowman &
Littlefield, 2000) and Annette Kolodny, *The Lay of the Land* (Chapel Hill: University of
North Carolina Press, 1975).

masculinized presence. When Wordsworth is led by mother nature to steal a boat, *father* nature rears up his head in admonition:

> a huge peak, black and huge
> As if with voluntary power instinct
> Upreared its head. I struck and struck again,
> And growing still in stature the grim shape
> Towered up between me and the stars, and still,
> For so it seemed, with purpose of its own
> And measured motion like a living thing,
> Strode after me.
>
> (*The Prelude* I: 378–84)

If the country is a contrary formation in its internal logic, as a gendered place, as aesthetic landscape (beautiful versus sublime), as social or physical space (wild versus cultivated), it is also a contrary to all that lies 'over against' it. The country (as Raymond Williams argues) stands against the city as its alternative, antagonist and counterpart.[3] It is the figure of nature to culture, of rustic past to citified present, of rural 'culture' to urban 'society' and 'civilization', of tradition to modernity. But as a dialectical concept, not a mere binary opposition, the country also contains and absorbs the city into itself as the name of a larger totality – the country as nation – a singular, unified collectivity of people, or the geographical region they occupy. That which opposes and stands apart becomes that which contains. The name of a place becomes the name of the people who dwell in it, and the name of the sovereign who rules over it. And this is a 'proper' name, not a common noun, that applies (as linguists have often noted) 'only to a single being (*God, Milton, London*)',[4] a specific person, place or thing. The proper name thus links identity with property, personhood with ownership, people with the land they belong to and that belongs to them. If that people achieve a collective identity as tribe or nation, the English people personified, for instance, as 'perfidious Albion', the place also takes on personhood: 'Britannia' doesn't just 'rule the waves'; she can suffer, bleed and make demands on her inhabitants. The mother- or father-land becomes the spatial, territorial incarnation of a collective person. We could speak of the 'country's two bodies', just as we do of the sovereign who

---

3 See 'Appendix' to Raymond Williams, *The Country and the City* (New York: Oxford, 1973), p. 307.
4 Oswald Ducrot and Tzvetan Todorov, *Encyclopedic Dictionary of the Sciences of Language*, trans. Catherine Porter (Baltimore: Johns Hopkins, 1979), s.v., 'Proper Names'.

becomes the figural, bodily personification of the people.[5] Thus 'king and country' is what one dies for, a double figure of person and place as representative of a single collective being.

'Country matters' means, then: (1) that the country makes a difference, *marks* a difference, in fact many differences, between parts and wholes, individuals and collectives, and distinctive forms of social space indicated by a host of vernacular oppositions – not just 'country and city', but country and court, country and county, country and town, village, house, farm, citizen, and (perhaps most potent of all) 'other countries'; (2) that the country is a material place, a real habitat composed of earth, stones, vegetation, animals and people, subject to physical re-shaping, destruction, and 'improvement'; (3) that the country is one of those endless, miscellaneous repertoires of 'matters', customs, habits, lore, sayings, skills, local knowledges, histories – in short, the archives of human cultures that happen to be located in or representative of rural areas.

The vast detail and intricacy of these subjects, each of which has a voluminous literature associated with it, is made even more intimidating by the limitations of an American perspective on England. How can someone who lacks the intimate sense of local history woven into personal memory capture the 'genius of a place' like England? Raymond Williams's classic, *The Country and the City* haunts any attempt to deal adequately, not just with the literary representation of the English countryside, but of any countryside whatsoever.[6] Williams weaves into his magisterial history of English literary landscapes a personal sense of place (not to mention a public commitment) that seems both necessary and inimitable. This writer's sense of place is mainly rooted in childhood memories of the Nevada desert and the foothills of the Sierra Mountains, a land of sagebrush, mesquite, and cactus, of arroyos, canyons, mesas, buttes and gulches. England's 'green and pleasant land' of heaths, meadows, wolds, copses, commons, downs, hedgerows, moors, fens, rivers and seashores[7] is almost as remote from this sensibility as Jerusalem, which may be the reason many Americans first come to the English countryside through its writers, especially its Romantic writers. In this text, the principal gateway to the country will be the poetry

5 Ernst Hartwig Kantorowicz, *The King's Two Bodies: A Study in Medieval Political Theology* (Princeton: Princeton University Press, 1957).

6 Raymond Williams, *The Country and the City*.

7 See Alan Everitt, *Landscape and Community in England* (London: The Hambledon Press, 1985), p. 16, for a topographical classification of the types of English countryside or *pays*.

of William Blake. Of all the Romantics, Blake is the poet who seems most alien to scenes of rural life. Resolutely opposed to 'natural religion', and what Jerome McGann called 'the Romantic ideology',[8] Blake is a poet of the city, or more precisely, of the *metropolis*, the unevenly expanding city that is invading the countryside. When Blake repairs to the countryside, to the coast of Felpham, for instance, he regards it as a 'three years slumber on the banks of the ocean' in which the muses can dictate new epic poems to him. When he attends to rural England, it is not to describe the picturesque beauties of the country, but to enumerate the *counties* as artificial creations of the human imagination:

> Here Los fixd down the Fifty-two Counties of England and Wales
> The Thirty-six of Scotland, & the Thirty-four of Ireland.
>
> (E 160; J 16:28–9)[9]

The counties of Britain are, for Blake, 'gates' that lead to 'all the Kingdoms & Nations & Families of the Earth', all descended from the scattered tribes of Israel:

> The Gate of Reuben in Carmarthenshire: the Gate of Simeon in
> Cardiganshire: & the Gate of Levi in Montgomeryshire.
>
> (E 160; J 16:35–6)

Blake's English countryside is a holy landscape, the centre of an anti-imperialist 'British Zionism' that envisions the unity of the human form in all races and regions of the world, as expressed in the figure of Albion ('all-be-one'), the sleeping giant whose 'couch of death' is the British Isles, and whose name resonates with the whiteness of the Dover cliffs.

> Then Albion rose up . . .
>
> . . . his face is toward
> The east, toward Jerusalems Gates: groaning he sat above
> His rocks. London & Bath & Legions & Edinburgh
> Are the four pillars of this Throne; his left foot near London
> Covers the shades of Tyburn; his instep from Windsor
> To Primrose Hill stretching to Highgate & Holloway
> London is between his knees: its basements fourfold

8 Jerome McGann, *The Romantic Ideology* (Chicago: University of Chicago Press, 1985).
9 All citations to Blake are from *The Complete Poetry and Prose of William Blake*, ed. David V. Erdman, newly revised edition (Garden City, NY: Anchor Doubleday, 1982), hereafter designated as 'E' followed by the page number. All the quotations are from Blake's poem 'Jerusalem', indicated by a 'J' followed by the plate and line number, or 'Milton', indicated by an 'M' followed by plate and line number.

His right foot stretches to the sea on Dovers cliffs, his heel
On Canterburys ruins; his right hand covers lofty Wales
His left Scotland; his bosom girt with gold involves
York, Edinburgh, Durham, & Carlisle & on the front
Bath, Oxford, Cambridge, Norwich; his right elbow
Leans on the rocks of Erins Land, Ireland ancient nation.

(E 140; M 39:32–45)

Blake is perhaps alone among the Romantics in achieving a totally comprehensive vision, not just of England, but of Britain, and its place in the world. He achieves this, of course, by sacrificing all local detail: Wales is 'lofty'; Dover has 'cliffs'. He only becomes specific about places when he is naming them, turning them into persons:

Cities / Are Men, fathers of multitudes, and Rivers & Mountains
Are also Men; every thing is Human.

(E 180; J 34:47–8)

and understanding those person / places not as passive regions or locales, but as active agents in a dynamic, terrifying drama, from the places of human sacrifice, which from Stonehenge to Tyburn's Tree still resonate with the cries of victims, to the new industrial cities and farms, where rural unrest and rick-burning were in the air:[10]

Hampstead Highgate Finchley Hendon Muswell hill: rage loud
Before Bromions iron Tongs & glowing Poker reddening fierce
Hertfordshire glows with fierce Vegetation! In the Forests
The Oak frowns terrible, the Beech & Ash & Elm enroot
Among the Spiritual fires: loud the Corn fields thunder along

(E 159; J 16:1–5)

Philippe de Loutherbourg's paintings of rural industry (e.g., *Coalbrookdale by Night*, 1801) convey the sense that whatever the 'Romantic countryside' was, it was not merely a pastoral retreat, but a site of radical, even violent transformation. Blake understands this as a revolutionary, even apocalyptic transformation. He calls the places 'by their English names', but understands 'English' to be the 'rough basement' of a built country-side whose 'eternal name' is Jerusalem.

There is a deep problem of perspective, then, in trying to see as a whole something called 'the country' (much less a place called 'England') in the

---

10 See David Erdman, *Blake: Prophet Against Empire* (Princeton: Princeton University Press, 1954), for a discussion of rural unrest.

Romantic period. If Blake cannot see the trees for the forests, the other Romantics generally focus on the individual trees at the expense of comprehensive coverage. The poetry of place, of what Wordsworth called 'the naming of places', of personal 'spots of time', of regions, countrysides and natural objects dominates literary and artistic production in this period. Constable is fond of painting portraits of specific trees, and Wordsworth insists on the particular at every turn:

> But there's a Tree, of many, one
> A single Field which I have looked upon.

Local histories like Gilbert White's *A Natural History of Selbourne* focus our attention not just on the broad contours of the landscape, but the ditches and minutiae of local flora and fauna. Edward Hasted's *History and Topographical Survey of the County of Kent* (1750–90) was, as its dates suggest, a lifetime's labour that deposited three million words on one county's landscape. The amount of natural and archaeological detail in the English countryside is rivalled by the amount of words and images that have been lavished on its analysis and description.[11]

And this is not merely a matter of describing what meets the eye in the present moment of observation. Perhaps because it is an island of modest, compact dimensions that has been under cultivation since prehistoric times, subject to repeated conquests, clearances and migrations, English topography is a rich palimpsest of history (perhaps rivalled only by the 'Holy Land' to which Blake compares it).[12] There has not been a primeval forest in England since the Mesolithic era (around 8,000 BC). The countryside is marked by stone age settlements, burial mounds, fortifications and ritual places; Teutonic outposts, Anglo-Saxon villages, Roman roads and forts, Norman castles, Cistercian abbeys, Reformation churches and Georgian hedgerows. Even where there is no mark of human habitation, one feels everywhere in England the sense that even the most remote areas have been visited, witnessed, cultivated and marked. There is no place in this island, as the mangled cliché goes, 'where the hand of man hath not trod'.

---

11 See also *Cary's New Itinerary* (London: John Cary, 1817), a reference book that, from the 1780s onwards, provides maps and mileages for every road and footpath in England.

12 If one compares England to the European mainland in this respect, it is notable that its population per square mile has been denser than any European nation since the Iron Age.

The Romantic period is the historical moment when awareness of the countryside as a deep palimpsest of inscriptions, traces, relics, fossils, ruins and monuments begins to dawn on English consciousness. It is also a moment of profound changes in the physical character of the English countryside – the beginnings of modern industry, road and canal systems, and agriculture. It is thus a period of a double 'marking' of the country: on the one hand, revolutionary transformations of the material landscape; on the other, a new awareness of the country, a 're-marking' on or noticing of the degree to which the land had been re-shaped by human and geological activity in the past. Landscape historians generally divide the history of the English countryside into three periods, punctuated by rapid, revolutionary transformations: (1) the Bronze Age (around 1600 BC) when the population rose from a few thousand to over a million people, and thousands of new settlements and hilltop fortifications appeared, along with field systems and a variety of weapons; (2) the long medieval period (eighth to twelfth centuries AD) when the great majority of English villages, with their familiar 'green and single street' pattern were created by the deliberate planning of feudal lords, along with the system of open or common fields; (3) the period of 'parliamentary enclosure' from the 1750s onward, 'a complete transformation, from the immemorial landscape of the open fields . . . into the modern checquer-board pattern of small, squarish fields, enclosed by hedgerows of hawthorn, with new roads running . . . across the parish in all directions'. During this period, as Raymond Williams notes, 'more than six million acres of land were appropriated, mainly by the politically dominant landowners' as a result of 4,000 Acts of Parliament.[13] Although the process of Enclosure had been going on since the thirteenth century, it reached a peak of intensity during the Romantic era.

This story of 'the making of the English landscape' was told for the first time in the era since the Second World War by the British geographer W. G. Hoskins in his book by that title, and it has remained (with some qualifications) the canonical narrative for half a century.[14] The one part of his story that survives unchallenged is his account of the impact of Enclosure, which has achieved mythic status (along with the industrial

13 Williams, *The Country and the City*, p. 96.
14 See W. G. Hoskins, *The Making of the English Landscape* (London: Hodder and Stoughton, 1955). The qualifications are those of Christopher Taylor, who provides notes and commentary on the 1988 re-issuing of Hoskins's classic text. Among the qualifications that would now have to be registered: for fairly transparent ideological reasons, Hoskins probably underestimated the impact of the four centuries of Roman

revolution) as the great transformative and modernizing revolution of the English countryside. Enclosure is mythic because it has been condensed into vivid, memorable images that were already familiar in the Romantic period, from Oliver Goldsmith's *Deserted Village*, especially as illustrated by Thomas Bewick's famous 1795 image of dispossessed country villagers leaving their homes, to Crabbe's *The Village*, which documented the painful truth of the modernized English countryside in contrast to the pretty fictions of the literary pastoral, to the peasant poet John Clare's laments for the vanishing heaths and patches of wilderness.

> Ye meadow-blooms, ye pasture-flowers farewell!
> Ye banish'd trees, ye make me deeply sigh
> Inclosure came, and all your glories fell:
> E'en the old oak that crown'd yon rifled dell
> Whose age had made it sacred to the view.
>
> (Clare, in Hoskins, 158)

Raymond Williams, in *The Country and the City*, warns against making too much of Enclosure in sentimental and nostalgic narratives of rural life as an ideal golden age destroyed by modernity:

> the idea of enclosures, localised to just that period in which the Industrial Revolution was beginning, can shift our attention from the real history and become an element of that very powerful myth of modern England in which the transition from a rural to an industrial society is seen as a kind of fall, the true cause and origin of our social suffering and disorder. But it is also a main source for that last protecting illusion in the crisis of our own time: that it is not capitalism which is injuring us, but the more isolable, more evident system of urban industrialism. (p. 96)

Another name for this myth is 'Romanticism', understood as a 'localizing' of the mythic fall from a golden age in a specific period in English cultural history from 1750–1850. One aspect of the Gothic revival that swept the English countryside in the Romantic period is a nostalgia for the pre-Enclosure period of feudal agriculture, when country lords ruled over a supposedly contented peasantry in organic, settled communities. A critic of the modernized countryside like Cobbett could seem simultaneously like a

---

settlement, with its extensive system of road building, fortification and clustered settlements, notably around the 'villa', from which the modern word for 'village' descends, and he overestimated the impact of the Saxon 'invasion' in the Dark Ages (England was not, as Hoskins believed, in a wild and primitive state, but thoroughly tamed by the Roman presence).

radical Jacobin in his hostility toward the absentee landlords, and like a Tory in his yearning for the organic, face-to-face relations of Merrie Englande.[15]

When Williams invokes 'capitalism' rather than the industrial trans-formation of the country as the 'true cause' of this fall, however, he may be invoking just another version of the Romantic myth. The groundwork for the critique of capitalism was, after all, being laid in this period, and not just by radicals like Blake and Shelley, but by conservatives such as Edmund Burke, who saw the country, the 'landed interest', as the main source of political opposition to the 'monied interest', the new class of capitalists and bourgeois intellectuals who were making a revolution in France. Although writing as an English socialist, Williams is too intellectually honest to pretend that Marxism had ever been any 'greener' in its politics than cap-italism. Written in the immediate aftermath of the attempt to re-stage a peasant-led 'Cultural Revolution' in Maoist China, *The Country and the City* is still caught up in the pastoral myth it attempts to criticize. It does succeed in historicizing that myth, decisively putting an end to the ever-repeated notion that some agrarian golden age 'that has come down to us from the days of Virgil' (p. 9) was passing away in their time – or in ours. Williams finds this mythic pattern repeated in the nostalgic invocations of vanished 'organic communities' that roll back into the past, as if we were riding on an escalator but could only see the step immediately behind us. But Williams was quite aware that he himself had not succeeded (nor did he want to succeed) in getting over the mystique of the country, the longing for a natural and native 'grounding' for moral and political certainty. Two hundred years after Wordsworth and Blake, the relation of 'the green and pleasant land' to the new social order Blake called 'Jerusalem' is still as urgent as it was for the Romantics. 'Nature' has never been a more potent issue than in our time, when the secret of life itself has been decoded, every natural organism and agricultural product may be re-designed and engin-eered, and when the countryside under the sway of advanced capitalism has almost completed the process of industrial transformation that began in the Romantic era. It is understandable, therefore, why it is so easy to think of Romanticism as the foundational moment of modern ecology and Green politics.[16]

15 See Kevin M. Gilmartin, *Print Politics: The Press and Radical Opposition in Early Nineteenth-Century England* (Cambridge: Cambridge University Press, 1996), for an excellent discussion of the complexity of Cobbett's position.
16 See Jonathan Bate, *Romantic Ecology* (London: Routledge, 1991), one of the founding texts of the emergent discipline of 'ecocriticism'.

While it is possible to trace sentiments about rural England back to Shakespeare and Chaucer, and to follow a development of pastoral and country-house writing from Sidney to Marvell to Pope, the *grounding* of those sentiments (if I may resort to a pun) in the real history of the earth, in the 'rocks and stones and trees' of rural England is a distinct development of the 'Romantic century' that stretches from the mid eighteenth to mid nineteenth century. In this period, a well-documented set of revolutions – industrial, social, political and technological – transforms England from a rural, agrarian economy into a world of commercial, industrial and imperial power. 'The accumulation of men in cities', as Wordsworth put it, the rise of new industrial towns, and the depopulation of the countryside, the acceleration of the enclosure of common fields and the disappearance of the English peasantry leads to a transvaluation of the countryside. As rural life seems to recede in the rear-view mirror of history it becomes all the more valuable, all the more in need of preservation, documentation, interpretation and representation in all the artistic media – painting, poetry, the novel, popular dioramas, tour guides, picture books – not to mention historical and scientific description. The end point of this process is the 'museification' of the entire English countryside, which seems at the threshold of the twenty-first century to have become one enormous theme park combining heritage industry with cultural and ecotourism. Hoskins's classic study, *The Making of the English Landscape*, written in the wake of the Second World War, at the threshold of its decline from a world power into a relatively minor nation with a glorious past and a picturesque countryside, is symptomatic of this transformation.

It is significant that E. P. Thompson's equally classic work of social history, *The Making of the English Working Class* (1966) takes its title from a book about the country. For one thing, the two histories are deeply intertwined. The working classes of England come into modern capitalism from the countryside; the depopulation of rural England, Enclosure, and the Industrial Revolution are all related events. 'Class' and 'country' are parallel concepts, deeply resonant with one another. 'Country people' are a kind of class, and work, labour, industry – planting and ploughing, herding, excavating, draining – are the kinds of activities that make a landscape what it is. 'Landscape' is, in fact, 'shaped land', whether shaped by physical transformation, or rendered as a 'view' or 'image' in some medium or other.

It would be tempting to conclude, then, that Romanticism simply *is* the aestheticization of nature and the countryside, or (even more broadly) its 'mediatization'. But perhaps the most potent mediation of the country articulated in this period is a political not an aesthetic one, namely, Edmund Burke's contention that political representation cannot be confined to men (women being out of the question) but must extend to the land itself, to landed property. Burke saw the representation of the country, of landed interests, as a crucial check and balance to the emergent interests of mobile capital and commerce. He thought the French Revolution had been led by the new class of volatile, energetic capitalists and urged that this 'monied interest' be countered by representing the sluggish, traditional tempera-ments of the 'landed interest'.[17]

What Burke's notion of 'representing the country' comes to in practice, of course, is representing the interests of an increasingly small elite of landed gentry who came into possession of most of the English countryside in this period. One name for the landscape aesthetic constructed by and for this class is 'the picturesque', a term that (like Romanticism itself) still endures as an ill-defined set of formulas for attractive objects and scenes. The relation between the picturesque and the Romantic could be charted as a short history of the way Romanticism has been defined in twentieth-century scholarship. Christopher Hussey's pioneering book on the subject makes it a centrally Romantic phenomenon, but one could find as many arguments that it is antithetical to 'High' Romanticism, with its elevated sentiments, and its tragic aesthetics of the sublime and the beautiful. The picturesque is often regarded as a kind of bourgeois affectation of good taste; it is closely associatied with kitsch and superficial tourism, and Wordsworth's famous repudiation of it still resonates. Nevertheless, it seems fair to say that the picturesque has begun to nudge out the grand thematics of the sublime in recent Romantic studies, asserting itself as a complex set of concepts and images that are woven in and out of the highly contested concept of Romanticism. At the very least, the resurgence of critical, historical interest in the picturesque is testimony to the 'pictorial turn' in contemporary Romantic studies, and in literary studies more gen-erally, which has made visual culture a crucial aspect of the study of verbal culture.

---

17 A similar division of representation between people and country is reflected in the lower and upper houses of the English Parliament and the House and Senate of the US Congress. Nebraska and New York have exactly the same number of senators, even though the latter has many times more inhabitants. When the senator (literally, the 'elder' or 'senex') speaks, he speaks for the country as land.

Perhaps the most fundamental thing to be said about it is that the concept of the picturesque is a thoroughly circular reduction of the countryside to a visual image: certain scenes remind the viewer of certain kinds of pictures (typically, landscape paintings by Claude Lorrain, Nicholas Poussin or Salvator Rosa), and those pictures in turn remind the viewer of certain kinds of scenes. William Gilpin, who gave the word its earliest English currency in 1768 defines it simply as 'that kind of beauty which would look well in a picture'.[18] Richard Payne Knight traces the entire circle in his *Analytical Inquiry into the Principles of Taste* (1805), as a product of the association of ideas:

> this very relation to painting, expressed by the word *picturesque*, is that, which affords the whole pleasure derived from association; which can, therefore, only be felt by persons, who have correspondent ideas to associate; that is by persons in a certain degree conversant with that art. Such persons being in the habit of viewing, and receiving pleasure from fine pictures, will naturally feel pleasure in viewing those objects in nature, which have called forth those powers of imitation and embellishment . . . The objects recall to mind the imitations . . . and these again recall to the mind the objects themselves.[19]

The appreciation of the picturesque in the arts and in nature, then, is a kind of feedback loop of visual cultivation and self-improvement. It is an elite, refined taste, available only to the connoisseur of art and nature. 'The peasant', notes Knight, 'treads . . . unheeded' over all the curious and interesting objects that excite this circuit of 'recollection' and 'enjoyment' (HW 348).

'Variety' and 'intricacy' are usually cited as the 'objective' criteria for the picturesque, as formulated by Knight's close friend, Uvedale Price, in his *Essay on the Picturesque* (1794):

> Intricacy in landscape might be defined [as] that disposition of objects which, by a partial and uncertain concealment, excites and nourishes

---

18 John Dixon Hunt and Peter Willis (eds.), *The Genius of the Place: The English Landscape Garden, 1620–1820* (New York: Harper & Row, 1975), p. 337.

19 *Ibid.* pp. 349–50. This is the best anthology of the many scattered writings on landscape and the picturesque. Hunt and Willis gather together the primary documents from the seventeenth century, including the English country-house poem, Milton's description of Paradise, as well as eighteenth-century reflections on gardening, landscape and rural scenery by Daniel Defoe, James Thomson, Alexander Pope, Joseph Addison, Henry Fielding, Joseph Warton and William Gilpin. For the sake of convenience, many of my references to the original writings on the picturesque will be to this anthology, hereafter referred to as 'HW'.

curiosity. . . As intricacy in the disposition, and variety in the forms, the tints, and the lights and shadows of objects, are the great characteristics of picturesque scenery; so monotony and baldness are the greatest defects of improved places . . . (HW 354)

The picturesque is thus defined contrastively, as the antithesis to the 'shaved' lawns and bald prospects of Capability Brown, whose massive 'improvements' to country estates in the late eighteenth century had, by the Romantic period, come to stand for a sterile and unnatural formula associated with a nakedly artificial beauty. It is also located, as Price argues, in a kind of middle location between Burke's categories of the beautiful and the sublime:

Picturesqueness, therefore, appears to hold a station between beauty and sublimity; and on that account, perhaps, is more frequently and more happily blended with them both than they are with each other. It is, however, perfectly distinct from either. (HW 354)

As should be evident, the picturesque was just definite enough to achieve independent status as an aesthetic category, and just vague enough to absorb almost any sentiment one wanted to attach to it. It was the perfect aesthetics for the political party known as the 'country Whigs' in the late eighteenth century, the party of Edmund Burke and James Fox. Progressive, liberal, nationalistic, the Whigs were suspicious of the court and the city, and above all, represented the country aristocracy that was chiefly responsible for the material re-shaping of the English countryside in the Romantic period. The picturesque was the ideal formula for synthesizing a vision of the nation as grounded in the country and expressed in the visual character of the landscape. It was a kind of 'trimmer's' aesthetic, identified with 'mixtures' of contrasting compositional elements, including the 'mixed' political constitution which balanced the powers of Church and State, Court and Country, City and Country, the House of Commons and the House of Lords.[20] As a national style, it could trace its pedigree to Milton's description of Paradise, 'a happy rural seat of various view', through Pope's Edenic vision of Windsor Forest, 'where unity in variety we see / And where, though all things differ, all agree', to Hogarth's *Analysis of Beauty*, which established the famous serpentine path or river as the emblem of variety and curiosity within the stabilizing framework of perspective. The

20 See Sidney Robinson, *An Inquiry into the Picturesque* (Chicago: University of Chicago Press, 1991).

national provenance of this landscape aesthetic was reinforced, despite its associations with Italian landscape painting, by contrast with French garden styles, which were seen as abstract, geometrical and artificial, right down to the details of topiary sculpture. The association of France with mathematical regularity, artificiality and political absolutism was a perfect foil to the 'English' aesthetic of irregularity, naturalness, informality and (of course) political liberty.[21]

In a very real sense, then, a central figure of Romantic aesthetics – the construction of the English countryside as an ideal combination of art and nature, an earthly paradise or garden 'walled in' by its providential coastline, reached right back into the seventeenth century, and, indeed, back to the origins of mankind.[22] 'All things begin and end in Albions rocky shore', noted Blake, registering the degree to which the English countryside had become a mythic entity in his time. But it is equally important to note that the picturesque, while it needed to trace its roots to an immemorial past (like the nation or country itself), was simultaneously a very modern phenomenon that was first articulated in the early Romantic period. Perhaps the best way to clarify this is to say that a long-lived aesthetic tradition (involving mixture, variety, intricacy) that could be traced back to the grotesqueries of Roman villa ornament, was given new life and a new name in the Romantic period. More specifically, this aesthetic category, which linked painting, landscape gardening, literary description and tourism, underwent a crisis in this period. It had scarcely been formulated as a distinct category when it immediately became associated with political radicalism, impractical idealism, Gothic excess and a formulaic body of touristic clichés that had to be overcome in favour of a more authentic encounter with the countryside. Rowlandson satirized the picturesque as a loony, middlebrow obsession (see his famous caricature of the picturesque traveller/painter, 'Dr Syntax in search of the picturesque'). Jane Austen pokes fun at pretentious landscape connoisseurs in *Northanger Abbey*, and dramatizes Elizabeth Bennett's good sense in *Pride and Prejudice* by showing her approval of Pemberley, Mr Darcy's well-managed country estate as a

---

21 See John Dixon Hunt, *The Figure in the Landscape: Poetry, Painting, and Gardening during the Eighteenth Century* (Baltimore: Johns Hopkins University Press, 1976).

22 Michael Drayton's *Poly-Olbion* (London: Humphrey Lownes, 1612; 1622), as its title suggests, is an extended song in praise of 'English variety', in which the rivers, mountains, valleys and indeed the entire topography of Britain are personified and dramatized in a series of historical narratives, lyrics of praise and singing competitions.

key moment in overcoming her prejudices against his apparent bad manners. Humphrey Repton, a prominent landscape gardener who had been attacked for his 'Brownian' tendencies by Price and Knight, counterattacked by ridiculing the intrusion into the placid English countryside of wild and unkempt 'scenes of horror, well calculated for the residence of Banditti' out of Salvator Rosa. Repton reminded people that what might be appealing in a painting or Gothic novel was not necessarily what was desirable in a real landscape design of a real place, and that the picturesque was as likely to become an oppressive system as any other fad that appropriated the authority of either 'the natural' or a pictorial genre to its cause, without respect for the individual character of a country scene – the 'genius of the place'.[23] Horace Walpole accused Knight of being a Jacobin who 'would level the purity of gardens . . . and as malignantly as Tom Paine or Priestley guillotine Mr. Brown'.[24] Under the pressure of the French Revolution, even the conservative, elitist rhetoric of Whig 'liberty' was likely to trigger a hostile reaction.

No matter how harshly it was criticized, however, the picturesque survives as one of the enduring legacies of the Romantic approach to country matters. It goes on to become the key principle in the work of the most influential of modern urban park designers, Frederick Law Olmsted, whose Central Park in New York, and its numerous relatives around North America, from San Francisco to Chicago to Montreal, democratizes the aristocratic form of the picturesque English landscape garden by eliminating the manor house as an (absent) sign of public ownership. It becomes the aesthetic motivation for a wide range of rural practices that go well beyond superficial tourism, and engage with a deeper sense of the temporality of the countryside inscribed in history and memory. Above all, it serves as the most potent ideological image of the countryside in its capacity to naturalize artificial conditions, and to manage contradictions. The great American earth artist Robert Smithson called the picturesque the 'dialectical landscape' in its mediations of the sublime and beautiful, wildness and order, creation and destruction, revelation and concealment, ownership and

---

23 See Stephen Daniels's defence of Price's commitment to responsible 'husbandry' in the management of the countryside. 'Humphrey Repton and the Improvement of Estate', in *Fields of Vision: Landscape Imagery and National Identity in England and the United States* (Princeton: Princeton University Press, 1993).

24 See Horace Walpole, 1796 letter to George Mason, in *Correspondence* (New Haven: Yale University Press, 1974). Discussed in Sidney Robinson, *Inquiry into the Picturesque* (Chicago: University of Chicago Press, 1991), p. 79.

destitution.[25] The picturesque is, in short, the aesthetic regime that stages the 'contra' character of country. It is perhaps the fundamental reason why all modern and postmodern notions of the countryside and the natural environment – and of space, place, and landscape, more generally – trace their genealogies to Romanticism.

There are three principal issues that must be considered in any account of the reframing of the English countryside by the Romantic picturesque. First is the question of the country as a socio-economic space whose real conditions are, in general, masked or softened by the picturesque aesthetic, so that beggars, gypsies, and 'rural vagrants' are not erased, but actually transformed into picturesque attractions, and rural labour is, as a rule, kept out of sight. Second is the question of time and the past, of memory and history inscribed on – and erased from – the rural landscape. Third is the re-enchantment of the country as an animate being with agency, desire and an autonomous existence – the 'genius of the place' for which Blake's name is Albion. We might summarize these topics in dialectical terms as the tensions between property and poverty, the legibility and illegibility of the past, and personal identity and impersonal nature. Let us take them up in that order.

The tensions between property and poverty

In the aftermath of the work of Raymond Williams, John Barrell, Ann Bermingham and numerous other scholars working within a materialist tradition, it has been impossible to view the Romantic picturesque without an awareness of its function as an ideological mystification. On the other hand, this explanation of the picturesque and of the Romantic view of the country does not 'explain away' the complexity and resilience of its specific aesthetic formulations.[26] The question arises: what are those poor folks *doing* in the Romantic landscape? What are the 'vagrant dwellers in the houseless woods', the Leech-Gatherer, the crazy women, and John Clare's gypsies up to? Or, more precisely, what are Romantic poetry, painting, tourism and other representational media up to in their fixation on figures

---

25 Robert Smithson, 'Frederick Law Olmstead and the Dialectical Landscape', in *The Writings of Robert Smithson: Essays with Illustrations* (New York: NY University Press, 1979).

26 I draw in much of what follows on Raimonda Modiano's brilliant essay, 'The Legacy of the Picturesque: Landscape, Property, and the Ruin', in *The Politics of the Picturesque: Literature, Landscape, and Aesthetics since 1770*, ed. Stephen Copley and Peter Garside (Cambridge: Cambridge University Press, 1994).

of destitution, abjection and ruination in the countryside? What pleasure lurks in the attention to these picturesque 'objects'? Is it the righteous indignation of a Cobbett or Blake? The melancholy and tragic dignity of Wordsworth? The intense sympathy and radical identification of Clare? Or is it the complacent pleasure of the picturesque tourist who congratulates herself on her distance from the less fortunate and treats the destitute figure as a compositional element (like ruins or an unmarked grave) that provides a nice contrast to scenes of natural beauty and abundance?

> Is this a holy thing to see,
> In a rich and fruitful land,
> Babes reduced to misery,
> Fed with cold and usurous hand?

The answer, in Blake's deepest, most mordant irony, is 'yes'. This is a 'holy sight', one that is all too typical, all too representative of what the sacred, fruitful countryside of England is – a place of continued human sacrifice, where Druid priests (as Wordsworth also saw) still dismember the human form, now on the altars of capital. The holy sight of already sacrificed human beings in the 'rich and fruitful land' is exactly the sort of 'contrast' on which the picturesque thrives. 'Invariably I have observed', notes Cobbett, 'that the richer the soil, and the more destitute of woods; that is to say, more purely a corn country, the more miserable the labourers.' Labourers 'invariably do best in the *woodland* and *forest* and *wild* countries. Where the mighty grasper has *all under his eye*, they can get but little.'[27]

The picturesque is a multiply articulated answer to Cobbett's observation. First, it avoids the rich (but boring) corn country and its workers. 'A working country is hardly ever a landscape', notes Williams, and the workers, whether ragged or bold, well-fed yeomen like the figures of G. R. Lewis's *Hereford, Dynedor, and the Malvern Hills* (1816) are not picturesque.[28] The picturesque takes us to the woodland, the forest and the wild, and it does not look at the workers who have prospered there, but the unemployed vagrants who have taken refuge or are (like the tourist) just passing through. And the tourist is, of course, by definition *not* 'the mighty grasper' who owns the land and exploits

---

27 Cobbett, *Rural Rides*, quoted in Williams, *The Country and the City*, p. 109. An excellent depiction of 'the mighty grasper' at work protecting his fields is a painting by William de Root entitled *Lincolnshire Landscape*. The painting shows a woman with a fistful of corn that she has gleaned from the leavings on the ground, fleeing from the angry squire galloping after her on horseback.

28 Copley & Garside (eds.), *The Politics of the Picturesque*, p. 18

the workers, but a free spirit, on holiday from business and the cares of property. The relation of tourist to the destitute is, therefore, one of simultaneous identification and dis-identification. Both the viewer and the viewed are idle, unemployed wanderers, both liberated from ownership and exchange. Their difference is marked visibly by spatial distance (the destitute must be in the 'middle distance' of the view, close enough to be observed and sketched, but not too close for comfort). It is marked invisibly by the peculiar complex of envy and superiority that characterizes the picturesque aesthetic at its most obnoxious. Jean Genet captures this complex perfectly in his description of French tourists in Barcelona from the point of view of the beggars they love to photograph:

> Foreigners in this country, wearing fine gabardines, rich, they recognized their inherent right to find these archipelagoes of poverty picturesque, and this visit was perhaps the secret, though unavowed, purpose of their cruise. Without considering that they might be wounding the beggars, they carried on, above their heads, an audible dialogue, the terms of which were exact and rigorous, almost technical.
> 'There's a perfect harmony between the tonalities of the sky and the slightly greenish shades of the rags.'
> '. . . something out of Goya . . .'
> 'It's interesting to watch the group on the left. There are things of Gustave Doré in which the composition . . .'
> 'They're happier than we are.'[29]

The picturesque stations the viewer as foreigner, and the Italian provenance of the English word, combined with the pictorial tradition that re-shapes the English countryside in the image of Italian landscape painting, suggests that, in a very real sense, the picturesque movement was the transformation of England's 'green and pleasant land' into a foreign country. The picturesque flourished during the period when wars with France prevented English tourists from visiting Europe, and turned their attention inward to the English landscape certainly reinforced the 'foreign' character of picturesque tourism, and made it ideal for colonial landscape representation as well. But Genet's most interesting observation is the note of envy: 'They're happier than we are.' Happier, presumably, because they have nothing to lose. They are free from property and care. The picturesque 'object', whether a ruined structure or a ruined person, has been liberated from economy and exchange value, and from use-value as well. The picturesque object is, the

---

29 Genet, *The Thief's Journal* (Paris: Olympia, 1959), p. 164.

precursor of the modernist 'found object', the concrete *thing* which has been discarded or orphaned and redeemed for aesthetic contemplation. Abject and unselfconscious, the picturesque object, like Wordsworth's Leech Gatherer, is both part of the landscape, and not part of it – the *punctum* or pleasurable 'pricking' that awaits the benign, non-acquisitive appropriation of the touristic gaze which will take possession of it without ownership or property.[30] It serves as a figure of the 'arrested desire' or wistfulness characteristic of picturesque affect. In Wordsworth's *Evening Walk*, the cattle gaze at 'tempting shades to them deny'd' and horses turn a 'wistful gaze' upon the swain. Even the animals are tourists. The winding, serpentine path of intricate variety, the partial concealment and elusiveness of the erotic tease, the 'roughness' which adds the spice of sublime violence and sadism to the picturesque, all contribute to a picturing of the country as the site of infinite desire – simultaneously wanting all, and wanting nothing. The destitute figure, like the country itself, is an idealized image of the tourist – happier than the tourist because uncompromised by property. The picturesque serves as a compensation, then, for the whole range of anxieties brought on by the transformation of the countryside: Enclosure, the draining of wealth from the country to the city, the loss of community, the rise of a working class and (more ominously) a destitute class, the spectre of revolution and the abolition of private property – all these and more haunt the picturesque image of longing for something whose face is the country. Not surprising, then, that this becomes the national and imperial icon of idealized nature/culture transactions, and that it moves so readily into New York's Central Park where it will serve as the front yard for a new aristocracy of Robber Barons in the nineteenth century.

The legibility and illegibility of the past

> For historians
> Commend me to these valleys.
> (Wordsworth, 'The Brothers')

The other great longing that haunts the Romantic image of the country is the desire of the past – the desire both to possess the past, and to bring it alive, the sense that the past itself somehow 'lives' in the country, calling to

---

30 Modiano notes that the unselfconsciousness of the destitute, their absorption in their own existence, and (supposed) obliviousness to the picturesque spectator links them to Michael Fried's aesthetic of anti-theatricality ('Legacy of the Picturesque', p. 200).

the beholder. 'There is a spirit in the woods', and it is that past. The past, it is said, is another country. But the country is also another past, a domain of history deeper, more archaic than the city, one that reaches into prehistory and natural history, before the ascent of man. More important, the country presents this deeper time as an immediate perception of the immemorial, the forgotten, the place where the past has disappeared without trace, while the city seems to assure us that the past has been secured for us in well-maintained monuments, museums and libraries. As a city falls into ruins, it 'becomes country' once again. The country itself is always and everywhere a chaotic archive of fragments, awaiting assemblage by the historical imagination, or falling back into an inscrutable oblivion.

For all the emphasis on 'reading' the landscape as if it were a legible textbook of memory, history and ideology, it is equally important to understand the way the countryside imposes an illegibility on the landscape, making things difficult to read, indecipherable, or even subjecting them to complete erasure. The picturesque is often seen as an aesthetic of surface, content with a superficial apprehension of 'pastness', without regard to the real, determinate past inscribed in relics, monuments and oral traditions. Wordsworth's poem 'The Brothers' opens with satirical remarks on 'tourists' who 'pencil in hand and book upon the knee / Will look and scribble, scribble on and look,' as oblivious to the country 'as if the earth were air, / And they were butterflies.' The remarks, however, are not Wordsworth's, but those of a country Priest who cannot understand why a young man, 'a moping Son of Idleness', has been tarrying for hours in the village churchyard where there are no inscriptions to be read:

> Why can he tarry *yonder?* – In our church-yard
> Is neither epitaph nor monument,
> Tombstone nor name – only the turf we tread
> And a few natural graves.

When the Priest approaches the young man, the latter complains of the illegibility of the graves:

> Your Church-yard
> Seems . . . To Say that you are heedless of the past:
> An orphan could not find his mother's grave:
> Here's neither head nor foot-stone, plate of brass,
> Cross-bones nor skull, – type of our earthly state
> Nor emblem of our hopes: the dead man's home
> Is but a fellow to that pasture-field.

And the Priest's reply is that

> We have no need of names and epitaphs;
> We talk about the dead by our fire-sides
> And then, for our immortal part! *We* want
> No symbols, Sir to tell us that plain tale:
> The thought of death sits easy on the man
> Who has been born and dies among the mountains.

Wordsworth both repudiates and embraces the picturesque in this dialogue, seeming to mock the tourist's superficial knowledge, but doing so from the standpoint of a country priest who fails to see that the young wanderer is a returned native of this spot, a former shepherd who has been at sea for twelve years – where he has been dreaming of the country:

> He, thus with feverish passion overcome
> Even with the organs of his bodily eye,
> Below him in the bosom of the deep,
> Saw mountains; saw the forms of sheep that grazed
> On verdant hills.

The mariner does not reveal himself to the Priest, but allows him to think of him as a tourist, while he hears the story of his own brother's death, as if told to a stranger. The mariner impersonates a picturesque traveller in order to hear the story of his brother – but why? Whatever his intention, the results of hearing this pathetic tale are clear. The mariner feels 'a gushing from his heart, that took away / The power of speech', as he realizes that 'This vale, where he had been so happy, seemed / A place in which he could not bear to live.' And so he gives up his plan to return to his home country, and returns to the sea 'a grey-headed Mariner'. He elects to be what he was pretending to be, a picturesque figure, a wanderer, a perpetual tourist – or an outcast.

This poem undermines the whole contrast between 'high Romantic argument' and the picturesque, between the tourist's superficial knowledge of the country and the native's sense of the past, based in an organic, oral community. The satire is directed as much at the forgetfulness of the deeply rooted country priest, who fails to recognize a native son of his place, and who is oblivious to many of the natural changes that have occurred in the valley. The wandering mariner's twelve-year absence has made him keenly aware of changes in the topography that have escaped the notice of local knowledge and oral tradition. For all the emphasis on 'landscape and memory', then, Wordsworth is equally emphatic about the landscape as a place of forgetting[31] – and about the peculiar sort of knowledge that can take the place of memory and history. I've called this a knowledge of 'pastness' as distinct from the past, and it seems fundamental to the picturesque as an aesthetic of surface, presence and immediacy. The picturesque tourist is on to something that eludes the knowing historian or antiquarian – an ahistorical phenomenology of the country that greets the 'onset of the image' as a moment of ecstatic newness.[32] When this newness is accompanied by a sense of pastness, it heightens the melancholy that seems built into the Romantic perception of the country – the sense that the past is finally irrecoverable, and that this is felt most intensely in the actual places where its traces remain, or are fading away. The mariner and his brother were 'the last of all their race', and the community that commemorates the illegible past is probably doomed to extinction as well. At this point, the country merges with its great natural antagonist, the sea, as a figure of trackless ever-shifting wastes that will bear no inscription and sustain no memory.[33]

Personal identity and impersonal nature: *genius loci*

> The Ancient Poets animated all sensible objects with gods or geniuses, calling them by the names and adorning them with the properties of woods, rivers mountains, lakes, cities, nations, and whatever their enlarged & numerous senses could perceive.   (Blake, *The Marriage of Heaven and Hell*)

It is a commonplace about Romanticism that it involves a return of magic, myth and superstition after the secular, rationalist interlude of the Enlightenment. Like all historical master-narratives, this one is a half-truth. In the country, it seems fair to say, the gods and geniuses never went away. They may have been reduced to ornamental statues in the poetical landscape gardens of Augustan England, or to verbal ornaments in the poetic diction of the so-called 'pre-Romantics', Collins, Thompson and Gray, with their personifications of seasons, times of day, and places, but they persist as a spirit of reverence and resistance in accounts of the country right through

---

31 See Simon Schama, *Landscape and Memory* (New York: A. A. Knopf, 1995), and my 'Holy Landscape', for a critique of Schama and a discussion of landscape and forgetting. *Landscape and Power*, 2nd edn (Chicago: University of Chicago Press, 2002).

32 Gaston Bachelard's *The Poetics of Space* (Boston: Beacon Press, 1964), is the classic reflection on this experience of phenomenological freshness.

33 Robert Pogue Harrison, unpublished paper on the sea, landscape and antiquity, presented at the 'Natural Histories' symposium, University of Chicago, January 2001. See also Sam Baker, 'Written on the Water: Romanticism and the Maritime Imaginary', Ph.D. Dissertation, University of Chicago.

the eighteenth century. By the end of the century, the classical nymphs and dryads of the Augustans have been joined – or supplanted – by the 'native' spirits of the Druids, Celts and Goths, but the classical gods make a comeback in the poetry of Keats, Shelley and Byron. The genius of the place, as Geoffrey Hartman notes, is simply a permanent possibility of poetry, a key to the rural genres of pastoral and georgic, and beyond that, something built into the encounter of human language with the non-human world.[34] Simply to name a place or a natural object is to 'animate' it with a 'god or genius', as Blake saw. But to affirm this sort of animism is not necessarily to fall back into superstition or magical thinking. It is not all that clear, for one thing, how literally the Greeks believed in their own myths.[35] More important, the very categories of superstition and magic are projections of a higher superstition called monotheism, which defines animism and nature worship as paganism. But pagans, as the word itself tells us, are simply 'country people', *paysans* whose childish beliefs are ridiculed by sophisticated city folk, and the priests of the one, invisible, transcendent God (who Blake calls Nobodaddy or Urizen). When Wordsworth, in one of his 'Poems on the Naming of Places', inscribes on a rock 'like a Runic Priest' the name of an absent lady friend whose laughter had once brought the surrounding mountains to life with echoes, the local vicar accuses him of 'reviving ancient idolatry'.[36]

So what are we to make of all the gods, geniuses, spirits, demons and fairies that come rushing back into the countryside during the Romantic period? First, it might be useful to make a distinction between the genius 'of' a place, and the genius 'in' a place. The latter formulation portrays the genius as a dweller in a place, like the figure in a landscape. The former is more difficult to grasp, and involves a picture of the place itself as a person, the landscape as a form or figure that faces the beholder. In its simplest, most secular form, this version of the genius loci is equivalent to the 'character' of a place, its distinctive features that make it singular, unique, deserving of a proper name, and deserving of respect by the intrepid farmer or improving landscapist. But this 'character', once acknowledged, can begin to take on a personality and a mind of its own, offering resistance to human intervention. These ambiguities are compounded by numerous others: is the genius of the place a benign 'tutelary' spirit to be invoked? Or a

---

34 Hartman, *Beyond Formalism* (New Haven: Yale University Press, 1970).
35 Paul Veyne, *Did the Greeks Believe Their Own Myths?* (Chicago: University of Chicago Press, 1988).
36 See Wordsworth, 'To Joanna'.

malevolent demon, a ghost that haunts an accursed site? Is it a natural thing that has 'put down roots', as we say of people who have lived in the same place for a long time, or an artificial construction, a bit of 'Runic' graffiti or a totemic figure, the *baalim* that guards the oasis?

The basic discovery of the Romantic period was that all these tropes of animated spaces, places and landscapes may be repressed by the 'conquering empire of light and reason', but they can never be destroyed. Romanticism is the return of the repressed natural/local genii, from Coleridge's 'tutelary spirit', the Albatross, to Keats's 'pretty . . . paganism'. But the return is not a matter of simply going back to a time before modernity or Enlightenment, but an *uncanny* return, in Freud's sense of the word. That is, the genius of the place seems to 'half' return, to come back shrouded in doubt and uncertainty, a liminal figure like that of Echo. Its return is invariably woven together with a sense of its departing; appearances are also vanishings, and presences are felt as absences. Romanticism grasps the horns of a dilemma that it bequeathes to modernity: it understands simultaneously that nature, figured as the country, is a human construction, a raw material to be shaped by our desires, and that nature is also a non-human counterpart, and antagonist – the contrary country that preceded us for eons, and will outlive us in the end. Among the picturesque relics and ruins being gathered in the countryside in this period are fossils, now understood for the first time (thanks to Charles Cuvier's paleontological research) as traces of an immeasurably 'deep time', what Wordsworth calls 'times abyss'. History, prehistory, primitivism and archaeological antiquity, the Romans, the Hebrews, the Egyptians, the "savages" of North America, Africa, Australia – all seem to rush forward into a common present, a *human* present, bracketed by the immemorial temporality of 'the country'. It's no wonder that country matters so much, to them and to us. For Romanticism is a movement of thought, and a 'structure of feeling' about the country, the environment, nature and the landscape that endures to the present day. That is to say: it is not just that some English men and women in the late eighteenth and early nineteenth centuries started to look at the country in a new way, but that their perception of the country is linked to ours and speaks to us across the intervening centuries. If Bruno Latour is right that we have never been modern, that can only mean that we have always been Romantic.

Romanticism and the wider world:
poetry, travel literature and empire

NIGEL LEASK

'Dear Mamma, only think, my cousin cannot put the map of Europe together – or my cousin cannot tell the principle rivers in Russia – or she has never heard of Asia Minor . . . How strange! – Did you ever hear of anything so stupid.'[1] Such is the exasperated response of the Bertram sisters to their 'poor relation' Fanny's geographical ignorance, in Jane Austen's 1814 novel *Mansfield Park*, illustrating the degree to which the new European 'planetary consciousness'[2] had permeated the educational expectations of polite Regency females. Of course, as a wide range of recent critics have argued, the Bertram household had a particular investment here, given that their family wealth depended on the exploitation of chattel slaves in the West Indian sugar colony of Antigua.[3] *Mansfield Park's* well-documented silences and ellipses concerning colonial slavery fail, as Katie Trumpener has shown, to disguise Austen's support for abolition of the slave trade, if not for the manumission of slaves. By the same token, the novel's moral condemnation of 'absenteeism' at home or abroad appeals to a new spirit of enlightened trusteeship in Britain's colonial transactions.[4]

Austen here overrides her family connections with Warren Hastings, former Governor-General of British Bengal and arch-exponent of the bad old colonial practices which are seen to have lost Britain her first empire,[5] In an indirect way her appeal also aligns itself with Edmund Burke's

---

1 Jane Austen, *Mansfield Park*, ed. James Kinsley and John Lucas (Oxford: Oxford University Press, 1970), p. 15.
2 The term is Mary Louise Pratt's, in *Imperial Eyes: Travel Writing and Transculturation* (London: Routledge, 1992), p. 9.
3 Edward Said, *Culture and Imperialism* (London: Chatto and Windus, 1993), pp. 95–115.
4 See Katie Trumpener, *Bardic Nationalism: The Romantic Novel and the British Empire*, (Princeton, NJ: Princeton University Press, 1997), pp. 174–92.
5 According to David Nokes, Austen's sister-in-law, Eliza Hancock, nominally Hastings' 'god-daughter', was actually his illegitimate daughter, but there is no conclusive evidence. David Nokes, *Jane Austen* (London: Fourth Estate, 1997).

denunciation of Hastings' 'geographical morality' (Burke's own phrase) in employing the techniques of 'oriental despotism' to govern British India in the previous decade. In the course of their landmark impeachment of Hastings between 1788 and 1795, Burke and his fellow-impeachers sought to define and stabilize a 'universal' British identity based on a blend of Christian capitalism, conservatism and social hierarchy, offering steadfast moral orientation *to* its colonies rather than being dis-oriented (or 'orientalized') *by* them. In this chapter I examine the extent to which travel writers and Romantic poets colluded in building the moral agenda of Britain's second empire, as well as scrutinizing the generic links between travel writing and imaginative literature.

It's symptomatic that Fanny Price's 'improvement' into adulthood at Mansfield is signalled by her reading of travel literature, specifically the narrative of Lord Macartney's 1792–4 embassy to China: 'You meanwhile will be taking a trip into China, I suppose', her cousin Edmund enquires in chapter 16, 'How does Lord Macartney go on? – (opening a volume on the table and then taking up some others). And here are Crabbe's *Tales*, and the *Idler*, at hand to relieve you, if you tire of your great book.'[6] Fanny's trip to China of course fails to settle her discomposure at Edmund's treacherous participation in the theatricals. Nonetheless, later in the novel, her inquisitive questioning of Sir Thomas concerning the Slave Trade (in contrast to Maria and Julia Bertram's indifferent 'dead silence')[7] reflects Fanny's growing moral vision, buttressed, we may assume, by her geopolitical reading. The development of Fanny's imperial ethic parallels her own journey in the course of the novel from the marginal space of her attic room in Mansfield Park to the moral centrality which she has assumed by the conclusion.

That Edmund Bertram considers Macartney a 'great book' for a young female reader like Fanny, a book from which (Austen's favourite authors) Crabbe and Dr Johnson offer light relief, is I think more than just an ironic exposé of Edmund's lofty expectations about what young women ought to read. In the Romantic decades, travel literature, both in the form of bulky collections of 'Voyages and Travels' adorning the library shelves of the wealthy,[8] and as single volumes in costly quarto or less expensive octavo,

---

6 Austen, *Mansfield Park*, pp. 140–1.
7 *Ibid.*, p. 178.
8 G. R. Crone and R. A. Skelton, 'English Collections of Voyages and Travels, 1625–1846', in Edward Lynam (ed.), *Richard Hakluyt and his Successors* (London: The Hakluyt Society, 1946), pp. 64–140.

provided metropolitan readers with their knowledge of the 'wider world', much of which was coming under the sway of British rule in the same years. Charles Batten's claim that by the end of the eighteenth century travel books were the most widely read division of literature, second only to novels and romances, seems credible.[9] Frequent reviews of new travel accounts with lengthy quotations in the 'highbrow' periodicals (Massimiliano Demata notes seventy-eight reviews of travel books in the *Edinburgh Review* alone between 1802 and 1815),[10] the enduring popular success of fictional travelogues such as Defoe's *Robinson Crusoe* or Swift's *Gulliver's Travels*, and, at the bottom end of the market, the chapbooks' mingling of romance with popular exoticism, or captivity narratives like the *Life of Sarah Shade* recently discussed by Linda Colley,[11] ensured that travel writing permeated all levels of eighteenth- and nineteenth-century culture. In the face of global competition from France and her allies, empire was a serious business impinging on the lives of Britons of all social classes; by the end of the Napoleonic Wars, in 1820, a staggering twenty-six per cent of the world's population were subject to British rule.[12]

With the inauguration of an official British 'exploration establishment' (marked by the foundation of the African Association in 1788), attempts were made to institutionalize travel writing in the service of empire. In the words of the editor of John Pinkerton's major seventeen-volume compilation of *Voyages and Travels* (1814), travel accounts written before 1768 (i.e. before Captain Cook's first Pacific voyage) 'are rather to be regarded as curious, than useful ... The old catalogues of pictures and statues, have sunk into obscurity before the new and important works, which illustrate the phenomena of nature, and display the politics and ethics, the agriculture and commerce, the state of the arts and sciences'.[13] Unmotivated patrician curiosity was increasingly subordinated to bourgeois utility in the interests of colonial expansion, a shift which helps to explain the patriotic imperative

9 Batten, *Pleasurable Instruction: Form and Convention in 18th Century Travel Literature* (Berkeley and London: University of California Press, 1978), p. 1.

10 'Travel Literature in the Edinburgh Review', in *British Romanticism and the Edinburgh Review: Bicentenary Essays*, ed. Massimiliano Demata and Duncan Wu (Houndmills: Palgrave Macmillan, 2002), p. 87.

11 *Captives: Britain, Empire, and the World 1600–1850* (London: Jonathan Cape, 2002), pp. 241–56.

12 C. A. Bayly, *Imperial Meridian: The British Empire and the World, 1780–1830* (London: Longman, 1989), p. 3.

13 *A General Collection of the Best and Most Interesting Voyages and Travels*, 17 vols. (London, 1814), vol. XVII, pp. xxviii, xxix.

underlying Fanny Price's 'serious' reading.[14] At the same time, as Deirdre Coleman has underlined in her important study *Romantic Colonization and British Anti-Slavery*, utility combined with anti-slavery ideology to produce a utopian colouring in much contemporary discourse: 'penal reformers and anti-slavery campaigners looked to Africa and New Holland as sites where slaves and convicts might be re-birthed as free people'.[15]

Relations between imperial ideology, the literature of travel, and emergent notions of literary value, were more problematic than is assumed by some post-colonial critics. Edmund Bertram's idea of a 'great book' certainly doesn't conform with the emergent romantic literary canon, influentially defined in 1823 by De Quincey as the 'literature of power'; 'Even books of much higher pretensions [than cookery books or encyclopaedias]' wrote De Quincey, 'must be excluded [from the 'literature of power] – as, for instance, books of voyages and travels, and generally all books in which the matter to be communicated is paramount to the manner or form of its communication'.[16] Although De Quincey draws here upon Kantian and Coleridgean aesthetics, a century earlier the Earl of Shaftesbury had made a similar discrimination in his attack on the contemporary rage for reading voyages and travels: 'Our relish or taste must of necessity grow barbarous, whilst barbarian customs, savage manners, Indian wars, and wonders of the *terra incognita*, employ our leisure hours, and are the chief materials to furnish out a library.'[17]

In a sense De Quincey's downgrading of travel writing to the status of a 'literature of knowledge' develops Shaftesbury's argument (against the post-Lockean privileging of travel as a paradigmatic discourse of empirical truth), that 'facts unably related, though with the greatest sincerity and good faith, may prove the worst sort of deceit. And mere lies, judiciously composed, can teach us the truth of things beyond any other manner.'[18] Better, then, to partition ably related *Fact* (history or science) from judicious and self-conscious *Fiction* (literature). Michael McKeon has argued that 'the Aristotelian separation of history and poetry, the factual and the probable, the singular

---

14 See my *Curiosity and the Aesthetics of Travel Writing, 1770–1840: 'From an Antique Land'* (Oxford: Oxford University Press, 2002).
15 Deirdre Coleman, *Romantic Colonization and British Anti-Slavery* (Cambridge: Cambridge University Press, 2005), p. 3.
16 'Letters to a Young Man whose Education has been Neglected', *London Magazine* 7 (1823), 332.
17 'Soliloquy; or, Advice to an Author' (1710), in *Characteristicks of Men, Manners, Opinions, Times*, ed. Lawrence Klein (Cambridge: Cambridge University Press, 1999), p. 153.
18 *Ibid.*, p. 154.

and the universal, is a revolutionary doctrine of great antiquity that lay like a time bomb in the cultural unconscious of the West'. Rediscovered by Romantic theorists like Coleridge and De Quincey, 'its doctrine of the universal truth of poetry [aided] in the formulation of the modern belief in the autonomous realm of the aesthetic'.[19]

A more typical eighteenth-century view of travel writing than Shaftesbury's, however, was that of Anglican moralist Vicesmus Knox, which Edmund Bertram would have had no trouble endorsing; 'no books of amusement whatever [are] so well adapted to young people [as travel books] . . . They interest the mind as much as a novel; but instead of rendering it effeminated and debauched, they make it usefully inquisitive, and furnish it with matter for reflection.'[20] Travel writing, feeding an appetite for the distant and the marvellous, may not in this view have been exactly *utilitarian*, but at least it was 'curious' in a constructively philosophical rather than a self-indulgent and 'fictional' sense. Jenny Mezciems puts the dominant eighteenth-century view of the matter succinctly: 'though the conventions of romance are strenuously avoided the material of romance is still there, whatever writer and reader may pretend'.[21]

Despite the 'exploration establishment's' official imprimatur, the immense popularity of travel writing during the Romantic period probably owed as much to the 'curiosity value' of tales of exotic adventure and survival, as its practical utility in promoting British expansionism. In a long draft for Book V of the *Five-Book Prelude* (1804), for example, William Wordsworth focused on Nature's agency in 'tak[ing] man into the bosom of her works – / Man suffering or enjoying' via the trope of the suffering traveller, drawing on the narratives of Christopher Columbus, the Elizabethan navigator Sir Humphrey Davies, Dampier and Mungo Park. Wordsworth focuses on heroic private suffering rather than imperial achievement; the fact that he eventually excluded the 130-line draft from the poem is telling.[22] Steve Clark goes so far as to suggest that 'travel writing's

---

19 Michael McKeon, *The Origins of the English Novel, 1600–1740* (Baltimore: Johns Hopkins University Press, 1987), p. 119.
20 Vicesimus Knox, *Essays, Moral and Literary* (1778), new edn, 2 vols. (Dublin, 1786), vol. I, p. 118.
21 Jenny Mezciems, ' "Tis not to divert the Reader": Moral and Literary Determinants in some Early Travel Narratives', in *The Art of Travel*, ed. Philip Dod (London: Frank Cass, 1982), p. 15.
22 *The Prelude, 1799, 1805, 1850*, ed. J. Wordsworth, M. H. Abrams, S. Gill (New York and London: Norton, 1979), pp. 496–9, lines 75–7 cited. Thanks to Carl Thomson for drawing my attention to this passage.

success as text, representation, may be predicated on what Pratt terms its "betrayal" of the imperial project, and testimony to failure'.[23]

In the light of these cautionary remarks, I'll suggest below that the influence of travel writing on the work of Romantic poets complicated, as often as it promoted, established ideologies of British imperialism. Travel narrative wasn't necessarily supportive of empire, any more than the Romantic poetry of travel. Most famously, Byron's *Childe Harold* lambasted Lord Elgin's removal of the Parthenon Marbles, taken to epitomize British imperial rapacity from Ireland to India, and *Don Juan* subjected contemporary discourses of orientalism, militarism and imperial expansion to a withering satirical assault. Even Fanny Price's travel reading recorded a major colonial fiasco; Staunton's book told how Macartney's embassy completely failed to secure trade concessions from China in the face of the Manchu Emperor Chien Long's indifference to vassals from an obscure northern island. Travel writing frequently represented the traveller in a transactional, reflexive and often vulnerable relationship to foreign places and people, and as such could be an unstable vehicle for promoting British expansionism.[24]

Travel writing, stadial theory and Romanticism

I want to turn now to the central importance afforded to travel writing in the epistemology of the eighteenth century, particularly in the intellectual crucible of the Scottish Enlightenment, keeping an eye on its subsequent epistemological demotion. To a large extent the genre enabled the emergence of the form of intellectual enquiry later known as 'anthropology', fundamental to the moral sciences of the enlightenment (in the older sense of 'mores', pertaining to human manners in general). Philosophers from Locke and Hume to Kant and Hegel frequently cited the evidence of travel writers to support axiomatic claims about human nature. In an age which valorized the evidence of the senses, the testimony of contemporary travellers was often considered more reliable than that of long-dead historians and chroniclers, evident in Edmund Burke's remarks to the Edinburgh historian William Robertson in 1777:

---

23 'Introduction', *Travel Writing and Empire: Postcolonial Theory in Transit* (London and New York: Zed Books, 1999), p. 5.
24 Mary Louise Pratt describes the 'utopian, innocent vision of European global authority' as a narrative of 'anti-conquest' (*Imperial Eyes*, p. 39). In my view this overestimates the coherence and teleology of imperial expansion in this period.

I have always thought with you, that we possess at this time very great advantages towards the knowledge of human Nature. We need no longer to go to History to trace it in all its stages and periods. History from its comparative youth, is but a poor instructour . . . But now the Great Map of Mankind is unrolld at once; and there is no state or Gradation of barbarism, and no mode of refinement which we have not at the same instant under our View.[25]

Burke here grasps the importance of travel writing for Scottish 'conjectural historians' like Lord Kames, Adam Ferguson and John Millar, who preferred contemporary travellers' accounts of savage societies to the (often non-existent) records of the early stages of their own civilization. True to Bacon's dictate *nullius in verba*, the eye-witness testimony of modern travellers was preferable to purely textual authority. But Burke's cartographic metaphor of 'the Great Map of Mankind' disguises the fact that the new anthropological knowledge was usually textually mediated, and travellers had to struggle to make their narratives creditable in a sceptical age. In his 1771 conjectural history of the distinction of ranks, the Glasgow philosopher John Millar weighed up the strengths and weaknesses of travel accounts in furnishing the modern historian with materials for a history of manners. He concluded that, unreliable as individual travellers often were, accumulative study of diverse narratives might permit objective truth to emerge. In fact too much scepticism concerning travellers' veracity might 'in a great measure destroy' the 'credibility of all historical testimony', for doubts about the testimony of travellers also applied to historical sources.[26] Implicit in Millar's remarks, as well as Burke's metaphor of history as the 'great map of mankind', is an intriguing parallel between geographical and historical distance, suggesting a powerful link between eighteenth-century exploration, travel writing and the rise of romantic historicism. As James Chandler puts it, 'in the literature of the period, one can see a new preoccupation with the dating of the cultural place, the location of the cultural moment', a preoccupation leading to the 'calibration of uneven temporalities' or differential rates of social progress.[27]

---

25 (9 June 1777), *The Correspondence of Edmund Burke*, vol. III, ed. George H. Guttridge (Cambridge: Cambridge University Press, 1961), pp. 350–1. See also Ronald Meek, *Social Science and the Ignoble Savage* (Cambridge: Cambridge University Press, 1976), p. 173.

26 *Observations Concerning the Distinction of Ranks in Society* (London: John Murray, 1771), p. xiv.

27 *England in 1819: The Politics of Literary Culture and the Case of Romantic Historicism* (Chicago and London: University of Chicago Press, 1998), pp. 108, 134.

Although the natural sciences would soon come to dominate the understanding of foreign peoples as well as places, particularly with the rise of Linnaean taxonomies and, later, the nineteenth-century biological understanding of race, in the earlier period observed social differences were still largely explained by climatic factors, epitomized by Montesquieu's *Spirit of the Laws* (1748).[28] Although this model of explanation was Eurocentric in the extent to which it favoured the manners of temperate regions over 'torrid zones', different religious and civic institutions were viewed as the products of contingent rather than essentialist racial or phenotypical factors. Moreover, climatic determinism implied that 'permeable' European travellers and colonizers themselves risked absorbing the traits of the societies in which they resided, often connected in British writing to anxieties that Britons might share the fate of 'creolization' suffered by French, Spanish and Portuguese settlers in the tropics. This fear underpinned much of the animus against 'nabobs' and 'planters' in metropolitan Britain, clearly evidenced in the impeachment of Warren Hastings in 1789–94. As I indicated above, the new imperial subjectivity which emerges in Britain in the Romantic decades strove to institute a new moral absolute, superior to the contingencies of 'geographical morality' influenced by relative cultural and climatic factors.

For Scottish stadial theorists like Adam Ferguson and John Millar,[29] the four socio-economic stages of hunting, pastoralism, agricultural and commerce, each marked by a distinct mode of production and system of 'manners', came to replace climate as the dominant explanatory model for historical change. Refined sensibility – characteristic of progressive, commercial Europe – was increasingly perceived to mark off the European subject from the inhabitants of less 'advanced' cultures. The historical march 'from Savages to Scotsmen'[30] was still not equivalent to achieving a secure cultural authority in a binary distinction between Europe and its Others, however. Fears concerning the corrupting influence of luxury in commercial societies, with a consequent dissolution of civic virtue, often counterbalanced the moral claims of progressivist theories, particularly

---

28 See Roxann Wheeler, *The Complexion of Race: Categories of Difference in Eighteenth-Century British Culture* (Philadelphia: Pennsylvania University Press, 2000), pp. 1–49.

29 See Ronald Meek, *Social Science and the Ignoble Savage* (Cambridge: Cambridge University Press, 1976). Meek argues that stadial theory peaked in the 1790s (p. 177). For a critique of 'economic reductionism' in Meek's book, see Mark Phillips, *Society and Sentiment: Genres of Historical Writing in Britain, 1740–1820* (Princeton: Princeton University Press, 2000), pp. 172–3.

30 This drollery is attributed to Walter Bagehot.

evident in Adam Ferguson's *History of Civil Society* (1767). Travel accounts which 'temporalized' distant cultures by reading them as 'classical' or 'feudal' were certainly relegating those cultures to a lower rung on the ladder of social progress. But on the other hand they often favourably compared the civic virtue of more 'primitive' cultures to the luxury and disaggregation of modern Europe, a major theme in utopian literature, one important 'spin-off' of European travel writing. Moreover, implicit in stadial theory was the notion that all cultures had implanted within them the germs of progressive development, and therefore didn't need to depend on benevolent colonial rule by more progressive societies to give them a leg up. Although stadial theory did unquestionably serve to underwrite imperial expansion and (increasingly) its supremacist ideologies, a degree of ambivalence always remained as long as it was possible to represent other cultures reflexively, in a critical relation to one's own.

Axiomatic to the role of refined sensibility in Scottish stadial theory was a linkage between social progress and the condition of women. As Mary Louise Pratt has indicated, travel narratives (produced by male as well as female writers) were just as susceptible to the discourse of sensibility as contemporary novels or poetry.[31] In the light of the correlation between social progress and refinement, however, the intensification of the traveller's subjectivity in travel writing (as opposed to the 'naïve empiricism' enjoined upon earlier travel writers in the Royal Society's 'Instructions for Travellers') had profound repercussions for the politics of subject–object orientation in cultural encounter. This is evident, for example, in Mary Wollstonecraft's *Short Residence in Sweden* (1796) when she writes 'I perceived that I could not give a just description of what I saw, but by relating the effect different objects had produced on my mind and feelings, whilst the impression was still fresh.'[32] By framing objective reportage with 'affective realism', Wollstonecraft's epistolary text gives a new autobiographical interest to the description of a foreign country. In so doing, it also registers the progressive British traveller's sensibility as superior to the 'unimproved' mind of the Norwegian farmers or provincial *petit-bourgeoisie* amongst whom she travelled. Wollstonecraft's troubled subjectivity is also notably more virtuous than the wavering affections of her unfaithful American lover Gilbert Imlay, to whom her letters are addressed, and

---

31 Pratt, *Imperial Eyes*, pp. 86–90.
32 *A Short Residence in Sweden*, ed. with intro. and notes by Richard Homes (Harmondsworth: Penguin, 1987), p. 62.

whom she believes has been corrupted by commercial speculation. In the end Wollstonecraft's hard-won claims to virtuous sensibility balance precariously on the edge of mental breakdown, itself the ultimate price of social over-refinement.

One of the most powerful mediators of Scottish stadial thought in the Romantic period was the Edinburgh Whig critic Francis Jeffrey. In an 1814 *Edinburgh Review* article on Byron's *Corsair* and *Bride of Abydos*, Jeffrey sought to weigh up the competing claims of history and geography as fit subjects for poetry. Jeffrey traced a historical cycle for poetry in which primitive passions were gradually refined and rationalised by more polished ('neo-classical') literature in modern commercial societies. Eventually, however, according to the logic of Jeffrey's conjectural history of poetic taste, 'a disdain and impatience of the petty pretensions and joyless elegancies of fashion will gradually arise: and strong and natural sensations will again be sought, without dread of their coarseness, in every scene which promises to supply them'.[33]

Like Shaftesbury, Jeffrey rather grudgingly engaged neo-classicism with the new vernacular canon which increasingly marked the taste of his contemporaries. He conceded that the romantic desire for 'natural passion' could discover inspiration in 'the feats of chivalry, and the loves of romance'[34] of the European Middle Ages. But echoing Burke's letter to Robertson cited above, Jeffrey noted the interchangeability of geographical and historical distance in the quest for the poetic sublime: 'The savages and barbarians that are still to be found in the world, are, no doubt, very exact likenesses of those whom civilization has driven out of it; and they may be used accordingly for most of the purposes for which their ancient prototypes are found serviceable.'[35] Jeffrey preferred British medievalism to exotic sources for poetry on the associationist grounds that the 'charm and fascination in what is ancient and long remembered' was absent from exotic travel accounts, with their strange gods and mythographical references. Hence 'Mr Southey . . . who has gone in search of strong passions among the savages of America, and the gods and enchanters of India, has had less success than Mr Scott, who has borrowed his energies from the more familiar scenes of European chivalry, and built his fairy castles with materials already tried and consecrated in the fabric of our old romances.'[36]

33 *Edinburgh Review* (April 1814), 198–229, 200.
34 *Ibid.*, p. 201.
35 *Ibid.*, p. 202.
36 *Ibid.*

In his well-known satirical essay of 1820 *The Four Ages of Poetry*, the work which goaded Shelley into composing the *Defence of Poetry*, T. L. Peacock went a step beyond Jeffrey in declaring that 'poetry cannot travel out of the regions of its birth, the uncultivated lands of semi-civilised men'.[37] For Peacock, the 'semi-barbarism' of Romantic poets is illustrated by Wordsworth's 'village legends [picked up] from old women and sextons', Byron's thieves and pirates, and the literary borrowings of Moore, Southey and Thomas Campbell, who 'extract from a perfunctory and desolate perusal of a collection of voyages and travels, all that useful investigation would not seek for and that common sense would reject'.[38] (Peacock, a senior employee of the East India Company, here expresses a belief which was shared by other members of the British 'exploration establishment', that the 'curious' interest of travel writing be subordinated to its utility.) Most scholars have seen Jeffrey's preferred antiquarian model for modern literature (rather than its geographical rival) dominating the Romantic literary field in general, evident in the medieval revival and the emergence of the historical novel. Nevertheless, Romantic historical consciousness was also permeated by exotic paradigms drawn from the travel writing of the second age of exploration, in the manner in which it conceived of historical distance and cultural alterity.

Wordsworth's 'Forsaken Indian woman' and Hemans's 'Traveller at the source of the Nile'

Although exoticism became something of a 'trademark' in the poetry of Southey, Byron or Thomas Moore, any sense of its general influence on Romantic poetry must be balanced by a countervailing preference for the familiar and unremarkable, most famously exemplified in the case of Wordsworth (indicated by Peacock's ironic remark, quoted above, about the poet's concern with 'old women and sextons'). In a marginal note to Payne Knight's *Analytical Inquiry*, Wordsworth expostulated against the commonplace use of ethnographic evidence in constructing philosophical propositions about human manners:

> What means all this parade about the Savage when the deduction as far as just may be made at our own firesides, from the sounds words

---

37 'The Four Ages of Poetry', in David Bromwich (ed.), *Romantic Critical Essays*, (Cambridge: Cambridge University Press, 1997), p. 208.
38 *Ibid.*, p. 208.

gesticulations looks &c which a child makes use of when learning to talk. But a Scotch Professor cannot write three minutes together upon the Nature of Man, but he must be dabbling with his savage state, with his agricultural state, his Hunter state, &c,&c.[39]

In addition to debunking the stadial theory of the Scottish Enlightenment, Wordsworth here questions the usefulness of gleaning moral truths about mankind from the anthropological accounts of distant travellers, when they might be gathered closer to home in 'the very world which is the world / Of all of us, – the place in which, in the end, / We find our happiness, or not at all!' (*Prelude* ix: lines 724–8).

Despite his well-known valorizations of the commonplace, however, Wordsworth was just as drawn as the 'Scotch Professors' to exotic travel accounts, writing in 1812 that 'the only modern Books that I read are those of travels, or such as relate to matters of fact'.[40] As Dorothy Wordsworth's *Recollections of a Tour made in Scotland* reveals, the discourse of exotic travel, as well as picturesque tourism, provided both Wordsworths with a frame of reference in describing their own frequent domestic excursions, especially evident in their 1803 foray into neighbouring Scotland. Wordsworth's geographical imagination had a distinct bias, as his friend Barron Field indicated in an 1828 letter to the poet where he commented 'all your travellers "step westward". You have no oriental poems.'[41] In this respect, Dorothy's *Recollections* echoed her brother's predeliction when she evokes Loch Lomond as 'an outlandish scene – we might have believed ourselves in North America', quoting Wordsworth's lines on American settlement from *Ruth*.[42] Such analogies with exotic American travel gave a sublime *frisson* to the more sedate activity of domestic tourism, connecting the peripatetic Wordsworths with explorers and colonizers on the margins of European expansion.

Dorothy's geographical analogy supports Alan Bewell's argument that Wordsworth's reading in exotic travel accounts contributed to the

39 E. A. Shearer, 'Wordsworth and Coleridge Marginalia in a Copy of Payne Knight's *Analytical Inquiry*', *Huntingdon Library Quarterly* 1 (1937), 73.
40 Quoted by Charles N. Coe in *Wordsworth and the Literature of Travel* (New York: Bookman Associates, 1953), p. 14. Coe indicates that thirty-eight-odd travel narratives inform Wordsworth's poetry, identifying sixty-four instances in forty-two separate poems, when a clear debt can be established (pp. 101–7).
41 Quoted in *Letters of William and Dorothy Wordsworth*, 2nd edn, *The Later Years*, ed. Alan G. Hill (Oxford: Clarendon Press, 1978), Part I, p. 695, n. 2.
42 *Recollections of a Tour made in Scotland*, intro., notes and photographs by Carol Kyros Walker (New Haven and London: Yale University Press, 1997), pp. 87–9.

overdetermined quality of many of the 'domestic' encounters described in poems like 'We Are Seven', 'The Discharged Soldier' or 'Resolution and Independence'.[43] Several recent critics have noted the colonizing imperatives which often seem to structure the epistemology of Wordsworthian encounter, not to mention the overtly imperialist sentiments aired in *The Excursion*.[44] Despite the persuasiveness of such interpretations, I'm more convinced by Bewell's argument that the younger, more 'experimental', poet tended to question rather than to endorse the paradigms of colonial encounter: 'in a radical inversion of the customary Enlightenment relationship between the observing *philosophe* and the observed population of silent marginalised peoples, Wordsworth makes the observer the observed and admonishes him for his dehumanising fictions'.[45]

Only two poems in *Lyrical Ballads* directly flag their indebtedness to travel books,[46] in both cases to recently published narratives of American travel. 'Ruth' (added to the 1800 second edition) footnotes an exotic reference to William Bartram's *Travels . . . in Florida* (1791), whilst 'The Complaint of the Forsaken Indian Woman' (published in 1798) cites its source as an anecdote in Samuel Hearne's *Journey from Hudson's Bay to the Northern Ocean* (1795), which is summarized in the poem's headnote. As Bewell indicates, this acknowledgement sets the poem apart from the other *Lyrical Ballads* (including 'Ruth') where 'instead of an outward movement, into the sphere of the exotic or into romance, Wordsworth returns these wanderers homeward and binds them to an English place'.[47] Like 'The Mad Mother' or 'The Thorn', 'The Complaint' is a dramatic monologue rather than an 'encounter poem' in the strict sense, and it's interesting that Wordsworth's anecdote is derived from Hearne's enthnography rather than any interest in the character of the traveller as suffering hero, as in the rejected draft of the *Five-Book Prelude* to which I referred above. The poem is based on Hearne's

---

43 *Wordsworth and the Enlightenment: Nature, Man, and Society in the Experimental Poetry* (New Haven and London: Yale University Press, 1989).

44 See Alison Hickey's 'Dark Characters, Native Grounds: Wordsworth's Imagination of Imperialism' in *Romanticism, Race, and Imperial Culture*, ed. Alan Richardson and Sonia Hofkosh (Bloomington and Indianapolis: Indiana University Press, 1996), especially p. 292, and David Simpson, 'Wordsworth and Empire – Just Joking' in *Land, Nation and Culture, 1740–1840: Thinking the Republic of Taste*, ed. Peter de Bolla, Nigel Leask and David Simpson (Basingstoke: Palgrave Macmillan, 2005), pp. 188–201.

45 Bewell, *Wordsworth*, p. 90.

46 Anna Seward's 'Elegy on Captain Cook' (1780), Helen Maria Williams's sonnets 'To the Torrid Zone' and 'The White Bird of the Tropics' (1795), and Cowper's 'The Castaway' (1799) are other examples of the many contemporary poems which acknowledge their sources in travel accounts.

47 Bewell, *Wordsworth*, p. 32.

story of a sick Chipeweyan woman who, separated from her baby and abandoned to die by her travelling family group, prepares for a lonely death. Hearne describes the episode in characteristically spare prose, adding only a brief moralising judgement:

> a custom so unnatural is perhaps not to be found among any other of the human race: if properly considered, however, it may with justice be ascribed to necessity and self-preservation, rather than to want of humanity and social feeling ... Necessity, added to national custom, contributes principally to make scenes of this kind less shocking to those people, than they must appear to the more civilised part of mankind.[48]

The Spartan fortitude of Native Americans was something of a cultural cliché in eighteenth-century Europe: Wordsworth's choice of subject-matter might have been dictated by the paradigmatic 'Scotch Professor' Adam Ferguson, who, drawing on the travel accounts of Lafitau, Charlesvoix and Colden, wrote in 1786 that amongst the North American Indians, 'the foundations of honour are eminent abilities and great fortitude; not the distinction of equipage and fortune'.[49] Wordsworth's poem belongs to the fashionable eighteenth-century genre of 'Dying Indian' poems, like Joseph Warton's 'The Dying Indian' (1755), Ann Hunter's 'North American Death Song' (written 1782, published 1802) or Thomas Gisborne's 'The Dying Indian's Ode' (1798), all poems which thematize the Native American's stoic fortitude in the face of suffering and death.

Wordsworth however challenges both his travelogue source and the conventions of the poetic sub-genre to which his poem belongs. Although the Indian woman's fortitude is initially asserted in lines 19–20 ('Then here contented will I lie! / Alone, I cannot fear to die')[50], her courage soon gives way to a longing for life, focused upon nostalgia for her absent child, a theme completely absent from Hearne's account of native women, who, if anything, appear prone to infanticide.[51] The Indian woman's fantasy of her

---

48 In *Travels, Explorations and Empires: Writings from the Era of Imperial Expansion, 1770–1835*, 5 vols., ed. Tim Fulford with Carol Bolton (London: Pickering and Chatto, 2001) vol. I, p. 172.
49 *Essay on the History of Civil Society*, ed. and intro. Duncan Forbes (Edinburgh: Edinburgh University Press, 1966), p. 89.
50 Wordsworth, *The Poems*, ed. John O. Hayden, 3 vols. (Harmondsworth: Penguin, 1977), vol. I, p. 276. Henceforth WP.
51 See *Travels, Explorations, and Empires*, vol. I, pp. 184–9. Hearne's comments on Native American infanticide indirectly link Wordsworth's 'Complaint' with 'The Thorn' and 'The Mad Mother', which both pick up the theme of indigenous British infanticide present in his traditional ballad source, 'The Cruel Mother'. See also Coe, *Wordsworth*, pp. 58–9.

baby suddenly grown to manhood, (in Wordsworth's version) rescuing her from lonely death, embodies the 'civilized' passions of domestic and familial affection cutting transversely through the Spartan ethic of 'primitive' group identification. Despite her acceptance of imminent death, the Indian woman still has something left to say, as she exhorts the wind to carry her message to her people; 'I should not feel the pain of dying, / Could I with thee a message send; / Too soon, my friends, ye went away; / For I had many things to say' (WP I, p. 277, lines 47–50). 'Universal' maternal passions – pity for one's child, rather than self-pity – here undercut the legendary stoicism of the American Indian in the face of death, so that the poem closes on a disturbed (and disturbing) note; 'My poor forsaken Child, if I / For once could have thee close to me, / With happy heart I then would die . . . But thou, dear Babe, art far away, / Nor shall I see another day.' (WP I, p. 277, lines 65–70).[52]

Wordsworth's poem thus qualifies Hearne's blandly 'philosophical' explanation that 'Necessity, added to national custom, contributes principally to make scenes of this kind less shocking' to Indians than to Europeans, by infusing the Indian woman with 'progressive' European maternal sensibility. 'The Complaint' may be an atypical poem in *Lyrical Ballads* by dint of its exotic setting, but Wordsworth's ethical universalism refuses any stadial account of cultural difference by attributing progressive sensibility to the 'primitive' woman. Indeed here the poet is less willing to typecast American Indians than the traveller from whom he borrows his anecdote. True to the desideratum of Wordsworth's 'Preface', in the poem's recasting of Hearne's original anecdote, the 'feeling therein developed gives importance to the action and situation, and not the action and situation to the feeling' (WP I, p. 872). Wordsworth's relationship to his travelogue source here is dynamic and critical, approaching his human subject via the inner sympathy of the poet rather than Hearne's ethnographic distance.

52 In the 1802 Preface Wordsworth groups 'The Complaint' with poems thematically concerned with death rather than maternal feelings (WP, vol. I, p. 871). However, in a letter to Coleridge dated 5 May 1809 he sketched a new classification of his poems, designating as a separate class 'those relating to Maternal feeling, connubial or parental'. In the 1815 collected edition the 'Complaint of the Forsaken Indian Woman' was classified among 'Poems of the Affections' and the last line changed from 'I feel my body die away / I shall not see another day!' to 'But thou, dear Babe, art far away, / Nor shall I see another day'. See Stephen Maxfield Parish, 'The Thorn: Wordsworth's Dramatic Monologues', *Twentieth Century Views: Wordsworth*, ed. M. H. Abrams (Englewood Cliffs, NJ: Prentice-Hall, Inc., 1972), p. 82.

At the same time, of course, by 'humanizing' one individual victim in the eyes of his readers, Wordsworth might also be seen to be exposing the *inhumanity* of savage manners in general, in so doing implicitly lending support to the moral reform of Native Americans as part of the coloniz-ing imperative. When the inhuman exposure of the sick and weak in Chipaweyan culture is juxtaposed with cognate practices in England, however (the subject of poems like 'Incidents on Salisbury Plain', as well as other *Lyrical Ballads* such as the 'Mad Mother' dealing with social margin-alization and dispossession), Wordsworth's indictment of primitive society turns against 'progressive' England as well. The juxtaposition again con-founds facile binaries dividing 'refined' Europeans from 'primitive' Native Americans, as well as more intellectually sophisticated 'conjectural histories' of mankind. Notwithstanding the colonizing ideology manifest in much of his later poetry, Wordsworth's ethical universalism here challenges Enlightenment categories of race, gender and class. Wordsworthian uniformitarianism proves to be a powerful critical tool when mapped back onto its contemporary contexts, including the travel accounts which informed the poet's dynamic sense of cultural comparison.

In conclusion, I turn to a lesser-known Romantic lyric, also based upon a source in contemporary travel writing, Felicia Hemans's 'The Traveller at the Source of the Nile' (1829).[53] Hemans's immense nineteenth-century popularity was in part related to her skill in deriving sentimental pathos from popular works of exotic travel writing. Like its companion poem 'The Flower of the Desert' (based on an episode in Mungo Park), 'The Traveller' poeticizes the trials and travails of a British male traveller in 'darkest Africa', offering a contrast to Hemans's more customary theme of the stoic suf-fering of national heroines in *Lays of Many Lands* (1826) or *Records of Women* (1828). Her poem is based upon a climactic passage in James Bruce's best-selling *Travels to Discover the Source of the Nile* (1790) in which the Scottish traveller basked in the 'sublime of discovery' at the Fountains of Gish, which he took to be the source of the Nile, undiscovered since ancient times. Evoking his hard-won moment of exaltation, Bruce wrote:

> Though a mere private Briton, I triumphed here, in my own mind, over kings and their armies; and every comparison was leading nearer and nearer to presumption, when the place itself where I stood, the object of

53 I refer to the text published in *Romantic Women Poets 1770–1838: An Anthology*, ed. Andrew Ashfield (Manchester and New York: Manchester University Press, 1995), pp. 190–1.

my vain-glory, suggested what depressed my short-lived triumph ... I found a despondency gaining ground fast upon me, and blasting the crown of laurels I had too rashly woven for myself.[54]

Bruce's mood-swing at Gish had proved faintly embarrassing to the British 'exploration establishment' when his book was published, to the extent to which it hardly endorsed a providentialist reading of British exploration.[55] (Bruce had visited Gish back in 1771, so neither could his narrative claim the status of 'writing to the moment' so important to the genre in the eighteenth century.) The quality of Bruce's account of his depression at Gish may be attributable to an amateur writer's attempt to master the contemporary discourse of sublime elevation and bathos, more successfully realized by Wordsworth in the famous Gondo Pass episode in book 6 of *The Prelude*. Bizarrely enough, he followed up this account of his depression with a farcical description of drinking the king's health with a cup of Nile water, likening himself to 'Don Quixote at that island of Barataria'.[56] The Quixotic allusion (amongst other implausibilities) would prove fatal to Bruce's credit as a travel writer, and his book was duly attacked for embroidering the truth; to the British public he was 'Macfable', one of the eighteenth century's most notorious 'travel liars'. In 1790 the *Analytical Review* 'deeply regretted' that 'a deluge of apparent improbabilities, inaccuracies, prejudices, conceits, contradictions, impotent witticisms, and stunning egotisms, had been poured over the mass of real information' which the book contained.[57]

With the increasing tendency of Romantic readers to appreciate travel books for their literary qualities rather than their utility or objectivity, however, Bruce's highly coloured narrative underwent a curious rehabilitation. What might be called the 'romantic reading' of Bruce is exemplified by Charles Lamb in an 1806 letter to Hazlitt:

> We just read through Bruce's Travels, with infinite delight where all is alive & novel & about kings & Queens & fabulous Heads of Rivers Abyssinian wars & the line of Solomon & he's a fine dashing fellow &

---

54 *Travels to Discover the Source of the Nile, in the years 1768–74*, 5 vols. (Edinburgh, 1790), vol. III, p. 597.

55 Hawkesworth's narrative of Captain Cook's *Endeavour* voyage raised similar embarrassment: see Jonathan Lamb's excellent remarks in *Preserving the Self in the South Seas, 1680–1840* (Chicago and London: University of Chicago Press, 2001), pp. 100–5.

56 *Travels*, vol. III, p. 598.

57 *Analytical Review* 9 (March 1791), 248.

intrigues with Empresses & gets into Harems of Black Women & was himself descended from Kings of Scotland: not farmers & mechanics & industry . . . [58]

Accommodating his literary judgements to the utilitarian claims of the 'exploration establishment', we saw De Quincey demoting travel writing to the status of a 'literature of fact', in which *content* was more important than literary form. In contrast, Lamb singles out a travel book which had been condemned for failing to meet the criteria of veracity (partly on account of stylistic exuberance) and rehabilitates it as an exemplar of De Quincey's privileged 'literature of power'. Evident here is a yawning abyss opening up between literary and scientific discourse, cutting through the 'integrated' text of eighteenth-century travel writing, and (by implication) leaving the genre in a subordinate relationship both to imaginative literature and new scientific disciplines like geography and anthropology.

Charles Lamb's reading of Bruce (like Coleridge's, whose 'Kubla Khan' is in part a meditation on Bruce's *Travels*)[59] transgresses the fact/fiction ontology of the emergent literary field in the interests of a supremacist literary imagination. The roots of this attitude may be traced to Lord Kames's notion of 'ideal presence' elaborated in his influential 1762 *Elements of Criticism*: 'it makes no difference whether the subject be a fable or a true history: when ideal presence is complete, we perceive every object as in our sight; and the mind . . . finds no leisure for reflection . . . history stands upon the same footing as fable: what effect either may have, depends on the vivacity of the ideas they raise; and, with respect to that circumstance, fable is generally more successful than history'.[60] Read in this light, Bruce's *Travels*, like all travel books, may labour under the disadvantage of its claims to be 'true history', but might nevertheless succeed (by dint of imaginative 'vivacity') to fulfil the criterion for fiction according to the post-Aristotelian idea of the universal truth of poetry. A version of Kames's 'ideal presence' seems to have grounded the claims of all subsequent 'literary' travel writers in the nineteenth and twentieth centuries who have tried to salvage the genre from its De Quinceyan demotion to the status of 'a literature of fact'.

---

58 *Letters of Charles and Mary Lamb,* ed. Edward Marrs (London and Ithaca: Cornell University Press, 1976), vol. II, p. 199. The allusion in the final part of the sentence is to Crevecouer's *Letters of an American Farmer,* which the Lambs had also been reading.

59 See my 'Kubla Khan and Orientalism: The Road to Xanadu Revisited' in *Romanticism* 4:1 (1998).

60 *Elements of Criticism,* 11th edn, with the Author's Last Corrections and Annotations (London, 1834), p. 37.

The problem remains, however, that (even in its postmodernist incarnation) travel writing can't quite cut the umbilical cord which connects it to the contingency of lived experience.

Bruce's Romantic rehabilitation is also evident in Hemans's choice of the 'fountains of the Nile' episode as the basis for her 1829 poem. In reworking her source, however (and in contrast to Wordsworth's 'Complaint'), she focuses exclusively on the traveller's troubled subjectivity, rather than upon any consideration of savage 'manners' in the style of enlightenment ethnography. Hemans's moralizing interest in Bruce is also quite distinct from Lamb's 'Romantic' reading, although any attempt to interpret her poem as simply reflecting her pro-imperial Tory politics is problematized by her critique of Bruce's masculinist 'sublime of discovery'. In the third stanza, Hemans writes 'The rapture of a conqueror's mood / Rush'd burning through his frame' (lines 13–14), comparing Bruce's elation at Gish to military vainglory. As in poems such as 'Casabianca' or 'Woman on the Field of Battle', the futility of masculine endeavour is criticized from a domesticated, female perspective: 'A shadow dark and strange / Breathed from the thought, so swift to fall / O'er triumphs hour – *and is this all?*' (lines 22–4).

Discarding the whole satirical 'Don Quixote at Barataria' passage, as well as Bruce's risky account of his Shandeyan antics at Gish, Hemans's poem develops his narrative of the sudden mood swing from a post-coital enjoyment of the 'coy fountains of the Nile' to melancholy *amor patriae* based on nostalgia for the traveller's native Scottish rivers: 'I remembered the magnificent scene in my own native country, where the Tweed, Clyde, and Annan rise in one hill; three rivers, as I now thought, nor inferior to the Nile in beauty, preferable to it in . . . cultivation . . . superior, vastly superior to it in the virtues and qualities of the inhabitants.'[61] This passage becomes the basis for Hemans's fifth and sixth stanzas;

> No more than this! – what seem'd it *now*
> First by that spring to stand?
> A thousand streams of lovelier flow
> Bathed his own mountain land!
> Whence, far o'er waste and ocean track,
> Their wild, sweet voices call'd him back.
>
> They call'd him back to many a glade,
> His childhood's haunt of play,
> Where brightly through the beechen shade

---

61 *Travels*, vol. III, pp. 640–1.

Their waters glanced away;
They call'd him with their sounding waves,
Back to his father's hills and graves.

(lines 25–36)

The feminized chorus of Annan, Clyde and Tweed now drowns out the exotic seduction of the 'distant' fountains of the Nile. Imperial conquest, discovery and masculine self-aggrandisement give way to the bittersweet melancholy – the 'wild, sweet voices' – of domesticated *amor patriae*. The traveller's 'alter'd heart within him died / With yearnings for his home!' (lines 45–6), leading to the sententious, Burnesian final couplet 'Oh happiness! How far we flee / Thine own sweet paths in search of thee!' (lines 53–4).

It would be a misreading of the poem, though, to conclude that Hemans wrote simply as a feminist critic of the 'goal-orientation' of masculine exploration, or of British imperialism in the broader sense. On the contrary, as the paramount patriot poet of late British Romanticism, Hemans works to define a newly conjugal imperial subject, based on sentimental ties of nostalgia and kinship which override 'geographical morality' of the Warren Hastings kind. In this poem memories of childhood, domestic love and picturesque British landscape reclaim the libertine Bruce's errant, unstable sensibility. A similar nostalgia is evident in Hemans's most famous lyric 'The Homes of England' with its picturesque shading of social difference in constructing a harmonious national ideal, or the lugubrious 'Graves of a Household' (with its anticipation of Rupert Brooke's 'some corner of a foreign field that is forever England') in the opening stanza; 'They grew in beauty, side by side, / They fill'd one home with glee; – / Their graves are sever'd, far and wide, / By mount, and stream, and sea' (lines 1–4).

In the companion piece to 'The Traveller', 'The Flower of the Desert', the eponymous moss rose reveals to the beaten, hunted explorer Mungo Park a new relationship between home and the imperial contact zone: 'Can that Being (thought I) who planted, watered, and brought to perfection, in this obscure part of the world, a thing which appears of so small importance, look with unconcern upon the situation and sufferings of creatures formed after his own image?'[62] God's love (for Hemans a projection of that feminine devotion which has the power to transcend male-induced suffering and conflict, as in her poem 'Woman on the Field of Battle') is omnipresent, no longer limited to the centripetal pull of the mother country.

---

62 *Travels in the Interior Districts of Africa* (London, 1799), p. 244.

Mungo Park's moss rose is like the hidden violet of Wordsworth's lyric 'She dwelt among the untrodden ways' plucked from rural obscurity into the service of empire. If 'The Traveller' softens and moralizes male errancy with its nostalgia for British home, the 'Flower of the Desert' takes comfort in the thought that home can be anywhere, even to the point of imbuing some corner of a dangerous foreign desert with the pious, sentimental comforts of the Homes of England. Hemans (in the words of Tricia Lootens) 'makes empire into a home, expanding affection in terms of latitude and longitude, until it reaches and symbolically appropriates the final resting place of the beloved and honoured dead'.[63] Hemans's poem foreshadows Lady Elizabeth Eastlake's resolution of the contradiction between domesticity and travel for nineteenth-century British wives and daughters of empire: 'wherever she goes, a little fertile patch of household comfort grows beneath [her] feet'.[64] Globalized British domesticity increasingly underpins Victorian imperial ideology, however repellent that would seem to a tradition of male travel writers like Richard Burton and Charles Doughty, or, in the twentieth century, T. E. Lawrence and Wilfred Thesiger.

In this chapter I have considered the importance of travel writing in connecting British writers and readers to the 'wider world', and examined some points of intersection between travel, empire and Romantic poetry. There seems, in conclusion, to be no fixed pattern of ideological affirmation or creative transformation evident in the cross-fertilization of travel writing and poetry. Wordsworth's 'Complaint of the Forsaken Indian Woman' questioned the authority both of its travelogue source and the Enlightenment's four-stage theory of social development in favour of a sentimental uniformitarianism which (at least by implication) challenged the complacency of progressivist theories of society. By contrast, the many geographical settings and stories of Hemans's poetry, gleaned from her wide reading of travel books, are homogenized into a gendered and sentimental geography productive of one major ideological strand of nineteenth-century British imperialism.[65]

---

63 Tricia Lootens, 'Hemans and Home: Victorianism, Feminine "Internal Enemies", and the Domestication of National Identity' in *Victorian Women Poets: A Critical Reader*, ed. Angela Leighton (Oxford: Blackwell, 1996), p. 17.

64 *Quarterly Review* 76 (June–September 1845), p. 105. See my *Curiosity and the Aesthetics of Travel Writing*, pp. 203–4 for further comments on this passage.

65 Nancy Moore Goslee, 'Hemans's "Red Indians": Reading Stereotypes' in *Romanticism, Race, and Imperial Culture*, p. 242.

With the eclipse of empiricism in the nineteenth century, travel writing (as the paradigmatic empiricist genre) suffered demotion in relation to poetry and the novel, although I have tried to show how the process of generic interchange continued nonetheless. The shift of attention which we have observed from an ethnographic focus (Wordsworth's dying Indian woman) to the traveller's subjectivity (Hemans's portrait of James Bruce at Gish) reflects a major trend in nineteenth-century travel writing itself, which increasingly discovered the (patriotic, pious or ironic) subjectivity of the European traveller to be more compelling than the empirical project of representing the foreign world through which he or she travelled. As geographers, anthropologists and naturalists increasingly sought to distinguish their scientific discourses from the 'impure' personal narratives of travel, a new brand of literary professionals like Dickens, Trollope, Stendhal, Flaubert, Stevenson, James, Edith Wharton and D. H. Lawrence worked to differentiate their travel books from tourist guides or scientific treatises. Twentieth-century criticism showed only lukewarm interest in a genre which seemed limited by its mimetic aspirations and lack of reflexivity. But as our notion of the literary canon is transformed by post-colonialism and the celebration of generic 'impurity' and cultural hybridity, travel writing has emerged from the shadow of its post-Romantic demotion into a new critical and intellectual limelight. This chapter has sought to explore some of the implications of that emergence for the study of Romantic literature.

The homes of England

MARGOT FINN

In the homes of England, Romantic writers struggled to fix the proper boundaries between publicity and privacy, seeking to elaborate new forms of domesticity that would allow houses and households to function at once as the locus of family life and the central hub from which an increasingly British state formation could radiate. Dissonance between public and private conceptions of the home is a hallmark of Romantic poetry and fiction, but so too is writers' insistence (often rehearsed in their own domestic histories) that only by rejecting neat binary distinctions between public and private spheres could the home effectively foster Romantic sensibilities and national well-being. The homes that emerge from Romantic writing are in consequence above all else historic homes: they figure as the domestic markers of a public history, not as havens from the changing outside world.

Economic, political and ideological developments all worked to underline the antinomies of domestic space in Romantic writing. The industrial and consumer revolutions disrupted established patterns of household use, introducing new modes of production, novel systems of political economy and an unprecedented, imperial range of household goods which writers struggled to accommodate in verse and fiction. By attempting to displace political power from its twin preserves in the aristocratic mansion and the Houses of Parliament, radical and patriotic popular political movements further problematized the home as a scene of literary life. Both the rise of Gothic fictions and the increasing prominence (and popularity) of women authors contributed decisively to these destabilizing developments. Gothic homes provided workshops in which Romantic writers hammered out domestic differences born of disparate national traditions of public and private life, forging new, modernizing domesticities that sought to marry English and Celtic conventions of interior space. The woman writer, resisting strict demarcations between public and private domains, was at once a symbol and an agent of the Romantic home's constant engagement with the world that lay beyond its walls.

Traditions of interpretation that identify the Romantic aesthetic with heroic self-absorption, alpine vistas and the sublime embrace of nature typically obscure the salience of the family and its household settings in Romantic writing. Odes to Napoleon, like odes to nightingales, are not conducive of domestic reflection; Coleridge's metaphysical concerns and Blake's Swedenborgian fixations typically resist the elaboration of homely themes. In shifting attention away from the canonical male poets, however, historicizing trends in scholarship have worked to recuperate the Romantic home. By fostering the exploration of a wider range of Romantic authors and encouraging scholars to locate literary texts within historical contexts, new historicism draws attention to 'actual literary communities as they functioned within their larger communities of time and space'.[1] Within the discipline of history itself, a prolonged obsession with industrial production – Blake's 'dark satanic mills' – has now given way to an emphasis on the rise of consumer culture, an historiographical shift that has lent household settings and the geography of social life new and salutary salience. Attention to gender – central both to new historicism and to the new economic history of consumerism – has further buttressed these developments. If the poetry and prose of the male Romantic canon flourished most profusely out of doors, the Romantic writings revealed by new historicism as often draw their inspiration from cabins, cottages, chateaux, castles and converted abbeys.

Reading Romanticism through a domestic optic, however, demands neither renunciation of the powerful claims of nature in this period nor denial of the impact of revolutionary politics. Rather, attention to the domestic sites of literary life reveals writers' repeated efforts to find a harmonious balance between the natural world and the built environment and exposes their preoccupation with relations of power in the home, the parish and the state. Gothic ruins and ruined cottages, Celtic cabins and metropolitan townhouses alike deny the Romantic home a secure location within a private domestic domain. Suspended precariously between natural decay and artificial refinement, the homes of England seldom subscribe to the 'separate spheres' paradigm of gender relations. Instead, their dominant imagery – lights and fires, doors and windows, beds and chairs, chinaware and textiles – speaks to the wider slippage between publicity and privacy that marked the literature and history of the Romantic era.

---

1 Marilyn Butler, 'Repossessing the Past', in Marilyn Butler, Paul Hamilton, Marjorie Levinson and Jerome J. McGann (eds.), *Rethinking Historicism: Critical Readings in Romantic History* (Oxford: Blackwell, 1989), p. 72.

Sites of labour: the cot

The cottage was the domestic style most readily accommodated by the Romantic male poets, but its literary purchase extended far beyond this select coterie of writers. Dove Cottage enjoys pride of place in the canonical geography of the Romantic home. Nested within the natural world, it served at once as a centre of sociability for the Lake poets and as the locus of their literary production. Here, as Kurt Heinzelman has argued, Dorothy and William Wordsworth worked to construct a domestic space in which exertion, affection and reflection were united in an organic whole. Allocating their household duties along lines that reflected the fluid labour regimes of neighbouring farming families, they elaborated a form of domesticity that departed both from emerging economic models of the proper division of labour between the sexes and from the cloying cult of domesticity with which Wordsworth was later to associate his home life in Grasmere.[2] Physically and metaphorically, Dove Cottage was always a porous container. Cold and draughty despite Dorothy's carpet-binding and mattress-making endeavours, the Wordsworths' home was open to a constant ingress and egress of pedlars, tradesmen, servants, neighbours, friends and family. Letters and newspapers supplemented this perpetual traffic of persons, ensuring that the cottage preserved in its domestic reincarnation key elements of the public function it had earlier served as a public house, the Dove and Olive Branch Inn.

Like Dove Cottage, the humble homes evoked in Wordsworth's poetry consistently eschew domestic enclosure, privileging instead the natural settings and the public face of family life. The home in 'Home at Grasmere' (1800–6) only rarely figures as a house: it is instead the 'passionate welcoming' offered by the overarching sky that renders Grasmere doubly domestic, enfolding the stone cottage within the wider embrace of nature to create 'a home / Within a home'. The opposition Wordsworth poses between the abandoned cottage of a profligate 'Scholar' dalesman and the 'delightful' dwelling of a neighbouring widower likewise celebrates what one might term the Romantic domestic exterior at the expense of modish styles of interior decoration. Married to a housewife whose 'industry / Was of that kind . . . which tended more / To splendid neatness, to a shewy,

2 Kurt Heinzelman, 'The Cult of Domesticity: Dorothy and William Wordsworth at Grasmere', in Anne K. Mellor (ed.), *Romanticism and Feminism* (Bloomington: University of Indiana Press, 1988), pp. 52–78.

trim / And overlaboured purity of house', the more worldly of the two farmers suffers economic losses, seduces his servant-girl, takes to drink, deserts the church and dies degraded by his grief and shame. In sharp contrast, the widower's cottage – 'the whole house . . . filled with gaiety' – testifies to its residents' rejection of the specious appeal of consumer novelties by incorporating natural goods and home produce into the architecture of daily life. Surrounded by rose-trees and entwined with jasmine, this home is adorned by 'Nature's care'. 'Laid open through the blazing window', the cottage willingly offers its interior up to Wordsworth's public scrutiny, revealing the farmer's eldest daughter at her spinning wheel, where she imparts to a younger girl the 'household work' learned as a child at her father's knee.[3] The imagery of 'Michael' (1800) reiterates these themes, underlining the public virtues of domestic labour. The 'aged' cottage lamp that allows Michael and his wife to work at their domestic fireside long into the night is 'famous in its neighbourhood, / And was a public symbol of the life / That thrifty Pair had lived'. Bereft of modern consumer goods, the cottage home's homeliness is best conveyed by natural metaphors. Illuminated by the ancient lamp, 'the House itself, by all/ Who dwelt within the limits of the vale, / . . . was named THE EVENING STAR'.[4]

Wordsworth's depiction of the happy cottage as a sociable site of natural productivity seamlessly integrated with its surrounding environment is rehearsed again and again by Romantic writers. In 'The Wish' (1808–19), John Clare constructs an idealized cottage that combines a range of distinct activities – eating, sleeping, reading and working – within its central parlour. Boasting a modest library shelved beside its snug fireside and a bed that serves as 'A neat appendage for a winter stove', Clare's cottage radiates warmth but nonetheless remains open to the natural world. Accoutred with 'things necessity would plan' rather than 'the pomp of gaudy furniture', his house promotes 'Each sweet production of the rural muse' by offering the poet 'delicious views' from its chamber windows.[5] For George Crabbe in 'The Poor and Their Dwellings' (1810), the openness of plebeian architecture is precisely its saving grace: in the absence of wealth, possessions and even family ties, forms of sociability associated with cottages that open out

3 *William Wordsworth: The Major Works*, ed. Stephen Gill (Oxford: Oxford University Press, 1984), pp. 174–99.
4 *The Poetical Works of William Wordsworth*, ed. E. De Selincourt (Oxford: Clarendon Press, 1952), pp. 84–5, lines 115, 129–31, 137–9.
5 *The Early Poems of John Clare 1804–1822*, ed. Eric Robinson and David Powell, vol. I (Oxford: Clarendon Press, 1989), pp. 45–6, lines 65, 100, 92, 80.

onto the street best foster the domestic affections. With its 'lockless Coffer and . . . lidless Hutch', the thatched dwelling of an indigent sailor offers no furnishings to attract the eye inside the home. But to its lone occupant, armed with a long-glass and peering through his window to the street beyond, the cot nonetheless affords a 'view complete'. Constructed to provide constant opportunities for conversation with passersby, it offers an effective antidote to the pauper's isolation, and thus works to maintain his precarious mental balance.[6]

More than merely local in its ambit and implications, the public character of cottage sociability ensures that even the most humble households are linked to the world of politics. When evening falls in Joanna Baillie's 'A Winter Day' (1790), an old soldier who has served his country in foreign wars totters to the threshold of a labourer's cottage to beg for food. Welcomed to a 'ready chair' set beside the blazing fireside, he shares a 'homely meal' and is offered a bed for the night. As evening advances, neighbours flock to the family's hospitable hearth, where the wife works at a spinning wheel, the husband weaves a willow-basket for her market produce and the patriotic soldier recounts 'tales of war and blood' before bedtime.[7] Here as in so much early Romantic writing, the home comfortably accommodates the outside world: in the well-ordered cottage, domestic life successfully incorporates the political, rather than featuring as its polar opposite. Burns captured the fundamental bond between the cot and the nation in 'The Cotter's Saturday Night' (1795), where the ultimate lesson taught by the domestic interior speaks to the strength of the state: 'From scenes like these, old Scotia's grandeur springs, / That makes her lov'd at home, rever'd abroad'.[8]

Although Romantic writers repeatedly celebrated happy cottage homes that were sited at the intersection of public and private or at the crossroads of culture and nature, they were fully alive to the perils of these liminal locations. As residents of cottages at home and abroad, Romantic authors endured cottages in which both the conspicuous presence of nature and the public character of private life were intensely problematic. Encounters with sheep, cattle and goats housed within cottage dwellings were a frequent

6 *George Crabbe: The Complete Poetical Works*, ed. Norma Dalrymple-Champneys and Arthur Pollard, 3 vols. (Oxford: Clarendon Press, 1988), vol. I, p. 523, lines 49–50.
7 Joanna Baillie, *Poems; Wherein It Is Attempted to Describe Certain Views of Nature and of Rustic Manners* (London: J. Johnson, 1790), pp. 10–15.
8 *Burns: Poems and Songs*, ed. James Kinsley (London: Oxford University Press, 1969), p. 121, lines 163–4.

occurrence for travellers in search of a night's lodging en route to sublime scenic vistas; mud, manure and rats were common accompaniments of cottage living in town and country alike. Journeying on the Continent in 1814, the Shelleys rested uneasily in quarters which, as Mary Shelley recorded in their shared journal, were 'not equalled by any discription [sic] I have heard of an Irish Cabin in filth & certainly the dirtiest Scotch cottage I ever entered was exquisitely clean beside it'.[9] More broadly and less prosaically, while the porous boundaries of humble homes in Romantic writing naturally lent themselves to beneficial forms of sociability, they also increased the family's vulnerability to hostile influences from the outside world. In *Frankenstein* (1818), Mary Shelley's monster rhapsodizes upon the domestic virtues displayed by a German cottage which is transformed into 'a paradise' by the 'luxury' of a fire on its domestic hearth. But the monster's ability to use this home as a 'school in which . . . I studied human nature' – by observing its occupants through a chink in the wall – soon demonstrates the perils of the cot's too public style of domesticity. Denied admission to the alluring family circle whose flimsy structure has exposed its daily activities to him, the enraged monster burns the cottage to the ground.[10]

If productive labour effectively animated the cottage economy, moreover, unemployment could all the more rapidly strip the home of both pragmatic purpose and domestic comfort. The disruption and dissolution of cottage life by economic and political developments were persistent tropes of Romantic writing. Crabbe's social criticism pairs the demise of cottage living with the rise of squalid tenements where stable family groups are replaced by promiscuous assemblages of paupers, whose only domestic comfort derives from possession of unmatched fragments of gaudy chinaware, the 'small consoling objects' cherished by men and women deprived of house and home. The dissolution of the cot reaches its apogee with the erection of 'Pauper-Palaces', the new workhouses designed to discourage the able-bodied poor from seeking relief from the parish. Denying paupers outdoor relief in their own homes, these enclosed institutions substitute Foucauldian symbols of discipline – clocks, locks, gates 'and all the Signs of Power' – for the open-hearted, open-door domesticity of pastoral writing. The absence of neighbourly relations compounds this loss of familiar domestic objects in the totalizing institution of the workhouse. As Clare

9 *The Journal of Mary Shelley 1814–1844*, vol. I: *1814–1822*, ed. Paula R. Feldman and Diana Scott-Kilvert (Oxford: Clarendon Press, 1987), p. 13.
10 Mary Shelley, *Frankenstein*, ed. M. K. Joseph (Oxford: Oxford University Press, 1969), ch. 12, pp. 110–11; ch. 15, p. 129.

asks rhetorically, 'Who can, when here, the social Neighbour meet? / Who learn the story current on the Street?' Figured as the least domestic of household spaces, poorhouses combine material 'Plenty, seldom found at home' with acute social and spiritual deprivation. Despite providing the poor with 'airy Rooms and decent Beds', the workhouse is 'the House they hate'.[11]

The erosion of cottage life, which Crabbe associates with the local politics of parsimonious parish elites, is situated within broader economic and political frameworks in Wordsworth's 'The Ruined Cottage' (composed 1797–8). Tracing the impact of the production crises that marked domestic handloom weaving during the industrial revolution by charting the successive stages by which a homely dwelling decays into a deserted hut, this poem reverses the natural imagery of Romantic domestic pastoral. When the weaver Robert enjoys full employment, his home displays an appropriate balance between nature and culture, public and private. Adorned with an 'outward garb of household flowers', the cottage welcomes passing travellers to its hearth and is the cheerful home of husband, wife and infant children. But when the collapse of handloom production forces his family onto the parish's meagre charity, the weaver enlists as a soldier and is removed to distant lands by service to the state. Wordsworth plots the progressive decline and eventual death of Robert's disconsolate family through the invasive entry into the very fabric of their home of plants and animals that were earlier instrumental in maintaining the cottage's economic viability and rustic beauty. Honeysuckle vines begin to crowd the doorway; sheep stray from the commons and stain the threshold of the house with tufts of wool discoloured by blood; damp seeps through the thatch, chilling the deserted wife to the breast, 'Even at the side of her own fire'.[12] Economic developments that remove industry from the home render plebeian households incapable of negotiating the competing claims made by interior and exterior worlds, unleashing natural forces of decay that the cottage, stripped of its productive and reproductive purposes, can neither contain nor withstand.

Subjected from one direction to the corrosive impact of industrialization, the Romantic cottage was eroded from the other by the sweeping tide of luxury brought into the English home by the consumer revolution. Humble cottages were a staple feature of Hanoverian pastoral, but from the later

11 *George Crabbe*, vol. I, ed. Dalrymple-Champneys and Pollard, pp. 525–32.
12 *William Wordsworth*, ed. Gill, pp. 31–44.

decades of the eighteenth century the cot was increasingly reconfigured as the cottage *ornée*. As middle- and upper-class men and women ensconced their families in elaborate, comfortable renditions of plebeian rural homes, architects 'exceeded themselves and each other in producing notions for cottages, summer-houses, dairies, cow-sheds, and conservatories that became more and more romantically extravagant as the years of classical restraint receded'.[13] Thomas De Quincey, who adopted Dove Cottage as his home when the Wordsworth family outgrew it, indulged Regency visions of domestic bliss that were far removed from the idyllic rustic pleasures of 'Home at Grasmere'. Declining to describe his home in terms of the mountains, shrubs and flowers that surround it, De Quincey in his *Confessions* (1821) insists instead that its comforts lie in the hearth-rugs, shutters and flowing curtains that protect its interior chambers from the elements outside. Luxurious commodities trump natural imagery in De Quincey's ideal home. Not merely tea, but 'an eternal teapot', graces his table; a laudanum receptacle, 'as much like a wine-decanter as possible', complements this fireside scene. Displaced from its rustic foundations and distanced from productive labour, Dove Cottage is transmogrified into a site of Oriental consumer excess. The cottage haunts De Quincey with nightmares of monstrous Asiatic interiors. Transposed by his drug-induced hallucinations from his home to 'Chinese houses, with cane tables', he observes with fascinated loathing as an Orientalized version of nature reclaims the cottage furnishings, rendering the feet of the sofa and tables literally 'instinct with life'.[14]

The Victorian period was to see the cottage rehabilitated for domesticity, as highly sentimentalized versions of enclosure increasingly supplanted De Quincey's fevered Oriental visions in the public mind. No longer troped as a site of productive labour, the cottage was now primed to migrate from the country to the city. 'In the nineteenth century, the city / metropolis mapped out and tamed its domestic territory as carefully as it mapped out and tamed its empire', Karen Sayer observes. 'At the same time, the rural working-class home was colonized by the (urban) bourgeoisie who, creating

---

13 Clifford Musgrave, 'Architecture and Interior Design', in Ralph Edwards and L. G. C. Ramsey (eds.), *The Regency Period 1810–1830* (London: The Connoisseur, 1958), p. 17.

14 Thomas De Quincey, *Confessions of an English Opium Eater*, ed. Alethea Hayter (Harmondsworth: Penguin, 1971), 'Introduction to the Pains of Opium', pp. 90, 93–5, and 'The Pains of Opium', pp. 108–10.

new cottages *ornée,* came to make them their own, ideal homes.'[15] Oriental influences were evident in the metropolitan cottages inspired by this urban wave of rural nostalgia, but they were not ascendant in them. Rather, medieval fantasies, in literature as in architecture, mediated the cottage's transformation: before it was absorbed entirely by the Victorian villa, the cot (like so many components of the Romantic domestic interior) had taken a Gothic turn.

Sites of power: the castle and converted abbey

Illuminated by Romanesque windows and adorned with mock-Tudor furniture, medievalized versions of the cottage *ornée* participated in a wider Gothic revival in which castles and converted abbeys enjoyed symbolic pride of place.[16] With the escalation of economic and political instability in the Napoleonic years, medieval institutions exerted increasing imaginative appeal in Britain and came to represent the glories of the national past in English, Scottish and Irish Romantic writing. Between 'Home at Grasmere' and *The Excursion* (1814), Wordsworth 'made the clamorous decision, following Burke, that the only sufficiently powerful safeguards lay in . . . the remnants of what he called the "feudal frame" of society'. Where natural landscapes and productive agrarian labour had served to ground social relations in the early poems, Lord Lonsdale's Lowther Castle – newly rebuilt in the Gothic style – featured as a bedrock of domestic tranquillity in Wordsworth's later writings.[17]

Gothic structures in which the successive phases of English national identity could be seen to unfold provided Romantic authors with a prime literary context for nostalgic rumination. The domestic appeal of castles and converted abbeys lay primarily in their political function, in the central place occupied by public power and sociability in medieval aristocratic residences. Byron's 'Elegy on Newstead Abbey' (n.d.) thus discounted his ancestral home's dilapidated fabric and celebrated its contribution to the history of English state formation. More honourable (even in decay) 'Than modern

---

15 Karen Sayer, *Country Cottages: A Cultural History* (Manchester: Manchester University Press, 2000), p. 2.
16 E. T. Joy, 'Furniture', in Edwards and Ramsey (eds.), *Regency Period,* p. 42.
17 Nigel Everett, *The Tory View of Landscape* (New Haven, CT: Yale University Press, 1994), pp. 162–70, citation from p. 167. Clive Wainwright details the strange history of Newstead Abbey as a Romantic interior in *The Romantic Interior: The British Collector at Home* (New Haven, CT: Yale University Press, 1989), pp. 284–6.

mansions, in their pillar'd state', the ruined abbey is superior 'to the guilded domes, / Or gewgaw grottos, of the vainly great'.[18] In 'Belvoir Castle' (1812), Crabbe maps the making of a modern English identity through the progressive architectural and decorative transformations of the Duke of Rutland's family seat. First erected by 'ancient Britons' who glory in their natural freedoms, the castle under Saxon rule acquires a 'frowning Hall' upon whose 'Rude Board the common Banquet steam'd'. Norman barons bring 'feudal pomp' to its gloomy halls, but Belvoir's Gothic domestication awaits the Renaissance, when 'gentler times' and 'soft'ning Arts' – not least the influence of 'Fair Ladies' – illuminate its dismal interior with lamps, highly polished floors and silver flagons.[19] The castle's changing public functions over time are reflected in its evolving interior spaces: the organic growth of British national identity is manifest in Belvoir's transition from dark baronial hall to illuminated aristocratic home. Scott's description of the Tower of Tillietudlem in *Old Mortality* (1816) likewise underlines the military imperatives of Lady Margaret Bellenden's home, offering a highly politicized rendition of domestic values. Lady Margaret's insistence that 'the great Turkey-leather elbow-chair, with the tapestry cushions' is a 'throne' which must 'never. . .be pressed by any less dignified weight' than that of the sovereign bespeaks a state-centred version of domesticity bereft of private comforts. The very foodstuffs upon her table signal public occupations rather than promoting the private pleasures of modern consumer culture. 'No tea, no coffee, no variety of rolls, but solid and substantial viands – the priestly ham, the knightly sirloin, the noble baron of beef, the princely venison pasty' are offered to her guests.[20] By emphasizing public manifestations of political power in historic homes and by arresting the castle's development in the centuries prior to the consumer revolution, Scott (like Crabbe before him) attempts to domesticate the Gothic interior without emasculating or Orientalizing it.

In this historic context, modernizing innovations often render the Gothic edifice habitable only at the expense of abdicating its public functions. When St Aubert revisits the 'Gothic hall' of his forebears in Radcliffe's *Mysteries of Udolpho* (1794), he is dismayed to find that the 'large table . . . where the master of the mansion loved to display his hospitality . . . was

---

18 *The Works of Lord Byron. Poetry*, vol. I, ed. Ernest Hartley Coleridge (London: John Murray, 1898), p. 117, stanza 2, line 2; p. 125, stanza 38, lines 1–2.

19 *George Crabbe*, ed. Dalrymple-Champneys and Pollard, pp. 331–5.

20 Sir Walter Scott, *The Tale of Old Mortality*, ed. Douglas S. Mack (London: Penguin, 1999), vol. I, ch. 9, pp. 76, 77–8; vol. I, ch. 11, p. 96; vol. I, ch. 12, pp. 99–100.

now removed'. Here too unhappily the 'arms and ancient banners of the family' have been displaced by 'frivolous ornaments . . . that denoted the false taste and corrupted sentiments of the present owner'.[21] Women, either as avid consumers or as objects of sexual consumption, feature conspicuously as the cause of the public home's fall from Gothic grace. In *Kenilworth* (1821) Amy Robsart's clandestine marriage to Leicester leads to a grand redecoration of Cumnor Hall that captures, in its Oriental imagery, her ambiguous moral position in the household. Velvet curtains fringed with gold, sky-blue wall hangings, Spanish carpets, Flemish tapestry and wainscots of dark Caribbean wood are the proper emblems of aristocratic power in this Renaissance prison-palace, but the hall's Oriental motifs smack worryingly of the seraglio. The canopied chair of state for Leicester and his countess sports 'cushions displayed in the Moorish fashion, and ornamented with Arabesque needle-work'; torches bearing wax candles are crafted to represent 'an armed Moor'; the bedroom lamps burn with perfumed oil.[22]

For Romantic authors of the Celtic fringe, domestic space was part and parcel of a wider spatial landscape marked by problematic boundaries between interior and exterior. Katie Trumpener has observed that the main plot device in Romantic tales situated outside England is 'the spatialization of political choices, presented as a journey of discovery through the British peripheries'.[23] In *The Wild Irish Girl* (1806), Sydney Owenson similarly opposes the virtues of Celtic Gothic domesticity to the dangerous allure of Continental and Eastern luxury consumer goods. With its tessellated pavements, open hearths, arched windows and princely devices, the Castle of Inismore conveys 'all the boundless extravagance and convivial spirit of ancient Irish hospitality' and captures the essence of Gothic 'domestic joys'. Set among rocks that rise to 'Alpine elevation' and boasting 'sublime objects' of savage beauty, the castle is a quintessential Romantic home, exhibiting 'nature in her most awful, most touching aspect'. But Owenson deploys the furnishings of her heroine's 'paradoxical boudoir' to signal the potential for sexual transgression in this crumbling Celtic stronghold. Amid oaken wainscots 'black with age', narrow casements, antique stools and a Gothic table, the rich new Turkey carpet, scarlet silk draperies, Etrurian

21 Ann Radcliffe, *The Mysteries of Udolpho*, ed. Bonamy Dobree (Oxford: Oxford University Press, 1998), vol. I, ch. 2, pp. 22–3.
22 Walter Scott, *Kenilworth: A Romance*, ed. J. H. Alexander (London: Penguin, 1999), vol. I, ch. 6, pp. 46–7.
23 Katie Trumpener, 'National Character, Nationalist Plots: National Tale and Historical Novel in the Age of Waverley', *ELH* 60 (1993), pp. 685–731, citation p. 693.

vases and London newspapers supplied by Glorvina's unwanted English suitor are incongruous and function to register Ireland's domination by an absentee Anglican Ascendancy, hostile to Irish traditions of Celtic decor and Gothic government.[24]

The task of domesticating the Gothic interior was not confined to historical Romantic writers, nor did the removal of Gothic tales from the exotic foreign geographical settings exploited by Owenson and Radcliffe serve to strip Romantic domestic interiors of their political significance. As Miranda Burgess argues, Austen's *Northanger Abbey* (1818) initiates a fictive process of 'domesticating Gothic: bringing the most visible conventions of the genre home from Italy, where Radcliffe has used them to distance the English reader from political instability; home from the turf of Wollstonecraft and the English Jacobins, who have assailed in Gothic novels and novelized polemic the justice of modern English politics and ancient tradition; home in the sense of a return to the domestic *and* national fold'.[25] In the abbey's refurbished chambers, Austen effects Catherine Morland's moral and consumer education – and hence completes her preparation for marriage and domestic life – by subjecting her to a crash course in Gothic interior design. Catherine, obsessed with the concocted medieval horrors of Romantic fiction, is incapable of appreciating the genteel interiors that mark the abbey as a domestic space suited to the Tilney family's wealth and status: 'the costliness or elegance of any room's fitting-up could be nothing to her; she cared for no furniture of a more modern date than the fifteenth century'. Persistently misreading Gothic domestic codes, she mistakes a black and yellow japanned cabinet – an obvious reference to the craze for chinoiserie stoked by the consumer revolution – for a Gothic receptacle of medieval manuscripts.[26]

Catherine's search for horrific sites of interiorized power in the home is repeatedly thwarted by General Tilney's fussy fascination with Northanger's furnishings: her Gothic visions of a patriarchal regime that has run amok in domestic tyranny are undercut by descriptions of the abbey's cheerful bedchambers and the general's tasteful choice of chinaware.

24 Sydney Owenson, Lady Morgan, *The Wild Irish Girl: A National Tale*, ed. Kathryn Kirkpatrick (Oxford: Oxford University Press, 1999), letter XII, pp. 101–2, letter V, p. 51, and letter XX, pp. 156–7.

25 Miranda Burgess, 'Domesticating Gothic: Jane Austen, Ann Radcliffe, and National Romance', in *Lessons of Romanticism: A Critical Companion*, ed. Thomas Pfan and Robert F. Gleckner (Durham, NC: Duke University Press, 1998), p. 399.

26 Jane Austen, *Northanger Abbey*, ed. Marilyn Butler (London: Penguin, 1995), vol. II, ch. 8, p. 159; vol. II, ch. 6, pp. 147–8.

Valued by Tilney for its 'elegance', Northanger's Staffordshire breakfast service is also selected 'to encourage the manufacture of his country . . .' By educating Catherine to prefer such domestic consumer patriotism over the adolescent pleasures of the imagined dungeon, Austen reconfigures and modernizes the public domesticity of the elite Gothic home. In Paul Morrison's Foucauldian reading of the novel's domestic interiors, 'far from being opposed to the dungeon as darkness is to light, the parlor reinscribes Gothic claustration in the mode of light or visibility, all the more effectively for eschewing the obvious mechanisms and paraphernalia of Gothic enclosure'. When Catherine has learned to decipher the symbolic messages conveyed by woollen carpets, English teapots and Rumford stoves she thus accepts a form of confinement that resides 'not in an economy of Gothic secrecy, but in a domestic sphere, at once social and psychological, in which there are no secret spaces, in which there is no escape from an openness that encloses'.[27]

Domestic sites: from stately home
to homely home

If *Northanger Abbey* attempts to reclaim the Gothic interior for a new, enclosed form of domesticity, containment is rarely achieved in the stately homes that form the prime locations of Austen's fiction. Literary critics have been too quick to equate Austen's careful attention to domestic space with a commitment to the home as 'a serene enclave set apart from change and flux', a separate sphere of privacy insulated from the demands of public life. *Mansfield Park* (1814) conventionally features in the secondary literature as Austen's most extended homage to domesticity, but its representations of the stately home continually stray beyond the boundaries of domestic decorum. 'Associating domesticity with tranquillity, comfort, and happiness, the language of *Mansfield Park* presents the reader with a domestic ideal', Aileen Douglas observes. 'In fact, we never actually witness domestic tranquillity in the novel': for Austen, domesticity functions as 'an ideal to be invoked, rather than a reality to be shown'.[28] Efforts to stage a sexually suggestive play within Mansfield's walls thus threaten to bring 'the end of all privacy and propriety' despite Sir Thomas Bertram's avowed desire for

---

27 Austen, *Northanger Abbey*, vol. II, ch. 7, p. 152; Paul Morrison, 'Enclosed in Openness: *Northanger Abbey* and the Domestic Carceral', *Texas Studies in Literature and Languages* 33:1 (Spring 1991), 11–12.

28 Aileen Douglas, 'Austen's Enclave: Virtue and Modernity', *Romanticism* 5:2 (1999), 152.

'domestic tranquillity, for a home which shuts out noisy pleasures'. Even Sir Thomas's success in halting the conversion of his private home into a public theatre by his progeny is at best a pyrrhic victory, for it fails to prevent his daughter's adulterous desertion of her husband's bed.[29]

Just as the cottage fostered forms of sociability that precluded the private enclosure of plebeian homes, so too elite patterns of visiting, tourism and travel ensured that the stately home was a public domestic space. Although large-scale country-house visiting developed only in the Victorian period, the Romantic era saw a significant increase in this practice among the gentry. Together, connoisseurs eager to display art treasures purchased on their Grand Tours and genteel tourists forced by revolutionary political upheaval to abandon continental travel ensured that 'a remarkable apparatus of country-house visiting grew up' throughout England from the 1790s.[30] Novelists eagerly put this new social phenomenon to literary use. In *Pride and Prejudice* (1813), it is Elizabeth Bennet's public tour of Darcy's stately home that precipitates the rapid cascade of plot developments which allow her, through marriage, to claim Pemberley as her private residence.[31]

In the national tales of Irish life popularized by Lady Morgan, Maria Edgeworth and Charles Maturin, travel to stately Irish homes provides especially rich opportunities for comparison between English Ascendancy and Irish Gothic forms of domestic life and government. Predicated on penal legislation that stripped Catholics of economic and political rights, the regime of Anglican Ascendancy established in the aftermath of the Glorious Revolution generated cultural antagonisms in Ireland that exercised a host of Romantic writers. Maturin's *Wild Irish Boy* (1808) presents a series of dramatic oppositions between native and foreign homes in which the corrosive social and cultural implications of Ascendancy politics are reinscribed in domestic architecture and furnishings. Like Owenson's *Wild Irish Girl*, Maturin's novel figures the deterioration of native paternalist relations through a castle set in the wilds of Connaught. Surrounded by bogs, this 'bold rude mass of structure' is a centre of public activity: enthroned on his over-sized wicker chair, the Catholic chieftain De Lacy conducts business

29 Jane Austen, *Mansfield Park*, ed. Kathryn Sutherland (London: Penguin, 1996), vol. I, ch. 16, p. 128; vol. II, ch. 1, p. 156.
30 Peter Mandler, *The Fall and Rise of the Stately Home* (New Haven, CT: Yale University Press, 1997), pp. 8–10, citation p. 9.
31 Jane Austen, *Pride and Prejudice*, ed. James Kinsley (Oxford: Oxford University Press, 1990), vol. III, ch. 1, pp. 185–96.

with his tenantry from his dinner table.[32] Neighbouring Ascendancy homes alert the reader to the despotic character of Protestant supremacy by their repeated violation of these Gothic norms of public life. At Hammond-house, public business is supplanted by private pleasures at the board, where the presence of a mistress and her bastard children reflects the home's degeneration from a locus of legitimate authority to 'a castle rackrent, an house of disorder and riot'. Nearby Montrevor House registers the futility of attempts to transplant English aristocratic culture to Irish soil. Incongruous, unnatural and Oriental decorative motifs mark the home's degeneration from a domestic site of public power to a dissipated scene of private vice. Returning in disgrace from London, the Montrevors initiate a frenetic campaign of redecoration that recapitulates the Ascendancy's doomed effort to remodel Irish culture, society and politics along English lines. Trees and shrubs crowd the entrance hall, accommodated in turf-tubs because the china vases in which they should properly be planted have cracked and broken in transit from the metropolis. In the state-rooms, naked walls stripped of venerable damask hangings await decoration with outlandish Egyptian antiquities; ill-fitting muslin window-shades painted to simulate Gothic casements lie useless beside the windows they should screen. An abortive exercise in aristocratic domesticity, Montrevor's redecoration, in Claude Fierobe's astute analysis, ensures that the ruling elite 'have lost forever any link with Irish soil and the nation's past and have become "fabrications", *trompe l'œil*, pastiches of foreign buildings, exotica . . . immutably alienated'.[33] To Maturin, for whom the house is a synecdoche for the householder, the demise of Gothic castles and the rise of stately homes in Ireland provide an object lesson in the political failure of the Act of Union.

For Irish novelists who rejected Maturin's dour assessment of Union, domesticating the Irish stately home was an essential task alike of imperial administration and colonial fiction. Maria Edgeworth's *The Absentee* (1812) constantly conflates the refurbishment of Irish aristocratic homes with the regeneration of Irish national life under English rule, and equates the decorative excesses of Orientalism with the debilitating consequences of absentee landlordism. In Edgeworth's writings, reformed gender relations

---

32 Charles Maturin, *The Wild Irish Boy*, 3 vols. (London: Longman, Hurst & Co., 1808), vol. I, pp. 180–4, citation p. 180.
33 Maturin, *Wild Irish Boy*, vol. I, pp. 221, 232–3; Claude Fierobe, 'Irish Homes in the Work of C. R. Maturin', in *The Big House in Ireland: Reality and Representation*, ed. Jacqueline Genet (Dingle: Brandon, 1991), p. 75.

are central to national renewal: only a reconstruction of feminine domestic taste can effect the absentee's return to his homeland. From the first page of the novel to its concluding paragraph, domestic furnishing transfixes Lady Colambre. Transplanted from her husband's Irish stately home to his London townhouse, she casts off her Celtic cultural moorings and falls prey to the seductive currents of metropolitan fashion. As her husband's mounting debts threaten to deprive their son of his inheritance, Lady Colambre drives the family fortunes deeper into crisis by attending only to the dictates of her London upholsterer. Feverish efforts to gain admittance to the highest circles of English society through lavish public entertainments in her home are mirrored by disastrous decorating agendas. Her reception rooms display an alarming combination of exotic styles, setting Turkish draperies, Alhambra hangings, seraglio ottomans and Chinese pagoda wallpaper against a background colour that bears the ludicrous sobriquet 'the belly-o'-the fawn'. Edgeworth, in contrast to Maturin, insists that Ireland's salvation lies in a rejection of neither English nor Irish standards of taste, but rather in a Romantic reconfiguration of Ascendancy and Celtic styles of domestic life. Initially refusing to return to Ireland because she detests 'the sight, the thoughts of that old yellow damask furniture, in the drawing-room at Clonbrony Castle', Lady Colambre is ultimately brought to acknowledge that she is 'always happier at home' and sets out for the family estate inspired 'to set the fashion of something better in that country'. With the castle's drawing-room chairs reupholstered in velvet embroidered with naturalistic flowers, the family's triumphal return to Ireland can exemplify Edgeworth's fond hope that under Union 'the fashion' will become 'not to be an Absentee'.[34]

As Edgeworth's derisive depictions of Orientalized metropolitan interiors attest, the inculcation of stable national identities was no less problematic in elite English mansions than in rude Celtic castles. Like the shifting and porous boundary between publicity and privacy, the balance between historic preservation and consumer modernization was fluid and unstable in the genteel homes of Romantic fiction. On the one hand, when Eastern passions were allowed to run riot, domestic disaster inevitably ensued. In Susan Ferrier's *Marriage* (1818, 1826), the thrusting tradesmen – 'loaded with china jars, monsters, and distorted tea pots' – who market Oriental goods in Lady Juliana's drawing room presage the dissolution of her marital home

---

34 Maria Edgeworth, *The Absentee*, ed. W. J. McCormack and Kim Walker (Oxford: Oxford University Press, 1988), ch. 2, pp. 12–14; ch. 14, p. 202; ch. 17, p. 266.

just as predictably as the Oriental interior of Lady Lindore's bedroom and boudoir – 'fitted up in a style that seemed rather suited for the pleasures of an Eastern sultana, or Grecian courtezan, than for the domestic comfort of a British matron' – signal her adulterous elopement. But precisely because Britain's identity as an imperial power entailed the incorporation of foreign lands and the comprehension of foreign cultures and commodities, the domestic interiors of the governing elite needed to accommodate and contain exotic motifs if they were to reflect the full panoply of British political authority at home and abroad. For Ferrier, this process of accommodation was best exemplified in the furnishings of country homes inhabited by the English gentry. In such houses, the domestic power of hereditary principles is so compelling that foreign and Oriental influences are safely absorbed as decorative devices, rather than precipitating domestic dissolution. 'Rose Hall was . . . perfectly English . . . for it wore the appearance of antiquity, without the too usual accompaniments of devastation or decay; neither did any incongruities betray vicissitudes of fortune, or change of owner', Ferrier observes in *Marriage*. 'The same old-fashioned respectability was also apparent in the interior of the mansion: . . . the spacious sitting room . . . had its due allowance of Vandyke portraits, massive chairs, and china jars, standing much in the same positions they had been placed in a hundred years before . . .'[35]

The secure incorporation of exotic products by the home is indeed a leitmotif of Romantic fiction, as John Galt's *Annals of the Parish* (1821) repeatedly demonstrates. When tea-drinking is first practised in Galt's fictional parish, the women who take to this new luxury resort not to their sitting rooms and parlours but to hedges, lanes, 'out-houses and by-places, just as the witches lange syne had their sinful possets and galravitchings'. Significantly, when tea-drinking is domesticated and moves into the manse, it loses its worrying sexual exclusivity, evolving from an activity practised defiantly out of doors by old biddies 'all cracking like pen-guns' to a convivial fireside activity shared by man and wife. Fully reconciled to this new form of consumption only when the pious widow Malcolm begins to retail tea from her home to support her needy family, Galt's narrator now seeks to cloak the luxurious connotations of this Eastern commodity with the language of domestic utility. When his wife purchases a silver teapot and ornamental chinaware to replace the wooden basins in which tea had been

---

35 Susan Ferrier, *Marriage, a Novel*, ed. Herbert Foltinek (London: Oxford University Press, 1971), pp. 131, 151, 264.

served in the hedgerows, she does so 'not . . . in a vain spirit of bravery . . . but because it was well known that tea draws better in a silver pot, and drinks pleasanter in a china cup, than out of any other kind of cup or teapot'.[36]

Far more troubling for Romantic writers than the adoption of exotic household commodities by the middling sort was the changing place of domestic labour in their homes. In castles and stately mansions, politics was a proper domestic employment of the governing elite, but for the swelling multitude of bourgeois households, the evolving claims of genteel, gendered domesticity placed new discursive limits on the glorification of household productivity. In cottages, the loss of domestic employment compromised the integrity of the home, but for more elevated households it was instead the retention of domestic labour that was fraught with difficulty and danger. Galt's protagonist takes as his second wife the daughter of an improving Ayrshire farmer who has 'a geni for management', and is quick to feel the troubling consequences of his choice. Filling the manse with 'the jangle and din' of spinning, carding, weaving and churning, the second Mrs Balwhidder converts her home into such 'a factory of butter and cheese' that her hapless husband thinks himself 'ruined and undone by her care and industry'.[37]

Women poets of middle-class life were especially vexed by the shifting definitions and valuations of productive labour in the Romantic household. For Anna Letitia Barbauld, domestic employments valorized the bourgeois home no less than they enriched the plebeian cot: in her early poetry, women's household work is vital not only to preserve the comforts of middle-class domestic life but also – and more crucially – to underpin the wider political order. Barbauld's 'Washing Day' (1797) insists upon the necessary linkage of private and public, interior and exterior in the well-ordered home. Here family and friends suffer a weekly expulsion from the warm circle of the domestic hearth precisely to ensure the maintenance of order and hospitality over time. Washing, rinsing, wringing, folding and starching 'chase . . . the very cat, / From the wet kitchen scared' and ensure that 'the friend / Whose evil stars have urged him forth to claim / On such a day the hospitable rites . . . In silence dines, and early slinks away'. Barbauld explicitly politicizes this household activity, comparing the travails

---

36 John Galt, *Annals of the Parish*, ed. D. S. Meldrum, 2 vols. (Edinburgh, 1936), vol. I, pp. 17, 29, 143.
37 *Ibid.*, vol. I, pp. 47–8, 196.

of the housewife who contemplates the 'sad disasters' of rain on washing day with the public ordeals suffered by 'Saints . . . stretched upon the rack, / And Montezuma . . . on burning coals . . .'[38] The growing ideological purchase of the 'science' of political economy, however, rendered such celebrations of public domestic labour in middle-class homes increasingly contentious. As political economists worked to distinguish unpaid household tasks from waged labour conducted in the marketplace, Barbauld's 'moral universe' was torn asunder. Later poems such as *Eighteen Hundred and Eleven* (1812), Josephine McDonaugh argues, indict the 'enchanted separation of spheres' prescribed by political economy for 'a lamentable privatisation of the domestic world, which renders it no longer capable of having the political and public function it holds in earlier work . . .'.[39] Male reviewers, fully alive to the gendered political implications of Barbauld's poetry, were swift to condemn her views. Savaged in the press for *Eighteen Hundred and Eleven*, Barbauld retired from the public sphere of publication.[40]

Conclusion

The resistance of women authors to strict demarcations between public and private realms is especially noteworthy in Romantic writing, but the poetry and fiction of this era were, more broadly, inspired by an appreciation of the inherent porosity of hearth and home to nature, politics and the market. In this respect, Felicia Hemans's most celebrated paeons to domestic life are – despite their much later date of composition and their focus on affluent households – of a piece with Wordsworth's early poems on plebeian cottage economy. 'The Homes of England' (1827), like 'Home at Grasmere', represents 'household love' through the devices of the Romantic domestic exterior rather than by cosy hearth-side scenes. Here Hemans defines 'The stately homes of England' not by their interior furnishings but by their ancestral trees, deer parks and watercourses, just as she describes humble cottages in terms of their orchards, brooks and bird life. Eliding distinctions between nature and culture, the trope of the Romantic domestic exterior

38 *The Poems of Anna Letitia Barbauld*, ed. William McCarthy and Elizabeth Kraft (Athens, GA: University of Georgia Press, 1994), pp. 133–5.
39 Josephine McDonaugh, 'Barbauld's Domestic Economy', in *Romanticism and Gender*, ed. Anne Janowitz (Cambridge: Cambridge University Press, 1998), pp. 62–77, citations pp. 66–7.
40 James Chandler, *England in 1819: The Politics of Literary Culture and the Case of Romantic Historicism* (Chicago: University of Chicago Press, 1998), pp. 114–20.

lent itself with ease to fictional and poetic efforts to conceptualize a domesticated public sphere. In Hemans's 'Domestic Affections' (1812), as in Wordsworth's 'Michael', the 'tranquil joys' where 'Domestic bliss has fix'd her calm abode' radiate outside the household, serving as a 'magnet-star' for the sons and fathers displaced from the home by 'the martial field, the troubled sea'.[41]

Surveying the title pages listed in the *Eighteenth-Century Short Title Catalogue*, John Brewer has drawn attention to 'the capacity of the public to absorb and represent the private' and has underlined the extent to which 'The "private" was "the other"' of the public in this period.[42] Attention to the content of poetry and prose writing suggests, however, that publicity was constitutive of Romantic private realms, rather than antagonistic or predatory to them. In Romantic representations of the domestic interior, productive labour, political power and even the natural world could comfortably cohabit. If the coffee house was the quintessential location of the public sphere in Restoration Britain, its central role in sustaining public discourse had, a century later, arguably been supplanted in literary works by the porous interior chambers of the domestic home.

The transition from the open, public domesticity so characteristic of Romantic writing to the cloying, claustrophobic private households of Victorian literature was never total. As Sharon Marcus has demonstrated in a wonderfully illuminating study of Victorian ghost stories, the terraced houses that came to dominate the later nineteenth-century domestic landscape were haunted by their very inability to enclose and secure their households over time and space.[43] By the 1830s, however, changes in the domestic scenes of literary life were increasingly conspicuous. The parlour, which now constituted the symbolic centre of the home, was far removed from the idealized, multipurpose chamber equipped for work and play sketched by John Clare in 'The Wish'. Cluttered 'with a profusion of things, things that are not primarily functional, that do not have obvious use-value, but rather participate in a decorative, semiotic economy', the parlours so

---

41 Felicia Hemans, *Records of Woman*, intro. Donald H. Reiman (New York: Garland, 1978), pp. 169–71; Felicia Hemans, *The Domestic Affections*, intro. Donald H. Reiman (New York: Garland, 1978), pp. 148–72.

42 John Brewer, 'This, That and the Other: Public, Social and Private in the Seventeenth and Eighteenth Centuries', in Dario Castiglione and Lesley Sharpe (eds.), *Shifting the Boundaries: Transformation of the Languages of Public and Private in the Eighteenth Century* (Exeter: University of Exeter Press, 1995), pp. 8–9.

43 Sharon Marcus, *Apartment Stories: City and Home in Nineteenth-Century Paris and London* (Berkeley: University of California Press, 1999), ch. 3.

copiously furnished by Victorian wives (and Victorian writers) privileged privacy over publicity, reproduction over production, and nurture over nature.[44] The seeds of this transformation of domestic space were themselves an ironic consequence of the Romantic movement's successful role in emancipating human desires from the imaginative and material constraints of the past,[45] but the fruit of this development was an increasingly strident renunciation of the Romantic domestic idiom. Charlotte Lucas, confessing her decision to marry the tiresome Mr Collins in *Pride and Prejudice*, speaks presciently to the appeal of the newly elaborated style of domesticity which was to triumph in Victorian writing. ' "I am not romantic you know" ', she explains to Elizabeth Bennet, ' "I ask only a comfortable home" '.[46]

---

44 Thad Logan, *The Victorian Parlour* (Cambridge: Cambridge University Press, 2001), p. 26.
45 See Colin Campbell, *The Romantic Ethic and the Spirit of Modern Consumerism* (Oxford: Blackwell, 1987), esp. p. 209.
46 Austen, *Pride and Prejudice*, vol. I, ch. 22, p. 96.

13

Writing, reading and the scenes of war

MARY A. FAVRET

To understand how war found its place in British literature in the late eighteenth and early nineteenth centuries, we might follow William Cowper's lead when, in *The Task* (1785) he organizes the scene of war around the figure of the post-boy.

> Hark! 'Tis the twanging horn! O'er yonder bridge . . .
> He comes, the herald of a noisy world,
> With spatter'd boots, strapp'd waist, and frozen locks,
> News from all nations lumb'ring at his back.
> True to his charge the close-pack'd load behind,
> Yet careless what he brings, his one concern
> Is to conduct it to the destin'd inn,
> And having dropp'd the expected bag – pass on.
> He whistles as he goes, light-hearted wretch,
> Cold and yet cheerful: messenger of grief
> Perhaps to thousands, and of joy to some . . . .[1]

The arrival of the post-boy (never named, but ever recognizable) opens Cowper's meditations in Book IV, 'The Winter Evening', where, half-convincingly, the poet cobbles out of 'Fireside enjoyments, home-born happiness' and 'sweet oblivion' a rural retreat from hostile weather and imperial hostilities (lines 140; 250). The arrival of the post-boy, however, daily disrupts Cowper's efforts to represent war retrospectively: 'Is India free?' he asks, prompted by seeing the mailbag; 'And does she wear her plumed / And jewelled turban with a smile of peace, / Or do we grind her still?' (lines 28–30).[2]

Cowper was awaiting the post-boy in the mid-1780s, before Britain had entered into its twenty-year contest with revolutionary and then

---

1 William Cowper, *The Task* in *Poetical Works*, ed. Humphrey Sumner Milford, 4th edn (London: Oxford University Press, 1967), Bk IV, lines 1–14, pp. 182–3.
2 Cowper refers to the notorious administration of Warren Hastings, Governor-General of Bengal, who would face impeachment for prosecuting unnecessary wars in India and using unscrupulous means to finance them.

Napoleonic France; but his response to the recently concluded war in North America and Britain's military endeavours across the globe lends its structure to a later generation attempting to construct an alternative theatre of war, within the geography of home rather than distant lands. The solitary youth with his makeshift uniform and purposive air, who arrives with fanfare and departs whistling, performs a national service while standing in for so many absent and always awaited young men gone to war. He offers the reader-poet fleeting contact – and consolation: however unexpected or disabling the burden he unloads, his comings and goings nevertheless inscribe a secure rhythm ordering the upheaval. And whatever the effect of his news, the young man performs his duty unscathed – *pace* mud and frozen locks. Indeed, the post-boy is more than a messenger, he is a figure of translation and condensation: disburdening his own body of a load of pain and grief, he converts the war into a matter of reading, its 'grief perhaps to thousands' packaged for consumption. As Cowper reports later, scanning the newspaper delivered from that bag, reading provides the 'loop-hole of retreat': 'The sound of war / Has lost its terrors 'ere it reaches me, / Grieves but alarms me not' (lines 100–2). In subsequent years, the 'terror' and 'alarm' thus muted would become for England the watchwords, if not the rationale, for war.[3] For now, the post-boy tells of a war made safe, regular and only intermittently present: an evening's performance.

Cowper's post-boy offers but one example of how a war fought on foreign ground and distant seas came home to England. He is a particularly rich example, comprising several of the strategies for representing war which would dominate literary production in the coming decades. The post-boy pops in and out of Romantic literature – heralding the opening of Wordsworth's 'Alice Fell, or Poverty'; ducking out of the door in Austen's *Sense and Sensibility*; manhandling letters in Lamb's 'Distant Correspondents'; or marking the passage of revolution and military glory in Hazlitt's late, evocative 'The Letter Bell'. In a fantastic moment he expands into De Quincey's imperial 'English Mail-Coach' ('Waterloo and Christendom!'). In a darker mood, the figure displays his alter ego: he is the solitary, nameless veteran who appears out of the blue in Wordsworth's *Prelude*; or, hobbling on crutches to deliver the crucial letter that transforms the fortunes of the

---

3 Coleridge stresses both these terms in 'The War and International Law', *The Friend* (1803), and 'Fears in Solitude' (1798), in Samuel Taylor Coleridge, *Collected Works*, 11 vols., ed. Barbara Rooke (London: Routledge and Kegan Paul; Princeton: Princeton University Press, 1967), vol. IV, pp. 265–7 and vol. I, pp. 468–73. They are crucial as well in the closing chapters of Walter Scott's *The Antiquary* (1816).

protagonists, he is the maimed soldier who haunts the finale to Charlotte Smith's *Old Manor House*. The post-boy's ubiquity attests to his picturesque ability to organize and soften the contours of history, but also to his contravening charge, to broadcast the disruptions of war. Taking Cowper's post-boy as a sort of literary herald, one learns how to recognize the appearance of war in the years to come. As Cowper's *Task* suggests, scenes of war would have some of the following features. First, they would display the curious intersection of spatial and temporal matters: because of their distance from the fighting, these scenes operate with a heightened sense of temporality, punctuated by intense moments, but also and therefore predicated on waiting. The geographical distance of war would be relayed through a complex set of temporal dispositions: space was felt through time. Scenes of war would also redistribute pains, noises and griefs between uniformed bodies (over there) and domestic bodies (here). They would focus on fleeting, solitary but immediately recognizable types. And they would tend to overwrite the burden of 'news' with the high-flying powers of imagination ('Is India free? does she wear her plumed / And jewelled turban . . .?'). Above all, as the global scope of war became more evident, the experience of war depicted in literature would locate itself more readily in the realm of the mind, rather than the body.

In part because of the displacement of war to the mental arena and to the act of reading itself, literary history has been slow to recognize how war governs much of Romantic literature. Scholars are used to viewing Romanticism through the lens of revolution, but as the contours of the period loosen, Romanticism appears as much the product of wartime as of that familiar dialectic, Revolution and Reaction. For most of the years between 1756 and 1815 England was fighting wars on four different continents, yet despite fears of invasion in 1797–8 and 1803, fighting never came to that sceptered isle. Such prolonged fighting abroad, experienced by most of the English public in mediated form, put its stamp on the period's writing in ways we have only begun to detect. Throughout the Romantic period, one can witness the slow dawning of an understanding that a foreign war was in fact something to be anticipated, willed or indeed read – as well as fought.

Wartime: reading, waiting

The modernity of this wartime is inextricable from the all-engrossing spectacle offered by the daily newspaper. A sense of 'wartime' emerged in the Romantic era with the public's unprecedented consumption of a kind of eventfulness, a situation Cowper realizes in the advent of the newsboy. If the newspaper and its distribution system helped give the wars both their temporal and narrative structure, it is illustrative to see how war reporting operated at the end of the eighteenth century, during the first modern war. Glancing at accounts of the Battle of the Nile in 1798, we see how the *London Times*, for instance, represented the war as episodic battles over timing and intelligence. Here is its first published account of 'Admiral Nelson's Victory' (August 1798) which appeared that October:

> The long-awaited news is come at last ... Yesterday morning, CAPTAIN SUTTON, of the *Prince of Wales* packet, which brought over the Hambourg mail, arrived at the SECRETARY OF STATE'S office, charged with a dispatch from SIR MORTON EDEN, at *Vienna*, which was delivered to him at Cuxhaven, after the Mail was on board. By this dispatch, which is dated the 15th of September last, we learn that on the third ult. the *Marine* cutter, with CAPTAIN CAPEL, ... arrived at *Naples*, with letters from the ADMIRAL for SIR WILLIAM HAMILTON. These letters contained advice that on the 8th of August our fleet attacked the enemy's ships near *Rosetta*; and his whole line of battle (consisting of 13 sail) was either sunk, taken or destroyed, excepting two ships.[4]

Before it describes the exploits of the valiant Nelson and his men, *The Times* suggests that such (long, complex) circulation of information organizes the scene of war, and that whoever commands intelligence commands that scene. The paper does not fail to point out the limits of Nelson's version, published the following day: it is 'too concise to satisfy the anxious curiosity of the Public'. To make up for the hero's deficiency, then, and to supplement the official account, *The Times* offers an array of its own 'private correspondence' over the course of the following week: letters from officers on various ships engaged in the battle and dispatches from a range of diplomatic centres (Naples, Madrid, Hamburg, Florence, Constantinople, Vienna, Basle), thereby fusing its ability to satisfy the public's demand for more compelling intelligence with its own organizing, global perspective on the war.

The Times constructs the war as a sort of national literacy event, contingent on the nation's ability to read in a specific way. It assumes an appreciation of certain facts (geographical and military), proper names (heroes, officers, ships) and relations (Briton vs. French, Italian, Turk, etc.) as they accumulate and develop meaning over the course of reading. Not to

4 *Times of London* (2 October 1798), p. 2.

be literate in this way is to be outside of the nation's experience of wartime. The novelists and poets of the period understood this state of affairs; thus in Jane Austen's *Persuasion*, the fundamental illiteracy of the Musgrove family – their negligence of the names of military posts, ships, officers – has the potential to disqualify them from participating in the nation. They are out of synch, consulting the navy lists only after peace is declared, whereas Anne Elliot, a devoted reader of war reports, is destined to fill a post of 'Domestic Virtue' and 'National Importance'.[5] Wartime creates itself out of continual, daily reading: the facts shift from day to day, from excerpt to excerpt, yielding the sense that no single instalment will deliver the truth and yet every snippet is crucial. Invested thus with suspense and continuity, war appears a plot ordained elsewhere but played out in the mind and body of the reader: the reader is not invited to interrupt the unfolding story but rather is compelled, out of what *The Times* calls 'anxious curiosity', to read on, revising his interpretation of events, until the (tragic or glorious) end. The very structure of Austen's novels such as *Pride and Prejudice* or *Northanger Abbey*, which prescribe a constant re-reading of events and relations, parallels the lessons of the newspapers' war correspondence, as do the Gothic novels of Ann Radcliffe, or poems such as Coleridge's 'Christabel' and 'Kubla Khan', Blake's *The Four Zoas*, or indeed Wordsworth's *The Prelude*, each of which announces at least an oblique relationship to war.

'The long-awaited news is come at last' – but never definitively. The punctuated eventfulness within dailiness that organized the public's experience of war accompanied a sense of living 'in the meantime', waiting for news of events that happened at a distance both geographical and temporal. As the newspapers made manifest, by the time a crucial victory had been reported in England, the British navy or army could have, in the meantime, suffered shattering defeat. The Navy lists could tell you that your son had not died as of a month ago, but they could not reassure you about time since. Moreover, though the reported events of war had always already happened, they were also open to revision. '[W]hat security can I have', Charles Lamb would ask, writing as Elia, 'that what I right now send you for truth shall not, before you get it, unaccountably turn into a lie?'[6] Or, as a poem in *The Morning Chronicle* mocked in 1804, news of victory could

---

5 Jane Austen, *Northanger Abbey and Persuasion*, The Oxford Illustrated Jane Austen, ed. R. W. Chapman, 3rd edn, 6 vols. (Oxford: Oxford University Press, 1923; rev. 1969; rpt 1988), vol. V, p. 278.

6 Charles Lamb, 'Distant Correspondents', in *The Complete Works and Letters of Charles Lamb* (New York: The Modern Library, 1963), p. 200.

spread like wildfire, but 'lo! What a change will a day or two show / For Truth now declares, we've scarced injur'd the foe.'[7] The lag-time built into scenes of war produced a deep anxiety about chronology. The sense of living 'in the meantime' gave birth to a fear that both history and future could be obliterated, and time left drifting in the present (but never present enough) wartime. On the one hand, living 'in the meantime' of war meant living in constant anticipation; simultaneously, and on the other hand, it meant living belatedly. Caught out of alignment with history, emotion itself would become intense, and intensely unmoored.

Military historians remind us that, for infantrymen and cavalrymen, warfare in the age of Napoleon consisted primarily of the tedium of waiting. Both Napoleon and Wellington figured out the strategic advantage of keeping troops busily in abeyance; in the Peninsular campaign of 1812, for example, 'only a minority of the [British] army as a whole would have smelt the smoke of battle in that, or any other year of the long war'.[8] Wartime meant the majority of the men were themselves waiting, oddly, for war to take shape. In this meantime between battles, feeling itself rose up to fill the limbo: 'It is a situation of higher excitement, and darker and deeper feeling, than any other in human life', writes one British soldier in Spain on the eve of battle.[9]

The home front too would discover its version of waiting in wartime, and fill it with affective power. Nina Auerbach makes the case for intense expectation as a structure of war when contemplating a passage from Pride and Prejudice: 'In presenting these drawing rooms full of women watching the door and watching each other', Auerbach observes, 'Jane Austen tells us what an observant, genteel woman has to tell about the Napoleonic Wars: she writes novels about waiting.'[10] If the charge against Austen's novels is that nothing happens, Auerbach provides a way of seeing that intensely felt eventlessness, that meantime, as itself an experience of the war. The reader is recruited into the position of waiting with great concentration for something decisive (in the figure of a man – or a post-boy) to arrive. One could as well extend this perception to a novel such as The Mysteries of

---

7 Anon., 'A New Song to an Old Tune,' in Betty T. Bennett (ed.), British War Poetry in the Age of Romanticism, 1793–1815 (New York and London: Garland Press, 1975), p. 329. The poem was first published in The Morning Chronicle, October 1804.
8 Rory Muir, Tactics and the Experience of Battle in the Age of Napoleon (New Haven and London: Yale University Press, 1998), p. 9.
9 Muir, Tactics, p. 7.
10 Nina Auerbach, Communities of Women (Cambridge, MA and London: Harvard University Press. 1978), pp. 38–9.

Udolpho (1794), where the agonized waiting, rimmed round with threats of violence, is less restrained than in Austen, resembling more closely the soldier's predicament; and where the heroine, carted through the very terrain of the war in Europe, yearns to find something decisive while imagining she sees corpses. A related but inverted logic applies to Walter Scott's heroes, who, like Darsie Latimer in *Redgauntlet*, learn the value of 'temporizing': not committing themselves, but anxiously waiting out the violence of military encounter. Their temporizing position is echoed by Robert Southey, speaking of military policy in 1811, where he argues for 'prudence' and 'forbearance' over 'rashness' in waiting out the response of the Continental powers to Bonaparte's incursions. 'To his [Napoleon's] oppression there must be a period: a day of retribution and freedom will at last arrive; . . . till [Prussia, Austria, Holland and Germany] shall be prepared to strike, at once and in concert, . . . *For that hour* England will anxiously watch; *at that hour* she will be prepared to put forth all her strength.'[11] Waiting out the periodicity of history – 'there must be a period' – provides Southey and Scott with a meantime wartime strategy. But not everyone had the confidence of their historicism.

As Scott's historical romances, Austen's own *Persuasion* and the newspapers themselves make clear, expectation can hardly be extricated from a conviction that the meaningful events have already occurred. For Wordsworth, writing a string of sonnets in October 1803, the anticipated threat of invasion coincides with the fear that nothing will happen because everything has already happened. He fears that time itself has been evacuated: 'The great events with which old stories ring / Seem vain and hollow'; 'such emptiness / Seems at the heart of all things'.[12] When Wordsworth tries to depict war, he habitually locates it at a great temporal remove, as in his 'Poems Dedicated to National Independence and Liberty', the Salisbury Plain poems, or 'Yew Trees': 'not loth to furnish weapons for the hands / Of . . . those that crossed the sea / And drew the sounding bows at Azincour . . .' (p. 146). Nor is he alone in trying to pull his experience of war into alignment with a select, but distant past: Southey, Scott, Hemans, Byron and many lesser known poets would gravitate to past and foreign battles in order to mine some affective relationship to the current war, in part from the sense that feeling had been drained from 'the present face of things' where, at

11 Robert Southey, Review of C. W. Pasley, *Essay on the Military Policy and Institutions of the British Empire*, *Quarterly Review* 5 (1811), 433–5.
12 William Wordsworth, 'October 1803', *Poetical Works*, ed. Thomas Hutchison, rev. edn Ernest de Selincourt (Oxford: Oxford University Press, 1936, rpt 1981), p. 245.

least for Keats's belated knight-at-arms, 'no birds sing'. For Byron, picking through the rubble of chivalry in *Childe Harold's Pilgrimage*, the question of belatedness would suffuse his response to the Peninsular campaign: Harold's very identity is cultivated from the charged affective limbo accompanying this sense of being unmoored from history. As Matthew Arnold would recognize years later, Byron's work offered the image of a 'passionate and dauntless soldier of a forlorn hope'.[13]

Perhaps the best figure for the conflicted position wartime produces between expectation and belatedness is the exile or wanderer. Charlotte Smith exploits this limbo in her long critique of the effects of war, 'The Emigrants' (1793), occasioned by the French exiles (primarily widows) then wandering the English countryside.[14] Pacing the downs above the sea in Sussex, the poet identifies her own position with that of the exiles: 'They, like me, / From fairer hopes and happier prospects driven / Shrink from the future and regret the past' (lines 150–2). Her exiles have lost both past and future, living between hope and dread, rushing and wandering. Their vantage explodes Cowper's loop-hole of retreat, where he snuggles in to read about distant violence, while 'Fancy, like the finger of a clock, / Runs the great circuit and is still at home.'[15] Smith pictures war as a scene where time – and wits – are deranged: 'when Nature seem'd to lose / Her course in wild distemperature, and aid, / With seasons all revers'd, destructive War.'[16]

Not knowing when, that is, how to mark the limits of the theatre of war, writers in wartime also did not know when, that is how, to feel about it. Some of the most evocative writing during wartime dramatizes this difficulty. Wordsworth's statement of his own 'Anticipation: October 1803' illustrates the difficulty concisely: prophesying an end both to anticipation and to the war itself, it echoes the noisy joy of biblical psalms in welcoming soldiers home. Yet the final lines falter from the anticipated assurance of happy retrospection when they imagine the dead and wounded:

> . . . the pain
> And even the prospect of our brethren slain,

13 Matthew Arnold, *Essays in Criticism, Second Series* (London: Macmillan, 1903), p. 202.
14 Charlotte Smith, *The Poems of Charlotte Smith*, ed. Stuart Curran (New York: Oxford University Press, 1993), pp. 131–63. Smith dedicates the poem to Cowper, citing the influence of *The Task*.
15 Cowper, *Works*, p. 185.
16 Smith, 'The Emigrants', in *Poems*, p. 156. The figure of derangement in response to war news reappears in Smith's 'The Forest-boy', *Poems*, pp. 111–16.

Hath something in it which the heart enjoys: –
In glory will they sleep and endless sanctity.

(lines 11–14)

The sonnet's final evocation of eternity does not cover over the question of what exactly the speaker anticipates: the end to anticipation and the possibility of retrospection? the 'something' enjoyable about brethren slain? the endlessness beyond anticipation? This 'Anticipation' which marks wartime does not know where it stands in time nor how or when it ought to be feeling.

Redistributing pain

Registering the agony of those waiting for news of war, we begin to realize how frequently war's pain is transferred from the body of the soldier to those Coleridge calls 'spectators and non-combatants', from battlefield to home.[17] Just as the newsboy dumps his load of grief or joy and moves on, 'indifferent', so the literature of the period redistributes the pains of war from the uniformed bodies of public servants to private, domestic bodies: not just to Cowper's cloistered reader but also, and more frequently, to women and children. In newspaper accounts and popular poetry especially, the scene of injury was the home front, where grieving mothers and widows would die from waiting or fall sick from news. The agonized feeling that rose to fill the emptiness of living 'in the meantime' could reach such a pitch that it reproduced, but also redirected, the effects of warfare.

This pattern marks a range of writing in the period, where the war widow with her orphan child had perhaps greater visibility in the press than the average fighting man.[18] Works by well-known writers – Mary Robinson's 'The Widow's House', Wordsworth's 'The Female Vagrant' and 'The Blind Highland Boy', Burns's 'Logan Water' or Smith's 'The Forest-Boy' – as well as such anonymous poems in newspapers and journals as 'The Widow', 'Anna's Complaint', 'Thomas and Kitty' – put the war widow centre stage in the theatre of war, her body both doubling and replacing the soldier's as the site of pain and devastation. 'The Widow', which appeared in *The Morning Post* in 1795 illustrates the common dynamic. Nancy, sleepless with worry, awaits the return of William, who has been pressed into service by the Royal Navy. At sea, William suffers euphemistically: 'Conquest no more

---

17 Coleridge, 'Fears in Solitude, Written in April 1798, During the Alarm of an Invasion', line 96. Coleridge, *Collected Works*, vol. I, p. 469.
18 Bennett, *War Poetry*, p. 52.

could heal poor WILLIAM's smart – / He spill'd the ruddy drop that warm'd his heart.' Back home, Nancy's grief is brought into violent synchrony with the sailor's fate: the verse relays the sequence (breast, drop, heart), this time translating euphemism into unequivocal death.

> Alternate Hope, alternate fear,
> In NANCY's constant bosom reign;
> In vain she dropp'd the pearly tear –
> Hope sooth'd her constant heart in vain,
> Her WILLIAM's fate was told; she heard and sigh'd
> Cast up to heav'n her eyes, then bow'd and died.[19]

The transfer of violence from sailor to widow displays the force of affection: aching love, rather than swords, guns or disease, is the agent of death. In Robert Merry's 'The Wounded Soldier' (1799), the transfer occurs less smoothly, confessing its open secret, that is, the extreme desire *not* to see the injured body of the military man. A wounded soldier makes his way home, filled with fear that his beloved Lucy will 'avert her eyes' from his 'horrid guise'. Arriving without warning at his parents' home, the soldier makes his presence known – with immediately fatal consequences. 'His mother shriek'd, and dropp'd upon the floor; / His father look'd to heav'n with streaming eyes, / And LUCY [conveniently present] sunk, alas! To rise no more'.[20] In near-parody, all eyes are directed away from the soldier's wounds, falling instead on the dead Lucy. In these poems and countless others, sentimental interest in the woman left behind dovetails with an effort to shield the reader from the monstrous sight of a wounded or dying man. As Wordsworth would make too plain in his own encounter with the Discharged Soldier, a governing impulse asked the war veteran 'not [to] linger in the public ways', but keep out of sight.[21]

Still the public ways were crammed with reminders that war's injury could not be contained by the domestic and sentimental. In a typical poem published in 1801 in both *The Morning Chronicle* and *The Courier*, the vulnerable widow is sent abroad, travelling to the site of her husband's grave and literally covering over his suffering with her own: 'Beneath the drifted snow she lay / A Corpse, upon the lone Heath's way.'[22] Thus, even as these

19 *Ibid.*, pp. 153–4.
20 *Ibid.*, pp. 242–5.
21 *The Prelude*, Bk IV, line 455; in Wordsworth, *Poetical Works*, p. 521.
22 Bennett, *War Poetry*, p. 269. Bennett locates a similar narrative structure in 'The Field of Battle' (1794) and Percy Shelley's 'Henry and Louisa' (1809). Bennett, *War Poetry*, pp. 60–1.

widows seem to deflect attention and pain from the fighting man, they shatter the fixed contours of the domestic sphere, undermining the logic that says war is fought at a distance in order to keep home safe. Joanna Baillie makes this explicit in her remarkable play, *Ethwald* Part 1, where the price of Ethwald's invincibility in the battlefield is seeing his childhood sweetheart, Bertha, wandering homeless and insane, dispossessed by the wars her lover has waged.[23] Although it is reasonable to explain the war widow's prominence simply as an effect of her visibility on the home front, ideological complexity must have given this figure a special charge. On the one hand, her vulnerable feminine body evokes domestic and chivalric sentiment, demands a restoration of domestic security and deflects our gaze from the image of the male body in pain. On the other hand, and simultaneously, she destroys the gendered subtext that divides the realm of the citizen-soldier from the realm of those he fights to protect. A similar equivocation, this time centred on a boy, makes Hemans's 'Casabianca' ('The boy stood on the burning deck') one of the more indelible representations of war in this period. Even historical accounts of battle, such as Southey's popular 'The Siege of Zaragoza [Saragossa]' work this substitution, putting the spotlight on heroic women in the midst of carnage, while blurring the image of the men who were slaughtered.[24] Frances Burney elaborates this provocative figure, overlaying the ambivalence of gender and home with that of national identity, in her last novel, *The Wanderer, or Female Difficulties* (1814), which incorporates the homeless woman of Radcliffe's Gothic and Smith's poetry into an explicitly wartime scenario. The wandering woman, the orphan and the boy emerge in this literature as, in part, alibis for a mortal adult male body. Dialectical emanations of the fiction of unassailable masculinity and nation, they evoke the failures of these fictions.

The wars clearly produced bodily alteration in a large proportion of the population, the result not only of fighting and disease abroad, but also of famine and poverty at home. Yet injury in the literature of the period usually appears singular: women wander alone, veterans sit by the roadside alone, boys die alone. Tremendous pressure condenses the pains of a nation

---

23 Baillie's *Count Basil* (1798) reverses this pattern.
24 Robert Southey, *History of the Peninsular Wars* in *Select Prose of Robert Southey*, ed. with intro. Jacob Zeitlin (New York: The Macmillan Company, 1916), pp. 374, 375–6, 378–9. James Gillray's print, *Spanish Patriots Attacking the French Banditti* (1808) has a similar emphasis.

onto a single representative type, perhaps in an effort to focus the sympathies of the public and imagine the nation as a unified body. Yet the effect, at least in these more pathetic instances, suggests a nation both isolated in its suffering and disintegrating. A counter movement would demand a similar sort of condensation but produce, in place of the feminized victim, the robust mother who could absorb the pains of war into her own body. Thomas De Quincey dreams up a remarkable version of such maternity when he reflects on the war period in 'The English Mail Coach'. The narrator brings to a woman news that her son has died in battle, but the paragraph swerves away from any report of 'the bloody trench':

> I lifted not the laurels from the bloody trench in which horse and man lay mangled together. But I told her how these dear children of England, privates and officers . . . rode their horses into the mists of death, (saying to myself, but not to *her*) and laid down their young lives for thee, O mother England! as willingly . . . as ever, after a long day's sport, when infants, they had rested their wearied heads upon their mother's knees, or had sunk to sleep within her arms.[25]

The violent scene finds rest in the mother's capacious, allegorical body. Britannia herself, the indomitable mother hailed in song and symbol, rose to special eminence in the war period. Conservative women writers such as Hannah More and Letitia Hawkins promoted the image of national maternity, not just as riposte to Wollstonecraftian feminism, but also as a rousing alternative to the haunting figure of the war widow.

More potent even than the mother in absorbing war's suffering was the military hero: Wellington, Howe, Nelson and Napoleon (as anti-hero); or, in a more cosmopolitan vein, Kosciusko, Pelayo or Hofer; or, in the mode of belatedness, King Alfred, Edward of Monmouth, and Henry of Marlborough. Indeed it was clear that these men were less bodies than names, the reading and reciting of which joined the public together in a common history and promised a future unprecedented in earlier eighteenth-century wars. While the heroes of the Seven Years' War, for instance, were widely known and celebrated, the wars at the turn of the century mobilized more names – appropriated from the past and other nations – and brought them to a greater audience. The immortality conferred on these names by a

---

25 Thomas De Quincey, 'The English Mail Coach', in *Confessions of an English Opium-Eater and Other Writings*, ed. Grevel Lindop (Oxford: Oxford University Press, 1985), p. 208.

burgeoning print culture reciprocally promised that the nation would survive. It is impossible to gauge adequately the extent to which these names galvanized the nation's sense of what war was, or how effectively they transcended the figure of the mangled, wounded body. (Though Nelson's injuries were common knowledge – busted eye, busted arm, a body beaten by illness – civic memorials, like West's famous painting of his death, always showed his body beautifully intact.) The remarkable popularity in this period of the singular, military hero, celebrated in epic, song, novel and drama also seems a pointed response to a new sort of war which, aspiring to be total, demanded vast armies of faceless commoners. When the innovations of the People's Army, mass conscriptions, and press gangs replaced professional armies; when 'the waste of the life of the combatants [became something] which . . . the power of the state [could] compel', titanic heroes rose up in a sort of compensatory fantasy of individualism.[26] Compressing the masses into larger-than-life action heroes, whose names the press would write in capitals, made representations of war more legible; it also radically under-represented the scale of injury. In this climate, Scott's solution in *The Lay of the Last Minstrel* (1805) to reduce warfare to a contest between two representative champions, mirrors a more general attempt to minimize public awareness of the sprawling and anonymous nature of war. Even artists less inclined to chivalric belatedness, such as the caricaturist James Gillray, would depict the world war, which involved dozens of countries and hundreds of thousands of warriors, as a clash of individuals, two oversized (but not always heroic) bodies vying for the globe.[27] Byron's *Don Juan*, in its ironic search for a hero, would mock this impulse, but also register its source in a war which offered neglect, anonymity and death in the place of fame and glory:

> But here I leave the general concern
> To track our Hero on his path of Fame;
> He must his laurels separately earn –
> For fifty thousand heroes, name by name,
> Though all deserving equally to turn
> A couplet, or an elegy to claim,

26 T. H. Green, *Principles of Political Obligation*, quoted in Michael Walzer, *Just and Unjust Wars: A Moral Argument with Historical Illustrations* (New York: Basic Books, 1977), p. 28. Georg Lukács takes up this issue in *The Historical Novel*, preface by Fredric Jameson (Lincoln and London: University of Nebraska Press, 1983), pp. 23–6.

27 James Gillray, 'The Plumb Pudding in Danger' (1805) or 'The Modern Prometheus, or the Downfall of Tyranny' (1814).

Would form a lengthy lexicon of Glory,
And what is worse still, a much longer story.[28]

Wartime's print culture conspires with the other technologies of modern war to obscure the names of the too numerous deceased. The desire to fix the experience of war in a single, iconic name influences the great heroic/ military biographies of the age (Hazlitt on Napoleon; Southey on Nelson), but also the pose of the Byronic hero (*the* Giaour, *the* Corsair) who stands resolutely apart from the masses. It even travels, in combination with the urge to domesticate war, to the complicated female figure of Joan of Arc (in Southey's popular epic and responses by Helen Maria Williams, Felicia Hemans and others).

The hero-as-name gives his life to his country in ways literal and figurative, his death standing in for, and making meaningful, countless others. But like the other figures attracting attention, the hero frequently if perversely serves to transfer the scene of injury away from the fighting. Consider the case of Nelson, England's most spectacular military hero who, after a string of iconoclastic naval victories, died in action in 1805 at Trafalgar, site of his greatest success. Dozens of biographies, songs and tributes followed Nelson's death, but Southey's *Life of Nelson* (1813) was the most influential monument, steeping the men of the nation in the life and character of this hero. Thirteen editions of Southey's *Life of Nelson* appeared before 1853; it was the most successful biography of the nineteenth century, required reading for soldiers, sailors and schoolboys who aspired to embody its lessons. Through Southey, Nelson's life became the fuel for empire. 'He has left us . . . a name and an example', Southey concludes, '[W]hich are at this hour inspiring thousands of the youth of England: a name which is our pride, and an example that will continue to be our shield and our strength.'[29] Southey's biography, much more than his predecessors', downplays Nelson's crippled body; injuries become the excuse to focus instead on the warrior's indomitable will, his sense of duty, and the talisman of both, Nelson's words. In the death scene, for instance, Nelson's demise is

---

28 George Gordon, Lord Byron, *Don Juan*, in *The Complete Poetical Works*, 7 vols., ed. Jerome McGann (Oxford: Clarendon Press and New York: Oxford University Press, 1980–93), Canto 8, stanzas XVII–XVIII. Compare the 'terrible presses' – alternately wine presses and printing presses – that consume multitudes in Night the Ninth of Blake's *The Four Zoas* in *The Complete Poetry and Prose of William Blake*, ed. David Erdman, rev. edn (Garden City, New York: Anchor Press/Doubleday, 1982), pp. 404–6.

29 Robert Southey, *The Life of Nelson* (London: John Murray, 1813), p. 290.

cushioned by an everlasting discourse: his 'last signal, ENGLAND EXPECTS EVERY MAN TO DO HIS DUTY!'; his last written words (a prayer and a diary entry); and his last spoken words, 'Thank God I have done my duty!'[30]

Yet Southey aims at more than converting the hero's suffering body into undying language; he wants to depict the violence of war as the cure for England's ills. The *Life of Nelson* understands itself as an antidote for a society Southey saw as 'poisoned' by a corrupt aristocracy and 'infected' by the plagues of colonial vice, especially illicit sexuality.[31] (The irony for the military man, of course, was that actual plagues and diseases were the leading cause of wartime fatalities; Nelson himself was made very ill serving in the East Indies.) The *Life of Nelson* showed the hero submitting temporarily to these metaphorical 'diseases' but then wresting himself free. A return to fighting helped soothe his tortured conscience and keep Nelson safe from vaguely foreign temptations; through his shining example, the men of England absorb a new purity to ward off moral, and therefore national decay. For a nation torn by factionalism and strife, Nelson's life, via Southey, could also offer a wholly transparent wholeness: 'All men knew [because the *Life of Nelson* insists] that his heart was as humane as it was fearless; that there was not in his nature the slightest alloy of selfishness or cupidity; but that with perfect and entire devotion, he served his country with all his heart and all his soul, and with all his strength.'[32] Nelson could not be anything but whole; his example, read 'at this hour' by thousands, made England, once ailing and broken, now healthy and entire.

In order for the hero's life, lost in battle, to heal the stricken nation, battle itself must be deemed therapeutic, even life-giving. Indeed, this is the note hit in the second half of the war, after Nelson's martyrdom. It rumbles through Coleridge's *The Friend*, where he diagnoses the public mind as having 'lost its tone and elasticity' while developing an 'unmanly impatience for peace'; the 'only remedy' for which, he writes, is the recommencement of war, which gains for England 'popular enthusiasm, public unanimity, and simplicity of object'.[33] The note sounds more softly in

---

30 Southey, *Nelson*, pp. 273–84. Compare this death scene with the detailed, clinical description in his primary sources, John Stanier Clarke and John MacArthur, *The Life of Admiral Lord Nelson, K. B.* (London: T. Caddell and Wm. Davies, 1809) and T. O. Churchill, *The Life of Lord Viscount Nelson* (London: Harrison and Rutter, 1810), esp. p. 84.

31 Tim Fulford, 'Romanticizing the Empire: The Naval Heroes of Southey, Coleridge, Austen and Marryat', *MLQ* 60 (1999), 168–78.

32 Southey, *Nelson*, p. 245.

33 Coleridge, *Collected Works*, vol. IV, pp. 264–5.

Austen's *Persuasion*, when Admiral Croft posits war as the solution to a young man's romantic vacillations. In these instances Coleridge and Austen chime with C. W. Pasley's popular *Essay on the Military Policy and Institutions of the British Empire* (1811) which uses Nelson's example to argue 'that the nation's moral and political health would be improved by imperial conquest on land and sea'.[34] The singular, national hero thus describes a teeter-tottering game: on the one hand his purity of resolve and self-sacrifice throw into relief the social and moral decay on the home front and in far-flung colonies, which his martyrdom then cures. Similarly the incoherent, faceless masses demanded by war are redeemed by his transcendent singularity. On the other hand, the hero supports the logic that says, by sending men's bodies off to be wounded, broken, killed, England will find itself a stronger, more robust and unified nation.

Nelson's example offers lessons in the redistribution of the ills of war while alerting us to the transfer of the agonistic scene from battlefield (or ship) to moral character.[35] For Southey, Nelson's battles with his adulterous love for Emma Hamilton or with his allegiance to the Neopolitan monarchs are solved by his victories at sea, and the narrative tacks between these paralleled scenes. In other Romantic texts, the parallel recedes, with the moral terrain – the battles of 'spirit', 'strength', 'ardour' and 'imagination' – emerging as *the* crucial scene of wartime. This is the terrain cultivated by some of the major male writers of the Romantic period, who, as Marlon Ross and others have demonstrated, fought to appropriate the military hero as the figure of their own poetic and moral efficacy.[36] But the field of war could be reassigned to the moral realm in ways that critiqued rather than duplicated a military ethos, especially in the 1790s when victories and heroes were hard to find. Coleridge's 'Fears in Solitude, Written in April 1798, During the Alarm of an Invasion' offers a paradigmatic argument for 'indolence' and 'love of nature' as the nation's best hope for winning the war, here understood as a fundamentally moral conflict. The ever-active military man cannot participate in the sort of self-reflection which the poet, writing in 1798, deems crucial for the proper moral reform – and thus

---

34 Fulford, 'Romanticizing', p. 185. Fulford details Pasley's close connection with Coleridge as well as Austen's and Southey's admiration for the soldier's book.
35 A similar case could be made for Wellington, whom the *Dictionary of National Biography* characterizes by 'his simplicity, straightforwardness, self-reliance, imperturbable nerve, and strength of will . . . [H]is aim was to do his duty, to "satisfy himself."' *DNB*, vol. XX, p. 1114.
36 Marlon Ross, *The Contours of Masculine Desire: Romanticism and the Rise of Women's Poetry* (New York: Oxford University Press, 1989), pp. 1–86.

survival – of his country. Indolence, or, as Wordsworth would call it, 'inviolable retirement', offers a 'meantime' alternative to the galvanizing tale of the military hero, and simultaneously makes that 'meantime' less anxious, more resourceful. In retirement the poet can cultivate the 'green and silent space', the 'quiet, spirit-healing nook' that Napoleon, but also public bellicosity, threaten.[37] Alongside a familiar Romantic valuation of local place (the dell, cottage and vale of the poem) runs a quietly reflective, conversational style of writing, alien to the rallying cry of the hero. These two elements together form Coleridge's own defence against invasion, not pacifism but an appeal to local attachments as a means for moral and national reformation. If, in the culture at large, as Gillian Russell has demonstrated, war associated itself with drama and performance, with roles that one could adopt and then discard, Coleridge was wresting war into the realm of natural sincerity.[38] The concern that warfare had become performative or inauthentic would surface later in the Ismail cantos of *Don Juan*, or Shelley's 'Mask of Anarchy'; but its flip side, the celebration of acting per se, supported the myth that grew up around such costumed, decorated heroes as Nelson or Wellington.

Coleridge, Wordsworth and others developed an intensely localized nationalism in response to a vastly diffuse global war, a tactic they learned from Cowper's *The Task*. The greater the reach of the war, the greater the recoil into small, desperately familiar places (see Coleridge's conversation poems, Wordsworth's 'Home at Grasmere' or more problematically, Hemans's early 'Domestic Affections').[39] In the literature of Romanticism, one of these desperately familiar places was, as 'Fears in Solitude' announces, the individual 'heart' or conscience; and its investigation would, for Coleridge, De Quincey and arguably Austen, constitute a patriotic act. In the subsequent years of victory and conquest, Coleridge's therapeutic mode would often be overwhelmed by aggressive military jingoism. Still, the insistence on moral purity and a totalizing, near-spiritual commitment to England did carry over into the forging of the Romantic military hero after

---

37 'Fears in Solitude', lines 1, 12, 86–9 in Coleridge, *Collected Works*, vol. XVI, *Poetical Works*, Part 1, ed. J. C. May, pp. 468–73.
38 Gillian Russell, *Theatres of War: Performance, Politics and Society 1793–1815* (Oxford: Oxford University Press, 1995).
39 This recoil did not hurt the war effort. Linda Colley points out that recruits in England, especially during the fears of invasion in 1798 and 1803, were promised 'that they would be able to serve alongside of friends and relations from their own village and county'. Colley, *Britons: Forging the Nation, 1707–1837* (New Haven: Yale University Press, 1992), p. 304.

Trafalgar, as Southey's Nelson demonstrates. Moreover, from the dark self-reflections of wartime in the 1790s, the subsequent generation would fashion its own distinctive heroes and heroines, loners warring against the self-complacency of post-Waterloo society. As Blake realized in 1804 in his epic *Milton*, war in the Romantic age was mutating into a moral, psychic, individual but still national affair, fought by new technologies of imagination and language.

> Bring me my Bow of burning gold:
> Bring me my Arrows of Desire:
> Bring me my Spear: O clouds unfold!
> Bring me my Chariot of fire!
> I will not cease from mental Fight,
> Nor shall my sword sleep in my hand:
> Till we have built Jerusalem
> In England's green & pleasant land.[40]

War systems

Acknowledging modern war's desire for mass enlistments, as well as its refusal to differentiate between soldiers and the civilian population, artists took an increased interest in and defence of the singular individual in wartime. Recognition of the global sweep of the war, meanwhile, lent new urgency to the cultivation of an interiority which comprehended the interior spaces of England itself, its homes and valleys, but also, and increasingly, its inner psyche. If, as Georg Lukács has argued, 'the inner life of a nation is linked with the modern mass army in a way it could not have been' prior to the French Revolution, the inner life itself cannot escape this militarized, nationalized context.[41] Thus, when we are given to see the workings of fear and faith in the poet; or the restlessness of the heroine in the drawing-room, we are seeing war in the Romantic era as much as when we are invited to worry about Napoleon, grieve with widows, condemn war speculators or read the Navy lists. All these scenes are comprehended by the meta-setting of wartime. Nevertheless, though living in wartime promoted the exploration, for instance, of new regions of interiority in a character's conscience, wartime in this period simultaneously supported an

---

40 William Blake, Preface to *Milton* in *Complete Poetry and Prose*, p. 95.
41 Lukács, *Historical Novel*, p. 24.

opposite but less familiar movement toward open spaces, vast systems and an impersonal yet passionate consciousness.

When William Blake takes to the skies in his mental Fight ('O clouds unfold! / Bring me my Chariot of fire') he is resisting the forces that 'depress Mental & prolong Corporeal war' (Milton, p. 95), but he is also advocating a new role for imagination in (and at) war. Like Coleridge, Blake locates war within the psyche, but instead of finding that psyche within 'the green and silent dell' or by the fireside, he constructs an aerial arena, where he can behold vast, intricate networks of relations and exchange. When, in Milton, he traces a topography of London, he is not exercising a free-flying fancy so much as projecting London as nerve centre of a system that extends globally: 'When shall Jerusalem return & overspread all the Nations / . . . thro' the whole world were reard from Ireland / To Mexico and Peru west, & east to China and Japan; till Babel / The Spectre of Albion frownd over the nations in glory & war . . . .' (Milton, pp. 99–100; plate 6). War calls forth the work of imagination; imagination mirrors war as a mental rather than corporeal activity. Only imagination provides the globally encompassing vision that holds together the local and the distant, metropolis and colony, not to mention the operations of capitalism, slavery, sexism, imperialism – all the interlocking systems of oppression which 'prolong corporeal war.' 'Striving with Systems to deliver individuals from these Systems,' Blake's heroes aim for the global, abstracted view in order to combat, at least mentally, the local pains of war (Jerusalem, p. 154; plate 11).[42] For Blake, the war cannot be understood without an awareness of these systems; and war is prosecuted through and for these systems.

As a means of representing war, Blake's ever-multiplying systems, linking conceptual and material concerns, have their analogues in other Romantic texts. One could argue that Scott's use of history provides a comparable awareness of vast interconnections, prompted by a desire to understand a world at war. While Blake's imagination moves spatially, Scott's works primarily through time.[43] But this aerial conception of war also shows itself in more partial ways when the artists of the period turn, as they obsessively do, to weather. Previous generations had followed Aristotle, Bouffon and others in reading weather as the characteristic of a particular place: a local

---

42 Saree Makdisi, Romantic Imperialism: Universal Empire and the Culture of Modernity (Cambridge: Cambridge University Press, 1998).
43 Later novels such as The Talisman and The Betrothed (1825), both set in the Crusades, make clear that Scott is thinking of the geographical as well as the historical underpinnings of modern war, extending beyond Britain to a larger world.

and therefore contained phenomenon, a *locus amoena*. By the late eighteenth century, however, one could envision weather as a global system of forces and exchanges, a cloudy battlefield of its own.[44] The very idea of forecasting tomorrow's weather or predicting next year's harvest required less a faith in God's providence than an assessment of impersonal forces operating elsewhere on the globe. Of course apocalyptic weather – earthquakes, floods, volcanic eruptions – was commonly enlisted to represent the revolution in France and its aftermath. But everyday weather was at least as significant – and ubiquitous – a means of representing and comprehending foreign war. In England especially, the weather was something tangible, like the newspaper, which arrived everyday with at least some hint of activity abroad. It promised the same interplay of suspense and continuity; it could be read. And yet its formless and erratic qualities reminded one of systems under no one's control; it was a far-flung agency, which no one individual controlled yet whose effects every one suffered – like war itself. Not surprisingly, weather proposed itself as perhaps the most common metaphor for representing distant conflicts and the movement of faceless forces across the globe.

'Army of clouds!' hails Wordsworth in 1808. 'Ye Winged host in troops / Ascending . . . as from a hidden world'.[45] Putting warfare into the sky took it out of the hands of mortals, into the realm of speculation:

> . . . were ye rightlier hailed, when first mine eyes
> Beheld in your impetuous march the likeness
> Of a wide army pressing on to meet
> Or overtake some unknown enemy? –
>
> . . .
>
> . . . Or are you jubilant,
> And would ye, tracking your proud lord the Sun,
> Be present at his setting; or the pomp
> Of Persian mornings would ye fill . . .?
>
> (lines 11–14, 23–6)

Raising war to this aerial, even imaginative level risks abdicating responsibility (who can change the weather?). It also risks reproducing the systems of abstraction which had unleashed violence on the planet, as Blake argued

---

44 Arden Reed, *Romantic Weather: The Climates of Coleridge and Baudelaire* (Hanover and London: University Presses of New England, 1983), pp. 20–52; and Vladimir Jankovic, *Reading the Skies: A Cultural History of English Weather, 1650–1822* (Chicago: University of Chicago Press, 2000), especially ch. 7.

45 Wordsworth, 'To the Clouds', *Poems*, p. 183.

and Felicia Hemans recognized. Her 'England's Dead' (1822) coordinates the aerial, imperial vantage with a worldwide map to the graves of the dead, fallen in wars of expansion and aggression. The aerial, systemic view, in other words, for all its ability to link distant events and forces, might sacrifice any critical purchase on military violence.

The difficulty for all these writers was finding sentient ground – a telling scene – for what appeared a free-floating, impersonal mechanism, removed from the immediate sensory experience of most of the British public. Bodies, names, homes; hearts, dells, post-boys: Romantic literature searched for that ground obsessively.

Regency London

SIMON DURING

The Regency is one of the few periods of British history to survive in popular memory: to confirm that all one needs to do is to scroll through the first thousand titles thrown up by a search for the term on the LibraryThing website.[1] What you'll find there is an epoch of aristocratic duels and décolletage, crowded with Byronic dandies gambling away fortunes in gentlemen's clubs, impetuously driving four-in-hand, dancing to the disturbingly erotic rhythm of the waltz, often against the backdrop of the sweeping streetscapes and neo-classical townhouses that John Nash brought to London's West End. This image is by no means new: one can trace its origins in contemporary caricatures of high life and scandals (with the Regent's mistresses as favourite targets) as well as in the 'silver-fork' school of novelists which from the late 1820s specialized in representations of Society for a middle-class readership. And it flowers in the Victorian reaction against what was perceived as Regency immorality. We can think, for instance, of William Thackeray's condescending representation of a superannuated Regency dandy – the 'Old Major' – in *Pendennis* (1848–50).

More recently a rival image of the period has emerged. Here the Regency becomes what E. P. Thompson called 'the heroic period of popular radicalism'.[2] This is no longer the Regency of Beau Brummell or Lady Caroline Lamb but of spy-plagued reformers, emerging out of poverty and social stasis to struggle against privilege in the face of government repression. It's a world which includes respectable figures such as the Benthamite, Francis Place, organizer of the Westminster electors and activist for parliamentary and educational reform, proprietor of one of the first shops in London to boast a plate glass window, and whose *Autobiography* is most graphic in its descriptions of how frequently girls from the labouring classes

---

1 For the LibraryThing website: www.librarything.com/
2 E. P. Thompson, *The Making of the English Working Class* (London: Penguin, 1968), p. 693.

in the London of Place's youth were compelled to turn to sex work, and of how important drink was to London's poor. And it contains figures such as Robert Wedderburn, a West Indian migrant, ex-slave, anti-clerical biblical scholar and Spencean preacher of revolution – a 'Black Prince' for his supporters; or the shoemaker Arthur Thistlewood, another follower of the brilliant propagandist, Thomas Spence who had polemicized for a redistribution of all property and the millennial restitution of primitive Christianity between the 1770s and his death in 1814. Ultra-radicals like Wedderburn and Thistlewood carried out their political work in London's 'free-and-easies' (debating and music societies established in plebeian public houses where pamphlets and newspapers were available) as well as in radical pubs like the Mulberry Tree in Moorfields and meeting places in the Soho backstreets like Thomas Evans's Archer Street club or Wedderburn's own short-lived breakaway chapel in nearby Hopkins Street.

This was a London unknown to the respectable upper and middling classes but one which could suddenly enter public view. It did so for instance in the symbolism of Spence's funeral, when supporters marched down Tottenham Court Road, distributing medallions and carrying the coffin along with 'scales as an emblem of Justice . . . containing an equal quantity of earth in each scale, the balance being decorated with white ribbons, to denote the innocence of his life and example'.[3] Or less peacefully in the shambolic attempt at insurrection organized for the last day of Bartholomew's Fair in 1817. Or in spectacles of cruelty such as when Thistlewood was hung in 1820 in front of a large crowd, many of whom had paid for their seats on coal-wagons. He was executed for his part in a plot (encouraged by government agents) to murder the Cabinet and decapitate its leaders. After being hung, Thistlewood was himself decapitated by a man in a mask wielding a long knife. The common hangman then lifted his bloody head to onlookers saying, 'Behold the head of Arthur Thistlewood, traitor.' In turn, a crowd later tried to castrate the hangman.

Both these images of the Regency – the romantic/aristocratic and the radical/populist one – are limited. They pass over the political reforms that were in fact carried out in the period, notably the legislation against slavery supported by London Evangelists like Zachery Macaulay and William Wilberforce and efforts to debrutalize the penal code by liberal lawyers like

3 This is cited from Thomas Evans, *A Brief Sketch of the Life of Spence* (Manchester, 1821), in Iain McCalman, *Radical Underworld: Prophets, Revolutionaries and Pornographers in London, 1795–1840* (Oxford: Clarendon Press, 1993), p. 99.

Samuel Romilly. Nor do they touch upon the everyday lives of most Londoners of the time – or even the most spectacular expressions of popular mood like the celebrations of Wellington's victories whose transparencies and illuminations so lit London that from afar it seemed on fire. Indeed, they have little to say about the most important cultural transformations of the period. Nor do they offer much insight into the material forces that were changing London in relation both to the rest of Britain, and to the world.

Regency London endures in these forms because this is a period of in-betweenness in British history. It stands between the oligarchic social order that had been set in place over a century before and a Victorian modernity to come; it's an interstice between deference and duty. By 1810 (the Regency's official starting point) the eighteenth-century quasi-confessional state (in which the Established Church, the justice system and the government formed an interlocking and almost impregnable apparatus of domination) was, if not dead, at least in dissolution. A series of events had unsettled the old order. Uneasy alliances between the middling and the plebeian classes became possible after the American and French Revolutions. Towns like Manchester and Birmingham based on new industries were growing rapidly – out of which the mass politics of the nineteenth century would appear. A wildly swinging economy led to new forms of inequality (and moments of ultra-profits for the landed gentry), not least after the agrarian protectionism of the 1815 Corn Law Act which turned city dwellers against the squirearchy. Dissent and Evangelicalism were becoming more influential. A series of blasphemy and sedition trials, of which William Hone's in 1817 attracted most public attention, indicated the political rise of free-thinking. Seemingly scientific modes of analysis and information gathering became associated with intellectual celebrities such as Jeremy Bentham, Thomas Malthus and David Ricardo, and controversial campaigns for non-denominational education, penal reform and a free market. The colonies became an attractive career option for the elite and America a tempting emigrant destination for the struggling.

On the other hand, the social order that we call Victorian had not yet been secured. Claims for parliamentary reform had not been conceded by the ruling class. The ideology of Christian duty, devotion and asceticism – the popularization of Evangelicalism – which undermined the power of the old alliance between Church and State, was only in its infancy. The state's role in securing minimum standards of public hygiene and education for all was an idea as yet unable to be persuasively articulated. The ugly suburban spread of the metropolis would only become an anxiety in the 1840s. Full-scale professionalization of middle-class careers lay in the future. Media with large-scale print runs (over 100,000) were a feature of the 1830s. Middle-class domestic life had not yet become nationally normative: that is, it had not displaced both aristocratic and plebeian styles in public consciousness. Britain did not yet see itself as a factory for the world. Imperial glories and responsibilities were not yet the stuff of popular media and imagination – even if they did surface in entertainments like those produced by Charles and Thomas Dibdin, or more serious works like William Wordsworth's *Excursion* (1804). So it is as an era in which neither elite nor non-industrial plebeian styles were under fetters that the Regency has retained its fascination.

Indeed an atmosphere of instability linked to urbanism and London is perceptible. It was as though the times – or, rather, history – were coming under the sway of new forces: not the Providence of conventional Christianity; not the slow progress of Enlightened philosophers; not the incrementally civilizing sway of commerce and sociability so often and so confidently asserted earlier in the century – but less predictable and familiar agencies. One such agency was fashion, which was becoming an autonomous domain conferring prestige at the same time that its secular rhythms were unsettling to many: the vindictive caricatures of, and pranks against, Robert Coates were a sign of that. (Coates was a self-displaying hanger-on of the circle around the Regent, known to the press as the 'amateur of fashion' but who transgressed Brummel's code of discrete and understated elegance.) After the Regency, of course, men's participation in fashion would be gradually reduced.

This atmosphere of instability can also be sensed in, say, the spread of millenarianism, or even (as a stabilizing reaction against it) in the widespread insistence on common sense with William Cobbett, the period's most successful journalist, being common sense's main champion. It can be sensed too in more minor forms like, for instance, the upsurge of bibliomania in the first three decades of the century – a somewhat ersatz turn to tradition in the form of literary collectibles. Or, for that matter, in the craze for hoaxes which ran through London around 1810, with Theodore Hook's 'Berners Street Hoax' the most widely publicized. Hook ordered cartloads of goods to be delivered to a rich woman's house causing traffic jams and consternation – an excessive heaping up of London's commodities and luxuries which was a lesson as much as a joke. A certain ungroundedness also lies behind the exoticisms that London embraced: Persian fashions in 1810 after a visit from the Persian envoy; Russian pants for men in 1814 in honour of the visiting Czar; literary and artistic imitations of Oriental styles by poets like Thomas Moore and Lord Byron; Egyptian interiors after *Household Furniture* (1807) by Thomas Hope whose Seymour Place house and art gallery (modelled on the ancient Greek *mouseion*, dedicated to worship of the Muses) was open to the public; Dean Mahomed's Hindostanee Coffee-House, London's first south Asian owned restaurant which aimed to offer a little piece of India to those who missed the place; shops that passed themselves off as bazaars such as Glidden's 'Cigar Divan' in Covent Garden, another imitation Oriental hangout for smokers, decorated with views of mosques and minarets.

But most of all this sense of instability was based in the gradual awareness that the economic order was changing in ways that both ungrounded society and shifted power from country to city, despite agrarian protectionism. Between 1797 and 1821 England did not adhere to the gold standard. This led to inflation as the government financed the war by printing money – and to an epidemic of banknote forgery. The unprecedented level of national debt was the subject of much doom-saying commentary. Then too, increasingly from the 1780s onwards, trade and industry rather than agriculture became, and were known to be, the primary motors of national prosperity, which meant that the cities rather than the country acquired symbolic as well as economic power. This economic activity was apparent in industrial centres like Manchester and Glasgow but also in the extraordinary extension of the London Docks, which made London the 'warehouse of the world'. Proponents of economic liberalism became increasingly influential, scoring major success such as the ending of the apprenticeship system (1813) and the final removal of the stigma against usury.

In 1798 Pitt had introduced income taxes to finance the wars; they were abolished in 1816 but the old Land Taxes were not restored so indirect taxes on labourer's consumption bore an undue weight of taxation. This helped fuel radicalism but also conspicuous consumption by an elite already enriched over the war period. It also encouraged speculation in foreign loans organized by City financers like the famous Nathan Rothschild, a patron of London's small Jewish community. In sum, such economic transformation led to a commingled sense of fearfulness, unpredictability, opportunity and weightlessness. Expressions of the giddying nature of contemporary economic life especially in London were commonplace. Let us take these lines from 'The Stock-Jobber's Lament' in James and Horace Smith's satirical *Horace in London* (1813) as characteristic:

> Fortune takes one behind her on a pillion;
> Another whom to-day she tumbles down,
> To morrow she may bless with half a million,
> And leave the first with scarcely half a crown.[4]

At street level, this sense of chanciness was exacerbated by the pervasive presence of state lotteries and by the campaigns mounted against them by figures as diverse as William Wilberforce and the reform journalist and man of letters, Leigh Hunt. Lotteries were advertised in popular pantomimes (Bish's Cornhill Lottery Office was featured in Charles Dibdin's Sadler's Wells harlequinade, *Thirty Thousand; or, Harlequin's Lottery* (1808)); lottery prints, including some specially produced for children, were distributed en masse on London streets and became important to the printing trade; lottery ballads were written by respected literary figures such as Charles Lamb; advertising parades for lotteries were a familiar component of metropolitan street life. So it is unsurprising that Samuel Coleridge ended his second *Lay Sermon* (1817), an appeal for society to return to the Bible as a moral standard, with an attack on the lotteries. And the state lotteries were in fact abolished in 1823 – as good an indication of the coming of a new moral regime as any.

It is a mark of this instability of cultural foundation and agency, partly caused by an increase of commercial activity, that Regency London increasingly became the object of representation, interpretation and inspection all on its own. London demanded such representation because, as a (seemingly) huge and chaotic metropolis, it needed ordering and mapping. London's capacity to confuse and riddle touched John Clare when he first visited it in 1820. He recalled the event in his idiosyncratic prose:

> as we approached it the road was lind wi lamps that diminishd the distance
> to stars this is London I exclaimd he laughd at my ignorance and only
> increased my wonder by saying we were yet several miles from it when we
> got in it was night and the next morning everything was so uncommon to
> what I had been used to that the excess of novelty confounded my instinct
> every thing hung round my confusd imagination like riddles unresolvd[5]

4 James Smith and Horace Smith, *Rejected Addresses and Horace in London*, ed. Donald H. Reiman (New York: Garland, 1977), p. 148.
5 John Clare, *John Clare by Himself*, ed. Eric Robinson and David Powell (Ashington; Manchester: Carcanet Press, 1996), p. 150.

Clare's confusion may have been partly caused by the gas lighting that was introduced on London's streets in the century's first decade and which, so contemporaries thought, was a competitor for the sun. Very far from Clare's innocent disorientation and wonder, a London auctioneer John Thompson, known as 'Memory-Corner', became notorious for his ability to draw from memory a map of any part of London down to details such as pumps, posts, trees and the bow-windows on the houses. Thompson's is an interiorized and miniaturized London as it were merely obsessionally under control.

At a national level, the new statistical modes of analysis uncovered accurate information about the city for the first time. The 1801 census ended age-old speculation about the city's population – it was just under a million. By 1821 it was over 1.3 million, increasing quickly but more slowly than the northern industrial cities. More importantly, however, the tendency to self-representation took a cultural turn: indeed in this period London increased its national and international cultural significance and self-regard while its economic importance relative to other British cities declined. As such London was seen as 'a center of publication and of intelligence for the whole empire'.[6] One sign of its place in the new cultural economy is to be found in the engraved illustrations of the city that flooded the market. Many were designed for hobbyists who interleaved (or 'grangerized') images of famous sites into information-crammed albums or books.[7] Among the books used for this purpose were Thomas Pennant's *Of London* (1790), Daniel Lysons's *Environs of London* (4 vols., 2nd edn, 1811) and James Peller Malcolm's *Anecdotes of the Manners and Customs of London* (1808), all of which created a web of historical associations through which the city could be experienced. Rudolph Ackermann's illustrated publications – especially *The Microcosm of London* (1808–10) were also grangerized. And Ackermann could also draw attention to a consumer's London experiencing boom times. The first issue of his monthly *Repository of Arts, Literature, Commerce, Manufactures, Fashions and Politics* (1809–28) contained five plates of retailing showrooms, including his own shop on the Strand; Harding, Howell and Company's Grand Fashionable Magazine on Pall Mall which sold everything from furs to French clocks and James Lackington's bookstore in

---

6 Cited in Jon P. Klancher, *The Making of English Reading Audiences, 1790–1832* (Madison, WI: University of Wisconsin Press, 1987), p. 32.
7 'Grangerized' after the Rev. James Granger who placed blank leaves into his *Biographical History of England* (1769) to which readers could paste their own collected engravings, thereby triggering a long-lasting fashion.

Finsbury Square – the Temple of the Muses, home to the book-remainder trade. Later issues of the periodical showed no less than nineteen plates of Morgan and Sanders's ware-room, where technological marvels such as Merlin's mechanical chair and Pitt's Cabinet Globe Writing Table were displayed for amusement and sale.

A more traditional London appeared through the fashion for watercolours, which reached its height around 1810 when 20,000 visitors attended the Watercolour Society's annual exhibition. Many of the images displayed there were of picturesque rural landscapes, but, for the first time, many were of cityscapes too. Another London still appeared in publications like *London Oddities; or, The Theatrical Cabinet: Being Neat Tit Bits for the Lovers of Humour and Eccentricity* (1823) in which items associated with popular comic actors were used to define a London mood. Indeed on the stage itself, pantomimes often presented their action on recognizable London sites: the city representing itself to itself in one of the liveliest modes of contemporary popular culture. The 1820 hit *Giovanni in London* offered a different theatrical London: the libertine Don Giovanni was too evil for Hell so the Devil sent him back to the wickedest city in the world: London. That was a trope which had already occurred to Percy Shelley, who had declared that 'Hell is a city much like London' in *Peter Bell the Third* (1819) an insight which was to be echoed by Byron in the Shooter's Hill stanzas in the English Cantos of his own *Don Juan* (1822).[8]

At the same time, London guidebooks for tourists from the country and abroad became rationalized: the dissenting publisher, Richard Phillips, who had been jailed in 1793 for selling Paine's *The Rights of Man* and was proprietor of the influential *Monthly Magazine*, produced the bestseller in this genre, *The Picture of London*, reprinting it almost annually before selling out to Longmans in 1812. Children were a market for representations of London too: texts like Priscilla Wakefield's *Perambulations in London and its Environs* (1809 and 1814) and Jane Taylor's *City Scenes* (3 editions in 1818) turned walking about London into scenes of instruction for middle-class children.

A variety of journalists also cashed in on curiosity about London, circulating new styles with which to inhabit – or just visit – the city. Of these the best known was Pierce Egan, whose *Life in London* was a major event when it appeared through 1820 and 1821. It stimulated imitations and an orgy of commodities: snuff boxes, shawls, handkerchiefs and so on. Almost

---

8 Percy Bysshe Shelley, *Poetry and Prose: Second Edition*, ed. Donald H. Ryman and Neil Fraistat (New York: W. W. Norton and Sons, 2002), p. 346.

every minor theatre produced its own dramatic adaptation of *Life in London*, the most successful being W. T. Moncrieff's ballad-opera version at the Adelphi on the Strand with a 300 night run and a reputed profit of £10,000. Egan himself had been a printer who, like many such, turned his hand to writing copy. He became a sports journalist for the *Weekly Despatch* (1801–), an eight pence halfpenny journal devoted mainly to crime, scandal and, after about 1810, sport. Egan first became famous as the author of *Boxiana* (1818), a history of boxing. He came to typify the 'Fancy', as the social world that aggregated around pugilism (then at the height of its popularity) was called. *Life in London* was illustrated by Robert and George Cruickshank, whose etchings contributed considerably to its success. A guide to London's tourist sites and the city's 'lower world' in a flimsy fictional setting, it is marked by its fascination with slang and its affirmation of London's het-erogeneity, self-consciousness and energy. London here is not so much an uninterpretable mystery, too vast for an individual to know (as it had sometime been represented since the late seventeenth century): it is transparent, or least easily mediated for a wide readership, just because, for Egan, it is constituted by energy, sociability and language rather than (for instance) poverty, crime, eccentricity. London is 'the faithful emporium of the enterprising, the bold, the timid . . . and where all can view themselves at full length, affording innumerable opportunities either to push forward, to retreat, to improve, or to decide' but also where '*superiority* on the one side always operates as a check upon *superiority* on the other'.[9]

The text's central characters – Corinthian Tom, swaggering son of a London businessman, and Jerry Hawthorn, shy son of a country squire – determine to experience all that London has to offer. Sometimes accom-panied by their friend Bob Logic in his dark glasses and, surprisingly, by their girlfriends, they visit, for instance, the Prince Regent's splendid Carl-ton House; the Royal Exchange (which elicits praise of the 'English Mer-chant'); Almacks (the Society assembly-rooms whose tickets were objects of intense desire); Newgate the prison (where the instrumentalities of justice in inner London were now concentrated); the pleasure-grounds of Vauxhall; a masquerade ball at the English Opera House; an exhibition of pictures at Somerset House (which elicits middlebrow praise of the portrait genre). And then scenes of low-life: an East End gin house; a prostitute's apartment

9 Pierce Egan, *Life in London: Or the Day and Night Scenes of Jerry Hawthorn, Esq. And His Elegant Friend Corinthian Tom Accompanied by Bob Logic, the Oxonian, in Their Rambles and Sprees through the Metropolis* (New York: D. Appleton and Co., 1904), p. 17.

where a waltz is danced; a dog-fight at Westminster Pit in Tothill Fields where the real-life monkey Jacco Maccacco defeats a dog; and the fictional 'back slum' drinking spot All-Max. High and low life episodes alternate. There is no doubt that Tom and Jerry are indulging in cultural slumming in the low-life scenes but they are also searching out the city's libidinal vitality. As Tom says, 'the lower orders know best how to enjoy themselves'. For Egan, real value is found in the freedom to cast off, and communicate across, social status – whether that is at All Max where blacks and whites, young and old, coal heavers and gentlemen tourists carouse together, or in the West End's Hyde Park where 'The Prince may be dressed as plain as the most humble individual in the kingdom; the *Tradesman* more stylish in his apparel than his Lordship; and the *Shopman* with as fine clothes on his person as a DUKE' (p. 119). Egan does not engage more radical responses to London's heterogeneous mix. He does not urge social equality or the loosening of social identity – the capacity to remain uncertain and socially suspended that (just a couple of years earlier) John Keats called 'negative capability'.[10] For him, difference between types and classes remained primary, and such differences formed a hierarchy. But this hierarchy of types did not lead to separation, nor was it based on scales of morals or tastes. Hierarchy without superiority is London's fabric, and only the tightly respectable lie beyond the pale of this London.

Leigh Hunt was another journalist who helped promote a new way of living in London. One of his more interesting efforts in this regard was the *Literary Pocket Book*, a profitable annual which he inaugurated in 1819 and edited for the publisher Charles Ollier for a couple of years. An expensive (5 s.), calf-bound book, it was designed to compete with calendars produced for businessmen. Its market was the aestheticized, reasonably affluent London (female) consumer: it was a tool for enjoying urban leisure. It contained information on charges for Hackney Cabs; lists of print and plaster-cast shops, circulating libraries and reading rooms and so on. The surviving artisan metropolitan holidays were listed, partly in nostalgia, partly as a push for an increase in labourers' leisure hours. Poems by Hunt's friends such as Keats and Shelley were first published there, though Keats at least is on record as despising the publication, calling it 'sickening stuff'.

One of its features was a section on 'Walks around London' not written by Hunt himself but based on a series of 'Suburban Essays' that he had

---

10 John Keats, *Letters of John Keats: A Selection*, ed. R. Gittings (Oxford: Oxford University Press), p. 43.

published in *The Examiner* in 1812. It presented outer villages/suburbs like Kilburn as models of the picturesque (at a time when painters and water-colourists like John Constable, John Varley and John Linnell were all working in the area). Hunt's London was a place where the pleasures of rural beauties were just as available as the delights of haunting the book-stalls round St Paul's or the melancholic pleasure of observing an under-taker 'singing and hammering in his shop' and thereby 'rapping death himself on the knuckles' as Hunt put in the first essay in another of his London series, this one on 'The Sight of Shops' published in *The Indicator* (1820).[11] Hence London could provide a reconstituted version of the Romantic pastoral – as in Hunt's verses on Hampstead in *The Examiner* in 1816. There his response to London's suburban landscape allows nature itself to be troped as leisure in jaunty, determinedly cheerful rhythm. The sublimity of Wordsworth's Lake District (to which he published his own *Guide* in 1810) belongs to another country.

If representations of London poured off the presses for audiences whose relation to the city was more motivated by pleasure, discovery and wonder than previously, that was largely because London was itself the centre of a cultural market of unprecedented vigour and complexity. This was a market that dealt in a wide variety of texts, art-objects, performances and leisure activities, each divisible into specialized kinds, and which imported talent from, and exported products to, the world. It also took shape in space and buildings – the theatres of course, but also sites like Savile House in Leicester Square or the Egyptian Hall in Piccadilly. Savile House, a London landmark, was rebuilt in 1806 to host a range of enterprises, among them an exhibition of Mary Linwood's famous needlework paintings, a bazaar, a shooting gallery, a concert room, a wrestling arena and a coffee house. Egyptian Hall was constructed in 1812 for William Bullock's Museum (which a couple of years earlier had moved down from Liverpool). Its highlights included taxidermic specimens, native artefacts from Cook's South Pacific voyages and a habitat display of a tropical rainforest with an Indian's hut. By 1819 it had become a site for all kinds of shows and exhibitions. It was here that Benjamin Haydon had his success showing his picture *Christ's Entry into Jerusalem* in 1820 for 1 s. a head; and where, the next year, the strongman, conjuror and archaeological excavator, Giovanni Belzoni, showed models of Egyptian antiquities from Abu Simbel.

11 Leigh Hunt, *Leigh Hunt as Poet and Essayist*, ed. Charles Kent (London: Frederick Warne & Co, n.d.), p. 203.

The most important components of London's variegated cultural market were journalism, drama, literature, art, shows, lectures and sport. Yet this market was characterized not so much by the specialization of its various sectors as by the interactions between them so as to animate activity across the whole. That is to say, in part at least, it fed on itself. Thus, for instance, in December 1814, Mary and Percy Shelley attended a show at the Lyceum. It was presented by a Mr Garnerin from France, famous as the world's first parachutist and concurrently appearing in a Joseph Grimaldi pantomime at Covent Garden. Garnerin's act was half a scientific lecture, half stage magic. Mary Shelley's memories of his performance – in which a portrait was electrified into life – formed a kernel of her novel *Frankenstein*, which, adapted for the theatre, itself became a theatrical hit.

The cultural market also fluidly engaged with non-market formations – especially politics and religion. Take the case of *The Examiner*, a weekly founded in 1808 by John and Leigh Hunt and which around 1816 was at the height of its influence. *The Examiner*'s mission was, as Leigh Hunt stated it later, 'to assist in producing Reform in Parliament, liberality of opinion in general (especially freedom from superstition) and a fusion of literary taste into all subjects whatsoever'.[12] Here the liberal reformist agenda fused with aesthetic taste on the basis of a sentimental literary sensibility, which itself depended on access to the urban cultural market that the paper belonged to and reported on. For *The Examiner*, taste was brought to bear on politics rather than, as for most of its rivals, politics guiding taste. In this move the cultural consumer effectively took control of the political subject. And from within the milieu that *The Examiner* helped shape emerged a series of claims that extended far beyond the market. This was the atmosphere in which individualistic figures like Haydon and Keats, lacking cultural status and, in Keats's case, strong social connections, could aspire to glory down generations. Or in which the paper itself could lobby for state support for the erection of public monuments of heroes like Captain Cook and John Locke: fame secured in lived-in space, and in a temporality that transcended commerce's rhythms.

The popular preacher offers another example of the market's ability to extend into non-commercial realms. Many London chapels were fundamentally business ventures. Congregations (often dominated by women) paid to hear sermons in approximately the same way as they might pay to

12 Leigh Hunt, *The Autobiography of Leigh Hunt* (London: Oxford University Press, 1928), p. 214.

go to theatre: by renting pews or by paying into the church plate. Even Robert Wedderburn's ultra-radical Hopkins Street chapel was (in part) a moneymaking venture: there one paid at the door. Popular preachers were celebrities. Their lithographic likenesses were widely circulated. Magazines reviewed their sermons, and in some cases, like John Hamilton Reynolds's 1817 series on 'Pulpit Oratory' in the *Yellow Dwarf*, offered satirical critique of them. Many popular preachers, whether in the Established Church or not, were tinged by what was still called enthusiasm. One of the most successful was the Scotsman, Edward Irving, whose cult was famous for speaking in tongues. A still more unorthodox theological enterprise was that of John Church who preached a form of antinomianism, a doctrine usually (but not only) attached to an extreme interpretation of the Calvinist doctrine of predestination as vividly described in James Hogg's *Private Memoirs of a Justified Sinner* (1824). From his Obelisk Chapel in St George's Fields, Church acquired admirers who stood by him even when, in 1817, he was imprisoned for performing mock marriages amongst transvestites in a gay brothel in Vere St – a public homosexual scandal in a period of intensifying prosecutions against sodomy. And it was in part against this vibrant theological entrepreneurialism that the Established Church, worried about its loss of reach and authority, lobbied for the so-called 'Million Act' (1819) which allocated a million pounds to build Anglican churches in the metropolis from public funds drawn from war reparations.

This cultural market needs to be distinguished both from street culture and from salon culture. London street life, marked by ceremonies and often by importunate demands for payment from the poor to the more comfortable, remained vital during the first decades of the century. But it was clearly under threat. Thus in 1815 a series of lithographs entitled *Vagabondia* was produced in the belief that, after the passage of legislation against begging, street mendicants would become extinct. Cruel pastimes like Bethnal Green's bullock hunt, in which a crowd of up to a thousand people chased a bullock, drew increasing criticism. And colourful ceremonies such as the May Day chimney sweep parade, in which the sweeps painted their faces pink and gold, frizzed their hair with powder (in imitation of the rich) and wore hats decorated with ribbons, foil and flowers, led by a 'Jack-in-the-Bush' – a dancing man disguised as a dancing bush – also came under attack, in this case because they were regarded as a form of begging which allowed masters to underpay their ill-treated employees. Campaigns against drunkenness, Sabbath-breaking, fortune telling and the sex trade by the Society for Suppression of Vice also had an impact on demotic street life. By the late 1820s in books like Hone's bestselling *Everyday Book* (1825–26) that life was beginning to be treated with a sentimental nostalgia.

On the other side, the salon culture associated with high society took place in exclusive meeting places during the (winter) Season. It was centred on aristocratic parties, largely organized around political and county affiliations, in which grandees and their families and friends mingled with celebrities and a favoured recipients of patronage like the poets Thomas Campbell and Thomas Moore. Gala occasions in this world – so-called 'routs' – were widely commented upon events. While the salons, as private spaces, were (like the chapels) often dominated by women, clubs like Whites and Brookes and Watiers (known as a haunt of dandies) were for men only. This was a world that, although a consumer of and resource for the cultural market too, remained reserved in relation to it, confident of its own political and economic power. It produced its own styles and values, and dealt in genealogical status, sexual charm, wit, elegance, male honour and conspicuous consumption. It could also form alliances with plebeian culture against the respectable middle class as it did in the Fancy where toughs like John Thurtell mingled with aristocrats and journalists. (Thurtell was arrested for murder in 1823, in a sensational crime case which became part of media history, since *The London Illustrated News* depicted it in ground-breaking illustrations.) From a literary-historical perspective, Lord Byron with his long-time refusal to make money from his poetry, his easy judgements of other's vulgarity and coxcombry (as of his friend Leigh Hunt), his physicality, his sense of homelessness in a society where lordship was increasingly caught between moral reformism and self-interested political reaction, offers most insight into salon culture. And those who at the height of the Regency boom joined London society without sufficient resources, like Byron's friend Scrope Davies – whose notebooks contain witticisms and citations designed to be spoken at parties 'spontaneously' – were in difficulties by the 1820s. Many such, like Beau Brummell (the exemplar of the dandy's understated, perfectionist style) and Davies himself, ended their lives shabbily on the Continent.

London was typified, then, by a cultural market that occupied a space outside of street and salon life, independently of the filiations and stratifications that had bound together an older, more agrarian Britain. When, in 1817, the Edinburgh journalists John Wilson and John Gibson Lockhart attacked the school of poets associated with Leigh Hunt in *Blackwood's Edinburgh Review* as 'Cockney' they were not attacking a particular poetic style as much as a milieu which they thought of as 'vulgar', 'affected', 'ignorant' and 'low'. That milieu was precisely that of London's cultural market whose reach and capacity for external and internal transactions was the real threat to the Scottish Reviewers. Of course, they were imitating the judgements of salon culture, an appropriating move which was to become commonplace among the British middle classes, becoming known as snobbishness by the 1840s. The irony was that *Blackwood's* itself was one of the most commercially successful and inventive journals of the epoch. Its attack on the Cockney school was as much an example of product differentiation as ideological or national disagreement.

Journalism and the theatre lay at the centre of the London cultural market. They were intricately connected, even if through a structure of opposition. After all, journalism was committed to the transitory, while the theatre was a realm of primary value, partly because Britain's national genius was a dramatist. Finally, however, the theatre was a business exploiting its capacity to entrance its audiences. Remembering the overpowering experience of a first visit to the theatre became almost a convention in memoirs of the period. Most periodicals (except the quarterlies) reported on London drama. Social relations between the green rooms of the major theatres and newspaper editors were close too. Indeed both journals and the theatre interacted with other sectors in the cultural market by providing publicity or resources – leisure technologies like the phantasmagoria (an advanced magic lantern show and topic of a Charles Mathews song and of newspaper stories) or low-grade exhibitions like that of the African woman, Sarah Bartman (aka the Hottentot Venus) who presented her body for inspection to paying customers, and whose unhappy career and resistance to those intervening in her life for the sake of her welfare was also the object of columns of newsprint. The stage magician, Henry, who was able to hire the Adelphi for a show that included traditional magic tricks, a cutting-edge optical illusion – the dissolving view – and an imitation of a Charles Mathews routine written for him by media professionals, was another case in point.

The two major cultural journalists of the period, Leigh Hunt and William Hazlitt, both made their name as theatre reviewers and Shakespeare fans: Hunt in his brother's weekly the *News* in 1805, and Hazlitt in London's leading Whig daily the *Morning Chronicle* in 1813. Hunt, under instructions from his brother John, was the first to write serious assessments of contemporary drama for a newspaper (rejecting the exchange of free tickets and advertising revenue for favourable notices), and mounting a campaign against John Kemble for his 'classical' formalism and affectation. Hazlitt went further: his reviews were written in two stages. First, before seeing a play he read it and wrote a critique of it, often drawing on his theory of the primacy of disinterest in human nature. He filed this and then, after seeing the performance, filed more copy consisting of impressionistic remarks on the acting, which was added to his textual critique. Armed with the authority granted by this principled technique, he helped make the career of Edmund Kean, who, after his debut playing Shylock at Drury Lane in January 1814, came to define the London stage in the period. For Hazlitt, Kean at his best revealed the truth of Shakespeare's tragic characters, and the ability of a man outside the sway of salon culture – a man of the people – to express that truth.

It was the print media that kept London's cultural market alive, both through commentary and through advertising. Regency journalism was fluid: periodicals opened and closed with bewildering speed, many only producing a few issues. Many were funded by printers or booksellers, but loose control of credit and the difficulties in finding start-up capital created endemic insecurity. The ordinary journalist was never far from the debtor's prison. Much copy was written by lawyers (John Hamilton Reynolds, Basil Montagu, Barron Field); or by government officials (Leigh Hunt was once a clerk in the War Office) or by imperial administrators (Lamb worked in East India House). Journalists moved from topic to topic (Hazlitt began as a parliamentary reporter), from market niche to market niche: Cyrus Redding, one of the period's most successful London journalists, moved from being a dogsbody at the daily *The Pilot* to being effective editor of the smart *New Monthly Magazine* via a period as an editor of a provincial paper.

Copyright barely existed. Material passed from book to periodical and back again and from periodical to periodical often without acknowledgement. All ideological formations, and especially the dissenting branches of Christianity, had their 'organs'. Yet innovation was prized. Each new periodical was a project, aiming at its own signature mode: print's prestige and reading's power to form styles and habits of life were uncontested. Each of the successful London cultural journals managed to assemble (admittedly overlapping) groups of contributors who produced a specific tone or take on the world. Several of them (Richard Cumberland's *The London Review* (1808); John Scott's *The Champion* (1814–17) and *London Magazine* (1820–9)) had a specifically London focus. Here too the logic of the period tended towards increased autonomization of cultural spheres. In the period 1817–19, for instance, no less than three weekly journals in a new genre appeared: the *Literary Gazette* (1817–62), the *Literary Journal* (1818–19) and the *Literary Chronicle* (1819–28). They concentrated on extracts from and commentaries on books, and information about authors, helping mark out a specific group of booklovers (even if 'literary' in a periodical's title did not mean it was aimed only at this community). A hierarchy of seriousness and cultural value, determined by periodicity and price, became consolidated by this mode of media organization. The quarterlies were more gentrified and careful than the monthlies (which for the most part specialized in miscellanies and catalogues) and the monthlies in turn contained more reflective pieces than the weeklies. Quarterlies and monthlies tend to solicit national readerships, which meant that in effect they were either London-centred or self-consciously regional like *Blackwood's*. The dailies tended to be small (four pages). They solicited close relations with readers through a letters column, and morning papers were more involved in culture and fashion than evening papers. Yet verses, say, could be found almost everywhere.

As to theatre: here a peaceful heterogeneity of audiences and genres was difficult to achieve partly because audiences confronted each other in physical space. In 1809 when a rebuilt Covent Garden opened after a fire, divisions between these audiences caused sixty-seven nights of riot known as the Old Price (OP) riots. Ultimately, this was a class war. The OPer's objected to the reduction in gallery seats to increase the number of luxurious boxes. It was also a war on behalf of public memory and rights. The protestors were responding to a threat to their traditional right of veto over their entertainment, and they called upon the whole repertoire of licensed disorder – including dressing in masquerade – to make their point. John Kemble, as manager, hired boxers, many of them Jewish, to protect his theatre – which raised anti-Semitic hackles. Although in the end Kemble had to compromise over prices, the economic rationality he represented won out, and the Regency audience was more docile than its predecessors. The elite retreated from the theatre, turning instead, for instance, to the opera at the grandest theatre of all, the Italian Opera House. Or to lectures. This was an age of the lecture (presented either publicly or privately): comic lectures (which had become popular in the 1760s) retaining their appeal; medical lecturers being regularly listed in the London guides, and artisan lecture series, like that developed by the tradesman Timothy Claxton being regularly inaugurated and as regularly terminated. Now established literary figures like Hazlitt, Coleridge, Thelwall, Henry Brougham and Campbell launched commercial lecture series too. More successfully still, the scientists Humphrey Davy and Michael Faraday became celebrities through lectures attended by the fashionable.

Behind this public culture lay another world enabling and shaping it: a world of more or less informal networks of sociability. This world, of course, did not extend far into the city's total population yet it is surprising how many people of all kinds were involved in these networks and how widely they spread, encroaching upon salon culture in one direction, and the radical underground in another. To cite two names at random, the distance between Byron's friend, the hostess Lady Blessington and the Jewish activist and blackmailer 'Jew' King was less than might be imagined when one considers these overlapping social circles.

These circles met in particular places and times, some more institutionalized than others. Most formal were clubs like the Guards Club that Wellington founded for officers returning from the wars or Major Cartwright's nationwide Hampden Clubs. Less formal were those like the literary club that the shoemaker Allen Davenport organized with fellow-workers to buy Cooke's edition of British Poets at 6d. a number from a hawker who plied the Edgeware Rd, or the group of working men who called themselves 'The Liberals' and who supported a small library, meeting twice a week to discuss literary, political and philosophical topics. A club like the bibliophile's Roxburgh Club lay somewhere in between. Most trades, and especially journalism and bookselling, encouraged social gatherings, whether at the workplace or at private rooms (though this distinction was not yet as rigid as it would become). Thomas Hill of the *Monthly Mirror* hosted a Sunday lunch attended at various times by Charles Mathews, Thomas Campbell, Theodore Hook, Leigh Hunt and Horace Smith. Rowland Hunter, a bookseller at St Paul's Churchyard, had a Friday party where William Godwin, Douglas Kinnaird (a magistrate and Byron's agent), Henry Fuseli and others met. Reformers like John Thelwall gathered at Richard Phillips's office at Bridge Street, Blackfriars.

Less formal sites of sociability were more important still. To limit the discussion to some literary figures: Samuel Rogers, the banker and poet, hosted breakfasts at his house in St James's Place, where salon culture intersected with the workaday literary world. It was there that Byron was introduced into London literary society in 1811. The Bedford Street house of the lawyer and illegitimate son of the Earl of Sandwich, Basil Montagu, was the centre of another circle, this one spreading into the world of Sir James Mackintosh who married into the Wedgwood family. Mackintosh, by the by, hosted dinners for Madame de Staël during her 1813 London visit, which was a major social and media event, conferring prestige on those who met the visitor. At Bedford Street too Hazlitt repeated one of his lectures from his first lecture series on English philosophy in front of Thelwall, Leigh Hunt, Lamb, Henry Crabb Robinson and others. Lamb's own Thursday evenings drew friends from East India House, lawyers, journalists from the *London Magazine* set, including the aesthete and poisoner Thomas Wainewright, and actors like John Liston, Joseph Munden and Fanny Kelly. Leigh Hunt's hospitality from the Vale of Health and then Lisson Grove collected together painters like Haydon, young poets like John Keats, publishers like Charles Ollier and musicians like Vincent Novello (himself the centre of a social circle). It was here that Keats met Shelley. When Hunt was imprisoned in Horsemonger Lane Gaol across the river in Surrey (1813–15) his cell became another meeting-place for reformers: Byron and Moore called, Hunt played shuttlecock with Jeremy Bentham, and Maria Edgeworth, James Mill, Hazlitt and the editor John Scott all came to pay respects. The merchant Charles Aders entertained William Blake in his Euston Square house, where Blake met Henry Crabb Robinson and where his amazing designs for an educational edition of Virgil were stoutly defended by Sir Thomas Laurence, the establishment portraitist.

These occasions could involve far more than conversation. Poets recited their verses. Lecturers recited their lectures. Music was played. Witty performances like Theodore Hook's ex-tempore versifying and punning were encouraged. And the houses themselves were often more than backdrops: they were manifestations of distinction and nurseries of taste. Rogers owned an excellent collection of art objects, specializing in Greek vases. Aders was a connoisseur of Italian and, more unusually, Northern European Renaissance painting – a taste which would circulate for decades by virtue of an avant-garde who came to know such work at his house. Maybe most important was Hunt's style – just because he was not rich, and lacked social status. His rooms were strewn with flowers in pots and vases, geraniums, myrtles and heart's-ease being his favourites. (He and his circle did much to encourage the modern love of cut flowers.) Plaster casts of cultural heroes like Homer (bought from the cast-maker Shout) were prominently displayed. A portrait of Milton hung from the wall. Flower-strewn wallpaper provided more ornamentation. A pianoforte, a real luxury, was available for expressive entertainment. Hunt's aestheticized interiors, designed for vernacular domestic life, became a symbol of Cockneydom (they are called 'Pleasure's Temple' in Keats's 'Sleep and Poetry', which admiringly describes them) and provided a precedent for a middle-class style that has endured down to our own day.[13]

---

13 John Keats, *The Complete Poems*, ed. John Barnard (London: Penguin, 1973), p. 92.

Most importantly, in these networks of sociability and distinction, careers and reputations were made. Ideas were exchanged and refined. Alliances were formed; enmities broke apart. Leigh Hunt and Benjamin Haydon may have disagreed about Christianity and publicly argued about the nobility of Africans but they fell out in a dispute over borrowed cutlery. In an important sense this was the fulcrum of London's cultural life: this is where that life was grounded in the place itself. Once the styles, ideas, words and images produced here entered the public domain they were, potentially at least, unmoored from their physical home. Indeed one can say that Regency London, both a self-imagined and a geographic place, both a centre defining a nation (or an empire) and a cluster of localities, existed most of all in the slippage between its (self-representing) cultural market and its physical topographies of cultural sociability.

PART III

★

HISTORIES: WRITING IN THE NEW MOVEMENTS

Rebellion, revolution, reform: the transit of the intellectuals

ANNE JANOWITZ

In late 1788 Louis XVI called the Estates General to meet in response to increasing agitation for reform. On 8 January 1789 Thomas Jefferson, observing the heightened political tensions, described the events and gave his benign opinion of their expected outcome: 'from the natural progress of things [the French] must press forward to the establishment of a constitution which shall assure to them a good degree of liberty'. The author of the American Declaration of Independence suggests as well in the same letter from Paris that the American events of 1775–83 had provided the energy for this 'illumination of the public mind as to the rights of the nation': 'Tho' celebrated writers of this and other countries had already sketched good principles on the subject of government, yet the American war seems first to have awakened the thinking part of this nation in general from the sleep of despotism.'[1] The American War had also, though Jefferson didn't state it, been a major source of the ongoing financial crisis of the French state.[2] Jefferson's letter was addressed to the distinguished London Dissenting Minister, Richard Price, an intellectual colleague in the culture of Enlightenment liberality. On 4 November 1789, Price delivered a sermon to the London Revolution Society to mark the centenary of the 1688 'Glorious Revolution', in which he claimed the kinship of parliamentary sovereignty between the 1688 Settlement and the recent occurrences in both America and France: 'After sharing in the benefits of One Revolution, I have been spared to be a witness to two other Revolutions, both glorious.'[3] Over the next few years, English radical writers frequently attached the term 'glorious' to the French Revolution to signal this international genealogy; most vivid was

---

1 Thomas Jefferson, 'To Richard Price', 8 January 1789, in *Jefferson Abroad*, ed. Douglas L. Wilson and Lucia Stanton (New York: Random House, 1999), p. 271.
2 William Howard Adams, *The Paris Years of Thomas Jefferson* (New Haven: Yale University Press, 1997), p. 256.
3 Richard Price, *A Discourse on the Love of our Country*, etc. (London: Cadell, 1789), p. 49.

William Wordsworth's description of his French journey of the summer of 1791, where he was greeted with fraternal joy by French citizens who recognized in the English their 'Forerunners in a glorious course'. Price's sermon opened a debate in Britain so politically volatile that authors of pamphlets associated with it would be variously feted, silenced, jailed, tried and hounded out of the country. Amongst the writings that engaged with Price's sermon were the most influential contemporary English-language pamphlets on the French Revolution: Edmund Burke's *Reflections on the Revolution in France* (1790) and Thomas Paine's *The Rights of Man* (1791).

In his letter to Price, Jefferson recognizes the image of the American War of Independence in the opening of the French Revolution, and Price found in it the family resemblance between 1688 and 1789. French reformers themselves who had, like Voltaire, idealized the civic freedoms of the English, reciprocated: Pierre Samuel Du Pont de Nemours, one of the aristocrat-reformers from the Assembly of Notables asserted that when the Assembly was called for the first time in 150 years, 'The King of France became a King of England.'[4] To Enlightenment thinkers, the Glorious Revolution, the American Revolution, and the French Revolution were all elements of an irresistible and international spread of 'the ardour for liberty', 'a general amendment beginning in human affairs; the dominion of kings changed for the dominion of laws, and the dominion of priests giving way to the dominion of reason and conscience'.[5]

But the language of reason and conscience was only one way of making the French events intelligible. In the summer of 1790, the English poet Helen Maria Williams sent a series of letters to her friends in England, which she then collected and published as a group. She writes of her visit to the now ruined Bastille:

> I requested to visit the Bastille; feeling a much stronger desire to contemplate the ruins of that building than the most perfect edifices of Paris. . . . We drove under that porch which so many wretches have entered never to repass, and, alighting from the carriage, descended without difficulty into the dungeons, which were too low to admit of our standing upright, and so dark that we were obliged at noonday to visit them with the light of a candle. We saw the hooks of those chains (14) by which the prisoners were fastened round the neck, to the walls of their cells; many of which, being below the level of the water, are in a constant

---

4 Simon Schama, *Citizens: A Chronicle of the French Revolution* (New York: Viking, 1989), p. 253.
5 Price, *Discourse*, p. 50.

state of humidity . . . Good God! – and to these regions of horror were human creatures dragged at the caprice of despotic power.[6]

Williams makes her observations in the terms of the literary conventions with which her friends would be familiar: Gothic romance and ruin imagery, supported by the rhetoric of 'sensibility' – that 'sympathetic going outwards of interiority' which Addison called 'a kind of quick and delicate feeling in the soul'. 'My love of the French Revolution', she writes, is a result of her faculty of 'sympathy', and 'therefore my political creed is entirely an affair of the heart; for I have not been so absurd as to consult my head upon matters of which it is so incapable of judging' (Letter IX, p. 66). Intimate yet public, Williams's letters politicize her readers by eliciting sympathetic *feelings*. In 'The Bastille', a poem written for her 1790 novel, *Julia*, Williams invokes the new world of liberty as a place where 'Freedom' will produce its authority through 'charm' rather than reason: 'Where this dark pile in chaos lies, / With Nature's execrations hurled, / Shall Freedom's sacred temple rise, / And charm an emulating world!'[7]

Both Jefferson and Williams write with radical ardour; Jefferson with the ardour of reason, Williams with the passion that strengthens in recoil from cruelty and injustice. Their expressive styles exemplify the complexity of radical Romanticism: the meeting place of Enlightenment reason and Romantic subjectivity, the discourses of civic entitlement and its subjective counterpart, the responsive interior life of the democratic self.

*

Accounts of the Atlantic democratic revolutions from the 1770s through the late 1790s are popularly classified as the American *rebellion* against colonial authority, the French constitutional and republican *revolution*, and the British struggle for political *reform*.[8] Though each of these political cataclysms began within domestic politics they were reciprocally influential as well, borne out of long histories of economic and political rivalry as well as intellectual and philosophical association in the formation of Enlightenment

---

6 Helen Maria Williams, *Letters from France*, 2 vols. (Dublin: Chambers, 1794), vol. I, pp. 14–15.
7 Helen Maria Williams, 'The Bastille', *Julia*, 2 vols. (London: 1790).
8 Jay Fliegelman, *Prodigals and Pilgrims: The Revolt Against Patriarchal Authority* (Cambridge: Cambridge University Press, 1982); Bernard Bailyn, *Ideological Origins of the American Revolution* (Cambridge, MA: Harvard University Press, 1967); Albert Goodwin, *The Friends of Liberty: The English Democratic Movement in the Age of the French Revolution* (Cambridge, MA: Harvard University Press, 1977), pp. 54–5.

principles of democratization. From natural rights arguments practically articulated by British Dissenters such as Joseph Priestley and Richard Price, American radicals had materials to hand for their founding principles and documents; twenty years later Priestley and Price advanced their own struggles for British reform by reference back to those principles, now authoritative because they had been enacted in the American Republic.[9]

The American colonies' agitational pamphlets and addresses against the powers of the Crown and in particular against taxation without representation, drew upon both the rational method learned from Locke and Voltaire and the visionary mode of Rousseau, as well as being broadly indebted to the political imagery of the Roman republic and narrowly and threateningly associated with seventeenth-century English republicanism. The documents of the American First Continental Congress, 1774, insisted that the colonists were entitled to the 'rights, liberties, and immunities of free and natural born subjects'. In France, after the oath at the Jeu de Paume, 20 June 1789, radical parliamentarians grew more and more interested in American constitutionalism, and welcomed political visitors such as Jefferson, who eagerly offered advice, and in so doing reinforced the historical precedence of the American republic.

In England, domestic reformers arguing for the extension of the franchise, extension of civic possibilities to non-conformists and Catholics, and the redistribution of parliamentary constituencies drew on American events and also turned to narratives of native democracy. These radical reformers revivified a long-standing English attachment to the symbol of the 'Norman Yoke', the oppression visited in 1066 by William the Conqueror. The American colonists invoked the same mythic symbol of a golden age of Anglo-Saxon freedoms often in the 1770s.

After 1789, as we have seen, radical intellectuals in Britain eagerly metaphorized the French Revolution as the new 'Glorious Revolution'. But the rapid pace of change in the French Revolution as it moved within months from establishing a constitutional monarchy to establishing a constitutional republic, threatened to collapse the analogy with 1688. In Britain the discussion became more heated about whether or not the 1688 Settlement had been founded on the traditional succession of kingship or on a more modern principle of parliamentary sovereignty, and whether it had, in fact, established these principles: 'First; The right to liberty of conscience in religious matters. Secondly; The right to resist power when abused. And,

---

9 Goodwin, *Friends of Liberty*, pp. 54–5.

Thirdly; The right to chuse our own governors; to cashier them for mis-conduct; and to frame a government for ourselves.'[10] The English, both those who embraced and those who feared the French Revolution found that they were drawn ever more frequently to the imagery of the 1649 regicide. To those who, like Edmund Burke, saw the French Revolution as the negation of the English traditions of custom and hierarchy, the idea of a constitutional monarchy brought into ever more sanguinary and terrible focus the image of the English Revolution, overtaking and obscuring that of the Glorious Revolution. Radical polemicists were wary of 'imagining the King's Death' in print, as that imagining itself had been a capital, treasonable offence since 1351, and such imagination had recently become reality in the execution of Charles I.[11] The re-emergence of the image of the regicide served as the motive for the Pitt Government's repressive legislation of 1794–8, which effectively suppressed radical activity and publication from the mid-1790s, and with it the drive for parliamentary and religious reform. The charge against Hardy, Thelwall and Tooke in the 1794 treason trial was precisely that they had 'compassed and imagined the death of the king'.[12]

Given the distinct political objectives of the radical groupings involved in the acts of rebellion, revolution and reform – acts which were only partially intelligible with reference to their international principles and hopes – it is not surprising that expressions of mutual admiration were also marked by signs of great anxiety, that identification was often followed by disavowal, and that radical idealization was often shadowed by vilification. In the early nineteenth-century movement for Parliamentary reform that led to the Reform Bill of 1832, the issues at stake of representation and re-drawing constituencies, conformed more closely to the needs of urban men who had enough property to pass a means test than to the principles that had ani-mated the earlier period of agitation. It was, in fact, the exclusions of the Reform Bill that led to the first self-organized working-class movement in Britain: Chartism.

Mary Wollstonecraft, writing from Paris in February 1793, only a few months after she had arrived, expressed her disenchantment: 'I am not become an Atheist, I assure you, by residing in Paris: yet I begin to fear that

---

10 Price, *Discourse*, p. 41.
11 John Barrell, *Imagining the King's Death: Figurative Treason, Fantasies of Regicide 1793–1796* (Oxford: Oxford University Press), p. 29.
12 Barrell, *Imagining the King's Death*, p. 127.

vice, or if you will, evil, is the grand mobile of action.'[13] The French Revolution provided a model, for good and ill, of what an apocalyptic overturning of the past might entail, but we should not see the impact of the French Revolution on British politics and culture as a one-directional movement, for though the domestic radical reform movement was politically stymied, it provided through Mary Wollstonecraft and Thomas Paine two of the most culturally radical positions of the nineteenth and twentieth centuries: the rights of man and the rights of woman as the bedrock of democratic sovereignty. In fact, the cultural radicalism of British culture formulated during the Revolutionary period is stunning for its long life through the nineteenth and twentieth centuries as well: rationally articulated feminism and sexual radicalism, land reform radicalism of urban plebeian radicals such as Thomas Spence, and international abolitionism, were powerful currents within the Atlantic radical reform movement.

The American Revolution began as a protest against abuses of British governmental principle, and ended in the establishment of a constitutional republic; the French Revolution began as a revolt against an unreformable old order, and though fractured by the Napoleonic imperium, established that the principles of democratic republicanism might be made to work in the world; and the British Reform movement began and continued as a flexible and mutating set of programmes for reform, which developed and changed in response to the circumstances in both America and France. It is also the case that the political pressures within the colonies, France and Britain engaged with other cultural and social campaigns going on alongside these prominent constitutional ones. In all three countries the issue of rights of the labouring classes, women's rights, and the place and meaning of both the Atlantic slave trade and the European abolition movement were alive and linked to the main political events, and political events produced effects in unsuspected spheres of debate and action. For example, English and American radicals celebrated the fall of the Bastille in 1789 as the literal ruin of the French State's unjust penal system. The ongoing British discussion about rights was made more immediate by the symbol of the Bastille, and in turn, catalysed the debate amongst English women about the specific nature of their natural and civic rights. Replies to the issue of women's rights also drew attention to and increased the visibility of women intellectuals within the larger pamphlet debates about revolution: the pamphlet

---

13 Janet Todd, *Mary Wollstonecraft: A Revolutionary Life* (London: Weidenfeld & Nicholson, 2000), p. 208.

writer Anna Barbauld was rebuked as a 'virago' and 'poissionière' 'proph-
etess' ready to exercise her 'talons', and a republican 'disciple of Paine'.[14]
The Unsex'd Females, Richard Polwhele's 1798 verse satire against Mary
Wollstonecraft and her disciples, scolds Mary Robinson for giving 'to Gaul
her Fancy'. For women intellectuals, the French Revolution opened a new
milieu within which to consider the meanings of women's political and
social experiences; for writers such as Polwhele, the French Revolution has
infected the very heart of British femininity.

Covering an even wider geographical orbit, as Peter Linebaugh and
Marcus Rediker have recently shown, sailors who worked the ships that
circumnavigated the Atlantic were the conduits for the transmission of
radical enlightenment thought to the eastern Atlantic, 'initiating pan-
Africanism [and] advancing abolition'.[15] The patterns of influence carried
by Atlantic plebeian radicals included the recognition of identity between
black and white labourers – the waged poor and the enslaved – the
transmission of strategies of rebellion, and political internationalism. The
organized abolition movement grew as a result in this period: the Société
des Amis des Noirs, established by the French-born American revolutionary veteran, Lafayette, was soon in correspondence with the British
abolitionist movement, together forming part of a pan-European anti-slave
trade initiative, which maintained its networks even while other political
issues threatened to dismantle them.[16]

The fact that the political and social campaigns were both internationalist
and nationalist through shared principles and competitive polities gave rise
as well to some stunning contradictions in principle and programme.
Thomas Jefferson, who spoke and acted in his most visionary and idealist
constitutionalist manner when living in France in the late 1780s, cut an
entirely different ideological figure twenty years later, when the Haitian
Revolution took off under Toussaint L'Ouverture. Jefferson had advocated
the abolition of slavery earlier, but by 1802, he was President of the
United States, a slave-holding nation, and he was as eager as any to
interrupt the model that the Haitians might offer to the American slave
community. Jefferson, eager for Napoleon to defeat the Haitians, offered
to 'furnish your army and fleet with everything, to reduce Toussaint to

---

14 *Letters of Horace Walpole*, ed. Padgett Toynbee, 19 vols. (Oxford: Clarendon Press,
   1925), vol. IX, p. 10; vol. XIV, p. 345; vol. XV, p. 25.
15 Peter Linebaugh and Marcus Rediker, *The Many-Headed Hydra: The Hidden History of
   the Revolutionary Atlantic* (London: Verso, 2000), p. 212.
16 Adams, *The Paris Years*, p. 270.

starvation'.[17] He soon proposed a prohibition on trading with revolutionary Haiti similar to the blockade of Cuba in the late twentieth century.

★

In their letters from France in 1789 and 1790, Jefferson writes with visionary idealism and Helen Maria Williams asserts the affective origin of her politics: together they offer one version of the 'Romanticism' of the period. But the Romanticism of the Democratic Revolutions was not principally an idealism, with its accompanying conceptual and stylistic conventions; rather, it was a set of lived experiences, which included work and writing and feelings, and perhaps for the first time in trans-Atlantic history, the transport of ideas from nation to nation. This was the daily reality of radical intellectuals who physically conveyed and enacted their commitments to political, social and cultural reform. Their political aspirations, cultural desires and personal experiments in living identify them as cultural as well as political revolutionary romantics, yoking, as Charles Taylor describes it, 'objectivity and sentiment'.[18] What distinguishes them from others who had much to say and do in the period is that they were not only all participants in an international culture of writing and pamphleteering, but as cosmopolitan radicals, they travelled to the places of radical activity as participant-observers.

It was indeed the case that from the opening days of the Revolution, English radical writers had opened up the language of politics to the romantic passionate conventions of natural description and affective vision. Anna Barbauld, who had been a demure advocate of dissenting enfranchisement in the 1780s, was excited by the news from France into a new and dramatic way of writing:

> Can you not discern the signs of the times? The minds of men are in movement from the Borysthenes to the Atlantic. Agitated with new and strong emotions, they swell and heave beneath oppression, as the seas within the Polar Circle, when, at the approach of Spring, they grow impatient to burst their icy chains.[19]

---

17 Joseph J. Ellis, *American Sphinx: The Character of Thomas Jefferson* (New York: Knopf, 1997), p. 246.
18 Charles Taylor, *Sources of the Self* (Cambridge, MA: Harvard University Press, 1989), pp. 185–98, passim.
19 Anna Barbauld, *Address to the Opposers of the Repeal* (London: Johnson, 1790), pp. 31–2.

Mary Robinson's 1790 revolutionary poem, *Ainsi va Le Monde* works the Gothic convention of ruin in similar terms to that used by Williams in her letter about a visit to the Bastille:

> Rous'd by oppression, *Man* his birth-right claims,
> O'er the proud battlements red vengeance flames;
> Exulting thunders rend the turbid skies; –
> In sulph'rous clouds the gorgeous ruin lies! – [20]

Though much of the literary production of the period 1789–93 radiates high passion, it is largely the passion of civic desire, in which the voice of polemicist and poet is a self-conscious medium for the imagined voice of the popular will. What is distinct and striking about the letters and reports sent home from the scenes of revolution by Mary Wollstonecraft, Thomas Jefferson, Thomas Paine and Helen Maria Williams is the access they give us to the individual's subjective experience of the revolutionary moment. At the same time, our four intellectuals were part of a shared sociality: they all met or exchanged writing with one another, dined at the homes and hotels associated with the cause of radicalism and constituted irregular intellectual and personal systems of knowledge and experience.

Mary Wollstonecraft, who is most familiar to modern readers as the rational feminist author of the *Vindication of the Rights of Woman*, was part of the London radical intelligentsia who congregated around the Dissenting Joseph Johnson's publishing house in St Paul's Courtyard. Wollstonecraft worked as Johnson's collaborator in editing the radical dissenting journal, the *Analytical Review*. Through her association with Johnson, she dined frequently with Johnson's writers. There she met Paine and Blake and the artist Henry Fuseli, with whom she wanted to construct a new kind of personal relationship, with more feelings than a simple friendship, less possessiveness than a marriage, and despite Fuseli's own marriage. Wollstonecraft went to France in December 1792 and stayed until 1795, in part to get away from the social politics of the Johnson milieu; and she lived there with Gilbert Imlay, a republican veteran of the American Revolution. She wrote about the revolution to help maintain herself and her child with Gilbert Imlay and she tried to help Imlay make the transition from American revolutionary to promoter of trade between France and the young United States.

---

20 Mary Robinson, *Poetical Works*, 3 vols. (London, 1806), p. 24.

Mary Wollstonecraft and Thomas Paine together brought the French Revolution to Britain in 1790 by strenuously developing the debate about 1688 into an unrestrained pamphlet war. Paine and Wollstonecraft had often dined and discussed politics at Johnson's London headquarters, where he gave frequent suppers for his 'sort of Menagerie of live Authors'.[21] Wollstonecraft's and Paine's coruscating critiques of Edmund Burke's defence of the *ancien régime*, discussed no doubt with each other and other guests of Johnson's such as Joseph Priestley and Richard Price and the cranky radical Gilbert Wakefield, prompted Pitt's legislation against seditious writings, resulting in Paine becoming an international refugee from the British State. Paine had been notorious well before 1789, however, chiefly as the author of *Common Sense* (1775), the pamphlet that was instrumental in the earliest period of the American rebellion. It was in North America that he met and later became friends with Thomas Jefferson, who himself went to France in 1784 as an ambassador of republican principles. Jefferson and Paine met again in Paris, and shortly before Jefferson returned to the United States in 1789, he and Paine met with French reformers to discuss the current drafts of the American Constitution as a model for a French charter.[22] Paine, having been driven out of England, stayed on, and served as a Deputy to the National Convention, delegated by Calais.

Like Wollstonecraft, and shortly Helen Maria Williams, Paine was a supporter of the Girondin current within the revolutionary movement, and both Paine and Williams were imprisoned for a time during the period of Jacobin supremacy. As Girondin supporters, Paine, Williams and Wollstonecraft were part of the group of Girondin-identified British women and men who congregated at White's Hotel in Paris, and who, in 1792, were part of the gala dinners celebrating each new event in the apparently secure journey to Parliamentary Democracy in France. Sunday 18 November 1792 was a night of dining and toasting, which included, along with toasts to the National Convention and The Republic of France, ones to Paine and to Helen Maria Williams, who apparently wrote for the evening a song in English to the 'tune of the Marseillaise'.[23] Helen Maria Williams, who eventually published eight volumes of *Letters from France*, detailing her ongoing experience of the French Revolution, was the companion and lover of John Hurford Stone, a leading member of the radical British in Paris, and

---

21 Todd, *Mary Wollstonecraft*, p. 152.
22 Adams, *The Paris Years*, p. 265.
23 Erdman, *Commerce des Lumières: John Oswald and the British in Paris, 1790–1793* (Columbia: University of Missouri Press, 1986), p. 230.

the Director of the British Club, whose meetings took place in White's. She would have been frequently in the company of Paine. Williams was linked to the heart of Girondin sociality as a regular visitor to Mme Roland's political salon. Wollstonecraft quickly became part of the expatriate community when she arrived in Paris. Another English person reported that at the dinner parties, 'Miss Wollstonecraft was always particularly anxious for the success of the Revolution.'[24]

Williams and Wollstonecraft were the leading English women intellectuals amongst those in Paris. Although the rather sterner Wollstonecraft ambiguously described Williams as one who Wollstonecraft would be more 'inclined' to 'love rather than admire', they became natural allies and friends.[25]

*

The lasting symbol of the French Revolution was the storming of the Bastille on 14 July 1789. The extraordinary emblematic resonance of the event can be measured by the fact that on Sunday 17 July, the King came to Paris and accepted the revolutionary cockade. In this way he signalled his acquiescence to the power of the National Assembly and the urban populace, for the tricolour placed the king's colour – white – between the colours of Paris.[26]

The spirit of the American Revolution permeated Paris that summer and autumn as the National Assembly planned a future for the French nation, and three important activists from the American Revolution – Jefferson, Paine and the French-born military leader, the Marquis de Lafayette – were all fascinated by and involved in formulating the imagery, discourse and principles of the Revolution.

When Jefferson arrived in Paris in 1784 as an Ambassador from the new American Republic, his diplomatic mission was to build trade relations between the two countries, and his personal authority rested on his having drafted the Declaration of Independence. If the English considered the Glorious Revolution the forerunner of French political change, Jefferson was certain that the American Revolution was the model for a democratic and republican world. Already back in France and a spokesperson for American principles, the returning war hero, the Marquis De Lafayette, quickly became

24 Todd, *Mary Wollstonecraft*, p. 210.
25 Mary Wollstonecraft, *Collected Letters*, ed. Ralph Wardle (Ithaca, NY: Cornell University Press, 1979), p. 225.
26 Georges Lefebvre, *The French Revolution* (London: Routledge, 2001), p. 120.

a partisan of French reform. Though his reputation was built as a military leader, his intellectual mentor was Jefferson.[27] It was Lafayette who designed the revolutionary cockade, and on the day after the Bastille was stormed, the National Assembly made him Commander of the National Guard.

In the spring of 1789, the maverick engineer-polemicist, Thomas Paine, joined these two founders of American republicanism in political discussion. As Paine saw it, the fall of the Bastille and the American Revolution were spiritually linked, and when, some years later, the Key to the Bastille was given as a gift to the President of the United States, George Washington, Paine wrote to him 'That the principles of America opened the Bastille is not to be doubted, and therefore the Key comes to the right place.'[28]

Jefferson's Paris letters are an extraordinary record of the opening of the French Revolution as it appeared to an American. His faith in popular power is evident throughout the winter of 1788 and the spring of 1789, as he writes of the bravery of the Parisians: 'They speak in all companies, in coffee-houses, in the streets, as if there was no Bastile: and indeed to confine all offenders in this way, the whole kingdom should be converted into a Bastile.'[29] Jefferson went daily to observe the proceedings of the Estates-General in May of 1789, and attempted to intervene in the conversion of the third estate into a 'commons'. He hoped that sections of the aristocracy and clergy would join the third estate and compel the King to sanction a bicameral legislature.[30] A month after the Bastille, Jefferson exhorted likeminded persons 'to besiege the throne of heaven with eternal prayers to extirpate from creation this class of human lions, tigers and mammouts called kings'.[31]

Jefferson's was the voice of Enlightenment idealism; Lafayette's was that of trained military prowess; Lafayette never entirely broke with his aristocratic links, and never accepted the end of French monarchy. Thomas Paine, more pragmatic than either Jefferson or Lafayette, was the man whose experience of 1789 attached him to the daily work of the revolution, in which he then participated fully until he was imprisoned in 1793.

In June 1789, Paine, Lafayette and Jefferson offered to Louis the plan for a Charter of Rights, which might 'gain time' for him while 'the public mind

---

27 Susan Dunn, *Sister Revolutions: French Lightning, American Light* (London: Faber & Faber, 1999), pp. 4–26.
28 Moncure Daniel Conway (ed.), *The Writings of Thomas Paine*, 4 vols. (New York: Putnam's, 1908), vol. III, p. vii.
29 'To David Humphries', 14 August 1787, *Jefferson Abroad*, p. 190.
30 Adams, *The Paris Years*, p. 281.
31 'To David Humphries', 14 August 1787, *Jefferson Abroad*, p. 191.

will continue to ripen and to be informed'.[32] In late 1789 Jefferson did not imagine a fully Republican France, but he felt that a written constitution would make a constitutional monarchy in France superior to that established in England's 1688 Settlement: 'In drawing the parallel between what England is, and what France is to be I forgot to observe that the latter will have a real constitution, which cannot be changed by the ordinary legislature; whereas England has no constitution at all.'[33]

Jefferson and Lafayette lived in the world of high politics and brilliant social occasions. Paine was the son of cottage-artisans, a product of the principles he promulgated: individualist, cranky and inventive. An intellectual–engineer, Paine was both a creator and an example of the American 'tinker' tradition: handymen who put their lives and a nation together with the skill of 'ingenuity' – the category that Adam Smith made vibrant and the American tinkers made material. Paine's great passions were the structure of political principles and the building of bridges. It was, in fact, his desire to sell to either the Americans or the French his model for a steel suspension bridge that sent him circulating through the radical geography.

Though he was a prophet of reason, Paine's experience and motivations were as often paranoiac and irrational. He was irascible, and fell out with most everyone (although never with Jefferson), leaving England for America after having been dismissed twice as an excise officer in 1774, where he wrote *Common Sense*, a document in the discourse of democratic simplicity. Paine's characteristic style was perfected in this pamphlet, a style that aimed to eschew ornamentation and allusion, accessible to any reader: 'In the following pages I offer nothing more than simple facts, plain arguments, and common sense'. Paine's style is the plain style – not ornamented or baroque, dissociated from the aristocracy, and filled with the dry humour of the yeoman thinker. Paine's writings both exemplified and shaped the trend towards simplicity in the last decades of eighteenth-century literary fashion, and they were significant as well in the romantic formulation of the popular. In England and France, Paine's best known radical work was his pamphlet, *The Rights of Man*, which was read and distributed in tens of thousands between 1791 and 1793. The expansion of popular print culture in England – prints, pamphlets, broadsides – meant that a new literate audience was being shaped into particular political positions through the worlds of taverns, street-meetings, and in the early 1790s, the radical

32 'To Rabaut de St. Etienne', 3 June 1789, *Jefferson Abroad*, p. 289.
33 'To Diodati', 3 August 1789, *Jefferson Abroad*, p. 293.

organization of the Corresponding Societies. Within a few years of the Bastille, the Corresponding Societies in England were addressing themselves to French revolutionary clubs, and formulating the genre of the 'friendly letter' written and read between groups of radicals on either side of the Channel. Paine's work was the motor that drove these radical internationalist exchanges.

In his debate with Burke, Paine asserted the primacy of principle over precedent, reason over custom, and the present over the past. Paine claims the autonomy of political generations from their forefathers, and this is modelled on the new romantic language of the growth of personal identity. Equality must work across time as well as space: 'Every generation is equal in rights to the generations that preceded it, by the same rule that every individual is born equal in rights with his co-temporary.'[34] But Paine's attention to internal processes does not prevent his polemic against the excesses of passion, and he accounts its impact as both political and literary. Past revolutions have been born of 'hatred' Paine writes, 'But in France we see a revolution generated in the rational contemplation of the rights of man' (p. 172). This is true for writing as well: 'When the tongue or pen is let loose in a phrenzy of passion, it is the man and not the subject that become exhausted' (p. 169).

William Blake, although unwilling to write to the radical audience in either an accessible language or through the pamphlet genre, nonetheless recognized and articulated the importance of Paine's *Rights of Man*, comparing Paine and Jesus: 'Is it a greater miracle to feed five thousand men with five loaves than to overthrow all the armies of Europe with one pamphlet?'[35] Blake points to the extraordinary power of writing in the period and the evanescence of any distinction between writing and intervening in politics. A warrant issued for his arrest, Paine fled into exile, apparently on the advice of Blake at a Johnson supper, and so began his career within the French revolutionary movement.

Paine's powers of persuasion were such that both the nations that embraced his writings in their first years of revolutionary enthusiasm became frightened of that power once their own had been consolidated. At the very end of 1793, the Jacobins imprisoned the man who had been elected to the National Convention and when he returned to the United States in 1802, he

---

34 Thomas Paine, 'The Rights of Man', in *The Complete Writings*, ed. Philip S. Foner, 2 vols. (New York: The Citadel Press, 1969), vol. I, p. 274.
35 William Blake, *Complete Writings*, ed. Geoffrey Keynes (Oxford: Oxford University Press, 1972), p. 391.

was repudiated as a 'loathsome reptile', an infidel and a drunk, 'His nose is a blazing star'.[36] Twenty years after having written the wildly popular *Common Sense*, Paine found a more sedate, even hidebound, polity.

Back in the United States, Jefferson continued his political career within the centres of power, and became President of the United States in the elections of 1800, his visionary idealism in thought living alongside his realpolitik in practice. Jefferson adapted to the situations in front of him. Paine, quite differently, was always outside the circles of power. The very image of the romantic revolutionary of the 1790s, Paine was left to his own devices and patents in his last years. After his death in 1807, however, he was reanimated as an American hero, and as the founder of American liberal political theory.

Jefferson and Paine brought the American Revolution to Paris as polemicists and diplomats and rejoiced in the fall of the Bastille. They hoped to see an extension of American principles of democracy in France, and for the two nations to be both trade and ideological allies. The Americans aimed as well to show in this ideological alliance their superiority to both the English past and present conceptions of constitutionalism. Nonetheless, the imagery of the Bastille quickly became part of English radical thought and imagery, first only through the radical correspondence between England and France, but later as an enduring symbol of authoritarian repression. In this light it is striking that the image of the Bastille should be summoned by the poet John Clare in 1849 to describe the Northampton Asylum where he lived in madness in the last years of his life, drawing on the idiom of 1790s English–French revolutionary zeal. Invoking the Franco-American images of Tom Paine and the liberation of the Bastille in a letter to his wife, Clare writes: 'this is the English Bastile a government Prison where harmless people are trapped & tortured till they die . . . when done & said with them truth is truth & the rights of man – age of reason & common sense are sentences full of meaning & the best comment of its truth is themselves'.[37]

*

The spirit of 1789 was quite different from that of the autumn of 1792 when, on 25 September, the National Assembly declared France a Republic, and

---

36 John Keane, *Tom Paine: A Political Life* (London: Bloomsbury, 1995), pp. 456–7.
37 John Clare, *Selected Letters*, ed. Mark Storey (Oxford: Oxford University Press, 1990), pp. 215–16.

from the winter months, when the King was guillotined. While Jefferson had returned to America in the very first days of the French Revolution, Mary Wollstonecraft and Helen Maria Williams were both living in Paris. They were part of the social and political world of those British expatriates who were trying to make sense of the capture and execution of the King, and wondering what this meant for the English reform movement within a constitutional monarchy. When Richard Price had delivered his sermon in 1789, welcoming the French Revolution, he described the King as 'no more than the first servant of the public, created by it, maintained by it, and responsible to it . . . and the term Majesty, which it is usual to apply to him, is by no means *his own* majesty, but the MAJESTY OF THE PEOPLE'.[38] In 1803, when Helen Maria Williams published Louis XVI's correspondence with an accompanying commentary, she cited for particular notice Louis' statement to Malesherbes: 'I shall undergo the fate of Charles the First; and my blood will flow, to punish me for having never shed any.'[39] The symbol of the ruined Bastille was replaced in British cultural imagery, with the more terrifying one of regicide: between 1789 and 1793 the abstract image of an office of kingship replaced by the particularized image of a man condemned to die, and the fears were felt on both sides of the Channel. John Barrell has explicated the intertwined representation of the doomed Louis XVI as the object of sentiment – the distraught family man, father, husband and sensible creature – and as the holder of an office that had to be destroyed for liberty to flourish. British radical commentators were unable and perhaps even unwilling to disentangle the image of Louis as a pitiable and transient individual from the impersonal, arbitrary and tyrannical power of kingship, as this distinction made more palpable the necessity of the abolition of the office to prevent further death sentence on those who occupied the office.[40] The language of sentiment indelibly marked this episode of the Revolution, and both Mary Wollstonecraft and Helen Maria Williams wrote within its conventions. Wollstonecraft was always struggling with her sentiment, trying to rationalize the power of passion as part of her reverence for rationality itself. Williams shifted away from the discourse of sentiment as her lived experience of the Revolution demanded the language of straightforward political analysis.

38 Price, *Discourse*, p. 25.
39 Helen Maria Williams (ed.), *The Political and Confidential Correspondence of Lewis the Sixteenth; with Observations on Each Letter*, 3 vols. (London: C. & G. Robinson, 1803), vol. III, pp. 71, 76.
40 Barrell, *Imagining the King's Death*, pp. 79–80.

For Wollstonecraft and Williams as for many others, the political, the sexual and the cultural aspects of this overturning of the *ancien régime* were so interfused that revolutionary love was part of the spirit of the age. Wollstonecraft had fallen in love with the painter Fuseli in the radical atmosphere of Joseph Johnson's dinner parties in London, and it was in the defeat of that passion that Wollstonecraft went to Paris in 1792 to observe the formation of a new world. As the recent author of *A Vindication of the Rights of Woman* (1792), Wollstonecraft arrived with sure intellectual credentials. In this volume, Wollstonecraft explores more closely the logic of reason that she had elaborated in *A Vindication of the Rights of Men* (1790), one of the first replies to Edmund Burke in the revolution controversy. In the *Vindication of the Rights of Woman*, Wollstonecraft makes a crucial argument that places reason above affect – virtue comes from reason, not feeling, and therefore if women are to be virtuous, they must have access to reason; that is, access to education, responsibility and the status of adults: 'It is a farce to call any being virtuous whose virtues do not result from the exercise of its own reason.'[41]

Wollstonecraft arrived in Paris as a radical intellectual, Imlay as a hero of the American Revolution. Like Jefferson, he was immediately concerned with establishing business contacts, and in their relationship Wollstonecraft was confronted with some of the practical consequences of the American events – the republic would not run on principles alone, but on the quotidian working out of commercial transactions.

The personal drama between Imlay and Wollstonecraft was played out in passionate and at times desperate letters from Wollstonecraft throughout 1793, as she managed poverty and a difficult pregnancy, to the increasingly disengaged Imlay. In 1793, Wollstonecraft worked on *An Historical and Moral View of the French Revolution*, published the next year in London by Johnson. Wollstonecraft's history offers a clear Enlightenment vindication of the revolutionary activities of 1792–3 while also evoking in the language of sensibility the resonance of a vanished aristocracy: 'How silent now is Versailles! – The solitary foot, that mounts the sumptuous staircase, rests on each landing-place, whilst the eye traverses the void, almost expecting to see strong images of fancy burst into life.'[42] Wollstonecraft's criticism of the state of brutality in 1793 is set out through the same affective language: 'Down fell the temple of

---

41 Mary Wollstonecraft, *Vindication of the Rights of Woman* (London: 1792), p. 11.
42 Mary Wollstonecraft, *Political Writings*, ed. Janet Todd (London: Pickering, 1993), pp. 341–2.

Despotism [the Bastille]; but – Despotism has not been buried in its ruins! – Unhappy country! – when will thy children cease to tear thy bosom?'

Helen Maria Williams wrote as a committed Girondin, with the emotion and imagery of revolutionary ardour. She first visited France in the summer of 1790, and after a visit to London, returned to Paris in 1791. As the Revolution in France progressed, the precedent of 1688 seemed less relevant to radical reformers in Britain, replaced by the image of a Britain sadly lagging behind its own principles of freedom. In her 1791 'Farewell for Two Years to England', Williams asks, 'Shall Albion mark with scorn the lofty thought, The love of Liberty, herself has taught?'[43] She was shocked by the reaction of the English to the events in France, and by the scaremongering of the press, and expressed herself in language which showed how sensibility might be the vehicle of political discernment:

> Are these the images of that universal joy, which called tears into my eyes, and made my heart throb with sympathy. Must I be told that my mind is perverted, that I am become dead to all sensations of sympathy, because I do not weep with those who have lost a part of their superfluities, rather than rejoice that the oppressed are protected, that the wronged are redressed, that the captive is set at liberty, and that the poor have bread.[44]

Wollstonecraft considered herself, because a rationalist, to be a more serious intellectual than Helen Maria Williams, but as Janet Todd rightly points out, Williams was much more fully committed to the Revolution, risked more, and suffered more acutely.[45] Though Williams cut a very different intellectual figure from Wollstonecraft, nonetheless the two not only shared the stage as brave women intellectuals but also as accomplished literary writers. Williams was a poet of some reputation in the 1780s and considered to be a gifted novelist as well. Like Wollstonecraft, Williams lived as a sexual revolutionary in France, her liaison with Stone well known, as he was the activist president of the British group that met in the evenings at White's Hotel.

The radical life of these women writers was not only about sexual freedom; it was also about the links between political and social freedom as well. Back in England, Horace Walpole recorded an evening at the London

---

43 Helen Maria Williams, *A Farewell, for Two Years, to England* (London: Cadell, 1791), p. 7.
44 Helen Maria Williams, *Letters from France . . . in the Years 1790, 1791, 1792, and 1793*, 2 vols. (Dublin: Chambers, 1794), Letter XXVI, p. 123.
45 Wollstonecraft, *Political Writings*, p. xxiii.

Hope & Crown on the anniversary of the Bastille being broken into by Government agents, and 'Eleven disciples of Paine [taken into] custody': 'Mrs. Merry, Mrs. Barbauld, and Miss Helen Maria Williams will probably have subjects for elegies.' Unconventional though Williams's experience of the French Revolution may have been, as conveyed to friends and then to a more general public back in England in her *Letters Containing a Sketch of the Politics of France* (1790–6), her rhetoric is elaborated through the conventions of sensibility, that late-eighteenth-century language which draws on the language of the heart, rather than the head, to investigate the things of the world. 'In my admiration of the revolution in France', she writes in 1790, 'I blend the feelings of private friendship with my sympathy in public blessings; since the old constitution is connected in my mind with the image of a friend confined in the gloomy recesses of a dungeon, and pining in hopeless captivity; while, with the new constitution, I unite the soothing idea of his return to prosperity, honour and happiness.'[46]

Williams had scope to participate with salon society as well, the setting which offered a place to women to engage in 'polite' discourse, which became from 1790 onwards, increasingly ardent in the political upheavals. Like Wollstonecraft, Paine and others who were part of the British Club in Paris, Williams's identification with the Girondins was predicated on the apparent congruence between 1688 and 1789. From the time of the Girondin expulsion from the National Convention, Williams and others were under threat of arrest, and Williams was taken to the Luxembourg prison on 12 October 1793. Williams remained a robust supporter of revolutionary principles despite the Terror and her own terror in the face of it, and brought out her second set of Letters in 1795. Williams apotheosized the defeated Girondins as 'a radiant constellation in the zone of freedom [who] diffused benignant beams over the hemisphere till extinguished by storms and darkness' (Letter III, vol. II). She was quite remarkable amongst her intellectual milieu for her ability to distinguish between the democratic aims of the Revolution and the disturbing violations of them. Unlike Wordsworth and others who came to believe that the errors of the French Revolution were immanent to its process, Williams remained clear-sighted about what democracy might offer all persons. After the Terror, 'I see again the dawn of that glorious light' that will dispel the 'gloomy history' recounted in the second volume of her letters. Unlike the later generation of

---

46 Helen Maria Williams, *Letters Written in France* (London: Cadell, 1796), 4 vols., vol. I, 1790, Letter IX, p. 72.

British intellectuals such as Hazlitt she did not glorify Napoleon nor consider him to be a saviour of the revolution. As her political commitments became more focused, Williams's language also lost much of its ornamentation and affective imagery. She shifts from being a sensitive observer to polemical partisan, and her writing becomes sparer and sharply analytical. As a first-hand account of the year 1790, Williams's narrative is strikingly vivid and throughout imbued with the language of aesthetic sensibility: for example, the spectacle on the anniversary of the fall of the Bastille is invoked: 'The ruins of that execrable fortress were suddenly transformed, as if with the wand of necromancy, into a scene of beauty and pleasure.' (Letter II, vol. I, p. 13.) But even while her rhetoric is steeped in the epithets of sensibility, she also draws on the more plain style language of revolutionary internationalism: 'It was a triumph of human kind; it was man asserting the noblest privileges of his nature; and it required but the common feelings of humanity to become in that moment a citizen of the world.' (Letter II, p. 9.)

All four of these intellectual travellers were citizens of the world. Though we are apt to think of Romanticism as a discourse of abstraction and idealization, Wollstonecraft, Paine, Jefferson and Williams all lived and tested their ideas in practice. As writers they aimed to write in a way that corresponded to the idea of the citizen rather than the subject, and forged styles that were practicable as well. Clarity of expression met the need for a language that would both explain the world and also body forth its emotional meaning, yoking together exact analysis with romantic utopianism. The immediacy of their letters and tracts, and the close relations between what they wrote, how they lived, and who they loved turned these down-to-earth romantics into romantic icons themselves, idealized in turn in the later twentieth century as forerunners in a glorious course of not only political but social and cultural rebellion, revolution and reform.

Changes in the world of publishing

ADRIAN JOHNS

The term 'publishing', used to denote a discrete and stable commercial practice, dates from the first quarter of the nineteenth century. It was only at that time that people began to refer to such entities as 'the world of publishing' at all. Less abstractly, it was also at that time that publishers themselves appeared on the scene in something like their modern guise, soon becoming the dominant force in the commerce of the book. Both developments were of the utmost importance for the creation, distribution and reception of literary work. The earliest example of the general usage given by the *Oxford English Dictionary* is attributed to Sir Walter Scott – a provenance that is almost too appropriate. Whilst it is unlikely that Scott, or any other individual for that matter, really inaugurated the usage, he was famously the author who made the most of the transformation that was captured by this shift. Scott exemplified, and was taken at the time to exemplify, the possibilities raised by such conjunctions of literary and commercial innovation. Those conjunctions are the subject of this chapter.

The years of Romanticism saw the English book trade change from a craft to something that might plausibly be called an industry. The trade expanded enormously, adopted new business techniques, embraced specialization, addressed a far larger and more diverse readership, and, toward the end of the period, embraced major technological change. It created new modes of public dialogue, including new literary forms. It also confronted a political situation in which real revolution did not seem at all inconceivable – a possibility to which the trade both contributed and had to respond. Not least, the revolutionary threat led to the imposition of police measures not seen in England since the days of the Stuarts, and some not even then. In addressing all these challenges, the trade helped to reshape the literature of the time.

Commercial genius, 1774–1830

By the last quarter of the eighteenth century the British book trade had enjoyed a long period of stability. A few firms grew into major enterprises, and the 1,800 or so titles published annually in 1740 had risen to over 5,000 fifty years later. A considerable proportion of this increase is accounted for by the expansion of commercial novel publishing (with temporary declines during the War of Independence and the French Revolution). Impression sizes, by and large, did not greatly increase, and novels retained an average impression size of around 500–800 well into the nineteenth century. Moreover, it is likely that the audience of readers reached by literary books (as opposed to newsprint) remained fairly static, or even declined. But in every other respect eighteenth-century statistics tell of a mature, not to say complacent, trade.[1] The levels of publication achieved by the late 1790s were then sustained into the early nineteenth century, but did not markedly increase further. There was no quantum leap in the number of editions associated with the introduction of mechanization; and edition sizes, too, with notable exceptions, remained at much the same level. Only right at the end of the 1830s would such a jump occur, apparently as a consequence not only of technology but also of an intense religious controversy that spurred a flurry of pamphleteering.[2]

Publishing had always been concentrated in London – indeed, it was virtually a metropolitan monopoly until the mid-eighteenth century. This continued to be the case, with the important exceptions of Edinburgh and, until 1800, Dublin. Distribution throughout the country took place via networks of booksellers, stationers, chapmen and others, the numbers of whom increased markedly over the century. There were over 1,000 retailers by the 1790s, and their catalogues reveal an ability to deal in new works of

---

1 J. Raven, *Judging New Wealth: Popular Publishing and Responses to Commerce in England, 1750–1800* (Oxford: Clarendon Press, 1992), pp. 32–3; J. Raven, 'The Novel Comes of Age', in P. Garside, J. Raven and R. Schowerling (gen. eds.), *The English Novel 1770–1829*, 2 vols. (Oxford: Oxford University Press, 2000), vol. I, pp. 15–121, esp. pp. 26–7, 35; W. St Clair, *The Reading Nation in the Romantic Period* (Cambridge: Cambridge University Press, 2004), pp. 88–9. St Clair's is by far the best account available of this subject.

2 S. Eliot, 'Some Trends in British Book Production, 1800–1919', in J. O. Jordan and R. L. Patten (eds.), *Literature in the Marketplace: Nineteenth-century British Publishing and Reading Practices* (Cambridge: Cambridge University Press, 1995), pp. 19–43, esp. p. 28–9; S. Eliot, *Some Patterns and Trends in British Publishing 1800–1919* (London: Bibliographical Society, 1994), p. 24; P. Garside, 'The English Novel in the Romantic Era: Consolidation and Dispersal', in Garside, Raven and Schowerling, *English Novel 1770–1829*, vol. II, pp. 15–103, esp. p. 38.

quality as well as chapbooks, schoolbooks and second-hand volumes. England's first guide to the trade, John Pendred's *London Printers, Booksellers and Stationers Vade Mecum* (1785), surveyed this expanding network in order to help London booksellers make the most of it.[3] Provincial printers grew in number too, but they remained devoted to jobbing work and local newspapers, with only occasional forays into book publishing. Few of them got their names on London imprints, Benjamin Collins of Salisbury being a rare exception. Nevertheless their newspapers did play a key role in advertising London's books. So did the first nationally circulated papers, which incorporated critical reviews. It was this distributive network that supplied literary goods to the developing consumer society across Britain.[4]

Within London itself, the trade had long been dominated by a relatively small and stable group of copyright-owning booksellers. These booksellers might compete against each other, but they also cooperated to preserve their collective near-monopoly of major publishing endeavours. Their prosperity resided in valuable copyrights like that of Pope's *Works*, which in 1767 was valued at £4,400. Such properties were divided into shares, which were traded at closed auctions in Paternoster Row. It was possible, for example, to own a 1/60 stake in Shakespeare's plays. Shareholders then collaborated to publish works in capital-intensive editions, sharing the risk among exclusive alliances that were originally called *congers* (after *conjure* – a reference to the confidentiality they nurtured). By the mid-1760s the patterns of ownership in these copies had become extraordinarily byzantine.[5] Their basis, however, was a matter of convention – and to some extent of intimidation – rather than statute law. The statutory copyright on them had in fact expired long before. But the grandees of the trade were united in assuming and asserting that the statute merely provided extra protection for an underlying property that was unwritten yet in principle perpetual.

3 J. Brewer and I. McCalman, 'Publishing', in McCalman (ed.), *An Oxford Companion to the Romantic Age* (Oxford: Oxford University Press, 1999), pp. 197–206, esp. p. 198. On the scale of the London trade see also E. Howe, *The London Compositor: Documents Relating to Wages, Working Conditions and Customs of the London Printing Trade 1785–1900* (London: Bibliographical Society, 1947), pp. 33–50, 53–7.

4 J. Feather, *The Provincial Book Trade in Eighteenth-Century England* (Cambridge: Cambridge University Press, 1985), pp. 28–31, 44–68 and *passim*; C. Y. Ferdinand, *Benjamin Collins and the Provincial Newspaper Trade in the Eighteenth Century* (Oxford: Clarendon Press, 1997), pp. 49–50; J. Feather, 'The Merchants of Culture: Bookselling in Early Industrial England', *Studies of Voltaire and the Eighteenth Century* 217 (1983), 11–21, esp. 12–13; J. Brewer, *The Pleasures of the Imagination: English Culture in the Eighteenth Century* (New York: Farrar Straus Giroux, 1997), pp. 132–3.

5 Raven, *Judging New Wealth*, p. 37; Brewer, *Pleasures of the Imagination*, p. 135.

George Robinson (1737–1801), for example – a prosperous late-century publisher – routinely declared in purchase documents that he had bought a certain copyright 'forever'. So whatever the situation might be *de jure*, this coterie ensured that *de facto* copyright remained secure. And the consequences extended to every aspect of printed culture – what could be bought, borrowed and read, from chapbooks to encyclopedias. In the 1770s, however, this system was challenged. When that happened, the legal concept of perpetual copyright collapsed with startling suddenness, leaving cartel and combination exposed as the bases of trade practice.[6]

The challenger who destroyed common-law literary property was a Scottish bookseller named Alexander Donaldson. Donaldson's career before the late 1750s had been exemplary of the pattern of collaboration and competition that obtained between London and Edinburgh. The son of a wealthy manufacturer, from 1751 he partnered Alexander Kincaid, a major Edinburgh bookseller, in producing learned and medical works. Kincaid was the Scottish participant in a long-running and highly profitable alliance with two Scots of the London trade, Andrew Millar and William Strahan. Through this alliance appeared most of the key works of the Scottish Enlightenment.[7] But Donaldson wished to take advantage of a recent ruling in Scotland that restricted copyright protection to the statutory terms laid out in the Act of Anne, and to reprint mainstays of the London trade such as Shakespeare and Thomson at prices that would dramatically increase their readerships. The partnership with Kincaid dissolved, and he launched himself into a career of reprinting a canon of works that the London booksellers still regarded as properties. Such titles included works by Defoe, Fielding, Locke and others. The Londoners denounced his practice as piracy, but Donaldson discounted their complaints, affirming both that Scottish jurisprudence, with its basis in Roman law, had no place for their presumptuous claims, and that he was striking a blow for Enlightenment. In 1763 he daringly opened a shop in London itself, selling his reprints for far less than their originals and defending the practice as upholding a public interest in the availability of affordable literature. After complex legal wrangles, in 1774 Donaldson's appeal against Thomas Becket, a London

6 G. E. Bentley, Jr., 'Copyright Documents in the George Robinson Archive: William Godwin and Others, 1713–1820', *Studies in Bibliography* 35 (1982), pp. 67–110, esp. p. 71; St Clair, *Reading Nation*, pp. 41–2, 77–81, 88–101.

7 R. B. Sher, *The Enlightenment and the Book: Scottish Authors and their Publishers in Eighteenth-century Britain, Ireland, and America* (Chicago, IL: University of Chicago Press, 2006), pp. 312–14.

copy-owner who had obtained an injunction against him for publishing Thomson's *Seasons*, came to the House of Lords. The Lords voted down the injunction, effectively demolishing the principle of perpetual common-law copyright. Overnight, the press reported, some £200,000-worth of what was 'yesterday thought property' had apparently been obliterated. The entire oligarchy of the trade were 'in a manner ruined'.[8]

The 1774 decision caused enormous trepidation in London's publishing circles. How could expensive projects be justified without security in copies? The Londoners asked Parliament for relief, but met with a distinct lack of sympathy.[9] Their conventional assumptions had lost their rationale for good, and they would have to live with the consequences. Donaldson's victory – coupled, a year later, by a similar verdict overthrowing the Company of Stationers' immensely valuable patent on almanacs – thus opened the way to enormous change. And the best modern study of the publishing history of the subsequent period has concurred, calling the result 'the most decisive event in the history of reading in England since the arrival of printing 300 years before'.[10] What followed may have been that profound, but it was not at all the spectacular collapse predicted by the trade's jeremiahs. Instead the next generation saw rapid expansion, the rise of the publisher, and the advent of specialists devoted to particular genres (for example, textbooks).[11] All were driven by a new state of affairs in which wealth could no longer be assumed to reside in a cache of old warhorses like Shakespeare, Thomson and Pope, publication of which could be reserved to the few. Instead it could be sought in new works, of which the number issued now increased dramatically. Or it might reside in the competitive printing of those same older works, in new formats, at reduced prices, and for vastly increased readerships. Alternatively, it might be found in pure publishing, with the old role of the bookseller being abandoned altogether. Others still specialized in wholesaling, or in novel forms of retailing, such as remaindering. And it should not be forgotten that for the London trade

---

8 M. Rose, *Authors and Owners: The Invention of Copyright* (Cambridge, MA: Harvard University Press, 1993), pp. 92–7.

9 W. Zachs, *The First John Murray and the Late Eighteenth-century London Book Trade* (Oxford: by Oxford University Press for the British Academy, 1998), p. 58.

10 St Clair, *Reading Nation*, p. 109.

11 J. Feather, *A History of British Publishing* (London: Routledge, 1988), p. 82–3; C. Blagden, 'Thomas Carnan and the Almanack Monopoly', *Studies in Bibliography* 14 (1961), 23–43; J. Topham, 'A textbook revolution', in M. Frasca-Spada and N. Jardine (eds.), *Books and the Sciences* (Cambridge: Cambridge University Press, 2000), pp. 317–37, esp. pp. 318–25.

carrying on as usual remained an option; it retained its ability to enforce by blacklisting and similar tactics a customary form of literary property that had no legal basis whatsoever. There were, it turned out, fortunes to be made, some of which proved enormous. But there was also great risk, and bankruptcies in the trade increased markedly. In short, the period began in a mood of radical uncertainty.[12]

Those prepared to experiment were often the ones to benefit the most from this new environment. Many were strangers to the London system, and not infrequently to London itself. A good example was the Scot John Bell (1745–1831). Bell had been another partner with Kincaid, but he too split with Strahan and Cadell (Millar's successor) after 1774. He then launched what became a 109-volume series of reprints between 1777 and 1793, entitled *The Poets of Great Britain*. Bell's project – described in its prospectus as 'the only complete uniform edition of the British Poets' – exploited the sudden release of poetry from protection to both literary and commercial effect. It innovated in typography, format and printing technique, creating virtually a new kind of book business to reach a new, broad readership. A rival projected by the traditional booksellers proved slower, smaller and less exhaustive, although Johnson's prefaces added lustre to the publication. It was also less innovative in commercial terms: for example, it was at first available only as an expensive complete set, whereas Bell's volumes were also sold separately at a variety of prices to different classes of customer. But these series (along with others less well known; Kincaid had initiated one as early as 1773) created a canon of English literary 'classics' from Chaucer to Cowper. The contents of this canon would then be fixed in place when, beginning in 1808, copyright terms were extended once again.[13]

Others resolved to create and exploit more specialist markets. Two of the outstanding examples were the market in children's books and that in Gothic fiction. John Newbery, who did most to create children's publishing, died in 1767, but his successors (among them Thomas Carnan, the destroyer of the Stationers' almanac patent) continued his strategy and it was under them that it bore fruit. In the period 1780–1820 they created a paradigmatic literature of 'instructive and entertaining' texts dedicated to 'moral

---

12 Raven, 'Novel Comes of Age', p. 90; Garside, 'English Novel', p. 47.
13 T. F. Bonnell, 'John Bell's *Poets of Great Britain*: The "little trifling edition" Revisited', *Modern Philology* 85 (1987), 128–52; S. Morison, *John Bell, 1745–1831* (Cambridge: Cambridge University Press for the author, 1930); M. J. M. Ezell, *Social Authorship and the Advent of Print* (Baltimore: Johns Hopkins University Press, 1999), p. 131; St Clair, *Reading Nation*, pp. 122–30.

didactics'. At first their books were small, cheap and plain; later, in the 1830s, their appearance would change completely with the introduction of mechanized binding.[14] Meanwhile the Minerva Press, created in Leadenhall Street by William Lane (c. 1745–1814) in 1790, pioneered the production of popular fiction on unprecedented scales, distributing it through Minerva's own library. Novel publishing had in any case been largely unaffected by the old share system, because novels were aimed at an immediate market, not at reprints, but still the initiative derived directly from the new dispensation. Not least, novels were particularly prominent among genres published by booksellers acting alone, not in the old-style alliances. But the 'Literary Museum, or Novel Repository' that Lane developed was particularly successful. In the 1790s he alone published a third of all new novel titles to appear, and Minerva remained the leading novel producer until 1826, when Henry Colburn, seeing an opportunity in a troubled period for the trade, came into his own. During that time Lane greatly contributed to the sense that reading was part and parcel of a consumer culture. He also published twice as many titles by women as by men, thus underscoring the contemporary identification of novels as a female form of literature. (Most novels were in fact authored by women until the 1820s.) It was largely his products that Austen satirized in *Northanger Abbey*.[15]

Some existing booksellers decided to move away from their traditional role altogether and concentrate solely on publishing. The term *publisher* consequently took on a new prominence and a new meaning. Longman was one of the first to see the possibilities; by the 1810s the firm had separated publishing from retailing entirely, in the process separating work from home (a distinctly modernizing move: earlier operations had conventionally been domestic). It became the leading conventional publisher of its generation. John Murray (1778–1843), inheritor of a successful bookselling–publishing concern, likewise moved west to Albemarle Street and turned the firm into one of the greatest publishers of the nineteenth century.[16]

14 C. Walsh, *A Bookseller of the Last Century* (London: Griffith etc., 1885), pp. 89–117; A. Fyfe, 'Young Readers and the Sciences', in M. Frasca-Spada and N. Jardine (eds.), *Books and the Sciences in History* (Cambridge: Cambridge University Press, 2000), pp. 276–90.

15 Raven, 'Novel comes of Age', pp. 79–80, 82, 87–8; Garside, 'English Novel', pp. 63, 74, 88–9; D. Blakey, *The Minerva Press 1790–1820* (London: Bibliographical Society, 1939), esp. pp. 16–25. Printers, too, specialized in this period: Howe, *London Compositor*, pp. 57–8.

16 Garside, 'English novel', p. 80; Feather, *History of British Publishing*, p. 120; Zachs, *First John Murray*, p. 250 (Zachs's book is about this John Murray's father).

Murray would devise the half-profits system for paying authors, which would remain the standard throughout the Victorian era. More than anyone else he epitomized the new figure of the nineteenth-century publisher.

As some firms concentrated on publishing, so others saw new opportunities in the old enterprises of retailing and wholesaling. One of the more evident changes was in sheer geography. As the fashionable heart of London moved westward, so the major booksellers followed, creating new centres in Piccadilly and Pall Mall to go along with the traditional foci of St Paul's Churchyard and Paternoster Row. One of the largest new shops, Hatchard's, was on St James's Street. Elsewhere could be found the remarkable 'Temple of the Muses' established by James Lackington in 1789 in Finsbury Square. Instead of selling a few books at high margins – the essence of the pre-1774 trade – Lackington perceived the possibility of selling many at low margins. In effect, he invented remaindering. The idea caught on, despite grumbling by the booksellers, and he was soon running the largest bookshop in the country. He made enough to retire to Devon in considerable luxury.[17]

Amid all this practical upheaval, however, one thing that showed less dramatic change was the stress laid by booksellers and publishers on civility. The book trade had long rested on a basis of conversations and social interactions, especially between authors – and would-be authors – and booksellers. Any 'print logic' guiding the development of the trade operated only through the practical pursuit of such civility, which had its own often quite complex conventions. This continued to be the case through industrialization. Indeed, its prominence perhaps even increased, if only because the prosperity of men like Murray enabled them to act as hosts to a more lavish extent. This needs to be recalled not only to qualify overly schematic talk of economic or technological determinism, but to balance the many stories about hack writers paid a pittance by rapacious booksellers. There were such writers and such booksellers – to the extent that the term debtor became habitually associated with the term author – but the economics that created such an image were shot through with sociability. Robinson exemplified how, in the midst of great change, booksellers could cling to the notion of commerce, domesticity and sociability going hand in hand. He was called 'the king of booksellers' by one contemporary (the title strikingly inapt for a leading supporter of Godwin and Paine), partly for keeping a

17 R. G. Landon, 'Small Profits do Great Things: James Lackington and Eighteenth-century Bookselling', *Studies in Eighteenth-Century Culture* 5 (1976), 387–99.

family 'villa' at Streatham at which he regularly entertained authors and other guests.[18] The Murrays too were known for their conviviality. In a business centrally concerned with opinion, eloquence, learning and communication, these were not peripheral customs. Authors and publications depended on them, Thomas Wakley's *Lancet* being an evident example. So, sometimes, did works left unpublished. Byron's memoirs are the outstanding example: after his death there was a private meeting in Murray's drawing room to decide whether to publish them. Murray himself hated the idea, but Thomas Moore thought that he would rather have them destroyed than risk their falling into the hands of Longmans. There was a violent argument, culminating in threats of duels, and the manuscript was thrust into the fire.[19]

The late eighteenth and early nineteenth centuries saw challenges to London and Edinburgh publishers from elsewhere. The burgeoning industrial towns became foci of literary productivity in their own right. With flourishing economies, booming populations and highly energetic local markets, booksellers in these towns could prosper into firms that lasted for generations.[20] Readers motivated by an intense ideology of self-help sought out improving reading matter, and booksellers rushed to meet the demand. Yet provincial publishing usually still meant publishing for a local readership. For literary authors it remained a second best. Wordsworth's *Lyrical Ballads* was famously ill-served by it when published by Joseph Cottle in Bristol in 1798 – although in fact his poetry never sold many copies wherever it originated. Virtually all novels, more to the point, continued to emanate from London (the proportion was still eighty-five per cent in the 1820s). Joseph Priestley may have published mainly in Warrington and Birmingham, but even he relied on a London distributor, the radical Joseph Johnson.[21]

More serious rivalry to London continued to come from Scotland. The intellectual vibrancy of the Scottish Enlightenment helped sustain

18 Bentley, 'Copyright Documents', p. 69.
19 J. W. Vail, *The Literary Relationship of Lord Byron and Thomas Moore* (Baltimore: Johns Hopkins University Press, 2001), pp. 226–7.
20 E.g., Liverpool: J. Secord, *Victorian Sensation: The Extraordinary Publication, Reception and Secret Authorship of 'Vestiges of the Natural History of Creation'* (Chicago: University of Chicago Press, 2000), pp. 193–9.
21 Feather, 'Merchants of Culture', pp. 14–15; R. E. Crook, *A Bibliography of Joseph Priestley* (London: Library Association, 1966), e.g. p. 116 for the example of the *Disquisitions Relating to Matter and Spirit*; G. P. Tyson, 'Joseph Johnson, an Eighteenth-century Bookseller', *Studies in Bibliography* 28 (1975), 1–16; Raven, 'Novel comes of age', p. 71; Garside, 'English Novel', p. 76.

substantial concerns in Edinburgh. After 1776, William Creech – protégé of Strahan, one-time apprentice to Kincaid and Bell, and successor to them as Scotland's leading bookseller – tried to establish a booksellers' association in Edinburgh to counter piracy within the community, but to limited effect. Creech had a commitment to medical and natural-scientific publishing that included Sinclair's huge *Statistical Account of Scotland*, and his premises became a centre for the sociability on which the Scottish Enlightenment depended. But his alliance with the Londoners cost him much of the esteem he enjoyed during his life. After his death in 1815 a new generation derided him for subservience to London interests. That new generation contrasted Creech's supposed timidity – representative of a time, as Lockhart wrote, when 'there was no such thing in Edinburgh as the great trade of Publishing' – to the enterprise and autonomy of Archibald Constable in their own day. In the event, Constable would continue to rely on eighteenth-century works as his firm's mainstay, but make fame and fortune out of the *Edinburgh Review* and Sir Walter Scott. The first modern best-sellers were *Waverley* (1814, issued in 40,000 copies over fifteen years) and *Rob Roy* (1818, in a first impression of 10,000); Cadell's Magnum Opus series of the Waverley novels, which used steam presses and stereotyping, hit print runs as high as 30,000.[22] But Constable would lose this fortune and more in his disastrous bankruptcy in 1826.[23]

From a similar starting point, Dublin's fortunes took a radically different turn. At the same time as denouncing Donaldson, the London booksellers had complained loudly of Irish piracy. The Dublin trade was flourishing at the time, and as a separate nation Ireland was certainly not subject to British copyright. Moreover, there was no literary property law in Ireland either, so in practice the only constraints on reprinting were customary and conventional. That should not be gainsaid: the trade banded together into a 'company of booksellers' that published some 200 editions in collaborative, anti-piratical union. But only if a prior edition had appeared in Dublin itself would a publication be deemed improper, and in practice much of the trade was devoted to reprinting London titles. Perfectly legal (if resented) as long as they remained in Ireland, such reprints became piracies as soon as they reached Britain. In fact, the extent of such importing seems to have been

22 Garside, 'English Novel', pp. 90–3, 102–3.
23 Sher, *Enlightenment and the Book*, pp. 355, 401–40; P. Garside, 'Rob's Last Raid: Scott and the Publication of the Waverley Novels', in R. Myers and M. Harris (eds.), *Author/Publisher Relations in the Eighteenth and Nineteenth Centuries* (Oxford: Oxford Polytechnic Press, 1983), pp. 88–118.

overstated by the Londoners – for the most part the Dubliners were interested in creating and addressing local markets (and, slightly later, those in the American colonies). Nonetheless, about seventy-five per cent of London novels from the later eighteenth century were reprinted in Dublin, sometimes with low standards of workmanship, and always at far lower retail prices.[24] So when the Act of Union was passed in 1800, one of the first consequences was the extension of British copyright to Dublin. The Irish publishing industry immediately fell into a calamitous decline.[25] The role of pirate lair would then be taken up by the United States, to which a sizable proportion of the Dublin book trade had emigrated. The origins of nineteenth-century debates over international copyright lay in this diaspora – and especially in its opportunistic appropriation of the Waverley novels, Byron's *Don Juan*, and Bulwer.[26]

In the meantime there were plenty of pirates to be found in London. Piracy was first identified as such toward the end of the seventeenth century, and had continued to be a thorn in the side of the London grandees ever since; the monopolists never had things entirely their own way. But a new generation after 1800 sought to make piracy a much greater force for cultural circulation and change. A convinced class of political and moral radicals, these men were dedicated to using print to distribute heterodox religious, philosophical and political views. Some, like Richard Carlile (1790–1843), would continue in radical causes as late as the Chartist era. Others, like George Cannon (1789–1854) and William Dugdale (c. 1800–68), later separated their lascivious works from political overtones and, in effect, invented modern pornography. Dugdale learned that trade from William Benbow, a one-time soldier who took to piracy to combat despotism and 'monopolising booksellers'.[27] The scope of this kind of activity extended far

24 W. MacDougall, 'Smugglers, Reprinters and Hot Pursuers: The Irish–Scottish Book Trade and Copyright Prosecutions in the Late Eighteenth Century', in R. Myers and M. Harris (eds.), *The Stationers' Company and the Book Trade 1550–1900* (Winchester: St. Paul's Bibliographies, 1997), pp. 151–83; Raven, 'Novel Comes of Age', p. 107; Sher, *Enlightenment and the Book*, pp. 443–502; J. W. Phillips, *A Bibliographical Inquiry into Printing and Bookselling in Dublin from 1670 to 1800* (Dublin: University of Dublin, 1981); M. Pollard, *Dublin's Trade in Books 1550–1800* (Oxford: Clarendon Press, 1989), pp. 168–9 and more generally pp. 66–226.
25 R. C. Cole, *Irish Booksellers and English Writers 1740–1800* (London: Mansell, 1986), pp. 152–4.
26 J. J. Barnes, *Authors, Publishers and Politicians: The Quest for an Anglo-American Copyright Agreement, 1815–1854* (London: Routledge and Kegan Paul, 1974), pp. 1–74.
27 I. McCalman, *Radical Underworld: Prophets, Revolutionaries and Pornographers in London, 1795–1840* (Cambridge: Cambridge University Press, 1988), pp. 204–31, 236; D. Saunders, 'Victorian Obscenity Law: Negative Censorship or Positive Administration?' in

beyond literature per se; the transformation in the social practice of medicine, for example, was accompanied and driven by successive levels of piratical reprinting. And in a context of piracy, the application of laws to attack opposition publications – for which see below – could have the unintended consequence of actually increasing their circulation. For instance, John Murray was reluctant to publish cheap editions of Byron's poems to address the new mass market, partly because he himself felt distaste for their expressed views. Piracies blossomed, however, especially when Lord Chancellor Eldon ruled (after careful perusal of the work) that it was immoral and hence undeserving of copyright protection. Much the same thing happened at Eldon's hands to William Lawrence's 1819 *Lectures on Physiology*, which, in pirated editions, contributed substantially to the profusion of materialist ideas. Shelley's *Queen Mab*, too, received most of its circulation in the form of piracies by political radicals. Inspired by the vastly greater readerships targeted by the pirates, in 1823 Byron himself switched to publishing through the radical John Hunt, who issued cantos of *Don Juan* in huge numbers at prices as low as a shilling.[28]

The era following the downfall of perpetual copyright coincided not only with this efflorescence of populist piracy but also, perhaps ironically, with the elevation of authorship to an unprecedented cultural status. Romantic notions of creativity rested on the idea that in writing a work an author vested it with something – an expression or a spirit – irreducibly identified with that author. It was, in short, an articulation of genius. That concept did not enjoy the kind of explicit status in England that it gained in Germany, and in practice not only were most novels (Austen's as well as Scott's) anonymous, but so was *Don Juan*.[29] But Wordsworth, among others, would

P. Hyland and N. Sammells (eds.), *Writing and Censorship in Britain* (London: Routledge, 1992), pp. 154–70; St Clair, *Reading Nation*, pp. 307–38.

28 O. Temkin, 'Basic Science, Medicine and the Romantic Era', *Bulletin of the History of Medicine* 37 (1963), 97–129; J. Goodfield-Toulmin, 'Some Aspects of English Physiology, 1780–1840', *Journal of the History of Biology* 2 (1969), 283–320; E. Jacob (ed.), *Reports of Cases Argued and Determined in the High Court of Chancery* (London: J. Butterworth and Son, 1828), pp. 471–4; *The Report of the Court of King's Bench . . . being the Mock Trials of Richard Carlile* (London: R. Carlile, 1822); W. H. Wickwar, *The Struggle for the Freedom of the Press, 1819–32* (London: G. Allen and Unwin, 1928), pp. 259–64; N. Fraistat, 'Illegitimate Shelley: Radical Piracy and the Textual Edition as Cultural Performance', *PMLA* 109:3 (May 1994), 409–23. St Clair, *Reading Nation*, pp. 680–91 provides data on *Queen Mab* and *Don Juan*.

29 M. Woodmansee, 'Genius and the Copyright', in Woodmansee, *The Author, Art, and the Market: Rereading the History of Aesthetics* (New York: Columbia University Press, 1994), pp. 34–55; Garside, 'English Novel', pp. 66–7; Raven, 'Novel comes of Age', p. 41.

base his campaign to revive perpetual copyright on the idea. Yet it was also possible to take the principle as a premise *against* such property, as did Wordsworth's antagonist, the radical publisher Thomas Tegg, who made his living by issuing reprints. Tegg argued that the public had an especial interest in the availability of works of genius, and that that interest must be set against the concerns of the author. Such arguments – which played out very publicly indeed – helped to create the impression that there was indeed a 'national literature' in which a public interest could be said to inhere.[30]

These developments affected the objects produced and distributed by the book trade. Perhaps the most familiar example is the decline of new commercial poetry; by the 1830s Edward Moxon largely had this market to himself.[31] In its place the essay became a dominant literary genre, and the periodical its dominant vehicle. If less drastic, the impact on novels was no less clear. The new publishers created uniform house 'looks' for their volumes, incorporating them into series with regular typographical and bibliographical styles. They were generally duodecimo in the eighteenth century, compact and suited for casual reading, but the format embodied their low cultural status and increasingly octavo came to be used in preference; as with so much else, this was inspired by Scott, in this case in *Ivanhoe* (1819).[32] A three-volume norm was also adopted that would last virtually to the end of the century. Retail prices were set high, and rose faster than inflation, culminating in the standard guinea and a half (31s. 6d.) for a three-decker. This mode of publishing was the true descendant of the old eighteenth-century London trade, content to sell small impressions at high prices. Relatively few copies were sold to private readers, as the three-deckers mainly went to libraries of various kinds. Contemporary complaints abounded that novels were padded to satisfy the format (*Frankenstein* being a clear case where this happened). But the norm also left a clear opening to pirates, not only in Britain but also – and in this case perhaps more importantly – abroad. From Paris (Galignani), Brussels (Baudry) and other European centres came skilfully printed unauthorized versions of the novels, elegant, readable, and far cheaper than the originals.[33]

---

30 R. G. Swartz, 'Wordsworth, Copyright, and the Commodities of Genius', *Modern Philology* 89:4 (1992), 482–509; William Wordsworth, *Prose Works*, ed. W. J. B. Owen and J. W. Smyser, 3 vols. (Oxford: Clarendon Press, 1974), vol. III, pp. 309–20.

31 L. Erickson, *The Economy of Literary Form: English Literature and the Industrialization of Publishing, 1800–1850* (Baltimore: Johns Hopkins University Press, 1996).

32 Raven, 'Novel Comes of Age', pp. 94, 96, 98, 103.

33 Garside, 'English Novel', pp. 90–3, 102–3; St Clair, *Reading Nation*, pp. 293–306.

Technological change: a printing revolution?

At the end of the eighteenth century the law, practices and constitution of the book trade had already changed profoundly, and its market had expanded enormously. But the actual machinery and customs of the paper-mill, printing house, bindery and bookshop remained remarkably similar to those of Shakespeare's day. If nothing else, the sheer expansion of the literary marketplace by the end of the eighteenth century had created a crying need for faster, cheaper and larger-scale production. Mechanization promised to meet that need. And it is clear that the extraordinary technological changes that occurred in the trade in the first half of the century were indeed called forth (sometimes by pirates) to further this existing trajectory, rather than creating it themselves. What happened could nevertheless plausibly be represented as a second printing revolution. As such, the questions it raises are comparable to those suggested by Gutenberg's invention. How was the new device apprehended by contemporaries in terms of existing possibilities? How did they put it to use such that it fostered a certain cultural impact? And how did they understand and represent that impact? Such thinking is justified by the status accorded to Gutenberg and Caxton themselves by men like Charles Knight, the great entrepreneur of steam printing, who went to Mainz to see the lavish commemoration of 400 years of printing in 1837 and made the steam press into his own icon of progress and civilization.[34]

The first thing to note is that prior to industrialization this was already an age when printing, presses, places and skills (including the speculative skills of the publisher) took on a variety of new forms, meanings and uses. And this process continued through the period of new technologies. In particular, a commitment to the value of presswork itself, often with an antiquarian cast, cut across any readily recognizable political or social lines. At one extreme we find a reactionary like Sir Samuel Egerton Brydges, whose private press issued what aspired to become an alternative canon of high literature – one based, professedly, not on copy-ownership and commerce but on imaginative integrity and noble descent. A dedicated bibliographical antiquarian, Brydges sought to rescue forgotten Tudor and Stuart poets (Drayton, Wither, Greene, Ralegh, etc.) from the shadow of Pope, that

---

34 C. Knight, *William Caxton* (London: C. Knight and Co., 1844), pp. 80–4.

great property of the Enlightenment book trade.[35] But for all its political and aesthetic conservatism, his Lee Priory press shared the artisans' commitment to craft skill, and was managed by a dedicated opponent of steam and stereotyping, John Johnson. That valuation of craftsmanship and community became all the more accentuated when the new technologies were taking hold in the 1820s; in the same generation the prices of hand presses fell and working-class printers found it possible to operate a printing house themselves, giving rise to a cheap, diverse and radical periodical and book literature without any real precedent. The work produced by these groups differed markedly in political and epistemological terms not only from that of the steam-press firms, but equally from that of the old metropolitan trade of Longman. And for some individuals the very practice of printing itself became an element in the articulation of genius. William Blake is today the best-known example (although he was little regarded at the time), whose anti-mechanical beliefs extended to making impression part of expression. But in fact a tradition could be identified of figures who boasted of setting type as they created their works; from the early modern period it would extend through eighteenth-century artisan poets and culminate in Victorian radicals like Spencer Hall. The idea was to demonstrate creative spontaneity, originality and authenticity. The newly invented typewriter would later remind Mark Twain strongly of this skill.[36]

The technological revolution in print took place alongside these changes. It is generally identified with the advent of the industrial steam press. Contemporaries did not call it a press at all, indeed, but a *machine*, the distinction being conscious and consistent.[37] There is good reason for this. When, after several abortive attempts to apply mechanized power to printing, Koenig's machine began operation at *The Times*, it increased impression-size tenfold. The change was extraordinary, and it took place literally overnight: the managers of the plant had kept the new machine hidden until the moment its first print-run was complete, fearing unrest among the printers about to be

35 A. Winter, *Mesmerized: Powers of Mind in Victorian Britain* (Chicago: University of Chicago Press, 1998), pp. 134, 374; S. E. Brydges, *The British Bibliographer*, 4 vols. (London: Triphook et al., 1810–14), vol. I, p. vi. For Brydges's biography see S. E. Brydges, *The Autobiography, Times, Opinions, and Contemporaries of Sir Egerton Brydges*, 2 vols. (London: Cochrane and M'Crone, 1834).
36 J. Viscomi, *Blake and the Idea of the Book* (Princeton: Princeton University Press, 1993), pp. 39–40 and *passim*; J. Johnson, *Typographia*, 2 vols. (London: Longman et al., 1824); Winter, *Mesmerized*, p. 374, n. 107; L. Gitelman, *Scripts, Grooves, and Writing Machines: Representing Technology in the Edison Era* (Stanford: Stanford University Press, 1999), pp. 204–5.
37 Dooley, *Author and Printer*, p. 78.

made redundant. That was in 1814; by 1827 *The Times* had a new generation of presses, capable of churning out 5,000 copies an hour. In such hands steam printing, along with the even newer railway, would facilitate the first national daily press. And a steam printing operation had to be of larger scale, and based on a larger capital investment, than anything in the craft culture of printing up to that time. So the social life of print stood to be transformed too. In effect, printing of this kind became a branch of factory culture.

But steam printing was not in fact the most significant innovation, and it could not have come to pass itself without other developments. The mechanization of papermaking was one. By the late eighteenth century it was increasingly evident that the supply of rags – the raw materials of the craft – was simply insufficient across western Europe. The expansion of printing had put intolerable strain on the system. It was not just that actual paper shortages occurred; a greater problem was that publishers could not be sure of finding large quantities at short notice, so were forced to keep substantial supplies in storage, thus locking up capital. Paper costs conspired with government-imposed stamp duties to make books more expensive than any period since the mid-fifteenth century. A remedy came with the advent of the papermaking machine, patented by Nicolas-Louis Robert in France in 1799. The sheer rate of production of the machine was remarkable – paper production was now measured not in reams per day, but in feet per minute. Similar machines installed by Henry and Sealy Fourdrinier in Hertfordshire in 1804 repeated the same performance commercially. Although it never enjoyed the public fame of the steam press, the papermaking machine had at least as great a role in the changes of this period. It was the paper-making machine, not the steam press, that Brunel justifiably hailed as 'one of the most splendid inventions of our age'. Even so, it was not until the 1820s that mechanical papermaking exceeded hand-papermaking in quantitative terms.[38]

Perhaps the most important development, however, was not strictly speaking one of mechanization at all. Eighteenth-century printers had often been able to afford only limited amounts of type. Reprints were therefore not literal copies, since forms could rarely be left standing from impression to impression. This simple reality had affected the nature and impact of book publishing, since it had compelled booksellers to make an entire

38 M. Plant, *The English Book Trade: An Economic History of the Making and Sale of Books* (London: George Allen and Unwin, 1939), p. 321; Garside, 'English Novel', p. 44, n.45. See in general R. L. Hills, *Papermaking in Britain, 1488–1988: A Short History* (London: Athlone, 1988), and D. C. Coleman, *The British Paper Industry, 1495–1860: A Study in Industrial Growth* (Oxford: Clarendon Press, 1958).

edition at one go, and store it expensively, sometimes for years, while it gradually sold off. In the early nineteenth century an old invention, repeatedly mooted, was at last taken up in a sustained fashion to address this situation. Stereotyping fixed the sheet in metal, allowing type to be redistributed without losing the form. Plates were combined with steam presses in 1815, after which they became a new standard for large-scale production of copies. It is significant that in many cases it was outsiders, not the London grandees, who embraced the technique most readily. The copies it produced ought, at last, to be truly identical – the realization of that dream of print uniformity ubiquitous since Gutenberg and key to the Enlightenment identification of print and progress, revived at this juncture by Charles Babbage. In practice, however, things were not quite so simple; stereotype plates could indeed be changed, and were. What prevented routine alterations were not so much technological limits as cultural and commercial ones. But stereotyping also had subtler effects; for example, it reintroduced a conventional equivalent to property, in the sense that it was rarely viable to re-compose a book once it had been stereotyped, so the owner of the plates became, in effect, a monopoly provider.[39]

Mechanization and stereotyping had profound consequences, particularly when carried out in conjunction. In an apt example, Babbage noted that a London print-run of *Chambers's [Edinburgh] Journal* became profitable only when stereotyped, steam-printed and distributed across the country by rail. This was steam literature *par excellence*: periodical, national and massive in its circulation. Its format and content, both of which were deliberately designed for steam printing, became a model.[40] The development of mass literacy relied substantially on industrial printing of this kind. Dickens's *Pickwick Papers* pioneered the stereotyped issue of part-novels in serials, along with the use of national advertising and distribution by rail. By the early 1840s popular novels were being printed industrially in parts, and published at a penny per issue.[41] All of these effects, which helped transform

39 A. C. Dooley, *Author and Printer in Victorian England* (Charlottesville: University Press of Virginia, 1992), pp. 4–5, 55–9, 76; St Clair, *Reading Nation*, pp. 182–5; A. Johns, 'The Identity Engine: Printing and Publishing at the Beginning of the Knowledge Economy', in L. Roberts, S. Schaffer and P. Dear (eds.), *The Mindful Hand: Inquiry and Invention from the Late Renaissance to Early Industrialization* (Chicago, IL: Edita/ University of Chicago Press, 2007), pp. 403–28.
40 C. Babbage, *On the Economy of Machinery and Manufactures*, 4th edn (1835), in Babbage, *Works*, ed. M. Campbell-Kelly, 12 vols. (New York: NYU Press, 1989), vol. VIII, pp. 190–1.
41 J. Sutherland, *Victorian Fiction: Writers, Publishers, Readers* (London: MacMillan, 1995), pp. 87–106.

a public culture into something like a mass culture, rested as much on innovative uses of technology as on intrinsic properties of the technology itself. Indeed, this much is very clear from representations of the industrial publishing enterprise itself, which were issued in steam-printed publications. Knight's journal *The Printing Machine* was emblematic: it made the printing machine into the emblem of progress *par excellence*.[42]

Printing was thus undergoing its own industrial revolution. Print runs ten or a hundred times as great as had ever previously been viable represented a quantitative leap of the same order as that associated with Gutenberg. The place of printing changed, just as had the place of publishing. What had hitherto been a workshop became something much more like a factory, subject to the pressures to uniformity lauded by the likes of Andrew Ure.[43] The press barons of the twentieth century would owe their baronies to the capital concentration required to use the new printing techniques introduced in the nineteenth. As with any revolution, however, this one sparked opposition. Mechanization threatened skills, and hence livelihoods. Processes like stereotyping provoked opposition from typefounders and compositors. 'Where are the heavy standard works, which used to afford constant employment to some of the largest houses in the trade?' they demanded in 1834. 'They have been stereotyped, and gone from the compositor's hand.'[44] Similarly, papermaking machines threatened the livelihoods of skilled men. The original purpose of such machines, indeed, had been not just to boost production, but to do so specifically by eliminating craft customs: 'disgusted, like me, by the bad conduct of the corporation of paperworkers', Robert's employer had decided 'to seek the means of fabricating paper without their aid'. The 'chapels' within printing houses had long been eroding, and in fact mechanization succeeded in this period partly because they were no longer the force they had been. (It is revealing that composing and typefounding, two areas in which artisans remained strong, were not mechanized for another generation or more, and not for want of potentially viable inventions; one promising device was bought up by an artisan who promptly took it out to sea and threw it overboard.) The first national union appeared in the 1840s, driven partly by anxieties about this process, and even entertaining proposals for utopian communities to house those made redundant.[45]

42 *The Printing Machine: A Review for the Many* I (15 February 1834).
43 A. Ure, *The Philosophy of Manufactures* (London: Knight, 1835).
44 Howe, *London Compositor*, p. 217.
45 L. N. Rosenbland, *Papermaking in Eighteenth-Century France: Management, Labor, and Revolution at the Montgolfier Mill, 1761–1805* (Baltimore: Johns Hopkins University Press, 2000), pp. 147–8; Plant, *English Book Trade*, pp. 294, 379–82.

Just as important as the uses of new machines were the ways in which they were *not* used. This is especially true in the realm of book publishing. The steam press played little direct role in this realm until the end of the period. The investment required to run mechanized presses was so substantial, and the accustomed runs for books so small, that their use was largely restricted to mass-circulation newspapers and periodicals. Stereotyping too remained the exception, not least because scarcely any novels were ever likely to be reprinted (the publishers' almost universal assumption was that the appeal of a novel would be transient, and that sales would be largely to libraries; so their investment must be recouped from one edition). As Babbage reported, 'stereotype plates can only be applied with advantage to cases where an extraordinary number of copies are demanded, or where the work consists of figures, and it is of great importance to ensure accuracy'. This kind of arrangement was rarely appropriate for novels, which long remained the preserve of hand presses. Even Cambridge University Press, which experimented with the technology for its enormous bible runs, did not adopt industrial techniques successfully for a generation.[46] Most novels were still set in movable type and printed on hand presses – even Scott's, with their huge runs. Under that kind of pressure, however, printing houses' customs changed: for Scott's novels, Ballantyne used twenty presses working round the clock.[47] Customs, in short, were resilient, but not unchangeable. And when the American reprinters got hold of Scott, it was not long before they put stereotyping to work.

Known and unknown publics: reading and regulation

The eighteenth century is often said to have created a new kind of public defined by the circulation of printed materials.[48] If so, it was a public of

---

46 Babbage, *On the Economy of Machinery and Manufactures*, p. 53; Secord, *Victorian Sensation*, pp. 52–3; D. J. McKitterick, *A History of Cambridge University Press. II: Scholarship and Commerce, 1698–1872* (Cambridge: Cambridge University Press, 1998), pp. 259–84.
47 Garside, 'English Novel', p. 39; Dooley, *Author and Printer*, p. 8.
48 The point of origin for what has become a vast literature is J. Habermas, *The Structural Transformation of the Public Sphere: An Inquiry into a Category of Bourgeois Society* (1962), trans. T. Burger and F. Lawrence (Cambridge: Polity, 1989). For surveys, see J. Brewer, 'This, That and the Other: Public, Social and Private in the Seventeenth and Eighteenth Centuries', in D. Castiglione and L. Sharpe (eds.), *Shifting the Boundaries: Transformation of the Languages of Public and Private in the Eighteenth Century* (Exeter: University of Exeter Press, 1995), pp. 1–21; R. Chartier, *The*

renters and borrowers. Most readers constituting that public did not buy the works they read, and a typical work had about thirty readers. Coffee-houses and inns remained places of reading as well as refreshment, and religious institutions both Anglican and nonconformist lent books too. But most of all the circulation of printed culture depended on what James Raven has called a 'library revolution'.

In the eighteenth century the provision of libraries expanded enormously. Based first in provincial bookshops, where customers might be permitted to borrow volumes for a fee before deciding whether to purchase them, circulating libraries developed into successful enterprises in their own right. By 1800 there were perhaps 1,000 in the provinces, and 100 in London alone; by the 1820s there were 1,500 in all. In Edinburgh, Bath and other large towns they grew into large, impressive premises, centres of conversation and sociability as much as of reading itself. The bigger ones issued printed catalogues listing thousands of titles, including history, geography and philosophy as well as novels. While the fees charged were probably sufficient to exclude the truly poor, circulating libraries nonetheless allowed many to read a far wider array of books than they could have afforded to buy. Most early nineteenth-century novels (Austen's, for example) were published primarily for these libraries. Subscription libraries were later and fewer (perhaps 100 by 1800), and concentrated on non-fictional works directed at the newly prosperous provincial merchant. On a yet smaller scale, book clubs in towns and villages across the country likewise permitted access to volumes, in their case generally polemical ones. The whole system would go on, *mutatis mutandis*, to permit the three-decker Victorian novels that would dominate literary publishing in the next period. In the meantime it encouraged a sense of participating in a nationally distributed sociability focused on the reading and discussion of the latest published works.[49]

Having identified the late eighteenth century as the high point of the public sphere, Jürgen Habermas proceeded to describe a transition in the

---

Cultural Origins of the French Revolution, trans. L. Cochrane (Durham, NC: Duke University Press, 1991); and T. C. W. Blanning, *The Culture of Power and the Power of Culture* (Oxford: Oxford University Press, 2002), pp. 103–82.

49 J. Raven, 'From Promotion to Proscription: Arrangements for Reading and Eighteenth-century Libraries', in J. Raven, H. Small and N. Tadmor (eds.), *The Practice and Representation of Reading in England* (Cambridge: Cambridge University Press, 1996), pp. 175–201; Brewer, *Pleasures of the Imagination*, pp. 176–86; T. Kelly, *Early Public Libraries* (London: Library Association, 1966), pp. 121–49; St Clair, *Reading Nation*, pp. 235–67.

succeeding decades as the high ideals and intellectual reciprocity of the public sphere gave way to the vulgarities and passivity of mass culture. A major transition in reading and readership did indeed occur in these decades. Audience sizes for periodicals and novels leapt; the economics and commercial practices of industrial printing both allowed and necessitated new kinds of literature; and contemporaries commented at length on the virtues and vices of the popular reading practices that suddenly seemed to spring into prominence, if not into actual existence. As a qualification to Habermas's scheme, however, it may be helpful to invoke a rather different distinction. That is the distinction between the (relatively) known public of the Enlightenment, constrained within all those libraries, coffee houses and clubs, and the 'unknown public' that Wilkie Collins famously sketched for the readers of Dickens's journal *Household Words* at the end of this period, in 1858. Collins articulated concerns that had begun to be felt much earlier. In particular, it was the mysterious quality of this new readership that made it seem both threatening and unpoliceable.

Collins's unknown public was not that of circulating libraries and book clubs. It had no such fixed abode at all. It was, he said, invisible and ineffable, served by an obscure literature that appeared in small quarto bundles of a few pages weekly. Ubiquitous throughout Britain, this 'locus-flight of small publications' reached readers in the millions. Those readers were unclassifiable and all but undetectable. But they were also crucial. 'It is perhaps hardly too much to say, that the future of English fiction may rest with this Unknown Public, which is now waiting to be taught the difference between a good book and a bad.'[50] The eighteenth century had recognized a fundamental distinction between people and public, which corresponded to a distinction between capricious passion and disinterested reason. This distinction now eroded. The public, as the decisive arbiter of taste and knowledge, was now showing far more of the attributes hitherto assigned to the people. It was massive, mobile, and unpredictable – and it read books that were suited to its nature, being cheap, heterodox and mass-produced. This unknown public gobbled up mechanically produced books and periodicals. Such was its collective economic clout that it shaped the very kinds of works publishers were prepared to create. Collins thought this class could lay no legitimate claim to the

---

50 W. Collins, 'The Unknown Public', *Household Words* 18:439 (21 August 1858), 217–22. See L. Huett, 'Among the Unknown Public: *Household Words, All the Year Round*, and the Mass-market Periodical in the Mid-nineteenth Century', *Victorian Periodicals Review* 38 (2005), 61–82.

constructively critical role of a public sphere – yet by sheer weight of numbers its illegitimate claim might well prove decisive.[51]

The roots of the unknown public lay in a rapid expansion of reading after 1780 among groups previously neglected by the metropolitan publishing trade – women, children and workers in particular. Many of these readers who have left traces portrayed themselves as autodidacts, exercising self-improvement despite cramped and dark quarters, lack of time, exhaustion and poverty. Many depended also on shared experiences of reading aloud. Thomas Carter, for example, a tailor in London, would read radical newspapers at a coffee house in the morning and recite the news to workers at his workplace afterwards. These were readers who read as 'intensively' as anyone in the early modern period.[52] Steam printing did not create such readers, but it helped multiply their numbers. This revived a long-standing concern that books innocuous enough in the restricted setting of the 'known' public (genteel, male, metropolitan, educated and politically quiescent) might become dangerous in the hands of an unknown audience feared to be proletarian, female as well as male, national and potentially revolutionary. So at the end of the period the steam press was used in an effort to swamp this audience with cheap periodicals containing 'nothing to excite the passions'. Steam-printed 'useful' knowledge would supplant Paine, Lamarck and La Mettrie by means of the *Penny Magazine* and *Penny Cyclopaedia*. In terms of sheer circulation, it was a great success: by 1832 the *Penny Magazine* was reaching a million readers. But its cultural effects were less certain.[53]

Collins's unknown public was not entirely a product of industrialized printing, although its scale was. The first laments about a splitting of the eighteenth-century public had occurred in periodicals of the 1790s, amid concerns about radical British Jacobinism. And in fact they reflected a recognition that even before then the Enlightenment concept of a cosmopolitan community had been something of a polite – if consequential – fiction. It may therefore be more useful to talk of several intersecting publics, of various degrees of familiarity, some of them antagonistic to the very ideal of

51 J. P. Klancher, *The Making of English Reading Audiences, 1790–1832* (Madison: University of Wisconsin Press, 1987), pp. 38–9, 44–5.
52 M. Lyons, 'New Readers in the Nineteenth Century: Women, Children, Workers', in G. Cavallo and R. Chartier (eds.), *A History of Reading in the West* (Cambridge: Polity Press, 1999), pp. 313–44, esp. 336–42; R. Wittmann, 'Was There a Reading Revolution at the End of the Eighteenth Century?' in Cavallo and Chartier (eds.), *History of Reading*, pp. 284–312, esp. p. 296.
53 Secord, *Victorian Sensation*, pp. 48–55.

cosmopolitan reason. The circulation practices, access protocols, civilities, reading conventions and consequences related to hand-press radicalism in the 1830s quite likely differed from those of steam periodicals like the *Penny Magazine*. But in the Romantic period any such unknown public could not be assumed to be passive or malleable. An irreducible multiplicity of reading practices both inspired attempts at disciplining and at the same time undermined those attempts.[54]

This is the context in which attempts at press regulation need to be seen. The initial expansion and diversification of the public had taken place in a regulatory environment markedly laxer than other western countries'. Since the lapse of licensing in 1695, no pre-publication monitoring had been instituted to replace it. Limits were established only by prosecutions for obscene, defamatory, blasphemous and seditious libel, all of these concepts being derived from older laws to preserve public order. Prosecutions under libel law had tended to be foregone conclusions, in part because juries decided only on the fact of publication, not on whether a work's content were indeed libellous. But this proved a fragile convention when John Wilkes challenged it in the 1770s, and the 1792 Libel Act vested the right to determine libellous content in juries. But that Act was intended as a repressive measure, part of what became the most sweeping system of press restraint imposed in Britain since at least the late seventeenth century. The British authorities were all too persuaded by the argument of Condorcet and, later, Hazlitt that the French Revolution was an almost deterministic consequence of the printing revolution.[55] So the 1790s saw a resurgence of attempts to limit its effects. The major piece of legislation overtly intended to restrict political publishing was the 1799 Seditious Societies Act. With this law the government required the registration of all presses and types, the inclusion of printers' names on title pages, and the keeping by those printers of logs detailing all their products. Such clauses had been on licensers' wish-lists in the Tory ascendancy of the mid-1680s, when they had been haphazardly implemented and had signally failed to prevent an English revolution; but only in the Romantic era were they actually imposed at all systematically. Habermas's identification of the 1790s as the moment when

---

54 See, for example, K. Gilmartin, *Print Politics: The Press and Radical Opposition in Early Nineteenth-century England* (Cambridge: Cambridge University Press, 1996), pp. 18, 39 and *passim*; P. Keen, *The Crisis of Literature in the 1790s: Print Culture and the Public Sphere* (Cambridge: Cambridge University Press, 1999).

55 M.-J.-A. Caritat, Marquis de Condorcet, *Outlines of an Historical View of the Progress of the Human Mind* (London: printed for J. Johnson, 1795).

the public sphere peaked in England is thus not without irony, since this was also the period when the country adopted its strictest ever policing of print.

It was also possible to suppress opposition views in less direct ways. For example, inns known to harbour suspicious newspapers could find their licences suspended, and retailers or hawkers could still be prosecuted under the old assumption that vending was equivalent to publishing (a view expressed explicitly in Lord Sidmouth's 1817 *Circular* directing magistrates to arrest such people). And when all these seemed not to work, the state need not even be the immediate instigator of action against publishers. In the 1820s private groups like the Constitutional Association for Opposing the Progress of Disloyal and Seditious Principles made it their business to pursue and prosecute Carlile unmercifully. Or as a last resort one could always try to buy off the radicals. The government tried to do this in earnest during the Queen Caroline affair in 1819–22, when the new King George IV sought to prevent his wife, whom he had long accused of adultery, from being crowned queen. Back in 1806 the then Prince of Wales had instigated a parliamentary inquiry to his allegation that she had produced an illegitimate child, only to suppress the report when it exonerated her. This report, universally christened 'the Book', then became the centrepiece of a wave of piratical reprintings and cod-chivalric imitations when Caroline returned in 1820, with the radical press using it freely to foment popular feeling in her favour. The authorities spent some £2,600 trying to buy off the pirates – Benbow alone got more than £200 in 1820 – only for them to bank the cash and publish anyway, with loud pronouncements of attempts to suppress the truth. The press regulation system virtually broke down in the welter of lewd and seditious print, which climaxed when Caroline was turned away from the Coronation. It declined only when she fortuitously died shortly afterwards.[56]

But the most effective method of restricting print was by taxing it. There was a broad appreciation that high pricing could severely curtail the effects of printed materials: Mary Shelley said that Pitt decided not to prosecute Godwin's *Political Justice* because 'a three guinea book could never do much harm among those who had not three shillings to spare'. On the other hand the danger perceived to attend Paine's pamphlets, which were produced by Godwin's bookseller, was largely a matter of their sheer cheapness.[57] The

---

56 McCalman, *Radical Underworld*, pp. 162–77.
57 St Clair, *Reading Nation*, pp. 624–5.

state intervened more effectively than by outright policing, therefore, by imposing stamp duties. These were technically part of the excise, and had been invented under Queen Anne as part of an endeavour to gain revenue. But there was always an allied intent to raise the prices of potentially dangerous publications and hence limit their readership. After the French Revolution, duties were used far more overtly to that end. Long set at 1d. per copy, in 1797 the duty was increased by 250 per cent, raising the price of a newspaper to the level of an artisan's daily wage.[58] Readers could partly circumvent such taxes by not purchasing what they read – they could rent copies at a pub or reading-room, for example – but those were at best mitigating strategies.

Opposition to these 'taxes on knowledge' grew more strident after Waterloo, as the concept took hold of the 'march of intellect'. The campaign was led by figures like William Cobbett, who created the 'unstamped' press in 1816, exploiting a loophole in the law that exempted news commentary from the tax to launch a weekly comprising the lead essay from his radical *Political Register* on a single, untaxed sheet, and later as an octavo pamphlet (this being taxed, but at only 3s. per impression). Cobbett claimed enormous sales – 200,000 for the first issue alone, and regularly 30,000 per week – and was soon being imitated. The result was a class of publication that did much to constitute disparate voices into something recognizable as a radical opposition. T. J. Wooler, William Hone, William Sherwin, Richard Carlile, John Wade, Thomas Davison and others – among them major proponents of radical piracy – launched their own weeklies. Local unstamped weeklies also started to appear. In 1819 the Government responded by passing a law that eliminated Cobbett's loophole and increased stamp duty. Only Cobbett's *Register*, Wooler's *Black Dwarf*, and Carlile's *Republican* staggered on. The 1819 suppression made the 'rights' of the press into a central radical cause. When the unstamped press resurfaced a generation later amid the Chartist campaigns, it would agitate, successfully this time, for a reduction of duties.[59] But in the meantime it must always be remembered that printing and publishing in the Romantic period operated under conditions of oversight and constraint unseen in the previous century and never again to be attempted.

In the end, the generation between *Donaldson vs. Becket* and the steam-powered bestseller demonstrated the continuing inseparability of law,

---

58 Feather, *History of British Publishing*, p. 86.
59 Gilmartin, *Print Politics*, pp. 65–113.

commercial practice, civility and literary culture. New circumstances permitted – in some cases almost forced – the development of commercial practices not hitherto envisaged. It was above all an age of experiment, the scope of which reached from workshop practices to the character of creativity. The material form and cost of literary works were likewise subjected to an extraordinary range of experimental trials. At the beginning of the period the figure of the publisher began to appear; yet the trade remained bound up in cartels originating much earlier, and swiftly renewed its commitment to long-term literary properties and restrictive practices. The ideas that reached a large audience did so, often, at the hands of risk-taking outsiders – pirates and reprinters, some of them outside the United Kingdom altogether. Many, like Babbage, inveighed against what they saw as the hidebound and illegitimate conspiracy of the main metropolitan trade against poorer readers, pointing to the much greater print-runs and cheaper prices prevailing on the Continent and in America. Yet the world of publishing emerged from the Romantic period addressing for the first time a mass middle-class audience – what might be called the first modern literary readership.

The new poetries

SUSAN J. WOLFSON

'What's new?'

Something, anyway, was stirring. Whether polemical 'experiment', flaunted 'innovation' or coded ally of political 'liberty', a new poetry was refusing imposed or inherited forms as tyranny, as strictures of outworn prestige, institution or just plain old bad habit. The signs were everywhere. 'I must Create a System, or be enslav'd by another Mans', declared Blake's Los (*Jerusalem*, plate 10). If Dryden argued that rhyme and metrical law were necessary to put 'bounds to a wilde over-flowing Fancy',[1] Wordsworth, though hewing to metre and often rhyme, recoiled from 'the bondage of definite form'.[2] He went so far as to equate 'all good poetry' with 'the spontaneous overflow of powerful feelings'. This last axiom is from his Preface to the second, signed edition of *Lyrical Ballads* (1800), a document that declared a refusal of 'known habits of association' in the production of and judgements about poetry.[3] Looking back in 1817, Coleridge marked a watershed in Wordsworth's 'awakening the mind's attention from the lethargy of custom' and from 'the film of familiarity' – not only in modes of perception, but in the very excitement of poetic events.[4] Shelley would soon raise the stakes in *A Defence of Poetry*, celebrating the power of poetry to transform everything within and without: poetry 'strips the veil of

---

1 *Of Dramatick Poesie. An Essay* (1668). *The Works of John Dryden*, 19 vols., ed. H. T. Swedenberg, Jr (Berkeley: University of California Press, 1961–79), vol. XVII, ed. Samuel Holt Monk (1971), p. 79.
2 'Preface to the Edition of 1815', in *The Prose Works of William Wordsworth*, ed. W. J. B. Owen and Jane Worthington Smyser, 3 vols. (Oxford: Clarendon Press, 1974), vol. III, pp. 26–39; the phrase quoted is on p. 34.
3 Preface to *Lyrical Ballads*, 1800, in *'Lyrical Ballads' and Other Poems, 1797–1800*, ed. James Butler and Karen Green (Ithaca and London: Cornell University Press, 1992), pp. 744 and 742. All quotations with reference to *Lyrical Ballads* are from this edition.
4 *Biographia Literaria, or Biographical Sketches of my Literary Life and Opinions* (1817), ed. James Engell and W. Jackson Bate (Princeton: Princeton University Press, 1983), vol. II, p. 7.

familiarity from the world' and, in correspondence, 'purges from our inward sight the film of familiarity which obscures from us the wonder of our being'.[5]

These declarations were more than visionary romance; they were political broadcasts. In 1819 the Italian police picked up reports of a resident British lord at the centre of 'a new secret Society, the *Società Romantica*' or '*Roma Antica*' (they weren't sure) and writing (they were sure) the 'poetry of this new school' in accord with 'certain rules, entitled Statutes of the Joyous Company' – a lawless conspiracy to promulgate 'the belief that man is subject to no religious or moral principle, but ought only to obey his natural instincts'.[6] The next year, the focus of all this surveillance, Lord Byron, was wryly noting yet another 'new school'. Expatriot from the centre of British revolutions, he affected perplexity about all the ferment 'in Germany, as well as in Italy':

> a great struggle about what they call '*Classical and Romantic*' terms which were not subjects of Classification in England – at least when I left it four or five years ago. – Some of the English scribblers, (it is true) abused Pope and Swift – but the reason was that they themselves did not know how to write either prose or verse but nobody thought them worth making a Sect of.[7]

Where the foreign struggle seemed to have high cultural stakes, the English version impressed Byron as no more than the latest run of an old story: new scribblers crediting themselves by abusing their elders, and declaring a sectarian revolution.

Amid this ferment, Byron himself wasn't easy to categorize. Some of his signatures were legibly classical: dramas set in the old unities of time, place and action; poetry, even the most extravagant, hewing to traditions of craft. 'Prose poets like blank-verse, I'm fond of rhyme, / Good workmen never quarrel with their tools', declares the poet of *Don Juan*'s crafty *ottava rima*

---

5 *Shelley's Poetry and Prose*, ed. Donald H. Reiman and Neil Fraistat (London and New York: Norton, 2002), p. 533. Shelley drafted his defence in 1821, but it wasn't published until 1840. All quotations are from this edition.

6 See the dossier in *The Works of Lord Byron, Letters and Journals*, ed. Rowland E. Prothero (London: John Murray, 1900), vol. IV, Appendix 6; I quote from pp. 458 and 460–2.

7 Postscript to the rejected dedication of *Marino Faliero* to Goethe; *Lord Byron: The Complete Poetical Works*, ed. Jerome J. McGann, 7 vols. (Oxford: Clarendon Press, 1980–93), vol. IV, pp. 546–7; *Marino Faliero*, ed. Barry Weller. I don't reproduce the scriptive elements. Byron is teasing the German anatomizing of Classical and Romantic by A. W. Schlegel, Staël, Schiller and Goethe himself. Conservative publisher John Murray probably rejected the dedication because the main body ridiculed Wordsworth and Poet Laureate Southey as state lackeys.

(Canto I.201, lines 1605–6), with a jibe at Wordsworth. Yet the large workmanship of this epic, blending narrative patter, picaresque adventure, and wild digressions on everything, was radically new, 'totally of its own species . . . at once the stamp of originality and a defiance of imitation', exclaimed Shelley to Byron himself; 'Nothing has ever been written like it in English – nor, if I may venture to prophesy, will there be . . . You are building up a drama, such as England has not yet seen'.[8]

As this totally unpredictable poetic architecture may suggest, what Byron termed 'subjects of Classification' were playing out on a modern terrain more various and contentious than any mere label such as 'Romantic' can convey. By 1820, the field sported a 'Lake School', a 'Cockney School', and a 'Satanic School'. In 1829, Edinburgh reviewer Francis Jeffrey surveyed another new district, 'Female Poetry'. While this last label was half-welcoming, half-patronizing, the earlier ones were disparaging, all radiations from cultural warfare. The new poetries, moreover, were not necessarily in accord with new politics. The most visible practitioner of liberal Miltonic blank verse in the Regency was Wordsworth (in *The Excursion*), and he was now Tory. A parvenu provoking Lord Byron to both classical and class contempt was suburban Keats, a Cockney comer with a passion for liberal revolutions but not his respect for Augustan poetics. Taking fire from mentor Leigh Hunt, Keats played with enjambed, avant-garde couplets, opening the pentametre line to lush, liberal expansions. Byron wanted to keep the heroic couplet registered as high style, whatever the modern tempo. In his preface to his pirate-romance, *The Corsair* (1814), he advertised an aim to revive 'the good old and now neglected heroic couplet' and he succeeded with a vengeance.[9] Jeffrey, with an affection for reform over radical innovation, rose to cheer the new 'spirit, freedom, and variety of tone' that Byron had infused into the worthy old measure, refitting it for 'all the breaks, starts, and transitions of an adventurous and dramatic narration'.[10]

If such freedom and variety might have had more in common with the temper of Keats's and Hunt's experiments than either they or Byron allowed, what distinguished the Hunt circle was a categorical disdain of worthy old measures. Writing in the wake of Jeffrey's praises, William Hazlitt smirked in *The Examiner* (the weekly paper edited by Hunt) that

8 *The Letters of Percy Bysshe Shelley*, ed. Frederick L. Jones, 2 vols. (Oxford: Clarendon Press, 1964), vol. II, pp. 357–8.
9 *Poetical Works*, vol. III, p. 149.
10 *Edinburgh Review* 23 (April 1814), 206.

Augustan poets Johnson and Pope would have been happy to render the blank verse of Milton's 'vaulting Pegasus into a rocking-horse' of couplet symmetries.[11] Keats reprised the sneer in *Sleep and Poetry*, the capstone of his debut volume, *Poems* (1817). Mocking the neo-classical Frenchified 'foppery and barbarism' of poets who 'sway'd about upon a rocking horse, / And thought it Pegasus' (lines 182, 186–7), he parodied the curriculum of prosody so

> closely wed
> To musty laws lined out with wretched rule
> And compass vile: so that ye taught a school
> Of dolts to smooth, inlay, and clip, and fit,
> Till, like the certain wands of Jacob's wit,
> Their verses tallied. Easy was the task:
> A thousand handicraftsmen wore the mask
> Of Poesy.
>
> (lines 194–201)

From such mechanical reproduction and mathematical precision, the new poets were truants, returning to old-school lessons only for fodder for satire.

Yet for all the vaunted modernity here, Keats had reservations about some new events, not the least, the goth fashion of 'strange thunders' (line 231). This seemed to him a Satanic school, not in the line of Southey's vision, but in a perverse, even anti-poetic flexing of mere strength,

> like a fallen angel: trees uptorn,
> Darkness, and worms, and shrouds, and sepulchres
> Delight it; for it feeds upon the burrs,
> And thorns of life.
>
> (*Sleep and Poetry*, lines 242–5)

Whether he meant Byronic gloom, or what Hunt called 'the morbidity that taints the productions of the Lake Poets' (Wordsworth chiefly), by early 1818 Keats was sighing in exasperation to 'coscribbler' J. H. Reynolds about all 'our Contemporaries . . . Wordsworth &c' (including Hunt). 'Let us have the old Poets' he exhorted, by which he meant the Elizabethans.[12] By

---

11 'On Milton's Versification', *Examiner* (20 August 1815); rpt *The Round Table*, 2 vols. (Edinburgh: Constable/London: Longman & Co., 1817), vol. I, p. 110.

12 Hunt, *Examiner* (13 July 1817), p. 443. Keats's friend and literary advisor Richard Woodhouse made a note that the lines refer to Byron (Stuart M. Sperry, 'Richard Woodhouse's Interleaved and Annotated Edition of Keats's 1817 *Poems*', *Literary Monographs*, vol. I, ed. Eric Rothstein and Thomas Dunseath (Madison, WI: University of Wisconsin Press, 1967), p. 145). Letter to J. H. Reynolds, 3 February 1818,

October it was Shakespeare whom he was championing as the model for his liberal 'camelion' poetics of 'no self', a mode he contrasted to the new poetic of 'the wordsworthian or egotistical sublime'.[13]

Byron's aristocratic irritation at new schools and his loyalty to old measures; Keats's ridicule of Augustan measures and his love of even older models for the new times; debates about urban versus rural, tradition versus innovation; Jeffrey's oscillations between admiration and contempt: Byron wasn't wrong about 'a great struggle'. It roiled with questions of national identification in the wake of the French Revolution and with anxieties about populist politics and insurgencies at home. Seemingly pastoral 'Lake Poets' could be suspected of channelling foreign influence into a charismatic domestic Methodism, a populist insurgency that by 1824 seemed so congruent with the appeal of the new poetry that the poets could be tagged 'Lake Methodists'.[14]

To Jeffrey, a Whig advocate of reform on behalf of middle-class consensus, divisive populism was a critical concern, and 'the new poetry' amounted to a dangerous counter-cultural activism, the worst excesses of the French Revolution brought home. Byron's irony about 'a Sect' was keyed to this register, which Jeffrey spoke loud and bold in the debut of the *Edinburgh Review* in 1802.[15] A nation's literary traditions, he did not hesitate to say in his opening salvo, demand the same vigilance as its religious institutions: 'Poetry has this much, at least, in common with religion, that its standards were fixed long ago, by certain inspired writers, whose authority it is no longer lawful to call in question' (p. 62). Ostensibly on Southey's metrical romance *Thalaba the Destroyer*, his essay's real target was the 1800 *Lyrical Ballads*, newly prefaced to expand the import of the brief Advertisement of the 1798 *Ballads* as modest 'experiments' in ascertaining 'how far the language of conversation in the middle and lower classes of society' could serve 'the purposes of poetic pleasure' (p. 738). The Preface was polemical, waving the flag at all those monitors who would 'establish a canon of criticism' in disdain of 'prosaisms' and their class locations. Contending there ought to be 'no essential difference between the language of

in *John Keats: A Longman Cultural Edition*, ed. Susan J. Wolfson (New York: Longman, 2007), pp. 99–100.

13 Letter to Richard Woodhouse, 27 October 1818, p. 214.

14 *Blackwood's Edinburgh Magazine* 14, 208. I am indebted to Jasper Cragwall's study of the parallel and frequently interactive culture of new poetry and new religion ('Lake Methodism', Princeton University dissertation, 2007).

15 *Edinburgh Review* 1 (October 1802), 62–83.

prose and metrical composition' (pp. 748–9), Wordsworth urged a revolution in poetic language. For his part, not only would he refuse hyper-poetic 'personifications of abstract ideas' and 'poetic diction' (artsy language); he would also elevate 'low and rustic life' for its converse with 'the beautiful and permanent forms of nature' remote from modern, urban 'social vanity' (pp. 747, 743–4).

To urban, urbane Jeffrey, such tenets were a splenetic sectarianism out to undermine literary institution: 'a *sect* of poets . . . has established itself in this country within these ten or twelve years . . . that they are *dissenters* from the established systems in poetry and criticism, is admitted, and proved indeed, by the whole tenor of their compositions'. He took it on himself to 'discharge', as if an agent of state surveillance, an 'inquisitorial office' against 'the nature and tendency of the tenets' (p. 63). Inquisition is no idle trope; Jeffrey's other vocation was law, and his tenure at the *Edinburgh* was succeeded by a career as advocate and judge. If Jeffrey is not out to try treason (as Tory-reformed Southey would do as Poet Laureate prosecutor of the 'Satanic School'), he did want to protect a mainstream cultural literacy that would advance the cause of political reform.[16] So he slaps down the sectarian eruption as adolescent acting out, the oldest act in the world, and without much to show at that: 'The disciples of this school boast much of its originality, and seem to value themselves very highly, for having broken loose from the bondage of ancient authority, and re-asserted the independence of genius'. The deft echo of Milton's republican-toned note on 'The Verse' of *Paradise Lost* ('an example set, the first in *English*, of ancient liberty recover'd to heroic poem from the troublesome and modern bondage of Riming'), prepares Jeffrey's *coup de grâce*: 'That our new poets have abandoned the old models, may certainly be admitted, but we have not been able to discover that they have yet created any models of their own' (pp. 63–4). But there were new models, as Jeffrey knew, and they conveyed a new, republican class consciousness.

He was not sanguine about the politics of language. To 'disdain to make use of the common poetical phraseology, or to ennoble their diction by a selection of fine or dignified expression', as these new poets made a point of doing, is more than a betrayal of the contract of 'art'; it is traffick in everything 'low and inelegant', purveying 'vulgar manners, in vulgar

---

16 Under Jeffrey's editorship the *Edinburgh Review* advanced the cause of parliamentary reform, and as Lord Advocate of Scotland Jeffrey would help shape the 1832 Scottish Reform Bill, which increased the electorate from 4,500 to 65,000.

language' to corrupt both 'common' practice and aspirations to anything 'noble' and 'dignified'.[17] Nothing if not critical, Jeffrey's class-inflected lexicon, from *ennoble* to *low* to *vulgar*, taps anti-Jacobinism for Whig consumption: 'A splenetic and idle discontent with the existing institutions of society, seems to be at the bottom of all their serious and peculiar sentiments', he said of the new poets; 'They are filled with horror and compassion at the sight of poor men spending their blood in the quarrels of princes, and brutifying their sublime capabilities in the drudgery of unremitting labour' (p. 71). New school of English poetry, or Anglicized French Revolution? The sarcasm didn't quite contain the ground of concern.

Splenetic, idle, discontented, peculiar or ridiculous, the new poetry was shaping up, in Jeffrey's view, as the avant-garde of social ferment. Southey's poetry in the 1790s turned sympathy to the most abject: prisoners, impressed sailors and slaves. *Lyrical Ballads* (in Hazlitt's wry retrospect) paraded 'a mixed rabble of idle apprentices and Botany Bay convicts, female vagrants, gypsies . . . peasants, pedlars, and village-barbers', all breaking out of old habits of representation (comic, villainous) to petition sympathy and a reflux of reflection on political injustice.[18] 'The clue to his *poetical* theory' (said Wordsworth's brother) 'may be found in his *political* principles; these had been democratical'. And in 1800, these were too much even for Whig MP Charles James Fox, who didn't like reading shepherd tales such as *Michael* and *The Brothers* in the same lofty measure as the poet's own meditations in *Tintern Abbey*: 'I am no great friend to blank verse for subjects which are to be treated of with simplicity'.[19] The affront to standard protocols was one Wordsworth fully theorized: having first cast *Michael* in the low form of balladry, he decided to democratize his blank verse, giving the poet solidarity with poetic shepherds, and compelling his readers to ponder the equation in dignity. No wonder Jeffrey warned that 'the mischief of this new system' is not 'depravation of language only; it extends to the

---

17 Jeffrey, *Edinburgh Review* 1, 64, 66–7. Jeffrey means to desynonymize *common* from *vulgar*. 'Plebeian; suiting to the common people; practiced among the common people', begins the entry on *vulgar* in Samuel Johnson's *Dictionary of the English Language* (London: Longman, 1755–73). For the complex registers of *vulgar* in the Romantic era, and with fine ear for political inflection, I am indebted to William Keach, 'Vulgar Idioms' (ch. 4 of *Arbitrary Power*).
18 'On the Living Poets', in *Lectures on the English Poets* (London: Taylor & Hessey, 1818), p. 321.
19 Christopher Wordsworth, *Memoirs of William Wordsworth*, ed. Henry Reed, 2 vols. (Boston: Ticknor, Reed, and Fields, 1851), vol. I, pp. 127, 172.

sentiments and emotions' (p. 66). He meant to hold the line, scotch the insurgency with categorical declarations of principles:

> The love, or grief, or indignation of an enlightened and refined character, is not only expressed in a different language, but is in itself a different emotion from the love, or grief, or anger of a clown, a tradesman, or a market-wench . . . The poor and vulgar may interest us, in poetry, by their *situation;* but never . . . by any sentiments that are peculiar to their condition, and still less by any language that is characteristic of it . . . not merely because poverty makes men ridiculous, but because just taste and refined sentiment are rarely to be met with among the uncultivated part of mankind. (pp. 66–7)

Wordsworth's refusal of this consensus about what interests 'us' reports one of the most radical disturbances of the 'new poetry' of the 1790s – stirring the poor and vulgar with aspirations.

Hazlitt's retrospect turned Jeffrey's historical diagnosis (the spark of the French Revolution) to satire. The *ancien régime* of English prosody had provoked the insurgency of 'something new and original', verse to turn the world 'topsy-turvy' and 'begin *de novo*'.

> Our poetical literature had towards the close of the last century, degenerated into the most trite, insipid, and mechanical of all things, in the hands of the followers of Pope and the old French school of poetry. It wanted something to stir it up, and it found that something in the principles and events of the French revolution . . . The change in the belles-lettres was as complete, and to many persons as startling, as the change in politics, with which it went hand in hand. There was a mighty ferment in the heads of statesmen and poets . . . all was to be natural and new. Nothing that was established was to be tolerated . . . rhyme was looked upon as a relic of the feudal system, and regular metre was abolished along with regular government.[20]

In 1818, the satire was pointed in part at the new-Toryism of 'the present poet-laureat and the authors of the Lyrical Ballads' (p. 320). But only in part. It also registers the political heat waiting to brand any polemically new poetry.

So effective was Jeffrey's censure, notwithstanding Wordsworth's Tory turn and emergence as England's national poet, that even in the 1820s, no Edinburgh bookseller would stock Wordsworth's volumes. If the 'new school' had proved no French Revolution, it was still too popular, and Jeffrey never stopped trying to discredit it. Writing on the 1807 *Poems*, he

---

20 'Living Poets', pp. 318–20.

concedes merit with one hand, and with the other continues to chastise: 'in spite of . . . occasional vulgarity, affectation, and silliness', the poems show 'a strong spirit of originality, of pathos, and natural feeling'. It was actually a respect for this spirit and a 'clear impression' of the poet's 'amiable dispositions and virtuous principles', he claims, that had focused his surveillance on the 'alarming innovation'.[21] But now five years have past, and what seemed alarming proved only immaturity, 'ideas of schoolboy imbecility and vulgar affectation, . . . coarse, inelegant, or infantine'. It is for the schoolboy that Jeffrey produces his adhesive label the 'Lake School', and ridicules its vulgar syllabus. 'It is possible enough, we allow, that the sight of a friend's garden-spade, or a sparrow's nest, or a man gathering leeches, might really have suggested to such a mind a train of powerful impressions and interesting reflections; but it is certain, that, to most minds, such associations will always appear forced, strained, and unnatural'; and the poetry 'will always have the air of parody, or ludicrous and affected singularity'. Even Coleridge would admit this effect, ten years on (at the time of Hazlitt's 'Lecture') calling it 'bombast'.[22]

Yet if Jeffrey could feel that he had disarmed the revolution in poetry of its potency, he worried that there might be a 'system' in the singularity. He wished 'no more encouragement', and wanted to persuade the poet 'to abandon' it (p. 216). So intent was he that he could only ridicule a simply titled *Ode*: 'This is, beyond all doubt, the most illegible and unintelligible' of all, he sighed in exasperation: 'We can pretend to give no analysis or explanation' (p. 227). The challenge of the poem later titled *Ode: Intimations of Immortality from Recollections of Early Childhood* was not any threat of political revolution. Its romance of 'liberty' was a spiritual revolution from adult life in time and history: a man cherishing the 'delight and liberty, the simple creed / Of childhood', cherishing even the child's 'obstinate questionings / Of sense and outward things' – the theme of stanza IX, which Jeffrey quoted entire to credit his perplexity.

By late 1814, when Jeffrey also had *The Excursion* on his desk, the French Revolution had been succeeded by Napoleonic imperialism. Amid this new world war, Wordsworth's new poetry looked just peculiar, no paragon of 'boldness and originality'. And so, the famous verdict:

> This will never do. It bears no doubt the stamp of the author's heart and fancy; but unfortunately not half so visibly as that of his peculiar system . . .

21 *Edinburgh Review* 11 (October 1807), 214–15.
22 Jeffrey, *Edinburgh Review* 11, p. 217–18; Coleridge, *Biographia*, vol. II, p. 136.

we give him up as altogether incurable, and beyond the power of criticism . . . a tissue of moral and devotional ravings . . . such a hub-bub of
strained raptures and fantastical sublimities, that it is often extremely difficult for the most skilful and attentive student to obtain a glimpse of the
author's meaning – and altogether impossible for an ordinary reader to
conjecture what he is about.[23]

If no one can understand him, this middle-ageing Laker is only impotent,
levelled with the clowns he meant to elevate. Even so, by 1814, Wordsworth's star was risen, and Jeffrey's zeal to scotch the influence confirmed,
even advertised, the tenacious modernity.

Inward turning

What Jeffrey discarded as a peculiar system was paradoxically involved with
a resonant communal voice, a dynamic on which Mary Wollstonecraft was
meditating in the *Monthly Magazine*, just before *Lyrical Ballads* appeared:

> The poet, the man of strong feelings, gives us only an image of his mind,
> when he was actually alone, conversing with himself, and marking the
> impression which nature had made on his own heart. – If, at this sacred
> moment, the idea of some departed friend, some tender recollection when
> the soul was most alive to tenderness, intruded unawares into his thoughts,
> the sorrow which it produced is artlessly, yet poetically expressed – and
> who can avoid sympathising?[24]

In this poetics of sympathy, the genres turned inward. Blake etched idiosyncratic prophetic visions; drama became (in Byron's phrase) '*a mental
theatre*';[25] narratives were organized by the flux of feeling and recollection.
Lyric, that prime mode of subjectivity, claimed all genres under the
principle Wordsworth articulated in the 1800 Preface: 'the feeling therein
developed gives importance to the action and situation'. When he added,
'The subject is indeed important!' the syntax was a double-play: 'subject' as
the feeling developed, and its agent, the feeling subject.[26] Wordsworth
spent half a century on an epic 'Poem on my own life', 'a thing

---

23 *Edinburgh Review* 24 (November 1814), 1–4.
24 'On Poetry, and Our Relish for the Beauties of Nature', *Monthly Magazine* (April 1797);
   The Works of Mary Wollstonecraft, ed. Janet Todd and Marilyn Butler, 7 vols.
   (New York University Press, 1989), vol. VII, p. 8.
25 So Byron states his aim to John Murray, 23 August 1821. *Byron's Letters and Journals*,
   ed. Leslie A. Marchand, 12 vols. (Cambridge: Harvard University Press, 1973–82),
   vol. VIII, p. 187.
26 *Lyrical Ballads*, p. 746.

unprecedented in Literary history that a man should talk so much about himself', he said in 1805, well into ten books of 'not much less than 9,000 lines', with two more books in the offing.[27] Sitting down to read *Tintern Abbey* once again, Keats revised his antipathy to the 'egotistical sublime', to find 'Genius' in the 'dark Passages'.[28]

In the Prospectus to *The Excursion* (a poem Keats rejoiced in), Wordsworth was not shy about trumping Milton on this score of dark sublimity, using his cascading iambics to propel the inner drama, with the mind as epic terrain and inspiration:

> Not Chaos, not
> The darkest pit of lowest Erebus,
> Nor aught of blinder vacancy – scooped out
> By help of dreams, can breed such fear and awe
> As fall upon us often when we look
> Into our Minds, into the Mind of Man,
> My haunt, and the main region of my Song.[29]

On the heels of *The Excursion*, an 'Essay, Supplementary to the Preface' to his self-canonizing collection of 1815 stated as a matter of course that the 'business of poetry' is to 'treat of things not as they *are*, but as they *appear*; not as they exist in themselves, but as they *seem* to exist to the *senses*, and to the *passions*'.[30] Even Hazlitt who, like Keats, derided the egotism (and, like Jeffrey, ridiculed *The Excursion*) thought Wordsworth 'the most original poet now living', this by force of an unabashed 'internal' poetry: 'he furnishes it from his own mind, and is his own subject'.[31]

The first venture in this new mode was *Lyrical Ballads*. Hazlitt recognized how poems such as *Tintern Abbey* and *Hart-Leap Well* (he quoted the last in full) had opened 'a finer and deeper vein of thought and feeling than any poet in modern times has done, or attempted'. Coleridge recollected the collaborative venture. His charge was to find emotional 'truth' in 'supernatural' circumstances, soliciting a reader's 'willing suspension of disbelief' as a contractual act of 'poetic faith'; Wordsworth performed the reciprocal,

---

27 To Sir George Beaumont, 1 May 1805, *The Letters of William and Dorothy Wordsworth*, ed. Ernest de Selincourt, *The Early Years, 1787–1805*, 2nd edn, rev. Chester L. Shaver (Oxford: Clarendon Press, 1967), pp. 586–7.
28 To J. H. Reynolds, 3 May 1818, *John Keats*, ed. Wolfson, p. 130.
29 *The Excursion, Being a Portion of The Recluse, A Poem* (London: Longman & Co., 1814), pp. xi–xii.
30 *Prose Works*, vol. III, p. 63.
31 Hazlitt, 'Living Poets', p. 309.

showing in 'things of every day' a glint of 'the supernatural' in 'the love-
liness and the wonders of the world before us'.[32] Coleridge produced the
magnificently haunting work that would be the volume's first and longest,
The Rime of the Ancyent Marinere. Nineteen poems by Wordsworth gave the
'every day' in a variety of genres: lyric, anecdote, quasi-dramatic monologue, conversation, and as capstone, *Tintern Abbey*. That short Advertisement of 1798 warned readers of a likely 'struggle with feelings of strangeness
and aukwardness' and advised that even those not bound by 'pre-established
codes of decision' might find the language 'too familiar, not of sufficient
dignity'.[33] The *Rime* forced the question. It was not new-modern, but new-
strange, bristling with antiqued diction, archaic spelling, idiosyncratic idiom
and a tale that defied, even parodied, easy moralizing. Even the simpler
poems involved subtle challenges. There was no 'poetic diction', no provision of 'gross and violent stimulants' to interest, no catering to 'craving for
extraordinary incident' or 'rapid communication of intelligence', sometimes
no resolution, no consolation, no lesson.[34]

A poetry of gaps and indirections, of understatements and silences,
required a new mode of reading, even a revolution of the kind that Jeffrey's
impatience with the *Ode* intuited but was in no mood of mind to theorize.
'If Poetry be a subject on which much time has not been bestowed',
Wordsworth proposed in the new Preface, any 'judgment' is useless. Such
time involves not only a 'long continued intercourse with the best models
of composition' but also a slow reading of 'the fluxes and refluxes of the
mind when agitated by the great and simple affections of our nature'.[35] To
make this time is to join a new democracy of sympathetic imagination.

Byron's celebrity: 'wholly new'

In little more than a decade, Byron would find community in a virtually
contradictory temper of the 'new'. Hot with sensation, energy, scandal and
ostentation, his poetry was dashed off quickly, and just as quickly devoured.
Paradoxically, he bucked new trends of taste, admiring Pope, writing heroic
couplets and Spenserian stanzas, while simultaneously flaunting a metropolitan, cosmopolitan, international idiom in contrast to Wordsworth's
regional and domestic nationalism. Wordsworth advocated plain language;

---

32 *Ibid.*, p. 309; Coleridge, *Biographia*, ch. 14 in vol. II, pp. 5–7.
33 *Lyrical Ballads*, pp. 738–9.
34 The phrases in quotation are all from the Preface of 1800; *ibid.*, p. 746.
35 Preface, *ibid.*, pp. 759, 745.

Byron's antidote was not the old poetic diction, but new ironies, parodies, and a 'flash' lexicon, slangy and colloquial.

Byron alone saw his name coined into currency: Byronism, Byronic, Byromania. No less than the dazzling poetry, Byron's newness was his celebrity: 'never did there exist before, and it is most probable, never will exist again, a combination of such vast mental power and surpassing genius, . . . the effect was, accordingly, electric' – so Thomas Moore recounted the dazzling debut of *Childe Harold's Pilgrimage* in 1812, quoting the amazement of Byron himself: 'I awoke one morning and found myself famous'.[36] The retro-title signalled a consciously decadent genre, a romance tuned to modern disillusion and ennui, to jaded alienation and theatrical melancholy. Jeffrey instantly hailed the 'power, spirit and originality' that prevailed over, even came into being by force of, multiple absences and negations: 'no story or adventure, . . . no incident of any kind', no 'regular order or connexion' to the reflections, no 'characters' other than the token Childe. And above all, 'no ordinary merit'. This litany of *no* credits to Byron what Wordsworth was also after in his modernism; but where Wordsworth seemed immature (and not to Jeffrey alone), Byron embodied 'plain manliness and strength . . . infinitely refreshing after the sickly affectations of so many modern writers'.[37] He was newer than 'new'.

Jeffrey's seduction was legion. After the fourth and final canto of *Childe Harold* appeared in 1818, John Wilson reviewed the whole uncannily democratic phenomenon: 'all mankind, the troubled and the untroubled, the lofty and the low, the strongest and the frailest, are linked together by the bonds of a common but inscrutable sympathy', a 'singular illusion'

> by which these disclosures . . . seem to have something of the nature of private and confidential communications . . . Who is there that feels, for a moment, that the voice which reaches the inmost recesses of his heart is speaking to the careless multitudes around him? . . . the words seem to pass by others like air, and to find their way to the hearts for whom they were intended, – kindred and sympathizing spirits, who discern and own that secret language.[38]

36 Thomas Moore, *Letters and Journals of Lord Byron: With Notices of His Life*, 2 vols. (London: John Murray, 1830), vol. I, p. 255.
37 *Edinburgh Review* 19 (February 1812), 46–7.
38 *Edinburgh Review* 30 (June 1818), 90; unsigned.

'The shadow double of the splendid Byronic hero', argues Peter Manning, 'is the alienated reader'.[39] Yet the paradox 'in the midst of all this', as Wilson puts it, is the 'prevailing' force of Byron's 'character' over all 'the waves of a common nature': in spite of themselves, 'the millions ... feel and acknowledge its strange and unaccountable ascendency'.[40]

This is a new poetry of glamour, and its glow, trumping all other consideration, crossed lines of class and gender. Joanna Baillie, Felicia Hemans and L. E. L. created Byronic heroines in transgressive, sometimes transvestite, figures. Labouring-class men were drawn to the principled, heartfelt alienation from the multiple oppressions of modern life: 'Byron attracts their sympathy by his sensuous fire and by the virulence of his satire against the existing social order', said Friedrich Engels.[41] William Hale White recalled his father reciting *Childe Harold* working as a compositor 'in a dingy printing office', and he wove this access of sympathy into his novel, *The Revolution in Tanner's Lane* (1887). 'Men and women who were accessible to no other poetry were accessible to his, and old sea-captains, merchants, tradesmen, clerks, tailors, milliners, as well as the best judges in the land, repeated his verses by the page', muses one soul (virtually reprising the parade in Jeffrey's jeremiad and Hazlitt's satire). Out of curiosity, he picks up *The Corsair*, and

> as he read his heart warmed, and he unconsciously found himself declaiming several of the most glowing and eloquent lines aloud ... Zachariah found in *The Corsair* exactly what answered to his inmost self, down to its very depths. The lofty style, the scorn of what is mean and base, the courage – root of all virtue – that dares and evermore dares in the very last extremity, the love of the illimitable, of freedom, and the cadences like the fall of waves on a sea-shore were attractive to him beyond measure.[42]

'Beyond measure' nicely reprises Jeffrey's admiration of Byron's innovations with the *Corsair*-couplet. In lofty style, Byron tapped into a world of human feeling, not in Wordsworthian commonality widely spread, but in the depths of a commonly alienated inmost self.

39 Manning, 'Childe Harold in the Marketplace: From Romaunt to Handbook', *Modern Language Quarterly* 52 (1991), 186.
40 Wilson, *Edinburgh Review* 30, 91–2.
41 *The Condition of the Working Class in England* (1845), trans. and ed. W. O. Henderson and W. H. Chaloner (Stanford: Stanford University Press, 1958), p. 273.
42 *Byron: The Critical Heritage*, ed. Andrew Rutherford (New York: Barnes & Noble, 1970), pp. 372, 370.

Don Juan (its hero in recurrent, anglicized rhyme with *new one*) was still more radically innovative: a mock-Homeric epic, with an affable hero instead of the old legendary rake; a colloquial narrator given to digressions on contemporary life, politics, manners, literature. Shelley, whose own poetic idiom could not have been more different, found it all 'astonishingly fine, . . . something wholly new & relative to the age'. The 'springy random haphazard galloping nature of its method', marvelled Virginia Woolf, with the acuteness of an experimenter in avant-garde, 'is a discovery by itself, . . . an elastic shape which will hold whatever you choose to put in it'.[43]

Hunting down the Cockneys

While Byron was working his new discoveries at home and then abroad, in 1817 a new periodical, *Blackwood's Edinburgh Magazine*, launched a serial assault on a new London-suburbanism: 'The Cockney School of Poetry', signed with the mark of 'Z'. The primary and perpetual target was Leigh Hunt and the culture, political and poetic, hosted by him and steadily promoted in his weekly, *The Examiner*. Soon in Z's sights was protégé Keats, and eventually Shelley and Byron, when social rank could no longer license bad morals. Z's first paper ridiculed Hunt's pretentious 'nobility of talent', of preening as a *'peer'* of Byron ('one of the most nobly-born of English Patricians'), or even rivalling untitled Wordsworth, who earns class capital for 'noble compositions' showing a 'dignified purity of thought and the patriarchal simplicity of feeling' to be found nowhere in Hunt's 'subaltern sneaking'.[44] If it was surprising for readers of the other Edinburgh review, Jeffrey's, to behold this 'Wordsworth', the disparity points up the volatility and political spin of judgements on the 'new'.

Even Hunt's circle was unconsolidated. Hunt adored Byron; Keats was cool to the self-dramatizing without mystery: 'Lord Byron cuts a figure', he said early in 1819, and couldn't see more to *Don Juan* than just another 'flash poem'.[45] Keats admired Wordsworth's 'dark Passages'; but Hunt, inviting Wordsworth to his 1814 *Feast of the Poets* to commend 'the greatness of [his]

---

43 Shelley, *Letters*, vol. II, p. 323; Woolf, *A Writer's Diary*, ed. Leonard Woolf (New York: Harcourt, 1954), p. 3.

44 'On the Cockney School of Poetry, No. I', *Blackwood's Edinburgh Magazine* 2 (October 1817), 40–1.

45 Keats to his brother and sister-in-law, 19 February 1819 (*John Keats*, ed. Wolfson, p. 240) and 18 September 1819, in *The Letters of John Keats, 1814–1821*, ed. Hyder E. Rollins, 2 vols. (Cambridge, MA: Harvard University Press, 1958), vol. II, p. 192; 'flash' is slang for 'slang'.

genius', chastised his 'solitary morbidities'. The objection was not political, like Jeffrey's; it was 'an excess that defeats the poet's intention', namely, poetic pleasure, Wordsworth's self-declared 'worthy *purpose*', after all. Turning 'our thoughts away from society and men altogether' to nourish an 'eremitical . . . reverie', Wordsworth was on a slippery slope 'to melancholy or indifference'.[46]

What did join the Hunt circle was its fresh poetic language and idiom – not Wordsworthian plain-speaking, but cheeky arty affectation, gushing sentiment. The rhymes were experimental, slant and jaunty, the themes anti-establishment, the tone colloquial, the repertoire an eclectic reading and mythology unstamped by university degrees. In a series in *The Examiner* in 1816, Hunt greeted the 'Young Poets' (Shelley, Reynolds, Keats) as 'a new school', and cheered the overthrow of standards that have 'prevailed among us since the time of Charles the 2d', upheld by 'merely versifying wits, and bead-rollers of couplets', as if working on an abacus.[47] His review of Keats's 1817 *Poems* elaborated this critique. Pope had 'little imagination, of a higher order, no intense feeling of nature, no sentiment, no real music or variety'. Even those 'of a truer poetical faculty, Gray, Thomson, Akenside, and Collins . . . were content with a great deal of second-hand workmanship, and with false styles made up of other languages and a certain kind of inverted cant'.[48]

This might sound like a sequel to Wordsworth's critique of 'poetic diction' in the Preface, but Z occluded the connection and instead rolled up his sleeves to break the news, in October 1817, of a 'new school of poetry which has of late sprung up among us', with delight in having 'the honour of christening it . . . THE COCKNEY SCHOOL'.[49]

> Its chief doctor and Professor is Mr Leigh Hunt, a man certainly of some talents, of extravagant pretensions both in wit, poetry, and politics, and withal of exquisitely bad taste, and extremely vulgar modes of thinking and manners in all respects . . . . He knows absolutely nothing of *Greek*, almost nothing of Latin, and his knowledge of Italian literature is confined to a few of the most popular of Petrarch's sonnets, and an imperfect acquaintance with Ariosto. (p. 38)

---

46 *The Feast of the Poets, with Notes, and other Pieces in Verse, by the Editor of the Examiner* (London: Crawthorn, 1814), pp. 89, 94–5; Wordsworth's Preface, *Lyrical Ballads*, p. 744; Hunt, *Feast*, p. 97.
47 *Examiner* (1 December 1816), p. 761.
48 *Examiner* (1 June 1817), p. 345.
49 'On the Cockney School of Poetry, No. I', p. 38.

Gender ridicule underpins the class put-downs. Reading Hunt, smirks Z, is like being coaxed into

> the gilded drawing-room of a little mincing boarding-school mistress, who would fain have an *At Home* in her house. Every thing is pretence, affect-ation, finery, and gaudiness. The beaux are attorneys' apprentices, with chapeau bras and Limerick gloves – fiddlers, harp teachers, and clerks of genius: the belles are faded fan-twinkling spinsters, prurient vulgar misses from school, and enormous citizens' wives. The company are entertained with lukewarm negus, and the sounds of a paltry piano forte.   (p. 39)

This is a feminine–effeminate culture, a farce of knock-off fashion, cheap libations, trade-class swells. The class insurgency behind the pretences of style sharpens the aim of Z's fourth paper (August 1818), a ridicule of Keats which pauses to read 'the Cockney School of Politics' out of 'the Cockney School of Poetry'.[50]

Satan's poets

Even noble poets, if impious, proved fair game for political attack. Not from the Scotch north but from the London court, another school received the heat of Tory Laureate Southey. His puffed up ode on George III's death, *A Vision of Judgement* (1821), had its own design of newness (as his Preface laboured to explain): blank hexameter as a bold new epic measure. But this prideful venture was rivalled by prosecution of a newly dubbed 'Satanic school' of poetry, led by 'men of diseased hearts and depraved imagi-nations', writing away in 'a Satanic spirit of pride and audacious impiety', not to mention caustic criticism of the present monarch. Though not named, Hunt, Shelley and Byron were clearly coded. The Laureate meant to defend the 'moral purity, the effect, and in its turn, the cause of an improvement in national manners' that had 'distinguished' the last half century of 'English literature', and he was hot to indict 'those monstrous combinations of horrors and mockery, lewdness and impiety, with which English poetry has, in our days, first been polluted!' Southey exercised his first vision of judgement on the chief begetter, Byron, the agent of 'a sin, to the consequences of which no limits can be assigned, and those conse-quences no after repentance in the writer can counteract. Whatever remorse of conscience he may feel when his hour comes (and come it must!)

---

50 'On the Cockney School of Poetry, No. IV', *Blackwood's Edinburgh Magazine* 3 (August 1818), p. 524.

will be of no avail.' Sure that 'moral and political evils are inseparably connected', Southey itched for immediate sentencing.[51]

Provoked by the Tory toadying, Byron lit off a counter-*Vision of Judgment* that not only renewed the case against the monarch and lampooned the sorry Laureate, but even put an amusingly urbane 'Sathan' into the celestial court. As this latest Byronic hero exquisitely satirizes Southey's pride, it also confirms what bothered the Laureate – the problematic influence of Byron's 'creations' (complained *London Magazine* in 1821) in managing a more than willing suspension of disapproval: 'what is striking in poetry is made a set-off against what is objectionable in morals'.[52] Ever since the French Revolution, Milton's Satan had been rehabilitated into noble political rebel, existential sufferer, and above all, sympathetic alienated poet. Childe Harold was the first, but not the only begotten son. Byron's heroes, Shelley's visionaries, Keats's poets, dreamers, and fallen Titans, Coleridge's exiles, even the nature-devoted Wordsworthian poet were in the train, sounding his phrases, inhabiting his epic agons, testing his scepticism. In the eyes of one of the first of these Romantic Satanists, Blake, Wordsworth was a confirmed traveller in this last register – even 'an *Atheist*' (Henry Crabb Robinson wrote to Dorothy Wordsworth in 1826): 'according to Blake Atheism consists in worshipping the natural world, which . . . properly speaking is nothing real, but a mere illusion produced by Satan'.[53]

The annuals and the she-poets

By the mid 1820s, Satanists Byron and Shelley were dead. So was Keats, and Scott long ago had left poetry for tales and novels. In the periodicals and papers – the *New Monthly* and *London* magazines, the *Literary Gazette* and later *The Athenum* – a new, eclectic generation was emerging, including 'poetess' stars, Felicia Hemans ('F. H.' or 'Mrs Hemans') and Letitia Landon ('Miss Landon' or 'L. E. L.'). Another hospitable site was the literary annual, a new venture for the gift-giving season, heralded in 1822 by *Forget Me Not, a Christmas and New Year's Present for 1823*. *The Literary Souvenir, or Cabinet of Poetry and Romance* soon followed, its strategic pricing at 12 shillings

---

51 *The Poetical Works of Robert Southey, Collected by Himself*, 10 vols. (London: Longman & Co., 1838), vol. X, pp. 205–6, 203–4, 206.
52 'Living Authors, No. IV: Lord Byron', *London Magazine* 3 (1821), p. 51.
53 *The Letters of William and Dorothy Wordsworth*, ed. Ernest de Selincourt, *The Later Years*, 2nd edn, rev. Alan G. Hill, 2 Parts (Oxford: Clarendon Press, 1978–9), Part 1, note on pp. 438–9.

garnering 6,000 sales in its first two weeks; the 1826 *Souvenir* was *The Corsair* of the day, with sales of 10,000. By 1831 there were more than sixty such productions. Not only could a 'poetess' profit financially and professionally from this market, but the generous pay breached the separate spheres, as poets Coleridge, Wordsworth, Lamb, Moore, Hood, Clare, Scott, Tennyson and even posthumous Shelley (his poetic remains resuscitated by his savvy widow) went annual. As the roster shows, all schools were welcome: radical and Tory, Satanic and saintly, male and female, noble and untitled. Even as Southey bitterly blamed the slow sales of his volumes on the annual rivalry, he joined up, consoling himself by always being listed as 'The Poet Laureate'. Scott thought it sheer madness when in 1828 he was offered £800 a year to edit *The Keepsake*; he declined, but accepted a handsome payment for a contribution. Wordsworth murmured against the 'degrading' and 'galling' culture of the 'splendid annual', those 'ornamented . . . greedy receptacles of trash', but he, too, managed to 'pocket [his] pride' and the pounds.[54]

The annuals favoured parlour-poetry, and the 'poetess' complied, but the new world of women's poetry was more various. The 'poetess' culture of the 1820s succeeded in no small part because of a discontinuity with the female generation of the 1790s, whose poems focused evangelical, dissenting, polemical vigour on public issues. Dissenting critic Anna Barbauld railed against the slave trade (as did conservative Hannah More). Helen Maria Williams wrote against the trade, against colonial imperialism, and on behalf of political 'liberty', whatever its rocky French career. Charlotte Smith, who made her name and her living (one of the first female poets to do so) with her serial publication in the culture of sentiment, *Elegiac Sonnets*, waxed political over the 1790s, first with *The Emigrants*, a cry against tyranny and warmongering, and then with anti-war and democracy-themed poems in later editions of *Elegiac Sonnets*. In 1810 Lucy Aikin published *Epistles on Women*, its good old neo-classical couplets sponsoring a fresh view of history from the perspective of maternal love and female culture.

---

54 For the annuals, see the books by Bradford Booth and Anne Renier (Booth, *A Cabinet of Gems* (Berkeley, CA: University of California Press, 1938) and Renier, *Friendship's Offering* (London: Private Libraries Association, 1964)); and Peter Manning's 'Wordsworth in the *Keepsake*', in *Literature in the Marketplace: Nineteenth-century British Publishing and Reading Practices*, ed. John O. Jordan and Robert L. Patten (Cambridge: Cambridge University Press, 1995). My quotations are from William Wordsworth to Samuel Rogers, *Letters, Later Years*, vol. II, pp. 275–6, and *The Letters of Dora Wordsworth*, ed. Howard P. Vincent (Chicago: Packard, 1944), p. 39.

Crying havoc at this eruption of new she-poetry, in 1798 Richard Pol-whele issued an Augustan-mode satire, evoking demonic patroness Lady Macbeth with his very title, *The Unsex'd Females*.[55] Ruing the eclipse of that 'female Muse' who, 'to NATURE true, / The unvalued store from FANCY, FEELING drew' (lines 50–1), he fulminated against the new freaks:

> Survey with me, what ne'er our fathers saw,
> A female band despising NATURE's law,
> As 'proud defiance' flashes from their arms,
> And vengeance smothers all their softer charms.
> I shudder at the new unpictur'd scene,
> Where unsex'd woman vaunts the imperious mien.
>
> (lines 11–16)

To resign the female-assigned 'power to please, / Poetic feeling and poetic ease' (lines 95–6) is to be branded 'unsex'd'. No reflexive sexist, Polwhele gets cover with an encomium to the old mid-century bluestocking salons, graced by poets Anna Seward (the 'Swan of Litchfield'), and Hannah More, who upheld Nature's law on the 'distinction of the sexes'.

Bluestocking Barbauld, already in Polwhele's cross-hairs for having for-saken 'her songs of Love, her Lyrics' for the polemical 'strain' (lines 91–2), reaped a whirlwind with *Eighteen Hundred and Eleven*, an anti-war, anti-imperialist satire in Augustan couplets, published the same year as Byron's *Childe Harold*. His *Romaunt* irked moralists and court loyalists, but achieved spectacular success; her satire provoked such sharp retaliation, not just for its theme but also for gender insurgency, that it all but ended her career. *Quarterly Review* was brutal: 'Mrs. Barbauld turned satirist! . . . We had hoped, indeed, that the empire might have been saved without the inter-vention of a lady-author.' The gender trespass was also a genre violation: 'Her former works have been of some utility; her "Lessons for Children", her "Hymns in Prose", her "Selections from the Spectator", . . . but we must take the liberty of warning her to desist from satire . . . any more pamphlets in verse.'[56] About a decade later, the *British Critic*, on the occa-sion of praising Hemans for 'painting the strength, and the weaknesses of her own lovely sex' and the 'womanly nature throughout all her thoughts and her aspirations', was still fuelling the Tory surveillance.[57] Keeping Hemans waiting in the wings, the article opened with an attack on the new

---

55 Unsigned, *The Unsex'd Females, A Poem* (London: T. Cadell and W. Davies, 1798).
56 *Quarterly Review* 7 (June 1812), pp. 309, 313; by John Wilson Croker (unsigned).
57 Art. VIII, *British Critic*, new series, vol. XX (July 1823), p. 52.

transgressors. In ridicule and disgust honed by every counter-authority, from divine creation, to modern science, to Shakespeare, they gave no quarter, even to Blue Stockings. 'We heartily abjure Blue Stockings', it began, in prelude to this rant:

> We make no compromise with any variation of the colour, from sky-blue to Prussian blue, blue stockings are an outrage upon the eternal fitness of things. It is a principle with us . . . We are inexorable to special justifications. We would fain make a fire in Charing-Cross, of all the bas blus in the kingdom, and albums, and commonplace books, as accessaries before or after the fact, should perish in the conflagration.
>
> Our forefathers never heard of such a thing as a Blue Stocking, except upon their sons' legs; the writers of Natural History make no mention of the name . . . Shakspeare, who painted all sorts and degrees of persons and things, who compounded or created thousands, which, perhaps, never existed, except in his own prolific mind, even he, in the wildest excursion of his fancy never dreamed of such an extraordinary combination as a Blue Stocking! No! it is a creature of modern growth, and capable of existing only in such times as the present. (p. 50)

The compounding of new Blue insurgency with parlour-culture albums and commonplace books suggests that the *British* was less interested in legislating a proper female poetry than in suppressing the advent altogether. The cause at base was the integrity of men of letters, 'our forefathers'.

Traditions of 'the new'

Yet it wasn't the Blues who were the real problem. It was the modern world in which all new poetry was coming to seem trivial, whimsical, irrelevant. Shelley was called to a *Defence of Poetry* by *The Four Ages of Poetry*, a satire published in 1820 by his friend T. L. Peacock. Peacock chronicled a fall from former grandeur to the new dispensation, an 'egregious confraternity of rhymesters, known by the name of the Lake Poets', fancying 'a new principle', seeing everything 'in a new light', and romancing 'what is called a new tone', yet managing to remain 'studiously ignorant of history, society, and human nature': 'Mr. Wordsworth picks up village legends from old women and sextons' or relays the 'phantastical parturition of the moods of his own mind'; 'Mr. Scott digs up the poachers and cattle-stealers of the ancient border. Lord Byron cruises for thieves and pirates', while 'Mr. Coleridge . . . superadds the dreams of crazy theologians and the mysticisms of German metaphysics'. Replete with 'barbarous manners, obsolete customs, and exploded superstitions', the new poetry was irrelevant: 'the rant of unregulated passion, the whine of exaggerated feeling, and the cant of factitious sentiment' had nothing to offer a modern world in which 'mathematicians, astronomers, chemists, moralists, metaphysicians, historians, politicians, and political economists' were setting the pace, producing new knowledges, and charting the lines of progress.[58]

Shelley got the jest, but he also knew that such views were dead serious Utilitarianism, and he met the challenge by concluding his *Defence* in a hyperbole that cancelled the court of contemporary opinion: 'Poets are the unacknowledged legislators of the World' (p. 535) – *Unacknowledged*, because their law derives from and abides in 'the eternal, the infinite, and the one' (p. 513), and only fleetingly in time and history. Yet for all this radical idealism, Shelley also wanted to credit the new poets with an 'electric life' amid the 'great and free developement of the national will' (p. 535), and in this inspiration, working as powerful mediators of new ideas. He had first written these sentences, and many other passages of the *Defence of Poetry* (as Jeffrey, Hazlitt, or Z. might have guessed) in a political pamphlet, *A Philosophical View of Reform*.

If Shelley was convinced that future vindication would credit the age's new poets, Byron wasn't so sure. In 1817 he told his publisher John Murray,

> *all* of us – Scott – Southey – Wordsworth – Moore – Campbell – I – are . . . upon a wrong revolutionary poetical system – or systems – not worth a damn in itself – & from which none but Rogers and Crabbe are free . . . the present & next generations will finally be of this opinion. – I am the more confirmed in this – by having lately gone over some of our Classics – particularly *Pope* – whom I tried in this way – I took Moore's poems & my own & some others – & went over them side by side with Pope's – and I was really astonished (I ought not to have been so) and mortified – at the ineffable distance in point of sense – harmony – effect – and even *Imagination* passion – & *Invention*.[59]

In 1819 Byron went public with a decalog in *Don Juan:*

> Thou shalt believe in Milton, Dryden, Pope;
> Thou shalt not set up Wordsworth, Coleridge, Southey;

---

58 *The Four Ages of Poetry*, in *Olliers Literary Miscellany* 1 (1820); rpt *Thomas Love Peacock: Memoirs of Shelley and other Essays and Reviews*, ed. Howard Mills (New York University Press, 1970), pp. 127–9, 132.
59 Byron, *Letters and Journals*, ed. Marchand, vol. V, p. 265. Murray's advisor William Gifford deemed this among the best things Byron ever wrote (*Letters and Journals*, ed. Prothero, vol. IV, note on p. 169).

Because the first is crazed beyond all hope,
    The second drunk, the third so quaint and mouthy:
With Crabbe it may be difficult to cope,
    And Campbell's Hippocrene is somewhat drouthy:
Thou shalt not steal from Samuel Rogers, nor –
Commit – flirtation with the muse of Moore.

                    (*Don Juan*, Canto I.205, lines 1633–40)

Milton, Dryden and Pope were the only certainties for Byron, even in this modern patter.

After nearly three decades at the *Edinburgh*, across the most tumultuous era since the English Civil Wars, Jeffrey took a breath at the end of a review in 1829 (his last year as editor) to ponder 'the perishable nature of modern literary fame':

> we have seen a vast deal of beautiful poetry pass into oblivion . . . The tuneful quartos of Southey are already little better than lumber: – And the rich melodies of Keats and Shelley, – and the fantastical emphasis of Wordsworth, – and the plebeian pathos of Crabbe, are melting fast from the fields of our vision. The novels of Scott have put out his poetry. Even the splendid strains of Moore are fading into distance and dimness, except where they have been married to immortal music; and the blazing star of Byron himself is receding from its place of pride . . . The two who have the longest withstood this rapid withering of the laurel, and with the least marks of decay on their branches, are Rogers and Campbell; . . . both distinguished rather for the fine taste and consummate elegance of their writings, than for the fiery passion, and disdainful vehemence, which seemed for a time to be so much more in favour with the public . . . If taste and elegance, however, be titles to enduring fame, we might venture securely to promise that rich boon to the author before us.[60]

This author was Hemans, and the he-poets in this gamble on the 'nature of modern literary fame' seemed to be those with the very qualities that Jeffrey, at the top of this essay, had been at pains to identify as 'Female Poetry', endorsed by the law of 'nature': fine taste, elegance, no vehemence, no fiery passion. Wordsworth, though destined to Laureateship after Southey, was anybody's guess in the crash of the poetry market in 1829. Even by 1826 *Literary Magnet* was lamenting that this 'poet of the most exalted genius' has 'been too much neglected, amid the rage for that tawdry and flaring class of poetry to which his severe but simple and amiable muse

---

60 Unsigned, *Edinburgh Review* 50 (October 1829), p. 47.

is so decided opposed'.[61] Shelley was a sectarian and coterie taste until mid-century; so was Keats, who in 1829 was better known as the frail fallen flower of Shelley's elegy, *Adonais*, than by his own out-of-print volumes. By the century's end, Jeffrey's 'Female Poets' would fade from the market, from literary histories, and would scarcely mark the canonical anthologies. We wouldn't hear of them again until the 1980s.

What of *Romantic*, our own term for the 'new' poetries? This present 'History of English Romantic Literature' still likes this old naming-convention for a cultural and a chronological span that does not always spell 'Romantic.' Like the labels used in the age it covers, it bears certain advocacies and enthusiasms, entails other antipathies and exclusions. If our stories today credit its new poetries with a generative role in the history of English Literature, the old stories keep us alert to what Romantic-era poets and their readers knew, and knew not, as 'new'.

61 *The Literary Magnet of Belles Lettres, Science, and the Fine Arts*, vol. IV (London: Wrightman & Cramp, 1826), p. 236.

Romanticism and poetic autonomy

PAUL HAMILTON

The symbiotic growth of critical and literary self-consciousness is so striking a feature of the Romantic period that many participants at the time and many subsequent commentators have thought it the historical key to understanding Romanticism. This mutual development is of course in line with the gradual democratization of print culture from the restricted court circulation of poetry up to the seventeenth century down to the global internet of our own day. But in Romanticism the *critical* interaction between writer and reader presided over the democratic function communication is now often assumed to possess necessarily. From around 1798, in Britain and mainland Europe, a new critical establishment leaps into being. Its characteristic idioms extend from the elliptical and highly theorized aphorisms of the early German Romantic journals to the anti-systematic *ad hominem* / *feminam* broadsides of British critics writing for politically partisan Reviews. Corresponding to this increased journalistic attention paid to literary pretensions is the professional self-consciousness of writers, especially poets, the characteristic reflexivity of whose writing to some extent pre-empts the critics, making the question of literary reception part of its subject matter. 'The poet, described in ideal perfection, brings the whole soul of man into activity', trumpets Coleridge's 1817 *Biographia Literaria*, the age's outstanding attempt to bridge both German and British traditions by advocating a literature philosophically encoding a conservative purpose and a philosophy radically open to literary extension.[1] But, as Shelley insisted a few years later, part of what poets thus activated was evidently a critical afterlife outlasting their own intentions for their work and bound to no single critical institution. Whether attributing a radical or conservative future to poetic writing, however, both Shelley and Coleridge must concede that it also summons into existence those contemporary

---

1 See Paul Hamilton, *Coleridge and German Philosophy: The Poet in the Land of Logic* (London: Continuum, 2007).

reviewing establishments actually interceding between poets and the audience they tried immediately to affect. Both poet and reviewer, in line with Coleridge's advice to Wordsworth, tried to create the taste by which literature ought to be enjoyed, competing for and shaping in the process the 'reading public'. Depending on your point of view, this reactive body either adapted its citizenry to new literary expectations or disallowed work that demanded the revision of its defining beliefs and social composition. The tension between writer and critic was one whose antagonisms were based on a shared acknowledgement of the critical mass inherent in literary production. Disagreements took place over the specific motivation involved, and over how far it was appropriate to systematize it, not over the question of whether or not literature invited its own critical extension. To understand this dynamic properly, however, we have to look carefully at the terms of debate.

The critical dynamic is most conspicuously in play in that commonplace of Romanticism, on whose existence very different schools of interpretation have continued to agree: its insistence on the autonomy of poetry. 'Poetry', in the inflated usage of the time, can refer to any creative art. But its peculiar awareness of its own artistic status is customarily taken to define aesthetic production. The emergent category of the aesthetic is characteristically self-conscious of its exemptions and privileges. Built into the constitution of mainstream Romantic poetry, it provides essential backing for almost all the manifestos of its poets. Exceptions exist, but their naïve successes tend either to prove the rule or to betray the artful effacing of an actual reflex-ivity. Aesthetic practice clinches the mutual implication, increasing in frequency throughout the eighteenth century, of two ideas: in the idea of being conscious of something is contained the idea of being sensibly affected or self-conscious. Romantic poetry, then, is sufficiently apprised of its own fictional status to make its licence or autonomy a critical part of what it is about.[2]

---

2 David Wootton summarizes the OED's catalogue of the 'birth of self-consciousness' in eighteenth-century usage in 'Unhappy Voltaire . . .', *History Workshop Journal* 50 (2000), 152–3; for the fate of the naïve under Romanticism, *From Schiller to Derrida* by Juliet Sychrava is helpful (Cambridge: Cambridge University Press, 1989). Simon Jarvis, in *Wordsworth's Philosophic Song: Poetic Thinking in Wordsworth* (Cambridge: Cambridge University Press, 2006), uses the French phenomenologist Michel Henry to recover a self-affective dimension given simultaneously in the consciousness of things. Poetry's uniquely intimate commerce with this primary self-awareness ensures its philosophical anteriority to subsequent ideological constructions of the self.

The meanings open to 'autonomy' here are many. Poetic autonomy could refer to a distinctive use of language inappropriate in any other discourse. It might describe criteria of coherence poems alone possess, or, conversely, point to poetry's exemption from standards of coherence obligatory in other modes of writing. As Coleridge tells a friend in 1802: 'Poetry justifies, as *Poetry* independent of any other Passion, some new combination of Language, & *commands* the exclusion of many others allowable in other compositions.'[3] At its most ambitious, Romantic poetry offers an ideal picture of the completeness other sciences were striving to achieve on their own terms, evincing a kind of exemplary independence. Consequently poetry becomes regarded as untranslatable; its unusual, artificial completeness requires an inviolable reciprocity of part and whole upon which any paraphrase would necessarily infringe. At the time and long afterwards this integrity was referred to as poetic organicism. To naturalize poetic artifice in this fashion as a 'second' nature (literally, a 'culture', or growth) ensured its independence within a natural world we apprehended, by contrast, with metonymic sparseness, piecemeal and not in its entirety. Whether poetry's 'second' nature legitimated or censured existing culture was a moot point for its critical reception. Certainly the reactionary associations 'naturalization' has for any critic who has read Roland Barthes are not necessarily appropriate here.[4] Finally and less ambitiously, or less metaphysically, poetic autonomy might simply refer to the genres and kinds in which poetry is written – lyric, epic, heroic, tragic.[5] Poetry resumes all the modes of qualifying for recognition of a distinctive literariness which would embarrass the compositions of the historian, the scientist or the philosopher.

What different readers at different times have made of the claim to poetic autonomy has varied enormously. Generally speaking, these reactions extend from neo-platonic acceptance of the ideal status of poetically free-standing myth, to the many forms of historical reduction or translation of poetic significance back into other discursive statements poetry is accused of having typically sublimated and deflected. In between lie the many

---

3 *Collected Letters of Samuel Taylor Coleridge*, ed. E. L. Griggs, 6 vols. (London: Oxford University Press, 1956–71), vol. II, p. 812.

4 See James Chandler, *Poetry as Second Nature: A Study of the Poetry and Politics* (Chicago and London: University of Chicago Press, 1984).

5 Kevis Goodman's *Georgic Modernity and British Romanticism: Poetry and the Mediation of History* (Cambridge: Cambridge University Press, 2004) provides a timely discussion of the discursive politics of Romantic genre through the (neglected) lens of Georgic.

interactions of writer and critic in which the poem is regarded as having irradiated the discourse which illuminates it. The merits and weaknesses of these opposed views are not the subject at issue here. Under examination is the persistent construction of poetic autonomy by a variety of intellectual means and cultural institutions that, on this issue, appear obliged to take their bearings from Romanticism. Up to and especially during the Romantic period, anthropological theories about the natural language of mankind tended to favour poetic idioms; histories of the originary genres of literature often discovered poetic sources; investigations of the authority of Biblical language allocated poetry a key role in legitimating a more historicist ('higher') Biblical criticism, and philosophy found the need to isolate an autonomous aesthetic sphere whose poetically symbolic discourse under-wrote an overall coherence philosophy desired but could not get on terms with itself.[6] We will characterize the *kinds* of argument invoked here, rather than pursue their historical detail, in keeping with this chapter's aim to provide a conceptual analysis of what is at stake in approaching Romanticism through its core belief in literary autonomy.

Much fine and still highly influential criticism in the second half of the last century – for which Meyer Abrams's *The Mirror and the Lamp* (1953) was a prime source – was dominated by the question of how poetry came by the linguistic materials rendering plausible its claims to be entitled to make rules for itself. Genetic explanations of poetic authority were thought to be in order because Romantic poetry and its supporting intellectual and scholarly traditions presented credentials. These assists could be as disreputable as Ossian's (James MacPherson's) fake ancient Scottish bardic poems, as speculative as Lord Monboddo's anthropology, as controversial and multivalent as Rousseau's *Discourses*. In the sort of language from which it derived, the common story ran, lay the source of poetry's power to command recognition and respect, a linguistic legislator rather than a humble refiner of existing usage. Poetry, it was argued, reproduced the primarily expressive character of original human utterance. Its apparent primitivism was offset by its authenticity, or its recovery of an essentially affective relationship to the world typical of a humanity as yet undiverted from its natural purpose or vocation. This retrospect was necessarily artificial and skilled, a licence to re-invent, one fraudulently but still inspirationally

---

6 Classic discussion of this can be found in P. Lacoue-Labarthe and J.-L. Nancy, *The Literary Absolute: The Theory of Literature in German Romanticism*, trans. P. Barnard and C. Lester (Albany, NY: SUNY, 1988). Jarvis's *Wordsworth's Philosophic Song* is a striking corrective.

exploited by MacPherson and later by the Romantically fashionable Thomas Chatterton's medieval revivals. More plausibly, poetry named an archaeological reconstruction or modern preservation of a defining orientation towards the world, one that had been obscured by subsequent forms of socialization and progress.

Rousseau's theories of the origin of language, the arts and of political society supported the poetic salvage of human nature, a potentially revolutionary exercise whose reputation rose and fell with his own. But Rousseau was influenced by and himself influenced numerous less controversial and poetically serviceable British thinkers from Shaftesbury, through the moral sense school and Scottish Enlightenment on to Wordsworth. The affective origins of language, minus Rousseau's political and cultural polemic, grew into a commonplace. Wordsworth's 'real language of men', a phrase which became almost a mnemonic for his Prefaces to *Lyrical Ballads* (1798–1802), condenses this variegated historical speculation but inflects it again with the Rousseauvian interest in the feasibility of recapturing an original human melody before it becomes lost in the social harmony and artifice of cultural institutions dictating what is to constitute acceptable human expression. A *new* institutionality can then be inaugurated, one geared once more to authentic human proportions and needs, although not immediately recognizable as such. Hence Wordsworth's ambitious, Rousseauvian-sounding claim that readers of his *Lyrical Ballads* 'will look round for poetry, and will be induced to inquire by what species of courtesy these attempts can be permitted to assume that title'. Hence, also, Percy Shelley's belief, according to *A Defence of Poetry* (written 1821), in a common 'cyclic poem', repeatedly historicized, never self-identical, rejuvenated by the poetic additions and critical reinterpretations of successive ages. Clearly, as Abrams argued, lyric form would gain 'distinct pre-eminence' in this context, and the Romantic habit of writing long poems in the Miltonic tradition of epic re-visioning becomes comparatively neglected, a neglect Abrams tries to repair in his later work, *Natural Supernaturalism* (1971), a book post-Kantian in its interests in the grand schemes of Kant's philosophical successors, especially Schelling and Hegel. Moments of extraordinary lyric intensity, as if modelled on Wordsworthian spots of time, cannot explain the art elaborating and plumbing the discursive spaces which stretch in between them and which even, by implication, criticize the spot of time's proclaimed self-sufficiency or power to disseminate affect ('fructifying' or 'renovating virtue', as successive versions of Wordsworth's *Prelude* have it) without further mediation.

Against genetic explanations of poetic authority we have to set the theorizing of the aesthetic. Poetry was justified not only by being traced back to an original, immediate, lyrical, human utterance; it was also adjudged philosophically significant. The German thinker, Alexander Baumgarten, is usually given credit for advancing in the middle of the eighteenth century a philosophical re-evaluation of the sensuous apprehension (aisthesis) more properly foregrounded in poetic than scientific discourse. The validity of poetically enlarging our experience became a basic assumption in the subsequent polemics of *Sturm und Drang* thinkers like Herder and Hamann, but was given its most systematic justification in Kant's 1790 *Critique of Judgement*, which Coleridge described to Crabb Robinson as 'the most astonishing' of his works.[7] Kant was very much influenced by Rousseau, but his reworking of what he found useful in him turned its back on the anthropology of poetry and its language. Instead, he developed the category of the aesthetic so that it legitimated formally poetry's philosophical purpose. Poetry now mediated the divide between our rational essence, as elusive in its way as Rousseau's state of nature, and the actual mixture of affect and reason ordinarily available to us. The aesthetic, with poetry as an obvious representative, offered a unique sensation of the fit between reason and experience. Poetry could figure or symbolize, through its formal perfection, the ethically desirable purposiveness, shared by our different faculties, which ensured the embodiment of rational imperatives. Friedrich Schiller, especially influential on Coleridge, developed Kant's severe ethic into a broader aesthetic education in which our integrated selves could be artificially enjoyed through creative illusion and play, setting a pattern for what ought to happen elsewhere.[8] The Kantian and still more confident post-Kantian investment in the significance of poetry's form of self-government has powered recent seminal expositions of Romanticism, such as the Kantian, formalistic histories of René Wellek, W. Wimsatt and Cleanth Brooks, and Abrams's post-Kantian adventure. Against them Marilyn Butler's *Romantics, Rebels and Reactionaries* (1981) set a much more detailed,

---

7 Alexander Baumgarten, *Aesthetica* (1750–8). See Henry Crabb Robinson, *Diary, Reminiscences, and Correspondence*, selected and ed. Thomas Sadler, 3 vols. (London: Macmillan, 1869), vol. I, p. 305. There is good short account of the implications of Baumgarten's theories for subsequent critical theory in Andrew Bowie, *Aesthetics and Subjectivity: From Kant to Nietzsche* (Manchester: Manchester University Press, 1990), especially the 'Introduction', pp. 1–15.
8 See Kant's *Critique of Judgement* and Schiller's *On the Aesthetic Education of Man* for the original accounts. Michael John Kooy's *Coleridge and Schiller* (London: Palgrave, 2001) is the latest account of the literary and philosophical bearing of Schiller on Coleridge.

dialogic and less philosophical history. At less of a tangent to their method, subsequent deconstructions of formalist readings themselves remained formalist for a while. It was either argued, by Harold Bloom, Geoffrey Hartman and followers, that almost all Romantic poetry (excepting Blake and a few others) ran shy of possible success, fearful of the apocalyptic, institutional devastation attending the unmediated vision its own autonomy might reveal. Or else, following the work of Paul de Man, it was accepted that poetic significance, if it is possible, must consist in the delivery of Kantian certainties, but the critical, deconstructive task was to expose their purely rhetorical character. The analysis of this rhetoric of Romanticism, though, gave way to a critique of aesthetic ideology: an unmasking of the political economy subtending that discursive economy within which the aesthetic and poetry can have the functions allocated them by Kant and Schiller. Critical theory is still in the early stages of responding to de Man's final uncovering of the literality, the dead typographical landscape, actually constituting that area beyond conventional signifying to which he thought Romantic symbolism – deconstructed – consigns ultimate human aspirations towards fulfilment.[9]

Deconstruction here begins to close with more overtly historicist attempts to demystify poetic autonomy. The alleged autonomy of poetry is discussed, especially in work now stemming from Jerome McGann's *The Romantic Ideology* (1983), as an aesthetic device by which inappropriately imaginary solutions to intractable social divisions can be passed off as present or actual experience.[10] *Tintern Abbey*'s 'still, sad music of humanity', one might argue in this vein, reconstituted, but now in empty Kantian form rather than Rousseauvian history, a natural state prior to social differentiation, one whose melody we can recognize as our own. Then with a more post-Kantian confidence, the rest of Wordsworth's poem builds a house for the actuality of this experience, a 'mansion' (as Keats also saw it) intended to

---

9 High points include Geoffrey Hartman, *The Unmediated Vision* (New Haven: Yale University Press, 1954); Harold Bloom, *The Visionary Company: A Reading of English Romantic Poetry*, rev. edn (Ithaca, NY: Cornell University Press, 1971); Paul de Man, *The Rhetoric of Romanticism* (New York: Columbia University Press, 1984) and *Aesthetic Ideology*, ed. with intro. Andrezj Warminski (Minneapolis and London: University of Minnesota Press, 1996); and the responses in *Material Events: Paul de Man and the Afterlife of Theory*, ed. Barbara Cohen, J. Hillis Miller, Andrezj Warminski and Tom Cohen (Minneapolis and London: University of Minnesota Press, 2000).

10 J. J. McGann, *The Romantic Ideology: A Critical Investigation* (Chicago and London: University of Chicago Press, 1983).

remain impregnable to external criticism: 'Nor perchance, / If I were not thus taught, should I the more / Suffer my genial spirits to decay . . .'[11]

This reading arguably ignores the sensuous foundation of Wordsworthian sublimity – 'Felt in the blood, and felt along the heart' – the rootedness in materiality, emphasized by the poem's story of growth, which refutes the idea that spirituality is generated out of anything other than bodily possibilities. Poetic autonomy, then, should not be dismissed in the Humean fashion of many new historicists as a dissembling strategy for manipulating matters of fact by re-describing them as relations of ideas. Rather, poetry finds a language for our sense of being produced by place and circumstance, a language whose self-originating fictions allow it to figure the workings anterior to articulacy itself, an animal determinism against which de Man's detached scenario is perhaps a protection. Poetic language describes not so much a genesis of self as a primal acquaintance with self, often baffling conscious expression, upon which subsequent development can build ('life and food / For future years'). In other words, some historicist reductions might be reproached for underestimating rather than over-estimating the coverage envisaged for poetic autonomy by its practitioners at the time. A defence of *Tintern Abbey*'s 'picture of the mind' might argue that Wordsworth's poetic afflatus gets at the pre-history any historical reading must assume but can never recover. Poetry then escapes from being entirely answerable to historical data because its vocation is instead to figure how we might come to be in possession of any history we can then recognize as our own. This autonomous power to express our pre-conceptual orientation towards the world is carefully theorized by Romantic philosophy from Kant's third *Critique* onwards, but necessarily escapes consideration by historicist methodologies unavoidably functioning, as it were, after the event. But then, the question arises, can *any* historical discourse gain a critical purchase on poetry? Is poetry constitutionally anachronistic? We shall see later that this dilemma too is entertained in Romantic poetry, compounding the difficulties as well as assisting in their solution. The structure of the problem is like the one celebrated by psychoanalysis: that of how we define an unconscious authority, responsible for conscious expression, but only indirectly accessible in the myths with which we construct that retrieval retrospectively. For Freud, Lacan and their critical followers, the Romantic problematic was a fertile precursor and source of

---

11 To J. H. Reynolds, 18 May 1818, *The Letters of John Keats*, ed. H. E. Rollins, 2 vols. (Cambridge, MA: Harvard University Press, 1958), vol. I, p. 181.

examples. Still more recently, Romantic anachronism has been variously theorized as giving salutary consistency to the idea of an exceptional case, or as figuring a virtual reality again offering its interpreter emancipatory possibilities outside historical orthodoxies.[12]

In any case, for our purposes here, the conclusion to be drawn is that it is obviously very hard to find established interpretations of Romanticism that are not basically situated in relation to Romantic poetry's claims to autonomy. Marxists had always attributed a more or less knowing complicity with political reaction to Romanticism's aesthetic sequestration of ultimate human values. But an internal distance salvaging art's criticism of the political life it inhabits was conceded in different ways by Marxists from Lukács to Althusser. Such optimism is now often replaced in new historicist criticism of Romantic writing by a post-Marxist belief (deriving from influential theorists like Adorno and Foucault) in the repressive tolerance or opportunistic production of the very idea of emancipation by the dominant power it notionally resists. Again, it is the poetry's autonomy that lets it contribute to this controlling function, and it is the autonomy of poetry that has to be rehabilitated for Romanticism to escape so pessimistic an overall scenario. Yet all these different outcomes for our own critical inheritance, whatever our choices between them, customarily revisit an original Romantic accreditation of poetry from which, in their different ways, they draw their strength. Latterly, this recursive habit has become more sensitive to the institutional conditions of poetry as 'an occupation and an art'. It is to these we now turn.[13]

Poetic autonomy and the critical establishment

Symbiotically linked to Romantic bids for the emancipation of poetry from the rule of other forms of understanding was the contemporary journalistic form of what René Wellek called the 'rise of literary history'. To preceding histories of English literature like Thomas Warton's (1774–81), or accounts of ascendant genres, like Clara Reeve's *The Progress of Romance* (1785), was

---

12 See James Chandler, *England in 1819: The Politics of Literary Culture and the Case of Romantic Historicism* (Chicago and London: University of Chicago Press, 1998) and Jerome C. Christensen, *Romanticism at the End of History* (Baltimore and London: Johns Hopkins University Press, 2000).

13 I deliberately echo the title of Peter Murphy's book, most helpful in this regard: *Poetry as an Occupation and an Art in Britain, 1760–1830* (Cambridge: Cambridge University Press, 1993).

added a kind of 'history of the present' written as the contemporary disciplining of discursive possibility by a combative and *engagé* reviewing establishment. For Dissenters, reviews under their editorial control, such as *The Monthly, Analytical, Critical* and *English Review* could furnish the cultural establishment or talking shop they were politically denied. Pitt's disciple, George Canning, on the other hand, could use his prominent association with the new *Anti-Jacobin* to further Government propaganda. Where the influential new Scottish reviews were concerned, probably more relevant is the predominantly legal training of the intelligentsia on which the Whig *Edinburgh* (1802), the Tory *Quarterly* (1809) and *Blackwood's Review* (1817) relied to convince audiences of their right to cultural adjudication. Others sought credibility by recruiting from London literary coteries or professional and occasional literati like William Hazlitt and Charles Lamb (although both also contributed to the *Edinburgh*), for whom reviewing helped concentrate very considerable creative endowments into their proper form. This new talent worked for recently launched or revived periodicals with unprecedented forensic assurance and zeal. Deference to the reviews concerning decisions as to what the middle class might buy and read, still a cultural short-cut, started then. Class loyalty or conflict was at play in judgements of the readability or unreadability of new work.[14] Then as now, what got read as literature was a key to the complicated workings of ideology in the period and its interaction with market forces. The timeliness of literary reputation and the significance of being in fashion increased proportionately. So did the practicability of having one's writing make a direct intervention in literary history. Confidence in immediate publicity encouraged poets to respond to preceding works in a knowing manner and to anticipate further responses to come. When the editor of the *Edinburgh Review* told the public of Wordsworth's *The Excursion* that 'This will never do', he clearly had in mind other candidates who would fit the bill, the bill here being the preservation of some kind of recognizable consistency of poetic succession to which new poems should properly add. But intertextuality, perhaps correspondingly, had also become a more prominently

14 See Jon Klancher's *The Making of English Reading Audiences, 1790–1832* (Madison: University of Wisconsin Press, 1987). Generally on the reviews, the following are helpful: Derek Roper, *Reviewing before the 'Edinburgh', 1788–1802* (London: Methuen, 1978); Marilyn Butler, 'Culture's Medium: The Role of the Review', in *The Cambridge Companion to Romanticism*, ed. Stuart Curran (Cambridge: Cambridge University Press, 1993), pp. 120–48; Mark Parker, *Literary Magazines and British Romanticism* (Cambridge: Cambridge University Press, 2000).

polemical affair within poems themselves: Coleridge's *Dejection: An Ode* reads Wordsworth's *Immortality Ode* severely, as Keats's *Endymion* does Percy Shelley's *Alastor*, and as Byron's *Don Juan* does just about everything else. We are dealing not just with the squibs and satires, the usual parodies shadowing most distinguishable styles and periods of literary production, but with something better described, in Harold Bloom's phrase, as 'strong misreading', in which the work of the first generation of English Romantic poets in an important way becomes the signified of the work of their immediate successors. As combative in their own fashion as the reviews, poems contributed a practical assertion or performance of poetic history; they made a fashionable poetic subject out of ongoing creative debate alive to the possibility of a quickly responsive literary review. The fact, better remembered, that the reviews did not always go the poets' way should not be allowed to obscure this emergent writerly tactic and the heightening of a sense of historical speed where literature was concerned.

Poetic and critical establishments interacted to the mutual enhancement of each other's authority. Poetic autonomy was supported by the continuity with which a series of reviews depicted literary history in relatively rapid motion. The reviews, in their turn, gained credibility as the arbiters of this part of culture because their judgement placed it within the larger map of 'letters' that they drew through their adjacent pronouncements on works of political, historical, economic and philosophical discourse. As William Hazlitt saw, periodical criticism was self-proliferating. His essay on 'The Periodical Press' in the *Edinburgh Review* of 1823 announces 'a truism on the subject, which, like many other truisms, is pregnant with deep thought, – *viz. That periodical criticism is favourable – to periodical criticism*. It contributes to its own improvement.'[15] Hazlitt thought the arts were not progressive, both because of their unscientific nature but also, especially in the case of poetry, because he suspected its political complicity with Legitimacy or the powers that be.[16] Its difference from science underpinned poetry's autonomy; but its power-loving dominant faculty, the imagination, tempted poetry to sell that independence for political favour. In this article, though,

---

15 'The Periodical Press', in *Complete Works of William Hazlitt*, ed. P. P. Howe, 21 vols. (London: J. M. Dent, 1930–4), vol. XVI, p. 212. There are good discussions of Hazlitt's relation to print politics in Parker, *Literary Magazines and British Romanticism*, 'Introduction' and ch. 2; and Kevin Gilmartin, *Print Politics: The Press and Radical Opposition in Early Nineteenth-Century England* (Cambridge: Cambridge University Press, 1996), pp. 227–34.
16 'Why the Arts are not Progressive', *Complete Works*, vol. XVIII, p. 6.

his paradox appears resolved. The range and answerability of review writing to public interest means, in Hazlitt's typically flamboyant historicist metaphor, that the Bastille of literary exclusiveness is prised open. The new public formed in the periodicals' popular revolution, though, is as attracted to a specifically literary form of illumination as was the old. 'The *Monarchism* of literature is at an end; the cells of learning are thrown open, and let in the light of universal day.'[17] It is the access to literary understanding that is democratized; literary distinction remains intact. Hazlitt, for example, believes that, despite appearances, the 'levelling Muse' he attributes to Wordsworth contrives to restore an elitist, esoteric literariness opposed to the popular entrée to the good things of culture Hazlitt favours. Hence, perhaps contrary to expectations, 'the secret of the Jacobin poetry and anti-jacobin politics of this writer is the same'.[18]

When the *Reviews* occasionally broke with the logic of the literary history that their even-handed treatment, democratic to Hazlitt's eyes, was meant to concede, things fell apart. John Gibson Lockhart of *Blackwood's* was accused by the *London Magazine*'s editor, John Scott, of playing fast and loose with his critical responsibilities. He had allegedly written separate articles for and against the same pieces by Wordsworth and Coleridge, making a nonsense of the history of their reception for which the *Reviews* had taken credit. For this offence of abusing the prerogative for controlling literary reputation, such high words were exclaimed that eventually Scott was called out by Jonathan Christie, *Blackwoods'* agent, and shot dead in a duel at Chalk Farm in north London. This lurid episode evokes the kind of confusion precipitated by a double-voicedness or irony quite tolerable in Byron's intertextual fun and games (the 'Eastern anti-Jacobin' who also voices Byron's patriotism in Book 3 of *Don Juan*, for example), but unacceptable or dishonourable as critical practice. The critical establishment's own drastic self-regulation in this incident strikingly demarcates the borders between poetic and critical licence. Within poetic performance, the drama of influence and innovation can be played out by the uncanny reversals and calculated anachronisms through which poets can still, spectacularly, accrue aesthetic capital – '. . . for they are all such liars / And take all colours, like the hands of dyers'. Subdued to what they work in, Romantic poets incur a self-corruption analogous to the journeyman work for the stage which Shakespeare's sonnet deprecates so disingenuously to

---

17 *Complete Works*, vol. XVI, p. 220.
18 *Complete Works*, vol. VII, p. 144.

the ears of a later audience now incapable of treating his dramas as other than cultural touchstones. From such ostensibly contaminated material, like him, they weave the texture of poetic success. The critical establishment, it appears, must rather guarantee the continuum of literary history. Only then may poetry creatively disrupt it. But the poetic autonomy the critics defend remains a discrete narrative of poetic history, one discourse among many, rather than a law unto itself. In this the critical establishment is democratic, its *Reviews* treating poetry on a par with other discourses and freeing criticism from the esoteric ruses of poetry itself.

Here we encounter a tension crucial for understanding the construction of poetic autonomy within Romanticism. The dialectic between poetry and criticism has a continuing relevance. The defining Romantic confrontation now looks as if it is produced by the difference between poetry as discourse and poetry as performance. As performance, poetry, sovereign and self-legislating, can encompass almost everything. The very idea that all things have their poetry stems from the Romantic hyperbole. We lack, Percy Shelley could claim in his defence of poetic significance (*A Defence of Poetry*), 'the poetry of life': a kind of imaginative suspension of scientific or ethical fixities and definites allowing us to reconsider their fitness to our entire existential orientation. The wonder accompanying this re-visioning of the quotidian leads to the formulations of a foundational theory of defamiliarization common to Wordsworth, Coleridge and Shelley. The carrying of sensation 'into the midst of thought itself', in Wordsworth's words, is the customary poetic enjoyment, much theorized since, of such poetic aspiration. That it is the product of an extraordinary ambition endemic to Romantic aesthetic practice can easily be forgotten.

An example egregiously foregrounding this ambitiousness, though, would be Coleridge's description in a letter of 30 May 1815 of the philosophical poem he had hoped Wordsworth might write, but which *The Excursion* had apparently fallen far short of. Coleridge's polemic slips in and out of focus, alternately asking for an exorbitant range of subject-matter ('the Totality of a System') and then for the poetic invention of a viewpoint making plausible its otherwise comically ambitious register, 'an insight in to the whole Truth'.[19] In the extension of his argument with Wordsworth in *Biographia Literaria* (published in 1817 but written around the same time), Coleridge's confidence in poetry's foundational authority looks for theoretical justification primarily in the post-Kantian philosopher, Friedrich

---

19 *Collected Letters*, vol. IV, p. 576.

Schelling, but actually reposes on critical empathy with the poetic performances of Shakespeare, Milton and Wordsworth himself. The philosophy remains implausible, indifferently expressed, tendentiously understood,
plagiarized; the critical prose internal to the performances it describes,
insisting on their untranslatableness, is what must carry conviction.
Complicating this verdict, though, remains the sense that Coleridge, like
Schelling, radicalized philosophy by advocating its literary embodiment.
Byron's declaration to his editor, John Murray, of his ambitions for his epic
Don Juan appears to parody Coleridge's explanation of unfettered poetic
significance, as indeed Byron does in the poem itself: 'The 5th. [Canto] is so
far from being the last of D.J. that it is hardly the beginning . . . I had not
quite fixed whether to make him [Juan] end in Hell, or in an unhappy
marriage, not knowing which would be the severest. The Spanish tradition
says Hell: but it is probably an Allegory of the other state.' But the desire for
an uninhibited poetic colonizing of everything is evident in the poem's
indiscriminately accommodating verse. It was *Don Juan* which prompted
Goethe to say: 'Our German aesthetical people . . . are always talking about
poetical and unpoetical objects; and in one respect they are not quite wrong,
yet at bottom no real object is unpoetical if the poet knows how to use it
properly.'[20]

Viewed from a position internal to its constitution, Romantic poetry
knows no bounds to its powers to reconceive and re-order experience.
Caught up within its language-game, the reader cannot escape Romantic
poetry's relentless power to translate failure into success. The major
philosophical strategies dominating its aesthetic, sublimity and irony, provide the reader with an epistemology in which to fall short of knowledge is
to acquire an expressive power offering an alternative take on the object
eluding knowledge. In sublimity, a sense of expanding subjectivity rushes in
to fill the void we fall into as our apprehension loses its grasp and slips off its
target. And, in the expectation that this should happen anyway to every
attempt to present some part of the world in all its contextual richness, we
may as well proffer our presentation of it ironically, telegraphing our
awareness of the insufficiency of our description and thus getting at sublime
expressiveness by more low-key, cynical means. This progression, from
sublimity to irony, drives the development of the aesthetic as it is theorized

---

20 *Byron's Letters and Journals*, ed. Leslie A. Marchand, 11 vols. (London: John Murray,
1978), vol. VIII, p. 78; J. P. Eckermann, *Conversations with Goethe* (London: J. M. Dent
and Sons, 1930), p. 211.

in Germany in the 1790s from Kant to Schlegel. But, informally, in practice, it also accounts for changes in the larger shapes of poetic ambition in England, prefigured by Laurence Sterne's *Tristram Shandy* and developed from Wordsworth and Coleridge to Byron and Keats. More speculatively, it also helps us understand that further emptying of poetic ambition in the settlement Romanticism makes with Victorian sentimentalism, anticipated this time in the work of a Felicia Hemans or an Elizabeth Laetitia Landon, consolidated in that of a Tennyson, a Browning or a Christina Rossetti.[21] Eventually, the importunate emotion of poetry no longer simply ironizes the linguistic conventions whose epistemological insufficiency it glosses; it subordinates their epistemological pretensions to be in good faith beneath a knowing primacy of feeling which leaves these conventions looking redundant and skeletal. *In Memoriam* ostensibly searches for an explanation of mortality aspired to unsatisfactorily in different discourses – theological, teleological, psychological – but then uncritically displaces this quest with its own performance of bereavement. The Romantic tension between performance and discourse has disappeared, just as the difference between elegizing and less imaginary relationships has been effaced in the process of making loss bearable.

Viewed from outside, however, and not as part of the stories and pictures it makes up about itself, the autonomy of Romantic poetry receives an entirely different kind of support. Poetry takes its place within the discursive map of the age, occupying the space allotted it between other discourses. The unique significance of the poetic solution of problems is to be granted, but understood by differentiating it from solutions produced within the space of the other discursive disciplines similarly recognized and reviewed by the intellectual establishment. Its autonomy is relative, not unconditional, functioning without prejudice to the claims of different knowledges. Like the imagination in earlier discursive maps, such as Francis Bacon's *The Advancement of Learning*, poetry can 'come to rule in its turn', but it does not rule absolutely. Romantic poetry's own self-descriptions – 'all / ye know on earth, and all ye need to know' – do often pretend to this absolutism, apparently opposing those democratic criteria of accountability typically

---

21 For Sterne's influence on Wordsworth see Mary Jacobus, *Tradition and Experiment in Wordsworth's 'Lyrical Ballads' (1798)* (Oxford: Oxford University Press, 1978). Jerome K. McGann, on whom I draw here, has written a classic account of the passage from sensibility and the sentimental into more modern poetic deployments in *The Poetry of Sensibility* (Oxford: Oxford University Press, 1996).

demanded by methodologies of the human sciences from the Early Modern period onwards.

Poetic autonomy's criticism of itself

Again, this way of looking at Romantic poetry, which understands it within the politics of discourse of its time, helps explain a continuing ambivalence in its interpreters. Romantic poetry's radicalism can appear undeniable: fundamentally, this art presents itself as essentially committed to innovation and transformation. If we are to believe its own publicity, it overleaps its boundaries, and, in its pretensions to a defamiliarized apprehension of everything prior to conceptualization, it appears foundational, promising a new heaven and a new earth. Equally, though, this power is premised on a literary absolutism that can just as easily appear constitutionally reactionary. A Coriolanus among discourses, poetry, for Hazlitt, must always prove 'right-royal', sympathizing with power rather than with the victims power oppresses, scornful of pleas for answerability or for it to show a consideration for the claims of other disciplines.[22] Coleridge's notional philosophical poem, as he commends it to Wordsworth, initially appears to be a socializing project, created out of its dialogue with different disciplines; but, in its formulation, it wavers between this intellectual cosmopolitanism and the belief that it alone, on its uniquely ideal plane, can solve the problems or reconcile the oppositions fissuring those other discourses. Keats, Hazlitt's friend, has numerous passages in his letters proclaiming a poetic self-sufficiency exempt from the claims of fact and reason. This confidence, however, is balanced or eroded by concessions one would expect from a poet who wanted to write 'on the liberal side of the question'. In this context, his *Hyperion* poems try to stage a progression from one kind of poetry to another, from the Titanic to the medicinal, the fanatical dream to the healing balm whose curative power facilitates rather than arbitrarily overrides our other discursive commitments. When the first *Hyperion* ends in Apollo's apotheosis, 'Knowledge enormous makes a God of me', Keats's words state precisely the tension between a knowledge, whose validity ought to be translatable to the benefit of all, and an absolute autonomy, whose exclusive esoteric experience alone seems able to realize that knowledge.

---

22 *Complete Works*, vol. IV, pp. 214–15.

Keats's poems in fact suggest that poetry acquires its therapeutic effect just through its controversial power to frame ideas of absolute authority while, simultaneously, implying that only in poetry can such notions of untrammelled autonomy be sensibly entertained. The result is to produce a demystifying self-consciousness that is double-edged. Poetry can be disgusted with its own hyperbole and linguistic inflation, exposed as the Titans are by Hyperion, 'To the most hateful seeing of itself'; or else it can use its sense of its own fictionality to criticize those ideas which can only achieve expression in poetry. Friedrich Schlegel explained or theorized this double-take as 'the irony of irony', a kind of parabasis, when the author steps aside from his or her work and comments on it *in propria persona* or as a Chorus not subject to but distinct from the fiction being acted out. The double irony comes from the paradox of being critical of poetry on criteria extraneous to the poetic discourse that nevertheless has invented them.

Many of Keats's poems contrive this puzzle, apostrophizing their own symbols and figures in a conspicuously disabused and detached voice. As Helen Vendler notes of Keats's 'Autumn', 'her hymns are sung in her absence'. The rupture is such that for other critics it looks like self-abuse, a devising of self-alienation marvellously expressive of Keats's social indigence but reflecting nothing to his or to poetry's credit.[23] In both cases, absolute poetic autonomy causes poetry to split, or become viviparous, dividing into itself and its cultured despisers, incorporating its own criticism in a manner that incensed the critical establishment on whose territory Keats's camp self-satire presumed. A passage from Keats's letters perhaps helps explain this at a safe distance from his poetic *en abyme*.

> Mr Lewis went a few morning[s] ago to town with Mrs Brawne they talked about me – and I heard that Mr L Said a thing I am not at all contented with – Says he 'O, he is quite the little Poet' now this is abominable – you might as well say that Buonaparte is quite the little Soldier – You see what it is to be under six foot and not a lord . . .[24]

A small man, Keats became understandably furious at being placed as 'quite the little Poet', but also, one imagines, because the remark prettifies the measured compensations poetry genuinely offered him. He is, after all,

---

23 Helen Vendler, *The Odes of John Keats* (Cambridge, MA: Harvard University Press, 1983), p. 294. Contrast Marjorie Levinson, *Keats's Life of Allegory: The Origins of Style* (Oxford: Basil Blackwell), pp. 220–1.

24 *The Letters of John Keats*, ed. H. E. Rollins, 2 vols. (Cambridge, MA: Harvard University Press, 1958), vol. II, p. 64.

passionately eloquent about those on many other occasions, happy to acknowledge them in appropriate sublime or ironic circumstances. Then, 'shapes of epic greatness are stationed around me'. Or, confronted by the prospect of repeating his brother's early tubercular death, his irony is poised – 'I always made an awkward bow'.[25] But his rage about the phrase 'quite the little Poet' is immediately linked in the letter with the comparable ridiculousness of 'quite the little Soldier' when applied to the less than tall Napoleon Bonaparte. The double irony here is that while Napoleon's importance is out of all proportion to his short stature, the illegitimate absolutism of his power, its *gloire*, is exposed precisely by its aptness to the poetic appreciation that rightly overcomes his physical shortcomings. Poetic glorification incriminates political authority when its own licence can provide a perfect parallel. And the same would be true of the sublime expression required by any unfair social ascendancy: whether that of the 'lord' invoked here, or that of the murderous brothers in *Isabella: or, the Pot of Basil*: their jealousy of social reputation is so indefensible that it fits perfectly the heroes of 'smokeable' romance – 'Why in the name of Glory were they proud?'[26] The poetry allows their pride to be condemned by its glorification.

Similarly, in the 1805 *Prelude*, Wordsworth draws a 'sympathy with power' (X:416) from the 'unintelligible chastisement' of the Terror during the French Revolution, when, again, unjustifiable political excess stimulates poetic sensibility to a sense of the autonomy only proper and authentic to it.[27] Coleridge, too, read poetic autonomy in this direction, contrary to Hazlitt, exonerating poetic absolutism instead of implicating it in analogous, unacceptable dictatorship or imposed Legitimacy where 'everything that is, is right'. In *Biographia Literaria* and elsewhere, Coleridge distinguishes between 'absolute genius' and 'commanding genius'. The latter is someone – a Nimrod, a Napoleon – who seeks to exert in real life an absolute authority that can only properly belong to art. In peaceful times, the 'perfect poem' the commanding genius exhibits can conform to the peaceful shape of 'palace or temple or landscape-garden'; but in stormier times, he forces the world to reflect his will through arbitrary violence. The

---

25 *Ibid.*, vol. II, p. 360.
26 *The Poems of John Keats*, ed. Jack Stillinger (Cambridge, MA: Harvard University Press, 1978); see the extended discussion of Keats's description of *Isabella* as 'smokeable' in James Chandler's *England in 1819*, pp. 395–402.
27 William Wordsworth, *The Prelude 1799, 1805, 1850*, ed. Jonathan Wordsworth, M. H. Abrams, and Stephen Gill (New York and London: Norton, 1979), 1805, X:416.

absolute genius, by contrast, always finds expression in the 'imagination' and 'spirit', and is, typically, a poet.[28]

These subtleties of poetic autonomy help formulate an alternative to Hazlitt's critique. Part of what poetic autonomy within Romanticism means, it now appears, is to be able to invent a critical self-regard which reflects upon concepts from other discourses which need poetry for their fullest expression or articulation. Another explanatory parallel might be the dialectic between Blake's symbiotic states of innocence and experience. Romantic poetry comparably suggests that its innocent fulfilments have to be organized by the understanding so as to register the fact that to live innocently in an experienced world either displays a culpable ignorance or a cynical corruption. Equally, not to feel the reproach that poetic autonomy casts on its mundane approximations is to forfeit a means for remaining alive to the contrasting slaveries and hegemonies under which we live. Often the contrast seems drawn too cleanly, and poetry's 'beautiful ideal-isms of moral excellence', as Shelley described his own *Prometheus Unbound*, look, to a non-Romantic eye, neglectful of the privileged culture on which they are premised. At its best, though, and Shelley's poetry would be a good example, Romantic poetry's self-critical dimension is inseparably bound up with the idea of its autonomy. This combination leaves a poetry agonized by the distance from the real world required for its satisfactions to be plausible and by the violations perpetrated when the enjoyment of such untrammelled self-legislation as its own is attempted outside the aesthetic dispensation. A man's life should be a perfect poem, as Milton thought, but Romantic poetry frequently mounts the sternest critique of this, its most desirable, end.

In his *An Essay on Criticism* (1711), Alexander Pope had attacked the pro-liferation of critics in his own day, predictably deploring this aspect of the popularization of high culture: 'Now one [fool] in verse makes many more in prose'. His response in that poem was to make the best criticism the prerogative of the poet. The poet who can use or imitate his great prede-cessors, as Virgil did Homer, necessarily surpasses the critical insights of prosaic theorists – 'And let your comment be the Mantuan Muse'. Pope insults critics as pseudo-doctors, 'modern 'pothecaries', anticipating by just over a century the idiom of the contumely to be heaped on Keats, the

---

28 Samuel Taylor Coleridge, *Biographia Literaria*, 2 vols., ed. James Engell and Walter Jackson Bate, *Collected Works VII* (London and Princeton: Princeton University Press, 1983), vol. I, pp. 31–3. See also *The Statesman's Manual* in *Collected Works VI*, pp. 65–6.

doctor's apprentice, by *Blackwood's Magazine*: 'It is a better and a wiser thing to be a starved apothecary than a starved poet; so back to the shop, Mr John, back to the "plasters, pills, and ointment boxes . . ."'.[29] Romantics like Keats, we can now see, argue in the other direction. Pope wants criticism to become exclusively performative, reducing to the excellence of prosody, poetic technique accessible only to the good taste of those internal to an exclusive classical culture. Keats, an apprentice here too, famously enjoyed his classicism at second hand, from Lemprière's *Classical Dictionary* and a host of translations. While Pope's poetic performance of critical precept in *An Essay on Criticism* resists being brought to critical reflection, Keats's critical reflections are encoded in poetic performance. The poetry typically asks the reader to produce a theory of itself. It can do even that, by being itself responsible for producing a defining critical resistance to its own expressions. Romantic poetry's internal, introspective recognition of its own authenticity *is* a critical self-consciousness. This genre proposes its own self-sufficiency, knows the dangers of structural affiliations with absolutism – those 'ancestral voices prophesying war' – and typically steps aside from its own perfection to suggest the critical demarcation of that success. Implied, enhanced, even, should be awareness of the close society of discourses and ways of being in the world entitled to exert their own claims and obligations.

The act of criticism or of bringing to reflection is the hallmark of Romantic philosophical activity from Kant to Hegel. This age is nothing if not critical. Equally, for philosophers like Schelling and then Coleridge, poetry was essential for grasping the productive unity of self and other that their philosophy hoped to demonstrate. In poetry this estranging, abstract philosophical groundwork was transformed into a familiar performance: in a recurrent Coleridgean formulation, the rules of imagination became the powers of growth and production. Hence, as suggested, Coleridge's *Biographia Literaria*, the most ambitious English essay in critical theory of its day, ascends, nervously, towards the climactic definition of a philosophically instrumental imagination and then, in its second volume, reverts confidently to collaborative poetic criticism and example.

Keats's criticism of art in art is no doubt partly what turned the critical establishment against him. In that he was doing what they did, isolating poetry and suspecting its licentious excess, he appears innocuous. But it is important to see that this reflection in fact carries poetic autonomy to a still

29 *Blackwood's Magazine* 3 (August 1818), pp. 519–24.

higher pitch, as it now presumes to appropriate even its own critical outside or limiting discursive exterior as part of the story it has to tell. This was the *Quarterly's* reviewer John Wilson Croker's quarrel with Leigh Hunt, who 'impudently presumed to seat himself in the chair of criticism, and to measure his own poetry by his own standard'. From this vanity Croker pardoned Keats, but only so as to describe his poetry's autonomy as sheer caprice – 'he writes it for its own sake'.[30] Unlike Coleridge, Keats does not spend a long time deferring to an authoritative critical discourse before practically internalizing it. He does not pay his critical dues. *Blackwood's* approved Coleridge's philosophical images of a magisterial criticism and viewed its too hasty translation into poetic affect as dangerous populism and vulgarization.

The feminization of Keats by reviewers, through socially diminishing judgements, prior to delivering the critical *coup de grâce*, associates him with another kind of social and cultural presumption they were keen to police.[31] Attacks on Romantic women poets can tell us still more about the current anxiousness to keep poetry in its place. Croker's infamous treatment of Anna Barbauld's poem *Eighteen Hundred and Eleven* in the *Quarterly* interestingly takes its stand on a match that he believes obtains between Barbauld's fault in straying outside her proper female sphere and the solecism of writing 'party pamphlets in verse'. Barbauld's poem appears to us now to be about the progressively civilizing influence of 'genius', which proceeds in imperialist manner from one age and geographical area to another. The trajectory of 'genius' recalls traditions of the progress of poetry, charted in late eighteenth-century poems as various as Thomas Gray's 'The Progress of Poesy', and then Blake's 'To Spring' with which he began his inaugural *Poetical Sketches*.[32] Their optimistic story has the migrant spirit of creativity settle finally upon England, home at last after various detours through other climes of classic and romance. Barbauld's sharp radicalism has this 'genius' move on from a clapped-out Europe to the Americas ripe for liberty. Croker, of course, registered the immediate political dissidence this betokened;[33] but his attack was based just as much upon the incompetence

---

30 *Quarterly Review* 19 (April 1818), pp. 204–8.
31 See Anne K. Mellor, *Romanticism and Gender* (London: Routledge, 1993), pp. 171–209.
32 'The Progress of Poesy: A Pindaric Ode', in *The Poems of Gray, Collins and Goldsmith*, ed. Roger Lonsdale (London: Longmans, 1969), pp. 155–77; 'To Spring', in *The Poems of William Blake*, ed. W. H. Stevenson, text by David V. Erdman (London and New York: Longmans and Norton, 1971), pp. 3–4.
33 *Quarterly Review* 7 (1812), pp. 309–13.

supposedly proved by the poetic character of Barbauld's feminine transgression into politics.

Recently, critics reviving interest in neglected women poets of the period have often attributed to them an agenda opposed to mainline Romantic ambition. But women poets, on their side, were also certainly aware of the formal symmetry between contemporary claims for the autonomy of poetry and the independence they themselves desired. Equally they knew they risked Croker's criticism of such free expression for promoting the overweening presumption of one discourse over all others. The way they elegize each other brings this out forcefully. Felicia Hemans clinches her memorial for Mary Tighe by turning Tighe's afterlife into a new poetic annexation: 'Now peace the woman's heart hath found, / And joy the poet's eye.'[34] In turn, Hemans is commemorated in one of the elegies written by Letitia Elizabeth Landon with a comparable conjunction of aspirations beyond the woman's and the poet's sphere, but here chastised and tragically culpable: 'The fable of Prometheus and the Vulture / Reveals the poet's and the woman's heart.' This is very different from the Hemans whose death is also lamented in Wordsworth's 'Extempore Effusion Upon the Death of James Hogg', the 'holy Spirit' who 'sunk into a breathless sleep'. Christina Rossetti continues the tradition of an actively posthumous female imagination in her own poems, but also in her elegy for Landon where, finally, 'true life is born of death' and 'new spring builds new heaven and clean new earth'.[35]

The apocalyptic tone heard here is tied more to realistic hopes for a less patriarchal audience in the future, and less to that apocalyptic language, associated predominantly with Blake, whose unmediated access to truth requires the passing away of all present institutions. As indicated earlier, influential schools of interpretation have been built upon the idea that Romanticism was running scared of (Bloom, Hartman) or magnificently sublimated (Abrams) its sense of a revelatory imaginative capability owing nothing to natural forms. In keeping with these readings, Wordsworth's textualization of the apocalyptic landscape he encountered in the Vale of Gondo – 'Characters of the great Apocalypse, / Types and symbols of

---

34 *Records of Woman, With Other Poems*, 2nd edn (Edinburgh and London: William Blackwood and T. Cadell, 1828), p. 163.

35 Hemans's and Landon's elegies are usefully anthologized, as is Barbauld's *Eighteen Hundred and Eleven*, in *Romantic Women Poets: An Anthology*, ed. Duncan Wu (Oxford: Blackwell, 1997). Rossetti's *L. E. L.* is included in *Victorian Women Poets: An Anthology*, ed. Angela Leighton and Margaret Reynolds (Oxford: Blackwell, 1995).

Eternity' (*Prelude*, 1805, VI:570–1) – holds at bay a truly millennial trans-formation. Otherwise, it might be argued again, that he catches at our primordial situation whose unconscious authority, in order to articulate us, must be structured like a language 'Of first and last, and midst, and without end' (VI: 572). Blake's deprecation of the world of generation grew out of his belief that nature was in any case an imaginative construction serving ideological ends. Women's writing of the period emphasizes this socio-logical rather than theological basis for apocalyptical writing. For example, Mary Shelley's novels *Frankenstein* and *The Last Man* are comparably rooted in enlivened feelings for natural possibilities dismissed as apocalyptic by the cultural and political establishments, conservative and radical, whose imaginative investment in one natural dispensation is offended by her imaginative construction of another.[36] Once more, the autonomy of lit-erature, here hyperbolically demonstrated in its representations of apoca-lypse, can function as a wake-up call to other discourses as yet unselfcritical of their own tendentiousness.[37]

To summarize, the autonomy of poetry advocated by Romanticism was advanced on several fronts. The poetic performances instantiating the poetic right to self-government draw on Enlightenment anthropology and Romantic philosophy and are supported by a burgeoning critical estab-lishment keen to accredit poetry as an important part of their own sphere of cultural legislation. However, Romantic poetry's own sense of autonomy brooks no restrictions and happily defamiliarizes other discourses if given the opportunity. It lays claim to a sense of objects prior to discursive con-ceptualization of them. The absolutism of poetry's ambition to reconceive the foundations of all other discourses offends democratic critical sensibil-ities. Equally, though, major Romantic poems themselves evolve a self-critical dimension in their telling by which they figure, paradoxically, an internal resistance to their own otherwise irresistible self-aggrandisement.

36 A good introduction to Mary Shelley's gendering of Romantic literariness is offered by Anne K. Mellor's *Mary Shelley: Her Life, Her Fiction, Her Monsters* (New York and London: Routledge, 1988).
37 See especially Harold Bloom, *Blake's Apocalypse* (Garden City: Doubleday, 1963), Geoffrey Hartman, *Wordsworth's Poetry 1787–1814* (New Haven: Yale University Press, 1964); M. H. Abrams, *Natural Supernaturalism: Tradition and Revolution in Romantic Literature* (New York: Norton, 1971). Morton Paley describes the conceptual variety and sectarian background to Romantic apocalyptic thinking in *Apocalypse and Millennium in English Romantic Poetry* (Oxford: Clarendon Press, 1999), and Steven Goldsmith offers a challenging political and ideological reading of Romantic apocalypse, and of its self-critical dimension, in *Unbuilding Jerusalem: Apocalypse and Romantic Representation* (Ithaca, NY: Cornell University Press, 1993).

Whether Romantic poetry's commentary on its own status makes for genuine self-criticism, or for a further unwarranted presumption of critical authority, is highly controversial. Various Romantic poets, especially women, are clearly castigated at the time for perpetrating the latter fault.

But the unfairness of the sexist attacks, like those on Keats, suggests an unwillingness to take criticism when it comes from a certain quarter, and does not confirm the implausibility of poetic criticism itself. The defamiliarization achieved by poetry's autonomous review of an entire cultural field may work in productive dialectic with reservations that it is to poetry that such an essential critical role has to be assigned. To the sceptics, the appointment of *poetry* as the Romantic ombudsman shows the calculated marginalization of this new enlightenment as a form of recreation, on artistic holiday from more serious matters. But this dialectic is central to critical theory now, thought by many to be the inevitable fate of art in modernity, and to be the necessary conclusion to be drawn by anyone working in the aesthetic tradition originating in Romanticism. By contrast, others have argued influentially that we should give up the concept of art altogether, and work with non-aesthetic categories, the assemblages of an avant-garde that has finally broken free of the confinement of the creative and the playful within aesthetic institutions.[38] Within this living debate, therefore, Romanticism is still profitably understood as being, among other things, the fullest expression of aesthetic possibility. Its standard-bearer in this respect is the autonomy of poetry.

---

38 For two usefully contrasting recent accounts of the legacy of the aesthetic, see Terry Eagleton, *The Ideology of the Aesthetic* (Oxford: Blackwell, 1990) and Isobel Armstrong, *The Radical Aesthetic* (Oxford: Blackwell, 2000).

Transformations of the novel – I

DEIDRE LYNCH

The novelist in the crowd

In the third volume of Mary Robinson's *Walsingham* (1797), the eponymous hero – who by this point has been disinherited, jilted and jailed, and whose existence, he observes, has been 'one perpetual scene of trial' – visits the Library on the North Parade at Bath. Walsingham's presence in this fashionable setting gives Robinson a pretext for putting fashion on trial and for assessing, in particular, how the smart set discuss novels. The results are discouraging. First, the visitors thronging the Library prove their sophistication by deriding the output of what they call 'the modern novel-mill'. Then real-life popular novelist of the late eighteenth century Courtney Melmoth arrives for a cameo appearance, in time to enable Robinson to tout his 'many excellent and beautiful productions', but also in time to experience the insolence of his potential readership.[1] In fact, modern novels are targeted for insult whenever Walsingham's memoirs deal with fashionable society, and, at their worst, those insults implicate the genre's very future. This is why, when, in this episode, a certain Lady Arabella wonders whether 'there will be any books in another century' and adds, giggling, that '[i]t would be monstrous comical if they should be totally exploded', the hero is goaded into making a characteristically Romantic claim for the causal relation between imaginative literature and historical change: the claim that literature brings into being the posterity that reads it. Robinson reminds her readers of the supposition that Jean-Jacques Rousseau was the 'author' of the French Revolution when Walsingham declares that were it not for such authors 'the earth had still been shackled by tyranny and superstition'.[2]

---

1 Mary Robinson, *Walsingham, or, The Pupil of Nature* (Peterborough, Ontario: Broadview, 2003), pp. 335; 336.
2 Robinson, *Walsingham*, pp. 339; 347.

Robinson's virtuous characters have been obliged before this to vindicate modern books – contemporary novels particularly. In *Walsingham*'s second volume the woman who visits the hero in his prison brings him novels by Courtney Melmoth, Frances Burney and Charlotte Smith and comments, in an only half self-deprecating way, on how she is 'old-fashioned enough' to value living writers as well as those in their sepulchres. Her comment chimes with one made in Smith's *Desmond*. In language recalling Desmond's critique of Edmund Burke for touting a politics that over-values prejudice and precedent, Smith's heroine, Geraldine Verney, contests the current habit of extending toward the mid-century works of Samuel Richardson 'a kind of hereditary prescriptive deference', at the expense of fictions of the present day.[3]

I begin with these self-referencing moments in *Desmond* and *Walsingham* because of the way they complicate both the standard account of 'the rise of the novel' and also the newer story that of late has come to supplement that familiar narrative of the genre's fortunes: the story of the Romantic-period upturn in rates of production and consumption that signalled the novel's 'quantitative' rather than qualitative rise.[4] In fact, as Robinson's Duchess of Riversford suggests with her reference to the 'novel-mill', readerly demand in the last three decades of the eighteenth century had soared, and to the point where novel writers seemed perforce to have adopted the techniques of industrialized mass reproduction. To many of the reviewers of the period, modern novels appeared, accordingly, not only to be purchased but also to be *made* in bulk, as if they were stamped out by machines. At the same time, as the examples from Robinson and Smith also suggest, such commentaries on the novel's popularity, or vulgarity, went hand in hand with a contrasting view of the novel's relation to modernity. That alternative view registers the consequences of the genre's consolidation, of those processes by which a diverse roster of prose fictions were retroactively unified under a common heading. It registers how by the last three decades of the century 'the British novel' had not only come to constitute a recognized category of writing (as registered by reviews and advertisements), but had also, repackaged, begun to acquire a history and canon of its own.

---

3 Robinson, *Walsingham*, p. 248; Charlotte Smith, *Desmond*, ed. Antje Blank and Janet Todd (Peterborough, Ontario: Broadview, 2001), p. 225.

4 'New novel titles are nearly three times more numerous in 1790 than in 1750, and the estimated total novel production, including all reprints, increased by a factor of four in the same period': James Raven, *Judging New Wealth* (Oxford: Clarendon Press, 1992), p. 38.

In 1775, for instance, the bookseller Francis Noble began to reprint *Roxana*, *Moll Flanders* and *Journal of the Plague Year* and packaged these texts – hitherto presented as autobiographies, histories or position papers on public policy – as the '*novels* of Daniel Defoe'. By making Defoe a 'novelist' Noble was not only contributing to the novel's making. He was also, crucially, helping to present the novel as a form whose best and classic days lay behind it, with its back list, and contributing to that 'hereditary prescriptive deference' of which Smith's heroine complains.

Encountering Walsingham's vindication of the Enlightenment purveyed by contemporary writing, one might be persuaded that the novelist was the instrument through which modernity had been and would be made. But one might as easily decide, especially after consulting the reviews, that by the century's end the novel was anything but a novelty. One might con-clude that, at this moment when novels appeared to enter the world in amorphous 'hordes' or 'swarms', the genre's fate – and at the exact moment that it attained the critical mass that made it a genre – was to go over the same ground again and again. To analyse such ambiguities in fiction's Romantic-era ascent to cultural hegemony, this chapter engages repeatedly with the sense of crowding that figures such as Robinson and Smith convey. By representing the bustle of the Library at Bath, Robinson brings home to her readers the fact that they too do their novel reading in a crowd. Self-consciousness in this half-arch, half-embarrassed style seems irresistible to many writers of this period, as if such moments of self-reflexivity gave them a way of acknowledging that the generic terrain of the novel had come into being as an already over-occupied territory. This chapter investigates those acknowledgements, and the writers' ways of intimating that a contem-porary preoccupation with old novels – and indeed a preoccupation with remembering old literature of all sorts – had created a situation in which current writing would perforce be crowded out by its precursors. Already in 1778 Burney prefaces *Evelina* by remarking the risks of pursuing a path previously traced by Johnson, Rousseau, Richardson, Fielding and Smollett: 'though they have rendered the path plain, they have left it barren'.[5] Such perceptions of overcrowding are, I shall argue, crucial to the transform-ations that, by the era of Walter Scott and Jane Austen, would produce 'the British novel' and bring it into being as a Romantic production.

---

5 Fanny Burney, *Evelina, or, the History of a Young Lady's Entrance into the World*, ed. Edward A. Bloom (Oxford: Oxford University Press, 1968), p. 9.

Given the High Modernist equation of woman and mass culture, it is predictable that modern scholars often treat the last three decades of the eighteenth century, an era when women novelists accounted for more new titles than ever before, as if they mattered only for their demonstration of 'the dark side of the reproductive power of printing and writing'.[6] Critical surveys of the novel frequently hurry past these decades to arrive more expeditiously at the works of Austen and Scott. The Waverley Series and *Emma* offer critics a sure foothold: compared with books such as *Walsingham* and *Desmond*, they feel reassuringly, solidly, literary. Nonetheless, Robinson, Smith and their late eighteenth-century contemporaries pioneer exactly the themes (investigations of perverse desire, the legacy, persons' relation to social context or 'the system'), the forms (novels of manners and Gothic romances) and the formal innovations (the free indirect discourse that an omniscient narrator employs to render a character's hidden mental life) that will remain central to novel writing through the nineteenth century. In many respects the later eighteenth-century novelist's achievements are the consequence of her reflections on these conditions of overcrowding and on the dislocations of the personal, the crises of self-possession and subjectivity, that they cause. The early history of the Romantic novel thus poses a particular challenge to scholars. It calls on us to move between a traditionally conceived history of literature and the history of the book market: between qualitative and quantitative registers of change and between the stories that the texts tell and the stories that the numbers tell.

For this reason it also calls on us to keep track of two sets of watershed dates. On the one hand, 1765 – when Horace Walpole reissued *The Castle of Otranto*, confessed to its authorship and thereby converted an antiquarian hoax into a renovated modern 'romance'; 1778 – the year of *Evelina* and the advent of what reviewers would herald as the 'Burney school' of novelists; and 1794 – when William Godwin in *Things As They Are, or The Adventures of Caleb Williams* brought into prominence the political novel, the form designed to expose how politics, in its new guise as ideology, insinuates itself into persons' most private dispositions. On the other hand, 1774 – when, in the case of Becket vs. Donaldson, the Law Lords' decision against booksellers' claims to perpetual copyright paved the way, in the immediate term, for a booming trade in reprints and, in the longer term, for new concepts of 'literature', 'literary tradition' and Britons' 'cultural heritage';

---

6 Ina Ferris, *The Achievement of Literary Authority: Gender, History, and the Waverley Novels* (Ithaca, NY: Cornell University Press, 1991), p. 42.

1779 – when subscribers to James Harrison's *Novelist's Magazine* began to acquire on the instalment plan complete 'libraries' of novels whose classic and classy credentials the *Magazine* had ratified by selecting them for reprinting; and 1784 – when William Lane founded his empire of circulating libraries and radically extended readers' access to fiction for hire.

These chronologies may be misleading, however. Both may place too much weight on proper names, whether authors' or booksellers'. To gauge how fiction changed as it came to be (in Anna Barbauld's words) 'furnished from the press, rather as a regular and necessary supply, than as an occasional gratification', it is more fruitful to think about crowds and about how, in this era of urbanization, a new mass politics, the Gordon Riots and the fall of the Bastille, crowds seemed as never before to swallow up individual identities and agency.[7] Thinking about crowd phenomena we approach more closely to how the novel market – and the genre's fortunes – appeared in the period, how they appeared out of control, because, in fact, no *one*, no individual, could control them.

Fashions in feeling and novels of manners

Entrepreneurs such as James Harrison encouraged their clients to consider their library acquisitions as cultural capital, badges of their refinement and upward social mobility. Lavishly illustrated, the works designed to 'recommend virtue' that Harrison's *Novelist's Library* preserved were also, it was hinted, books to furnish a room.[8] The canon-making creating and elevating 'the' novel thus participated in the paradoxes of the period's new consumerism. It registered the unsettling effect that new spending patterns had on old understandings of the cultural pecking order. Although much fiction of the period presents itself as the equipage necessary for tasteful lifestyles or even as a source of inside information on the lives of the genteel, within its pages it frequently represents gentility as something mere money cannot buy. Indeed, well into the nineteenth century, novel reading will provide British culture with its chief example of the contagiousness of consumer desire *and* provide consumers with the mechanism that they will use to distance themselves from other people's vulgar, overly conspicuous consumption. The readerly pleasure afforded to those whose consumerism

---

7 Anna Laetitia Barbauld (ed.), *The British Novelists* (London: F. C. and J. Rivington, 1810), vol. I, p. 38.
8 Robert D. Mayo, *The English Novel in the Magazines, 1740–1815* (Evanston, IL: Northwestern University Press, 1962), p. 366.

takes the refined form of transactions with books hinges, repeatedly in the history of the novel, on novelists' satiric portraits of their characters' *mis*-readings: those practised by the parvenu who misconstrues status symbols or by the fashion victim whose quest for personal distinction leaves her looking exactly like everyone else. Frances Burney's *Cecilia* (1782) thus includes in its survey of London's fashionable follies the sect of the Insen-sibilists, who, in the wake of their discovery that it is vulgar and common to be pleased, forego happiness and yet continue to pay for the theatre tickets that enable them to be visibly disgusted in all the best places. The novel's peculiar, love–hate relation to consumerism was crucial to the thematic and formal innovations that novelists of manners such as Burney introduced into the genre. Crucial too was the legacy of sentimentalism, a phenom-enon whose relation to the late eighteenth-century marketplace merits some analysis.

The eighteenth century made contradictory claims for sentiment – con-ceiving of feelings both as a currency that passed from person to person and as exclusive properties that proved the possessor's refinement. Sentimental fiction – through its modelling of a language of the heart and its compiling of the cor-respondence (to recall a pun that Samuel Richardson doted on) that it casts as the most appropriate vehicle for such expressions of sincerity – exemplifies and enacts the virtues of connection. Richardson's *Clarissa* harries its reader not only into yielding its suffering heroine the tribute of the tears but also into pooling those tears with those shed by men and women of feeling within the text. Sympathy operates as a solvent. It breaks down the barriers segregating one person's emotions from another's and the barriers segregating book from world. For the generation of nov-elists after Richardson, who shift novels away from the well-shaped, providential plots favoured by their predecessors, and towards plotting that takes what shape it can claim from a protagonist's desire for attachment and affiliation, the chronicle of fellow feeling becomes the medium for new modes of social scansion. In Henry Mackenzie's *The Man of Feeling* (1771), for instance, Old Edwards recounts to Harley, the hero, a heart-wrenching story that begins with Edwards's eviction from his farm at the hands of a covetous landlord, moves to his capture by a press gang, and ends with his witnessing of the atrocities that an equally covetous British Army commits in the Indies. Flogged for refusing to assist in torturing an 'old Indian', Old Edwards is nursed by the man he spared, who assures the Englishman that he must have an 'Indian heart'. Individuals have opportunities to emote across borders in the Man of Feeling's milieu. In this milieu, too, local deeds have, willy-nilly, global implications.[9] In the last third of the eighteenth century, numerous novelists arrange to embed sentimental scenarios within a new travelogue form. Philanthropic ramblers, who take hearts and wallets on their travels, abound in a novelistic landscape that now, thanks in part to the conviction that sensibility can supply the framework for cross-cultural investigations, takes in wider, trans-national vistas.

But these efforts to parse the local and global and to use feeling to both annul and mark the differences separating diverse sectors of the social body (philanthropists, on the one hand, and those who regale them with tales of woe, on the other) coexist with an alternative conception of sensibility. That capacity for feeling is also cast as the exclusive property of an exceptional being. Minutely annotating their protagonists' blushes, making liberal use throughout their texts of ellipses and dashes which suggest how very much remains *unsaid*, the sentimental novelists often suggest that feeling is too natural and artless, too private and individual, to be adequately conveyed by language – an artificial medium and, worse, an irrevocably social one. In *Julia de Roubigné* (1779), Mackenzie, in his guise as the 'editor' of a correspondence that records Julia's guilty love, her husband's lust for vengeance and her childhood sweetheart's experience of the Caribbean slave economy, complains of the difficulty he has had in determining the proper sequence in which to present these letters: 'they are made up of sentiment, which narrative would destroy'. The *Critical Review* had earlier written of *The Man of Feeling* that 'there is not indeed fable [plot] enough in this volume to keep up the attention of the majority of novel readers'.[10] Within the emergent code that identified novel reading's popularity with its debasement, this was a compliment.

Ironically, though, from the 1770s through the 1790s the forms and rhetorics of sentimental effusions proved to be especially amenable to mass replication and marketing. Mackenzie's *Julia* is, of course, merely one in a crowd of alternately bowdlerizing and jacobinizing rewritings of Rousseau's *Julie* and, as such, might appropriately be aligned with the numerous imitations of Laurence Sterne's *A Sentimental Journey* and continuations of Goethe's *Werther* that also exasperated reviewers in these decades. Examination of the period's magazines, which marketed sentimental fiction

9 Henry Mackenzie, *The Man of Feeling*, ed. Brian Vickers (Oxford: Oxford University Press, 2001), p. 70.
10 Henry Mackenzie, *Julia de Roubigné*, ed. Susan Manning (East Lothian: Tuckwell Press, 1999), p. 5; *Critical Review* 31 (June 1771), 482–3.

as well as fashion news to their readers, also belies the claim that the appreciation of sensibility was confined to the discerning few. Indeed magazines like the *Lady's* (founded 1770) were eager to boost their output of that fiction which was now demanded 'as a regular and necessary supply'. Relying on their semi-official exemption from copyright, they made it simple for amateur contributors to conflate composing and copying and to submit as their own fictions that had long since been published elsewhere. Under such conditions, sensibility perforce became a watchword for the hackneyed and ersatz, as well as for the sincere. A contributor to a 1793 periodical lamented this irony in an address to Sterne's narrator and alter ego: 'Yorick! indignant I behold / Such spendthrifts of thy genuine gold!'[11]

It was, in part, by engaging such ironies in the story of feeling that a series of fictions that extends from *Evelina* through the works of Charlotte Smith, to Maria Edgeworth's *Belinda* (1801) established the characteristic settings, story lines and formal devices of the novel of manners. They made that story one of inner meaning and developed a new syntax for inexpressible psychological processes. At the same time, they arranged matters so that this inward turn of the novel would become visible only against a backdrop constituted by scenes of consumption – by a market that promised fashion-conscious consumers that, with the right purchases, they might redesign themselves from the outside in. In later eighteenth-century print culture, romance and commerce commingled comfortably: the engraver Thomas Stothard's illustrations for the works reprinted in *The Novelist's Magazine* did double duty promoting the latest fashions; Edward Burney both illustrated his cousin's works and designed fashion plates for ladies' pocket books. In the meantime, the novelists whose works Stothard and Burney illustrated addressed head on just this confusion of amatory and consumer desire and of inner and outer worth.[12] The heroines of the courtship novels written under the Romantic mandate which valorizes literature as the vehicle of intimate, inner truths typically occupy the mortifying position in which Edgeworth's Belinda is found when, attending a modish masquerade, she overhears the one man she admires complain of how, during the last social season, Belinda Portman was '"hawked about every where ... Belinda

---

11 'To Sensibility', in Simon Olivebranch [pseud.], *The Looker-On: A Periodical Paper*, vol. III (London: G. G. and J. Robinson, 1795), p. 216; originally published 23 June 1793.
12 On Burney and Stothard, see Neil McKendrick et al., *The Birth of a Consumer Society* (Bloomington: Indiana University Press, 1982), p. 47 n. 42.

Portman, and her accomplishments, ... were as well advertised, as Packwood's razor strops"'.[13] Almost fifty years later readers will listen in as Jane Eyre laments Rochester's determination to outfit her in the latest fashions – ' "I will not be your English Céline Varens" ', she declares – and expresses her alienation from the version of herself she confronts when she faces that finery. Those continuities suggest the longevity of that political project which Nancy Armstrong ascribes to the novel and which consists in contrasting domestic woman who is all inner life with an aristocratic woman wholly devoted to bodily display.[14] They also suggest, however, that, in order to valorize those emotional depths, the novel must write the heroine's story as one of mistaken identity – she must appear as those *other* women do – and it must arrange to give the reader, whose discernment is thereby flattered, the inside knowledge that might remedy that mistake. The vehicle of that knowledge is frequently free indirect discourse, the device through which a third-person narrator mimes the unspoken mental life of a character, and the stock in trade of Burney (in works postdating the epistolary *Evelina*), Smith, Edgeworth and, of course, Jane Austen.

All these novelists satirize social emulation: the fashion victim whose pursuit of self-gratification in the theatre of consumerism leaves her (like *Cecilia*'s Insensibilists) without much of a self to call her own. At the same time, all thrust their heroines into that milieu that puts the unique and personal at risk. The crowd – the throng of minor characters whom a heroine encounters in public places, who spy on her actions, misrepresent her intentions or even become the physical obstacle preventing her from catching the eye of the man she loves – serves as a figure for all that complicates the exercise of individual agency.

Sentimental fiction is often said to be a casualty of the reaction against the French Revolution – finished off by critics and parodists who connected social disorder to unrestrained desire and felt it was particular folly to let 'women plead their feelings' (to quote the magistrate who, in Mary Wollstonecraft's *The Wrongs of Woman* (1798), crushes the heroine's hopes for a release from her marriage).[15] Correspondingly, the formal

---

13 Maria Edgeworth, *Belinda*, ed. Kathryn J. Kirkpatrick (Oxford: Oxford University Press, 1994), p. 25.

14 Charlotte Brontë, *Jane Eyre*, ed. Margaret Smith (Oxford: Oxford University Press, 1975), pp. 272–7; Nancy Armstrong, *Desire and Domestic Fiction* (New York: Oxford University Press, 1987).

15 Wollstonecraft, *The Wrongs of Woman*, ed. Gary Kelly (Oxford: Oxford University Press, 1976), p. 198.

transformations that, after the 1790s, redeemed the novel from its degraded position in the generic hierarchy have been attributed to the revisionary efforts made by conservative novelists. Redeeming fiction from sentimental conventions which, if they had not actually caused the Revolution, had certainly gone stale, and preparing the ground for nineteenth-century realism, these authors are said to have disciplined feeling by putting it under social supervision. They pointedly ensured, for instance, that the letters that had been self-expressive sensibility's vehicle would be marginalized within their novels, introduced as evidence, perhaps, but no longer made the medium of a plot's unfolding. They lodged authority not with individual characters but with the reassuringly impersonal omniscient narrator whose voice was that of the social consensus.[16]

A longer view, however, might suggest a differently inflected account of the fate of the rhetoric of sensibility. One might recall that sensibility had from the start led a double life, in representing both what was distinctively individual and what was conventionally commonplace, and one might consider how the free indirect discourse of the Burney school remedied that impasse. It made the personal effects – the sense of self – conveyed in fiction a more personal, a more exclusive and privatized property than ever before. In novels that hinge on the ironic discrepancy between a heroine's true self and the misconstructions that 'the world' puts on appearances, reader and character are drawn together by a sympathetic bond of secret-sharing. That bond feels flatteringly exclusive, and that knowledge of character seems an arcane knowledge imparted in confidence, thanks to the irony that the fiction mobilizes. Playing to the insecurities of a reader all too aware of doing her reading in a crowd, it distinguishes this discriminating reader from those who take the heroine at face value. Ironies sort out readers and their readings. Possessive pleasures of just this sort are provided by the handling of point of view in *Sense and Sensibility* (1811) – to cite merely one of the instances in which Jane Austen helped put the finishing touches on sentiment's makeover. Austen ensures that it is Elinor Dashwood, whose romantic disappointment remains for much of the novel a secret to which the reader alone is privy, who is privileged as her real heroine, and not Elinor's sister Marianne, whose pathos-filled letters to Willoughby connect her to the sentimental

---

16 For these arguments see Marilyn Butler, *Jane Austen and the War of Ideas*, 2nd edn (Oxford: Oxford University Press, 1987), and Nicola Watson, *Revolution and the Form of the British Novel, 1790–1825* (Oxford: Clarendon Press, 1994).

tradition, and whose demonstrativeness makes her story public property for the gossips. Elinor feels more deeply, but does not express her feelings in her letters.

Paring down the social panoramas and crowded canvasses favoured by her predecessors in the novel of manners, Austen nonetheless discerned the appeal that the form exerted for a culture of copies. Novels of manners engage the problem of identifying real feeling in a context where all, potentially, are adept in the formulae of polite exchange, and the problem of sorting out the self's authentic desires from those that are merely the fashion. This relocation of narrative interest so that it lies less with the individual's preservation of her virtue and lies more, in what, retroactively, we call a Romantic manner, with our querying of her desire, is especially visible in the 1790s. In that decade, fictions of all stripes seem to discover new modes of desiring: moving beyond the exploration of desire in relation to prohibitions that are removed or satisfactions that are obtained, they engage desire as perversity, self-torment and a secret to be extracted. This engagement produces such figures as Caleb Williams, whose effort to associate himself with a project of impartial truth-telling is belied by his eroticizing of the dangers of his enterprise; or Miss Milner in Elizabeth Inchbald's *A Simple Story* (1791) who, unwilling to content herself with love merely, sets out to acquire proof that she is beloved in spite of her faults; or Robinson's Walsingham, a self-styled 'involuntary seducer', who, reluctantly but reliably, does violence to the ladies he loves. Much literary history has traced how novels (Gothic fiction especially) register, often punitively, the crystallizing of new sexual identities at the end of the century, when, as Michel Foucault suggested, a new sub-race of transgressors, different from libertines of the past, carried their infamy before a newly professionalized medical establishment: *Walsingham* in particular might plausibly join Matthew Lewis's 1796 *The Monk* (whose interest in transvestism it shares) as documentary evidence of this process.[17] But one might in addition remark the reassurance that such explorations of what might be individual about desire supply for a culture troubled by the growth of consumerism and by the increasing impersonality of the satisfactions the market provided.

17 Robinson, *Walsingham*, vol. IV, p. 73; Michel Foucault, *The History of Sexuality: Volume One*, trans. Robert Hurley (New York: Vintage, 1980).

Confession and public polemic in the memoir-novel

If the early novels of manners aim to privatize the truths of the self, other new forms of fiction register in a different manner the threat a culture industry in overdrive poses to the boundaries of the individual. Intent on intervening into public sphere debate, the 'Jacobin' novels of the 1790s especially, discern in this threat an opportunity – to 'write a tale that shall constitute an epoch in the mind of the reader'.[18] Working, as the Burney school do, with the legacy of sentimentalism, the Jacobins also cast subjectivity as the structuring principle for fiction. But, fascinated with political persuasion, they often do so in works whose in-set narratives dramatize the act of polemicizing and render personal relationships as a clash of philosophies. Rescripting the grand narratives of political and social history as the private histories of *mental* revolutions, they make first-person narration their vehicle of choice. Subjectivity in this context therefore takes the form of a voice that is heard directly. It is not what it is in the novels of manners, where the recourse to the free indirect style seems predicated on the notion that the very act of communication involves a diminution of consciousness – it is not a voice that one may overhear only. In fact, the memoir novels penned by Godwin (e.g. *Things As They Are*; *St Leon* (1799)), and by writers inspired by his example, Mary Hays (*Emma Courtney* (1796) and *The Victim of Prejudice* (1799)) and the American Charles Brockden Brown (*Wieland* (1798), *Arthur Mervyn* (1799), and *Memoirs of Carwin the Biloquist* (1804)) mobilize the autobiographical and intimate in strangely extroverted, public ways.

The redeployment of first-person narration that shapes these texts, and which likewise inspires Edgeworth in *Castle Rackrent* (1800), in the Lady Delacour section of *Belinda*, in *Ennui* (1809) and in *Harrington* (1817), represents, in part, this era's belated engagement with the legacy of Defoe. Thus, though ostensibly writing at the end of the sixteenth century, Godwin's St Leon refers in his memoir to stories of 'wretched mariners' that sound much like Defoe's and indeed enacts his Robinsonade in a superlatively solitary key: having found the secret of immortality, St Leon is forced to see himself as belonging to a species entirely distinct from that of other humans, his own mortal children included.[19] These memoir

18 William Godwin, *Caleb Williams, or, Things as They Are*, ed. Maurice Hindle (London: Penguin, 1988), p. 350.
19 William Godwin, *St Leon: A Tale of the Sixteenth Century*, ed. William D. Brewer (Peterborough, Ontario: Broadview Press, 2006), p. 323.

novels also recreate the rhetorical instability that undermines the Defoe protagonists' claim to be just what and who they say they are. What interests Defoe's turn-of-the-century readers is the strangely self-cancelling manner in which his narrator tells all, the way in which the subjectivity of this narrator becomes hollowed out by the weight of history. In 1832 Godwin recalled how he had prepared to write *Things As They Are* by rereading now-classic novels and noted that he had done so without feeling in 'danger of servilely copying my predecessors', so sure was he that he possessed 'a vein of thinking that was properly my own'; but a counter-example that belies this confidence in individual distinction is supplied by his narrator, Caleb, who begins his 'memoirs with the idea of vindicating my character', and finds that 'I have now no character that I wish to vindicate'.[20] In Edgeworth's hands, as the memoirs of the Irishmen 'honest' Thady and Lord Glenthorn (Christy Donoghoe before he was changed at nurse) suggest, that precariousness of personality can represent a specifically colonial disease.

The unsettling effects of these memoirs derives not only from the way in which their inscriptions of the self are self-defeating (in a stronger sense than is usual) but also from their oddities of tone. The Jacobins, especially, manage to sound simultaneously melodramatic and cerebral, high-minded and ludicrously indiscreet. This is because their protagonist brings a verit-able science of the passions to bear on the case history of his own mind. His 'metaphysical dissecting knife' readied, he is an anatomist of his self. Made up of three sets of letters, exchanged, respectively, between the heroine and her confidante, the man-of-the-people hero and his confidant, and the aristocratic villain and his brother rake, Thomas Holcroft's *Anna St Ives* (1792) looks formally conservative compared to the fictions of his political fellow-travellers. Nonetheless, the reaction this book's Lovelacean villain has to the memorandum that his fiancée Anna writes up for him – which, the product of her determination to 'shew my heart unveiled, undisguised', recounts the history of her erotic preference for the son of her father's steward – predicts how Holcroft's contemporaries would see the memoir fictions. Clifton writes that Anna's 'unabashed justification of all she has said ... thought and ... done [is] not to be paralleled in the records of female extravagance'.[21] The boldest of the decade's interrogations of

---

20 Godwin, *Caleb Williams*, pp. 351; 337.
21 Thomas Holcroft, *Anna St Ives*, ed. Peter Faulkner (Oxford: Oxford University Press, 1970), pp. 260; 272. The phrase 'metaphysical dissecting knife' is Godwin's: *Caleb Williams*, p. 51.

public/private boundaries, Mary Hays's *Memoirs of Emma Courtney*, was upon publication excoriated for just this failure, to be abashed. Emma's memoirs contribute to that generic hybrid developed by numerous eighteenth-century women writers as they transposed educational treatises into fictional form. Her story, which makes much of her reading, first in fiction, then in sterner stuff, and then, fatefully, in the *Julie* of Rousseau, resembles those narratives in demonstrating how a mode of education that carries the mark of gender and serves to give a woman 'a sexual character' will invariably prove a mis-education. Hays's experiment in genre mixing went further, however. The epistolary sections of Emma's memoir incorporate the forlorn love letters Hays herself had written to the Cambridge mathematician William Frend. That mingling of the author's autobiography with fiction about an autobiographer enables Hays to explore the relationship between personal experience and the social conventions – narrative paradigms – through which the personal is understood. The author's self-exposure thus raises exactly the questions about how the paper world of representation relates to action which the term *political novel* implies.[22]

To the reading public of 1796, however, Hays's experiment with form looked like immodesty, and nothing more. A comparable response greeted *The Wrongs of Woman* after Godwin's biography of Wollstonecraft tactlessly clarified the parallels between the affair Wollstonecraft's heroine, tellingly named Maria, has with Darnford and the one Wollstonecraft had had with Gilbert Imlay.[23] But in their indiscreet autobiographical dimensions Emma's and Maria's stories should each be seen as rigorously consummating the logic of the memoir novel, precisely through this looping back that applies to the authors themselves the form's pivotal insight. For all their protagonists' isolation and egotism (the effects of the first-person form), these are works in which, unremittingly, the social surfaces in the most private recesses of character. *Things As They Are* thus portrays ideology's internalization in Caleb, whose vindication of his character unravels as he trades roles with his aristocratic persecutor: Caleb identifies with the latter's power to oppress and passes on to him his role as victim. Wollstonecraft and Hays lay bare Maria's and Emma Courtney's internalization of a script of erotic

---

22 On political novels, see Tillotama Rajan, 'Wollstonecraft and Godwin: Reading the Secrets of the Political Novel' in *The Supplement of Reading* (Ithaca, NY: Cornell University Press, 1990).

23 Wollstonecraft's and Hays's experiments with confessional form are debunked in Elizabeth Hamilton's satiric tale of Bridgetina Botherim, the would-be romantic heroine of *Memoirs of Modern Philosophers* (1800).

victimhood – associated in both cases with the authors' own reading of Rousseau – which predisposes women for betrayal.

Notably, the two women novelists authorize their heroines' self-revelations by casting them as the fulfilment of their maternal duty. They legitimate their memoirs of disastrous romance as vehicles of a younger generation's education: Emma addresses hers to her adopted son; Maria, to her daughter. That the memoir is made to double as a letter to the future, a future that may be emancipated from things as they are, suggests the novelists' desire to salvage the notion of progress, their exploration of psychological blockage notwithstanding. At the same time, however, this reframing of their experience entangles education and inheritance in a way that reinforces the resemblance that connects Hays's and Wollstonecraft's texts to a line of female-authored sentimental fiction that extends from *Evelina* to *A Simple Story* and that makes maternal guilt the central, melancholy lesson of a daughter's education. The interpretive crux for much of this fiction concerns a heroine's relation to her dead or a lost mother, a mother who has not properly passed on the lessons that are the sole inheritance she can give her child or who has not properly passed on, period. When the mother dies too soon, either her daughter is dispossessed of the educational legacy that would enable her to survive, or she dies herself in attempting to emulate that impossible example of virtuous self-effacement. Alternatively, when the mother sins, her daughter's very existence keeps alive the memory of her illicit sexuality.[24] By associating themselves with a maternal inheritance to be transmitted to posterity, Hays's *Emma* and Wollstonecraft's *The Wrongs of Woman* look backward as well as forward and represent themselves as successors to this line of novels. This means that the vision of progress and the valorization of the judgement of the informed individual that are embedded in their address to the future clash with a sense of the weight of history and of past generations. Enlightened rationality and Gothic melancholy become the recto and verso of the same page.

Gothic crises of self-possession

Within Jacobin and sentimental writings alike, then, the problem of literary precedent and the problem of the legacy are hard to tell apart. The terms of

---

24 See April Alliston, 'The Value of a Literary Legacy: Retracing the Transmission of Value through Female Lines', *Yale Journal of Criticism* 4 (1990), 109–27.

reference that determine how a late eighteenth-century heroine employs her experience loom out of another's past or are supplied by books (as the many heroines of the 1790s whose lives are changed by their fateful readings of Rousseau can attest). It was left to the period's Gothic fictions to develop the repertory of stock situations that thereafter would betoken the horrors of such reiteration. Under tutelage offered by Walpole's *Otranto* and, more influentially, by Clara Reeve's *The Old English Baron* (1777) and Sophia Lee's *The Recess; or, A Tale of Other Times* (1783–5), the public quickly grew accustomed to haunted castles, cavern prisons incarcerating inmates whose existence had been forgotten, portraits of dead ancestors and time-worn, musty manuscripts. Those settings and props supplied a shorthand for conveying the powers of the past: the past's refusal to go away, notwith-standing a linear scheme for ordering time that declared certain forms of violence and doctrinal compulsion to have been superseded by the advent of a Protestant civil society. Gothic fictions – through their representation of the staying power of things (heirlooms and houses) and through the resistance to continuous narration that they manifest at a formal level – present a past that is something more malign than a mere prologue to the enlightened present. (In the Gothic, the past does not stay past; instead, we might say, the dead who do not know their place start crowding out the living.) And, although Walpole, when prefacing *Otranto*, touted the innovations informing his 'modern' romance, the fact is that his novelty also assisted in a romance revival. *Otranto* and its successors demonstrate how Gothic romance served Romantic-period culture as a site for exploring the more troubling implications of the eighteenth century's invention of the vernacular literary canon and also of the 'hereditary prescriptive deference' that British Literature's now firmly canonized past masters might exact.

Audiences came to this form for more of the strange delights of artificial grief provided by sentimental fiction. They also came for the pleasures of regression: to be enthralled by the superstitions discouraged by an age of reason. At the same time, by virtue of their very popularity, their capacity to simultaneously put thousands of readers on the rack of suspense, Gothic novels appeared, especially to detractors, to be the pre-eminent instanti-ation of modern media. They appeared to participate in a quintessentially modern project of crowd control. In the nightmarish visions a pundit like Coleridge conjures up when he considers the individual who is subjected to, and entranced by, mass culture, William Lane's stable of Minerva Press authors figure prominently. Such oneiric accounts of reading as mass experience are both projected onto the Gothic and projected by it.

Participating in the reflexivity prompting so many contemporaries to write about reading, Gothic writers arrange it so that their audiences invariably encounter their doubles within the texts they consume, in the guise of characters who while away their nights reading old romances that tell hair-raising tales of supernatural occurrences. Their protagonist is typically forced to live over again what her progenitors have already experienced, and their reader is not exempted from such repetition compulsions.

The powers the late eighteenth century ascribed to the book are fore-grounded in multiple ways by Ann Radcliffe. Her subject in works such as *The Romance of the Forest* (1791) or *The Mysteries of Udolpho: A Romance* (1794) is, as for the novelists of manners, the mortification undergone by a friendless heroine adrift in the marriage market. But Radcliffe uses her war-torn, banditti-ridden settings in ways that unveil the potential for terror that subsists within women's everyday social intercourse: she leaves open the possibility that this reference to mortification might be literalized. Radcliffe's subject is also, again as for the novelist of manners, the drama of inner feeling – which she treats in a manner that typifies how the Gothic simultaneously recreates archaic romance and deploys the literary tech-niques associated with a new species of novel. The swashbuckling adven-tures and mysterious encounters with the other-worldly which compose the Radcliffean plot are filtered through the heroine's consciousness, shifted onto a register of privacy to which the author's free indirect discourse gives the reader access. And, crucially, Radcliffe's habit of inserting into her prose the poetry that her protagonist composes extemporaneously allies this heroine's exceptional sensibility with her literacy. Punctuated with these lyric effusions, and embellished as well with epigraphs extracted from that poetic canon which, in the wake of the Lords' decision in Becket vs. Donaldson, was being repackaged as every Briton's cultural heritage, these novels (like those of Smith, Robinson, Lewis and, later, Scott) come to resemble the period's anthologies and to approximate their social functions. Novels 'interspersed with pieces of poetry' (to quote the promotional lan-guage of their title-pages) invite consumers to distinguish themselves from the mass of novel-readers, for to tolerate the author's suspension of a spine-tingling plot, to savour the poetic beauties supplied in its place, is to manifest one's taste.[25]

25 Leah Price, *The Anthology and the Rise of the Novel* (Cambridge: Cambridge University Press, 2000), pp. 91–7.

Still, this lyricizing of the novel represents something more than a bid for the literariness that might elevate the novel in the generic hierarchy. It has a second effect, since the epigraphs to the chapters seem, in appearing out of nowhere, and in their detachment from an originating context, *apparitions*. Similarly, for the characters, to be possessed of a poetic imagination is almost by definition to be haunted: the moods of reverie that inspire their verse, arrive unbidden, as inexplicable forces. The texts' pieces of poetry are framed thereby as equivalents of the other-worldly communications that are standard plot elements: equivalents of the spectral voices that boom from the beyond or the enigmatic music that a Gothic protagonist hears from her prison and whose origin she is unable to determine. British Literature – at the very moment of its inception, when developments in copyright were helping invent the literary tradition by inventing the public domain – is here rendered a ghostly presence. In this way, even as they enlisted under the banner of 'romance' and allied themselves with the native, premodern or Gothic origins of modern national cultures (with, in Scott's words, the tale of tradition that celebrated 'the early valour of the fathers or the tribe'), Gothic novels put the concept of literary lineage under scrutiny.[26] Giving Sir Philip Sidney, one father of romance, a new lease on life when she introduces him as a character into *The Recess*, Lee emphatically links the novelist's enterprise to the revivalism of the Romantic period's nascent discipline of literary history. But because of the atmosphere of oppression that pervades Lee's book and because of the many proofs that her rewriting of Stuart dynastic history offers of the deadliness of a legacy, only the finest line comes to separate the literary historian's effort to possess the heritage of the dead from the effort of the dead to haunt and to possess the living.

The Gothic's presentation of the predicament of characters whose experience is mediated by precedent and who are hemmed in by others' stories thus doubles as commentary on the conditions of production afflicting novelists at the overcrowded end of the eighteenth century. In telling ways, when late eighteenth-century authors account for the provenance of their 'romances' they take pains to dissociate the narratable from the prosaic present: story is framed as the product of a dream – as in Walpole's account of the prehistory of *Otranto* – or as an antiquarian windfall, one which has tumbled out of the archive of 'other times'.

26 Sir Walter Scott, 'Essay on Romance', in *Miscellaneous Prose Works*, vol. VI (Edinburgh: Robert Cadell, 1834), p. 148.

A belated example, *Frankenstein* explains its own existence by calling up both pretexts: this book began life (Mary Shelley's 1831 Introduction states) in a dream and in others' books, the 'volumes of ghost stories . . . [that] fell into [Shelley's] hands'. Tracing his career of scientific vainglory back to its origin, Frankenstein proffers a parallel account of beginnings: for him, the fateful moment occurred when a work of medieval alchemy made an untimely appearance on the eighteenth-century stage and 'fell into' his hands.[27]

In just this manner – by interesting itself in the afterlife of words, by driving home the lesson that one can never predict the consequences of reading – the Gothic elaborated one idiom that we draw on still to specify what it means to live 'in' a society or to be 'inside' a culture. When it told tales of how superstition proved contagious for travellers who stumbled into ancient castles and were disastrously affected by their exposure to their echoing halls, or when it created mesmerizing villains, the Gothic engaged that strange mixture of activity and passivity which is at stake when persons are under an influence. Engagement with such themes has the effect of dissociating guilt and complicity from questions of intention and account-ability. The longevity of the Gothic – its place of pre-eminence in contemporary culture – might have to do with how it thereby renders self-possession both a more desirable and more unattainable goal than ever.

Conclusion: novel sociology

Of course, for critics committed to chronicling the rise of the novel, Gothic fiction, not least because it was a crowd-pleaser, stands for all that went awry with fiction in the century's closing decades. For those critics, this late eighteenth-century embrace of the supernaturally unreal and this self-consciousness about the contrivances of plotting make for a regrettable hiatus in the history of the realism that is supposed to define the novel. That lapse, we have been told, is remedied only when Austen and Scott consign to oblivion such clichés of romance (and perhaps, in addition, consign to oblivion the Jacobins' assaults on common sense or the senti-mentalists' bad faith) . These two novelists restore 'normal' psychology and 'normal' history and introduce a new ethnography of everyday life in the homeland.

27 Mary Shelley, *Frankenstein, or, The Modern Prometheus*, ed. Maurice Hindle (Harmondsworth: Penguin, 1992), pp. 6; 45.

This canonizing account bestows on Austen and Scott an immunity to fashionable influences. It intimates that these nineteenth-century novelists did their imagining in solitude, far from the madding crowds in circulating libraries. But rather than delineate the novel's late eighteenth-century history as a story of a lapse that interrupts a rise, one might note, instead, how consistently the narrative structures that writers from 1770s through the 1790s elaborated in order, alternately, to highlight and to suspend individual agency have been called on to specify 'the way we live now' – in the aftermath of that modern reorganization of the polity that sees powers of domination shift from sovereign 'persons' to 'social' institutions. Noting this, we might recognize in, for instance, the Gothic's trademark explorations of influence, unintended complicity and crowd experience the link which connects the late eighteenth-century remembering of romance to an Enlightenment history of the modern fact and the nascent social sciences. Along these lines Christopher Herbert has excavated the Gothic aspects of the nineteenth century's oft-remarked interest in the social environment, emphasizing how the concept of 'culture' that was elaborated in this period out of the legacy of the Scottish Enlightenment depends on invisible forces, on supersensible (empirically unverifiable) concepts of 'affinities' or 'influences'. Throughout their modern history, theorists of 'culture' and 'society' habitually resort to a metaphorics of ghostliness to identify the principles of coherence that produce collective patterns of feeling and behaviour and to report on the determinism exerted by socio-cultural 'contexts'. Practitioners of the social 'sciences' conjure up supernatural presences – ghosts and vampires – so as to supply themselves with displaced representations of what is otherwise impossible to image.[28]

It is no accident then, this work suggests, that a phantom that would be at home in the Castle of Otranto performs a crucial office in the capitalist system vindicated in *The Wealth of Nations*: there Adam Smith conjures up an 'invisible hand' to incarnate the force that orchestrates the actions of individual agents and makes them into a social body – that makes this society more than the sum of its parts. It is no accident, either, that, in an episode near the close of his story, St Leon sets out to bring relief to a Hungarian nation afflicted by famine and discovers that his work as a corn factor does not improve but instead brings havoc to the nation's economy: Godwin's sixteenth-century hero is obliged to discover the central lesson of

---

28 Christopher Herbert, *Culture and Anomie: Ethnographical Imagination in the Nineteenth Century* (Chicago: University of Chicago Press, 1991).

nineteenth-century political economy – the discipline that, following Smith, will locate the essence of socio-economic history in the unintended consequences of individuals' acts of agency.

St Leon, Caleb Williams, Walsingham (the 'involuntary seducer') and Victor Frankenstein all mean to benefit mankind but leave trails of corpses in their wake. Their careers suggest the obsession with unintended crime that is a hallmark of late eighteenth-century fiction in its Gothic and Jacobin modes. That obsession registers the era's quandaries – ones that, as I have shown, later eighteenth-century novelists who were conscious of beating a well worn track had special reason to contemplate – over what it means to exercise agency in the overcrowded context that is *a society*, where no one can anticipate or control the risks incurred in his inevitable encounters with others.[29]

And to a comparable extent such quandaries also preoccupy the two novelists credited with getting the genre back onto a realist track. Walter Scott's fascination with the friction between ideals of individual responsibility and notions of history as a mass experience peoples his narratives with heroes who are, as Alexander Welsh notes, perversely ready to subject themselves to the examination of the law and invite their own arrest: the Waverley hero declares himself a member of the social body whenever he acknowledges that punishment is in his own interest.[30] Jane Austen's characters are likewise deprived of the luxury of thinking of themselves as 'blameless': by setting her novels in confined localities, Austen creates worlds in which the smallest blunders have the potential to do large-scale social damage. Austen's and Scott's investigations of how social life dislocates individual agency are usually heralded as testimony to how, come the nineteenth century, novelistic realism once again managed to overthrow romance, but their interest in the limits of agency might as plausibly be seen as a legacy that these two writers receive from the sentimental, Jacobin and Gothic novelists surveyed in this chapter. After all, Scott opens *Waverley* (1814) with a moment of intertextuality that works, much as Walsingham's visit to the library did, to reconfirm that for modern novelists (as one reviewer had put it as early as 1773) there was no avoiding 'treading in each other's steps'. When Scott's narrator claims that 'Waverley' is 'an

29 On the role of this concept of 'unlimited liability' in the histories of the law and the novel, see Sandra Macpherson, 'Lovelace, Ltd.', *English Literary History* 65 (1998), 99–121.
30 Alexander Welsh, *The Hero of the Waverley Novels, With New Essays on Scott* (Princeton: Princeton University Press, 1992), pp. 213–41.

uncontaminated name', one without any historical baggage, he fibs. As Scott knows, and knows his readers know, his hero's namesakes can be encountered in both Smith's *Desmond* and Jane West's *The Loyalists* (1812). With this fib and appeal to a readerly sense of the déjà vu and déjà lu, Scott also acknowledges how his female predecessors have taught him to take the overcrowded conditions of modern novel-writing in his stride.[31]

31 Review of *The Fashionable Friend: A Novel, Critical Review* 36 (September 1773), p. 235; Walter Scott, *Waverley*, ed. Claire Lamont (Oxford: Oxford University Press, 1986), p. 3.

Transformations of the novel – II

INA FERRIS

At the beginning of the year which was to witness the reconfiguration of Great Britain into the United Kingdom of Great Britain and Ireland, Joseph Johnson published an anonymous novel titled *Castle Rackrent* (1800). To contemporaries the title might well have signalled a satire on Gothic romance, an instance of the eighteenth-century type of moral fiction known as the anti-romance. It was followed, however, by an awkwardly precise subtitle ('An Hibernian Tale Taken From Facts and From the Manners of the Irish Squires Before the Year 1782') that points forward rather than backward, and heralds the reshaping of the novelistic field in the early decades of the nineteenth century. The innovation effected by Edgeworth's tale has been variously named by literary historians both British (e.g. 'provincial novel', 'regional fiction') and Irish (e.g. 'Big House novel', 'colonial novel'), but what makes *Castle Rackrent* a suggestive starting point for thinking about the post-1800 novel in the British Isles is less its specifically inaugural status than its symptomatic positioning of fiction in the literary field. Setting her novel in a relationship of adjacency to what Mary Poovey has termed 'the modern fact',[1] Edgeworth inserts her Hibernian Tale in a modern matrix of historical chronology ('Before the Year 1782'); emerging knowledge genres (empirical 'facts', sociological 'manners'); and social analysis ('Irish squires'). This kind of deliberate self-alignment with non-fictional genres was crucial to the changing status of the novel in the period, working in complicated ways to achieve for this still largely suspect fictional form a significant measure of literary authority by the 1820s.

The key to this assumption of authority by novelistic genres was that fiction did not simply parasitically attach itself to the more prestigious knowledge genres but actively participated in a larger middle-class project of their transformation on behalf of a precisely modern allegiance to what

---

1 *A History of the Modern Fact: Problems of Knowledge in the Sciences of Wealth and Society* (Chicago and London: University of Chicago Press, 1998).

Castle Rackrent called 'the present times'. Edgeworth framed her first novel with a preface sharply distancing the text from the 'professed historians' and 'critics' who sustained the dignity of an older heroic history; instead, she allied it with 'the public' and with familiar, unofficial forms of history writing (e.g. anecdote, memoir, letters, diaries) that were reshaping the field of history itself at the turn of the century.[2] In a complex dynamic of legitimation, early nineteenth-century fiction 'novelized' the genres of reason and high culture even as it harnessed fiction's own distinctive powers for the work of national consolidation in a period of massive upheavals both at home and abroad. This does not mean the novel achieved literary authority either rapidly or easily. Throughout the period novel reading continued to be characterized in periodicals under the suspect signs of debased taste, wasted time and delusion, especially when it came to the 'female readers' widely understood to be its main practitioners.[3] The proverbial (and fleshy) Minerva Press reader, devouring 'sensational trash' on her sofa, stood for the novel reader in this degraded mode, with commentators routinely warning against the dangers to domestic and social order of her asocial ('unfeminine') self-indulgence. Thus linked to the promiscuous powers of print – endless multiplication, anonymous circulation, unfocused desire – novels were seen as consumptive goods, the disposable ephemera of an increasingly commercialized economy fed in no small measure by the mechanical printing press.

But at the same time, a new and newly powerful critical discourse pioneered by the *Edinburgh Review* began to recognize in novelistic fictions a power potentially allied to its own middle-class ambitions, and took increasing heed of the existence of a large – and impressionable – readership outside its protocols. As they engaged in constructing their own national authority, high culture quarterlies and monthlies set about paying more serious attention to novels, including them within the terms of their discourse rather than regarding them primarily as occasions for mockery, dismissal and diatribe. While the scissors-and-paste format of the eighteenth-century review remained in place, spurts of analytic content (formal, historical and theoretical) began to punctuate the standard plot summaries and lengthy extracts. Socially useful 'proper' novels were distinguished from the 'rubbish' of the dubious 'ordinary' novel; taxonomies of

---

2 *Castle Rackrent and Ennui*, ed. Marilyn Butler (London: Penguin, 1992), p. 61.
3 Robert Uphaus, 'Jane Austen and Female Reading', *Studies in the Novel* 19 (1987), 334–45; Jacqueline Pearson, *Women's Reading in Britain 1750–1835: A Dangerous Recreation* (Cambridge: Cambridge University Press, 1999).

novelistic 'kinds' were tentatively defined; individual reviews were framed by theoretical or historical discussions of the genre.[4] Novels thus were starting to be construed as objects of critical intelligence (hence potentially legitimate inhabitants of the literary field) and seen as participants in the formation of a responsible reading public for the post-revolutionary nation. Edgeworth was a pivotal figure in this process of absorption and legitimation, extolled in particular by the highly influential *Edinburgh Review*, which saw her performing the same kind of sober work as itself in training middle-class British readers in the virtues of prudence, order and rationality and in impressing on them the lessons of the new knowledge of political economy. Repeatedly highlighting the 'utility' of her work, Francis Jeffrey reinforced Edgeworth's own early generic move by declaring her tales 'works of more serious importance than much of the true history and solemn philosophy that comes daily under our inspection'.[5]

These decades, as Homer Obed Brown has argued, were definitive in the 'institution' of the British novel, setting in place a history and a canon whose contours had begun to emerge in the final decades of the eighteenth century.[6] As they sorted through eighteenth-century novels, early nineteenth-century commentators constructed a genealogy for 'the English novel' whose main outlines remain familiar (Richardson, Fielding, Smollett, Sterne et al.), although later periods were to restrict and more fully narrativize the loose and ramshackle lists produced at this time by pioneering figures like Anna Laetitia Barbauld ('On the Origin and Progress of Novel Writing', 1810) and John Dunlop (*The History of Fiction*, 1814). The consequential move, however, was the drawing of a line between past and present – the 'invention' of the eighteenth-century novel as a category distinct from current practices of fiction – because this made possible a *history* for the genre (as well as enabling the historical novel itself as a fictional form). The publishing industry reinforced such authorizing activities by publishing major collections of English novels edited by respected literary names, notably Barbauld's own fifty-volume *The British Novelists; with an Essay, and Prefaces Biographical and Critical* (1810) and Sir Walter Scott's ten-volume *Ballantyne's Novelist's Library* (1821–4) for which he wrote a series of important critical introductions. But scholarly trappings and the fiction

---

4 Ina Ferris, *The Achievement of Literary Authority: Gender, History, and the Waverley Novels* (Ithaca, NY: Cornell University Press, 1999), ch. 1.
5 Review of *Fashionable Tales*, *Edinburgh Review* 20 (July 1812), 100–1.
6 *Institutions of the English Novel From Defoe to Scott* (Philadelphia: University of Pennsylvania Press, 1997), ch. 6.

industry came together most spectacularly – and influentially – at the end of this period when Robert Cadell decided to publish Scott's Waverley Novels in the collected edition known as the Magnum Opus (1829–33). This was at once a cheap mass-market edition, issued in five-shilling monthly volumes, and an annotated and revised authorial edition, whose form and critical apparatus, as Jane Millgate has stressed, for the first time conferred on a contemporary author 'a treatment normally accorded only to the achievements of the great masters of the past'.[7]

In an important way, the scene of novel reading was shifting from the sofa to the study, but the regendering of the novel and the professionalization of fiction (not to mention the novel's bid for monumental status in something like the Magnum Opus edition of the Waverley Novels) went hand in hand with a novelization of the learned and professional genres on whose discourse the cultural authority of novels depended. If *Blackwood's Magazine* could declare that the novel has 'risen to a rank in the world of letters little if at all inferior to the most dignified productions of scholars and poets', the *Edinburgh Review* could equally declare that novels had come to rival non-fictional forms as sources of 'information' and celebrate 'how greatly the sphere of the Novel may be extended, and how capable it is of becoming the vehicle almost of every species of popular knowledge'.[8] The learned genre crucially at stake in this dance of reciprocal colonization was historiography, and the pivotal figure was Walter Scott, whose enormously successful historical novels, starting with the publication of *Waverley* in 1814, were widely seen as a challenge (or affront, depending on the reviewer) to standard historiography. For those on the novelizing side, standard history was typically identified with an old political history tied to a dynastic model of the nation and to an outdated understanding of historical agency and event. By contrast, the Waverley Novels were presented as bringing onto the discursive scene a new national history whose central task was to make visible (in a period phrase) 'the condition and opinions of a people'. It was not that Scott was an innovator in historical thought – his debt to the Scottish Enlightenment model of history was explicit – but that his novels rewrote narrative history in light of the thematic of modernity developed by the Scottish school, opening up new scenes of historical inquiry and forging

7 *Scott's Last Edition: A Study in Publishing History* (Edinburgh: Edinburgh University Press, 1987), p. vii.
8 'Remarks on Mandeville', *Blackwood's Magazine* 2 (January 1818), 403; [T. H. Lister], 'The Waverley Novels', *Edinburgh Review* 55 (April 1832), 77.

a potent new synthesis of theory and narrative through which to articulate national concerns.

The proliferation of historical and national fictions in this period – Scott's is only the most prominent instance – testifies to the generic uncertainty of history writing itself, positioned somewhere between philosophy and the novel, as it sought to turn itself into a modern genre in a commercial economy. Its own transitional status thus left open spaces for historical speculation on the part of neighbouring genres. If in the eighteenth century it was philosophy that had most famously poached on history's terrain, by the turn of the nineteenth century fictional narrative was moving into the position of equivocal rival and complement. By the late eighteenth century, fiction and historiography increasingly overlapped in their understanding of the historicization of everyday life, as history drew on sentiment and private 'experience' as much as on public 'action' in its own narratives.[9] By so blurring the line between fiction and non-fiction within itself, historiography placed fictional genres like the novel in new and closer relation. In an important way the innovations of romantic fiction are a direct consequence of this new reciprocity of encounter with nonfictional genres, not just those of history but also those of moral and political philosophy, antiquarianism, science, and geography (such as travel writing).

Through such intergeneric links the novel achieved visibility as a *public* genre. Engaged in the debates that agitated post-revolutionary Britain, it entered the contentious zone of publicity and publication Paul Magnusson has dubbed 'public Romanticism', which replaced the more limited and consensual zone of the liberal eighteenth-century public sphere.[10] The 1790s had initiated this process, with writers from all sides of the political spectrum harnessing the powers of fiction to pursue public arguments in the heated struggle over the shape of the British nation in that decade. Meshing genres of reason and theory (e.g. political philosophy, political economy, theology) with narrative fictional genres (e.g. romance, moral tale, court-ship novel), writers of the 1790s like William Godwin, Mary Wollstonecraft and Hannah More altered the public possibilities of fiction. 'It was a new and startling event in literary history', wrote Hazlitt in 1830 in a review of William Godwin, 'for a metaphysician to write a popular romance'.[11] What

---

9 Mark Phillips, *Society and Sentiment: Genres of Historical Writing in Britain, 1740–1820* (Princeton: Princeton University Press, 2000).
10 *Reading Public Romanticism* (Princeton: Princeton University Press, 1998), ch. 1.
11 'Mr. Godwin', *Edinburgh Review* 51 (April 1830), 145.

was 'startling' in Godwin's work, as Hazlitt's specification of 'popular romance' indicates, was not the conjoining of philosophy and fiction – the eighteenth century had developed a variety of philosophical fictions – but the choice of the lowly mode of romance. Philosophical tales typically placed ideas in a narrative matrix of wit and allegory, that is, placed them in relation to an alternative play of mind; by contrast, popular romances such as Godwin's *Caleb Williams* (1794) and *St Leon* (1799) placed ideas in intimate and affective relation to subjectivity and interiority, generally destabilizing both in the process. Post-1800 novelists were to follow both tactics, but the main point is that their fictions assumed public resonance through techniques of generic hybridization and contestation learned from the aggressive interventions of the 1790s.

All this comes into play in the national tale, one of the most significant new genres to emerge in the aftermath of the formation of the United Kingdom.[12] An Anglo-Irish and female-authored genre, it was produced in direct response to the 'incomplete union' of Great Britain and Ireland forged by the Act of Union. Explicitly political and generally committed to the liberal cause of Catholic Emancipation (whose delay made the Union a continuing sore spot on both sides of the Irish Sea), it was nonetheless not confined to any one political modality, admitting the Romantic Jacobinism of Lady Morgan (*The Wild Irish Girl, O'Donnel, Florence Macarthy, O'Briens and O'Flahertys*); the Whig reformism of Maria Edgeworth (*Ennui, The Absentee, Ormond*); the Tory pessimism of Charles Robert Maturin (*The Milesian Chief*); and the O'Connellite anger of John Banim (*The Anglo-Irish of the Nineteenth Century*). Definitive of the genre was an acute sense of national grievance: an assertion of Irish 'claim' that exerted pressure on the new national compound of the United Kingdom. Lady Morgan (Sydney Owenson), whose celebrated 1806 novel, *The Wild Irish Girl: A National Tale*, named the genre, stressed the point of grievance when she defined her romance as a 'fictitious narrative, founded in national grievances, and borne out by historical fact'.[13] Importantly, while the fictional roots of Morgan's innovation lay in the debased female romances of the Minerva Press like Mrs Patrick's *The Irish Heiress* (1797) or Regina Maria Roche's *Children of the Abbey* (1796), her own definition underscores the more prestigious generic mix of fiction, politics and history.

---

12 Katie Trumpener, *Bardic Nationalism: The Romantic Novel and the British Empire* (Princeton: Princeton University Press, 1997).
13 'Prefatory Address', *The Wild Irish Girl*, rev. edn (London, 1846), p. xxvi.

Exploiting a dense intertextuality that would characterize the national tale, Morgan's inaugural text locates the genre from the outset amidst public genres of national import. *The Wild Irish Girl* is a story of a courtship largely conducted as an initiation into and discussion of the question of Ireland both for the English protagonist and for the targeted reader. It not only includes political and historical discussions within the narrative but accompanies the main text with an extensive set of footnotes (in several languages) citing histories, antiquarian writings, travels, philosophical treatises, political analyses and so on. Moreover, it explicitly positions itself in relation to a very specific discourse, that of the Irish tour. A liberal, civic genre, the early nineteenth-century Irish tour derived from Arthur Young's landmark eighteenth-century agricultural *Tour of Ireland*, which sought to bring Ireland within the purview of modern understanding. In the uneasy aftermath of the Act of Union, rational confidence yielded to post-revolutionary anxiety, but the tour continued to be firmly anchored in a reassuring English enunciation. The key move of the national tale was to dislodge this enunciation, to displace the metropolitan traveller-figure from the point of vantage. Even as Anglo-Irish national tales remained concili-atory in relation to the English reader – indeed, the generic goal was to 'secure' the insecure Union – this now meant unsettling English genres and English readers before returning them to equilibrium.

Fiction itself provided the lever for such unsettling, specifically the old romance trope of encounter, now activated on behalf of modern civic concerns to move the visitor more fully into a land that had been simply traversed in standard travels. Morgan's romance tells the story of a young Englishman of the landed classes who reluctantly comes to Ireland, his mind filled with negative stereotypes of the Irish derived from travel writings. In the remote estates owned by his father in the west of Ireland, he literally falls into an enchanting enclave of Gaelic culture maintained by what is left of the Irish family dispossessed by his own ancestors. Here he encounters a remarkable trio of figures, most notably Glorvina, the Wild Irish Girl of the title, who initiates him into an erotic (if chaste) pastoral world while instructing him in Irish difference, as she teaches him Irish and recounts Irish history from the other side. Importantly, entry into this world is possible only on the basis of disguise (as is the way in romances): the hero must estrange himself from himself in order to be educated and regener-ated. In the end proper identities are resumed, and the novel concludes with a conciliatory marriage across difference in which romance and politics trope one another in an allegorical moment of utopian harmony fusing traditional and legal claims to land, Irish right and English rule. Strategically for an Anglo-Irish text, the future is identified neither with England nor with Ireland but with the passage between the two (the couple will live in both countries). This 'Glorvina solution'(in Robert Tracy's happy phrase) was to become conventional not only in national tales but in much nineteenth-century fiction as well.[14]

Morgan represents the way that early nineteenth-century women writers helped to redefine the place of fiction in public discourse and highlighted its active role in the formation of the modern nation. Unlike Morgan, most did so through the domestic novel, whose role in such formation gained prominence as the debate over the nation became focalized through the figure of femininity. Late eighteenth-century discourse had resituated patriotism in the private sphere, making women its primary bearers, thereby allowing writers like Hannah More to seize the opportunity to rewrite British home space in newly feminized terms.[15] More's only novel for the middle classes, *Coelebs in Search of a Wife* (1809) appeared relatively late in her career, but it grew out of the pedagogic/patriotic discourse she had influentially helped to develop in the 1790s. This discourse, largely focused through questions of gender, propriety and education, underpins a series of domestic fictions in the first decades of the nineteenth century, ranging from Amelia Opie's quirky thought experiment, *Adeline Mowbray, or the Mother and Daughter* (1804) to Mary Brunton's severely titled *Self-Control* (1810) and *Discipline* (1814), not to mention Jane Austen's sardonic take on such discourse in *Northanger Abbey* and *Sense and Sensibility* (1811). But under pressure from revitalized publication out of the British peripheries, the social-ethical notion of domesticity was becoming increasingly understood in relation to an emerging modern notion of 'culture' as the distinctive way of life of a people. 'Manners' now took shape in relation to specific geographies and temporalities rather than being seen in relation to general virtues and models of sociability. In many ways, such specification increased the difficulties middle-class femininity had to negotiate, for if women were to be moral connectors between places, capable of harmonizing complex national unions such as that of the early nineteenth-century United Kingdom, they had to be lifted out of the particularity of place. National

---

14 Robert Tracy, 'Maria Edgeworth and Lady Morgan', *Nineteenth-Century Fiction* 40 (1985), 1–22.
15 Anne K. Mellor, *Mothers of the Nation: Women's Political Writing in England, 1780–1830* (Bloomington: Indiana University Press, 2000), ch. 1.

sentiment, however, was becoming more and more invested in the native place – the dearly loved spot, Burke's 'little platoon'[16] – at whose heart stood a rooted, quasi-maternal figure. Such tensions took on added resonance for women writers from the peripheries, who typically sought to coordinate an abstract British identity with a localized Scottish or Irish (more rarely Welsh) one. Working out of such asymmetries, they exemplify an incipient modern historical-cultural consciousness that infused categories of nation, place, home and femininity with a newly charged sense of nationality, at once thickening the time inhabited by individual subjects and rendering more problematic the codes regulating them as public beings.

Certainly, most women writers from the British peripheries remained committed to the ethos of domesticity, as anxious as their English counterparts to promulgate the rational-prudential model of conduct sustaining a modern commercial and imperial society. But to write from within a peripheral consciousness was to have a double vision and hence to denaturalize, if not to reject, taken-for-granted systems like domesticity. Indeed the managerial energies of modern domesticity often came to seem all the more attractive. Thus Elizabeth Hamilton's popular *Cottagers of Glenburnie* (1808) rewrote Hannah More's famous cottage tracts not by repudiating her values, which it endorsed, but by overlaying class with national difference. Hamilton's matron, Mrs Mason, sets out to convert slovenly Scottish villagers to middle-class discipline, and her project ends, for the most part, in success. What captured the attention of Hamilton's first readers, however, was not the successful Englishing of the village but the detailed evocation of a particular form of life, along with the recalcitrance of the villagers, whose punchy dialect responses entered the more general vocabulary. Hamilton's proto-ethnographic comparatist model allowed her to coordinate Scottish and English 'manners' on the same grid, but the concreteness of her representation of the Scottish village meant that it emerged less as an abstract 'problem' accessible to an analytic intelligence than as a specific 'world' often opaque to such an intelligence.[17] The narrative thus moves out of the homogeneity of ethical or political space, so that even as Hamilton's text remains primarily invested in a

---

16 *Reflections on the Revolution in France*, ed. Conor Cruise O'Brien (London: Penguin, 1968), p. 135.
17 This point draws on James Chandler's model of 'the historical situation' in *England in 1819: The Politics of Literary Culture and the Case of Romantic Historicism* (Chicago and London: University of Chicago Press, 1998).

universalizing moral idiom, it gestures toward the differentiation of a historical understanding.

Even when domestic novels from the peripheries sported the abstract titles characteristic of didactic fiction, as in Susan Ferrier's *Marriage* (1818), a consciousness of nationality (albeit not always a national consciousness) tended to cut across domestic conventions and to modify their bearings. Ferrier's tale of female education deploys the standard two-heroine motif, and makes a familiar argument for the positive value of a modest, rational femininity over against the negative powers of flashy and irrational women of fashion. But the predictable valorization of the domestic sphere is played out in relation to a complicated interplay between Scotland and England in which both countries manifest themselves in different kinds of spaces, blocking any impulse toward identification of a unitary or integral 'national character'. Moreover, even as the novel activates an art/nature binary to underwrite its 'natural' Scottish heroine (who exemplifies a Wordsworthian attachment to native place), it pries apart gender and nature by insisting on a non-biological understanding of motherhood and foregrounding national hybridity. Women, nature and the British nation appear in less than transparent relation, pointing to the way in which women's novels from the British peripheries tended to trouble the English domestic forms they at the same time practised.

In particular, they placed under scrutiny notions of family and inheritance, experimenting with configurations and modalities outside origin and tradition in the attempt to imagine new forms of domesticity for the modern nation. Christian Isobel Johnstone's *Clan-Albin: A National Tale* (1815) offers a striking instance. A contemporary tale of a small Highland community devastated by the Clearances, it both overlaps with ethnographic studies such as Anne Grant's *Essays on the Superstitions of the Highlanders of Scotland* (1811) and rewrites the Highland tour from the inside out. On the one hand the novel conforms to the rational–didactic mode, valorizing an improving rational heroine and a domesticated modern hero (who reads Hannah More to unruly troops); on the other, it draws powerfully on folk and oral tradition to create an alternative and intensely matrocentric order at whose centre stand two ancient pre-modern matriarchs (one high, one low in rank). In a utopic ending, these aged women preside over the new community that re-forms on the site of the ruined one. In a now renovated glen, a progressive modernity has banished feudal bondage, replacing it with a communal 'family' of misfits and leftovers from various parts of the British isles: remarried widows, orphans, old soldiers, and so on. Significantly, it contains few of the old clan that once inhabited the glen, as Johnstone tries to conjugate a new Britain out of the old, putting this and that together in ideal (and idealized) relation.

Similar attempts to rethink the constitution of family and nation shaped the Anglo-Irish national tales. Edgeworth's *Ennui* (1809) and *The Absentee* (1812) pose questions of maternal desire and national order, exploring maternity as deviant energy and worrying broad issues of gender, the body and social order as they pursue a tangled argument for modern nationhood as a formation outside birth and inheritance yet obscurely tied to both. In terms of the enlightened landlordism Edgeworth espoused (and practised when running her father's estate), nations were primarily rational economic units, but at the same time her fictions suggest that nations consistently exceeded such modellings, at least in the case of Ireland. In her novels the nation remains an equivocal category: at once a choice and a duty, a project and an inheritance. Most of all, it is cast as a potentiality rather than a history, and here she differs sharply from her compatriot Morgan who (attached as she was to Gaelic, as well as to English, lines of Irish history) was more attracted to nationalist and historical models. Morgan too, however, critiqued the notions of inheritance underwriting such models. Indeed, she came to interrogate the 'natural' articulation of woman and nation her own *The Wild Irish Girl* had done much to inscribe. In a significant revision, her later tales such as *O'Donnel* and *O'Briens and O'Flahertys* rewrite the natural, pastoral national heroine as a performative figure, by no means 'natural' but nonetheless national. Working out of French models of a cosmopolitan and undomestic femininity (Stael's *Corinne* is a key intertext), Morgan constructs a hybrid and mobile heroine whose intensely theatricalized being deliberately refuses the ethics of intimacy and interiority marking the English domestic heroine. Operating in the interstices of culture and under various names, this heroine resists identification – Beavoin O'Flaherty of *The O'Briens and the O'Flahertys* is a striking instance – and she is linked to a principle of sociality outside both family and nation, one attached to informal associations of obscure sanction such as confraternities, operating well outside the (literal) view of central authority.

From various directions, then, domestic novels and national tales opened up speculative spaces even as they continued to work inside the political terms of national settlement. But if these incipiently historical and culturalist narratives established the novel as a public genre and inaugurated its move into the literary field, it was the intervention of a male novelist that spectacularly accelerated the genre's achievement of literary authority and decisively altered what it was henceforth possible to do in novelistic fictions.

Reinventing historical romance as the modern historical novel in *Waverley* (1814), Walter Scott explicitly built out of the work of female writers from the peripheries, naming Edgeworth, Hamilton and Anne Grant as predecessors in the postscript to his first novel. Like them Scott was committed to securing the British nation state across difference, and his first novel follows the conventions and tactics of the national tale, from its travel plot to the displacement of the hero to the motif of courtship as cultural initiation. But his was a historical sensibility in a way that theirs was not, and this profoundly altered the valence of the fiction.

The Waverley Novels fused romance, theory and scholarship into a potent new narrative synthesis that for the first time articulated a fully historicist vision (the self-conscious sense of living in history) in fiction. Shifting the novel out of the immediacy of didactic-ethical space from which genres like the domestic novel and the national tale had launched themselves directly into the middle of contentious public discourse, Scott transferred it to a historical-analytic space that defined itself not so much as an intervention in as a reflection upon the current state of the polis. Out of a variety of historical and romance discourses, he forged a flexible and capacious narrative driven by a dialectic of consolidation and differentiation. This narrative at once validated the modern imperial nation as the positive culmination of evolutionary historical process and placed in question the very modernity it embodied as, in novel after novel, Scott turned to the past to give affective charge to the myth of modern Britain as the passage out of violence into civil society.

But the ideological power of the Waverley Novels lay more fully in the form than in the content of their narration. Governed by an impersonal and self-consciously modern third-person narrator, Scott's historical fictions achieved their effect by a constant oscillation between the 'wide' view of this narrator, whose understanding of historical process allowed for the placing of events in meaningful relation to each other and to his own time, and the 'narrow' view of those immersed in the historical action and through whose perspective the narrative events were focalized. Behind this proto-ethnographic narrative situation lay two late eighteenth-century historical genres that crucially shaped Scott's imagination: philosophical conjectural history and antiquarian 'curiosities'. Very differently placed as historical discourses in the culture but equally serious enterprises for Scott, these two forms of history operated at distinct levels: the distanced, high plateau of generalization, and the close-up, lowly field of details and fragments. Out of their interchange Scott generated a distinctively Romantic form of history as an oscillation between recovery (the antiquarian imperative of preservation and recreation for which the past is something to be loved) and analysis (the philosophical imperative for which the past is something to be understood).

Such a doubled history produced the national past as two very different kinds of sites, and the tension between them constitutes the dynamic of Scott's historical investigation. The Postscript to the very first of his Waverley Novels identifies as the catalyst for his novelistic project the rapid pace of recent change in Scotland, drawing for its vocabulary on both the analytic-explanatory vocabulary of the Scottish school and the antiquarian's language of lost traces and preservation. The nation thus appears on the one hand as the site of impersonal economic and socio-political forces (commerce, law, policy); on the other, it emerges as the product of distinct social customs (faith, hospitality, honour) and their associated affects. The juxtaposition of the two points to the specifically modern anxiety at the heart of the Waverley Novels, an anxiety that made them resonate not just for Scott's immediate British contemporaries but for a wide – and multinational – readership throughout the nineteenth century. As impersonal site, a nation becomes a subject of history in its own right (a 'nation' spins its history from itself in a way that a 'kingdom' does not), but in assuming such an identity, a nation subsumes the identity and agency of other subjects on its terrain. Particular social formations, specific communities and individual subjectivities appear only as ephemera tossed up by a national dynamic operating at the level of deep structure.

Straddling the border between deep structure and transient forms, the historian for Scott looked both to the larger patterns of historical change and to evanescent social formations. And his profound sense of the precariousness and disappearance of the latter engenders the melancholy that underlies the writing of history in the Waverley Novels (for all Scott's jokes about Dryasdust historians). This melancholy of history conditions, in turn, the interplay of romance and history in these novels, as *Waverley* itself makes almost schematically visible. Romance figures not simply as adolescence but as the attempt to hold on to a specifically human (not to say humanist) promise in the face of an inhuman history; hence Edward Waverley surrenders his swerve into romance with a 'sigh' when he declares 'the romance of his life was ended, and . . . its real history had now commenced'.[18] For the masculine

---

18 *Waverley; or, 'Tis Sixty Years Since*, ed. Claire Lamont (Oxford: Oxford University Press, 1986), p. 283.

subjectivity on which the Waverley plot of initiation focuses resignation is the mood of entry into modern history. Through this plot the hero discovers himself as *already* the subject of history. Waverley's travels in the peripheries, in contrast to those of national tale heroes, reveal to him the English gentleman he always was, and the key moment in the novel's closural sequence is not the conciliatory cross-cultural marriage but the preservation of a site of romance for modern British sensibility through the sentimental restoration of a Jacobite mansion. Only through such artifactual acts can the modern sensibility endure the resignation of historical consciousness.

The Waverley Novels are thus a key moment in the founding of historical tourism as much as in the invention of the modern historical novel, and both the material practice and the discursive literary form respond to the sense of emptiness within modern time to which, ironically, the vital and crowded representations of Scott were among the first to bear witness. Over and over again (and often anachronistically), the Waverley Novels rehearse the fraught entry of a particular social formation into modernity, foregrounding moments of disruption and displacement when a premodern order finds itself jolted out of its habitual ways of being. Such moments make acutely visible the unevenness of the terrain of history, and one of the key effects of Scott's thick evocation of the heterogeneities of the past was to alert readers to the differentiated structure of any historical moment, including their own present moment. In an important way these novels read historical process as dislocation, haunted by the spectre of alienation, and nowhere more so than in their famous 'middling' heroes, those bearers of historical progress who tend to become ever more insubstantial and ghostly as their narratives approach the historical future they themselves have been heralding (e.g. Henry Morton in *Old Mortality*, Wilfrid Ivanhoe in *Ivanhoe*). At the same time, however, their tales operate within a narration governed by the 'wide' view of the modern historian. For Scott's contemporaries the voice of this narrator, reassuringly impersonal, sane and balanced, was the voice they identified as the signature of 'history'. Coordinating concrete events and general laws to produce the sense of a national story, this narrator established the horizons that allowed for semantic weight and made history itself the very form of intelligibility for much of the rest of the century.

Scott's historical novel assumed an unprecedented dominance, so that novelists throughout Great Britain and not only in his immediate vicinity of Edinburgh (the second most important publishing venue after London) found themselves working in what Ian Duncan has aptly termed 'Scott's shadow'.[19] But the mode of historical fiction established by *Waverley* did not go unchallenged; indeed Scott himself experimented with more tangled models of historical process and more difficult notions of modernity in his post-*Waverley* fictions, ranging from early tales like *The Antiquary* (1816) and *Rob Roy* (1817) to late entries such as *The Fair Maid of Perth* (1828). Nonetheless, the Author of Waverley loomed over the novelistic field as a paradigmatic figure, his fame obscuring alternative models of historical fiction (often directly contesting his own) which appeared throughout the period but tended to cluster in the 1820s. These counter-fictions take a wide range of forms: small-scale annalist and chronicle forms (e.g. John Galt's *Annals of the Parish* (1821), *The Provost* (1822), *The Entail* (1823)); psychically inflected historical Gothic (e.g. William Godwin's *Mandeville* (1817), Charles Robert Maturin's *The Milesian Chief* (1812) and *Melmoth the Wanderer* (1820)); novels of insurgency (e.g. James Hogg's *The Three Perils of Woman* (1823), Michael Banim's *The Croppy* (1828)); speculative counterfactual histories (e.g. Mary Shelley's *Valperga* (1823)). Where they converge is in a refusal of the assumption that historical truth inheres in the subsumption of events into a larger whole that coincides with national-historical 'progress'.

Eschewing the impersonal and detached perspective of the Scott narrator, along with his smooth narrative flow, such counter-fictions tend to be angular, agitated and melodramatic. They move into the foreground darker senses of historical process, as in history as trauma (*Mandeville*), erasure (*Milesian Chief, Valperga*), or oppression and sadism (*Melmoth the Wanderer*). Typically, they do so by overwriting the already written. Charles Robert Maturin's *The Milesian Chief* (1812), for example, reinvents the national tale as Irish Gothic, refusing its conciliations to define colonial history as usurpation, guilt and terror. This extravagant and bitter tale of Irish rebellion defines Irish Gothic in critical relation to dominant models of historical understanding from the start, throwing humanist models of memory and history into crisis by moving them into the limit-zone. Working in a more rational and sentimental idiom but equally displacing dominant readings, Mary Shelley's *Valperga: or, The Life and Adventures of Castruccio, Prince of Lucca* (1823) rewrites the figure of femininity that underwrote Scott's account of the passage into modernity as the accession of national liberty. Arguing, by contrast, that the modern imperial state is rooted in the suppression of liberty, Shelley builds on the eighteenth-century female tradition of speculative fictional histories exemplified by

19 *Scott's Shadow* (Princeton: Princeton University Press, 2007).

narratives such as Sophie Lee's *The Recess* (1783–5) to focus on two imaginary women whom she places inside the historical record (the 'public histories') of early modern Tuscany.[20] As supplementary figures, the heroines of *Valperga* figure both what is left out of such official histories and what fractures them from within, but most of all Shelley deploys the perspective from the interstices to place in question the ready alignment of public and private that underwrote domesticity as the base of the nation.

Equally resistant to the notions of national and social order achieving purchase in the period, the quirky fictions of James Hogg take the Romantic novel at once further back and further forward, bypassing the Enlightenment models that continued to shape novels such as *Valperga*. Hogg's incorporation of oral and folk idioms brings into the novel pre-modern modes of narration; at the same time, his generic incongruities, disjointedness and grotesquerie anticipate registers of postmodern narrative. Paradoxically (but in keeping with longstanding novelistic tradition) his own print narratives refuse ultimate seriousness either to print genres (e.g. the novel, the periodical) or to the professional literary culture in which Hogg himself was deeply engaged. The productions of the Author of Waverley (whom he distinguished from his old friend Wattie Scott) gave specific focus to his mistrust, and Hogg countered the Waverley Novels on their own ground by writing over Scott's Jacobite and Covenanter tales in his own *Brownie of Bodsbeck* (1818) and *Three Perils of Woman* (1823). Openly agitated and partial, these are 'minor' histories from intensely local perspectives, conjuring up a very physical world of enormous confusion, sudden events and strange disconnections. Hogg contested not just Scott's account of Scottish history – the elision of Culloden in *Waverley*, for example – but also the narrative form and scholarly–editorial apparatus that made Scott the definitive voice of history for the period. Among other things, Hogg's extraordinary *Memoirs and Confessions of a Justified Sinner* (1824) is an exercise in historical critique, its twigging of both the modern editor of the Sinner's memoirs and the Edinburgh literati (who seek literally to unearth the body of the past) effecting a sardonic reading of the protocols of modern historical understanding being set in place in his time.

At once a wayward enactment and repudiation of the attraction to 'remains' that was redefining what it meant to do history and to publish the past in the period, Hogg's prankish text moves into the foreground the

---

20 *Valperga: Or, the Life and Adventures of Castruccio, Prince of Lucca*, ed. Tilottama Rajan (Peterborough, ON: Broadview Press, 1998), p. 439.

struggle with history that impelled the novel's most powerfully innovative energies in the Romantic period. At the same time it draws attention to the Romantic novel's divided ambitions and ambivalent relationship to official literary culture. Seeking to harness for itself the cultural power of modern fact and to transform itself into a properly public genre in the new British polity, novels in the period allied themselves with sober genres of higher status. But at the same time, as the counter-impulses to Scott's historical novel and to the domestic novel indicate, fictions continued to resist the regulative protocols to which they thereby became subject. The fractious making of the new United Kingdom out of parts that were themselves unsettled and very often recalcitrant put into motion a dynamic of drive and counter-drive that was not simply political (in the strict sense) but peculiarly novelistic. Cobbled together out of various genres and seeking legitimacy, novels remained at the same time popular fictions, impelled by impulses irreverent and fanciful, as well as speculative and combative. Thus even as they placed themselves within the literary field and sought to operate on serious public terrain, it was the suspect power inhering in their status as fictions that allowed them to keep questions of public import from hardening into premature settlement.

Theatre, performance and urban spectacle

JULIE CARLSON

The theatre world of the English Romantic period gives us phenomenal access to the fantasies and daily realities of a people living through one of the Western world's most revolutionary periods. The content of what is presented on stage, the manner and places of its presentation, the types of person creating it, and commentary on its reception all provide extraordinary access to cultural ferment in the period and insight into how a people processes current events through theatrical means. Even the legal terminology that designates London theatrical scenes in this period – legitimate vs. illegitimate theatre – suggests an artistic forum in transition. It also accurately suggests how politics is addressed through aesthetic media. This is in large part because what animates theatrical discussion is debate over national representation, a concern deepened by reflections on the French Revolution and the abolition of slavery with their impassioned descriptions of what and who best represent 'the English' in an emerging democracy.

While concerns over representation emerge in discussions of all forms of art in this period (and in all periods of art), they are particularly salient in descriptions of Romantic theatre. At once aesthetic form and social forum, theatre requires an elaborate coordination of artistic, financial, technical and audience demands that, in this period, is distinguished by two pressures. First, each of these domains is not only in enormous flux but is also described as being so in ways that dramatize clashes between established and innovative or radical interests. Second, discourse on Romantic theatre is the first to portray spectatorship as a problem *for* artistic and political representation. One of the major contributions of Romantic theatre to cultural studies generally is the way that it voices ambivalence about materializing dreams. A second is the connection it forges between so-called visual and popular cultures.

Such major claims for the importance of Romantic theatre in its day or ours underscore another form of disjuncture between representation and visibility. For most of the history of literary histories of English Romanticism, theatre has been largely invisible in accounts of its literary and social successes. At most, theatre is recognized as occupying some of the period's best essayists, but even then the fame of that writing often depends on its construction of a separation between drama and theatre. For the most part, no play has been deemed worthy of substantial critical attention, and Romanticism as a movement has long been characterized as undramatic and antitheatrical. Renewed attention to Romantic theatre in the past two decades has restored much of the vibrancy, vitality and heterogeneity of theatre culture in this period – so much so that it is hard to imagine how or why theatre ever was perceived as marginal to the period's cultural activity or self-perception. Recalling its marginality illustrates another service offered to the study of Romanticism by theatre. Since almost everything about it has been deemed antithetical to the spirit of this age, attending to theatrical matters allows us to perceive 'Romanticism' in the making.

Two interlocking claims structure the ensuing discussion of the theatre world of late Georgian England. First, theatre is the optimal site in this revolutionary culture for exploring the interaction between aesthetic and political change. Not only is each of the period's major social revolutions represented in and by contemporary plays but also the material practices and subgenres of theatre are seen as reflecting these changes and are used as categories for evaluating them. For example, commentary on the French Revolution depicts its action, heroes and plots as not only theatre but also engaged in a struggle over traditional and insurgent dramatic forms (i.e. tragedy vs. melodrama and farce). Discourse regarding the abolition of slavery turns on evoking sympathy for others whose nobility is perceptible to the degree it is skin-paint deep. Arguments for women's liberation intensify discursive campaigns to downplay the sexuality and physicality of female bodies on stage in order to promote more respectable notions of a public woman. Outcries against mechanization, itself responsible for the proliferation of stage machinery in this period, foreground the resistance of high culture to things material. In short, all the various forms of representation through which this theatre stages and interprets cultural events are themselves sites of contestation in this age.

The second claim is that theatre's non-sense-making features – its status as entertainment and increasingly spectacular means of recreation – begin to be seen as instrumental to achieving political change. In part, this is because stage censorship still prohibits direct commentary on current events, so that political messages have to assume indirect, historically displaced, or spectacular form.[1] In part, it is because the Romantic stage is an avowed theatre of illusion, not yet of realism, whose aim is to body forth possibility by not fully fleshing it out. Theatre's non-reflective and anti-mimetic approach to staging reality occasions conflicted commentary over what viewers are seeing or should see on stage. At one extreme, the rage for spectacle that is said to distinguish these audiences is depicted as occluding all the value of an evening's entertainment. At the other, precisely theatre's status as entertainment is credited with refreshing and consolidating a people torn by class division and weary of complicated oratorical wrangling. Such discursive struggles over how theatre convenes a public or what mass entertainment offers an individual or the concept of individuality remain useful lessons in our current discussions regarding the state of the arts. In its promotion of a separation between page and stage, reading and viewing, discourse on Romantic theatre foregrounds elite culture's ostensible antipathy to embodied activity.

Conditions of theatre viewing

The short answer to what underlies the nature and experience of late Georgian London theatre is struggles over 'legitimacy'. The term settles little definitively but is fundamental to the operations of this theatre, not merely because its status as a legal designation of theatre is on its way out in this period. In the most basic terms, legitimacy applies to the two designated 'patent' or 'royal' theatres that exercise a duopoly over the spoken drama in London – Drury Lane and Covent Garden. (The summer theatre, The Haymarket, is also deemed legitimate in this period.) This duopoly stems from a decision made by Charles II in 1662 to grant exclusive rights to perform drama in London to Thomas Killigrew and William Davenant, that over time was then extended to those theatres. A subsequent act of theatre legislation, the 1737 Licensing Act, reinforced the duopoly and coordinated legitimacy with censorship. This act continued to restrict London theatrical entertainment to the borough of Westminster and the royal residences but required all texts of plays to be submitted to the Office of the Lord Chamberlain for censorship two weeks prior to their performance. The main targets of the Examiner of Plays – John Larpent for the period 1788 to 1824, George Colman the Younger from 1824 to 1836 – concerned references

---

1 See Leonard W. Conolly, *The Censorship of the English Drama, 1737–1824* (San Marino: Huntington Library, 1976).

to politics, topical events, religion or sex, the restrictions on political expression intensifying after 1790. Much of the interest of this theatre stems from the fact that it is the only arena of literary activity still subject to censorship, the state having abolished censorship of the press in 1695. This means that direct political commentary in the patent theatres must be read elsewhere than in the lines.

Illegitimate theatre basically refers to performances at venues (often designated 'minor') where spoken drama, especially tragedy and comedy, is officially proscribed. It encompasses London playhouses outside Westminster, such as the Surrey, Coburg, Adelphi, Olympic, Sadler's Wells, and a set of genres that circumvent spoken dialogue through nonverbal appeals to ear and eye – pantomime, harlequinade, melodrama, burlesque, extravaganza, equestrian spectaculars, burletta. These distinctions become extremely porous during this period as the ways to circumvent the law grow increasingly ingenious. In the case of burletta, which combines music with recitative, precious little distinguishes it from spoken drama. For patent and minor theatres in this period constitute overlapping and interconnected, rather than opposing, cultures with benefits from that overlap accruing to both sides of the official division. Illegitimate theatres become so successful at encroaching on legitimate dramatic terrain, especially on Shakespeare, that 'respectable' audiences often prefer to attend there. At the same time, patent theatres take several cues from the popularity of the minors. Performances of melodrama, pantomime and romance overshadow performances of tragedy and comedy in terms both of frequency of offering and spectacular appeal. Indeed, the rage for spectacle usually ascribed to a lowering of the social composition of patent theatre audiences is equally the result of attempts to lure back the large audiences attending the minors for the pleasures of their visual appeals. The degree of cross-over between legitimate and illegitimate domains means that the duopoly is effectively abolished some two decades before it is officially revoked in the Theatre Regulation Act of 1843, a fact well documented in testimony before the parliamentary 1832 Select Committee on Dramatic Literature.[2] But its nominal existence aids in forging a lasting association between visual and popular forms of art.

---

2 See *Report from the Select Committee on Dramatic Literature: with the minutes of evidence*, 1832; repr. in the Irish University Press Series of British Parliamentary Papers, ed. Marilyn L. Norstedt (Shannon, Ireland, 1968).

Say, then, that one decides to attend an evening at Drury Lane in the 1790s. That playgoer enters a space that would appear quite foreign to our conceptions of theatre. Both it and Covent Garden in the 1790s are cavernous, frequently dangerous, noisy and fully lit spaces that offer wildly heterogeneous viewing experiences. If our playgoer attends an evening at Drury Lane before 1794, s/he enters an auditorium that seats 2,500 persons and, after the Henry Holland renovations of 1794 (and up until 1812), seats 3,611. Either before or after 1794 and for the next two decades, that auditorium remains illuminated throughout the evening by chandeliers holding candles, gas lighting becoming available only after 1817. Where s/he sits in the auditorium determines who and what s/he sees in a fairly literal fashion. With growing exceptions, the higher orders sit in the front and side boxes; the critics and professional men, civil servants, tradesmen and a general cross-section of the middling classes in the pit and lower gallery; working people, including servants, journeymen, apprentices, sailors and their women-folk, in the upper gallery. These seating arrangements affect the quality of one's apprehension of the action on stage as well as critics' assessments of the overall quality of action on it. Persons in the upper galleries frequently cannot see or hear what is happening on stage. Those in more favourable positions often have their vision blocked by columns, ladies' hats, dealings with orange-sellers, prostitutes, or the occasional theatre brawlers. Theatre criticism of the period constantly laments the negative effects on acting of these 'preposterously large' spaces.[3] Among the effects that they condemn are exaggerated gestures and facial features and the intensification of spectacle, all said to be compensating for the inability to hear what is being said on stage.

This heterogeneity of viewing experience is both inadvertent and part of the evening's design.[4] A full programme at the patent theatres entails a mixture of genres, emotions and acting styles. At a minimum, our playgoer would see a mainpiece (five-act tragedy, comedy or full-length operatic piece) and afterpiece (farce, burletta, pantomime). For a benefit, s/he would see even more kinds of pieces. Adding to the variety of the evening, which can last anywhere from four to seven hours, are the recitation of a prologue and epilogue (if the mainpiece is a new composition), three pieces of music by the orchestra before the curtain opens, music at the end of the night, and

---

3 The phrase is Joanna Baillie's.
4 See Jeffrey N. Cox, 'Spots of Time: The Structure of the Dramatic Evening in the Theater of Romanticism', *Texas Studies in Literature and Language* 41:4 (1999), 403–25.

dancing, music or recitations in the conventional seven-minute interval between acts. As such variety and spectatorial stamina indicate, a coherent, emotionally unified experience is not the goal of this theatre.

Comprehensive handlists make it possible to specify what mainpiece and afterpiece(s) our playgoer would see on any given night at Drury Lane.[5] Yet the information that they provide is often at odds with interpretive historical accounts. On the one hand, the lists substantiate the critical assessment that late Georgian playgoers favour melodrama, Gothic tragedy, sentimental comedy and dramatizations of novels, especially of Scott. On the other, they remind us that summaries of taste not only are dictated by who is doing the summarizing but also by a focus on what is new rather than what is actually being performed nightly throughout a period – as if playgoers do not have a substantial taste for the familiar. These handlists indicate a strong probability that the mainpiece would feature some standard of the dramatic repertory: a tragedy or comedy by Shakespeare or a play by Nicholas Rowe, Thomas Otway, Thomas Southerne, John Dryden, William Congreve, George Farquhar, Joseph Addison, Oliver Goldsmith or George Colman, the Elder. Contemporary offerings might involve a play by Elizabeth Inchbald, Richard Cumberland, Thomas Holcroft, the Dibdins, Richard Sheridan, Hannah Cowley or George Colman, the Younger – in these cases, probably either an original comedy or farce or a translation or adaptation of any number of plays from Germany and France. Odds are good too that one of these new pieces is authored by a woman – the period between 1788 and 1800 giving rise to an unprecedented proliferation of dramatic writing by women with more than ninety women writing dramas between 1789 and 1823.[6] What our playgoer is not likely to see is a tragedy or comedy by any of the major Romantic poets, all of whom wrote for the stage, unless s/he caught the twenty-night run, starting 24 January of 1813, of Coleridge's *Remorse* (a revision of the rejected *Osorio* of 1796–7) or was on hand for the pirated production of Byron's *Marino Faliero* that ran for seven nights beginning with 25 April 1821. The virtual absence of these poets' plays on stage has played a leading role in

---

5 See Charles Beecher Hogan (ed.), *The London Stage, 1660–1800: A Calendar of Plays, Entertainments, and Afterpieces*, 5 vols., Part 5: *1776–1800* (Carbondale, IL: Southern Illinois University Press, 1968); Allardyce Nicoll, *A History of English Drama, 1660–1900*, 5 vols., vol. IV: *Early Nineteenth Century Drama, 1800–1850* (Cambridge: Cambridge University Press, 1955).

6 See Ellen Donkin, *Getting into the Act: Women Playwrights in London, 1776–1829* (London: Routledge, 1995).

'proving' drama's decline, a view that is aided by their having written about theatre after their own writings for theatre have been rejected.

Equally suspect in corroborating the longstanding claim that drama is in decline during this period is the second major ingredient of theatre – actors. Here the logic of decline is proportional rather than defensive: their rise equals drama's decline. By all accounts, this period represents one of the highpoints for acting in the history of British theatre – a height that, in the case of Sarah Siddons, is arguably unsurpassed. Deemed the Kemble era, during which siblings John Kemble and Sarah Siddons rule the stage, theatre reaches new levels in quality of acting, respectability associated with it, and quality of the respectability that characterizes these two classic Romantic actors. Their status as stars, moreover, must be viewed in relation to two contradictory features of acting in this transitional period of theatre. On the one hand, up until 1800 patent theatres rely on resident, or stock, companies, not the actor-manager star system that characterizes the nineteenth century. Under this system, stars like Kemble and Siddons must envision themselves as part of an ensemble, for all of whom playwrights, even if they write with a particular actor in mind, must devise suitable roles. But increasingly Kemble and Siddons find themselves having to contend not just with other possible stars (Dorothy Jordan, Eliza O'Neill, Robert Elliston) but also with new kinds of theatrical celebrity that threaten to eclipse even the substance of their brilliance. Among such sensations are the child actor, William Henry West Betty, known as Master Betty or the 'Infant Roscius', who not only forced Kemble and Siddons to retire from acting during the height of his fame in 1804 and 1805 but inspired a series of infant prodigies on stage. Then there is the 'quintessential Regency celebrity' and 'unquestioned King of English Clowns', Joseph Grimaldi, who ruled both patent and minor stages – often saving the former financially.[7] Or that phenomenal Romantic tragedian, Edmund Kean, the force of whose charge threatens to eclipse even the language of eclipse by shifting the referent to electricity. Or the box-office appeal of characters in black-face who keep theatres in the black even while England is profiting from the slave trade.

But spectacle is the dimension of this theatre that is most frequently ascribed to the drama's decline. Though there is a long history of anxiety over stage business, during this period spectacle is seen as overwhelming

---

7 Jane Moody, *Illegitimate Theatre in London, 1770–1840* (Cambridge: Cambridge University Press, 2000), p. 209, see pp. 208–20; on Bettymania, see Julie A. Carlson, 'Forever Young: Master Betty and the Queer Stage of Youth in English Romanticism', *SAQ* 95:3 (1996), 575–602.

everything else that is happening on stage. Several developments in stagecraft are seen as shifting the balance of theatrical power from verbal to visual. The most important involve transformations in set and scene design, initiated with the hiring of Philippe Jacques de Loutherbourg at Drury Lane in 1771 and intensified by the enlargement of both patent theatres.[8] The sheer size of the stage and its distance from spectators require that they are given more, larger, and more spectacular things to see. Even the exaggerated gestures and facial expressions adopted by actors and castigated by critics are dwarfed by the cataracts, volcanoes, storms, historic battle scenes, animals, Gothic cathedrals, Incan temples, tribal rituals, court pageantry and funeral processionals making their way on stage. For such attractions, the patents often borrow on the expertise of the minors – Astley's horses, Sadler Wells' pageants and Charles Dibdin's aquatic inventions – honed by the law that compels illegitimate theatre to substitute visual for verbal effects.

A second major innovator, William Capon, hired by Covent Garden in 1794 after painting scenery for the minors, responds to a growing demand for authenticity in setting and costume. In this realm, technological developments coincide with developments in historiography, antiquarianism and ethnography. Set designs expand the world that theatre is capable of reflecting, transporting spectators to 'exotic' climes (Peru, India, Jamaica, Fatteconda) or former times (primitive, medieval, Elizabethan). They also transform theatrical hierarchies, scenic display frequently being highlighted on stagebills and described by reviewers as the most interesting thing in the play. To a lesser degree, costume follows suit. If the majority of actors still appear in contemporary dress, the wardrobe of the period reveals two contradictory trends: growing attempts to appear in the fashions of their story's time or locale; increasing naturalism in hair, dress and style. Some aspects of this transition make the period's stagecraft resemble, not necessitate, closet agendas. Virtually anything in this theatre of illusion can be made to appear natural; at the same time, illusion comes to be apprehended as a constituent of reality whose appearance also changes with the times. Other aspects highlight the compensatory logic of the closet. For, given the combined power of spectacle and acting in this period, advocates of drama might need to cordon off page from stage as the word's only means of defence.

---

8 See Sybil Rosenfeld, *Georgian Scene Painters and Scene Painting* (Cambridge: Cambridge University Press, 1981).

Reviewing

Until recently, Romantic commentary on theatre has been the most prized aspect of the period's theatrical activity and has referred primarily to the essays and newspaper reviews written by well-known Romantic writers. These are the materials that made their mark by erecting the distinction between stage and page. Keep in mind that the best-known Romantic writers about theatre – Charles Lamb, Leigh Hunt and William Hazlitt – were close friends of the poets who suffered rejection as playwrights, and that Coleridge, P. B. Shelley and Byron also produced important theories of drama. All of these men are self-declared advocates of imagination and poetry who worry aloud about the capacity of theatre to circumscribe dreams and to render society materialistic, mechanical and mindless. It would be foolish to discredit their writings on theatre, which remain justly celebrated and famously complex. But it is prudent to interrogate the antagonism that they establish between poetic and visual cultures, supplement their views with those by writers who are less 'Romantic', and underscore the, well, performative nature of their pronouncements. Their accounts not only mean to produce the types of character that they claim to be receiving from either the stage or page but reveal the advantages of repeatedly declaring things in decline. High culture frequently gets a boost from ostensibly low times. How better to know when, or that, it is high?

A fairer picture starts to emerge if we add to the canonical list of writers on theatre the now virtually canonical writings of Joanna Baillie and Elizabeth Inchbald. Besides being the most respected Romantic playwright of either gender, Baillie rivals premier theorists of theatre in the comprehensiveness of her account of the psychological and moral efficacy of theatre through her commitment to staging the invisible processes that motivate and undermine action. Inchbald is the first British critic of either gender commissioned to record her observations on the 125 plays selected to comprise *The British Theatre*. We should also include in our survey of theatre commentary the relatively neglected writings of Thomas Holcroft, Hannah Cowley, Thomas Lovell Beddoes and Jane Scott as well as the countless signed or anonymous articles printed in some 160 newspapers, magazines and journals devoted to the theatre alone between 1800 and 1830, especially *The Examiner, Morning Chronicle, Champion, The Times, News, Tatler, Dramatic Censor* and *Morning Post*. In both its content and placement alongside major news of the day, this 'Theatrical Intelligence', as it is usually headlined, best captures the vibrant interaction between theatrical and socio-political commentary.

Despite this striking variety, several threads of discussion keep surfacing. The best-known revolves around closet drama or mental theatre, embodied in the counterintuitive claim that theatre is no longer the appropriate venue for drama. The argument is usually ascribed to Lamb, Coleridge and Hazlitt, who contend that 'poetry and the stage do not agree together' because 'in the glare of the scenes, with every wished-for object industriously realized, the mind becomes bewildered in surrounding attractions'.[9] That these men are some of the period's best writers *for* theatre as well as champions of it is one of the paradoxes that make study of Romantic theatre so rich. In the case of Lamb and Hazlitt, the paradox is resolved by recognizing their primary target: the closeting of Shakespeare, for otherwise they treat theatregoing with enthusiasm. Scholars have construed this operation as a way to protect the genius of Shakespeare, under the logic that, because genius is immaterial, Shakespeare cannot be faithfully represented on stage. The accompanying view, that Shakespeare's status as England's cultural centre means that he can no longer be seen as well-represented by theatre, indicates a shift in the period's apprehension of where imagination resides and a major parting of the way between modes of spectatorship and vision. It also demonstrates these critics' political savvy. Because Shakespeare is frequently appropriated by illegitimate forces and touted as the source and sanction for radical causes, bardolators construe the transcendence of Shakespeare as proving that he is above party politics and theatre altogether.

A second consequence of the alleged priority on closet drama is a discursive and material expansion of the spaces construed as closets and the kinds of sensibility housed in them. In the most extensive version, closet space is made synonymous with domestic space and seen to support several forms of female drama: most respectably, a penchant for private theatricals credited to aristocratic women (the Margravine of Anspach and the Countess of Buckinghamshire), but also perceptions of the private sphere as the setting for female histrionics, the source of domestic tragedy, and a less exoticized theatre of war. Baillie not only thematizes the connections

---

9 *The Complete Works of William Hazlitt*, ed. P. P. Howe, 21 vols. (London: J. M. Dent and Sons, 1930–4), vol. V, p. 276; S. T. Coleridge, *Lectures 1808–19: On Literature*, 2 vols., ed. R. A. Foakes, vol. V in *The Collected Works of Samuel Taylor Coleridge*, Bollingen Series 75 (Princeton: Princeton University Press, 1986). See also Charles Lamb, 'On the Tragedies of Shakespeare, Considered with Reference to Their Fitness for Stage Representation' (1811), in *The Works of Charles and Mary Lamb*, ed. E. V. Lucas, 4 vols. (London: Methuen, 1903–5).

between domesticity and warfare in her tragedies on love (*Basil*) and remorse (*Henriquez*) but reforms closet space in her Introductory Discourse and subsequent prefaces to *A Series of Plays on the Passions*. For her, closet is neither opposed to stage nor hostile to it. Nor does her focus on the passions imply that interior processes are invisible and thus unstageworthy. It 'belong[s] to tragedy' to 'unveil the human mind under the dominion' of 'strong and fixed passions' *in* public theatres that, at most, need to be reconstructed so that spectators can see this more distinctly.[10] Moreover, delight in spectacle to her does not imply a coarsening of taste or lack of imagination. 'Love' for 'striking contrasts of light and shadow; for splendid decorations and magnificent scenery; is as inherent in us as the interest we take in the representation of the natural passions and characters of men.'[11] Others, like Byron and P. B. Shelley, advocate closet drama for the way that it sets in motion the futurity of action. For them, writing for the closet signifies writing for the time when theatre and world are more amenable to visionaries.

A second thread of discussion concerns the proper constitution, reception and evaluation of character, a concern that itself reflects significant changes in late Georgian theatre conditions: an increasing number of women performing on stage and writing for it; a more diversified audience in terms of gender, class and race; growing awareness of the 'others' that threaten Britain's empire over its geographical empire; anxiety regarding the status of any individual in democratic and mass culture. Drama and theatre criticism in this period is profitably viewed as a form of conduct manual in its establishment of proper codes of behaviour and appearance, especially for women and the middle classes. Accounts of Shakespeare's characters are directed at reforming female character, the interaction of social classes, and adjudicating the proper balance between reality and idealism in minds, persons or society. Drama criticism also serves as specific stage-conduct manuals for actors, through which critics delineate their visions of how actors should assume their various characters. Such projects occasion the contradictory critical tones that render writings on theatre at once the most genial and lethal form of literary criticism in this period. Literally the space of play, theatre is also the locale of subject formation, social transformation and the latest information on current events. Theatrical Intelligence also

10 Joanna Baillie, *The Dramatic and Poetical Works* (1851) (Hildesheim, NY: Georg Olms Verlag, 1976), pp. 10, 233.
11 *Ibid.*, p. 232.

registers profound ambiguity over what forms of identity theatre enjoins and reflects: generic or particular, mass or individual, stupefied or energized, enslaved or free.

Accounts of the most famous actors of the day enter into broader social commentary by portraying them as illustrating warring categories of identity. The two male leads, Kemble and Kean, are said to represent clashing eras (ancient, modern), class affiliations (patrician, plebian), and aesthetic sensibilities (classic, Romantic; beauty, sublimity) that are then mapped onto contemporary events and offered as aids to spectators in the process of acquiring new social and gender identities. As 'tragedy personified', 'Mrs Siddons' embodies a wide range of fe/male options: sublime beauty, suffering femininity, public woman as mother, and actress as queen mother. Siddons's portrayal of Lady Macbeth epitomizes the powerful linkage that her enactments of more conventional wives (Belvidera, Lady Randolph, Calista and Mrs Beverly) establish between suffering and commanding femininity. No wonder Burke's Marie Antoinette is modelled on Siddons. Such a woman can bring down the house without ever protesting her confinement by home.

Accounts of these actors also accentuate tensions in conceptions of how theatre forms and informs individuals. If Siddons, Kemble and Kean are said to exemplify 'woman', 'English', 'patrician' or 'Jacobin', what makes them exemplary is that they are exceptional – a fact that fuels the public's desire to know them and their characters in all their rich interiority and particularity. Yet this inquisitiveness regarding what makes a being exceptional is at odds with the dominant mode of representing character: as a type made discernible through stylized gestures and standardized routines. Underlying these conflicts are fundamental questions regarding the ends of theatrical self-formation. What identities does theatre fashion? Group? Individual? Animal? Is its psychology one of surface or depth? Moreover, to where does group pleasure transport the individual: indifference? violence? higher or lower planes? These discussions occasion contradictory assessments of the service to society that is provided by theatre, ranging from the disservice proclaimed by closet advocates to claims that it is a better form of church than church advanced by theatre enthusiasts.

Grounds for the moral justification of theatre also run the gamut from it being a site of rational entertainment or moral reform to diversion, recreation, sociability and gossip. Influencing the latter set of depictions is widespread disillusionment over the sufficiency of reason for achieving social coherence. After the 1790s, writers are likely to praise playhouses for their capacity to 'scatter egotism and collect sociality', to 'rally us round the standard of our common humanity', a standard intentionally lowered by those disheartened over witnessing the terrors of independent intellect.[12] In this regard, the suspension of disbelief associated with theatre provides relief from the notion that reason is best suited to making a group cohere. Perhaps spectacle, music, banality are. But this affirmation of theatre's sociable nature again confronts its limits in the representation of Shakespeare, who apparently can only remain the source of a person's or people's cultural identity as long as he is not envisioned by or in a crowd. Because for many people Shakespeare is at the heart of personal identity, of some of one's earliest and dearest attachments, one's sense of self is threatened by having to witness other people's conceptions of him. Even by the greatest actors, 'representation of the character on the stage almost uniformly interferes with our conception of the character itself'.[13] This self-protectiveness regarding Shakespeare reaches new heights, i.e., depths, when the 'African Roscius' Ira Aldridge performs Othello at Covent Garden in April 1833. Even before his debut, 'Friends' need to circulate a handbill defending his right to audience fair play, but Aldridge's Othello is granted only two appearances, since a black man performing Shakespeare is deemed 'not very creditable to a great national establishment'.[14]

Urban spectacles

Strong evidence for the power of late-Georgian theatre exists outside the bounds demarcated by legitimate and illegitimate drama. Whether found in the streets, civic spaces, state spectacles or personal theatrics, this theatre goes even farther than traditional forms in accentuating the public's delight in spectacle – both viewing it and becoming one.[15] Popular forms of drama, like the juvenile drama or the penny gaffs, serve constituencies excluded even from illegitimate theatre. The one targets youth, especially boys, who

12 *Leigh Hunt's Dramatic Criticism, 1808–31*, ed. Lawrence Huston Houtchens and Carolyn Washburn Houtchens (New York: Columbia University Press, 1949), p. 316; William Hazlitt, *Hazlitt on Theatre*, ed. William Archer and Robert Lowe (New York: Hill and Wang, 1895), p. 143.

13 Hazlitt, *Hazlitt on Theatre*, pp. 50–1.

14 Passage from *The Times* cited in Herbert Marshall and Mildred Stock, *Ira Aldridge: The Negro Tragedian* (Carbondale and Edwardsville: Southern Illinois University Press, 1968), p. 121.

15 See Jacky Bratton, *New Readings in Theatre History* (Cambridge: Cambridge University Press, 2003), pp. 133–70.

purchase materials to construct miniature theatres at home that are modelled on current offerings at the major theatres, the other presents clandestine performances, often mounted in old storefronts, warehouses and
pits, to poor and illiterate audiences ranging from several hundred to a
thousand people. London streets themselves offer an array of theatricalized
spaces in which passers-by gain access to other places, races and times. De
Loutherbourg's Eidophusikon is one example, constructed in 1781 as a
miniature moving stage on which is depicted scenes from history or nature.
It spawns the many diorama and panorama that present scenes of natural
disasters, famous battles, major cities, monuments and landmarks, or
spectacular landscapes at different seasons. Other sites have more erotic
charges, such as Dr Graham's Temple of Hymen, complete with the first-
ever Celestial or Magnetico-electrico bed. These relatively permanent sites
are located in a street life that frequently combines things to buy with things
to see – as the new practice of window shopping embodies. Urban bazaars
house picture galleries and various exhibitions alongside of their consumer
wares. Places of amusement, like Ranelagh and Vaux-Hall, thrive on the
variety and notoriety of their shows.

It is difficult to say when making a spectacle of one's self first became
popular, given that it remains a prime tactic of elite cultures and the earliest
stage of identity formation. But the process gains a particular shape and
urgency when the right to dominate political or entertainment arenas
becomes a matter of votes or sales rather than bloodlines or established
names. Techniques from legitimate theatre aid public personae in fashioning their claims to visibility and credibility. The demand for *Lives* of
various actors shows the possibilities of constructing a public persona at
odds with the facts. 'Lord Byron' epitomizes this appeal, the variety of
whose literary alter egos testify to the theatricality of his ego and its
inspiration for countless others. Before him, several theatrical women trade
in the parts that cohere as his career: Siddons and the publicity of a private
life, Mary Robinson and sex appeal, Emma Hart Hamilton and her Attitudes. These techniques trickle down to the populace, inspiring audience
members to model themselves on celebrity images.

Nowhere is the circulation between theatre and life more pronounced
than in various dramas of state that characterize this period. These scenes
theatricalize public life and coordinate styles of performance and spectatorship with modes of self- and group-fashioning. The process is especially
visible in two famous court cases, the seven-year impeachment proceedings
in the House of Lords against Warren Hastings, convicted by the Commons

in 1786 of high crimes and misdemeanours while serving as Governor-General of India, and the Treason Trials of 1794, in which eleven men, including John Thewall, Thomas Hardy, John Horne Tooke and Thomas Holcroft, are accused of high treason for seditious activities involving the London Corresponding Society and the Society for Constitutional Reform. These trials demonstrate the fluidity between legal and theatrical arenas and have long been read as highpoints of urban theatre – commentators stressing the long wait for tickets, the threat to limb and fashion in attending, and the way that theatrical categories influence the reporting of events. Of particular interest is how these trials inaugurate new trends in the intersections between drama and law. One trend prompts us to see melodrama first as a legal performance that then gets adopted by theatre – the introduction of stage melodrama in England, usually attributed to Thomas Holcroft's *A Tale of Mystery* of 1802, occurring a decade after these trials. Another shows how these trials produce not just high (melo)drama but famous new plays and adaptations, Sheridan's *Pizarro*, which inserts the most famous speech that Sheridan delivers during the Hastings trial into the play, being the most popular play of the entire 1790s.

The Hastings trial highlights two key manoeuvres that become standard legal-theatrical fare throughout the century, both of which concern the nature of evidence as presented in Sheridan's Begums speech.[16] One pertains to the content of this speech, the recognition that conviction favours feeling over fact. In accusing Hastings of turning a son against his mother and grandmother, Sheridan links evidence to those feelings that appear self-evident, chief among them filial piety and the desire of (Indian) women to live in sequestration. A second concerns delivery, the strength of conviction that is felt to attend body language. Sheridan's closing tableau involves his collapsing into Burke's arms with the words, 'My Lords, I have done.' The Treason Trials replay such successes, the attorney for the accused, Thomas Erskine, being a master at swooning and at accentuating the domestic distress felt by these poor men's wives and babies. Even more substantially, the charge itself concerns theatre, the statutory definition of high treason being 'when a man doth compass or imagine the death of our lord the king'.[17] Of a theatrical nature, too, is establishing the guilt or innocence of Hastings, for what kind of person is a company man?

16 See Daniel O'Quinn, *Staging Governance: Theatrical Imperialism in London, 1770–1800* (Baltimore: Johns Hopkins University Press, 2005), pp. 164–221.
17 John Barrell, *The Spirit of Despotism: Invasions of Privacy in the 1790s* (Oxford: Oxford University Press, 2006).

Two other forms of state drama illustrate contradictions between spectacle and popularity in the theatre of public life. The first occurs within legitimate theatre but spotlights the role of the audience in directing public affairs – the Old Price Riots of 1809, the last great theatre riot in English history and the 'most important event in London (and perhaps Britain) in the autumn and early winter of 1809'.[18] For sixty-seven nights, spectators stopped or severely disrupted the show on stage by staging their own drama, complete with costumes, props, music, signs, dances, races on the pit benches, mock fights and general mayhem. Their protest targeted several innovations associated with the reopening of Covent Garden after extensive renovations resulting from fire: the rise in ticket prices, the number and exclusivity of private boxes, and the amount of money paid to the Italian singer, Angelica Catalani. The riot stresses the complicated interactions between radical and conservative objectives, since the rioters were protesting innovation in the name of tradition, England, and their right to view Shakespeare at a reasonable price. At the same time, the riots speak to the changeability and interchangeability of role, class and identity in theatre, 'King John' Kemble being cast (and castigated) as the revolutionary reduced to dumbshow, and the spectators not only running the show but making it reflect their version of the proper constitution of England. At other times, spectators take to the streets after seeing a play, inspired by what they have seen to protest at once the staged and real-life treatment of servants, slaves, apprentices or sailors.

The coronation(s) of George IV in 1820 accentuates the spectacle of state power and its powers of replication. For the coronation not only ushers in a more opulent, aristocratic manner of government mis/rule but a repeat performance that rivalled the original event in grandeur and surpassed it in the numbers of person able to view it and employed in constructing it. In August 1820 Robert Elliston produced and played the lead in The Coronation at Drury Lane, a ninety-minute replica of the coronation that ran for 104 performances and included a facsimile of the interior of Westminster Abbey and Hall and a procession of around 400 authentically costumed actors. Ostensibly staging the peaceful transfer of power in a revolutionary age, it reflects the influence of illegitimate theatrics on royal stages, such documentary pageants being a mainstay of the minors. It also displays theatre's power to document reality as a theatrical arena, to train spectators to see

---

18 Marc Baer, Theatre and Disorder in Late Georgian London (Oxford: Clarendon Press, 1992), p. 16.

pomp as a circumstance of power, and to challenge the legitimacy of that power. The coronation/ *The Coronation* produced many sequels, one being Scott's pageant for George IV in 1822, but a more immediate one being the third major trial of the period, the divorce proceedings against Queen Caroline. This latter production accentuates another sobering reality, that leading ladies can be rich, independent, liberated and still essentially powerless.

Whether we look, then, at legitimate theatres, venues of London theatricality, or the history of literary history's aversion to theatre in the Romantic period, we encounter the major role that theatre played in this period's individual and group life. Current enthusiasm for performative models of identity can flatten out claims for the specificity of Romantic theatre's share (or indeed of any theatre's share) in identity formation, but I would argue for two ongoing legacies. Given that Romantic theatre is not only situated in a revolutionary age but also was itself often characterized as too radical, material, or insurgent for literary representation, it stresses the highly political nature of so-called culture wars and how suspect are the demarcations that separate legitimate from illegitimate spaces, voices or interests. Moreover, with its heightened attention to the differences between viewing and reading drama, Romantic theatre foregrounds the practice of ascribing particular aesthetic pleasures to particular individuals and groups – even of reducing certain groups to the entertainment industry. When we argue that sitting in front of a screen (whether silver, TV or PC) impedes vision and renders a citizenry passive, we re-enter the discourse theatre of Romanticism. And when we posit that gaining media visibility indicates cultural legitimacy, we gloss over darker realities portrayed on and by this stage. Discourse on Romantic theatre depicts the formation of the equation by which 'popular' means delight in spectacle, immediacy, distraction and 'respectable' means preference for reading, contemplation and the beauty of truth. But it depicts this equation as a fantasy that also seriously restricts the domain of fantasy.

The epigenesis of genre: new forms from old

TILOTTAMA RAJAN

Preliminaries

Discarding the 'classical' theory of genre, Friedrich Schlegel wrote provocatively that there is only one genre or as many genres as texts. Similar claims for the power of texts to create their own rules were made by William Wordsworth, Victor Hugo and Friedrich Schelling.[1] The diversification of genres, the insistence at times that every text is *sui generis*, and the definition of poetry (by Percy Shelley for example) as a faculty not confined to literature, might suggest that the Romantics attached no value to literary genre. But Schlegel's notion of a single genre – a progressive universal 'poetry' which he also called the 'novel' – and his insistence that we need a theory of genre,[2] imply that genre remained important to a period that branched out from the 'central genres' to 'extended literature'[3] and to a sense of literature itself as extending into and engaging with other cultural domains. I suggest here that genres imply an approach to aesthetic education. Thus the idea of a pre-established number (whether three or eight), and the arrangement of these kinds of subject-matter in a hierarchy, both

---

1 Friedrich Schlegel, *Literary Notebooks 1797–1801*, ed. Hans Eichner (Toronto: University of Toronto Press, 1957), p. 110; William Wordsworth, 'Essay Supplementary to the Preface', in *Literary Criticism of William Wordsworth*, ed. Paul M. Zall (Lincoln, NE: University of Nebraska Press, 1966), p. 182; Victor Hugo, *Preface to 'Cromwell'* (1827) (Paris: Garnier Flammarion, 1968), p. 107; Friedrich Schelling, *The Philosophy of Art* (1803/4), ed. and trans. Douglas W. Stott (Minneapolis, MN: University of Minnesota Press, 1989), p. 239. For elaboration see my 'Theories of Genre', in *The Cambridge History of Literary Criticism*, vol. V: *Romanticism*, ed. Marshall Brown (Cambridge: Cambridge University Press, 2000), pp. 226, 230–6.
2 Percy Shelley, *A Defence of Poetry* (1821), in *Shelley's Poetry and Prose*, ed. Donald H. Reiman and Sharon Powers (New York: Norton, 1977), pp. 478–508; Schlegel, *Philosophical Fragments*, trans. Peter Firchow (Minneapolis, MN: University of Minnesota Press, 1991), p. 31.
3 The terms are those of Alistair Fowler, *Kinds of Literature: An Introduction to the Theory of Genres and Modes* (Cambridge, MA: Harvard University Press, 1982), p. 17.

subtend particular ways of disciplining the subject and constructing literature as a discipline. In this sense, the Romantics' unfixing of genres or 'kinds' from the canonicity of lyric, drama and epic challenges the restriction of literature itself to certain 'kinds' of experience learned through apprenticeship to a curriculum of genres. Indeed the very shift from a formal theory of genre, and the blurring of the line between genre and mode, are part of this challenge. This de-formalization is connected to the space made in aesthetics for individual genius or, less romantically, new technologies of the self facilitated by the proliferation of print culture. But since genres are social contracts, the fact that cognitive and cultural re-formation occurs through *genre* is significant. Genres do not arise autonomously but as part of a network of allusions and differences. In this sense genre, as Julia Kristeva says of intertextuality, situates 'the text within history and society, which are then seen as texts read by the writer, and into which he inserts himself by rewriting them'.[4]

The Romantic or 'modern' practice (as Schlegel also calls it) thus moves from a formal to a more contingent and hybrid notion of genre as historically produced and still in process. The vestiges of an older education through genre can be seen in Blake, Wordsworth and Keats who (like Spenser and Milton) begin with lyric and proceed to more epic forms, sometimes paying lip-service to drama. Yet Keats, who lays out this curriculum in 'Sleep and Poetry' (1816), does not complete his aesthetic, any more than his medical, education. Halfway through the mansion of genres, he breaks off his apocalyptic epic *Hyperion* and reconstructs it in *The Fall of Hyperion* (1819) as a permanent ruin. A parallel curriculum was forming for women writers who began with educational manuals and children's stories, proceeding to the novel of manners. Mary Wollstonecraft's *Original Stories From Real Life* (1788) marks her initial interpellation into this system,[5] containing the complexity of narrative she later confronted in *The Wrongs of Woman, or Maria* (1798) within the moralism of the story as epigrammatic narration. But if genres codify the kinds of experience through which writers engage with the world, and if generic *Bildung* proceeds from

---

4 Julia Kristeva, *Desire in Language: A Semiotic Approach to Literature and Art*, trans. Leon Roudiez (New York: Columbia University Press, 1980), p. 65.
5 I use the term interpellation in Louis Althusser's sense, to refer to the process of 'hailing' by which an individual finds his place in social and kinship structures which are ideologically constructed, and represent 'the imaginary relationship of individuals to their real conditions of existence' ('Ideology and Ideological State Apparatuses' (1969), *Lenin and Philosophy and Other Essays*, trans. Ben Brewster (New York: Monthly Review Press, 1971), pp. 162, 170–7).

preliminary genres to ones that assume a cultural responsibility, these latter are varied, constructed in dialogue with each other, and often introduced (like *Wrongs* itself) as experiments yet to be completed.

In short, the cultural discipline subtended by the system of genres was in flux by the Romantic period. First, the diversity of Romantic writing is at odds with Goethe's claim that lyric, epic and drama are the '*Naturformen der Dichtung*', the natural forms of poetry.[6] Second, this triad itself has a merely residual status for the Romantic philosophers who systematically theorize genre. For both Friedrich Schelling and G. W. F. Hegel, thinking genre historically and not just logically results in an emergent model, in which the attempt to contain difference by leading new genres stemmatically back to old ones mutates into far more rhizomatic genealogies.[7] For instance the German Romantics generally see the novel as a modern form of epic, as later elaborated by Georg Lukács. Yet this only means that the epic is an alibi for bringing into the archive genres that are decidedly non-epic: annals, biographies, travel-writing, confessions and oriental tales.[8] As in the rhizome, it is then impossible to distinguish the root-genre from branches that put down roots and become new points of inception. Nevertheless the unruliness of Romantic genre has often been disciplined by our own critical biases. For a long time Romanticism was synecdochically represented by the lyric, as it was credited with definitively replacing the triad epic/tragedy/comedy with that of epic/drama/lyric.[9] Lyric was thus the dominant mode – if not genre – of a Romanticism that internalized the quest romance (in Keats's *Endymion* and Shelley's *Alastor*), or lyricized an array of forms including the ballad, the epic (in Wordsworth's *The Prelude* (1805)), and drama (in Percy Shelley's *Prometheus Unbound*).[10] The New Critics further promoted lyric by analysing even narrative poetry in lyric segments, though they rescued Romanticism from its devaluation by the moralism of

---

6 Cyrus Hamlin, 'The Origins of a Philosophical Genre Theory in German Romanticism', *European Romantic Review* 5:1 (1994), 10–13.

7 An example is Schelling's discussion of epic, *Philosophy of Art*, pp. 223–47.

8 Georg Lukács, *The Theory of the Novel: A Historico-Philosophical Essay on the Forms of Great Epic Literature*, trans. Anna Bostock (Cambridge, MA: MIT Press, 1971); Schlegel, *Notebooks*, pp. 54, 163–4, 33.

9 Irving Ehrenpreis, *The 'Types Approach' to Literature* (New York: King's Crown Press, 1945), p. 16.

10 On lyric, see my 'Romanticism and the Death of Lyric Consciousness', in *Lyric Poetry: Beyond New Criticism*, ed. Patricia Parker and Chaviva Hosek (Ithaca, NY: Cornell University Press, 1985), pp. 194–207; on quest-romance see Harold Bloom, 'The Internalization of Quest Romance', in *The Ringers in the Tower: Studies in Romantic Tradition* (Chicago: University of Chicago Press, 1971), pp. 13–37.

F. R. Leavis in associating lyric with complex thought rather than pure feeling. Rather than questioning the lyric synecdoche, the historicism of the mid-eighties critiqued it as the Romantic ideology: an ideology of inwardness, Kantian disinterestedness and the avoidance of history. That critique held regardless of whether lyric was a trope for transcendence or for a Heideggerian slow thought that was equally seen as aestheticist.[11]

More recently, these two inversely related reductions of Romanticism to lyric – and the resulting partition of poetry and the novel between Romanticism and Victorianism – have been qualified by an interest in prose fiction before 1830. However, in one of the most powerful attempts to read genre as an epistemic and not simply literary category, Clifford Siskin sees lyric and the novel (or 'novelism') as two arms of an ideological apparatus that makes Romanticism a key stage in modernity. In his argument, lyric contains the productivity of 'writing' (analogous to what Roland Barthes calls 'text') within Literature: the narrower 'discipline that took writing as its professional work'. While Literature is professionalized and aestheticized as lyric, in the form of the novel it has the role of ensuring that the aesthetic serves the public sphere.[12] In this scheme lyric retains its pre-eminence, as Romanticism both prefigures the disciplinary role of the Victorian novel and privatizes Literature through lyric.

Arguably this emphasis on lyric has less to do with Romanticism than with the way Robert Browning and J. S. Mill constructed Shelley and Wordsworth, and with the Victorian formation of English Studies in universities as a discipline linked to the history of the nation. The current retrojection of the epistemic category of Literature onto the Romantics, moreover, reflects an ideology that derives *its* professional authority from reading texts through the *topoi* of cultural capital, social construction and the middle class. I suggest by contrast that in the Romantic period Literature had yet to emerge as a discipline with a defined curricular core, and that its diversity has paraliterary ramifications for disciplinarity and society different from those that follow from reducing Romanticism to lyric and the novel. Even as a canon Romanticism was constructed by exceptions: in their

---

11 See Jerome J. McGann, *The Romantic Ideology: A Critical Interpretation* (Chicago: University of Chicago Press, 1983); Marjorie Levinson, *Wordsworth's Great Period-Poems* (Cambridge: Cambridge University Press, 1986).
12 Clifford Siskin, *The Work of Writing: Literature and Social Change in Britain, 1700–1830* (Baltimore, MD: The Johns Hopkins University Press, 1998), pp. 14, 20, 103–54, 172–92. I capitalize the word Literature when using it, as Siskin does, to refer to an ideological and epistemic category rather than an empirical corpus.

time the six 'major' poets were not famous, with the exception of Byron, who was infamous. This place made by Romanticism for difference is facilitated by three shifts in the cognitive environment of texts, which affect genre and provide tools for its rethinking. In this context, it may be useful to approach Romantic genre not through the conventional formal triad(s) but through more fundamental generic 'radicals' or '*Grundhaltungen*'.[13] I will go on to suggest three such radicals that are distributed across the formal divisions between prose, poetry and non-fiction prose: extensive (long and usually narrative) genres; intensive (brief, intense, at times psychically compacted) genres; and genres-in-progress.

Three contexts for genre

The first context or cognitive environment for rethinking genre is 'writing', the term Siskin uses to describe the expansion of print after 1700 and the effects of this new technology on texts.[14] The Renaissance had seen a proliferation of subgenres produced by vernacularization, but literature remained a formal affair because the first print revolution did not breach the boundaries of class and gender.[15] But after 1780 'writing' and the reading it generated multiplied the books by women and the range of printable subject matters. This demographic expansion also affected male writers. For not only did it lead someone like William Godwin to move from historical romance in *St Leon* (1797) to the domestic novel in *Fleetwood* (1805), and to the domestic as part of *history*; indirectly it also created the very possibility of 'minor literature'. Minor literature, as Gilles Deleuze and Felix Guattari define it, includes the effect that minorities have on majorities: the texts written in a major language by majorities who discover their own minority.[16] John Thelwall's *The Peripatetic* (1793), which combines verse and prose, literature and journalism, is a quasi-poem/novel that resists the professionalization of poetry often attributed to the Lake Poets. It could not

13 The term is used by Karl Viëtor. See Claudio Guillen, *Literature as System: Essays Towards the Theory of Literary History* (Princeton, NJ: Princeton University Press, 1971), pp. 117–18.
14 Siskin, *Work*, pp. 2, 14. For a more qualified view of the hegemony of professionalization in the Romantic period see Gary Kelly, *English Fiction of the Romantic Period: 1789–1830* (London: Longman, 1989), pp. 252–4.
15 Robert Southey is one of the first to construct a parallel if lower canon of working-class poets in *Lives and Works of the Uneducated Poets* (1831) (London: Humphrey Milford, 1925).
16 Gilles Deleuze and Felix Guattari, *Kafka: Toward a Minor Literature*, trans. Dana Polan (Minneapolis, MN: University of Minnesota Press, 1986), p. 16.

have been written without an acceptance of minor literature as more than just the preparatory exercise that previously allowed for the practice of minor genres such as the sonnet. This notion also allows us to include as literature such work as Coleridge's notebooks and marginalia (which he toyed with seeing as a book). That 'writing' results in work that does not employ the technology of print that Siskin associates with it is only apparently paradoxical. For the notebooks are a response – in handwriting – to the proliferation of the print archive, which then calls into question the very genres of publishable writing. In this sense writing resembles the more recent phenomenon of 'text' as conceived by the *Tel Quel* group. 'Text' is not just a shift in the relation of author to work but affects what comprises literature, thus reaching into the very 'organizing structure of disciplinarity'.[17]

A second context for generic change involves travel and the related phenomenon of translation, literal and cultural. Antoine Berman describes German Romanticism as a culture of translation, where the experience of the foreign extends beyond curiosity to open up 'a relationship with the "Other", and with an otherness in oneself'.[18] Though travel literature existed before Romanticism, travel often took the form of the grand tour, which Byron repeats in *Childe Harold's Pilgrimage* (1812–18), only to abandon it for a more peripatetic journeying in the more generically amorphous *Don Juan* (1819–24). The grand tour (bleakly revisited at the end of Mary Shelley's *The Last Man*) is a form of cultural capitalism in which the elite of states whose economic power is recent visit countries, particularly Italy, that are in decline but are venerated for historical reasons.[19] It is homologous to the apprenticeship in set genres that earlier constituted literary training. What changed in the Romantic period were the travellers, parameters of, and motives for travel. The grand tour had been part of a masculine education. Now women such as Wollstonecraft travelled to countries (such as Sweden) that did not provide a predictable cultural dividend. Their travel (and that of the Shelleys and Coleridge) was not tourism, which is posited on a return home that 'domesticates the ... critical possibilities' of a changed

17 John Mowitt, *Text: The Genealogy of an Antidisciplinary Object* (Durham, NC: Duke University Press, 1992), p. 24.
18 Antoine Berman, *The Experience of the Foreign: Culture and Translation in Romantic Germany*, trans. S. Heyvaert (Albany, NY: State University of New York Press, 1984), pp. 4, 35.
19 Louis Turner and John Ash, *The Golden Hordes: International Tourism and the Pleasure Periphery* (London: St Martin's Press, 1976), p. 29.

perspective, so that 'wandering can be . . . enclosed [and] understood'.[20] For Wollstonecraft, who went on business for her faithless lover, travel – so often linked to colonization – became vulnerability. It precipitated forms of inner experience, such as melancholia, only theorized much later by feminist psychoanalysis, and it thus radicalized the very category of 'sensibility'. Some travellers (Percy Shelley, Keats and Helen Maria Williams) never came home. Others returned at a cost evident in Mary Shelley's submission to the novel of manners after her experiments in Italy with science fiction in *Frankenstein* (1818), feminist history in *Valperga* (1823), and apocalypse in *The Last Man* (1826), not to mention a breaching of the very boundaries between what can and cannot speak its name in the cryptically personal *Mathilda* (1819), a novella about incest which was not published until the twentieth century.

For Godwin who, in his eccentric and inventive *Lives of Edward and John Phillips, Nephews of Milton* (1817), traces the mixture of decline and opportunity in the shift from High Literature to Grub Street, cultural travel is linked to the burgeoning print archive. Godwin focuses on the nephews' 'writing' and on John Phillips's translations of oriental material and his wandering away from a Miltonic, classical education. His *St Leon* shows the consequences of travel: the inflection of the historical novel by a mode that allows space to expand time, so that the genre itself travels uncertainly beyond the identity Scott was to give it as a form of nationalism. Travel is a material influence on, and a metaphor for, the migratory status of genres, as well as a context for tensions between domestication and innovation. Travel opened up new philosophical horizons for Coleridge. For women writers it created new epistemic opportunities. Elizabeth Hamilton, in her *Letters of a Hindoo Rajah* (1796), travelled vicariously through her brother and took epistolary fiction out of the narrow domesticity often allotted to the female mind into social history. If epistolarity allowed Hamilton and Williams to engage the larger world under the cover of a female genre, the fact that Williams let the genre travel from fictitious to real history helped other writers more definitively to enter the masculine spheres of politics and history.

A third context for generic change involves developments in biology, the discipline named by F. A. Lamarck in 1802. For genre (deriving from *genus*) refers to both literary and natural kinds. The parallel can be seen in Goethe,

---

20 Georges Van Den Abbeele, *Travel as Metaphor: From Montaigne to Rousseau* (Minneapolis, MN: University of Minnesota Press, 1992), pp. xx, xvii.

whose attempt to hold on to the *Naturformen der Dichtung* is repeated in his desire for an *Urpflanz* or ur-plant, and whose ultimately much more complicated theory of metamorphosis in plants has future consequences for a theory of literary kinds.[21] The word genre is also connected to 'gender' and 'engendering'. These etymological links, also present in the German word *Gattung*, inscribe the very concept of genre in the problems of genesis and change. Biological models for genre have been criticized for projecting the determinism of Darwinian evolution onto literature (particularly in the work of Brunetière and J. A. Symonds), as well as because they confuse the more open system of the history of species with an individual life cycle of growth and decline.[22] But evolution is not the only way of narrativizing what the nineteenth-century biologist Treviranus called 'the Science of Life', and the nineteenth century's shift from taxonomy to a *history* of species is important precisely for the problems not resolved by its narrative models, and thus for the space it creates for anomalies. In this period 'epigenesis' gradually replaced 'preformation' as an account of how organisms develop. As important, embryology was absorbed into the larger field of natural history which has implications for literary historiography. Epigenesis, as a result, became an account not just of how an organism develops but also of the emergence of new species. And new species could develop laterally or regressively in ways that compromised the progress science sought to project onto natural 'history'.

The term epigenesis goes back to William Harvey, who distinguishes it from 'metamorphosis' (or preformation). In the latter the organism develops through the unfolding of a pre-existent form in the germ, while in epigenesis the embryo develops in stages, forming structures not originally in the egg (as in the growth of an acorn into an oak tree, or analogously of the epic into the novel). In the early modern period, however, both are closed theories: in preformation nothing can develop that was not originally there, but in epigenesis development follows an internal logic also based only on the original material. That the theories are variants of each other is suggested by the fact that 'metamorphosis', used by Harvey to describe preformation, is elaborated by Goethe with reference to the kind of example

---

21 Johann Wolfgang von Goethe, 'The Metamorphosis of Plants' (1790), in *Scientific Studies*, ed. and trans. Douglas Miller (New York: Suhrkamp Publishers, 1988), pp. 76–97; see also his discussion of *Gestalt* in *Scientific Studies*, pp. 63–6, and his discussion of plant monstrosities, p. 106.

22 David Fishelov, *Metaphors of Genre: The Role of Analogies in Genre Theory* (University Park, PA: Pennsylvania State University Press, 1993), pp. 23, 35.

Harvey uses for epigenesis.[23] On the other hand, when late eighteenth-century science returned to epigenesis it was to account for the manifestly varied forms of species. Moreover, the problem is not just one of genesis but also of judgement. Or as Immanuel Kant says, 'the forms of nature are so manifold' that natural phenomena cannot always be judged by existing rules.[24] Kant evokes nature in order to theorize aesthetic judgement, at a time when the emerging field of anthropology opened up by travel was causing a reassessment of natural and cultural phenomena as a closed set. When J. F. Blumenbach (the German anthropologist and physiologist, one of whose students was the explorer Alexander von Humboldt) abandoned preformation for epigenesis, it was thus to explain both the emergence of different species and the development of hybrids.[25] While Blumenbach's *De generis varietati humani nativa* (1795) sought to account for the various races by tracing them to an origin from which they had degenerated, its interest also lies in the role it accords climate and mode of life in the production of new varieties. It is only a short step from natural to cultural explanations of generic mutation. This step had already been taken by the German philosopher and cultural anthropologist J. G. Herder. Questioning his own preformationist theory of genre with regard to the lyric, Herder also sees the 'shape' of genre, the shape of shape itself, as constantly changing, and sees the offshoots as equal in importance to the 'root', given that we cannot draw our 'standards from only *one* kind' and '*one* people'.[26]

For his part, Blumenbach allowed that the 'formative force' might be diverted from its *telos* by the production of monsters, hybrids and varieties. It is true that he struggled to derive the varieties of mankind from an original (white) race. He also saw hybrids as unable 'to propagate . . . their new ambiguous shape sprung from anomalous venery',[27] so that eventually variations and deviations die out. However, Romantic biologists soon

---

23 See W. F. Bynum, E. J. Browne, and Roy Porter (eds.), *Dictionary of the History of Science* (Princeton, NJ: Princeton University Press, 1981), p. 127; Wilbur Applebaum, *Encyclopedia of the Scientific Revolution: From Copernicus to Newton* (New York: Garland, 2000), pp. 213, 523. For a larger discussion of the reciprocal involvement of science and the arts see Robert J. Richards, *The Romantic Conception of Life: Science and Philosophy in the Age of Goethe* (Chicago: University of Chicago Press, 2002).

24 Immanuel Kant, *Critique of Judgment*, trans. J. H. Bernard (New York: Hafner, 1951), p. 16.

25 Timothy Lenoir, *The Strategy of Life: Teleology and Mechanics in Nineteenth-Century German Biology* (Chicago: University of Chicago Press, 1989), pp. 17–20.

26 J. G. Herder, *Selected Early Works, 1764–1767*, ed. and trans. Ernst A. Menze and Karl Menges (University Park, PA: Pennsylvania State University Press, 1992), pp. 70–1.

27 J. F. Blumenbach, *On the Natural Varieties of Mankind* (3rd edn, 1795) (New York: Bergman, 1969), p. 195.

discovered that hybrids *were* fertile, and that monstrosity could start its own lineage.[28] Blumenbach himself admitted that the structure of an organism might be permanently modified by its environment, and John Hunter – the surgeon and physiologist who inspired Coleridge's *Theory of Life* (1816) – not only saw monstrosities as normal but argued (like Goethe) that 'supernumerary parts' might be 'so complete in their formation, as to become', over time, a 'part of the whole'.

Romanticism thus saw the revision of normalizing taxomonies by the fact of undiscovered phenomena in nature. Indeed Hunter proposes three models for change in species: evolution or preformation, in which nothing develops that is not there initially; metamorphosis, where the parts are also there from the outset but shift in 'form, action, &c.'; and epigenesis, in which new parts are 'formed as they [are] wanted'. The three models explain different kinds of development, but may also overdetermine change in the same organism.[29] Indeed the models are really ways of interpreting change. Whereas preformation would conservatize the epistolary novel by deriving it from the verse epistle, metamorphosis would allow the shift by which a poetic form becomes novelistic to connote a more categorical change. A further model allows us to imagine change in species not as occurring along a ladder but through a form of lateral 'bushing' or speciation. This 'allopatric' theory reflects the beginnings of a kind of anthropology within biology: 'new species arise in *very small* populations that become isolated from their parental group' and develop rapidly at the periphery, then reconstituting dominant genres.[30] From this perspective the epistolary novel could be seen as produced through the very isolation of women writers whose contribution then permanently troubles the identity of the novel as what Hegel calls the 'bourgeois epic'.[31]

More important than the models is the need they suggest to open up the ways mutation is interpreted and classified. This last point is of enormous *future* significance, given the symbiosis between aesthetics and science in the work of Kant, Hegel, Coleridge, Goethe and others. For although theory in nineteenth-century Britain lags behind literature, developments in biology

---

28 Lenoir, *Strategy*, p. 19; J.H. Green, *Vital Dynamics: The Hunterian Oration Before the Royal College of Surgeons* (London: William Pickering, 1840), p. 83.
29 John Hunter, *Essays and Observations on Natural History, Anatomy, Physiology, Psychology, and Geology*, 2 vols. (London: John Van Voorst, 1861), vol. I, pp. 247, 239–45, 204; Goethe, *Scientific Studies*, pp. 111–17.
30 Fishelov, *Metaphors*, pp. 247–51.
31 G. W. F. Hegel, *Aesthetics: Lectures in Fine Art*, trans. T. M. Knox, 2 vols. (Oxford: Clarendon Press, 1975), vol. II, p. 592.

make it possible at an archeological level not only to rethink the system of genre epigenetically (as adding new forms where needed), but even to rethink what constitutes the aesthetic organism. That there are natural forms worth discussing though they fail the test of creative evolution is significant given Romantic scientists' comparisons of nature to an artist.[32] From J. B. Robinet in the eighteenth century to the German Idealist *Naturphilosophen* natural history is seen aesthetically as a *Bildung* or process of development that proceeds to perfection, but through a series of 'abortions', in the phrase used by Coleridge's friend, the physician and Idealist philosopher J. H. Green. While Green's scheme is teleological, more important is the place it makes for the incomplete, for failed or botched forms. This incompletion may be seen regressively, as in the idea explored by Green, that monstrosity occurs when the resumption of phylogeny in ontogeny fails, and the 'development of the embryo' is 'arrested' at an earlier stage of its evolution. Or it may be viewed progressively, for instance by Coleridge, who sees lower forms as posing problems solved higher up the scale of nature, as 'parts' emerge whose 'full purpose' grows clear only later.[33]

The impact of these developments is evident in Hegel, who worked on both natural history and art. Hegel wanted to see art as the 'adequate embodiment of the idea' achieved by classicism. But he found classical perfection limiting, and was more interested in the 'idea's' failure to articulate itself in the modes of art that he called 'symbolic' and 'romantic'. Symbolic art, in which the form and content fail to coalesce because the 'idea' is deficient, and romantic art, whose dis-integration results from the fact that external forms are insufficient to convey the idea, are two forms of incompletion, like the regressive and progressive.[34] Inasmuch as its evolution is incomplete, the 'bad determinacy' of the symbolic is no more than a symbolic resolution of underlying contradictions (in Fredric Jameson's Lacanian use of 'symbolic'). The Gothic would in this sense be a symbolic form with supernumerary parts whose role becomes clear only later, and whose distortions are the 'gigantic shadows which futurity casts upon the present'.[35] As I shall suggest throughout this chapter, Romanticism's most important contributions to genre were metageneric: they consist not only of

32 Green, *Vital Dynamics*, pp. 30, 130.
33 Green, *Vital Dynamics*, p. 40; S. T. Coleridge, *Shorter Works and Fragments*, ed. H. J. and J. R. de J. Jackson, 2 vols. (Princeton, NJ: Princeton University Press, 1995), vol. II, p. 1194.
34 Hegel, *Aesthetics*, vol. I, pp. 76–80.
35 Shelley, *Defence*, p. 508.

adding genres but also of rethinking the very limits of acceptable kinds of literature.

Extensive genres

Given this diversification of genres, what happens to the central genres in a period that is technically committed to the schema epic/lyric/drama, but sees the beginnings of the modern curricular trinity novel/poetry/drama? From Boileau onwards, criticism tried to contain genre in triads: a notion that collaborated with the Romantic fondness for dialectic. But the supplementary permutations of this triad suggest the futility of its desires to limit and segregate genres. Romantic genre has a hybridity we overlook if we focalize it through a single mode. While epic may have been lyricized in *The Prelude*, it is novelized in *Don Juan*, where poetry travels into the realm of the social. But if *Don Juan* is a novel, could one not also see Wordsworth in *The Prelude* as novelizing his narrowing of the epic into the aesthetic? Or as exposing lyric to demographic pressures through lyrical 'ballads' that engage poetry with the genres of everyday life? Romantic genres extend into each other, forming temporary syntheses or dissensions. Unlike the generic hybrids of the Renaissance, these are not just compounds of existing genres but entirely new inter-genres such as lyrical drama, the 'quasi-novel', or Schlegel's 'symphilosophy' and 'sympoetry'.[36]

Among the key *principles* for approaching Romantic genre is a sensitivity to this hybrid, aleatory quality – which in turn reflects the heuristic as much as descriptive status of genres. As suggested, we might also consider intersecting the formal division between prose and poetry with one between extensive and intensive genres. Lukács introduces the term 'extensive' to describe texts with a range of characters and events located in space. Epic is an 'extensive totality', whereas the novel is extensive without being totalizing. But what *is* the novel in the Romantic tradition on which Lukács draws? For Schlegel, who 'detest[s] the novel as . . . a separate genre', novels include poems and plays. The novel is the genre of the Romantic or modern, also defined as 'progressive universal poetry' (in the older sense of poetry as 'making'). As such it is a principle of experience involving openness and heterogeneity and, as Mikhail Bakhtin says, a reorientation of time towards the present and future rather than the past. Lukács for his part alludes to the Romantic notion of the novel as

36 Kelly, *English Fiction*, pp. 252–60; Schlegel, *Fragments*, p. 34.

'combining all genres' including those alien to literature. He describes the novel as a 'polemical' genre in contention with itself: a 'fusion of hetero-geneous ... components' which is 'abolished over and over again'.[37] Although I will limit 'novel' to prose fiction, these non-formal definitions allow poems to possess narrativity (or spatial and temporal extension), but uncouple prose fiction from the disciplinary mechanisms of the novel as interpellation into a *plot* that contains narrative's discontents within the closure of a beginning and end.

On the one hand, novelizing other extensive genres allows *poetry* to be removed from its current esotericism and seen as producing the novel. 'The Thorn' – which could be approached 'intensively' as a short story trau-matically cut off from narrative development, but could also be placed in the more extensive network of the *Lyrical Ballads* – can be read with the earliest experiments in naturalism in Mary Hays's *Victim of Prejudice* (1799), or as laying the grounds for the sensation novel. If the 'outward form' of the novelistic genre consists in the biographical,[38] Percy Shelley's *Alastor* (1815) could be viewed as novel and not just elegy. The poem, then, would be 'progressive', by which Schlegel implies a concern with the unfolding of events in time and thus with the real. Finally, reading poetry or poetic drama under the eclectic rubric of 'narrative' – as a story situated in its own telling, that could be told otherwise and remains unconcluded – allows poetry to be read as 'text'. Reading *Cain* (1821) as tragedy binds it to a mimesis that chastises Cain's questioning of God's law, although Byron defers any hypostasis of the plot by making the play a closet drama. Instead we could approach it as an assemblage of narrative materials that interrupts the dramatic action with a speculative excursion into other worlds that precede and follow that of the Bible. Cain's tragedy would then be only one possible outcome to the text's metaphysical story, which could be narrati-vized differently in other possible intellectual worlds.

On the other hand, progressive universal poetry also merits unpacking as a description of the *novel*. Schlegel's concept, repeated by Percy Shelley,[39] implies that genres of experience are linked in an ongoing, open-ended

---

37 Lukács, *Theory*, pp. 43, 46, 79, 84, 91; Schlegel, *Dialogue on Poetry and Literary Aphorisms*, trans. Ernst Behler and Roman Struc (University Park, PA: Pennsylvania State University Press, 1968), p. 101; Mikhail Bakhtin, *The Dialogic Imagination: Four Essays*, trans. Caryl Emerson and Michael Holquist (Austin: University of Texas Press, 1981), pp. 7, 13–15.

38 Lukács, *Theory*, p. 77.

39 Shelley, *Defence*, p. 494.

curriculum. If 'progressive' is connected to reality, 'poetry' gives the novel a creative role that goes against the disciplinary division of romance and novel reluctantly urged by Clara Reeve but blurred by Godwin.[40] As a 'novel' in the Romantic sense, Hays's *Memoirs of Emma Courtney* (1796) polemicizes the *Bildungsroman* by putting epistolarity and the memoir into mutual contention. While the memoir educates us into real life, the epistolary romance (addressed to future as well as past correspondents), struggles to reimagine female *Bildung* through a negative dialectic of realism and romance. Hays's novel can also be seen as autonarration: a form that mixes personal life, ideas and fiction so as to put its imagination at risk through a life aware of its social construction.[41] Combining these genres, her novel is a poetry that is progressive in the sense of still working itself out.

The novel as poetry can be set against Siskin's subsuming of the genre into 'novelism', given the initially liberating but finally consumerist expansion of the market for novels. Novelism has three aspects which do not all coincide with what Bakhtin, following Schlegel, calls 'novelization'.[42] The first is its association with the new (or 'news'), with a sense of literary history itself as 'developmental innovation' rather than 'imitative decline'. But the second is the *English* novel's association with '*modern disciplinarity*' and the constitution of nationalism in a 'newly united kingdom'. Hence a third aspect is that the ascendancy of the novel 'naturalizes' what it includes as new: 'When writing becomes just like hunting and shooting', though novels are still dangerous 'we know how to handle them.'[43] But we should be wary of prematurely Victorianizing the Romantic novel. For its conflicting subgenres are still being proliferated through writing rather than disciplined by criticism.

To be sure, the Regency period sees the beginnings of the interest in governmentality associated with modernity.[44] Scott's progress from ballads

40 Clara Reeve, *The Progress of Romance, Through Times, Countries, and Manners* (1785) (New York: Facsimile Text Society, 1930), pp. 110–11; William Godwin, 'Of History and Romance', in *Things as They Are; or The Adventures of Caleb Williams*, ed. Maurice Hindle (Harmondsworth: Penguin, 1988), p. 368.

41 Tilottama Rajan, 'Autonarration and Genotext in Mary Hays, *Memoirs of Emma Courtney*', in *Romanticism, History, and the Possibilities of Genre*, ed. Tilottama Rajan and Julia Wright (Cambridge: Cambridge University Press, 1999), pp. 213–39.

42 Schlegel, *Fragments*, p. 10; Bakhtin, *Dialogic Imagination*, p. 5.

43 Siskin, *Work*, pp. 175, 185.

44 The term is Michel Foucault's, and indicates the study of the technologies and theoretical accounts according to which people are governed ('Governmentality', in Graham Burchell, Colin Gordon and Peter Miller (eds.), *The Foucault Effect: Studies in Governmentality* (Chicago: University of Chicago Press, 1991), pp. 87–104).

and romances to the historical novel participates in the Scottish Enlightenment's constitution of Britain as a commercial nation through the relegation of the Highlands past to the mode of nostalgia. Scott also masculinizes prose fiction by regulating romance within the novel. Austen takes up women's share in this narrowed genre by finessing the novel of manners as the production of proper ladies, thus helping to govern the nation by dividing the novel along the lines of gender. In this newly gendered economy, even the exception can be said to prove the rule. Thus Caroline Lamb's *Glenarvon* (1816), a pseudo-historical novel, may seem to transgress the boundary between female manners and masculine history. But Lamb's harlequin romance about Byron specifically enacts a novelism that allows literary experiment to be consumed as trash. Conflating Byronism and the 1798 Irish uprising, she sensationalizes the political radicalism of the Jacobin novel and the radical genre of autonarration so as to reduce transgression to mere fashion. Lamb paradoxically re-establishes propriety by showing that she has no manners, by writing a generically confused novel that proves women's unfitness to do the work of history.

Still, this partition of the novel into the separate spheres of history and manners is misleading. The novel of manners was not named until 1866 and was not initially popular:[45] We have perhaps retrojected its canonization onto Romanticism in absorbing the period into the 'Nineteenth Century'. Two decades before *Emma* (1815), Eliza Fenwick's *Secrecy; or The Ruin on the Rock* (1795) inscribes the novel of manners in a more tangled dialogue of discourses through Caroline's failure to become an Austenian narrator. The later Romantic period witnessed Scott's growing fame, but also Mary Shelley's creation of a feminist historical novel intertextually engaged with the work of her parents and husband in *Valperga*. Nor can the historical novel be neatly gendered: Scott's view of history as evolution is rebuked by Godwin's *Mandeville* (1819), which interiorizes history as its own psychoanalysis through the trauma of an individual who never emerges into history. New genres are constantly being invented. Moreover, any given work migrates through more than one genre. As Lukács says of this period, genres 'cut across one another . . . and become traces of authentic or false searching' for an aim 'no longer clearly . . . given',[46] constituting the work of genre as extensive but not totalisable.

45 Barbara Brothers and Bege K. Bowers, 'Introduction', in Bowers and Brothers (eds.), *Reading and Writing Women's Lives: A Study of the Novel of Manners* (Ann Arbor: UMI Research Press, 1990), pp. 5, 9.
46 Lukács, *Theory*, p. 41.

Intensive genres

Given the many extensive genres in Romanticism, what happens to lyric, or more broadly 'intensive' genres? In the Bourdieuvian genealogy currently popular, lyric has been given a conservative role in the reproduction of culture. Through Wordsworth's troping of lyric as georgic (the middle term in an older triad that leads from pastoral to epic), the wise passiveness of the aesthetic is legitimized as work, and the poet becomes a producer of symbolic capital for an emergent middle class that is aesthetically educated in disinterestedness and sensibility. In Wordsworth's poetry, often the primal scene of these analyses, the revolutionary consciousness of social ills is thus contained in the still life of the 'lyrical' ballad. More generally, it is argued, lyric merely seems to create a feeling *subject*, but in fact serves the disciplinary apparatus of society.[47] Gender also plays a role in this story. For just as the novel after Scott contains its ties to women's writing in romance subplots, so too the professionalization of lyric reappropriates for masculine use what had become a female genre by the 1800s. Thus a potentially dangerous negative capability in 'sensibility' is channelled into manageable and marketable affects, withheld from cognitive development or social intervention by the very brevity of lyric.

This account has considerable validity, as is evident from the functioning of lyric analogues in other genres as part of a culture of amateurism that forgets the revolutionary ferment of the 1790s. Thus the development of the essay in England as the preferred form for criticism goes hand in hand with a continuation of the medieval guild-university in Oxbridge, as distinct from the Humboldt university in Germany or the technical schools in France. Like the lyric, the essay is a liberal form that contains openness as closure. Though it has the potential to create a space withdrawn from knowledge as science (as Theodor Adorno argues),[48] the essay canonized by and in *British* literary history through its emphasis on Hazlitt and Lamb aestheticizes its subjects, and commodifies thought as leisure.

---

47 Siskin, *Work*, pp. 22, 129; Thomas Pfau, *Wordsworth's Profession: Form, Class and the Logic of Early Romantic Cultural Production* (Stanford, CA: Stanford University Press, 1997), pp. 3, 9, 12, 15, 92, 228–30.
48 Theodor Adorno, 'The Essay as Form', in *The Adorno Reader*, ed. Brian O'Connor (Oxford: Blackwell, 2000), pp. 92–110. Adorno writes of the essay as a withdrawal from 'method' that is not amateurism or belles-lettrism: 'Thought acquires its depth from penetrating deeply into a matter, not from referring it back to something else' (p. 99).

But this story also raises questions, both ideological and empirical. First there is the cultural agenda embedded in making lyric a metonym for poetry. For while the shift from the triad epic/lyric/drama (in Romantic criticism) to the modern triad novel/poetry/drama seemingly expands from lyric to poetry, it has latterly concealed a reduction of poetry to lyric. The reasons are ostensibly curricular: in survey courses like 'The Nineteenth Century', poetry is more efficiently represented by short items. Condensed into lyric it then becomes, like lyric, a commodity circulated in miscellanies and anthologies, and thus itself miscellaneous. The rarifying of poetry as lyric and its reduction to a sound bite are part of the marginalizing of what it earlier represented in the name of a reality principle of which current historicisms are as much a mirror effect as a critique. What poetry once represented (and thus the critical acts it made possible) includes both its earlier sense as imaginative writing, and the capacity for difficult, often ontological or epistemological, thought. So thoroughly is lyric cathected with Sartre's bifurcation of poetry and prose along the lines of withdrawal versus social engagement,[49] that it can be seen as a *faux genre*. Lyric has become a receptacle for values we question, and an antithetical term in the reshaping of our cultural Imaginary.

Perhaps for this reason we should speak of a range of intensive genres of which lyric – particularly the Greater Romantic Lyric – is only one. Lyric itself does not prescribe an aesthetic ideology simply because it has been so used in liberal or colonialist pedagogy. The equation of the Romantic lyric with aesthetic ideology seems to be a result of its narrowing to the lyrics of Wordsworth (though even they could be seen as experimenting, sometimes ironically, with aestheticization). But broadly speaking, lyric as a paradigm for what Siskin calls 'deep knowledge', simply allows for the careful probing of moments overlooked in more extensive critical forms such as cultural studies. In this vein, Adorno sees lyric as a 'rupture' from a world in which experience is reduced to reification and categorical subsumption.[50] In Keats's 'Ode on Melancholy' the naming of a new psychic place, through its protection in a form read in silence and slow thought, uses the aesthetic attitude to elevate to the level of what Kant calls reflective judgement an emotional complex that eludes its temporary formalization in an ode, and that is more unsettlingly explored in Mary Shelley's *Mathilda*. Brief forms

---

49 Jean-Paul Sartre, *What is Literature?*, trans. Bernard Frechtman (Gloucester, MA: Peter Smith, 1978), pp. 6–8, 29–30.
50 Adorno, 'Lyric and Society', *The Adorno Reader*, pp. 211, 215; Siskin, *Work*, pp. 131–40.

withdraw from interpellating 'the intellect on the model of a . . . work ethic', and allow for reflection and puzzlement. But they should not be abstracted from their dialogical relation with a writing largely comprised of extensive genres. Any 'single' work, as Adorno says, is 'vulnerable to the charge of . . . ideology',[51] and lyric has been particularly subject to a reading practice that creates the work of art as fetish-object.

I adapt the term 'intensive genres' partly from Allen Tate's distinction between 'extension' and 'intension', which defines the latter as the failure to achieve a 'tension' between structure and texture. Tate sees a connotative inwardness and obscurity in intention as overwhelming the drive to extension or denotation,[52] which involves a more public form of statement. Lukács (drawing on Hegel's distinction of inwardness from its objectification) also speaks of 'intensive' as opposed to 'extensive totalities'.[53] The importance of Lukács's distinction lies in its implicit decoupling of inwardness from the totality now used to conservatise Romantic subjectivity. If there are extensive genres that are not totalizing (such as the novel), there must also be forms of inwardness that eschew totality for a more amorphous subjectivity. These forms highlight the problematic place of intensity in extensive genres such as the novel. Given an epistemic shift that legitimized feelings as objects of enquiry, one of Romanticism's metageneric contributions is thus the possibility of the brief as intensive rather than epigrammatic or preliminary. Coleridge's late poetry makes a radically new place for the brief as the obscure, the abject: material cut off from narrative development. Alternatively, in the case of a poem such as his 'Time Real and Imaginary', totality itself, as formalization, marks the text as dissociated from itself.[54] These same features of cryptic compactness and formalisation can be seen in short stories such as Mary Shelley's 'Transformation' (1830), which register a darker side to the tale. Whereas Amelia Opie's 'tales' – Simple Tales (1806), Tales of Real Life (1813) – show a domestic modesty about large ventures and are prose equivalents for the lyrical construction of the subject in Wordsworth's ballads, Shelley's short stories are the uncanny, allegorical remnant of her submission to middle-class life

51 Adorno, 'The Essay', p. 93.
52 Allen Tate, 'Tension in Poetry' (1938), in Essays of Four Decades (Chicago: Swallow Press, 1968), pp. 62–4.
53 Lukács, Theory, p. 46.
54 See Tilottama Rajan, 'Coleridge, Wordsworth, and the Textual Abject', in Rhetorical and Cultural Dissolution in Romanticism, ed. Thomas Pfau and Rhonda Ray Kercsmar, South Atlantic Quarterly 95 (1996), pp. 797–820.

after her return to England – their very brevity reflecting the trauma of realism.

Genres-in-progress

The archeological shifts facilitated by Romanticism return us to the impact of biology on genre. For as J. H. Green notes, natural history is a 'preface and portion of the history of man', with ramifications for history (and literary history). Embryology studies the organism in its life history, while natural history deals with the interconnecting life of multiple species. But what does 'life' mean? As already noted, from Robinet to the *Naturphilosophen* natural history is constructed as a progressive universal poetry. Nature is thus a single organism that perfects an 'original prototype' through time.[55] But the process is full of contingencies. It may be allopatric or metamorphic or subject to retardation. It may carry within it the traces of past traumas or obstructions yet to be worked through. Thus 'progressive' may simply mean ongoing or incomplete. Or as Hegel says, in rethinking cultural through natural history, spirit in its 'restless fermentation' is still struggling to clarify itself, and 'strives to imagine . . . a meaning for the shape' or a 'shape for the meaning'.[56]

Biology therefore leads to a uniquely new sense of literature as historically unfinished. Romanticism is famous for having legitimized fragments as 'tendencies, ruins, and raw materials'.[57] But the fragment is not the only form of incompletion. Keats's *Fall of Hyperion* makes re-vision the intensive centre of an epic extensiveness that can no longer be totalized. More literally, editorial work on Wordsworth shows how much he too was constantly revising. He did not publish the *Prelude*, and held on endlessly to 'The Ruined Cottage', which migrates among lyric, narrative and abject – the sentimental tale of Margaret published as Book 1 of *The Excursion* being only one uneasy redaction of the text. It is Romanticism that has made possible an embryology of texts that justifies the study of earlier versions, so as to inscribe texts in the (psychic) history of their own metamorphoses and displacements. The period also saw (in the museums of Hunter and Blumenbach) the first anthropological collections of everything that might be a 'portion' of the history of man, from the remains of other species to

---

55 Green, *Vital Dynamics*, pp. 57, 103–6.
56 Hegel, *Aesthetics*, vol. I, pp. 338, 440, 448.
57 Schlegel, *Fragments*, pp. 1, 20–1.

fossils. As tainted as these collections may be by cultural bias, they provide generic validation for such projects as collecting Coleridge's marginalia and publishing his notebooks.

Unpublished work foregrounds textuality as radically incomplete. But publication too was not yet tied to the notion of final authorial intention entrenched by the development of the speed press, which allowed for manuscripts to be delivered complete rather than in instalments. Authors therefore did not have to see their books as final. Texts often begin or end with promises of a further volume: for instance Shelley's *Defence*, Wollstonecraft's *Vindication of the Rights of Woman* (1792), and her study of the French Revolution (of which she promises 'two or three more volumes'). Genres themselves may be in progress. Closet drama can be seen as a form of 'writing' not ready to be performed. In Hegel's terms, its disjunction between inside and outside could be either symbolic (due to a lack of internal clarity) or romantic (due to the difficulties of externalizing a vision that is internally clear). Shelley points to the second possibility when he links the 'lyrical drama' of *Hellas* to the 'unfinished' state of history, which prevents the 'subject in its present state' from being 'treated otherwise than lyrically'.[58]

We can conclude with a genre whose current popularity may have much to do with its being 'in progress'. Critics have found the Gothic difficult to fix as conservative or radical, especially given its use for both masculine sado-masochistic fantasies and female subversion, as well as for an unstable cross-dressing between these opposites (in Charlotte Dacre's *Zofloya* (1806) or Percy Shelley's *Zastrozzi* (1811)). Jerrold Hogle suggests that the Gothic is a collective crypt for conflicting contemporary discourses – mercantile, scientific, familial, political – that cannot yet be culturally processed.[59] Registering the trauma of this overdetermination in the wake of the French Revolution (which Blake psychoanalysed as conflating Orc and Urizen), the Gothic is the presently deformed possibility of future transformations – a genre, like so many others, that invites embryological reading as conflictedly progressive and regressive. As the case of the Gothic suggests, an embryology rather than a formalism or thematics of genre may in the end be the most significant contribution of Romantic genre viewed as a practical poetics.

---

58 Shelley, 'Preface' to *Hellas* (1821), in *Poetry and Prose*, p. 408.
59 Jerrold Hogle, 'Frankenstein As Neo-Gothic: From the Ghost of the Counterfeit to the Monster of Abjection', in *Romanticism, History, and the Possibilities of Genre*, ed. Rajan and Wright, pp. 178–9.

23

The literature of the new sciences

JAN GOLINSKI

Introduction

The period of the late eighteenth and early nineteenth centuries, familiar to students of literature as the age of Romanticism, has been named by some historians of science 'the second Scientific Revolution'. The suggestion is of a transformation comparable in significance to the seventeenth-century movement in which Galileo, Descartes and Newton played prominent roles. In the earlier period, the earth had been recognized as a planet orbiting the sun, and natural philosophy reshaped by applying experimental and mathematical methods. The later period saw the emergence of new scientific disciplines, including geology, biology and physiology, and the reconfiguration of existing ones, especially physics and chemistry. Changes in disciplinary practices coincided with fundamental changes in scientific institutions. In Britain, the period also saw vigorous development of new means of popularization and new audiences; science attained a higher profile in the eyes of the general public than it had hitherto enjoyed. Scientific ideas circulated in general literate culture, communicated by public lectures in London and the provinces and periodicals and books addressed to middle-class readers. They even achieved a currency in working-class circles through the efforts of journalists, publishers and educators. The 'scientist' – to adopt the new term, first proposed by William Whewell at a meeting of the British Association for the Advancement of Science in 1833 – was a figure in the public eye.[1]

1 Stephen G. Brush, *The History of Modern Science: A Guide to the Second Scientific Revolution, 1800–1950* (Ames: Iowa State University Press, 1988); Jan Golinski, *Making Natural Knowledge: Constructivism and the History of Science* (Cambridge: Cambridge University Press, 1998), pp. 66–78. I would like to thank Tim Fullford for his careful reading of this chapter, and the organizers and participants at the conference on 'Romanticism and Empirical Method', at Queen Mary and Westfield College, University of London, 2–3 March 2001, for the stimulus of their ideas.

The fact that the public audience for science expanded significantly during this era undermines the notion that science and literature were already segregated into the 'two cultures', famously lamented by C. P. Snow.[2] This chapter will not present a picture of the rise of an autonomous, specialist scientific worldview and the retrenchment of literary culture from engagement with scientific ideas. Rather, scientific and literary intellectuals will be shown to have shared a single cultural realm, exchanging concepts and metaphors and focusing jointly on certain issues of pressing concern. I shall propose that the agenda of learned discourse was substantially shaped by the political climate of the times, especially the almost continuous state of war between Great Britain and France, from 1793 until 1815, and the steady (and at times violent) pressure for an extension of political rights to the unenfranchised majority of the population. The campaign for wider political rights, resisted in part because of establishment fears that the upheavals of the French Revolution would jump the Channel, attained partial success with the passage of the first Reform Act in 1832. The whole period was characterized by a fundamental polarization of political opinion, dividing members of the different social classes, and setting reformers against conservatives within the literate middle class. The opening up of these profound political differences in the 1790s made for the 'end of the Enlightenment' in Britain and the fragmentation of what seemed in retrospect like a fairly homogeneous public sphere of intellectual and social discourse.

In the first section of the chapter, I briefly survey the transformation of Enlightenment public science into the more extensive but more fragmented enterprise of the early nineteenth century. I then examine in turn four themes that featured centrally in scientific discourse of the period. These are, first, the appreciation of certain forces in the natural world as instances of the 'sublime'; second, the growing sense of a very lengthy past in the history of the earth and other planets; third, the new awareness of the processes of life in their chemical, electrical and physiological dimensions; and, fourth, the emergence of the figure of the scientific hero as a mediator between specialists and the wider public. Each of these themes was prominent in the scientific writings circulating within society at large. In each case, also, political issues reflecting the serious social tensions of the period were just beneath the surface of scientific discourse, influencing the form it took in middle-class and working-class communities.

2 C. P. Snow, *The Two Cultures and the Scientific Revolution*, intro. Stefan Collini (Cambridge: Cambridge University Press, 1993).

The reformation of public science

By the 1830s, after decades in which the intellectual legacy of the Enlightenment had been fiercely contested, the public dimension of scientific activity had changed significantly from the situation prevailing in the eighteenth century. Small, self-organized societies devoted to learning and improvement had been a commonplace phenomenon throughout enlightened Europe; the reactionary scare of the 1790s placed many of those in Britain under unprecedented strain. In 1795, Prime Minister William Pitt introduced the first of a series of parliamentary measures against 'seditious meetings', requiring all groups for intellectual debate to be licensed and forbidding them to discuss religion or politics. A lurid exposé by W. H. Reid, published in 1800, claimed that London was a hotbed of 'infidel societies', propounding subversive doctrines under the influence of the writings of Voltaire, Thomas Paine, William Godwin and Joseph Priestley.[3] Wariness and suspicion undermined the ideals of enlightened public science, of which Priestley had been the best-known spokesman. Priestley had insisted that the diffusion of learning should advance popular enlightenment, extirpating 'all error and prejudice' and putting an end to 'all undue and usurped authority'.[4] When he emigrated to America, following the ransacking of his house in Birmingham by a loyalist mob in 1791, the most vigorous defender of public science as a motor of progress and enlightenment was silenced.

From the crucible of the 1790s, new forms of public science emerged. New institutions extended the size of middle-class audiences. New publications – periodicals and books – served an expanding readership, which included significant numbers of women. In many settings, however, the enlightened aspiration for social progress through the diffusion of knowledge was censored or denounced. Humphry Davy, who stood at the apex of scientific lecturing in London in the 1800s, as professor of chemistry at the Royal Institution, emphasized in his lectures how science lent support to social and religious authority. In his inaugural lecture in January 1802, Davy renounced 'delusive dreams concerning the infinite improveability of man' and reassured his elite audience that the natural philosopher would always 'be averse to the turbulence and passion of hasty innovations, and will

---

3 William Hamilton Reid, *The Rise and Dissolution of the Infidel Societies of this Metropolis* (London: J. Hatchard, 1800).
4 Joseph Priestley, *Experiments and Observations on Different Kinds of Air*, 2nd edn, 3 vols. (London: J. Johnson, 1775–7), vol. I, pp. xiii–xiv.

uniformly appear as the friend of tranquillity and order'. In his *Elements of Agricultural Chemistry* (1813), he proffered a sanitized vision of social progress, in which advances in the sciences would be passed down 'from the higher classes of the community . . . to the labouring classes', and recruited natural theology to reinforce the language of stability and order.[5]

Elsewhere, however, the traditions of enlightened scientific communication and education lived on, encouraging the emergence of new publications and forms of instruction. William Nicholson, a writer and teacher of chemistry, brought out his *Journal of Natural Philosophy, Chemistry and the Arts* in 1797. Nicholson's *Journal* presented an accessible mix of original research reports and news of lectures and meetings of scientific societies. It established the model for a scientific periodical accessible to a broader readership than the somewhat intimidating *Philosophical Transactions* of the Royal Society. The following year, it was joined by the rival *Philosophical Magazine*, edited by the Scottish journalist and printer Alexander Tilloch. In 1813, another Scot, Thomas Thomson, published the *Annals of Philosophy*, which forced a merger between Nicholson's and Tilloch's publications in an increasingly crowded field. Further competitors and consolidations followed, but the seed planted by Nicholson had taken root. In the first three decades of the nineteenth century, a commitment to public education was still seen by many as integral to the advancement of science. These publications spoke to the proliferation of scientific and learned societies throughout the land, such as the Literary and Philosophical Societies established in many provincial cities. Scientific content was also increasingly to be found in general periodicals from the beginning of the century. The *Edinburgh Review*, from its first appearance in 1802, reflected the outlook of the Scottish universities, in which the sciences were treated as part of general letters and discussed in connection with political and moral issues. Geology, botany, chemistry and exploration were all treated in the *Edinburgh Review*, which subjected scientific writings – as much as literary ones – to informed criticism. When the rival *Quarterly Review* appeared in 1809, countering the *Edinburgh*'s Whig orientation with a metropolitan Tory alignment, it was obliged also to provide scientific coverage. The two periodicals each claimed a circulation of 12,000 copies during the years

---

5 Humphry Davy, 'Discourse Introductory to a Course of Lectures on Chemistry', in *The Collected Works of Humphry Davy*, ed. John Davy, 9 vols. (London: Smith, Elder, 1839–40), vol. II, pp. 323, 326; Davy, *Elements of Agricultural Chemistry*, in *Works of Davy*, vol. VII, p. 197.

1812–14; they only began to lose their dominant position to new rivals in the middle-class market after the end of the Napoleonic wars.[6]

By the 1820s, the Scottish Whig Henry Brougham, a frequent contributor to the *Edinburgh Review*, was beginning to organize public education initiatives that extended beyond the middle-class readership of the literary journals. Brougham's *Practical Observations upon the Education of the People* (1825) spoke on behalf of the growing movement to found mechanics' institutes, where working people could be educated to help them improve their prospects in society. Within a few years, institutes were founded in Edinburgh, Newcastle, Carlisle, Derby and many other cities, all of them featuring such sciences as chemistry prominently in their curricula. The movement was a highly controversial one, inevitably reawakening conservative fears of the social upheaval that popular education might produce. Brougham's foundation of the Society for Diffusion of Useful Knowledge (in 1828) again raised these concerns among the elite. Brougham was a middle-class reformer who disavowed any aims of radical social change, but Tories feared his efforts would prepare the ground for the subversive propaganda of agitators like Richard Carlile, a publisher of atheistic and materialist tracts aimed at the working class. Participants in the mechanics' institute movement provoked this reaction by criticizing the exclusive orientation of the scientific establishment toward a middle-class audience. For example, the short-lived periodical, *The Chemist*, published for just over a year between 1824 and 1825, did not hesitate to attack Davy as representative of 'a sort of royal science'. The journal was edited by Thomas Hodgskin, a writer and activist associated with popular education and the mechanics' institutes. Davy was unrelentingly denounced in its pages for having 'no appearance of labouring for the people' and indeed excluding them from his lectures. 'Fortunately, however', *The Chemist* insisted, 'the spirit of the age does not accord with the views of the dandy philosophers' like Davy. For those associated with this journal, the spirit of the Enlightenment lived on: science should be a democratic enterprise, available to all, as it had been in the age of Priestley, Benjamin Franklin and other heroes.[7]

While the idea that scientific communication should serve the cause of general enlightenment still had its defenders, the chastening experience of

---

6 Jan Golinski, *Science as Public Culture: Chemistry and Enlightenment in Britain, 1760–1820* (Cambridge: Cambridge University Press, 1992), pp. 252–5; Marilyn Butler, 'Culture's Medium: The Role of the Review', in Stuart Curran (ed.), *The Cambridge Companion to British Romanticism* (Cambridge: Cambridge University Press, 1993), pp. 120–47.
7 *The Chemist* 1 (1824), vii; 2 (1824–5), 47.

the 1790s had made return to the era of Priestley and Franklin impossible. Public science was now deeply divided along social and political lines. Those who were fearful of social change looked for reassurance that scientific ideas did not carry subversive implications, that they rather reinforced the conception of an ordered and lawful nature, presided over by an omnipotent God. On the other hand, intellectuals who sought social reform frequently saw education as an indispensable tool to channel the aspirations of the working class into self-improvement. Science could play its part in fitting working men and women for respectable employment, but only if it was not so obviously aligned with Anglican theology as to exclude Dissenters and others who resented the power of the established church. To conservatives, the reformers seemed to be sailing far too close to the wind, encouraging the appalling excesses of the radical materialists and atheists, who had been suppressed in the 1790s but were making their voices heard again by the 1820s. Thus, scientific knowledge was invested with the hopes and fears of different groups in a period of prolonged social tension. Readings of the religious implications of science frequently reflected this social context; and, as we shall see, even its aesthetic dimension was often politicized.

The natural sublime

The 'sublime' has been much discussed by scholars of literature and the arts in the Romantic period. The term was frequently used at the time in discussions of philosophy and literary criticism. It named an effect deliberately cultivated by visual artists, poets and prose writers. As a key aesthetic category, it linked the products of human art with the nature they represented. Human creations might be sublime on their own account, but, applied to the arts, the term generally referred to the natural phenomena whose power they communicated. Scientific lecturers and writers sought to elicit feelings of the sublime in their audiences – just as visual artists and poets might – with various ends in view. Invocations of the sublime, for example in descriptions of the dramatic scenery of foreign lands, might serve to inspire further efforts to conquer nature, to subdue it to human knowledge. On the other hand, the sublime was also a way to draw attention to the enigmas of the natural world, sometimes with the suggestion that they would continue to elude human curiosity. As a feature of nature – nature in certain aspects or moods – the sublime evoked the theological dimension of natural philosophy. In certain ways, it pointed to functions previously fulfilled by the deity in scientific discourse, but no longer so explicitly specified. It served as a reminder of the powers and terrors of nature, of the ways it challenged the human desire to know and perhaps of its ineluctable mysteries.

Discussions of the sublime in English took their point of departure from Edmund Burke's *Philosophical Enquiry into the Origin of our Ideas of the Sublime and the Beautiful* (1757). Burke established the sublime as counterpart to the beautiful in the vocabulary of aesthetic appreciation. The experience was that of astonishment, Burke claimed, 'and astonishment is that state of the soul, in which all its motions are suspended, with some degree of horror'. 'Whatever therefore is terrible, with regard to sight', he went on, 'is sublime too, whether this cause of terror, be endued with greatness of dimensions or not.'[8] Examples included dangerous animals, the ocean, darkness or vast spaces. Other instances of the sublime displayed the power of nature and, indirectly, of the divinity: earthquakes and thunder, for example. From Burke onwards, sublimity was distinguished from straightforward beauty in descriptions of natural scenery or weather events. In the 1790s, discussions of the 'picturesque' by William Gilpin and Uvedale Price put forward a third aesthetic category to be differentiated from Burke's two. Some English readers also became aware of the analysis by Immanuel Kant in his *Critique of Judgment* (1790), which significantly altered the terms in which the sublime was understood. Kant's list of sublime phenomena was similar to Burke's: 'Bold, overhanging, and as it were threatening rocks; clouds piled up in the sky, moving with lightning flashes and thunder peals; volcanoes in all their violence of devastation; the boundless ocean in a state of tumult; the lofty waterfall of a mighty river, and such like . . .'[9] But the German philosopher inserted an element of reflection into appreciation of the sublime, insisting that astonishment and terror alone did not suffice to produce the effect – only when they were succeeded by a feeling of intellectual mastery of fear by comprehension of the underlying phenomena. What was truly sublime was not the power of nature itself but the power of the human mind to grasp it. To quote Kant: 'Sublimity therefore does not reside in anything of nature, but only in the mind, in

8 Edmund Burke, *A Philosophical Enquiry into the Origin of our Ideas of the Sublime and the Beautiful*, ed. James T. Boulton (Oxford: Basil Blackwell, 1987), p. 57.
9 Immanuel Kant, *Critique of Judgment*, trans. Werner S. Pluhar (Indianapolis: Hackett, 1987), p. 120.

so far as we can become conscious that we are superior to nature within, and therefore to nature without us.'[10]

Although Kant's work was not widely read in Britain, his manoeuvre of inserting mental reflection into the aesthetics of the sublime was matched by British commentators. It permitted writers to discriminate between a discerning apprehension of the powers of natural phenomena and a merely irrational – even superstitious – fear of them. This did not, however, resolve the theological ambiguities of the term's connotations. The orthodox construed the sublimity of nature as a sign of the deity. In his 1802 lecture, Davy concluded that chemistry 'must be always more or less connected with the love of the beautiful and the sublime; . . . [being] eminently calculated to gratify and keep alive the more powerful passions and ambitions of the soul'.[11] Thus, God could be approached through sublime phenomena, which were apprehended by the intellectual function of the mind, rather than being the object of primitive superstition. For religious sceptics, on the other hand, the inherent powers of nature or the vast expanses of the earth's history pointed to the absence of God. For them, sublimity was a characteristic of the human mind that was able to grasp this profound vacancy and to master the fear it instilled.

Chemistry, in Davy's view, was a sublime science because it revealed the fundamental unity of natural forces, all of them derived from electricity. Geology exhibited the immensely powerful forces of earthquakes and volcanoes, and was generally seen as opening up the sublime vista of ages past. Meteorology was another science that offered a plentiful fund of sublime phenomena for representation and interpretation. The popular fear of unusual meteoric sights, such as auroras, ball lightning, tornadoes and peculiar cloud formations, had been denounced as superstition since the early eighteenth century. Enlightened opinion had sought to tame these terrors by reducing the weather to normal fluctuations of temperature and other variables, recorded as a matter of routine. The sublimity of atmospheric phenomena was nonetheless continually evoked in written and visual representations. The drawings and paintings of William Hodges, prepared during Captain James Cook's second Pacific voyage in 1772–5, derived much of their impact from meticulous rendering of weather conditions. John Reinhold Forster's account, *Observations made during a Voyage round the World* (1778), matched Hodges's images with detailed verbal

---

10 Kant, *Critique of Judgment*, p. 123.
11 Davy, 'Discourse', in *Works of Davy*, vol. II, p. 325.

records of the same meteorological phenomena. In Tahiti, the cloud-shrouded peaks loomed mysteriously over Hodges's pastoral scenes; off the coast of New Zealand, he portrayed threatening waterspouts in a storm-darkened landscape in the style of Salvator Rosa.[12] Alexander von Humboldt later referred to the emotional impact of these scenes, which 'awakened throughout Northern Europe a deep interest mingled with a sort of romantic longing'.[13] Hodges, Forster and other artists of exploration succeeded in rousing feelings of the sublime with their representations of exotic overseas locations. They used the sublimity of weather phenomena as a resource for this purpose, evoking the mysteries of atmospheric events while purporting not to succumb to the irrational superstition that had previously surrounded them.

The balancing act was typical of invocations of the meteorological sublime. The Quaker meteorologist Luke Howard recorded an unusual phenomenon witnessed with his family on the cliffs at Folkestone in July 1820. With the sun behind them, facing into a bank of low mist, the group observed their shadows projected onto the misty screen. A halo surrounded the shadow of the group as a whole, and another each person's head. An individual separating from the group acquired a halo around his own shadow, from his own point of view, but not from the others'. Howard concluded: 'The whole phenomenon was highly curious and interesting; and the facility with which each of the party could either appropriate the *glory* to himself or share it with the company present, suggested to me some reflexions of a *moral* nature – in which, however, I shall not anticipate the reader.' The moral reflections presumably concerned the importance of mutuality and the limitations of an egotistic view of the world. The incident demonstrated how sublime weather phenomena could convey to the enlightened observer a morally uplifting message rather than the degrading nostrums of superstition.[14]

Thunder and lightning were rather more problematic in this respect than clouds and haloes. Their terrors were less easily dispelled, and the attempts to control them were more politically loaded in the context of arguments

12 Bernard Smith, *European Vision and the South Pacific*, 2nd edn (New Haven, CT: Yale University Press, 1985), pp. 55–71; B. Smith, 'Coleridge's Ancient Mariner and Cook's Second Voyage', *Journal of the Warburg and Courtauld Institutes* 19 (1956), 117–54.

13 Alexander von Humboldt, *Views of Nature: Or Contemplations on the Sublime Phenomena of Creation*, trans. E. C. Otté and Henry G. Bohn (London: Bohn, 1850), p. 419.

14 Luke Howard, *The Climate of London, Deduced from Meteorological Observations*, 2 vols. (London: W. Phillips, 1818–20), vol. II, p. 346.

over the legacy of the Enlightenment. From Franklin's days, experimental philosophers had identified lightning with the static electricity familiarly generated and transmitted by human hands. As Priestley saw it, a heavenly power had been brought to earth by the electrical philosophers – testimony to the ability of human reason to bring nature under its sway. For Franklin and Priestley, control of lightning was associated with the power of progressive enlightenment to challenge despotic authority.[15] Davy shied away from the political implications, but did not hesitate to lay claim to command of these natural forces; he listed electricity among the means by which man was enabled 'to interrogate nature with power, not simply as a scholar, passive and seeking only to understand her operations, but rather as a master, active with his own instruments'.[16] The moral dangers of such a stance were reflected in the treatment of atmospheric electricity in Mary Shelley's *Frankenstein* (1818). Shelley, who was acquainted with Davy's reputation and writings, portrayed the hazards of a Promethean attempt to control the forces of nature. In her novel, thunderstorms and lightning appear as forces of destiny, partially identified with the monster created by Frankenstein, but also manifesting the relentless powers of nature itself. Frankenstein records how he was seduced into the study of natural philosophy by witnessing an oak tree blasted by lightning. His studies reach their culmination with the infusion of a 'spark of being' into the creature he has manufactured. Storms accompany each subsequent appearance of the creature, as it demands restitution for its solitary state and begins to exact its revenge on its creator. At the end, it is Frankenstein who is left 'blasted' in the wastes of the Arctic, his scientific ambitions horribly thwarted.[17]

Mary Shelley's fantasy can be read as a warning of the moral dangers of enlightened intellectual hubris, or even as an allegory of its potential to stir up social unrest.[18] The hazardous power of atmospheric electricity – partially and insecurely controllable by man – stands for the capacity of nature to avenge trespasses upon its domain. This is a message of continuing relevance to modern science and technology, as the enduring

15 Simon Schaffer, 'Natural Philosophy and Public Spectacle in the Eighteenth Century', *History of Science* 21 (1983), 1–43.
16 Davy, 'Discourse', in *Works of Davy*, vol. II, p. 319.
17 Mary Shelley, *Frankenstein, or the Modern Prometheus*, 3 vols. (London: Lackington, Hughes, Harding, Mavor, and Jones, 1818).
18 Chris Baldick, *In Frankenstein's Shadow: Myth, Monstrosity and Nineteenth-Century Writing* (Oxford: Clarendon Press, 1987).

popularity of Shelley's novel attests.[19] In other manifestations, however, the natural sublime is a source of reassurance in the novel: mountainous and pastoral scenery signify the benevolent aspects of nature to which Frankenstein is insensitive. It is because he is largely indifferent to these forms of the natural sublime that he succumbs to the temptation to try to improve on nature's own processes of reproduction. In tracing his fate, Shelley's novel explores the ambiguities of the natural sublime, its capacity for encoding both the raw terrors of nature and the powers of the human mind to subdue it. Her emblematic story captures how the natural sublime had come, in certain respects, to stand in for the deity – comforting the humble, warning the proud and jealously guarding the cosmic mysteries.

The abyss of the past

One manifestation of the natural sublime that exhibited its ambiguities in an acute form was the great length of the history of the earth being revealed by the science of geology.[20] The newly disclosed abyss of time past was regarded by some as inspiring a greater reverence for the creator, whose design had been realized over an unimaginably long period. For others, the prospect of a lengthy history of the world, unfolding according to natural laws, tended to dispense with the need to invoke the deity. Abraham Werner's influential teachings at the mining academy at Freiberg in Saxony were generally seen as encouraging the former interpretation. Werner's 'Neptunist' geology outlined the long-term effects of erosion in forming the landscape, assigning the origins of rock strata to successive deposits laid down at the bottom of a primeval ocean. Those who saw Neptunist geology as reconcilable with the Biblical account of the flood believed it opened up the sublime prospect of an extended period of divine creativity in the history of the earth. Fossils and minerals appeared as the keys to this inspiring vision. As the former radical James Parkinson put it, in his monumental *Organic Remains of a Former World* (1811), 'By widening the views of the natural philosopher, . . . by showing him a glimpse of other creations, more just and more grand sentiments also must be excited of the

---

19 Jon Turney, *Frankenstein's Footsteps: Science, Genetics and Popular Culture* (New Haven, CT: Yale University Press, 1998).

20 Martin J. S. Rudwick, *Bursting the Limits of Time: The Reconstruction of Geohistory in the Age of Revolution* (Chicago: University of Chicago Press, 2005).

immensity of animated nature and of the power of the great Creator of all things.'[21]

Attempts to render the geological sublime conformable with Christian theology were, however, called into question by the rise of alternatives to the Wernerian system. The 'Vulcanist' geology of the Scottish natural philosopher James Hutton ascribed a crucial role to the processes of heat and fire in creating rock formations, recognizing discontinuities in the surface strata caused by deeper rocks being thrust upwards by the earth's internal heat. More importantly, Hutton saw these natural forces as operating continuously through immense periods of time, raising rock formations that would in turn be eroded away in an eternal cyclical process. In a phrase that became notorious, he claimed he perceived 'no vestige of a beginning – no prospect of an end'. Hutton's dizzying vista of a history without beginning or end was perceived as a direct challenge to Christian notions of the creation and the apocalypse. His model undermined scripture and suggested an alternative vision of the history of the earth, in which landscapes and continents were formed by natural processes operating over an indefinite expanse of time.[22]

Hutton's systematic exposition of his ideas, *The Theory of the Earth* (1795), lengthy and indigestible as it was, sounded alarm bells among those more inclined to defend religious orthodoxy. The Irish chemist and meteorologist Richard Kirwan, in his *Geological Essays* (1799), charged Hutton with an uncontrolled imagination, 'the sublime talent of fascinating *Invention*', which could all too easily seduce the public.[23] The danger was accentuated by the translation of Hutton's ideas into a more accessible idiom by his former student John Playfair, in his *Illustrations of the Huttonian Theory* (1802). Responding to this, the Swiss-born chemist Jean André Deluc, in his *Elementary Treatise on Geology* (1809), charged Hutton with 'sapping the very foundation on which the great edifice of society has always rested . . . in short, abandoning men to themselves'.[24] Deluc advocated a geology that was more reconcilable with the scriptural doctrine of creation. The

---

21 Alexander M. Ospovat, 'The Work and Influence of Abraham Gottlob Werner: A Re-evaluation', *Actes du XIIIe Congrès International d'Histoire des Sciences, 1971* 8 (1974), 123–30; James Parkinson, *Organic Remains of a Former World*, 3 vols. in 1 (London: Sherwood, Neely, and Jones, 1811), p. 12 (punctuation modified).

22 Denis R. Dean, *James Hutton and the History of Geology* (Ithaca, NY: Cornell University Press, 1992).

23 Richard Kirwan, *Geological Essays* (London: T. Bensley, 1799), p. v.

24 Jean André Deluc, *An Elementary Treatise on Geology* (London: F. C. and J. Rivington, 1809), pp. 4–5.

Edinburgh Review, on the other hand, had welcomed Playfair's *Illustrations* for his 'eloquent language, . . . well calculated to fascinate the imagination, by the novelty and sublimity of the conceptions'.[25] From the *Edinburgh*'s point of view, the geological sublime was neither to be feared nor ridiculed, but rather enlisted as an inspiring vision of how human reason could encompass the chasm of historical time. A similar thought appears to have motivated Percy Shelley's use of Hutton's ideas to invoke the sublimity of the deep past in his poem 'Mont Blanc' in 1816.[26]

Predictably, Davy's lectures on geology, given to the Royal Institution in 1805, did not align him with Scottish Whigs or English radicals. While he criticized the kind of geology that remained enthralled by scripture, he was scornful of the speculative excesses he perceived in both Huttonian and Wernerian systems. Davy invoked the sublime as a kind of veil drawn by the deity across the depths that human knowledge was not permitted to penetrate. He admonished Hutton that man 'was not intended to waste his time in guesses concerning what is to take place in infinite duration'. Balancing his accounts, Davy also criticized Deluc for his 'vain attempts to penetrate into mysteries that have been wisely concealed from us', Werner for his desire 'to satisfy the ardent imagination of students', and Kirwan for 'the lighter ebullitions of his fancy'.[27] The sublimity of the past, Davy suggested, should be respected as an impenetrable mystery. He warned of the dangers of crossing the bounds set for human knowledge and the risks of seducing the public imagination to pursue this goal. Ironically, in other fields of his scientific endeavours, such as electrochemistry, Davy was judged guilty of exactly these faults. It was the perception of his willingness to trespass on the domain of forbidden knowledge – and to use his public fame in support of his efforts – that led Mary Shelley to use him as a model for her character Waldman, the charismatic chemistry professor who inspires Victor Frankenstein.

As the interior depths of the earth disclosed the abyss of times past, the vacancy of outer space began to reveal an even more lengthy history. A key idea was the 'nebular hypothesis', the notion that stars and planets could be

25 [Anon.], Review of Playfair, *Illustrations of the Huttonian Theory*, *Edinburgh Review* 1 (1802), 201–16, p. 214.

26 Nigel Leask, 'Mont Blanc's Mysterious Voice: Shelley and Huttonian Earth Science', in Elinor S. Shaffer (ed.), *The Third Culture: Literature and Science* (Berlin: Walter de Gruyter, 1998), pp. 182–203.

27 Humphry Davy, *Humphry Davy on Geology: The 1805 Lectures for the General Audience*, ed. Robert Siegfried and Robert H. Dott (Madison: University of Wisconsin Press, 1980), pp. 45, 54, 56.

formed by natural processes of gravitational attraction operating on primeval clouds of dust and gas. The discovery of dozens of nebulae in the heavens opened up the sublime prospect of the formation of solar systems like our own by the action of natural laws. The hypothesis was put into general circulation in the fourth edition of Pierre Simon de Laplace's *Exposition du système du monde* (1813). By the 1830s, it had several prominent Whig defenders in Britain. William Whewell's Bridgewater Treatise, *Astronomy and General Physics* (1833), insisted the nebular hypothesis could be reconciled with belief in a divine being who acted over a very long period of time. The hypothesis was viewed as complementary to Huttonian geology by Playfair and the younger geologist Charles Lyell, both of whom distinguished a scientific belief in historical development from illegitimate and unprofitable speculations about the creation. It was in this context that the hypothesis was presented by the Glasgow astronomer John Pringle Nichol, in his *Views of the Architecture of the Heavens* (1837).[28]

Many Whigs who were comfortable with the idea that divine creativity had extended over a long history of the physical formation of the earth nonetheless refused to contemplate a concurrent process of biological evolution. Since respectable opinion had rounded on Erasmus Darwin's evolutionary speculations in the 1790s, ideas of the transmutation of species had been exiled to the radical fringe. Discussions of biological evolution threatened to reduce the origins of humanity itself to natural processes, a doctrine associated with the most extreme materialism and atheism of the Enlightenment. Such ideas were nonetheless to be found in the radical working-class press from the 1820s. Subversive journalists such as Richard Carlile and Charles Southwell advocated the materialist philosophy of the Baron d'Holbach and the transmutationist theories of Jean-Baptiste Lamarck.[29] By the 1830s, it was becoming harder to draw the line between respectable contemplation of the history of the earth and the disreputable doctrines of biological evolution. Some middle-class geologists acknowledged that a progressive trend in the development of living things was evidenced by the fossil record; others, including Lyell, continued to deny this. Progressive development might be regarded as a further tribute to the

---

28 Simon Schaffer, 'The Nebular Hypothesis and the Science of Progress', in James R. Moore (ed.), *History, Humanity, and Evolution* (Cambridge: Cambridge University Press, 1989), pp. 131–64; J. H. Brooke, 'Nebular Contraction and the Expansion of Naturalism', *British Journal for the History of Science* 12 (1979), 200–11.

29 Adrian Desmond, 'Artisan Resistance and Evolution in Britain, 1819–1848', *Osiris* (2nd ser.) 3 (1987), 77–110.

powers of the deity, exerted periodically to bring forth new kinds of life, for instance by the comparative anatomist Richard Owen in the 1840s. Owen regarded each stage in the progressive development of the vertebrates as a successive realization of the 'archetype', a kind of ideal plan in the divine mind. Other anatomists, however, perceived the same phenomena as evidence for materialist theories of the transmutation of species. Robert Knox, an extramural lecturer in Edinburgh and later in London, and Robert Grant, professor at University College London, found their evolutionary teachings echoed in the radical press while they were ostracized by respectable society.[30]

The appearance of the anonymous *Vestiges of the Natural History of Creation* in 1844 revealed how contemplation of the abyss of the past had descended into fiery discord. Deeply divided opinions about the extent of divine involvement in the history of life on earth could no longer be sheltered under the ambiguities of the sublime. Although the hidden author of *Vestiges*, the publisher and journalist Robert Chambers, was a friend of Scottish Whigs like Nichol and the phrenologist George Combe, his text attained a scandalous notoriety by explicitly proposing materialist theories of the origin and development of life. The book advanced conjectures on the formation of living beings from non-living matter and their progressive evolution by natural causes. The nebular hypothesis and the findings of comparative anatomists found their place alongside embryological fantasies and questionable experiments on the spontaneous generation of life. Chambers's work succeeded with readers who were inspired by a new kind of sublime vision: that of the progressive development of life – including human life – under the auspices of natural laws. Respectable authorities who were unwilling to accept this conclusion, such as the Cambridge geologist Adam Sedgwick, feared the way had been opened to atheism and thoroughgoing materialism. *Vestiges* was vehemently attacked by Sedgwick and others on these grounds. To the Anglican scientific establishment, it seemed that the veils of sublime mystery had been torn away from the vision of the past. The abyss of time threatened to yawn wide and swallow

---

30 Evelleen Richards, '"Metaphorical Mystifications": The Romantic Gestation of Nature in British Biology', in Andrew Cunningham and Nicholas Jardine (eds.), *Romanticism and the Sciences* (Cambridge: Cambridge University Press, 1990), pp. 130–43; Philip H. Rehbock, 'Transcendental Anatomy', in Cunningham and Jardine (eds.), *Romanticism*, pp. 144–60; Adrian Desmond, *The Politics of Evolution: Morphology, Medicine and Reform in Radical London* (Chicago: University of Chicago Press, 1989).

the existing order of society, founded as it was believed to be on a general faith in stable divine government.[31]

The powers of life

When talk of biological transmutation surfaced in Britain in the 1830s, it drew energy from a dispute about the nature of living beings that had erupted periodically since the 1790s. Although evolution was little discussed in the intervening decades, the question of the properties of life was never entirely off the agenda. The spectre of materialism – frequently denounced but never entirely suppressed – hovered over the debate about vital powers throughout the period. Respectable opinion sought to demarcate living from non-living things, to show that life required an infusion of extraordinary powers into matter and could not originate naturally. On the other side of the question were those who wanted to close the gap between animate and inanimate worlds, to demonstrate that life was a natural outcome of material organization without any addition of superior powers. The dispute between 'transcendentalists' and 'immanentists' was implicit in discussions of biological properties such as respiration and animal electricity.[32] Investigations of human nervous physiology and mental attributes were especially fraught in this connection, since they seemed to bear upon the question of the existence of an immaterial soul. In each domain, newly revealed experimental phenomena were subject to disputed interpretations, as the problem of the powers of life defied conclusive resolution.

In the 1790s, the question of vital powers arose in connection with pneumatic medicine. Priestley, author of the materialistic *Disquisitions Relating to Matter and Spirit* (1777), had also bequeathed to science his discoveries of several new gases, soon investigated for their potential medical utility. In the mid 1790s, pneumatic medicine was taken up by the physician Thomas Beddoes, who had been ejected from the Oxford chemistry chair for his radical associations and sympathies. Beddoes recruited the young Davy to assist with dispensing gaseous therapy at his Pneumatic Institution, established in Bristol in 1797. The most notorious episode there, in 1799,

---

31 Robert Chambers, *Vestiges of the Natural History of Creation and Other Evolutionary Writings*, ed. James A. Secord (Chicago: University of Chicago Press, 1994); Secord, *Victorian Sensation: The Extraordinary Publication, Reception, and Secret Authorship of Vestiges of the Natural History of Creation* (Chicago: University of Chicago Press, 2000).
32 L. S. Jacyna, 'Immanence or Transcendence: Theories of Life and Organization in Britain, 1790–1835', *Isis* 74 (1983), 310–29.

concerned the breathing of nitrous oxide. After Davy experienced hallucinations and a feeling of blissful intoxication from respiring the gas, friends
and supporters of Beddoes flocked to Bristol to try it out. The poets Samuel
Taylor Coleridge and Robert Southey were among those who enjoyed the
ecstatic feeling of freedom and mental excitement that the gas induced.
Davy's recorded response to his own experience suggested that the gas
offered a means of transcending normal bodily conditions; it seemed to
transport him to a world of ideas independent of matter: 'My emotions
were enthusiastic and sublime ... with the most intense belief and
prophetic manner, I exclaimed to Dr. Kinglake, "*Nothing exists but thoughts! –
the universe is composed of impressions, ideas, pleasures and pains*"'.[33]

To most observers, however, the nitrous oxide experiments suggested a
different conclusion, namely the dependence of mental states on the body's
physical condition. Taken at face value, the incident showed that the mind
could be altered by chemical means, lending support to the materialists'
position that it was a function of the physical organization of matter. Davy
himself had written an 'Essay to Prove the Thinking Powers Depend on the
Organization of the Body' in a private notebook in the 1790s. In slightly
guarded comments at the end of the decade, he and Beddoes welcomed the
prospect, held out by nitrous oxide, of a chemical solution to the problems
of health and happiness. For conservative commentators who lined up to
criticize the Bristol 'enthusiasts', the materialist motivation of the project
was obvious and its claims for the effectiveness of the gas had to be resisted.
The *Anti-Jacobin Review* ridiculed the 'Pneumatic Revellers' in a poem
published in 1800, which set the tone for a number of other satirical attacks.
The satirists asserted that the notion that nitrous oxide could be the material
agent of general enlightenment was nothing but fantasy. The supposed
effects of the gas were dismissed as collective delusion. Tellingly, little
further research was done on nitrous oxide for decades and its anaesthetic
effects – later so widely exploited – were not recognized until the 1840s.[34]

Many of the same doctors who explored the potential of pneumatic
medicine were also interested in therapeutic applications of electricity,
which offered a candidate for the principle of life itself. In the 1790s, Luigi
Galvani's discovery that movement could be produced in a dissected frog by
apparently transmitting electrical impulses generated enormous interest in

33 Humphry Davy, 'Researches, Chemical and Philosophical, Chiefly Concerning
   Nitrous Oxide', in *Works of Davy*, vol. III, pp. 289–90; Golinski, *Science as Public
   Culture*, pp. 166–9.
34 Golinski, *Science as Public Culture*, pp. 171–3.

the role of electricity in animal life.[35] The attention of the public was drawn to the vital function of electricity by the spectacular experiments of Galvani's nephew, Giovanni Aldini, in London in 1803. On one widely reported occasion, the body of a recently hanged criminal was brought to a private anatomy theatre, where a group of surgeons watched as wires from an electrical battery were applied to the corpse. Aldini reported that the body's muscles twitched and an eye opened, so 'as almost to give the appearance of re-animation'. After another attempt at revival, Aldini noted, 'vitality might, perhaps, have been restored, if many circumstances had not rendered it impossible'.[36] It was expedient to be cautious because the implications of what had been attempted were staggering: control of electricity might place in human hands the power to bring the dead back to life. Mary Shelley later acknowledged the importance of such incidents in inspiring her conception of *Frankenstein*.

The issue of vital processes was of central concern to Coleridge during the decade of the 1790s, and his reflections were symptomatic of the difficulties raised by the legacy of materialism. Even while associating with Beddoes's Bristol circle and endorsing its philanthropic aims, he withheld support from what he took to be its underlying materialism. At the end of 1796, he wrote to the radical poet John Thelwall, taking him up on his argument that the principle of life was a kind of subtle matter like air or electricity. He also commented on the ideas of Dr John Ferriar, who had been writing about the 'vital principle' in the *Memoirs* of the Manchester Literary and Philosophical Society. Ferriar's view constituted an alternative to the materialism of which Priestley and Erasmus Darwin were identified as spokesmen.[37] But, as Coleridge came to understand, talk of the vital principle and identification of it with electricity or subtle matter, did not

---

35 Naum Kipnis, 'Luigi Galvani and the Debate on Animal Electricity, 1791–1800', *Annals of Science* 44 (1987), 107–42; Stuart Strickland, 'Galvanic Disciplines: The Boundaries, Objects, and Identities of Experimental Science in the Era of Romanticism', *History of Science* 33 (1995), 449–68; Giuliano Pancaldi, *Volta: Science and Culture in the Age of Enlightenment* (Princeton, NJ: Princeton University Press, 2003).

36 John Aldini, *An Account of the Late Improvements in Galvanism* (London: Cuthell and Martin, and J. Murray, 1803), pp. 193–5.

37 Ian Wylie, *Young Coleridge and the Philosophers of Nature* (Oxford: Clarendon Press, 1989), pp. 33–6, 44, 57–60, 124–9; James Averill, 'Wordsworth and Natural Science: The Poetry of 1798', *Journal of English and Germanic Philology* 77 (1978), 232–46, pp. 239, 245; Trevor H. Levere, *Poetry Realized in Nature: Samuel Taylor Coleridge and Early Nineteenth-Century Science* (Cambridge: Cambridge University Press, 1981), pp. 208–9; Nicholas Roe, '"Atmospheric Air Itself": Medical Science, Politics, and Poetry in Thelwall, Coleridge, and Wordsworth', in Richard Cronin (ed.), *1789: The Year of the Lyrical Ballads* (Basingstoke: Macmillan, 1998), pp. 185–202.

suffice to keep materialism at bay. While vitalism seemed like an alternative to materialism, since it acknowledged an exogenous principle in addition to the organizing capabilities of matter itself, questions remained as to whether the vital principle was itself a kind of matter and whether it operated within the realm of natural law. The London surgeon John Abernethy concluded that firmer lines of demarcation had to be drawn. Lecturing to the Royal College of Surgeons in 1815, he distinguished three entities: the material body, the vital principle (a 'subtle, mobile, invisible substance, superadded to the evident structure of . . . matter') and the immaterial soul.[38] Abernethy's position was scornfully dismissed as 'bombast' by the *Edinburgh Review* and fiercely criticized by his former student William Lawrence in 1816. Lawrence denounced the idea of a separate principle of life as a philosophical mystification, akin to ancient notions of an 'anima'. He insisted that life could be understood as a phenomenon of organized matter, and enlisted the support of the great French physiologist Xavier Bichat for this assertion. Abernethy responded by charging his opponent with materialism and atheism for his attribution of vital powers to matter itself. In turn, Lawrence denied that medical findings had any implications for theological issues: 'An immaterial and spiritual being', he remarked, 'could not have been discovered among the blood and filth of the dissecting room'.[39]

This widely publicized debate gave fuel for both sides of the dispute about vital powers. Lawrence's dismissal of an exogenous principle of life was adopted by other reforming physicians, such as John Elliotson, a professor at the University of London from 1831; it also encouraged evolutionists like Elliotson's colleague Grant. Bichat had proposed that human mental processes were elaborations of simple organic properties like sensibility. The suggestion was that the human mind could be viewed as an evolutionary outcome of animal development. Such a conception appealed to writers in the radical underground press. Richard Carlile wrote that, 'instead of viewing ourselves as the particular objects of the care of a great Deity, . . . we should consider ourselves but as atoms of organised matter'.[40]

---

38 John Abernethy, *Part of the Introductory Lecture for the Year 1815* (London: Longman, 1815), p. 39. On the dispute, see Jacyna, 'Immanence or Transcendence'; Levere, *Poetry Realized in Nature*, pp. 45–52; Owsei Temkin, 'Basic Science, Medicine, and the Romantic Era', in Temkin, *The Double Face of Janus and Other Essays in the History of Medicine* (Baltimore: Johns Hopkins University Press, 1977), pp. 345–72.

39 William Lawrence, *Lectures on Physiology, Zoology, and the Natural History of Man* (London: J. Callow, 1819), p. 7.

40 Carlile quoted in Jacyna, 'Immanence', p. 326.

On the other hand, it was precisely to oppose this kind of radical materialism that Coleridge and other conservative writers swung to Abernethy's side. In lectures given in 1818–19, the poet declared that Bichat's definition of life – 'the sum of all the functions by which death is resisted' – was 'the vilest form . . . of modern materialism'.[41] Organization had to be seen as the consequence of life, not its cause. Life was the result of a vital principle that transcended normal material causation. Only on this basis, Coleridge held, could morality be sustained. If human beings were reduced to organized matter, there would be no foundation for elevating them above base natural instincts, no grounds for human aspirations to transcend the animal level.

The birth of the scientific hero

The cultivation of a sense of the sublimity of nature provided an aesthetic basis for communicating scientific discoveries to a broad public audience. Among the issues raised by the popularization of science, the abyss of time and the enigma of life posed particularly acute problems for traditional religious doctrine. The emergence of a new kind of public scientific culture provided the conditions for bringing these questions to light and also made them especially fraught and urgent. Members of the social elite were well aware that the recruitment of a large public audience had made radical ideas much more dangerous. Enlargement of the public for scientific knowledge injected a fear of social instability into the discussion of problematic issues in the sciences.

Central to the new relationship between the sciences and their public audience was a new image of the man of science: the scientific hero. In various ways, the public persona of the male natural philosopher was reconstructed in this period. Certain individuals achieved conspicuous celebrity by virtue of their standing with public audiences. The scientific hero shared some features of the poetic or artistic 'genius', as this figure was coming to be understood. In science, as in literature and the arts, the genius was distinguished by a mysterious quality exceeding normal human capabilities. As Simon Schaffer has written, 'Genius began to be understood not as a peculiar capacity possessed by a creative artist, but as the power which possessed him'.[42] Signs of possession by this power included an ability to

41 Coleridge, *The Philosophical Lectures of Samuel Taylor Coleridge*, ed. Kathleen Coburn (New York: Philosophical Library, 1949), p. 356.
42 Simon Schaffer, 'Genius in Romantic Natural Philosophy', in Cunningham and Jardine (eds.), *Romanticism*, pp. 82–98, p. 83.

sense intuitively the sublime forces of nature. The public personae of many men of science came to be identified with their emotional responses to natural phenomena. In addition to genius, the scientific hero possessed a capacity for strenuous exertion and bodily suffering. Among the features that might distinguish him were dauntless self-experimentation or gruelling travel. The scientific hero was a passionate as much as a calculating being, attuned to the powers of nature on an emotional as well as an intellectual level, though no less masculine for all his depth of feeling. He suffered considerably in the quest for knowledge and was morally enhanced thereby.

In the 1760s, Priestley had explained how natural philosophy ought to improve the moral standing of those who studied it. 'A philosopher', he remarked, 'ought to be something greater, and better than another man'. Contemplation of God's works 'should give a sublimity to his virtue ... [and] expand his benevolence', so that natural philosophers could become 'great and exalted beings'.[43] To this conception of the elevating power of nature, the Romantic era added an increased appreciation of its sublime forces and their impact on the receptive individual. As Schaffer notes, however, philosophers' cultivation of their receptivity to natural powers seemed morally troubling to many commentators. In Germany, Kant and Goethe led resistance to the notion that insight into nature could follow from indulgence of the imagination or the emotions. In England, Edmund Burke set the terms in which pneumatic medicine and galvanism were satirized as varieties of 'enthusiasm', rather than acknowledged (as their devotees claimed) as sources of natural inspiration.[44]

Notwithstanding the satirical attacks on his work at Beddoes's Pneumatic Institution, Davy went on to show that space did exist in British public life for a man to fashion himself as a scientific genius. While he ceased to display mind-altering gases, he developed a passionate style of self-presentation to his audiences, apparently giving way to transports of rhetorical intensity as he dilated on the beauties of the divine design or the sublimity of natural forces. In the words of one perceptive observer of his lectures, Davy 'presented most strongly to the popular observation the attributes of genius'.[45] These attributes included a heightened sensitivity to natural scenery, a generous dedication to the public good and heroic powers of bodily

---

43 Joseph Priestley, *The History and Present State of Electricity with Original Experiments*, 2nd edn (London: J. Dodsley, J. Johnson and J. Payne, and T. Cadell, 1769), p. xviii.
44 Schaffer, 'Genius'; Golinski, *Science as Public Culture*, pp. 176–87.
45 Harriet Martineau, *The History of England during the Thirty Years' Peace, 1816–1846*, 2 vols. (London: Charles Knight, 1849–50), vol. I, p. 594.

endurance. Davy's last writings, *Salmonia* (1828) and *Consolations in Travel* (1830), exhibited his scenic sensibilities and his awe of the infinities of time and space. His invention of the miners' safety lamp was taken to show his selfless benevolence toward humanity at large. Reckless trials of the effects of gases on his own physiology were followed by no less painful submission to the effects of electrical currents and sparks applied to parts of his body. He sustained permanent injury to his right hand from a laboratory explosion. During an episode of serious illness in 1807, the chemist's female admirers thronged around his residence anxious for news. The sufferings of Davy's body in the pursuit of knowledge had become central to his public persona as a hero of science.[46]

Each aspect of Davy's heroic image was shared by other experimenters of his time. In the obituary *éloges* presented to the Paris Institut to mark the passing of distinguished savants, their sensitivity to the powers of nature was particularly noted. Individuals were repeatedly shown to have been inspired in the quest for knowledge by experiencing the sublime emotions elicited by natural scenery.[47] The sublime forces of nature were also invoked in celebrations of technological genius, for example in the poems of Erasmus Darwin, where the ability to tame those forces was lauded in panegyrics of leading industrialists like James Watt and Matthew Boulton.[48] A powerful desire to benefit humanity in general was ascribed to Watt in biographies and eulogies following his death in 1819; it became central to the creation of his image as a heroic genius of industrial innovation.[49] Similarly, the promoter of vaccination, Edward Jenner, was celebrated as a scientific hero for his benevolence and humane genius in numerous portraits on canvas, in print, on medals and in sculpture.[50] Finally, Davy's self-sacrificing galvanic experiments were matched or exceeded in their painfulness by

---

46 Jan Golinski, 'Humphry Davy's Sexual Chemistry', *Configurations* 7 (1999), 15–41; David Knight, 'The Scientist as Sage', *Studies in Romanticism* 6 (1967), 65–88.

47 Dorinda Outram, 'The Language of Natural Power: The *éloges* of Georges Cuvier and the Public Language of Nineteenth-Century Science', *History of Science* 26 (1978), 153–78.

48 Maureen McNeil, 'The Scientific Muse: The Poetry of Erasmus Darwin', in L. J. Jordanova (ed.), *Languages of Nature: Critical Essays on Science and Literature* (London: Free Association Books, 1986), pp. 159–203.

49 C. MacLeod, 'James Watt, Heroic Invention and the Idea of the Industrial Revolution', in Maxine Berg and Kristine Bruland (eds.), *Technological Revolutions in Europe* (Cheltenham: Edward Elgar, 1998), pp. 96–116; David Philip Miller, '"Puffing Jamie": The Commercial and Ideological Importance of Being a "Philosopher" in the Case of the Reputation of James Watt (1736–1819)', *History of Science* 38 (2000), 1–24.

50 Ludmilla Jordanova, *Defining Features: Scientific and Medical Portraits, 1660–2000* (London: Reaktion Books, 2000), pp. 87–127.

those of the German experimenters, Johann Wilhelm Ritter and Alexander von Humboldt, who repeatedly subjected their own bodies to electrical currents.[51]

Although Davy developed the heroic potential of travel to only a limited degree, gruelling travel was central to the lifelong self-fashioning of other scientific heroes, especially Humboldt. Humboldt's reputation was gained in the course of his journey in the Amazon basin, the Andes and the pampas in the years 1799 to 1804, recorded in the massive *Voyage aux régions équinoxiales du nouveau continent* (1805–34), which eventually reached thirty volumes. His long-laboured account comprised tables and innovative diagrammatic representations of the vast quantity of data he had assembled from astronomical, magnetic, meteorological and geological instruments. In stunning maps and images, Humboldt presented his findings on the distribution of plant and animal life, climatic zones, geological formations and geographical features. He combined this with a verbal narrative in which his physiological and emotional reactions were highlighted, in order to match the instrumental record against the sufferings of his own body, and to convey to readers the aesthetic dimension of the natural environment.[52] The style owed something to the example of Georg Forster (son of J. R. Forster), with whom Humboldt had travelled in the Low Countries, France and England in 1790. It was also deployed in his popular *Ansichten der Natur* (1808), where Humboldt explained: 'Descriptions of nature affect us more or less powerfully, in proportion as they harmonize with the condition of our own feelings. For the physical world is reflected with truth and animation on the inner susceptible world of the mind.'[53] The Humboldtian style of exploration became enormously influential through the popularity of its written descriptions, for example in the portion of his monumental work translated as the *Personal Narrative of Travels to the Equinoctial Regions of*

---

51 Walter D. Wetzels, 'Johann Wilhelm Ritter: Romantic Physics in Germany', in Cunningham and Jardine (eds.), *Romanticism*, pp. 199–212; Stuart Strickland, 'The Ideology of Self-Knowledge and the Practice of Self-Experimentation', *Eighteenth-Century Studies* 31 (1998), 453–71.
52 Michael Dettelbach, 'Humboldtian Science', in N. Jardine, J. A. Secord and E. C. Spary (eds.), *Cultures of Natural History* (Cambridge: Cambridge University Press, 1996), pp. 287–304; Malcolm Nicolson, 'Alexander von Humboldt and the Geography of Vegetation', in Cunningham and Jardine (eds.), *Romanticism*, pp. 169–85; Mary Louise Pratt, *Imperial Eyes: Travel Writing and Transculturation* (London: Routledge, 1992), pp. 111–43; Susan Faye Cannon, *Science in Culture: The Early Victorian Period* (New York: Dawson, 1978), pp. 73–110.
53 Humboldt, *Views of Nature*, p. 154.

the New Continent (1814–29).[54] Charles Darwin packed a copy of this book during his own travels in South America. Other scientific explorers, including Lyell and Joseph Hooker, were also inspired by the heroic endurance and emotional sensitivity of the German traveller.[55]

Humboldt provided his contemporaries with an influential model of the scientific hero, but not the only one. Contemporary ideas of genius also shaped the public images of the industrialist Watt, the experimental philosopher Michael Faraday, and even the long-deceased Isaac Newton, none of whom travelled very much.[56] Thomas Carlyle, whose *On Heroes, Hero-Worship and the Heroic in History* (1841) did more than any other work to popularize Romantic notions of genius in Britain, was scornful of the idea that true genius existed in the contemporary sciences. In his essay 'Signs of the Times' (1829), he pointed to the social and institutional machinery by which learning was advanced and communicated: 'No Newton, by silent meditation, now discovers the system of the world from the falling of an apple; but some quite other than Newton stands in his Museum, his Scientific Institution, and behind whole batteries of retorts, digesters and galvanic piles imperatively "interrogates Nature", – who, however, shows no haste to answer.'[57] Carlyle's remarks drew attention to the ways in which the influence ascribed to individual genius overlooked the trends toward routine training in research skills and concentration of resources in leading institutions. In view of this, it may be that the emphasis on individual genius was at least as much a reaction to contemporary social changes as a reflection of them. The market for public science made heroes of a few individuals, like Davy, and placed substantial resources at their disposal. At the same time, the culture of celebrity allowed these individuals to present themselves as rising above the level of the masses, being possessed of special imaginative insights into nature and its powers. A similar point has been

---

54 Nicolaas Rupke, 'A Geography of Enlightenment: The Critical Reception of Alexander von Humboldt's Mexico Work', in David N. Livingstone and Charles W. J. Withers (eds.), *Geography and Enlightenment* (Chicago: University of Chicago Press, 1999), pp. 319–39.

55 Roger Cardinal, 'Romantic Travel', in Roy Porter (ed.), *Rewriting the Self: Histories from the Renaissance to the Present* (London and New York: Routledge, 1997), pp. 135–55.

56 Geoffrey Cantor, 'The Scientist as Hero: Public Images of Michael Faraday', in Michael Shortland and Richard Yeo (eds.), *Telling Lives in Science: Essays on Scientific Biography* (Cambridge: Cambridge University Press, 1996), pp. 171–93; R. R. Yeo, 'Genius, Method, and Morality: Early Victorian Images of Sir Isaac Newton', *Science in Context* 2 (1988), 257–84.

57 Thomas Carlyle, *Selected Writings*, ed. Alan Shelston (Harmondsworth: Penguin, 1971), p. 66.

made about the images of poets and men of letters, whose individual creativity and imaginative power was hailed the more as they became more subject to the demands of a commercial market for writers' work. Against the background of the expanding literary marketplace, writers came to view themselves as 'artists', uniquely endowed individuals who were independent of material interests.[58]

Conclusion

The commercial market for public education and scientific writing was fundamental to the circumstances in which ideas circulated in British society in the early nineteenth century. An understanding of the prevailing social and political circumstances is essential to a grasp of this culture as a whole, in which scientific ideas took their place. Enough has been said here to show that the notion that science was comprehensively opposed by literary intellectuals is quite inaccurate. Coleridge was deeply inspired by Davy's chemical investigations. Percy and Mary Shelley reacted rather differently to specific trends in scientific thought in the 1810s, Percy enthusiastically exploring the radical implications of geology and vitalism, while Mary composed her brilliant allegory on the dangers of scientific hubris. Wordsworth maintained a significant interest in sciences such as geology during his poetic career.[59] These and other thinkers responded to specific scientific issues as part of their overall intellectual life. The conception that science was a single entity to be judged as a whole – for or against – simply did not exist for them. 'Science', in fact, still meant something like 'organized knowledge', rather than being identified as a specific set of beliefs and practices concerning the natural world. Many intellectuals struggled to retain a sense of learning as a whole throughout this period. Whewell's terminological innovation – 'scientist' – was resisted by many, who disapproved of the narrowing of outlook that it seemed to suggest. It was precisely because the sciences were not isolated from other cultural domains that the problems raised by materialism, for example, were so disturbing.

---

58 Raymond Williams, *Culture and Society* (Harmondsworth: Penguin Books, 1963), pp. 48–64; Marilyn Butler, *Romantics, Rebels, and Reactionaries: English Literature and Its Background, 1760–1830* (New York: Oxford University Press, 1982), pp. 69–93.

59 Wylie, *Young Coleridge*; Levere, *Poetry Realized in Nature*; Averill, 'Wordsworth'; John Wyatt, *Wordsworth and the Geologists* (Cambridge: Cambridge University Press, 1995); Anne K. Mellor, *Mary Shelley: Her Life, Her Fiction, Her Monsters* (New York: Routledge, 1989).

To isolate science from other areas of learning would be to view this period too much in the light of subsequent arguments about the 'two cultures'. Rather, I have argued here that a deeply polarized political climate was pervasive in its effects on intellectual discussion, and that it led people to very discriminating judgments on specific scientific ideas. Science could neither be ignored nor dismissed; its content called for sustained intellectual engagement and assessment. In a setting where scientific specialists maintained a lively relationship with public audiences, and in which science was commonly treated in general literary publications, a high level of awareness of these questions was taken for granted. The themes of providence and divine design of the natural world provided the vocabulary for legitimating scientific discoveries in relation to established religion. The reconciliation could be accomplished by a variety of routes, but it came under severe strain when sensitive issues arose such as the length of geological history, the possibility of biological evolution, or the material basis of life. In these areas, everyone was aware of the potential for radical appropriation of certain ideas and development of their materialistic or atheistic implications. Individuals responded to the possibility in ways that reflected their own political and social outlooks. Science, in other words, was no monolith but a highly contested domain, which intersected in multiple ways with creative literary work in a complex politicized field. Readers today need to recapture a sense of the intricacy and fluidity of this situation.

The making of child readers

KATIE TRUMPENER

Around 1800, William Pitt Scargill recalls in *Recollections of a Blue-Coat Schoolboy* (Harvey and Darton, 1829), 'very little attention was paid to the reading of boys'.[1] In the absence of 'rational books' (p. 74) designed for children, pupils at Christ's Hospital read chapbooks during recreation hours. Even in school, 'while we appeared to be learning our lessons, we were amusing ourselves with Robinson Crusoe or Jack the Giant Killer' (p. 92), concealed amid grammars and dictionaries. When a pupil was sent to change the dormitory nurse's novel at a nearby circulating library, he skimmed it on the way home, and might be allowed to take it into dinner. 'Sometimes three or four of us would sit together on the steps of the grammar-school, poring over the same book, and reading with most astonishing rapidity page after page'. Together, the boys 'contrived to obtain possession of the whole story'; 'however imperfectly picked up' (p. 76), it was retold whenever 'four or five' met in one bed for hours of 'irregularities' (p. 74): clandestine, nocturnal story-telling sessions.

As a child, Samuel Taylor Coleridge escaped school-fellows' taunting by chapbook reading, yet the stories so haunted him that his father burnt them.[2] For Scargill's schoolboys, chapbooks function rather as social glue, counterbalancing a curriculum of rote memorization and Latin recitation. These boys immerse themselves indiscriminately in the popular narratives of the chapbook and lending-library novels, parts of a common literary repertoire; such narratives generate both book-reading and oral experiences for the same readers.

---

1 William Pitt Scargill, *Recollections of a Blue-Coat Schoolboy or, A View of Christ's Hospital* (rpt Wakefield: S. R. Publishers and New York: Johnson Reprint Corporation, 1968), p. 74. Where germane, publisher's name and publication date are cited directly in the text. Unless otherwise specified, the works thus cited are published in London.
2 Letter to Thomas Poole, 9 October 1797. *Collected Letters of Samuel Taylor Coleridge*, ed. Earl Leslie Griggs, 10 vols. (Oxford: Clarendon Press, 1956), vol. I: *1785–1800*, pp. 207–9.

What Scargill's memoir evokes is an interstitial moment around 1800. During the 1740s, John Newbery reinvented children's literature by commercializing children's publishing and inaugurating a new epoch of juvenile consumption. In the late eighteenth century, Samuel Johnson chided Hester Thrale for raising her children on Newbery books instead of romances. Unswayed by Thrale's invocation of the 'numerous editions and quick sale of *Tommy Prudent* or *Goody Two-Shoes*', Johnson found Newbery's books 'too trifling' to engage young minds.[3] By the time Scargill attended Christ's Hospital (1794–1802), Newbery books had apparently waned in influence, and the early nineteenth-century rediscovery of juvenile readers not yet begun. In 1805, John Harris's runaway success with Sarah Catherine Martin's *Comic Adventures of Old Mother Hubbard and Her Dog* – selling 10,000 copies in months, 20 editions within the year – would renew publishers' interest in children's books, sparking increasingly fierce competition for the juvenile book market. Like the novels skimmed at Christ's Hospital, *Old Mother Hubbard* reached adult and child readers alike.[4] The competing 'Novelties for the Nursery' quickly published by Benjamin Tabart, John Marshall, William Darton, Mary Jane and William Godwin – usually brightly illustrated and drawn, as *Mother Hubbard* had been, from oral or chapbook sources like nursery rhymes or fairy tales – marked themselves specifically as works for children.

Romantic writers belonged to the first generations raised on Newbery's books and the self-consciously literary, book-centred and commercial forms of children's writing Newbery inaugurated. Their reactions to the Newbery revolution varied widely. Neither marked nor sold commercially, William Blake's *Songs of Innocence and Experience* offered a radical critique of market forces and the new culture of childhood.[5] In memorializing an older body of chapbooks and fairy-tales as imaginative fodder for child readers, William Wordsworth's *Prelude* implicitly polemicized against new regimes of children's literature and child-rearing.[6] Yet other Romantics saw intriguing

3 Geoffrey Summerfield, *Fantasy and Reason: Children's Literature in the Eighteenth Century* (Athens, GA: University of Georgia Press, 1984), p. 36.
4 Iona and Peter Opie, *The Nursery Companion* (Oxford: Oxford University Press, 1980), p. 5.
5 Blake's *Songs* was not widely read until the late nineteenth century, yet it had a sustained, if indirect impact on Romantic juvenile writing through Ann and Jane Taylor, the period's most popular children's poets. See my 'City Scenes: Commerce, Utopia and the Birth of the Picture Book', in *The Victorian Illustrated Book: New Explorations*, ed. Richard Maxwell (Charlottesville: University of Virginia Press, 2002), pp. 332–84.
6 One of Wordsworth's *Lyrical Ballads*, fittingly, circulated as an anonymous children's chapbook, 'The Little Maid and the Gentleman; or, We are Seven' (York: J. Kendrew,

aesthetic, moral and political possibilities in the new juvenile literature, and became active in writing, producing and disseminating it. The Godwins' work as children's publishers and booksellers, for instance, has been read both as exemplifying the new, market-driven approach to children's writing, and as a utopian alternative to it. As Romantic writers revisited Newbery's children's books, reviled or revised Newbery's bookselling strategies, indeed, they fed a second revolution in children's literature.

The Romantic era, arguably, saw the making of a new class of child readers alongside the making of the working classes. Romantic authors – and booksellers – imagined children in terms still recognizable in our own day: as psychologically inward, observant and self-observant, commercially savvy, modern. And at least in subterranean ways, their very acquisition of literacy, and initiation into literary reading also exposed them to some of the debates we associate with Romanticism: debates over the politics of consumption, the price of modernization, the nature of tradition.

Novels for the nursery

Amid 'the multitude of books professedly written for children', Anna Laetitia Barbauld complains in 1787, not one is 'adapted to the comprehension' of very small children: clearly printed and 'telling simple domestic stories'.[7] Later writers expand on this complaint. Maria Edgeworth's *Continuation of Early Lessons* (1815) demonstrates the vicissitudes of reading comprehension, as children recite Thomas Gray, Alexander Pope and William Collins, without understanding the poems they have memorized.[8] Jefferys Taylor's *Harry's Holidays: or the Doings of One, Who Had Nothing to Do* (Baldwin, Craddock and Joy, 1818; 2nd edn, 1819) shows problematic reading habits creating child Quixotes. Given *Rasselas* for his birthday, young Harry only skims it, 'in the hope of meeting with something he called interesting'

---

c. 1820). Gerald Gottlieb and J. H. Plumb (eds.), *Early Children's Books and their Illustration* (New York: Pierpont Morgan Library/Boston: David Godine, 1975), p. 180.

7 Anna Laetitia Barbauld, 'Advertisement', *Lessons for Children, from Two to Three Years Old* (London: J. Johnson, 1787), pp. 2–3.

8 Mitzi Meyers, 'Reading Rosamond Reading: Maria Edgeworth's "Wee-Wee Stories" Interrogate the Canon', in Elizabeth Goodenough et al. (eds.), *Infant Tongues: The Voice of the Child in Literature* (Detroit: Wayne State University Press, 1994), pp. 57–79. Yet in *The Juvenile Story-Teller: A Collection of Moral Tales, for the Amusement and Education of Young Masters and Misses* (London: James Imray, 1805), prim Billy and Betsy Worthy renounce the fair to memorize poetry at home.

(p. 72), reads Aesop too quickly to grasp its morals, and over-identifies with the more gripping *Robinson Crusoe*.[9] Such fables are manifestos for a new children's literature, its lessons anchored in everyday events, its didacticism couched as novelistic realism. If young readers cannot assimilate existing literary classics (even those traditionally given children), they must have works, indeed novels, of their own.

Eighteenth-century juvenile reading consisted not only of catechisms, tracts, primers, but of chapbook versions of ghost and crime stories, fairy-tales, and popular adult novels like *Crusoe* and *Gulliver's Travels*.[10] Sold at markets and fairs throughout Britain by itinerant 'chapmen', (licensed peddlers who traversed the country on regular routes, carrying a wide range of wares), these inexpensive little books were central to the rise of mass (and juvenile) literacy, and formative for generations of British writers, from John Bunyan to James Boswell, George Crabbe and John Clare.[11] In the 1690s (after the expiration of the Act restricting printing), chapbook publishing proliferated into a major London industry, concentrated near London Bridge and in Holborn, with several publishers located around St Paul's Churchyard, venerable site of one of England's first publishing presses. In the 1740s, in turn, when Newbery founds the first 'juvenile library' (or children's bookstore), he establishes its permanent home at 20 Ludgate Street, at the corner of St Paul's Churchyard.[12]

As James Janaway's widely read *A Token for Children: Being An Exact Account of the Conversion, Holy and Exemplary Lives, and Joyful Deaths of Several Young Children* (1671) underscores, early modern juvenile works were often preoccupied by death and divine vengeance. Newbery replaced this emphasis on suffering as a catalyst for Christian conversion with a new, secular interest in children's thinking and everyday experiences. As announced on the frontispiece to the earliest extant (1760) edition of Newbery's first book for children, *A Little Pretty Pocket-Book* (1744), Newbery

---

9 On contemporary *Crusoe* reception, see Samuel F. Pickering, *Moral Instruction and Fiction for Children, 1749–1820* (Athens, GA: University of Georgia Press, 1995), p. 59.

10 Warren W. Wooden, *Children's Literature of the English Renaissance*, ed. Jeanie Watson (Lexington: University Press of Kentucky, 1986); Patricia Demers, *Heaven upon Earth: The Form of Moral and Religious Children's Literature, to 1850* (Knoxville: University of Tennessee Press, 1993); Margaret Spufford, *Small Books and Pleasant Histories: Popular Fiction and its Readership in Seventeenth-Century England* (Athens, GA: University of Georgia Press, 1981); Victor E. Neuburg, *The Penny Histories: A Study of Chapbooks for Young Readers over Two Centuries* (New York: Harcourt, Brace and World, 1968).

11 Spufford, *Small Books*, pp. 6–7; Summerfield, *Fantasy*.

12 F.J. Harvey Darton, *Children's Books in England: Five Centuries of Social Life* (1932; Cambridge: Cambridge University Press, 2nd edn, 1970), p. 138.

books combined 'Instruction with delight', echoing the stated aim of most adult fiction of the period. Newbery, indeed, began publishing children's books during a breakthrough decade for the British novel (given major works by Samuel Richardson, Tobias Smollett and Henry Fielding), and some Newbery books – including *The History of Little Goody Two-Shoes* (1765), possibly written by Newbery regular Oliver Goldsmith – conjoin the fabular structure of exemplary tales with novelistic social and psychological details. Yet most remain closer to miscellanies, drawing on material from chapbooks, oral tradition and contemporary magazines, from jokes and topical satire to fairy-tales and nursery rhymes.[13]

Newbery's *The Fairing: or, a Golden Toy; for Children of all Sizes and Denominations* (first advertised edition 1765, first extant copy 1767) thus traverses the fairgrounds, describing the surging crowd, introducing various vendors, and showcasing literary wares. Ballad singers perform songs. The crowd hears 'Dick Whittington' (in a version straight from period chapbooks), then 'Puss-in-Boots', and declares a preference for the less fantastical Whittington: 'fairy Tales should never be read but on Fair Days, when People are inclined to have their Heads stuffed with Nonsense'.[14] *The Fairing* itself offers highly assorted literary fare: poems, nursery rhymes, cautionary tales, song lyrics, allusions to Henry Fielding, Shakespeare, Edward Young and other Newbery books, even cameo appearances by previous Newbery protagonists (Giles Gingerbread mans the fair's gingerbread stand).

The Fairing's hodge-podge of materials, Newbery's preface insists, mirrors the fair's hurly-burly and heterogeneous wares:

> as this Book is a Metaphor, or Simile, or Description, or Picture of a Fair, it must be like a Fair . . . one entire Whole, but a whole Heap of Confusion . . . . Pray, put this book in the Front of your Library, and take Care you don't rub off the Gold on the Covers. (pp. v–vi)

Newbery presents his book as the literary equivalent of gilt-covered gingerbread, which can either be eaten at the fair or hung on cottage walls; although offering instant gratification, *The Fairing* is also a carefully produced, self-consciously literary work, designed for a permanent place in eighteenth-century book collections and children's bookshelves.

---

13 Newbery's short-lived *Lilliputian Magazine* (1751–2), the earliest known English-language children's periodical, juxtaposes Bible stories, a didactic serial, verses, songs and a travel narrative echoing *Crusoe* and *Gulliver*.

14 John Newbery, *The History of Little Goody Two-Shoes and The Fairing* (rpt New York: Garland, 1977), *Fairing*, p. 115.

Newbery books are designed for mass consumption – but also as collectors' items and prize books.[15] Drawing on chapbook formats, stories and illustrations, Newbery's books repackaged them in a distinctive new way. Always small and unbound, chapbooks varied widely in organization, typeface, style and degree of illustration. Newbery adopts the chapbooks' small size. Yet his elaborate title-pages, carefully produced pictures (often copperplate or newly cut woodblocks) and bindings (leather, vellum or cardboard, hand coloured; sometimes featuring decorative paper) offer a far more consistent and cultivated look.[16] While chapbooks addressed the widest possible audience, the style and price of Newbery's books suggest middle-class readers.[17]

Chapbooks were sold by itinerant vendors; Newbery supplanted the chapbook as the main form of children's reading. Developing innovative new methods of commissioning, packaging, publicizing and distributing children's books, he single-handedly transformed an 'irregular and tentative' branch of publishing into a profitable, well-established sector of the book trade.[18] His juvenile books, heavily and ingeniously advertised, sold thousands of copies annually. *Little Pretty Pocket-Book* was advertised with a tie-in toy ('Price of the Book alone 6d., with Ball or Pincushion 8d.'); another was 'Given gratis by J. Newbery (only paying one Penny for the binding)'.[19] Newbery publication also referred incessantly to Newbery's juvenile library and children's books, even to the patent medicine Newbery produced. In *Fables in Verse* (1757), a character enters a Bath bookstore 'to read one of Mr. *Newbery's* little Books'; characters in *The Twelfth Day Gift* (1767) repeatedly pull 'one of Mr. Newbery's books' from their pockets.[20] Little Goody Two-Shoes is orphaned when her father falls ill in a place where

15 In *The Mother's Gift: or a Present for all Little Children who are Good*, 2nd edn (London: Carnan and Newbery, 1770), a philanthropist awards a whole library to the child demonstrating the best character and reading abilities.
16 Darton, *Children's Books*, p. 137.
17 M. F. Thwaite, 'Introduction', in John Newbery, *A Little Pretty Pocket-Book* (New York: Harcourt, Brace & World, 1967), pp. 1–49: 47. In the 1790s, anti-Jacobins like Hannah More attempted to reclaim the chapbook for popular education; their tracts address a broad adult and juvenile audience with rudimentary reading skills.
18 M. F. Thwaite, *From Primer to Pleasure: An Introduction to the History of Children's Books in England, from the Invention of Printing to 1900* (London: The Library Association, 1963), p. 40. Such transformations had a human price. Partly through Newbery's commissions and financial backing, Christopher Smart established himself as a professional writer, eventually marrying Newbery's stepdaughter. Yet Newbery's relentless pressure on Smart to produce probably hastened the latter's breakdown.
19 Thwaite, 'Introduction', pp. 2, 23.
20 Charles Welsh, 'A Bookseller of the Last Century, Being Some Account of the Life of John Newbery' (1885), rpt in John Rowe Townsend (ed.), *John Newbery and His*

Newbery's star nostrum is tragically unavailable; learning to read, she teaches literacy to others by singing a song 'which may be found in the *Little Pretty Play Thing*, published by Mr. NEWBERY', and devising alphabet games resembling Newbery's commercial reading-aids.[21]

Absorbing chapbook conventions, yet constructed around subplots to justify self-advertisement, Newbery's narratives help shape a tradition of children's miscellanies and framed story-collections. Newbery's successor Elizabeth Newbery had huge success with her 1787 adaptive translation of Arnaud Berquin's *Looking Glass for the Mind* (selling 20,000 copies by 1800) and her pioneering 1791 juvenile edition of *Thousand and One Nights*. Both influenced a new breed of juvenile guide-books (whose fictionalized frame-stories of child travellers lend narrative interest to fact and overview) and anthologies like John Aikin and Anna Barbauld's 1792–6 *Evenings at Home* (whose domestic frame-narrative gathers disparate materials into 'evenings' worth of reading).

Yet other juvenile narratives mirrored the forms of the adult novel. Mary Ann Kilner's *Adventures of a Pincushion* (John Marshall, c. 1780) and *Memoirs of a Peg-Top* (John Marshall, 1783), Thomas Day's *History of Little Jack* (John Stockdale, 1788), and Dorothy Kilner's *Life and Perambulations of a Mouse* (John Marshall, c. 1790) experiment with picaresque and circulation novels: children, mice, pincushions or peg-tops are moved through the world, comparing, stumbling, learning as they go. Gathering fictional letters from a child writing home from school, Dorothy Kilner's *First Going to School, or the Story of Tom Brown and His Sisters* (Tabart, 1804) developed a juvenile epistolary novel. Animal stories like Sarah Trimmer's *Fabulous Histories. Designed for the Instruction of Children, respecting the treatment of animals* (Longman, Robinson and Johnson, 1786, later known as *History of the Robins*), Dorothy Kilner's *The Rational Brutes; or, Talking Animals* (Vernor and Hood, 1799), and Arabella Argus's *Adventures of a Donkey* (William Darton, 1815) mirrored adult sentimental fiction, using close observation and empathetic identification with fellow creatures to inculcate charity and morality. Eliza Fenwick's *Lessons for Children or, Rudiments of Good Manners, Morals, and Humility* (J. Godwin and Co., 1813) refunctions sentimental novels like Henry Mackenzie's *Man of Feeling* (1771) and Richardson's *Pamela* (1740). Fenwick's first story breaks off at an exciting moment because a

---

Books: Trade and Plumb-cake for Ever, Huzza! (Metuchen, NJ: Scarecrow Press, 1994), pp. 29–113: 106–7.
21 Newbery, *The History of Little*, p. 33.

careless boy in the frame story left his new book for the dog to chew into illegibility, leaving boy and reader dangling and frustrated. In a later *Lesson*, conversely, an imprudent boy wins his father's forgiveness by offering him his diary; as in eighteenth-century epistolary fiction, this reading of the intimate record softens both reader and reader-in-the-text.

Thomas Day's *Sandford and Merton* (1783–9) alternates between frame and interpolated stories, yet (as in Fielding or Goldsmith), the frame characters remain the true protagonists. Edgeworth's *Early Lessons* (1801) follows children over a series of episodes and tales, laying equal emphasis on local lessons and cumulative maturation. Although derived partly from religious catechisms, the dialogue form popular in didactic juvenile writing potentially allowed both vivid characterization and the dramatization of the child's intellectual and moral socialization, in the increasing convergence and harmonization of initially opposed standpoints.[22]

By 1800, most children's books favoured the psychological over the picaresque. Discarding the heterogeneity and polyglossia of the Newbery miscellany for moral and social tales of domestic life, they focused minutely on quotidian interactions, petty jealousies, altruistic moments.[23] The education of children through the surmounting of physical dangers and other extreme or strange situations, gives way to sentimental situations enabling their slow acquisition of moral sense. This shift from circulation to accumulation offers a narrative correlative to the contemporaneous shift from itinerant chapbook selling to stationary juvenile libraries. Late eighteenth-century tales propel children around the city, country or world. Early nineteenth-century moral tales show children fixed in place but gaining inner depth, as they absorb servants' life narratives or learn compassion for family members.

The conflicts driving these miniature *Bildungsromane* – as children quarrel with playmates, pry into others' business, or master their own greed – mirror adult courtship novels, in which vicissitudes of attraction, expectation, disappointment and fulfilment strengthen character and sensibility. Girls' stories like S. W. [Elizabeth Kilner]'s *A Puzzle for a Curious Girl*

---

22 On the relationship between juvenile tales and novels, see my 'Tales for Child Readers' in Richard Maxwell and Katie Trumpener (eds.), *The Cambridge Companion to Fiction of the Romantic Period* (Cambridge: Cambridge University Press, 2008), pp. 178–90.

23 Mary Mister's *The Adventures of a Doll, Compiled with the Hope of Affording Amusement and Instruction* (London: Darton, Harvey and Darton, 1816) recapitulates this transformation: moving from London toy shop to rural Wales, it subsumes picaresque circulation into the local colour and regional identifications of Romantic national tales.

(Tabart, 1803) parallel *Evelina*, *Northanger Abbey* and *Pride and Prejudice* in the way their heroines advance hypotheses about social relationships, while their narratives foreground the acquisition of interpretive skills and the limits of female detective work.[24] Like sentimental novels for adults, such tales extol reading for fostering emotional inwardness, identification and communion with others: in Eliza Fenwick's *Infantine Stories, Composed Progressively, In Words of One, Two and Three Syllables* (Tabart, 1810) young siblings forced indoors by rain take turns reading aloud, weeping together over a sad story of miscreant sons and broken-hearted father.

In *The Juvenile Spectator*, by 'Arabella Argus' (Darton, 1810), conversely, two sisters scream and fight over a book, which the younger did not want to read but nonetheless 'claimed as *her* property'.[25] When children purchase or possess books, 'individual' reading sparks unpleasant power-struggles, displays of selfishness, jealousy and mimetic desire. Books represent shared intellectual property. Yet when books are bought and sold in stores, as Romantic children's authors are uncomfortably aware, their commodity status potentially undermines their educational and moral mission. Newbery's commercialization of the juvenile book trade formed the historical precondition for the development of modern children's literature. That trade's commercial character and practices remains not only a central subject but a recurrent moral anxiety for children's literature. The psychic history of juvenile reading, meanwhile, remains closely intertwined with the material history of children's books.

At the corner of St Paul's Churchyard

Although John Newbery died in 1767, the juvenile library at St Paul's Churchyard continued to operate for several decades, passing from Newbery's son Francis Newbery and stepson Thomas Carnan, to his nephew's widow, Elizabeth Newbery, to her manager John Harris and then to his successors. Along with the existing stock, each new owner took over

24 Before a 1988 find prompted reattribution to Elizabeth Kilner, works by S. W. were traditionally attributed to Sarah Wilkinson. Marjorie Moon, *Benjamin Tabart's Juvenile Library. A bibliography of books for children published, written, edited and sold by Mr. Tabart, 1801–1820* (Winchester, Hampshire: St Paul's Bibliographies and Detroit, MI: Omnigraphics, 1990), p. 69.
25 'Arabella Argus', *The Juvenile Spectator*, vol. I, rpt in Jonathan Cott (ed.), *Masterworks of Children's Literatures*, 7 vols. (New York: Chelsea House, 1984), vol. IV, pp. 331–424: 343.

Newbery's tradition of self-advertisement.[26] In an otherwise unmotivated episode in Elizabeth Newbery's adaptation of *Looking-Glass for the Mind*, a girl who loses her mother on the way to market is thus comforted by a 'good old woman' who tells her 'pretty stories', criticizes children's penchant for supernatural tales, inquires what books she has read, and is reassured that the girl's books are all bought at the corner of St Paul's Churchyard.[27]

'At Harris's, St. Paul's Churchyard, / Good children meet a sure reward', promises *Dame Partlet's Farm, Containing an Account of The Great Riches She Obtained by Industry, The Good Life She Led, and Alas, Good Reader! Her Sudden Death* (John Harris, 1804). For only a penny, a child can purchase

> a little book
> With covers neat, and cuts so pretty,
> There's not its like in all the city;
> And that for twopence he could buy
> A story-book would make one cry;
> For little more a book of riddles:
> Then let us not buy drums and fiddles,
> Nor yet be stopt at pastry-cooks,
> But spend our money all in books;
> For when we've learnt each book by heart
> Mamma will treat us with a tart.
>
> (A2)

A Visit to the Bazaar (Harris, 1818) puts Harris's bookshop and St Paul's Churchyard on its cover. The Bazaar's bookseller offers an excellent selection, the text explains. Yet one father hesitates to buy from her, for as he reminds his son, 'I always make a point of buying all your books at the corner of St. Paul's Church-yard'. Luckily, the bookseller can reassure him that all her books came originally from 'Mr. Harris, in St. Paul's Church-yard'.[28] Newbery's *Fables in Verse* mentioned the Bath bookshop carrying the Newbery line. Here, the juvenile library stands at the centre of a

---

26 Marjorie Moon (ed.), *John Harris's Books for Youth 1801–1843: A Check-List* (Cambridge: Marjorie Moon and A. J. B. Spilman, 1976), p. 1; Welsh, 'A Bookseller', p. 50. A bookstore operated in this location until the late 1880s. Townsend (ed.), *John Newbery*, p. 157.

27 'Anabella's Journey to Market', in Arnaud Berquin, *The Looking-Glass for the Mind; or, Intellectual Mirror, Being an Elegant Collection of the Most Delightful Little Stories, and Interesting Tales, Chiefly translated from that much admired Work, L'Ami des Enfans* (1794 edn; rpt Wakefield: S. R. Publishers and New York: Johnson Reprint Corp., 1969), pp. 8–15: 12–13.

28 *A Visit to the Bazaar* (1818; Tokyo: Holp Shuppan, 1981), pp. 75–6.

bookselling network; Harris's name, taste and list serve as guarantees to purchasing parents, even when selecting books in a different location. Newbery's Juvenile Library, then its much-repeated address, gradually become trademarks, which continue to vouch for the Library's books, wherever they are sold.[29] Newbery's self-advertising techniques, meanwhile, were widely imitated by children's writers and publishers across the English-speaking world.[30] Newbery's marketing strategies proved as transportable, adaptable and durable as his titles themselves.

By the early nineteenth century, the bookstore promotion was a set-piece of juvenile literature. The country tourists in S. W.'s [Elizabeth Kilner's] 1805 *A Visit to London* thus spend a day (and short chapter) on 'A Visit to the Juvenile Library'. Upon hearing that Mrs Sandby wishes to augment her children's 'well-chosen' but 'small' library, her London friend Mrs Barsfield accompanies her to the juvenile library 'she has always dealt at', where she has always been 'very well served'.[31] In the *Visit*'s early editions, published by Tabart, they visit Tabart's Juvenile and School Library in New Bond Street, with Benjamin Tabart himself (shown in an engraved illustration) on hand to serve them. After William Darton took over Tabart's copyright on this and other children's volumes, early Darton editions of *A Visit to London* had the Sandbys visiting 'Darton's Juvenile Library, Holborn Hill', and Mr Darton advising customers.[32]

As a reward for her diligence in reading and learning, Mrs Sandby's daughter is permitted to select numerous books for herself and for friends. And while the Sandbys stock up on or exclaim over various games, toys and juvenile books, the chapter quickly becomes an annotated shopping list of Tabart (and in later editions, Darton) products.

29 See also James Raven, 'Memorializing a London Bookscape: The Mapping and Reading of Paternoster Row and St. Paul's Churchyard, 1695–1814', in R. C. Alston (ed.), *Order and Connexion. Studies in Bibliography and Book History: Selected Papers from The Munby Seminar* (Woodbridge, Suffolk: Boydell and Brewer, 1994), pp. 177–200.

30 In Isaiah Thomas's 1786 American version of a 1750 Newbery original, *Nurse Truelove's Christmas Box, or, The Golden Plaything for Little Children, By which they may learn the Letters as soon as they can speak, and know how to behave so as to make every Body love them* (1789 edn; rpt Chicago: Toby Rubovits, 1934), the hero proves his goodness by reading Thomas's line of Newbery reprints: 'Why he got all the little books by rote that were sold at Mr. *Thomas's* in *Worcester*, when he was but a very little boy.' 'The History of Master Friendly', pp. 19–26: 20. See also John Rowe Townsend, 'The Newbery Books in America' in Townsend (ed.), *John Newbery*, pp. 150–4.

31 S. W. [Elizabeth Kilner], *A Visit to London, Containing a Description of the Principal Curiosities in the British Metropolis* (London: Benjamin Tabart, 1808), p. 148.

32 Moon, *Benjamin Tabart's Juvenile Library*, p. 76. The chapter disappears from later Darton editions.

Maria's eyes sparkled with pleasure, as she entered the famous Juvenile Library ... 'Oh, mamma,' exclaimed she, 'here is *Mental Improvement* and *Leisure Hours* by Mrs. Wakefield. Be so good as to buy them for us. You know how much we were pleased with Mrs. Wakefield's *Juvenile Anecdotes*.'[33]

At the visit's end, Mrs Barfield gives Maria a gift-book. In the Darton edition, the book chosen is S. W.'s *A Visit to a Farm House* (Tabart, 1804, also reprinted by Darton), companion to the volume Maria herself inhabits.

Another 1805 Tabart book, Eliza Fenwick's *Visits to the Juvenile Library; or, Knowledge Proved to be the Source of Happiness*, unfolds an equally self-referential and self-congratulatory paean to the juvenile book trade. Mrs Clifford, who spent her youth caring for her aged nurse, tragically loses her own daughter to a vengeful kidnapping relative.[34] Yet this 'most excellent lady' overcomes her bereavement to become guardian to five orphans, newly arrived from the West Indies. Yet the baleful influence of their illiterate black nurse Nora blocks Mrs Clifford's initial attempts to educate and acculturate the Mortimers. Imagining reading and writing 'only to be acquired by excessive suffering', Nora encourages the children's distaste for education as for 'dull disagreeable England' (pp. 13–14). Thus when Mrs Clifford brings the Mortimers books, and offers to take them to Tabart's Juvenile Library, the orphans claim not to be interested.

'I don't like books,' said Arthur ... 'I always grow low spirited when I am obliged to read,' said Richard ... And little Louisa rose from her stool, and said, with a half crying and very passionate face ... 'Nora said you would make us read, and write, and work until we should all be quite wretched.'

(pp. 9, 10)

But Tabart's soon changes their minds. Shown a picture of this 'admirable repository of knowledge and amusement' (p. 18), the Mortimers yearn to visit this 'large bookseller's shop' (p. 18), even if 'they were ashamed to say so' (p. 21); that night, they 'dreamt of being carried to *Tabart's Juvenile Library*' (p. 31). Then new friends enthusiastically recommend and generously lend out an extensive collection of Tabart books. Their conversations repeatedly endorse Elizabeth Kilner's oeuvre.

33 S. W. (Elizabeth Kilner?), *A Visit to London* (Philadelphia: Benjamin Warner, 1817; American reprint of the Darton edn), p. 82. Here as elsewhere, Darton retains the general Tabart wording, substituting more recent book titles.
34 Eliza Fenwick, *Visits to the Juvenile Library* (1805; rpt New York: Garland, 1977), p. 3.

Howard. – 'Then here is a book called *A Visit to a Farm House*; which, if you read it with attention, will amuse you exceedingly, and make you . . . acquainted with English farming . . .'

   Soames. – '. . . I have one which I will lend . . . *A Puzzle for a curious Girl*. I heard my Mamma say yesterday it was one of the best books that was ever written for children, and that even no grown person could read it without being improved by it.' (pp. 38–9)

Although strongly reminiscent of publishers' blurbs, the stilted conversation of these highly literate children fires the Mortimers' imaginations, and they begin to read Tabart books like Kilner's *Visit to London*. Even Nora is discovered trying to learn to read, to keep pace with her beloved charges. Now rueing their days as 'sad tyrants to the poor Negro woman' (p. 73), the Mortimer children teach her to write, enabling her to send letters home to the West Indies. Finally, the children visit London and Tabart's, to see for themselves the store's 'endless varieties' (p. 61) and many attractions (including, on winter days, a warming fire for shoppers).

Notwithstanding they had heard so much said in praise of the Juvenile Library, they found it far exceeded their utmost expectations. *What, all these books written for children!* they were ready to exclaim . . . They took up first one book and then another, examined the globes, peeped into the boxes of dissected maps, and wished again and again, that they could carry the whole shop away with them. (pp. 61–2)

At Tabart's, Mrs Clifford's charitable pity is excited by a meanly dressed girl delivering an allotment of hand-coloured pictures and picking up another hundred. She proves to be Mrs Clifford's long-lost daughter. Tabart's Juvenile Library facilitates mental improvement for the young, literacy for the ignorant or foreign-born, and renewed family bonds. It also serves as meeting ground for children of varying abilities, backgrounds and classes. Yet while leisured children come to purchase and consume books, less fortunate children assist in their physical manufacture (including the eye-straining job of hand-colouring). Fenwick's conversion narrative shows ill-bred children emerging out of mental torpor and emotional dependence (linked implicitly to slavery, explicitly to colonialism and ignorant nurses), won over to reading and English culture by exposure to a new breed of juvenile literature and of children's bookstore.

The improving Tabart volumes the Mortimers discuss and purchase, meanwhile, includes 'a very entertaining history called the *Life of Carlo*' (p. 94) – written by Fenwick herself. In the 1780s and 90s, Elizabeth Kilner's famous aunts, Mary Ann and Dorothy, followed Newbery's precedent, larding their juvenile works with praise for their own and each other's books. During the first years of the nineteenth century, children's books further intensified their penchant for self-reflection, self-reference and self-promotion, given renewed economic competition over the children's book business. Kilner's and Fenwick's meta-narratives appear in 1805, the same year as *Old Mother Hubbard*, hence at a moment of major transformation for children's bookselling and juvenile libraries.

The same year, moreover, William Godwin and his second wife Mary Jane (who had previously written and edited children's works for Tabart's) opened their own juvenile library – under Mary Jane's name, lest the spectre of freethinkers influencing children rouse scandal or official scrutiny. Their City Juvenile Library sold a range of toys, maps and writing materials along with books they published themselves.[35] High-mindedly, the Godwins paid their staff above-average wages, while keeping the store unheated, even in winter. Eliza Fenwick extolled the fire that warmed Tabart's customers. During her brief stint as manager of the Godwin's bookstore, in contrast, she complained to Mary Hays she had 'sold myself into slavery'.[36]

Despite its chill, the City Juvenile Library functioned as an important gathering place for various schools and generations of Romantic intellectuals. Despite his interest in the Library, Coleridge never delivered the juvenile volume he promised Godwin. The list of actually published volumes is nonetheless illustrious. The Godwins' *Old Mother Hubbard*-style illustrated books included Charles Lamb's pseudonymous *The King and Queen of Hearts* and ten-year-old Mary Shelley's *Mounseer Nongtongpaw* (1808), their moral tales the first English translation of Johann David Wyss's *Swiss Family Robinson* (published as *The Family Robinson Crusoe*, 1814) and *Stories of Old Daniel, or Tales of Wonder and Delight* (1807) by Margaret King

---

35 An anonymous 1813 tip to the Home Office (apparently never acted on) denounced Godwin as the City Juvenile Library's true owner, who intended to infiltrate the schools with subversive democratic ideas. Godwin's front-man, Thomas Hodgkins, embezzled from the bookstore, contributing to its financial troubles. To Horace Smith, it appeared just 'an inferior shop for stationery and children's books'. Summerfield, *Fantasy*, p. 246. Yet it stocked many children's books from France, drawing Mary Jane Godwin's friends in the French émigré community and prompting the shop's renaming as The City French and English Juvenile Library. William St Clair, *The Godwins and the Shelleys: The Biography of a Family* (Baltimore: Johns Hopkins University Press, 1989), pp. 284–5. On period resistance to Godwin, see Donelle Ruwe, 'Guarding the British Bible from Rousseau: Sarah Trimmer, William Godwin, and the Pedagogical Periodical', *Children's Literature* 29, ed. Elizabeth Lennox Keyser and Julie Pfeiffer (New Haven: Yale University Press, 2001), 1–17.

36 Claire Tomalin, Preface to Fenwick, *Visits*, p. x.

Moore (Lady Mount Cashell).[37] Their list also included an English grammar by William Hazlitt, Charles and Mary Lamb's *Tales from Shakespear* (1807) and *Mrs Leicester's School* (1809), Charles Lamb's *Adventures of Ulysses* (1808) and (under the pseudonym 'Edward Baldwin') William Godwin's own *Fables Ancient and Modern* (1805) and *The Pantheon* (1806), this last a profound influence on John Keats.[38]

Self-consciously parodying Newberyian self-advertising, the Godwins' *Dramas for Children* (1809) depict a girl and a footman discussing the purchase, at 'the Juvenile Library in Skinner-street', of Baldwin's *Pantheon* (the footman finds it hard to follow); a Quixotic governess becomes so absorbed in reminiscing about juvenile book buying at Skinner Street, praising and reading aloud from Baldwin's *Fables*, that she fails to notice the arrival of burglars.[39] In real life, the Godwins' utopian experiment was unable to prevail over Newbery's commercial model of children's bookselling. Indeed despite the backing of many of the period's major writers – and repeated financial bailouts from supporters ranging from Thomas Wedgwood to the young Percy Shelley – the Godwins' shop repeatedly approached bankruptcy.[40]

Geoffrey Summerfield, nonetheless, sees the Godwins manifesting a 'philistine and grubbily commercial view of the business of publishing books for children', indistinguishable from commercial competitors, which compromised the works they commissioned.[41] Summerfield particularly deplores Godwin's request that Lamb delete from *Adventures of Ulysses* references to cannibalism, the Cyclops' vomit and his gouged-out eye. 'It is strange with what different feelings an author and a bookseller looks at the same manuscript', Godwin wrote Lamb. 'The author thinks what will conduce to his honour: the bookseller what will cause his commodities to sell.'[42] Lamb omitted the vomit, but refused further changes: 'As an author I say to you, an author, Touch not my work. As to a bookseller I say, Take

---

37 To honour her former governess, Mary Wollstonecraft, Moore adopted the pen-name 'Mrs Mason' (the governess in Wollstonecraft's *Original Stories*). Stephanie Hutcheson, 'Preface', Margaret King Moore, *Stories of Old Daniel, or Tales of Wonder and Delight* (2nd edn 1810; rpt Wakefield: S. R. Publishers and New York: Johnson Reprint Corp., 1969), pp. vii–xiii.
38 William St Clair, 'William Godwin as Children's Bookseller', in Gillian Avery and Julia Briggs (eds.), *Children and Their Books: A Celebration of the Work of Iona and Peter Opie* (Oxford: Oxford University Press, 1989), pp. 165–79: 173.
39 *Dramas for Children, Imitated from the French of L. F. Jauffret, by the Editor of Tabart's Popular Stories* (London: M. J. Godwin, 1809), p. 14.
40 St Clair, *The Godwins*, esp. pp. 279–98.
41 Summerfield, *Fantasy*, p. 244.
42 Cited *ibid.*, p. 255.

the work as it is, or refuse it.' Lamb himself, however, does not present macabre touches as suitable for child readers. Instead, he too advances commercial arguments: as the proven market for Gothic novels and *Tales of Terror* suggests, 'Such things sell.'[43]

Despite Godwin's 'almost rhapsodic tribute to the unconstrained imaginative life of the chap-book romances', Summerfield argues, he endorsed 'the prosy didacticism of those who were intent on "forming" children's minds' (p. 246). This didactic strain, Summerfield insists, originates with Newbery, whose insistence on 'promoting socially advantageous virtues' (p. 82) and self-interested philistinism inaugurated that struggle between fantasy and improvement, which Summerfield and other commentators see as the central axis of Romantic-era children's literature. Their accounts typically quote Lamb's invective against 'the cursed Barbauld crew' whose works have 'banished all the old classics of the nursery'. Yet in original context, a 1802 letter to Coleridge, Lamb's comments indict a novelty-driven book market as much as the new women authors.

> *Goody Two-Shoes* is almost out of print. Mrs. Barbauld's stuff has banished all the old classics of the nursery. The shopman at Newbery's hardly deigned to reach them off an exploded corner of the shelf when Mary asked for them. Mrs. Barbauld's and Mrs. Trimmer's nonsense lay in piles about . . . Is there no possibility of averting this sore evil? Think what you would have been now, if, instead of being fed with tales and old-wives' fables in childhood, you had been crammed with geography and natural history!
>
> Hang them! – I mean the cursed Barbauld crew, those blights and blasts of all that is human in man and child.[44]

Lamb suggests not that the old classics have vanished entirely from the nursery, but that children's booksellers no longer sell them. Those classics, moreover, encompass not only traditional oral or chapbook material – 'tales and old-wives' fables' – but self-promoting Newbery books like *Goody Two-Shoes*. Having introduced a new commodity logic to the manufacture and sale of children's books, Newbery juvenile libraries (and their descendants) become reluctant to sell even their own, now-venerable wares; instead, they favour newer, drier and more popular fare.

An anonymous 1820 *London Magazine* essay, 'The Literature of the Nursery' echoes Lamb's lament. The Mother Hubbard books, now archaic, extended

---

43 Letter to William Godwin, 11 March 1808. *Collected Works and Letters of Charles Lamb* (New York: Modern Library, 1935), p. 766.
44 Letter to Samuel Taylor Coleridge, 23 October 1802. *Ibid.*, pp. 726–8: 727.

oral and chapbook literature not only in their popular materials, but in their preoccupation with the consumption of food as the imaginative centre of childhood orality. Before them, the Newbery books, fashioned to resemble fair gingerbread, had built an audience for education by appealing to primal childish appetites. In retrospect, these gilt-covered books represent a gold standard, now undermined by the 'profligate publications' of once-venerable children's publishers.[45] John Marshall's physical move from Aldermary Churchyard to Fleet Street, from church-yard to media centre, epitomizes the transition from a children's literature still linked to oral and chapbook tradition to a vulgar commercial writing whose patina of smartness and contemporaneity derives from city street-slang. The chapbook, whose often blurry illustrations forced readers to imagine for themselves, have been replaced by glossy picture books, whose 'flashy' (p. 482) images present people, animals and places as glamorous, 'fashionable' (p. 483) commodities, teaching children to scorn the relative 'modesty of nature' (p. 433). If chapbooks, then Newbery books, hastened the decline of oral literature by circulating it in print form, post-1805 nursery books destroy the timeless aura and carrying power of legend by fixing their characters as slick modern images.

In the early nineteenth century, the renewed commercialization of children's literature created new anxieties about the propriety of juvenile reading and the status of the book as personal property, while reactivating old anxieties about the social transformations and economic displacements which had accompanied the establishment of the children's book trade, over half a century earlier. Particularly given the post-1805 renaissance of nursery rhyme and fairy-tale 'nursery literature', Romantic children's books remain preoccupied with the earlier banishment of the chapbook, with the lost world of the chapmen, with a half-forgotten orality. When Romantic children's books evoke orality as a developmental phase or sentimentalize the relationship between old and young, they work, not least, to understand children's relationship to new modes of interiority, the emergence of the children's book as a commodity, and their own transitional status as printed books meant partly to be read aloud.

Oral greed, literate moderation

Charles Lamb was wrong, in 1802, to predict the imminent disappearance of *Goody Two-Shoes*. By 1804, Tabart offered a version in a Nursery Tales series,

45 'The Literature of the Nursery', *London Magazine* 2:11 (November 1820), 478–83: 479.

along with Cinderella, Children in the Wood, Jack the Giant-Killer, and Robin Hood – in whose company it appeared as part of popular oral tradition, not an alternative to it. In 1804 Harris published *Dame Partlet's Farm*, an extended sequel to *Goody Two-Shoes*, and in 1808 *The Alphabet of Goody Two Shoes; By Learning Which, She Soon Got Rich*. Both spin-offs link Goody's pedagogy to orality. *The Alphabet* begins with food words. A is an apple put in a pie, B Biddy who made the pastry, C a cheese nibbled by mice,

> D was Dick Dump,
> Who did nothing but eat,
> And who would leave book, and play,
> For a nice bit of meat.
>
> (p. 4)

For young children, alimentary pleasure challenges reading in its claim on the passions. Yet those who abandon food to read their horn-books are rewarded by being given food to read about: an immediate, physical hunger (or greed) is assuaged indirectly, through the mediation of print.[46]

Dame Partlet's Farm and Mary Belson Elliott's *Goody Two Shoes, Exemplifying the Good Consequences of Early Attention to Learning and Virtue* (Darton, c. 1830) present food experiences and memories as foundational to the acquisition of literacy. Elliott's Goody teaches poor children by having them use her hand-carved letter blocks to spell out the food they have just eaten for dinner. Together, they assemble the letters to spell b-r-e-a-d, apple-pie; potatoes; beef; mutton and turnips, 'all of which they spelled with the greatest accuracy' (p. 21). Goody's 'rattletrap' blocks enact literacy's democratizing potential: the rural poor use their own version of movable type to describe the materials of their lives. Yet the instructor also makes tactical use of the poor's preoccupation with food and satiety; they move from being orally fixated, hungry for bodily sustenance, to being literate, hungry for intellectual stimulus.

In *Dame Partlet's Farm*, reading and sustenance form cornerstones of a utopian political economy, itself the legacy of Goody Two Shoes. An impoverished widow and mother of six, Dame Partlet was also 'a very near relation of that renowned person GOODY TWO SHOES, so well known to every good child who has read those pretty books sold at the corner of St. Paul's Church-yard, London' (A3). In Newbery's tradition of one book

---

46 Nineteenth-century alphabets featured letters eating one another. See Patricia Crain, *The Story of A: The Alphabetization of America From 'The New England Primer' to 'The Scarlet Letter'* (Stanford: Stanford University Press, 2001).

puffing and selling another, one literary character begets another. Yet those who teach literacy also beget new lines of intellectual descent, ink thicker than blood. An early beneficiary of Goody's reading lessons, Dame Partlet becomes one of the village's best readers, helps others to read, and uses Goody's methods to teach her numerous children:

> when they were at breakfast, and at dinner or supper, she made them spell what they had on the table . . . so that they learned a great deal without Dame Partlet losing time from her household affairs: The little ones would spell *salt, milk, tea, bread, cheese, chair, stool, bed*, &c. and the next *butter, cabbage, oatmeal*, and such words . . .   (pp. 27–8)

This pedagogy, rooted in food and domestic life, is supplemented by books the Rector purchases 'at the Corner of St. Paul's Church Yard' (p. 33) as New Year's presents for Dame Partlet and deserving child scholars. Dame Partlet reads her gift copy of *The Sick Man's Friend* to ailing villagers. Her study of almanacs and herbals make her the village's foremost healer. And on winter evenings, she gathers village children in her 'instructive habitation' to hear 'such a number of little tales and histories' (p. 35). Learned, helpful, industrious, she rises to become a woman of property. Yet her epitaph memorializes her, above all, for feeding the needy and rewarding learning with food. She sends 'her apples and her pears' to children who say their prayers, gives cheesecake or pie to those who never told a lie, custard or tart 'to those who learnt their book by heart'. Particularly good scholars were 'ever welcome to her kitchen, / For cake and sweetmeats she was rich in' (pp. 66–7).

Newbery linked the children's book to the fair-bought gilt gingerbread, prized for its potential deliciousness and its display potential. Early nineteenth-century authors present literacy – and the intellectual appetites it engenders – as an extension of and alternative to bodily nourishment. *Aunt Ann's Lesson-Book, for Very Young Children. In Words of One and Two Syllables, By a Friend to Little Children* (Harvey and Darton, 1822) contrasts oral greed with literacy's deferred but lasting gratifications. In 'A Pretty Book', two boys are given sixpence. Frank 'bought a cake', ate it, 'and the cake was gone'. But Henry bought 'a pretty book . . . and the next day he had his book, and the next day, and the next. A whole year after, he still had his book. Indeed, I believe he has his pretty book at this moment' (p. 5).

Many Romantic cautionary tales show 'dunces' doomed to regression or arrested development, caught in infantile forms of orality. Yet in Barbauld's *Lessons for Children from Three to Four Years Old* (J. Johnson, 1788), good scholars internalize the pressure to read by developing eating disorders. Three boys at school receive cakes from their mothers. A 'clever fellow' who 'loved his book' and 'got to be first in his class', Harry gets a cake because his mother is impressed with how well he has 'learned his book' (pp. 14–15). The cake is delicious, but Harry gorges himself so full he almost dies. Harry's school-fellow, nicknamed Peter Careful, is sent a cake after writing 'his mamma a very neat pretty letter – there was not one blot in it all' (p. 21). Anxious not to make himself sick, as Harry has, Peter hoards his cake, until it grows stale, and must be thrown away; he is sick at heart, but nobody else 'was sorry for him' (p. 24). Billy, who receives a cake simply because his mother 'loved him dearly, and he loved her dearly' (p. 24), shares it with his schoolmates, saving only one little piece for tomorrow. But when an 'old blind Fiddler', crying with loneliness and hunger, comes to play for the boys, Billy gives him the last piece. 'And the Fiddler thanked him, and Billy was more glad than if he had eaten ten cakes' (p. 30).

Literacy and orality meet here on several levels. Parents whose love seems conditional on the acquisition of literacy produce exemplary young readers and writers addicted to infantile, secretive forms of orality. Feeling the pressure to excel, to read without halting, to write without a blot, these schoolboys yearn for cake's unconditional sweetness, a substitute for parental affection to be gorged, hidden or hoarded. This mode of youthful literacy internalizes school's competitiveness and alienation; Harry and Peter develop a proprietary relationship to the book, and a painful, secretive, oedipalized, relationship to orality. The schoolboy loved for himself, in contrast, treats school as an extension of his loving home, sharing easily with schoolmates – and compassionate towards a broken, bardic representative of oral tradition.[47]

---

47 Elizabeth Turner's retelling in *The Daisy, or Cautionary Tales for Children* (London: Harris, 1807) omits Barbauld's school setting and links between literacy, love and greed, while preserving the contrast in eating habits and social outlooks. Lamb's 'Dissertation upon Roast Pig' lambasts Barbauld's parable. Young Elia, returning to school with his aunt's parting plum-cake, is accosted by a gray-headed beggar. Without money to give him, Elia, 'in the vanity of self-denial, and the very coxcombry of charity, school-boy-like', instead hands him the cake. Temporarily 'buoyed up . . . with a sweet soothing of self-satisfaction', Elia quickly finds his 'better feelings' returning, regretting his own 'impertinent spirit of alms-giving' and mentally cursing 'that insidious, good-for-nothing, old grey impostor' (*Complete Works*, pp. 108–13, all p. 112). Coleridge's 1808 'Lecture on Education', similarly, critiques Edgeworthian moral tales for inducing not goodness but 'goodyness', charity that is really vanity. Summerfield, *Fantasy*, p. 257.

From old wives' tales to publishers' lists

In Germany, Friedrich Kittler has argued, literacy became oedipally charged around 1800, as mothers took a newly central – yet self-abnegating – role in feeding their infants and teaching their children to read; when Romantics wrote poetry or glorified oral tradition, they were inspired by half-repressed memories of their mother's half-suppressed voice.[48] In Romantic-era Britain, Elizabeth Kowaleski-Wallace suggests, the education of children often involved an implicit (re)education of mothers, who set aside their own needs and interests to become hovering, involved interlocutors, framing juvenile explorations.[49]

Romantic children's literature idealizes mothers, nurses and school-mistresses as agents of literacy. Yet it also demonstrates how the struggle for literacy can escalate into a battle of wills between recalcitrant child learner and punitive adult teacher. In Dorothy Kilner's *The Village School* (2 vols., John Marshall, 1787–98?), 'Ben Heady would never be persuaded to look into his book at all', while Nancy Dawdle frets and cries into hers, then rubs her tears 'about with her fingers, till, in several places, she quite made holes in the paper, and also made her book illegible' (vol. II, p. 48). In her *Histories of More Children than One; Or Goodness Better than Beauty* (John Marshall, 1795), a young boy reads daily lessons aloud to his mother but balks unexpectedly at 'thought': 'he would not either spell it, or tell what it was without spelling it, but stood like a dunce with his book in his hand, crying and sobbing badly'.[50] Unable to persuade with reason, Mary Strictum ties her son to a tree for hours, until he relents. The next day, he is unusually eager at his lesson, preparing it so it 'might be quite perfect'; what he most fears is that his mother 'would not trouble herself to teach him any more' (p. 18). In Mary Belson Elliott's *Precept and Example; or, Midsummer Holidays* (Darton, 1811), a boy who defers learning his lessons is reproved by his mother until he weeps, begging her renewed confidence. Determined to draw reluctant children across the threshold of literacy, female teachers sometimes resort to force, breaking the child's spirit or threatening the withdrawal of love or pedagogic attention.

48 Friedrich A. Kittler, 'The Mother's Mouth', *Discourse Networks 1800/1900*, trans. Michael Metteer with Chris Cullens (Stanford: Stanford University Press, 1990), pp. 25–69.
49 Elizabeth Kowelski-Wallace, *Their Father's Daughters: Hannah More, Maria Edgeworth, and Patriarchal Complicity* (New York: Oxford University Press, 1991), esp. pp. 112–17.
50 Dorothy Kilner, *Histories of More Children than One* (rpt London: Baldwin, Cradock and Joy; N. Hailes and John Marshall, 1822), p. 5.

Elizabeth Kilner's Mrs Sandby, Fenwick's Mrs Clifford succeed more easily, by using the juvenile library to develop a love of reading; the allure of children's books, commercially displayed, helps minimize ambivalence about literacy, preserving domestic equilibrium. The familial struggles Dorothy Kilner anatomized lose their claustrophobic intensity if the juvenile library is introduced as a third, mediating or triangulating force, if the terrain of reading moves from the nursery or schoolroom's relative isolation to the attractive public setting of the children's bookstore.

The juvenile library is ascribed a similar mediating role in the ongoing struggle over children's literature, between those who see children as inheritors and future transmitters of a traditional oral repertory, and those who envision child readers raised solely on improving modern children's books. Anthologies like *Mother Goose's Melody; or, Sonets [sic] for the Cradle: Containing the Most Celebrated Songs and Lullabies of the old British Nurses* (Francis Power, 1791, perhaps reprinting an earlier Newbery book) had long worked to dignify nursery rhymes as national literary heritage. In *The Parental Instructor; or, A Father's Present to his Children* (Edinburgh: Oliver and Boyd, c. 1820?), conversely, a boy who asks his father to tell 'the tale of Cinderella, Ass-skin, Tom Thumb, or Bluebeard' draws scorn instead; this penchant for 'frivolous books', 'childish tales' whose 'chimeras' cannot yield any 'benefit' are pardonable only 'in a child, who requires to be rocked asleep by his nurse'.[51]

Working to reconcile these apparently irreconcilable positions, many Romantic texts celebrate a sentimental rapprochement between generations, showing the oral narratives of the old providing moral education for the young. *Stories of Old Daniel*, Moore explains, was inspired by a real-life Old Daniel, whose tales amused village children and taught them to understand each other. Moore's own aim is to encourage children's 'love of reading' and 'that love of literature, which procures *the most independent of all employments, and the most durable of all pleasures*'. To this end, she has

> thought it expedient to suppress some of his stories, to alter others, and to supply him with several which he never heard of. I have also taken the liberty of making great improvements in his mode of expression, as I do not perceive any advantage children can derive from an acquaintance with vulgar or provincial praises . . . When Daniel's diction is only simple, and

51 Rpt in Leonard De Vries (ed.), *Flowers of Delight, Culled from the Osborne Collection of Early Children's Books* (New York: Pantheon, 1965), pp. 91–3: 91.

not absolutely improper, I have endeavoured to preserve it, as it sometimes renders his narrations more interesting.[52]

As a child, the narrator hears a benevolent old man's moral tales and life adventures; as an adult, the narrator transmits these stories, yet changes them fundamentally in the cause of literacy. Jane Porter lovingly remembers the fairy stories she learned, as a 'little prattling child . . . between the knees of my grandfather's white-haired Robin'.[53] Yet if she regrets the passing of such tellers, she also regrets how old wives' tales haunted their listeners, years after the telling. Her own tales are conceived on a different, didactic model.

Mary Belson Elliott refuses altogether the burden of oral tradition. In *Peggy and her Mammy* (Darton, 1819), an orphan repays the care of her poor elderly foster-'mammy' by buying her a comfortable chair. A closing tableau of devotional reading emblematizes the grateful bond and mutual admiration between generations: Susan rests 'her aged form in her new chair' while Peggy, 'in soft accents, read a chapter from the Bible . . . Peggy was never tired of admiring the dame in her new station. Susan was never weary of blessing the grateful little being who had procured her so great a comfort in her old age' (pp. 57–8). Yet the story rechannels, even reverses traditional transmission process, in which stories, songs or oral tradition pass from old to young.

Such stories form the context for Elizabeth Newbery's Berquin adaptation, whose old woman intrudes into the narrative to denounce old wives' tales, and frame the advertisement for Newbery's products. The literary repertoire of old chapbook and old nurse is to be replaced by modern children's literature – and the old dame herself ostensibly endorses this shift. In Fenwick's *Mary and her Cat. In Words not exceeding Two Syllables* (Darton, 1819), Old Nurse Brown

lov-ed Ma-ry dear-ly, and Ma-ry lo-ved her nurse dear-ly, and she u-sed ve-ry of-ten to go to the cottage, where some-times she would read to her

---

52 [Author's] Preface, Moore, *Stories of Old Daniel*, pp. iii–iv.
53 Jane Porter, *The Two Princes of Persia: Addressed to Youth* (Crosby and Letterman, 1801), p. xii. In Maria Edgeworth's *Harrington* (1817), in contrast, nursery stories condemn young hearers to years of anxiety and prejudice. Sir Richard Phillips sees 'nurse's stories', circulated even in enlightened families and public schools, as pervading 'all ranks' with the 'lowest superstition'; 'imbibed in infancy' and 'confirmed through the entire period of youth', their impression remain the strongest and most 'universally operative'. *A Morning's Walk from London to Kew*, 2nd edn (London: J. and C. Adlard, 1820), pp. 68–9.

nurse, and some-times nurse Brown would tell sto-ries to her, or to sing old songs, such as she had learn-ed from the books that are sold at Mr. Dar-ton's shop, on Hol-born Hill, where all kinds of books that can a-muse or in-struct chil-dren are to be bought.   (pp. 4–5)

While still the teller and singer of traditional narratives, the nurse no longer embodies oral tradition: her repertoire derives completely from the juvenile library. Whether Mary reads or the nurse sings, old and young draw on exactly the same print tradition.

Romantic children's books promote the children's bookshop as an institution able to circumvent or forestall pedagogical struggles, as the solution to cultural anxieties about the disappearance or extirpation of oral tradition, indeed about the printing press itself as an agent of social change. Print, these books insist, need not represent the death of oral tradition, but can speed its dissemination and transmission, ensure its preservation. Elliott imagined a girl reading to an old woman; Fenwick shows old woman and young girl meeting on shared ground, thanks to Mr Darton's shop.

The promise of children's literature and juvenile libraries, then, is the suspension of generational conflict, the levelling of generational differences. Elliott's *Precept and Example* paints a grimmer picture. Here children reunited with their mother after years at school must internalize a rigid, unstated code of reading and book-buying. It is not enough, they learn, to memorize random scraps of poetry by rote and in haste, as at school; instead, they must fathom poems' meanings and recite them clearly. When their mother announces she will send to London for Darton's new, improved 'puzzle maps', Charlotte should not show impatience that delivery may take a week, nor suggest the local bookseller might have 'some that will do'. Although his books and educational toys may be 'near at hand', it is worth waiting while Darton sends 'the best of its kind' (p. 35). Darton's parcel arrives quickly, but Charlotte is not given anything from it, even to look at. For 'knowing her objections to suspense', her mother

> thought it best to buy what picture-books her little girl might fancy at Mr. Kingsley's, in the village, who had a great variety of cheap ones, not more than a penny each.
>
> 'Penny books!' exclaimed the offended scholar; 'dear Mamma, you are but joking; I should be sorry to read such silly stories.'
>
> 'Sorry!' repeated her Mamma, 'what, when you can get them in a few minutes, while you feel such a longing for them; besides, you forget the pretty gilt covers.'   (pp. 37–8)

As much as her chagrin and 'tears of mortification', Charlotte's scornful refusal of the penny books suggest she has learned her lesson. Nonetheless, her punishment continues, her 'fond parent' deriving 'the most grateful pleasure' from Charlotte's manifestations of 'self-denial' (p. 41).

> When the new books were produced, her eyes indeed naturally turned towards them, but she remained quietly on her chair, at too great a distance from the table to distinguish their frontispieces, which she heard so much extolled by her brother. At length she was invited to go forward and look at them; she obeyed joyfully, but attempted not to touch one, and waited with the greatest patience . . . (p. 41)

What Charlotte learns is the ability to delay gratification. Other Romantic children's books postulated deferral as the precondition, price and psychic reward of literacy. Elliott's sadistic tale advocates deferral to ratify an emerging hierarchy of metropolitan over provincial bookstores. Some books are better than others. Elaborate frontispieces are better than gilt covers. London's juvenile libraries are preferable to the local bookseller. With its juvenile library puff, Elliott's venal fable represents one logical consequence of the Newbery revolution, which deployed self-advertising and product placement, gilt covers and elaborate frontispieces to upstage the chapbook and put the chapmen out of business.[54]

---

54 Research for this chapter was conducted at the Osborne Collection of Early Children's Books, Toronto Public Libraries; the Lilly Library, Indiana University – Bloomington; the British Library; Bodleian Library, Oxford; Beinecke Rare Book Library, Yale; Special Collections, Regenstein Library, University of Chicago; Rutherford and Coutts Libraries, University of Alberta. James Chandler, Deidre Lynch, Maureen McLane, Richard Maxwell and Donelle Ruwe made helpful suggestions, as did auditors at CalTech, Wesleyan, Duke, Rice, Harvard, Oxford, Sussex, Bosphorus University and the 2001 NASSR conference. Special thanks to Leslie McGrath (Osborne Collection) and to Sabine Volk and Patricia Demers, inspired teachers who awakened my interest in early children's literature.

PART IV

★

THE ENDS OF ROMANTICISM

Representation restructured

FRANCES FERGUSON

John Stuart Mill, in his essays on Jeremy Bentham and Samuel Taylor Coleridge, observes that 'these two men', though 'they agreed in being closet-students', 'were destined to renew a lesson given to mankind by every age, and always disregarded – to show that speculative philosophy . . . is in reality the thing on earth which most influences' mankind.[1] Mill, in the first instance, stresses the points of contrast between the two. Thus, he paints Bentham as a figure who continually challenged the truth of standard formulations and was unwilling to accept views simply because they were customary and Coleridge as one who saw 'the long duration of a belief' to be 'at least proof of an adaptation in it to some portion or other of the human mind' (p. 100). Yet Mill's account also helps to bring out certain similarities in their projects: both were crucial participants in a massive change in the understanding of representation that occurred within their lives and those of their Romantic contemporaries. When Mill refers to the Germano-Coleridgean legacy, he points to Coleridge's role in bringing to England a specific appreciation for the Kantian claim that humans are not passive recipients of sensory experience but rather active originators of representations that make the perception of objects possible. The consequence, for Coleridge as for many others of Romantic-era England, was that human psychology, understood as the study of the basic laws of human nature, developed a powerful centrality. Bentham, meanwhile, for all the emphasis that Mill rightly puts on his insistence upon 'facts' as opposed to human sentiments, was so far from claiming a transhistorical nature for those facts that he produced classifications designed continually to rework the data registered in experience and develop fresh facts. In the Romantic period various writers brought important modern senses of 'representation' – political, epistemological and aesthetic – into relation with one another.

---

1 John Stuart Mill, *Mill on Bentham and Coleridge*, ed. and intro. F. R. Leavis (Cambridge: Cambridge University Press, 1980), p. 39.

In the process, the political overtones of the word 'representation' ceased to be merely metaphorical. 'Representation' came, in the work of Bentham and Percy Shelley and others, to involve more than a depiction of reality and began to include achieving a notion of activism in expression itself. This claim for the efficacy of speech, indeed, led Shelley to go so far as to identify poets as the 'unacknowledged legislators of the world'.

Perhaps the most direct route to appreciating the contribution of Romantic-era writers in altering our understanding of representation is to introduce Raymond Williams's *Culture and Society* into evidence. There Williams proceeds from what might seem like fairly small-scale materials – the change in the uses of five key words – *industry, democracy, class, art* and *culture*. Yet in detailing the specific nature of the changes in the understanding of those words, Williams enables us to see that a representational change of enormous dimensions has taken place. As he makes clear, eighteenth-century empiricism continually foregrounded individual testimony about experience as a route to knowledge. While it had once seemed important to personify abstract ideas such as Sin, Death and Fear to make them more readily available for individual human perception and to insist upon the primacy of individual traits (with 'industry', for example, being a 'particular human attribute', p. xi), Williams traces a progress in which individuals may act as individuals but must also situate themselves in relation to the collective products of their time. 'Culture' is not, thus, merely an abstraction. Instead, the term marks the degree of agency that individuals have come to ascribe to their own productions and to the collective productions of their societies. Individuals perceive and act as persons; but they also come to engage in a kind of dialogue with 'industry, democracy, class, art, and culture', in which individuals must learn to interpret these collective entities and to develop techniques for making them more susceptible to human aims. When the word 'imagination' no longer refers to the faculty of receiving images and instead comes to involve the capacity to have such a vivid sense of absent things as to make it seem as if they were present, representation comes to involve more than testimony about one's immediate experience. It speaks of past and future as well as the immediate present, and it thus becomes an intimate part of the process of recognizing what Mill called the 'laws of the existence and growth of human society' (p. 129).

The palpable expansion of the representational field involves two direct consequences. First, Romantic writers regularly find themselves speaking of the different appearances of the same ideas, as when Wordsworth describes, in the first of his 'Essays upon Epitaphs', the 'subtle progress by which both in the natural and the moral world, qualities pass insensibly into their opposites, and things revolve upon each other'.[2] Second, Romantic writers depict remarkably split accounts of their own positions. Thus, Burke can speak of his opposition to the French Revolution and its animating ideas and at the same time can imagine being proved to have been on the wrong side of the debate, recognizing in anticipation the possibility of a time in which those 'who persist in opposing this mighty current in human affairs, will appear rather to resist the decrees of Providence itself, than the mere designs of men'[3]; and Mary Shelley can depict Victor Frankenstein as a character who has learned to damn himself for having created his monster: 'Cursed (although I curse myself) be the hands that formed you!'[4]

In these formulations, the expansion of the representational field to include past, present and future might seem to contribute to a sense of irresolvable ambiguity or contingency, on the one hand, or tragic irony, on the other. Yet basic political questions emerge as Romantic thinkers attempt to discern the direction of the growth of human society. As Williams points out, Romantic writers like the Wordsworth of the Preface to *Lyrical Ballads* can claim to be simply a man speaking to men, and can suggest that true poetic achievement is to represent the life of all persons rather than the private opinions of a self-expressive lyric speaker – only to run into a practical difficulty about a poet's accepting criticism from that degraded entity called the 'public'. Indeed, Coleridge advocates the development of a special segment of the population – a 'clerisy' paid to specialize in preserving and analyzing the knowledge that makes it possible to respond appropriately to the moral imperatives of one's age. And this sense of the importance of directing public opinion led to a suspicion of Bentham's arguments on behalf of 'numerical majority' that Mill and Matthew Arnold later foregrounded in their insistence that it was important to achieve self-education and to repudiate what Mill called 'the despotism of Public Opinion'. By contrast with writers like Pope and Swift who had known how to put a fine point on their partisanship, Romantic writers attempted to use

---

2 'Essays upon Epitaphs, I', in *The Prose Works of William Wordsworth*, ed. W. J. B. Owen and Jane Worthington Smyser (Oxford: Clarendon Press, 1974), vol. II, p. 53.
3 Quoted in a discussion of Burke's capacity to 'return . . . upon himself', in Matthew Arnold, *Essays in Criticism*, intro. G. K. Chesterton (London: Dent, 1966), pp. 17–18. See Edmund Burke, *Further Reflections on the Revolution in France*, ed. Daniel E. Ritchie (Indianapolis: Liberty Fund, 1992), pp. 254–5.
4 Mary Shelley, *Frankenstein*, ed. James Rieger (Indianapolis: Bobbs-Merrill, 1974), p. 96.

their understanding of the human capacity for representation as a way of transcending their merely personal opinion.

From one perspective, the British Romantics consolidated and extended trends that had become important for their eighteenth-century predecessors. First, they took the periodical essay of Addison and Steele and Johnson, and published long-running reviews that treated the essay as a distinctive genre. Inflected by the urgency of the deadline (however changeable it might be), the essays of the periodical reviews provided a platform both for commenting on the occurrences of daily private and public life and for passing judgements on actual persons and literary work. Second, they extended the notion of public opinion that Jürgen Habermas has traced to Addison and Steele.[5] No longer was it to be the case that literature emerged as the expression of the political views of a writer allied with a patron. Following the precedent of Addison and Steele, literature now took itself to represent a republic of letters that not only expressed political views but also submitted them for the approval of a new constituency, readers largely unknown to the authors whose work they read. Third, following on the attention that Locke and Hume had devoted to the impact of language on thought, they developed both brief and extensive systematic accounts of language – from Wordsworth's thoughts on poetic diction and tautology, to Coleridge's descriptions of primary imagination, secondary imagination and fancy, to Bentham's *Theory of Fictions*, and to Hazlitt's *New and Improved Grammar of the English Tongue*.

These various different kinds of attention to representation – essayistic evaluation, the contribution of acceptance by an audience, and detailed analysis of the differences between one use of language and another – help to indicate the extent to which the Romantics restructured representation. They developed a writing that explicitly saw itself as centrally including commentary. As Jerome McGann has usefully observed in his *Romantic Ideology*, the Coleridgean notion that the writer/critic was a member of the clerisy, a commentator on and analyst of other texts in the manner of a religious scholar, dictated both the shape of various texts (such as 'The Rime of the Ancient Mariner', which presented itself as already containing its own scholarly apparatus) and the sense of the importance of criticism.[6] Romantic

---

5 Jürgen Habermas, *The Structural Transformation of the Public Sphere: An Inquiry into a Category of Bourgeois Society*, trans. Thomas Burger with the assistance of Frederick Lawrence (Cambridge, MA: The MIT Press, 1991).

6 Coleridge's heuristics of the clerisy undergoes transformation and emerges in the form of Arnold's account of the positive effects of the French Academy, which, in his view,

writers might see themselves, as Coleridge did, as giving 'lay sermons' that linked current political events and literature to Biblical scripture; others might see themselves as providing commentary without the benefit of much recognizable religious belief and thus without the benefit of a clearly anointed text, a holy scripture, as the central focus for their commentary. Indeed, a writer like De Quincey regularly organized his essays by noticing something as insubstantial as his own emotional reaction, and continually sifting it for an explanation. The reaction to a detail, rather than an elaborate account of a literary tradition, becomes the best evidence for the significance of the text. It constitutes what we might think of as second-order representation to talk about the importance that we ascribe to an event by saying we have remembered it for years.

To observe that Romantic texts continually use testimony about an individual's emotional reaction is merely to suggest how far they were in sympathy with the basic tendencies of Kant's deontologizing gesture, his constant insistence that, since human beings could only know things and situations through their representations (and could not know things in themselves), one could not simply read off the meanings of things but had to evaluate them in the situations in which one encountered them. If there were no constant, directly available things on which to hang descriptions of experience, so there were no directly identifiable values for things. This point might seem to be one that merely concerns questions of knowledge. Yet the Kantian revolution that Coleridge and others brought to Britain was one that altered the notion of the relationship between a concept and an example. In the process, it ratcheted up the claim on representations, and required them to provide the basis for searching them for their own hidden springs and motives. Texts were not to be seen as straightforward testimony of perceptions and insights that were taken to be accurate. Instead, as De Quincey was particularly adept at insisting, reactions came to be crucial; they became the primary evidence of how a text might not merely communicate a tale but distribute its emphases. What people have come to associate with Romantic subjectivity and emotional response can, perhaps, be best represented by De Quincey's exhortation to his reader (in 'On the Knocking at the Gate in *Macbeth*') 'never to pay any attention to his understanding when it stands in opposition to any other faculty of his

enables 'A Frenchman . . . [to have] to a considerable degree, what one may call a conscience in intellectual matters', *Essays in Criticism*, p. 39.

mind'.[7] De Quincey's view is that 'the mere understanding, however useful and indispensable, is the meanest faculty in the human mind, and the most to be distrusted' (vol. III, p. 150). Indeed, he goes so far as to maintain that the representations of daily life that rely exclusively on the understanding are like drawings produced without any reliance on perspective. Someone trying to draw the houses on a street, he says, and relying exclusively on the understanding, which includes no intuitive knowledge of the laws of vision, will draw the houses so that they appear to be 'all tumbling down together'. Drawing without the representational tool of perspective, in De Quincey's account, produces a situation in which 'the understanding is positively allowed to obliterate the eyes, as it were'. And the person attempting to draw on the basis of his mere understanding without having recourse to perspective 'does not know what he has seen (and therefore, *quoad*, his consciousness has *not* seen) that which he *has* seen every day of his life' (vol. III, p. 151).

De Quincey's basic point extends well past a claim about the relationship between vision and drawing. Indeed, it constitutes an attempt to introduce all the elements of what increasingly came to be known as psychology, the study of the patterns of distortion with which our representations regularly supplement the understanding so as to capture 'that which [we have] seen every day of [our lives]'. That interest in the psychological introduces an emphasis on what we see – as opposed to what we think we ought to see. While commentators on the law, for instance, had long tried to eliminate an identification between spectators at an execution and the convicted criminal who stood for execution, De Quincey implicitly suggests that such an identification can never be expunged. Moreover, he would argue, the very effort to see only with the understanding – the rational version of the moral judgement that sorts actions and objects into good and bad, acceptable and unacceptable – is a mistaken aim. Thus, he begins by asserting that our reactions should not so much be restrained as noticed: 'All action in any direction is, best expounded, measured, and made apprehensible by reaction' (vol. III, p. 153).

That notion of reaction as exposition, measurement and apprehensible form for action distinguishes the understanding of action that De Quincey and other Romantic writers proceed from. Indeed, the notable decline in the pre-eminence of drama in the period – as it becomes closet drama rather

7 Thomas De Quincey, *The Works of Thomas De Quincey*, gen. ed. Grevel Lindop; vol. III, *On Murder*, ed. Robert Morrison (Oxford: Oxford University Press, 2006), p. 150.

than action presented on the stage – marks the considerable difference from the Aristotelian account of drama as the presentation of a complete action and the use of a chorus as a regular commentary on that action. Powerful dramas continue to be written in the Romantic period, but they frequently do not accommodate themselves to a stage. Yet here it is worth insisting that the closetedness of Romantic drama (its not being easily open to performance in front of an audience) does not merely involve the difficulty of using dramatic techniques for presenting such things as the story of Prometheus with its manifestly monumental scale. Instead, the Romantic attention to reaction makes action look as though it is connected to virtually all writing – and, indeed, to all experience. The actions of Macbeth and Lady Macbeth prompt perceptible reactions, but then so do newspaper accounts of murders, the sights that one unexpectedly encounters in a walk (such as the sea of daffodils that Wordsworth comes across and makes the stuff of lyric poetry), and a host of everyday occurrences.

Action, in the new dispensation of the Romantics, is not so much recounted by a witness as it is inferred from the evidence at a scene – or by a tense combination of the two (as in Wordsworth's 'Hart-leap Well', 'Michael' and 'The Thorn'). Indeed, something like De Quincey's account of notorious murders brilliantly anticipates the techniques of modern suspense as someone like Hitchcock will come to deploy them. For in his handling, the story no longer revolves around the crime in and of itself. Instead, a crime scene establishes that something happened, but it quickly comes to be seen as the occasion for a kind of resonance between the perspective of the murderer and the perspective of those who react with horror to the scene and then attempt to piece together exactly how the murderer must have proceeded. In both 'On the Knocking at the Gate in *Macbeth*' and 'On Murder Considered as One of the Fine Arts', we have a practical demonstration of at least one version of what Romantic irony means. For him, the circumstantial evidence that composes a crime scene does not merely identify a killer who can be brought to justice; it also enables one to trace out what that killer must have done and, in the process, what he must have thought.

This is as much as to say that De Quincey foregrounds the psychological, which he treats as a universalizing impulse that does not confine us simply to the moral choices that we would endorse and hope to make ourselves. If for Freud men and women are not only men or only women but persons who continually discover themselves in and as one another, De Quincey cares about pursuing the researches into what might be thought of as sympathy for the devil in such a way as to demonstrate the importance of the imagination as a power of identifying the reality and availability even of the choices we would reject. Thus, Shakespeare's *Macbeth* is for him an important instance of the power of imaginative literature to cause us to see the limits of the most commonplace moral judgements:

> Murder, in ordinary cases, where the sympathy is wholly directed to the case of the murdered person, is an incident of coarse and vulgar horror; and for this reason, – that it flings the interest exclusively upon the natural but ignoble instinct by which we cleave to life ... This instinct, therefore, because it annihilated all distinctions, and degrades the greatest of men to the level of 'the poor beetle that we tread on', exhibits human nature in its most abject and humiliating attitude. (vol. III, p. 151)

'But', he later observes, 'in the murderer, such a murderer as a poet will condescend to, there must be raging some great storm of passion ... which will create a hell within him; and into this hell we are to look'. With this gesture, De Quincey makes Shakespeare's play specifically, and great literature generally, do the work of what he calls 'a sympathy of comprehension', in which we enter into undesirable feelings and 'are made to understand them' (vol. III, p. 152). Maxims of conduct, such as the Ten Commandments, may recommend choices that ought to prevail. But it is, in De Quincey's treatment, the province of literature to move from the prescriptive to the descriptive and to recount not merely what has happened but what must have been necessary for individuals to have become the authors of catastrophes. Williams, the murderer whom he mentions in 'On the Knocking at the Gate in *Macbeth*' and whom he dwells upon in 'On Murder Considered as One of the Fine Arts', creates a world in which slight gestures become crucial. The knowledge of the murders hangs over the entire story, and makes each detail look as though it had come to have a previously unsuspected importance. Each item comes to seem necessary: the murderer's request that a shopkeeper provide him with 'a pair of unbleached cotton socks', which would require the victim 'to face round to the rear, and at the same moment to raise his eyes and his hands to a level eighteen inches above his own head'; the night watchman's report of a suspicious person lurking outside the shop occurring within the murderer's earshot, so that he could adapt his own movements; the young serving girl's knocking at the door that the family could no longer answer. Each trivial detail has come to appear a *sine qua non*.

De Quincey's essays on literature and murder – and the literature of murder – simultaneously accomplish two things: they lend what

Wordsworth would have called 'a radiance' to the everyday, and they create an appreciation for radical evil in the person of the murderer clever enough to have been capable of instantaneously intuiting the means of achieving a difficult end, the murder of persons who, entirely predictably, are eager to preserve their own lives. While Wordsworth used reflective observation to claim the importance of 'the meanest flower that blows', De Quincey makes circumstantial evidence both lead to the identity of the murderer and the murderer's thought processes and underscore the significance of trivial actions and effects. Yet if De Quincey's evocation of the nearly infinite complexity of the minute actions that must accumulate for a murder to be successfully accomplished bespeaks the intensity of the motivation of a murderer, those studies in something like dispassionate psychology are allied with a remarkable new approach to biographical sketches that emerges in the period.

Both De Quincey and Hazlitt are masters of the new biographical mode. In De Quincey's *Recollections of the Lakes and the Lake Poets* and in Hazlitt's 'On My First Acquaintance with Poets' and 'Charles Lamb', for instance, we encounter biographical sketches that are more reviews than histories.[8] Plutarch had recounted the life stories of various historical characters in the effort to sift their strengths and to recognize the tragic flaws that made them the victims of their own success. Boswell had, more recently, provided enthusiastic documentation of much of Samuel Johnson's behaviour over a period of years. What De Quincey's and Hazlitt's sketches introduce is something yet again: a tension between, on the one hand, each writer's recollection of his own youthful idealization of the writers who seemed to him to epitomize all that was best and most interesting in contemporary thought and, on the other, the now disillusioned sense of the ways in which those writers fail to provide life models. As De Quincey recounts his admiring friendship and his falling out with Wordsworth, as Hazlitt details Coleridge's inability to accomplish all that each of them had expected from him, the point of biography changes. Plutarch had scanned the lives of the ancient Greeks and Romans for life lessons from history, as if they could be read off by individuals in other ages. Romantic biographical sketches, like the Romantic readings of Shakespeare that uncover the psychology of dramatic characters, seek the keys to individual psychology less in traits like Alexander's ambition and rage than in modest revelatory circumstance.

8 William Hazlitt, *The Complete Works*, ed. P. P. Howe (London: J. M. Dent and Sons, 1930), vol. V, p. 144.

Coleridge, in Hazlitt's description, walks in a 'tangential' manner that comes to emblemize his thought; Charles Lamb, in De Quincey's account, instantaneously descends from his high stool at his Leadenhall desk to greet the young man coming to meet him, negotiating great awkwardness in his effort to be hospitable to his unknown guest.

The modesty of the subjects of Romantic poetry and the resolutely modest incidentals of only privately epochal meetings converge in this new biographical mode. As Hazlitt says of the new literature that so gripped him, the Romantic poets 'founded a new school on a principle of sheer humanity, on pure nature void of art', setting out with the 'paradox' that 'all things are by nature equally fit subjects for poetry; or that if there is any preference to be given, those that are the meanest and most unpromising are the best, as they leave the greatest scope for the unbounded stores of thought and fancy in the writer's own mind'. Indeed, Hazlitt's almost breathless catalogues of the merits and defects of writers whom he considers at a rush suggest how lives are no longer to be recounted in terms of grand historical design. Instead, he identifies a new 'school of affectation' that Joanna Baillie has profited from, in which she makes 'moral puppets' of 'her grown men and women, pulls the wires, and [makes them] talk virtue and act vice, according to their cue and the title prefixed to each comedy or tragedy, not from any real passions of their own, or love either of virtue or vice'.

What Hazlitt objects to in Baillie and other affected authors is precisely the fact that action is presented in terms of preconceived patterns, as if moral or aesthetic judgements were valuable only in so far as they could be repeated. The paradox of moral and aesthetic judgements as he presents them is that they are representative only when they do not reply on precedents. He thus argues against the kind of criticism in which the critic's object 'is not to do justice to his author . . ., but to do himself homage, and to show his acquaintance with all the topics and resources of criticism' and the kind of coffee-house talk in which people simply echo received opinion of old vintage or recent coinage. The new representativeness, as Hazlitt presents it, is originality. Moreover, literary originality resembles the kind of psychological distinctiveness that De Quincey traces and that Byron enacts. It cannot be striven for or won, but is instead the ability to be oneself so thoroughly that one escapes the condition of becoming a puppet to another person's model.

Indeed, this originality comes to be especially prized insofar as it cannot be aimed at. Hazlitt repeatedly describes action of all kinds as a process beyond the reach of the conscious will. Even a commitment to art that rests on a belief in one's future fame has this element of unconsciousness to it. For, as Hazlitt puts it, that conception of fame cannot really count as an ordinary motive: 'Fame itself is immortal, but it is not begot till the breath of genius is extinguished . . . This, indeed, is one test of genius and of real greatness of mind, whether a man can wait patiently and calmly for the award of posterity, satisfied with the unwearied exercise of his faculties, retired within the sanctuary of his own thoughts; or whether he is eager to forestall his own immortality, and mortgage it for a newspaper puff.' Genius, on his account, involves the ability to have an attachment to an art that is self-affirming, and does not rely on other incentives. And while that description might, from some perspective, look like the kind of mystified description of genius that ignores the social and political realities of literary practice, it is instead precisely the reverse. Genius, as the resistance to external incentives – or even the inability to feel them, is not unconscious greatness in the most rhapsodic sense of the word. Rather, it registers the difference between conscious and unconscious motives, and opens Romantic writing to the kind of analysis that Freud would later produce (while giving substantial credit to Romantic poets for his insights). The preoccupation of various Romantic writers with sleep, dreams and death bespeak this interest in determining how one understands the importance of thoughts and actions outside the control of the conscious will.

Hazlitt's rejection of a pattern-language for accomplishment helps to clarify certain recurrent movements in the way that he and De Quincey write about their exact and near contemporaries. For the refusal to see individuals as following out narratives forged by others involves seeing originality as inevitable, rather than something to be sought. Everyone is, ultimately, original, because the emphasis on originality that had been initiated with Young's *Conjectures on Original Composition* involved having individuals see themselves both as part of a societal project and as distinctive in the terms in which psychoanalysis will treat individuals as distinctive (in inflecting the commonalities that make it plausible to talk about categories like narcissism and borderline personalities with a consciousness of the uniqueness of the paths through which individuals arrive at their distinctive personalities).

Hazlitt thus presents biographical sketches that foreground two elements: first, the sense of the immediate and formative impact that a character like Coleridge had on him and second, the sense of long-term assessment. For while Harold Bloom and Walter Jackson Bate have characterized the Romantic period as a moment in which writers particularly came to struggle with an 'anxiety of influence' and a sense of the 'burden of the past' in relation to their predecessors, it seems more accurate to observe that Hazlitt and De Quincey did not have to work hard at avoiding becoming the figures like Coleridge and Wordsworth whom they so admired in their youth.[9] Their descriptions of meetings with poets, of the kind that Hazlitt and De Quincey produce with consummate skill, register what it is like to see the experience of meeting someone as a life-altering event. They are examples of what Hazlitt calls 'gusto' and what De Quincey calls 'reaction', but they do not revolve around the kind of intense identification and disappointment that Bloom ascribes to them. For, even though Hazlitt and De Quincey continually interlard their descriptions of the earlier generation of Romantic writers with ruminations on themselves, they do not do so because they are engaged in treating Coleridge and Wordsworth as role models. Instead, the reactions to these persons come to be revelatory about the persons who are recording them. Thus, Hazlitt breaks off his account of an early meeting with Wordsworth to say, 'So I have loitered my life away, reading books, looking at pictures, going to plays, hearing, thinking, writing on what pleased me best. I have wanted only one thing to make me happy – but wanting that, have wanted everything.' What he describes is a sense of emptiness and longing that characterizes not just him and Coleridge. Instead, longing becomes the condition of the new accumulative mode in which one continually tries to assess the poems and paintings and persons whom one encounters and also one's place in one's own experience. If Gilles Deleuze will later describe the importance of ethical thought as capturing the notion of our 'being worthy of what happens to us', Hazlitt already captures that ambition along with the sense of its failure.

The second aspect of the Romantic biographical mode that we should consider is its constant pressure of assessment. Hazlitt, for example, in 1823 delivers himself of a remarkably ambivalent recollection of Coleridge's physical presence: 'His mouth was gross, voluptuous, open, eloquent; his chin good-humoured and round; but his nose, the rudder of the face, the index of the will, was small, feeble, nothing – like what he has done.' For Hazlitt provides his physiognomical account of Coleridge less to register an always apprehensible truth than to emphasize the alterations in our estimations of things that we have seen over a period of time. Doing justice to a

---

9 W. Jackson Bate, *The Burden of the Past and the English Poet* (New York: W. W. Norton and Company, 1970); Harold Bloom, *The Anxiety of Influence: A Theory of Poetry* (New York: Oxford University Press, 1973).

poem or a painting, like doing justice to a person, is not simply a matter of being fair rather than rivalrous or self-absorbed. It is instead a matter of disclosing the inherent observational flaws in the observer, of paying tribute and showing the limitations of one's own abilities to acknowledge. Thus, Hazlitt's self-anatomizing about his emotional emptiness underscores the importance of the awakening of his understanding: 'My soul has indeed remained in its original bondage, dark, obscure, with longing infinite and unsatisfied; my heart, shut up in the prison-house of this rude clay, has never found (nor will it ever find) a heart to speak to – but that my understanding also did not remain dumb and brutish, or at length found a language to express itself, I owe to Coleridge.'

In this treatment, persons are not typical – not representative of types. Their important feature is not their personal histories but their capacity for making the history of the persons they meet. They are not role models but precipitators of the history of the future, and they are remembered from that future as if their subsequent importance had almost been perceptible in the moment. Yet if Hazlitt and De Quincey would agree in describing personal reaction as a measure of the power of the persons and things reacted to, their expansive sense of the role of criticism in continually taking the measure of persons and things in the world is part and parcel of the Romantic consciousness of the simultaneous importance and insufficiency of the self. Wordsworth's 'Ode, Intimations of Immortality from Recollections of Early Childhood' (composed 1802–4) may have established one touchstone for this consciousness in its plangent account of how 'The things which I have seen I now can see no more', but Hazlitt and De Quincey's sense of the fragility of their own personal experience makes it clear that Wordsworth's report is not merely personal. It has become the universal account of the inadequacy of the personal in its effort to assess the value of experience. Criticism may involve cultivating the ability to measure a host of things against one another – the personalities of one's contemporaries, the various different literary productions of the age, but its authority is repeatedly called into question by the recognition that these assessments unwrite themselves. The very experience of reworking an essay or a poem – indeed, the very experience of rereading an essay or a poem – is the experience of registering the mutability of one's own reactions.

Yet while Hazlitt and De Quincey epitomize the Romantic flowering of criticism with its reliance on – disappointment in – the evaluations that persons make in the process of having and noticing their emotions, by the time they wrote Jeremy Bentham had already engaged himself with the question of how to develop evaluations that would escape the narrowest possible empirical claims about what things really were and would also be unreliant on the merely personal. Hazlitt's portrait of Bentham in 1825 in *The Spirit of the Age* is thus a particularly interesting essay because it displays the limits of Hazlitt's sympathy with and understanding for Bentham's project. For Hazlitt, all that is right and all that is wrong with Bentham begins and ends in the fact that his 'influence is purely intellectual'. Noting that Bentham is 'honoured most outside of England', he attributes this fact of Bentham's reception to his having 'devoted his life to the pursuit of abstract and general truths', so that his work has met with enthusiasm in 'Paris or Peru', but has not been at home in his home country (vol. XI, p. 5).

Bentham, in Hazlitt's portrait, is not a man of his own time or place. He 'has never mixed himself up with personal intrigues or party politics', and produces 'reasonings' which, 'if true at all, are true everywhere alike' (vol. XI, p. 5). Indeed, Bentham is so far removed from a personal approach that he is capable of delivering remarks that Hazlitt sees as exaggerating the importance of his own theories: 'He has been heard to say (without any appearance of pride or affectation) that "he should like to live the remaining years of his life, a year at a time at the end of the next six or eight centuries, to see the effect which his writings would by that time have had upon the world"' (vol. XI, p. 7). To Hazlitt such a remark sounds like a pure piece of deluded self-importance:

> Alas! His name will hardly live so long! Nor do we think, in point of fact, that Mr. Bentham has given any new or decided impulse to the human mind. He cannot be looked upon in the light of a discoverer in legislation or morals. He has not struck out any great leading principle or parent-truth, from which a number of others might be deduced; nor has he enriched the common and established stock of intelligence with original observations . . . One truth discovered is immortal, and entitles its author to be so; for, like a new substance in nature, it cannot be destroyed. But Mr. Bentham's *forte* is arrangement; and the form of truth, though not its essence, varies with time and circumstance . . . His writings are, therefore, chiefly valuable as *books of reference*, as bringing down the account of intellectual inquiry to the present period, and disposing the results in a compendious, connected, and tangible shape . . .   (vol. XI, p. 7)

Bentham's strength lies in his having methodized thought, but such method, Hazlitt opines, involves a loss for moral thought. Bentham has, in the process of making his arrangements, lost track of 'moral truth', for which 'a calculation of consequences is no more equivalent to a sentiment, than a *seriatim* enumeration of square years or feet touches the fancy like the sight of the Alps or Andes' (vol. XI, p. 9).

In the course of offering this assessment of Bentham, Hazlitt describes Bentham as having tried to capture 'the truth, the whole truth, and nothing but the truth' without regard to the 'capacity of the agent, and to his fitness for apprehending or attaining' an object (vol. XI, p. 9). And he goes on to challenge Bentham's calculation of pleasure by asserting that it fails to take into account the importance of the good, 'that which approves itself as such on reflection, or the idea of which is a source of satisfaction' (vol. XI, p. 9). There is, perhaps, no more succinct statement of the opposition between Bentham's thinking and Hazlitt's and the Germano-Coleridgean aspect of English Romanticism. For Hazlitt is defending the importance of philosophy as a personal project – a continuing effort to refine the faculty of reflection and engage in the kind of soul-making that Keats attributed to Wordsworth. Bentham, on the other hand, eschews the project that underwrites Hazlitt's version of criticism, and dismisses it as essentially metaphysical, and committed to returning to constant restatements of 'the contradiction and anomaly in the mind and heart of man' that yield 'some tastes that are sweet in the mouth and bitter in the belly', to 'how things affect the mind' (vol. XI, p. 9).

For while Hazlitt aims to develop an account of human nature that will accommodate individual human reflection and will make criticism the project of continually sifting literary, philosophical and artistic production for the things that most reward reflection, Bentham dedicates himself to devising systems that will not rely on conscious reflection and will instead find ways of displaying the value of actions in relation to an entire if temporary social group. From this perspective, Bentham's 'arrangement' thus comes to look more than merely mechanical. It is, instead, a means of capturing and displaying the relative values of choices and actions that do not continually refer themselves back to individual persons as individual persons, with greater or lesser degrees of sensibility, imagination and fancy. For Bentham sees himself as producing ways of making visible the effective operation of what had remained for Adam Smith the largely invisible hand of the workings of social groups.

Thus, while Hazlitt's way of proceeding ultimately involves projecting an account of human nature against which individuals are judged (so that a Bentham or a Coleridge comes to look like an extraordinarily accomplished individual who nevertheless fails in certain crucial ways to embody humanity in his own person), Bentham requires far less of persons and of humanity. For his method enables him to avoid seeking the deep commonalities in individual experience and reflection and to bypass the attempt to worry the relationship between his writing and his audience that animated Coleridge's *Lay Sermons*, which divided their (actual and projected) audiences into the upper, middling and lower classes of society.

The most concrete instance of Bentham's exercises in social arrangement occurs in his Panopticon writings, in which he adapted the educational experiments of Andrew Bell and Joseph Lancaster to analyse individual actions in relation to the operation of the larger group.[10] Bell in Madras and Lancaster in England and America had devised methods for delivering education to the masses. Claiming that they could educate as many as 1,000 pupils simultaneously, they inaugurated what they called the monitorial system, in which groups of students would be called upon to produce answers *seriatim*, to spell a word or announce a sum. Every correct answer would entitle a pupil to continue in the educational game, and to accrue the windfall profit of ranking above other students who, by virtue of their mistakes or omissions, were eliminated. The crucial feature of these educational strategies was that they provided a narrowly defined account of the action to be performed and coordinated all similar actions (in spelling or arithmetic or whatever subject) with one another to produce a rank order. By contrast with Rousseau's techniques for quizzing his pupil Emile so as to educe the underlying rationale for his every decision, the monitorial system did not seek the foundations of its pupils' choices. Instead, it aimed at creating practical structures that would identify the relative value of the answers that any individual student was able to produce, and eliminated the notion of individual approval, the reflection of a particular teacher on a pupil or even a pupil's reflective approval of himself.

In Bentham's elaboration of the monitorial system, which he pursued in his writings on Chrestomathia (which he glossed as *'conducive to useful learning'*) and in his Panoptic writings (in which he developed schemes for the ready supervision of many by one), various features of the monitorial system became particularly prominent. First, Bentham minimized the role of opinion by treating each of his groups as a concrete transcendental, in which everyone was evaluated by everyone else under something like rules of a game. These social structures were objective, in that they did not rest

---

10 Joseph Lancaster, *Improvements in Education* (Clifton, NJ: Augustus M. Kelley Publishers, 1973); Andrew Bell, *The Madras School: or, Elements of Tuition* (London: Routledge/Thoemmes Press, 1993).

on emphasizing a general set of views, whether political or religious. As Hazlitt observed, Bentham 'never mixed himself up with personal intrigues of party politics'. And this ability to rise above politics bespoke not just a personal tendency but a highly articulated philosophical position. He instead emphasized a strong and palpable sense of context for individual belief and opinion, and claimed that no truth was a truth in isolation from the context in which it appeared. If this approach was not, in Hazlitt's sense, 'universal', in that it failed to capture the varieties of individual human nature, it offered a universal technique for analyzing the distinctions to be made between the relative values of one fact and another, and thus the relative values of the persons able to produce the scarcer, hence more valuable, facts. Second, he abandoned the project of describing the commonalities of human experience and sought instead to identify persons as distinct from other persons. As his schemes worked themselves out in practice, the trials of knowledge proceeded until all ties were eliminated. There was always one and only one who was first in the class. Third, Bentham focused on acts rather than characters, and thus lightened the burden of action. Where Hazlitt might review his own talents and accomplishments only to bemoan his failure to achieve emotional satisfaction, Bentham did not focus on individual deficits by comparison with an ideal of complete personhood. Instead, he imagined that demonstrating to persons that they could act, that they had acted, and that those actions had value was the most effective means of bringing about personal reformation. In his treatment, one did not need to worry about the deviousness of the criminal nature that concerned Hazlitt when he argued that 'criminals, for whose controul laws are made, are a set of desperadoes, governed only by their passions' (vol. XI, p. 11). For he imagined that social structures might be devised that easily prompted actions that were not reliant on the passions, and that they thus might provide new ways for even criminals to see themselves and be seen with new capacities, as rehabilitated. Individuals no longer needed to review their entire histories to come to know the truth of their souls, but instead came to see the evaluations of their actions through the evaluations of the concrete transcendental structure.

The first major implication of the Benthamite approach for literary representation was that meaning became harder to locate in an individual consciousness. In his ground-breaking *Theory of Fictions*, Bentham propounded the importance of the notion of sentence meaning, the view that sentences rather than words constitute the unit in which language should be analysed. One could not, he thought, produce a set of definitions for words and simply combine them to translate a given sentence. Rather, the sentence was itself the context of the individual words, the complex that gave them their values. That view went a long way toward explaining the significance of the fact that one could cite other people's remarks without subscribing to them, and toward lightening the burden of insufficient belief that might make hypocrisy look like a constant threat. For words, like names, could no longer exactly be conceived in terms of objects with certain stable properties. Instead, Bentham's emphasis on the seriality of his social structures and of sentences made it clear that the analysis of language could now yield a sense of the variability of almost any given word.

Understanding an action or a word as a choice one made within the context of a social structure or a sentence meant that one no longer saw oneself as responsible for providing deep universal truths out of the fragility of one's own nature.

To see the force of this point is to see that Benthamite utilitarianism did not set itself in opposition to literature but instead had rather deep affinities with the growing Romantic opposition to foregrounded meaning. If Hazlitt had objected to Baillie's writing as affected because it offered up patterns of action and belief that characters were made to take up, the Benthamite approach was simply more thorough-going in its objection to didacticism. Didacticism, conceived as the effort to promulgate particular beliefs in literary works, came to seem less like an unpleasant option and more like an unavailable one. When Shelley announced in his Preface to *Prometheus Unbound*, that 'didactic poetry is my abhorrence', he was not so much objecting to Benthamite facts as participating in a scepticism about the constancy of meaning over contexts that Bentham had himself significantly contributed to. Shelley took issue with many of Bentham's specific suggestions for reform, but he nevertheless took up Bentham's most important claim, that the apprehension of politics – or anything else – must now rely on systematic accounts, which attempt to explicate individual positions in the light of a concretely transcendental view.

Indeed, writing to Leigh Hunt about his *A Philosophical View of Reform*, Shelley said that the *View* was 'intended for a kind of standard book for the philosophical reformers politically considered, like Jeremy Bentham's something, but different & perhaps more systematic'.[11] The significance

---

11 Percy Bysshe Shelley, *Letters*, ed. Frederick L. Jones (Oxford: Clarendon Press, 1964), vol. II, p. 201. This passage is one that I was alerted to by James Chandler's extraordinary essay 'Representative Men, Spirits of the Age and Other Romantic Types', in *Romantic Revolutions: Criticism and Theory*, ed. Kenneth R. Johnston, Gilbert

of political views could no longer emerge from a simple process of succession in which writers like Bacon, Spinoza, Hobbes, Bayle and Montaigne 'regulated the reasoning powers, criticized the past history, exposed the errors by illustrating their causes and their connection, and anatomized the inmost nature of social man' and were succeeded by metaphysicians like Locke, Berkeley, Hume and Hartley, who promulgated views that were 'correct, popular, simple, and energetic, but not profound'.[12] Nor could it rest simply on the opposition between warring political factions in any given moment. For Shelley was already reaching towards a structural understanding of history, in which both political actions and literary works would come to be evaluated. If the simple fact of the social ills that most people laboured under exposed the limitations of the political philosophers, those limitations lay less with their ideas than with their transmissibility, the difficulty of their being palpable and perceptible to more than a small portion of the population.

Shelley went on, in 'A Defence of Poetry; or Remarks Suggested by an Essay Entitled: "The Four Ages of Poetry" by Thomas Love Peacock', to provide an account of poetry in which the imagination itself sounds remarkably like an analogue to Bentham's concrete transcendental systems.[13] He began by describing reason and imagination as two classes of mental action that might be conceived as distinct from one another, identifying reason as 'the principle of synthesis' which 'has for its objects those forms which are common to universal nature and existence itself' and imagination as the 'principle of analysis' which 'regards the relations of things simply as relations, considering thoughts not in their integral unity but as the algebraical representations which conduce to certain general results' (p. 480). As he continued to describe reason as 'the enumeration of quantities already known' and imagination as 'the perception of the value of those quantities, both separately and as a whole', it became clear that he did not need to treat criticism as the analytical supplement to poetry, because he saw poetry itself as already analytical. Thus, it could mark 'the before unapprehended relations of things' in the poetic expression of 'the influence of society or nature upon [the poets'] own minds' (p. 482).

Chaitin, Karen Hanson and Herbert Marks (Bloomington: Indiana University Press, 1990), pp. 104–32; see especially pp. 120–2.

12 Chandler, 'Representative Men', p. 121.

13 Percy Bysshe Shelley, Shelley's Poetry and Prose, ed. Donald H. Reiman and Sharon B. Powers (New York: W. W. Norton, 1977), pp. 478–508.

While Bentham sought to evaluate individual actions in relation to systematic social action, Shelley repeatedly described poetry as lending 'systematic form' to social imagination, as he claimed that the *Divina Commedia* and *Paradise Lost* had done for modern mythology. Poetry thus had as little use for a poet's expressions of his own ideas of right and wrong as Bentham had for statements of opinion. For the moral importance of poetry, which Shelley expands to include both measured and unmeasured writing, lies in the pressure that its structuring imagination places on even the ideas of its makers. Thus, even a poem like *Paradise Lost* that 'has been a chief popular support' of a narrowly defined religious doctrine of rewards and punishments is important for providing such a powerful structure as to revalue even the ideas that it may be seen to express. For the capacity of poets to be more 'sensible' than other men 'to pain and pleasure' involves their creating structures that transmute even their own views (thus enabling even a writer like Wordsworth to serve the spirit of liberty even more than he was conscious of). 'Poets', Shelley concludes,

> are the hierophants of an unapprehended inspiration, the mirrors of the gigantic shadows which futurity cast upon the present, the words which express what they understand not; the trumpets which sing to battle, and feel not what they inspire; the influence which is moved not, but moves. Poets are the unacknowledged legislators of the world.　　　　(p. 508)

26

Romantic cultural imperialism

SAREE MAKDISI

It is astonishing to consider that a literary movement typically associated with daffodils and waterfalls might have had a secret obsession with imperial domination in the East; that there might have been a strange connection between the sleepy hillsides of England's Lake District – Romanticism's spiritual home – and scenes of conquest in India, Egypt and Palestine. But scholars have gradually come to recognize that most of the major writers of the Romantic period (with the notable exception of William Blake) had at least a passing flirtation with the most prominent cultural component of imperialism, namely, Orientalism – if not a full-blown Orientalist phase – and that almost all had some kind of interest in the larger imperial project, of which Orientalism was merely one manifestation among others. Indeed, for many of the period's writers the Orient (which by the end of the eighteenth century had become the focal point of Britain's imperial energies) provided not just an important point of reference for cultural or political difference, but an essential scene in the formation of a literary career ('stick to the East', Byron once famously advised Thomas Moore). The early part of the Romantic period witnessed, for example, the publication of Sir William Jones's translations from (and imitations of) poetry in Arabic, Persian and Sanskrit, William Beckford's *Vathek*, Robert Bage's *Fair Syrian*, Samuel Taylor Coleridge's *Kubla Khan*, Robert Southey's *Thalaba the Destroyer* and *Curse of Kehama*, Cornelia Knight's *Dinarbas*, Walter Savage Landor's *Gebir*, Richard Johnson's *Oriental Moralist*, Elizabeth Hamilton's *Letters of a Hindoo Raja* and Charlotte Dacre's *Zofloya*, not to mention the virtually endless matrix of references to 'Oriental despotism' in the surge of political pamphlets in the 1790s. To this already ample supply would be added in later decades the somewhat redefined Orientalism of, for example, Byron's Turkish Tales, *Childe Harold* and *Don Juan*, Thomas Moore's *Lalla Rookh*, Percy Shelley's *Ozymandias*, *Revolt of Islam* and *Alastor*, and Thomas De Quincey's *Confessions of an English Opium-Eater*.

At least until the 1990s, however, such Orientalism had generally been thought of by literary historians and scholars of British Romanticism as something of a minor sideshow compared to the 'real' literature of the period, especially the nature poetry of Wordsworth and the Lake poets – which had come to be seen as definitively Romantic, precisely because of its apparent detachment from foreign scenes. In the 1990s, scholars began exploring the Orientalist and imperialist themes in Romanticism, but much of the scholarship was concerned with the later part of the period, and with the explicitly Orientalist work of, for example, Byron, Moore and De Quincey. The earlier period was, however, already all-pervasively obsessed with the East, as the turbans, harems, genies, seraglios, sultans, viziers, eunuchs, slavegirls, janissaries, snake charmers, fakirs and imams made familiar by two or three generations of European Orientalist mythmaking gradually found their way out of Arabic and Indian writing ('genuine' or otherwise – and it was mostly otherwise) and into English literature.

However, the Orient provided much more than merely a thematic stage for British Romanticism. The period's obsession with the East was so extensive that it can hardly have been the case that Orientalism was merely one of Romanticism's many sideshows. Much of the period's interest in Orientalism actually had little or nothing to do with the Orient itself (even the Orient as a cultural and political construction rather than an actual place[1]), which suggests that it fulfils a function other than the exploration of foreignness as such. Indeed, the persistent presence of Orientalist references, gestures and subtexts, even in forms of discourse that on the face of it have nothing to do with the East at all – for example, Nature poetry – suggests that Orientalism helped to define political, social and cultural practices in areas far removed from the East itself, and that it played a much more important role in the emergence of Romanticism than has hitherto been generally acknowledged.

In the 1950s the French cultural historian Raymond Schwab went so far as to say that the emergence of Romanticism was actually inspired – set in motion – by the European 'discovery' of the East in what he calls the Oriental Renaissance of the late eighteenth century – a claim that for many years had surprisingly little impact on the way scholars of British Romanticism conceived of their object of study.[2] Yet Schwab's assertion has considerable

---

1 See Edward Said, *Orientalism* (New York: Vintage, 1979).
2 Raymond Schwab, *The Oriental Renaissance* (New York: Columbia University Press, 1984).

analytical power. A wave of translations of Eastern texts, beginning with the Zend-Avesta, the Bhaghavad-Gita and others, opened up whole new vistas of the imagination for European artists and writers. The 'discovery' of the East helped to define Europe's dramatically changing relationship with the peoples and cultures being drawn into one or another of the great European empires.[3] This relationship both determined and was determined by the political and cultural exigencies of European empire-building projects, of which the most extensive was the British: over 150 million people were brought under British imperial control between 1790 and 1830 alone.

The imperial relationship between Britain and its others sometimes inspired and sometimes compelled British writers to articulate what it was that made Britain different. That is, it prompted the emergence of a new imperial British subjectivity against the Afro-Asiatic objects of British rule: a process that was at times exhilarating and at times threatening. In this sense, Orientalism can be thought of as a collective version of the highly per-sonalized individual experience of the sublime.[4] Just as the experience of the sublime, in the realm of aesthetics and philosophy, enables the constitution of an individual phenomenological 'self' as against some profound force (natural or otherwise), Romantic period Orientalism helped to enable the constitution of a collective cultural and political identity, the definition of an imperial culture as against its civilizational 'others'. This indicates the nature of the relationship between the newly developing Orientalist experience of the East and the more specifically *individual* experience of the sublime that has come to be associated with Wordsworthian Romanticism. Romanticism may, in effect, be thought of as the discourse emerging from and articulating both encounters (collective and individual) at once.[5] Or, more broadly speaking, it may be recognized as a discourse of otherness which comprehends Orientalism along with other forms of exoticism.[6]

The nature of the relationship between, on the one hand, the civiliza-tional encounter between Britain and its imperial others in the East, and, on the other hand, the individual encounter of 'self' and 'other' in arenas often far removed from the Orient itself requires a little further elaboration. The

---

3 See, however, Martin Bernal, *Black Athena: The Afroasiatic Roots of Classical Civilization* (New Brunswick, NJ: Rutgers University Press, 1987).
4 See Schwab, *Oriental Renaissance*, p. 18. Here it becomes essential to bear in mind Edward Said's critique of Schwab, and the political / historical corrective he applies to Schwab's argument. See Said, *Orientalism*, pp. 5–6.
5 Schwab hints at such an understanding of Romanticism; see p. 18.
6 Or so I argue in *Romantic Imperialism* (Cambridge: Cambridge University Press, 1998).

Romantic period witnessed the consolidation of both bourgeois individualism – the cornerstone of modern cultural politics and political culture –
and a new modern imperial project; each emerged in relation to the other.
On the one hand, the consolidation through the Romantic period of the
solitary self as the dominant cultural, aesthetic and political category owed
as much to the changing nature of the large-scale British encounter with
'other' cultures as it did to small-scale individual encounters with the
'otherness' of, for example, typically Romantic scenes of natural (or at least
rural) seclusion, beauty and sublimity; or the somewhat less typical but still
also Romantic scenes of individual subjective encounters with the plebeian
multitude (best exemplified by Book VII of Wordsworth's *Prelude*). And, on
the other hand, all these forms of encounter – in which the dialectic of self
and other functioned in essentially the same way – would have been
impossible, or would have taken an entirely different form, without the
cultural, aesthetic and political category of the solitary self. Thus, we might
argue that the imperial politics of otherness in the Romantic period were as
essential to the construction and consolidation of the bourgeois subject as
the latter was to them, for it was in the sovereignty of the Empire that the
sovereignty – the empire – of the self was confirmed.

This explains why that version of Orientalism that began to emerge in the
mid to late 1780s cannot meaningfully be separated from highly politically
charged discussions of the status and rights of the individual, and from a
process of self-definition that extended far beyond the explicit concern with
scenes of colonial otherness. For imperialism provided one of the essential
ideologies – or, more precisely, what Raymond Williams called a structure
of feeling – for all forms of cultural expression in the Romantic period; its
logic was virtually inescapable.[7] Imperialist culture ultimately enabled the
constitution of a viewing subject from whose philosophical, aesthetic and
phenomenological standpoint the culture of (Western) modernity could be
understood and defined for better or for worse – as against, for example, the
sublime panoramas of Oriental splendour and/or decay that had emerged in
the earlier eighteenth century, accelerated through the work of Sir William
Jones, were realigned by poets like Robert Southey, and would reach a kind
of crisis in Byron and De Quincey (to mention only a few of the dozens of
writers experimenting with Orientalist themes through the eighteenth
century and on into the Romantic period). The existential 'anxieties of

---

7 See Nigel Leask, *British Romantic Writers and the East: The Anxieties of Empire*
(Cambridge: Cambridge University Press, 1992).

empire' that scholars such as Nigel Leask have so carefully elaborated in terms of Britain's obsession with the East were not, in other words, limited to the East itself. Especially in the early part of the Romantic period, these are the anxieties attendant upon the constitution of the bourgeois subject, a process whose primary concern was (by definition) ultimately not the 'other', but rather the highly politicized concept of the self.

What we can distinguish as a specifically Romantic form of Orientalism is therefore characterized not merely by certain anxieties of empire, but by a set of philosophical and political obsessions with the self (the citizen, the author, the professional, the *moral agent* essential to, for example, Malthus's revolutionary theory of the population principle). Thus the explosion through the Romantic period of writing on self-determination and the rights of the sovereign individual must be recognized as a profoundly Orientalist discourse – even when it had literally nothing to do with the experience of the East, Orientalism still provided a vital structuring principle. For most writers in the Romantic period were more interested in the constitution and legitimation of the self from whose standpoint the East could (and would) ultimately be viewed and controlled than they were in the Orient as such. The Orient was important for them because it could be mobilized as an imaginary site in which to project various political and ideological modes of being – despotism, idleness, femininity and luxury, as well as a certain kind of religious enthusiasm – which were understood to be incompatible with the forms of selfhood and subjectivity essential to Romanticism.

The Romantic version of Orientalism had its roots in the period's political radicalism, and it would make its way into poetry through the early radical affiliations of writers such as Wordsworth, Coleridge and Southey. At play throughout the corpus of 1790s radicalism – in the work of John Thelwall, Tom Paine and Mary Wollstonecraft, among others – was the consistent conflation of the enemies of the radical cause, the (real) aristocratic enemy and an (imaginary) Oriental enemy, in which the faults of the former were rewritten and overcoded in terms of the faults of the latter – and the faults of both were gendered as 'feminine'. In other words, the supposed characteristics of Oriental society and culture were in radical writing projected on to the aristocracy ('the proud and polished, the debauched, effeminate, and luxurious', as Thelwall put it[8]), while at the same time the Orient became

---

8 John Thelwall, 'Rights of Britons', in *The Politics of English Jacobinism: Writings of John Thelwall*, ed. Gregory Claeys (University Park, PA: Pennsylvania State University Press, 1995), p. 473.

seen as the ideological locus of aristocratic degeneration, and the Oriental seraglio the dark cousin of the aristocratic palace.

In the work of radical writers in the early Romantic period, the systematic Orientalization of the residual culture of the British aristocracy was used in order to depict a dire threat to the emergent social order and its new notions of propriety grounded in merit and right, rather than inheritance and privilege. The aristocratic/Oriental nexus was gendered, saturated with a discourse of femininity, and elaborated as a threat not only to a specifically masculine-gendered 'virtue', but to the very possibility of constituting a bourgeois subject, a masculine citizen (whether male or female hardly mattered for some, though admittedly not all, radicals). For in radical political writing, the rights of the 'manly' citizen were shown to be incompatible with the seraglio, and with the East in general, for the same reason that they were supposed to be incompatible with a declining aristocratic economy also supposedly characterized by 'unnatural' despotism, idleness and luxury. Radical writers in the early Romantic period deployed the trope of Asiatic despotism (and the scene of the seraglio in particular) in order to articulate their arguments in favour of the 'manly' rights of what was thought of as a specifically Western mode of citizenship. This mode of citizenship was taken to be not only incompatible with the East, but structurally at odds with it, and the radical articulation of the rights and duties of citizenship rested upon an unyielding contrast with the 'unnatural' contagion threatened from the East.

This point is perhaps best illustrated with reference to the question of style. For example, at the very beginning of *A Vindication of the Rights of Woman* – a text that so obviously ought to have nothing to do with the Orient that its profound Orientalism stands out all the more starkly – Mary Wollstonecraft dismisses 'those pretty feminine phrases' and 'that weak elegancy of mind, exquisite sensibility, and sweet docility of manners, supposed to be the sexual characteristics of the weaker vessel'. She refuses to 'polish' her style, and hoping 'rather to persuade by the force of my arguments than to dazzle by the elegance of my language', she says that she will not waste her time 'in rounding periods, or in fabricating the turgid bombast of artificial feelings'. She declares that she 'shall be employed about things, not words!' and hence that she will do her best 'to avoid that flowery diction which has slided from essays into novels, and from novels into familiar letters and conversations'.[9] Wollstonecraft dismisses 'those pretty

9 See Mary Wollstonecraft, *A Vindication of the Rights of Woman* (1792; rpt Harmondsworth: Penguin, 1992), pp. 82–3.

feminine phrases', and 'that weak elegancy of mind', not just because they are 'supposed to be the sexual characteristics of the weaker vessel', but also, as she announces in the very opening sentences of the *Vindication*, because they conform to the 'true style of Mahometanism'.[10] For Wollstonecraft, it seemed obvious that Islam (which here stands in for the Orient more generally) was the pre-eminent and most notorious source of that flowery diction, that dazzling (but bewildering and entrapping) elegance, that weak, effeminate language, those 'pretty superlatives, dropping glibly from the tongue', which 'vitiate the taste, and create a kind of sickly delicacy that turns away from simple unadorned truth', that 'deluge of false sentiments and overstretched feelings, stifling the natural emotions of the heart', which 'render the domestic pleasures insipid, that ought to sweeten those severe duties, which educate a rational and immortal being for a nobler field of action'. What must be accounted for, however – beyond asking what a seemingly gratuitous denigration of Islam could have had to do with the struggle for women's rights in England – is just why it must have seemed so important to Wollstonecraft to specify at such length and in such detail her stylistic distance from the Orient in the opening pages of her *Vindication*.

By the 1790s, Oriental tales, stories, essays, poems and histories were understood to be so defined by the very kind of language so roundly dismissed by Wollstonecraft as to make them, from the sober, objective, rational standpoint being claimed by radicals such as Wollstonecraft at best inappropriate sources of genuine knowledge, and at worst dangerous repositories of 'those emotions which disturb the order of society, and engross the thoughts that should be otherwise employed'.[11] Martha Conant argues that by the end of the eighteenth century, the stock Oriental (or pseudo-Oriental) tale included a fairly stable set of components, including slight characterization, vaguely Asiatic scenery, and 'a picturesque background of strange Eastern customs, sometimes enriched by allusions to religious or philosophical beliefs, often by lavish use of magic and enchantment'. She points out that Oriental or pseudo-Oriental nomenclature 'aids in producing the desired effect of remoteness', and the language would usually have been 'coloured by oriental phraseology', generally 'figurative and inflated'.[12] By the end of the eighteenth century, however, the norms of exoticism had changed considerably, and few, if any,

---

10 *Ibid.*, pp. 82, 80.
11 *Ibid.*, p. 114.
12 See Martha Conant, *The Oriental Tale in the Eighteenth Century* (New York: Columbia University Press, 1908), pp. 226–7.

successful Romantic Orientalist texts threatened to drown their readers in the unfathomable deluge of words supposedly typical of Oriental style.

In fact, the most successful Orientalist tales or pictures in the Romantic period – of which Byron would later claim to provide the finest 'samples' – depended upon a sometimes jarring discrepancy between, on the one hand, the work's quasi-Oriental allusions, styles, images and themes; and, on the other hand, a distancing apparatus consisting of notes or ironic qualifications and subversions of the supposedly Oriental material, which, according to Nigel Leask, would pull the reader back to a secure location, 'away from a dangerous proximity to the image, in order to inscribe him/her in a position of epistemological power; nothing other than the commanding vision of imperialist objectivity'.[13] Given the prominence that it has, Wollstonecraft's denunciation of over-embellished language and style, flowery diction and artificial bombast is not merely a gratuitous gesture; nor is it simply a rejection simply of the usefulness of such a style. It is, rather, a rhetorical tactic designed to emphasize her distance from the 'turgid bombast' of Eastern manners typically associated with the Oriental tale, and therefore her contrary position as an objective rational exponent of a discourse of rights, in which artificiality and excessive figural language have no place – and which Orientals would be incapable of understanding.

Wollstonecraft's *Vindication* offered, however, an almost entirely new conception both of the East and of its antagonistic opposite, the West. The East had not previously been thought of in such systematically feminized terms. Much of the seventeenth- and earlier eighteenth-century English writing on the East seems purely pragmatic and commercial, quite disinterested in political and cultural matters, and barely interested at all in contemporary Oriental life (Lady Mary Montagu's Turkish Embassy letters provide a notable exception). It was precisely the *lack* of 'art and design', i.e., sophistication, that defined Eastern culture for many earlier writers.[14] 'Dirt and Nastiness',[15] rather than elaborate artificiality, crude bestial lust rather than the arts of seduction, characterize native life, reflecting the primitive earthiness – even naturalness – that were taken to be characteristic of

---

13 Nigel Leask, '"Wandering through Eblis"; Absorption and Containment in Romantic Exoticism', in Tim Fulford and Peter Kitson (eds.), *Romanticism and Colonialism: Writing and Empire, 1780–1830* (Cambridge: Cambridge University Press, 1998), pp. 164–88.

14 See, for example, Henry Maundrell, *A Journey from Aleppo to Jerusalem, at Easter*, AD 1697 (London, 1697), p. 39.

15 *Ibid.*, p. 9.

Eastern culture. Thus, the 'art and design' that signified civilization for earlier writers, would systematically come to be seen as quintessentially Oriental features (as in the way that Wollstonecraft refers to them) only in the Romantic period. Indeed, 'art' itself would come to assume its increasingly negative connotations toward the end of the eighteenth century partly because of its association with the new conception of the East (as the site of art and seduction) along with which it was redefined. This in itself explains a great deal of the emphasis that was placed by Romantic period writers on 'naturalness' *as opposed to* art.

Even in British writing from as late as the mid-eighteenth century there was still a strong distinction between an intoxicating femininity and the Orient itself, which Romantic-period radicals would collapse into each other. If, for example, Robert Wood, in his monumental 1753 tome on the ruins at Palmyra, in Syria, could readily reconcile 'fondness of shew and magnificence'[16] with the 'severe character of masculine beauty' that he associates with Queen Zenobia, by Wollstonecraft's time such 'shew and magnificence' would definitively be recognized as a token of that languorous femininity linking together the East and the degenerate aristocracy of the West – such as Wollstonecraft saw in the European aristocratic officer class, made up of 'idle superficial young men, whose only occupation is gallantry, and whose polished manners render vice more dangerous, by concealing its deformity under gay ornamental drapery'.[17]

Such a link between the aristocratic and the Oriental was not unique to Wollstonecraft, of course. A similar gesture was essential to Tom Paine's attack on Burke's *Reflections on the Revolution in France* in *Rights of Man*.[18] In arguing that Burke 'is not affected by the reality of the distress touching his heart, but by the showy resemblance of it striking his imagination', that Burke 'pities the plumage, but forgets the dying bird', Paine is able to reconfigure his opponent as a fawning servant of kings and priests, for whom 'shew and magnificence' constitute a kind of substitute reality, an imaginative world to be accessed (as the narrator of Walter Scott's *Waverley* would put it a few years afterwards) via magic carpets and flying sentry-boxes. 'Accustomed to kiss the aristocratical hand that hath purloined him from himself', Paine writes of Burke, 'he degenerates into a composition of art, and the genuine soul of nature forsakes him. His hero or his heroine

---

16 See Robert Wood, *The Ruins of Palmyra, otherwise Tedmor, in the Desart* (London, 1753), pp. ii, 8–9.
17 Wollstonecraft, *Vindication*, p. 97.
18 See Olivia Smith, *The Politics of Language 1791–1819* (Oxford: Clarendon Press, 1984).

must be a tragedy-victim expiring in show, and not the real prisoner of misery, sliding into death in the silence of a dungeon'.[19] Paine refuses 'to follow Mr Burke through a pathless wilderness of rhapsodies, and a sort of descant upon governments, in which he asserts whatever he pleases, on the presumption of its being believed, without offering evidence or reasons for so doing'. He insists that 'before anything can be reasoned upon to a conclusion, certain facts, principles, or data, to reason from must be established, admitted, or denied', and that Burke's flowery, imaginative, and hence pseudo-Oriental discourse is not compatible with such reasoning.

For both Paine and Wollstonecraft the real problem with those 'polished manners' that 'render vice more dangerous, by concealing its deformity under gay ornamental drapery', is not merely a matter of morality. The problem with such false showiness is not simply that it substitutes the 'plumage' for the 'dying bird', the 'showy resemblance' for the 'reality of distress', the 'tragedy-victim dying in show' for the 'real victim of misery', a pretend reality (of 'art', 'show' and 'tragedy') for genuine reality (the reality of 'facts, principles, and data'). Rather, the problem is that artificiality and show corrupt the 'genuine soul of nature', and allow an individual to be 'purloined' from himself. 'Vice' is rendered 'more dangerous, by concealing its deformity under gay ornamental drapery', not just because it is more difficult for others to recognize in us, but above all because it is more difficult for us to recognize in ourselves. Showy style, elaborate forms of writing, excessive figuration, inflated phraseology – in short, the essential elements not just of Burke's *Reflections* as read by Paine and Wollstonecraft, but of what had come to be seen as essential components of Oriental style, the ultimate 'pathless wilderness of rhapsodies' – are bad not just because they prevent us from engaging with 'facts, principles, and data'; they are bad because they prevent genuine self-knowledge, self-awareness, and self-control. 'Art' is here distinguished from reality by the same mechanisms enabling 'us' (but not the Oriental peoples) to distinguish excess from simplicity, idleness from vigour, unfounded assertion from reasoned argument, the artificial from the natural, the useless from the useful, the unmanly from the manly, and hence, ultimately, the East from the West: our others from our selves.

In this context, then, the question of style is an immediately political question. Or rather, aesthetics and politics are collapsed into each other in the question of style. One's style defines one's location on a political terrain

19 See Paine, *Rights of Man*, p. 51.

constructed in and through language. According to Paine and Wollstone-craft, self-control and self-knowledge – and hence self-affirmation, self-constitution, self-determination – are rendered equally impossible by despotism, which denies it, and by excess, which precludes it (as Malthus would argue at around this time, scarcity rather than abundance is the key to self-control and ultimately to an accompanying political economy based on the moral principle of self-restraint).[20] And this holds true as much in a stylistic or aesthetic sense as it does in a practical one: genuine self-expression, self-knowledge, self-control are stifled or precluded as much by turgid and bombastic – or pretty and superlative – prose as they are by the effects of political dictatorship or military hierarchy. This is because for Romantic period radicals such as Paine and Wollstonecraft the contours of individual freedom must be defined by voluntary self-regulation, self-limitation, self-denial – a rejection of figurative and verbal, as well as bodily and sensual, excess – rather than by externally enforced regulation, limitation and denial. While the radicals' lengthy excurses on style, and in particular their refusal of 'polish' and 'art' in the name of natural simplicity and forthright 'manly' honesty, is ultimately intended as a rejection of the politics of the old regime as repre-sented by Burke, it articulated through the systematic repudiation of the excess, luxury and idleness of the East. The critique of the *ancien régime* represented by Burke, in other words, takes the shape of an attack on Oriental style, and the celebration instead of a newly found Western style, enabling of the constitution of self-regulating sovereign Western subject.

The concept of the sovereign Western subject would prove essential to the work of the empire-builders of the nineteenth century. But for them it was a concept to be put to use for a greater cause, namely, the Empire itself, especially for the Empire seen as a project whose avowed aim was to help and instruct that slovenly Eastern object of imperial rule to learn (eventu-ally) to become a subject himself. For the struggle of the radicals of the Romantic period however, the liberty of the sovereign individual subject *was* the objective. Moreover, the knowledge/power of the individual self, or subject, would also serve as the central cognitive orienting node for a simultaneously political and aesthetic project that emerged directly from the currents of 1790s radicalism, albeit one that engaged not in the field of politics in the narrow sense, but rather the field of cultural production which enables and sustains political action. I refer to Wordsworthian

20 See Thomas Malthus, *An Essay on the Principle of Population* (1798; rpt Oxford: Oxford University Press, 1993).

Romanticism. For in proposing a new aesthetic form in *Lyrical Ballads*, Wordsworth was also proposing an explicitly political intervention, in which style serves at once as an auxiliary for the aesthetic/political project and as an analogue for it.

Just as Wollstonecraft and Paine had done only a few years earlier, Wordsworth needs to preface his revolutionary poems with some account of the politics of their style. For if, he writes in the *Preface*, 'there will be found in these volumes little of what is usually called poetic diction', that is because Wordsworth rejects that diction and the style associated with it. Here, in other words, Wordsworth is reactivating the very same matrix of dualisms so thoroughly explicated by Wollstonecraft and Paine only a few years earlier, and for precisely the same purpose: the necessarily simultaneous political and aesthetic project to 'redeem' (i.e., bring into being by articulating) a properly bourgeois notion of subjectivity, largely by contrasting it with the supposed failings of the East.[21]

Wordsworth's struggle is therefore to rescue Poetry from being merely 'a matter of amusement and idle pleasure', as though a taste for Poetry were 'as indifferent as a taste for Rope-dancing, or Frontiniac or Sherry'.[22] It is a struggle, in the face of 'idleness and unmanly despair',[23] to create an explicitly 'manly'[24] style, in order to show the Reader how to equip himself with the kind of 'sound and vigorous mind'[25] ultimately required for fully appreciating Wordsworth's own poetry. For, though it derives from them, great poetry is not simply 'the spontaneous overflow of powerful feelings', of which the most powerful is the experience of the sublime. Rather, 'it takes its origin from emotion recollected in tranquillity: the emotion is contemplated till by a species of reaction the tranquillity gradually disappears, and an emotion, similar to that which was before the subject of contemplation, is gradually produced, and does itself actually exist in the mind'.[26] Emotion and excitement, on their own, suggest 'an unusual and irregular state of the mind', in which 'ideas and feelings' do not 'succeed each other in accustomed order'; and in powerful Poetry 'there is some danger that the excitement may be carried beyond its proper bounds'.

21 See Wordsworth, fragment on the sublime, in Wordsworth, *Selected Prose* (Harmondsworth: Penguin, 1988), pp. 263–74; and *Essay, Supplementary to the Preface*, in *Selected Prose*, pp. 387–413, 408–9.
22 Wordsworth, *Preface*, p. 257. This passage is from the 1802 edition.
23 *Ibid.*, p. 257. This passage is also from the 1802 edition.
24 *Ibid.*, p. 263.
25 *Ibid.*, p. 266.
26 *Ibid.*, p. 266.

However, Wordsworth adds, 'the co-presence of something regular', that is, metre and rhyme, 'cannot but have great efficacy in tempering and restraining the passion by an intertexture of ordinary feeling'.[27] The rigorous new style that Wordsworth seeks to create, then, draws its rigour and power precisely from the fact that, because of rhyme and metre, it is 'regular and uniform, and not, like that which is produced by what is usually called poetic diction, arbitrary and subject to infinite caprices upon which no calculation whatever can be made'. In the latter, Wordsworth explains, 'the Reader is utterly at the mercy of the Poet respecting what imagery or diction he may choose to connect with the passion', whereas in the former – his own poetry – the metre obeys certain laws, 'to which the Poet and Reader both willingly submit because they are certain'.[28]

The kind of poetry to which Wordsworth aspires, then, is one that would allow for the greatest expression of emotion, while at the same time keeping that emotion firmly regulated and uniform, under strict linguistic control. Such poetry is a celebration of self-control, of the capacity of an elevated mind to assert, through the highly regulated language of 'good' poetry, control over what would otherwise be merely disorganized feelings, however powerful ('bad' poetry, on the other hand, is bad because it surrenders such self-control in a gush of 'gross and violent stimulants'). Powerful poetry thus re-enacts in language the experience of the sublime. It is, in other words, a celebration of the substitution of raw natural emotion for a re-produced emotion, a simulacral reproduction whose condition of possibility is self-control. Thus it is a celebration, a 'calling forth' and 'communication', of *power*.[29]

Indeed, as Wordsworth would explicitly claim in the *Essay, Supplementary to the Preface of Lyrical Ballads*, for all the poet's own power and capacity for linguistic self-control, for all his skill at expressing pathos and sublimity, 'without the exertion of a co-operating *power* in the mind of the Reader, there can be no adequate sympathy with either of these emotions: without this auxiliary impulse, elevated or profound passion cannot exist'.[30] To be moved by passion, Wordsworth continues, requires an effort on the part of the Reader, which is why he must be of 'sound and vigorous mind'. If the genius of the Poet represents 'an advance, or a conquest', Wordsworth asks, 'is it to be supposed that the reader can make progress of this kind, like an

27 *Ibid.*, p. 264.
28 *Ibid.*, p. 262.
29 See *Essay*, p. 410.
30 Wordsworth, *Essay*, p. 409. Emphasis in original.

Indian prince or general – stretched on his palanquin, and borne by his slaves? No; he is invigorated and inspirited by his leader, in order that he may exert himself; for he cannot proceed in quiescence, he cannot be carried like a dead weight'. Therefore, Wordsworth concludes, 'to create taste is to call forth and bestow power, of which knowledge is the effect; and *there* lies the difficulty'.[31] The difficulty, in other words, lies in creating not just a new kind of taste, but an altogether new kind of reader, an explicitly *Western* reader, who – unlike an Indian general addicted to an easy life of indulgence – is capable of the vigorous self-discipline that Wordsworth says his poetry requires, and, indeed, calls forth as an expression of 'power, of which knowledge is the effect'.

Ultimately, Wordsworth's argument most clearly dovetails with Wollstonecraft's and Paine's Orientalism on the question of self-control, and on the extent to which that self-control is necessarily synonymous with the knowledge/power of the subject. In both cases, the power/knowledge of the subject is contrasted with the world of objects surrounding him, over which he seeks to gain control and mastery precisely by being able to express it, know it, represent it. Especially given the visual register that so dominates Wordsworth's passages on aesthetic philosophy, as well as his poetry, the subject's power/knowledge is exerted over a landscape whose primary defining feature is that it is outside him, *exotic* at once in the sense that it is alien and in the sense that it is external, its externality and alienness being, in fact, mutually constitutive, together enabling the constitution of the viewing subject. This is why there is such a startling continuity between Romantic landscape aesthetics and the emergent cultural politics of imperialism. Why else, in describing his nature poetry, would Wordsworth find himself obliged to fall back on the otherwise seemingly inappropriate political and military vocabulary of 'conquest', in which the reader too must participate – must be interpellated – if the conquest is to be successful?

Poetry, for Wordsworth, is the highest form of knowledge; and hence it expresses the highest form of power. In his hands, Poetry becomes explicitly an imperial discourse. The Poet's power over the landscape, over the exotic object-world, over the visual field in general, is synonymous with his ability to know and to represent it; just as, for the great prophets of nineteenth-century British imperialism, the empire's power over its possessions would be precisely synonymous with its knowledge of them. Whereas, for Cromer, for Lawrence, for Balfour, the knowing subject can demonstrate

---

31 *Ibid.*, pp. 409–10. Emphasis in original.

his knowledge/power through his ability to construct and elaborate a reasoned argument, the Oriental object of his vision (and hence of his rule) is incapable of such argument and has to rely instead on impulse, caprice, wiliness, seduction, assertion, mere persuasion. The Poet, for Wordsworth, must express not raw emotion, not 'the spontaneous overflow of powerful feelings', with the attendant danger of unbounded excitement – for *that* is the hallmark of the enthusiastic Oriental – but rather, 'emotion recollected in tranquillity', that is, emotion reconstructed, reconsidered, re-presented through the controlling, restraining regularity of law-obeying rhyme and metre.

Here the power/knowledge of the self-controlling, self-knowing, self-representing sovereign subject confronting an exotic landscape is precisely analogous to the power/knowledge of the empire whose sovereignty is derived from its ability to know, to control and to represent its others. If the most successful Orientalist art and literature of the Romantic period would combine exposure to otherness with a turn back towards a position of 'imperialist objectivity', guaranteed by control over the forms of representation (linguistic or visual or both), Wordsworth's poetry works in precisely the same way. It is a celebration of the power of the observing subject; it 'calls forth and bestows power, of which knowledge is the effect'. In the sovereign subject emerging in this period, Romantic aesthetics and political ideology – particularly but not exclusively the emergent ideology of a new form of imperialism, one of whose driving forces would be the capacity to represent otherness – become quite inseparable. The future imperialism would rely at its most basic level on the structure of dualistic otherness that was elaborated in the discourse of radicalism and in the Wordsworthian Romanticism that emerged alongside it – for both of which Orientalism would prove an essential constitutive feature.

Orientalism, then, was hardly just a thematic 'sideshow' for Romantic poetry. It saturated most forms of writing in the Romantic period – it even became something of a structuring principle for cultural thought. Not all writers from the period worked out this problematic in just the way that Wordsworth did, of course. Nor were all poets in the period as convinced as was Wordsworth of the viewing or narrating subject's fully synthesized combination of knowledge and power (or rather his *claim* that the subject ought to combine these attributes – for Wordsworth himself often explored, most famously in 'Tintern Abbey', the actual fragility and transitoriness of the self that in other contexts he claimed could wield such command over the visual field and the cultural realities which it expressed). John Clare, for example, shared none of Wordsworth's convictions about the power of the self. His poetry explores, on the contrary, the tenuousness of selfhood, its fleeting capacity for ensuring any kind of stability in a world so otherwise evidently out of control. 'I am – yet what I am, none cares or knows', says the narrator of one of Clare's greatest poems ('I Am'); 'I am the self-consumer of my woes; – / They rise and vanish in oblivion's host, / Like shadows in love's frenzied stifled throes: – / And yet I am, and live – like vapours tossed / Into the nothingness of scorn and noise'. None of Clare's narrators stabilize long enough for one to imagine them calling forth and bestowing 'power, of which knowledge is the effect'. Quite the contrary: Clare was uninterested in such power and its correlative forms of knowledge, and in the whole discourse of imperial conquest to which they correspond. At face value, this might be attributed to the madness for which he would be condemned to an asylum in later life (where he wrote 'I Am' and much of his greatest poetry). Yet Clare was not the only writer in the Romantic period who was unconvinced of the self's capacity to bestow the combination of knowledge and power that so invest Wordsworth's poetry.

Much of John Keats's greatest poetry, for example, actually offers – in anticipation of Clare – an exploration of the vulnerability and weakness of the individual self, a meditation on the fragility of individual subjectivity. As with Clare, this might be explained by the state of Keats's health, his sense of the proximity of death, his awareness that, as he put it in his final letter, he was already 'leading a posthumous existence'. Keats's Odes explore the tentative nature of our existence, the limits of the 'sole self', and the desolation of a life lived on the banks of the virtual Lethe to which Keats seemed so often to return: that combination of death and erasure of memory that might be seen as the only true deliverance from the tortured confines of selfhood. Given that these themes were ones to which he returned throughout his career, however, it is remarkable that even Keats was able, at least on one occasion, to fall back on the conflation of empire and subjectivity that was similar to the one that Wordsworth had already articulated. For in his 1816 poem 'On First Looking into Chapman's Homer', Keats explicitly compares the sudden unveiling of the new literary world made available to him by that volume to the prospect made available to the gaze of the imperial adventurer. Delving into Chapman's Homer, Keats writes, opened up a whole new way of imagining himself in relation to the outer world:

> Then I felt like some watcher of the skies
> When a new planet swims into his ken;

> Or like stout Cortez when with eagle eyes
> He star'd at the Pacific – and all his men
> Look'd at each other with a wild surmise –
> Silent, upon a peak in Darien.

Here we find once again the alignment of subjective viewpoint and imperial outlook that Wordsworth elaborated in the *Supplementary Essay*. It is as though the only language available to convey the feelings attendant on the discovery of a new literary world made available through translation was the language of imperial conquest. It hardly matters that it was actually Balboa, rather than Cortez, who saw the Pacific from Darien: the point for Keats is that the prospect of new readings is like the prospect of future conquest, as expressed in the 'wild surmise' of Cortez (i.e., Balboa) and his men, as they stare out across the Pacific. If in 'Sleep and Poesy' Keats would express his desire to 'overwhelm / Myself in poesy', here in 'Chapman's Homer' the pressures are reversed: Keats loses all his fragility and weakness and stands with Cortez in the position of a conquering hero: the self stands supreme, vigilant, powerful and knowing. 'Keats's text is a private dream of self-elevation', Vincent Newey argues, pointing to the poem's invocation of Cortez; 'his desire for advancement and the possession of space enacts at the individual level the core impulses of a competitive and expansionist – incipiently imperialist – society'.[32] But, in addition to the question of imperial perspective, there is something else at stake in Keats's invocation of imperialism in his celebration of Homer.

After all, if the Romantic period may be said to have originated with the wave of translations into English that emerged from the endeavours of (and were largely subsidized by) the East India Company, it should hardly be cause for surprise that a translation should engender feelings of excitement at the discovery of a foreign literary terrain. Far more significant in this instance, then, is the fact that the translation in question was not from one of the Asiatic languages, but rather from Greek. What it made available for Keats was thus not merely a new perspective on a world yet to be conquered, but *also* the perspective of the conquering European looking out over a non-European world; what Keats could find in his identification with Homer, in other words, was a sense of what made conquering Europeans worthy of their imperial missions, or what it was that separated European conquerors from non-European conquered people.

---

32 Vincent Newey, 'Keats, History and the Poets', in Nicholas Roe (ed.), *Keats and History* (Cambridge: Cambridge University Press, 1995), pp. 165–93.

Indeed, the Romantic obsession with Greece unfolded precisely under circumstances in which Europeans were trying to differentiate themselves from non-Europeans. Hellenism – which Keats also expresses in his poem on first encountering the Elgin marbles – became a kind of shorthand to distinguish 'we' Europeans from all those unworthy peoples awaiting the deliverance from superstition and darkness that European imperialism would so often claim to provide. This is exactly the sentiment underlying and motivating Shelley's proclamation in the preface to *Hellas* that in the ancient Hellenic civilization Europeans could find not merely a model to imitate but rather the very basis of what it was that differentiated their superior culture from the inferior culture of the Oriental world:

> The apathy of the rulers of the civilized world to the astonishing circumstance of the descendants of that nation to which they owe their civilization, rising as it were from the ashes of their ruin, is something perfectly inexplicable to a mere spectator of the shows of this immortal scene. We are all Greeks. Our laws, our literature, our religion, our arts have their roots in Greece. But for Greece – Rome, the instructor, the conqueror, or the metropolis of our ancestors, would have spread no illumination with her arms, and we might have been savages and idolaters; or, what is worse, might have arrived at such a stagnant and miserable state of social institution as China and Japan possess.

Shelley here deploys an explicitly imperialist language to articulate what it is that differentiates Europeans (particularly the British, as the supposed inheritors of the torch passed from Greece to Rome and on to the West) from non-Europeans generally and Asiatics specifically. In this sense Hellenism is offered at once as a justification for imperial conquest and as the basis for an essentialized European subjectivity that could be claimed to have resisted all change for hundreds of years: in other words, exactly the opposite kind of subject (reasonable, daring, knowledgeable, conquering) from that other essentialized identity that also proved so important to the cultural justification of empire, namely, the degraded Oriental. Thus it should come as no surprise that when the visionary traveller of Shelley's *Alastor* arrives in the East, what he finds is utter desolation and barrenness. The East that emerges from Shelley's work is silenced, a place where the images of 'dead men / Hang their mute thoughts on the mute walls around'. It falls, presumably, to the European to breathe life into this barren landscape, to restore it to sound and vitality.

Again, not all Romantic period writers accepted the argument in favour of Western cultural superiority – and its attendant cultural and political orientation – with as little hesitation as Shelley. Even Byron, who would ultimately give his life to the cause of Greek independence, retained considerable scepticism with regard to the increasingly aggressive European stance toward the East. Not only did Byron, earlier in his career, flee to the East precisely to get away from what he perceived to be the limitations of the culture of Western modernity which privileged and defined itself against a pre- or anti-modern East, he also immortalized that gesture of escapism in much of his greatest poetry, including *Childe Harold* and *Don Juan*. Indeed, the East offered Byron a space from which to critique Europe and the nascent culture of Eurocentrism. Nowhere in Byron's work does one find expressed the sense that Europeans are culturally superior to Asiatics. On the contrary, throughout his body of writing one can trace a sense of ease at crossing between cultures, the joy of passing from one to the next – and even the expression of a desire to be able to 'pass' as someone who could be from *any* culture rather than one particular culture – as so many of Byron's characters seem to be able to do. Byron's poetry at its best consistently returns to the desire to maintain cultural fluidity and movement, rather than seeking shelter in a rigid sense of opposition to 'other' cultures, by claiming, for example, that 'we' are Greeks, and 'they' are therefore barbarians.

Nowhere does Byron articulate the scale of his resistance to cultural Eurocentrism more passionately than in 'The Giaour'. Although we now approach the poem almost inevitably via its visual rendering in Eugene Delacroix's classic 1826 Orientalist painting, *The Combat of the Giaour and Hassan*, which was inspired by Byron's poem, and hence we might be tempted to think of it automatically in Orientalist terms (i.e., based on the opposition of East and West), the figure of the Giaour himself is in Byron's poem hardly a self-identified Westerner. He is, rather, a perpetual exile, not at home in either East or West: perfectly appropriate for someone whose only identifying label is provided by a *Turkish* word signifying '*foreigner*'. As identified by the narrative voice of the monk who explains his encounter with the Giaour, the latter is of an uncertain origin, and really ought not to be allowed to stay on in the monastery that has given him shelter for so many years:

> 'Tis twice three years at summer tide
> Since first among our freres he came;
> And here it soothes him to abide
> For some dark deed he will not name.
> But never at our vesper prayer,
> Nor e'er before confession chair

Kneels he, nor recks he when arise
Incense or anthem to the skies,
But broods within his cell alone,
His faith and race alike unknown.
The sea from Paynim land he crost,
And here ascended from the coast;
Yet seems he not of Othman race,
But only Christian in his face:
I'd judge him some stray renegade,
Repentant of the change he made,
Save that he shuns our holy shrine,
Nor tastes the sacred bread and wine.
Great largess to these walls he brought,
And thus our abbot's favour bought;
But were I prior, not a day
Should brook such stranger's further stay,
Or pent within our penance cell
Should doom him there for aye to dwell.[33]

On this account, the Giaour is a universal outsider, traversing a world of cultural, religious and political differentiations, refusing to assimilate, and constantly being judged as alien and un-belonging by those who are more comfortably at home in the territories through which he merely passes. Perhaps this sense of perpetual alienation is something that Byron found it easy to identify with. But such a standpoint, already so exceptional in Byron's own lifetime, would become increasingly unusual as the nineteenth century wore on, and more and more Britons sought shelter in the sense of cultural and political distinctions – premised on the opposition to otherness – that seemed to remove and privilege them over the Asiatic others whom they would go on ruling for decades to come.

33 'The Giaour' in *The Poetical Works of Lord Byron* (London: John Murray, 1847), p. 71.

Romanticism and religious modernity: from natural supernaturalism to literary sectarianism

KEVIN GILMARTIN

> Man must & will have Some Religion.
> William Blake, *Jerusalem*

Since Blake issued his injunction 'To the Deists',[1] readers have contested the measure and the character of religion to assign British Romantic writing. While perhaps not as pivotal as it once was to definitions of Romanticism, religious faith remains a central issue in critical commentary, and seems to impinge especially on qualitative responses to the Romantic achievement. Thus the competing claims of Classical and Romantic art have generated sharply negative accounts of the latter's spiritual designs, most famously in T. E. Hulme's treatment of Romanticism as 'spilt religion'. By contrast, the dialectics of Enlightenment and Romanticism sometimes yield more positive treatments of Romantic faith as a return from excessive scepticism and materialism. In this sense, the period chronology that authorizes a literary history of Romanticism has religious implications. Romanticism becomes a spiritual dispensation, an individual or coterie struggle to come to terms with the eclipse of shared Christian doctrines. The rough narrative is familiar. A corrosive phase of rational enquiry and sceptical critique (Enlightenment) undermines the established articles of Christian faith, condemning a generation or two of (Romantic) poets to contemplate the ruins of belief. Their individual desires for renewed consecration or enchantment get articulated in radically imperfect aesthetic, psychic and social forms. Romantic poetry is fragmentary because it is conditioned by deteriorating systems of belief; Romantic poetry is lyric and solipsistic because it solicits individual adherence in the absence of a knowable community of believers.

---

1 William Blake, *Jerusalem*, in *The Complete Poetry and Prose of William Blake*, ed. David Erdman, rev. edn (New York: Anchor Books, 1982), Plate 52.

For Hulme, the process was a regrettable consequence of Enlightenment. The 'perverted rhetoric' of rationalism suppressed an instinctual human theism which then found its way out in an 'abnormal direction': 'You don't believe in a God, so you begin to believe that man is a god. You don't believe in Heaven, so you begin to believe in a heaven on earth. In other words, you get romanticism.'[2] Yet not all readers have been so contemptuous of the earnest humanism associated with a Romantic recuperation of transcendental impulses in more mundane terms. Romantic lyric or epic meditations on spiritual impairment, typically worked out in relation to Milton's *Paradise Lost*, have been treated as intellectually honest and finally enabling confessions of imperfect human faith. Here, the vexed and fragmentary modalities of Romantic art become a consummate form of *period* expression, setting the terms for a protracted transition from Enlightenment scepticism to more settled forms of Victorian belief and doubt. Among the many powers Romantic poetry has been assigned, two in particular – the capacity for visionary and prophetic insight, and the ability to console or heal – have led commentators back to the terms of Christian tradition, even where the Romantic role in that tradition gets associated with a longer history of secularization.

Critical attenuations of faith

Well before the historical contours of 'Romanticism' were defined, major authors from the period seemed to assert a claim upon belief. As early as 1879, Matthew Arnold launched a campaign to rescue William Wordsworth from the spiritual and philosophical system of the 'Wordsworthians'. In advancing something like our own canon of major poems, his 1879 Preface to *Poems of Wordsworth* distinguished the '*poetic* truth' of a sheer joy in natural affection from the sonorous pieties of *The Excursion* (1814). The Wanderer's response to the bitterly disillusioned Solitary seems to Arnold to betray not poetry but a 'doctrine such as we hear in church':[3]

> An assured belief
> That the procession of our fate, howe'er
> Sad or disturbed, is ordered by a Being

2 T. E. Hulme, 'Romanticism and Classicism', in *Speculations: Essays on Humanism and the Philosophy of Art*, ed. Herbert Read (London: Routledge and Kegan Paul, 1924), pp. 117–18.
3 Matthew Arnold, 'Wordsworth', in *Selected Prose*, ed. P. J. Keating (Harmondsworth: Penguin, 1970), pp. 378–9.

Of infinite benevolence and power;
Whose everlasting purposes embrace
All accidents, converting them to good.[4]

According to Lionel Trilling, a leading American heir of Arnoldian cultural critique, the Wordsworthians had by 1950, and the occasion of the centenary of Wordsworth's death, lamentably disappeared from anywhere but the university. Ironically, Trilling suggested that a decline in public interest might be accounted for by the fact that Wordsworth was 'too Christian a poet' for modern taste. At the same time, the ascendancy of *The Prelude* (1850) at the expense of *The Excursion* seems to have alleviated concerns about the doctrinal limitations of Wordsworthian faith. In fact, Trilling made his striking case for 'a Judaic quality' in Wordsworth through a contrast with overtly Christian poets like Dante, Donne or Hopkins, for whom 'the specific Christian feeling and doctrine is of the essence of their matter'. What there was of religion in Wordsworth – charity, community, submission to mystery, the sense of burden and the search for peace – was perhaps more elusive than doctrine but it became central to the cultural mission that Trilling and other mid-century critics were preparing for poetry.

Trilling argued what Hulme would not allow, that the residual and diminished presence of Christian belief in Romantic expression was a positive and constructive achievement. In part he accomplished this by deriving Wordsworth's belief from a latitudinarian rather than corrosively sceptical eighteenth century, a mitigated Enlightenment that was concerned to develop 'the ethical and social aspects of Christian belief' at the expense of what Arnold considered to be dogma. Romanticism contributed to this 'sort of attenuation of religion' by making 'the sense of transcendence and immanence so real and so attractive'. And by tracing Wordsworth's 'mysticism' in particular to 'the intensity with which [the poet] experienced his own being', rather than to any reaching upward to the divine, Trilling helped set the terms for the later twentieth-century rise of Wordsworth's reputation. A heightened and even sacrilized response to ordinary experience links this Wordsworth with literary modernism (Elliot, Joyce, Lawrence, Faulkner), and connects the latitudinarian eighteenth century with liberal modernity. Yet the difficulty of Trilling's case is clear. The same secularization

---

4 William Wordsworth, *The Excursion*, in *Poetical Works*, ed. Thomas Hutchinson, new edn, rev. Ernest De Selincourt (Oxford: Oxford University Press, 1936), Book 4, lines 12–17.

narrative that lends Wordsworth a precocious modernity also diminishes his availability, since it issues in a twentieth century that does not like Wordsworth because it 'does not like the Christian ... virtues'.[5] And the line from Arnold to Trilling also suggests how such late works as *The Excursion* came to be eclipsed in the development of a canonical Wordsworth, and a canonical Romanticism, that was held to mitigate rather than reclaim Christian doctrine.

The broader Romantic contours of a sacralized Wordsworthian sense of personal being were left to be worked out in the decades after Trilling's centenary reflections by M. H. Abrams, Geoffrey Hartman, Harold Bloom, Earl Wassermann and others. While there are good reasons to be sceptical about the historical terms in which this generation of interpreters cast Romantic belief, they exercised a decisive influence upon the development of Romantic studies in the United States especially, and their influence extends (by way of reaction) through later historicist reassessments. Working in the long shadow of A. O. Lovejoy's challenge to 'Romanticism' as an analytically useful concept, they reasserted the coherence and unity of English Romantic expression, and helped secure the status of a few decades of literary history as a credible and even exalted field of study. They consolidated a canon of six male poets, with Wordsworth ascendant and Blake fully admitted, and in so doing narrowed the range of Romantic literary achievement by privileging lyric and visionary epic, eliding fiction and including some essayists (William Hazlitt, Leigh Hunt, Charles Lamb, Thomas De Quincey) who were felt to ratify claims about the power of imagination and the prophetic spirit of the age. Romantic poetry became an acutely self-conscious, post-Enlightenment exploration of the interchange between the perceiving mind and the perceived world. It fulfilled itself in dislocated forms of apocalyptic vision – doubly dislocated, because Romantic apocalypse was experienced in human and natural rather than divine terms, as redemptive consciousness, and because millennial expectations were conditioned by a sobering yet imaginatively enabling disenchantment with the political designs of the French Revolution.

Reclaiming visionary Romanticism as a spiritual exercise did not yield agreement on the extent to which an apocalypse transferred to consciousness or to nature actually sustained Christian faith. For Bloom, English Romantic poetry was 'a kind of religious poetry' that issued directly from a

---

5 Lionel Trilling, 'Wordsworth and the Rabbis', in *The Opposing Self: Nine Essays in Criticism* (New York and London: Harcourt Brace Jovanovich, 1955), pp. 104–9, 126.

Protestant faith that was itself 'astonishingly transformed by different kinds of humanism or naturalism'.[6] Abrams dwelt more closely on the historical problems this kind of argument raised. Developing a framework of 'progressive secularization' that involved 'the assimilation and reinterpretation' rather than suppression of religious ideas, he found 'integrity and courage' rather than idle nostalgia in the Romantic development of a 'secularized form of devotional experience'.[7] To his credit, Hartman was more cautious about resting claims for Romantic spiritual modernity on a straightforward secularization thesis, but he too identified the period with 'a time when art frees itself from its subordination to religion or religiously inspired myth, and continues or even replaces these'. At the same time, there was an altogether darker cast to his sense of Romantic vision. Where other critics have seemed to indicate that prophetic ambition could fulfil itself in imagination, Hartman's account of a Wordsworthian *consciousness of self raised to apocalyptic pitch* attended more closely to nature as a constraining power and to the poet's curious 'avoidance of apocalypse' in *The Prelude*. The result is not a fully realized poet-prophet, but a post-Enlightenment seeker more plausibly limited by nature and humanity, and more modestly concerned to justify poetic faith in 'the possibility of his renovation through daily and natural means'.[8]

These accounts of English Romantic poetry as a dislocated Protestant spiritual exercise have invited any number of critiques, and the trend has been towards a diminished attention to religion rather than alternative accounts of its pivotal role in Romantic expression.[9] The new historicism shifted attention to what Jerome McGann (in a contrarian project hinging on Byron) termed the 'wholly secular sense' of Romantic revelation,[10] and to the specific social and historical conditions that are obscured when

6 Harold Bloom, *The Visionary Company: A Reading of English Romantic Poetry*, rev. edn (Ithaca: Cornell University Press, 1971), pp. xvii, xxiv.
7 M. H. Abrams, *Natural Supernaturalism: Tradition and Revolution in Romantic Literature* (New York and London: Norton, 1971), pp. 12–13, 65–6, 338.
8 Geoffrey Hartman, 'Romanticism and "Anti-Self-Consciousness"', in *Romanticism and Consciousness: Essays in Criticism*, ed. Harold Bloom (New York and London: Norton, 1970), p. 52, and *Wordsworth's Poetry, 1787–1814* (New Haven: Yale University Press, 1964), pp. 17, 53, 61.
9 Although see Steven Goldsmith, *Unbuilding Jerusalem: Apocalypse and Romantic Representation* (Ithaca, NY: Cornell University Press, 1993), Robert Ryan, *The Romantic Reformation: Religious Politics in English Literature, 1789–1824* (Cambridge: Cambridge University Press, 1997), and Daniel E. White, *Early Romanticism and Religious Dissent* (Cambridge: Cambridge University Press, 2006).
10 Jerome J. McGann, *The Romantic Ideology: A Critical Investigation* (Chicago: University of Chicago Press, 1983), p. 131.

imagination departs from politics and community. In this sense, the secular narratives of social and political history have tended to supplant religious tradition in recent accounts of Romanticism. Thus Alan Liu has replaced Hartman's 'mystic pilgrimage' with a less teleological and less transcendental 'worldly tour'. The terms 'history, nature, self' become the coordinates for a Wordsworthian 'three-body problem', troubling Abrams's model of a secularized but still spiritually yearning Romanticism that absorbed the divine principle of an Augustinian triad (God, nature, man) into the two other worldly terms.[11]

Yet to focus too narrowly on these dialectical refutations of the case for a natural supernaturalism would be to overlook just how thoroughly subsequent scholarship, and Romantic-period writing itself, exceeds and undermines any model of Romanticism as a lyrical expression of the apocalyptic imagination. One aim of this chapter will be to reopen the question of Romanticism and religion now that *The Excursion* and a host of other authors, genres and texts have returned to scholarly attention, without assuming that the literature of the Romantic period gestured forward in one direction, nor that Romanticism provides the decisive clue as to how our own experience of modernity came into being. English literary Romanticism as a discrete aesthetic project worked out across two generations by a visionary company of male poets has given way to an interest in the many other voices that found expression in the Romantic period, and to a clearer recognition of aesthetic and intellectual differences within the old canon of major poets. Furthermore, the trend towards a more finely grained literary history, and towards more material models of literary transmission, has made the notion of a generalized radical Protestant tradition passed down from Milton to Blake, Wordsworth, John Keats and Percy Shelley seem untenably thin and incomplete. A similar trend towards internal differentiation has taken place in eighteenth-century studies, further complicating any notion of Romanticism as an attempt to recover faith in the aftermath of a period of corrosive scepticism and rationalism. This is particularly true for the English case, where Enlightenment enquiry and sociability were not always decisively secular, and instead took place within the institutional framework of the Dissenting congregations and the established Church.[12] Continuities across the notional boundary between the two periods have also become more evident, particularly where

---

11 Alan Liu, *Wordsworth: The Sense of History* (Stanford: Stanford University Press, 1989), pp. 4, 513–15, and Abrams, *Natural Supernaturalism*, pp. 89–90.
12 See Sheridan Gilley, 'Christianity and Enlightenment: A Historical Survey', *History of European Ideas* 1 (1981), 103–6, and Roy Porter, 'The Enlightenment in England', in *The*

Wordsworth, Blake, Shelley and others extended Enlightenment inquiries into the primitive sources of human belief and into non-Christian sacred traditions.

Reclaiming the church

One of the real difficulties about attempting to knit Romanticism together within a generalized radical Protestant tradition is that this tends to flatten out the complex social and cultural history of religion in the period. While political revolution remains the preferred context for Romantic studies, the era was also marked as by upheavals in faith and worship, with results that conditioned literary expression as forcefully as any recoil from Enlightenment scepticism. For most British subjects, formal religious experience was still dominated by the Church of England, whose identity derived less from any particular doctrine than from its distinctive liturgy and episcopal structure, and its privilege as the established national church. If not absolute, this privilege did involve overwhelming social and political dominance: the Test Acts of 1673 and 1678 and the Corporation Act of 1661 combined to exclude most Roman Catholics and Nonconformists from participation in national and local government, the universities, and the army and navy, unless they were prepared as a matter of occasional conformity to receive communion in the Church of England. Anglican establishment did less for practical piety. While historians have challenged easy assumptions about a moribund late Georgian Church, biding its time for a Victorian renewal of purpose, it remains clear that the effectiveness of Anglican worship was compromised by a system of underpaid curates and widespread absenteeism and pluralism among the parish clergy.

Anglican privilege came at the further price of the assimilation of Church hierarchy into state networks of patronage and influence. Over the course of the eighteenth century, the clergy became more wealthy and more closely identified with the landed classes, typically functioning as magistrates and leaders in rural society. 'In their approach to their work and their style of life they were not so much religious specialists as gentlemen who happened to be ordained.'[13] Jane Austen, herself the daughter and sister of Anglican clergymen, amply registered the opportunities and liabilities this

Enlightenment in National Context, ed. Roy Porter and Mikulas Teich (Cambridge: Cambridge University Press, 1981), p. 6.

13 James Obelkevich, 'Religion', in *The Cambridge Social History of Britain, 1750–1850*, vol. III: *Social Agencies and Institutions*, ed. F. M. L. Thompson (Cambridge: Cambridge University Press, 1990), p. 313.

condition afforded. And while her fiction may not treat the extremes of an Erastian church, it does map a middle range of clerical positions, from the vulgar careerism of Mr Elton in *Emma* (1816) and the comic sycophancy of Mr Collins in *Pride and Prejudice* (1813) to Edmund Bertram's more earnest, if not especially pious, sense of duty in *Mansfield Park* (1814). In an essential way, Austen's distinctive vision of a moral order embodied in the social life of the rural gentry was made possible by the integration of the pastoral, clerical and disciplinary functions of the Church into the propertied classes.

In conjunction with her conservatism, the social framework for Austen's fiction also suggests how a Church with little doctrinal baggage might then take on a campaigning role in the political crisis of the 1790s. Trends through most of the eighteenth century had been latitudinarian, as social stability seemed to mitigate the political considerations that first excluded those unwilling to swear oaths of supremacy and allegiance. By the 1780s Dissenting sects were agitating with increased confidence against their disabilities. Yet their campaign foundered in the aftermath of the French Revolution, as a resurgent High Church toryism and fears of popular unrest reinforced a commitment to establishment as a necessary element of social order. Charles James Fox's bill for repeal of the Test and Corporation Acts was soundly defeated in the House of Commons in 1790, and the situation remained unfavourable until the post-war crisis passed. Relief for Nonconformists was finally achieved in 1828, followed shortly by Catholic emancipation in 1829. These dates teasingly align with the rough outlines of the Romantic period, and while the case should not be overstated, it is worth considering how Romantic expression developed in England within the precise historical contours of official retrenchment on matters of Church authority and public worship. The point is reinforced by a paradox in the course of political controversy. While arguments about divine sanction were declining in formal political theory, in ways that are consistent with a theory of secularization, religion did not disappear from the polemical field, but instead tended to migrate into social claims about the role of faith in securing social hierarchy, moral restraint, and popular contentment.[14] Anglicans by no means monopolized these developments, nor did they have an exclusive hold upon related trends towards lay activism and religiously sanctioned popular education. But the Church did clearly advance with a

---

14 Robert Hole, *Pulpits, Politics and Public Order in England, 1760–1832* (Cambridge: Cambridge University Press, 1989), pp. 1–7, 84–5, 127–37.

heightened sense of urgency about the role of belief in securing social and political order.

The movement of the Lake poets from youthful radicalism to mature conservatism was conditioned by their growing commitment to the social and cultural, rather than narrowly spiritual or doctrinal, mission of the Church of England.[15] The religious trajectory of William Wordsworth is the most difficult to assess, in part because there is so little agreement about the extent of his early radicalism in matters of faith: the manuscripts and published poems of the 1790s have yielded assessments ranging from infidel pantheism to a muted Christian Trinitarianism.[16] The case for a more adventurous early pantheism can indicate a sharp break to later orthodoxy, and pious revisions to *The Prelude* after 1805 are often called in as evidence. But the social and cultural rather than spiritual character of Wordsworth's late commitment to the Church of England may indicate the persistence of earlier metaphysical speculations, suggesting as well that Arnold was a fit intermediary for his later reputation. Robert Ryan has argued that 'the poet's return to Christian practice and belief required no significant recantation, ... but rather involved a quiet personal reintegration into the local and national religious community from which he had kept his distance'.[17]

These interpretive problems have helped restore *The Excursion* to scholarly attention. If Book 6 opens with a strikingly uncomplicated expression of what Arnold considered mere doctrine – 'Hail to the State of England! And conjoin / With this a salutation as devout, / Made to the spiritual fabric of her Church' – it is worth noticing that this twin invocation of Church and state introduces not pious meditation but a more concrete mapping of national community in space and time:

> And O, ye swelling hills, and spacious plains!
> Besprent from shore to shore with steeple-towers,
> And spires whose 'silent finger points to heaven';
> Nor wanting, at wide intervals, the bulk
> Of ancient minster lifted above the cloud
> Of the dense air, which town or city breeds

15 David Pym, 'The Ideas of Church and State in the Thought of the Three Principal Lake Poets: Coleridge, Southey, and Wordsworth', *Durham University Journal* 83 (1991), 19.

16 For a review of the literature and a vigorous case for the poet's consistent Christianity, see William A. Ulmer, 'The Christian Wordsworth, 1798–1800', *Journal of English and Germanic Philology* 95 (1996), 336–58.

17 Ryan, *The Romantic Reformation*, pp. 94–5, 98.

To intercept the sun's glad beams – may ne'er
That true succession fail of English hearts,
Who, with ancestral feeling, can perceive
What in those holy structures ye possess
Of ornamental interest, and the charm
Of pious sentiment diffused afar,
And human charity, and social love.[18]

In his *Ecclesiastical Sketches* (1822), Wordsworth responded to the renewed challenge of Catholic agitation by affirming his public commitment to the Church as source of 'social love' within the national community, and noted the coincidence between his own historical sonnet sequence and Robert Southey's more conventional prose history, *The Book of the Church* (1824). Southey had for years been campaigning on behalf of the Anglican establishment in the *Quarterly Review* and elsewhere, and his version of a usable Christian past was both more openly polemical, excoriating 'the pestilent errors of these distempered times', and more direct about the need to defend the 'Church Establishment' against radical claims on the grounds that it had 'materially improved' the 'temporal condition of all ranks'.[19]

Where Southey may pose the extreme instance of Lake School migration to Tory Anglicanism, the case of Samuel Taylor Coleridge is complicated by his early exposure to radical Dissent at Cambridge. This inflected his own early political radicalism to the extent that he seriously considered entering the Unitarian ministry in the late 1790s. His Bristol lectures of 1795 were particularly uncompromising in their assault upon religious establishment: 'He who sees any real difference between the Church of Rome and the Church of England possesses optics which I do not possess – the mark of antichrist is on both of them.'[20] A return to the Church and to Trinitarianism over the course of the next decade was motivated in part by a conviction that Enlightenment reason and infidelity were responsible for the corrosive designs of the French Revolution and an increasingly plebeian domestic radical movement. In this sense, an intimate connection between politics and religion remained the consistent element in Coleridge's career, and his early experience with radical religion made him one of the period's most resourceful if often paradoxical campaigners against it. Unitarian

---

18 Wordsworth, *The Excursion*, in *Poetical Works*, Book 6, lines 6–8, 17–29.
19 Robert Southey, *The Book of the Church*, 2 vols. (London: John Murray, 1824), vol. I, pp. 1–2.
20 Samuel Taylor Coleridge, *Lectures 1795: On Politics and Religion*, ed. Lewis Patton and Peter Mann (Princeton: Princeton University Press, 1971), p. 210.

circles had exposed him to the German higher criticism, and to historical and mythological approaches to scriptural analysis that, while susceptible to radical purposes, were also more flexible and accommodating than the polemical forms of comparative religion associated with Volney and the French Enlightenment. In carrying his exposure to the higher criticism with him through his return to orthodoxy, Coleridge contributed centrally to the nineteenth-century development of a new and more critically informed apologetics for Anglican doctrine.[21] And he remained throughout his life the most consistently theological and scriptural of the Lake poets. It is easy to see for example how his theory of imagination challenged empiricism by aligning human perception with a divine act of creation.

Yet the major engagement with religion in Coleridge's career was a sequence of publications – *The Friend* (1809–10), the two *Lay Sermons* (1816–1817), *Aids to Reflection* (1825), and *On the Constitution of the Church and State* (1829) – that were meant to exemplify even as they advanced the modern role of the Christian intellectual.[22] Taken together, these form the most comprehensive Romantic account of a stabilizing social and cultural mission for the Church of England. Coleridge joined Southey in lamenting the corrosive moral effects of commercial development, and he seized upon the post-war economic downturn as an opportunity for cautionary prophetic address to elites. The *Statesman's Manual* recommended scripture as 'the main lever by which the moral and intellectual character of Europe has been raised to its present comparative height', and urged the leading classes to secure their own elevation by taking the Bible as 'the best guide to political skill and foresight'. *A Lay Sermon* then advised the middle classes that Christian education alone, rather than political economy or radical reform, could alleviate the excesses of a commercial spirit: 'If we are a Christian nation', Coleridge concluded, 'we must learn to act nationally as well as individually, as Christians.'[23]

On the Constitution of Church and State was nominally motivated by parliamentary discussions of Catholic emancipation, but it became Coleridge's most systematic effort to reconstitute the Church of England as an authentic

21 E. S. Shaffer, *'Kubla Khan' and the Fall of Jerusalem: The Mythological School in Biblical Criticism and Secular Literature, 1770–1880* (Cambridge: Cambridge University Press, 1975), pp. 24–7, 32–4.
22 Marilyn Butler, *Romantics, Rebels, and Reactionaries: English Literature and its Background, 1760–1830* (Oxford: Oxford University Press, 1981), p. 87.
23 Samuel Taylor Coleridge, *Lay Sermons*, ed. R. J. White (Princeton: Princeton University Press, 1972), pp. 3, 31, 228.

'National Church'. Distinguished from the 'Church of Christ', this institution was to be embodied in the form of a 'Clerisy' or 'permanent, nationalized, learned order' that included not only divines but 'the learned of . . . all the so called liberal arts and sciences'. In theorizing a clerisy as the active ministry of a National Church, Coleridge wanted to provide his own guiding and stabilizing intellectual labour with a secure endowment and an acknowledged social purpose. Properly constituted as 'the *third* great venerable estate of the realm', and invested again with the property and educational mission it had lost to the Reformation, the clerisy would organize and soothe contending national interests.

> The proper *object* of the *National* Church is civilization with freedom; and the duty of its ministers, could they be contemplated merely and exclusively as officiaries of the National Church, would be fulfilled in the communication of that degree and kind of knowledge to all, the possession of which is necessary for all in order to their CIVILITY.[24]

While Coleridge's idea of the clerisy has figured prominently in theories of professionalism and intellectual labour, the case for his direct impact on the material organization of intellectual life is problematic. Nineteenth-century reforms of the Anglican clergy would surely have proceeded in any case, and the development of the professions outside the Church tended to diverge from a ministerial model, undermining his vision of a unified professional field with divinity at its head. Indirect or personal influence is perhaps easier to argue but more difficult to measure. Coleridge's influence has often been exaggerated, in ways that more earnestly recapitulate his own mischievously obscure treatments of influence and effect. But he did establish a style of public utterance that echoed down through the Victorian sages, and his case for moral management by an intellectual third estate was favourably received among a number of prominent nineteenth-century thinkers, including Thomas Arnold, William Gladstone and F. D. Maurice. For Romanticism, his effort to theorize his own discursive activity as a portion of the Church offers a salutary reminder that literary anxieties about public influence in the period did not merely betray a frustrated seepage of poetic ambition into fantasies about priestly or prophetic authority, but instead registered a pertinent debate about the role of the Church in an age of revolution, reaction and reform.

---

24 Samuel Taylor Coleridge, *On the Constitution of Church and State*, ed. John Colmer (Princeton: Princeton University Press, 1976), pp. 42, 46, 54, 69, 125.

Dissenting communities

A leading antitype to Coleridge's state affiliated cleric can be found in his own unreconstructed youthful self. Before snapping the 'squeaking baby-trumpet of Sedition', Coleridge joined radical inheritors of the mantle of Old Dissent in sympathizing with American rebellion, welcoming French revolution and advocating thoroughgoing reforms of Church and state at home. Derived from the religious struggles of the seventeenth century, Old Dissent was a loose designation that encompassed Presbyterians, Congregationalists, Baptists and sometimes Quakers too. And as the memory of revolution was contested again in the 1790s, Dissenting nonconformity became a leading catalyst not only for radical protest but for Anglican and Evangelical counter-mobilization. Establishment suspicions understandably fell upon the radical wing of Dissent, but this was in fact a diverse spiritual tradition, initially linked by Calvinist inclinations in theology and worship, and by a shared seventeenth-century experience of persecution which only gradually gave way to reluctant and politically disabling toleration. Over the course of the eighteenth century, congregations developed and fragmented, and while many Baptists became absorbed in Evangelical enthusiasm, Presbyterians tended to migrate instead towards a more 'rational' Arminianism, accepting the universal availability of salvation and the effectiveness of good works, and orienting themselves progressively towards social and political reform. Unitarianism emerged as rational tendencies extended to a Socinian rejection of Christ's divinity. Unitarian congregations assumed a leading role in the progressive wing of Nonconformity, and in many ways formed the activist core of the late Enlightenment in England. Rational Dissent risked public outrage in its early sympathy with the French Revolution and its later opposition to the Napoleonic wars, and the link between Dissent and political protest was secured by the work of such leading intellectuals as the moral and political philosopher Richard Price and the natural scientist, linguist and political philosopher Joseph Priestley. Such figures became flashpoints in the early stages of the reaction to the French Revolution: Price's *Discourse on the Love of Our Country* (1789) triggered Edmund Burke's hostile response in the *Reflections on the Revolution in France* (1790), and Priestley's house and laboratory were destroyed by a mob in 1791, motivating his emigration to America a few years later.

Rational Dissent was in many respects an elite formation. Congregations grew wealthy and influential in a number of provincial cities, even as the Anglican clergy assimilated itself to property and power in the countryside. Yet having conceded this relative privilege, it would be a mistake to allow the prominence of major figures like Price and Priestley to eclipse the more ordinary and diffused, and in many cases female, practices of education, communication and sociability that sustained the community of Dissent over the course of the eighteenth century, and belied a reputation for merely individualist commitment to human reason. In 'My First Acquaintance with Poets', William Hazlitt recalled the 'custom' by which a scattered community of Dissenting ministers exchanged visits 'in each other's neighbourhoods'. Recalling his own father's engagement in this practice, he credited it with forging 'a line of communication' that helped sustain 'the flame of civil and religious liberty'.[25] As it converges on the figure of Coleridge, Hazlitt's essay deliberately marks a number of fissures within English Romantic expression. Above all, by calling attention to fragile strands of continuity within Dissenting communities, the second generation writer reflects critically on the shock of being introduced to a first generation poet just as that poet is found to break the line of communication and prove his own unreliability by refusing a career in the Unitarian ministry.

The sociability Hazlitt fondly recalled was embodied above all in the Dissenting academies, and while the quality and advanced character of these institutions can be exaggerated, the best of them did challenge curricular tradition by extending instruction from the classics into modern languages, history, mathematics, chemistry and natural history.[26] First designed to train Dissenting ministers in the face of official exclusion from grammar schools and the two major universities, the academies wound up having a much wider cultural influence. The imaginative life and the politics of John Keats have been persuasively tied to his experience at the Enfield academy.[27] The experience of the Aiken family at Warrington and elsewhere was a still more exemplary instance of the way an advanced Dissenting culture of public expression and sociability extended opportunities to talented women as well as men. As a tutor in the highly regarded Dissenting academy at Warrington, the elder John Aiken provided his children with a superior education. His daughter, Anna Laetitia Aiken (later Barbauld), became a distinguished poet, essayist, critic and anti-slave trade

---

25 William Hazlitt, 'My First Acquaintance with Poets', in *The Complete Works of William Hazlitt*, ed. P. P. Howe, 21 vols. (London and Toronto: J. M. Dent and Sons, 1933), vol. XVII, p. 107.

26 Michael Watts, *The Dissenters*, vol. II, *The Expansion of Evangelical Nonconformity* (Oxford: Clarendon Press, 1995), pp. 274–8.

27 Nicholas Roe, *John Keats and the Culture of Dissent* (Oxford: Clarendon Press, 1997).

activist, and with her husband, Rochemont Barbauld, a Warrington student, she went on to run another successful Dissenting academy at Palgrave.[28] Her brother John was driven out of a successful career as physician because of his public opposition to the Test and Corporation Acts, and then entered upon a prolific literary career in London as an editor, biographer and historian, and as co-founder with Richard Phillips in 1796 of the *Monthly Magazine*, a leading organ of liberal, nonconformist, middle-class opinion in politics and culture. Two of John's sons, Arthur and Charles, attended the Barbauld's Palgrave school, and his daughter, Lucy Aiken, who was instructed at home, went on to become an influential essayist, historian and poet. In doing so she joined a brilliant cohort of Romantic-period women writers with Dissenting connections, including Mary Hays, Helen Maria Williams, Mary Wollstonecraft, Jane Taylor and Amelia Opie.

While the sense of exhaustion haunting Hazlitt's reminiscences about Unitarian sociability can be accounted for in part by his own political disenchantment, rational Dissent did confront serious obstacles. The era of the American Revolution had been an expansive one for English Dissent, and the mutation of Presbyterianism into Unitarianism towards the end of the eighteenth century helped consolidate an articulate and increasingly affluent community of liberal opinion. Yet as leading figures aged or emigrated they were not always replaced by a younger generation of activists and thinkers, or they were replaced in ways that significantly departed from the movement's core beliefs – there is the example of Hazlitt himself, and there is Jeremy Bentham's secular reworking of the utilitarianism of Joseph Priestley. The failure of the campaign against the Test and Corporation Acts in the 1790s signalled a period of retrenchment, during which the community of rational Dissent remained vital within itself but did not always achieve the wider social and spiritual impact it envisioned. And in matters of political organization, the renewed parliamentary reform movement that developed spectacularly in the years after Waterloo tended to express secular rather than spiritual impulses.

Evangelical revival

As the older Dissenting congregations tended just to hold their numbers or even to decline during the Romantic period, growth and expansive activism

---

28 For a nuanced account of the range of Barbauld's literary, aesthetic and public interests, see White, *Early Romanticism and Religious Dissent*, pp. 34–86.

was achieved elsewhere, in a more emotional register and often at the lower end of the social scale, with the rise of Evangelical piety. 'The failure of the humane, civilized, and sophisticated versions of Christianity offered by the Unitarians and Quakers to attract a mass following contrasts with the success of the Evangelical version of Christianity in winning wholesale conversions . . . in England and Wales and throughout the world.'[29] If Evangelicalism was the most dynamic form of English piety, it was also remarkably diverse, extending from the Baptist congregations of Old Dissent and an ambiguously positioned Methodism to spiritual revival within the Anglican Church. These movements were loosely joined by a vivid sense of sin and depravity, an enthusiastic expression of faith through energetic preaching, an acute concern for personal salvation and conversion, and a commitment to the sufficiency of scripture and to personal habits of pious reading and reflection.

Methodism was in many ways the most startling expression of Evangelical revival, and while from the time of his conversion in 1738 John Wesley worked to keep his movement within the Church of England, the years after his death in 1791 witnessed not only the break with Anglicanism but also a whole series of expulsions and sectarian divisions, resulting from the efforts of the original Wesleyan Connexion to manage growth and to organize a formal Methodist ministry out of the unruly traditions of itinerancy and lay preaching. Growth was explosive: between Wesley's death and 1850, Wesleyan Methodism alone grew sixfold, reaching over 350,000 members. Other Methodist denominations increased too, with much of the expansion coming in rural areas and among cottagers, labourers, artisans and shopkeepers. Even as the Wesleyan Connexion and other sects instituted formal clerical orders, the old emphasis on itinerancy and lay agency in preaching and organization did not disappear, nor did the spontaneity and emotionalism of Methodist worship. Indeed, it was the formation of Primitive Methodists in 1812 that introduced American style camp-meetings and came to be associated with the most energetic forms of religious showmanship.[30] Throughout the period of its rise, elites tended to respond with contempt to the enthusiasm and drama of Methodist worship, and blamed the movement for the spread of egalitarian feeling and political unrest. The controversy over the movement's political valance is far from

29 Watts, *The Dissenters*, vol. II, p. 100.
30 *Ibid.*, pp. 30–5, 132–46, and Obelkevich, 'Religion', in *The Cambridge Social History of Britain*, vol. III, pp. 324–5.

settled, as historians weigh its disruptive emotions and essentially democratic message about sin and salvation against the professed quietism and conservatism of most Methodist leaders, and the arguably stabilizing effect of its practices among ordinary believers.

Within the Church of England, Evangelical tendencies were similarly ambiguous in the way they joined a campaigning and often inclusive activism with conservative commitments to hierarchy and social order. Once the Methodists had withdrawn, Evangelicism became a distinct interest within the Church, limited in its numbers but energetic in its spirit, based in the middle class but keen to secure aristocratic patronage and unleash reformist energy upon the morally degenerate poor. Long-standing currents of seriousness and respectability within middle-class life were powerfully reinforced by the Evangelical revival, as habits of piety and emotional expression were brought firmly within the orbit of the family, offering women in particular a new sense of moral purpose that often extended anxiously into public life. Where Southey and Coleridge have long been associated with the later Victorian sage, it is only recently that scholars have come to appreciate the role of late eighteenth-century Evangelicals, and Hannah More especially, in the development of a prophetic and reformist and arguably feminist social discourse that later issued in the novels of Elizabeth Gaskell and George Eliot.[31] The Evangelical movement achieved its disproportionate social impact not through the conversion of the Anglican clergy, where numbers have been estimated at perhaps one in ten by 1800, but instead through the enterprise of lay activists, notably William Wilberforce and the members of the Clapham Sect. Their characteristic machinery of associations, meetings, publications, and subscriptions transformed public life even as it was often devoted to conservative campaigns for moral restraint and social stability. An estimation of the Evangelical impact upon literature depends appreciably on what counts as literature. To be sure, none of the major Romantic writers experienced Evangelical conversion. Yet it is easy to see how Evangelical piety resonated through an age of sensibility to the Romantic lyric poet's heightened emotional register and acute sense of personal impairment, and suggestive arguments have been made, for example, about Wordsworth's 'almost Wesleyan devotional intensity'.[32]

31 Christine Krueger, *The Reader's Repentance: Women Preachers, Women Writers, and Nineteenth-Century Social Discourse* (Chicago: University of Chicago Press, 1992).
32 Stephen Prickett, 'The Religious Context', in *The Romantics*, ed. Stephen Prickett (London: Methuen, 1981), pp. 125–31. But see Stuart Curran, *Poetic Form and British*

And other canons come into view, with their own dynamic fields of literary production and reception, when we recognize the extraordinary impact that Evangelical revival had upon the public culture of the period. Beginning soon after his conversion in 1784, Wilberforce worked tirelessly on behalf of the campaign to abolish the slave trade throughout the British Empire. The Abolition movement had strong roots in Quaker activism, and extended from the older Dissenting communities to the reinvigorated Anglicanism associated with Wilberforce and his Evangelical collaborators. Vigorous pamphleteering was just one vector of a sustained print campaign to expose the human tragedy of slavery and the social and moral costs of England's role in the slave trade. While the declamatory rhythms and polite sensibilities of Hannah More's poem 'Slavery' (1788) were perhaps typical of abolitionism in verse, Alan Richardson has shown that the literature was astonishingly wide-ranging, including 'ballads and songs, . . . epistles and essays, eclogues and elegies, odes and brief epics, satires, [and] tales'. His catalogue of the 'distinct and overlapping traditions' that informed anti-slave trade activism provides a vivid register of the specific communities and lines of transmission that were involved in the period's religious activism:

> A loosely affiliated succession of Bristol poets and a closely bound group of Liverpool writers and reformers, a self-consciously female line running from Eliza Knipe to Letitia E. Landon, a radical group including John Thelwall, George Dyer, and the young Robert Southey and a reformist group writing for children, and a white Creole tradition that takes in writers as diverse as the colonial historian Bryan Edwards and the satirist John Wolcott ('Peter Pindar').[33]

Far from restricting herself to the question of slavery, Hannah More joined Sarah Trimmer and other female activists in contributing to the development of a more dispersed but no less influential Evangelical moral reform movement, with its infrastructure of Sunday schools, subscriptions, vice societies and tract publication. The aim was to expose the irregularities of elites, to mobilize middle-class moral enterprise and (by extension) shape the missionary sensibilities of a newly emerging leading class, and above all

---

Romanticism (Oxford: Oxford University Press, 1986), pp. 57–9, for the view that Romantic poetry was perhaps more influenced by less emotional, and even less Christian, Enlightenment patterns of learned hymnody.

33 Alan Richardson, 'Introduction', in *Slavery, Abolition and Emancipation: Writings in the British Romantic Period*, vol. IV: *Verse* (London: Pickering and Chatto, 1999), p. xi.

to root out the depravities of popular culture and inculcate the lower orders with Christian principles of industry and subordination. Evangelical activists contributed decisively to the process by which reading became an *ordinary* habit in this period, moving down the social scale, and spreading through a culture of personal reflection, testament, diary keeping, and domestic prayer and Bible reading. Again, the range of printed matter associated with this movement was impressive, extending from prayer books and catechisms through pious fiction and biography to broadsheet ballads and devotional allegories in verse and prose. Its scale was unprecedented. More claimed to have circulated two million tracts through her Cheap Repository within the first year of its founding in 1795, providing the English middle class with its first concerted experience of the mass distribution of reading matter.[34] Although initiative was supposed to be reserved for elites, literacy was no more easy to contain than spiritual revival, and some Sunday schools in particular developed a distinct working-class character,[35] even as they helped train generations of articulate activists whose lives were by no means restricted to subordinate Christian piety.

Elite critics of Evangelical activism lined up on the right as well as the left, and Wilberforce and More were both treated with suspicion by such reactionary High Church publications as the *Anti-Jacobin Review*. Yet as the 1790s proceeded, the Evangelical mission among the poor became increasingly attractive to elites who might have had little sympathy for moral reform in earlier decades. Evangelical Anglicanism was particularly well-situated for public patronage since it joined establishment credentials with a powerful conviction about human corruption that seemed to many to have been borne out by the French Revolution. Indeed, over the course of this period Christian principles of innate depravity suffused the moral literature addressed to children and to a populace just entering upon literacy. Experimental treatments of childhood in William Blake's *Songs of Innocence and of Experience* (1794) and Wordsworth's 'We Are Seven' can be understood as challenges to the Evangelical management of personal disposition and literary response.[36]

---

34 Richard Altick, *The English Common Reader: A Social History of the Mass Reading Public, 1800–1900* (Chicago: University of Chicago Press, 1957), p. 76.
35 Thomas Walter Laqueur, *Religion and Respectability: Sunday Schools and Working Class Culture, 1780–1850* (New Haven: Yale University Press, 1976).
36 Alan Richardson, *Literature, Education, and Romanticism: Reading as Social Practice, 1780–1832* (Cambridge: Cambridge University Press, 1994), pp. 14–15, 64–77.

Religious underworlds and alternative beliefs

Some of the same historical developments that invigorated the Evangelical wing of the Anglican Church and contained the energies of rational Dissent also contributed to a dynamic and largely urban underworld of plebeian radical belief, informed by a variety of heterodox religious and political traditions. While it would be a mistake to assume consistency in any of the arenas of Christian belief discussed so far, the radical underworld was especially fragmented and syncretistic, a place where imperfectly trans-mitted seventeenth-century Puritan traditions met a downwardly mobile radical Enlightenment and the galvanizing impact of the French Revolution. The enthusiastic prophecies of Richard Brothers and Joanna Southcott were only the most visible instances of a strain of millennial enthusiasm that ran right through the Romantic period, and while popular apocalypse was by no means new to Britain, counter-revolutionary mobilization ensured that such expectations were treated with renewed rigour and alarm. Given the secular and arguably more systematic development of parliamentary reform agitation in the period, one of the most striking features of plebeian protest was its capacity to join sceptical infidelity and popular strains of blasphemy, folk magic and anti-clericism with Protestant traditions of antinomian belief and millennial prophecy. As Iain McCalman has shown, 'a long history of convergence between millenarian religious ideas and popular forms of scep-ticism or materialism' came together in this period in a vibrant if essentially unstable London radical underworld. In his weekly periodical *Pig's Meat* (1793–5) and elsewhere Thomas Spence drew on the most radical implications of John Locke and Thomas Paine even as he seasoned his land reform plan with the language of Biblical prophecy and Puritan millenarianism.[37]

A more narrowly canonical Romantic scholarship might have ignored this radical underworld except that it issued magnificently in the work of an indisputably major figure, William Blake. While the precise nature of Blake's Dissenting heritage remains obscure, popular radical enthusiasm clearly informed the language and prophetic spirit of the illuminated books of the 1790s, and was sustained through such later epic works as *Milton* (c. 1804–11) and *Jerusalem* (c. 1804–20). No other major Romantic period writer can be so fully understood within a framework of Christian tradition, and Blake has provided evidence for interpretive claims about a post-Enlightenment

---

37 Iain McCalman, *Radical Underworld: Prophets, Revolutionaries and Pornographers in London, 1795–1840* (Cambridge: Cambridge University Press, 1988), pp. 63–6.

recuperation of faith in the life of the imagination. Certainly, he conducted an unyielding campaign against the spiritually destructive effects of rationalism and materialism:

> The Spectre is the Reasoning Power in Man; & when separated
> From Imagination, and closing itself as in steel, in a Ratio
> Of the Things of Memory. It thence frames Laws & Moralities
> To destroy Imagination! the Divine Body, by Martyrdoms & Wars

> Teach me O Holy Spirit the Testimony of Jesus! let me
> Comprehend wonderous things out of the Divine Law
> I behold Babylon in the opening Street of London, I behold
> Jerusalem in ruins wandering about from house to house
> This I behold the shudderings of death attend my steps
> I walk up and down in Six Thousand Years: their Events
>   are present before me.[38]

Yet as these lines from *Jerusalem* indicate, by insisting upon the sustained and ordinary availability of prophetic inspiration, and by drawing prophetic rhythms from a range of scriptural and antiquarian sources (including Robert Lowth's ideas about the Bible as primitive literature), Blake produced a visionary poetry that cannot be mistaken for anything in Wordsworth, Coleridge or Shelley. There was more of 'the opening Street of London' in his work, and less of the natural world and personal reflection. Blake himself argued this distinction in his marginal response to Wordsworth's 1815 *Essay, Supplementary to the Preface*: 'Imagination is the Divine Vision not of The World nor of Man nor from Man as he is a Natural Man but only as he is a Spiritual Man Imagination has nothing to do with Memory.'[39] To argue this distinction is not to reinforce longstanding assumptions about his solitary genius or retreat to a party of one. On the contrary, prophetic ambition and antinomian resistance to moral law were just two of the many currents of radical enthusiasm that flowed through Blake's work, as he pursued a common popular tendency to travel in and out of heterodox subcultures.[40]

While Blake was moved more by sectarian enthusiasm than Enlightenment reason, he was no more exclusive than other radical visionaries of the

---

38 William Blake, *Jerusalem*, in *Complete Poetry and Prose*, ed. Erdman, Plate 74, lines 10–19.
39 Blake, *Complete Poetry and Prose*, p. 666.
40 Jon Mee, *Dangerous Enthusiasm: William Blake and the Culture of Radicalism in the 1790s* (Oxford: Clarendon Press, 1992), pp. 57–60.

period, and turned the critical resources of scepticism and materialism to his own ends. The opening lines of Plate 11 of *The Marriage of Heaven and Hell* (1790) set out from a comparative mythological method that was often taken to undermine Christian scripture by challenging its source and uniqueness: 'The ancient poets animated all sensible objects with Gods or Geniuses, calling them by the names and adorning them with the properties of woods, rivers, mountains, lakes, cities, nations, and whatever their enlarged & numerous senses could perceive.' Yet the sense here of an original condition of perceptual wholeness, which opens out on Blake's distinctive epistemological understanding of the Christian fall, suggests that the authority of revelation cannot be entirely discredited. After a turn through Enlightenment anti-clericism – 'Priesthood' forms when the ancient animation of nature deteriorates into 'system' – the plate concludes not by dissolving belief but rather by reclaiming a radical Christian dispensation: 'Thus men forgot that All deities reside in the human breast.'[41] In this instance, Blake's ability to appropriate sceptical historical methods for his own spiritual purposes recalls Coleridge's apologetic inflection of the higher criticism, though with a very different political valance. And it suggests one important way in which English Romantic discourse was a late Enlightenment or post-Enlightenment formation: critical resources that had fuelled scepticism and infidelity tended to spill out into more ambiguous and multivalent reflections on the history and sociology of religious belief.

Harsh repressive conditions certainly contributed to this redirection of infidelity. In the politically charged atmosphere of the 1790s, the first two parts of Paine's *Age of Reason* (1794–5) were considered a blasphemous attack on faith of any kind, though they are better understood as a late expression of English Deism, concerned to critique atheism as well as revealed Christianity, and to defend the idea of a supreme being reached by unaided human reason and close observation of the natural world. The danger of the work lay not just in its fierce anti-clericism and thoroughgoing attack on scripture, but in the way Paine's forceful vernacular prose reached beyond the elite confines of a declining Deist tradition. Daniel Isaac Eaton was convicted of blasphemous libel for his 1811 edition of Part 3 of the *Age of Reason*, and Richard Carlile, Paine's most energetic second-generation disciple, was similarly prosecuted in 1819. In 1792 Joseph Johnson brought out an English translation of a still more explosive text in the radical canon of

---

41 Blake, *The Marriage of Heaven and Hell*, in *Complete Poetry and Prose*, Plate 11.

infidelity, Constantin Volney's *The Ruins, or, A Survey of the Revolutions of Empires*. Couching his argument as an allegorical dream vision, Volney drew on comparative historical methods to trace the rise of priestly imposition, and in Chapter Fifteen, 'The New Age' (often brought out separately in pamphlet form), he portentously linked the rise of religion with the division of society into two classes, laboring producers and parasitic elites. Volney and the radical materialist Baron d'Holbach were central influences on Percy Shelley's *Queen Mab* (1813), an unrelenting verse and prose attack on institutional religion and priestcraft, which Shelley learned to regret when it was later picked up by pressmen such as Carlile and transmitted to later nineteenth-century working-class radicalism. In *Frankenstein* (1818), Mary Shelley registered the impact of the *Ruins* more ambiguously by including it among the books that shaped the creature's moral development.

Although conservative Anglicans routinely warned that any radical departure from Church doctrine would end in materialism and atheism, Percy Shelley and others went on to negotiate the hazardous political climate of the post-Napoleonic era by absorbing a whole range of unorthodox beliefs as well as doubts. Esoteric and Orientalist sources including Sir William Drummond's seasonal interpretations of primitive myth and the sexual theories of early human worship associated with Sir William Jones and Richard Payne Knight came to inform the progressive and erotic visions of a distinct circle of second-generation Romantic writers. The progressive, sensual and self-consciously cultivated vision of the circle of writers gathered around Shelley while he lived at Marlow in the summer of 1817 was epitomized in Shelley's own *Revolt of Islam* (1817) and in Thomas Love Peacock's *Rhododaphne* (1817), and it extended through the work of Leigh Hunt to poems by Keats and Byron as well. At this point an earlier generation of poets became the polemical vector for contests over comparative mythology and countervailing scriptural tradition. As Marilyn Butler has suggested, the 'cult of sexuality' at Marlow allowed the younger Romantic writers to situate themselves against their immediate forebears and against 'an institutionalized Christianity that was part of the apparatus of State'. It is not easy to decide whether, in the period of the emergence of a more plebeian radical mass platform, and in the wake of the pointed controversies of the 1790s, esoteric spiritual sources yielded a style of dissent that deflected open conflict. Butler argues that mythological experiment did in fact express rather than conceal a critique of Christian doctrine, though she allows that the repressive episodes of 1817 and 1819 contributed to the shift to 'a more abstract, less immediately political critique of Christianity' among the second generation poets.[42] Byron's literary fashioning of a satanic self-image and his reworking of Christian fable in works such as the verse drama *Cain, A Mystery* (1821), while no doubt shrewd if volatile marketing devices, were similarly disposed to extend generational conflict and challenge establishment complacency in the years after Waterloo.

As if to confirm the widening gap between the Lake School and the Marlow circle on matters of faith, Robert Southey's epic forays into orientalism and comparative religion trace a more aggressive retreat from anything like a critical response to Christianity. Where *Thalaba the Destroyer* (1801) accommodated a sympathetic treatment of Islam within an alternative framework for belief, *The Curse of Kehama* (1810) painted a more sinister portrait of Hinduism as a violent form of superstition that undergirded a ruthlessly hierarchical society, and the poem has been aligned with contemporary defenses of the work of Evangelical missionaries in India.[43] Again, if there are arguably attenuations of Enlightenment scepticism in all of these poetic developments, this should not obscure crucial rifts within the field of Romantic writing. The case for an internally differentiated Romanticism is vividly realized in Wordsworth's notorious response to Keats in 1817, after hearing the young poet recite the 'Hymn to Pan' from *Endymion* (1818): 'a Very pretty piece of paganism'.[44] Ironically, Keats was partly influenced in his turn to myth by Book 4 of *The Excursion*, where the Wanderer treats primitive belief positively, as an innate human response to the presence of the divine in nature, but also carefully distinguishes an authentic Christian dispensation from 'bewildered' paganism.[45]

Romantic sectarianism

Even allowing for the omissions that are required to produce a literary canon knit together by natural supernaturalism, there is a doubtful lack of historical specificity about the religious traditions said to have been at work

---

42 Marilyn Butler, *Romantics, Rebels, and Reactionaries*, p. 136, and 'Myth and Mythmaking in the Shelley Circle', *ELH* 49 (1982), 67–8. My discussion of the Marlow circle is indebted to Butler's work; see also her chapter titled 'Orientalism' in *The Penguin History of Literature: The Romantic Period*, ed. David B. Pirie (Harmondsworth: Penguin, 1994), pp. 395–447.

43 Nigel Leask, *British Romantic Writers and the East: Anxieties of Empire* (Cambridge: Cambridge University Press, 1992), p. 26, and Butler, 'Orientalism', pp. 409–10, 415–16.

44 See *The Keats Circle: Letters and Papers, 1816–1878*, ed. Hyder Edward Rollins, 2nd edn (Cambridge, MA: Harvard University Press, 1965), vol. II, pp. 143–4.

45 Wordsworth, *The Excursion*, in *Poetical Works*, Book 4, line 934; see Roe, *John Keats and the Culture of Dissent*, pp. 76–7.

in a shared Romantic displacement of apocalyptic vision into human consciousness and literary imagination. In a perceptive discussion of Christian metaphor that allows for salient differences within the old Romantic canon, Leslie Brisman suggests the level of abstraction that a spiritually unified Romanticism requires. 'One generalization about the "direction" of Romantic religious metaphor will, I think, hold. It has been remarked of Byron that he was certainly a Calvinist even if was not a Christian, and in general the Romantics were radical Protestants (of varying degrees and kinds of radicalism) even if they were not Christians.' The layered qualifications here seem to exclude very little, while eliding constitutive differences within the English Protestant tradition. In particular, one of two Romantic 'qualities or habits of mind' that Brisman derives from radical belief, 'enthusiasm',[46] was itself a source of friction within English Protestant tradition, particularly where more conservative forms of Evangelical piety diverged from rational Dissent. And the esoteric mythologies of Shelley and Keats can be understood as a concerted departure from radical Protestant tradition. Younger poets with liberal and progressive sympathies learned to look beyond the proscribed idioms of Dissent, and beyond Christianity itself, to express their own distinctive form of resistance to the Anglican portion of a reactionary British state.

In his essay 'On Court-Influence' William Hazlitt offers a usefully contrarian though no less partial account of the fortunes of radical Protestantism within Romantic literary tradition. First published in January 1818 in John Hunt's radical weekly *The Yellow Dwarf*, the essay enters the controversy over Robert Southey's acceptance of the poet laureateship by interrogating 'the sincerity of the present laureate in his change of opinion'. Hazlitt concludes that Southey was, like Edmund Burke, motivated less by 'interest in the grossest sense' than by the 'magic charm' of royal favour. The sinister operations of court influence and elite opinion are also found lurking behind recent attacks by Southey and Coleridge on rational Dissent, and Hazlitt counters with a vigorous defense of sectarian traditions as 'the nurseries of public spirit, and independence, and sincerity of opinion': 'A thorough-bred Dissenter will never make an accomplished Courtier. The antithesis of a Presbyterian Divine of the old school is the Poet-laureate of the new'. Dissenting virtue eventually comes to rest in the figure of Hazlitt's own father, and there is something deeply moving about his

---

46 Leslie Brisman, 'Mysterious Tongue: Shelley and the Language of Christianity', *Texas Studies in Language and Literature* 23 (1981), 390–1.

acknowledgement that political consistency was not a matter of warm enthusiasm, but instead issued from a sectarian 'hardness of manner and cold repulsiveness of feeling'. The complex literary typology is extended further when the cool reserve of Dissent is in turn contrasted with the passionate eloquence that 'blazed out' in Edmund Burke's *Reflections*. While the essay does slip into the darkly elegiac tone that characterized much of Hazlitt's political writing after Waterloo, a sense that the Dissenting character might have 'worn itself out' does not diminish its value as a polemical counterweight to the inconsistency of the Lake School: 'This is better than the life of a whirligig court poet.'[47] Hazlitt's essay shows how radical Protestant tradition could haunt the Romantic literary community as a spectre of difference rather than shared principle. As so often in his fiercely dialectical prose, distinctions proliferate, and the case against Burke and Southey is accompanied by a host of bristling distinctions about the relative value of faith and doubt, reason and sensibility, poetry and prose.

Protestant tradition was essentially a *sectarian* tradition of conflict and controversy, so it should come as no surprise that it energized Romantic writing as much through particular differences as through any comprehensive spiritual design. Before there was 'Romanticism' there were a host of contemporary sectarian literary designations, conceived in antagonism and sustained in debate. Of these, Southey's assault on the Satanic school of Shelley and Byron was the most overtly concerned with matters of faith, but the controversial development of the Lake and Cockney schools also impinged centrally on religious matters, and Southey had himself been attacked by Francis Jeffrey early in his career as the leader of a Dissenting sect in poetry. Taken together, these contested designations again suggest a framework of real and imagined religious difference, closely linked with matters of social organization and political commitment that were transforming faith and worship in the period. Yet the fractious development of Romantic-period belief is not likely to stop Romanticists from invoking it as a unifying principle, and Robert Ryan's *Romantic Reformation* is a distinguished late instance of the way religious interpretation converges on an account of 'the Romantic writers as participants in a single literary movement'.[48] Yet for all its force Ryan's case for a liberating Romantic reformation risks underestimating religion as a controlling and conservative

---

47 William Hazlitt, 'On Court-Influence', in *Complete Works of William Hazlitt*, ed. Howe, vol. VII, pp. 233, 239–42.
48 Ryan, *Romantic Reformation*, pp. 11, 28–9.

force, and may be less convincing than his insistence that religious impulses in the literature of the period, far from registering escapist or transcendental tendencies, were a crucial vector for social and political engagement. Spiritually motivated engagement divided and distinguished the writers of the Romantic period as often as it drew them together in a coherent literary movement. If faith has to some extent been displaced from the centre of critical discussions of Romanticism, its pivotal role in the social and cultural history of the period ensures that it will remain present in any finely grained account of British Romantic literature.

Is Romanticism finished?

JEROME MCGANN

I

Villon and Borgia – Sidonia, Lovelace, Becky Sharp, Heathcliff, and, supremely, the Divine Marquis Himself! How much better these demonic creatures than the Pale Galilean who tormented them with the platitudes of his wretched moral codes and those 'forms of worship' Blake banished forever to a darkness deeper than Stygian, wider than Chaos. How much better and – better yet, Thank Somebody! – how much worse!

(A. C. Swinburne to D. G. Rossetti, 1 April 1866, Easter Sunday)

Is Romanticism finished? Such is the question posed for me by the editor of this volume. Cultural observers like ourselves, the essayists in this book, have a certain professional investment in answering that question negatively. 'Certainly not, Romanticism flourishes, its forms are central to the best that has been known and thought etc. etc.' And if that way of thinking has been, if it *be*, but a vain belief, how often have our spirits turned to it – how often, in how many days and ways!

'Is Romanticism finished?' No? YES, according to one of our age's defining cultural spokespersons. It is and always has been and always will be. Death and loss are the glory of a Romantic imagination. 'Romanticism is a doomed tradition, yet a perpetually self-renewing one.'[1] It's been a long-lived and persuasive view – Romanticism as the land of the last and the lost. Look up, there's that great Romantic figure, Prometheus. Byron chains him to his rock 'perpetually' – no escapes wanted here! – but though tightly bound by what Byron elsewhere calls 'the electric chain of [that] despair', the Titan is nonetheless, we are assured, 'making death a victory'.

Byron's friend Shelley, let us recall, read that text of Byron's with wonder and with horror. However grand the figure of Byron's Prometheus, for Shelley it would never do. He wrote his masterpiece, *Prometheus Unbound*,

---

1 Harold Bloom, *The Ringers in the Tower* (Chicago: University of Chicago Press, 1971), p. 326.

to install a very different Promethean idea. Byron's Prometheus is 'a symbol and a sign / To mortals of their fate and force': doomed, enduring, and – most impressive of all – *seeing* it all with immense clarity and defiance. Shelley's Prometheus is a symbol and sign of something else: how the clarified mind can gain its liberty without, as in Aeschylus, making a truce with ruling power. You cast spells to establish an 'empire' of the free. The spells are moral imperatives: suffer woe, defy power (so far, acceptably Byronic, but then), forgive wrong, and most of all 'love and bear [and] hope, till hope creates/ From its own wreck the thing it contemplates'.

Between Shelley's and Byron's ideas of forgiveness, love and hope falls the shadow of their very different imaginations of Prometheus, their different Romanticisms.

We shall have to revisit, later, that scene of mountain gloom and mountain glory. For now let's turn away and cast our eyes along the roads descending from those primal Romantic texts. Carlyle, following Shelley, inveighs against what he saw as the 'Everlasting Nay' of Byronism. A bit later Arnold, with his schoolmasterly condescension, would refigure the Shelleyan spells as the beautiful wings of ineffectual angels. Later still, as we remember, men like Hulme, Babbitt, Leavis, Eliot and a New Critical academy have worse things yet to say until – it's around 1935 – Romanticism seemed finished, at least as a dominant cultural and pedagogic formation. Not just Byron and Shelley but all of it ('Thank Somebody!', as Swinburne used to say).

Yet as we know, it rose again like some 'unfather'd vapour', or perhaps more like the Gothic revenant conceived in Romanticism's famous summer of 1816. Looking at Romanticism in 1935 it would have seemed, like Blake's Albion, sick, languishing, plague-struck; but soon 'the fierce Americans rushing together in the night . . . play around the golden roofs in wreaths of fierce desire' (*America*, Plate 15). America to the rescue! W. J. Bate, Northrop Frye, M. H. Abrams, Carl Woodring, Earl Wasserman, Harold Bloom, Geoffrey Hartman. And after those heroes, the names are legion. Perpetually doomed, perpetually self-renewing.

Why in the world would one think it might be finished? That's to say, dead in no glorious sense: unimportant, irrelevant – *to the point* only because beside the point.

The world is a large place, diversely populated. Let's put our question to someone who might see the matter from another part of this large world. Let's ask J. M. Coetzee. His answer comes in (and as) his novel, *Disgrace* (1999).

II

The novel's central character, David Lurie, is an academic, a literary scholar – a Romanticist, in fact. His career is framed on one end – before the novel begins – with a book about Wordsworth, and on the other end – the period of the novel's action – with an opera focused on Byron. Perfect. The book is organized around the Twin Towers – the ultimate dialectic – of the Romantic Movement in England.

Disgrace unfolds a complex and in my view an entirely original interpretation of Byron. Coetzee also develops an interpretation of European Romanticism. The most selfconscious of writers, he clearly locates this reading of traditional Romantic thought-forms in a Euro-African context. That nexus is important to remember, in the context of this book, because the politics of a Romantic ethos is a long-standing cultural and even scholarly issue. Nadine Gordimer famously criticized Coetzee in her 1984 review of *The Life and Times of Michael K* for what she saw as his 'revulsion against all political and revolutionary solutions' to the problems of South Africa.[2] She might well judge *Disgrace* in the same way. However that may be, Coetzee's works are through and through politically and historically aware, and this novel is no exception.

Disgrace seems a deliberate attempt to show how difficult it must be for a contemporary western imagination to make 'a passage to Africa', as E. M. Forster might have said. Coetzee organizes his investigation of this subject around Lurie's romanticized character, which is the lens framing and focusing what we see. The matter is relevant to my central subject because the book ties its investigation directly to Lurie's effort to 'change [his] life'. He despairs of making such a change – that *is* the story of the book – but in his despair he appears to discover, to us and perhaps even to himself, the point where a change might begin – might even, by the last page of the book, be imagined by the reader to *have* begun, though just barely. 'Might' and 'Just barely', we say, because David Lurie, the novel's diaristic narrator, is an immensely deceiving and self-deceived man.

We trace the argument for the possibility of change along two lines, one related to Lurie's daughter Lucy, the other to Bev Shaw, Lucy's friend who runs the animal shelter that has virtually no function except to put down an exploded population of unwanted dogs. Both lines of argument are

2 Nadine Gordimer, 'The Idea of Gardening: *Life and Times of Michael K*', in *Critical Essays on J. M. Coetzee*, ed. Sue Kossew (New York: G. K. Hall, 1998), p. 143.

explicitly linked to the novel's Byronic themes via the opera Lurie is trying to write. In that Byronic horizon – parodic and ludicrous as Coetzee represents the matter – Lurie is of course Byron, Lucy is the avatar of his daughter Allegra, and Bev is Byron's famous 'last attachment', Teresa Guiccioli. These 'identifications' are complicated by the novel's nuanced sets of doppelgängers, not the least conspicuous of its Romantic features.

Before I sketch Coetzee's Byronically organized double argument, then, let me clarify my view of his fictive method and, ultimately, his polemical purposes. The book is narrated by Lurie as a meticulous and supremely self-conscious autobiographical record. That narrative procedure is a second-order sign of Lurie's colossal self-absorption. So acute is his condition that, as the book opens, he seems nearly consumed with self-loathing. He masks his despair in various ways. His apparent candour and openness, his ironical wit, his quick erotic responsiveness: all are defences for hiding himself from himself and from real contact with others. Coetzee turns the whole of the surface of the text over to Lurie so that Lurie will expose himself to us, the book's readers. For it is we who are this novel's main interest and object of attention, and in this respect we touch another Byronic quality in the book. Like *Les Fleurs du mal* and its precursor texts from Byron and, through Byron, from Poe, *Disgrace* is fashioned as a test of the reader, whose hypocrisy is suspected, perhaps even assumed. Invited to judge this clearly disgraceful man, the reader gets drawn into a trial of his or her own moral and political ideas.

Not many of the book's reviewers glossed its running meditations on Byron and the ethos of Romanticism. One of the few who did was Ranti Williams, who remarks briefly on the book's 'obvious analogy' to Byron's life. The Byronic allusions, Williams says, are 'false notes in an otherwise laceratingly true book'.[3] But it's clear to me that Williams has scarcely come to terms with the Byronic 'analogy' Coetzee develops. Williams seems to think the analogy is simply to Byron's notorious despair, to the legend of his sexual libertinage, and to the 1816 'disgrace' and subsequent exile, when Byron and the Countess Teresa Guiccioli met and fell in love. Much is involved in these allusions, which are worked into the novel in complex and subtle ways. Two are especially consequential.

First of all, the book specifically asks the reader to interpret all these matters, indeed the entirety of the Byronic legend, in terms of Byron's

3 Ranti Williams, 'A Man's Salvation' (review of J. M. Coetzee, *Disgrace*), *Times Literary Supplement*, 25 June 1999, p. 23.

(famous) devotion to animals. This is an interpretive line that was often followed, though in a sentimental mode, in the nineteenth century. Byron's verses to his dog Boatswain served the nineteenth century as a point of reference for a sympathetic view of the man who was otherwise so mad, bad and dangerous to know. In this reading, Boatswain is an example of that 'one virtue' by which the 'thousand crimes' of Byron's life are to be measured and judged. Coetzee's novel makes a startling return upon that now-largely-ignored byway of the Byronic legend. Lurie's despair takes him back across the wasteland of his self-delusions where, in a far more stern reprise of Byron's tale of Mazeppa, Lurie is forced to a zero-degree point of self-assessment. The critical moment comes when his daughter Lucy tells him she will become a *'bywoner'* by giving herself to the native African Petrus, who once worked for her. She will become one of Petrus's wives, or concubines, to gain his protection, and she will give Petrus her land as part of the bargain. In this way she will manage to keep her house and continue to live where she wants to live, in Africa – but in Africa on African, not European, terms. When she tells her father her plan his despair is perfected:

> 'How humiliating', he says finally. 'Such high hopes, and to end like this.'
> 'Yes, I agree, it is humiliating. But perhaps that is a good point to start from again. Perhaps that is what I must learn to accept. To start at ground level. With nothing. Not with nothing but. With nothing. No cards, no weapons, no property, no rights, no dignity.'
> 'Like a dog.'
> 'Yes, like a dog.'[4]

In the end Lurie will himself begin to step along this path cleared for him by his remarkable daughter. He will become the book's *dog man*, the phrase Petrus ironically applies to himself at the start of the novel.

It's clear that Coetzee is aware of the Byronic 'analogy' behind all this. Less clear is whether he also means the analogy to suggest a reinterpretation of the Byronic legend. Given the way the novel uses its running Byronic materials, however, such a reinterpretation is inevitable. Coetzee's book implicitly argues that Byron's (and Lurie's) sexual transgressions are senti-mentalized evasions of a more deeply imbedded set of allegiances. For example, Coetzee's book resuscitates the legend of Byron's devotion to Boatswain – and his love for animals generally – in order to read that European legend in a new and, for this place and time, a better and deeper

---

4 J. M. Coetzee, *Disgrace* (London: Secker and Warburg, 1999), p. 205.

way. The romantic sign of the loving and faithful dog gets disgraced in Coetzee's book. For the story shows with painful clarity how the dog is a white cultivation in the South African world – a key instrument for defending white property. The slaughter of Lucy's dogs is carried out with particular brutality because the animals are heavily coded symbols of white power. Lurie's final vocation – to perform the service of the dead for these wretched and exploited animals – emblemizes the poetic (and piteous) justice being meted out in the book.

Which brings us to the second interesting Byronic strain in the novel. Lurie's initial idea is to set his Byronic opera during Byron's lifetime – a musical recreation of the famous 'last attachment', Teresa and Byron's love affair that ran from 1819 until 1824. As Lurie unravels his slow and painful self-exposure, however, his conception of his opera changes radically. When he is finally able to begin writing, the central figure has become Teresa, not Byron. The opera is set decades later – Byron is long dead – in the last period of Teresa's dogged devotion to 'Mio Byron', whose memory she cherished to the end. This part of the Byron legend has, like Boatswain, lost nearly all its sentimental aura for contemporary culture – or rather, its sentimental aura has turned sour and undergone a thorough disgrace. At least the young Teresa was beautiful! The years took away that beauty and left her a ludic and distinctly unromantic figure, plunged in a self-deceived folly of love and in wacko efforts to capture it again through séances and table-rapping.

But Coetzee recovers precisely this Teresa for us, this foolish old lady, stripped of her romantic charms. She is short, she has (to use the Byronic term) grown dumpy. And in Lurie's disgraceful opera she will sing for the dead dog Byron, not to the romantic piano and in her youthful voice, but in cracked and aged strains, accompanied by a banjo, 'plink! Plunk!' In the novel her avatar is explicitly Beth Shaw, Lurie's own 'last attachment', this touching woman – 'touching' in every sense, as we see in her animal shelter – who actually finds Lurie someone to have sex with and to trust with her loved animals. Like Lurie's daughter Lucy, the revenant of Byron's daughter Allegra, Bev gets doubled in Lurie's parodic opera as the contemporary model for, or image of, a Teresa stripped of all apparitional charms conjured by a narcissistic male imagination.

At a crucial moment in the story Lurie's narrative exposes how both women haunt Lurie's fantasy life as merged female forms. In a maudlin moment of self-pity, Lurie imagines himself beyond hope, utterly loathsome, incapable of anything honest. He is too old, he thinks, too committed to European ideas of 'honour'. He then pursues his thought in a comical and unserious mode – as if he were thinking like a character in his travesty opera: 'That is why he must listen to Teresa. Teresa may be the last one who can save him. Teresa is past honour . . . She has immortal longings, and sings her longings. She will not be dead' (p. 209). Those are double-voiced words, of which this subtle book has many. That double-voicing goes right past the ironical Lurie, the diaristic narrator. But the reader is asked to hear this voicing and the unexpressed significance of the passage: Who must be listened to, who is past honour, who will not be dead? Lucy? Bev? David Lurie? Us? What of us after all, the white readers specifically addressed by this book so cunningly sent to us decked in its white white cover?

Both women are symbols and signs of the novel's benevolent decon-struction of the romantic dreams that David Lurie's European heritage has kept him so desperately cherishing. Wrecked as they are in this book, the dreams hold on now in their disgraced material forms, dog-faithful to things that appear 'nothing' at all to Lurie's lurid and ludic romantic imagination. One of those nothings is Lurie himself, loathed, self-loathed, loathsome: yet to Bev Shaw, someone she will trust and even have sex with, knowing exactly what he is and has been. Bev seems to have a kind of dream of Lurie, as if he were or might be (or might have been) someone else, just as Lucy has a dream of becoming 'African'. What we are asked to see is that both of these are completely conscious dreams, cherished with great clarity of mind. Bev and Lucy are very practical even with their dreams.

Coetzee surely means us to think of Wordsworth as we read to the end of this book. Lucy's name, in context, can hardly have been undeliberated. But unlike Bev, who cherishes her animal dreams with a kind of Wordsworthian simplicity, Lucy is no Wordsworthian figure. With all of her father's hard-edged mental awareness, she appears like some new Byronic hero *determined* to gain her desire by sheer force of will.

And indeed this book never strays far from its Byronic representations. Early on, for example, when Lurie undergoes his trial and disgrace, he clearly affects the Byronic Hero, posed in his cynical and withering ironies – 'proud as Lucifer', as my mother used to say. Poe, Baudelaire and Nietzsche (among many others – painters, musicians, writers, philosophers) loved and made much of this image of Byron. It was their principal tool for exposing what Baudelaire famously called the 'hypocrite reader'. Coetzee recovers that image in order to bring a similar judgement against current Euro-American white avatars of those nineteenth-century readers. The argument comes principally in the third of the book that takes place entirely under a 'white' horizon of European ideas, mores and social institutions.

The central event here is the university board of inquiry's meeting to interrogate Lurie and make a disciplinary recommendation. Lurie opens the proceedings by pleading guilty and asking to have sentence passed on him. The board is displeased and under pressure from the parodic feminist Farodia Rassool it demands more. They want him 'to express contrition' (p. 54). When Lurie complies with this demand as well, he is asked whether his statement 'reflect[s] your sincere feelings' (p. 54). He refuses to answer, arguing that the state of his 'heart' is not the business of the board of inquiry. His admission of wrongdoing and his expression of 'regret' are, he tells the board, 'as far as I am prepared to go' (p. 55).

The situation is exquisitely Byronic in a full Baudelairean sense. Coetzee is fashioning the inquisition of Lurie into an exposure of the varieties of European, and specifically Romantic, hypocrisy. Rassool says to her colleagues that 'we [must be] crystal clear in our minds [about] what Professor Lurie is being censured for', and her colleague Mathabane replies on the board's behalf: 'In our own minds I believe we are crystal clear' (pp. 50–1). The remark is both a philosophical paradox and a joke on Mathabane and his self-righteous inquisitors, who are no more clear in their minds than Lurie is. Rassool wants blood, Mathabane wants institutional justification, Hakim wants compromise. The academic meeting is another of the book's symbols and signs, a western travesty of a truth commission, and the entire scene amounts to a conscious, critical investigation of the Romantic idea – or ideology – of 'sincerity'. 'You want me to demonstrate [my] sincerity' (p. 55), Lurie says, but he refuses this demand. The refusal forces the reader to see two matters: first, Lurie's continued determination not to 'know himself' or to inquire into himself; and second, the board's reciprocal determination to deceive itself about its own 'sincerity', honour and clarity of purpose.

The immediate index of the board's righteousness and hypocrisy is a narrative fact: like Lurie, its members show no practical interest in the girl who is at the centre of the case. She does not exist for them – indeed, Lurie himself barely exists. Later in the book, when the African context of the story gets elaborated, the world of Petrus, Bev and Lucy will throw into sharpest relief the vacancy of this white enclave and its devotion to its western 'crystal' clarities.

Coetzee's book is thus in great measure a satiric investigation of a wide range of Romantic ideologies – from Wordsworthian sincerity, on one end, to Byronic intellectual flamboyance on the other. Its point of departure is, however, distinctly Byronic, not Wordsworthian. Two advantages come from taking this procedure. First, because Byronic satire is confessedly a 'spoiler's art' – a critical engagement with error undertaken from a complicit point of view – Coetzee and Byron will both set their moral norms in a world beyond the range of what they or their work could pretend to understand. The second advantage, a corollary of the first, gives a local habitation and a name to that world elsewhere. It is the world of the reader – in this case, the white Euro-American reader directly addressed by Coetzee's book.

More than any of the Romantics except Blake, Byron writes poetry that puts readers to a test of their own minds and ideas. In this respect his is a consciously rhetorical poetry even as it is, unlike Blake's, a poetry of Romantic self-expression. When Coetzee recalls and exploits that paradoxical stylistic method in his diaristic novel, then, we readers are all laid under an implicit interrogation because we are all invited to make moral judgements about the book's characters and events. This is a difficult and challenging book exactly because our clearest surrogates are Lurie's academic inquisitors. 'Crystal clarity' is a cherished western demand, as is the 'sincerity' of one's critical purposes. Reading this book, like reading Byron, suggests that these twin ideals may no longer come into play until they are brought into complete disgrace.

III

Coetzee's way with Byron, and with Romanticism in general, is a sceptical one. In this respect it has much in common, we may think, with the aesthetic practices of Romantic artists. If Romanticism is perpetually 'doomed' and perpetually 'self-renewing', those reciprocities draw on a common energy source: imaginative scepticism. Blake's programme is explicitly to 'go to Eternal Death' via the 'Buildings of Los(s)'. Romantic imaginations are restless and self-critical, constructing and reconstructing forms of life in order to examine and establish their limits, thence moving on to other, unrealized or undared possibilities. 'Something evermore about to be'; 'I change, but I cannot die'. These are Romantic scepticisms cast as benevolent apprehensions. When the apprehensions grow dark and fearful, the impulse 'To strive, to seek, to find, and not to yield' may turn to question and perplexity, but it does not lessen: 'Was it a vision or a waking dream? / Fled is that music – do I wake or sleep?' Byron's Promethean defiance takes a sceptical stand toward any given order of the world. The defiance may appear *Sturm und Drang* – as in the early tales and *Childe Harold* – or it may come in the ironically Faustian mode that dominates the later work, pre-eminently *Don Juan*.

But Romantic scepticism is most impressive when it turns upon its own resources. In *Prometheus Unbound*, as noted earlier, Shelley marshals his sceptical critique of Byronic defiance, on one hand, and of 'the advocates of injustice and superstition' on the other. Wordsworth's greatest victories are equivocal: 'If this be but a vain belief'; 'Not without hope we suffer and we mourne'. The self-scepticism of Shelley – in 'The Triumph of Life', in 'Julian and Maddalo' – is even more direct and unflinching – like Byron's candid 'I have been cunning in mine overthrow / The careful pilot of my proper woe'.

To summarize Romantic ideology in this way barely does justice to the movement's artistic achievements. Nonetheless, we monitors of culture make these summaries all the time, as we should and must. In doing so, however, we put our critical work in peril of choosing forms of worship from the poetic tales we are missioned to preserve. We should guard against turning Romantic scepticism from a mode of experience – exemplary in its way and its limits – into a code of morals. I make these summaries here because they throw into relief the sharp difference between any form of Romantic scepticism and the scepticism fuelling Coetzee's work.

Disgrace puts its critique of Romanticism in Byronic terms, I think, exactly because it wants to locate its critique at an extreme of the Romantic sceptical tradition. The progressivist Wordsworthian imagination, pursuing (however vainly) sincerity and clear vision ('crystal clarity'), has been left far behind – like David Lurie's first book – as if it were some distant point of Romantic departure. We are past even Keats's fearful 'Purgatory blind' and plunged into the shattered Byronic world where 'there woos no home, nor hope, nor life, save what is here'. 'What is here' is white Romanticism – variously disgraceful, empty-headed, well-meaning, stupid and dull, comical and moving, wilful, determined, even often admirable. But whatever its tonal condition, in this contemporary African frame of reference it appears to us peripheral at best, at worst irrelevant.

Peripheral, irrelevant – but not finished. Why? How?

We want to address those questions by first addressing them to Romanticism considered as a 'doomed . . . but perpetually self-renewing' tradition. A rhetorical phrase like that – not to say a ponderous and pretentious phrase – recalls many Romantic texts celebrating death and self-generated rebirth. But what if, as in Hardy, death loses its sting by losing its grandeur. And what if, in consequence, the idea of self-renewal undergoes a sea change – as happens '"According to the Mighty Working"' of certain hard, Hardian reflections upon something evermore about to be:

> This never truly being,
> This evermore becoming,
> This spinner's wheel onfleeing
> Outside perception's range.
>
> (lines 9–12)

Byron's infamous despair has always been useful exactly as the limit case it defines for the Romantic imagination. (Gendered female, the limit would be the remarkable Letitia Elizabeth Landon, whose contemporary fame and infamy we are only now beginning to recover.) Poe and Baudelaire, Bronte and Melville, Kierkegaard and Nietzsche: all remount their self-renewing Romanticisms from the desperate position Byron initially staked out, and from which he generated, in gestures of satanic pride, his figures of personal triumph. Shelley's critical turn on Byron, as we've seen, sought to renew his Romantic flight by casting it in mythic and impersonal terms – as if 'Romanticism' were itself a kind of transcendental Being and not the subjective *élan* of a Byronic pilgrim.

Shortly after Shelley's masterpiece, and quite independently, Felicia Hemans made her own anti-Byronic move. After reading the fourth canto of *Childe Harold* and reflecting on what the *Quarterly Review* lamented as 'the course which literature . . . seem[s] lately to be taking',[5] Hemans proposed a restoration of the works of art in England (so to say). This came as her polemical poem *The Sceptic* (1820), which aims to counter the rites of passage of Byron's limit-case Romanticism. The poem is very like Shelley's in imagining the source of Romantic self-renewal beyond any mortal individual. Where Shelley casts spells of enlightenment, however, Hemans imagines her transmortal resource as Christian redemption.

Although Hemans's poem undertakes the whole corpus of Byron's work, it alludes specifically to *The Prisoner of Chillon*, *Manfred*, various lyrics (including 'Prometheus'), and all of *Childe Harold*. It focuses on Canto IV, however, as we realize in the climax of her poem where Hemans writes an

---

5 The review is quoted extensively following the edition of the poem printed in *The Works of Mrs. Hemans with a Memoir of her Life by her Sister* (Edinburgh and London: William Blackwood and Sons, 1844), vol. III, pp. 1–26 (for the quotation see p. 26). Citations to the poem are given in the text by page number from this edition.

elegy for the Princess Charlotte to offset the dark elegy for the princess that climaxes Byron's canto.[6] Hemans's princess is a complex Christ figure whose death locates a 'perpetually renewed' system of Christian redemption. The death in childbirth of the Princess Charlotte and her son refigures the *imitatio Christi* in a maternal form. In Byron, by sharp contrast, that myth of a perpetual light shining upon us was seen as historical and transitory – in Byronic terms, meteoric alone. If 'its promise seemed / Like star to shepherds' eyes', Byron says, "Twas but a meteor beamed'.[7]

The most interesting feature of Hemans's counter-Byronic poem is not the Christian myth she proffers but the manner in which the myth appears to us. The central argument of the poem is that 'the sceptic' is a creature whose proud self-assurance will collapse in fear when the moment of death comes upon him. According to Hemans, such a person needs the promise of Christian happiness to face and endure what Byron calls our 'funereal destiny'. Byron read Hemans's poem and disagreed with what she argued. He subsequently wrote to John Murray – his as well as Hemans's publisher at the time – and commented that in arguing thus Hemans was 'quite wrong. Men died calmly before the Christian era, and since, without Christianity . . . . A deathbed is a matter of nerves and constitution, and not of religion' (letter to Murray, 7 June 1820). That thought runs through all of Byron's work, which brings an imperative to face and outface every form of funereal destiny. In Manfred's famous last words: 'Old man, 'tis not so difficult to die.'

The most important issue at stake here is not, however, either factive – does the Byronic sceptic die in terror? – or ideological – whose case is strongest, the fideist Christian's or the sceptical agnostic's? When Hemans writes against Byron her form of worship comes as a poetic tale, and that makes all the difference. Her poem locates not a sceptical deficiency but the exact form of Hemans's Romanticism. This form comes to us as an affective representation – a 'Romantic' form, a poem of sincerity. It is not the Byronic sceptic who works out his salvation in fear and trembling in this poem, it is the faithful Christian. 'Byron' and 'The Sceptic' are magical mirrors giving Hemans access to that dreadful Christian situation within which Hemans's

6 Since writing this chapter (in 2000, shortly after *Disgrace* was published), Anne Hartman, Nanora Sweet and Barbara Taylor have all written important essays on *The Sceptic*. These can be found (along with some other interesting essays and critical materials) in the online Romantic Circles Electronic Edition *The Sceptic: A Hemans–Byron Dialogue*, published in 2004 (www.rc.umd.edu/editions/sceptic/).
7 *Childe Harold's Pilgrimage*, Canto 4: stanza 170.

special Romanticism exfoliates: the Romanticism of maternal fear and anxiety. What terrifies in Hemans's poem is less that the sinner will fall into the hands of an angry God than that a frail mortal will be hurled to the edge of the Christian God's world with no resources at all – alone, like some Blakean lost boy or girl. Hemans conjures a place of abandonment

> Where the lone sufferer dies without a friend,
> He whom the busy world shall miss no more
> Than morn one dewdrop from her countless store,
> Earth's most neglected child . . .
>
> (p. 17)

As Hemans imagines 'the parting mind' coming upon that Christian place, the verse heaves over into the intense interrogative mode that organizes its climactic passages:

> Tell her, what shall burst
> In whelming grandeur on her vision first,
> When freed from mortal films? – what viewless world
> Shall first receive her wing, but half unfurl'd?
> What awful and unbodied beings guide
> Her timid flight through regions yet untried?
>
> (p. 15)

> Whence, then, shall strength, which reason's aid denies,
> An equal to the mortal conflict rise?
> When, on the swift pale horse, whose lightning pace,
> Where'er we fly, still wins the dreadful race,
> The mighty rider comes – O whence shall aid
> Be drawn, to meet his rushing undismay'd?
>
> (p. 16)

Hemans's Christian imagination foreknows these nightmares, but it is her identification with the abandoned mother and child – Princess Charlotte and her infant – that give them a romantic habitation and a name. From that same sympathetic identification comes the poem's resolving conception: 'Aided by Him [Jesus]', the soul departs life in confidence, 'Call'd to the hope of glory' (p. 17).

Hemans's 'comforter' is not the self but a being beyond the self, a mythic (Christian) enginery structurally akin to Shelley's secular mythic resource. Like *Prometheus Unbound*, however, the success of Hemans's poem is not a function of its ideological commitments. The Christian mythos is a kind of template on which Hemans inscribes a complex act of Romantic self-expression, as we see in a passage like the following:

> When fled the hope through all thy pangs which smiled,
> When thy young bosom, o'er thy lifeless child,
> Yearn'd with vain longing – still thy patient eye,
> To its last light, beam'd holy constancy!

(p. 18)

The peculiar management of these paradoxes clearly forecasts the way Tennyson will typically work his poetry of cliché, most tellingly in *In Memoriam*. In this moment of fled hope, vain longings and dying light, Hemans imagines the Princess Charlotte as a new *Pietà* – here not a figure of depthless grief but of perfect constancy. The figure seems fashioned as a polemically symbolic counter-sign set against the stern and 'impenetrable Spirit' of Byron's 'Prometheus'.

The most moving aspect of such lines, however, and of Hemans's poem in general, lies in their romantic self-exposure. In making her poetical case against Byron's fierce romantic subjectivity, she succeeds only (only?) in laying bare her heart's core of fears. Byron knew she had directed her poem at him and he knew she had mistaken the secrets of his heart. But so far as her poem is concerned, it hardly matters that he was right. If the 'comforter' realized in *The Sceptic* is anything but cold, her sympathy, like Shelley's angelic visions, dances on its own grave. Hemans's 'argument' comes in questions, her resolutions rest in paradoxes. The text is naked.

> But for the vision of the days to be,
> But for the comforter, despised by thee,
> Should we not wither at the Chastener's look,
> Should we not sink beneath our God's rebuke,
> When o'er our heads the desolating blast,
> Fraught with inscrutable decrees, hath pass'd,
> And the stern power who seeks the noblest prey,
> Hath call'd our fairest and our best away?
> Should we not madden when our eyes behold
> All that we loved in marble stillness cold,
> No more responsive to our smile or sigh,
> Fix'd – frozen – silent – all mortality?

(p. 17)

These rhetorical questions are romantic, not classical: though directed at Byron and 'the course which literature . . . seem[s] lately to be taking', the questions turn back upon Hemans. For that literary course is, in the end, exactly her own. Imagining an answer to Byron, she draws a sketch of her emotional life. 'Comforter, where is thy comforting?' The questions also (necessarily) turn back on Hemans's immediate act of writing, which is thus called to invoke, in a perfectly romantic style, the spectre of its inadequacy and failure. We see this most clearly when Hemans's maternal imagination refigures *Childe Harold*'s Roman ruins as her lost loves. Byron's Rome is a monumental romantic elegy for the works and days of imagination conceived as a record of past greatness. Hemans's paedophilia translates that text from a lamentable past to the fearful future – the sepulchral vision concealed in her cherished 'homes of England'.

IV

'Is Romanticism finished?' Well, not exactly. But now its works are being composed in a different key, as *Disgrace* and numerous other contemporary fictions and poems suggest. We cannot take any of our Romantic heritage on its own polemical terms – Hemans, Blake, Byron, Shelley – any of it. This is not at all to dismiss it, in the manner of Hulme, Leavis, Eliot. Rather, we come to value it exactly for the insights fostered in its blind commitments.

To counter the unreasoning confidence of the ideology of Enlightenment, Coleridge instituted a famous Romantic definition of 'poetic faith' as the 'willing suspension of disbelief'. The word 'willing' is crucial, reminding us as it does that Coleridge was quite alive to the illusive fragility of cherished beliefs. So his Romantic way was to choose consciously to enter worlds that are quite *un*believable by any enlightened standard. This brave and foolish choice, a fundamental Romantic move, would be altogether preposterous were it not done in that wilful way. The wilfulness is the Romantic critique of the ideology of Enlightenment – which is to say, it is made from a position as sceptical of itself as of its critical object. Hemans's critique of 'the sceptic' succeeds exactly because the poem's consciously chosen belief structure gets stripped bare in its critical unfolding – more 'disgraced' even than David Lurie partly because more consciously deliberate in her action.

In an age of 'spin', hypocrisy and aggressive moral certitude – our dregs of early Romantic sincerity and imagination – we are arrested by art forms grounded, like Coetzee's, in what may appear to us as a willing suspension of *belief* rather than disbelief. Typically these forms turn to comedy, satire, parody – even pastiche. An art perhaps first completely explicated in

Brecht's 'epic theatre'. But Coetzee's pitiless treatment of Lurie and his European academic cronies is a kind of zero-degree act of sympathy with them and the audience of (western) readers – ourselves – these figures reflect. Do we judge and recoil from Lurie? We have made much, in our imperial day, of the need to sympathize with 'The Other'. Yet here is the most intimate Other of our alienated selves – this 'serial rapist', as I have heard it said of him and of his antitype Lord Byron. Baudelaire's 'Au Lecteur' remains as pertinent as ever: 'Hypocrite lecteur, mon semblable, mon frère.'

Certain early Romantics stand that kind of modern and postmodern cold better than others. The more developed the scepticism and the self-questioning – the more we are able to see and engage with such features in their work – the more available these artists are to us. 'Is Romanticism finished?' The question is purely – in both senses – academic. Romantic works flourish all about us in popular and highbrow art, music, writing. Indeed, it is this vigour of a present world that forces the question. Does our scholastic and critical interest in Wordsworth or Keats, etc., have a public function at the present time? Are we purveying antiquities to an E-Bay world? Is it a goblin market?

The answer to those questions, I believe, should be 'yes, that is precisely our case'. We handle these antiquities with care – we take them to our heavens – not because of their virtues but because they are our responsibility. It doesn't matter whether or not we think them deserving of this care or who takes an interest in them or why. As scholars we owe them all our care in any case. Not as one owes a debt but as one owes a human obligation, compelled by love and duty, whether the objects seem – to us, to others, to themselves – deserving or not 'on the merits'. Rizpah's love – not blind to fault or deceived, but consciously chosen exactly because virtue – not least the virtue of such works – is so uncertain.

Queer as it seems in the world of globalized capital, scholarship will go on with its memorial activities, as classical scholars have long since done with works even more unbelievable than the works of Modernity. (Think about Achilles and the other Greek heroes. Heroes? Yes, of course, but also monsters.) Something important is gained when we willingly suspend our disbelief in Shakespeare and Rousseau, the Bible and the Upanishads, and consciously enter a sympathetic relation to their weakened and alienated condition. Byron called it an act of 'mobility', Keats called it 'negative capability' – and in each case the move is consciously represented under the sign of what Byron also called a 'spoiler's art'. That kind of sympathy, a latter-day form of Socratic self-questioning, is the unfinished – possibly the unfinishable – business of Romanticism. 'Perhaps that is a good point to start from again. Perhaps that is what I must learn to accept. To start at ground level. With nothing. Not with nothing but. With nothing.' Or, as a twentieth-century latterday Romantic famously put the matter: with 'Nothing that is not there and the nothing that is'.

Chronology

1768   Maria Edgeworth born
Sterne dies
Encyclopædia Britannica published (1768–71)
Sterne, *A Sentimental Journey*

1769   Denis Diderot, *The Paradox of Acting* (1769–73, pub. 1830)
Napoleon Bonaparte born
James Watt's first patent for a steam engine
Sir Joshua Reynolds, *Discourses on Art* (1769–90)

1770   Captain James Cook lands at Botany Bay
Thomas Chatterton's suicide
Ludwig van Beethoven born
Georg William Friedrich Hegel born
James Hogg born
William Wordsworth born
Goldsmith, *The Deserted Village*

1771   Walter Scott born
Dorothy Wordsworth born
Tobias Smollett dies
James Beattie, *The Minstrel* (1771–4)
Henry Mackenzie, *The Man of Feeling*
Smollett, *Humphrey Clinker*

1772   Mansfield Decision denies a legal basis for slavery in England
Samuel Taylor Coleridge born
Johann Herder, *On the Origin of Language*

1773   Boston Tea Party
Francis Jeffrey born
James Mill born
Anna Laetitia Barbauld, *Poems*
Goldsmith, *She Stoops to Conquer*

1774   Donaldson vs. Becket re-establishes limits on copyright
Accession of Louis XVI of France
Robert Southey born
Goldsmith dies
John Wesley, *Thoughts on Slavery*
Johan Wolfgang von Goethe, *The Sorrows of Young Werther*
Hannah More, *The Inflexible Captive*

1775   War begun with American Colonies
Jane Austen born
Charles Lamb born
Joseph Turner born
Johnson, *A Journey to the Western Isles of Scotland*
Richard Brinsley Sheridan, *The Rivals*
Robert Wood, *An Essay on the Original Genius and Writings of Homer*
(posthumous)

1776   American Declaration of Independence
John Constable born
David Hume dies
Smith, *An Inquiry into the Nature and Causes of the Wealth of Nations*
Edward Gibbon, *The History of the Decline and Fall of the Roman Empire*
(1776–88)
Thomas Paine, *Common Sense*

1777   Thomas Chatterton, 'Rowley' Poems (posthumous)
Sheridan, *The School for Scandal*

1778   Franco-American Alliance signed at the Second
Continental Congress
Britain declares war on France
William Hazlitt born
Rousseau dies
Voltaire dies
Burney, *Evelina*
Rousseau, *Reveries of a Solitary Walker*

1779   Britain declares war on Spain, begins war with Mahrattas (1779–82)
David Hume, *Dialogues Concerning Natural Religion*
Johnson, 'Prefaces' to *The Works of the English Poets* (1779–81)
William Cowper and John Newton, *Olney Hymns*

1780   Anti-Catholic Gordon Riots erupt after the Catholic Relief Act (1778)
removes restrictions on Catholic land ownership, military
membership and inheritance
Yorkshire Petition seeks Parliamentary reform

1781   Warren Hastings removes Raja of Benares from power, confiscates
treasure of the Nabob of Oudh
Friedrich Schiller, *The Robbers*
Immanuel Kant, *Critique of Pure Reason*
Rousseau, *Confessions*

1782   Lord North's ministry falls
Independent Irish parliament under Henry Grattan
Frances Burney, *Cecilia*
Edward Cowper, *Poems*
Pierre Choderlos de Laclos, *Les Liaisons dangereuses* (*Dangerous Liaisons*)
Joseph Priestley, *A History of the Corruptions of Christianity*

1783   American independence recognized at Peace of Versailles
Fox–North (Whig–Tory) coalition in Parliament
William Pitt the Younger's first ministry
William Blake, *Poetical Sketches*
George Crabbe, *The Village*

1784   Pitt's India Act restricts the East India Company's autonomy
James Leigh Hunt born
Johnson dies

Diderot dies
Pierre Beaumarchais, *The Marriage of Figaro*
Capt. James Cook, *A Voyage to the Pacific Ocean*
More, *The Bas Bleu; or, Conversation*
Charlotte Smith, *Elegiac Sonnets*
Jacques-Louis David, *The Oath of the Horatii*

1785   Edmund Cartwright invents the power loom
Thomas de Quincey born
Thomas Love Peacock born
Cowper, *The Task*
Boswell, *A Journal of a Tour to the Hebrides*

1786   William Beckford, *Vathek*
Burns, *Poems, Chiefly in the Scottish Dialect* published at Kilmarnock
Mozart, *The Marriage of Figaro*
Helen Maria Williams, *Poems*

1787   Society for Effecting the Abolition of the Slave Trade founded
American Constitution signed
James Johnson, *The Scots Musical Museum* (1787–1803, with anonymous contributions from Burns)
Wollstonecraft, *Thoughts on the Education of Daughters*

1788   George III's first attack of insanity
Centenary of the Glorious Revolution
First Fleet establishes penal colony in New South Wales
George Gordon (later Lord) Byron born
More, *Slavery, a Poem*
Ann Yearsley, *A Poem on the Inhumanity of the Slave-Trade*
Charlotte Smith, *Emmeline*
Wollstonecraft, *Original Stories from Real Life*

1789   Convening of the Estates General to deal with financial crisis in France; the Tennis Court Oath; the Bastille falls; Declaration of the Rights of Man
Jeremy Bentham, *Introduction to the Principles of Morals and Legislation*
Blake, *Songs of Innocence* and *The Book of Thel*
William Bowles, *Fourteen Sonnets Written Chiefly on Picturesque Spots during a Journey*
Charlotte Brooke, *Reliques of Irish Poetry*
Olaudah Equiano, *The Interesting Narrative of the Life of Olaudah Equiano*
William Lisle Bowles, *Fourteen Sonnets, Elegiac and Descriptive*

1790   Adam Smith dies
Blake, *The Marriage of Heaven and Hell*
Burke, *Reflections on the Revolution in France*
Radcliffe, *A Sicilian Romance*
Wollstonecraft, *A Vindication of the Rights of Men*

1791	American Bill of Rights ratified
	Church and King Riots aimed at Joseph Priestley's beliefs concerning religious toleration and his political radicalism lead to the destruction of much property, including Priestley's house
	Louis XVI captured at Varennes
	Mozart dies
	Boswell, *The Life of Samuel Johnson*
	Burns, 'Tam o' Shanter'
	Paine, *The Rights of Man*
	Radcliffe, *The Romance of the Forest*
1792	Royal Proclamation against seditious writings issued by George III; *The Rights Of Man* banned and Paine charged with sedition
	Continental allies invade France; September massacres; declaration of the French Republic; imprisonment of French royal family
	Wordsworth in France
	Percy Shelley born
	Charlotte Smith, *Desmond*
	Samuel Rogers, *The Pleasures of Memory*
	Wollstonecraft, *A Vindication of the Rights of Woman*
1793	Trial and execution of Louis XVI; France declares war on Britain; the Terror; execution of Marie Antoinette
	Scottish treason trials
	Blake, *Visions of the Daughters of Albion* and *America: a Prophecy*
	William Godwin, *An Inquiry Concerning Political Justice*
	Wordsworth, *An Evening Walk* and *Descriptive Sketches*
1794	Suspension of Habeas Corpus in England; reformers jailed without charges
	Robespierre executed; end of the Terror; the Directorate
	Gibbon dies
	Blake, *Songs of Innocence and Experience*, *Europe: A Prophecy* and *The Book of Urizen*
	Coleridge, 'Monody on the Death of Chatterton'
	Erasmus Darwin, *Zoonomia*
	Godwin, *Caleb Williams*
	Thomas Paine, *The Age of Reason*
	Radcliffe, *The Mysteries of Udolfo*
1795	Britain gains Ceylon and Cape of Good Hope
	Seditious Meetings Act and Treasonable Practices Act ('Two Bills')
	Speenhamland system established to alleviate rural poverty through wage normalization
	Thomas Carlyle born
	John Keats born
	Boswell dies
	Macpherson dies

Blake, *The Book of Los* and *The Book of Ahania*
Coleridge, *Conciones ad Populum*
More, *Cheap Repository Tracts* (1795–8)
Friedrich Schiller, *Letters on Aesthetic Education* and *On Naive and Sentimental Poetry*
Southey, *Poems*

1796   Attempted French invasion of Ireland
The Insurrection Act in Ireland imposes harsh penalties (execution or transportation) for participating in unlawful oaths; permits searches for arms and punishments without trial
Napoleon's successful campaign in Italy
Burns dies
Robert Bloomfield, *The Farmer's Boy*
Burke, *A Letter to a Noble Lord* and *Two Letters on a Regicide Peace*
Burney, *Camilla*
Coleridge, *Poems on Various Subjects* and *The Watchman*
Johann Gottlieb Fichte, *Foundations of Transcendental Philosophy*
Mary Hays, *Memoirs of Emma Courtney*
Matthew Lewis, *Ambrosio, or The Monk*
Mary Robinson, *Sappho and Phaon*
Southey, *Joan of Arc*
Thelwall, *The Rights of Nature Against the Usurpation of Establishments*

1797   Wordsworth and Coleridge become neighbours in Somerset, begin their historic collaboration
Burke dies
Walpole dies
Wollstonecraft dies
Coleridge, *Poems*
Radcliffe, *The Italian*

1798   Irish Rebellion; French army lands in Ireland
The Battle of the Nile
The *Athenaeum* publishes fragments by founders Friedrich and A.W. Schlegel, and by Novalis, and Schleiermacher (1798–1800)
Baillie, *Plays on the Passions*
Charles Brockden Brown, *Wieland*
Coleridge, 'Fears in Solitude', 'France: an Ode' and 'Frost at Midnight'
Richard Lovell and Edgeworth, *Practical Education*
Godwin, *Memoirs of the Author of a Vindication of the Rights of Women*
Lamb, *Rosamund Gray*
Thomas Malthus, *An Essay on the Principle of Population*
Charlotte Smith, *The Young Philosopher*
Wollstonecraft, *Maria, or the Wrongs of Woman*
Wordsworth and Coleridge, *Lyrical Ballads* (published by Joseph Cottle in Bristol)

Wordsworth launches poem 'on his own mind', a work that will be posthumously published as *The Prelude* in 1850

1799   Combination Act passed, forbidding trade unions

French Directorate falls; Napoleon made First Consul

Brown, *Ormond, Arthur Merwyn* and *Edgar Huntley*

Thomas Campbell, *The Pleasures of Hope*

Mary Hays, *The Victim of Prejudice*

More, *Strictures on the Modern System of Education*

1800   Act of Union with Ireland

Cowper dies

Anne Bannerman, *Poems*

Edgeworth, *Castle Rackrent*

Mary Robinson, *Lyrical Tales*

Wordsworth and Coleridge, much-expanded second edition of *Lyrical Ballads*

1801   George III refuses to support Catholic Emancipation; Pitt resigns

Hogg, *Scottish Pastorals*

Southey, *Thalaba*

1802   Treaty of Amiens with France; Napoleon elected First Consul for life

Darwin dies

Edinburgh Review begins publication; Francis Jeffrey christens the 'Lake School of Poetry'

William Cobbett begins the *Political Register* (1802–35)

Bannerman, *Tales of Superstition and Chivalry*

Coleridge, 'Dejection: An Ode'

Edgeworth, *Belinda*

Lamb, *John Woodvil*

Amelia Opie, *Poems*

Scott, *Minstrelsy of the Scottish Border*

Wordsworth begins composition of what will become 'Ode: Intimations of Immortality'

1803   Capture of Delhi

Napoleon interns all British civilians in France; war resumed with France

Darwin, *The Temple of Nature*

Hazlitt, *An Essay on the Principles of Human Action*

1804   Henry Addington resigns; Pitt becomes Prime Minister

Napoleon becomes Emperor

Priestley dies

Kant dies

Blake, *Milton* and *Jerusalem*

Edgeworth, *Popular Tales*

Wordsworth completes the Immortality Ode

1805	Samuel Palmer born
	Godwin, *Fleetwood*
	Scott, *The Lay of the Last Minstrel*
	Southey, *Madoc*
	Turner, *The Shipwreck*
	Wordsworth completes the thirteen-book version of what will later be called *The Prelude*
1806	Lord Grenville becomes Prime Minister
	Pitt dies
	Fox dies
	Charlotte Smith dies
	Edgewoth, *Leonora*
	Sydney Owenson (Lady Morgan), *The Wild Irish Girl*
1807	Slavery abolished in England, but not in colonies; slave trade ended
	Resignation of Grenville; Portland becomes Prime Minister
	Hazlitt, *A Reply to the Essay on Population*
	Byron, *Hours of Idleness*
	Hegel, *The Phenomenology of Spirit*
	Charles and Mary Lamb, *Tales from Shakespear*
	Charles Maturin, *The Fatal Revenge*
	Thomas Moore, *Irish Melodies*
	Wordsworth, *Poems* (2 vols.)
1808	Spanish uprisings
	Hunt becomes editor of *The Examiner*
	Goethe, *Faust* pt I
	Felicia Browne (née Hemans), *Poems, England and Spain*
	Lamb, *Specimens of the English Dramatic Poets*
	Scott, *Marmion*
1809	Portland resigns; Perceval becomes Prime Minister
	Paine dies
	Alfred Tennyson born
	Charles Darwin born
	Quarterly Review founded
	Blake, *A Descriptive Catalogue*
	Byron, *English Bards and Scotch Reviewers*
	Campbell, *Gertrude of Wyoming*
	Coleridge, *The Friend*
	Edgeworth, *Tales of Fashionable Life* (1809–12)
	Wordsworth, *The Convention of Cintra*
1810	Scott, *The Lady of the Lake*
	Percy Shelley, *Zastrozzi*
	Southey, *The Curse of Kehama*
	Wordsworth, *A Topographical Description of the Country of the Lakes*

1811	Regency begins as George III is declared mentally unfit to rule
	Luddite movement begins in response to mechanization of the textile industry
	Austen, *Sense and Sensibility*
	Barbauld, *The Female Speaker*
	Hunt, 'The Feast of the Poets'
	Lamb, 'On the Tragedies of Shakespeare'
	Scott, *The Vision of Don Roderick*
	Mary Tighe, *Psyche* (privately printed 1805)
	Percy Shelley, *On the Necessity of Atheism*
1812	Spencer Perceval assassinated; Lord Liverpool becomes PM
	America declares war on Britain
	Robert Browning born
	Charles Dickens born
	Byron, *Childe Harold's Pilgrimage* (1812–18)
	Crabbe, *Tales in Verse*
	Edgeworth, *The Absentee*
	Percy Shelley, *An Address, to the Irish People*
1813	Edmund Kean's first appearance at Drury Lane
	Austen, *Pride and Prejudice*
	Byron, *The Bride of Abydos* and *The Giaour*
	Coleridge, *Remorse*
	Hogg, *The Queen's Wake*
	Scott, *Rokeby*
	Percy Shelley, *Queen Mab*
1814	Fall of Paris; Napoleon abdicates
	Wars with America ended by the Treaty of Ghent
	Austen, *Mansfield Park*
	Burney, *The Wanderer*
	Byron, 'Ode to Napoleon Bonaparte', *The Corsair* and *Lara*
	Scott, *Waverley*
	Percy Shelley, *A Refutation of Deism*
	Southey, *Roderick*
	Wordsworth, *The Excursion*
1815	Onset of industrial depression
	Corn Bill forbids the importation of foreign corn, favouring landlords
	Battle of Waterloo; Napoleon's surrender and exile; Restoration of Louis XVIII
	Holy Alliance between Russia, Austria and Prussia
	Byron, *Hebrew Melodies, The Siege of Corinth* and *Collected Poems*
	David Ricardo, *An Essay On the Low Price of Corn and the Profits of Stock*
	Scott, *The Lord of the Isles, The Field of Waterloo* and *Guy Mannering*
	Wordsworth, *The White Doe of Rylstone* and *Poems*

1816	Spa Fields riot dispersed, radical leaders jailed
	Byron leaves England
	Sheridan dies
	Austen, *Emma*
	Coleridge, 'Christabel', 'Kubla Khan', *Lay Sermons* and 'The Pains of Sleep'
	Hunt, 'Young Poets'
	Maturin, *Bertram*
	Peacock, *Headlong Hall*
	Scott, *The Antiquary*, *The Black Dwarf* and *Old Mortality*
	Shelley, *Alastor, or, the Spirit of Solitude; and other Poems*
	Southey, *The Lay of the Laureate*
	Wordsworth, 'Thanksgiving Ode'
1817	Jane Austen dies; her authorship is announced by her brother Henry
	The Shelleys join Byron in Italy
	Blackwood's Magazine founded
	Byron, *Manfred*
	Coleridge, *Biographia Literaria* and *Sibylline Leaves*
	Edgeworth, *Ormond* and *Harrington*
	Hazlitt, *The Characters of Shakespeare's Plays*
	Keats, *Poems*
	Scott, *Rob Roy*
	Southey, *Wat Tyler* (pirated)
1818	Habeas Corpus restored
	Austen, *Northanger Abbey* and *Persuasion*
	Hazlitt, *Lectures on the English Poets*
	Keats, *Endymion*
	Scott, *The Heart of Mid-Lothian*
	Mary Shelley, *Frankenstein* (anonymous)
	Percy Shelley, *The Revolt of Islam* and 'Ozymandias'
1819	British East India Company colonizes Singapore
	Peterloo Massacre occurs outside Manchester when a large public meeting calling for Parliamentary Reform is attacked by troops
	The so-called 'Six Acts' criminalize radical meetings and publications
	Queen Victoria born
	Walt Whitman born
	John Ruskin born
	Byron, *Don Juan* (1819–23)
	Campbell, *Specimens of the British Poets* (7 vols.)
	Crabbe, *Tales of the Hall*
	Felicia Hemans, *Tales and Historic Scenes in Verse*
	Keats composes his Great Odes
	Théodore Géricault, *The Raft of the Medusa*
	John Polidori, *The Vampyre*

Scott, *The Bride of Lammermoor*, *The Legend of Montrose* and *Ivanhoe*

Wordsworth, *Peter Bell* and *The Waggoner*

1820 Accession of George IV; 'Queen Caroline Affair' questions the legitimacy of Caroline's claim to the throne

Revolts in Spain, Portugal and Naples against the Bourbon monarchies

London Magazine founded

John Clare, *Poems Descriptive of Rural Life* and *The Village Minstrel*

Victor Hugo, *Les Orientales*

Keats, *Lamia, Isabella, The Eve of St Agnes, and other Poems* and *Hyperion*

Maturin, *Melmoth the Wanderer*

Peacock, 'The Four Ages of Poetry'

Percy Shelley, 'Ode to the West Wind', *Prometheus Unbound*, *The Cenci*

Scott, *The Abbott* and *The Monastery*

1821 Greek War of Independence begins

Keats dies

Napoleon dies

Joanna Baillie, *Metrical Legends of Exalted Characters*

John Constable, *The Hay Wain*

De Quincey, Confessions of an English Opium Eater

Hazlitt, *Table-Talk*

Percy Shelley, *A Defence of Poetry*, 'Adonais' and 'Epipsychidion'

Scott, *Kenilworth*

1822 Matthew Arnold born

Percy Shelley dies

Byron, Hunt and Percy Shelley publish in *The Liberal*

1823 Charles Babbage first presents a paper on a 'difference engine' to the Royal Society

War between France and Spain

Radcliffe dies

Felicia Hemans, *The Vespers of Palermo*, *The Siege of Valencia* and *Tales and Historic Scenes* (2nd edn)

Lamb, *Essays of Elia*

Mary Shelley, *Valperga*

Scott, *Quentin Durward*

1824 Byron dies

Beethoven, Symphony No. 9 (Choral)

Hogg, *Private Memoirs and Confessions of a Justified Sinner*

Owenson, *The Life and Times of Salvator Rosa*

Scott, *Redgauntlet*

Percy Shelley, *Posthumous Poems* (ed. Mary Shelley)

1825 Stock market crash (so-called 'Panic of 1825') leads to closure of several banks, financial crisis

Barbauld, *Works*
Hazlitt, *The Spirit of the Age, or, Contemporary Portraits*
Laetitia Elizabeth Landon, *The Troubadour: Poetical Sketches of Modern Pictures, and Historical Sketches*
Selections from Samuel Pepys' diary (1660–9) published

1826   James Fenimore Cooper, *The Last of the Mohicans*
Mary Shelley, *The Last Man*

1827   Greek Independence; Treaty of London puts pressure on Turks to free Greeks
Blake dies
Beethoven dies
Wordsworth, *Poems* (5 vols.)
Scott acknowledges authorship of the *Waverley* novels

1828   Repeal of the Test and Corporation Acts permits Dissenters to hold official posts
Turks agree to withdraw from Greece
University College London opens
Carlyle, 'Essay on Burns'
Coleridge, *Poetical Works*
Felicia Hemans, *Records of Woman with Other Poems*
Hunt, *Lord Byron and Some of His Contemporaries*

1829   Catholic Emancipation Act allows Catholics to hold official posts
Honoré de Balzac, *Les Chouans*
Carlyle, 'Signs of the Times'
James Mill, *An Analysis of the Phenomena of the Human Mind*
Peacock, *The Misfortunes of Elphin*

1830   Death of George IV and accession of William IV
July Revolutions in France
Christina Rossetti born
Hazlitt dies
Carlyle, 'On History'
Lamb, *Album Verses*
Charles Lyell, *Principles of Geology*
Palmer, *Coming from Evening Church*
Tennyson, *Poems, Chiefly Lyrical*

1831   Lord John Russell introduces a Reform Bill in House of Commons
Charles Darwin departs on the *Beagle*
Coleridge's last meeting with Wordsworth
Benjamin Disraeli, *The Young Duke*
Hegel, *Lectures on the Philosophy of History*
Peacock, *Crotchet Castle*
Mary Prince, *The History of Mary Prince*
Scott, *Castle Dangerous*

1832   The Representation of the People Bill (First Reform Act)
        passes in Parliament
        Scott dies
1834   Coleridge dies
        Lamb dies
        Thelwall dies

Bibliographies

CHAPTER 1 BIBLIOGRAPHY

Primary works

Aikin, John (ed.), *The Monthly Magazine and British Register* (1796–1826), 'Question: Ought Sensibility to be cherished, or repressed?', *The Monthly Magazine* 2 (October 1796).

Blair, Hugh, *Lectures on Rhetoric and Belles Lettres*, ed. Linda Ferreira-Buckley and S. Michael Halloran, Carbondale, IL: Southern Illinois University Press, 2005.

Sermons, vol. II, Edinburgh: W. Strahan, 1780.

Boruwlaski, Joseph, *Memoirs of the Celebrated Dwarf Joseph Boruwlaski, a Polish Gentleman*, 2nd edn, trans. S. Freeman (a revision of the translation by A.J. Des Carrières), Birmingham: J. Thompson, 1792.

Boswell, James, *Boswell's London Journal, 1762–63*, 2nd edn, ed. Frederick A. Pottle (Edinburgh: Edinburgh University Press, 2004).

Byron, Lord, *Poetical Works*, ed. Frederick Page, London: Oxford University Press, 1970.

Chambers, Ephraim, *Cyclopedia: or an Universal Dictionary of Arts and Sciences*, 5 vols., London: W. Strahan, 1778–88.

Cheyne, George, *The Natural Method of Cureing the Diseases of the Body and the Disorders of the Mind Depending on the Body*, London: Geo. Strahan, 1742.

Diderot, Denis, and Jean le Rond d'Alembert, *Encyclopédie, ou Dictionnaire raisonné des sciences, des arts, et des métiers*, vol. XV, Paris, 1765.

Home, Henry, Lord Kames, *Elements of Criticism*, ed. Peter Jones, Indianapolis: Liberty Fund, 2005.

Principles of Equity, 2nd edn, Edinburgh, 1767.

Hume, David, *A Treatise of Human Nature*, ed. David Fate Norton and Mary J. Norton, Oxford: Oxford University Press, 2000.

James, Robert, *A Medicinal Dictionary; including physic, surgery, anatomy, chymistry, and botany*, London: T. Osborne, 1743–5.

Johnson, Samuel, *The Rambler* (1750–2), ed. W.J. Bate, John M. Bullitt and L.F. Powell, *The Yale Edition of the Works of Samuel Johnson*, vol. III, New Haven, CT: Yale University Press, 1969.

Mackenzie, Henry, *et al.*, *The Lounger* (1785–7).

Mackintosh, James, journal entry for August and September 1811, BL Add. MSS. 132r–132v.

More, Hannah, *Strictures on the Modern System of Female Education. With a view of the principles and conduct prevalent among women of rank and fortune*, 2 vols., London: T. Cadell, 1799.

Orton, Job, *Memoirs of the Life, Character and Writings of the Late Reverend Philip Doddridge*, Salop, 1766.

Reeve, Clara, *The Progress of Romance*, 2 vols., Colchester, 1785.

Richardson, Samuel, *The Correspondence of Samuel Richardson*, ed. Anna Laetitia Barbauld, 6 vols., London, 1804.

Smith, Adam, *Lectures on Rhetoric and Belles Lettres*, ed. J. C. Bryce, Indianapolis: Liberty Fund, lecture XX, 1985.

    The Theory of Moral Sentiments, ed. D. D. Raphael and A. L. Macfie, Indianapolis: Liberty Fund, 1982.

Smollett, Thomas (ed.), *The Critical Review; or, Annals of Literature* (London, 1756–90).

Sterne, Laurence, *The Beauties of Sterne: including all his pathetic tales, and most distinguished observations on life*, London, 1782.

    A Sentimental Journey and Other Writings, ed. Ian Jack and Tim Parnell, Oxford: Oxford University Press, 2003.

Stuart, Gilbert, *The Beauties of the English Drama, digested alphabetically* [. . .], 4 vols., London, 1777.

The Monthly Review (1749–89), rpt ed. Benjamin Christie Nangle, 2 vols., Oxford: Clarendon Press, 1934. [Enfield, William, review of *Edwin and Julia* (anon.), *The Monthly Review* (April 1775).

Trotter, Thomas, *A View of the Nervous Temperament; being a practical Enquiry into the increasing prevalence, prevention and treatment of those diseases*, London: Longman, Hurst, Reeves & Orme, 1807.

Warton, Joseph, *Essay on the Writing and Genius of Pope*, London: M. Cooper, 1756.

Whytt, Robert, *Observations on the Nature, Causes, and Cure of those Disorders which have been commonly called Nervous, Hypochondriac, or Hysteric*, Edinburgh: J. Balfour, 1765.

Secondary works

Ellis, Markman, *The Politics of Sensibility: Race, Gender and Commerce in the Sentimental Novel*, Cambridge: Cambridge University Press, 1996.

Frye, Northrop, 'Towards Defining the Age of Sensibility', *ELH* 13 (1956), 144–52.

Johnson, Claudia L., *Equivocal Beings: Politics, Gender, and Sentimentality in the 1790s: Wollstonecraft, Radcliffe, Burney, Austen*, Chicago: University of Chicago Press, 1995.

McGann, Jerome, *The Poetics of Sensibility: A Revolution in Literary Style*, Oxford: Clarendon Press, 1996.

Mullan, John, *Sentiment and Sociability: The Language of Feeling in the Eighteenth Century*, Oxford: Clarendon Press, 1988.

Phillips, Mark Salber, *Society and Sentiment: Genres of Historical Writing in Britain, 1740–1820*, Princeton: Princeton University Press, 2000.

CHAPTER 2 BIBLIOGRAPHY

Primary works

Addison, Joseph, and Richard Steele, *The Spectator*, ed. and intro. Donald F. Bond, 5 vols., Oxford: Clarendon Press, 1965.

Barbauld, Anna, 'The Origin and Progress of Novel-Writing', in *The British Novelists*, London, 1810.

Beattie, James, *The Minstrel; or, The Progress of Genius. A Poem*, London: Printed for Edward and Charles Dilly, 1772, 1774.

The Works of James Beattie, ed. Roger Robinson, 10 vols., London and Bristol: Routledge/Thoemmes Press, 1996.

Blackwell, Thomas, *Letters Concerning Mythology*, London, 1748.

Blair, Hugh, *Lectures on Rhetoric and Belles Lettres*, London: W. Strahan & T. Cadell, 1783.

'A Critical Dissertation on the Poems of Ossian, the Son of Fingal' (1765), in Howard Gaskill (ed.), *The Poems of Ossian*, Edinburgh: Edinburgh University Press, 1996, pp. 343–401.

Boswell, James, *Boswell's Life of Johnson*, ed. George Birkbeck Hill, rev. L. F. Powell, 6 vols., Oxford: Oxford University Press, 1931; 1971.

Brooke, Charlotte, *Reliques of Irish Poetry*, Dublin: George Bonham, 1789.

Brown, Thomas, *Lectures on the Philosophy of the Human Mind*, 4 vols., Edinburgh: W. and C. Tait, 1820.

Burns, Robert, *The Poems and Songs of Robert Burns*, ed. James Kinsley, 3 vols., Oxford: Oxford University Press, 1968.

Chatterton, Thomas, *Selected Poems*, ed. Grevel Lindop, Manchester: Carcanet Press, 1986.

Coleridge, Samuel Taylor, *Poetical Works*, ed. E. H. Coleridge, Oxford: Oxford University Press, 1912.

Combe, William, *The First [Second and Third] Tour of Dr. Syntax*, New York: Routledge, 1878.

The Tour of Doctor Prosody, in Search of the Antique and the Picturesque, Through Scotland, the Hebrides, the Orkney and Shetland Isles, London, 1821.

Ellis, George, *Specimens of Early English Metrical Romances, Chiefly Written During the Early Part of the Fourteenth Century*, 3 vols., London: Longman, 1805.

Ferguson, Adam, *An Essay on the History of Civil Society, 1767*, ed. and intro. Duncan Forbes, Edinburgh: Edinburgh University Press, 1966.

Gray, Thomas, and William Collins, *Poetical Works*, ed. Roger Lonsdale, Oxford: Oxford University Press, 1977.

Grose, Francis, *The Antiquarian Repertory: a Miscellany, intended to preserve and illustrate several remains of old times*, 4 vols., London, 1775–84.

The Antiquities of England and Wales, 6 vols., London: S. Hooper, 1773–87.

The Antiquities of Ireland, 2 vols., London: Hooper & Wigstead, 1797.

The Antiquities of Scotland, 2 vols., London: Hooper & Wigstead, 1797.

A Classical Dictionary of the Vulgar Tongue, London, 1785.

Hazlitt, William, *Selected Essays of William Hazlitt*, ed. Geoffrey Keynes, London: Nonesuch Press, 1930.

Heber, Richard, *Bibliotheca Heberiana*, London, 1834.

Hecht, Hans (ed.), *Songs from David Herd's Manuscripts*, Edinburgh: William J. Hay, 1904.

Home, Henry, Lord Kames, *Essays upon Several Subjects Concerning British Antiquities*, Edinburgh: A Kincaid, 1747.

Hume, David, *The History of Great Britain*, 4 vols., Dublin: John Smith, 1755-7.

Hurd, Richard, *Letters on Chivalry and Romance*, London: A. Millar, 1762.

Jones, Edward, *Musical and Poetical Relicks of the Welsh Bards, Preserved by Tradition, and Authentic Manuscripts, From Remote Antiquity*, London, 1784.

Johnson, James (ed.), *The Scots Musical Museum*, Edinburgh, 1787-96.

Johnson, Samuel, *A Dictionary of the English Language*, 2 vols., London: Longman, 1755.

Keats, John, *The Letters of John Keats 1814-1821*, ed. Hyder Edward Rollins, 2 vols., Cambridge: Cambridge University Press, 1958.

Poetical Works, ed. H. W. Garrod, Oxford: Oxford University Press, 1956.

Lennox, Charlotte, *The Female Quixote, or, The Adventures of Arabella*, ed. Margaret Dalziel, Oxford: Oxford University Press, 1989.

Lonsdale, Roger (ed.), *Thomas Gray and William Collins: Poetical Works*, Oxford: Oxford University Press, 1977.

Mackenzie, Henry, *The Works of Henry Mackenzie*, 8 vols., intro. Susan Manning, London and Bristol: Routledge/Thoemmes Press, 1996.

Macpherson, James, *Fragments of Ancient Poetry, Collected in the Highlands of Scotland and Translated from the Galic or Erse Language*, Edinburgh: Hamilton and Balfour, 1760.

The Poems of Ossian, ed. Howard Gaskill, Edinburgh: Edinburgh University Press, 1996.

Maturin, Charles, *The Milesian Chief: A Romance*, London: Henry Colburn, 1812.

Peacock, Thomas Love, *The Novels of Thomas Love Peacock*, ed. David Garnett, London: Rupert Hart-Davis, 1948.

Percy, Thomas, *Reliques of Ancient English Poetry*, 3 vols., London: J. Dodsley, 1765.

Pennant, Thomas, *A Tour in Scotland, MDCCLXIX*, Perth: Melven Press, 1979.

Radcliffe, Ann, *Gaston de Blondeville, or, The Court of Henry III Keeping Festival in Ardenne: a romance of St. Alban's Abbey: a metrical tale with some poetical pieces, to which is prefixed a memoir of the author with extracts from her journals*, London: H. Colburn, 1826.

Ramsay, Allan, *The Ever Green: Being a Collection of Scots Poems*, Edinburgh, 1724.

The Tea-Table Miscellany, Edinburgh, 1723.

Reeve, Clara, *The Progress of Romance, Through Times, Countries and Manners . . .* , 2 vols. (in one), Colchester: W. Keymer, 1785.

'Preface to the Second Edition', in *The Old English Baron: A Gothic Story*, ed. James Trainer, Oxford: Oxford University Press, 1977.

Ritson, Joseph, *Ancient Engleish Metrical Romanceës*, London: Bulmer and Company, 1802.

Scott, Walter, *Ivanhoe*, ed. Graham Tulloch, Edinburgh: Edinburgh University Press, 1998.

Letters of Sir Walter Scott, ed. H. J. C. Grierson, 12 vols., Edinburgh: Edinburgh University Press, 1932.

Minstrelsy of the Scottish Border (1801–3; 1830), 4 vols., Edinburgh and London: William Blackwood and Sons, 1902, vol. IV, pp. 3–79.

The Miscellaneous Prose Works of Sir Walter Scott, 28 vols., Edinburgh: Robert Cadell, 1834–6.

'Preface' to 'The Lay of the Last Minstrel', in *The Poetical Works of Sir Walter Scott*, Oxford: Oxford University Press, 1917, p. 1.

'Report of the Committee of the Highland Society on the Poems of Ossian. Drawn up by Henry Mackenzie, Esq. And the Poetical Works of James Macpherson Esq.; with Notes and Illustrations by Malcolm Laing Esq.', *The Edinburgh Review* 6:12 (July 1805), 429–62.

'Specimens of early English Metrical Romances, chiefly written during the early Part of the Fourteenth Century. By George Ellis, Esq. And Ancient Engleish Metrical Romanceës, selected and published by Joseph Ritson', *Edinburgh Review* 7:14 (January 1806), 387–413.

Waverley; or, 'Tis Sixty Years Since (1814), ed. Claire Lamont, Oxford: Clarendon Press, 1981.

Sinclair, John, *The Statistical Account of Scotland 1791–1799*, Edinburgh: William Creech, 1791–9.

Smellie, William, *Account of the Institution and Progress of the Society of Antiquaries of Scotland*, Edinburgh: William Creech; London: Thomas Cadell, 1782.

Smollett, Tobias, *The Works of Tobias Smollett, M. D. with Memoirs of His Life / to which is prefixed a view of the commencement and progress of romance by John Moore*, 8 vols., London: B. Law, 1797.

Southey, Robert, *Madoc*, London: Longman, 1805.

Thomson, James, *The Seasons and the Castle of Indolence*, ed. James Sambrook, Oxford: Clarendon Press, 1972.

Walpole, Horace, *The Castle of Otranto*, ed. W. S. Lewis, Oxford: Oxford University Press, 1964.

Warton, Thomas, *The History of English Poetry from the Eleventh to the Seventeenth Century*, London: Ward, Lock and Tyler, 1872.

Watson, James, *A Choice Collection of Comic and Serious Scots Poems, Both Ancient and Modern*, Edinburgh: J. Watson, 1706–11.

Wordsworth, William, *Lyrical Ballads*, 2 vols., London: Longman, 1800.

Wordsworth's Literary Criticism, ed. Nowell C. Smith, Bristol: Bristol Classical Press, 1980.

Wordsworth's Poems of 1807, ed. Alun R. Jones, London: Macmillan, 1987.

Secondary works

Bann, Stephen, *The Inventions of History*, Manchester: Manchester University Press, 1990.

Romanticism and the Rise of History, New York: Twayne Publishers, 1995.

Benjamin, Walter, *Illuminations*, ed. and intro. Hannah Arendt, trans. Harry Zohn, London: Fontana, 1968; 1973.

Bronson, Bertrand H., *The Ballad as Song*, Berkeley & Los Angeles: University of California Press, 1969.

Buchan, David, *The Ballad and the Folk*, London: Routledge & Kegan Paul, 1972.

Dorson, Richard M., *The British Folklorists: A History*, London: Routledge & Kegan Paul, 1968.

Duff, David, *Romance and Revolution: Shelley and the Politics of Genre*, Cambridge: Cambridge University Press, 1994.

Ferris, Ina, 'Pedantry and the Question of Enlightenment History: The Figure of the Antiquary in Scott', *European Romantic Review* 13 (2002), 273–83.

　The Romantic National Tale and the Question of Ireland, Cambridge: Cambridge University Press, 2002.

Fielding, Penny, *Literature and Orality: Nationality, Culture, and Nineteenth-Century Scottish Fiction*, Oxford: Clarendon Press, 1996.

Fowler, David C., *A Literary History of the Popular Ballad*, Durham, NC: Duke University Press, 1968.

Freud, Sigmund, 'Notes upon a Case of Obsessional Neurosis (the "Rat Man")', *Case Histories*, vol. II, ed. Angela Richards, Harmondsworth: Penguin Books, 1979.

Gaskill, Howard (ed.), *Ossian Revisited*, Edinburgh: Edinburgh University Press, 1991.

Goode, Mike, 'Dryasdust Antiquarianism and Soppy Masculinity: The Waverley Novels and the Gender of History', *Representations* 82 (2003), 52–86.

Groom, Nick, *The Making of Percy's Reliques*, Oxford: Clarendon Press, 1999.

Jameson, Fredric, *The Political Unconscious: Narrative as a Socially Symbolic Act*, London: Methuen, 1981.

Johnston, Arthur, *Enchanted Ground: The Study of Medieval Romance in the Eighteenth Century*, London: Athlone Press, 1964.

Klancher, Jon, *The Making of English Reading Audiences, 1790–1832*, Madison, WI: University of Wisconsin Press, 1987.

Levine, Joseph M., *The Battle of the Books: History and Literature in the Augustan Age*, Ithaca and London: Cornell University Press, 1991.

Lewis, Jayne Elizabeth, *Mary Queen of Scots: Romance and Nation*, London and New York: Routledge, 1998.

Moore, Dafydd, 'Ossian, Chivalry and the Politics of Genre', *British Journal of Eighteenth-Century Studies* 23:1 (Spring 2000), 21–35.

Muensterberger, Werner, *Collecting: An Unruly Passion: Psychological Perspectives*, Princeton, NJ: Princeton University Press, 1994.

Piggott, Stuart, *Ruins in a Landscape: Essays in Antiquarianism*, Edinburgh: Edinburgh University Press, 1976.

Stafford, Fiona, 'Introduction: The Ossianic Poems of James Macpherson', in Howard Gaskill (ed.), *The Poems of Ossian*, Edinburgh: Edinburgh University Press, 1996, pp. v–xix.

Stafford, Fiona, and Howard Gaskill (eds.), *From Gaelic to Romantic: Ossianic Translations*, Amsterdam: Rodopi, 1998.

Stewart, Susan, *Crimes of Writing: Problems in the Containment of Representation*, New York & Oxford: Oxford University Press, 1991.

　On Longing: Narratives of the Miniature, the Gigantic, the Souvenir, the Collection, Durham, NC: Duke University Press, 1999.

Sutherland, Kathryn, 'The Native Poet: The Influence of Percy's Minstrel from Beattie to Wordsworth', *Review of English Studies* NS 33 (1982), 414–33.

Sweet, Rosemary, 'Antiquaries and Antiquities in Eighteenth-Century England', *Eighteenth-Century Studies* 34:2 (2001), 181–206.

'A Social Tie', unpublished paper presented to the University of Edinburgh History seminar, January 2001.

Trumpener, Katie, *Bardic Nationalism: The Romantic Novel and the British Empire*, Princeton, NJ: Princeton University Press, 1997.

Watkins-Jones, A., 'Bishop Percy, Thomas Warton, and Chatterton's Rowley Poems 1773–1790 (Unpublished Letters)', *PMLA* 50(1) (1935), 769–84.

CHAPTER 3 BIBLIOGRAPHY

Primary sources

Bentham, Jeremy, *Bentham's Political Thought*, ed. Bhikhu Parekh, New York: Barnes and Noble, 1973.

Deontology, Together with a Table of the Springs of Action, and the Article on Utilitarianism, ed. Amnon Goldworth, Oxford: Clarendon Press, 1983.

Burke, Edmund, *Philosophical Enquiry into the Origin of Our Ideas of the Sublime and the Beautiful*, ed. Adam Phillips, Oxford: Oxford University Press, 1998.

Coleridge, Samuel Taylor, *The Friend*, in *The Collected Works of Samuel Taylor Coleridge*, vol. IV, ed. Barbara E. Rooke, Princeton, NJ: Princeton University Press / London: Routledge and Kegan Paul, 1969.

Lay Sermons, in *The Collected Works of Samuel Taylor Coleridge*, vol. VI, ed. R.J. White, Princeton, NJ: Princeton University Press / London: Routledge and Kegan Paul, 1972.

'Letter to the Morning Post: 14 October 1800', *Essays on His Time in the Morning Post and the Courier*, in *The Collected Works of Samuel Taylor Coleridge*, vol. III, ed. David V. Erdman, Princeton, NJ: Princeton University Press / London: Routledge and Kegan Paul, 1978.

On the Constitution of the Church and State, in *The Collected Works of Samuel Taylor Coleridge*, vol. X, ed. John Colmer, Princeton, NJ: Princeton University Press / London: Routledge and Kegan Paul, 1976.

The Watchman, in *The Collected Works of Samuel Taylor Coleridge*, vol. II, ed. Bart Winer, Princeton, NJ: Princeton University Press / London: Routledge and Kegan Paul, 1970.

De Quincey, Thomas, *The Logic of Political Economy*, vol. X, *The Works of Thomas De Quincey*, New York: Hurd and Houghton, 1878.

Godwin, William, *The Enquirer: Reflections on Education, Manners, and Literature*, London: G. G. and J. Robinson, 1797.

Enquiry Concerning Political Justice, ed. Isaac Kramnick, Harmondsworth: Penguin, 1985.

Hume, David, 'Of the Populousness of Ancient Nations', in *Essays Moral, Political, and Literary*, Oxford: Oxford University Press, 1971.

Malthus, Thomas, *An Essay on the Principle of Population: Text, Sources and Background, Criticism*, ed. Philip Appleman, New York: Norton, 1976.

Mill, James, *Elements of Political Economy*, 2nd edn, London: Baldwin, Cradock, and Joy, 1824.

Ricardo, David, *The Principles of Political Economy and Taxation*, ed. Donald Winch, London: J. M. Dent and Sons, 1973.

Shelley, Percy Bysshe, 'Defense of Poetry', *Shelley's Poetry and Prose*, eds. Donald H. Reiman and Sharon B. Powers, New York: Norton, 1977.

'A Philosophical View of Reform', in *The Complete Works of Percy Bysshe Shelley*, vol. VII (New York: Scribner's, 1930).

Smith, Adam, *An Inquiry into the Nature and Causes of the Wealth of Nations*, Oxford: Clarendon Press, 1976.

Southey, Robert, Rev., *An Essay on the Principles* [sic] *of Population*, in *The Annual Review and History of Literature for 1803*, London: Printed for T. N. Longman and O. Rees by T. Gillet, 1804, vol. II, p. 296.

Essays, Moral and Political, 2 vols., London: John Murray, 1823.

Wordsworth, William, *Wordsworth's Poetical Works*, ed. Thomas Hutchinson and Ernest De Selincourt, Oxford and New York: Oxford University Press, 1936.

Secondary sources

Blaug, Mark, *Ricardian Economics: A Historical Study*, New Haven: Yale University Press, 1958.

Calleo, David P., *Coleridge and the Idea of the Modern State*, New Haven: Yale University Press, 1966.

Carnall, Geoffrey, *Robert Southey and His Age: The Development of a Conservative Mind*, Oxford: Clarendon Press, 1960.

Caygill, Howard, *Art of Judgement*, London: Basil Blackwell, 1989.

Colmer, John, *Coleridge: Critic of Society*, Oxford: Clarendon Press, 1959.

Connell, Philip, *Romanticism, Economics and the Question of Culture*, Oxford: Oxford University Press, 2001.

Deane, Seamus, *Foreign Affairs: Essays on Edmund Burke*, Notre Dame: University of Notre Dame Press, 2005.

Eastwood, David, 'Robert Southey and the Intellectual Origins of Romantic Conservatism', *English Historical Review* 411 (1989), 308–31.

'Ruinous Prosperity: Robert Southey's Critique of the Commercial System', *The Wordsworth Circle* 25 (1994), 72–6.

Ferguson, Frances, 'Malthus, Godwin, Wordsworth, and the Spirit of Solitude', in *Literature and the Body: Essays on Population and Persons*, ed. Elaine Scarry, Baltimore: Johns Hopkins University Press, 1988.

Foucault, Michel, *The Order of Things: An Archeology of the Human Sciences*, New York: Random House, 1970.

Furniss, Tom, *Edmund Burke's Aesthetic Ideology: Language, Gender, and Political Economy in Revolution*, Cambridge: Cambridge University Press, 1993.

Gallagher, Catherine, *The Industrial Reformation of English Fiction: Social Discourse and Narrative Form, 1832–67*, Chicago: University of Chicago Press, 1985.

Goodman, Kevis, *Georgic Modernity and British Romanticism: Poetry and the Mediation of History*, Cambridge: Cambridge University Press, 2004.

Guillory, John, *Cultural Capital: The Problem of Literary Canon Formation*, Chicago: University of Chicago Press, 1993.

Harrison, Gary, *Wordsworth's Vagrant Muse: Poetry, Poverty, and Power*, Detroit: Wayne State University Press, 1994.

Hilton, Boyd, *The Age of Atonement: The Influence of Evangelicism on Social and Economic Thought, 1785–1865*, Oxford: Clarendon Press, 1988.

   Corn, Cash, Commerce: Economic Policies of the Tory Governments, 1815–1830, Oxford: Oxford University Press, 1977.

Janowitz, Anne, *Lyric and Labor in the Romantic Tradition*, Cambridge: Cambridge University Press, 1998.

Kaufman, David, *The Business of Common Life: Novels and Classical Economics Between Revolution and Reform*, Baltimore: Johns Hopkins University Press, 1985.

Kennedy, William F., *Humanist versus Economist: The Economic Thought of Samuel Taylor Coleridge*, Berkeley: University of California Press, 1958.

Langer, Cary F., *The Coming of Age of Political Economy, 1815–1825*, New York: Greenwood, 1987.

Mahieu, D. L., 'Malthus and the Theology of Scarcity', *Journal of the History of Ideas* 40 (1978), 467–74.

Marshall, Alfred, *The Memorials of Alfred Marshall*, ed. Alfred Pigou, London: Macmillan, 1925.

McDonagh, Josephine, *De Quincey's Disciplines*, Oxford: Clarendon Press, 1994.

McLane, Maureen N., *Romanticism and the Human Sciences: Poetry, Population, and the Discourse of the Species*, Cambridge: Cambridge University Press, 2000.

Meek, Ronald, *Economics and Ideology and Other Essays: Studies in the Development of Economic Thought*, London: Chapman and Hall, 1967.

Mirowski, Philip (ed.), *Natural Images in Economic Thought: Markets Red in Tooth and Claw*, New York: Cambridge University Press, 1994.

O'Brien, D. P., *The Classical Economists*, Oxford: Clarendon Press, 1975.

Packham, Catherine, 'The Physiology of Political Economy: Vitalism and Adam Smith's Wealth of Nations', *Journal of the History of Ideas* 63 (2002), 465–81.

Pfau, Thomas, *Wordsworth's Profession: Form, Class, and the Logic of Early Romantic Cultural Production*, New York: Cambridge University Press, 1993.

Poovey, Mary, *A History of the Modern Fact: Problems of Knowledge in the Sciences of Wealth and Society*, Chicago: University of Chicago Press, 1998.

   Making a Social Body: British Cultural Formation, 1830–1864, Chicago: University of Chicago Press, 1995.

Shapiro, Barbara, *A Culture of Fact: England, 1550–1720*, Ithaca, NY: Cornell University Press, 2000.

Siskin, Clifford, *The Work of Writing: Literature and Social Change in Britain, 1700–1830*, Baltimore: Johns Hopkins University Press, 1998.

Spiegelman, Willard, *Majestic Indolence: English Romantic Poetry and the Work of Art*, New York: Oxford University Press, 1995.

Thompson, E. P., *Making of the English Working Class*, New York: Vintage, 1966.

Thompson, Noel W., *The People's Science: The Popular Political Economy of Exploitation and Crisis, 1816–1834*, Cambridge: Cambridge University Press, 1984.

Tribe, Keith, *Land, Labor and Economic Discourse*, London: Routledge and Kegan Paul, 1978.

Waterman, A. M. C., *Revolution, Economics and Religion, 1798–1833*, Cambridge: Cambridge University Press, 1991.

Williams, Raymond, *Keywords*, New York: Oxford University Press, 1985.

Winch, Donald, 'Higher Maxims: Happiness Versus Wealth in Malthus and Ricardo', in *That Noble Science of Politics*, ed. Stefan Collini, Donald Winch and John Burrow, Cambridge: Cambridge University Press, 1983.

　Riches and Poverty: An Intellectual History of Political Economy in Britain, 1750–1834, Cambridge: Cambridge University Press, 1996.

　ed., *The Principle of Political Economy and Taxation*, London: J. M. Dent and Sons, 1973.

CHAPTER 4 BIBLIOGRAPHY

Primary works

Anon., Letter to the *Gentleman's Magazine* 47 (March 1777), 105.

Anon., Review of *Essays Moral, Philosophical, and Political, Monthly Review* 46 (1772), 382–3.

Anon., Review of the *Waverley Novels* and *Tales of My Landlord, Edinburgh Review* (January 1832), 61–79.

Austen, Jane, *Emma*, ed. Terry Castle, World's Classics, Oxford: Oxford University Press, 1998.

Bacon, Francis, *Novum Organum With Other Parts of The Great Instauration* (1620), trans. Peter Urbach and John Gibson, Chicago: Open Court, 1994.

Barbauld, Anna Laetitia (ed.), *The British Novelists*, 50 vols., London: F. C. & J. Rivington, 1810.

Belcher, William, *Intellectual Electricity, Novum Organum of Vision, and Grand Mystic Secret . . . : being an experimental and practical system of the passions, metaphysics and religion, really genuine: accompanied with appropriate extracts from Sir Isaac Newton, Dr. Hartley, Beddoes, and others: with medical observations rising out of the subject / by a rational mystic*, London: Lee and Hurst, 1798.

Blake, William, *The Poetry and Prose of William Blake*, ed. David V. Erdman with commentary by Harold Bloom, New York: Doubleday, 1970.

Byron, George Gordon, Lord Byron, *Byron's Letters and Journals*, ed. Leslie A. Marchand, 13 vols., London: John Murray, 1973–94.

　Lord Byron: The Complete Poetical Works, ed. Jerome J. McGann, 7 vols., Oxford: Clarendon Press, 1980–93.

Coleridge, Samuel Taylor, *The Collected Works of Samuel Taylor Coleridge*, ed. Kathleen Coburn, 16 vols., Bollingen Series, vol. XIV, *Table Talk*, ed. Carl Woodring (2 vols.), Princeton, NJ and London: Princeton University Press/Routledge, 1971–2001.

Condillac, Abbé de, *Dictionnaire des synonymes*, ed. Georges LeRoy, *Oeuvres philosophiques de Condillac*, vol. III, Paris: Presses Universitaires de France, 1947–51.

　Philosophical Writings of Etienne Bonnot, Abbé de Condillac, trans. Franklin Philip and Harlan Lane, Hillsdale, NJ: Lawrence Erlbaum, 1982.

Godwin, William, *Things As They Are; or, The Adventures of Caleb Williams* (1794), ed. Maurice Hindle, London: Penguin, 1988.

Hays, Mary, *Appeal to the Men of Great Britain in Behalf of Women* (1798), ed. Gina Luria, New York: Garland, 1974.

Hume, David, *Enquiries Concerning the Human Understanding and Concerning the Principles of Morals*, ed. L. A. Selby-Bigge and P. H. Nidditch, 3rd edn, Oxford: Clarendon Press, 1902; 1975.

Johnson, Samuel, *A Dictionary of the English Language*, ed. Anne McDermott, 1st and 4th edns, CD-ROM, Cambridge: Cambridge University Press, 1996.

Kant, Immanuel, 'An Answer to the Question: "What is Enlightenment?"', in *Kant's Political Writings*, ed. Hans Reiss, Cambridge: Cambridge University Press, 1970, pp. 54–60.

Malthus, Thomas Robert, *An Essay on the Principle of Population* (1798), ed. Philip Appleman, New York: Norton, 1976.

Martin, Benjamin, *Philosophia Britannica or A New and Comprehensive SYSTEM of the Newtonian PHILOSOPHY, ASTRONOMY and GEOGRAPHY*, 2 vols., London: C. Micklewright and Co., 1747.

Rousseau, Jean-Jacques, *The Confessions of Jean-Jacques Rousseau Newly Translated into English*, 2 vols., Philadelphia and London: J. B. Lippincott Company, 1891.

Smith, Adam, *The Theory of Moral Sentiments* (1759), ed. D. D. Raphael and A. L. Macfie, Glasgow Edition of the Works and Correspondence of Adam Smith, 6 vols., Oxford: Clarendon Press, 1976.

Watts, Isaac, *The Improvement of the Mind: or, A supplement to the Art of logick: containing a variety of remarks and rules for the attainment and communication of useful knowledge, in religion, in the sciences, and in common life*, London: J. Brackstone, 1741.

Wordsworth, William, *Lyrical Ballads* (1798), ed. R. L. Brett and A. R. Jones, London: Methuen, 1965.

Wordsworth, William, and Wordsworth, Dorothy, *The Letters of William and Dorothy Wordsworth: The Early Years, 1787–1805*, ed. Ernest de Selincourt and rev. Chester L. Shaver, 2 vols., Oxford: Oxford University Press, 1967.

Secondary Works

Bazerman, Charles, *Shaping Written Knowledge: The Genre and Activity of the Experimental Article in Science*, Madison, WI: University of Wisconsin Press, 1988.

Born, Daniel, *The Birth of Liberal Guilt in the English Novel: Charles Dickens to H. G. Wells*, Chapel Hill, NC: University of North Carolina Press, 1995.

Brown, Marshall, 'Romanticism and Enlightenment', in *The Cambridge Companion to British Romanticism*, ed. Stuart Curran, Cambridge: Cambridge University Press, 1997, pp. 195–219.

Cassirer, Ernst, *The Philosophy of Enlightenment*, trans. Fritz C. A. Koelin and James P. Pettegrove, Boston: Beacon Press, 1955.

Foucault, Michel, 'What is Enlightenment?' in *The Foucault Reader*, ed. Paul Rabinow, New York: Pantheon, 1984, pp. 32–50.

Guillen, Claudio, *Literature as System: Essays Toward the Theory of Literary History*, Princeton, NJ: Princeton University Press, 1971.

Haney, John Louis (ed.), *Early Reviews of English Poets*, New York: Burt Franklin/Lenox Hill, 1904; 1970.

Haslett, Moyra, *Byron's* Don Juan *and the Don Juan Legend*, Oxford: Clarendon Press, 1997.

Hayes, Julie C., 'Fictions of Enlightenment: Sontag, Süskind, Norfolk, Kurzweil', *Bucknell Review: A Scholarly Journal of Letters, Arts and Sciences* 41:2 (1998), 21–36.

Kelly, Kevin, *Out of Control: The Rise of Neo-Biological Civilization*, Reading, MA: Addison-Wesley, 1994.

Knight, Isabel F., *The Geometric Spirit: The Abbé de Condillac and the French Enlightenment*, Yale Historical Publications, Miscellany 89, New Haven: Yale University Press, 1968.

McGann, Jerome, *The Romantic Ideology: A Critical Investigation*, Chicago: University of Chicago Press, 1983.

Reiman, Donald (ed.), *The Romantics Reviewed: Part A, The Lake Poets*, 2 vols., New York and London: Garland, 1972.

Simpson, David, *Romanticism, Nationalism, and the Revolt Against Theory*, Chicago: University of Chicago Press, 1993.

Siskin, Clifford, *The Historicity of Romantic Discourse*, New York: Oxford University Press, 1988.

'Novels and Systems', *Novel* 34:2 (Spring 2001), 202–15.

The Work of Writing: Literature and Social Change in Britain 1700–1830, Baltimore: Johns Hopkins University Press, 1998.

'The Year of the System', in *1798: The Year of Lyrical Ballads*, ed. Richard Cronin, Basingstoke: Macmillan, 1998, pp. 9–31.

Sullivan, Alvin (ed.), *British Literary Magazines: The Romantic Age, 1789–1836*, Westport, CT: Greenwood Press, 1983.

Williams, Raymond, *Writing in Society*, London: Verso, 1983.

Woof, Robert (ed.), *William Wordsworth: The Critical Heritage*, vol. I, London and New York: Routledge, 2001.

CHAPTER 5 BIBLIOGRAPHY

Primary works

Account of the Proceedings of a Meeting of the Inhabitants of Westminster, in Palace-Yard, Monday, Nov. 26, 1795, London: Citizen Lee [1795].

Account of the Proceedings of a Meeting of the London Corresponding Society, held in a Field near Copenhagen House, Monday, Oct. 26, 1795, London: Citizen Lee [1795].

Ambulator: or, a Pocket Companion in a Tour round London, London: J. Scratcherd, 1796.

[Bowles, John], *Letters of the Ghost of Alfred, addressed to the Hon. Thomas Erskine, and the Hon. Charles James Fox*, London: J. Wright, 1798.

The British Critic

Burke, Edmund, *The Works of the Right Honourable Edmund Burke*, new edn, 14 vols., London, F. and C. Rivington, 1815–22.

Burney, Fanny, *Camilla: or, A Picture of Youth*, ed. Edward A. and Lillian D. Bloom, Oxford: Oxford University Press, 1983.

Colquhoun, Patrick, *A Treatise on the Police of the Metropolis*, 3rd edn, London: C. Dilly, 1796.

O'Byrne, Alison, 'Walking, Rambling, and Promenading in Eighteenth-Century London: A Literary and Cultural History' (unpublished Ph.D. thesis, University of York, 2003).

Phillips, Michael, 'Blake and the Terror 1792–93', *The Library*, 6th ser., 26:4 (December 1994), 263–97.

Roper, Derek, *Reviewing before the Edinburgh*, London: Methuen, 1978.

Stevenson, John, 'The London Riots of 1794', *International Review of Social History* 16 (1971), 40–58.

Popular Disturbances in England 1700–1780, London and New York: Longman, 1979.

Tames, Richard, *Bloomsbury Past: A Visual History*, London: Historical Publications, 1993.

Taylor, George, *The French Revolution and the London Stage 1789–1805*, Cambridge: Cambridge University Press, 2000.

Winchester, Simon, *The Map that Changed the World*, London: Penguin, 2002.

CHAPTER 6 BIBLIOGRAPHY

Primary works

Burns, Robert, *The Poems and Songs of Robert Burns*, ed. James Kinsley, Oxford: Oxford University Press, 1968.

Hogg, James, *The Stirling/South Carolina Research Edition of the Collected Works of James Hogg*, 20 vols., ed. Douglas S. Mack and Gillian Hughes, Edinburgh: Edinburgh University Press, 1995–.

Macpherson, James, *The Poems of Ossian and Related Works*, ed. Howard Gaskill, Edinburgh: Edinburgh University Press, 1996.

Scott, Walter, *The Edinburgh Edition of the Waverley Novels*, 30 vols., ed. David Hewitt, Edinburgh: Edinburgh University Press, 1993–2008.

Secondary works

Brown, Ian, Thomas Owen Clancy, Susan Manning and Murray Pittock (eds.), *The Edinburgh History of Scottish Literature*, Vol. II: Enlightenment, Britain and Empire (1707–1918), Edinburgh: Edinburgh University Press, 2007.

Brown, Mary Ellen, *Burns and Tradition*, Urbana: Illinois University Press, 1984.

Carruthers, Gerard, and Alan Rawes (eds.), *English Romanticism and the Celtic World*, Cambridge: Cambridge University Press, 2003.

Chandler, James, *England in 1819: The Politics of Literary Culture and the Case of Romantic Historicism*, Chicago: University of Chicago Press, 1998.

Christensen, Jerome, *Romanticism at the End of History*, Baltimore: Johns Hopkins University Press, 2000.

Clive, John, *Scotch Reviewers: The Edinburgh Review 1802–1815*, Cambridge, MA: Harvard University Press, 1957.

Craig, Cairns, *Out of History: Narrative Paradigms in Scottish and English Culture*, Edinburgh: Polygon, 1996.

Craig, David, *Scottish Literature and the Scottish People, 1680–1830*, London: Chatto & Windus, 1961.

Crawford, Robert, *Devolving English Literature*, Oxford: Clarendon Press, 1992.

ed., *Robert Burns and Cultural Authority*, Edinburgh: University of Edinburgh Press, 1997.

The Scottish Invention of English Literature, Cambridge: Cambridge University Press, 1998.

Crawford, Thomas, *Burns: A Study of the Poems and Songs*, Edinburgh: Oliver and Boyd, 1960.

Society and the Lyric: A Study of the Song Culture of Eighteenth Century Scotland, Edinburgh: Scottish Academic Press, 1979.

Davis, Leith, *Acts of Union: Scotland and the Literary Negotiation of the British Nation 1707–1830*, Stanford: Stanford University Press, 1998.

Davis, Leith, Ian Duncan and Janet Sorensen (eds.), *Scotland and the Borders of Romanticism*, Cambridge: Cambridge University Press, 2004.

Demata, Massimiliano, and Duncan Wu (eds.), *British Romanticism and the Edinburgh Review: Bicentenary Essays*, New York: Palgrave, 2002.

Duff, David, and Catherine Jones (eds.), *Scotland, Ireland, and the Romantic Aesthetic*, Lewisburg, PA: Bucknell University Press, 2007.

Duncan, Ian, *Scott's Shadow: The Novel in Romantic Edinburgh*, Princeton: Princeton University Press, 2007.

Ferris, Ina, *The Achievement of Literary Authority: Gender, History, and the Waverley Novels*, Ithaca, NY: Cornell University Press, 1991.

Fielding, Penny, *Writing and Orality: Nationality, Culture, and Nineteenth-Century Scottish Fiction*, Oxford: Clarendon Press, 1996.

Fontana, Biancamaria, *Rethinking the Politics of Commercial Society: The Edinburgh Review 1802–1832*, Cambridge: Cambridge University Press, 1985.

Garside, Peter, and Rainer Schöwerling, *The English Novel 1770–1829: A Bibliographical Survey of Prose Fiction Published in the British Isles*, Vol. II: *1800–1829*, Oxford: Oxford University Press, 2000.

Gaskill, Howard (ed.), *Ossian Revisited*, Edinburgh: Edinburgh University Press, 1991.

Gifford, Douglas, *James Hogg*, Edinburgh: Ramsay Head, 1976.

Goslee, Nancy Moore, *Scott the Rhymer*, Lexington: University Press of Kentucky, 1988.

Gottlieb, Evan, *Feeling British: Sympathy and National Identity in Scottish and English Writing, 1770–1832*, Lewisburg: Bucknell University Press, 2007.

Hart, Francis Russell, *Lockhart as Romantic Biographer*, Edinburgh: Edinburgh University Press, 1971.

Hayden, John O. (ed.), *Scott: The Critical Heritage*, New York: Barnes & Noble, 1970.

Hechter, Michael, *Internal Colonialism: The Celtic Fringe in British National Development, 1536–1966*, Berkeley: University of California Press, 1975.

Hont, Istvan, and Michael Ignatieff (eds.), *Wealth and Virtue: The Shaping of Political Economy in the Scottish Enlightenment*, Cambridge: Cambridge University Press, 1983.

Hook, Andrew, *Scotland and America: A Study of Cultural Relations, 1750–1835*, Glasgow: Blackie, 1975.

Irvine, Robert, *Enlightenment and Romance: Gender and Agency in Smollett and Scott*, Oxford and Bern: Peter Lang, 2000.

Jones, Catherine, *Literary Memory: Scott's Waverley Novels and the Psychology of Narrative*, Lewisburg: Bucknell University Press, 2003.

Kidd, Colin, *Subverting Scotland's Past: Scottish Whig Historians and the Creation of an Anglo-British Identity, 1689–c. 1830*, Cambridge: Cambridge University Press, 1993.

Klancher, Jon, *The Making of English Reading Audiences, 1790–1832*, Madison, WI: University of Wisconsin Press, 1987.

Lee, Yoon Sun, *Nationalism and Irony: Burke, Scott, Carlyle*, New York: Oxford University Press, 2004.

Lincoln, Andrew, *Walter Scott and Modernity*, Edinburgh: Edinburgh University Press, 2007.

Livingston, Donald W., *Hume's Philosophy of Common Life*, Chicago: University of Chicago Press, 1984.

Low, Donald A. (ed.), *Robert Burns: The Critical Heritage*, London: Routledge and Kegan Paul, 1974.

Mack, Douglas S., *Scottish Fiction and the British Empire*, Edinburgh: Edinburgh University Press, 2006.

MacQueen, John, *The Enlightenment and Scottish Literature*, 2 vols., Edinburgh: Scottish Academic Press, 1982, 1989.

Manning, Susan, *Fragments of Union: Making Connections in Scottish and American Writing*, Houndmills: Palgrave, 2002.

   The Puritan-Provincial Vision: Scottish and American Literature in the Nineteenth Century, Cambridge: Cambridge University Press, 1990.

Maxwell, Richard, 'Inundations of Time: A Definition of Scott's Originality', *ELH* 68:2 (2001), 419–68.

McCracken-Flesher, Caroline, *Possible Scotlands: Walter Scott and the Story of Tomorrow*, New York: Oxford University Press, 2005.

McGuirk, Carol, *Robert Burns and the Sentimental Era*, Athens, GA: University of Georgia Press, 1985.

McIlvanney, Liam, *Burns the Radical: Poetry and Politics in Late Eighteenth-Century Scotland*, East Linton: Tuckwell, 2002.

McNeil, Ken, *Scotland, Britain, Empire: Writing the Highlands, 1760–1860*, Columbus, OH: Ohio University Press, 2007.

Miller, David, *Philosophy and Ideology in Hume's Political Thought*, Oxford: Clarendon Press, 1981.

Miller, Karl, *Cockburn's Millennium*, Cambridge: Harvard University Press, 1976.

   Electric Shepherd: A Likeness of James Hogg, London: Faber & Faber, 2004.

Millgate, Jane, *Walter Scott: The Making of the Novelist*, Edinburgh: Edinburgh University Press, 1984.

Murphy, Peter, *Poetry as an Occupation and an Art in Britain, 1760–1830*, Cambridge: Cambridge University Press, 1993.

Nairn, Tom, *The Break-Up of Britain: Crisis and Neo-Nationalism*, London: NLB, 1981.

Phillips, Mark Salber, *Society and Sentiment: Genres of Historical Writing in Britain, 1740–1820*, Princeton: Princeton University Press, 2000.

Pittock, Murray G. H., *The Invention of Scotland: The Stuart Myth and the Scottish Identity, 1638 to the Present*, London: Routledge, 1991.

Poetry and Jacobite Politics in Eighteenth-Century Britain and Ireland, Cambridge: Cambridge University Press, 1994.

Potkay, Adam, *The Fate of Eloquence in the Age of Hume*, Ithaca, NY: Cornell University Press, 1994.

Redekop, Magdalene, 'Beyond Closure: Buried Alive with Hogg's *Justified Sinner*', *ELH* 52:1 (Spring 1985), 159–84.

Robertson, Fiona, *Legitimate Histories: Scott, Gothic and the Authorities of Fiction*, Oxford: Clarendon Press, 1994.

Russett, Margaret, *Fictions and Fakes: Forging Romantic Authenticity, 1760–1845*, Cambridge: Cambridge University Press, 2006.

Schoenfield, Mark L., 'Butchering James Hogg: Romantic Identity in the Magazine Market', in *At the Limits of Romanticism: Essays in Cultural, Feminist, and Materialist Criticism*, ed. Mary Favret and Nicola Watson, Bloomington: Indiana University Press, 1994, pp. 207–24.

Sher, Richard B., *Church and University in the Scottish Enlightenment: The Moderate Literati of Edinburgh*, Princeton: Princeton University Press, 1985.

    The Enlightenment and the Book: Scottish Authors and their Publishers in Eighteenth-Century Britain, Ireland and America, Chicago: University of Chicago Press, 2006.

Simpson, Kenneth G., *The Protean Scot: The Crisis of Identity in Eighteenth-Century Scottish Literature*, Aberdeen: Aberdeen University Press, 1988.

Simpson, Kenneth G. (ed.), *Burns Now*, Edinburgh: Canongate, 1994.

Siskin, Clifford, *The Work of Writing: Literature and Social Change in Britain, 1700–1830*, Baltimore: Johns Hopkins University Press, 1998.

Skoblow, Jeffrey, *Double Tongue: Scots, Burns, Contradiction*, Newark, NJ: University of Delaware Press, 2001.

Sorensen, Janet, *The Grammar of Empire in Eighteenth-Century British Writing*, Cambridge: Cambridge University Press, 2000.

Stafford, Fiona, *The Sublime Savage: A Study of James Macpherson and the Poems of Ossian*, Edinburgh: Edinburgh University Press, 1988.

Stewart, Susan, *Crimes of Writing: Problems in the Containment of Representation*, New York: Oxford University Press, 1991.

Sutherland, Kathryn, 'Fictional Economies: Adam Smith, Sir Walter Scott and the Nineteenth Century Novel', *ELH* 54:1 (1987), 97–127.

Trumpener, Katie, *Bardic Nationalism: The Romantic Novel and the British Empire*, Princeton: Princeton University Press, 1997.

Welsh, Alexander, *The Hero of the Waverley Novels: With New Essays on Scott*, Princeton: Princeton University Press, 1992.

Wickman, Matthew, *The Ruins of Experience: Scotland's 'Romantick' Highlands and the Birth of the Modern Witness*, Philadelphia: University of Pennsylvania Press, 2007.

Wilt, Judith, *Secret Leaves: The Novels of Walter Scott*, Chicago: University of Chicago Press, 1985.

Womack, Peter, *Improvement and Romance: Constructing the Myth of the Highlands*, Basingstoke: Macmillan, 1989.

Youngson, A. J., *The Making of Classical Edinburgh, 1750–1840*, Edinburgh: Edinburgh University Press, 1966.

CHAPTER 7 BIBLIOGRAPHY

Primary texts

Ashfield, Andrew, and Peter de Bolla (eds.), 'Irish Perspectives', in *The Sublime: A Reader in British Eighteenth-Century Aesthetic Theory*, Cambridge: Cambridge University Press, 1996.

Barry, James, *The Works of James Barry, Esq., Historical Painter*, London: T. Cadell and W. Davies, 1809.

Brooke, Charlotte, *Reliques of Irish Poetry*, Dublin: George Bonham, 1989.

Bunting, Edward, *A General Collection of the Ancient Irish Music*, Dublin: W. Power, 1796.

Burke, Edmund, *A Philosophical Enquiry into the Origin of our Ideas of the Sublime and Beautiful* (1757), London: Routledge & Kegan Paul, 1958.

    Reflections on the Revolution in France (1790), ed. Conor Cruise O'Brien, Harmondsworth: Penguin, 1975.

Croker, Thomas Crofton, *Researches in the South of Ireland, Illustrative of the Scenery, Architectural Remains, and the Manners and Superstitions of the Peasantry* (1824), intro. Kevin Danagher, Dublin: Irish University Press, 1968.

Edgeworth, Maria, *The Absentee* (1812), ed. W. J. McCormack and Kim Walker, London: Penguin, 1987.

    Castle Rackrent, an Hibernian Tale (1800), ed. George Watson, Oxford: Oxford University Press, 1964.

    Ormond (1817), ed. Claire Connolly, London: Penguin, 2000.

Hardiman, James, *Irish Minstrelsy, or Bardic Remains of Ireland* (1831), Shannon: Irish University Press, 1971.

Mangan, James Clarence, 'Autobiography', in *Prose*, Dublin: Irish Academic Press, 2003.

    Selected Poems of James Clarence Mangan, ed. Jacques Chuto *et al.*, Dublin: Irish Academic Press, 2003.

Maturin, Charles Robert, *Melmoth the Wanderer, A Tale* (1820), ed. Althea Hayter, Harmondsworth: Penguin, 1977.

    The Milesian Chief: A Romance (1812), New York: Garland Publishing, 1979.

    The Wild Irish Boy (1808), New York: Garland Publishing, 1979.

Moore, Thomas, 'Prefatory Letter on Music', to *Irish Melodies* (1807–28), *The Poetical Works of Thomas Moore*, London: Frederick Warne, n.d.

[Moore, Thomas], *Memoirs of Captain Rock, the Celebrated Irish Chieftain*, London: Longman, 1824.

Morgan, Lady, *Florence McCarthy, A National Tale*, London: H. Colborn, 1818.

    The O'Briens and the O'Flahertys: A National Tale (1827), intro. Mary Campbell, London: Pandora Press, 1988.

    O'Donnel, A National Tale (1814), London: Downey & Co., 1895.

Owenson, Sydney, [Lady Morgan], *The Wild Irish Girl* (1806), ed. Claire Connolly and Stephen Copley, London: Pickering & Chatto, 2000.

Toland, John, 'A Specimen of the Critical History of the Celtic Religion and Learning, Containing an Account of the Druids', in *A Collection of Several Pieces of Mr. John Toland*, London, 1726.

Walker, Joseph Cooper, *Historical Memoirs of the Irish Bards*, London: T. Payne & Son, 1786.

Zimmerman, Georges Denis, *Songs of Irish Rebellion: Political Street Ballads and Rebel Songs*, Dublin: Figgis, 1967.

Secondary works

Connolly, Claire, 'Irish Romanticism, 1800–1830', in Margaret Kelleher and Philip O'Leary (eds.), *The Cambridge History of Irish Literature*, vol. I, Cambridge: Cambridge University Press, 2006.

Deane, Seamus, *Strange Country: Modernity and Nationhood in Irish Writing Since 1790*, Oxford: Clarendon Press, 1997.

Dunne, Tom, 'Haunted by History: Irish Romantic Writing, 1800–1850', in Roy Porter and Mikulas Teich (eds.), *Romanticism in National Context*, Cambridge: Cambridge University Press, 1988.

Ferris, Ina, *The Romantic National Tale and the Question of Ireland*, Cambridge: Cambridge University Press, 2002.

Gibbons, Luke, *Gaelic Gothic: Race, Colonization and Irish Culture*, Dublin: Attic Press, 2004.

Kilfeather, Siobhan, 'Gothic Novel', in J. W. Foster (ed.), *The Cambridge Companion to the Irish Novel*, Cambridge: Cambridge University Press, 2006.

Killeen, Jarlath, *Gothic Ireland: Horror and the Irish Anglican Imagination in the Long Eighteenth Century*, Dublin: Four Courts Press, 2005.

Leerssen, Joep, *Remembrance and Imagination: Patterns in the Historical and Literary Representation of Ireland in the Nineteenth Century*, Cork: Cork University Press, 1997.

Lloyd, David, *Nationalism and Minor Literature: James Clarence Mangan and the Emergence of Irish Cultural Nationalism*, Berkeley: University of California Press, 1987.

McCormack, W. J., *From Burke to Beckett: Ascendancy, Tradition and Betrayal in Irish Literary History*, Cork: Cork University Press, 1997.

Trumpener, Katie, *Bardic Nationalism: The Romantic Novel and the British Empire*, Princeton: Princeton University Press, 1997.

Vance, Norman, 'Romanticism in Ireland: 1800–1837', in *Irish Literature Since 1800*, London: Longman, 2002.

CHAPTER 8 BIBLIOGRAPHY

Primary works

Barbauld, Anna Laetitia, *The Works of Anna Laetitia Barbauld, with a Memoir by Lucy Aikin*, 2 vols., Boston: David Reed, 1826.

Behn, Aphra, *The Works of Aphra Behn*, ed. Janet Todd, Columbus: Ohio State University Press, 1996.

Blair, Hugh, *Sermons*, London: T. Allman, 1832.

Britton, John, *Sheridan and Kotzebue*, London, 1799.

Bulwer, Edward Lytton, *England and the English*, ed. Stanley Meacham, Chicago and London: University of Chicago Press, 1970.

Burke, Edmund, *Reflections on the Revolution in France*, ed. Conor Cruise O'Brien, Harmondsworth: Penguin, 1976.

Carlyle, Thomas, *Critical and Miscellaneous Essays*, 5 vols., London: Chapman and Hall, 1905.

De Quincey, Thomas, *The Collected Writings of Thomas De Quincey*, 14 vols., ed. David Masson, Edinburgh: Adam and Charles Black, 1890.

De Staël, Germaine, *Germany*, 3 vols., London: John Murray, 1813.

Gibbon, Edward, *The History of the Decline and Fall of the Roman Empire*, 7 vols., London: Bell and Daldy, 1872.

Hazlitt, William, *The Complete Works of William Hazlitt*, 21 vols., ed. P. P. Howe, New York: AMS Press, 1967.

Imlay, Gilbert, *The Emigrants*, ed. Robert R. Hare, Gainesville, FL: Scholars' Facsimiles and Reprints, 1964.

Moore, Thomas, *The Poetical Works of Thomas Moore*, ed. A. D. Godley, Oxford: Oxford University Press, 1915.

Murphy, Arthur (trans.), *Tacitus: Historical Works*, 2 vols., London and New York: Dent and Dutton, 1907.

Preston, William, 'Reflections on the Peculiarity of Style and Manner in the Late German Writers whose Works have appeared in English, and on the Tendency of their Productions', *Transactions of the Royal Irish Academy*, vol. VIII, Dublin, 1802.

Price, Richard, *Political Writings*, ed. D. O. Thomas, Cambridge: Cambridge University Press, 1991.

Reid, William Hamilton, *The Rise and Dissolution of Infidel Societies in this Metropolis*, London: J. Hatchard, 1800.

Shelley, Percy Bysshe, *The Esdaile Notebook*, ed. Kenneth Neil Cameron, London: Faber and Faber, 1964.

Thelwall, John, *The Politics of English Jacobinism: The Writings of John Thelwall*, ed. Gregory Claeys, University Park, PA: Penn State University Press, 1995.

Warton, Thomas, *The History of English Poetry*, ed. Richard Price, 3 vols., London: Thomas Tegg, 1840.

Wordsworth, William, *The Prose Works of William Wordsworth*, 3 vols., ed. W. J. B. Owen and Jane Worthington Smyser, Oxford: Clarendon Press, 1974.

Young, Arthur, *The Example of France, a Warning to Britain*, Dublin, 1793.

Secondary works

Anderson, Benedict, *Imagined Communities: Reflections on the Origins and Spread of Nationalism*, rev. edn, London and New York: Verso, 1991.

Bainbridge, Simon, *Napoleon and English Romanticism*, Cambridge: Cambridge University Press, 1995.

Blackall, Eric A., *The Emergence of German as a Literary Language, 1770–1775*, 2nd edn, Ithaca and London: Cornell University Press, 1978.

Butler, Marilyn, *Romantics, Rebels and Reactionaries: English Literature and its Background, 1760–1830*, Oxford and New York: Oxford University Press, 1982.

Cafarelli, Annette, 'Rousseau and British Romanticism: Women and the Legacy of Male Radicalism', in *Cultural Interactions in the Romantic Age: Critical Essays in Romantic Literature*, ed. Gregory Maertz, Albany: SUNY Press, 1998.

Carlson, Julie A., *In the Theatre of Romanticism: Coleridge, Nationalism, Women*, Cambridge: Cambridge University Press, 1994.

Chandler, James K., *England in 1819: The Politics of Literary Culture and the Case of Romantic Historicism*, Chicago and London: University of Chicago Press, 1998.

  Wordsworth's Second Nature: A Study of the Poetry and Politics, Chicago and London: University of Chicago Press, 1984.

Colley, Linda, *Britons: Forging the Nation, 1707–1837*, New Haven and London: Yale University Press, 1992.

Craciun, Adriana, and Kari Lokke (eds.), *Rebellious Hearts: British Women Writers and the French Revolution*, Albany, NY: SUNY Press, 2001.

Crawford, Robert, *Devolving English Literature*, Oxford: Clarendon Press, 1992.

Dart, Gregory, *Rousseau, Robespierre and English Romanticism*, Cambridge: Cambridge University Press, 1999.

Deane, Seamus, *The French Revolution and Enlightenment in England, 1789–1832*, Cambridge, MA and London: Harvard University Press, 1988.

Duffy, Edward, *Rousseau in England: The Context for Shelley's Critique of the Enlightenment*, Berkeley, Los Angeles, London: University of California Press, 1979.

Durey, Michael, *Transatlantic Radicals and the Early American Republic*, Lawrence, KS: University Press of Kansas, 1997.

Gamer, Michael, *Romanticism and the Gothic: Genre, Reception, and Canon Formation*, Cambridge: Cambridge University Press, 2000.

Helgerson, Richard, *Forms of Nationhood: The Elizabethan Writing of England*, Chicago and London: University of Chicago Press, 1992.

Hill, Christopher, 'The Norman Yoke', in *Puritanism and Revolution: Studies in the Interpretation of the English Revolution of the Seventeenth Century*, London: Secker and Warburg, 1958.

Hobsbawm, E. J., *Nations and Nationalism Since 1780: Programme, Myth, Reality*, Cambridge: Cambridge University Press, 1990.

Kelly, Gary, *Women, Writing and Revolution, 1790–1827*, Oxford: Clarendon Press, 1993.

Kohn, Hans, *Nationalism, Its Meaning and History*, rev. edn, New York: Van Nostrand, 1971.

Lease, Benjamin, *Anglo-American Encounters: England and the Rise of American Literature*, Cambridge: Cambridge University Press, 1981.

McDonald, Joan, *Rousseau and the French Revolution, 1762–1791*, London: Athlone Press, 1965.

Mitchell, W. J. T., 'Influence, Autobiography and Literary History: Rousseau's *Confessions* and Wordsworth's *The Prelude*', ELH 57 (1990), 643–64.

Newman, Gerald, *The Rise of English Nationalism: A Cultural History, 1740–1830*, New York: St Martin's Press, 1987.

Roddier, Henri, *J.-J. Rousseau en Angleterre au XVIIIe siècle*, Paris, 1947.

Ruland, Richard (ed.), *The Native Muse: Theories of American Literature*, Vol. I, New York: Dutton, 1976.

Segeberg, Hanno, 'Germany', in *Nationalism in the Age of the French Revolution*, ed. Otto Dann and John Dinwiddy, London and Ronceverte: Hambledon Press, 1988.

Simpson, David, *The Politics of American English, 1776–1850*, Oxford and London: Oxford University Press, 1986.

  Romanticism, Nationalism, and the Revolt Against Theory, Chicago and London: University of Chicago Press, 1993.

Stokoe, F. W., *German Influence in the English Romantic Period, 1788–1818. With Special Reference to Scott, Coleridge, Shelley and Byron* (1926), New York: Russell and Russell, 1963.

Surel, Jeannine, 'John Bull', in *Patriotism: The Making and Unmaking of British National Identity*, vol. III, ed. Raphael Samuel, London and New York: Routledge, 1989.

Trumpener, Katie, *Bardic Nationalism: The Romantic Novel and the British Empire*, Princeton: Princeton University Press, 1997.

Voisine, Jacques, *J.-J. en Angleterre à l'époque romantique: les écrits autobiographiques et la légende*, Paris, 1956.

Watson, Nicola J., *Revolution and the Form of the British Novel, 1790–1825: Intercepted Letters, Interrupted Seductions*, Oxford: Clarendon Press, 1994.

Weinbrot, Howard D., *Britannia's Issue: The Rise of British Literature from Dryden to Ossian*, Cambridge: Cambridge University Press, 1993.

Wellek, René, *Immanuel Kant in England, 1793–1838*, Princeton: Princeton University Press, 1931.

CHAPTER 9 BIBLIOGRAPHY

Primary works

Byron, George Gordon Lord, *Byron: The Complete Poetical Works*, 7 vols., ed. Jerome McGann, Oxford: Clarendon Press, 1980–92.

  Byron's Letters and Journals, 13 vols., ed. Leslie Marchand, Cambridge, MA: Harvard University Press, 1973–94.

Guiccioli, Teresa, *Lord Byron's Life in Italy*, trans. Michael Rees, ed. Peter Cochran, Newark, DE: University of Delaware Press, 2005.

Hemans, Felicia, *Felicia Hemans: Selected Poems, Letters, Reception Materials*, ed. Susan J. Wolfson, Princeton: Princeton University Press, 2000.

  Poetical Works, Philadelphia: Grigg and Elliott, 1844.

Hunt, Leigh, *Autobiography*, ed. J. E. Morpurgo, London: Cresset, 1969.

  Stories from the Italian Poets, Paris: Galignani, 1846.

  'Young Poets', *The Examiner*, 1 December 1816.

Jameson, Anna, *Diary of an Ennuyée*, Boston: Osgood, 1875.

Keats, John, *Complete Poems*, ed. Jack Stillinger, Cambridge, MA: Harvard University Press, 1982.

Novello-Cowden Clarke Collection, The, Leeds: Brotherton Library, 1955.

Rogers, Samuel, *Italian Journal*, ed. J. R. Hale, London: Faber and Faber [1956].

Scott, Sir Walter, *Prose Works*, 3 vols., Edinburgh: Cadell, 1841.

Shelley, Mary, *The Mary Shelley Reader*, ed. Betty T. Bennett and Charles E. Robinson, Oxford: Oxford University Press, 1990.

Valperga: Or, the Life and Adventures of Castruccio, Prince of Lucca, ed. Michael Rossington, Oxford: Oxford University Press, 2000.

Shelley, Percy Bysshe, *Complete Poetical Works*, ed. Thomas Hutchinson, London: Oxford University Press, 1929.

Poetry and Prose, ed. Donald H. Reiman and Neil Fraistat, New York: Norton, 2002.

Sismondi, J. C. L. de, *History of the Italian Republics*, London: Longman, 1832.

Staël, Germaine de, *Corinne, or Italy*, trans. Avriel H. Goldberger, New Brunswick: Rutgers University Press, 1987.

Wordsworth, William, *The Poems*, 2 vols., ed. John O. Hayden, Harmondsworth: Penguin, 1982.

Secondary works

Bieri, James, *Percy Bysshe Shelley: A Biography: Exile of Unfulfilled Renown, 1816–1822*, Newark, DE: University of Delaware Press, 2005.

Brand, C. P., *Italy and the English Romantics*, Cambridge: Cambridge University Press, 1957.

Butler, Marilyn, *Romantics, Rebels and Reactionaries: English Literature and its Background 1760–1830*, Oxford: Oxford University Press, 1982.

Cavaliero, Roderick, *Italia Romantica: English Romantics and Italian Freedom*, London, I. B. Tauris, 2005.

Chapman, Alison and Jane Stabler (eds.), *Unfolding the South: Nineteenth-Century British Women Writers and Artists in Italy*, Manchester: Manchester University Press, 2003.

Cox, Jeffrey N., *Poetry and Politics in the Cockney School: Keats, Shelley, Hunt and their Circle*, Cambridge: Cambridge University Press, 1998.

Dekker, George, *The Fictions of Romantic Tourism: Radcliffe, Scott and Mary Shelley*, Stanford: Stanford University Press, 2005.

Doody, Margaret, *Tropic of Venice*, Philadelphia: University of Pennsylvania Press, 2006.

Eglin, John, *Venice Transfigured: The Myth of Venice in British Culture, 1660–1797*, New York: Palgrave, 2001.

Eisler, Benita, *Byron: Child of Passion, Fool of Fame*, New York: Knopf, 1999.

Gilbert, Sandra M., 'From *Patria* to *Matria*: Elizabeth Barrett Browning's Risorgimento', in *Victorian Women Poets: A Critical Reader*, ed. Angela Leighton, Oxford: Blackwell, 1996.

Grosskurth, Phyllis, *Byron: The Flawed Angel*, London: Hodder and Stoughton, 1997.

Holmes, Richard, *Coleridge: Darker Reflections, 1804–1834*, New York: Pantheon, 1998.

Hornsby, Clare (ed.), *The Impact of Italy: The Grand Tour and Beyond*, London: British School of Rome, 2000.

Moe, Nelson, *The View from Vesuvius: Italian Culture and the Southern Question*, Berkeley: University of California Press, 2002.

Mizukoshi, Ayumi, *Keats, Hunt and the Aesthetics of Pleasure*, Basingstoke: Palgrave, 2001.

O'Connor, Maura, *The Romance of Italy and the English Political Imagination*, New York: St Martin's, 1998.

Pascoe, Judith, *Romantic Theatricality: Gender, Poetry and Spectatorship*, Ithaca: Cornell University Press, 1997.

Pite, Ralph, *The Circle of our Vision: Dante's Presence in English Romantic Poetry*, Oxford: Oxford University Press, 1994.

Priestman, Martin, *Romantic Atheism: Poetry and Freethought, 1780–1830*, Cambridge: Cambridge University Press, 1999.

Roe, Nicholas, *Leigh Hunt: Life, Poetics, Politics*, London: Routledge, 2003.

St Clair, William, *That Greece Might Still Be Free: The Philhellenes in the War of Independence*, London: Oxford University Press, 1972.

Siegel, Jonah, *The Haunted Museum: Longing, Travel and the Art-romance Tradition*, Princeton: Princeton University Press, 2005.

Thompson, James R., *Leigh Hunt*, Boston: Twayne, 1977.

Watson, Lorna, *The Errant Pen: Manuscript Journals of British Travellers to Italy*, La Spezia: Agorà, 2000.

Zuccato, Edoardo, *Coleridge in Italy*, Cork: Cork University Press, 1996.

CHAPTER 10 BIBLIOGRAPHY

Primary works

Cary, John, *Cary's New Itinerary*, London: John Cary, 1817.

Cobbett, William, *Rural Rides in the Counties of Surrey, Kent, Sussex, Hampshire, Wiltshire, Gloucestershire, Herefordshire, Worcestershire, Somersetshire, Oxfordshire, Berkshire, Essex, Suffolk, Norfolk, and Hertfordshire: with economical and political observations relative to matters applicable to, and illustrated by, the state of those counties respectively*, London: W. Cobbett, 1830.

Drayton, Michael, *Poly-Olbion*, Part 1 and Part 2, London: Humphrey Lownes, 1612, 1622.

Hunt, John Dixon and Peter Willis (eds.), *The Genius of the Place: The English Landscape Garden, 1620–1820*, New York: Harper & Row, 1975.

Secondary works

Bachelard, Gaston, *The Poetics of Space*, Boston: Beacon Press, 1964.

Bate, Jonathan, *Romantic Ecology*, London: Routledge, 1991.

Copley, Stephen and Peter Garside (eds.), *The Politics of the Picturesque: Literature, Landscape, and Aesthetics since 1770*, Cambridge: Cambridge University Press, 1994.

Daniels, Stephen, *Fields of Vision: Landscape Imagery and National Identity in England and the United States*, Princeton: Princeton University Press, 1993.

Erdman, David, *Blake: Prophet Against Empire*, Princeton: Princeton University Press, 1954.

Everitt, Alan, *Landscape and Community in England*, London: The Hambledon Press, 1985.

Hoskins, W. G., *The Making of the English Landscape*, London: Hodder and Stoughton, 1955.

Hunt, John Dixon, *The Figure in the Landscape: Poetry, Painting, and Gardening during the Eighteenth Century*, Baltimore: Johns Hopkins University Press, 1976.

Kolodny, Annette, *The Lay of the Land*, Chapel Hill: University of North Carolina, 1975.

McGann, Jerome, *The Romantic Ideology*, Chicago: University of Chicago Press, 1985.

Mitchell, W.J.T. (ed.), *Landscape and Power*, 2nd edn, Chicago: University of Chicago Press, 2002.

Modiano, Raimonda, 'The Legacy of the Picturesque: Landscape, Property, and the Ruin', in *The Politics of the Picturesque: Literature, Landscape, and Aesthetics since 1770*, ed. Stephen Copley and Peter Garside, Cambridge: Cambridge University Press, 1994.

Robinson, Sidney, *An Inquiry into the Picturesque*, Chicago: University of Chicago Press, 1991.

Schama, Simon, *Landscape and Memory*, New York: A. A. Knopf, 1995.

Smithson, Robert, 'Frederick Law Olmstead and the Dialectical Landscape', in *The Writings of Robert Smithson: Essays with Illustrations*, New York: New York University Press, 1979.

Williams, Raymond, *The Country and the City*, New York: Oxford, 1973.

CHAPTER II BIBLIOGRAPHY

Primary works

Anon., review of James Bruce, *Travels to Discover the Source of the Nile*, *Analytical Review* 9 (March 1791).

Austen, Jane, *Mansfield Park*, ed. James Kinsley and John Lucas, Oxford: Oxford University Press, 1970.

Bruce, James, *Travels to Discover the Source of the Nile, in the years 1768–74*, 5 vols., Edinburgh, 1790.

Burke, Edmund, *Correspondence*, vol. III, ed. George H. Guttridge, Cambridge: Cambridge University Press, 1961.

Cooper, Antony Ashley, Earl of Shaftesbury, *Characteristicks of Men, Manners, Opinions, Times*, ed. Lawrence Klein, Cambridge: Cambridge University Press, 1999.

De Quincey, Thomas, 'Letters to a Young Man whose Education has been Neglected', *London Magazine* 7 (1823).

Eastlake, Elizabeth, Lady, *Quarterly Review* 76 (June–Sept 1845).

Ferguson, Adam, *Essay on the History of Civil Society*, ed. and intro. Duncan Forbes, Edinburgh: Edinburgh University Press, 1966.

Hearne, Samuel, *Journey from Hudson's Bay to the Northern Ocean* (1795), in *Travels, Explorations and Empires: Writings from the Era of Imperial Expansion, 1770–1835*, 5 vols., ed. Tim Fulford with Carol Bolton, London: Pickering and Chatto, 2001.

Hemans, Felicia, 'The Traveller at the Source of the Nile', in Andrew Ashfield, *Romantic Women Poets 1770–1838: An Anthology*, ed. Andrew Ashfield, Manchester and New York: Manchester University Press, 1995.

Home, Henry, Lord Kames, *Elements of Criticism*, 11th edn, with the Author's Last Corrections and Annotations, London, 1834.

Jeffrey, Francis, review of Byron's *Corsair* and *Bride of Abydos*, *Edinburgh Review* (April 1814), 198–229.

Knox, Vicesimus, *Essays, Moral and Literary* (1778), new edn, 2 vols., Dublin, 1786.

Lamb, Charles, *Letters of Charles and Mary Lamb*, ed. Edward Marrs, London and Ithaca: Cornell University Press, 1976.

Millar, John, *Observations Concerning the Distinction of Ranks in Society*, London: John Murray, 1771.

Park, Mungo, *Travels in the Interior Districts of Africa*, London, 1799.

Peacock, Thomas Love, 'The Four Ages of Poetry', in *Romantic Critical Essays*, ed. David Bromwich, Cambridge: Cambridge University Press, 1997.

Wollstonecraft, Mary, *A Short Residence in Sweden*, ed. with intro. and notes by Richard Homes, Harmondsworth: Penguin, 1987.

Wordsworth, Dorothy, *Recollections of a Tour Made in Scotland*, intro., notes and photographs by Carol Kyros Walker, New Haven and London: Yale University Press, 1997.

Wordsworth, William, *The Poems*, ed. John O. Hayden, 3 vols., Harmondsworth: Penguin, 1977.

The Prelude, 1799, 1805, 1850, ed. Jonathan Wordsworth, M. H. Abrams and Stephen Gill, New York and London: Norton, 1979.

Wordsworth, William and Dorothy, *Letters of William and Dorothy Wordsworth*, 2nd edn, *The Later Years*, ed. Alan G. Hill, Oxford: Clarendon Press, 1978.

Secondary works

Batten, Charles, *Pleasurable Instruction: Form and Convention in 18th Century Travel Literature*, Berkeley and London: University of California Press, 1978.

Bayly, C. A., *Imperial Meridian: The British Empire and the World, 1780–1830*, London: Longman, 1989.

Bewell, Allan, *Wordsworth and the Enlightenment: Nature, Man, and Society in the Experimental Poetry*, New Haven and London: Yale University Press, 1989.

Chandler, James, *England in 1819: The Politics of Literary Culture and the Case of Romantic Historicism*, Chicago and London: University of Chicago Press, 1998.

Clark, Steve, 'Introduction', *Travel Writing and Empire: Postcolonial Theory in Transit*, London and New York: Zed Books, 1999.

Coe, Charles N., *Wordsworth and the Literature of Travel*, New York: Bookman Associates, 1953.

Coleman, Deirdre, *Romantic Colonization and British Anti-Slavery*, Cambridge: Cambridge University Press, 2005.

Colley, Linda, *Captives: Britain, Empire, and the World, 1600–1850*, London: Jonathan Cape, 2002.

Crone, G. R. and R. A. Skelton, 'English Collections of Voyages and Travels, 1625–1846', in Edward Lynam (ed.), *Richard Hakluyt and his Successors*, London: The Hakluyt Society, 1946.

Demata, Massimiliano, 'Travel Literature in the Edinburgh Review', in *British Romanticism and the Edinburgh Review: Bicentenary Essays*, ed. Massimiliano Demata and Duncan Wu, Houndmills: Palgrave Macmillan, 2002.

Goslee, Nancy Moore, 'Hemans' Red Indians: Reading Stereotypes' in *Romanticism, Race, and Imperial Culture*, ed. Alan Richardson and Sonia Hofkosh, Bloomington and Indianapolis: Indiana University Press, 1996.

Hickey, Alison, 'Dark Characters, Native Grounds: Wordsworth's Imagination of Imperialism', in *Romanticism, Race, and Imperial Culture*, ed. Alan Richardson and Sonia Hofkosh, Bloomington and Indianapolis: Indiana University Press, 1996.

Bibliographies

Hulme, Peter, and Tim Youngs (eds.), *Cambridge Companion to Travel Writing*, Cambridge: Cambridge University Press, 2003.

Lamb, Jonathan, *Preserving the Self in the South Seas, 1680–1840*, Chicago and London: University of Chicago Press, 2001.

Leask, Nigel, *Curiosity and the Aesthetics of Travel Writing, 1770–1840: 'From an Antique Land'*, Oxford: Oxford University Press, 2002.

'Kubla Khan and Orientalism: The Road to Xanadu Revisited', *Romanticism* 4:1 (1998).

Lootens, Tricia, 'Hemans and Home: Victorianism, Feminine "Internal Enemies", and the Domestication of National Identity', in Angela Leighton (ed.), *Victorian Women Poets: A Critical Reader*, Oxford: Blackwell, 1996.

McKeon, Michael, *The Origins of the English Novel, 1600–1740*, Baltimore: Johns Hopkins University Press, 1987.

Meek, Ronald, *Social Science and the Ignoble Savage*, Cambridge: Cambridge University Press, 1976.

Mezciems, Jenny, '"Tis not to divert the Reader": Moral and Literary Determinants in Some Early Travel Narratives', in *The Art of Travel*, ed. Philip Dod, London: Frank Cass, 1982.

Phillips, Mark, *Society and Sentiment: Genres of Historical Writing in Britain, 1740–1820*, Princeton: Princeton University Press, 2000.

Pratt, Mary Louise, *Imperial Eyes: Travel Writing and Transculturation*, London: Routledge, 1992.

Said, Edward, *Culture and Imperialism*, London: Chatto and Windus, 1993.

Simpson, David, 'Wordsworth and Empire – Just Joking', in *Land, Nation and Culture, 1740–1840: Thinking the Republic of Taste*, ed. Peter de Bolla, Nigel Leask and David Simpson, Basingstoke: Palgrave Macmillan, 2005.

Wheeler, Roxann, *The Complexion of Race: Categories of Difference in Eighteenth-Century British Culture*, Philadelphia: University of Pennsylvania Press, 2000.

CHAPTER 12 BIBLIOGRAPHY

Primary works

Austen, Jane, *Mansfield Park*, ed. Kathryn Sutherland, London: Penguin, 1996.

Northanger Abbey, ed. Marilyn Butler, London: Penguin, 1995.

Pride and Prejudice, ed. James Kinsley, Oxford: Oxford University Press, 1990.

Baillie, Joanna, *Poems; Wherein It Is Attempted to Describe Certain Views of Nature and of Rustic Manners*, London: J. Johnson, 1790.

Barbauld, Anna Letitia, *The Poems of Anna Letitia Barbauld*, ed. William McCarthy and Elizabeth Kraft, Athens, GA: University of Georgia Press, 1994.

Burns, Robert, *Burns: Poems and Songs*, ed. James Kinsley, London: Oxford University Press, 1969.

Byron, Lord, *The Works of Lord Byron, Poetry*, vol. I, ed. Ernest Hartley Coleridge, London: John Murray, 1898.

Clare, John, *The Early Poems of John Clare, 1804–1822*, 2 vols., ed. Eric Robinson and David Powell, Oxford: Clarendon Press, 1989.

Crabbe, George, *The Complete Poetical Works*, 3 vols., ed. Norma Dalrymple-Champneys and Arthur Pollard, Oxford: Clarendon Press, 1988.

De Quincey, Thomas, *Confessions of an English Opium Eater*, ed. Alethea Hayter, Harmondsworth: Penguin, 1971.

Edgeworth, Maria, *The Absentee*, ed. W. J. McCormack and Kim Walker, Oxford: Oxford University Press, 1988.

Ferrier, Susan, *Marriage, a Novel*, ed. Herbert Foltinek, London: Oxford University Press, 1971.

Galt, John, *Annals of the Parish* (1821), ed. D. S. Meldrum, 2 vols., Edinburgh: J. Grant, 1936.

Hemans, Felicia, *The Domestic Affections*, intro. Donald H. Reiman, New York: Garland, 1978.
Records of Woman, intro. Donald H. Reiman, New York: Garland, 1978.

Maturin, Charles, *The Wild Irish Boy*, 3 vols., London: Longman, Hurst & Co., 1808.

Owenson, Sydney (Lady Morgan), *The Wild Irish Girl: A National Tale*, ed. Kathryn Kirkpatrick, Oxford: Oxford University Press, 1999.

Radcliffe, Ann, *The Mysteries of Udolpho*, ed. Bonamy Dobree, Oxford: Oxford University Press, 1998.

Scott, Sir Walter, *Kenilworth: A Romance*, ed. J. H. Alexander, London: Penguin, 1999.
The Tale of Old Mortality, ed. Douglas S. Mack, London: Penguin, 1999.

Shelley, Mary, *Frankenstein*, ed. M. K. Joseph, Oxford: Oxford University Press, 1969.
The Journals of Mary Shelley 1814–1844, vol. I: *1814–1822*, ed. Paula R. Feldman and Diana Scott-Kilvert, Oxford: Oxford University Press, 1987.

Wordsworth, William, *The Major Works*, ed. Stephen Gill, Oxford: Oxford University Press, 1984.
The Poetical Works of William Wordsworth, 2nd edn, ed. E. De Selincourt, Oxford: Clarendon Press, 1952.

Secondary works

Barnard, Toby, *Making the Grand Figure: Lives and Possessions in Ireland, 1641–1770*, New Haven, CT: Yale University Press, 2004.

Berg, Maxine, *Luxury and Pleasure in Eighteenth-Century Britain*, Oxford: Oxford University Press, 2005.

Brewer, John, 'This, That and the Other: Public, Social and Private in the Seventeenth and Eighteenth Centuries', in *Shifting the Boundaries: Transformation of the Languages of Public and Private in the Eighteenth Century*, ed. Dario Castiglione and Lesley Sharpe, Exeter: Exeter University Press, 1995, pp. 1–21.

Burgess, Miranda, 'Domesticating Gothic: Jane Austen, Ann Radcliffe, and National Romance', in *Lessons of Romanticism: A Critical Companion*, ed. Thomas Pfau and Robert F. Gleckner, Durham, NC: Duke University Press, 1998, pp. 392–412.

Butler, Marilyn, 'Repossessing the Past', in *Rethinking Historicism: Critical Readings in Romantic History*, ed. Marilyn Butler, Paul Hamilton, Marjorie Levinson and Jerome McGann, Oxford: Blackwell, 1989, pp. 64–84.

Campbell, Colin, *The Romantic Ethic and the Spirit of Modern Consumerism*, Oxford: Blackwell, 1987.

Chandler, James, *England in 1819: The Politics of Literary Culture and the Case of Romantic Historicism*, Chicago: University of Chicago Press, 1998.

Douglas, Aileen, 'Austen's Enclave: Virtue and Modernity', *Romanticism* 5:2 (1999), 147–60.

Everett, Nigel, *The Tory View of Landscape*, New Haven, CT: Yale University Press, 1994.

Fiérobe, Claude, 'Irish Homes in the Work of C. R. Maturin', in *The Big House in Ireland: Reality and Representation*, ed. Jacqueline Genet, Dingle: Brandon, 1991, pp. 71–84.

Heinzelman, Kurt, 'The Cult of Domesticity: Dorothy and William Wordsworth at Grasmere', in *Romanticism and Feminism*, ed. Anne K. Mellor, Bloomington: University of Indiana Press, 1988, pp. 52–78.

Impey, Oliver, *Chinoiserie: The Impact of Oriental Styles on Western Art and Decoration*, London: Oxford University Press, 1977.

Joy, E. T., 'Furniture', in *The Regency Period 1810–1830*, ed. Ralph Edwards and L. G. C. Ramsey, London: The Connoisseur, 1958, pp. 39–51.

Leask, Nigel, *British Romantic Writers and the East: Anxieties of Empire*, Cambridge: Cambridge University Press, 1992.

Logan, Thad, *The Victorian Parlour*, Cambridge: Cambridge University Press, 2001.

Mandler, Peter, *The Fall and Rise of the Stately Home*, New Haven, CT: Yale University Press, 1997.

Marcus, Sharon, *Apartment Stories: City and Home in Nineteenth-Century Paris and London*, Berkeley: University of California Press, 1999.

McDonagh, Josephine, 'Barbauld's Domestic Economy', in *Romanticism and Gender*, ed. Anne Janowitz, Cambridge: D.S. Brewer, 1998, pp. 62–77.

McKendrick, Neil, John Brewer and J. H. Plumb, *The Birth of a Consumer Society: The Commercialization of Eighteenth-Century England*, Bloomington: University of Indiana Press, 1982.

Mellor, Anne K., *Romanticism and Gender*, London: Routledge, 1993.

Morrison, Paul, 'Enclosed in Openness: *Northanger Abbey* and the Domestic Carceral', *Texas Studies in Literature and Languages* 33:1 (Spring 1991), 1–23.

Musgrave, Clifford, 'Architecture and Interior Design', in *The Regency Period, 1810–1830*, ed. Ralph Edwards and L. G. C. Ramsey, London: The Connoisseur, 1958, pp. 15–36.

Phillipson, Mark, 'Byron's Revisited Haunts', *Studies in Romanticism* 39 (Summer 2000), 303–22.

Sayer, Karen, *Country Cottages: A Cultural History*, Manchester: Manchester University Press, 2000.

Smith, R. J., *The Gothic Bequest: Medieval Institutions in British Thought, 1688–1863*, Cambridge: Cambridge University Press, 1987.

Trumpener, Katie, 'National Character, Nationalist Plots: National Tale and Historical Novel in the Age of Waverley', *ELH* 60 (1993), 685–731.

Vickery, Amanda, *The Gentleman's Daughter: Women's Lives in Georgian England*, London: Yale University Press, 1998.

'Golden Age to Separate Spheres: A Review of the Categories and Chronology of English Women's History', *The Historical Journal* 36:2 (1993), 383–414.

Wainwright, Clive, *The Romantic Interior: The British Collector at Home*, New Haven, CT: Yale University Press, 1989.

Worthen, John, *The Gang: Coleridge, the Hutchinsons and the Wordsworths in 1802*, New Haven, CT: Yale University Press, 2001.

CHAPTER 13 BIBLIOGRAPHY

Primary works

Arnold, Matthew, *Essays in Criticism, Second Series*, London: Macmillan, 1903.
Austen, Jane, *The Oxford Illustrated Jane Austen*, ed. R. W. Chapman, 3rd edn, Oxford: Oxford University Press, 1923; rev. 1969; rpt 1988.
Baillie, Joanna, *Ethewald Pt 1* and *Count Basil*, in *Dramas in Three Volumes*, London: Longman, Rees, Orme, Brown, Green, & Longman, 1836.
Bennett, Betty T. (ed.), *British War Poetry in the Age of Romanticism, 1793–1815*, New York and London: Garland Press, 1975.
Blake, William, *The Four Zoas* and *Milton*, in *The Complete Poetry and Prose of William Blake*, ed. David Erdman, rev. edn, Garden City, New York: Anchor Press/Doubleday, 1982.
Byron, George Gordon, *The Complete Poetical Works*, 7 vols., ed. Jerome McGann, Oxford: Clarendon Press and New York: Oxford University Press, 1980–93.
Churchill, T. O., *The Life of Lord Viscount Nelson*, London: Harrison and Rutter, 1810.
Clarke, John Stanier, and John MacArthur, *The Life of Admiral Lord Nelson, K. B.*, London: T. Caddell and Wm Davies, 1809.
Coleridge, Samuel Taylor, *The Collected Works of Samuel Taylor Coleridge*, 11 vols., ed. Barbara Rooke, London: Routledge and Kegan Paul and Princeton: Princeton University Press, 1969–2001.
Cowper, William, *The Task* in *Poetical Works*, ed. Humphrey Sumner Milford, 4th edn, London: Oxford University Press, 1967.
De Quincey, Thomas, 'The English Mail Coach', in *Confessions of an English Opium-Eater and Other Writings*, ed. Grevel Lindop, Oxford: Oxford University Press, 1985.
Godfrey, Richard T., James Gillray and Mark Hallett, *James Gillray: The Art of Caricature*, London: Tate Publishing, 2001.
Hemans, Felicia, *Selected Poems, Letters, Reception Materials*, ed. Susan Wolfson, Princeton: Princeton University Press, 2000.
Lamb, Charles, 'Distant Correspondents', in *The Complete Works and Letters of Charles Lamb*, New York: The Modern Library, 1963.
Pasley, Charles W., *Essay on the Military Policy and Institutions of the British Empire*, London: T. Egerton, 1813.
Radcliffe, Ann, *The Mysteries of Udolpho*, ed. Bonamy Dobree, London: Oxford University Press, 1966.
Scott, Walter, *The Edinburgh Edition of the Waverley Novels*, ed. P. D. Garside *et al.*, Edinburgh: Edinburgh University Press and New York: Columbia University Press, 1998–.
Smith, Charlotte, *The Poems of Charlotte Smith*, ed. Stuart Curran, New York: Oxford University Press, 1993.
Southey, Robert, *History of the Peninsular Wars*, in *Select Prose of Robert Southey*, ed. and intro. Jacob Zeitlin, New York: The Macmillan Company, 1916.

The Life of Nelson, London: John Murray, 1813.

Review of C. W. Pasley, *Essay on the Military Policy and Institutions of the British Empire*, *Quarterly Review* 5:10 (1811), 433–53.

Wordsworth, William, *Poetical Works*, ed. Thomas Hutchison, rev. edn Ernest de Selincourt, Oxford: Oxford University Press, 1936; rpt 1981.

Secondary Works

Auerbach, Nina, *Communities of Women*, Cambridge and London: Harvard University Press, 1978.

Bainbridge, Simon, *British Poetry and the Revolutionary and Napoleonic Wars: Visions in Conflict*, Oxford and New York: Oxford University Press, 2003.

Bewell, Alan, *Romanticism and Colonial Disease*, Baltimore and London: Johns Hopkins University Press, 1999.

Christensen, Jerome, *Romanticism at the End of History*, Baltimore and London: Johns Hopkins University Press, 2000.

Colley, Linda, *Britons: Forging the Nation, 1707–1837*, New Haven: Yale University Press, 1992.

Favret, Mary A., 'Everyday War', *English Literary History* 72 (2005), 605–33.

'War in the Air', *Modern Language Quarterly* 65 (2004), 631–59.

Fulford, Tim, 'Romanticizing the Empire: The Naval Heroes of Southey, Coleridge, Austen and Marryat', *Modern Language Quarterly* 60 (1999), 161–96.

Hahn, H. George, 'The Progress of Patriotism and Biography: The Battle of Trafalgar in Southey's *The Life of Nelson*', *War, Literature and the Arts* 9 (1997), 67–82.

Jankovic, Vladimir, *Reading the Skies: A Cultural History of English Weather, 1650–1822*, Chicago: University of Chicago Press, 2000.

Kroeber, Karl, *British Romantic Art*, Berkeley, Los Angeles and London: University of California Press, 1986.

Liu, Alan, *Wordsworth: The Sense of History*, Stanford: Stanford University Press, 1989.

Lukács, Georg, *The Historical Novel*, preface by Fredric Jameson, Lincoln and London: University of Nebraska Press, 1983.

Makdisi, Saree, *Romantic Imperialism: Universal Empire and the Culture of Modernity* (Cambridge: Cambridge University Press, 1998).

Muir, Rory, *Tactics and the Experience of Battle in the Age of Napoleon*, New Haven and London: Yale University Press, 1998.

Ross, Marlon, *The Contours of Masculine Desire: Romanticism and the Rise of Women's Poetry*, New York: Oxford University Press, 1989.

Russell, Gillian, *Theatres of War: Performance, Politics and Society, 1793–1815*, Oxford: Oxford University Press, 1995.

Shaw, Philip, *Romantic Wars: Studies in Culture and Conflict, 1789–1822*, Aldershot, Hampshire: Ashgate, 2000.

Waterloo and the Romantic Imagination, Basingstoke, Hampshire and New York: Palgrave Macmillan, 2002.

Walzer, Michael, *Just and Unjust Wars: A Moral Argument with Historical Illustrations*, New York: Basic Books, 1977.

Watson, J. R., *Romanticism and War: A Study of British Romantic Period Writers and the Napoleonic Wars*, Basingstoke, Hampshire and New York: Palgrave Macmillan, 2003.

CHAPTER 14 BIBLIOGRAPHY

Primary works

Ambulator; or a Pocket Companion to a Tour round London, London, 1796.

Ackermann, Rudoph, *The Microcosm of London*, London: Ackermann, 1808–1810.

Blessington, Marguerite, *The Magic Lantern; or, Sketches of Scenes in the Metropolis*, 2nd edn, London: Longman, Hurst, Rees, Orme, and Brown, 1823.

Bulwer, Edward, *Pelham; or the Adventures of a Gentleman*, 3 vols., London: Henry Colburn, 1828.

Davis, Michael T., Iain McCalman and Christina Parolin (eds.), *Newgate in Revolution: An Anthology of Radical Prison Literature in the Age of Revolution*, London: Continuum, 2005.

Disraeli, Benjamin, *Vivian Grey*, 3 vols., London: Henry Colburn, 1826.

Egan, Pierce, *Life in London: Or the Day and Night Scenes of Jerry Hawthorn, Esq. and his Elegant Friend Corinthian Tom Accompanied by Bob Logic, the Oxonian, in Their Rambles and Sprees through the Metropolis*, New York: D. Appleton and Co., 1904.

Farington, Joseph, *The Diary of Joseph Farington*, ed. Kenneth Garlick and Angus Macintyre, New Haven: Yale University Press, 1978.

Haydon, Benjamin Robert, *Life of Benjamin Robert Haydon: Historical Painter, from his Autobiography and Journals*, ed. Tom Taylor, London: Longman, Brown, Green, and Longmans, 1853.

Hunt, Leigh, *The Autobiography of Leigh Hunt*, ed. J. E. Morpurgo, London: The Cresset Press, 1949.

Lysons, Daniel, *The Environs of London: being an historical account of the towns, villages, and hamlets, within twelve miles of that capital; interspersed with biographical anecdotes*, 2nd edn, London: T. Cadell and W. Davies, 1811.

Malcolm, James Peller, *Anecdotes of the Manners and Customs of London during the eighteenth century: including the charities, depravities, dresses, and amusements, of the citizens of London, during that period; with a review of the state of society in 1807; to which is added, a sketch of the domestic architecture and of the various improvements in the metropolis; illustrated by forty-five engravings*, 2nd edn, London: Longman, Hurst, Rees, and Orme, 1810.

Mathews, Anne, *Memoirs of Charles Mathews, Comedian*, 4 vols., London: Richard Bentley, 1839.

Pennant, Thomas, *Of London*, London: Robert Faulder, 1790.

Place, Francis, *The Autobiography of Francis Place*, ed. Mary Thale, Cambridge: Cambridge University Press, 1972.

Reynolds, John Hamilton, *Selected Prose*, ed. Leonidas M. Jones, Cambridge, MA: Harvard University Press, 1966.

Robinson, Henry Crabb, *Diary, Reminiscences, and Correspondence of Henry Crabb Robinson*, 4 vols., London: Macmillan, 1869.

Schopenhauer, Johanna, *A Lady Travels: Journeys in England and Scotland, from the Diaries of Johanna Schopenhauer*, trans. and ed. Ruth Michaelis-Jena and Willy Merson, London: Routledge, 1988.

Smith, James, and Horace Smith, *Horace in London: consisting of imitations of the first two books of the Odes of Horace*, London: J. Miller, 1813.

Taylor, Jane, *City Scenes: Or A Peep Into London. For Children*, London: Harvey & Darton, 1818.

Wakefield, Priscilla, *Perambulations in London and its Environs . . . [with] a short account of the surrounding villages. In letters, designed for young persons*, London: Harvey & Darton, 1809.

Wilson, Harriette, *Harriette Wilson's Memoirs of Herself and Others*, London: Douglas, 1825.

Secondary works

Adburgham, Alison, *Silver Fork Society: Fashionable Life and Literature from 1814–1840*, London: Constable, 1983.

Altick, Richard D., *The Shows of London*, Cambridge, MA: Harvard University Press, 1978.

Arnold, Dana, *Re-presenting the Metropolis: Architecture, Urban Experience and Social Life in London, 1800–1840*, Aldershot, Ashgate, 2000.

Byrd, Max, *London Transformed: Images of the City in the Eighteenth Century*, New Haven: Yale University Press, 1978.

Copeland, Edward, 'Crossing Oxford Street: Silverfork Geopolitics', *Eighteenth-Century Life* 25 (Spring 2001), 116–34.

Cox, Jeffrey N., *Poetry and Politics in the Cockney School: Keats, Shelley, Hunt and their Circle*, Cambridge: Cambridge University Press, 1998.

Donohue, Joseph, *Theatre in the Age of Kean*, Oxford: Basil Blackwell, 1975.

Dyer, Gary, 'Thieves, Boxers, Sodomites, Poets: Being Flash to Byron's Don Juan', *PMLA* 116:3 (May 2001), 562–79.

Fox, Celina, *London: World City, 1800–1840*, New Haven: Yale University Press, 1992.

Franzero, Carlo Maria, *A Life in Exile: Ugo Foscolo in London, 1816–1827*, London: W. H. Allen, 1977.

Gronow, R. H., *Captain Gronow: His Reminiscences of Regency and Victorian Life 1810–60*, ed. Christopher Hibbert, London: Kyle Cathie, 1991.

Hemingway, Andrew, 'Art Exhibitions as Leisure Class Rituals in Early Nineteenth-Century London', in *Towards a Modern Art World in Britain, c.1715–c.1880*, Studies in British Art 1, ed. Brian Allen, New Haven: Yale University Press, 1995.

Hone, J. Ann, *For the Cause of Truth: Radicalism in London 1796–1821*, Oxford: Oxford University Press, 1982.

Horwood, Richard, *The A to Z of Regency London*, London and Lympne Castle, Kent: H. Margary in association with Guildhall Library, 1985.

Hyde, Ralph, *Panoramania*, London: Barbican Gallery, 1988.

Low, Donald A., *The Regency Underworld*, Stroud: Sutton Publishing, 1999.

McCalman, Iain, *Radical Underworld: Prophets, Revolutionaries and Pornographers in London, 1795–1840*, Oxford: Clarendon Press, 1993.

Moers, Ellen, *The Dandy: Brummell to Beerbohm*, Lincoln: University of Nebraska Press, 1978.

Morley, John, *Regency Design, 1790–1840: Gardens, Buildings, Interiors, Furniture*, New York: H. N. Abrams, 1993.

Norton, Rictor, *Mother Clap's Molly House: The Gay Subculture in England, 1700–1830*, 2nd edn, Stroud: Chalford Press, 2006.

Ogborn, Miles, *Spaces of Modernity: London's Geographies, 1680–1780*, New York: Guilford Press, 1999.

Parissen, Stephen, *Regency Style*, London: Phaidon, 1992.

Porter, Roy, *London: A Social History*, London: Penguin, 1996.

Rendell, Jane, *The Pursuit of Pleasure: Gender, Space and Architecture in Regency London*, New Brunswick, NJ: Rutgers University Press, 2002.

Roe, Nicholas, *Fiery Heart: The First Life of Leigh Hunt*, London: Pimlico, 2005.

Russell, Gillian, 'Spouters of Washerwomen: The Sociability of Romantic Lecturing', in *Romantic Sociability, Social Networks and Literary Culture in Britain, 1770–1840*, ed. Gillian Russell and Clara Tuite, Cambridge: Cambridge University Press, 2002.

Sales, Roger, *Jane Austen and Representations of Regency England*, London: Routledge, 1994.

Thompson, E. P., *The Making of the English Working Class*, New York: Viking, 1963.

Timbs, John, *Walks and Talks about London*, London: Lockwood, 1865.

Wood, Marcus, *Radical Satire and Print Culture, 1790–1822*, Oxford: Oxford University Press, 2002.

CHAPTER 15 BIBLIOGRAPHY

Primary works

Barbauld, Anna, *Address to the Opposers of the Repeal*, London: Johnson, 1790.

Blake, William, *Complete Writings*, ed. Geoffrey Keynes, Oxford: Oxford University Press, 1972.

Clare, John, *Selected Letters*, ed. Mark Storey, Oxford: Oxford University Press, 1990.

Jefferson, Thomas, *Jefferson Abroad*, ed. Douglas L. Wilson and Lucia Stanton, New York: Random House, 1999.

Paine, Thomas, *The Writings*, ed. Moncure Daniel Conway, 4 vols., New York: Putnam's, 1908.

Price, Richard, *A Discourse on the Love of our Country*, etc., London: Cadell, 1789.

Robinson, Mary, *Poetical Works*, 3 vols., London: 1806.

Walpole, Horace, *Letters*, ed. Padgett Toynbee, 19 vols., Oxford: Clarendon Press, 1925.

Williams, Helen Maria, *A Farewell, for Two Years, to England*, London: Cadell, 1791.

Julia, 2 vols., London: 1790.

Letters from France, 2 vols., Dublin: Chambers, 1794; photoreprint of 5th edn, 1796, published Demar, NY: Scholars' Facsimiles and Reprints, 1975.

Letters Containing a Sketch of the Politics of France, London: G. G. and J. Robinson, 1795–6; photoreprint Demar, NY: Scholars' Facsimiles and Reprints, 1975.

Williams, Helen Maria (ed.), *The Political and Confidential Correspondence of Lewis the Sixteenth; with Observations on Each Letter*, 3 vols., London: C. G. Robinson, 1803.

Wollstonecraft, Mary, *Collected Letters*, ed. Ralph Wardle, Ithaca, NY: Cornell University Press, 1979.

   Political Writings, ed. Janet Todd, London: Pickering, 1993.

   Vindication of the Rights of Woman, London, 1792.

Secondary works

Adams, William Howard, *The Paris Years of Thomas Jefferson*, New Haven: Yale University Press, 1997.

Bailyn, Bernard, *Ideological Origins of the American Revolution*, Cambridge, MA: Harvard University Press, 1967.

Barrell, John, *Imagining the King's Death: Figurative Treason, Fantasies of Regicide, 1793–1796*, Oxford: Oxford University Press, 2000.

Dunn, Susan, *Sister Revolutions: French Lightning, American Light*, London: Faber & Faber, 1999.

Ellis, Joseph J., *American Sphinx: The Character of Thomas Jefferson*, New York: Knopf, 1997.

Erdman, David, *Commerce des Lumières: John Oswald and the British in Paris, 1790–1793*, Columbia: University of Missouri Press, 1986.

Fliegelman, Jay, *Prodigals and Pilgrims: The Revolt against Patriarchal Authority*, Cambridge: Cambridge University Press, 1982.

Goodwin, Albert, *The Friends of Liberty: The English Democratic Movement in the Age of the French Revolution*, Cambridge, MA: Harvard University Press, 1977.

Keane, John, *Tom Paine: A Political Life*, London: Bloomsbury, 1995.

Lefebvre, Georges, *The French Revolution*, London: Routledge, 2001.

Linebaugh, Peter, and Marcus Rediker, *The Many-Headed Hydra: The Hidden History of the Revolutionary Atlantic*, London: Verso, 2000.

Schama, Simon, *Citizens: A Chronicle of the French Revolution*, New York: Viking, 1989.

Todd, Janet, *Mary Wollstonecraft: A Revolutionary Life*, London: Weidenfeld & Nicholson, 2000.

CHAPTER 16 BIBLIOGRAPHY

Primary works

Babbage, C., *On the Economy of Machinery and Manufactures*, 4th edn (1835), in Babbage's *Works*, 12 vols., ed. M. Campbell-Kelly, New York: NYU Press, 1989, vol. VIII.

Brydges, S. E., *The Autobiography, Times, Opinions, and Contemporaries of Sir Egerton Brydges*, 2 vols., London: Cochrane and M'Crone, 1834.

   The British Bibliographer, 4 vols., London: Triphook et al., 1810–14.

Caritat, M.-J.-A., Marquis de Condorcet, *Outlines of an Historical View of the Progress of the Human Mind*, London: for J. Johnson, 1795.

[Carlile, R.], *The Report of the Court of King's Bench . . . being the Mock Trials of Richard Carlile*, London: R. Carlile, 1822.

Bibliographies

Collins, W., 'The Unknown Public', *Household Words* 18:439 (21 August 1858), 217–22.

Jacob, E. (ed.), *Reports of Cases Argued and Determined in the High Court of Chancery*, London: J. Butterworth and Son, 1828.

Johnson, J., *Typographia*, 2 vols., London: Longman et al., 1824.

Knight, C., *William Caxton*, London: C. Knight and Co., 1844.

Printing Machine: A Review for the Many 1 (15 February 1834).

Ure, A., *The Philosophy of Manufactures*, London: Knight, 1835.

Walsh, C., *A Bookseller of the Last Century*, London: Griffith etc., 1885.

Wordsworth, W., *Prose Works*, 3 vols., ed. W. J. B. Owen and J. W. Smyser, Oxford: Clarendon Press, 1974.

Secondary works

Barnes, J. J., *Authors, Publishers and Politicians: The Quest for an Anglo-American Copyright Agreement, 1815–1854*, London: Routledge and Kegan Paul, 1974.

Bentley, G. E., Jr, 'Copyright Documents in the George Robinson Archive: William Godwin and Others, 1713–1820', *Studies in Bibliography* 35 (1982), 67–110.

Blagden, C., 'Thomas Carnan and the Almanack Monopoly', *Studies in Bibliography* 14 (1961), 23–43.

Blakey, D., *The Minerva Press, 1790–1820*, London: Bibliographical Society, 1939.

Blanning, T. C. W., *The Culture of Power and the Power of Culture*, Oxford: Oxford University Press, 2002.

Bonnell, T. F., 'John Bell's *Poets of Great Britain:* The "little trifling edition" Revisited', *Modern Philology* 85 (1987), 128–52.

Brewer, J., *The Pleasures of the Imagination: English Culture in the Eighteenth Century*, New York: Farrar Straus Giroux, 1997.

  'This, That and the Other: Public, Social and Private in the Seventeenth and Eighteenth Centuries', in Castiglione and Sharpe (eds.), *Shifting the Boundaries*, pp. 1–21.

Brewer, J., and I. McCalman, 'Publishing', in *An Oxford Companion to the Romantic Age*, ed. I. McCalman, Oxford: Oxford University Press, 1999, pp. 197–206.

Castiglione, D., and L. Sharpe (eds.), *Shifting the Boundaries: Transformation of the Languages of Public and Private in the Eighteenth Century*, Exeter: University of Exeter Press, 1995.

Cavallo, G., and R. Chartier (eds.), *A History of Reading in the West*, Cambridge: Polity, 1999.

Chartier, R., *The Cultural Origins of the French Revolution*, trans. L. Cochrane, Durham, NC: Duke University Press, 1991.

Cole, R. C., *Irish Booksellers and English Writers, 1740–1800*, London: Mansell, 1986.

Coleman, D. C., *The British Paper Industry, 1495–1860: A Study in Industrial Growth*, Oxford: Clarendon Press, 1958.

Crook, R. E., *A Bibliography of Joseph Priestley*, London: Library Association, 1966.

Dooley, A. C., *Author and Printer in Victorian England*, Charlottesville: University Press of Virginia, 1992.

Eliot, S., *Some Patterns and Trends in British Publishing 1800–1919*, London: Bibliographical Society, 1994.

'Some Trends in British Book Production, 1800–1919', in *Literature in the Marketplace*, ed. J. O. Jordan and R. L. Patten, Cambridge: Cambridge University Press, 1995, pp. 19–43.

Erickson, L., *The Economy of Literary Form: English Literature and the Industrialization of Publishing, 1800–1850*, Baltimore: Johns Hopkins University Press, 1996.

Ezell, M. J. M., *Social Authorship and the Advent of Print*, Baltimore: Johns Hopkins University Press, 1999.

Feather, J., *A History of British Publishing*, London: Routledge, 1988.

'The Merchants of Culture: Bookselling in Early Industrial England', *Studies of Voltaire and the Eighteenth Century* 217 (1983), 11–21.

The Provincial Book Trade in Eighteenth-Century England, Cambridge: Cambridge University Press, 1985.

Ferdinand, C. Y., *Benjamin Collins and the Provincial Newspaper Trade in the Eighteenth Century*, Oxford: Clarendon Press, 1997.

Fraistat, N., 'Illegitimate Shelley: Radical Piracy and the Textual Edition as Cultural Performance', *PMLA* 109:3 (1994), 409–23.

Frasca-Spada, M., and N. Jardine (eds.), *Books and the Sciences in History*, Cambridge: Cambridge University Press, 2000.

Fyfe, A., 'Young Readers and the Sciences', in M. Frasca-Spada and N. Jardine (eds.), *Books and the Sciences*, Cambridge: Cambridge University Press, 2000, pp. 276–90.

Garside, P., 'The English Novel in the Romantic Era: Consolidation and Dispersal', in *The English Novel, 1770–1829*, ed. P. Garside, J. Raven and R. Schowerling, vol. II, Oxford: Oxford University Press, 2000, pp. 15–103.

'Rob's last raid: Scott and the Publication of the Waverley Novels', in R. Myers and M. Harris (ed.), *Author/Publisher Relations*, Oxford: Oxford Polytechnic Press, 1983, pp. 88–118.

Garside, P., J. Raven and R. Schowerling (eds.), *The English Novel, 1770–1829*, 2 vols., Oxford: Oxford University Press, 2000.

Gilmartin, K., *Print Politics: The Press and Radical Opposition in Early Nineteenth-Century England*, Cambridge: Cambridge University Press, 1996.

Goodfield-Toulmin, J., 'Some Aspects of English Physiology, 1780–1840', *Journal of the History of Biology* 2 (1969), 283–320.

Habermas, J., *The Structural Transformation of the Public Sphere: An Inquiry into a Category of Bourgeois Society* (1962), trans. T. Burger and F. Lawrence, Cambridge: Polity, 1989.

Hills, R. L., *Papermaking in Britain, 1488–1988: A Short History*, London: Athlone, 1988.

Howe, E., *The London Compositor: Documents Relating to Wages, Working Conditions and Customs of the London Printing Trade, 1785–1900*, London: Bibliographical Society, 1947.

Huett, L., 'Among the Unknown Public: *Household Words, All the Year Round*, and the Mass-market Periodical in the Mid-Nineteenth Century', *Victorian Periodicals Review* 38 (2005), 61–82.

Hyland, P., and N. Sammells (eds.), *Writing and Censorship in Britain*, London: Routledge, 1992.

Johns, A., 'The Identity Engine: Science, Stereotyping, and Skill in Print', in L. Roberts, S. Schaffer and P. Dear (eds.), *The Mindful Hand*, Chicago, IL: Edita/University of Chicago Press, 2007, pp. 403–28.

Jordan, J. O., and R. L. Patten (eds.), *Literature in the Marketplace: Nineteenth-century British Publishing and Reading Practices*, Cambridge: Cambridge University Press, 1995.

Keen, P., *The Crisis of Literature in the 1790s: Print Culture and the Public Sphere*, Cambridge: Cambridge University Press, 1999.

Kelly, T., *Early Public Libraries*, London: Library Association, 1966.

Klancher, J. P., *The Making of English Reading Audiences, 1790–1832*, Madison: University of Wisconsin Press, 1987.

Landon, R. G., 'Small Profits do Great Things: James Lackington and Eighteenth-century Bookselling', *Studies in Eighteenth-Century Culture* 5 (1976), 387–99.

Lyons, M., 'New Readers in the Nineteenth Century: Women, Children, Workers', in G. Cavallo and R. Chartier (eds.), *History of Reading in the West*, Cambridge: Polity, 1999, pp. 313–44.

MacDougall, W., 'Smugglers, Reprinters and Hot Pursuers: The Irish-Scottish Book Trade and Copyright Prosecutions in the Late Eighteenth Century', in R. Myers and M. Harris (eds.), *The Stationers' Company*, Winchester: St Paul's Bibliographies, 1997, pp. 151–83.

McCalman, I., *Radical Underworld: Prophets, Revolutionaries and Pornographers in London, 1795–1840*, Cambridge: Cambridge University Press, 1988.

McCalman, I. (ed.), *An Oxford Companion to the Romantic Age*, Oxford: Oxford University Press, 1999.

McKitterick, D. J., *A History of Cambridge University Press. II: Scholarship and Commerce, 1698–1872*, Cambridge: Cambridge University Press, 1998.

Morison, S., *John Bell, 1745–1831*, Cambridge: Cambridge University Press for the author, 1930.

Myers, R., and M. Harris (eds.), *Author/Publisher Relations in the Eighteenth and Nineteenth Centuries*, Oxford: Oxford Polytechnic Press, 1983.

The Stationers' Company and the Book Trade 1550–1900, Winchester: St Paul's Bibliographies, 1997.

Phillips, J. W., *A Bibliographical Inquiry into Printing and Bookselling in Dublin from 1670 to 1800*, Dublin: University of Dublin, 1981.

Plant, M., *The English Book Trade: An Economic History of the Making and Sale of Books*, London: George Allen and Unwin, 1939.

Pollard, M., *Dublin's Trade in Books, 1550–1800*, Oxford: Clarendon Press, 1989.

Raven, J., 'From Promotion to Proscription: Arrangements for Reading and Eighteenth-century Libraries', in J. Raven, H. Small and N. Tadmor (eds.), *The Practice and Representation of Reading*, Cambridge: Cambridge University Press, 1996, pp. 175–201.

Judging New Wealth: Popular Publishing and Responses to Commerce in England, 1750–1800, Oxford: Clarendon Press, 1992.

'The Novel Comes of Age', in P. Garside, J. Raven and R. Schowerling (eds.), *The English Novel, 1770–1829*, vol. I, Oxford: Oxford University Press, 2000, pp. 15–121.

Raven, J., H. Small and N. Tadmor (eds.), *The Practice and Representation of Reading in England*, Cambridge: Cambridge University Press, 1996.

Roberts, L., S. Schaffer and P. Dear (eds.), *The Mindful Hand: Inquiry and Invention from the Late Renaissance to Early Industrialization*, Chicago, IL: Edita/University of Chicago Press, 2007.

Rose, M., *Authors and Owners: The Invention of Copyright*, Cambridge, MA: Harvard University Press, 1993.

Rosenbland, L. N., *Papermaking in Eighteenth-century France: Management, Labor, and Revolution at the Montgolfier Mill, 1761–1805*, Baltimore: Johns Hopkins University Press, 2000.

Saunders, D., 'Victorian Obscenity Law: Negative Censorship or Positive Administration?', in P. Hyland and N. Sammells (eds.), *Writing and Censorship*, London: Routledge, 1992, pp. 154–70.

Secord, J. A., *Victorian Sensation: The Extraordinary Publication, Reception and Secret Authorship of 'Vestiges of the Natural History of Creation'*, Chicago: University of Chicago Press, 2000.

Sher, R. B., *The Enlightenment and the Book: Scottish Authors and their Publishers in Eighteenth-century Britain, Ireland, and America*, Chicago: University of Chicago Press, 2006.

St Clair, W., *The Reading Nation in the Romantic Period*, Cambridge: Cambridge University Press, 2004.

Sutherland, J., *Victorian Fiction: Writers, Publishers, Readers*, London: MacMillan, 1995.

Swartz, R. G., 'Wordsworth, Copyright, and the Commodities of Genius', *Modern Philology* 89:4 (1992), 482–509.

Temkin, O., 'Basic Science, Medicine and the Romantic Era', *Bulletin of the History of Medicine* 37 (1963), 97–129.

Topham, J., 'A Textbook Revolution', in M. Frasca-Spada and N. Jardine (eds.), *Books and the Sciences*, Cambridge: Cambridge University Press, 2000, pp. 317–37.

Tyson, G. P., 'Joseph Johnson, an Eighteenth-century Bookseller', *Studies in Bibliography* 28 (1975), 1–16.

Vail, J. W., *The Literary Relationship of Lord Byron and Thomas Moore*, Baltimore: Johns Hopkins University Press, 2001.

Viscomi, J., *Blake and the Idea of the Book*, Princeton: Princeton University Press, 1993.

Wickwar, W. H., *The Struggle for the Freedom of the Press, 1819–32*, London: G. Allen and Unwin, 1928.

Winter, A., *Mesmerized: Powers of Mind in Victorian Britain*, Chicago: University of Chicago Press, 1998.

Wittmann, R., 'Was there a Reading Revolution at the End of the Eighteenth Century?', in G. Cavallo and R. Chartier (eds.), *History of Reading in the West*, Cambridge: Polity, 1999, pp. 284–312.

Woodmansee, M., *The Author, Art, and the Market: Rereading the History of Aesthetics*, New York: Columbia University Press, 1994.

Zachs, W., *The First John Murray and the Late Eighteenth-century London Book Trade*, Oxford: by Oxford University Press for the British Academy, 1998.

CHAPTER 17 BIBLIOGRAPHY

Abrams, M. H., *The Mirror and the Lamp: Romantic Theory and the Critical Tradition*, New York: Norton, 1953.

  Natural Supernaturalism: Tradition and Revolution in Romantic Literature, New York: Norton, 1971.

'Structure and style in the Greater Romantic Lyric' in H. Bloom (ed.), *Romanticism and Consciousness: Essays in Criticism*, New York: Norton, 1965, pp. 201–32.

Attridge, Derek, *Peculiar Language: Literature as Difference*, Ithaca, NY: Cornell University Press, 1988.

Behrendt, Stephen C., and Harriet Kramer Linkin (eds.), *Romanticism and Women Poets: Opening the Doors of Reception*, Lexington, KY: University of Kentucky Press, 1999.

Bloom, Harold, 'The Breaking of Form', *Deconstruction & Criticism*, New York: Seabury Press, 1979, pp. 1–37.

'The Internalization of Quest-romance', in H. Bloom (ed.), *Romanticism and Consciousness: Essays in Criticism*, New York: Norton, 1970, pp. 3–23.

Bloom, Harold (ed.), *Romanticism and Consciousness: Essays in Criticism*, New York: Norton, 1970.

Booth, Bradford, *A Cabinet of Gems*, Berkeley: University of California Press, 1938.

Brown, Marshall, 'Romanticism and Enlightenment', in *The Cambridge Companion to British Romanticism*, ed. Stuart Curran (Cambridge: Cambridge University Press, 1993), pp. 25–47.

Butler, Marilyn, *Romantics, Rebels, and Reactionaries*, Oxford: Oxford University Press, 1982.

Chandler, James K., *England in 1819*, Chicago: University of Chicago Press, 1998.

Christensen, Jerome, *Lord Byron's Strength: Romantic Writing and Commercial Society*, Baltimore, MD: Johns Hopkins University Press, 1993.

Collings, David, *Wordsworthian Errancies: The Poetics of Cultural Dismemberment*, Baltimore, MD: Johns Hopkins University Press, 1994.

Cox, Jeffrey N., '*Lamia, Isabella*, and *The Eve of St. Agnes*', in *The Cambridge Companion to John Keats*, ed. Susan J. Wolfson, Cambridge: Cambridge University Press, 2001, pp. 53–68.

Poetry and Politics in the Cockney School: Keats, Shelley, Hunt and their Circle, Cambridge: Cambridge University Press, 1998.

Curran, Stuart, *Poetic Form and British Romanticism*, Oxford: Oxford University Press, 1986.

'Romantic Poetry: Why and Wherefore?', in *The Cambridge Companion to British Romanticism*, ed. Stuart Curran, Cambridge: Cambridge University Press, 1993, pp. 216–35.

'Romantic Poetry: The I Altered', in *Romanticism and Feminism*, ed. Anne K. Mellor, Bloomington, IN: Indiana University Press, 1988, pp. 185–207.

Shelley's Annus Mirabilis: The Maturing of an Epic Vision, San Marino, CA: Huntington Library, 1975.

Curran, Stuart (ed.), *The Cambridge Companion to British Romanticism*, Cambridge: Cambridge University Press, 1993.

Dawson, P. M. S., 'Poetry in an Age of Revolution', in *The Cambridge Companion to British Romanticism*, ed. Stuart Curran, Cambridge: Cambridge University Press, 1993, pp. 48–73.

Dyer, Gary, 'Thieves, Boxers, Sodomites, Poets: Being Flash to Byron's *Don Juan*', *PMLA* 116:3 (May 2001), 562–78.

Eilenberg, Susan, *Strange Power of Speech: Wordsworth, Coleridge, and Literary Possession*, Oxford: Oxford University Press, 1992.

Fay, Elizabeth, *Becoming Wordsworthian: A Performative Aesthetic*, Amherst: University of Massachusetts Press, 1995.

Ferguson, Frances, *Wordsworth: Language as Counter-spirit*, New Haven, CT: Yale University Press, 1977.

Galperin, William H., *The Return of the Visible in British Romanticism*, Baltimore, MD: Johns Hopkins University Press, 1993.

  Revision and Authority in Wordsworth: The Interpretation of a Career, Philadelphia: University of Pennsylvania Press, 1989.

Glen, Heather, *Vision and Disenchantment: Blake's 'Songs' and Wordsworth's 'Lyrical Ballads'*, Cambridge: Cambridge University Press, 1983.

Goodman, Kevis, *Georgic Modernity and British Romanticism: Poetry and the Mediation of History*, Cambridge: Cambridge University Press, 2004.

Goodridge, John, and Bridget Keegan, 'John Clare and the Traditions of Labouring-class Verse', in *The Cambridge Companion to English Literature, 1740–1830*, ed. T. Keymer and J. Mee, Cambridge: Cambridge University Press, 2004, pp. 280–95.

Hartman, Geoffrey, *Wordsworth's Poetry, 1787–1814*, New Haven: Yale University Press, 1964.

Jacobus, Mary, *Romanticism, Writing, and Sexual Difference*, Oxford: Clarendon Press, 1989.

  Tradition & Experiment in Wordsworth's 'Lyrical Ballads' (1798), Oxford: Clarendon Press, 1976.

Jones, Steven E., *Satire and Romanticism*, New York: St. Martin's Press, 2000.

Kandl, John, 'The Politics of Keats's Early Poetry', in *The Cambridge Companion to John Keats*, ed. Susan J. Wolfson, Cambridge: Cambridge University Press, 2001, pp. 1–19.

Keach, William, *Arbitrary Power: Romanticism, Language, Politics*, Princeton, NJ: Princeton University Press, 2004.

  Shelley's Style, New York: Methuen, 1984.

Keats, John, *John Keats: A Longman Cultural Edition*, ed. Susan J. Wolfson, New York: Longman, 2007.

Keymer, Thomas, and Jon Mee (eds.), *The Cambridge Companion to English Literature, 1740–1830*, Cambridge: Cambridge University Press, 2004.

Kucich, Greg, 'Keats, Shelley, Byron, and the Hunt Circle', in *The Cambridge Companion to English Literature, 1740–1830*, ed. Thomas Keymer and Jon Mee, Cambridge: Cambridge University Press, 2004, pp. 263–79.

Levin, Susan, *Dorothy Wordsworth and Romanticism*, New Brunswick, NJ: Rutgers University Press, 1987.

Levinson, Marjorie, *Keats's Life of Allegory: The Origins of a Style*, Oxford: Basil Blackwell, 1988.

Magnuson, Paul, 'The Lake School: Wordsworth and Coleridge', in *The Cambridge Companion to English Literature, 1740–1830*, ed. Thomas Keymer and Jon Mee, Cambridge: Cambridge University Press, 2004, pp. 227–43.

Manning, Peter, *Byron and his Fictions*, Detroit, MI: Wayne State University Press, 1978.

  'Childe Harold in the Marketplace: From Romaunt to Handbook', *MLQ* 52 (1991), 170–90.

  Reading Romantics: Text and Context, Oxford: Oxford University Press, 1990.

'Wordsworth in the *Keepsake*' in *Literature in the Marketplace: Nineteenth-century British Publishing and Reading Practices*, ed. John O. Jordan and Robert L. Patten, Cambridge: Cambridge University Press, 1995, pp. 44–73.

McGann, Jerome J., *Byron and Romanticism*, ed. James Solderholm, Cambridge: Cambridge University Press, 2002.

The Poetics of Sensibility: A Revolution in Literary Style, Oxford: Oxford University Press, 1996.

Mee, Jon, 'Blake and the Poetics of Enthusiasm', in *The Cambridge Companion to English Literature, 1740–1830*, ed. Thomas Keymer and Jon Mee, Cambridge: Cambridge University Press, 2004, pp. 194–210.

Mellor, Anne K., *Romanticism and Gender*, New York: Routledge, 1992.

'Women's Political Poetry', in *Mothers of the Nation: Women's Political Writing in England, 1780–1830*, Bloomington: Indiana University Press, 2000.

Page, Judith W., *Wordsworth and the Cultivation of Women*, Berkeley: University of California Press, 1994.

Pascoe, Judith, '"Unsex'd females": Barbauld, Robinson, and Smith', in *The Cambridge Companion to English Literature, 1740–1830*, ed. Thomas Keymer and Jon Mee, Cambridge: Cambridge University Press, 2004, pp. 211–26.

Pinch, Adela, *Strange Fits of Passion: Epistemologies of Emotion*, Stanford, CA: Stanford University Press, 1996.

Rajan, Tilottama, *Dark Interpreter: The Discourse of Romanticism*, Ithaca, NY: Cornell University Press, 1980.

Renier, Anne, *Friendship's Offering*, London: Private Libraries Association, 1964.

Roe, Nicholas, *John Keats and the Culture of Dissent*, Oxford: Clarendon Press, 1997.

Rosenberg, Harold, *The Traditions of the New*, New York: McGraw-Hill, 1965.

Ross, Marlon B., *The Contours of Masculine Desire: Romanticism and the Rise of Women's Poetry*, Oxford: Oxford University Press, 1989.

Schor, Esther, *Bearing the Dead: The British Culture of Mourning from the Enlightenment to Victoria*, Princeton, NJ: Princeton University Press, 1994.

Scrivener, Michael Henry, *Radical Shelley*, Princeton, NJ: Princeton University Press, 1982.

Simpson, David, 'Romanticism, Criticism and Theory', in *The Cambridge Companion to British Romanticism*, ed. Stuart Curran, Cambridge: Cambridge University Press, 1993, pp. 1–24.

Wordsworth and the Figurings of the Real, Atlantic Highlands, NJ: Humanities Press, 1982.

Wordsworth's Historical Imagination, New York: Methuen, 1987.

Sperry, Stuart M., 'Toward a Definition of Romantic Irony in English Literature', in *Romantic and Modern: Revaluations of Literary Tradition*, ed. George Bornstein, Pittsburgh, PA: University of Pittsburgh Press, 1977, pp. 3–28.

Stabler, Jane, *Byron, Poetics and History*, Cambridge: Cambridge University Press, 2002.

Transitions: Burke to Byron, Barbauld to Baillie, 1790–1830, Basingstoke: Palgrave, 2002.

Swann, Karen, '*Endymion*'s Beautiful Dreamers', in *The Cambridge Companion to John Keats*, ed. Susan J. Wolfson, Cambridge: Cambridge University Press, 2001, pp. 20–36.

'Literary Gentlemen and Lovely Ladies: The Debate on the Character of *Christabel*', *ELH* 52 (1985), 397–418.

Sweet, Nanora, and Julie Melnyk (eds.), *Felicia Hemans: Reimagining Poetry in the Nineteenth Century*, New York: Palgrave, 2001.

Wasserman, Earl R., *Shelley: A Critical Reading*, Baltimore, MD: Johns Hopkins University Press, 1971.

Wolfson, Susan J., *Borderlines: The Shiftings of Gender in British Romanticism*, Stanford, CA: Stanford University Press, 2006.

    Formal Charges: The Shaping of Poetry in British Romanticism, Stanford, CA: Stanford University Press, 1997.

    'Romanticism and the Measures of Meter', *Eighteenth-Century Life* 16 ns 3 (1992), 221–46.

    'What's Wrong with Formalist Criticism?', *Studies in Romanticism* 37 (Spring 1998), 77–94.

Wolfson, Susan J. (ed.), *The Cambridge Companion to John Keats*, Cambridge: Cambridge University Press, 2001.

Wu, Duncan, 'Keats and the "Cockney School"', in *The Cambridge Companion to John Keats*, ed. Susan J. Wolfson, Cambridge: Cambridge University Press, 2001, pp. 37–54.

    Wordsworth: An Inner Life, Oxford: Basil Blackwell, 2002.

CHAPTER 18 BIBLIOGRAPHY

Primary works

Blake, William, *The Poems of William Blake*, ed. W. H. Stevenson, text ed. David V. Erdman, London and New York: Longman and Norton, 1971.

Byron, George Gordon, Lord, *Letters and Journals*, ed. Leslie A. Marchand, 11 vols., London: John Murray, 1978.

Coleridge, Samuel Taylor, *Biographia Litteraria*, 2 vols., ed. James Engell and Walter Jackson Bate, *Collected Works VII*, London and Princeton: Princeton University Press, 1983.

    Collected Letters of Samuel Taylor Coleridge, ed. E. L. Griggs, 6 vols., London: Oxford University Press, 1956–71.

    The Statesman's Manual in *Collected Works VI*, London and Princeton: Princeton University Press, 1972.

Eckermann, J. P., *Conversations with Goethe*, London: J. M. Dent and Sons, 1930.

German Aesthetic and Literary Criticism, ed. H. B. Nisbet, David Simpson, Kathleen Wheeler, 3 vols., Cambridge: Cambridge University Press, 1984–5.

Gray, Thomas, *The Poems of Thomas Gray, William Collins and Oliver Goldsmith*, ed. Roger Lonsdale, London: Longmans, 1969.

Hazlitt, William, *The Collected Works of William Hazlitt*, 21 vols., ed. P. P. Howe, London: Dent, 1930–4.

Hemans, Felicia, *Records of Woman, With Other Poems*, 2nd edn, Edinburgh and London: William Blackwood and T. Cadell, 1828.

Kant, Immanuel, *Critique of the Power of Judgement*, trans. Paul Guyer and Eric Matthews, Cambridge: Cambridge University Press, 2000.

Keats, John, *The Letters of John Keats*, ed. H. E. Rollins, 2 vols., Cambridge, MA: Harvard University Press, 1958.

The Poems of John Keats, ed. Jack Stillinger, Cambridge, MA: Harvard University Press, 1978.

Leighton, Angela, and Margaret Reynolds (eds.), *Victorian Women Poets: An Anthology*, Oxford: Blackwell, 1995.

Pope, Alexander, *An Essay on Criticism* in *The Poems of Alexander Pope: A One-volume Edition of the Twickenham Text with Selected Annotations*, ed. John Butt, London: Methuen, 1963.

Reeve, Clara, *The Progress of Romance* . . ., 2 vols., Colchester: W. Keymer, 1785.

Schiller, Friedrich, *On the Aesthetic Education of Man, In A Series Of Letters*, ed. and trans. Elizabeth M. Wilkinson and L. A. Willoughby, Oxford: Clarendon Press, 1967.

Shelley, Percy Bysshe, *A Defence of Poetry* (1821).

Warton, Thomas, *The History of English Poetry, from the close of the eleventh to the commencement of the eighteenth century* . . . 4 vols., London, 1774–81.

Wordsworth, William, *The Prelude 1799, 1805, 1850*, ed. Jonathan Wordsworth, M. H. Abrams and Stephen Gill, New York and London: Norton, 1979.

Wu, Duncan (ed.), *Romantic Women Poets: An Anthology*, Oxford: Blackwell, 1997.

Secondary works

Abrams, M. H., *Natural Supernaturalism; Tradition and Revolution in Romantic Literature*, New York: Norton, 1971.

Armstrong, Isobel, *The Radical Aesthetic*, Oxford: Blackwell, 2000.

Bloom, Harold, *Blake's Apocalypse*, Garden City: Doubleday, 1963.

The Visionary Company: A Reading of English Romantic Poetry, rev. edn, Ithaca, NY: Cornell University Press, 1971.

Butler, Marilyn, 'Culture's Medium: The Role of the Review', *The Cambridge Companion to Romanticism*, ed. Stuart Curran, Cambridge: Cambridge University Press, 1993, pp. 120–48.

Chandler James, *England in 1819: The Politics of Literary Culture and the Case of Romantic Historicism*, Chicago and London: University of Chicago Press, 1998.

Wordsworth's Second Nature: A Study of the Poetry and Politics, Chicago and London: University of Chicago Press, 1984.

Christensen, Jerome C., *Romanticism at the End of History*, Baltimore and London: Johns Hopkins University Press, 2000.

Cohen, Barbara, J. Hillis Miller, Andrzej Warminski and Tom Cohen (eds.), *Material Events: Paul de Man and the Afterlife of Theory*, Minneapolis and London: University of Minnesota Press, 2000.

Conrad, Peter, *Shandyism: The Character of Romantic Irony*, Oxford: Blackwell, 1978.

de Man, Paul, *Aesthetic Ideology*, ed. with intro. Andrzej Warminski, Minneapolis and London: University of Minnesota Press, 1996.

The Rhetoric of Romanticism, New York: Columbia University Press, 1984.

Eagleton, Terry, *The Ideology of the Aesthetic*, Oxford: Blackwell, 1990.

Gilmartin, Kevin, *Print Politics: The Press and Radical Opposition in Early Nineteenth-Century England*, Cambridge: Cambridge University Press, 1996.

Goldsmith, Steven, *Unbuilding Jerusalem: Apocalypse and Romantic Representation*, Ithaca, NY: Cornell University Press, 1993.

Goodman, Kevis, *Georgic Modernity and British Romanticism: Poetry and the Mediation of History*, Cambridge: Cambridge University Press, 2004.

Hamilton, Paul, *Coleridge and German Philosophy: The Poet in the Land of Logic*, London: Continuum, 2007.

Metaromanticism: Aesthetics, Literature, Theory, Chicago and London: University of Chicago Press, 2003.

Hartman, Geoffrey, *The Unmediated Vision*, New Haven: Yale University Press, 1954.

Wordsworth's Poetry 1787–1814, New Haven: Yale University Press, 1964.

Jacobus, Mary, *Tradition and Experiment in Wordsworth's 'Lyrical Ballads' (1798)*, Oxford: Oxford University Press, 1978.

Jarvis, Simon, *Wordsworth's Philosophic Song: Poetic Thinking in Wordsworth*, Cambridge: Cambridge University Press, 2006.

Klancher, Jon, *The Making of English Reading Audiences, 1790–1832*, Madison: University of Wisconsin Press, 1987.

Kooy, Michael John, *Coleridge and Schiller*, London: Palgrave, 2001.

Lacoue-Labarthe, P. and J.-L. Nancy, *The Literary Absolute: The Theory of Literature in German Romanticism*, trans. P. Barnard and C. Lester, Albany, NY: SUNY, 1988.

Levinson, Marjorie, *Keats's Life of Allegory: The Origins of a Style*, Oxford: Basil Blackwell, 1988.

McGann, J. J., *The Poetry of Sensibility*, Oxford: Oxford University Press, 1996.

The Romantic Ideology: A Critical Investigation, Chicago and London: University of Chicago Press, 1983.

Mellor, Anne K., *Mary Shelley: Her Life, Her Fiction, Her Monsters*, New York and London: Routledge, 1988.

Romanticism and Gender, London: Routledge, 1993.

Murphy, Peter, *Poetry as an Occupation and an Art in Britain 1760–1830*, Cambridge: Cambridge University Press, 1993.

Paley, Morton, *Apocalypse and Millennium in English Romantic Poetry*, Oxford: Clarendon Press, 1999.

Parker, Mark, *Literary Magazines and British Romanticism*, Cambridge: Cambridge University Press, 2000.

Roper, Derek, *Reviewing before the 'Edinburgh', 1788–1802*, London: Methuen, 1978.

Simpson, David, *Irony and Authority in English Romantic Poetry*, London: Macmillan, 1979.

Vendler, Helen, *The Odes of John Keats*, Cambridge, MA: Harvard University Press, 1983.

Wellek, René, *A History of Modern Criticism: 1750–1950*, 8 vols., New Haven and London: Yale University Press, 1955–1992.

The Rise of Literary History, Chapel Hill: University of North Carolina Press, 1941.

CHAPTER 19 BIBLIOGRAPHY

Primary works

Brown, Charles Brockden, *Arthur Mervyn; or, Memoirs of the Year 1793* (1799), ed. Warner Berthoff, New York: Holt, Rinehart and Winston, 1965.

Wieland; and Memoirs of Carwin the Biloquist (1798 and 1804), ed. Jay Fliegelman, New York: Penguin, 1991.

Burney, Frances, *Cecilia, or, Memoirs of an Heiress* (1782), ed. Peter Sabor and Margaret Anne Doody, Oxford: Oxford University Press, 1988.

Evelina, or, The History of a Young Lady's Entrance into the World (1778), ed. Edward A. Bloom, Oxford: Oxford University Press, 1968.

Edgeworth, Maria, *Belinda* (1801), ed. Kathryn J. Kirkpatrick, Oxford: Oxford University Press, 1994.

Castle Rackrent; and, Ennui (1800 and 1809), ed. Marilyn Butler, London: Penguin, 1992.

The Works of Maria Edgeworth, 12 vols., ed. Marilyn Butler and Mitzi Myers, London: Pickering and Chatto, 1999–2000.

Godwin, William, *Caleb Williams* (1794), ed. Maurice Hindle, London: Penguin, 1988.

Collected Novels and Memoirs of William Godwin, 8 vols., ed. Mark Philp, London: Pickering and Chatto, 1992.

St Leon: A Tale of the Sixteenth Century (1799), ed. William D. Brewer, Peterborough, Ontario: Broadview Press, 2006.

Hamilton, Elizabeth, *Memoirs of Modern Philosophers* (1800), ed. Claire Grogan, Peterborough, Ontario: Broadview Press, 2000.

Hays, Mary, *Memoirs of Emma Courtney* (1796), ed. Eleanor Ty, Oxford: Oxford University Press, 1996.

The Victim of Prejudice (1799), ed. Eleanor Ty, 2nd edn, Peterborough, Ontario: Broadview Press, 1998.

Holcroft, Thomas, *Anna St. Ives* (1792), ed. Peter Faulkner, Oxford: Oxford University Press, 1970.

Inchbald, Elizabeth, *A Simple Story* (1791), ed. J. M. S. Tompkins, Oxford: Oxford University Press, 1988.

Lee, Sophia, *The Recess, or, A Tale of Other Times* (1783–5), ed. April Alliston, Lexington: University Press of Kentucky, 2000.

Lewis, Matthew, *The Monk* (1796), ed. Howard Anderson, Oxford: Oxford University Press, 1995.

Mackenzie, Henry, *Julia de Roubigné* (1779), ed. Susan Manning, East Lothian: Tuckwell Press, 1999.

The Man of Feeling (1771), ed. Brian Vickers, Oxford: Oxford University Press, 2001.

Radcliffe, Anne, *The Mysteries of Udolpho* (1794), ed. Bonamy Dobrée, Oxford: Oxford University Press, 1998.

The Romance of the Forest (1791), ed. Chloe Chard, Oxford: Oxford University Press, 1991.

Reeve, Clara, *The Old English Baron: A Gothic Story* (1777), ed. James Trainer, Oxford: Oxford University Press, 2003.

Robinson, Mary, *Walsingham, or, The Pupil of Nature* (1797), ed. Julie A. Shaffer, Peterborough, Ontario: Broadview Press, 2003.

Smith, Charlotte, *Desmond* (1792), ed. Antje Blank and Janet Todd, Peterborough, Ontario: Broadview Press, 2001.

The Works of Charlotte Smith, ed. Stuart Curran, London: Pickering and Chatto, 2005–7.

Walpole, Horace, *The Castle of Otranto: A Gothic Story* (1764–5), ed. W. S. Lewis, Oxford: Oxford University Press, 1996.

Wollstonecraft, Mary, *Mary, and The Wrongs of Woman* (1788 and 1798), ed. Gary Kelly, Oxford: Oxford University Press, 1976.

The Works of Mary Wollstonecraft, 7 vols., ed. Marilyn Butler and Janet Todd, London: Pickering and Chatto, 1989.

Secondary works

Alliston, April, 'The Value of a Literary Legacy: Retracing the Transmission of Value through Female Lines', *Yale Journal of Criticism* 4 (1990), 109–27.

Armstrong, Nancy, *Desire and Domestic Fiction: A Political History of the Novel*, New York: Oxford University Press, 1987.

Brown, Marshall, *The Gothic Text*, Stanford: Stanford University Press, 2005.

Butler, Marilyn, *Jane Austen and the War of Ideas*, 2nd edn, Oxford: Oxford University Press, 1987.

Clemit, Pamela, *The Godwinian Novel: The Rational Fictions of Godwin, Brockden Brown, Mary Shelley*, Oxford: Clarendon Press, 1993.

Clery, E. J., *The Rise of Supernatural Fiction, 1762–1800*, Cambridge: Cambridge University Press, 1995.

Downie, J. A., 'The Making of the English Novel', *Eighteenth-Century Fiction* 9 (1997), 249–66.

Duncan, Ian, *Modern Romance and Transformations of the Novel: The Gothic, Scott, Dickens*, Cambridge: Cambridge University Press, 1992.

Ellis, Markman, *The Politics of Sensibility: Race, Gender and Commerce in the Sentimental Novel*, Cambridge: Cambridge University Press, 1996.

Favret, Mary A., *Romantic Correspondence: Women, Politics and the Fiction of Letters*, Cambridge: Cambridge University Press, 1993.

'Telling Tales about Genre: Poetry in the Romantic Novel', *Studies in the Novel* 26 (1994), 281–300.

Ferris, Ina, *The Achievement of Literary Authority: Gender, History, and the Waverley Novels*, Ithaca: Cornell University Press, 1991.

Gamer, Michael, *Romanticism and the Gothic: Genre, Reception, and Canon Formation*, Cambridge: Cambridge University Press, 2000.

Garside, Peter, James Raven and Rainer Schöwerling, *The English Novel, 1770–1829: A Bibliographical Survey of Prose Fiction Published in the British Isles*, 2 vols., Oxford: Oxford University Press, 2000.

Gilroy, Amanda, and Wil Verhoeven, 'Introduction: The Romantic-Era Novel: A Special Issue', *Novel: A Forum on Fiction* 34 (2001), 147–62.

Henderson, Andrea, 'Commerce and Masochistic Desire in the 1790s', *Eighteenth-Century Studies* 31 (1997), 69–86.

Johnson, Claudia L., *Equivocal Beings: Politics, Gender, and Sentimentality in the 1790s*, Chicago: University of Chicago Press, 1995.

Jane Austen: Women, Politics, and the Novel, Chicago: University of Chicago Press, 1988.

Kelly, Gary, *English Fiction of the Romantic Period, 1789–1830*, London: Longman, 1989.

Lynch, Deidre Shauna, *The Economy of Character: Novels, Market Culture, and the Business of Inner Meaning*, Chicago: University of Chicago Press, 1998.

'Gothic Libraries and National Subjects', *Studies in Romanticism* 40 (2001), 29–48.

Mayo, Robert D., *The English Novel in the Magazines, 1740–1815*, Evanston, IL: Northwestern University Press, 1962.

Price, Leah, *The Anthology and the Rise of the Novel*, Cambridge: Cambridge University Press, 2000.

Rajan, Tillotama, 'Wollstonecraft and Godwin: Reading the Secrets of the Political Novel', in *The Supplement of Reading*, Ithaca: Cornell University Press, 1990.

Raven, James, *Judging New Wealth: Popular Publishing and Responses to Commerce in England, 1750–1800*, Oxford: Clarendon Press, 1992.

Siskin, Clifford, 'Periodicals, Authorship, and the Romantic Rise of the Novel', in Clifford Siskin, *The Work of Writing: Literature and Social Change in Britain, 1700–1830*, Baltimore: Johns Hopkins University Press, 1998, pp. 155–71.

Spacks, Patricia Meyer, *Desire and Truth: Functions of Plot in Eighteenth-Century English Novels*, Chicago: University of Chicago Press, 1990.

Taylor, Richard C., 'James Harrison, *The Novelist's Magazine*, and the Early Canonizing of the English Novel', *Studies in English Literature* 33 (1993), 629–43.

Trumpener, Katie, *Bardic Nationalism: The Romantic Novel and the British Empire*, Princeton: Princeton University Press, 1997.

Watson, Nicola, *Revolution and the Form of the British Novel, 1790–1825*, Oxford: Clarendon Press, 1994.

Watt, James, *Contesting the Gothic: Fiction, Genre and Cultural Conflict, 1764–1832*, Cambridge: Cambridge University Press, 1999.

CHAPTER 20 BIBLIOGRAPHY

Primary works

Austen, Jane, *The Works of Jane Austen*, 9 vols., gen. ed. Janet Todd, Cambridge: Cambridge University Press, 2005–8.

Banim, John, *The Anglo-Irish of the Nineteenth Century: A Novel*, London, 1828.

Banim, Michael, *The Croppy: A Tale of the Irish Rebellion of 1798* (1828), New York: Garland, 1978.

Barbauld, Anna Laetitia (ed.), *The British Novelists; with an Essay, and Prefaces Biographical and Critical*, 50 vols., London, 1810.

Brunton, Mary, *Discipline*, Edinburgh, 1814.

  Self-Control: A Novel in Two Volumes, Edinburgh, 1810.

Burke, Edmund, *Reflections on the Revolution in France* (1790), ed. Conor Cruise O'Brien, London: Penguin, 1968.

Dunlop, John, *The History of Fiction*, London, 1814.

Edgeworth, Maria, *The Absentee* (1812), ed. W. J. McCormack and Kim Walker, Oxford: Oxford University Press, 1988.

  Castle Rackrent; and, Ennui (1800; 1809), ed. Marilyn Butler, London: Penguin, 1992.

  Ormond (1817), ed. Claire Connolly, London: Penguin, 2000.

  The Works of Maria Edgeworth, 12 vols., ed. Marilyn Butler and Mitzi Myers, London: Pickering and Chatto, 1999/2000.

Ferrier, Susan, *Marriage* (1818), ed. Herbert Foltinek, Oxford: Oxford University Press, 1986.

Galt, John, *Annals of the Parish*, Edinburgh, 1821.

The Entail: or the Lairds of Grippy (1822/3), ed. Ian A. Gordon, Oxford: Oxford University Press, 1984.

Ringhan Gilhaize: or The Covenanters (1823), ed. Patricia J. Wilson, Edinburgh: Scottish Academic Press, 1984.

Godwin, William, *Mandeville: A Tale of the Seventeenth Century in England* (1817), ed. Pamela Clemit, *Complete Novels and Memoirs of William Godwin*, vol. VI, London: Pickering and Chatto, 1992.

Hamilton, Elizabeth, *Cottagers of Glenburnie: A Tale for the Farmer's Inglenook* (1808), New York: Garland, 1974.

[Hazlitt, William], 'Mr. Godwin', *Edinburgh Review* 51 (April 1830), 144–59.

Hogg, James, *The Brownie of Bodsbeck* (1818), ed. Douglas S. Mack, Edinburgh: Scottish Academic Press, 1976.

> *The Private Memoirs and Confessions of a Justified Sinner: Written by Himself, With a Detail of Curious Traditionary Facts and Other Evidence by the Editor* (1824), ed. P. D. Garside, Edinburgh: Edinburgh University Press, 2002.

> *The Three Perils of Woman* (1823), ed. Antony Hasler and Douglas S. Mack, Edinburgh: Edinburgh University Press, 2002.

[Jeffrey, Francis], Review of Edgeworth, *Fashionable Tales*, *Edinburgh Review* 20 (July 1812), 100–26.

Johnstone, Christian Isobel, *Clan-Albin: A National Tale* (1815), ed. Andrew Monnickendam, Glasgow: Association for Scottish Literary Studies, 2003.

[Lister, T. H.], 'The Waverley Novels', *Edinburgh Review* 55 (April 1832), 61–79.

Maturin, Charles Robert, *Melmoth the Wanderer* (1820), ed. Douglas Grant, Oxford: Oxford University Press, 1989.

> *The Milesian Chief: A Romance*, London, 1812.

Morgan, Lady (Sydney Owenson), *Florence Macarthy: An Irish Tale*, London, 1818.

> *The O'Briens and the O'Flahertics: A National Tale*, London: 1827.

> *O'Donnel: A National Tale* (1814), New York: Garland, 1979.

> *The Wild Irish Girl: A National Tale* (1806), ed. Claire Connolly and Stephen Copley, London: Pickering and Chatto, 2000.

> *The Wild Irish Girl*, rev. edn, London, 1846.

Opie, Amelia, *Adeline Mowbray; or the Mother and Daughter* (1805), ed. Shelley King and John B. Pierce, Oxford: Oxford University Press, 1999.

> 'Remarks on Mandeville', *Blackwood's Magazine* 2 (January 1818), 402–8.

Scott, Walter, *The Waverley Novels*, 48 vols., Edinburgh, 1829–33.

> *Waverley; or, 'Tis Sixty Years Since* (1814), ed. Claire Lamont, Oxford: Oxford University Press, 1986.

Scott, Walter (ed.), *Ballantyne's Novelist's Library*, Edinburgh, 1821–4.

Shelley, Mary, *Valperga; or, The Life and Adventures of Castruccio, Prince of Lucca* (1823), ed. Stuart Curran, New York and Oxford: Oxford University Press, 1997.

Secondary works

Bann, Stephen, *Romanticism and the Rise of History*, New York: Twayne Publishers, 1995.

Brown, Homer Obed, *Institutions of the English Novel From Defoe to Scott*, Philadelphia: University of Pennsylvania Press, 1997.

Burgess, Miranda, *British Fiction and the Production of Social Order, 1740–1830*, Cambridge: Cambridge University Press, 2000.

Butler, Marilyn, Introduction, *Castle Rackrent; and, Ennui*, London: Penguin, 1992, pp. 1–54.

Chandler, James, *England in 1819: The Politics of Literary Culture and the Case of Romantic Historicism*, Chicago and London: University of Chicago Press, 1998.

Dennis, Ian, *Nationalism and Desire in Early Historical Fiction*, London: Macmillan, 1997.

Duncan, Ian, *Modern Romance and Transformations of the Novel: The Gothic, Scott, Dickens*, Cambridge: Cambridge University Press, 1992.

  Scott's Shadow, Princeton: Princeton University Press, 2007.

Ferris, Ina, *The Achievement of Literary Authority: Gender, History, and the Waverley Novels*, Ithaca: Cornell University Press, 1991.

  The Romantic National Tale and the Question of Ireland, Cambridge: Cambridge University Press, 2002.

Fielding, Penny, *Writing and Orality: Nationality, Culture, and Nineteenth-Century Scottish Fiction*, Oxford: Clarendon Press, 1996.

Garside, Peter, James Raven and Rainer Schöwerling, *The English Novel, 1770–1829: A Bibliographical Survey of Prose Fiction Published in the British Isles*, 2 vols., Oxford: Oxford University Press, 2000.

Kelly, Gary, *English Fiction of the Romantic Period*, London: Longman, 1989.

Lynch, Deidre, 'Gothic Libraries and National Subjects', *Studies in Romanticism* 40 (2001), 29–48.

Magnusson, Paul, *Reading Public Romanticism*, Princeton: Princeton University Press, 1998.

Millgate, Jane, *Scott's Last Edition: A Study in Publishing History*, Edinburgh: Edinburgh University Press, 1987.

Pearson, Jacqueline, *Women's Reading in Britain, 1750–1835: A Dangerous Recreation*, Cambridge: Cambridge University Press, 1999.

Phillips, Mark, *Society and Sentiment: Genres of Historical Writing in Britain, 1740–1820*, Princeton: Princeton University Press, 2000.

Poovey, Mary, *A History of the Modern Fact: Problems of Knowledge in the Sciences of Wealth and Society*, Chicago and London: University of Chicago Press, 1998.

Rigney, Ann, *Imperfect Histories: The Elusive Past and the Legacy of Romantic Historicism*, Ithaca: Cornell University Press, 2001.

Robertson, Fiona, *Legitimate Histories: Scott, Gothic, and the Authorities of Fiction*, Oxford: Clarendon Press, 1994.

Tracy, Robert, 'Maria Edgeworth and Lady Morgan', *Nineteenth-Century Fiction* 40 (1985), 1–22.

Trumpener, Katie, *Bardic Nationalism: The Romantic Novel and the British Empire*, Princeton: Princeton University Press, 2000.

Uphaus, Robert, 'Jane Austen and Female Reading', *Studies in the Novel* 19 (1987), 334–45.

Watson, Nicola J., *Revolution and the Form of the British Novel, 1790–1825: Intercepted Letters, Interrupted Seductions*, Oxford: Clarendon Press, 1994.

Welsh, Alexander, *The Hero of the Waverley Novels: With New Essays on Scott*, Princeton: Princeton University Press, 1992.

CHAPTER 21 BIBLIOGRAPHY

Primary works

Baillie, Joanna, *The Dramatic and Poetical Works* (*1851*), Hildesheim, NY: Georg Olms Verlag, 1976.

Coleridge, Samuel Taylor, *Lectures 1808–19: On Literature*, 2 vols., ed. R. A. Foakes, vol. V, in *The Collected Works of Samuel Taylor Coleridge*, Bollingen Series 75, Princeton: Princeton University Press, 1986.

Hazlitt, William, *The Complete Works of William Hazlitt*, ed. P. P. Howe, 2 vols., Toronto and London: J. M. Dent and Sons, 1930–4.

  Hazlitt on Theatre, ed. William Archer and Robert Lowe, New York: Hill and Wang, 1895.

Hunt, Leigh, *Leigh Hunt's Dramatic Criticism, 1808–31*, ed. Lawrence Huston Houtchens and Carolyn Washburn Houtchens, New York: Columbia University Press, 1949.

Lamb, Charles, 'On the Tragedies of Shakespeare, Considered with Reference to Their Fitness for Stage Representation', in *The Works of Charles and Mary Lamb*, ed. E. V. Lucas, London: Methuen, 1903–5.

Secondary works

Altick, Richard Daniel, *The Shows of London*, Cambridge, MA: Harvard University Press, 1978.

Baer, Marc, *Theatre and Disorder in Late Georgian London*, Oxford: Clarendon Press, 1992.

Bate, Jonathan, *Shakespearean Constitutions: Politics, Theatre, Criticism, 1730–1830*, Oxford: Oxford University Press, 1989.

Boaden, James, *Memoirs of the Life of John Philip Kemble, Esq., Including a History of the Stage, from the Time of Garrick to the Present Period*, 2 vols., London: Longman, Hurst, 1825.

  Memoirs of Mrs Siddons: Interspersed with Anecdotes of Authors and Actors, 2 vols., London: Henry Colburn, 1827.

Bolton, Betsy, *Women, Nationalism and the Romantic Stage: Theatre and Politics in Britain, 1780–1800*, Cambridge: Cambridge University Press, 2001.

Bratton, Jacky, *New Readings in Theatre History*, Cambridge: Cambridge University Press, 2003.

Bratton, Jacky (ed.), *Acts of Supremacy: The British Empire on Stage, 1790–1930*, Manchester: Manchester University Press, 1991.

Brody, Jennifer Devere, *Impossible Purities: Blackness, Femininity, and Victorian Culture*, Durham and London: Duke University Press, 1998.

Buckley, Matthew S., *Tragedy Walks the Streets: The French Revolution in the Making Of Modern Drama*, Baltimore: Johns Hopkins University Press, 2006.

Burroughs, Catherine, *Closet Stages: Joanna Baillie and the Theater Theory of British Romantic Women Writers*, Philadelphia: University of Pennsylvania Press, 1997.

Burroughs, Catherine (ed.), *Women in British Romantic Theatre: Drama, Performance and Society, 1790–1840*, Cambridge: Cambridge University Press, 1991.

Burwick, Frederick, *Illusion and the Drama: Critical Theory of the Enlightenment and Romantic Era*, University Park: Pennsylvania State University Press, 1991.

Carlson, Julie A., *In the Theatre of Romanticism: Coleridge, Nationalism, Women*, Cambridge: Cambridge University Press, 1994; pbk 2007.

Cox, Jeffrey N., *In the Shadows of Romance: Romantic Tragic Drama in Germany, England, and France*, Athens: Ohio University Press, 1987.

Cox, Jeffrey N. (ed.), *Slavery, Abolition, and Emancipation in the British Romantic Period*, vol. V, *The Drama*, London: Pickering & Chatto, 1999.

Cox, Jeffrey N., and Michael Gamer (eds.), *The Broadview Anthology of Romantic Drama*, Toronto: Broadview Press, 2003.

Crochunis, Thomas C. (ed.), *Joanna Baillie, Romantic Dramatist: Critical Essays*, London and New York: Routledge, 2004.

Davis, Tracy C., *The Economics of the British Stage, 1800–1914*, Cambridge: Cambridge University Press, 2000.

Davis, Tracy C., and Ellin Donkin (eds.), *Women and Playwriting in Nineteenth-century Britain*, Cambridge: Cambridge University Press, 1999.

Donkin, Ellen, *Getting into the Act: Women Playwrights in London, 1776–1829*, London: Routledge, 1995.

Donohue, Joseph W., Jr, *Dramatic Character in the English Romantic Age*, Princeton: Princeton University Press, 1970.

Gamer, Michael, *Romanticism and the Gothic: Genre, Reception, and Canon Formation*, Cambridge: Cambridge University Press, 2000.

Hadley, Elaine, *Melodramatic Tactics: Theatricalised Dissent and the Marketplace, 1800–1885*, Stanford: Stanford University Press, 1995.

Hays, Michael, and Anastasia Nikolopoulu, *Melodrama: The Cultural Emergence of a Genre*, New York: St Martin's Press, 1996.

Marshall, Herbert, and Mildred Stock, *Ira Aldridge, the Negro Tragedian*, Carbondale and Edwardsville: Southern Illinois University Press, 1958.

Mayer, David, *Harlequin in His Element: The English Pantomime, 1806–1836*, Cambridge, MA: Harvard University Press, 1969.

Moody, Jane, *Illegitimate Theatre in London, 1770–1840*, Cambridge: Cambridge University Press, 2000.

Moody, Jane, and Daniel O'Quinn (eds.), *Cambridge Companion to British Theatre, 1730–1830*, Cambridge: Cambridge University Press, 2007.

O'Brien, John, *Harlequin Britain: Pantomime and Entertainment, 1690–1760*, Baltimore: Johns Hopkins University Press, 2004.

Oettermann, Stephan, *The Panorama: History of a Mass Medium*, trans. Deborah Lucas Schneider, New York: Zone Books, 1997.

O'Quinn, Daniel, *Staging Governance: Theatrical Imperialism in London, 1770–1800*, Baltimore: Johns Hopkins University Press, 2005.

Pascoe, Judith, *Romantic Theatricality: Gender, Poetry, and Spectatorship*, Ithaca: Cornell University Press, 1997.

Richardson, Alan, *A Mental Theatre: Poetic Drama and Consciousness in the Romantic Age*, University Park: Pennsylvania State University Press, 1988.

Roach, Joseph, *Cities of the Dead: Circum-atlantic Performance*, New York: Columbia University Press, 1996.

Rosenfeld, Sybil Marion, *Temple of Thespis: Some Private Theatres and Theatricals in England and Wales, 1700–1820*, London: Society for Theatre Research, 1978.

Russell, Gillian, *The Theatres of War: Performance, Politics and Society, 1793–1815*, Oxford: Clarendon Press, 1995.

Schofield, Mary Anne, and Cecilia Macheski, *Curtain Calls: British and American Women and the Theater, 1660–1820*, Athens and London: Ohio University Press, 1990.

Simpson, Michael, *Closet Performances: Political Exhibition and Prohibition in the Dramas of Byron and Shelley*, Stanford: Stanford University Press, 1998.

Simpson, Michael (ed.), *Romantic Drama in Place, Texas Studies in Literature and Language* 41:4 (1999).

Southern, Richard, *Changeable Scenery: Its Origin and Development in the British Theatre*, London: Faber, 1951.

Swindells, Julia, *Glorious Causes: The Grand Theatre of Political Change, 1789–1833*, Oxford: Oxford University Press, 2001.

Taylor, George, *The French Revolution and the London Stage, 1789–1805*, Cambridge: Cambridge University Press, 2000.

West, Shearer, *The Image of the Actor: Verbal and Visual Representation in the Age of Garrick and Kemble*, London: Pinter Publications, 1991.

Worrall, David, *The Politics of Romantic Theatricality, 1787–1832: The Road to the Stage*, New York: Palgrave Macmillan, 2007.

　Theatric Revolution, Oxford: Oxford University Press, 2005.

CHAPTER 22 BIBLIOGRAPHY

Primary works

Blumenbach, Johann Friedrich, *On the Natural Varieties of Mankind* (1795), rpt New York: Bergman, 1969.

Coleridge, Samuel Taylor, *Shorter Works and Fragments*, ed. H. J. and J. R. de J. Jackson, 2 vols., Princeton, NJ: Princeton University Press, 1995.

Godwin, William, 'Of History and Romance', in *Things as They Are; or The Adventures of Caleb Williams*, ed. Maurice Hindle, Harmondsworth: Penguin, 1988.

Goethe, Johann Wolfgang von, *Scientific Studies*, ed. and trans. Douglas Miller, New York: Suhrkamp Publishers, 1988.

Green, Joseph Henry, *Vital Dynamics: The Hunterian Oration Before the Royal College of Surgeons*, London: William Pickering, 1840.

Hegel, Georg Wilhelm Friedrich, *Aesthetics: Lectures on Fine Arts*, 2 vols., trans. T. M. Knox, Oxford: Clarendon Press, 1975.

Herder, J. G., *Selected Early Works, 1764–1767*, ed. and trans. Ernst A. Menze and Karl Menges, University Park, PA: Pennsylvania State University Press, 1992.

Hugo, Victor, *Preface to 'Cromwell'* (1827), Paris: Garnier Flammarion, 1968.

Kant, Immanuel, *Critique of Judgment* (1791), trans. J. H. Bernard, New York: Hafner, 1951.

Reeve, Clara, *The Progress of Romance, Through Times, Countries, and Manners* (1785), rpt New York: Facsimile Text Society, 1930.

Schelling, Friedrich, *The Philosophy of Art* (1803/4), ed. and trans. Douglas W. Stott, Minneapolis, MN: University of Minnesota Press, 1989.

Schlegel, Friedrich, *Dialogue on Poetry and Literary Aphorisms*, trans. Ernst Behler and Roman Struc, University Park: Pennsylvania State University Press, 1968.

    Literary Notebooks, 1797–1801, ed. Hans Eichner, Toronto: University of Toronto Press, 1957.

    Philosophical Fragments, trans. Peter Firchow, Minneapolis, MN: University of Minnesota Press, 1991.

Shelley, Percy Bysshe, *A Defence of Poetry*, in *Shelley's Poetry and Prose*, ed. Donald H. Reiman and Sharon Powers, New York: Norton, 1977.

    'Preface' to *Hellas*, in *Shelley's Poetry and Prose*, pp. 407–10.

Southey, Robert, *Lives and Works of the Uneducated Poets* (1831), London: Humphrey Milford, 1925.

Wordsworth, William, 'Essay Supplementary to the Preface' (1815), in *Literary Criticism of William Wordsworth*, ed. Paul M. Zall, Lincoln, NE: University of Nebraska Press, 1966.

Secondary sources

Adorno, Theodor, 'The Essay as Form', in *The Adorno Reader*, ed. Brian O'Connor, Oxford: Blackwell, 2000.

    'Lyric Poetry and Society', in *The Adorno Reader*.

Althusser, Louis, 'Ideology and Ideological State Apparatuses' (1969), in *Lenin and Philosophy and Other Essays*, trans. Ben Brewster, New York: Monthly Review Press, 1971.

Applebaum, Wilbur, *Encyclopedia of the Scientific Revolution: From Copernicus to Newton*, New York: Garland, 2000.

Bakhtin, Mikhail, *The Dialogic Imagination: Four Essays*, trans. Caryl Emerson and Michael Holquist, Austin: University of Texas Press, 1981.

Benjamin, Walter, *The Origin of German Tragic Drama*, trans. John Osborne, London: Verso, 1992.

Berman, Antoine, *The Experience of the Foreign: Culture and Translation in Romantic Germany*, trans. S. Heyvaert, Albany, NY: State University of New York Press, 1984.

Bloom, Harold, 'The Internalization of Quest Romance', in *The Ringers in the Tower: Studies in Romantic Tradition*, Chicago: University of Chicago Press, 1971.

Brothers, Barbara, and Bege K. Bowers (eds.), *Reading and Writing Women's Lives: A Study of the Novel of Manners*, Ann Arbor: UMI Research Press, 1990.

Bynum, W. F., E. J. Browne and Roy Porter (eds.), *Dictionary of the History of Science*, Princeton, NJ: Princeton University Press, 1981.

Deleuze, Gilles, and Felix Guattari, *Kafka: Toward a Minor Literature*, trans. Dana Polan, Minneapolis, MN: University of Minnesota Press, 1986.

Ehrenpreis, Irving, *The 'Types Approach' to Literature*, New York: King's Crown Press, 1945.

Fishelov, David, *Metaphors of Genre: The Role of Analogies in Genre Theory*, University Park, PA: Pennsylvania State University Press, 1993.

Foucault, Michel, 'Governmentality', in Graham Burchell, Colin Gordon and Peter Miller (eds.), *The Foucault Effect: Studies in Governmentality*, Chicago: University of Chicago Press, 1991.

Fowler, Alistair, *Kinds of Literature: An Introduction to the Theory of Genres and Modes*, Cambridge, MA: Harvard University Press, 1982.

Guillen, Claudio, *Literature as System: Essays Towards the Theory of Literary History*, Princeton, NJ: Princeton University Press, 1971.

Hamlin, Cyrus, 'The Origins of a Philosophical Genre Theory in German Romanticism', *European Romantic Review* 5:1 (1994), 3–14.

Hogle, Jerrold, 'Frankenstein as Neo-Gothic: From the Ghost of the Counterfeit to the Monster of Abjection', in *Romanticism, History, and the Possibilities of Genre: Re-forming Literature, 1789–1837*, ed. Tilottama Rajan and Julia Wright, Cambridge: Cambridge University Press, 1999.

Kelly, Gary, *English Fiction of the Romantic Period: 1789–1830*, London: Longman, 1989.

Kristeva, Julia, *Desire in Language: A Semiotic Approach to Literature and Art*, trans. Leon Roudiez, New York: Columbia University Press, 1980.

Lenoir, Timothy, *The Strategy of Life: Teleology and Mechanics in Nineteenth-Century German Biology*, Chicago: University of Chicago Press, 1989.

Levinson, Marjorie, *Wordsworth's Great Period-Poems*, Cambridge: Cambridge University Press, 1986.

Lukács, Georg, *The Theory of the Novel: A Historico-Philosophical Essay on the Forms of Great Epic Literature*, trans. Anna Bostock, Cambridge, MA: The MIT Press, 1971.

McGann, Jerome J., *The Romantic Ideology: A Critical Interpretation*, Chicago: University of Chicago Press, 1983.

Mowitt, John, *Text: The Genealogy of an Antidisciplinary Object*, Durham, NC: Duke University Press, 1992.

Pfau, Thomas, *Wordsworth's Profession: Form, Class and the Logic of Early Romantic Cultural Production*, Stanford, CA: Stanford University Press, 1997.

Rajan, Tilottama, 'Autonarration and Genotext in Mary Hays' *Memoirs of Emma Courtney*', in *Romanticism, History, and the Possibilities of Genre*, ed. Tilottama Rajan and Julia Wright, Cambridge: Cambridge University Press, 1999.

'Coleridge, Wordsworth, and the Textual Abject', in *Rhetorical and Cultural Dissolution in Romanticism*, ed. Thomas Pfau and Rhonda Ray Kercsmar, *South Atlantic Quarterly* 95 (1996), 797–820.

'Romanticism and the Death of Lyric Consciousness', in *Lyric Poetry: Beyond New Criticism*, ed. Patricia Parker and Chaviva Hosek, Ithaca, NY: Cornell University Press, 1985.

'Theories of Genre', in *The Cambridge History of Literary Criticism*, vol. V: *Romanticism*, ed. Marshall Brown, Cambridge: Cambridge University Press, 2000.

Richards, Robert J., *The Romantic Conception of Life: Science and Philosophy in the Age of Goethe*, Chicago: University of Chicago Press, 2002.

Sartre, Jean-Paul, *What is Literature?*, trans. Bernard Frechtman, Gloucester, MA: Peter Smith, 1978.

Siskin, Clifford, *The Work of Writing: Literature and Social Change in Britain, 1700–1830*, Baltimore, MD: The Johns Hopkins University Press, 1998.

Tate, Allen, 'Tension in Poetry' (1938), in *Essays of Four Decades*, Chicago: Swallow Press, 1968.

Turner, Louis, and John Ash, *The Golden Hordes: International Tourism and the Pleasure Periphery*, London: St Martin's Press, 1976.

Van Den Abbeele, Georges, *Travel as Metaphor: From Montaigne to Rousseau*, Minneapolis, MN: University of Minnesota Press, 1992.

CHAPTER 23 BIBLIOGRAPHY

Primary works

Abernethy, John, *Part of the Introductory Lecture for the Year 1815*, London: Longman, 1815.

Aldini, John, *An Account of the Late Improvements in Galvanism*, London: Cuthell and Martin, and J. Murray, 1803.

[Anon.], Review of Playfair, *Illustrations of the Huttonian Theory*, *Edinburgh Review* 1 (1802), 201–16.

Burke, Edmund, *A Philosophical Enquiry into the Origin of our Ideas of the Sublime and the Beautiful* (1757), ed. James T. Boulton, Oxford: Basil Blackwell, 1987.

Carlyle, Thomas, *Selected Writings*, ed. Alan Shelston, Harmondsworth: Penguin Books, 1971.

Chambers, Robert, *Vestiges of the Natural History of Creation and Other Evolutionary Writings* (1844), ed. James A. Secord, Chicago: University of Chicago Press, 1994.

Coleridge, Samuel Taylor, *The Philosophical Lectures of Samuel Taylor Coleridge*, ed. Kathleen Coburn, New York: Philosophical Library, 1949.

Davy, Humphry, 'Discourse Introductory to a Course of Lectures on Chemistry' (1802), in *The Collected Works of Humphry Davy*, ed. John Davy, 9 vols., London: Smith, Elder, 1839–40, vol. II, pp. 311–26.

Elements of Agricultural Chemistry (1813), in *Works of Davy*, vol. VII, pp. 169–391.

Humphry Davy on Geology: The 1805 Lectures for the General Audience, ed. Robert Siegfried and Robert H. Dott, Madison: University of Wisconsin Press, 1980.

Deluc, Jean André, *An Elementary Treatise on Geology*, London: F. C. and J. Rivington, 1809.

Howard, Luke, *The Climate of London, Deduced from Meteorological Observations*, 2 vols., London: W. Phillips, 1818–20.

Humboldt, Alexander von, *Views of Nature: Or Contemplations on the Sublime Phenomena of Creation*, trans. E. C. Otté and Henry G. Bohn, London: Bohn, 1850.

Kant, Immanuel, *Critique of Judgment* (1790), trans. Werner S. Pluhar, Indianapolis: Hackett, 1987.

Kirwan, Richard, *Geological Essays*, London: T. Bensley, 1799.

Lawrence, William, *Lectures on Physiology, Zoology, and the Natural History of Man*, London: J. Callow, 1819.

Martineau, Harriet, *The History of England during the Thirty Years' Peace, 1816–1846*, 2 vols., London: Charles Knight, 1849–50.

Parkinson, James, *Organic Remains of a Former World*, 3 vols. in 1, London: Sherwood, Neely, and Jones, 1811.

Priestley, Joseph, *Experiments and Observations on Different Kinds of Air*, 2nd edn, 3 vols., London: J. Johnson, 1775–7.

The History and Present State of Electricity with Original Experiments, 2nd edn, London: J. Dodsley, J. Johnson and J. Payne, and T. Cadell, 1769.

Reid, William Hamilton, *The Rise and Dissolution of the Infidel Societies of this Metropolis*, London: J. Hatchard, 1800.

Shelley, Mary, *Frankenstein, or the Modern Prometheus*, 3 vols., London: Lackington, Hughes, Harding, Mavor, and Jones, 1818.

Secondary works

Averill, James, 'Wordsworth and Natural Science: The Poetry of 1798', *Journal of English and Germanic Philology* 77 (1978), 232–46.

Baldick, Chris, *In Frankenstein's Shadow: Myth, Monstrosity and Nineteenth-Century Writing*, Oxford: Clarendon Press, 1987.

Brooke, J. H., 'Natural Theology and the Plurality of Worlds: Observations on the Brewster-Whewell Debate', *Annals of Science* 34 (1977), 221–86.

'Nebular Contraction and the Expansion of Naturalism', *British Journal for the History of Science* 12 (1979), 200–11.

Brush, Stephen G., *The History of Modern Science: A Guide to the Second Scientific Revolution, 1800–1950*, Ames: Iowa State University Press, 1988.

Butler, Marilyn, 'Culture's Medium: The Role of the Review', in Stuart Curran (ed.), *The Cambridge Companion to British Romanticism*, Cambridge: Cambridge University Press, 1993, pp. 120–47.

Romantics, Rebels, and Reactionaries: English Literature and Its Background, 1760–1830, New York: Oxford University Press, 1982.

Cannon, Susan Faye, *Science in Culture: The Early Victorian Period*, New York: Dawson, 1978.

Cantor, Geoffrey, 'The Scientist as Hero: Public Images of Michael Faraday', in Michael Shortland and Richard Yeo (eds.), *Telling Lives in Science: Essays on Scientific Biography*, Cambridge: Cambridge University Press, 1996, pp. 171–93.

Cardinal, Roger, 'Romantic Travel', in Roy Porter (ed.), *Rewriting the Self: Histories from the Renaissance to the Present*, London and New York: Routledge, 1997, pp. 135–55.

Clubbe, John, 'The Tempest-toss'd Summer of 1816: Mary Shelley's Frankenstein', *The Byron Journal* 19 (1991), 26–40.

Cooter, Roger, and Stephen Pumfrey, 'Separate Spheres and Public Places: Reflections on the History of Science Popularization and Science in Popular Culture', *History of Science* 32 (1994), 237–67.

Cunningham, Andrew, and Nicholas Jardine (eds.), *Romanticism and the Sciences*, Cambridge: Cambridge University Press, 1990.

Dean, Denis R., *James Hutton and the History of Geology*, Ithaca, NY: Cornell University Press, 1992.

Desmond, Adrian, 'Artisan Resistance and Evolution in Britain, 1819–1848', *Osiris* (2nd ser.) 3 (1987), 77–110.

The Politics of Evolution: Morphology, Medicine and Reform in Radical London, Chicago: University of Chicago Press, 1989.

Dettelbach, Michael, 'Humboldtian Science', in N. Jardine, J. A. Secord and E. C. Spary (eds.), *Cultures of Natural History*, Cambridge: Cambridge University Press, 1996, pp. 287–304.

Gillispie, C. C., *Genesis and Geology: A Study in the Relations of Scientific Thought, Natural Theology, and Social Opinion in Britain, 1790–1850*, Cambridge, MA: Harvard University Press, 1951.

Golinski, Jan, 'Humphry Davy's Sexual Chemistry', *Configurations* 7 (1999), 15–41.

Making Natural Knowledge: Constructivism and the History of Science, Cambridge: Cambridge University Press, 1998.

Science as Public Culture: Chemistry and Enlightenment in Britain, 1760–1820, Cambridge: Cambridge University Press, 1992.

Grant, R., 'Hutton's Theory of the Earth', in L. J. Jordanova and R. S. Porter (eds.), *Images of the Earth: Essays in the History of the Environmental Sciences*, Chalfont St Giles: British Society for the History of Science, 1979, pp. 23–38.

Inkster, Ian, 'Science and Society in the Metropolis: A Preliminary Examination of the Social and Institutional Context of the Askesian Society of London, 1796–1807', *Annals of Science* 34 (1977), 1–32.

Inkster, Ian, and Jack Morrell (eds.), *Metropolis and Province: Science in British Culture, 1780–1850*, London: Hutchinson, 1983.

Jacyna, L. S., 'Immanence or Transcendence: Theories of Life and Organization in Britain, 1790–1835', *Isis* 74 (1983), 310–29.

Jordanova, Ludmilla, *Defining Features: Scientific and Medical Portraits, 1660–2000*, London: Reaktion Books, 2000.

Kipnis, Naum, 'Luigi Galvani and the Debate on Animal Electricity, 1791–1800', *Annals of Science* 44 (1987), 107–42.

Knight, David, 'The Scientist as Sage', *Studies in Romanticism* 6 (1967), 65–88.

Leask, Nigel, 'Mont Blanc's Mysterious Voice: Shelley and Huttonian Earth Science', in Elinor S. Shaffer (ed.), *The Third Culture: Literature and Science*, Berlin: Walter de Gruyter, 1998, pp. 182–203.

Levere, Trevor H., *Poetry Realized in Nature: Samuel Taylor Coleridge and Early Nineteenth-Century Science*, Cambridge: Cambridge University Press, 1981.

MacLeod, Christine, 'James Watt, Heroic Invention and the Idea of the Industrial Revolution', in Maxine Berg and Kristine Bruland (eds.), *Technological Revolutions in Europe*, Cheltenham: Edward Elgar, 1998, pp. 96–116.

McNeil, Maureen, 'The Scientific Muse: The Poetry of Erasmus Darwin', in L. J. Jordanova (ed.), *Languages of Nature: Critical Essays on Science and Literature*, London: Free Association Books, 1986, pp. 159–203.

Mellor, Anne K., *Mary Shelley: Her Life, Her Fiction, Her Monsters*, New York: Routledge, 1989.

Miller, David Philip, '"Puffing Jamie": The Commercial and Ideological Importance of being a "Philosopher" in the Case of the Reputation of James Watt (1736–1819)', *History of Science* 38 (2000), 1–24.

Money, John, 'Joseph Priestley in Cultural Context: Philosophic Spectacle, Popular Belief and Popular Politics in Eighteenth-Century Birmingham', *Enlightenment and Dissent* 7 (1988), 57–81; 8 (1989), 69–89.

Morrell, J. B., 'Professors Robison and Playfair and the "Theophobia Gallica"', *Notes and Records of the Royal Society of London* 26 (1971), 43–63.

Morus, Iwan, Simon Schaffer and James Secord, 'Scientific London', in Celina Fox (ed.), *London – World City, 1800–1840*, New Haven, CT: Yale University Press, 1992, pp. 129–42.

Nicolson, Malcolm, 'Alexander von Humboldt and the Geography of Vegetation', in Andrew Cunningham and Nicholas Jardine (eds.), *Romanticism and the Sciences*, Cambridge: Cambridge University Press, 1990, pp. 169–85.

Ospovat, Alexander M., 'The Work and Influence of Abraham Gottlob Werner: A Reevaluation', *Actes du XIIIe Congrès International d'Histoire des Sciences, 1971* 8 (1974), 123–30.

Outram, Dorinda, 'The Language of Natural Power: The *éloges* of Georges Cuvier and the Public Language of Nineteenth-Century Science', *History of Science* 26 (1978), 153–78.

Pancaldi, Giuliano, *Volta: Science and Culture in the Age of Enlightenment*, Princeton: Princeton University Press, 2003.

Pratt, Mary Louise, *Imperial Eyes: Travel Writing and Transculturation*, London: Routledge, 1992.

Reed, Arden, *Romantic Weather: The Climates of Coleridge and Baudelaire*, Hanover, NH: University Press of New England, 1983.

Rehbock, Philip H., 'Transcendental Anatomy', in Andrew Cunningham and Nicholas Jardine (eds.), *Romanticism and the Sciences*, Cambridge: Cambridge University Press, 1990, pp. 144–60.

Richards, Evelleen, '"Metaphorical Mystifications": The Romantic Gestation of Nature in British Biology', in Andrew Cunningham and Nicholas Jardine (eds.), *Romanticism and the Sciences*, Cambridge: Cambridge University Press, 1990, pp. 130–43.

Richards, Robert J., *The Romantic Conception of Life: Science and Philosophy in the Age of Goethe*, Chicago: University of Chicago Press, 2002.

Roe, Nicholas, '"Atmospheric Air Itself": Medical Science, Politics, and Poetry in Thelwall, Coleridge, and Wordsworth', in Richard Cronin (ed.), *1789: The Year of the Lyrical Ballads*, Basingstoke: Macmillan, 1998, pp. 185–202.

Rudwick, Martin J. S., *Bursting the Limits of Time: The Reconstruction of Geohistory in the Age of Revolution*, Chicago: University of Chicago Press, 2005.

Rupke, Nicolaas, 'A Geography of Enlightenment: The Critical Reception of Alexander von Humboldt's Mexico Work', in David N. Livingstone and Charles W. J. Withers (eds.), *Geography and Enlightenment*, Chicago: University of Chicago Press, 1999, pp. 319–39.

Schaffer, Simon, 'Genius in Romantic Natural Philosophy', in Andrew Cunningham and Nicholas Jardine (eds.), *Romanticism and the Sciences*, Cambridge: Cambridge University Press, 1990, pp. 82–98.

'Natural Philosophy and Public Spectacle in the Eighteenth Century', *History of Science* 21 (1983), 1–43.

'The Nebular Hypothesis and the Science of Progress', in James R. Moore (ed.), *History, Humanity, and Evolution*, Cambridge: Cambridge University Press, 1989, pp. 131–164.

'Priestley's Questions: An Historiographical Survey', *History of Science* 22 (1984), 151–83.

Secord, James A., *Victorian Sensation: The Extraordinary Publication, Reception, and Secret Authorship of* Vestiges of the Natural History of Creation, Chicago: University of Chicago Press, 2000.

Smith, Bernard, 'Coleridge's Ancient Mariner and Cook's Second Voyage', *Journal of the Warburg and Courtauld Institutes* 19 (1956), 117–54.

European Vision and the South Pacific, 2nd edn, New Haven, CT: Yale University Press, 1985.

Snow, C. P., *The Two Cultures and the Scientific Revolution*, intro. Stefan Collini, Cambridge: Cambridge University Press, 1993.

Strickland, Stuart, 'Galvanic Disciplines: The Boundaries, Objects, and Identities of Experimental Science in the Era of Romanticism', *History of Science* 33 (1995), 449–68.

'The Ideology of Self-Knowledge and the Practice of Self-Experimentation', *Eighteenth-Century Studies* 31 (1998), 453–71.

Temkin, Owsei, 'Basic Science, Medicine, and the Romantic Era', in Temkin, *The Double Face of Janus and Other Essays in the History of Medicine*, Baltimore: Johns Hopkins University Press, 1977, pp. 345–72.

Turney, Jon, *Frankenstein's Footsteps: Science, Genetics and Popular Culture*, New Haven, CT: Yale University Press, 1998.

Wetzels, Walter D., 'Johann Wilhelm Ritter: Romantic Physics in Germany', in Andrew Cunningham and Nicholas Jardine (eds.), *Romanticism and the Sciences*, Cambridge: Cambridge University Press, 1990, pp. 199–212.

Williams, Raymond, *Culture and Society*, Harmondsworth: Penguin Books, 1963.

Wyatt, John, *Wordsworth and the Geologists*, Cambridge: Cambridge University Press, 1995.

Wylie, Ian, *Young Coleridge and the Philosophers of Nature*, Oxford: Clarendon Press, 1989.

Yeo, R. R., 'Genius, Method, and Morality: Early Victorian Images of Sir Isaac Newton', *Science in Context* 2 (1988), 257–284.

CHAPTER 24 BIBLIOGRAPHY

Primary works

The Alphabet of Goody Two Shoes; By Learning Which, She Soon Got Rich, London: John Harris, 1808.

'Anabella's Journey to Market', in Arnaud Berquin, *The Looking-Glass for the Mind; or, Intellectual Mirror, Being an Elegant Collection of the Most Delightful Little Stories, and Interesting Tales, Chiefly translated from that much admired Work, L'Ami des Enfans*, 1794 edn [Elizabeth Newbery], rpt Wakefield: S. R. Publishers and New York: Johnson Reprint Corp., 1969, pp. 8–15.

'Argus, Arabella', *Adventures of a Donkey*, London: William Darton, 1815.

Juvenile Spectator, London: Darton, 1810; vol. I rpt in Jonathan Cott (ed.), *Masterworks of Children's Literatures*, 7 vols., New York: Chelsea House, 1984, vol. IV, pp. 331–424.

Aunt Ann's Lesson-Book, for Very Young Children. In Words of One and Two Syllables, By a Friend to Little Children, London: Harvey and Darton, 1822.

Barbauld, Anna Letitia, *Lessons for Children from Three to Four Years Old*, London: J. Johnson, 1788.

Lessons for Children, from Two to Three Years Old, London: J. Johnson, 1787.

Coleridge, Samuel Taylor, *Collected Letters of Samuel Taylor Coleridge*, ed. Earl Leslie Griggs, 10 vols., Oxford: Clarendon Press, 1956.

Dame Partlet's Farm, Containing an Account of The Great Riches She Obtained by Industry, The Good Life She Led, and Alas, Good Reader! Her Sudden Death, London: John Harris, 1804.

Day, Thomas, *History of Little Jack*, London: John Stockdale, 1788.

de Vries, Leonard (ed.), *Flowers of Delight, Culled from the Osborne Collection of Early Children's Books*, New York: Pantheon, 1965, pp. 91–3.

Elliott, Mary Belson, *Goody Two Shoes, Exemplifying the Good Consequences of Early Attention to Learning and Virtue*, London: Darton, c. 1830.

Peggy and her Mammy, London: Darton, 1819.

Precept and Example; or, Midsummer Holidays, London: Darton, 1811.

Fenwick, Eliza, *Infantine Stories, Composed Progressively, In Words of One, Two and Three Syllables*, London: Benjamin Tabart, 1810.

Lessons for Children or, Rudiments of Good Manners, Morals, and Humility, London: M. J. Godwin and Co., 1813.

Mary and her Cat. In Words not Exceeding Two Syllables, London: Darton, 1819.

Visits to the Juvenile Library; or, Knowledge Proved to be the Source of Happiness, London: Benjamin Tabart, 1805; rpt New York: Garland, 1977.

Godwin, William (pseud. 'Edward Baldwin'), *Fables Ancient and Modern*, London: M. J. Godwin, 1805.

The Pantheon, London: M. J. Godwin, 1806.

Godwin, William and Mary Jane, *Dramas for Children, Imitated from the French of L. F. Jauffret, by the Editor of Tabart's Popular Stories*, London: M. J. Godwin, 1809.

The Juvenile Story-Teller; A Collection of Moral Tales, for the Amusement and Education of Young Masters and Misses, London: James Imray, 1805.

Kilner, Dorothy, *First Going to School, or the Story of Tom Brown and His Sisters*, London: Benjamin Tabart, 1804.

Histories of More Children than One; Or Goodness Better than Beauty (1795); rpt London: Baldwin, Cradock and Joy; N. Hailes and John Marshall, 1822.

Life and Perambulations of a Mouse, London: John Marshall, c. 1790.

The Rational Brutes; or, Talking Animals, London: Vernor and Hood, 1799.

The Village School, 2 vols., London: John Marshall, 1787–98?.

Kilner, Mary Ann, *Adventures of a Pincushion*, London: John Marshall, c. 1780.

Memoirs of a Peg-Top, London: John Marshall, 1783.

S. W. [Elizabeth Kilner?], *A Puzzle for a Curious Girl*, London: Benjamin Tabart, 1803.

A Visit to a Farm House, London: Darton, 1804.

A Visit to London, Containing a Description of the Principal Curiosities in the British Metropolis, London: Darton, 1805.

A Visit to London, London: Benjamin Tabart, 1808.

A Visit to London, Philadelphia: Benjamin Warner, 1817 [American rpt of Darton edn].

Lamb, Charles, *Collected Works and Letters of Charles Lamb*, New York: Modern Library, 1935.

'The Literature of the Nursery', *London Magazine* 2:11 (November 1820), 478–83.

'The Little Maid and the Gentleman; or, We are Seven', York: J. Kendrew, c. 1820.

Martin, Sarah Catherine, *Comic Adventures of Old Mother Hubbard and her Dog*, London: John Harris, 1805.

Mister, Mary, *The Adventures of a Doll, Compiled with the Hope of Affording Amusement and Instruction*, London: Darton, Harvey and Darton, 1816.

Moore, Margaret King (Lady Mount Cashell), *Stories of Old Daniel, or Tales of Wonder and Delight*, 2nd edn 1810; rpt Wakefield: S. R. Publishers and New York: Johnson Reprint Corp, 1969.

Mother Goose's Melody; or, Sonets [sic] for the Cradle: Containing the Most Celebrated Songs and Lullabies of the old British Nurses, London: Francis Power, 1791.

The Mother's Gift: or a Present for all Little Children who are Good, 2nd edn, London: Carnan and Newbery, 1770.

Newbery, John [author or editor], *Fables in Verse*, London: John Newbery, 1757.

  The History of Little Goody Two-Shoes and The Fairing, rpt New York: Garland, 1977.

  'The History of Master Friendly', *Nurse Truelove's Christmas Box, or, The Golden Plaything for Little Children, By which they may learn the Letters as soon as they can speak, and know how to behave so as to make every Body love them*, 1789 edn; rpt Chicago: Toby Rubovits, 1934, pp. 19–26.

  A Little Pretty Pocket-Book (1744); rpt New York: Harcourt, Brace & World, 1967.

  The Twelfth Day Gift, London: John Newbery, 1767.

The Oriental Moralist or the Beauties of the Arabian Nights Entertainment, London: Elizabeth Newbery, 1791.

Phillips, Sir Richard, *A Morning's Walk from London to Kew*, 2nd edn, London: J. and C. Adlard, 1820, pp. 68–9.

Porter, Jane, *The Two Princes of Persia: Addressed to Youth*, London: Crosby and Letterman, 1801.

Scargill, William Pitt, *Recollections of a Blue-Coat Schoolboy or, A View of Christ's Hospital* (1829); rpt Wakefield: S. R. Publishers and New York: Johnson Reprint Corporation, 1968.

Taylor, Jeffreys, *Harry's Holidays: or the Doings of One, Who Had Nothing to Do*, London: Baldwin, Craddock and Joy, 2nd edn, 1819.

Turner, Elizabeth, *The Daisy, or Cautionary Tales for Children*, London: Harris, 1807.

Trimmer, Sarah, *Fabulous Histories. Designed for the Instruction of Children, Respecting the Treatment of Animals* [*History of the Robins*], London: Longman, Robinson and Johnson, 1786.

A Visit to the Bazaar (1818); rpt Tokyo: Holp Shuppan, 1981.

Secondary works

Crain, Patricia, *The Story of A: The Alphabetization of America From 'The New England Primer' to 'The Scarlet Letter'*, Stanford: Stanford University Press, 2001.

Darton, F. J. Harvey, *Children's Books in England: Five Centuries of Social Life* (1932); Cambridge: Cambridge University Press, 2nd edn, 1970.

Demers, Patricia, *Heaven upon Earth: The Form of Moral and Religious Children's Literature, to 1850*, Knoxville: University of Tennessee Press, 1993.

Gottlieb, Gerald and J. H. Plumb (eds.), *Early Children's Books and their Illustration*, New York: Pierpont Morgan Library / Boston: David Godine, 1975.

Kittler, Friedrich A., *Discourse Networks 1800/1900*, trans. Michael Metteer with Chris Cullens, Stanford: Stanford University Press, 1990.

Kowelski-Wallace, Elizabeth, *Their Father's Daughters: Hannah More, Maria Edgeworth, and Patriarchal Complicity*, New York: Oxford University Press, 1991.

Meyers, Mitzi, 'Reading Rosamond Reading: Maria Edgeworth's "Wee-Wee Stories" Interrogate the Canon', in Elizabeth Goodenough *et al.* (eds.), *Infant Tongues: The Voice of the Child in Literature*, Detroit: Wayne State University Press, 1994, pp. 57–79.

Moon, Marjorie, *Benjamin Tabart's Juvenile Library: A Bibliography of Books for Children Published, Written, Edited and Sold by Mr. Tabart, 1801–1820*, Winchester, Hampshire: St Paul's Bibliographies / Detroit: Omnigraphics, 1990.

Moon, Marjorie (ed.), *John Harris's Books for Youth, 1801–1843: A Check-List*, Cambridge: Marjorie Moon and A. J. B. Spilman, 1976.

Neuburg, Victor E., *The Penny Histories: A Study of Chapbooks for Young Readers over Two Centuries*, New York: Harcourt, Brace and World, 1968.

Opie, Iona and Peter, *The Nursery Companion*, Oxford: Oxford University Press, 1980.

Pickering, Samuel F., *Moral Instruction and Fiction for Children, 1749–1820*, Athens, GA: University of Georgia Press, 1995.

Raven, James, 'Memorializing a London Bookscape: The Mapping and Reading of Paternoster Row and St. Paul's Churchyard, 1695–1814', in R. C. Alston (ed.), *Order and Connexion. Studies in Bibliography and Book History: Selected Papers from The Munby Seminar*, Woodbridge, Suffolk: Boydell and Brewer, 1994, pp. 177–200.

Ruwe, Donelle, 'Guarding the British Bible from Rousseau: Sarah Trimmer, William Godwin, and the Pedagogical Periodical', *Children's Literature* 29, ed. Elizabeth Lennox Keyser and Julie Pfeiffer, New Haven: Yale University Press, 2001, 1–17.

Spufford, Margaret, *Small Books and Pleasant Histories: Popular Fiction and its Readership in Seventeenth-Century England*, Athens, GA: University of Georgia Press, 1981.

St Clair, William, *The Godwins and the Shelleys: The Biography of a Family*, Baltimore: Johns Hopkins University Press, 1989.

'William Godwin as Children's Bookseller', in Gillian Avery and Julia Briggs (eds.), *Children and Their Books: A Celebration of the Work of Iona and Peter Opie*, Oxford: Oxford University Press, 1989, pp. 165–79.

Summerfield, Geoffrey, *Fantasy and Reason: Children's Literature in the Eighteenth Century*, Athens: University of Georgia Press, 1984.

Thwaite, M. F., *From Primer to Pleasure: An Introduction to the History of Children's Books in England, from the Invention of Printing to 1900*, London: The Library Association, 1963.

Townsend, John Rowe, 'The Newbery Books in America', in Townsend (ed.), *John Newbery and His Books: Trade and Plumb-Cake for Ever, Huzza!*, Metuchen, NJ: Scarecrow Press, 1994, pp. 150–4.

Trumpener, Katie, 'City Scenes: Commerce, Utopia and the Birth of the Picture Book', in *The Victorian Illustrated Book: New Explorations*, ed. Richard Maxwell, Charlottesville: University of Virginia Press, 2002, 332–84.

'Tales for Child Readers', in Richard Maxwell and Katie Trumpener (eds.), *The Cambridge Companion to Fiction of the Romantic Period*, Cambridge: Cambridge University Press, 2008.

Welsh, Charles, 'A Bookseller of the Last Century, Being Some Account of the Life of John Newbery' (1885), in John Rowe Townsend (ed.), *John Newbery and His Books*, Metuchen, NJ: Scarecrow Press, 1994, pp. 29–113.

Wooden, Warren W., *Children's Literature of the English Renaissance*, ed. Jeanie Watson, Lexington: University Press of Kentucky, 1986.

CHAPTER 25 BIBLIOGRAPHY

Primary works

Bentham, Jeremy, *Chrestomathia*, ed. M. J. Smith and W. H. Burston, Oxford: Clarendon Press, 1984.

The Panopticon Writings, ed. Miran Bozovic, London: Verso, 1995.

Coleridge, Samuel Taylor, *The Collected Works of Samuel Taylor Coleridge*, Princeton: Princeton University Press, 1969–2001.

Hazlitt, William, *The Complete Works of William Hazlitt*, ed. P. P. Howe, London: J. M. Dent and Sons, 1932.

Mill, John Stuart, *Mill on Bentham and Coleridge*, ed. F. R. Leavis, Cambridge: Cambridge University Press, 1980.

Quincey, Thomas de, *The Works of Thomas de Quincey*, Oxford: Oxford University Press, 2006.

Shelley, Mary Wollstonecraft, *Frankenstein*, ed. James Rieger, Indianapolis: Bobbs-Merrill Company, 1974.

Shelley, Percy Bysshe, *Shelley's Poetry and Prose*, ed. Donald H. Reiman and Sharon B. Powers, New York: W. W. Norton and Company, 1977.

Wordsworth, William, *The Prose Works of William Wordsworth*, ed. W. J. B. Owen and Jane Worthington Smyser, Oxford: Clarendon Press, 1974.

Secondary works

Barrell, John, *Imagining the King's Death: Figurative Treason, Fantasies of Regicide, 1793–1796*, Oxford: Oxford University Press, 2000.

Bolla, Peter de, *The Discourse of the Sublime: History, Aesthetics and the Subject*, Oxford: Basil Blackwell, 1989.

Butler, Marilyn, *Jane Austen and the War of Ideas*, Oxford: Oxford University Press, 1987.

Canuel, Mark, *Religion, Toleration, and British Writing, 1790–1832*, Cambridge: Cambridge University Press, 2002.

Chandler, James, *England in 1819: The Politics of Literary Culture and the Case of Romantic Historicism*, Chicago: The University of Chicago Press, 1998.

Christensen, Jerome, *Romanticism at the End of History*, Baltimore: Johns Hopkins University Press, 2000.

Dart, Gregory, *Rousseau, Robespierre and English Romanticism*, Cambridge: Cambridge University Press, 1999.

Ferguson, Frances, *Solitude and the Sublime: Romanticism and the Aesthetics of Individuation*, New York: Routledge, 1992.

Franta, Andrew, *Romanticism and the Rise of the Mass Public*, Cambridge: Cambridge University Press, 2007.

Galperin, William, *The Return of the Visible in English Romanticism*, Baltimore: Johns Hopkins University Press, 1993.

Goodman, Kevis, *Georgic Modernity and British Romanticism: Poetry and the Mediation of History*, Cambridge: Cambridge University Press, 2004.

Halevy, Elie, *The Growth of Philosophic Radicalism*, trans. Mary Morris, Boston: The Beacon Press, 1955.

Hartman, Geoffrey H., *Wordsworth's Poetry, 1787–1814*, New Haven: Yale University Press, 1971.

Hofkosh, Sonia, *Sexual Politics and the Romantic Author*, Cambridge: Cambridge University Press, 2006.

Jacobus, Mary, *Romanticism, Writing, and Sexual Difference: Essays on* The Prelude, Oxford: Oxford University Press, 1994.

Janowitz, Anne, *Lyric and Labour in the Romantic Tradition*, Cambridge: Cambridge University Press, 1998.

Jarvis, Simon, *Wordsworth's Philosophic Song*, Cambridge: Cambridge University Press, 2007.

Johnson, Claudia L., *Equivocal Beings: Politics, Gender, and Sentimentality in the 1790s: Wollstonecraft, Radcliffe, Burney, Austen*, Chicago: The University of Chicago Press, 1995.

Keach, William, *Arbitrary Power: Romanticism, Language, Politics*, Princeton: Princeton University Press, 2004.

Kelley, Theresa M., *Reinventing Allegory*, Cambridge: Cambridge University Press, 1997.

Klancher, Jon, *The Making of English Reading Audiences, 1790–1832*, Madison: University of Wisconsin Press, 1987.

Levinson, Marjorie, *The Romantic Fragment Poem: A Critique of a Form*, Chapel Hill: University of North Carolina Press, 1986.

Liu, Alan, *Wordsworth: The Sense of History*, Stanford: Stanford University Press, 1989.

McLane, Maureen N., *Romanticism and the Human Sciences: Poetry, Population, and the Discourse of the Species*, Cambridge: Cambridge University Press, 2006.

McGann, Jerome J., *The Romantic Ideology: A Critical Investigation*, Chicago: The University of Chicago Press, 1985.

Pfau, Thomas, *Romantic Moods: Paranoia, Trauma, and Melancholy, 1790–1840*, Baltimore: Johns Hopkins University Press, 2005.

Pinch, Adela, *Strange Fits of Passion: Epistemologies of Emotion, Hume to Austen*, Stanford: Stanford University Press, 1999.

Richardson, Alan, *Literature, Education and Romanticism: Reading as Social Practice, 1780–1832*, Cambridge: Cambridge University Press, 1994.

Russett, Margaret, *De Quincey's Romanticism: Canonical Minority and the Forms of Transmission*, Cambridge: Cambridge University Press, 1997.

Simpson, David, *Romanticism, Nationalism, and the Revolt against Theory*, Chicago: The University of Chicago Press, 1993.

Siskin, Clifford, *The Work of Writing: Literature and Social Change in Britain, 1700–1830*, Baltimore: Johns Hopkins University Press, 1998.

Smith, Olivia, *The Politics of Language, 1791–1819*, Oxford: Clarendon Press, 1984.

Taylor, Barbara, *Mary Wollstonecraft and the Feminist Imagination*, Cambridge: Cambridge University Press, 2003.

Trumpener, Katie, *Bardic Nationalism: The Romantic Novel and the British Empire*, Princeton: Princeton University Press, 1997.

Tuite, Clara, *Romantic Austen: Sexual Politics and the Literary Canon*, Cambridge: Cambridge University Press, 2002.

Whale, John, *Imagination under Pressure, 1789–1832: Aesthetic, Politics, and Utility*, Cambridge: Cambridge University Press, 2005.

Williams, Raymond, *Culture and Society, 1780–1850*, New York: Harper and Row, 1966.

Wolfson, Susan, *Formal Charges: The Shaping of Poetry in British Romanticism*, Stanford: Stanford University Press, 1999.

CHAPTER 26 BIBLIOGRAPHY

Primary works

Bate, Jonathan, *'I am:' The Selected Poetry of John Clare*, New York: Farrar, Strauss & Giroux, 2003.

Bromwich, David (ed.), *Edmund Burke: Speeches on Empire, Liberty and Reform*, New Haven: Yale University Press, 2000.

Erdman, David (ed.), *Complete Poetry and Prose of William Blake*, New York: Anchor Books, 1997.

Fitzgerald, Maurice (ed.), *Poems of Robert Southey*, Oxford: Oxford University Press, 1909.

Hamilton, Elizabeth, *Translations of Letters of a Hindoo Rajah*, Peterborough, Ontario: Broadview Press, 1999.

Hayden, John (ed.), *William Wordsworth: The Poems*, New Haven: Yale University Press, 1981.

Jackson, H. J. (ed.), *Samuel Taylor Coleridge: The Major Works*, Oxford: Oxford University Press, 2000.

Leader, Zachary, and Michael O'Neill (eds.), *Percy Bysshe Shelley: The Major Works*, Oxford: Oxford University Press, 2003.

McGann, Jerome (ed.), *Lord Byron: The Major Works*, Oxford: Oxford University Press, 2000.

Paine, Thomas, *Rights of Man*, Harmondsworth: Penguin, 1984.

Stillinger, Jack (ed.), *John Keats: Complete Poems*, Cambridge, MA: Harvard University Press, 1991.

Wollstonecraft, Mary, *A Vindication of the Rights of Woman*, Harmondsworth: Penguin, 2004.

Wordsworth, William, *Selected Prose*, Harmondsworth: Penguin, 1988.

Secondary works

Barrell, John, *The Infection of Thomas De Quincey: A Psychopathology of Imperialism*, New Haven: Yale University Press, 1991.

Fulford, Timothy, and James Kitson, *Romanticism and Colonialism: Writing and Empire, 1780–1830*, Cambridge: Cambridge University Press, 1998.

Leask, Nigel, *British Romantic Writers and the East: Anxieties of Empire*, Cambridge: Cambridge University Press, 1992.

Makdisi, Saree, *Romantic Imperialism: Universal Empire and the Culture of Modernity*, Cambridge: Cambridge University Press, 1998.

William Blake and the Impossible History of the 1790s, Chicago: University of Chicago Press, 2003.

Mehta, Uday, *Liberalism and Empire: A Study in Nineteenth-Century Liberal British Thought*, Chicago: University of Chicago Press, 1999.

Richardson, Alan, and Sonia Hofkosh, *Romanticism, Race and Imperial Culture*, Bloomington: Indiana University Press, 1996.

CHAPTER 27 BIBLIOGRAPHY

Primary works

Austen, Jane, *Emma*, ed. Richard Cronin, Cambridge: Cambridge University Press, 2005.

Mansfield Park, ed. John Wiltshire, Cambridge: Cambridge University Press, 2005.

Pride and Prejudice, ed. Pat Rogers, Cambridge: Cambridge University Press, 2006.

Blake, William, *The Complete Poetry and Prose of William Blake*, ed. David Erdman, rev. edn, New York: Anchor Books, 1982.

Burke, Edmund, *Reflections on the Revolution in France*, ed. J. G. A. Pocock, Indianapolis, IN: Hackett, 1987.

Byron, George Gordon, Lord, *Cain, A Mystery*, London, 1821.

Coleridge, Samuel Taylor, *Lay Sermons*, ed. R. J. White, Princeton: Princeton University Press, 1972.

Lectures 1795: On Politics and Religion, ed. Lewis Patton and Peter Mann, Princeton: Princeton University Press, 1971.

On the Constitution of Church and State, ed. John Colmer, Princeton: Princeton University Press, 1976.

Hazlitt, William, *The Complete Works of William Hazlitt*, ed. P. P. Howe, 21 vols., London and Toronto: J. M. Dent and Sons, 1933.

Keats, John, *Endymion*, London, 1818.

Paine, Thomas, *The Age of Reason*, London, 1794–95.

Peacock, Thomas Love, *Rhododaphne: or the Thessalian Spell*, London, 1818.

Price, Richard, *A Discourse on the Love of Our Country*, in *Political Writings*, ed. D. O. Thomas, Cambridge: Cambridge University Press, 1992.

Shelley, Mary, *Frankenstein*, ed. Maurice Hindle, Harmondsworth: Penguin, 2003.

Shelley, Percy, *Queen Mab*, in *The Complete Poetry of Percy Bysshe Shelley*, vol. II, ed. Donald H. Reiman and Neil Fraistat, Baltimore, MD: Johns Hopkins University Press, 2004.

The Revolt of Islam, London, 1817.

Slavery, Abolition and Emancipation: Writings in the British Romantic Period, 8 vols., ed. Peter J. Kitson and Debbie Lee, London: Pickering and Chatto, 1999.

Southey, Robert, *The Book of the Church*, 2 vols., London: John Murray, 1824.

The Curse of Kehama, London, 1810.

Thalaba the Destroyer, 2 vols., London, 1801.

Spence, Thomas, *Pig's Meat* [1793–5].

Volney, Constantin, *The Ruins, or, A Survey of the Revolutions of Empires*, London, 1792.

Wordsworth, William, *The Excursion*, in *Poetical Works*, ed. Thomas Hutchinson, new edn, rev. Ernest De Selincourt, Oxford: Oxford University Press, 1936.

Secondary works

Abrams, M. H., *Natural Supernaturalism: Romantic Tradition and Revolution in Romantic Literature*, New York and London: Norton, 1971.

Arnold, Matthew, 'Wordsworth', in *Selected Prose*, ed. P. J. Keating, Harmondsworth: Penguin, 1970.

Bloom, Harold, *The Visionary Company: A Reading of English Romantic Poetry*, rev. edn, Ithaca: Cornell University Press, 1971.

Brisman, Leslie, 'Mysterious Tongue: Shelley and the Language of Christianity', *Texas Studies in Language and Literature* 23 (1981), 389–417.

Butler, Marilyn, *Romantics, Rebels, and Reactionaries: English Literature and its Background, 1760–1830*, Oxford: Oxford University Press, 1981.

'Myth and Mythmaking in the Shelley Circle', *ELH* 49 (1982), 50–72.

Goldsmith, Steven, *Unbuilding Jerusalem: Apocalypse and Romantic Representation*, Ithaca, NY: Cornell University Press, 1993.

Hartman, Geoffrey, *Wordsworth's Poetry, 1787–1814*, New Haven: Yale University Press, 1964.

Hole, Robert, *Pulpits, Politics and Public Order in England, 1760–1832*, Cambridge: Cambridge University Press, 1989.

Hulme, T. E., 'Romanticism and Classicism', in *Speculations: Essays on Humanism and the Philosophy of Art*, ed. Herbert Read, London: Routledge and Kegan Paul, 1924.

Krueger, Christine, *The Reader's Repentance: Women Preachers, Women Writers, and Nineteenth-Century Social Discourse*, Chicago: University of Chicago Press, 1992.

Laqueur, Thomas Walter, *Religion and Respectability: Sunday Schools and Working Class Culture, 1780–1850*, New Haven: Yale University Press, 1976.

Leask, Nigel, *British Romantic Writers and the East: Anxieties of Empire*, Cambridge: Cambridge University Press, 1992.

McCalman, Iain, *Radical Underworld: Prophets, Revolutionaries and Pornographers in London, 1795–1840*, Cambridge: Cambridge University Press, 1988.

McGann, Jerome, *The Romantic Ideology: A Critical Investigation*, Chicago: University of Chicago Press, 1983.

Mee, Jon, *Dangerous Enthusiasm: William Blake and the Culture of Radicalism in the 1790s*, Oxford: Clarendon Press, 1992.

Obelkevich, James, 'Religion', in *The Cambridge Social History of Britain, 1750–1850*, vol. III: *Social Agencies and Institutions*, ed. F. M. L. Thompson, Cambridge: Cambridge University Press, 1990.

Porter, Roy, 'The Enlightenment in England', in *The Enlightenment in National Context*, ed. Roy Porter and Mikulas Teich, Cambridge: Cambridge University Press, 1981.

Pym, David, 'The Ideas of Church and State in the Thought of the Three Principal Lake Poets: Coleridge, Southey, and Wordsworth', *Durham University Journal* 83 (1991), 19–26.

Richardson, Alan, *Literature, Education, and Romanticism: Reading as Social Practice, 1780–1832*, Cambridge: Cambridge University Press, 1994.

Roe, Nicholas, *John Keats and the Culture of Dissent*, Oxford: Clarendon Press, 1997.

Ryan, Robert, *The Romantic Reformation: Religious Politics in English Literature, 1789–1824*, Cambridge: Cambridge University Press, 1997.

Shaffer, E. S., *'Kubla Khan' and the Fall of Jerusalem: The Mythological School in Biblical Criticism and Secular Literature, 1770–1880*, Cambridge: Cambridge University Press, 1975.

Specter, Sheila A. (ed.), *The Jews and British Romanticism: Politics, Religion, Culture*, New York: Palgrave, 2002.

Trilling, Lionel, 'Wordsworth and the Rabbis', in *The Opposing Self: Nine Essays in Criticism*, New York and London: Harcourt Brace Jovanovich, 1955.

Ulmer, William A., 'The Christian Wordsworth, 1798–1800', *Journal of English and Germanic Philology* 95 (1996), 336–58.

Watts, Michael, *The Dissenters*, vol. II, *The Expansion of Evangelical Nonconformity*, Oxford: Clarendon Press, 1995.

White, Daniel E., *Early Romanticism and Religious Dissent*, Cambridge: Cambridge University Press, 2006.

CHAPTER 28 BIBLIOGRAPHY

Primary works

Byron: The Complete Poetical Works, 7 vols., ed. Jerome McGann, Oxford: The Clarendon Press, 1980–92.

Coetzee, J. M., *Disgrace*, London: Secker and Warburg, 1999.

Erdman, David V. (ed.), *The Complete Poetry and Prose of William Blake*, commentary by Harold Bloom, newly rev. edn, Berkeley: University of California Press, 1982.

Hardy, Thomas, *The Complete Poems*, ed. James Gibson, Variorum Edition, London: Macmillan, 1979.

Shelley, Percy Bysshe, *Shelley's Poetry and Prose*, ed. Donald H. Reiman and Neil Fraistat, 2nd edn, New York: Norton, 2002.

Sweet, Nanora, and Barbara Taylor (eds.), *The Sceptic: A Hemans–Byron Dialogue*, in *Romantic Circles Electronic Editions*, www.rc.umd.edu/editions/sceptic/

The Works of Mrs. Hemans with a Memoir of her Life by her Sister, 7 vols., Edinburgh and London: William Blackwood and Sons, 1844.

Secondary works

Abrams, M. H., *The Mirror and the Lamp: Romantic Theory and the Critical Tradition*, New York: W. W. Norton, 1953.

Babbitt, Irving, *Rousseau and Romanticism*, Boston: Houghton Mifflin, 1919.

Bate, Walter Jackson, *From Classic to Romantic*, Harper and Row, 1946.

Baucom, Ian, and Jennifer Kennedy (eds.), *Afterlives of Romanticism*, South Atlantic Quarterly 102:1 (Winter 2003).

Bloom, Harold, *The Anxiety of Influence: A Theory of Poetry*, New York: Oxford University Press, 1973.

The Ringers in the Tower, Chicago: University of Chicago Press, 1971.

The Visionary Company: A Reading of English Romantic Poetry, New York: Doubleday, 1961.

Eliot, T. S., *The Use of Poetry and the Use of Criticism: Studies in the Relation of Criticism to Poetry in England*, Cambridge, MA: Harvard University Press, 1933.

Frye, Northrop, *Fables of Identity: Studies in Poetic Mythology*, New York: Harcourt, Brace, and World, 1963.

Frye, Northrop (ed.), *Romanticism Reconsidered: Selected Papers from the English Institute*, New York: Columbia University Press, 1963.

Gordimer, Nadine, 'The Idea of Gardening: *Life and Times of Michael K*', in *Critical Essays on J. M. Coetzee*, ed. Sue Kossew, New York: G. K. Hall, 1998, pp. 139–44.

Hartman, Geoffrey, *The Unmediated Vision: Wordsworth, Hopkins, Rilke, and Valery*, New Haven: Yale University Press, 1954.

Hulme, T. E., *Speculations: Essays on Humanism and the Philosophy of Art*, New York: Harcourt, Brace, and Co., 1924.

McGann, Jerome, *Byron and Romanticism*, Cambridge: Cambridge University Press, 2002.

The Romantic Ideology, Chicago: University of Chicago Press, 1983.

Wasserman, Earl, *The Finer Tone*, Baltimore: Johns Hopkins University Press, 1967.

Wilson, Carol Shiner, and Joel Hafner (eds.), *Re-Visioning Romanticism, British Women Writers, 1776–1837*, Philadelphia: University of Pennsylvania Press, 1994.

Woodring, Carl, *Politics in English Romantic Poetry*, Cambridge, MA: Harvard University Press, 1970.

Index